Inclusion Strategies That Work!

Third Edition

This book is dedicated to all of my students throughout the years.

Together we have learned so much.

The world awaits, welcomes, and applauds your brilliance and perseverance to succeed.

Continue to connect with me on LinkedIn.

Inclusion Strategies That Work!

Research-Based Methods for the Classroom

Third Edition

Toby J. Karten

CORWIN
A SAGE Company

CORWIN
A SAGE Company

FOR INFORMATION:

Corwin
A SAGE Company
2455 Teller Road
Thousand Oaks, California 91320
(800) 233-9936
www.corwin.com

SAGE Publications Ltd.
1 Oliver's Yard
55 City Road
London EC1Y 1SP
United Kingdom

SAGE Publications India Pvt. Ltd.
B 1/I 1 Mohan Cooperative Industrial Area
Mathura Road, New Delhi 110 044
India

SAGE Publications Asia-Pacific Pte. Ltd.
3 Church Street
#10-04 Samsung Hub
Singapore 049483

Acquisitions Editor: Jessica Allan
Associate Editor: Kimberly Greenberg
Editorial Assistant: Cesar Reyes
Production Editor: Melanie Birdsall
Copy Editor: Jared Leighton
Typesetter: C&M Digitals (P) Ltd.
Proofreader: Caryne Brown
Indexer: Beth Nauman-Montana
Cover Designer: Michael Dubowe
Marketing Manager: Amanda Boudria

All clip art courtesy of Art Explosion 600,000.

Printed in the United States of America

A catalog record of this book is available from the Library of Congress.

ISBN: 978-1-4833-1990-2

This book is printed on acid-free paper.

MIX
Paper from responsible sources
FSC www.fsc.org
FSC® C014174

15 16 17 18 10 9 8 7 6 5 4 3 2 1

Inclusion Strategies That Work!

Research-Based Methods for the Classroom

AT A GLANCE

Contents

List of Inclusive Activities and Worksheets

for Teachers and Students

Preface

Teachers and students are sometimes caught up in the special education paradigm, with a San Andreas Fault separating effective research practices from classroom implementation. I hope this book facilitates learning for students with and without disabilities by jump-starting teachers with research-based strategies for inclusive classrooms. As you proceed through the chapters and activities, please note that I often italicize the base word *abilities* in the word dis*abilities* to highlight that it is not about what students *cannot* do; instead, the focus in inclusive classrooms must be on students' strengths—what they *can* do. Educators owe students the opportunity to achieve their maximum potential. This need not be a complicated process if professionals are trained and equipped with the right tools that focus on students' abilities. Step-by-step practices are explained in each chapter, with guided student and teacher activities for internalizing strategies. This text explains what research says about the inclusion of children as well as inclusive content, focusing on the achievement of productive student outcomes in diverse classrooms. Knowledge is retained by *doing*, so the words in this text leap off their pages with activities for inclusive classrooms, as shown below. A goal of this book is to help you tackle your list of inclusionary concerns.

PRIOR INCLUSION CONFUSION

Historical Sample of Inclusionary Concerns	My List of Inclusionary Concerns
1. What's inclusion?	
2. I won't do inclusion.	
3. I don't know how to do inclusion.	
4. Who's included?	
5. Can I have training for inclusion?	
6. I need more planning time.	
7. It's not working.	
8. More direct skill instruction is needed.	
9. What's differentiated instruction?	
10. When do I retire?	

Available for download at **www.corwin.com/inclusionstrategies**

The first chapter begins by establishing the reason for inclusion. Research and legal considerations are detailed and examined with text and cooperative assignments to help readers understand more about the impact of the Individuals with Disabilities Education Act (IDEA) amendments and response to interventions (RTI) entering classrooms. The impact on the classroom made by the Americans with Disabilities Act (ADA), Section 504 of the Rehabilitation Act of 1973, and the Common Core State Standards (CCSS) is also investigated. The second chapter explains some of the special terminology along with the negative effects that labeling has on students with and without disabilities. Experiential simulations and resources for more dis*ability* awareness are included. The third chapter delineates how knowledge of special education strategies benefits students with and without exceptionalities. Expansive interactive strategies and techniques ask the reader to process strategic concepts through varied activities.

The text moves on to discuss the individualized education program (IEP), demystifying the document with practical guidelines that include basic IEP elements and ways for teachers to provide and document goals with classroom modifications that accommodate and honor individual needs. The text also addresses social issues as an integral part of the curriculum, including ways for teachers to improve student behavior. Emotional intelligences, self-advocacy, functional behavioral assessments, and interpersonal reflections are all major components of successful inclusive classrooms, as shown with academic and social connections.

None of these inclusive principles would work without teachers co-planning structured lessons with clear-cut objectives, universal design for learning (UDL), differentiated instruction (DI) principles, and thinking about assessments through understanding by design (UbD). Sample collaborative classroom dilemmas are examined. The chapter on co-teaching tries to blur the lines between special and general education teachers to merge their sometimes separate worlds. The longest chapter in the book, Chapter 7, is about using the three Rs of reading, 'riting, and 'rithmetic, with an abundance of student templates that focus on teaching the basics. Content areas of physical education, art, music, science, and social studies complement this chapter, along with thematic interdisciplinary lessons. Learning more about study skills is next, along with retention, comprehension, and accountability issues with assessments. Teachers can reflectively examine classroom scenarios, questioning whether *fair* translates to *equal* and how effort, progress, and achievement factor into the grading and overall assessment process.

Chapter 10 focuses on how parents and families need to be part of the inclusive team, communicating and working together with teachers. Parents, families, and guardians are teachers' allies who should be valued as members of the school planning team. Establishing an ongoing system of home–school communication benefits all.

The technology chapter includes sample classroom activities and resources that teachers and students can use to maximize inclusive performance. Examples include how technology assists students with varying disabilities in leading more productive lives and how technology does not replace but augments curriculum topics.

The last chapter of the book reiterates the benefits of revisiting concepts to ground learning in memory. Reflections direct educators to plan lessons with clear-cut objectives in which they teach, move on, and then review. Reviewing is not taking a step backward but cementing or concretizing student learning. Educational mirrors benefit all!

At the end of the book, readers are given descriptive, clear, and informative dis*ability* tables that delineate possible causes, characteristics, and educational strategies that work with many disabilities, from attention deficit hyperactivity disorder to autism spectrum, physical disabilities, emotional disorders, and more, with the changes from DSM-5 offered. A compilation of acronyms is given for quick reference. There are also many organizations and references offered in the bibliography to seek out for further investigation.

This third edition of *Inclusion Strategies That Work! Research-Based Methods for the Classroom* offers updated research-based practices and connects them to inclusive classrooms to reflect ongoing changes in the special education (SE) and general education (GE) fields with a greater thrust toward high student outcomes in a digitally connected world. Hence, it includes access to many interactive documents for instruction, documentation, assessment, and professional practice. It is no ordinary book that is intended to collect dust on your shelf. It is a book whose binding will be well worn, since it is meant to be used and reused. Existing materials touch upon many of these topics, but this compilation of materials houses not only the characteristics and dynamics of dis*abilities,* but also vital and feasible strategies and good practices that teachers of all students can use in their classrooms. The text pragmatically explains how research meshes with inclusion when prepared teachers are at the helm.

Acknowledgments

I would like to acknowledge all of my colleagues, friends, and family who answered countless questions and offered endless encouragement to complete this text.

Specific acknowledgment is given to the teachers whose dedicated collaboration is making inclusion a successful reality for all very *abled* students!

More specifically, thanks to Marc and Adam, the two sources of my personal inspiration and the rocks I can lean on. Life has purpose with the two of you by my side. Zelda, Al, and Stephan, I love you as well and always will.

Thanks to all the professionals at Corwin who are part of the production team as well as to the peer reviewers at distinguished universities who carefully scrutinized the text. The first edition was made possible with the assistance of my first editor, Robb Clouse, who read an electronic query and *tastefully* acted upon it. Thank you to Jessica Allan, senior acquisitions editor, who is a constant supporter of my work to share the best practices. Additional thanks to these Corwin liaisons, associate editor Kimberly Greenberg, editorial assistant Cesar Reyes, production editor Melanie Birdsall, copy editor Jared Leighton, proofreader Caryne Brown, indexer Beth Nauman-Montana, cover designer Michael Dubowe, and marketing manager Stephanie Trkay.

About the Author

Toby J. Karten is an experienced educator who has worked in the field of special education since 1976. She has taught students who received a continuum of services throughout the years, ranging from residential settings to self-contained classrooms and inclusive environments. She has an undergraduate degree in special education from Brooklyn College, a master's degree from the College of Staten Island, a supervisory degree from Georgian Court University, and an honorary doctorate from Gratz College. Being involved in the field of special education for four decades has afforded Ms. Karten an opportunity to help many children and adults from elementary through graduate levels around the world. Along with being an author of several inclusion resources, inclusion coach, and educational consultant, Ms. Karten has designed face-to-face and online graduate courses entitled "Skills and Strategies for Inclusion and disAbility Awareness," "From Challenge to Success: ADHD, LD, and the Spectrum," "Interventions for Students With Dyslexia and Other Reading Differences," and "Collaborative Practices for Inclusive Schools." She is an adjunct professor at Monmouth University and works with the Regional Training Center in New Jersey, Pennsylvania, and Maryland as a course trainer and graduate instructor for The College of New Jersey and Gratz College. She has presented at local, state, national, and international workshops and professional conferences. Ms. Karten has been recognized by both the Council for Exceptional Children and the New Jersey Department of Education as an exemplary educator, receiving two "Teacher of the Year" awards.

Ms. Karten is married and has a son as well as a few dogs. She enjoys teaching, reading, writing, artwork, and—most of all—learning. As the author of this book, she believes that inclusion does not begin and end in the classroom but is a philosophy that continues throughout life. Hence, inclusion is not only research-based but life-based as well!

1

Examining the Research Base and Legal Considerations in Special Education, CCSS Connections, and the Reasons for Inclusion

DISABILITY LEGISLATION

Legislation has changed the way society thinks about disabilities and has also driven research to find better ways for schools to deliver appropriate services to children in the least restrictive environment (LRE). Basically, students have the right to a free, appropriate public education (FAPE) that addresses their diverse needs. Teachers must understand what legislation and research say about students with differing abilities in regard to the curriculum, instruction, Common Core State Standards (CCSS), assessment, and transitional skills. In addition, since the CCSS have been adopted by a majority of states and are applicable to students with and without disability classifications, there is a huge emphasis on improving both the academic and functional outcomes of students with disabilities through research-based interventions. This chapter offers the legislative underpinnings that compel educators to connect evidence-based practice to learning. Disability laws, standards-based reforms, and strategic research about disabilities are detailed in this chapter, beginning with the reasons that we need to do inclusion.

■ INTRODUCTION: WHY DO INCLUSION?

AFFECTIVE COMPARISON

Directions: Think of a time when you were excluded from an academic or social activity as a child or an adult. List the emotions you experienced as a result of this exclusion. Contrast this experience with a time when you were included or allowed to participate with others, and list those emotions under the appropriate heading as well.

Inclusion Versus Exclusion	
Inclusion	**Exclusion**

Available for download at **www.corwin.com/inclusionstrategies**

Now think of teaching a student who has similar exclusionary emotions and compare them to the ones you listed under the "Exclusion" column and how he or she would feel about school. How could you learn if you were experiencing these exclusionary emotions? Is there a moral here?

The primary reason for inclusion is the list of positive inclusive emotions. The Latin root of inclusion is *includo*, meaning to embrace, while the Latin root of exclusion is *excludo*, meaning to separate or shut out. Unfortunately, in their haste to include students, administrators in some school districts created the impression that inclusion is just a way to save money, with the unintended outcome that it burdens teachers. Educational players now realize that inclusion will not succeed without the proper scaffolding. Most teachers are skeptical because there is no script or template to follow for inclusion. Even though inclusion has been at the forefront for a while, it is still in its infancy and will continually evolve. Opposing dialogues and anti-inclusionary attitudes exist. Some school staff and community members question student placements in general education classrooms, wondering if this is another educational tide and if the general education classroom is always the best placement for increasing student academic achievement (Crowson & Brandes, 2010; Dawkins, 2010). Overall, inclusion is a way of life and a preparation for adulthood. It supports the civil rights of all learners. Inclusion may not be the most appropriate placement for meeting all students' needs, yet it should be considered the first viable option. At times, inclusion involves a combination of push-in and pull-out services with an array of staff that includes general and special education teachers, teaching assistants, and related staff such as occupational therapists (OTs), physical therapists (PTs), speech-language pathologists, mobility trainers, teachers of the deaf and hard of hearing, behavioral interventionists, and other consultative experts. The determination of a student's least restrictive environment placement is based foremost on each student's individual levels.

ESTABLISHING LEGISLATIVE KNOWLEDGE

Courting Issues

Laws were designed to protect people with disabilities by giving them access to the same societal opportunities as those accessible to people without disabilities. To segue to a more detailed examination of the special education (SE) laws and research, you are invited to answer the following true-or-false questions.

LEGISLATIVE KNOWLEDGE: TRUE OR FALSE?

_____ 1. Eighteen percent of the school-age population has a disability.

_____ 2. Cooperative learning is a competitive teaching strategy.

_____ 3. Right angles of learning refer to measuring the classroom.

_____ 4. About 5 to 6 percent of the school-age population has a learning disability (LD).

_____ 5. Section 504 of the Rehabilitation Act has been in effect since 1983.

_____ 6. FAPE stands for Federally Approved Programs for Education.

_____ 7. The Individuals with Disabilities Education Act (IDEA) is an educational program that protects children ages five to twenty-one.

_____ 8. Teachers can call for a new individualized education program (IEP) meeting anytime they need additional support.

_____ 9. A student who is not classified can be considered for Section 504 protection.

_____ 10. There are thirteen specific disability categories under IDEA for students from ages three to twenty-one.

_____ 11. The Americans with Disabilities Act (ADA) protects individuals with physical or mental impairments that may limit a major life activity.

_____ 12. People with an intellectual disability are more likely to have children who also have cognitive impairment.

Available for download at **www.corwin.com/inclusionstrategies**

Inclusion Web

Special education laws demand that the general education classroom be looked at as the first placement option and the least restrictive environment for students with disabilities. The web below outlines more particulars about inclusion.

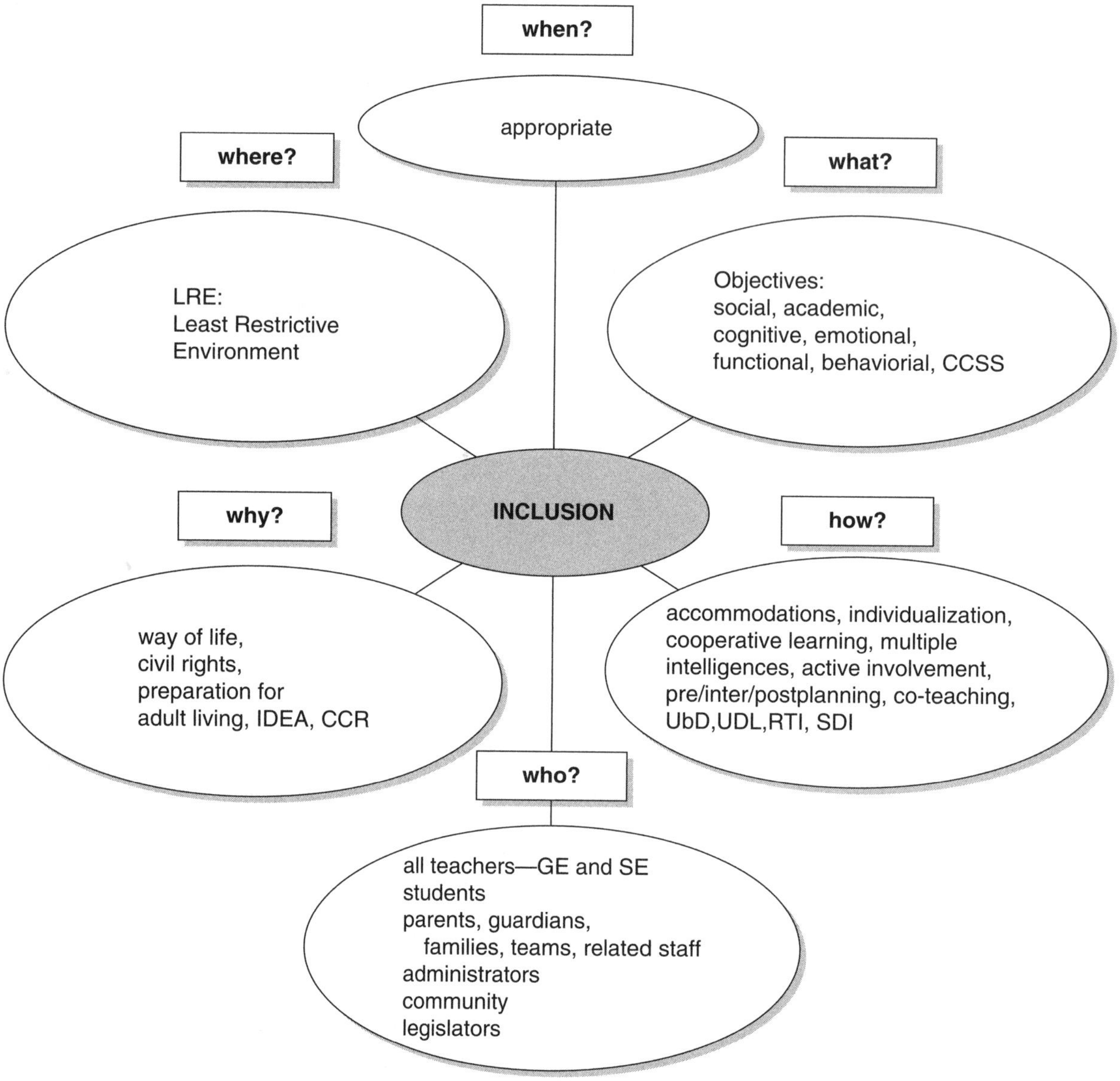

The true-or-false activity might have been frustrating if you did not have background knowledge about special education or related laws. Compare it to the spelling pretest given to students who have no prior knowledge of the words. Teachers sometimes begin a content area assuming children have prior knowledge.

Moral: All students do not have the same background knowledge or experience. Learning should be at an optimum level while frustrations should be kept to a minimum since they only interfere with and thwart the learning process. Ascertaining what students know before the lesson proceeds then helps to guide instruction. (See page 7 for answers to the true-or-false statements.)

Research about cooperative learning affirms its social and academic advantages (Jenkins, Antil, Wayne, & Vadasy, 2003; Johnson & Johnson, 1975; Kagan, 1994; Slavin, 1990; Ferguson-Patrick, 2012). Positive social interactions increase as students work collaboratively toward a common goal. Academically, students are willing to spend more time learning from each other rather than from the teacher, resulting in better educational outcomes with often challenging curricula.

The CCSS offer rigorous standards for students to achieve college- and career-ready skills. The Partnership for 21st Century Skills advocates collaboration, communication, critical thinking skills, and creativity. When students with special needs are placed in inclusive environments, they are afforded the opportunity to achieve these standards side by side with their age-level peers who will hopefully one day be their coworkers. Cooperative communication bridges students to adulthood since it is a prerequisite for future employment relationships. Getting along with others is a skill that schools can foster through cooperative learning. Team skills, increased self-esteem, improved peer interaction, and higher task completion with learning assignments are some of the benefits that are yielded when structured, heterogeneous cooperative groups work together in classrooms. Overall, cooperation is a functional skill for educators and peers in inclusive classrooms to repeatedly foster and model.

Special education services are provided without cost to the students and families under all three laws: IDEA, ADA, and Section 504. Under IDEA, the least restrictive environment is first the general education classroom unless the severity of the disability prohibits that placement. The intention of this next legislative review is to increase your knowledge of SE laws and to walk the cooperative talk.

JIGSAWING READING

To review the basic terminology and legislation in the field of special education, cooperative groups should equitably divide the legislative readings on the following pages to collectively share knowledge and then answer six out of ten listed questions under the heading "Cooperative Legislative Review." This jigsaw technique is a cooperative learning strategy where teachers direct students to learn and share content with each other. Having a choice of which questions to answer empowers the student under the teacher's auspices. Teachers monitor learners and drift to different groups, clarifying questions and concerns while addressing individual and group thought processes. The following readings summarize pertinent facts about legislation, along with past, present, and future concerns about special education and the rights of people with disabilities.

Cooperative Division

1. Everyone reads the IDEA/ADA/504 comparison.

   Then, equitably divide the following:

2. Details about the least restrictive environment

3. Description of thirteen disability categories under IDEA

4. History of the ADA

5. Civil rights for people with disabilities

6. Past, present, and future concerns

Available for download at **www.corwin.com/inclusionstrategies**

ANSWERS TO TRUE/FALSE

1. F—Approximately 13 percent of all children and youth ages three to twenty-one
2. F—Noncompetitive
3. F—It's a hierarchy of learning objectives.
4. T—Students falling under the LD category vary from state to state (e.g., Kentucky has a low of 2.9 percent while Massachusetts has a high of 7.35 percent).
5. F—1973
6. F—Free, appropriate public education
7. F—Ages three to twenty-one (Under IDEA Part C, from birth to age three those eligible for services include students with developmental delays, e.g., physical development, cognitive development, communication, social or emotional development, or adaptive [behavioral] development.)
8. T
9. T—Examples include a child with asthma (staff trained to administer EpiPen), diabetes (glucose monitoring with trained personnel, access to water and bathroom), food allergies (safe snacks available), juvenile arthritis (word processor, scribe), attention deficit hyperactivity disorder (ADHD) (modified schedule, homework decreased, reduced or minimized distractions). Review this site for more 504 ideas: www.ncld.org/students-disabilities/iep-504-plan/developing-successful-504-plan-k-12-students
10. T
11. T—Life activities include walking, speaking, working, learning, caring for oneself, eating, sleeping, standing, lifting, bending, reading, concentrating, thinking, and communicating.
12. F—Children can be affected by the limitations, but their mothers' illnesses during pregnancy and use of drugs or alcohol are major contributors.

SOURCE: Holler and Zirkel (2008), Mauro (n.d.), Pierangelo and Giuliani (2010), and the National Center for Education Statistics (2013).

IDEA of 1990 & Individuals with Disabilities Education Improvement Act of 2004 (IDEIA)	ADA of 1990 & Americans with Disabilities Act Amendments Act of 2008 (ADAAA)	Section 504 of the Rehabilitation Act of 1973/ Impact of ADAAA
Children ages three to twenty-one with disabilities listed below are eligible for a free and appropriate public education in the least restrictive environment. IDEA is a statute that funds special education programs under the following categories: • Autism • Deafness • Deafness–blindness • Hearing impairments • Intellectual disabilities • Multiple disabilities • Orthopedic impairments • Other health impairments • Emotional disturbance • Specific learning disabilities • Speech or language impairments • Traumatic brain injury • Visual impairments Under IDEA Part C, states may choose to add a 14th category of developmental delay for students ages three to nine who exhibit significant physical, cognitive, behavioral, emotional, or social differences in development in comparison with children of the same age and for students from birth to age three. The IDEA defines an IEP, which provides written statements about current academic and functional levels. Long-term and short-term objectives are required for students who take alternate assessments. Accommodations, modifications, and evaluation criteria are listed for each child.	Civil rights law that protects people with disabilities from discrimination in public services if reasonable accommodations can be provided by state and local governments. Physical or mental impairment has to substantially limit one or more life activities (walking, breathing, seeing, hearing, speaking, learning, working, caring for oneself, eating, sleeping, standing, lifting, bending, reading, concentrating, thinking, or communicating). A word such as *concentrating* qualifies a student with attention issues, such as a child who may have a diagnosis of ADHD. Disability determinations are made without regard to mitigating measures (e.g., medication, appliances, medical supplies, low-vision devices [not eyeglasses or contacts], prosthetics, hearing aids, and mobility devices). Person must have a record and be regarded as having such impairment. This does not include transitory or minor disabilities that have a duration of six months or less. Prevents employment discrimination against individuals with disabilities who meet other job qualifications. Helps to ensure public access to transportation and communication.	Civil rights law that stops discrimination against people with disabilities in public and private programs or activities that receive public financial assistance. Services under 504 protection include special education and general education with appropriate related services, accommodations, and aids. ADAAA extended more eligibility for K–12 students under Section 504. Before ADAAA, students with 504 plans accounted for about 1.2 percent of national school-age children. 504 plans include but are not limited to students with ADHD, diabetes, food allergies, and other learners who qualify for eligible services (Holler & Zirkel, 2008). Similar to IDEA but can include students and staff of all ages who may not be covered under IDEA classifications. Disability has to limit student's ability to learn or perform other major life activities. Students who use illegal drugs are not eligible for 504 plans. Lists mitigating measures (e.g., low vision [except contact lenses or eyeglasses], hearing aids, cochlear implants, and assistive technology). Includes reasonable accommodations and modifications.

IDEA of 1990 & Individuals with Disabilities Education Improvement Act of 2004 (IDEIA)	ADA of 1990 & Americans with Disabilities Act Amendments Act of 2008 (ADAAA)	Section 504 of the Rehabilitation Act of 1973/ Impact of ADAAA
Present levels of academic achievement and functional performance (PLAAFP) are written in students' IEPs as snapshots of each child's current status and progress. The word *functional* refers to routines of everyday living that are nonacademic and better prepare students with disabilities for postschool adjustments. Implementation of early intervening services by local education agencies (LEAs) to include professional development for educators and for related staff to deliver scientifically based academic and behavioral interventions (e.g., literacy, services, and supports). Limitation of related services for devices that are surgically implanted (e.g., cochlear implants). Supplementary aids and services are provided in general education classes as well as extracurricular and nonacademic settings. IEPs are based on each child's unique, individual needs.	Can include special education students who are employed in community jobs or those people with disabilities visiting schools. Can refer to private, nonsectarian schools. The Office of Civil Rights (OCR) enforces Title II of the ADA, which extends the prohibition against discrimination to public schools, whether or not they receive public funding. Expanded definition of *substantially limited* rather than mandating a severe or significant restriction. The definition of major life activities says that the impairment needs to limit only one major activity in order to be considered as an ADA disability, although it may limit more as well. Amendments of ADA affect 504 plans in forms and procedures, increasing the number eligible of students in Grades K–12 protected under Section 504.	Limited amount of money a school district can spend if the services are too costly since, unlike IDEA, there are no provisions that districts be reimbursed. State and local jurisdictions are responsible. Requires a plan with a group that is knowledgeable about the unique needs of the student. Specifies educational benefits, aids, services, class, and assessment modifications (e.g., reading test questions aloud, behavior intervention plans, and preferential seating). Periodic reevaluations. Like IDEA, local education agencies must provide impartial hearings for parents who disagree with the identification, placement, or evaluation. Do not need both an IEP and a Section 504 plan if student qualifies for services under both since one way to meet 504 requirements is to comply with IDEA. General education teachers must implement provisions of Section 504; their refusal would mean district could be found noncompliant.

Least Restrictive Environments

According to IDEA, FAPE must be provided in the LRE, which is first the general education classroom setting because of the academic and nonacademic benefits along with the effects of that placement on other children. Special education services are linked to both academic and functional goals in what is then deemed the LRE. The assumption under the law is that every child with a disability is educated in the general education classroom; if this is not the case, then the school district must provide documentation for why this should not occur. A continuum of some alternative placements is determined on an individual basis with planning, interventions, and documentation of effectiveness merited in all environments. The goal is to go down the continuum to more restrictive environments only as necessary based on student levels and to move up the continuum to full inclusion as appropriate.

Least Restrictive Environment Options

- *General education classroom* with moderate support—for example, consultation periods; in-class support by a special education teacher or other trained personnel for part of the day; or perhaps two teachers, general education (GE) and special education, co-teaching and co-planning lessons for all children in the classroom. The two teachers (GE and SE) and related staff may work together in an inclusion setting to help students with responses to the curricula through strategic planning, specified interventions, and data that monitor ongoing benchmark assessments.

- *Pull-out programs* to support or replace some subjects that may be taught in a resource room. Academic subjects such as reading, language, science, social studies, or mathematics may be taught or supported in another setting within the school. The student fully participates in all other classroom content areas and activities with peers and follows the rest of the class schedule, with maximum social integration. This combination of services allows for periods of direct skill instruction along with social and academic inclusion with peers.

- *Special education classroom* in a neighborhood school with the possibility of mainstreaming for certain subjects, academic and social goals delineated, and adequate supports provided in the general education classroom and all other settings. Special class placement can also be self-contained.

- *Special school* if education cannot be provided in the neighborhood school.

- *Home instruction* if the student's needs cannot be met in the school due to social, academic, physical, or medical issues.

- *Residential placement* that is provided in a setting other than the neighborhood school or home, which can include instruction in hospitals or residential institutions. Even though a placement such as a hospital is considered one of the most restricted environments, it may actually be the least restrictive setting for someone with a mental illness if it is deemed the most appropriate one to serve that individual's needs.

IDEA has four parts, with these inclusive elements:

Part A: General Provisions. This part includes the purpose of special education law, definitions of terms, and congressional findings.

Part B: Assistance for Education of All Children with Disabilities. This part includes the state formula grant program, eligibility, evaluations, IEPs, funding, procedural safeguards, and preschool grants.

Part C: Infants and Toddlers with Disabilities. This part delineates early intervention programs for infants and toddlers with disabilities along with findings and policies.

Part D: National Activities to Improve Education of Children with Disabilities. Included here are discretionary programs, state improvement grants, supporting and applying research, personnel preparation, parent training and information centers, technical assistance, technology development, and disseminating information.

When IDEA was reauthorized in 2004 as IDEIA, major reauthorization points focused on linking goals with academic and functional outcomes that are connected to research-based responses to intervention (RTIs). There was also an allowance to remove benchmarks and short-term objectives from a student's IEP unless that student is participating in an alternate assessment aligned to alternate achievements (This exemption usually applies to a student with a very significant cognitive impairment who responds markedly differently to stimuli or has overall difficulties in communicating or providing a response). States may include benchmarks, but it is not federally mandated. Some states include benchmarks for subjects for which students are receiving replacement instruction rather than the subjects where students have full inclusion since the standards and objectives in the general education curriculum are then looked at as those students' goals. Students with disabilities are offered more rigorous academic content though grade-level CCSS. The standards are connected to IEPs and 504 plans, with specially designed instruction (SDI) outlined in a student's IEP. Even though at times students with disabilities share classifications, each disability involves heterogeneous characteristics, with each student possessing unique needs. Since each student has individual characteristics, the level of support and services as well as the instructional strategies are unique to each student. The Council of Chief State School Officers (CCSSO) and the National Governors Association Center for Best Practices (NGA Center) released criteria for college- and career-readiness (CCR) standards that are intended for *all* students, including students who have IEPs. The standards are accessible at www.corestandards.org.

IEP-CCSS Organizer

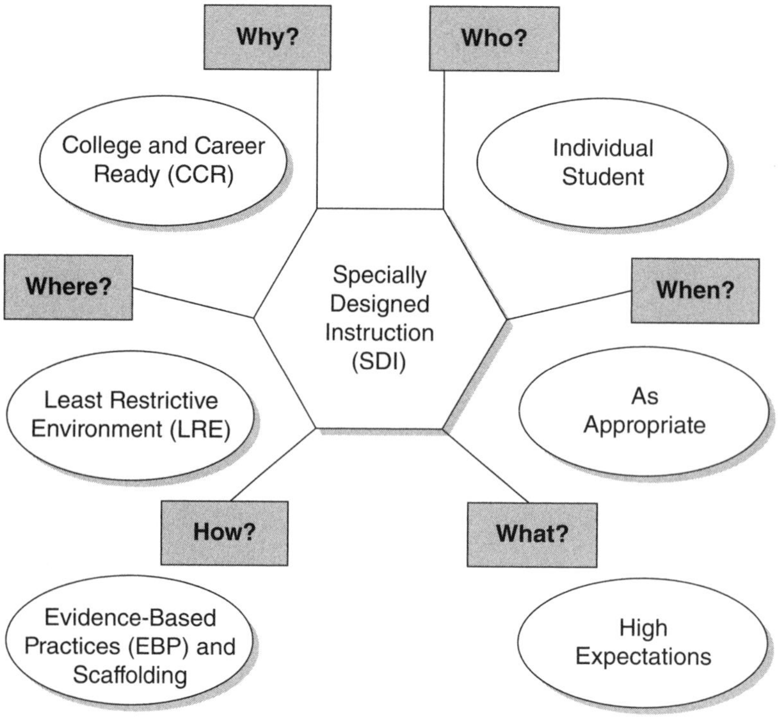

SOURCE: Karten (2014c). Please refer to Resource C for an explanation of acronyms.

Overall, as with IDEA, parents, guardians, families, school personnel, and students are integral collaborative players in this process who must always consider and focus on matching all students' strengths to meet the CCSS with appropriate IEP services.

Some examples of appropriate IEP services can include the following:

- Braille for a student with blindness or visual impairment
- Behavioral intervention plan for a student with significant behavioral issues
- Communication and language supports for a student with deafness or hearing impairment; a student who is nonverbal; or a student who may have articulation, receptive, or expressive language needs
- Appropriate assistive technology services and devices needed by the student, though not always required by the district (e.g., a portable word processor or an instructional assistant serving as a scribe for a student with dysgraphia, although beneficial, may not be part of every school district's standard procedure)
- Occupational or physical therapy for students (e.g., assistance with routines, structure, gait, balance, and/or handwriting)

As always, the present level of performance reflects how a child's disability impacts both his or her participation and progress in the general education curriculum. To qualify for services, a child's educational performance must be adversely affected as a result of the disability. The levels of academic achievement and functional performance are the crucial foundations for the development of the IEP since they drive the appropriate services needed to address, improve, and remediate the impact of a disability on a student's performance. Families are notified of student progress through periodic reports (e.g., quarterly intervals). Most important, IDEA directs IEP teams to implement instructional programs that have proven track records based on peer-reviewed research that gives merit to a program's effectiveness in both academic and behavioral domains. That means that schools are not arbitrarily using a program, but rather there is a research-based reason for that choice.

Appropriate accommodations for standardized assessments should not modify or alter test results, but should provide valid assessments that truly yield information on what the test is intended to measure. The frequency, location, and duration of all services are stated in the IEP. The consortia for the CCSS—the Partnership for the Assessment of Readiness for College and Careers (PARCC) and the Smarter Balanced Assessment Consortium (SBAC)—offer manuals with accessibility features and accommodations that are available for standardized testing at www.parcconline.org. Some of these adaptations are available to all students, such as the line reader, zoom magnification, and pop-up glossary in PARCC, while other accommodations are identified in advance and specific to individual students' needs, such as changing the foreground or background color, answer masking, and extended time. Smarter Balanced offers a conceptual framework that outlines universal tools that are available to all students, such as breaks, digital notepads, glossaries, math tools, and more. Student-specific accommodations include but are not limited to bilingual dictionaries, scribes, American Sign Language (ASL), separate settings, paper copies, read-alouds, and more. Teams determine the accommodations a student with an IEP or a 504 plan needs, which are then delineated in a personal needs profile. The National Center and State Collaborative (NCSC) and Dynamic Learning Maps (DLM) developed alternate assessments for students with the most significant cognitive disabilities that, like PARCC and SBAC, are state adopted. These assessments are linked to grade-level expectations for students to achieve a high academic outcome through prescriptive testing that offers diagnostic information to guide instruction during the school year. The goal is to prepare students with significant cognitive disabilities for viable postsecondary outcomes. If a student takes one of these assessments, it indicates that the grade-level curriculum is not appropriate (e.g., if the student has a significant intellectual disability, which affects less than one percent of all students).

Accessibility takes many forms. It may mean supporting high-quality, intensive professional development for personnel who work with children with disabilities, including training-related services personnel, teacher assistants, and paraprofessionals. Accessibility could also mean using technology for children with disabilities, whether print, digital, graphic, audio, or video formats. The National Center on Accessible Instructional Materials (aim.cast.org) provides accessible instructional materials, such as digital textbooks.

Accessibility can also mean providing Braille or text-to-speech formats for those students who require such services. To facilitate movement from school to postsecondary activities, transition services within a results-oriented process should be used to the maximum extent possible and include further recommendations for continuing education, independent living, and community participation. Transitional plans are federally required for students of age sixteen and offered earlier if warranted.

The overall philosophy is to help students with disabilities meet challenging state academic achievement standards and at the same time yield high functional achievements. Services for the homeless, foster children, children with disabilities in the military, and English learners (ELs) are also addressed. Reducing misidentification of children with disabilities by encouraging direct skill instruction is something that IDEA strongly advocates.

Highlights of IDEA include the following:

- Attorney fees are awarded to local education agencies if a parent's case is determined frivolous or improper based on legal precedents. The law is written so as to put most of the liability on the parent's attorney for pursuing a frivolous suit. There is also a two-year time limit to file, starting from the date the local educational agency knew of the issue in question. Information is kept confidential.

- With reference to learning disabilities, IDEA says a discrepancy between achievement and intellectual ability is not the sole indicator for LD classification. It allows for a process that determines if the child is responding to interventions. This targets students who are functioning below classroom standards to receive help, even though no discernible discrepancy may be revealed between tested intelligence and school performance. It focuses on early identification with assistance through early intervention services before the specific determination of a learning disability. RTIs (that is, responses to intervention) include monitoring and assessing students to determine levels, modifying classroom programs, and intervening with the appropriate evidence-based programs, strategies and resources, instead of referring students for automatic LD identification. RTIs merit the provision of appropriate early intervention services in natural environments to meet the needs of individual children. RTIs are implemented differently in many states, with a problem-solving approach that includes three overall tiers of interventions:

    1. Core (whole class) receives instruction and monitoring to determine needs and effectiveness of instruction

    2. Targeted (small groups) for students who need more strategic interventions identified

    3. Intensive (small groups, 1:1) for students with more chronic needs who require frequent monitoring of rigorous interventions

- IEP team members can be excused from attending meetings if all agree attendance is deemed unnecessary beforehand. The IEP team will obtain that member's input prior to the meeting (e.g., parent or guardian signs off with

LEA agreement that the member's area of the curriculum or related services are not being modified or discussed in the meeting).

- Schools should try to consolidate meetings, such as combining reevaluations with IEP team meetings.

- There is a federal timeline of sixty days allowed for evaluation, unless states have enacted other timelines, a parent or guardian enrolls the student in another school district, or a parent or guardian does not produce the student for evaluation.

- Changes to a child's IEP do not require another meeting if the LEA and parent or guardian of the child agree.

- An IEP can be amended or modified without redrafting the entire IEP.

- Alternative means of meeting participation and communication are allowed, such as video conferences, conference calls, and email (e.g., parent(s) and guardian(s) must give informed consent prior to an initial evaluation in which case e-mail could be an acceptable mode).

- Families have the right to obtain one free independent evaluation for each school evaluation (or reevaluation) if they believe that the evaluation conducted by qualified school personnel was inappropriate. If a school district does not agree to pay for an independent evaluation, then a hearing officer is obtained to determine whether or not another evaluation is warranted. If a private evaluation is conducted, the school district considers the findings but does not necessarily have to agree with or implement the recommendations.

- The act reduces paperwork burdens on teachers by conducting reviews of processes and forms and expanding the use of technology in the IEP process.

- It reduces the number of times a copy of procedural safeguards is given to parents or guardians. Copies are now required only once a year unless parents request them again.

- The use of positive discipline and other behavioral assessments and classroom approaches is required to prevent emotional and behavioral violations from recurring.

- The discipline code has been changed to a case-by-case basis to ensure the safety and appropriate educational atmosphere in the schools under the jurisdiction of the local educational agency. The act allows schools to expel students without first determining whether the behavior was linked to the child's disability. The behavior might involve drugs, bringing weapons to school, or causing bodily harm. Students can be removed for up to forty-five school days with instruction in another setting (e.g., interim alternative educational setting, or IAES).

- The incidence, duration, and type of disciplinary actions must be recorded and a determination must be made whether misbehaviors resulted from a failure of the IEP.

• The act sets up procedures that require the state educational agency (SEA) to develop a model form to assist parents in filing a complaint and a due process complaint notice.

• Due process hearings are delayed while all parties attempt to meet to resolve problems. Parties are not allowed to raise issues at due process hearings that were not raised in the original complaint.

• The LEA must conduct a Child Find to ensure and provide equitable services to children with disabilities who attend private schools within the LEA, without regard to where the children may reside (Office of Special Education Programs, 2005). Part C of IDEA refers to children from birth to age three.

• The act strengthens the role and responsibility of parents and ensures that families have meaningful opportunities to participate in the education of their children at school and at home.

Resources for Further Updates

American Recovery and Reinvestment Act of 2009: www.ed.gov/policy/gen/leg/recovery/factsheet/idea.html

Council for Exceptional Children: www.cec.sped.org

Dynamic Learning Maps: dynamiclearningmaps.org

Elementary and Secondary Education Act: www.ed.gov/esea

National Center and State Collaborative: www.ncscpartners.org

Parent Advocacy Coalition for Educational Rights (PACER) Center: www.pacer.org

Partnership for the Assessment of Readiness for College and Careers: www.parcconline.org

Smarter Balanced Assessment Consortium: www.smarterbalanced.org

Response to Intervention and Literacy Collaborative: www.lcosu.org/documents/PDFs/RtI_in_Literacy_Collaborative_Schools.pdf

U.S. Department of Education, Building the Legacy: IDEA 2004: idea.ed.gov

Wrightslaw: www.wrightslaw.com

DISABILITY CATEGORIES UNDER INDIVIDUALS WITH DISABILITIES EDUCATION ACT (IDEA)

In order to receive funds under Part B of IDEA, states must ensure that a free and appropriate public education is provided to children within thirteen disability categories at no cost to the parents, guardians, and families, in conformity with the individualized education program.

Exact classification language of each state is decided after it looks at federal regulations and does its alignment. As the U.S. Department of Education points out, the federal role in education is limited as per the 10th Amendment. Education policy is determined at state and local levels. School districts across the United States have many interpretations of and ways to implement federal disability laws. Sometimes states use different terms, but it is not the label that is important; it is matching the criteria under that disability category. Labels are just for eligibility. There is an enormous disadvantage for students when certain words and a condition title are needed to describe and convey a disability, rather than a person. Again, some states use different terms, as words develop negative connotations, but criteria remain the same and are aligned with federal regulations, with varying state interpretations and school applications.

IDEA Categories

Autism

This is a developmental disability significantly affecting verbal and nonverbal communication and social interaction, generally evident before age three, that adversely affects educational performance. It was added to IDEA in 1990.

Deafness

This is a hearing impairment so severe that a child is impaired in processing linguistic information through hearing, with or without amplification, resulting in adverse effects on educational performance.

Deaf-Blindness

These are simultaneous hearing and visual impairments, the combination of which causes such severe communication and other developmental and educational problems that a child cannot be accommodated in special education programs solely for children with deafness or blindness.

Hearing Impairment

This is an impairment in hearing, whether permanent or fluctuating, that adversely affects a child's educational performance but is not included under the definition of deafness.

Intellectual Disability

This requires significantly subaverage general intellectual functioning that exists concurrently with deficits in adaptive behavior, manifests during the developmental period, and adversely affects a child's educational performance. The former term *mental retardation* is no longer a category under the federal law due to its negative connotation. This change resulted from a legislative statute, Rosa's Law (2010), brought on by Rosa Marcellino, a nine-year-old girl with Down syndrome.

Multiple Disabilities

These are simultaneous impairments (such as intellectual disability/blindness or intellectual disability/orthopedic impairment), the combination of which causes such severe educational problems that the child cannot be accommodated in a special education program solely for one of the impairments. The term does not include children with deaf-blindness.

Orthopedic Impairment

This is an orthopedic impairment so severe that it adversely affects a child's educational performance. The term includes impairments caused by a congenital anomaly, such as clubfoot or the absence of a limb. Impairments caused by disease include poliomyelitis or bone tuberculosis and impairments from other causes such as cerebral palsy, amputations, and fractures or burns that might cause contractures (loss of joint motion).

Other Health Impairment

These impairments include having limited strength, vitality, or alertness due to chronic or acute health problems, such as attention deficit hyperactivity disorder, a heart condition, tuberculosis, rheumatic fever, nephritis, asthma, sickle cell anemia, hemophilia, epilepsy, lead poisoning, leukemia, diabetes, and Tourette syndrome (listed as a chronic or acute health problem under IDEA 2004), that adversely affect a child's educational performance.

Emotional Disturbance

This is a condition that adversely affects educational performance and exhibits one or more of the following characteristics over a long period of time and to a marked degree:

- An inability to learn that cannot be explained by intellectual, sensory, or health factors
- An inability to build or maintain satisfactory interpersonal relationships with peers and teachers
- Inappropriate types of behavior or feelings under normal circumstances
- A general or pervasive mood of unhappiness or depression
- A tendency to develop physical symptoms or fears associated with personal or school problems

The term includes children who have schizophrenia. The term does not include children who are socially maladjusted unless it is determined that they have a serious emotional disturbance.

Specific Learning Disability

This is a disorder of one or more of the basic psychological processes involved in understanding or using spoken or written language, which may manifest itself in an imperfect ability to listen, think, speak, read, write, spell, or do mathematical calculations. The term includes such conditions as perceptual disabilities, brain injury, minimal brain dysfunction, dyslexia, and developmental aphasia. The term does not include children who have learning problems that are primarily the result of visual, hearing, or motor disabilities; intellectual disability; emotional disturbance; or environmental, cultural, or economic disadvantage.

Speech or Language Impairment

This is a communication disorder such as stuttering (childhood onset fluency disorder), impaired articulation, a language impairment, or a voice impairment that adversely affects a child's educational performance.

Traumatic Brain Injury

An acquired injury to the brain caused by an external physical force resulting in total or partial functional disability, psychosocial impairment, or both that adversely affects educational performance. The term does not include brain injuries that are congenital or degenerative or brain injuries induced by birth trauma. Added to IDEA as a category in 1990.

Visual Impairment, Including Blindness

A visual impairment includes both partial sight and total blindness that even with correction adversely affects a child's educational performance.

SOURCE: Center for Parent Information and Resources (2012).

The following is a mnemonic to help remember all thirteen IDEA disabilities:

All very determined students deserve infinitely more opportunities than school has ever offered.

All (autism)
very (visual impairment)
determined (deafness)
students (speech and language impairment)
deserve (deaf-blindness)
infinitely (intellectual disability)
more (multiple disabilities)
opportunities (orthopedic impairment)
than (traumatic brain injury)
school (specific learning disability)
has (hearing impairment)
ever (emotional disturbance)
offered (other health impairments).

HISTORY OF THE AMERICANS WITH DISABILITIES ACT

The Americans with Disabilities Act (1990) was designed to prohibit discrimination against people with disabilities by state and local governments and provide equal opportunities in the following areas:

- Public accommodations
- Employment
- Transportation
- Telecommunications
- State and local governments

ADA's intent was to afford people with disabilities the same opportunities as everyone else to lead full and productive lives. Its goal was to break down barriers for people with disabilities, which stop them from achieving emotional and social independence. As a civil rights act, its enforcement enables our society to benefit from the skills and talents that people with disabilities have always possessed but have been thwarted from demonstrating. The overall goal in schools is to offer reasonable accommodations for students with disabilities to achieve the same results and be given the same benefits as students without disabilities.

The ADA Amendments Act (2008) defines disability as an impairment that substantially limits major life activities such as breathing, seeing, hearing, speaking, learning, caring for oneself, working, eating, sleeping, bending, lifting, communicating, thinking, reading, and concentrating. Included here are examples of major bodily dysfunctions that directly impact major life activities related to the circulatory, respiratory, digestive, and reproductive systems, along with the functions of the neurological system, brain, cell growth, immune system, bowel, and bladder. If the impairment is temporary, such as a nonchronic condition of a short duration, that person is not covered under ADA. For example, someone with a broken leg would not qualify. Disabilities that are six months or less in duration do not qualify. In addition, ADA states that a person must have a record of impairment, thereby including someone recovering from a chronic or long-term impairment such as mental illness or cancer. The definition expands further by including someone who is regarded as having such impairment. This involves determining how others regard or look at someone with a disability. ADA would protect someone who might have a facial disfigurement such as cleft palate from being denied employment because of workers' reactions. It would also allow an individual who has motor impairments due to cerebral palsy to perform a job that someone might incorrectly assume he or she cannot cognitively perform due to the person's discriminatory perception of that individual. The U.S. Equal Employment Opportunity Commission (EEOC) and the Supreme Court had made many decisions that were reversed by the ADAAA's definition of "substantially limits," with ADAAA being less rigorous.

In addition, the conditions are looked at without regard to the ameliorative effects of medication, medical supplies or equipment, prosthetics, assistive technology, reasonable accommodations or auxiliary aids, or behavioral or adaptive neurological modifications. This means that the underlying impairment is looked at without considering the effects of the extra devices; just the disability itself is addressed.

An individual is deemed qualified for a job position if he or she possesses the skills, education, or other job requirements of the position, with or without reasonable accommodation. This basically prohibits discrimination against individuals with disabilities in the private sector. Courts are currently interpreting this law on an individual basis.

Examples of reasonable accommodations include the following:

- Modifying a work schedule
- Providing menus in Braille or having a waiter reading the menu to a customer who is blind (the former allows for more independence)
- Installing numbers in Braille in office or hotel elevators and outside rooms
- Allowing seeing-eye dogs in public facilities
- Providing a sign interpreter at theater performances if the theater is given sufficient notice by someone with a hearing impairment
- Providing assistive listening devices and effective means of communication to families, friends, or associates of individuals seeking access to a service, program, or activity of a public entity, such as Video Remote Interpreting (VRI) communication for people who are deaf through webcams or videophones
- Training personnel to administer insulin to people with diabetes
- Removing existing barriers if it is readily achievable and can be done without much difficulty or expense (For instance, if a ramp or elevator could not be built because the business is not profitable enough, curbside service could be provided to people with disabilities. However, not every building or each part of every building needs to be accessible.)
- Accommodations could be as simple as lowering a paper towel dispenser, widening a doorway, or providing special parking spots

Courts levy penalties against a business if it shows bad faith in complying with ADA. Acts of bad faith might include deliberately ignoring a person's request, hostile acts, or refusing voluntary compliance. The Justice Department considers the size and resources of individual businesses before civil penalties are issued. Complaints must be valid. For example, refusing employment to someone because he or she suffers from depression, has HIV/AIDS, or has a history of alcoholism would be discrimination based upon societal stereotypes, not the person's ability to perform a job. However, someone with myopia or hypertension is not covered by ADA because the condition is correctable (e.g., with eyeglasses and medication). If a person needs to use a seeing-eye dog, the owner of a restaurant cannot arbitrarily deny admittance to the dog and the patron who is blind. Similarly, if the venue is given ample notice, sign language interpreters must be provided at theaters and other public gatherings for people who cannot hear.

Court cases continually wrestle with the meaning of the word *disability.* In 1998, a golfer with a birth defect in his right leg, Casey Martin, was allowed to ride a golf cart instead of walking the course in tournament play. At the time, the Professional Golfers' Association thought that Mr. Martin would have an unfair advantage over other golfers, but the Supreme Court determined that a golf cart was a reasonable accommodation, since Casey Martin suffered from fatigue and walking the course would have been an additional burden for him. In May 2004, the Supreme Court allowed George Lane, a man in a wheelchair who was a defendant ordered to testify, and Beverly Jones, a court reporter with a mobility impairment, to sue the state of Tennessee for monetary damages since they needed to appear in a second-floor courtroom in a building without elevators. In this ruling, it was determined that there was a failure to provide people with disabilities access to the courts. Other cases concern seniority issues being honored (e.g., a person with a disability cannot take the job of a worker without a disability who has higher seniority), whether someone's health might be impacted by a certain job (e.g., working with chemicals if one has a preexisting medical condition), being granted testing accommodations at the graduate level, claiming too much noise interfered with passing a nursing exam for someone with a mental impairment, and whether someone who has chronic fatigue syndrome can adequately perform a job. Topics also include the possibility of granting indefinite periods of leave or open-ended schedules. Reasonable accommodations mean that with the accommodation in place the person is able to perform all of the job requirements. Safety is sometimes a mitigating factor; for example, someone who is blind cannot successfully claim discrimination because he or she is not hired as an airline pilot.

ADA enters school settings by guaranteeing that staff, parents, families, and students with disabilities have access to school plays, conferences, graduation ceremonies, and more. It translates to guaranteeing the same access to students with disabilities as peers without disabilities (e.g., a librarian assisting a student in a wheelchair so he or she has access to books on higher shelves or allowing a student who has cerebral palsy to be a cheerleader). There are no special education rules in ADA; however, it does have an impact on education. Overall, as a civil rights act, ADA protects persons with disabilities in the private sector and school settings by guaranteeing reasonable accommodations, services, aids, and policies as it works in alignment with other state and federal laws.

CIVIL RIGHTS FOR STUDENTS WITH DISABILITIES UNDER SECTION 504

Section 504 of the Rehabilitation Act of 1973 generally refers to adjustments in the general education classroom but can include other educational services as well. It states

> No otherwise qualified individual with a disability in the United States . . . shall, solely by reason of her or his disability, be excluded from the participation in, be denied the benefits of, or be subjected to discrimination under any program or activity receiving Federal financial assistance. (Quoted in Duncan & Ali, 2010, para. 2)

Public school districts, institutions of higher education, and other state and local education agencies are required to provide the protections found in Section 504. Both ADA and Section 504 are enforced by the Office for Civil Rights (OCR), while IDEA is enforced by the Office of Special Education and Rehabilitative Services (OSERS). Both are divisions of the U.S. Department of Education. ADA does not limit the rights or remedies available under Section 504. Students with IEPs may also have 504 plans, while students with 504 plans do not necessarily have IEPs.

For a person to be classified as having a disability, he or she must have a record of a physical or mental impairment that limits one or more major life activities and be regarded as having such an impairment. A life activity includes functions such as caring for oneself, performing manual tasks, walking, seeing, hearing, speaking, breathing, learning, and working, along with the additions in ADAAA (2008), which include eating, standing, sleeping, lifting, bending, reading, communicating, thinking, and concentrating. In addition, other life activities not included in 504 can also be protected. Trained personnel who have particular knowledge of the strengths, abilities, and unique needs of the students conduct the evaluation of students with disabilities to determine placements. The information is not solely based on one assessment and must assess the student's need, not the impairment. For example, a student with blindness cannot be asked to count the number of hands raised but would need to be given an alternate kinesthetic accommodation to test his or her ability to actually count, not his or her ability to see the hands. Placement decisions come from varying sources, including teacher recommendations along with aptitude and achievement tests, and they must take into account cultural, social, physical, and adaptive needs.

Like IDEA, Section 504 states that every effort must be made to educate students with their nondisabled peers if the academic and social needs can be met there. Appropriate education for a student with a disability might include placement in a general or special education class with or without supplementary services or related services. Specific recommendations must include strategies and delineate accommodations. Disability documentation needs to be provided, and necessary accommodations must be requested. Individuals who qualify for Section 504 protection can fall under any of the thirteen IDEA classifications or other classifications such as the following examples (this is not an exhaustive list):

ADHD

AIDS

Arthritis

Asthma

Cancer

Cerebral palsy

Diabetes

Emotional/psychiatric disability

Epilepsy

Hearing impairment/deafness

Learning disability

Visual impairment/blindness

Strategies, names of implementers, monitoring dates, and general comments are examples of elements included in 504 plans. If a student qualifies for services under IDEA, that student does not need both an IEP and a Section 504 plan. The reason is that one way to meet 504 requirements is to comply with IDEA. General education teachers must implement provisions of Section 504, or that district may be found to be noncompliant with the federal law. Again, the general education teacher needs to review the 504 plans of students to effectively implement appropriate educational services. School districts must properly identify and evaluate students with disabilities who need services, supplying an educational plan under Section 504, which is then protected by procedural safeguards. In this scenario, teachers also need proper instruction and preparation to meet an individual child's needs if that child has a 504 plan. Parents and guardians, building administrators, teachers, support staff, and the Section 504 coordinator are involved in developing the plan. The coordinator may be a principal, guidance counselor, special education director, supervisor, or another appointed qualified staff member. A 504 plan can simply include strategies like breaking down long-term projects into smaller sequential steps, sending home a duplicate set of texts, or maybe sitting a child nearer to the center of instruction (e.g., chalkboards or interactive whiteboards). It may also include training staff how to use an EpiPen (to inject emergency allergy medication) or allowing a child with diabetes more frequent breaks or access to unlimited water. Overall, health and learning plans are determined and outlined in 504 plans.

Section 504 laws apply to elementary, secondary, and postsecondary schools. Trained personnel who assess the needs, not the impairments, must conduct evaluations in order to determine placement. Placement decisions consider the maximum extent to which the student can be educated with his or her peers without disabilities. This may be accomplished with and without supplementary and related services but must be subject to periodic reevaluations. Parents and guardians are informed about all placement and evaluation actions and may examine their child's records. Students may not be denied access to any nonacademic activities, such as clubs, transportation, athletics, and counseling, based on their disability.

PAST, PRESENT, AND FUTURE CONCERNS

Special education was not always accepted in the larger school community. Before the passage of Public Law 94-142 (Education of the Handicapped Act) in 1975, students with disabilities did not receive the most appropriate services. After the act was passed, students were entitled to receive a free and appropriate public education designed to meet their unique needs. The result of this law was the development of specialized programs and services. However, nowhere does the law explain what "appropriate" means or use the word *inclusion.* Approximately 20 years later, it was discovered that these separate programs were actually excluding students with disabilities from exposure to the general education curriculum and not preparing them for successful community integration. IDEA (1997) advocated people-first language—looking at the student first and then the disability. After all, students should not be defined by what they cannot do; rather, their strengths should be highlighted. IDEIA (2004) includes responses to intervention as a part of the evaluation for identifying a student with a specific learning disability. RTI is not mandated but offered as an option, instead of solely using the discrepancy model, which involves revealing a discernible discrepancy between tested intelligence and school performance. Therefore, more accountability is now placed on the types of instruction, programs, and interventions offered. Yes, students have differences, but now classrooms must proactively offer appropriate interventions before automatically labeling a student. Sometimes it's the instruction, not the disability, that's the culprit in cases of lower performance.

Today's thrust is toward inclusion and improving student outcomes with appropriate interventions, but concerns exist. Debates between teachers and administrators occur on topics such as time for planning and collaboration, types of supports and assessments given, honoring the CCSS and IEPs, how to divide instructional time to provide equally for all groups of learners, behavioral concerns, assessment, and accountability issues. Often teachers are so overwhelmed by their busy days that they are unable to preplan, evaluate, and assess lessons with cooperating teachers. In the ideal world, common planning time should be allotted in both general and special education teachers' schedules, giving them the time to design and evaluate lessons. Consistent constructive review of both successful and unsuccessful teaching methodology is an integral inclusionary factor. Response to interventions has entered classrooms, but just who determines what constitutes an effective intervention and assessment is still an issue. The reliability and validity of programs require further determination.

Teachers are seldom unwilling to include students, but some lack the training or experience regarding what strategies, programs, or academic or behavioral scaffolding need to be provided so that they do not sacrifice any one group of learners. Specially designed instruction is imperative for students who have IEPs. Accountability for student performance raises the following question among teachers, students, parents, administrators, and learners:

"Does fair mean equal?" If students or families declare, "It is not fair," please share the following definition. A fair is a place where you go on rides and buy cotton candy—any questions?

Several studies (Mostert & Crockett, 2000; Norris & Schumacker, 1998; Skiba et al., 2008) revealed that, in the past, schools have disappointed former special education students with ineffective interventions. Research highlights that aligning the content standards with assessments and appropriate instruction results in higher learning outcomes for all students, with and without disabilities (Browder, 2006; Thurlow, 2003; Wiener, 2005).

Inclusion is a fabulous concept, but the pragmatics involved do not always result in its proper implementation. Inclusion has sometimes actually resulted in exclusion. Students with disabilities who are included in a general classroom are at times overwhelmed by the pace, complexity, and amount of work they are expected to do, and prior knowledge they are assumed to have. Special educators should be integral members of the larger school community, but this is often not the case. All students and educators possess the ability to make integral, productive contributions to the classroom. As delineated in Chapter 6 on collaboration, special education and general education teachers and related staff work as partners to instruct all students, with ability levels ranging from nonverbal students to those who are gifted, to ensure the individualization of programs and services in shared inclusive classrooms.

General education teachers want all students to succeed, but they need more direction and training on how to differentiate instruction without sacrificing any one group of students. Inclusion has sometimes dangerously erased direct skill instruction that was formerly given in separate classrooms. Public Law 94-142, the grandmother of IDEA, originally called the Education of All Handicapped Children Act and passed by Congress back in 1975, was designed to provide services to students whose academic needs were not being met in the general education classroom. Today, unless the dynamics of the general education classroom are changed, these academic, social, cognitive, and emotional needs will still not be met. RTI can and should be used to monitor progress and adjust interventions accordingly, yielding benefits for all learners who are struggling with the curricula, not just those learners who receive special education (Chambers, 2008). Interventions are offered in general education classrooms first, before students are assumed to require special education services. The thinking here is that perhaps it is the instruction that is the issue, rather than the student's disability. Many families, administrators, educators, related staff, and students have concerns and sometimes diverse desires, interpretations, and ways to think about both general and special education deliveries, services, and interventions.

Upcoming legislation will address the full funding of IDEA, since current funding is only 16 of the 40 percent promised in the IDEA Full Funding Act. This will assist with the recruitment and the retention of quality staff, according to Senator Harkin. The IDEA Fairness Act proposes for parents to receive reimbursement for expert witnesses and for tests or evaluations if parents prevail during due process hearings. Read more about both acts at www.help.senate.gov/newsroom/press/release/?id=49395c2f-ea55-4133-8556-827b2e521a62&groups=Chair. Other legislation on the horizon involves additional training for educators to recognize dyslexia, the need for more research, greater understanding of learning disabilities, and considering RTI under ESEA, instead of IDEA.

Somewhere in *edutopia*, a happy balance needs to be achieved with interventions to determine what kind, to what extent, how, where, and who will deliver the interventions. *Special education is headed in the right direction.* With more fine-tuning, this transitional stage will effectively ride the now turbulent waves. Education never worked well with a one-size-fits-all philosophy. Inclusion is a great idea if it is properly implemented but should not be considered the only option if the child's academic and social needs are not being met by placement in the general classroom. Accountability along with appropriate identifications, interventions, and funding is essential. Special education is an *evolutionary*, not a *revolutionary*, process. Significantly reducing the bureaucracy, paperwork, and litigiousness that too often spring from disagreements over implementation of the law; settling school discipline issues; figuring out how to continually and appropriately fund IDEA; and determining just which academic and behavioral interventions are appropriate ones are not simple issues.

At times, an abundance of paperwork has scared many teachers away from continuing in the field, since quite often the time required in order to comply with writing IEPs and data reports, attend meetings, and keep on top of changes in legislation is deducted from much-needed student instruction. In the attempt to "get it right," administrators, families, general and special education teachers, and all students can be frustrated by the sometimes confusing system, which makes it harder to focus on helping students with disabilities achieve academic and social success. Some of the revisions in IDEA (2004) address that (e.g., reducing the number of meetings, allowing revision consent by email, and combining meetings). Education is a complex issue for parents, guardians, teachers, administrators, all staff members, and children of all abilities. Further IDEA reauthorizations will hopefully continue to advocate ways to incorporate appropriate services for students with disabilities, honoring individual student levels and grade-level CCSS.

COMMON CORE STATE STANDARDS

Special education teachers in many states face further challenges as they try to balance and align the standards with students' IEPs and the Common Core State Standards. Educators feverishly think of ways that students with disabilities can achieve mastery or progress toward those standards. The curriculum is not diluted for any group of students but taught in subskills that reflect the standards in smaller, more palatable bites. Individual strategies, materials, and accommodations are geared toward achieving higher outcomes for all students.

Both GE and SE teachers require a greater knowledge of the CCSS and the strengths of students with disabilities who are now expected to achieve standards and outcomes. Ignoring improvements toward achievements is simply not an option for any group of students. However, bridging the gap between current levels and desired outcomes is imperative. Inclusion is marching onward, with everyone honoring abilities and ways to increase academic, behavioral, social, emotional, and functional levels in all domains.

The CCSS are implemented across the grade levels and disciplines for all students, including those students with special learning needs who often present a different set of skills and knowledge. The goal of the CCSS English language arts (ELA) standards is to prepare learners for reading, writing, and communication skills beyond their school years, to be college- and career-ready. There are anchor and grade-specific standards for reading, writing, speaking and listening, and language. The CCSS for reading include, but are not limited to, honing students' skills and knowledge to infer and reason, cite textual evidence, interpret words and phrases, and compare points of view in a range of literature, informational text, and diverse formats. The vast choices include short stories, novels, news articles, poems, myths, essays, plays, technical texts, historical documents, and digital sources from Grades K–12 for literature and informational text, including both the understanding and the evaluation of fiction and nonfiction genres. Beginning in Grade 6 and continuing to Grade 12, the reading and writing standards are divided into two sections: one for English classes and one that relates the literacy skills to history, social studies, science, and technical subjects. Specific standards are denoted for the content teachers of students in Grades 6–8, 9–10, and 11–12. Grades 6–12 literacy standards are integral parts of other content areas, beyond the exclusive focus of English classes. Therefore, reading and writing is a cross-disciplinary responsibility. As the CCSS site states, the reading standards in history, social studies, science, and technical subjects are intended to complement the specific content demands of the disciplines, not to replace them. This includes but is not limited to citing text to support reading and writing; analyzing primary and secondary documents; determining the meaning of symbols, phrases, diagrams, and data; and interpreting historical, scientific, and technical academic and domain-specific vocabulary. The writing standards invite students to compose pieces that include supportive evidence from texts to organize thoughts, revise writing, and reflect on writing across the disciplines.

In Grades K–8, domains organize the math standards, while Grades 9–12 are organized by conceptual categories. Each grade level builds on the standards in the earlier grades and expands prior student knowledge and skills with increasing proficiency. There are eight mathematical practices that represent the expertise that teachers must help their students develop, beginning in kindergarten and onward to 12th grade. These are practices and proficiencies that connect to specific grade-level content to help students solve math problems.

The following charts denote CCSS ELA and math codes, categories, and domains.

Codes	English Language Arts (CCSS.ELA)	
RF	*Reading foundational skills*	Print concepts and phonological awareness (K & Grade 1)
		Phonics and word recognition (Grades K–5)
		Fluency (Grades K–5)

Codes	English Language Arts (CCSS.ELA)	
RL	*Reading literature*	Key ideas and details (K–12) Craft and structure (K–12) Integration of knowledge and ideas (K–12) Range of reading and level of complexity (K–12)
RI	*Reading informational text*	Key ideas and details (K–12) Craft and structure (K–12) Integration of knowledge and ideas (K–12) Range of reading and level of complexity (K–12) *Standards for Literacy in History/Social Studies, Science, and Technical Subjects* in Grades K–5 are integrated in the reading while Grades 6–8, 9–10, and 11–12 are subject specific
W	*Writing*	Text types and purposes (K–12) Production and distribution of writing (K–12) Research to build and present knowledge (K–12) Range of writing (K–12) Integrated in specific subject areas in Grades 6–12
SL	*Speaking and listening*	Comprehension and collaboration (K–12) Presentation of knowledge and ideas (K–12)
L	*Language*	Conventions of standard English (K–12) Knowledge of language (begins in Grade 2) Vocabulary acquisition and use (K–12)

CCSS Mathematics		Grades
CC	Counting and cardinality	K
OA	Operations and algebraic thinking	K–5
NBT	Number and operations in base ten	K–5
NF	Number and operations in fractions	3–5
MD	Measurement and data	K–5
G	Geometry	K–12
RP	Ratios and proportional relationships	6–7
NS	Number systems	6–8
EE	Expressions and equations	6–8
F	Functions	8–12
SP	Statistics and probability	6–12

Math (Grades 9–12) high school standards include these categories and additional skills under each one.

Number and Quantity	Algebra	Functions	Modeling (connected to all categories)	Geometry	Statistics and Probability

NOTE: For a complete review with the exact language of the ELA and Math Common Core State Standards, consult www.corestandards.org. Review the appendices for a wealth of information.

Challenges arise when students with and without exceptionalities enter inclusive classrooms with different background knowledge, skills, motivation, and instructional experiences or successes. In addition, when the students progress to upper grades and the focus shifts from learning to read to reading to learn, problems may arise in finding the main ideas, supporting details, predictions, inferences, and summaries (Jitendra, Burgess, & Gajria, 2011).

The following vignettes offer CCSS scenarios across the grade levels for students with IDEA classifications.

ELA Decoding Goal

Using his knowledge of phonics and syllabication, Angel, a student with dyslexia, will decode two-syllable words that contain short and long vowel sounds and consonant blends, achieving eighty percent accuracy on running grades and quizzes each week, for twelve consecutive weeks. Angel will practice these skills at home (*partners IEP and CCSS goals with the family to strengthen and value reading skills in both environments*).

Math Problem Solving Goal

By the end of the school year, Brittany, a student with a learning disability, will solve one-digit multiplication problems and identify the correlating division facts with eighty-five-percent accuracy on curriculum-based quizzes and tests. Brittany will record her progress (*establishes student metacognition*) and be offered positive, realistic, and consistent feedback.

Reading—Literature and Informational Standards

Isabella, a girl with an intellectual disability, will make predictions and inferences by identifying details and text examples to achieve eighty percent accuracy on oral and written questions related to nonfiction text at her instructional level at the end of sixteen weeks of direct explicit instruction within a small-group setting. Isabella will require a trained peer to work with her three times a week to reread the text to highlight and color-code the appropriate details and to connect those details to specific narration (*modeling of skills, cooperative learning, repetition, reinforcement, peer mentoring, increased social and communication skills*). Isabella will also be offered high-interest, low-level text and text-to-speech options.

Dylan, a student with autism, will make predictions and inferences by identifying details and text examples with eighty-five percent accuracy at the end of twelve weeks of explicit reading, comprehension instruction. Dylan will also require weekly consultation or collaboration with behavioral, occupational, and speech-language therapists, a visual schedule, increased verbal prompts, and social stories to ensure task completion.

ELA Writing Goal

Jacob, a student with emotional disturbance, will produce clear and coherent writing in which the development, organization, and style are appropriate to the task, purpose, and audience. Jacob will receive two forty-minute counseling sessions with the school psychologist each week. Jacob will use organizational writing frames as planners (*offers a writing road map to structure and sequence his thoughts*). Positive reinforcement for efforts as well as achievements will be offered (*increases student motivation*). Weekly personal writing conferences will be scheduled with the teacher (*proactive ongoing communication*).

SOURCE: Adapted from Karten (2014a, 2014b, 2014c).

The Dynamic Learning Maps Essential Elements offers statements of knowledge and skills linked to the grade-level academic expectations identified in the Common Core State Standards for students with the most significant cognitive disabilities. These essential elements can be accessed at dynamiclearningmaps.org/content/essential-elements.

The educational goals of students with disabilities are just as valid as those of other students. High expectations of the CCSS need to be developed for all students in the classroom, but without proper supports, children and teachers can become lost and frustrated by the system. Sometimes, wonderfully conducted research offering promising techniques seems difficult or impossible to pragmatically translate into classrooms composed of students with mixed abilities. However, keep in mind that the ultimate goal is successful outcomes for all.

COOPERATIVE LEGISLATIVE REVIEW

Directions: As a review of these readings, choose either Option 1 or Option 2.

Option 1: Cooperatively answer six of the following ten questions on a separate piece of paper. Circle the question numbers you will be answering. Each person should write down the answers (true cooperative learning).

Option 2: If your group has access to online sites, cooperatively divide and answer all five questions by visiting the legislative sites listed below. Then, share your responses.

Rationale for collaborative options: Choosing questions or assignments to answer or complete empowers learners. Questions are teacher-guided, but students gain some control and responsibility as self-regulated learners. Within your classrooms, these types of choices can be offered from early grades onward to continually develop and foster independent learning and increased student responsibility. In addition, completing assignments collaboratively fosters interpersonal and team skills.

Option 1

1. Describe three laws that protect persons with disabilities.
2. Relate a Common Core State Standard to a student who has one of the thirteen IDEA categories.
3. Who can benefit from a 504 plan?
4. Think of a disability scenario that falls under the protections of the ADA.
5. Compare and contrast the benefits and pitfalls of inclusion.
6. If you could amend any of the laws, what changes would you make?
7. Where do you see special education going in the next 10 years?
8. Explain how children with disabilities can benefit from inclusion.
9. How can general education teachers influence a child's classroom success?
10. Do you think special education is going in the right direction? Support your response with current research.

Option 2: Legislative Web Quest

1. Identify and briefly describe three major disability laws that affect students in school settings.
2. Share how you plan to connect IEP elements to the CCSS.
3. Briefly describe two court cases and their implications for inclusive environments. Twenty choices are listed below.
4. Identify the elements listed in a student's transitional plan.
5. What rights do families have in formulating IEP documents?

Use these websites for your responses: www.wrightslaw.com, www.cec.sped.org, IDEA.ed.gov, www.ada.gov, and hhs.gov/ocr/civilrights/resources/factsheets/504.pdf.

Court Cases	Main Concepts
1. *Pennsylvania Association for Retarded Children v. Commonwealth of Pennsylvania*, 1972	Students with disabilities are not excluded from appropriate educational opportunities
2. *Mills v. Board of Education of the District of Columbia*, 1972	Need to provide whatever specialized instruction will benefit the child, with due process and periodic review (precursor of IDEA)
3. *Board of Education of the Hendrick Hudson Central School District v. Rowley*, 1982	FAPE (Free Appropriate Public Education)
4. *Brookhart v. Illinois State Board of Education*, 1983	Passing state tests to receive high school diplomas
5. *School Board of Nassau County, Florida v. Arline*, 1987	Defenses under 504—reasonable accommodations
6. *Honig v. Doe*, 1988	Suspension and expulsion
7. *Timothy W. v. Rochester, New Hampshire School District*, 1989	Proof of benefit not required; there is zero reject
8. *Sacramento City Unified School District, Board of Education v. Rachel H.*, 1994	LRE—educational and nonacademic benefits weigh in as well (e.g., social, communication)
9. *Gadsby v. Grasmick*, 1997	States to ensure compliance with IDEA
10. *Sutton v. United Airlines, Inc.*, 1999	Disability defined with corrective devices
11. *Cedar Rapids v. Garret F.*, 1999	Related services
12. *Toyota Motor Manufacturing, Kentucky, Inc. v. Williams*, 2002	Substantial limitation in major life activity under ADA
13. *AW ex rel. Wilson v. Fairfax County School Board*, 2004	Manifestation determination—Did the disability impact the student's ability to control the behavior?
14. *Schaffer ex rel. Schaffer v. Weast*, 2005	Burden of proof in a due process hearing on party seeking relief
15. *Arlington Central School District Board of Education v. Murphy*, 2006	Entitles parents to recover fees paid to expert witnesses if they prevail
16. *Winkelman v. Parma City School District*, 2007	A parent acting as his or her child's lawyer in IDEA actions but is not a licensed attorney
17. *Board of Education of City of New York v. Tom F.*, 2007	Reimbursement for private education if student was not enrolled in public school
18. *Forest Grove School District v. T. A.*, 2009	Reimbursement for private special education services when a public school fails to provide FAPE
19. *Doug C. v. Hawaii*, 2013	Validated the procedural requirement of parental attendance at an IEP meeting
20. *Brown v. Board of Education*, 1954	Separate education facilities are inherently unequal; ended legal segregation in public schools.

IMPLICATIONS OF THE ELEMENTARY AND SECONDARY EDUCATION ACT

Let me begin this section with a few questions before we delve into the meaty implications of the Elementary and Secondary Education Act (ESEA). When George W. Bush reauthorized ESEA as No Child Left Behind (NCLB) at the turn of the millennium, panic permeated throughout school districts, with teachers asking questions such as

If my students do not perform well on the standardized tests, will I be fired?

Decades later, teachers ask questions such as

How will my students with disabilities achieve the grade-level standards?

In the future, teachers may ask,

Whatever happened to the good old days when we had time for things other than tests, such as fun learning activities?

Now let's review the history of the Elementary and Secondary Education Act of 1965. In the years 2001 to 2002, ESEA was updated as NCLB and signed into law by President George W. Bush, with the intention that it would provide a better education for all children. Schools would be held more accountable for results. In addition, methods of teaching and teacher qualifications would be more heavily scrutinized. Focus was on improving the academic achievement of all students, allowing everyone access to future progress and lifelong achievements, including those from the highest- to the lowest-income schools. The expanded definition includes the application of rigorous, systematic, and objective procedures to obtain reliable and valid knowledge relevant to educational activities and programs (in the amended Section 9101-37 of ESEA). This includes rigorous data analysis with multiple measurements, observations, controls, and designs. Peer-reviewed academic journals are valued over educator magazines or practitioner journals. Children with disabilities are included in district testing, allowing for a small percentage of students with more significant cognitive impairments to receive alternative assessments.

As this book is going to press, the ESEA and IDEA are due for reauthorization. The Consortium for Citizens with Disabilities (CCD) offers the following recommendations for the reauthorization of the ESEA:

1. All students are considered general education students, with an integration of ESEA, IDEA, and Section 504 of the Rehabilitative Act to ensure that students with disabilities receive a free and appropriate public education. *Note:* Educational decisions will be affected if RTI is under IDEA or ESEA domains.
2. Students are prepared to leave high school either college or career ready.
3. Both general and special education teachers are highly qualified to identify student needs and appropriately deploy evidence-based practices to

teach and assess grade-level content and diverse learners. This includes but is not limited to academic, social, emotional, and behavioral factors, with universal design for learning (UDL) honored for instruction and assessments.

4. Learners who struggle are identified and serviced with appropriate instruction and interventions.
5. If a growth model is utilized, students of all levels are included, with expectations held high for all students.
6. Individual education programs are agreements that list the specific skills, services, and supports that students receive while the ESEA assessments provide academic accountability.
7. Meaningful family engagement empowers families to be advocates for their child with the appropriate tools, training, and technical assistance provided to allow them to make informed and appropriate contributions.
8. Both IDEA and ESEA require funding that provides public schools with the necessary resources to meet the needs of all students.

SOURCE: Consortium for Citizens With Disabilities (2010).

The Time for Innovation Matters in Education Act (TIME) advocates grants to promote school reforms with rigorous learning in core subjects, enrichment, and increased time for teacher planning. Proponents want increased learning time (ILT) for disadvantaged students in low-performing, high-poverty schools that may be receiving supplemental educational services (SES) from outside and private agencies to create high-quality extended learning time (ELT) within the same school district. There is a strong intention to increase positive school experiences of students within their communities. This increase of nontraditional school hours is intended to benefit disadvantaged students who need more support.

Hopefully, all students with disabilities will continually be offered a free appropriate public education in their least restrictive environment with the correct level of scaffolding to increase performance levels. The bar needs to be continually raised for students of all ability levels.

Investigate further by visiting www.timeandlearning.org/time-innovation-matters-education-act, www.ed.gov/nclb/landing.jhtml, and www.copaa.org/?page=ESEA.

Now, back to those original questions and some answers:

If my students do not perform well on the standardized tests, will I be fired?

No, but the types of programs, instructional strategies, and accommodations and the frequency, duration, and location of interventions, assessments, and evaluations will be reviewed and revised to determine just why the learning gaps exist. The focus needs to be on how to better deliver targeted curriculum standards—not pointing fingers but promoting remediation.

How will my students with disabilities achieve the grade-level standards?

It's about increasing the outcomes for students with disabilities. Value what benchmark tests reveal in terms of instruction and curricular focus. Increase formative assessments to guide instruction rather than valuing only summative evaluations. Benchmark tests reveal the effectiveness of strategies and interventions, with students' responses telling administration and staff what standards need to be addressed, along with the resources and deliveries that require fine-tuning.

Whatever happened to the good old days when we had time for things other than tests, such as fun learning activities?

With creativity, perseverance, and diligence regarding the curriculum standards, teachers will realize that assessments do not replace fun but accompany tangible learning results. The distribution of time to concentrate on learning does not translate to the deletion of other activities but must correlate with the standards and all subjects. Then the message is transmitted to students that learning is fun and not just about the test! Accountability is crucial but can be accomplished only if it accompanies higher student motivation.

Accountability Questions to Ponder

- How is increased accountability for students with disabilities a step in the right direction?
- What is the impact of the reauthorization of ESEA on individual students who come from different ability groups?
- How will a revised ESEA affect IDEA's current provisions?
- What impact will sanctions have on schools that serve students with disabilities?
- Will teachers teach to the test, or can all subjects be equally balanced?
- What will the educational picture look like in the next few decades?

(Answers can and will vary.)

TRANSLATING RESEARCH INTO LEARNING STRATEGIES THAT WORK

Research and Professional Literature Says the Following:

- Structured, well-delivered, research-based interventions positively influence student performance within inclusive environments, honoring high expectations and best practices for all students (Beattie, Jordan, & Algozzine, 2006; Damasio, 2003; Karten, 2007d; LeDoux, 2002; McNary, Glasgow, & Hicks, 2005; Sousa, 2007).

- Successful quality inclusion programs involve team approaches with collaborative efforts from schools and families, allowing for flexibility to perceive when something works well and adaptation to change it when it does not work (Willis, 2009; Karten, 2014c).

- Inclusion generally uses five methods to help students succeed in a general education classroom. These five methods include

  1. collaborative consultation,
  2. cooperative teaching and other team arrangements,
  3. curricula and instructional strategies,
  4. accommodations and adaptations, and
  5. training general education teachers to accommodate diversity (Hallahan, Kauffman, & Pullen, 2012).

- Social skills do not come naturally to students with autism and must be directly taught if they are going to be mastered (e.g., what to explicitly do and say in each situation) (Baker, 2005).

- The stages of backward design—or *understanding by design* (UbD)—involve identifying the desired results first, determining acceptable evidence, and then planning experiences and instruction accordingly. This includes the acquisition of important information and skills, making meaning of the content, and then effectively transferring that learning beyond the school (Wiggins & McTighe, 2005).

- Teachers must understand the role of culture in human development and schooling in order to make good decisions about classroom management and organization (Rothstein-Fisch & Trumbull, 2008).

- "A teacher can be ten times more effective by incorporating visual information into a classroom discussion. . . . Our brains have more receptors to process the images coming in than the words we hear" (Burmark, quoted in Association for Supervision and Curriculum Development [ASCD], 2002).

- Teachers need to present new information in smaller chunks and offer strategic stopping points for demonstration, descriptions, summarization, discussion, and predictions. Teachers also need to take steps to establish and communicate learning goals and track student progress as they interact with that new knowledge (Marzano, 2007).

- "Students need to know that they're accepted. I had one student with a learning disability; everyone told him what was wrong with him, but no one tried to help him realize what was good in him" (Tomlinson, quoted in ASCD, 2002).

- "Students need multiple opportunities to meet standards, and those opportunities should include differentiated instruction, accommodations and modifications, and opportunities for advanced learners" (Harris, quoted in ASCD, 2002).

- Teacher efficacy (thinking that you will influence students' successes), collaborative relationships, mentoring/advocacy, and community building are essential components of inclusive classrooms (Cramer, 2006).

- The people who work in the school building (e.g., principal, assistant principals, educators, instructional assistants, and all staff) along with the students' families are the actual inclusive experts who know the students the best (Hammeken, 2007).

- Schools that do not have forward-thinking programs for students with special needs are usually the ones with families who are not advocates for their children (Tramer, 2007).

- The absence of interventions in the early school years has a negative impact on the academic, emotional, social, and behavioral growth of students with reading and behavior disorders (Levy & Chard, 2001; Raver, 2003; Trout, Epstein, Nelson, Synhorst, & Hurley, 2006).

- Universal design of curriculum and instruction offers learning alternatives to students with and without disabilities and provides a framework for both creating and implementing lessons that value flexible goals, methods, and assessments (Pisha & Stahl, 2005). (For more information, visit the Center for Applied Special Technology website at www.cast.org.)

- Discussion, communication, connection, and learning in context helps learners in inclusive classrooms develop better literacy and numeracy competencies along with higher cognitive skills (Chorzempa & Lapidua, 2009; Graham & Harris, 2005; Hyde, 2007; Karten, 2009; Steen, 2007).

- "The public wants schools to hold kids accountable, but they also want schools to recognize that kids are kids" (Johnson, 2003, p. 37).

- Co-teachers who work together in inclusive classrooms collaboratively improve student outcomes with the mastery of the curriculum standards and emotional growth (Friend & Cook, 2003; Karten, 2007d; Nevin, Cramer, Voigt, & Salazar, 2008).

- In many schools, there is a lack of communication after the writing of the IEP and little if any communication or support from the special education teacher for the regular education teacher (Costley, 2013)

- Learning that is associated with students' interests and experiences is more likely to be retrieved from students' prior knowledge (Allsopp et al., 2008a; Karten, 2007d, 2008a, 2009).

- "Having opportunities to make choices in academic tasks can provide the environmental predictability needed to minimize inappropriate behaviors of students, while strengthening appropriate responses and increased levels of engagement. . . . For students with EBD [emotional behavioral disability], predictability and control may be critical concepts and skills that are necessary for appropriately coping with the environment" (Jolivette, Stichter, & McCormick, 2002, p. 24).

- Research-based instruction yields information on how children learn and how teachers need to teach with continual screening of essential skills, early interventions, progress monitoring, and data-driven decisions (Russo, Tiegerman, & Radziewicz, 2008).

- Students with special needs require academic and social support with effective accommodations, modifications, and guidance to achieve educational and emotional gains in inclusive settings—for example, differentiation of instruction that honors individual student strengths, needs, and potentials (Beattie et al., 2006; Karten, 2014c; Littky, 2004; McKinley & Stormont, 2008; Salend, 2005; Tomlinson, 2008).

MY PRAGMATIC RESEARCH INVESTIGATION

My research says . . .
Source:

Available for download at **www.corwin.com/inclusionstrategies**

INCLUSION AND THE STUDENT WITH DIS*ABILITIES*

When *inclusion* replaced the word *mainstreaming*, many teachers and professionals embraced the idea while others thought if they resisted it enough, it might go away. Mainstreaming had students included in classrooms for subjects they were more prepared for. Inclusion says, Let's include the students and provide the supports that will make it work. There are no guidelines, but listed on the next page are several ways students, teachers, and peers can fit in. As the book progresses, all of these will be delineated further, with specific curriculum classroom applications.

ACTIVITY: EIGHTEEN INCLUSIVE PRINCIPLES

Each person puts his or her name on an index card or Popsicle stick that is then randomly pulled from a hat, can, or jar to reveal the numbered inclusion ideas listed below. Each number on the list can also be clapped to focus attention, thereby adding a musical/rhythmic component. This procedure establishes equity in the classroom and stops the "ooh-ooh" child from volunteering to read everything or answering all of the questions. It also wakes up sleepers. In the classroom, sensitivity and variation can be used to help students with reading difficulties. For example, have students with and without reading difficulties select the Popsicle sticks to be part of the activity. Instead of determining who reads, intermittently ask some students to paraphrase statements, so they are not embarrassed by reading words that are too difficult in front of the class. Always mix it up by asking the best readers in the class to do nonreading activities as well.

(Continued)

(Continued)

Eighteen Inclusive Principles

1. Ask for help.
2. Differentiate content (what you are teaching) from process (how you teach—delivery and strategies).
3. Work with specialists as a team to modify and adapt the curriculum to meet the special needs of students while allowing for flexibility in scheduling.
4. Teach students how to learn by offering lessons in study skills along with the curriculum.
5. Get the whole class involved so that everyone is working together to help each other by establishing a team mentality.
6. Use cooperative learning and let peers work together to develop friendships.
7. Know when to change course.
8. Increase your own dis*ability* awareness.
9. Be aware of the physical classroom setup.
10. Provide directions in written form for children with auditory problems and in verbal form for those with visual difficulties.
11. Teach to strengths while avoiding weaknesses to minimize frustrations (e.g., honor students' favored intelligences after informal inventories).
12. Help students by giving them methods for organizing their written work.
13. Collect files containing additional higher-level materials and activities for students who require more challenges.
14. Allow students to work on various assigned tasks.
15. Be aware of multiple intelligences.
16. Value opinions of families and community.
17. Model appropriate behavior.
18. *Believe in yourself and your students!*

Available for download at **www.corwin.com/inclusionstrategies**

INCLUSION IS . . . ACROSTIC

Directions for Inclusion Acrostic Activity: Write a word that describes inclusion next to each letter below. You can use whatever words you desire, but a suggestion for one of the Ns is the word *naturally*. Hopefully, including others can become something automatic and natural—a way of life.

Acrostic writing is sometimes used to focus thoughts and enhance creativity.

I

N

C

L

U

S

I

O

N . . . ATURALLY

Available for download at **www.corwin.com/inclusionstrategies**

Success Stories

Whatever happened to that kid? Remember the one who wouldn't sit still in class and kept jumping around from activity to activity without completing the specified requirements? Well, that child grew up and became a dancer who loves to express herself through body movements. Or that child might be a CEO who supervises others, multitasking and delegating the details to subordinates. Whatever happened to that child who doodled all day in class? Well, that child may now be a renowned architect or engineer who just designed an incredible building or new prototype for an ingenious car. Maybe the fidgety child who could never sit still learned to work with his hands, create sculpture, be a chef, or even work as a sign language interpreter. Maybe the child who had trouble making friends is now a guidance counselor or child psychologist. Maybe the child who has Down syndrome is now gainfully employed and has learned to live independently. Maybe the child who couldn't stop talking is now a lawyer or a journalist. What about the child who could barely read at grade level? Well, that child may now love e-books and has figured out how to decipher the written word by using different learning strategies. That child also may have gone on to college. Sure, the child might have needed a remedial reading and writing course, but with strong perseverance and support from friends, educators, and family, that child may never give up on her goals. That child may have graduated with a college diploma and is now gainfully employed. Maybe that child never went to college but is now taking adult education courses to learn more. Maybe that child learned a trade and is now a whiz with computers. Or maybe that child is an electrician or a plumber. Maybe that child learned to focus on her strengths and abilities. Maybe that child was helped by a teacher who successfully found a way to include her in the classroom. Maybe that child was included in society, not because it was the law but because it was the right thing to do. Legislation and research support inclusion, but educators are the ones who must support the child by turning the rhetoric into successful classroom practice.

2

Understanding Complicated Special Education Terminology and the Effects of Labels

The purpose of this chapter is to investigate the special education (SE) terminology and how others view and treat people with disabilities. Through the years, children and adults with disabilities have had to overcome the "handicapping" attitudes of society. Varying societal acceptance of differences can either thwart or foster academic and social development. This chapter offers more knowledge about special education labels and gives practical activities that teachers can use to help themselves and others to better view people with exceptionalities as valuable individuals. Experiential activities to increase understanding of learning, sensory, emotional, and physical differences are included, along with ample reflections for both staff and students. Overall, those with disabilities should be treated as people first; thereby, the student is not defined by what he or she cannot do but by his or her strengths and potential.

DIS*ABILITY* INTROSPECTION

Before we begin our DA (dis*ability* awareness) journey, it is vital to continually emphasize the importance of introspection for staff, families, and students. *Self-awareness and accurate reflections are incredibly effective catalysts to personal, social, academic, and cognitive growth.* You need to know where you've been before you can continue onward. Including students in classrooms means understanding them as well.

Defining Normal

> Moral or question for discussion: "Who or what defines the word *normal*?"

Some of *Merriam-Webster's* synonyms for *normal* include words such as *conformity, standard, average, typical, regular,* and *usual.* The origin of *normal* is actually a carpenter's square for measuring right angles. Later on, we'll discover some "right angles" teachers can use to help students learn.

NORMAL JOURNAL ENTRY

Describe a normal teacher interacting with a normal child. Please note that interpretations of this assignment will vary depending on individual definitions of the word *normal.*

What Exactly Is Normal?

Normal food ________________________________

Weird food ________________________________

Normal clothes ________________________________

Weird clothes ________________________________

Normal book ________________________________

Weird book ________________________________

Normal movie ________________________________

Weird movie ________________________________

Normal music ________________________________

Weird music ________________________________

Normal hobby ________________________________

Weird hobby ________________________________

Normal teaching ________________________________

Available for download at **www.corwin.com/inclusionstrategies**

BEING TREATED DIFFERENTLY

Spinach Helped Popeye: How It Feels to Be Special

A waitperson who served spinach to a child would most likely be greeted with a grimace as opposed to a smile. If the spinach was replaced with ice cream, then the scenario would be quite different. Even though the child may never have tasted spinach, the reaction will likely be strongly negative.

Attitudes toward people with disabilities are a little like spinach—strong and sometimes based on misunderstandings.

> People need to know how it feels to be *special* and how being treated differently can lead to attitudinal barriers and the internalization of negativity.

No matter how great one's self-worth, individuals are constantly influenced by how others perceive and act toward them. Some members of society fear diversity or think it might rub off on them or their children. Society is not born in an instant but influenced by various materials such as movies, books, and magazines that frequently portray "perfect people" in a "perfect world." Sometimes one must gradually acquire a taste for spinach in order to fully appreciate it. Didn't it make Popeye strong? The following questions have no answer key, but consider how you would respond.

DISABILITY REFLECTIONS

1. Is physical beauty important in our culture?
2. Do young children think disabilities can be cured?
3. How do the media portray people with disabilities?
4. Do adults and children feel uncomfortable around someone with a disability?
5. Do attitudes toward those with disabilities need improvement?

Available for download at **www.corwin.com/inclusionstrategies**

> **Moral:** Even though someone with a disability forgets about it, others remind him or her through sometimes careless, unintentional remarks and unwelcoming stares. It's often not just the words themselves but the manner of delivery that can be hurtful. People with a disability can be aware of not only their disability but the associated stigma as well. Attitudes toward children in inclusive settings are no exception.

In Vogue: Wind-Blown Education—Negative Connotations of Words

There are many trends within the field of education. As the wind blows in, a new term is created and then often thrust upon classroom teachers. Thank goodness we have come a long way from the early 1900s when "ugly laws" did not allow people who were considered deformed in some way (e.g., a person with a physical disfigurement) to be seen in public lest they be fined. No one today would argue that those "prettier people" who made and enforced the laws were truly the ugly ones! Society evolves, and positive changes result. Special education, in particular, undergoes continual changes. After many years, the use of certain words is no longer in vogue or fashionable since eventually they develop negative connotations. The names of classifications, syndromes, disorders, and existing strategies are constantly being altered. Perhaps as this book is revised, the names will again change, but the following describes former and present *special* terminology.

The list of names arising out of differing schools of thought and trends will continually grow. Outdated special education terminology, no longer in vogue, follows. Think of other more positive terms you can replace them with before using words such as these.

moron	imbecile	crippled
idiot	handicapped	victim
retard	mongoloid	afflicted

Moral: Some of the names have been changed to protect the innocent.

Trends in the field of special education include new classifications with an educational pendulum that is continually shifting back and forth. The word *handicapped* has been replaced with words such as *impaired* and *disabled,* and *retarded* with the terms *cognitive, developmental, or intellectual disability.* Some thought the word *handicapped,* derived from "cap in hand," as in someone who begs, was derogatory, and it has dropped out of common use. Even The Arc (formerly the Association for Retarded Citizens) kept its acronym due to familiarity, but it does not want to be associated with the word *retarded.* The public seems to catch on to these words as the terms change. *Retarded* at one time just meant slow, but now it has a negative connotation. Even the word *special* can be condescending when used to describe someone with a disability.

A revised fifth edition of the *Diagnostic and Statistical Manual of Mental Disorders* (DSM-5) (American Psychiatric Association, 2013), which contains descriptions, symptoms, coding, common language, and criteria for health professionals, clinicians, researchers, and other related providers to diagnose mental disorders, offered several changes to the names and classifications of many disorders. The DSM-5 has revisions in criteria and coding, using a dimensional system that includes levels of functioning (LOF) as mild, moderate, or severe. There is a disorder section known as neurodevelopmental disorders, which includes intellectual disabilities, communication disorders, autism spectrum disorder, attention deficit hyperactivity disorder (ADHD), specific learning disorders, and motor disorders (including tic disorders). An intellectual disability (formerly known as *mental retardation*) has three domains—conceptual, social, and practical—that impact how individuals cope with everyday tasks. The conceptual domain involves academic skills such as reading, writing, math, memory, and reasoning. Social judgments, empathy, and friendships are included in the social domain, while self-management, personal care, responsibility on the job, organizing school tasks, managing money, and other self-help skills are included under the practical domain. Global developmental delay serves as a temporary diagnosis for those under age five if all three domains are not established at that age. Under the communication subsection of neurodevelopmental disorders, expressive and mixed receptive-expressive are now listed under language, while social (pragmatic) communication excludes autism spectrum if there are restricted/repetitive behaviors/interests/activities. Autism spectrum disorder has subsumed the pervasive developmental disorder (PDD) section from DSM-IV, including autism and Asperger's. Obsessive-compulsive disorder was removed from the section on anxiety disorders and given its own chapter, while disruptive impulse control and conduct disorders (e.g., oppositional defiant disorder [ODD], intermittent explosive disorder [IED], conduct disorder [CD], antisocial personality disorder, pyromania, kleptomania) were expanded. ADHD was broadened to include symptoms documented prior to age twelve instead of age seven. There is also a new section grouping similar disorders, ODD and IED. In addition, dyslexia and dyscalculia are acknowledged as valid terms in DSM-5. The mixed episode for bipolar and related disorders was replaced with mixed specifier and more clear descriptors. Depressive disorders include disruptive mood dysregulation (DMDD) to capture those children who do not meet the mania descriptor.

There is also consideration for overlapping characteristics, as sometimes a fine line separates one disorder or label from another. Comorbidity—the co-occurrence of one or more conditions in the same individual—is common for students with emotional and behavioral disorder (Hallahan, Kauffman, & Pullen, 2012). As an example, ADHD and conduct disorder can coexist with depressive disorders in DSM-5. Comorbidity exists for many other disorders/labels as well. Tourette syndrome is often connected to ADHD and obsessive-compulsive disorder. Benn Foss (2013), author of the *Dyslexia Empowerment Plan*, states how people in "the Nation of Dyslexia" carry a passport that allows easy entry into the bordering countries of "the Nations of Dyscalculia, Dysgraphia, and ADHD." Of course, as with all disabilities, it is essential to remember that a disability never mirrors an individual even if one or more disability characteristics or labels are shared.

MERITS OF INDIVIDUALITY

People-first language emphasizes that the child, not the disability, is the focus. For example, rather than saying "the autistic kid," it's preferable to say "the child with autism." The difference might seem merely semantic, but the key point is that the disability should not scream at you. It is only one component of a person's makeup.

The next exercises emphasize the importance of individuality, not labels.

WE'RE ALL INDIVIDUALS: PLOTTING STRENGTHS AND WEAKNESSES

Directions: Rate your personal strengths and weaknesses on this graph (with 10 being the highest), and then connect the dots to form your profile.

10						
9						
8						
7						
6						
5						
4						
3						
2						
1						
	Singing	Writing	Spelling	Dancing	Being a Friend	Drawing

Available for download at **www.corwin.com/inclusionstrategies**

Physically Seeing That Differences Exist

To further understand this concept, move to stations by posted signs in the room numbered 1 to 8. Continue movement to different stations, noting one another's similarities and differences. Descriptors can be varied to match the interests of learners in Grades K–12.

Station #1
Anyone who loves chocolate

Station #2
Anyone who is great at Sudoku

Station #3
Person who easily remembers directions

Station #4
Anyone who has glasses or contacts to see better

Station #5
People who speak two or more languages

Station #6
Anyone who is part of a book club

Station #7
Someone who has a pet

Station #8
Anyone for whom three or more descriptors fit

Moral: We're all different!

DIS*ABILITY* AWARENESS CLASSROOM SUGGESTIONS

1. Develop positive and sensitive attitudes about all students.
2. Understand that there are different types of disabilities, including:
   - *Visible*—someone using a wheelchair, sign language, hearing aids, or looking different in physical appearance
   - *Hidden*—someone with a learning disability, emotional difficulties, epilepsy, a heart condition, asthma, diabetes, sickle-cell anemia, or another disability not easily seen by looking at the person
3. Focus on what individuals *can* do instead of the disability alone. Be aware that people and the environment itself can transform a disability into a handicap.
4. Emphasize that a disability might mean that some students *learn and see things differently*.
5. Use *people-first language*: "I know someone who has difficulty with _____" (seeing, hearing, learning, walking). Do not say "the ADHD kid" or "the blind girl" since the disability should not define the person.
6. People with disabilities like to be *accepted and included by their peers*, such as receiving a birthday or holiday party invite or even going shopping together.
7. Contact family and individual disability organizations to provide more information about particular disabilities. Invite guest speakers when appropriate.
8. Do not assume that people with a disability cannot do something. *Let them be the judge of their own capabilities.* Ask first.
9. Don't be afraid to be yourself. *Treat someone with a disability with the same respect that you would want.* You can be friends with someone with a disability if you like the person, not because you feel you have to just because the person has a disability.
10. You can ask someone about his or her disability, but it is the person's choice to talk about it or not.

Available for download at **www.corwin.com/inclusionstrategies**

What I Need to Know About Dis*abilities*

(Use the following list with your younger students.)

- Everyone has differences.
- We should treat someone with a disability the same way we would like to be treated.

- Don't be afraid to be yourself!
- You can be friends with someone with a disability if you like the person, not because you feel you have to just because the person has a disability. Pity helps no one!
- People and places can be the handicaps for someone with a disability.
- Our kind attitudes will make a difference!
- Disabilities do not define people. The disability is just a small part of the whole person, like a petal on a flower.
- Focus on strengths, what people can do, their abilities!

Available for download at **www.corwin.com/inclusionstrategies**

LEARNING FLOWERS: CLASSROOM GARDEN

Directions: Create your own *special* flower with unique characteristics, including *positive* statements about students with differences, or personalize your flower to tell something about yourself. Samples are shown below. Collectively, the flowers compose a garden, just like children who can bloom all year. Remember that each flower represents a complex person, and if the person has a disability, it is only one petal of the entire flower. With the right strategies planted, inclusive education can bring sunshine and growth to all.

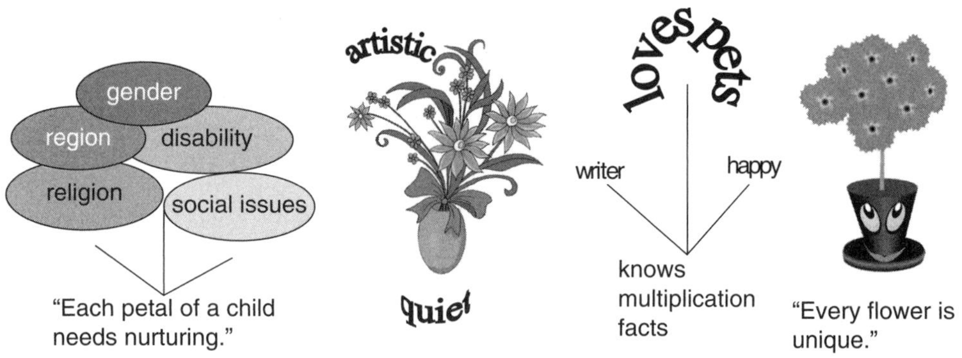

My Flower:

Available for download at **www.corwin.com/inclusionstrategies**

Simulated Activities

(Always place safety issues foremost in importance and exercise reason regarding which activities best suit the maturity levels of your students.) The Native American expression, "You can better understand what someone is saying by walking a mile in his or her moccasins," explains the purpose of these activities. Additional knowledge can also be gained from individual disability organizations and government agencies.

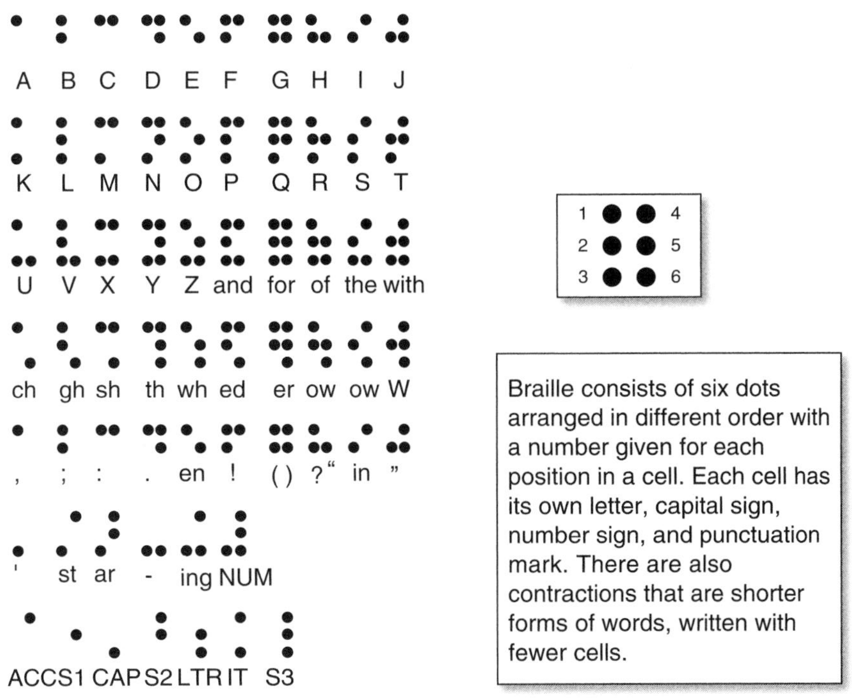

SOURCE: Copyright © 2000, John J. G. Savard. Used by permission.

Visual Needs

- Students can learn the Braille alphabet, feeling the textures of cells.
- Blindfold selected seated children in class while they are using the chalkboard.
- Use a six-tray muffin pan with tennis balls inserted as one kinesthetic way to copy the Braille alphabet, or use an egg carton cut in half.
- Write words to a poem in a tiny font, *such as this*, to distort the words.
- Ask students to close their eyes while seated at an assembly or in the lunchroom.
- Purchase magnification pages and games for your classroom, such as tactile checkers, low-vision or Braille Monopoly and Scrabble, or Sudoku puzzles with bold numbers or Braille, from organizations such as American Foundation for the Blind (AFB).
- Ask a speaker who is blind to talk to the class. As a thank-you, give him or her flowers and send a digital recording of the class's appreciation.
- Infuse the latest technology (e.g., *AFB Access World Magazine*, available at www.afb.org/aw/main.asp).

Hearing Reflections

- Give students oral directions while playing loud background music.
- Ask students to listen to a quiet story, one that you "read" to them without talking, to see if they can follow the plot with pictures or lip reading.
- Play static on a radio to simulate sounds hearing aids might produce.
- Explain the difference between listening and hearing.
- Turn off the sound of a closed-captioned movie.
- Tell students to cover their ears for three of every ten minutes for an hour.
- Teach students how to finger-spell, or invite a sign language interpreter to explain gestures and teach the class to sign some sentences. Be certain that when the students ask questions, they speak slowly and face the presenter. Overemphasizing lip reading might also be insulting. Remember to tap the person who needs to lip-read gently on the shoulder when addressing him or her so that the person can focus attention before you begin speaking.
- Have the class research possible reasons for hearing loss at different ages and discuss the graph below, which indicates how high decibel levels cause hearing loss over time. Talk about how wearing earplugs when people are involved in loud activities is *sound* advice for maintaining hearing.

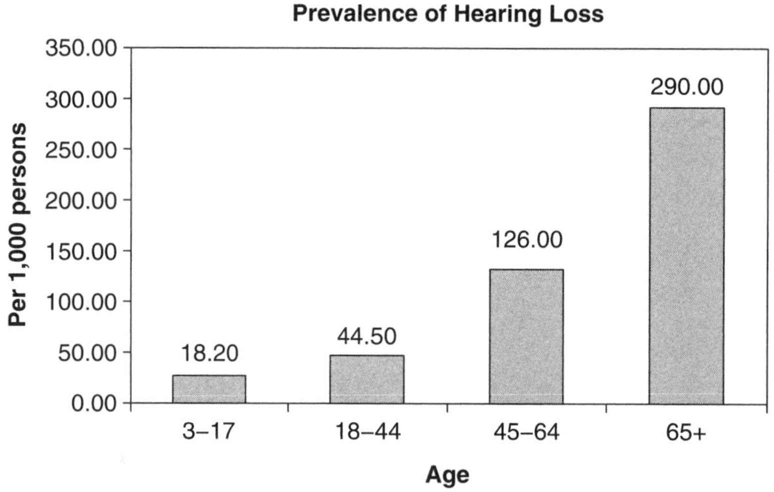

Decibel (dB) level	How this dB level can affect a person's hearing
110	Repeated over and over, everyday exposure for more than 1 minute risks permanent hearing loss.
100	Unprotected exposure—without earplugs—for less than 15 minutes is recommended as the maximum.
85	Prolonged exposure to noise at or above this decibel level can cause gradual hearing loss over time.

Now here are the decibel levels of things you might use or be around every day:

Snowmobile—100dB

Firecracker—150 dB

Heavy traffic—85 dB

Motorcycle—95 dB

Loud stereo at highest volume—105 dB

Normal speaking—60 dB

Whisper—30 dB

Moral: *Use your ears soundly!*

SOURCE: National Institute on Deafness and Other Communication Disorders (2011).

Communication Thoughts

- Speech involves your brain, chest, nose, mouth, and muscles in your face.
- Speech disorders can be caused by hearing loss or other factors.
- Speech therapy by skilled therapists with consistent home practice can help.
- If a child has an articulation problem, it will sound like talking with your tongue touching the roof of your mouth. "Thpeeking incowectly ith orful."
- If a student experiences childhood-onset fluency disorder, or stuttering, she will repeat sounds a lot, while stammering means the child is repeating words. The child might cough periodically, which is another type of interruption of speech or thought. "Ssspeaking in-in-in-c-c-correctly is aw-aw-aw-aw-ful."
- Voice disorders can mean that there is hoarseness, poor projection, breathiness, and differences in pitch. Some of these disorders can be caused by neurological factors, trauma, or even voice abuse, like too much yelling.
- A child with a language problem knows what he wants to say, but can't put all of the words in the correct order. "Tough speaking not happy."
- Students who are nonverbal and some who have intellectual or multiple disabilities may need training on how to use communication boards, such as this one, to help let their needs be known.

SOURCE: Copyright © 1981–2004, Mayer-Johnson, Inc. Used with permission.

If a student has verbal apraxia of speech or developmental verbal dyspraxia, then he or she may display difficulties with motor and speech-planning skills (e.g., tongue placements, phrasing, or sequencing). Speech may range from intelligible to partially intelligible.

This handout from Super Duper Publications offers more information about the distinctions between the two: www.superduperinc.com/handouts/pdf/50_Aprax_Speech.pdf. The chart on the facing page offers insights to help teachers and students understand more about speech and language differences they may encounter in inclusive classrooms. Always collaborate with your school's speech-language pathologist (SLP) for classroom interventions, resources, and appropriate interventions.

MOVING TO SOUNDS AROUND

Directions: This activity shows that learning to communicate would be difficult if the appropriate words were missing and a new system needed to be learned. After being given brief instructions with these auditory prompts, can you *motorically* respond appropriately?

Finger snapping	→	Touching your forehead
Clapping	→	Running in place
Beeping	→	Backward arm circles
Bell ringing	→	Hopping on one foot
Playing maracas	→	Circling hips

Available for download at **www.corwin.com/inclusionstrategies**

What are some skills included in this activity?

Moving to Sounds Around involves the following:

1. Concentration
2. Memory
3. Listening
4. Auditory processing
5. Socialization
6. Kinesthetic movement to productively channel classroom energy (great to do after a long period of sitting)
7. Reminding students that learning about sounds can be fun!

Emotional Concerns

Often students with behavioral issues cannot express themselves vocally through acceptable means and will act out in negative ways that offend both

Speech and Language Terms	Descriptions	Classroom Examples	What to Do
speech	Involves voice, articulation, and fluency (smoothness of the speech)	Student may stutter, hesitate, mispronounce words, or avoid or minimize dialogue with others for fear of embarrassment.	Coordinate with speech-language pathologist (SLP) to visit and consult with teachers to offer practice exercises in the classroom and at home; be patient and do not finish student sentences.
language	Using sounds, symbols, and words to communicate with others	Student may have better receptive language (understanding) than expressive language.	Ask student to paraphrase what was said, or give student informal oral or written assessments to confirm understandings; offer more visuals.
pragmatics	Rules of language usage and social conversing	Student may have difficulties in cooperative learning activities or conversing at lunch or at recess, changing topics, or sharing thoughts.	Again, coordinate with SLP, inviting him or her to observe, monitor, and intervene with the student in natural classroom environment and other social situations.
semantics	Rules involving the content of language with vocabulary and communication	Student may have difficulties with idioms and sarcasm.	Be specific in directions, and preteach new vocabulary in readings and subjects; play with words and sentences on index cards, sentence strips, and recordings.
syntax	Rules with grammar and ordering of words	Student may have difficulties in writing or logically conveying thoughts in sentences.	Use direct skill instruction with rules of grammar; teach student to diagram sentences, clearly labeling or color-coding parts of sentences, (e.g., subject/predicate, objects, nouns, verbs).
morphology	Rules involving how words are formed (e.g., smaller parts/ morphemes)	Student may leave out word endings; may not understand about structural analysis (e.g., prefixes and suffixes).	Use guided practice with identification of word parts in isolation and text in all genres; compose a three-columned wall chart of different prefixes and suffixes that students continually add to as they discover words; teach and review meaning of commonly used prefixes and suffixes across the curriculum.
phonology	Rules of language and how sounds are organized	Student may mispronounce words and lose understanding across content areas.	Break up words into syllables and phonemes as needed; offer daily structured teaching, practice, and application of the sounds of letters by modeling rules and exceptions; give pre and posttest inventories to gauge progress.

teachers and classmates. Avoid this kind of isolation by proactively allowing the child to have more space or an opportunity to remove himself or herself from tense situations.

This type of disability is often one of the most misunderstood since it is usually a hidden one, not visible. It is a broad topic with many individual concerns, and it requires tremendous sensitivity and training. Emotions can range from depression and withdrawal to mood swings and outbursts with little warning, like a volcano that suddenly explodes.

Safety issues are of the utmost importance for all children. If a child is being volatile, it is important to secure a safe environment for all students and to instruct other children on how to behave. A list of appropriate behavioral classroom rules can be posted and discussed ahead of time with the entire class. Role-playing hypothetical situations can prepare and alert students to possible scenarios. Peer-mediation training and channeling anger through activities such as yoga or art is also effective. Understand that some days are better than others for kids who need more guidance with their behavior.

EMOTIONAL SCENARIO

Directions: Cooperatively choose at least one of the following ten statements:

1. I'm going to count to ten.
2. I will take a deep breath and relax.
3. There's no need to get upset; I can handle this.
4. Violence never solved anything.
5. I better not blow this out of proportion.
6. I'm in control.
7. There must be something I can learn from this.
8. I know I can get mad, but it won't help.
9. There's definitely some humor in this.
10. I'd better figure out what to do.

Now think of a hypothetical classroom situation whose resolution could be the statement you've chosen. Act out the scenario.

Available for download at **www.corwin.com/inclusionstrategies**

Learning Differences

- Ask students to solve thirty difficult math problems in a five-minute period, or require them to read a passage and answer questions containing vocabulary at least two reading levels above their independent level. Then ask them how they felt when they could not complete the assignment.
- Demonstrate how to make a pinwheel using origami, giving rushed directions with ineffective modeling.
- Play a song in a different language, and then ask your students to write about what they just heard.
- Require students to memorize ten unfamiliar science or social studies words in an unreasonably short amount of time.
- Ask meth to eard entsences uchs sa hits to misutale a reabgin pisorber. (Translation: Ask them to read sentences such as this to simulate a reading disorder).

Physical Insights

- Have students write or catch a ball with their nondominant hand.
- Ask children to tie their shoes while wearing mittens.
- After having students take turns sitting in a wheelchair for about an hour, ask them to express how it felt to watch their nondisabled peers while being immobile.
- Arrange for a speaker with a physical disability to talk with the class.
- Give each student a small square paper to fold into quarters and ask them to hold it against their forehead. Then instruct them to write their name on the paper using their nondominant hand (pencils are recommended). This activity causes brain confusion and simulates fine-motor difficulties. The reversals and illegible handwriting simulate someone who has fine-motor difficulties or perceptual difficulties that are evidenced by poor handwriting.
- Remind students that these were only simulations but to think about how frustrated they felt.

Negative Effects of Labeling: Edible Simulation—Background Information for Teachers

This edible simulation involves five groups: apple, chocolate, lemon, pretzel, and nut people. Collectively, each group describes its characteristics with guided questions below. Reflections include how stereotypes impact the learning environment. Teacher expectations of a child who is included, or how classmates view someone who is different, may very well be based on preconceived thoughts about a group and may not allow for individual differences within that group or label. The objective of the activity is to help students think about the negative effects of labeling people with specific categories or disabilities. For example, all students with ADHD are not the same, nor do all people with learning, physical, or emotional needs have the exact same characteristics or require the same delivery of services or strategies. Labeling is sometimes used for budgetary purposes to allocate funding for specific disability groups. Hopefully, concrete, edible accompaniments will make these insightful analogies more pleasant to digest.

EDIBLE SIMULATION

Directions for Students: You are a(n) ____________________ (apple, chocolate, lemon, pretzel, or nut) person. Describe yourself by listing your characteristics. What do other people think about you? If you could talk, what would you say? Describe how you can be combined with other edibles, but during this simulation, you may eat only from the category you have chosen and speak only to your food group.

Characteristics of a __________ person:

What people think about a __________ person:

What a ___________ person would say:

Who/what can a _______________ person be combined with?

Available for download at **www.corwin.com/inclusionstrategies**

Food for thought: Placing individuals into specific categories or disabilities can be harmful to all.

THINKING ABOUT DIS*ABILITIES*

After participating in some of these activities, answer the following questions:

1. How did you feel when you couldn't ________?
2. What were you thinking as you watched or heard others?
3. Would you like to try the activity again?
4. What strategies helped you cope?
5. What have you learned?
6. Would you recommend this exercise to a friend? Why or why not?
7. What's the difference between this simulated activity and the experience of someone who has an actual disability?
8. What effect does labeling have on individuals?

Available for download at **www.corwin.com/inclusionstrategies**

VIEWING DIFFERENCES IN BOOKS AND MOVIES ■

Books and movies help increase students' exposure and sensitivity to differing abilities. After reading a book or viewing a movie, invite students or your colleagues to discuss the theme and concepts presented. Students can draw pictures in a storyboard or digital presentation, write essays, and talk about the characters, plots, settings, and story endings with each other. Invite them to share what they have learned about people's abilities in written, oral, visual, and dramatic reports. Aside from reading and writing connections, the objective is to understand that people with disabilities can and do lead successful and productive lives. School staff can also share insights gained from the literature and movies in professional learning communities. See www.corwin.com/inclusionstrategies for a list of recommended books and movies.

From the Mouths of Babes

These two letters from fourth-grade students in response to disability awareness classroom presentations delineate how such programs positively influence a child's perception of someone with a disability.

Dear Mrs. Karten,

I learned today what it is like if you can't read, see, or can't learn as fast. I also learned that you should not make fun of someone because of those things. They could be just as good as you. Can't wait to see you next time!

From,

L. M.

Dear Mrs. Karten,

You did a wonderful job today. You taught me a lot. I had felt sorry for people with a disability. But I never let it show because in the last visit you said, "People don't want to be treated any differently because they have a disability." Your lesson really paid off because a girl in my Hebrew class has a disability and now I know the perfect way to treat her (the same as anyone else).

Love,

F. L. (please come back soon)

■ DIFFERENT CHOICES

MY THOUGHTS

Directions: Think about how you would act toward a student who . . .

- needed more attention from the teacher.
- wanted things repeated a lot.
- required more time to do math problems.
- could not see well.
- had sloppy handwriting.
- could not hear some sounds.
- had trouble sitting quietly.
- could not read the same level text as the rest of the class.
- did not have enough time to complete a test.
- tried his or her best but kept failing tests.
- did less homework than other students.
- was unable to take notes.

How will you help that person? I will ______________________.

Available for download at **www.corwin.com/inclusionstrategies**

Question for adults and older students to ponder: Does fair translate to equal?

Activities for Classroom Digestion

Role-play these situations:

1. Pretend a child has a cut on his or her finger.

   Solution: Place a Band-Aid on the finger.

2. Pretend a student had a fight with his or her parents.

   Solution: Place a Band-Aid on the finger.

3. Pretend a child failed a test.

   Solution: Place a Band-Aid on the finger.

Moral/Fact: Band-Aids do not fix all problems. Differences exist, but they are handled in various ways by students and teachers.

Shake It Up!

The next few activities try to concretely increase students' awareness that they should not judge people by superficial facts or appearances or if they do not have that person's prior experiences.

In this first activity, the teacher places the following items in three separate, identical empty coffee cans: a dollar bill in can #1, twenty pennies in can #2, and one quarter in can #3. The teacher then shakes each can and asks the class, "Which one do you think is worth more?" The moral here is that the more valuable things are not always the easiest to identify and also may be the quietest. What you hear or see on the outside does not tell the whole story!

In the second activity, the teacher again places items in three separate, identical empty coffee cans. Now, can #1 has a dollar bill, can #2 has one hundred pennies, and can #3 has four quarters. The teacher then shakes each can and asks the class, "Which one do you think is worth more?" The moral here is that you don't always know what's on the inside by what you see or hear on the outside. In this case, the cans are all equal but in different ways. People are equal in different ways, too!

In the third activity, the teacher places equal amounts of rice grains in a coffee can, an opaque orange juice container, and a paper bag. Use your best judgment here with quantity—no need to count! The teacher then asks the students, "What do you think is on the inside of these containers?" Elicit student responses and then have a class discussion. The moral here is that even though these things appear different on the outside, the contents or insides of each are the same. Every person on this planet has the same worth, regardless of what he or she looks like on the outside.

In the fourth activity, ask the students what they think is worth more: rice or money. Discuss how if a hungry person were left on a deserted island, the rice would be worth more than the money if he or she were starving for food! The moral here is that each person has different needs. *Shake it up!* teaches about the value of money, and people too. We're the same in some ways, and different as well! People *can be like cans:* Some are just *a little shaky.* Others are willing to *shake it up!* (Karten, 2008a).

SHAKE IT UP! STUDENT WORKSHEET

Activity #1: Circle the one that you think is the most valuable:

Can #1 Can #2 Can #3

Activity #2: Circle the one that you think is the most valuable:

Can #1 Can #2 Can #3

Activity #3: What do you think is on the inside of these containers?

Coffee can ______________________________

Juice container ______________________________

Paper bag ______________________________

Activity #4: Circle the one that is worth more.

Rice Money

Something to think about: What do you think it means when someone says, "You can't judge a book by its cover"?

I think it means ______________________________

______________________________.

Available for download at **www.corwin.com/inclusionstrategies**

DIS*ABILITY* STATEMENTS TO PONDER

Directions: Write either true or false by the following statements:

______ 1. A person with one arm can be a physical therapist.

______ 2. A teenage girl with Down syndrome can have highlights put in her hair.

______ 3. A person who is blind can *read* a visual dictionary.

______ 4. Someone with dyslexia can go to college.

______ 5. A person with prosthetic legs can be a contestant on *Dancing With the Stars*.

______ 6. A child with autism can be successfully employed.

______ 7. An artist can have no hands.

______ 8. Someone with an intellectual disability can have children of his or her own.

______ 9. A person who is blind can *see* what you mean, or even climb Mt. Kilimanjaro.

______ 10. People with disabilities need opportunities to show their abilities.

All of the above statements are true.

Available for download at **www.corwin.com/inclusionstrategies**

Keep in mind: When in doubt, apply sensitivity and common sense!

PREPARATION FOR SUCCESSFUL INCLUSION ■

"_________ **might need help with** _________" is a preparatory statement that can erase the shock or tendency to shy away from someone who is different. Teachers can alert, instruct, and guide students by modeling and informing a class on specific appropriate ways they can help classmates and others.

Dis*ability* Charts (Resource A)

Some of the barriers that prevent children from leading productive lives as members of the adult community are lack of exposure to the grade-level curriculum, lower expectations, untrained teachers, and negative societal attitudes. Teachers, students, administrators, communities, and families must be equipped with appropriate knowledge to circumvent unplanned inclusion that inevitably leads to failure. Preparation, sensitivity, and more knowledge for all are crucial.

The dis*ability* charts at the back of the book (Resource A) list possible causes of some common disabilities and syndromes, characteristics of people who have these conditions, educational strategies to use, and resources to help you. Please note that dis*abilities* are heterogeneous and that *each of these charts describes a syndrome or disorder, not a specific child.* In addition, some characteristics and strategies may be shared and overlap with others. Remember that clinicians are trained to make diagnoses. The information in the charts is intended to broaden knowledge and does not make anyone informed enough to diagnose. Diagnoses and labels are serious things! Information for the charts in Resource A was obtained from field experts, the individual disability organizations listed, the Council for Exceptional Children (CEC), professional journals, the Center for Parent Information and Resources, and diagnostic criteria from DSM-5. Contact these references for additional personal and professional perspectives and more resources about specific disabilities.

> Teachers who know individual disability characteristics can effectively apply appropriate strategies that match children's individualized education programs.

Wow! That sure was a loaded sentence but not an impossible task. Instructional learning strategies help students of all abilities.

Directions: Complete the disability web and business card activities on the following pages.

CHOOSE YOUR LEARNING WEB

Directions: As a way to absorb, reflect, and apply the knowledge on the pages in Resource A listing different syndromes' characteristics and possible causes and educational strategies for coping with them, choose one of the disabilities that you would like to discover more about, and fill in the blank with its name. Use the information previously given, your prior knowledge, cooperative help from peers, the disability tables in Resource A, and other available research to answer these questions.

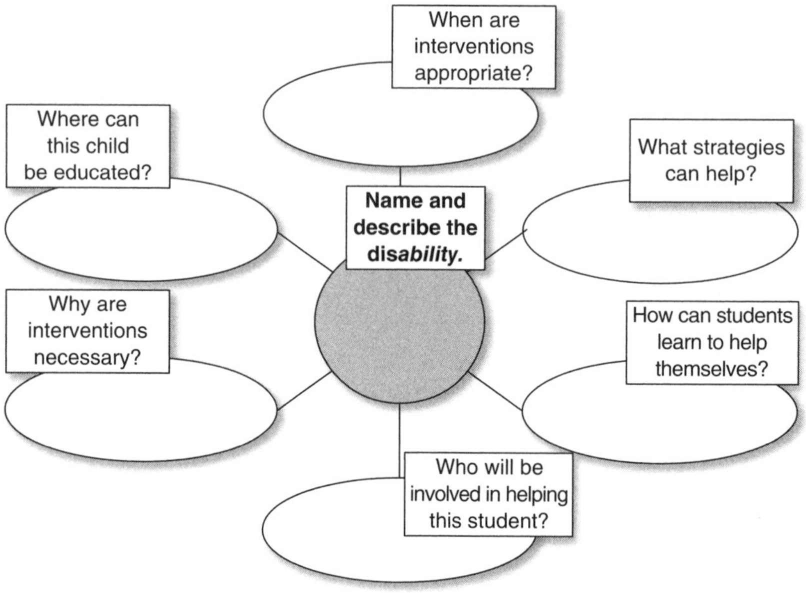

Available for download at **www.corwin.com/inclusionstrategies**

FOCUSING ON ABILITIES

Knowing different characteristics of various dis*abilities* helps teachers appropriately modify lessons. Most important, concentrating on students' strengths rather than weaknesses instills greater self-confidence, thereby encouraging learning. More progress can always be achieved through focusing on abilities, not *dis*abilities.

Suppose someone with a certain dis*ability* was to open a business. What would it be?

BUSINESS CARD ACTIVITY

Directions: After selecting a dis*ability,* cooperatively create a business card for possible employment that a child with __________ might be suited for when he or she reaches adulthood and enters the community. Place the specified characteristics on the corresponding locations of an index card or larger paper. The criteria described in the template below focus on positive traits, since *disability does not translate to inability.*

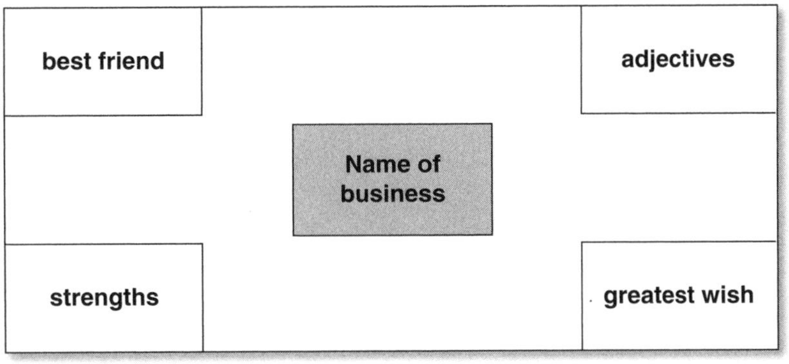

Sample Business Cards

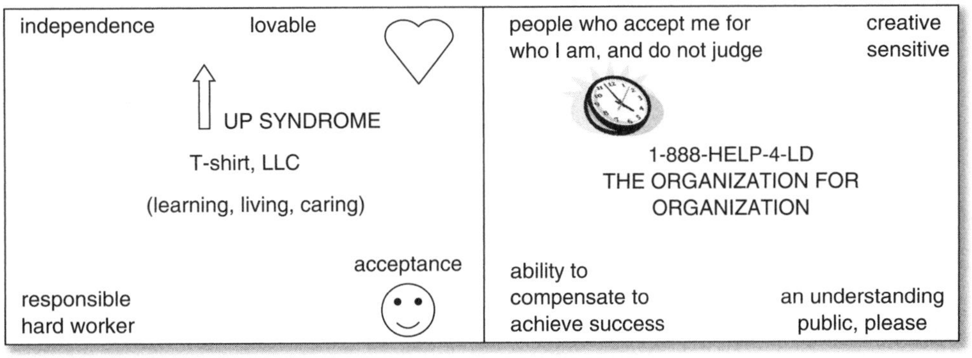

Available for download at **www.corwin.com/inclusionstrategies**

Some Biographical Readings and Research

Read biographies in texts or online about people with disabilities who have accomplished great things in their lives. See www.corwin.com/inclusion strategies for a list of recommended readings and research.

SEASAW ACTIVITY OF PEOPLE WITH ABILITIES

Directions: Collectively list famous scientists, entertainers, artists, sports figures, advocates, and writers with physical, learning, cognitive, and behavioral disabilities. Other categories could include political figures and fictional characters in books or movies.

S (Scientists)

E (Entertainers)

A (Artists)

S (Sports figures)

A (Advocates, with or without disabilities)

W (Writers)

More Categories

Political Figures

Fictional Characters

See www.corwin.com/inclusionstrategies for a list of inspiring people.

Life offers different choices to accommodate differences. The many stores in a shopping mall and the vast selection of languages offered on Google Translate denote the diversity of our global population. The universe is not made up of clones with robotic blueprints but people with unique fingerprints. Simply put: Different vehicles accommodate different people, but all transport them to the places they need to go. As long as the destination is safely reached, who has the right to judge one's needs or choices in life? A child with differing abilities must be understood as just that: a child with diverse and unique needs who is then educated within a school system and when appropriate an inclusive classroom.

Education needs to make adjustments for learning, sensory, emotional, behavioral, developmental, communication, and physical differences as individual levels are identified. Students require specially designed instruction with different ways to show what they know. *Ableism,* which involves thinking that people with disabilities are not as capable as those without disabilities, exists in schools and many other settings. Additional experiences with students with disabilities, increased knowledge from literature and research, and infusing more positive role models with disabilities into content areas will alter those attitudes (Storey, 2007).

JUST THINK: HOW MANY WAYS CAN YOU . . . ?

read a book	research a topic	shop	multiply numbers	sing a song
do laundry	cook a meal	communicate with a friend	interpret educational legislation and research	hear a conversation
appreciate flowers	vary teaching objectives	exercise	talk	include students in classrooms

Available for download at **www.corwin.com/inclusionstrategies**

3

Establishing Successful Inclusive Classrooms

Knowing more about the legislation, research, and often complicated terminology leads to this next topic of determining ways teachers meet individual student needs in their classrooms. These pedagogical strategies teach students at their ability levels with expansive instructional techniques, using sound learning principles as well as different modalities to appeal to multiple intelligences, interests, and knowledge backgrounds. Classroom learners benefit with specially designed instruction (SDI) and interventions that have initials such as UbD (understanding by design), UDL (universal design for learning), DI (differentiated instruction), and PBL (project- or problem-based learning) . Thinking ahead about outcomes and being prepared with differentiated lessons and resources involve proactively planning and valuing just how desired lesson goals will reach students. As delineated in this chapter, appropriate content and teaching yield more effective student results, making us all more *abled*! Templates for teacher-friendly implementation are included.

STRATEGIES THAT WORK WITH ALL LEARNERS

Special education strategies are applicable for all classroom populations. Sometimes in teachers' haste to thrust knowledge upon students and deliver the curriculum, students are not becoming metacognitive learners. In today's classrooms, knowing how to be a learner is essential. It is also unfair for teachers to ask all students to achieve the same competencies if the means of instruction and assessment are not varied. When included, some students also need to learn how to follow routines and know what to do when the routines change as well—dealing with transitions from one subject to the next or from one school to the next and preparing for meaningful postsecondary choices. Diverse strategies develop competencies and create lifelong learners who view school as a place for successes, not failures. These experiences are then translated into productive adult choices. With proper methodology, inclusive classrooms benefit all.

Imagine entering a classroom where supportive, structured, research-based education allowed learners to effectively demonstrate their knowledge. Ingredients include relevant and meaningful instruction with diverse learning strategies that capitalize upon students' strengths. Now imagine: What if such a classroom did not exist?

THE "AUDUBONIMABLE"* CLASSROOM

All of the birds decided that they needed to improve their status in the world, so they organized a school. The principal, Ms. Audubon, drew pictures and classified each type of bird. From the school's beginning, many disputes developed among the administration, community, teachers, students, and families, thwarting any educational successes.

The peacocks thought that they were the smartest since they had the brightest multitude of colors. The owls didn't attend because basically they didn't give a hoot about learning. The mockingbirds laughingly thought the whole thing was a joke, while the hummingbirds constantly made noises in class and would not listen to Ms. Audubon.

Parents of other animals heard about the birds' attempts to soar above their young and decided to fill out applications for their offspring, but the birds would not allow their admission. The bird administration refused to give the camel an inch and would not permit the giraffe to stick its neck where it didn't belong. They simply tweeted at the other animals and told them if they were admitted, they would be like fish out of water and never achieve flying colors. They even made the deer homeless since they broke ground for the new school on the deer's land.

Eventually, some of the birds graduated from the school but were never successful in life since the only subject they had been taught was flying. Sadly, Ms. Audubon had chosen a curriculum that parroted the birds' needs but ignored the rest of the universe.

Questions for Discussion

- What do you think about this *abominable* classroom?
- Is it possible for educators to successfully teach students of all abilities together in one classroom?
- How can educators help students achieve *flying colors*?

*John James Audubon, known for his study of birds in the early 1800s, was not a success in school because he spent too much time outside watching and painting birds. This parable *stretches* his name and describes an *abominable* time when schools did not value other strengths, ignoring different ways of being smart. Today, the National Audubon Society works hard for the preservation of wildlife, while classrooms also work hard to preserve and cultivate individual minds and interests.

Available for download at **www.corwin.com/inclusionstrategies**

Moral: This classroom is for the birds since a homogenous, one-size-fits-all approach is an abomination. Alternatively, diverse classrooms can help prepare all learners for life.

EFFECTIVE INGREDIENTS

Hopefully, this book will give teachers palatable skills to appetizingly serve to hungry students who deserve more of an entrée than an *abominable* classroom. Educational practices can be compared to baking a cake.

What's involved in baking a cake?

1.
2.
3.
4.
5.

What's involved in effective education?

1.
2.
3.
4.
5.

Special TIPS

The following acronym, TIPS, highlights four major school considerations:

Topic (concrete vs. abstract concepts, unfamiliar subjects vs. material review, amount of prior knowledge, complexity, number of lessons in a unit, interest)

Individuals (including teachers, students, administrators, parents, guardians, and related staff; encompasses supportive attitudes, skills, experiences, teaching styles, and family views; awareness of dis*ability* characteristics with sensitivity preparation for teachers, students, and all staff; ongoing legislative parties; community advocates; and academic and emotional support to go with learners' motivations and cognitive levels)

Planning (goes beyond choosing a topic to how you are going to teach it using cooperative learning, learning stations, varying objectives/strategies, repeated exposure to subject matter, multiple intelligences, UbD to think about outcomes at the onset, UDL to honor existing differences and brain networks, and PBL to value student inquiry; possible modifications required, matching instruction with individual needs and assessment methods; includes both formal and informal reviews before, during, and after lesson to determine mastery level and instructional plans)

Setting (physical classroom design, either in general education classroom or setting for smaller groups or individual students; texts, curriculum materials, school/district policies, class size, distractions, and environments that are conducive to adaptations)

Available for download at **www.corwin.com/inclusionstrategies**

APPLYING DIVERSE STRATEGIES

It is difficult to apply diverse strategies without reflecting on these educationally action-packed words.

VERB-DRIVEN EDUCATION

assessing exploring researching discussing documenting evaluating monitoring

analyzing refining revising reflecting practicing learning socializing generalizing

applying observing anticipating communicating interacting role-playing instructing rewarding informing modeling encouraging enhancing fostering embracing developing

Questions to Consider

- Whom are you teaching?
- What are you teaching?
- How will you teach it?
- Did it work?

Directions: Choose ten of these verbs and use them to write an effective educational paragraph, including **TIPS** above!

Available for download at **www.corwin.com/inclusionstrategies**

VALUABLE AND APPLICABLE THINGS TO DO IN ALL CLASSROOMS ON A DAILY BASIS

1. Establish prior knowledge.
2. Plan lessons with structured objectives, allowing inter or postplanning that delineates goals and desired student outcomes.
3. Proceed from the simple to the complex by using discrete task analysis, which breaks up the learning into its parts.
4. Use a step-by-step approach, teaching in small bites with much practice and repetition for students who require this framework.
5. Reinforce abstract concepts with concrete examples, such as looking at a map while walking around a neighborhood or reading actual street signs.
6. Think about possible accommodations and modifications that might be needed, such as using a digital recorder for notes, reading math word problems aloud, or if necessary reducing or enriching an assignment.
7. Incorporate sensory elements—visual, auditory, and kinesthetic-tactile ones—across the disciplines.
8. Teach to strengths to help students compensate for weaknesses, such as encouraging a child to hop to math facts if the child loves to move about but hates numbers.
9. Concentrate on individual children, not syndromes.
10. Provide opportunities for success to build self-esteem.
11. Give positives before negatives.
12. Use modeling with both teachers and peers.
13. Vary types of instruction and assessment with multiple intelligences, learning centers and stations, cooperative learning, project-based learning, and universal designs.
14. Relate learning to children's lives using interest inventories.
15. Remember the basics, such as teaching students proper hygiene, respecting others, effectively listening, reading directions on a worksheet, and the three Rs: Reading, 'Riting, and 'Rithmetic.
16. Establish a pleasant classroom environment that encourages students to ask questions and become actively involved in their learning.
17. Increase students' self-awareness of levels and progress.
18. Effectively communicate and collaborate with families, students, and colleagues while smiling (It's contagious!).

STRATEGIC CCSS APPLICATIONS

Scenario 1: Kindergarten Class

This inclusion class has learners with and without disabilities. Students have academic and behavioral differences, with higher and lower levels of independence exhibited. Some students require additional scaffolding to identify the main ideas in spoken and written text, others need more assistance with fine motor tasks, and two other students with autism spectrum disorder require coaching and modeling to appropriately communicate ideas and effectively interact with peers and adults within whole class, small groups, and one to one.

The teacher addresses these Common Core State Standards for English Language Arts (CCSS.ELA):

Reading Foundational Skills: Fluency

CCSS.ELA-Literacy.RF.K.4: Read emergent-reader texts with purpose and understanding.

Informational Text: Key Ideas and Details

CCSS.ELA-Literacy.RI.K.1: With prompting and support, ask and answer questions about key details in a text.

CCSS.ELA-Literacy.RI.K.2: With prompting and support, identify the main topic and retell key details of a text.

Speaking and Listening

CCSS.ELA-Literacy.SL.K.2: Confirm understanding of a text read aloud or information presented orally or through other media by asking and answering questions about key details and requesting clarification if something is not understood.

CCSS.ELA-Literacy.SL.K.3: Ask and answer questions in order to seek help, get information, or clarify something that is not understood.

The Next Generation Science Standards (NGSS)

Life Sciences—Interdependent Relationships in Ecosystems: Animals, Plants, and Their Environments.

K-LS1-1: Use observation to describe what plants and animals (including humans) need to survive.

Inclusion Plans: The kindergarten teacher establishes students' prior knowledge about the attributes of living and nonliving things with class discussion and everyday examples. The teacher reads *Are You Living? A Song About Living and Nonliving Things* by Laura Purdie Salas and the book *What's Alive?* by Kathleen Weidner Zoehfeld. Together the class identifies the main idea of the text, reviewing the pictures and listening to the songs as the teachers record responses to questions in a graphic organizer—a columned chart of the differences between living things (e.g., all living things need water; plants need light but do not require food like animals; a living thing breathes, moves by itself, grows/changes, and reproduces). Learners then cut out and sort pictures and one-syllable words in cooperative groups and watch related animated videos on butterflies, endangered species, and habitats. Some pictures are placed into simpler shapes, such as a circle or square, to lessen the fine-motor cutting requirements. Specific cooperative roles and peer interactions are defined, modeled, and monitored. Community connections occur when the students take virtual field trips to zoos and animal parks.

Scenario 2: Elementary Reading Class

The teacher introduces a novel to a third-grade inclusion class with students who have a wide range of reading levels: five students have specific learning disabilities, some students have difficulties decoding multisyllabic words, others struggle with inferential-type comprehension questions, and other learners are reading at or above grade level. In addition, several students have attention and focusing issues. Another student is on the autism spectrum, needing assistance to follow the rules of conversation. This student also has highly restricted fixated interests; for example, he loves dogs.

The teacher addresses these Common Core State Standards for English Language Arts (CCSS.ELA):

Key Ideas and Details

CCSS.ELA-Literacy.RL.3.1: Ask and answer questions to demonstrate understanding of a text, referring explicitly to the text as the basis for the answers.

CCSS.ELA-Literacy.RL.3.2: Recount stories, including fables, folktales, and myths from diverse cultures; determine the central message, lesson, or moral and explain how it is conveyed through key details in the text.

CCSS.ELA-Literacy.RL.3.3: Describe characters in a story (e.g., their traits, motivations, or feelings) and explain how their actions contribute to the sequence of events.

Craft and Structure

CCSS.ELA-Literacy.RL.3.4: Determine the meaning of words and phrases as they are used in a text, distinguishing literal from nonliteral language.

Inclusion Plans: The teacher relates the learning to children's lives and the CCSS. ELA by selecting *Lewis and Clark and Me: A Dog's Tale* by Laurie Myers to read with the class. The illustrations appeal to students reading below grade level since the visuals concretize the text. The short chapters hold the attention of learners who have concentration and attention difficulties. The excerpts from Lewis's journals motivate higher-level learners, who are offered a *Lewis and Clark Webquest* enrichment assignment to cooperatively complete at zunal.com/process.php?w=2459. Sponge activities are available for all learners to investigate

Sacagawea, William Clark, Meriwether Lewis, plants, animals, and Native American tribes. Students appropriately use technology tools as they create dialogue in a digital comic strip format for the characters using Comic Creator at www.readwritethink.org/files/resources/interactives/comic/. Learners also design illustrated brochures about the expedition, write interactive letters, and complete research reports. This easily fits in with the social studies curriculum and writing standards. The student on the autism spectrum and his third-grade peers enjoy this novel since it is told through the perspective of Lewis's dog. The student with autism also reads with a peer mentor who received tips on how to appropriately engage the mentee in conversation. Some learners are reading independently, some are working cooperatively in literature groups, and other students are receiving direct skill instruction from a co-teacher who pushes in at this time to model how to cite text-based evidence in response to comprehension questions. Students keep track of their reading progress each day. The teacher prepared a packet of reading and writing templates. All students receive instruction as a whole class with minilessons generated from the novel and the same reading packet, but they are assigned different skill pages (e.g., identifying syllable types in text vocabulary, structural analysis of words, summarizing chapters, illustrating scenes with captions, diagramming story elements, identifying main idea and cause and effect, defining words, writing sentences with similes and metaphors, and filling in a timeline of Lewis and Clark events). The teacher incorporates visual, auditory, and kinesthetic-tactile elements (e.g., students write vocabulary words with raised glue, scribe words in salt trays, listen to digital prerecorded passages, and are offered energizing brain-break activities. The Lewis and Clark rubric that outlines academic and behavioral expectations is prepared and distributed to the students and signed by a family member at the outset of the unit. Portfolios that contain vocabulary and comprehension quizzes along with dated class and homework assignments are kept and reviewed by students and teachers during individual conference time. The work is also shared with families, who are encouraged to support and celebrate the learning.

Scenario 3: Middle School Seventh-Grade Science Class

The science teacher plans a lesson on habitats and niches for a general education science class that has eight students with IEPs, three students with 504 plans, and fourteen other students who vary in motivation, prior scientific knowledge, and reading and writing levels. Some learners need enrichment, while other learners require additional monitoring to ensure task completion. The teacher is concerned that, if she slows down her pace and spends time offering remediation, she will not cover the curriculum. The general education (GE) teacher wants all of her students to think and act like scientists, regardless of their prior knowledge, and to ask questions to develop solutions to real-world problems to honor Next Generation Science Standards (NGSS). There are also a few students in the class without IEPs or 504 plans who have behavioral issues that require the teacher to extract time from the science instruction for disciplinary reminders.

The teacher addresses these Common Core ELA Standards that relate to her science curriculum:

Key Ideas and Details

CCSS.ELA-Literacy.RST.6-8.2: Determine the central ideas or conclusions of a text; provide an accurate summary of the text distinct from prior knowledge or opinions.

CCSS.ELA-Literacy.RST.6-8.3: Follow precisely a multistep procedure when carrying out experiments, taking measurements, or performing technical tasks.

Craft and Structure

CCSS.ELA-Literacy.RST.6-8.4: Determine the meaning of symbols, key terms, and other domain-specific words and phrases as they are used in a specific scientific or technical context relevant to *grades 6–8 texts and topics*.

CCSS.ELA-Literacy.WHST.6-8.2. Write informative/explanatory texts, including the narration of historical events, scientific procedures/experiments, or technical processes.

Inclusion Plans: The middle school science teacher plans a collaborative project-based unit with students working in cooperative groups to investigate an ecosystem in a location other than their own city. Specific requirements are offered to outline the living and nonliving things in the population, how ecological factors either limit or increase population growth, and the patterns noted. Students access science vocabulary terms (e.g., *abiotic* and *biotic* with definitions and images on Quizlet at quizlet.com/34166732/ecosystems-flash-cards/). This assists students with differing reading levels and prior knowledge to achieve the CCSS.ELA requirements. Students activate the text-speech tools, create digital flashcards, and self-check their knowledge by creating multiple choice and fill-in tests. This list serves as a word bank of the domain-specific vocabulary for the students, with opportunities to decode the words both in context and in isolation. Students are assigned cooperative roles within each group as *Resource Researcher, Animal Artist, Environmental Expert, Survival Specialist, Interaction Investigator,* and *Population Person.* Positive behavioral support on the tool ClassDojo (www.classdojo.com) motivates students and reinforces good behavior with immediate feedback points. The teacher provides approved online articles for the students to read in science centers from the following sites: www.nsta.org/middleschool, news.sciencemag.org, and www.newsela.com. Articles chosen from Newsela allow the teacher to differentiate the Lexile levels with the click of a button. Science writing frames and transitional and sensory word lists are offered to the learners. Each person in the cooperative group fills out a dated log of progress achieved. In addition to an individual written report, as the final presentation, students post their group's work as a PowerPoint, Prezi, Glogster, or ShowMe on a teacher-created Edmodo page.

Scenario 4: High School Algebra I Class

The math class has several students with ADHD and specific learning disabilities (SLD) and a student with visual impairment. The majority of the class needs frequent reminders to take notes during the lesson, demonstrating a range of impulsive, fidgety, and/or inattentive behavior. This is the second year that five of the students have taken Algebra I. This is the algebra teacher's first year teaching, and she has no prior experience implementing strategies that assist students with ADHD. There is an assistant in the room, assigned to help the student with visual impairments, but the assistant has limited knowledge of algebra.

The GE teacher plans to address these Common Core State Standards for Math to create equations that describe numbers or relationships and to reason with equations:

> CCSS.Math.Content.HSA.CED.A.1: Create equations and inequalities in one variable and use them to solve problems. *Include equations arising from linear and quadratic functions, and simple rational and exponential functions.*
>
> CCSS.Math.Content.HSA.CED.A.2: Create equations in two or more variables to represent relationships between quantities; graph equations on coordinate axes with labels and scales.
>
> CCSS.Math.Content.HSA.CED.A.3: Represent constraints by equations or inequalities, and by systems of equations and/or inequalities, and interpret solutions as viable or nonviable options in a modeling context. *For example, represent inequalities describing nutritional and cost constraints on combinations of different foods.*
>
> CCSS.Math.Content.HSA.REI.B.3: Solve linear equations and inequalities in one variable, including equations with coefficients represented by letters.

Inclusion Plans: The student support team shares students' IEPs and 504 plans with the GE algebra teacher and the instructional assistant before the first class. The staff uses this learner profile for collaborative notes.

Learner Profile					
Student Name, Date of Birth, and Grade	**Strengths: VAKT (Visual, Auditory, and Kinesthetic-Tactile) Learning Styles and Multiple Intelligences**	**Interests: School/ Outside**	**Objectives: Academic, Social/ Emotional, Behavioral, Physical, and Communication**	**Inclusion Action Plan, Accommodations, Modifications, and Recommendations**	**Timeline for Reviewing Results**

SOURCE: Karten (2013).

The GE teacher is offered resources and practical strategies from special education (SE) staff and online sources (e.g., www.helpguide.org/mental/adhd_add_teaching_strategies.htm). The teaching assistant is also offered introductory algebra resources to preview before the class lessons (e.g., www.purplemath.com/modules/ and www.mathsisfun.com/algebra/introduction.html). The GE teacher and instructional assistant formulate a plan to share responsibilities to provide the appropriate scaffolding with specially designed instruction for students with SLD, ADHD, and the student with visual impairment. The pair decides that the instructional assistant will monitor students' behavior during the GE teacher's direct skill instruction. The content teacher also shares the vocabulary, big ideas, and essential elements of the lessons with the instructional assistant at the outset of each unit, which she in turn previews with the students. The teacher posts these Standards for Mathematical Practices, using text with a large font, as a visual wall reminder for the class:

Standards for Mathematical Practices

CCSS.Math.Practice.MP1: Make sense of problems and persevere in solving them.

CCSS.Math.Practice.MP2: Reason abstractly and quantitatively.

CCSS.Math.Practice.MP3: Construct viable arguments & critique the reasoning of others.

CCSS.Math.Practice.MP4: Model with mathematics.

CCSS.Math.Practice.MP5: Use appropriate tools strategically.

CCSS.Math.Practice.MP6: Attend to precision.

CCSS.Math.Practice.MP7: Look for and make use of structure.

CCSS.Math.Practice.MP8: Look for and express regularity in repeated reasoning.

Students tally the corresponding math practice standard addressed during each lesson. The GE teacher and instructional assistant communicate and follow structured routines with physical organization of the classroom environment (e.g., notebooks are set up and checked; "Do Nows" and exit cards are in the schedule each class; and supplies are available on a strategy table that students access with materials such as markers, rulers, Post-it notes, graph paper, algebra tiles, and calculators for the students to use). The students are offered opportunities to move about the room in an activity entitled "Clockwork Algebra," with color-coded questions and answers taped to classroom walls that the students solve and check with peers. Some students are provided flowcharts and step-by-step checklists to assist with factoring, the categorization of the roots of quadratic functions based on the discriminant, determining the end behavior of polynomial functions, and other concepts that are broken down into their steps. The teacher begins with lower-level questions to determine prior knowledge, avoid frustrations, create a foundation for higher-level questioning, and for the students to make mathematical connections. The assistant enlarges the text pages for the student with visual impairment; all wall materials are large enough for the student to see clearly, and visual clutter is reduced. Worksheets and written assignments with detailed text are digitally recorded for the student with visual impairment and those students with SLD who have lower reading levels. The algebra teacher uses a *whole-part-whole* approach (e.g., teaching systems of equations, graphical representations, and determining a solution algebraically). Direct skill instruction is given to the whole class; students then cooperatively expand their knowledge with "Think-Pair-Share" and "Solve a Problem" activities, and then gather as a whole to communicate discoveries. Both the teacher and instructional assistant circulate to monitor on-task behavior and to ensure accurate answers whether the students are working independently or in small groups. Students who need remediation before, during, or after a lesson access online tutorials (e.g., www.khanacademy.org/math/algebra, www.purplemath.com/modules/, mathforum.org/library/topics/algebra/, and illuminations.nctm.org). Students keep math journals with three entries required each week. The following "Tic-Tac-Toe Choice Board" on a unit of systems of equations and inequalities is completed to offer differentiation and empower students.

Tic-Tac-Toe Choice Board		
Write a fairy tale or fable with constraints that model a given system of inequalities.	Make a poster using hands-on materials or Glogster that outlines the possible answers to a system by graphing.	Set up a word problem that involves a community to model a given system of equations.
Design a lesson plan with handouts to teach "special systems" using digital tools.	STUDENT CHOICE Teacher approval required.	Describe a local, national, or global business situation that would require the solving of a system of equations.
Create a poem, rap song, or interpretive dance to explain the steps of solving by linear combination.	Explain how a solution relates to the graph and solving by linear combination. Use of online tools is optional.	Write three systems that have one, zero, and infinite solutions. Solve and explain to another group.

SOURCE: Adapted from a math lesson by Michelle Doris, HS algebra teacher.

Afterward, educators reflect on their lesson as shown with the questions in the next table.

Educator Reflections: *Do I/We . . .*	Always	Sometimes	Never
1. provide students with appropriately leveled interest-based learning experiences?			
2. provide guided learning experiences that help students to set goals?			
3. encourage students to ask questions in welcoming classroom environments?			
4. consistently schedule time for open classroom discussions and small-group and individual conferencing?			
5. think of ways of developing self-directed learners?			
6. value student participation and progress?			
7. offer and apply models of problem-solving steps?			
8. actively offer metacognitive strategies and guidance?			
9. observe and assist students as appropriate to help but not provide too much support?			
10. connect the CCSS to students' lives?			

SOURCE: Adapted from Karten (2009).

Available for download at **www.corwin.com/inclusionstrategies**

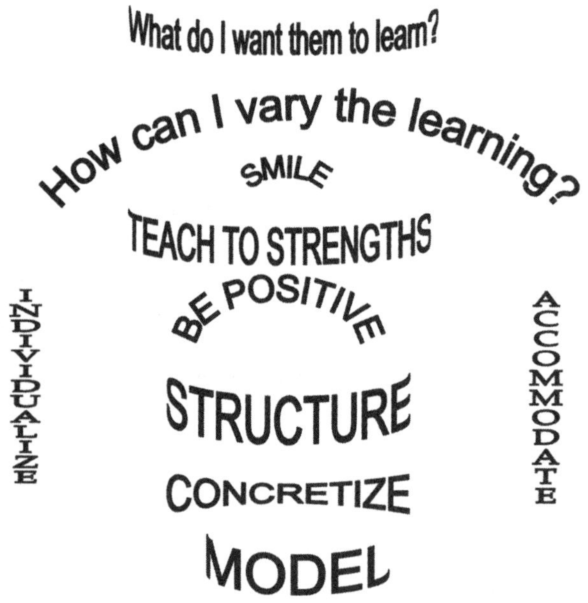

Knowing Students and What to Teach

Knowing what students already know can help the teacher gauge prescriptive instruction with clear-cut objectives. Basically, all students are learning but on their individual levels within the same classroom. Teachers must be aware of levels of learning before instruction begins.

Independent Level

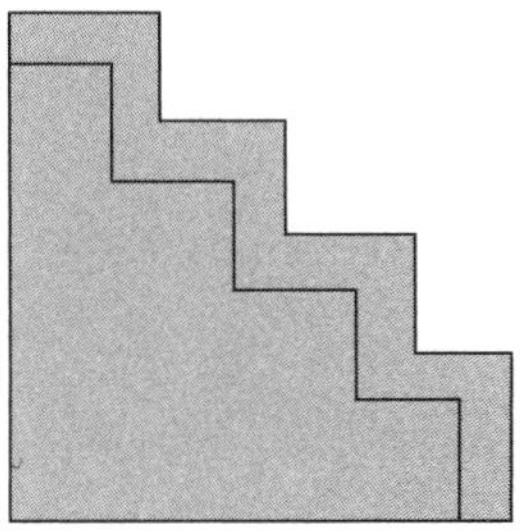

Student does not need instruction and can accomplish tasks independently, given direction and intermittent teacher reinforcement. Teacher first informally checks if prior knowledge is correct and periodically monitors.

Classroom Examples: Early learners orally respond to comprehension questions after listening to a read-aloud of *Arrow to the Sun*. Elementary students completed a unit about Native Americans and are asked to fill in a chart telling about the lives of different groups of Native Americans in the early colonies. The classroom text is used for information. Secondary students learning about manifest destiny have prior knowledge of Jackson's policy of Indian removal and the Native American treaties that were signed and reference primary documents for additional information.

Instructional Level

A student needs the teacher's guidance to understand concepts and cannot independently complete assignments without specific instruction.

Classroom Examples: The younger student is sorting pictures of living and nonliving things. The teacher clarifies the critical attributes of living things. An elementary-level student is reading a grade-level story with new vocabulary words. The story includes similes and metaphors, which the teacher needs to explain. The student then writes his or her own story using figurative language. A biology class learns about mitosis, meiosis, and sexual reproduction with direct instruction of domain-specific vocabulary (e.g., gametes, zygotes, and haploid/diploid numbers through context clues, visuals, lab lessons, and stations).

Frustration Level

Learning is way too difficult for the student and can lead to shutdown, frustrations, and unwillingness to complete assignments for fear of failure. In most cases, students are missing prerequisite knowledge.

Classroom Examples: The early learner may be unable to complete the construction of a number line. The student needs to have multiple daily experiences with one-to-one correspondence, such as counting aloud while pointing to each number. The elementary student could not divide by two-digit divisors because he or she lacked understanding of the concepts of multiplication and division or did not know basic math facts. The student needs to work on independent or instructional levels, reviewing basic facts, and proceed with clear-cut explanations, step-by-step instructions, and modeling. The secondary-level geometry student needs to derive the equation of a circle of given center and radius by using the Pythagorean theorem, but the student does not have a command of the steps involved.

Teachers must continually assess prior, inter-, and post-knowledge levels!

ESTABLISHING PRIOR KNOWLEDGE

PREASSESSMENT GUIDELINES FOR TEACHERS

Tell everything you know about ______________ [TOPIC].

Sample Curriculum Questions

Who ____?
Where ____?
Why ____?
When ____?
How ____?
What ____?

Grades K–2

What is a community?

Where do earthworms live?

How do you spell . . . ?

Grades 3–5

Why does it rain?

Where did the Pilgrims land? Show your answer on a map of the United States.

Which of the following dictionary guidewords will help you locate the word *learn*?

- FRIEND—FUNNY
- LIGHT—LOUD
- LAUGH—LIP

Grades 6–8

Identify and list the contributions of this civilization:

When was World War II? What implications did it have for Germany and the world?

How would you solve this problem? $2a + 6 = 16$

Grades 9–12

What are the main bonds that elements use to form compounds?

Explain the significance of this quote from *A Midsummer Night's Dream*: "Lord, what fools these mortals be!"

Identify the geographical division between Asia and Europe on a world map.

What are appropriate ways to prepare for and behave on a job interview?

Available for download at **www.corwin.com/inclusionstrategies**

After the preassessment, which outlines varying levels of prior student knowledge, the teacher can address the different learning needs of the class. Students are divided into cooperative groups, working together to understand more about any given curriculum topic. This is also a time when teachers individually conference with students or offer remediation or enrichment for small-group instruction, sharing responsibilities with related staff and co-teachers, if present. The goal is for the learning to occur on appropriate individual instructional and/or independent levels, with necessary supports.

Some Cooperative Group Ideas

- A group of students write from picture prompts on any topic, using a variety of genre and writing techniques, giving each picture a meaningful caption. As appropriate, online resources are accessed. For example, a visual dictionary can be accessed at www.visualdictionaryonline.com.
- Other students could use textbooks to create timelines of historical dates, define/review vocabulary, or answer content-related questions with research. Investigate Dipity, an online digital timeline tool, accessed at www.dipity.com.
- Another group might design a product using auditory, visual, and tactile/kinesthetic learning styles, or complete assignments at classroom stations, maybe role-playing academic or social situations or debating viewpoints.
- Students could answer or design curriculum-related WebQuests, given approved sites to work from. Investigate zunal.com and questgarden.com.

Divided-Column Charts

Divided charts are quick classroom guides to levels. The first column asks for background knowledge about any subject and, at a quick glance, helps the teacher assess varying classroom levels while at the same time dispelling any myths or incorrect information. The second column, telling what students know, is vital because the students' questions, needs, and concerns are identified, thereby letting instruction fit students' levels. The final TBC (to be continued) column is left blank, since further study, research, and experiences later add to this column. Cooperative roles such as these are then assigned:

Recorder (writes on chart paper for class gallery walk)

Reader (shares findings with other groups)

Focuser (ensures that group members concentrate on the task)

Goodies person (gathers the chart paper, tape, markers, etc.)

Processor (helps others apply thoughts to the assigned task)

Encourager (compliments and acknowledges contributions of others)

To establish equal, simultaneous, and individual participation, each person records the answers on individual charts. The recorder transcribes the final copy on larger paper that will be posted in the classroom, allowing the entire class to see each group's response in a gallery walk. In this scenario, children are learning alongside each other, under the teacher's direction.

Curriculum connection is shown with a sample topic on dis*abilities.* The positive effects of prior knowledge are evident, from courses in biology (Ozuru, Dempsey, & McNamara, 2009) to teachers' perceptions about inclusion (Symeonidou & Phtiaka, 2009), or in reading with patterns in books such as repetition, alphabetical progression, and counting, since schema are more predictable within students' prior experiences and knowledge (Zipprich, Grace, & Grote-Garcia, 2009). Charts like these help establish students' independent, instructional, and frustration levels on any topic. The last column (TBC) is revisited after the unit of learning is completed and can also be an assessment tool. Using three-columned learning or preassessment questions establishes prior knowledge before learning misconceptions are evidenced by both teachers and students. The ultimate goal is to prevent incorrect prior knowledge from interfering with the learning process.

PRIOR KNOWLEDGE ABOUT *SPECIAL* EDUCATION

Directions: Levels of learning also refers to teachers and related staff who have varying prior knowledge and experiences on how to instruct an inclusive class. Knowing the obstacles, resources, strategies, and available administrative supports help staff to ensure student success. Write things you know about dis*abilities*, special education, and inclusion strategies in the first column. In the second column, list all of your concerns and topics you would like to know more about. Leave the last column vacant; this is the one you will revisit later on to determine whether needs and questions in the second column were addressed.

Special Education Inclusion Disabilities	**? Tell me more about that.**	**TBC (To Be Continued)**
Independent Level	Instructional Level	Assessment Level

PREASSESSMENT AT A GLANCE

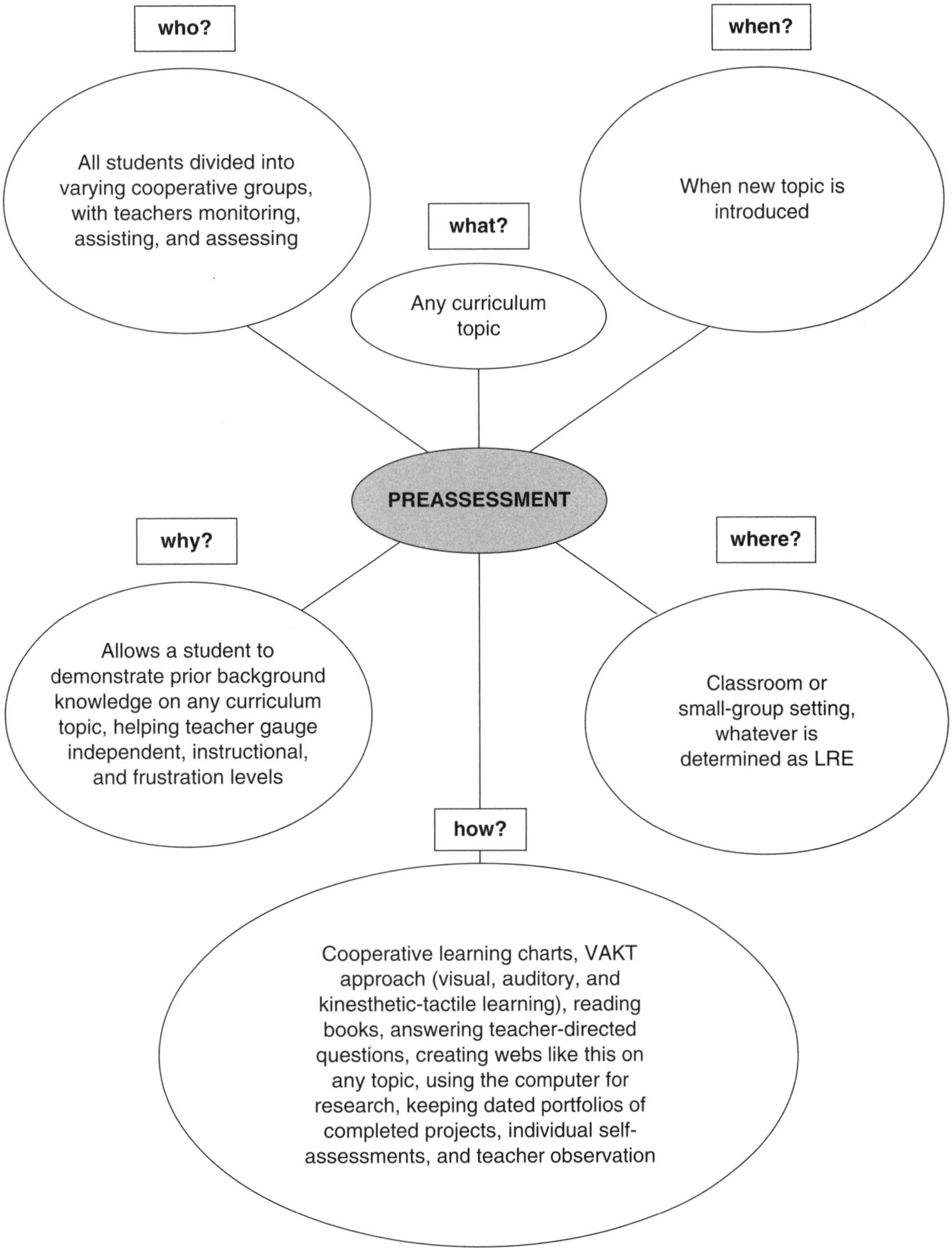
who?
All students divided into varying cooperative groups, with teachers monitoring, assisting, and assessing
when?
When new topic is introduced
what?
Any curriculum topic
PREASSESSMENT
why?
Allows a student to demonstrate prior background knowledge on any curriculum topic, helping teacher gauge independent, instructional, and frustration levels
where?
Classroom or small-group setting, whatever is determined as LRE
how?
Cooperative learning charts, VAKT approach (visual, auditory, and kinesthetic-tactile learning), reading books, answering teacher-directed questions, creating webs like this on any topic, using the computer for research, keeping dated portfolios of completed projects, individual self-assessments, and teacher observation

Available for download at **www.corwin.com/inclusionstrategies**

Scoring With Metacognition (Knowing What You Know)

Where do you begin? *Awareness* is definitely the first step. A massive dose of *metacognition* for all involved parties is highly recommended. Without motivation and a good measure of perseverance, reaching any goal is a bit like running on a treadmill, as your destination remains the same. Basic education involves learning objectives but must also include effective anticipatory sets that motivate, entice, and encourage students to listen and learn. Without the right attitude, even the best research-proven strategies will fail. Questions to ponder include the following:

Why are the students there?

Why are the teachers there?

There will be a difference in the learning outcomes if students perceive themselves as *school prisoners rather than eager participants* in the learning process. This attitude applies to the teaching staff as well. Again, metacognition is critical.

Students can keep track of their own grades and behavior in their portfolios and decide on future goals. They need to ask themselves, How am I doing? Do my grades and behavior show improvement? What is my goal? Learning success is the ultimate goal of all education.

Being goal-oriented is the reason hockey fans scream deliriously as the puck reaches the net and the team scores a goal. But what is the goal of special education or perhaps of all education? Those who enjoy math might love deciphering the following mathematical self-correcting exercise to discover the goal of *special* education.

THE GOAL OF *SPECIAL* EDUCATION ■

Directions: Solve each mathematical problem and place the correct letter above each blank. Numbered answers correspond to the order of the letters in the alphabet as shown in the code below. Try to think of different mathematical problems without duplicating the ones on this page to complete the rest of the sentence. The message reveals the goal of *special* education.

_T_ _O_ ____ ____ ____ ____ ____ ____ ____

5 × 4   12 + 3   32 ÷ 2   6 × 3   60 ÷ 12   4 × 4   10 ÷ 10   9 × 2   30 ÷ 6

____ ____ ____ ____ ____ ____ ____ ____ ____ ____ ____ ____ ____ ____

9 ÷ 3   16 ÷ 2   3 × 3   9 + 3   20 – 16   36 ÷ 2   40 ÷ 8   2 × 7   10 × 2   30 ÷ 2   3 × 4   5 × 1   18 ÷ 18   –5 + 9

____ ____ ____ ____ ____ ____ ____ ____ ____ ____

8 × 2   12 + 6   3 × 5   –8 + 12   63 ÷ 3   27 ÷ 9   10 × 2   54 ÷ 6   11 × 2   3 + 2

____ ____ ____ ____ ____ ____ ____ ____ ____ ____ ____

63 ÷ 7   30 – 16      3 + 2   9 × 2 – 2   12 ÷ 2 – 1   7 × 2   100 ÷ 25   100 ÷ 20   9 + 5   1000 ÷ 50

L I V E A S

____ ____ ____ ____ ____ ____

M E M B E R S

____ ____ ____ ____ ____ ____ ____

O F T H E A D U L T

____ ____ ____ ____ ____ ____ ____ ____ ____ ____

C O M M U N I T Y.

____ ____ ____ ____ ____ ____ ____ ____ ____

A	B	C	D	E	F	G	H	I	J	K	L	M	N	O	P	Q	R	S	T	U	V	W	X	Y	Z
1	2	3	4	5	6	7	8	9	10	11	12	13	14	15	16	17	18	19	20	21	22	23	24	25	26

Self-Checking Exercises

The preceding exercise assumed specific prior mathematical knowledge. Comfort levels along with time taken to complete the exercise may vary, as will individual motivation and frustration. The self-checking component allows students of all ages to gain their own feedback before teachers correct their mistakes. Adding this type of self-correcting exercise is also interdisciplinary, connecting math skills with reading. Mathematical problems will vary depending on student levels of learning. It's an excellent avenue to reinforcing computational skills while reading about the main idea in the science, social studies, art, music, or language domains.

NUMBERS + LETTERS + WORDS = RETENTION OF MEANINGFUL IDEAS

DISCOVERING THE ANSWER: ALPHABETICAL MESSAGE

Pick a curriculum topic and design your own alphabetical message.

A	B	C	D	E	F	G	H	I	J	K	L	M	N	O	P	Q	R	S	T	U	V	W	X	Y	Z
1	2	3	4	5	6	7	8	9	10	11	12	13	14	15	16	17	18	19	20	21	22	23	24	25	26

Available for download at **www.corwin.com/inclusionstrategies**

MOTIVATING AND PERSONALIZING LEARNING CHOICES

It's amazing that some children are so turned off to learning. Even though education is compulsory, physical attendance alone does not constitute attention. If a student does not possess the drive or desire to learn, frustrated teachers perform to empty audiences. When interests are heightened, meaningful learning connections are made and greater understanding achieved. When teachers ask children what they like, learning can be personalized, allowing students to become more involved in their learning. Not every lesson can be tailored to each child's likes, but perhaps making personal connections can awaken a present body but dormant mind, letting motivation be a precursor of learning.

When a teacher is selecting a reading book, it is important to know what a student likes. For example, if a child loves dogs but dislikes reading, picking a compelling story such as *Old Yeller, Sounder,* or *Where the Red Fern Grows* will increase the odds that this particular student will be more drawn into the reading process. Interest inventories can also help in the writing process.

Teachers who always assign writing topics are not allowing students to pick topics from within. Topics from within are the ones students will more freely write about. Although some writing assignments are mandatory, always giving students prompts is not allowing for the impromptu creativity that personal topics yield. For example, introducing a unit on poetry has more merit if initially you allow students to share their favorite poem and then ask them to mirror that style. Knowing what students like actively involves them in their own learning destiny and will lead to future retention.

Interest Inventories

Teachers can motivate learners to make necessary connections to their own lives to achieve lasting insights. Some curriculum connections in Grades K–12 follow.

K–3

- Draw, cut out, or gather pictures of their favorite things from magazines or approved online sources.
- As appropriate, offer word banks, clip art, or picture/visual dictionaries.
- If help is needed with handwriting, configuration strategies, stencils, computer programs, templates for words, digital recordings, or scribing to a peer can be used as scaffolding techniques to improve the appearance of the printed word or to let interests be shared without requiring the handwriting component. Investigate Keyboarding Without Tears at www.hwtears.com/kwt and collaborate with an occupational therapist for strategies.

4–6

- Use an interest inventory for selecting writing topics during the year (see page 93).
- If possible, try to acknowledge students' likes and dislikes in the lessons.
- Have students periodically review inventories that they fill out at the beginning of the year, which can be conveniently kept in their writing folder to see if interests changed.
- Students exchange thoughts with peers by sharing ideas.
- Inventories can be turned into a class graph.

7–8

- Students create their own categories.
- Design a cartoon, advertisement, or chart based on interests.
- Create a poem, short story, news article, word search, picture book, or slide show.

9–12

- Compare students' interests to family/school surveys.
- Form cooperative writing groups based on student interests.
- Match interests with a variety of genres in reading and writing across all subjects.
- Collaborate with teachers of other disciplines to create interdisciplinary lessons that acknowledge and honor students' interests to increase motivation and time on task.

Another great advantage of interest inventories is their ability to draw students closer together. Students discover things about their peers they might never find out with the "heads-forward" learning approach. Socially, students become more interpersonal by sharing introspections. Teachers who complete and share the same interest inventory are making a meaningful bond that connects them to their students. Even teachers and students can have things in common. Learning about each other is very *interesting*. Overall, there are many merits to asking, "What do you like?"

"WHAT DO YOU LIKE?"

A Few of My Favorite Things

FOOD	PERSON	PLACE
BOOK	MOVIE	TV SHOW
SEASON	PET	CAR
SONG	SUBJECT	TIME

Exploring Potential With Many Ways of Being Smart

Howard Gardner and his colleagues, working on a research project at the Harvard Graduate School of Education (infed.org/mobi/howard-gardner-multiple-intelligences-and-education) expanded the idea of intelligences to multiple domains such as logical thinking, linguistics, music, movement, interpersonal activities, and self-knowledge. As Gardner notably pointed out, intelligence is not always as quantifiable as measuring someone's height. According to this school of thought, since measurement of intelligence is not always exact, classroom teachers can help students learn to tap into their stronger intelligence, maximizing what they are good at, rather than instructing or assessing through weaknesses. This theory helps teachers and students achieve more successes.

What Is Intelligence? Solving Problems, Creating Products—Information

- We each have capabilities in varying degrees that are influenced by exposure and specific training.
- Students with disabilities need to work through their strengths (stronger intelligences to improve weaker ones). For example, children with learning disabilities who are weaker in verbal-linguistic and logical-mathematical intelligences may be stronger in visual-spatial and bodily-kinesthetic ones. Instruction then addresses individual differences via assignments, delivery, and assessments.
- Teachers must also be aware of their own preferred (stronger) intelligences as well as their weaker ones, since sometimes teachers will shy away from their more uncomfortable ones. For example, I rarely sing in front of a class, due to what I perceive as my weaker intelligence (musical-rhythmic). Yet I would encourage my students to display their own competence in the musical area and be aware of classroom sounds.

MULTIPLE INTELLIGENCES OF STUDENTS

Depending on the students' stronger or preferred intelligences, these are some of the classroom behaviors that teachers may see. Nothing is this clear-cut since students may have two or three favorite intelligences, but usually weaker ones are most evident.

Knowing students better helps teachers plan more productive lessons, tapping into student strengths. "Only multiple intelligences (MI) hold the power and potential for instructors or educators to develop flexible and broad enough methodologies and approaches to address a diverse audience with differing skill sets or potentials" (McFarlane, 2011, para. 6).

Verbal-Linguistic

- This student is adept at offering excuses. He or she can convince you that the dog ate the homework.

- Even though verbal skills are child's preference, he or she may be overly sensitive to criticism or sarcastic remarks.
- This student may use acronyms or mnemonics to memorize written information.

Logical-Mathematical

- This student prefers a high degree of organization in a structured classroom.
- He or she is usually not comfortable in chaotic settings.
- This student is likely to be computer literate.

Visual-Spatial

- This student can be overwhelmed or frustrated by print-only material or long written assignments.
- He or she often visualizes learning concepts.
- This student prefers concrete, semiconcrete, or semiabstract levels of presentations.
- He or she may be a doodler. Determine if doodling interferes with learning before modifying behavior, since doodlers very often multitask and are actually listening.

Musical-Rhythmic

- This student has high sensitivity to classroom sounds (e.g., quiet noises), human voices, and rhythmic patterns.
- He or she may tap fingers, hum, or whisper during silent reading.

Bodily-Kinesthetic

- This student has difficulty sitting still for long periods of time.
- He or she may be distracted by the movement of others.
- This student will remember what is done rather than what is said.

Naturalistic

- This student pays attention to minute details, relationships, and sensory information.
- He or she learns best when knowledge is connected to prior topics.
- This student is quite aware of his or her place among the surroundings.

Interpersonal

- This student learns best when allowed to interact with others.
- He or she enjoys cooperative learning, peer editing, and team-building activities.

Intrapersonal

- This student needs wait time to respond to questions and reflect on learning.
- He or she responds well to empowerment activities with choices in assignments.
- This student likes journals or writing notebooks for personal thoughts.

Existentialist

- This student asks questions as a critical thinker and problem solver.
- He or she likes to reflect on reasons for learning and the nature of tasks.
- This student responds well to open discussions, quotes, questionnaires, and surveys.
- He or she thinks beyond sensory data.

Multiple Intelligences Resources to Check Out

Armstrong, T. (2003). *You're smarter than you think: A kid's guide to multiple intelligences.* Minneapolis, MN: Free Spirit Publishing. (Dr. Armstrong's website is www.ThomasArmstrong.com.)

Armstrong, T. (2009). *Multiple intelligences in the classroom.* Alexandria, VA: Association for Supervision and Curriculum Development.

Gardner, H. (2006). *Multiple intelligences: New horizons.* New York, NY: Basic Books.

Project Zero: www.pzweb.harvard.edu.

MULTIPLE INTELLIGENCES SURVEY

Directions: Place the numbers 1 to 9 in the following boxes to rank your preferable intelligences, with "1" as your favorite intelligence and "9" as your least favorite intelligence. This will help you think about how you learn best.

Verbal-Linguistic

Interpersonal

Bodily-Kinesthetic

Naturalistic

Intrapersonal

Musical-Rhythmic

Visual-Spatial

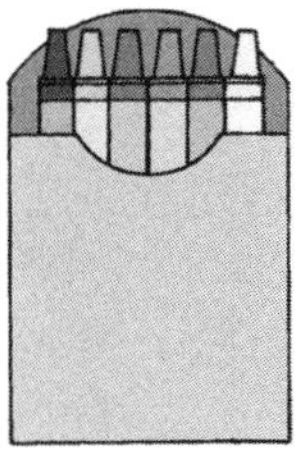

Logical-Mathematical

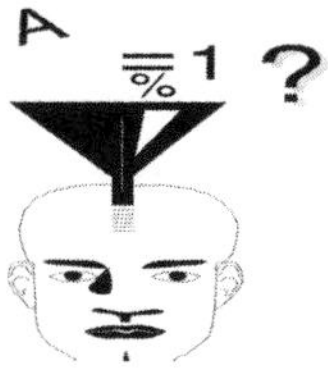

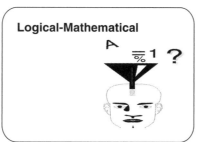

Existentialist

■ LEARNING ANALYSIS

Education requires preparation that analyzes each step of the learning process. The old adage "Rome was not built in a day" can most definitely be applied to many learning situations.

A CUPFUL OF LEARNING

Illustrated below is a step-by-step drawing that transforms an oval into a cup. Draw the previous steps in the boxes at the right of each drawing. Repeating the prior steps each time yields further retention.

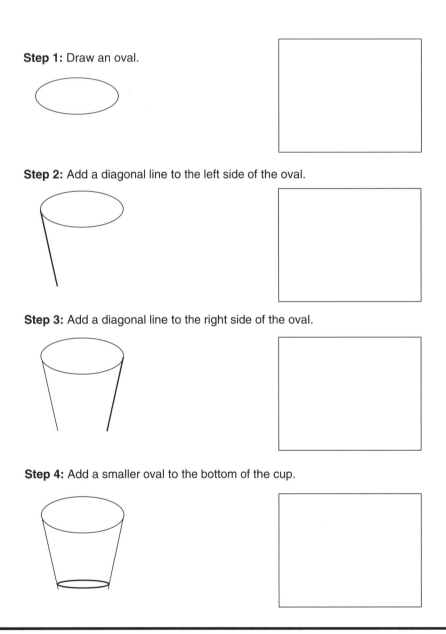

Step 1: Draw an oval.

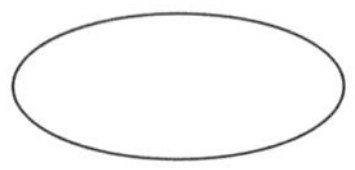

Step 2: Add a diagonal line to the left side of the oval.

Step 3: Add a diagonal line to the right side of the oval.

Step 4: Add a smaller oval to the bottom of the cup.

APPLYING THE STEP-BY-STEP PROCESS TO LEARNING SITUATIONS

Suppose you were trying to teach a first grader how to write the letter "b."

Step 1: Draw a line.

Step 2: Place your pencil point about $\frac{2}{3}$ of the way down the line.

Step 3: Add a small circle from that point to the bottom of the line.

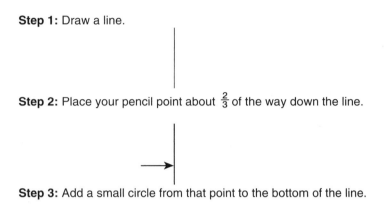

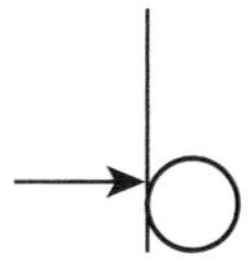

Available for download at **www.corwin.com/inclusionstrategies**

Sample Curriculum Connections

Reviewing each step along the way helps students to reach the end product. Whether a student is drawing a cup or writing the letter *b*, outlining individual skills involved can ensure mastery and further retention. Even though this is the old stick-and-ball method, the underlying principle is to help students with letter formation and directionality. To further assist learners, rules can be verbalized while using wide-lined paper at first, before paper with smaller, more confined lines is given. Again, breaking up the learning requires systematically outlining different components involved in lessons that some learners automatically grasp; others need this type of instruction to master the same principles. For example, if a student's goal was to count objects one through ten, then at first that student may just practice counting and identifying sets of one to four objects, then add sets of five to seven, and ones with eight to ten objects, with review and repetition of all numbers from one to ten to reinforce and periodically maintain the counting skills. Yes, it requires more time, but the results are worth it because the former type of instruction, which does not match individual needs, is an unproductive use of student and teacher time and effort. Better to master some steps than to be overwhelmed and frustrated by the entire lesson and gain no skills at all. Specific grade-level examples of step-by-step applications follow.

K–2

Putting on a coat. Washing hands. Tying a shoe. Writing a heading on a paper. Drawing a picture of the student's neighborhood. Putting a group of words in alphabetical order. Counting how many syllables or phonemes are in a word. Classifying the shapes of objects. Identifying what sounds letters, digraphs, or diphthongs have. Ordering numbers. Making eye contact during conversations.

3–5

Dividing with two or more steps involved, with a one-digit divisor into a three-digit dividend. Identifying the subject of a sentence. Estimating the product of 2 three-digit factors. Writing a paragraph about a favorite book. Telling what a plant needs to grow. Finding the greatest common factor of two numbers. Identifying the parts of words: prefixes, suffixes, and root words. Summarizing a book, chapter by chapter. Learning about weather or ecosystems. Working cooperatively with peers.

6–8

Using a microscope. Finding the mean, median, mode, and range of a set of numbers. Editing work. Diagramming a sentence into its subject and predicate. Identifying the direct and indirect objects of sentences. Describing the layers of the earth. Writing a five-paragraph essay. Finding the latitude and longitude of a city, or applying other map skills such as a scale of miles. Demonstrating appropriate daily hygiene. Creating a time frame for completing a long-range assignment.

9–12

Graphing a linear algebraic equation. Balancing chemical equations. Setting up a research paper. Writing a haiku. Identifying types of analogies. Describing how the stock market works. Telling how a bill becomes a law. Determining the correct change to be received in a store. Filling out a bank deposit slip. Traveling with public transportation. Writing a résumé. Transitioning to postsecondary settings.

APPLYING A STEP-BY-STEP APPROACH TO LEARNING

Directions: Think of particular content or functional areas and how tasks can be broken up into their learning components for the students in your class who require this type of assistance. As appropriate, use the CCSS.ELA-Anchor and Mathematical Practice Standards along with grade-level standards. Review these sites for standards-based connections: www.corestandards.org and www.masteryconnect.com/learn-more/goodies.html. Possibilities are endless, while results can be fruitful for all.

Topic: ____

Description of academic/functional objective:

____

____

____

____

Step 1: ____

Step 2: ____

Step 3: ____

Step 4: ____

Step 5: ____

Sample Activity: Adding Mixed Numbers

LEARNING ANALYSIS WORKSHEET

Teachers review each step or skill and determine its components, deciding what accommodation/ modification might be needed. Simply put, it's step-by-step teaching and learning. This grid is more than just task analysis, since teachers and students identify and strengthen exact areas of need within lessons. When teachers concretely keep track of steps, students are noticed and rewarded for incremental accomplishments. Students who are more advanced can apply the skill of adding mixed numbers to a group activity such as selecting a favorite recipe and doubling or halving it. If appropriate for age and skill sets, peer tutors can use the *Learning Analysis* tool.

CCSS: 5.NF.1: Add and subtract fractions and mixed numbers with unlike denominators using area models.

Steps	Yes/ Not Yet	What Happened?	Accommodation/ Modification
1. Copy problem in notebook.	Y	Checked for accuracy	
2. Decide if fractions need common denominators.	Y	Identified fractions with different denominators	
3. Find common denominators.	Y	Able to find lowest common multiples	
4. Add fractions.	NY	Added denominators as well and combined whole numbers as part of the numerators	Separate whole numbers and fractions.
5. Reduce fractions or change to improper fractions.	NY	Cannot change improper to mixed numbers or vice versa	Review mixed-number conversions.
6. Add whole numbers.	Y	Accurately performed task at familiar level	
7. Combine whole numbers and fractions.	NY	Inverted fractions	Fraction circle manipulatives, semiabstract presentation level, more guided and then independent practice

LEARNING ANALYSIS WORKSHEET

Objective/Activity: ______________________________

CCSS Connection: ______________________________

Steps	Yes/Not Yet	What Happened?	Accommodation/ Modification

Student(s) ______________________________

____

____

____

Additional comments on how inclusive learner(s) performed: ______________________________

____

____

____

____

CONCRETIZING LEARNING

After you have established the student's prior knowledge and interests and analyzed the learning steps and frequency, it is time for concretization.

Levels of Presentation

Concrete: Using a real object to demonstrate a concept (e.g., using a sneaker to teach how to tie a shoe or a meter stick to teach metrics, having students follow along on a tablet while learning keyboarding skills, seeing a rock imprinted with a fossil or a cut tree to show the age rings inside, or using actual coins to count change).

Semiconcrete: Using a representation of an object to demonstrate a concept (e.g., using Cuisenaire rods, algebra tiles, and other manipulatives in math; cutting up an apple to represent fractions; or using a model of a heart in a biology class).

Semiabstract: Using a picture of an object to illustrate a word or concept (e.g., magazine pictures or clip art of words with initial or final consonants, artwork depicting events in American history, a diagram showing labels of microscope parts, U.S. Civil War timeline, reproduction of a historical diary entry, or a cut-up map of the world to teach about plate tectonics)

Abstract: Teaching a concept from the textbook, without any visual or concrete accompaniment (e.g., using math worksheets or simply lecturing to students).

Cutting Up and Tossing the World

Concept to Be Demonstrated: Approximately three-quarters of the world is water, and one-quarter is land. To reinforce or concretize this concept, the teacher presents it on a semiconcrete level.

Examples: The teacher brings an apple to school and cuts it into four parts, sets aside three of those parts, and compares them to the water or blue part of the world. Later on, an assessment on this topic can include a circle, which students are asked to divide and label to represent the earth's water and land. These edible fractions now solidify the *global* learning. An inflatable globe is then tossed and caught for fifty trials while students record and chart the results of where their right index finger landed (water or land). Think of your own lesson to concretize.

SOURCE: Cassidy (1994).

The tossing activity was a component of a Special Science Teams program developed at Rutgers, The State University of New Jersey, funded by the National Science Foundation and Research for Better Schools.

TEACHER'S CONCRETE PLANNER

Concept to Be Demonstrated: ____________________

Level of Presentation: (concrete, semiconcrete, semiabstract, abstract)

Step-by-Step Procedure

____

____

____

____

____

____

Evaluation/Assessment

____

____

____

____

____

____

Follow-Up

____

____

____

____

____

____

LEARNING DESIGNS

Universal Design for Learning (UDL)

UDL refers to universal design for learning, which advocates having learning options and accommodations already in place instead of waiting until student or educator needs arise. Universal design (UD) initially entered society as an acronym that referred to architectural accessibility; for example, curb cuts on sidewalks or an inclined ramp for those in wheelchairs also helps parents or caretakers with baby carriages and strollers or a person navigating the city on a skateboard or motorized scooter. Another example is closed captioning. Although initially intended to help those with hearing impairments, it universally appeals to people who speak another language with its written transcriptions as well as people with dyslexia who are learning to read. Classrooms with UDL practices vary presentations, expressions, and engagements with built-in flexibility for students' differing strengths. There is a wide array of resources, strategies, deliveries, sensory approaches, and advocacy for differentiation available right away, rather than waiting and then frantically scrounging for ideas, resources, and approaches when the needs arise.

Examples of UDL include but are not limited to the following list:

- Setting up sections in the inclusive classroom as quieter study areas
- Establishing sponge activities and ongoing projects for students who master assignments before their peers (e.g., ongoing classroom newspaper or poetry corner, writing, reading, math, science, social studies, art, or music stations with delineated activities prepared)
- Understanding that some students need to move about to release excessive energy; setting up approved spaces and activities for students to productively channel what may otherwise be deemed inappropriate behavior (e.g., word walls, sensory opportunities, or brain breaks)
- Transcribing novels and worksheets into Braille or larger font prior to the placement of a student with visual impairments or blindness
- Teaching sign language to the whole class
- Valuing multiple intelligences for instruction and assessment
- Having talking websites and digital texts (e.g., Digital Accessible Information System [Daisy], available at www.daisy.org/accessibility; Bookshare, available at www.bookshare.org; Learning Ally, available at www.learningally.org)
- Setting up a strategy table with items such as pencil grips, page blockers, highlighters, counters, kneaded erasers, Koosh balls, transitional word lists, headphones, magnification pages, calculators, Post-its, index cards, manipulatives, and more

Classroom Application of Universal Design Principles With Access to All	
Descriptions	**Objectives**
Content-related visual dictionaries and thematic clip art	To help students better understand vocabulary by offering semiabstract connections for written works and sometimes abstract texts, helping students to visualize the concepts
Textbooks and literature on tape (e.g., Daisy Talking Books, LeapFrog) or ones with same content, with perhaps larger font, different vocabulary, or fewer words on each page	Easier to comprehend stories and information to honor the age, integrity, and independence of all learners, even if hearing, visual, or reading levels may vary due to physical, sensory, perceptual, or learning differences
Cut-up tennis balls on the bottoms of chairs	Lower extra noises and distractions and assist students with attention issues
Increased technology (e.g., SMART Boards, word prediction programs, sound field amplification systems, swivel chairs)	Helps with note taking and focusing, especially beneficial for students with fine motor, attention, and hearing concerns such as dysgraphia, ADHD, limited hearing, and auditory processing disorders
Lesson plans that consider individual students' needs, likes, and dislikes (e.g., more strategies built into lessons to help students with learning, such as outlines, graphic organizers, color coding, or infusing interest inventory responses into lessons)	Motivate and connect students to learning on their instructional level rather than their frustration level. Allow students with perceptual or processing issues to understand concepts and give better organizational skills to all students. Assist with guided notes that later serve as study guides, which students independently review.
Treating all students with dignity	Higher student self-esteem, which translates to taking ownership of learning and attempting even more difficult tasks, whether the student is nonverbal, has learning challenges, or is gifted
Computer technology UDL (www.cast.org) Picture Exchange Communication System (PECS), curriculum-related software sites (e.g., www.funbrain.com)	Helps all students gain access to information, allowing for individual communication, sensory, physical, and cognitive levels (e.g., talking Web sites, math and reading software, worksheets and graphic organizers, curriculum-connected visuals, animated graphics, along with PowerPoint slide presentations)
Portable, handheld, speaking electronic dictionaries (e.g., Franklin Speller)	Allow all learners to hear the information to reinforce the written word. In addition to helping those students who are blind or have dyslexia, increase understandings of vocabulary in literature and curriculum without having the words, or encoding, decoding, or reading levels interfere with conceptual understanding
Modeling lessons with increased praise	Reinforces academic, social, emotional, and behavioral levels of students to increase motivation, self-esteem, self-efficacy, and academic focus

SOURCE: Adapted from Karten (2008a).

Differentiation of Instruction

Differentiation of instruction (DI) approaches consider student levels, prior knowledge, interests, and strengths to vary the content, process, and results during planning, instruction, and assessment stages. DI includes appropriate and meaningful tasks, flexible groupings, and tiered instruction. It is interrelated with students' multiple intelligences, universal designs, interests, levels, and learning profiles to offer both accommodations and challenges to the diverse learners who are present in inclusive classrooms. Options include but are not limited to preparing sponge and anchor activities, technology, choice boards, and rubrics. It is a time when learners complete tasks as a class, in small groups, and individually, with and without staff assistance. Differentiation values diverse levels of learning, whether remediation or enrichment is required. The classroom environment has a multitude of resources available, from leveled books to math manipulatives, art/music supplies, and materials that value both struggling and advanced learners. Differentiation of instruction considers diverse ways that teachers instruct and a multitude of ways that learners demonstrate their knowledge. DI incorporates a variety of assessment tools—from informal to standardized ones—that can range from students performing a puppet show to writing an essay and the many choices in between for students with and without IEPs or 504 plans. Differentiation values students with different skill levels, cultures, interests, and abilities. Peruse the *Differentiated Lesson Unit* to connect it to a lesson with consideration for the baseline knowledge, more advanced level, and challenging assignments for the students who are present in an inclusive class. You are invited to fill in additional thoughts for the subject/unit, concepts, domains, instructional objectives, motivations, student activities, co-teaching models, grouping, strategies, assessments, scaffolding, accommodations, enrichment, remediation, and follow-ups.

DIFFERENTIATED LESSON UNIT

Subject: **Unit:** **Concepts:**	
Domains	Educators collaboratively differentiate the learning for a unit of study with planned enrichments and reinforcements
Instructional **Objectives and Standards**	Baseline Knowledge: Advancing Level: More Challenging Assignments:
Motivation and Connections	Based on learner profiles
Student Activities	Cubing, tic-tac-toe boards, anchor and sponge activities, learning contracts, compacting, cooperative groups, independent practice, centers, technology . . . along with multiple means of engagement and representation
Co-Teaching Models	Staff and assistants bouncing ideas off each other, parallel teaching, one leading/one assisting, small groups/1:1, stations/centers, consultation
Grouping: **Whole Class, Small Group, and 1:1**	Set up an ongoing structured system of groups within the classroom (instead of pullout). Recommend 10–12 min. twice a week for review, on-level, and challenging assignments with smaller groups of students—sending a strong communication for students to be prepared and not wait for the day before the test to ask questions to gain clarifications. This prevents misconceptions from escalating. This ongoing classroom setup communicates the importance of review for *all* students and offers the students with IEPs more in-class support without singling them out. It also enables more advanced students to continue their learning at higher levels.
Instructional Strategies Assessments	
Scaffolding and Accommodations	
Enrichment and Remediation	
Follow-Up/ Revisitation Plans	
Other ideas and comments:	

SOURCE: Karten (2013).

Available for download at **www.corwin.com/inclusionstrategies**

Understanding by Design

This approach to thinking about the curriculum offers a framework set up in stages, focused on several core concepts that are correlated with what students are expected to know for specific disciplines or skills. UbD involves thinking about the overall learning outcomes at the outset, rather than proceeding with a lesson and then setting up assessments that might focus on trivial or irrelevant information. Stages are delineated as follows:

Stage 1: Desired results of what students will ultimately understand—the BIG picture

Stage 2: Indicators of real-world learning applications or assessment evidence

Stage 3: The instructional learning plan steps

In addition, UbD advocates continual reflection on the design of learning by means of fine-tuning assessments and examining results, the quality and quantity of work, and appropriate student engagement with curriculum standards and desired skills. It involves designing diagnostic and formative assessments to yield effective, meaningful student accomplishments that encourage eventual independent transfer of learning based on essential evidence and thoughtfully designed activities.

Source to Review

Wiggins, G., & McTighe, J. (2005). *Understanding by design* (2nd ed.). Alexandria, VA: Association for Supervision and Curriculum Development.

The next model serves as an example of a UbD lesson on inclusion for preservice educators.

Stage 1: Preservice educators will understand the complexities involved in designing an inclusive lesson, answering the following questions:

- What will I do if I am teaching a lesson to students with a range of reading levels?
- How will I document students' progress?
- How will I honor students' academic and functional objectives?

Stage 2: Evidence and indicators of the learning will be 80 percent mastery of the curriculum lesson objectives for students in inclusive fieldwork settings, thereby demonstrating knowledge and skills through research, discussion, planning, teamwork, curriculum-based oral and written assessments, student work samples, pre and postassessments, data review, and observation.

Stage 3: This stage includes instruction that honors multiple intelligences, cooperative learning activities, peer mentoring, and establishing prior knowledge, with learning objectives in three levels of mastery under the qualifiers of baseline, more advanced, and challenging academic and functional objectives with different levels of reading texts and appropriate vocabulary pretaught. Student portfolios, work samples, and data are monitored and reviewed to gauge progress and instructional pacing across disciplines.

PROBLEM- AND PROJECT-BASED LEARNING CONNECTIONS

Problem-based learning uses open-ended strategies that value student inquiry. Students are transitioned into active learning roles as they make meaningful connections to relevant content. PBL includes authentic problem solving with educator and student collaboration, engagement, and reflection. Other vital PBL ingredients include extensive instructional planning with monitoring that offers formative and ongoing feedback (Ertmer & Simons, 2005). Findings confirm the potential of PBL for effective interaction (Belland, Glazewski, & Ertmer, 2009).

The initial driving questions presented are broad enough, acting as a springboard for motivating students to develop their own questions and investigations. The following questions offer examples of some PBL connections across the grade levels:

How can we get others to exercise daily?

How do the seasons affect living things?

How can we get from here to there?

How can we safely use digital tools?

How does the government affect my family's life?

How is sound produced?

How does art help people?

How can our class and school impact the local or world community?

Design a restaurant that includes healthful menu choices. Consider location, hours of operation, start-up costs, and advertising.

What is involved in producing a play in a local theater?

What math skills assist specific professionals (e.g., scientists engineers, teachers, doctors, nurses, architects, cartographers, astronauts, chefs, biologists, chemists)?

Teachers connect PBL with what students already know to reach the desired outcomes. It invites meaningful applications of content and skills. Project-based learning is similar to problem-based learning, but differences may include the length of time devoted to the project and whether it is a hypothetical problem or a project related to a real-world authentic task or setting. Both PBLs involve student engagement, inquiry, collaboration, communication, critical-thinking skills, and creativity.

Consult these resources for additional PBL ideas:

Buck Institute for Education: bie.org

Edutopia: www.edutopia.org/project-based-learning

Zunal Webquest: zunal.com/process.php?w=120599

KINESTHETIC CONNECTIONS

Kinesthetic and tactile learning simply means moving, feeling, experiencing, touching, or manipulating learning objects to reinforce abstract concepts. Kinesthetic refers to body movements, while tactile pertains to the sense of touch. Examples include clay models of elements' electrons, neutrons, and protons; skywriting the shapes of letters with their fingers in the air; writing spelling words in salt; using raised glue to write the letters in words; using Cuisenaire rods, algebra tiles, yarn, or magnetic numbers; writing syllables on index cards; doing scientific experiments; and so on. Researchers have shown that exercise and physical activity meaningfully affect reading, spelling, math achievement, and memory, reducing stress and depression and increasing overall learning performance (Jensen, 2000; Mitchell, 2009; Ratey, 2008). Dissociated information will be better remembered if it has been repeatedly demonstrated in a concrete, meaningful way with movements that facilitate cognition, interpersonal connections, and class cohesiveness. Sometimes breaking away from the learning with meaningful activities actually improves comprehension, with opportunities for more attention after completing a physical activity. Perhaps that's why television programs have commercials every fifteen minutes or so and then return to the scheduled programming!

Do remember that safety is paramount with appropriate levels of class management and student engagement that match students' individual IEP goals, interest levels, and recommended physical activity, for example, adapted physical education (PE), occupational therapy (OT), or physical therapy (PT) for students' fine or gross motor skills. Overall, the brain attends to *moving* physical activities!

The next concrete activity uses "meetballs." People need to arrange in small circles of eight to ten and have a soft foam ball.

Meeting With Meetballs

Yes, that is spelled correctly. It's a way to remember names rather than wearing those stickers that say, "Hello, My Name Is _______." It beats walking into a store or restaurant and being personally greeted by total strangers because you have forgotten to remove the adhesive label. "Meetballs" help you meet others!

MEETBALL RECIPE

Directions: Form circles of eight to ten people and have them randomly toss a soft, round object (e.g., a Koosh Ball or Nerf ball) to each other. When someone receives the ball, the person says his or her name. The tossing continues until everyone feels confident about remembering each other's names. The next step is to try to remember a person's name and toss the ball to that person as you say the name. Adding more soft objects to simultaneously toss and repeating or reversing the order varies the game. If everyone already knows each other's names, personal information or answers to content- or curriculum-related questions can be shared when the ball is caught. Sample curriculum connections follow.

Kinesthetic Curriculum Connections

Toss a ball around a classroom and ask students of varying ages and grade levels the following:

What do you think about inclusion?

How did imperialism change the world?

What words begin with the consonant blend *tr?*

How can math help you be successful in life?

Who is your favorite character from literature?

When do earthquakes occur?

Why were Native Americans displaced by colonists?

What are the factors of the number fifty-four?

How should you dress for a job interview?

Use the word *advantageous* in a meaningful sentence.

Name some careers that incorporate geometry.

People Finders are another way to mobilize and think about learning concepts while interacting with one another. The *special* People Finder that follows is a perfect example of kinesthetic learning that leads to discussions on any given topic. Students rotate around the classroom, finding a peer who can sign a given descriptor (see below). Teachers or students design People Finders on just about any curriculum topic.

A SPECIAL PEOPLE FINDER

Directions: Have participants circulate about the room and find someone who would sign his or her name by the appropriate descriptor. Continue until all lines are filled.

________________ can read a newspaper while listening to the radio.

________________ believes IEPs are useful tools.

________________ thinks special education is heading in the right direction.

________________ likes frequent vacations.

________________ thinks a person who is blind can go bowling.

________________ sometimes needs things repeated several times.

________________ doesn't have a junk drawer at home.

________________ likes to use landmarks to find his or her way.

________________ has experienced a physical disability.

________________ thinks inclusive classrooms can be successful ones.

________________ has experienced frustrations with children.

________________ would like more planning time to implement ideas.

________________ makes lists to remember things.

________________ is very grateful for digital spelling, grammar, and dictionary tools.

________________ cannot assemble a swing set.

________________ hates to mow the lawn.

________________ thinks education needs more accountability.

________________ believes in the same standards for all children.

________________ does not read directions.

________________ has better receptive than expressive language.

________________ dislikes this People Finder.

ECLECTIC PEOPLE FINDER CURRICULUM CONNECTIONS

Directions: Find someone who would sign his or her name by the following descriptors:

________________ knows why the American Civil War began.

________________ can name the steps in photosynthesis.

________________ knows the percent for the fraction two-fifths.

________________ can identify the protagonist in *Macbeth*.

________________ can name the final consonant of this picture:

________________ knows the name of the planet closest to the sun.

________________ can describe an isthmus.

________________ knows the number of U.S. presidents.

________________ can tell what a mathematical product is.

________________ knows who painted the *Mona Lisa*.

________________ can say where the Olympic Games began.

________________ can identify three countries in Africa.

________________ can list the thirteen original colonies.

________________ can name two adverbs.

________________ has read a historical novel.

________________ can hum "The Star-Spangled Banner."

________________ can hop on one foot for thirty seconds.

________________ knows what the commutative property is.

________________ can spell two homonyms for *there*.

________________ can graph an inequality.

________________ can ____.

Learning Strides

Kinesthetic cards are used to introduce a unit or topic or as a review of previously taught information. Learning material this way helps fidgety learners who need acceptable ways to channel excess motor energy. Socially, students are interacting with each other, instead of experiencing the "all heads facing forward while learning" mentality. Relinquishing control of the learning, the teacher then becomes more the facilitator of knowledge than the disseminator. Classrooms might be noisier, but they are filled with the sounds of learning as students move about at the same time.

SAMPLE CURRICULUM CONNECTIONS FOR MATCHING KINESTHETIC CARDS

Directions: Teachers or students place questions and answers on two differently colored index cards. Cards are then shuffled and distributed to each student in the classroom, some receiving answers and the others receiving question cards. Students then walk around, finding an answer for their social studies or science question, synonyms for vocabulary words, or maybe a solution to an equation.

synonym for happy	content
How do you say, "My house is your house" in Spanish?	Mi casa es su casa.
A novel by Toni Morrison	*Beloved*
Name of this shape 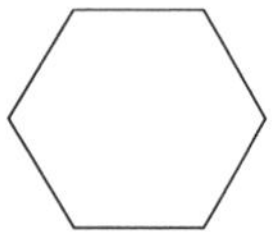	hexagon

Playing charades with vocabulary words on index cards also works across subject areas.

More Kinesthetic Examples to Help Learning Jump Off the Page

Kinesthetically Teaching the Circumference of Circles

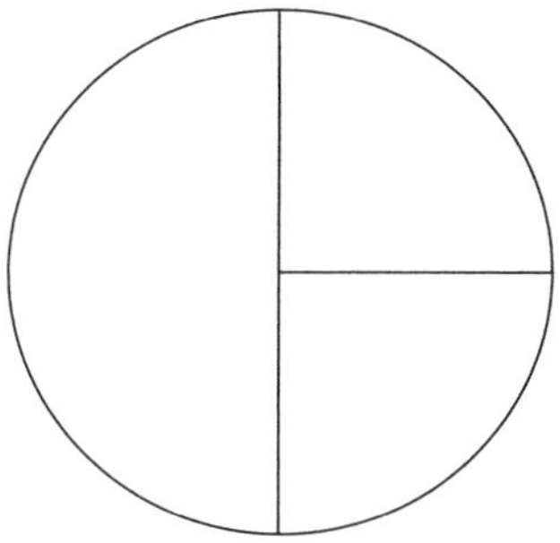

Form a circle while sitting on the floor, with one person in the middle identified as the *center*. Then toss a foam ball from the center person to someone sitting on the outer circle or the *arc*. Each time the ball is passed to the person in the center, a *radius* is created. To illustrate the kinesthetic definition of *diameter*, pass the ball over the head of the person in the middle to someone else. Draw circles with radii and diameters for further concretization of these concepts. The teacher will then model how multiplying the diameter by π (pi), or 3.14, will yield the *circumference*, or distance around the circle. Students check this out by taking a piece of yarn to measure around the circle and comparing that measurement to the product received when the diameter is multiplied by π. More advanced students verify that for any circle, when you divide the circumference by the diameter, it will equal π. Students can use other circular objects, such as paper plates or coins. Some students will need more guidance, while others will independently complete more intricate problems, such as figuring out the radius based on the circumference.

Kinesthetically Teaching New Vocabulary Words, Learning About Characters in a Fictional Book or Historical Figures

Cooperatively create dramatic skits. While preparing demonstrations, notice how much extra learning is involved. Suddenly students will ask, "Can we use the textbook or story for more information?" Eureka! Try pantomiming vocabulary words, settings from novels, and so on.

Kinesthetically Teaching How to Follow Directions

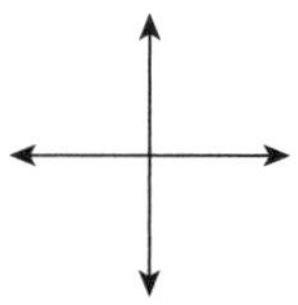

Display a compass rose on the interactive board and point to specific directions, such as north, south, east, and west. On a simpler level, just call the arrows up, down, left, or right. For more complexity, southwest, southeast, northeast, and northwest can be added. Ask everyone to stand up and point their arms in the direction that a leader indicates or says. As students progress, the teacher can then instruct them to point to or say the opposite direction. It's a quick way to release energy while listening and following directions. When the students sit down, notice how much more attentive they are.

Kinesthetically Helping Students to Spell and Decode Words

Writing letters in the air, in a bowl of salt, or with Ziploc bags filled with paint or shaving cream, or clapping hands or tapping fingers or feet to letters and syllables are other ways to learn letters and word parts.

Kinesthetically Teaching Left-to-Right Progression in Reading

A student creates a sentence by writing one word on each index card. Then cards can be rearranged or different ones can be inserted in the original sentence, changing and expanding the meaning or creating questions. Here are some examples: "I like ice cream." "Do you like ice cream?" "I do like ice cream." Verbs, nouns, adjectives, and adverbs can be placed on different-colored index cards, along with punctuation marks.

Kinesthetically Teaching the Song "B-I-N-G-O"

Students sometimes have a difficult time learning when to clap without singing. Select five students and give them each one letter card. Students will hold up their letter card each time that letter is sung. When it is time to delete that letter and clap, that student sits down (in place). The class then claps each time they come to a seated student.

Kinesthetically Teaching Angles

Students in groups of three are each given a card with a point on it labeled A, B, or C. They are then asked to collectively form an angle with two students stretching out their arms as rays in opposite directions while a third student is the vertex, naming each angle A, B, or C. Each time the vertex is changed, the angle is renamed. Other variations can include more students as arrows to represent rays, line segments with students' fists as endpoints, or outstretched arms to indicate that the line continues in one or both directions. Squares and rectangles will have four vertices, and other polygons such as hexagons will be two groups of three with differently labeled points. The *point* is that the kinesthetic possibilities here are *endless*!

Kinesthetically and Digitally Surveying Class Responses to Find Out What Students Know

When teachers want to simultaneously ascertain the understanding of the whole class, they can ask students to respond to written or oral multiple-choice questions by holding up an appropriate number of fingers that correspond to their answer choice (e.g., pointer finger for choice *a*, pointer and middle finger held up together for choice *b*, three fingers for choice *c*, four fingers for choice *d*, or holding up a fist to indicate *I don't know*). Teachers can use this approach, offer classroom response systems with student clickers, ask students to go to designated areas of the room to indicate a response, or simply have clear communication boards holding marked worksheets when delivering interactive quizzes online (e.g., www.brainpop.com, using a *Who Wants to Be a Millionaire?* format, or self-created curriculum-based verbal queries to establish prior or postknowledge). These types of quick informal assessments then assist teachers in gauging what instruction or skills to repeat or how to divide students in the class into review, maintenance, or accelerated learning teams and groups. If there are two teachers or an instructional assistant in the room, he or she could record kinesthetic student choices, whether they are higher- or lower-tech ones.

CAN I KINESTHETICALLY TEACH THIS?

(Remember that kinesthetic teaching means students will be moving, feeling, experiencing, touching, or manipulating learning objects or representations of concepts.)

Think of a Curriculum Topic: ____________________

Kinesthetic Plan (A Walk-Through Lesson):

Objective: ____________________

____

____

____

____

Materials: ____________________

____

____

____

____

Procedure: ____________________

____

____

____

____

Follow-up: ____________________

____

____

____

____

SENSORY APPROACHES AND LEARNING MODALITIES

Modalities refer to the way that sensory information is used to learn. People usually process information through cues directed at visual, auditory, and kinesthetic modalities. Generally, individuals learn by seeing, hearing, touching, doing, and moving. Sometimes one sense of learning is stronger than another. Modalities affect how you interpret reality and communicate with others. Senses are the main tools you use to learn about your environment.

Teachers can incorporate sensory elements into lessons to *reinforce learning and the retention of concepts.* If a student is weak or deficient in one modality, teachers can reinforce the learning by presenting facts through a different one. For example, a teacher may provide more visuals to someone with hearing impairments or more auditory stimuli to a student with visual needs. I once arranged for a speaker who is blind to talk to a fifth-grade class about her disability. She was well received by the class, who gave her flowers and a digitally recorded thank-you message to show their appreciation!

Some still remember the lunchroom smell of their elementary school's cafeteria. What about the smell of those old mimeograph sheets? Quite pungent! My son's friend claimed that when he studied, he wore a certain cologne, and then when he took the test, he wore it again to trigger his memory. There are also schools of thought about the healthy effects of aromatherapy, for example, reduced stress, anxiety, and depression (See health.howstuffworks.com/wellness/natural-medicine/aromatherapy/aromatherapy.htm). Think about all those thriving candle shops!

Children can be helped to learn through many modalities. Tracing letters in the air or in a bowl of salt can reinforce in a tactile way handwriting skills more effectively than just using paper and pencil. Seeing a documentary about World War II can make more of an impression on students than just reading textbook pages. High school science without laboratory experiments, studying art without experiencing different media, talking about music instead of listening to it, or reading about exercise without sweating has less learning merit. Learning theorist Helen Irlen (2008) talks about the power of different colors to help students remember and process information better, such as when different-colored highlighters are used. Colored overlays on reading material block out distractions and help some students read better. Even having learners write their work on yellow lined paper or copying and distributing worksheets and tests on colored paper assists students. Moving students away from window glare beneficially removes distractions. Auditory factors also come into play under the topic of sensory influences. Even *quiet sounds* in the environment will sometimes distract learners who are never bothered by their own extra noises. Some students with autism and other disabilities require sensory integration therapy. Wearing a weighted vest offers some students more comfort. Sensory awareness is an important learning component, whether it assists with the understanding of otherwise abstract concepts or heightens or reduces personal connections. Staff need to honor individual preferences and sensory differences by connecting academic and environmental factors. "Touchable" learning can be as meaningful as those wooden blocks we eagerly manipulated in childhood.

For more information about sensory integration for children with and without disabilities, investigate *The Out-of-Sync Child* by Carol Kranowitz and *Parenting a Child With Sensory Processing Disorder* by Christopher Auer and Susan Blumberg.

Concretizing Conceptual Relationships

Using sensory modalities reinforces the abstract. Manipulating three different-sized objects easily concretizes the concepts of small, smaller, and smallest or large, larger, and largest, allowing degrees of differences to be seen in similar objects. For example, apples, oranges, and balls all have spherical shapes, although not everything round can be eaten. Understanding the difference between two words such as *hard* and *harder* can be demonstrated with a bar of soap and a rock, by tactilely concluding that one can dig his or her fingernail into the soap, but not into the rock. Gathering their own classroom items, students can classify them according to different sensory similarities or differences to develop higher-level thinking skills. Students simply fold lined paper into three columns, listing items, similarities, and differences under appropriate headings. Higher-level relationships can be investigated, while complexities across grades and levels of learners can vary.

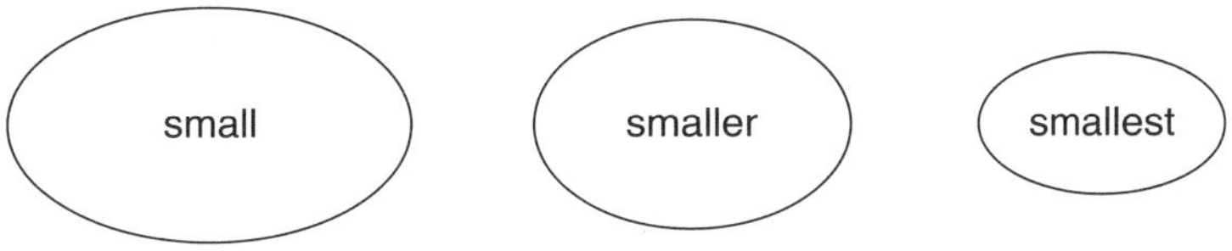

SELF-DISCOVERY CHART

Items	Similar	Different
Pencil, chalk, marker	All used for writing	Materials, texture, width, color, malleability

SENSATIONAL PARTY: WHAT DO I SEE, HEAR, SMELL, TASTE, AND TOUCH?

Directions: Design a *sensational* party. Pick a setting and list what you might see, hear, smell, taste, or touch. Senses help us to visualize learning, understand relationships, and thereby concretize many otherwise abstract (or *sense-less*) concepts.

Possible Settings

Beach	Carnival	Laboratory	Battlefield
Park	North Pole	Museum	Video Arcade
Baseball Field	Football/Hockey Game	12th Century	Parthenon
Rainforest	Library	Safari	Other

Sights	Sounds	Smells	Tastes	Touch

Visualization: Abstract Thinking

Visualizing concepts is a way to internalize and concretize otherwise abstractly presented facts, rather than just being recipients of boring lectures or dry textbook facts. Imagining encourages role-play, with learning protagonists. Close your eyes and imagine!

Imaginable Curriculum Connections

Social Studies: Imagine that you are a slave, living in the colony of Virginia in the year 1740, being put up for auction. Look around and describe your thoughts.

Science: You are a plant with roots too small for your pot. How do you feel? What are your needs? Describe your greatest wish.

Math: You are a number that is a multiple of seven, but less than one hundred. Who are your friends? Place yourself in several computational word problems and solve them.

Reading: You are the best friend of a story's main character. What activities do you do together? Where would you vacation? Tell how you would change the plot.

Think of your own learning visualizations:

Imagine . . .

4

Next, Writing and Applying the Individualized Education Program

This chapter offers more information on what to include in individualized education programs (IEPs), as well as ways to effectively implement and document them in individual classrooms. Guidelines for using and writing effective IEPs that align with the curriculum will benefit all students. The children of today are tomorrow's workforce and need the right skills to make productive contributions. The delivery of the IEP, as shown in this chapter, need not be frustrating or complicated. It is a plan for teachers, parents, guardians, students, and all staff who must act as allies working toward the achievement of written, agreed-upon, realistic school goals.

After the passage of the Individuals with Disabilities Education Improvement Act (IDEIA) in 2004, goals written in IEPs, although still individualized, became more aligned with the general education (GE) curriculum with evidence-based practices and instruction. This requires a planning process that advocates higher expectations for students with IEPs. It involves the general education curriculum and all that then follows in life, through an educational program in both academic and functional skills that prepares students to be part of society. Legislation for students with disabilities has evolved throughout the decades, beginning with Public Law (PL) 94-142 in 1975 and progressing to the Individuals with Disabilities Education Act (IDEA) in 1990, then to amendments in 1997, with more improvements and reauthorizations in 2004 and future reauthorizations on the horizon. IEPs before the 2004 reauthorization are compared to present practices in the chart that follows.

WHAT EXACTLY IS AN IEP?

- Written plan for a child who is eligible for special education services
- Based on student's individual needs

Prior IEP mind-sets, before 2004 reauthorization	Present IEP mind-sets, now based on legislative impacts
Less inclusion of students with disabilities in GE curriculum standards and classroom objectives	Common Core State Standards (CCSS) aligned with the needs of students in inclusive classrooms
Deficit-driven instruction based on what students cannot do, often inadvertently highlighting students' weaknesses	Growth paradigm for what students can and will achieve, based on strengths and research-based strategies to achieve desired outcomes
Students with disabilities were more often omitted from district and statewide testing	Students with disabilities are part of the accountability picture with district and statewide assessments, unless students have severe cognitive disabilities and must take alternate assessments
Separate GE & special education (SE) programs and facilities for students, with less collaboration between staff	Increased collaboration between GE and SE programs and staff within inclusive environments; consultative services with common threads intertwined and woven across disciplines, facilities, and programs
Modifications automatically offered, sometimes assuming that students can't get it, before asking, "How will they get it?"	Exploration of accommodations versus modifications without the automatic dilution of outcomes, saying, "We'll figure out a way that the students will get it!"
More time for other activities involving daily living and functional skills	Focus on academic skills, test preparation, and data collection and interpretation for instruction
Lack of research-based criteria before the recommendation of IEP services and programs; increased referrals for special education	More use of research-based interventions in classrooms even before IEPs are written, taking proactive response to intervention (RTI) steps instead of waiting for students to fail or automatically testing and labeling students

- Requires development of specialized instruction and services with reviews and revisions
- States the present level of academic achievement and functional performance (PLAAFP), or present level of performance (PLOP, i.e., current reading, math, spelling, language, perceptual, and social skills are delineated)
- Incorporates psychoeducational evaluations, including observation and discussion with the students, teachers, staff, parents, and guardians
- Includes input from parents and guardians concerning developmental history
- Integrates all home and school reports

- Bases decisions about placement on current levels of performance, which are determined by multidisciplinary instructional support groups and teams, not the availability of services

- Considers environmental and ecological circumstances, including how and where skills will be both learned and applied within school and outside, in community settings

- Determines the extent to which the student can participate in general educational programs

- Provides necessary aids, supports, and related services

- Lists accommodations and modifications, including frequency, location, and duration of services

- Incorporates parent and guardian participation and communication in both planning stages and reporting child's progress

- Includes general and special education teachers

- Includes any teachers or staff considered by the school district or families to be beneficial to the student's success in school in IEP planning

PRACTICAL GUIDELINES FOR USING AND WRITING THE IEP

- All parties who work with student must read the IEP to effectively apply appropriate strategies, unless parents or guardians prohibit certain people from accessing the document, as allowed in some states.

- IDEA does not use the term *inclusion*; however, it does require school districts to place the students in the least restrictive environment (LRE) to the maximum extent appropriate, alongside their nondisabled peers, unless the nature or severity of the disability is such that success in the general education classroom cannot be achieved even with the use of supplementary aids or services.

- If the IEP cannot be implemented in the regular or general education classroom of the school the child would attend if not disabled, then that classroom is not the LRE placement for that child. It would render the general education classroom inappropriate.

- The student's needs are the basis for his or her placement.

- Supplementary aids and services, such as a note taker, instructional assistant, computer, communication boards, or Braille, are specifically described in the IEP.

- A child can receive related medical services unless it would require the direct supervision of a physician and cause an undue burden on the district. Examples of appropriate services are catheterizations or feeding tubes administered by a trained school nurse.

- Both educational and nonacademic benefits to the student with a disability must be considered in placement decisions.

• Students are exempt from a standardized assessment if it is stated in the IEP; that is, alternative means of assessment with modified achievement standards are permitted for a small percentage of those students with IEPs who, even with accommodations, cannot participate in the standardized testing. States must then ascertain these students' proficiencies on alternative assessment tests to demonstrate that learning has taken place. These alternative evaluations are based on modified achievement standards with assessments then developed by individual states.

• IDEIA states that when a student reaches the age of sixteen, the IEP must include a statement of transitional-service needs. This statement can also be included at a younger age, if it is appropriate to that child's individual needs. The statement focuses on postschool goals, but most important, it stipulates what educational experiences or vocational training will best suit a particular child's program. The Division of Vocational Rehabilitation Services (DVRS) for each state and the Division on Career Development and Transition (www.dcdt.org), part of the Council for Exceptional Children (CEC, www.cec.sped.org), offer technical consultation and assistance for vocational training and guidance with employment issues. Transition services are detailed in students' IEPs, with specific statements about adult plans. Community involvement, related services, employment, functional living skills, and the establishment of connections with outside agencies are included. Skills need to be included in the IEP to prepare the student to reach this goal. For instance, academic, self-help, personal hygiene, other independent-living skills, plans for community integration, or vocational training are objectives that may be applicable. Whether their decision involves continued education or entry into the workforce, teenagers can also be helped with the transition to life after high school through learning opportunities such as life-skills classes in school settings.

• The IEP provides an appropriate educational experience for each student, with effective communication between home and school. It includes continuity of services based on students' present levels of performance with consideration of the future. There is a zero-reject clause, meaning that no child with a disability can be excluded from education. The evaluation must also consider the student's culture, language, and background.

• Noncompliance with the law means that states and school districts will face consequences for ignoring the mandates outlined in IDEA.

> The federal law mandates what information must be included in the IEP, but each state or individual school system decides what the IEP paperwork will look like. There is no standard IEP form, as evidenced by its varying appearance in different states and districts. IDEA revisions aimed at reducing paperwork by clarifying that no additional information is necessary in the IEP beyond what federal regulations require.

The individualized document is collaboratively planned with input from the following stakeholders:

- Special education teachers
- General education teachers
- Parents or guardians
- Administrators
- Team members known in some states with initials such as CST (Child Study Team), SST (Student Study Team), IST (Instructional Support Team), MET (Multidisciplinary Evaluation Team), or MDT (Multi-Disciplinary Team). Members of these teams usually include a social worker, learning disabilities teacher consultant, and a school psychologist.
- Case manager, who may be a member of the team
- Speech/language therapist
- Other related staff members, such as speech-language pathologists, occupational and physical therapists, orientation-mobility trainers, behavioral interventionists, counselors, sign-language interpreters, and inclusion coaches
- Student (if age and input are appropriate)

Inclusive IEP Elements

- Present levels of academic achievement and functional performance
- Individualized goals and benchmarks as major components of what you want the child to achieve. The Individuals with Disabilities Improvement Education Act of 2004 eliminated benchmarks and short-term objectives, which are now required only for those students with severe cognitive disabilities. States can include them but are not required to do so.
- Emphasis on student outcomes rather than compliance
- Modifications and supplementary aids or services needed in the general or special classroom along with supports for extracurricular/nonacademic activities
- Method and schedule for reporting student's progress, for example, quarterly reports such as report cards
- Related services that can include but are not limited to speech therapy, occupational therapy, physical therapy, or appropriate technology
- Behavioral plan and interventions
- Extended school year (ESY) if appropriate to maintain skills
- Statement of transitional services mandated at age sixteen or older; can develop appropriate future goals if student is younger
- Extent of participation in district and state assessment programs and graduation requirements
- Signed parental/guardian consent and signatures of all who planned the IEP

APPROPRIATE GOALS AND SKILLS TO CONSIDER WHEN WRITING AN IEP

Based on student data of present level of performance, measurable academic and functional goals such as the following ones are written. Consideration is given to where the student is functioning in comparison to the grade-level standards and what specially designed instruction, with accommodations and modifications, is required for the student to be successful. Goals are then formulated with realistic expectations of what the student will achieve in the upcoming year.

Phonics/Word Identification. Reading multisyllabic words, identifying consonant clusters, decoding grade-level word lists, academic-specific vocabulary in literature and informational text, street signs, and isolating prefixes and suffixes.

Reading Comprehension. Locating the main idea; knowing the elements of a story (setting, characters, plot, resolution); inferential reading skills (cause and effect, sequencing events, prediction of outcomes); ordering from a menu; and reading a newspaper or online article (e.g., interpreting current events, finding out the weather, reading classifieds, selecting a time and location for a movie, and more).

Mathematics. Counting objects, ordering numbers, finding patterns, computations with all operations, fractions, measurements, understanding and unraveling word problems, identifying geometric shapes, solving algebraic expressions, telling time, getting change in a store, and figuring out the answers to vertex-edge problems.

Science. Seasons; plants; senses; nutrition; scientific methods such as hypothesis or observation; reading a periodic table; balancing formulas; and relating scientific principles to concrete daily activities in physics, chemistry, health, and more.

Social Studies. Community, map skills, world history, civil rights, economics, cultural awareness, character education, and global connections.

Language. Listening, speaking, capitalization, punctuation, grammar, categorizing words, writing paragraphs, letter writing, essays, research reports, poems, figurative language, and responding to prompts with speculative essays.

Computers. Identifying computer parts, keyboarding, bolding text, preparing a résumé, writing a research report, finding clip art, and paraphrasing and citing online sources.

Study Skills. Attending to the teacher, taking notes, bringing home appropriate books, preparing for tests and long-range assignments, organizing work area, maintaining a daily list of completed assignments, and communicating needs.

Motor Skills

Gross Motor. Sitting or standing balance, sitting upright in a wheelchair, activities with multiple motor movements, appropriate touching, throwing a ball, and laterality.

Fine Motor. Manuscript or cursive handwriting or lettering, holding a pencil or crayon, cutting, folding paper, writing within given parameters, and using utensils.

Communication Skills

Vocalizations, articulations, gestures, receptive (understanding) and expressive (speaking) language, following directions, using proper volume when speaking, exhibiting conversation skills, and expressing ideas verbally and nonverbally.

Cognitive

Auditory. Remembering and processing information, discriminating between sounds of letters, understanding cues from environmental sounds such as a fire drills, retelling a story using the correct sequence, and filtering out background noises from essentials.

Visual. Matching colors and shapes, seeing likeness and differences of similar letters (b, d, p), classifying pictures or written words into categories, understanding figure-ground relationship, following a written line of print, lining up math problems, forming images to improve visual memory, and recognizing patterns.

Preparation for Adult Living

- Knowing home address and number
- Reading circulars
- Shopping in a store
- Writing a letter
- Talking on a phone
- Holding utensils
- Proper hygiene
- Reading road signs
- Using a telephone directory
- Reading a map
- Developing interpersonal skills
- Sequencing daily events
- Maintaining a calendar
- Signing a check
- Balancing a checkbook
- Using a calculator
- Counting change

- Being punctual
- Reading bus or train schedules
- Identifying emergency signs
- Using conversational skills
- Establishing eye contact
- Interacting appropriately with peers and strangers
- Being goal-oriented
- Walking around a shopping mall
- Ordering food in a restaurant
- Understanding safety issues with items such as household appliances, toasters, stoves, or irons
- Applying first-aid skills
- Texting, e-mailing, and safely communicating online

Social Goals

Better Interpersonal Skills. Saying thank you, respecting the rule that one person speaks at a time, smiling, increasing positive interactions with peers, working effectively in cooperative groups, engaging in conversation, and peer tutoring.

More Self-Control and Self-Awareness of Behavior. Keeping a journal, exhibiting appropriate behavior in stressful situations, using a problem log, thinking before reacting, substituting an acceptable response, charting or graphing daily moods, and giving more positive peer- and self-references.

Appropriate Classroom and School Behavior. Staying seated, raising hand in class, using appropriate voice volume, following classroom routine, walking quietly in the hallway, sitting properly on the bus, and being prepared and motivated to learn.

Behavioral Considerations

- Using proactive strategies that reinforce appropriate behavior and teach problem solving
- Determining if misbehavior is related to the disability (e.g., a child with epilepsy would not be expelled from class for having seizures)
- Adapting curriculum and instruction to meet individual needs
- Teaching thinking skills and giving specific direction on how students can cope with emotions, stress, and peers
- Remembering that the educational and social skills need to be consistently delivered over a long period of time and continually reinforced since learning is evolutionary
- Including a home-to-school component where parents and families feel empowered to coordinate school efforts with family education and supports
- Supervising and encouraging students to participate in recreational and extracurricular activities at school and in communities that promote social competencies

- Continuing instruction on how to resist peer pressure
- Providing interim alternative educational setting (IAES) for students with chronic behavioral problems (e.g., carrying a gun to school, using illegal drugs, engaging in behavior that is harmful to self and others), permitting the school personnel to place the student in another setting for up to forty-five school days. Interventions should begin in the IAES while following the student's IEP. Services then need to be continued to the next placement with appropriate coordination between the settings.
- Intervening to address behaviors and factors that led to disciplinary action
- Ongoing staff development with all school personnel involved
- Emphasizing positive interventions over punitive ones

HOW TO TRACK AND DOCUMENT IEPs

The IEP is a procedural safeguard that is meant to benefit all learners. Just like a recipe that might need more salt or less sugar, the IEP is a living document that can be amended. Teachers, parents, families, guardians, administrators, support staff, and students act as a team and a cohesive group rather than sparring partners engaged in seeking alternative goals and objectives. Everyone benefits when the IEP is vigilantly planned, followed, supported, shared, and translated to the classroom. Goals and skills attained can be reviewed at interim periods during the school year, such as quarterly marking periods, with parents and guardians being informed of their children's progress as outlined in the IEP. When teachers have made a dedicated effort to support the advancement of a student's individual needs, they cannot be held accountable for a student's lack of progress or regression when they have diligently applied the educational interventions. Teachers can document students' partial progress in their lessons, with varying student accommodations.

Deliberately ignoring or refusing to address a child's needs as outlined in an IEP means that the school district is not being compliant with agreed-upon IEP decisions. When progress does not occur, then many variables must be reviewed; the educator is a contributing but not sole factor in a student's advancement. If changes need to be made, staff, team members, families, and—if appropriate—students reconvene and adjust programs, services, frequency of services, accommodations, and more. If parents or family support systems are still dissatisfied with placement, progress, or enforcement, then all parties can continually meet to plan for more effective changes or ask for mediation, bringing in an objective third party not involved in the disagreement. If another school meeting or mediation still does not solve the matter, then parents or guardians can ask for a due process hearing where both families and school personnel present their sides of the matter and views on the issues in contention. If parents or guardians believe that the IEP is still being violated, a complaint can be filed with the state education agency (SEA), which must try to resolve the complaint within sixty days, unless extreme circumstances exist. IDEA improvements now allow local or state education agencies to be awarded attorneys' fees if a parent's complaint is deemed frivolous, unreasonable, or without foundation. A frivolous case is determined by legal precedent. This differs from the past practice of allowing parents who win cases only to recoup attorneys' fees.

IEP CHALLENGES

Parents of students who are culturally and linguistically diverse are often not full participants in the IEP process and face barriers such as limited English proficiency, a disparity in communication style, low acculturation level, attitude toward the disability, and lack of knowledge about the school structure and IEP process (Jung, 2011). Culturally mindful schools invite family input, exhibiting sensitivities that value cultural differences while sharing the IEP information. Cultural barriers need to be erased and replaced with school practices that allow families of all cultures to be valued IEP partners in implementing steps toward student progress.

In addition, as the academic rigor and accountability demands increase, educators often keep an eye on ensuring that the curriculum is covered, finding it difficult to monitor individual student levels. High school teachers are sometimes challenged in finding the best ways to include students with disabilities (Johnson & Thurlow, 2003; Yell, Katsiyannis, & Collins, 2012). Teachers must be provided with the preparation, training, and support to assist students with IEPs to perform well on assessments that are aligned with the CCSS (Powell & Stecker, 2014). This requires administrators to grant teachers planning time to consult and collaborate with co-teachers, related staff, students, and families and the time to review the data.

IMPLEMENTING ADAPTATIONS BY CHARTING LESSONS

Both GE and SE teachers monitor how their lessons align with accommodations, modifications, and goals listed in a student's IEP and grade level CCSS. If interventions, adaptations, or strategies are not working, then it should be reported to the IEP team so that changes can be recommended. In today's legislative thrust toward increased accountability, the curriculum standards are expected to be mastered, but first some scaffolding or accommodations must be given to students who need this interim support. This may involve a combination of services that includes but is not limited to instruction within smaller skill-focused classroom groups or individualized instruction within or outside of the general education classroom setting. A response to intervention (RTI) model with tiered classroom groups is often put into place before an IEP is written to ensure that the appropriate instruction has been given. The ultimate goal is to raise student levels and competencies. Monitoring the progress of student achievements with the interventions then guides instruction. Data are collected, analyzed, and attached to evidence-based instruction for evaluating the success of the intervention and deciding what further adaptations or specialized services and supports are required. This process guides how students respond to interventions. Data collection and all other components of formulating and implementing IEPs are often time consuming, but it is essential that the goals and adaptations—either accommodations or modifications—be driven by and connected to individual student performance data. There are several online IEP programs that assist school staff in the formulation of individualized education programs. Examples include IEP Planet (iep4.iepplanet.com) and IEP Direct (www.iepdirect.com/iepdotnet/hub/index.html). Read on for further IEP considerations.

Students with more severe cognitive impairments are also expected to achieve progress but on levels that offer alternative assessments and, sometimes, modified expectations toward mastery of the curriculum standards. This chart offers a glimpse of the types of classroom adaptations that can be documented.

MODIFICATIONS/ACCOMMODATIONS CHART

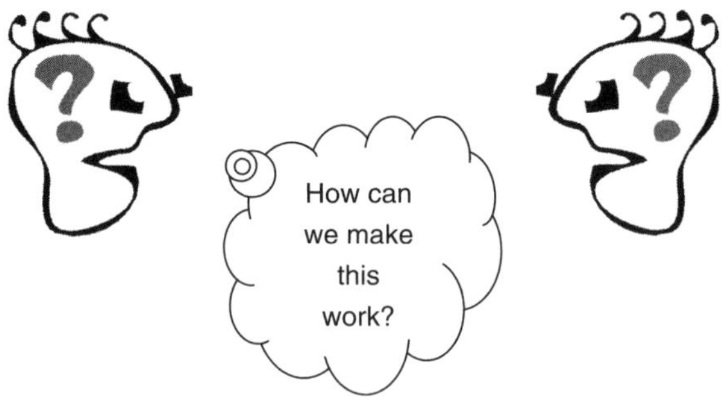

Modifications/Accommodations
G—Grading modified
S—Seating
HW—Homework modified/reduced
P—Preteaching
R—Reteaching/repetition
A—Assessment varied/simplified
SG—Study guide
V—Visuals
T—Extra time, or wait time for tasks
BP—Behavior plan
C/T—Computer/technology
M—Alternate materials
OW—Oral/written presentations
MS—Multisensory techniques
TGS—Team and group support
HFI—Home/family involvement
B—Buddy system
NT—Note-taking system
LOV—Learning objective varied
O+—Other modifications
MBHE—Modified, but high expectations

Subject:

Teachers:

Students	Accommodations/ Modifications	Assessments/Dates Mastery Level	Comments

Related Services: ______________________________

Teachers observe and review children's progress during class lessons and chart individual modifications. For effective class management, this table can document progress for ten students or record progress of one child over a period of time.

Content Area: ______________________________

Objectives: ______________________________

____

Student(s) (name/ initials) and/or dates	**Able to fully participate in the same lesson as peers**	**Needs modified expectations or extra materials to accomplish lesson's objective**	**Can independently participate in a different but related assignment in the room**	**Requires supervision/ assistance to complete or attend to assignments**	**Cannot proficiently complete task in classroom even with support**	**Brief comments; observations; needs; modifications; notes; visual, auditory, kinesthetic, or tacticle concerns; future plans**

MOCK IEP (IT'S EDUCATIONALLY PRUDENT!)

WHAT? + HOW? = PLAN

Directions: Act out an IEP meeting. The IEP may be for an actual or hypothetical student. If it is for a real student, the name must be changed to respect confidentiality. Include current academic and functional levels, an LRE statement, academic and social goals, strategies, accommodations, modifications, levels of mastery hoped to have been achieved, behavioral plans, transitional services, assistive technology needed, along with location, frequency, and duration of placement. Consideration needs to be given to the curriculum and the delivery process, including what you want to teach and how it will be accomplished and assessed. Please refer to Chapter 1 for additional IEP insights about IDEA requirements, specially designed instruction (SDI), and CCSS connections. Remember to include only academic goals that disability impacts. For example, if the student demonstrates attention and study-skill difficulties that have an impact on reading but has excellent reading comprehension, then it would not be appropriate to include reading comprehension objectives since it is not an area of deficit. In this case, study-skill strategies and attending to tasks are more appropriate goals. View the sample IEP goals given along with listed components, understanding how the student's present level of academic achievement and functional performance leads to goals that are aligned with curriculum standards, which then lead to appropriate services with necessary accommodations. The IEP should also list related services and explain the extent to which the student will or will not participate with nondisabled children in the *regular*, or what I prefer to call *general education*, classroom (since SE is not an *irregular* classroom, if that is what a student needs) and other school activities. Include the child's strengths, results of evaluations, and a plan for reporting progress to parents and guardians. Also include the type of professional training and support needed for all staff members to effectively implement the IEP. Remember that each person acts as a member of a team, collectively deciding how to individualize instruction for each child's unique needs while possessing high expectations for all students. Collecting baseline data is crucial in determining the effectiveness of educational interventions. This can include but is not limited to teacher observation; informal written or oral quizzes and tests; curriculum-based assessments (CBAs); student work samples; and family, parent, or guardian input. Keeping track of learning then requires a comparison of students' work and levels of proficiency.

Overall domains to consider include the following:

- Cognitive/Academic
- Speech/Language/Communication
- Social/Emotional/Behavioral
- Fine and Gross Motor Skills/Adaptive Behavior

Other student variables to consider include the following:

- *Limited language proficiencies.* English learners (ELs) require more visuals and academic support with modified or supplemental curriculum materials that have the same content but different reading levels to appropriately honor interests and ages.
- *Communication needs.* Students with autism may need augmentative communication and a picture exchange communication system (PECS). A student with deafness may need a sign language interpreter or more visuals to accompany abstract concepts. Teachers need to regularly consult and collaborate with the speech and language pathologist for classroom connections.
- *Visual impairments.* Students may need Braille, magnification of text or worksheets, or additional tactile curriculum connections (e.g., standing in a circle with yarn used to demonstrate the concepts of diameter and radius).

- *Physical or mobility differences*. Students may need a scribe for dysgraphia, a word prediction program or portable keyboard and word processor to ease fine motor requirements, modified goals for physical education, or alternate access to classroom and school facilities. Consult with your OT and PT staff for their input.
- *Emotional/behavioral differences*. Students may require behavioral intervention plans (BIPs) to address areas such as impulsivity, defiance, compulsivity, depression, aggression, increasing self-awareness, ways to improve peer interactions, and more. BIPs state behavior desired and plans or steps for achieving that behavior as an outcome. Consultation may include working with a guidance counselor, school psychologist, behavioral interventionist, and of course students and families.
- *Attention difficulties*. Students may need a seating change to thrive, along with lessons that match interests, closer proximity to the instruction, rewards and praise for time on task, reinforcement of attending behavior, allowance for more kinesthetic classroom movements, or assistive listening devices.
- *Autism (with more cognitive impairments)*. Students may need additional adult or structured peer support with daily routines; simplified commands with visual cues; sensory motor breaks; adapted physical education, art, and music programs; behavior modification plans; coordination with the speech/language pathologist to improve receptive and expressive language (e.g., verbal requests, dialogue, social reciprocity, pragmatic language, and increased modeling with more concrete presentations to explain abstract ideas); additional time; and paced lessons.
- *Learning differences*. Students may require interventions with structured reading programs (e.g., *Orton-Gillingham, System 44, Read 180, Jolly Phonics, Fast Forward,* and *Wilson Language*) for decoding and encoding needs; direct skill instruction with comprehension skills; direct teaching of social skills; praise for approximations toward standards; guidance with information processing and organizational and study skills; and more guided instruction before independent assignments are given. Ask the student to paraphrase understandings.

The following people's input should be considered in your *educationally prudent* IEP meeting:

- Parents/guardians
- Students
- General education teachers
- Special education teachers
- School psychologists
- Social workers
- Speech/language therapists
- Learning disabilities teacher consultants
- School guidance counselors
- Physical therapists
- Occupational therapists
- Behavioral interventionists
- Inclusion coaches
- Assistive technology staff
- Administrators
- Instructional assistants/paraprofessionals/teacher assistants
- All other support staff for related services

The following is a review of important IEP elements to consider in individualized education programs. The first chart has the duos, trios, quartets, and pentatonic initials, while the second one has the translations for the initialized SE terms.

(Continued)

(Continued)

PLAAFP or PLOP	RTI	CBA	AT	EL
BIP	LRE	FBA	LD	FAPE
EIS	ESY	FERPA	CI	OHI
TS	GE	SE	STOs	TGIF

Translation of initials that often enter IEPs:

Present level of academic achievement and functional performance Present level of performance	Response to interventions	Curriculum-based assessments	Assistive technology	English learners
Behavioral intervention plan	Least restrictive environment	Functional behavioral assessment	Learning differences	Free and appropriate public education
Early intervention services	Extended school year	Family Educational Rights and Privacy Act	Communication impaired	Other health impairments
Transitional services	General education	Special education	Short-term objectives as per state requirements	Thank goodness inclusion's feasible!

Available for download at **www.corwin.com/inclusionstrategies**

Recommended Resources for Staying Current on IEP Requirements

Council for Exceptional Children: www.cec.sped.org

Goalbook—Success for Every Student: goalbookapp.com

IEP Direct: www.iepdirect.com/iepdotnet/hub/index.html

IEP4U: www.iep4u.com

U.S. Department of Education: www.ed.gov/index.jhtml

Wrightslaw: www.wrightslaw.com

5

Introducing Social, Emotional, and Behavioral Issues Into the Curriculum

Physical inclusion in the general education classroom, which may be outlined as part of a student's IEP, does not guarantee social acceptance. This chapter provides teacher tips and practical strategies regarding how to address complex and diverse social, emotional, and behavioral issues to build more successful classrooms. As delineated in this chapter, with proper guidance, teachers can help students connect to themselves, others, the curriculum, and—most important—life!

CONNECTING COGNITIVE AND AFFECTIVE SKILLS

Whether a child with special needs is in a preschool or elementary, middle, or high school inclusion class, he or she faces the academic demands of the curriculum and social expectations with peers. For example, a student with a learning disability, emotional disturbance, autism, or ADHD may not be aware that if he or she displays inappropriate behavior, it will isolate peers. Working in cooperative science or literature groups may present challenges for students who have emotional, social, and behavioral issues, leaving some students unable to effectively complete assignments. A student with a learning disability is sometimes more concerned that the other students do not know that he or she is not on par with the rest of the class. So rather than ask questions to clarify misunderstandings in a math or history class, the student may keep silent or act out. A student with autism may require direct skill instruction to monitor the volume of his or her voice, respectfully wait for a peer or teacher to finish speaking or for assistance on how to display social reciprocity. Students without disabilities also need instruction on how they can increase the comfort level of students with disabilities to maximize and normalize peer interactions (e.g., talking at eye level to a student in a wheelchair or speaking face to face at a typical pace to a peer who may be lip reading). Overall, it is nonnegotiable that student differences be both accepted and embraced regardless of whether student level requires repetition or enrichment.

Balancing both cognitive and affective skills is essential, since academics and socialization are two vital classroom ingredients. The Collaborative for Academic, Social, and Emotional Learning (CASEL), accessed at www.casel.org, declares that social and emotional learning, such as self-management, social awareness, relationships, decision-making skills, and attitudes and beliefs about self, others, and school, impact academics. Research findings about students in school-based social and emotional learning (SEL) programs indicate improved social and emotional skills, improved attitudes about self and others, improved behavior, increased helping behaviors, reduced aggression and emotional distress, and gains in academic achievement (Durlak, Weissberg, Dymnicki, Taylor, & Schellinger, 2011).

Teachers need to know how social, emotional, and behavioral factors often influence student performance. Sometimes how much students learn is dependent on how they feel while they are learning. Teachers and staff within inclusive environments set the learning stage to assist students with academics as well as manage internal thoughts to heighten confidence levels. Students need to view themselves as competent and capable of achievements. At times negative internal thoughts interfere with academics and how to get along and assist each other.

This next Pinterest-like tic-tac-toe board offers students a menu of topics that they can choose to talk or write about. Although these topics are not listed in the curriculum standards, they often affect academic performance. As appropriate, guidance counselors, teachers, and related staff should set up student-conference times to invite discussion.

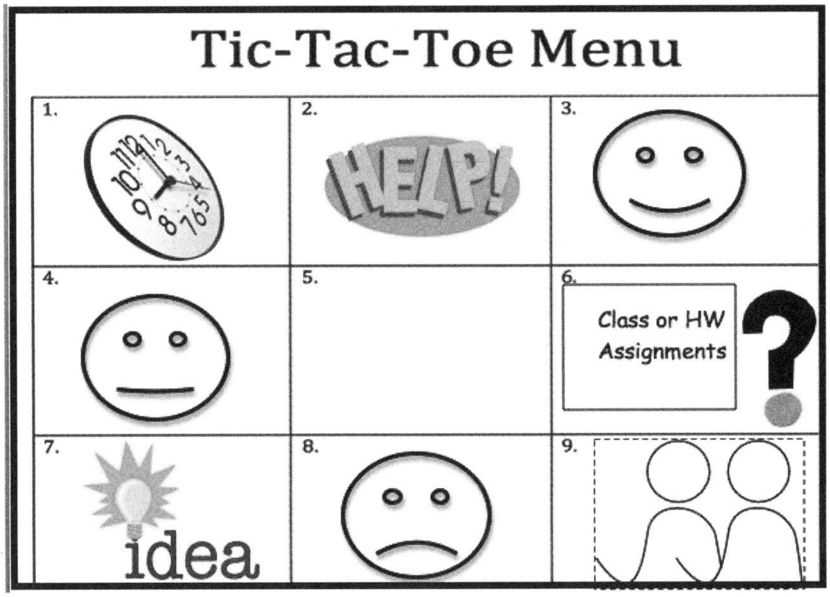

Available for download at **www.corwin.com/inclusionstrategies**

1. Time management
2. Situation where help is needed
3. Something that makes you smile
4. Something that you don't care about
5. Open-ended choice
6. Homework or class assignments
7. An idea
8. Something that makes you sad
9. A person you know

Understanding the Whole Child

Students with special needs are at times confused by the many rules. The hidden curriculum of how to act sometimes escapes them. Questionable self-esteem and lack of security or safe havens in their lives impact academic performance. Socially, students with disabilities struggle to be accepted by their peers, who will often tolerate students with differences in their academic classroom setting but exclude them from their social circles. Other students' and teachers' perceptions, attitudes, and knowledge affect how successful the inclusion experience will be (Burke & Sutherland, 2004; Kniveton, 2004; Siperstein, Parker, Bardon, & Widaman, 2007). Students with disabilities are more likely to be bullied, have fewer friends, and participate in fewer extracurricular activities (Palmer, Heyne, Montie, & Abery, 2011). Very often, students with special needs still have separate sports teams, cluster together at their own table in the school cafeteria, or hear about other kids' sleepovers or birthday parties but are not invited. In our haste to provide the best possible education, we sometimes overlook some of the detrimental social, emotional, and behavioral implications when children face rejection and isolation, regardless of school policies against harassment and bullying. In the face of the judgmental attitudes of peers who are seeking their own niche in the classroom hierarchy, children may lose self-esteem when they are not free to be themselves. Physical inclusion alone does not translate into successful social or academic outcomes. School administrators, classroom teachers, and related staff need to set up nonnegotiable school and classroom norms that are continually reinforced.

In addition, some children are exposed to unfair situations at an early age. There is sometimes no equity in the distribution of safe, protective, and nurturing environments. Poor attendance, behavioral issues, and generally apathetic attitudes compound the resulting low academic performance. If nobody cares about these students, why should they care about themselves? Although students rarely vocalize this sentiment, it is ingrained in their every movement and the choices they make in their lives concerning school, family, friends, everyday decisions, and future goals. School staff can stop this cycle of failure by being supportive adults who figure out how to make a difference in students' lives.

Other children have behavioral issues that interfere with the learning of their classmates, and they need set disciplinary actions and workable plans within an inclusion setting. Sometimes students just need gentle reminders or private signals to increase their awareness to focus on more positive behavior, without facing embarrassment in front of peers. Because academics and socialization are often interrelated, instruction and practice are necessary for both areas.

Social issues that educators can help students improve on include the following:

1. Setting goals
2. Self-control
3. Managing stress and frustrations
4. Self-acceptance
5. Honesty
6. Motivation
7. Sense of responsibility
8. Feeling capable
9. Willingness to accept and help others
10. Having conversations (eye contact, tone of voice)
11. Social greetings and appropriately approaching others
12. Knowing about personal space
13. Cooperating with adults, students, and parents or guardians
14. Thinking about consequences
15. Dealing with anger
16. Effective work habits
17. Positive peer relationships
18. Understanding nonverbal communication
19. Making generalizations
20. Monitoring progress

SOURCE: Vision Management Consulting (n.d.) and McIntyre (n.d.).

Check out www.corwin.com/inclusionstrategies for a list of sources for some social and behavioral tips for teachers in schools and for educators to share with families.

ADDRESSING EMOTIONAL INTELLIGENCES ■

Relationships and emotional processes affect how and what we learn (Vega, 2012). Howard Gardner's theory of multiple intelligences speaks about different intelligences, including two emotional intelligences, *intra*personal and *inter*personal. Intrapersonal intelligence requires building self-knowledge, while interpersonal intelligence describes how people relate to others. Some children and adults feel more comfortable working alone to self-check and reflect upon their progress, while others prefer to be part of a group, with peers collaborating together.

Intrapersonal Activities

- Keeping a journal
- Self-created graphs of progress
- Writer's notebook
- Self-checking activities
- Independent study under teacher's auspices
- Setting goals
- Personalizing learning
- Interest inventories
- Individual projects
- Portfolios
- Poetry
- Keeping a to-do list
- Teaching and encouraging relaxation techniques (yoga, deep breathing, counting slowly)

Interpersonal Activities

- Cooperative learning
- Study buddies
- Tutoring or mentoring a classmate
- Teams
- Board games
- Group projects and classroom centers
- Collaborative reports
- Plays
- Planning a class/school function
- Debates and discussions
- Helping others with conflicts
- Empowering students as consultants (give them an official clipboard)

Explore these resources to help students to develop more self-awareness:

The Girl Who Never Made Mistakes by Mark Pett and Gary Rubinstein

I Like Myself! by Karen Beaumont

Stand Tall, Molly Lou Melon by Patty Lovell

Students with Disabilities Advocate Best for Themselves
(Available at www.ldonline.org/article/6359/)

The Way I Feel by Janan Cain

When Sophie Gets Angry—Really, Really Angry… by Molly Bang

Cooperative learning offers an alternative to lecturing and seatwork, while effectively promoting social skills. Cooperative grouping in inclusive classrooms needs to value heterogeneous yet structured groups. Some ideas and models can be viewed at www.teach-nology.com/currenttrends/cooperative_learning/kagan.

In cooperative learning situations, students interact with peers in a positive way to achieve a cooperative academic outcome. This is different from group learning, which just has children physically working together, since with cooperative learning, each student is more responsible and accountable. Cooperative learning is not just grouping kids together but offering more learning structure while encouraging interpersonal skills, such as collaborative planning and reports.

*P*ositive Interdependence—

Everyone is actively involved in completing the assignment.

*I*ndividual Accountability—

Each person documents his or her own work.

*E*qual Participation—

All children are given responsible voices.

*S*imultaneous Interaction—

During a given time period, all students are learning.

NOTE: Spencer Kagan at www.KaganOnline.com has many resources on cooperative learning.

BEHAVIORAL APPROACHES FOR EDUCATORS

Self-Advocacy Skills

Students with self-advocacy skills are able to express their interests and take active roles in decisions regarding current and future placements. Self-advocacy involves an awareness of levels of learning, being actively assertive in getting help, and being part of the team that plans objectives. A student who attends an IEP meeting and gives input is practicing self-advocacy by communicating his or her opinions. A child who looks at both the positives and negatives of a situation, records his or her own grades, plots behavior, decides on transition plans, or records assignments on weekly and monthly calendars is exhibiting self-advocacy skills. A student on the autism spectrum who understands how his or her anxiety level affects performance is also exhibiting self-advocacy skills. The following is a checklist you can use with students to help them develop self-advocacy.

SELF-ADVOCACY CHECKLIST

Name ______________________________ Date ______________________________

My checklist of ways to help me learn more about ______________________________.

Place a check next to each idea you think will help you in school.

___ Listening more with intent to remember
___ Knowing what topic is coming next
___ Reading over my notes
___ Asking parents/other adults to help, such as when reviewing work at home
___ Activities that require moving around instead of sitting at a desk
___ Teacher repeating directions
___ Someone to read more difficult words
___ Dividing a large test into smaller parts
___ Being familiar with test format
___ Seeing a written sample of an assignment
___ Knowing expectations
___ Having an outline
___ Study groups
___ Working with a partner
___ Making a chart or graph
___ Knowing why the lesson is important
___ Using a graphic organizer
___ Knowing key points or main ideas
___ Rewriting notes
___ Calculator or manipulatives
___ Study guide
___ Highlighter
___ Extra time in class to complete work
___ Mnemonics (a word or sentence made up to help me remember a lot of information)
___ Digital tools
___ Seating change
___ Knowing lesson vocabulary beforehand
___ Activities/games that help me understand and play with the info
___ More visuals like pictures and graphs
___ Keeping myself more organized
___ Using other reading materials
___ Reviewing a behavior chart
___ Other help or support I need: ______________________________

Please note: If students are nonreaders or struggling readers, then as an alternative, students can work with an adult (e.g., teacher, assistant, or family member) to fill out a checklist that has fewer options, more pictures, and more explanations. As another option, to invite more metacognition and collaboration, allow students to collaboratively fill out or self-create checklists in study-skill groups with peers. The following student pledges, to be duplicated and recited daily, ask students to take an oath to be integral players in their learning outcomes, valuing individual identity and interactions with others.

STUDENT PLEDGE

(To be recited with enthusiasm!)

I know it's the (morning / afternoon)

And we're (still yawning / leaving soon)

But this is my promise for (today / now)

When I will (say / vow)

That I will do my best

And it's not said in jest

To really care

And be sincere

To listen and learn

And respect each in turn

We all have many a need

But we all can succeed

If we use our mind

And to each other be kind

So here I am in school

Where not only teachers rule

But it's each student

That needs to be prudent

If I have a positive attitude

I could master math, reading,
and even latitude

The implications are great

I decide my own fate

So I'll give it my best try

And that's no lie

It's my promise, no fingers crossed

I'll ask questions when I'm lost

I'll care about this stuff

Even when the going gets tough

And I think I'll even smile

May as well, I'll be here a while
(Karten, 2007d, p. 64)

Available for download at **www.corwin.com/inclusionstrategies**

Younger learners or students with lower vocabulary or reading levels can view digital movies or candid snapshots of themselves during classroom learning and then write behavioral captions or numerically rate their level of attention. Students can also increase social, emotional, and behavioral metacognitive levels by reading or repeating a simpler pledge such as this one:

I can
Plan
And say
Each day
There are a lot of facts I need
That will feed
My budding brain
And I won't complain

I will be fine
I won't whine
I will always try
And that's no lie
Because being smart
Is an art
So I promise to grow
To be a kid who'll know!
(Karten, 2007d, p. 65)

Available for download at **www.corwin.com/inclusionstrategies**

FUNCTIONAL BEHAVIORAL ASSESSMENT

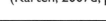

Educators are faced with the difficult task of teaching diverse students within the same classroom. When this diversity is complicated or accompanied by behavioral issues, then teaching can often become a harrowing experience. Functional behavioral assessments (FBAs) offer a concrete alternative that asks teachers and students to look at inappropriate behaviors and discover the reasons for their occurrence.

A student who is refusing to do work may be frustrated by work that is too difficult, or perhaps may just be uninterested in the assignment. Teachers who identify the underlying reasons for certain behaviors can then develop and implement appropriate classroom interventions.

The following FBA questions must be answered:

1. Is the behavior related to a skill deficit?
2. Is the student acting out for more attention?
3. Is the student trying to avoid or escape an assignment or task?
4. Is the task too demanding or boring?
5. Does the student consider rules, routine, or expectations irrelevant?

SOURCE: Center for Effective Collaboration and Practice (2001).

After the problem is identified and documented through observation and recording behavior in a variety of settings, educators and students think of a solution that addresses changing the behavior—*not just controlling it!* Punishments such as homework slips or detention may control only the symptom, not the cause. By getting to the root of a problem, teachers can even hypothesize instances when the behavior is likely to occur and determine how classrooms can be modified to manipulate antecedents. These types of pupil-specific interventions increase motivation for more appropriate behaviors and offer students opportunities for intrinsic as well as extrinsic rewards. The psychologist B. F. Skinner was a proponent of *operant conditioning,* which rewards children for steps taken toward their goals with positive reinforcers that serve as immediate feedback (see www.instructionaldesign.org/theories/operant-conditioning.html). Functional behavioral assessments lead to the development and implementation of strategies for improving behavior. Whether or not students have formal FBAs, teachers and students can keep anecdotal records and chart appropriate behaviors in order to evaluate the effectiveness of behavioral plans and interventions.

Charting Daily Behavior

The following questions, charts, and tables help students and teachers to both analyze and evaluate behavior. Before charts are filled in, the teacher and student together must decide which behavioral goals need improvement, such as the following:

- Paying attention to the teacher with body language and eye contact
- Using appropriate language
- Getting along with other classmates
- Following written/oral directions
- Staying on task, doing what needs to be done
- Treating other students with respect
- Completing homework
- Taking turns in conversations

The student consistently needs to be aware of his or her individual goal, which is always stated in *positive language.* Remember, although undesired behaviors exist, always write exactly what you wish the student to achieve, not the behavior you wish the student to extinguish. For example, rather than saying, "Stop sleeping in class," you can restate it as, "Concentrate or focus on classroom lessons." Charts such as this one help teachers, students, and parents see patterns of behavior as well as what might trigger events.

Charting Behaviors

HOW I WAS TODAY

Time/Day	WOW 5 points	Good 4 points	Better 3 points	OK 2 points	????? 1 point	
Totals	______ +	______ +	______ +	______ +	______ =	______ Total Points
Name ______________________________						

Available for download at **www.corwin.com/inclusionstrategies**

"?????" means that the behavior is questionable and needs to be both improved and discussed. It allows the teacher to ask the student questions, for example, "Why did you _______?" or "When you _______, what were you thinking?" The student can also fill out a "What's Going On?" form if it's appropriate (see later in this chapter). Younger children may need shorter time increments tracked.

A VISUAL TOOL FOR EARLY OR CONCRETE LEARNERS

TIME/DAY	WOW!	GOOD CHOICE	Needs ? Reminders	Poor Choices

Available for download at **www.corwin.com/inclusionstrategies**

Daily behavioral charts such as these can be duplicated and used to make students more aware of their behavior. It is deliberately small, so other classmates won't notice. Daily copies are held by the student or teacher or kept on index cards. A teacher can check off or initial appropriate ratings for each time slot, period, or day and then help the student total daily points. Even though this might be difficult to implement in busy, full-sized classrooms, the time spent is well worth it. Some children need this type of concrete structure to improve behavior, making them more aware of their own patterns and choices. The extra positive attention may well extinguish prior inappropriate behaviors. I once offered this type of behavioral chart to a sixth-grade student on the autism spectrum who decided that he wanted to revise my chart by creating his own hand-drawn figures in a comic strip format with dialogue. He asked me if that was OK. My response was, "No, that is not OK, it is terrific!" He then *owned his behavior*, since the strategies were his, not mine.

Next Step: Daily/Weekly Graphing

?????, OK, Better, Good, and WOW are given points from one to five, respectively, which are then totaled for the week or day, charted onto graph paper, and held in a separate student folder as a running record. For example, if a child has five WOW days in a row for six daily time slots, it is conceivable that the weekly score could be plotted as high as 150, since a daily score of thirty (five points each in six time slots) multiplied by five days would equal 150. The lowest score for the week would be thirty, since ????? ratings are worth one point each. Younger learners can also be assigned points such as four for the WOW column and decreasing to three, two, and one. Together, the teacher and student total the weekly or daily behavioral points and plot them onto the graph paper. By creating a visual that strings several days together, children will not be upset if they have an off day, since they are able to look at the whole picture with one glance and see that those days are just part of the bigger picture. Once a desired behavior improves, the goals can be enhanced, added to, or changed, as agreed upon with student, teacher, and/or family/parent conferencing and collaboration.

Graphing concretizes the acceptable behavior, creates more metacognition, and establishes a trusting, positive relationship between a student and teacher that consistently *values, recognizes, and rewards students' achievements in a structured manner.* If necessary, children can also graph daily points. Younger students can count check marks in each "happy face" time slot or use simpler, larger graphs.

WEEKLY GRAPHING

Points **Weekly Graphing**

Points																													
150																													
145																													
140																													
135																													
130																													
125																													
120																													
115																													
110																													
105																													
100																													
95																													
90																													
85																													
80																													
75																													
70																													
60																													
50																													
40																													
30																													

Dates:______________________________

Name:______________________________

TRANSITIONAL SERVICES

What do I want to be when I grow up? is a question children continually ask themselves. Some students may also need help just to realize that not every day of their lives will be monitored. Transitional planning involves helping students make decisions that will lead to successful lives as productive members of their community—a plan for the future. That is the purpose of the common core standards, which prepare students for college and or a career, making viable postsecondary options available. Transitional plans honor students' choices, goals, and dreams yet also outline and delineate possible barriers and strategies. Transitional plans focus on capitalizing upon students' strengths and abilities to circumvent possible challenges along the adult road ahead, whether it is a paved or bumpy one. They center on postschool outcomes, postsecondary education decisions, vocational training, and overall school-to-community-to-life connections with appropriate academic, social, emotional, and behavioral skills.

Transitional Elements for Students to Consider

1. Current academics and appropriate preparatory classes
2. Vocational training or employment internships
3. Related agencies and services (e.g., guidance counselor, Social Security benefits or aid for qualifying college students, voting, employment opportunities) and places to go for more help
4. Community integration and social skills
5. How to develop self-advocacy skills; being assertive, not aggressive or passive
6. Likes, dislikes, stronger and weaker intelligences
7. How to secure outside living arrangements
8. Extent of family involvement (e.g., support in navigating systems and services)
9. Future educational planning or postsecondary schools
10. Available technology services
11. Transportation options
12. Money management ideas and planning
13. Health care: dentists, doctors (internists, audiologists, ophthalmologists, psychiatrists), physical therapists, and nutritionists
14. Independent living skills
15. Work ethic with colleagues and employers; organizational skills, such as updating a résumé or being punctual
16. Appearance and hygiene

17. How to develop better interpersonal and intrapersonal skills
18. Transferring classroom learning to the outside world.

Overall, transition plans for students' future aspirations! Inventory your students to survey their levels and gauge their interests. Then outline appropriate plans to move forward and upward with their skills. See www.corwin.com/inclusionstrategies for a list of transitional resources and tools.

WAYS TO TEACH SOCIAL SKILLS

In order for educators to provide appropriate interventions, they must understand how students perceive their places in the world and why students might misbehave. *All behavior has meaning,* whether it is evident to teachers or not. Sometimes it's a way for children to achieve a sense of belonging or control. Other times it's for the attention, whether positive or negative, just so they are noticed. Social skills can be taught and organized.

Teachers can

- Establish trust by consistently listening to concerns without judging
- Outline class rules and consequences with the students, working within a structured, well-organized classroom
- Separate the behavior from the child, letting the student know that he or she is valued, but not approve of a given behavior
- Understand how a student might perceive a given situation by exploring his or her perspective and listen to the student for more insights
- Engage in structured role-playing or have the student fill in dialogue for hypothetical social situations on blank comic strips

Available for download at **www.corwin.com/inclusionstrategies**

- Model appropriate behavior and language
- Remain calm, despite the immediate reaction, avoiding power struggles
- Try to talk to the student privately about his or her negative behavior

- Allow for constructive movement times as a release
- Have high expectations for all children
- Establish an ongoing method of communication with other teachers
- Include parents or guardians in a child's school progress and try to map out effective behavioral plans that can be used in both home and school environments
- Have a sense of humor
- Use student worksheets such as "What's Going On?" and specific behavioral charts to help students be more aware of their own behavior
- Reward and individualize appropriate desired behaviors with stickers, notes, positive talks, looks, or just more smiles

☺☺☺☺☺☺☺☺☺☺☺☺☺

"The Friendship Corner," where one child holds a card with the word *mouth* and may speak while the other children listen (holding the cards with ears), is a concrete way to resolve conflicts and develop listening skills in the primary grades.

ONE PERSON SPEAKS AT A TIME

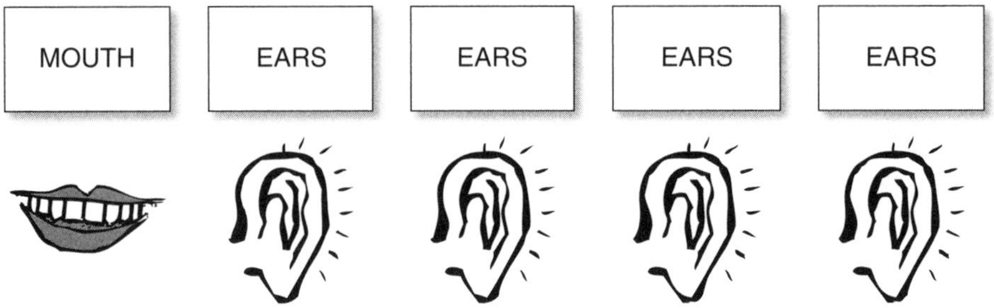

Available for download at **www.corwin.com/inclusionstrategies**

Peer mediation/conflict resolution programs are effective strategies for helping students in higher grades gain these same valuable insights.

"What's Going On?" is a tool that models how teachers can structure a writing exercise to build organized communication. Younger learners could verbally complete the following phrases with an older student or scribe. Students are empowered since they are not required to answer every question but are given choices for their responses in order to have them reflect on their behavior, perhaps diffuse their anger, and be more aware of their emotions.

WHAT'S GOING ON?

Directions: Read all of the words on the next two pages, and then fill in at least five blanks you would like to tell more about.

Name ______________________________

Well, this is what happened:

First, ______________________________

____

Then, ______________________________

____

My friends ______________________________

____

My family ______________________________

____

The world seems ______________________________

____

Keep Going!

I love it when ______________________________

____

I hate it when ______________________________

____

Sometimes I am confused when ______________________________

____

One day I want to ______________________________

____

Keep Going!

Next time, ______________________________

____

I need ______________________________

____

I wish ______________________________

____

____

(Continued)

(Continued)

OK, Here's My Plan

First, I will ____

____

____

I'll try to ____

____

____

I'll try not to ____

____

____

I'll get help from ____

____

____

I'll help myself ____

____

____

I won't get upset when ____

____

____

My plans include ____

____

____

Other things I need to say: ____

____

____

Available for download at **www.corwin.com/inclusionstrategies**

SOCIAL CIRCLES

Continually reexamining personal contacts helps students reflect on relationships in their lives.

Directions: The students place names of people fitting descriptors in concentric circles. Names of people nearest to them are in the closest circles, while further circles contain people who should be kept at a distance. Circles like these concretize abstract emotions for students with poor social judgments as well as for some with cognitive difficulties, while increasing personal reflections for all. For classroom instruction, teachers can model their own social circle, showing students that there are many people around us, each having a different place in our lives. By including more personal information about their own lives, teachers are also telling students that they are willing to share information, which may serve as a catalyst for children to follow, establishing a trusting and communicative relationship. At the same time, it helps students concretely understand a variety of social interactions they encounter and that there are appropriate distances for different people.

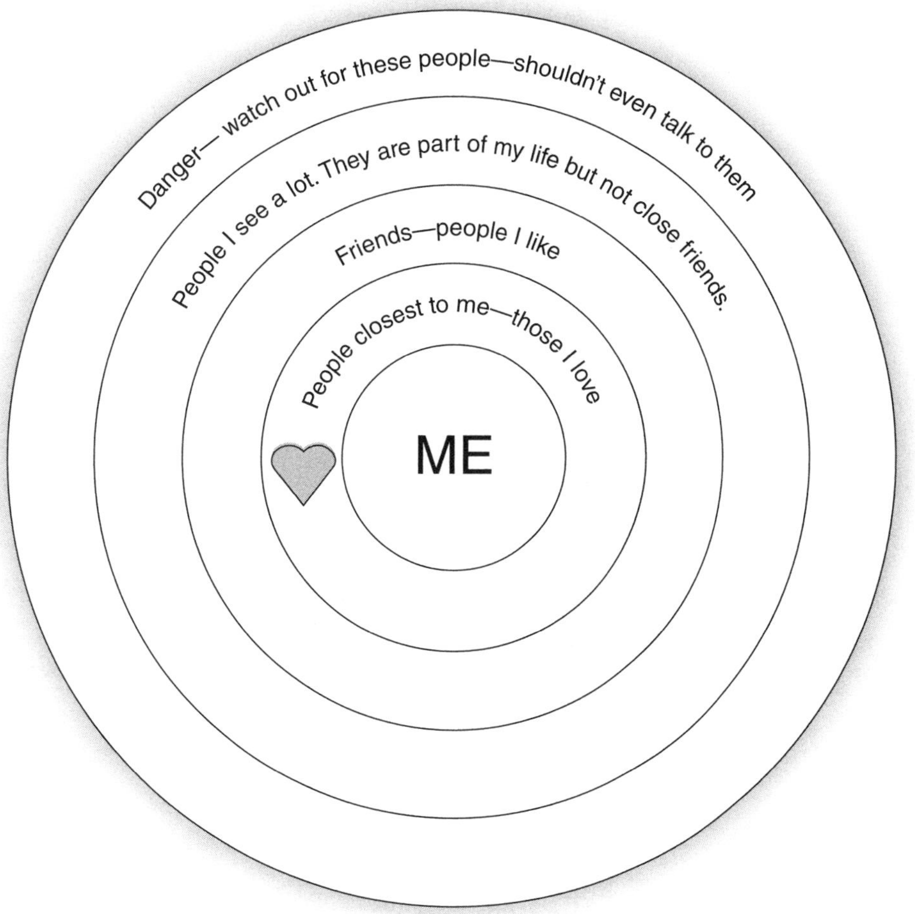

SOURCE: Adapted from O'Brien and Forest (1989).

■ CLASSROOM CLIMATE

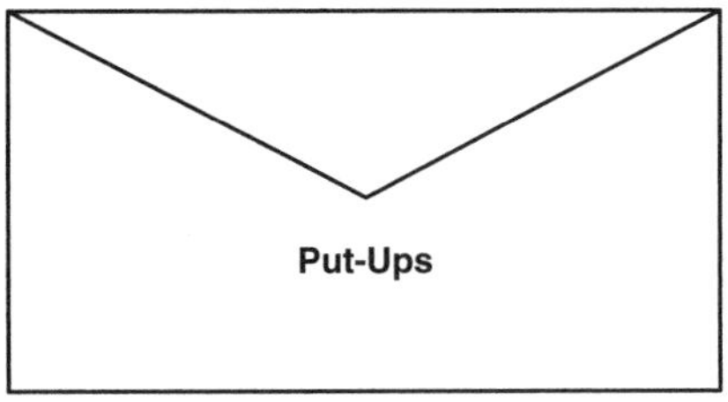

Just as critics write reviews that make or break restaurants, Broadway shows, movies, and books, opinions also influence children and teachers. Teachers want complimentary evaluations by administrators, while children seek good grades, praise, and recognition from peers and adults in their lives. Students who are constantly criticized or put down by a teacher, peer, or family member may form negative self-images that thwart future successes. The obverse, positive recognition, can enhance a person's self-worth. One way to accomplish this is to use a "Put-Up Envelope," which can house positive statements. It allows students to recognize one another's good deeds by writing positive comments. These comments can be read daily or weekly, depending on the number. A pad and pencil, kept nearby, allow for these *uplifting* comments to be recorded.

Moral: Put-ups can be used in individual classrooms to establish an environment that is conducive to learning, by recognizing the *good* things about one another. It is suggested that the teacher always be the reader of the comments since he or she has the option of deleting anything negative and adding more positive remarks to boost the self-esteem of a child who thought nobody noticed or cared. Everyone beams when given a compliment! Even academics can improve in a classroom that focuses on *positivity.* It changes the adage, "If you have nothing nice to say, say nothing," to...

"Say nice things!"

A Touch of Lucky Charms

I often think of one student of mine who would leave school not knowing if his family would be evicted from their home that day or which father would be present. The one thing I could offer him was a bowl of Lucky Charms* each morning because that was his favorite cereal. The custodian provided the milk. It was not much, but in his eyes it was a sign that someone cared.

There is no giant eraser that makes the ugliness disappear, but teachers can make the school hours as nonthreatening and productive as possible.

*The actual cereal was Froot Loops, but it was his "lucky charm."

Five Helpful Factors

1. Develop rapport with students.
2. Sharpen academic skills while involving students in positive school experiences.
3. Increase students' self-awareness of their goals and strides.
4. Create and implement a plan that includes appropriate interventions while defining specific support that will be available.
5. Be ready with a bowl of Lucky Charms!

6

Reaching and Co-Teaching Your Students

Many inclusion classrooms today value co-teaching to meet the needs of children with disabilities. Servicing students through this model, rather than pull-out programs, affords students with disabilities increased exposure to the grade-level curriculum alongside their peers with the expertise and monitoring offered by two trained educators. Special education (SE) and general education (GE) teachers, along with administrators, support staff, students, and families, are all stakeholders who collaborate to achieve successful student outcomes. As shown in this chapter, classroom lessons and objectives are shared, structured, and differentiated to offer whole-class, small-group, and individualized instruction from the preschool to adolescent level for students who may have different learning levels and cultural backgrounds. This model allows students to achieve attainable academic and social gains within inclusive general education classrooms. Collaboration among staff, students, and families ensures responsible communication and the division of roles to achieve higher student outcomes. Read on for more specifics.

EDUCATIONAL COLLABORATION ■

The days of a closed door and the philosophy of "doing my own thing" have been replaced by a revolving classroom door that brings new meaning to the adapted phrase, "No teacher is an island." General and special education teachers need to share ownership in all phases of the learning objectives for their students: planning, instructional delivery, offering extra help, accommodations or modifications, and assessments. A full commitment to inclusion requires administrative support and scaffolding that allow co-teachers and instructional/teacher assistants sufficient planning time and opportunities for frequent communication to evaluate and assess the effectiveness of interventions. All staff must be informed of children's levels, needs, and accommodations as outlined in their individualized education programs (IEPs) since students require a carryover of services across all settings, from the math, English, social studies, and science classrooms to physical education, art, music, and world language classes as well as on the bus, at chorus or band practice, on the track or field, or at lunch. *Communication and coordination ensure consistency of academic, social, and behavioral programs.*

Effective inclusion sometimes means two or more teachers or staff members working together in a classroom, sharing responsibilities for both general and special education students. Co-teaching has often been compared to a marriage, with two personalities spending a considerable amount of time together. In today's society, one often spends more time with one's co-worker than one's spouse. For premium effectiveness, the professional assignments should be compatible ones that match staff who have similar or complementary approaches. Harmonious pedagogical relationships yield beneficial student outcomes. What follows are "prenuptials"—what to consider before co-teaching.

BUILDING PRODUCTIVE RELATIONSHIPS

Educational Prenuptials

Focusing on common issues and pedagogical concerns predetermines whether some collaborative relationships will be successful educational marriages. It is intended to lead to good discussions between co-teachers and staff and to prepare everyone for realistic situations that they may find themselves in one day. Professional compatibility helps!

WHAT'S IMPORTANT IN MY CLASSROOM?

Directions: Circle only five descriptors that you think are the most important for learning.

1. Listening skills
2. Following written directions
3. Communication skills
4. Reading comprehension
5. Vocabulary development
6. Following classroom routines and rules
7. Math computation
8. Study skills
9. Written expression
10. Self-confidence
11. Organizational skills
12. Concentration
13. Logical thinking
14. Performing assignments carefully
15. Remembering information
16. Completing work on time
17. Positively interacting with peers
18. Behaving appropriately in classroom groups
19. Working independently
20. Knowing how to get help

Something to ponder: These twenty items can be weaknesses of children with learning disabilities (difficulties with language, word decoding, reading comprehension, abstract concepts, social skills, organization, and so on).

It would be wonderful to say that every co-teaching and instructional assistant relationship will be tremendously beneficial for the general education and special education staff and all classroom students involved. Yes, it would be a wonderful statement, but one that would totally lack veracity. As we well know, it's a big world filled with many people who have varying personalities, ages, years on the job, background experiences, mind-sets, educational foundations, attitudes about teaching, desires to instruct students with and without differences, degrees of flexibility and amenability, and support systems. That's probably why it is a diverse country and world with partnerships that work between or within spouses, families, communities, states, countries, businesses, global affiliations, lifelong friends, and acquaintances.

Now with that stated, let's turn to our options and see how co-teaching and working with staff and colleagues can be realistically implemented in an inclusive school. We'll also consider what to do if that classroom situation is one that you would not choose to be part of but have to live with. In this case, your only option will be to learn how to make *inclusive lemonade.* The next table lists situations that are ideally inclusive, some that are not so ideal, and some simple ideas for what to do to make it all work better. When co-teaching and staff relationships are harmonious, it's like an educational marriage or family made in heaven, with both students and pedagogy benefiting from the experience. Perhaps you will find some of these listings and scenarios familiar and can vouch for their effectiveness, while others that you have not experienced will help guide you on the path to more productive co-teaching and healthier relationships that work for all collegial partners and students.

INCLUSIVE PARTNERSHIPS

Ideal Situation

From the first day that the general education and special education teacher meet, they feel that they have known each other their whole lives. After the second week, they are finishing each other's sentences, and even dressing alike in the same colors and styles, regardless of the fact that their gender differs. It does not matter who leads the lesson or who follows with the lesson: each supports the other teacher. There is no one person who appears or needs to be in charge. The class and teacher assistant are inspired and guided by the two teachers who are waltzing through the lessons to deliver the curriculum standards. Students with and without IEPs are thriving and passing all assessments given. Sometimes there is whole-group instruction, while other times there are small groups, individualized instruction, and combinations of all types of learning. There are stations and centers set up, allowing students to circulate about and cooperatively perform tasks and other sponge activities. No one knows who has an IEP and who does not. Planning, delivery, grading, and all classroom tasks are equally shared. When there are disagreements or differing opinions, they are privately discussed and ironed out, with sound compromises made. The paraprofessional is given information about the students' levels beforehand, with knowledge about the abilities of the students, classroom management ideas, and ways to best deliver the inclusive strategies.

By the way, everyone is smiling 90 percent of the time—both students and adults—with the administration offering praise and accolades, thinking about duplicating the successes next year. All families are delighted with the inclusiveness and progress of the students. Other teachers applaud what's happening in this classroom, while students exhibit high levels of comfort with their peers; no one thinks that he or she is better than the next person, either students or teachers.

Not-So-Ideal Situation

The classroom tension cannot be cut with a machete. When anyone walks into the room, he or she wants to turn around and leave. If one teacher says, "Yes," the other one says, "No." The students with special needs are clustered together and will work only with each other, not their peers without IEPs. The special education teacher is handed the lesson plans each week and never asked for his input on the content, process, delivery, or assessments for the lessons. Most times, the general education teacher leads the lesson and is annoyed when the special education teacher opens his mouth to try to get the students to reflect on or to discuss what was taught. There are visuals offered on PowerPoints, but the pacing is way too rapid for the students to grasp, with vocabulary and depth of content that exceeds students' reading levels and prior knowledge about the topic. There are no connections with functional academics or meaningful and concrete ways for students to absorb the learning. Overall, most students with IEPs are so frustrated that they prefer instruction outside the classroom, since they are experiencing high levels of anxiety and humiliation from not being able to keep up with their peers. A few have even expressed that they cannot learn because they are *special*. The teacher assistant tries to help ease the situation but is not sure of what to do, where to stand, or whom to help. The administration is aware of the situation and tells both teachers to work it out.

By the way, no one is smiling, and few are learning. Most students are in the skill-and-drill mode, wanting to succeed on tests rather than gain intrinsic knowledge. Fun is a rare commodity for all parties.

What to Do to Make It Better

First, when feasible, administrators need to honor teachers' requests to work together. Would you choose to marry someone you had little respect for, hoping that oil and water will mix nicely together? When faced with a situation you have not chosen, try to remember the bottom line, which is to help students succeed, and work backward from there, figuring out the elements that are necessary to make that happen. Remove the personal frontal attacks and concentrate on how to increase communication with more planning time. Share students' successes, and try to find something to respect in the other person. Make it about the students, not about you. Share knowledge and strategies with all staff, both teachers and assistants. Be allies and try to create common ground with each other, students, families, and administrators. Create a united front in the classroom and teacher's lunchroom. Practice yoga and count to ten, twenty, thirty…one hundred, and more! Smile as well, with your head held high. It might be contagious! Read on for more ideas.

A few co-teaching options follow:

1. Whole-Class Instruction

All students are taught together, with teachers bouncing ideas off of each other, both creating and modeling academic dialogue.

Classroom Examples:

SE teacher: "Wow! I cannot believe that people were treated that way as slaves during the triangular trade in the early 17th century. Would you like to have lived then?"

GE teacher: "No way! I am so happy that things are different today. Now class, why don't we create a list comparing and contrasting what things were like then, hundreds of years ago, to how they are now in a democracy with personal freedoms."

One teacher leads the discussion while the other teacher creates a table in a Word document that records students' responses as they appear on an interactive board. The teacher assistant circulates about the room, encouraging students to look through their textbooks for details. Roles can vary, as will length of the discussion and which teacher assists or leads. No one monopolizes the lesson, and each adult's input is valued. Guided notes are distributed to students with attention issues, dysgraphia, or visual impairments as well as other students who would like to check the accuracy of their note taking.

2. Class Division

Students work with teachers in parallel groups, independently, or in cooperative groups with peers while teachers and staff monitor, instruct, assist, and circulate to ensure accurate completion of assignments, clarify understanding, and reinforce behavior. Groups can be skill and/or interest based.

In the next scenario, two groups are created, each instructed by a different teacher—one SE and one GE teacher—while one student receives individualized instruction from a teacher assistant or a trained peer mentor.

Classroom Examples: Students walk in and complete the "Do Now," which asks them to find the slope of a line using the formula that was covered in the previous lesson. The students hold up their worksheet answers to the teachers, which they have placed in clear communicators. The teachers quickly discover that out of twenty-eight students, approximately 65 percent of the class has the correct answer, while 35 percent of the class needs further instruction. The GE teacher helps the students who require more instruction and explains vertical and horizontal rises, while the SE teacher gives a few enrichment problems to the eighteen students who understand what to do with additional graphing of distance and slope problems. The assistant or peer mentor is working with a student who has more intellectual challenges, creating a visual dictionary of slopes (e.g., ski slopes, driveways, playground slides, ramps by the school for people in wheelchairs or people wheeling baby carriages). The student also draws and measures his own slopes, with trained peer mentors from either group assisting with the measurements, by plotting up and down points to represent the vertical (y) and horizontal (x) coordinates. The visual is then shared with the whole class at a later time. After the two groups have had time to master given assignments, the class gathers together as a whole, discusses the learning outcomes, and then moves on to the next lesson. Scenarios will vary, as will group sizes, assignments, and which teachers work with which groups. The atmosphere is an accepting collegial one in which students' levels are continually assessed, potentials are honored, and differences in learning pace and teachers' personalities are respected. Exit cards are given before students leave with a question related to the lesson just taught to reassess if some students need additional instruction before proceeding to the next lesson.

3. Learning Activity Centers

This option can be offered to introduce a thematic unit, motivate students to delve into the learning after instruction, as an authentic cooperative assignment, or to assess students' application of concepts. While students are completing assigned lessons, the teacher(s) circulate(s) about the classroom, offering social, academic, emotional, and behavioral assistance to both gauge and clarify understandings.

Classroom Examples: After learning about what plants need in order to grow, students are offered opportunities to demonstrate what they know in stations and tasks such as the following, with technology options:

- *Performance Station:* skit, song, dance, commercial, Go Animate, digital storytelling
- *Picture This Station:* bubble dialogue, captioned illustrated picture, Glogster, Scriblitt, Popplet, Pinterest
- *Research Station:* info on approved websites (e.g. Webquest on Zunal .com), texts, magazines
- *Teacher Station:* Students design instruction and a test on material studied using Quizlet or ShowMe.
- *Word Station:* crossword puzzles, word searches, charades, Wordle, Tagxedo, mindmaps, Discovery Education

More delineation of these stations is shown in the reading section on pages 214–228. Results could include songs about chlorophyll; cartoons with the sun or water as protagonists; open-ended, multiple-choice, or essay tests; crossword puzzles; and additional research. The best part is that students are constructively discovering more concepts as teachers and students *plant* the ideas with collaborative classroom *roots!*

SURVEY OF TEACHING STYLES THAT PROMOTE PRODUCTIVE RELATIONSHIPS

(To Circumvent Possible Oil-and-Water Relationships Between Teachers)

Directions: Write some brief thoughts about the following topics:

Classroom Modifications and Accommodations (Varying learning objectives, requirements, instructional materials)

Curriculum Concerns

Varying Classroom Rules/Organization Preferred

Instructional Style

Assessment Methods/Grading

COLLABORATING AS A TEAM ■

Teaching for Two

- Think ahead, *planning* and organizing the content, considering materials, environment, and individual needs of students.
- Use *multiple approaches* to teaching, based on the needs of the students, curriculum difficulty, and comfort levels of teachers. Abandon the "all heads face forward and listen" approach; try more cooperative learning, research projects, and awareness of multiple intelligences.
- Be kind to each other and students. Remember that all changes and relationships take time to develop. Learning is *evolutionary.* Although teachers may have different expertise in the subject matter, different favorite movies, or be from Generation X or Y, they usually possess the same professionalism and desire to help all children succeed. Give it time to work, and stay focused on achieving class objectives and IEP goals for all students.
- General education and special education teachers are helping *all students* in the classroom through different types of classroom grouping. Examples can include both of the teachers teaching the lesson together or dividing the class into smaller groups while the same or alternate content is taught. That means that sometimes the GE teacher may be teaching the group that needs extra help while the SE teacher may be instructing the more advanced group, or vice versa. In an ideal co-teaching classroom, the roles would be interchangeable ones, meaning that each teacher is responsible for all students. Other options can have students involved in cooperative learning, classroom learning stations, and independent work, while both teachers assist, supervise, and instruct both general and classified groups of students.

C ooperation
O ngoing
P re/Inter/Post
L essons
A ssessments
N eeds

C urriculum addressed
O pen to ideas
T eam working together
E veryone involved
A ccommodations given
C ohesive
H ierarchy of modifications

A Review of Thoughtful Inclusion by Working Together

The co-teachers and, if applicable, related staff are in the classroom, with one (GE or SE) teaching and the other one assisting by verbally or physically supporting instruction.

- Staff can also be instructing separate groups within the same classroom or simultaneously rotating about to support learners while providing clarification to students completing individual assignments.

- Both teachers are responsible for the planning, instruction, and assessment for all students.
- Students work independently and cooperatively at their learning levels under collaborative staff auspices with modeling.
- Centers with ongoing projects are available to students.
- The staff keeps anecdotal records and document modifications and accommodations. Nothing elaborate is necessary, even a dated composition book works.
- Classroom reflection exists for students, staff, and administration.
- Communicate with next year's teachers, related staff providers, students, and families to bridge learning and behavioral objectives.

Unfortunately, this is not always the scenario in all school districts. At times, districts have the SE teacher exclusively write the IEP, while the GE is left to plan, instruct, and assess with minimally trained instructional assistants. In addition, scheduling issues may require that the SE teacher be there for only part of the instructional period since he or she supports students in different classes and/or grades during the day. Planning and instruction then become challenging for all. If a not-so-perfect scenario exists, then staff must ask for more qualified support from administrators and case managers, specifically naming what personnel, materials, or scheduling will be needed. When a dedicated GE teacher holds the child's best interest in his or her heart but is not given the proper supports to make the plan work, then the lesson in inclusion becomes one of exclusion and frustration. Working together means everyone is on the same team. GE and SE, when combined in collaborative classrooms, equal EE (excellent education) for all!

Collaborative Tips to Remember

1. Involve all staff, students, and families.
2. Share information and ideas.
3. Remember that everyone benefits!

Teaching for Results

Educational diets include a variety of concepts, using different presentations. Yes, repetition is crucial to retaining facts, but learning must proceed before boredom occurs. What would happen if the only computational skills students learned about were the addition and subtraction of whole numbers? Suppose they never tasted multiplication or division. If fractions, decimals, and percentages were permanently deleted from their diet, wouldn't they develop educational malnutrition? For example, I always thought Roman numerals were too difficult for weaker math students, so I would skip them and move on to what I deemed more beneficial. One day I introduced them, and the students were thrilled. They had always seen these odd letters or numbers in books, on clocks, dates, and movies, but never understood them. Once I started teaching them, I saw how much was involved. XXXIV as 34 is really teaching 10 + 10 + 10 + (5 – 1). Now students are adding and subtracting and learning how to expand numbers. Within a diverse classroom, learners of all abilities must be challenged.

Simple Point: Do not teach to mastery or saturation if students are frustrated by the concepts. Expose students to learning material in varying degrees with tweaked objectives. Sometimes you will need to move on, and then repeat the concepts at a later time, creating a spiraling curriculum. Keep track of which students require more instruction for mastery or must gain additional skills to move on, and then offer support, extra examples, and assistance as needed, but never assume that education cannot be tasted by all!

CLASSROOM DYNAMICS

The next activity explores classroom dynamics from a student's point of view. It typifies how classrooms are faced with the dilemma of educating many different levels within the same room. Within ten minutes of instruction, everyone will try to use the chart below to solve the algebra story problem.

During the classroom simulation, one person tries to teach the lesson, remaining calm, supportive, and focused despite unusual comments and actions from those who have taken the assigned roles of *circles, squares, ovals,* and *rectangles.* Later on, all can reflect upon this experience.

Classroom Simulation

SHAPELY DESCRIPTORS

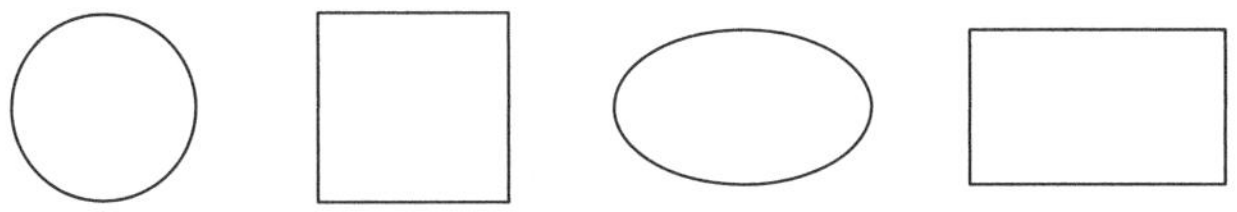

- Circles love to raise their hands to answer questions, but their responses are completely unrelated to the questions.
- Squares are highly intelligent but quite arrogant and intolerant of others' errors.
- Ovals need things repeated several times to gain understanding of oral directions.
- Rectangles smile a lot but are totally clueless unless a visual accompanies spoken words.

Story Problem: In a boy's bank, there is a collection of nickels, dimes, and quarters that amounts to $3.20. There are three times as many quarters as nickels, and five more dimes than nickels. How many coins of each kind are there?

(Continued)

(Continued)

Amount ×		**Value***		
Let n = number of nickels	n	.05	5	$5n$
Let $3n$ = number of quarters	$3n$	.25	25	25(3n)
Let $n + 5$ = number of dimes	$n + 5$	.10	10	$10(n + 5)$
*Multiply by 100 to make computations easier; then set up the equation: $5n+25(3n)+10(n+5)=\$320$ $5n+75n+10n+50=320$ $90n+50=320$ $-50 - 50$ $\frac{90n}{90}=\frac{270}{90}$ (Answer: 3 nickels, 9 quarters, 8 dimes) $.15 + $2.25 + .80 = $3.20				

Reflection

How can a teacher strategically plan to meet the needs of this diverse group?

The teacher can . . .

Available for download at **www.corwin.com/inclusionstrategies**

Measuring Learning Ingredients With Right Angles

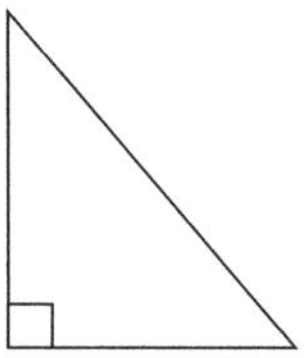

Obviously, teachers cannot present all students with the same breadth of material if prior knowledge and academic levels differ within the classroom. The *right angle* approach reaches and teaches all learners at their appropriate instructional levels, with a plan for successful outcomes. Some students achieve all objectives, while others obtain partial mastery, working at their individual instructional levels.

The basis for calling this concept *right angle on learning* is the fact that not only is it the "right" approach, but there are also 90 degrees in a right angle. So how does this relate to inclusive classes? Shouldn't we think of 100 percent of learners achieving the objectives, not the figure 90? What happens to the other 10 percent of learners? Well, those students are the ones who are achieving mastery of each tiered objective in the lessons. Using specified objectives, teachers and staff plan lessons based upon prior knowledge and levels of the students. The goal of 90 percent of learners mastering objectives allows for 10 percent uncertainty for borderline or varying levels, since there are different degrees of learning. Percentages for objectives will vary, but stagnation is never an option. Remember that not everyone will begin on the same level, yet incremental learning improvements are gains and building blocks for more learning. All students are learning when teachers are using the *right angle!*

Curriculum Connections—Samples of Ways to Apply Right Angles

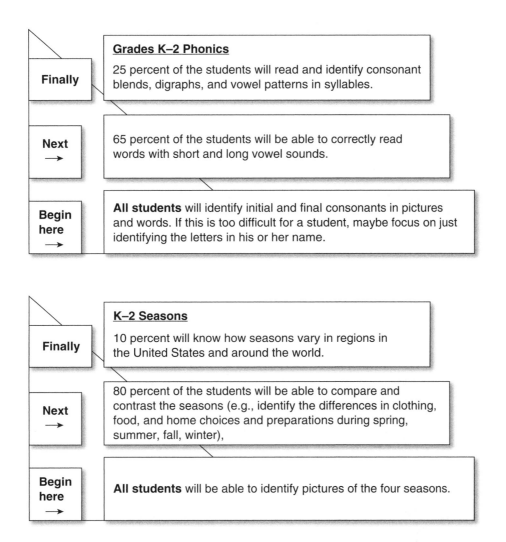

Grades K–2 Phonics

Finally — 25 percent of the students will read and identify consonant blends, digraphs, and vowel patterns in syllables.

Next → — 65 percent of the students will be able to correctly read words with short and long vowel sounds.

Begin here → — **All students** will identify initial and final consonants in pictures and words. If this is too difficult for a student, maybe focus on just identifying the letters in his or her name.

K–2 Seasons

Finally — 10 percent will know how seasons vary in regions in the United States and around the world.

Next → — 80 percent of the students will be able to compare and contrast the seasons (e.g., identify the differences in clothing, food, and home choices and preparations during spring, summer, fall, winter),

Begin here → — **All students** will be able to identify pictures of the four seasons.

Finally

Grades 3–5 Word Analysis

15 percent of the students will read and identify words from lists two grade levels above, achieving at least 80 percent mastery.

Next →

75 percent of the students will demonstrate structural analysis by identifying suffixes, prefixes, and base words of grade-level lists of words.

Begin here →

All students will identify parts of compound words, read grade-level word lists, and clap to identify the number of syllables in words. Objective for some is to just repeat clapping pattern.

Finally

Grades 6–8 Natural Resources

30 percent of the students will know how the Earth's resources are protected and threatened.

Next →

60 percent of the students will be able to use a map to locate geographic places in the world where resources are found.

Begin here →

All students will be able to identify a natural resource.

Finally

Grades 9–12 Writing

20 percent of the students will use metaphorical writing in creative stories with varying genres.

Next →

70 percent of the students will be able to write a five-paragraph narrative with correct capitalization, punctuation, spelling, and cohesive organization of thoughts.

Begin here →

All students will write a well-planned paragraph with a main idea and supporting details. If this is still too difficult, some students could use digital recorders and dictate thoughts.

Applying Right Angles

Now think of any curriculum topic and make divisions for learning objectives, using the triangular template below. Fill in approximate percentage levels in the boxes below.

Topic ____

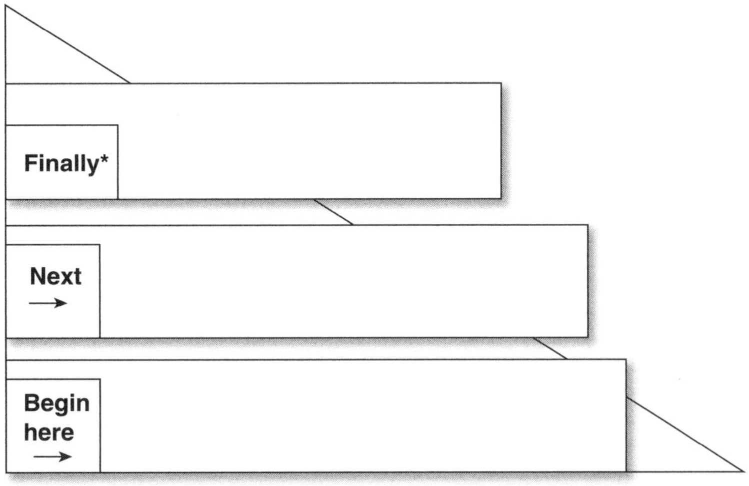

*Please note that there really is no "finally," because the learning will be revisited at another time, in another way, shape, or form. Even right angles need remeasuring!

Applying Right Angles in Your Classroom

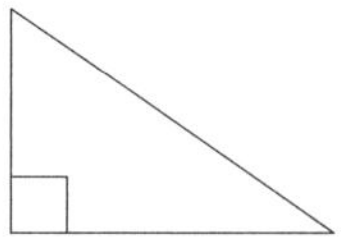

Questions You Might Ponder

1. How can classes be learning-related concepts, with different complexities?
2. What about classroom management?
3. Can one teacher divide the class into focused groups?
4. Do I need a large protractor to do this right angle stuff?

It's simple, if you think about your classroom in the following ways:

1. Everyone is learning together in one room.
2. Different thought processes and (independence, instructional, or frustration) levels exist within the same room.
3. Teaching everyone does not mean that everyone is learning the same breadth of material at the same time.
4. The ultimate goal is progress for all, based on individual needs.
5. Always keep mastery in mind for all, with appropriate pacing and scaffolding as strategic tools, never expecting too little from your students or yourself!

How? Some Suggestions

Think of how your lessons can be composed of these three different stages:

1. Whole

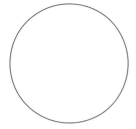

2. Part

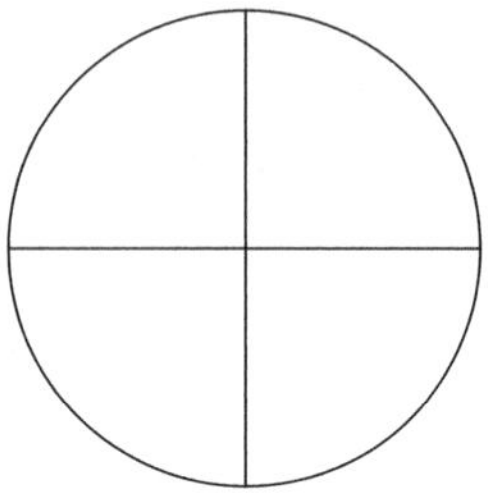

3. Whole

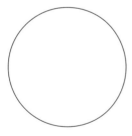

Available for download at **www.corwin.com/inclusionstrategies**

Classroom Structure

First:

Whole

1. Whole

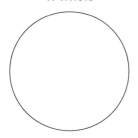

Everyone in the class could

- Listen to the same story, poem, or mathematical word problem
- Look at the same picture prompt related to the content
- Chorally read or write a story together on chart paper
- Have a group discussion about ...
- Be introduced to science and social studies vocabulary
- Preview and discuss what skill(s) the lesson will focus on (e.g., digraphs and diphthongs, scientific method, time lines, decimals, finding the main idea, determining cause/effect, how to improve writing by substituting words)
- Be involved in a teacher demonstration or experiment, handling concrete objects or lesson-related manipulatives

Next:

Part

2. Part

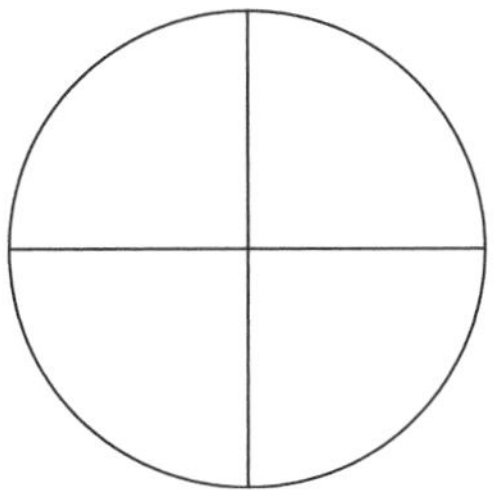

Students can work with smaller groups, partners, or individually

- Completing an assigned reading or writing task
- Creating a product based on what was learned (e.g., poem, story, short skit, illustrating captioned pictures, crossword puzzle, word search, solving given problems, reenacting an experiment, researching on the computer, reading and learning more about . . .)
- Completing various activities from text, dividing assignments on matching colored paper (e.g., green, blue, yellow, white) for better classroom management, having students complete one of each color on their own or in groups
- Learning under teacher's auspices, which now exists for all students

During this time, the teacher walks around supervising or instructing smaller groups or individual students while recording observations and individual needs evidenced.

Then:

Whole Again

3. Whole

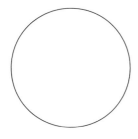

Together the class becomes a whole unit again, while individual students, teachers, partners, and groups share

- What else they learned or discovered about the topic from a book, computer, other student, teacher, or by themselves
- A finished product created
- What they now know, giving specific details
- What they still wonder about
- Questions about the material presented

It's basically a time for all learners to celebrate their discoveries and progress with each other, while validating and reflecting on their own learning.

Finally

Again, remember that *finally* is a term used just for now, because ________.*

*Answer: Learning always needs to be revisited at another time or in another way, shape, or form. Just because something was taught three months, three weeks, three days, three hours, three minutes, or three seconds ago does not mean that it has been remembered by all students. Reviewing increases retention of prior concepts. Students may need that 100 percent mastery on some concepts to move on in that topic or subject. Afford them the opportunity to revisit the concepts, since they now have increased prior knowledge to capitalize on.

Three-Question Lesson Design: Objectives, Not Objections!

Lesson design requires asking these three simple questions:

1. What are you going to teach?	→	OBJECTIVE
2. How are you going to teach it?	→	PROCEDURE
3. Did it work?	→	ASSESSMENT

> Special education can be special for all, if teachers consider the following factors. Remember that not every lesson requires all of these ingredients, but perhaps being cognizant of their importance will allow these objectives to evolutionarily diffuse into the repertoires of all teachers. Think how these points fit into a lesson.

SPECIAL LESSON OUTLINE

Topic:
Desired goals (social, academic, emotional, behavioral, physical, communicative, and cognitive):
Baseline knowledge:
Motivating activity:
Visual, auditory, and kinesthetic-tactile sensory elements:
Critical and creative thinking skills:
Interpersonal activity and cooperative roles:
Curriculum connections:
Universal design for learning (UDL) considerations:
Possible accommodations:
Parallel activity:
Anticipated roles of general educator, special educator, instructional assistant, student, peers, family, specialists, related services, and administration:
Adult, peer, and self-assessments:
Closure:
Revisitation dates:

Available for download at **www.corwin.com/inclusionstrategies**

INCLUSION DILEMMAS

Directions: Read over the descriptions of these students. Then explain how diverse learning strategies and educational plans will meet academic, emotional, social, and behavioral needs. Include things such as sensory components, concretization, accommodations, inclusion tips, right-angled objectives, elements in the special lesson design, and other related appropriate services.

Students

Friendship is a second-grade student who has auditory and visual-perceptual difficulties that interfere with her learning. Friendship can be quite personable but can also create disturbances in the classroom when confronted with difficult assignments. She can scream loudly and have tantrums that disrupt the other children. What strategies can her teachers use to address her problems and the needs of the other students in the classroom?

Sweet Sara is a fourth-grade student with Down syndrome. She has excellent home support and is well liked by her classmates, who eagerly include her in their school activities. Sara loves playing baseball during gym and is delighted when she is part of a team. At times, abstract assignments present difficulties for Sara. She is currently unable to keep pace with the rest of the class as they are learning two-digit multiplication. She is also experiencing difficulties on the bus and in the cafeteria with other children teasing her. What would be your plan for addressing academic and social concerns?

Taylor Mills will be in Ned Nice's sixth-grade social studies class. Taylor can read fluently and independently answer questions on a third-grade level. Heidi Helpful is a special education teacher who will be working with Ned Nice. How do you think Taylor will be able to handle the class, especially the textbook? What type of appropriate adaptations can be made for Taylor during class? How can Ms. Helpful and Mr. Nice work together to help Taylor?

Arthur, a twelve-year-old boy, has autism. He is in a sixth-grade class, with an instructional assistant who helps him. At times, Arthur is inattentive and distracted by his own thoughts, missing the facts and concepts presented in lessons. His poor study skills affect his test performance, since he is disorganized. He works well with peers in cooperative groups, often modeling what other children do, but rarely carries on conversations unless he chooses the topic (he loves talking about animals). Home support is inconsistent, with his mom stating that he is difficult to handle. Long-range projects are rarely completed. What behavioral and academic strategies will improve Arthur's school and home performance?

Kind Calvin is an eighth-grade boy who has learning disabilities. His tested intelligence level is low, but he is performing on grade level in math computations, language, and reading, with in-class support. He is able to memorize social studies and science facts but cannot grasp higher-level concepts that require creative or critical thought; most of his learning requires a concrete level of presentation. He was introduced to beginning algebra but needs more remediation in this area. Calvin has a strong desire to learn and has excellent parental support at home. Calvin loves sports and will effortlessly devote a great deal of his time to being a participant in or observer of athletic events. What recommendations would you make for Calvin's high school program?

(Continued)

(Continued)

Tammy Talker is a seventh-grade student with average intelligence. She has a mild hearing loss and often reads lips. Tammy's word decoding skills are excellent. She can accurately pronounce and spell most seventh-grade words but has a poor grasp of word meanings. Tammy has difficulty understanding critical-thinking questions; her inferential reading skills are on a fourth-grade level. Tammy loves to draw and is learning to creatively express herself in written form. Socially, Tammy Talker is well liked by peers and will focus excessive attention on friends and classroom dynamics, often missing the crucial elements of classroom instruction. Her mom thinks that Tammy's younger sister is smarter, more trustworthy, and a nicer child than Tammy, who is well aware of her mom's sentiments. What academic and social recommendations could be offered by the general education teacher and instructional support team to help Tammy be successful?

Rollercoaster Ryan is a fifteen-year-old tenth-grade boy who is athletically inclined. He has a strong desire to succeed on his teams in wrestling and football. He wants to do well in the classroom, but his learning and emotional difficulties interfere with his progress. He gets frustrated very easily with schoolwork and tends to slack off, usually playing video games incessantly. He craves attention, whether negative or positive. One minute he's having a good day, and the next minute, he's having a bad day; therefore, he is set off easily. What type of program and classroom strategies would you recommend for Ryan?

Available for download at **www.corwin.com/inclusionstrategies**

How to Meet Student Needs

Friendship: Most important is to find out Friendship's reason for her misbehavior. Are the tantrums related to frustrations from difficult classroom assignments? Determine the extent of perceptual difficulties and use kinesthetic ways of instruction. Try setting up a behavioral intervention plan that rewards Friendship's appropriate strides. Teach social skills in small groups, gradually increasing the number of students in the group. Enlist the help of the guidance counselor, if available. Instruct peers about appropriate ways that they can help Friendship with social and academic issues.

Sweet Sara: Children on the bus and in the cafeteria who are bothering Sara need to be identified and given direct sensitivity instruction through guided character education awareness. Activities are needed to help them gain more insights on how and why they can and should help, rather than tease, Sara. Enlist a bus buddy and train and empower chosen peers to offer help and support at lunch, recess, and in other social situations to include Sara. Social relationships need to be taught to Sara as well, letting her know whom she can turn to for more support. A step-by-step learning approach is needed with delineated objectives in all academics, presented at a concrete level of instruction. Perhaps as others in math are learning two-digit multiplication, Sara can sort, classify, and count manipulatives in groups or again work with a trained peer mentor.

Taylor Mills: The textbook needs to be used as a reference, supplementing it with reading materials on Taylor's level containing the same subject matter. Perhaps the text can also be made available on audio, through organizations and resources such as Learning Ally (www.learningally.org), SOLO Literacy Suite—Read OutLoud or Write OutLoud (donjohnston.com/solo), BMI Educational Services (www.bmionline.com), Bookshare (www.bookshare.org), or Daisy Talking Books (www.daisy.org). Heidi Helpful and Ned Nice can pre-teach vocabulary and concepts, so Taylor can follow along better in class. Homework assignments also need to be modified and simplified. Both teachers need to assess Taylor's progress through benchmark assessments, varying types of grading criteria with multiple intelligence approaches, giving Taylor ample, diversified opportunities to demonstrate what she knows, and not penalizing her for reading difficulties.

Arthur: Arthur needs organizational support, breaking long-term projects into smaller increments. The instructional assistant can help him refocus attention with a private, agreed-upon signal to increase eye contact and to watch the gestures of the teacher to pick up on cues. The teacher's and assistant's proximity need to vary to improve Arthur's concentration and to promote independence. Cooperative grouping needs to be structured, holding Arthur consistently accountable. Use his interest in animals for independent reading and writing assignments and to reward completed academics. Connect his mom with support groups to help manage her wide range of emotions and gain helpful insights from others. Coordinate with his mom and multidisciplinary teams as well, establishing a behavioral support plan for home and school. Offer much praise for Arthur's improvements.

Kind Calvin: Capitalize on Calvin's strong motivation and excellent parental support by giving him extra practice to improve inferential reading skills. Use manipulatives such as algebra tiles (illuminations.nctm.org/Activity.aspx?id=3482) or hands-on equations (www.borenson.com) to concretize abstract concepts. Conduct a learning analysis to determine Calvin's prior knowledge of topics. Use sports as a motivator, trying to relate it to lessons when appropriate. Have Calvin develop self-advocacy skills and a transitional plan that includes future goals. Recommend a high school program that includes athletics, extra help, and peer tutoring, if available.

Tammy Talker: Foremost, Tammy's social issues call for increasing her self-esteem and praising her strides, since family dynamics are complicated. The instructional support team needs to help the GE teacher present learning to Tammy on a semi-abstract level, letting pictures concretize concepts. Provide more outlines, visuals, and handouts. Allow Tammy opportunities to illustrate answers, capitalizing on her strong visual-spatial intelligence. Use a visual dictionary and teach on her instructional, not frustration, level. Here are a few sources for accompanying curriculum-related visuals: visual.merriam-webster.com, www.infovisual.info, pics.tech4learning.com, www.snappywords.com, and www.clipart4schools.com. Usborne Publishers has visual dictionaries in many languages on topics ranging from physics to ancient civilizations at www.usborne.com/default.asp. Since Tammy likes her peers, include more cooperative learning assignments. The GE teacher will need to vary Tammy's objectives due to her fourth-grade reading level. If Tammy is lip reading, the teacher should face her when giving directions, speaking slowly and clearly in a conversational voice. Have a few swivel chairs in the classroom for Tammy to easily view peers without being singled out as different, or try to seat the class in group configurations that allow her maximum access to face students. Check with the school nurse, home, and team members to be certain that she is receiving the maximum technology available for her hearing difficulties (e.g., a sound-field amplification system).

Rollercoaster Ryan: Determine the reason for misbehavior, having Ryan increase his metacognition while plotting progress to decrease frustration. Use sports as an outlet and reward, perhaps incorporating Premack's principle (e.g., eat your veggies and then you can have dessert). Incorporate more kinesthetic learning approaches into classroom instruction. Coordinate with home to decrease video games, and replace them with appropriate technology and online sites and digital programs that augment the curriculum (e.g., www.funbrain.com, www.studyisland.com, www.khanacademy.org, mathforum.org, or www.homeworkspot.com/high/english). Allow Ryan the option to attend his IEP meeting and be his own advocate. Include transitional skills and behavioral interventions in his IEP as well.

MORE LESSON CONCERNS

Preschool Students

Increased exposure to socialized learning experiences at an early age is critical for future school successes. IDEA includes Child Find, whereby states must actively seek out and plan for the education of young children with special needs (e.g., advertising on local television, newsletters) who may not have entered the school system yet. "According to the U.S. Department of Education (2008), in 2007 a total of 707,848 children aged 3–5 years with disabilities were served under IDEA, Part B and over 240,000 children were served in early childhood settings with their typical peers more than eighty percent of the time" (Cross, Salazar, Dopson-Campuzano, & Batchelder, 2009, p. 1). Although early childhood educators have open minds and hearts, many are still anxious about their ability to respond fully to the needs of students with disabilities. Individualized considerations support each child's needs for learning and their family's wishes and concerns (Watson & McCathren, 2009). Such programs try to afford preschoolers with special needs equal beginnings through early individualized interventions that target cognitive, language, communication, behavior, social, emotional, and physical developments.

When early educators actively involve students in a variety of learning activities, the children become more curious to explore the world. Using appropriate curricula, materials, and procedures is a position that is supported further by the National Association for the Education of Young Children (www.naeyc.org) and the Council for Exceptional Children's Division for Early Childhood (www.dec-sped.org). Their joint position advocates that inclusion be for every infant and young child along with his or her family, giving them the right to participate in a broad range of activities within many environments and contexts, regardless of abilities.

Family involvement and guidance are essential ingredients, as is a play-based arena of assessment, with teachers observing and recording needs. Play activities must allow enough space to promote active engagement and opportunity for more learning at home and in school settings. This includes exposure to social and early academic skills and increased reflection that promote full involvement with high expectations for functional, cognitive, social, behavioral, perceptual, emotional, and physical opportunities to achieve standards alongside peers. A progress-monitoring portfolio is an effective way to illustrate growth and the development of specific skills and to depict the mastery of skills for young children (Stockall, Dennis, & Rueter, 2014).

Early educators have the important task of effectively instructing young students who are entrusted to their care. It is not a task that can be taken lightly, since teaching smaller children is a large undertaking. Creating a climate of acceptance and excellence is nonnegotiable for preschoolers in inclusive classrooms. The following factors are necessary ones to consider:

- Transitions (e.g., from early intervention to preschool or to grade-level kindergarten standards)
- Embedded, developmentally appropriate academics and responsive teaching in language-rich environments
- Critical thinking skills and appropriate social interactions
- Development of autonomy
- Individual student needs, interests, and strengths within student's zone of proximal development (ZPD)
- Valuing differentiation as the norm, with enrichment and remediation
- Proactive versus reactive approaches (e.g., UDL; See www.cast.org)

The High Scope curriculum values active participatory learning for young students to explore ideas and solve problems. There are categories that encompass approaches to learning with considerations for social, emotional, and physical development, along with increased skills in language, literacy, communication, creative arts, science, technology, social studies, and mathematics. Key developmental indicators (KDI) across the content include an array of fifty-eight indicators, such as initiative, self-identity, problem solving, cooperative play, community roles, spatial awareness, alphabet knowledge, body awareness, shapes, measuring, decision making, and more. A complete KDI list is available at www.highscope.org/Content.asp?ContentId=566.

Preschool educators provide young students with excellent early beginnings for a sound foundation that is expanded on in elementary and secondary grades.

Gifted Education

> The list below offers some heterogeneous characteristics and strategies for recognizing the *gifts* all learners offer. Some students are also considered twice exceptional, exhibiting unusual strengths yet some weaknesses that directly impact their learning.

- Learners may excel or show interest in some topics or skills but be weaker in or dislike others. For example, some may be better in science compared to writing, have better math skills than physical coordination, or be excellent in verbal skills but poor writers. Interdisciplinary approaches and those that reflect multiple intelligences take this into consideration by appealing to stronger areas to improve weaker ones.

- Cognitive skills do not always match social maturity. Be cognizant of the whole child, thinking of a child's hobbies and interests and letting academics mesh with appropriate social development.

- Classrooms with instruction that values varying background knowledge and differing motivations, curiosity, and thinking skills give students a greater opportunity to learn. Ongoing stations or learning centers offer a vast variety of directed activities across the curriculum in math, music, science, art, reading, writing, and social studies. Set up stations that allow for differing learning rates while fostering independent cognitive skills and individual creativities, such as chess centers, artists' studios, composers' land, time zones, and authors' world.

- Share realistic expectations with students while they keep dated portfolios as evidence of their academic achievements.

- Remember to continually offer organizational support, and always encourage further critical thinking skills with opportunities for vertical advancement.

- Include positive family communication and home support.

- Understand that some students may also be twice exceptional, having areas that they excel in and weaker ones as well (e.g., excellent readers with poor attention or organizational skills).

- Know that sometimes educators need to accelerate, accommodate, and of course appropriately individualize lessons to differentiate curriculum, instruction, and assessments.

Joseph Renzulli outlines three interrelated concepts concerning giftedness. They include above average ability, creativity, and task commitment to acquire and demonstrate knowledge. Renzulli emphasizes how these three factors, along with personality and environment, impact gifted behaviors (See "Three-Ring Conception of Giftedness," accessed at www.gifted.uconn.edu/sem/semart13.html).

Just as staff differentiates lessons for students who need remediation, lessons must be differentiated for students with more advanced skills who are educated in inclusive classrooms. Continually provide students with opportunities to nurture and expand their skills, such as involvement in cooperative and independent project activities that offer challenges.

Recommended Resources

The Association for the Gifted (TAG), Division of the Council for Exceptional Children: www.cectag.org

The Knowledge Master Open: www.greatauk.com/

National Association for Gifted Children (NAGC): www.nagc.org

Thinking Cap Quiz Bowl: www.thinkingcapquizbowl.com/thinkingcap

Twice-Exceptional Online Newsletter: www.2enewsletter.com

Cultural Concerns for Special Learners

There are a large number of minority students in special education, due to language difficulties, unfair assessments, poverty, and different cultural values, experiences, and family backgrounds. These diverse groups of students may or may not have special education needs and thereby may suffer from prejudices that yield inappropriate educational services.

Culturally responsive educators need to inwardly reflect and check their personal assumptions and biases to offer students appropriate, mindful, and culturally responsive instruction and communications (Dray & Wisneski, 2011). It is essential that English learners be offered opportunities to capitalize on their strengths instead of being viewed through a deficit model because they differ from the class or school norm. Educators need to collaborate with staff and families to gain valuable insights about students who have linguistic differences (Liasidou, 2013).

There is no legislation that can outlaw the negative connotations of being different from others. Self-awareness is the first step. The survey below allows teachers an opportunity to reflect upon their own self-awareness before they address the needs of diverse learners within their classrooms.

CULTURAL SELF-ASSESSMENT

Directions: Beside each of the following ten statements, indicate whether you believe it is **A**lways, **S**ometimes, or **N**ever true.

1. ___ I have an awareness of my own cultural heritage.
2. ___ I am willing to learn about others.
3. ___ I am willing to learn from others.
4. ___ I believe that being different is okay.
5. ___ Cooperative activities encourage the acceptance of differences.
6. ___ All people are the same.
7. ___ Planned classroom lessons in various content areas can address different cultures.
8. ___ Cycles of oppression continue throughout generations.
9. ___ Textbooks are generally written from a Eurocentric point of view.
10. ___ Evaluation techniques should be the same for all students.

Available for download at **www.corwin.com/inclusionstrategies**

Special Needs of Cultures

Some disability groups consider themselves separate *cultures,* with a different way of life, and prefer not to fit in with the *mainstream* culture. Interviewing parents, guardians, children, disability support groups, and community members validates that student's culture and says that differences are okay. In addition, schools must evaluate students in their native language to see if a disability exists, without letting a student's language proficiency interfere with the testing. Interpreters also must be provided for parents and families during all phases of the special education process, from notification to evaluation, allowing parents and guardians comfortable levels of planning input during all school contacts.

Taking it a step further, we can learn not only *about* other cultures but *from* them as well. Prejudice involves looking at others who are different from the mainstream in negative ways, or prejudging them. *Both children and adults need to increase their own sensitivity and awareness to learn from others.*

> Increased self-awareness activities are valuable for both students and school staff. Incorporate programs that value character education, and include prejudice-reduction activities, which help students develop positive attitudes toward cultures and diversity.

USE YOUR SENSES TO THINK ABOUT PREJUDICE

Looks like	Sounds like	Tastes like	Smells like	Feels like

Available for download at **www.corwin.com/inclusionstrategies**

Resources to Explore

Anti-Defamation League: www.adl.org

Dave's ESL Café: www.eslcafe.com

Interesting Things for ESL Students: www.manythings.org

Multicultural Resources: www.teachersfirst.com/multicult.htm

Southern Poverty Law Center— Teaching Tolerance: www.tolerance.org

USC Shoah Foundation—IWitness: iwitness.usc.edu/SFI

TEEN CULTURE

Teens have a distinct culture as well. Many children, including teenagers, think that the sun rises and sets just for them. As the mother of an adolescent, I was faced with the dilemma of giving my son his personal space with room to grow and, at the same time, demanding his daily itinerary. It is a turbulent time for a teenager, and for a teenager with a disability, it is a doubly difficult time. Adolescents generally strive to be the same as their peers, but an adolescent with a disability feels much more pressure to belong. Trusting and letting go is a difficult task for any parent. Handling tough issues, such as independence, relationships, dating, and sexuality, is compounded by this ever-complicated world we live in. Judgments and social decisions are influenced by hormones, cyberspace, the media, tweeting, and differing societal views on fitting in. In this complex world, all children are not afforded the same financial or emotional opportunities. Sometimes societal and peer pressure can further complicate the process of leaving childhood to enter the almost-adult world. Dr. Stanley Greenspan's book *The Child With Special Needs* delineates the importance of not overloading an adolescent's experiences. He explains that if things become complex too quickly, with too much to process and comprehend, a child may become disorganized rather than able to handle abstract situations.

Students with LD who are in middle and high school classes may not have demonstrated mastery of prerequisite skills. This in turn interferes with higher-level curriculum demands and thinking skills (Bulgren, Graner, & Deshler, 2013), with many students experiencing frustration. Even though students may be older, the same basic learning strategies apply. Teachers need to use higher-interest-level, age-appropriate curriculum materials, along with step-by-step multisensory approaches that include kinesthetic-tactile, visual, and auditory elements. Establishing prior knowledge with lessons appealing to multiple intelligences, and ones including cooperative learning principles, honors the diverse academic and social levels and needs of teens. Universal design for learning, project-based learning, and understanding by design need to enter the inclusive adolescent classroom to connect with future goals and the needs of diverse students.

Unfortunately, not all children get to pick their experiences. That's where involved adults can help students handle whatever cards are dealt. Making choices that will affect the rest of their lives is not easy. Suddenly, adolescents are asked to seriously think about what they plan on doing *when they grow up.* Erik Erikson's (1968) theory on psychosocial development identified adolescents going through a stage labeled *identity versus role confusion* in middle school and high school, while Piaget's (1952) stages of cognitive development identified difficulties that adolescents encounter with formal operations dealing with abstract thoughts and reasoning to solve problems. Even though these psychological icons did not live in the 21st century, their schools of thought are still applicable to teenagers today, who are continually trying to find their places in the world and within their own bodies, while learning concepts coupled with societal expectations become more challenging. This is a time when the grown-up world places more demands on adolescents' performance in school, at home, and in their community as they prepare for life beyond school walls. If adolescents have good role models, decision making is then an easier task due to situational osmosis. Drugs, depression, suicide, and violence are unfortunately all issues of concern for adolescents. Depression is the most common emotional issue during adolescence, with students feeling worthless, moody, and isolated (Snowman, McCown, & Biehler, 2009). Educators, guidance counselors, and positive community involvement can direct adolescents during these turbulent times.

Teachers can model problem-solving techniques, with systematic questioning for academic and social areas, offering teens options for appropriate discussions, reflections, and applications. This means teaching social skills to students on the autism spectrum as well as understanding the adolescent needs of a student with intellectual, communicative, emotional, social, or behavioral differences. Adolescents in inclusive classrooms with and without disabilities require honed information-processing skills, learning how to attend better to organize, synthesize, and generalize abstract concepts. Educators must also help students to *know what they know.* Assist them with ways to better access and retain information by increasing self-advocacy skills through guided experiences that help them to realize just how they learn best (e.g., by recopying notes, talking into a digital recorder, reviewing online sources, working with peer mentors, having study sessions, using more visuals, and more).

Students need to be reminded that good values along with solid academics will open many doors, and when maturation kicks in, decision making will be an easier task. Setting up positive channeling activities helps avoid the negative choices some teenagers make as a result of peer pressure. This may require strategies that range from social journals to social scripts. Giving an adolescent a pat on the shoulder also goes a long way! Teach, but listen, respect, and encourage each adolescent to value himself or herself as well!

See www.corwin.com/inclusionstrategies for a list of resources for teens and adults.

7

The Common Core State Standards and Using the Three Rs to Guide Instruction and Assessment

When I was a newlywed a few decades ago, my poor husband was regularly greeted by the new casserole of the week. Well, I remember thinking, if I threw in a little of this and that, with an extra can of something in the pantry, sprinkled it with parmesan cheese, and then baked it in a preheated 375-degree oven, wouldn't it be delicious? Now, in this age of curriculum standards, information explosion, data collection, and ongoing assessments, classrooms cannot become that dreaded casserole. The purpose of this chapter is to help teachers stick to and complement the educational basics: reading, writing, and math. This translates to providing students with and without disability classifications with the academic knowledge and skills that prepare students for a greater range of postsecondary options for college and careers. Included are student templates to reinforce concepts across the disciplines while at the same time giving merit to the three Rs, thereby yielding higher student performance.

FIRST R: READING ■

Reading is a complex process for some students whose brains are not automatically wired to read. Students with and without disabilities need to interact with increasingly complex texts. When reading instruction takes an eclectic approach, both word identification and comprehension skills are honored. This method offers high expectations for students as they climb the reading ladder on their instructional, not frustration level. *Phonological awareness,* the awareness of the sound structure of the spoken word, includes the ability to distinguish among the smallest units of speech, such as the syllables in a word and their individual phonemes. Phonological awareness is taught using controlled texts and grade-appropriate literature. Some students with disabilities benefit from a multisensory approach for word decoding and comprehension, since they may process language differently or have varying attention, behavioral, sensory, and learning needs. Although reading novels teaches the joy of delving into a story, some students require direct skill instruction with structured reading activities for the application of skills. Literacy rises if reading material is related to a child's life, increasing both retention and motivation. It is recommended that a developmental reading assessment (DRA) or another type of informal reading inventory be administered, since it offers staff insights into the reading accuracy, fluency, comprehension levels, and reading interests of students. Then, one should administer the same inventory at set times during the year, such as each marking period, to indicate student progress and guide instruction. As students read, the responses are looked at to determine the types of errors (e.g., insertions, substitutions, omissions, or repetitions), time taken to read, and general comprehension of nonfiction and fiction passages to ascertain independent and instructional reading levels. Increasing academic vocabulary for informational and literary texts may require approaches that value repetition, have accompanying visuals, and perhaps offer embedded text-to-speech features. The nonnegotiable bottom line is that increased skills with reading, writing, listening, and speaking are attainable when best practices with universal design for learning (UDL) approaches are continually infused.

Word Identification

Word decoding and identification involves several components, such as understanding vowel patterns, syllabication rules, context clues to identify unfamiliar vocabulary words, structural analysis, and dictionary skills, along with computer language tools such as how to use a spell-checker or thesaurus.

Five Reading Strategies to Help Identify Unfamiliar Words

1. Vowel and consonant patterns identified
2. Syllabication rules applied
3. Context clues discovered
4. Structural analysis understood
5. Words defined

An example of these five reading ingredients is delineated in the boxed sentence below.

FIGURING OUT WORDS

The aromatic smell coming from the kitchen was a culinary dream to the patrons as they eagerly and ecstatically awaited their meal.

Vowel Rules and Consonant Patterns

Short *e*: smell, ecstatically. Long *e* using *ea:* dream, eagerly

Consonant blends: ec**st**atically has *st* blend, and pa**tr**ons has *tr* blend

Syllabication Rules

kit-chen ec-stat-ic-al-ly cu-li-nar-y

Context Clues

An aromatic smell and a culinary dream must mean that something good is being created in the kitchen since people are eagerly and *ecstatically* awaiting their meal.

Structural Analysis

Aromatic has the base word *aroma,* with a suffix, *-tic,* added. *Eager* has the suffix *-ly* added, which makes it into an adverb, *eagerly. A-wait-ed* can be broken up into three parts, with a prefix, base word, and suffix.

Words Defined

I'm still not certain of what *ecstatically* means, so I think I'll use my online dictionary, thesaurus, or electronic speller. More examination and application of these rules continues.

Remember that all learning needs to be repetitive for further retention.

"EXAMINING WORDS CLOSELY" WORKSHEET

Primary and reading teachers can consistently model this strategy, selecting one reading rule at a time. As students gain understanding of each rule, select more words so they can practice applying it.

Explanation of Strategic Reading Rules

1. Sound out the word by looking at vowel and consonant patterns. For vowels, this means *a, e, i, o, u,* or any combination of these letters at the beginning, middle, or end of words. Vowels may be short, long, *r* controlled, or combined with another vowel. Consonants also blend (*fl*ag) or have *digraphs*—two letters with one sound (such as *wh, sh, th, ch*). Digraphs can also combine with other consonants (lu*nch*).
2. Try to say one syllable at a time; each syllable needs at least one vowel.
3. Find the parts of words by looking for the root words, prefixes, and suffixes.
4. Use context clues by reading surrounding words in the sentence to guess the meaning. Understand the sentence in relation to the passage.
5. Find the word's meaning and pronunciation in the dictionary or with a digital tool.

Using the above five strategies, choose ten words that appear in a book and examine them closely. Explain which strategy you would apply to help read each word.

Word	Strategy Used
1.	
2.	
3.	
4.	
5.	
6.	
7.	
8.	
9.	
10.	

GUIDED QUESTIONS TO HELP STUDENTS INCREASE PHONEMIC AWARENESS

Words are made up of basic units of sound called phonemes. These sound units are formed by letters that are combined in different ways. The following guided questions can help students of all ages learn about phonics and how to pronounce unfamiliar words.

Isolation of a Sound

What is the beginning sound in *success?*
What is the ending sound in *planning?*

Discriminating Among Sounds

Which of the following words has a different beginning sound from the others?

assessment accommodations outcomes

Blending Sounds

What word would you have if you put the following sounds together?

s / c / a / n

Matching Sounds to Words

Is there a *p* sound in *cooperate?*

Matching Words to Words

Do *curriculum* and *connections* begin with the same sound?
Find two words that have the same *er* sound as in *learning.*

Dissecting or Identifying Sounds as You Stretch Words

What sounds do you hear in the word *study?*

Rhyming Sounds

Think of two words that rhyme with *study.* Make rhyming charts, such as the following:

at	putty
mat	study
rat	buddy
flat	muddy

Deleting a Phoneme

What word would be left if the *s* were taken out of *self?*

Adding a Phoneme

What would be the resulting word if a *p* were added to *art?*

Available for download at **www.corwin.com/inclusionstrategies**

Moral: Phonemic knowledge is essential!

TROUBLESOME WORDS THAT ARE CLOSE BUT NOT CLOSE ENOUGH

Over the course of several years, I recorded students' misread words in the context of reading literature. Compare the pronunciation differences between the two lists on the following pages. Misread phonemes can definitely thwart reading comprehension! After all, peppercorn and popcorn have similar letters, but there's quite a difference in taste.

sweet butter	sweat bitter
barter goods	butter goods
calm down	clam down
interpret this	interrupt this
watch out	witch out
imagine that	manage that
change it	charge it
applause	applesauce
immediate family	intermediate family
selling lemonade	spelling lemonade
it's the beginning	it's the being
hot meal	hot metal
delay	daily
Idaho	Iowa
bought	brought
aviator flies planes	aviator flies plants
it's a threat	it's a treat
in the groove	in the grove
steep valley	step valley
invitation	invasion invention

sweet butter	sweat bitter
buckskin	duckskin
angels in the sky	angles in the sky
grandmother's sixtieth birthday	grandmother's sixteenth birthday
commanded orders	committed orders
sturdy table	study table
what a price	what a prize
inch through the mob	itch through the mob
read a fairy tale	read a fair tailor
shouts of people	shots of people
stitch of clothing	switch of clothing
Denise	Dennis
started	stared
assign work	assassin work
flowers smelled	flowers smiled
yoga class	yogurt class
hundreds place	hundredths place
context clues	contact clues
skills developed	skulls developed

Classroom Reading Identification Suggestion

Students need more awareness of the mistakes they make in their reading so they do not repeat word errors. Misreading words directly impacts a student's comprehension when substituted words are not close in meaning. Daily time should be set aside for individual oral reading. Teachers can rotate about to individually read with some students, while others are silently reading or involved in classroom assignments. Within a half-hour period, a teacher can comfortably meet with five students for five-minute periods to record individual reading sheets. If this is done with five different students each day, the whole class can read with the teacher each week. Other options include utilizing digital recorders for students to record their passages, allowing teachers to make corrections to be shared with students at a later date. The worksheet on the next page can then be shared with the students and parents as part of their "readacognition" (awareness of their reading program). Students regularly read the words on these sheets to ascertain types of errors, reinforcing corrections.

READACOGNITION: WORDS I NOW KNOW

Name ______________________________

Date	Word I Said	Correct Word

HOW STUDENTS LEARN BY MANIPULATING LETTERS

Instead of repeatedly writing misspelled words or rereading word errors, students learn more about words and their phonemes by actually manipulating letters. Students cut out the letters below and then use these letter cards to tactilely reinforce letter sounds. As a teacher calls out various words, students who each have their own set of laminated cards form the words and make corrections without erasers. Students can also write letters on index cards. Teachers can increase difficulties, depending on students' levels. For example, fat, fate, late, inflate, deflate, and inflated might be one sequence read, or in, win, tine, wind, twin, and twine. Possibilities for words to use are endless.

a	**a**	**a**	**a**
b	**b**	**b**	**b**
c	**c**	**c**	**c**
d	**d**	**d**	**d**
e	**e**	**e**	**e**
f	**f**	**f**	**f**
g	**g**	**g**	**g**
h	**h**	**h**	**h**
i	**i**	**i**	**i**
j	**j**	**j**	**j**

k	k	k	k
l	l	l	l
m	m	m	m
n	n	n	n
o	o	o	o
p	p	p	p
q	q	r	r
r	r	s	s
s	s	t	t
t	t	u	u
u	u	v	v
w	w	x	x
y	y	z	z

(Continued)

(Continued)

Teachers can laminate these cards for students to cut out and store in their own letter envelopes. Since students are physically manipulating the letters, the sensory impression will lead to further retention. Repeated practice works!

Try manipulating the cut out letters to make the words in the list below.

Spelling Rules

1. Teach spelling patterns.
2. Teach in small units.
3. Provide sufficient practice and feedback.
4. Select appropriate words.
5. Maintain previously learned words.
6. Teach for transfer of learning.
7. Motivate students to spell correctly.
8. Include dictionary training.
9. Use visuals.
10. PRAISE strides!

ad
red
read
reading
or
row
word
words
he
helps
we
hen
when
you
to
ouch
touch
he
the
let
letters

Available for download at **www.corwin.com/inclusionstrategies**

Check Out These Websites

Achieve 3000: www.achieve3000.com

International Dyslexia Association: www.interdys.org

International Reading Association: www.reading.org

Jolly Phonics: jollylearning.co.uk

Orton-Gillingham: www.ortonacademy.org

Reading Online: www.readingonline.org

Solo Literacy Suite: donjohnston.com/solo/

System 44 and Read 180: system44.scholastic.com/pdf/research/S44R180_Special_Ed.pdf

Wilson Language Training: www.wilsonlanguage.com

STOP TO MANIPULATE LETTERS

How many words can you make out of this sign?

1.
2.
3.
4.
5.
6.
7.
8.
9.
10.
11.

Students can manipulate letters in games such as Scrabble, Boggle, crossword puzzles (www.puzzlemaker.com), jumbles, word searches, and other fun word games.

Possible Answers

1. spot
2. so
3. top
4. tops
5. to
6. pot
7. pots
8. post
9. opt
10. opts
11. sop

WORD ANALYSIS CHART

Words can be dissected into their *affixes,* or word parts. The columned table below zeroes in on prefixes, suffixes, base words, and the two parts of a compound word. Increasing student awareness of how words are formed allows learners to transfer decoding skills to their reading. The chart below lists examples of words, with specific page numbers listed from the novel *The House on Mango Street,* by Sandra Cisneros. Primary-grade teachers need to focus on one affix, or part of speech, at a time, modeling extensively before requiring students to do this type of activity. Creating a classroom wall chart is also recommended.

Prefixes	Base Words	Suffixes	Compound Words	Page Number
			down stairs	3
	care	ful		3
			butter flies	33
			lunch room	54
			lunch time	54
	burn	ing		59
	luck	y		62
re	build	ing		67
			lip stick	67
			repair man	71
	damp	ness		70
	danger	ous		82
dis	appear	ing		95
	bare	ly		103
			for ever	110

MY WORD ANALYSIS CHART

Directions: As you finish reading for the day, fill in words in the columns below.

Name: ____

Title of Book: ____

Prefixes	Base Words	Suffixes	Compound Words	Page Number

READING COMPREHENSION

Some children have a rapid oral reading pace but poor comprehension. Read the following educational passage and fill in reading skills below.

> The days of the teacher sitting in front of the classroom with all student eyes facing forward have long passed. Teachers are currently encouraged to de-emphasize lecturing and concentrate more on active approaches in their classrooms. Less time is now spent on reading from textbooks and having students regurgitate isolated facts. Strict memorization without developing analytical skills will only serve students useless information that is unrelated to real-world problems. In contrast, developing critical thinking skills can be carried across all curriculum areas. It is hoped that all teachers will adapt this win–win approach to their individual educational environments.

Directions: Match each statement with the correct reading skill listed in the box below.

1. Students need active learning.

 ____

2. Memorizing isolated facts is ineffective for learning.

 ____

3. Teachers will become facilitators, rather than disseminators, of knowledge.

 ____

4. The writer has read extensive educational research.

 ____

5. Teachers must help students to become critical thinkers.

 ____

Main Idea	Cause and Effect	Predictions
Inference	Sequencing	Summarizing

In the next activity, after being given short reading passages, students are asked to work backward, thinking of their own questions, rather than answering teacher-created ones. It is recommended that the teacher first model an example with the entire class and have students use the "Think of a Question" template. Primary students could use a graphic organizer with fewer words and clouds or bubbles to separate different types of questions; this would achieve the same goal of increasing reading comprehension.

THINK OF A QUESTION

Name: ____

Directions: After you have read the pages your teacher assigned, think of questions that relate to these reading skills. Exchange your questions with a classmate.

Main Idea

This is the *most important idea of the story.* Asking about the main idea might involve using words such as *who, what, when, where, why,* or *how.* The main idea may be found anywhere in a paragraph, from the first to the last sentence. Sometimes it is not specifically stated with exact words, so you must figure it out. Discover the main idea and reword it into a question.

Main Idea Question:

____

____

Details

These are *facts that tell more about the main idea.* Suppose you just read a paragraph whose main idea was: *Dogs are great pets.* The paragraph also states that a Labrador retriever is a lovable breed that can be trained to bring in a newspaper. The sentence about a Labrador is a supporting detail for the main idea. Such details may be specific names, dates, locations, directions, or perhaps descriptive words. Choose a detail and reword it into a question.

Details Question:

____

____

Predictions

Stop reading and write a prediction question such as the following (with the blanks filled in). What will happen next if ________? When will __________? How will _________? Where will _________? Predictions deal with the future. If you have finished reading a book or passage, what might a sequel be about? What might happen to the characters?

Prediction Question:

____

____

(Continued)

(Continued)

Inferences

These are tough kinds of questions. Take a step beyond the written words you have read and write about *what the author implied or hinted at but did not actually state in so many words*. Your inference needs to be supported by what you just read, by noting an example, comparison, mood, or maybe a relationship between events and details presented.

Inference Question:

____

____

Sequencing

Order in the reading! Words such as *first, next, later, after,* and *finally,* along with other story clues, help to indicate the sequence. Questions might involve asking, What happened before ______? after ________? during _________?

Last, But Not Least, a Sequencing Question:

____

____

CLASSIFYING WORDS

As you read a novel, notice how nouns, verbs, adjectives, and adverbs add spice to otherwise bland sentences. List different kinds of words in appropriate columns, with the page number next to each one. Try to imitate the writing style of authors you read, and use different kinds of words in your own writing. Remember that reading and writing are "relatives," with words as the common blood they share. Words can jump off pages and be stored in a word mind-bank!

Nouns	Verbs	Adjectives	Adverbs
• Naming word: a ____, an ____, the ______ • Some may end in *er,* or *tion, sion,* or *ness.* • Nouns indicate a person, place, thing, or idea.	• They can indicate an action, expression, or occurrence. Examine your verbs. • Many verbs end with *s, es,* or *ing.* • Verbs also have a past tense.	• Used with a noun or pronoun to describe it • Can be found between an article and a noun—the *friendly* girl, *another* table, a *delicious* apple, *five brown* horses • Adjectives answer the questions: What kind? Which one? How many?	• Tell about verbs, adjectives, and other adverbs • Sometimes end in *ly.* Adverbs express cause and manner, and to what degree. For example, "He ran well. She is extremely capable." • Adverbs answer the questions, How? (degree, manner) When? (time) Where? (place)
learner p. 5	learning p. 8	creative p. 12	skillfully p. 17
class p. 23	instruct p. 30	pleasing p. 38	constantly p. 38
imagination p. 55	shared p. 62	several p. 75	now p. 105

CLOZE READING EXERCISES

Cloze exercises delete important words, asking students to substitute their own. As a modification, a word box can be included. If students give inappropriate words, the level of reading or subject matter may be too difficult. If students do not use a word box, more than one answer is acceptable. As a further accommodation, some students may need the sentences and words read aloud to them, so the teacher can ascertain comprehension rather than word identification level.

The following passages are examples of cloze exercises. Word boxes are included, but appropriate free responses are also welcomed.

Learning Disabilities

1. ______________the processes and strategies.
2. Allow students to demonstrate learning in ________________ways.
3. Teach ____________-regulation and give positive feedback.
4. Provide opportunities for extended ____________ and _____________.
5. Adjust ______________loads and _____________ requirements.

Word Box (1–5)

a. accommodations	b. self	c. practice	d. multiple
e. work	f. time	g. model	h. application

Attention Deficit Hyperactivity Disorder

1. Can display ______________ and/or __________________
2. _____________ with poor delay of ___________________
3. Increased _______________ of task performance
4. Diminished _______________________ behavior
5. Give students ________________support
6. Maintain a ______________________
7. Arrange the ____________________to facilitate attention

Word Box (6–12)

i. impulsivity	j. inattention	k. gratification
l. schedule	m. variability	n. hyperactivity
o. environment	p. rule-governed	q. organizational

DESIGN A CLOZE EXERCISE

Directions: Cooperatively design a cloze passage on any topic. First, pick vocabulary words, and write them in the boxes at the bottom of the page. Then, write sentences in the large blank box below, substituting blanks where the words would be filled in. Sentences must tell more about topic.

Word Box

Available for download at **www.corwin.com/inclusionstrategies**

Consult this site to create your own cloze exercise: edhelper.com/cloze.htm.

Compartmentalizing Reading

Works of fiction have these story ingredients: characters, setting, problem/plot, and resolution. The graphic organizer "Story Stuffing," which appears a little further on, helps students visually separate these story elements and ensures ongoing comprehension as plots develop. The graphic organizer "Vocabulary Review" concretely helps learners compartmentalize their thoughts by having them write the word's definition, the sentence with the vocabulary word from the story's context, and their own sentence using the same vocabulary word. Students can also draw pictures of key vocabulary words in the sentence and identify synonyms, antonyms, and analogies. This type of organizational support for reading assists students in mastering the Common Core State Standards for English Language Arts (CCSS.ELA).

Classroom book clubs are another way to improve reading comprehension, vocabulary development, and word identification. Adding a social dimension through cooperative grouping draws even the most reluctant reader into a book. Specific reading requirements are given to a group of at least five children who together review the same novel, showing their understanding in different ways. By working with peers under the teacher's direction, students become actively involved in their own course of learning as they eagerly share their knowledge, learning from each other under the teacher's auspices. Collectively they achieve a grade, while individually they are each accountable for a packet of materials. At first, it is recommended that everyone in the class read the same novel, so the teacher can extensively model the skills that will be required in cooperative reading assignments. Simply put, students need to crawl before they can successfully walk or run, or in this case, before they can branch off from the teacher to read cooperatively. When I was the inclusion teacher in an English class, everyone read *The Lion, the Witch, and the Wardrobe,* by C. S. Lewis. While the class read the same book together, each child was responsible for completing his or her own reading packet. After that, children in the class were given a choice of one out of five novels: *I Got a "D" in Salami; Dogsong; The Twenty-One Balloons; The Legend of Jimmy Spoon;* and *In the Year of the Boar and Jackie Robinson.* After students made their book choice (based on interest and reading levels), book clubs were cooperatively required to read their chosen book and complete collated assignments that consisted of the following duplicated pages. The general education teacher and I rotated among the groups to monitor understanding and fill out "readacognition" sheets. Digital recordings were also available as an option for the class to listen to as they read independently or in groups.

Classroom Templates

Teacher Directions for Novel Book Club Reading Packets

Appropriate variations can be given for grade levels and students' individual academic or social needs. Workload and time requirements can also be modified, yet simultaneously connected to the CCSS.ELA anchor and grade level standards accessed at http://www.corestandards.org/ELA-Literacy/. Read on for more directions and reading templates that combine literature with direct skill instruction.

1. *Chapter Summary Pages*—Students list the main idea of each chapter in well-constructed, detailed sentences. (The number of pages depends on how many chapters are in the book. For example, seven sheets with three summaries per page would be enough to summarize twenty-one chapters.)

2. *Vocabulary Review Pages*—These contain definitions of chosen vocabulary, sentences from the story using the words, and students' own sentences showing word meaning. (Ten sheets with two vocabulary words on each page would be enough for twenty vocabulary words.)

3. *Reading Graph*—Students are asked to date, grade, and plot what they think about a book, giving it a grade such as WOW (85–100), GOOD (70–85), OK (55–70), ???? (35–55)—not sure what's going on, or ——— (5–35)—so bad that there's no comment for the book.

   Quite often, students might not want to give a book a chance, but by plotting their reading reactions on a daily basis, they can visually identify which parts interest them most before dismissing a book.

4. *Story Stuffing Page*—This graphic organizer is used to increase students' knowledge that every story has these essential ingredients: characters, setting (where and when), plot, climax (turning point or zenith), and ending or resolution. Students can continue to fill out this template as more events unfold or details and characters emerge.

5. *Word Analysis Page*—This page asks students to identify affixes with specific prefixes and suffixes, base words, and compound words. Students then become less fearful of those long words, since they can now identify the meaning and pronunciation of longer words by breaking them apart.

6. *Columned Nouns, Verbs, Adjectives, Adverbs*—Students find words in their chosen novels and place them in appropriate categories, depending on how they are used in specific sentences. This page becomes much easier to fill out after the teacher has guided them through it in the novel they read together. Book club members can work together to cooperatively identify the parts of speech at any time while reading the novel.

7. *Readacognition*—Students periodically read with teacher and review vocabulary words their group has chosen.

STORY STUFFING

Characters

(Who?)

Setting

(Where? When?)

Plot/Climax

(How did it happen? What's the problem? What's the exciting part?)

Resolution

(Tell about the ending.)

VOCABULARY REVIEW

Words/Definitions From the Story/Text That I Now Know:

Word: ______________________________

Definition: ______________________________

____

Word: ______________________________

Definition: ______________________________

____

Sentences From the Story That Use Vocabulary Words:

____

____

____

____

____

____

____

____

____

____

My Own Sentences Using Vocabulary Words:

____

____

____

____

____

____

____

____

____

____

CHAPTER SUMMARIES

Story Title: ______________________________

Author: ______________________________

STUDENT CRITIQUE: GRADE YOUR BOOK CHAPTER BY CHAPTER

Directions: Place date of your reading under each vertical line and grade your book, scoring it from 5 to 100 according to the descriptions in the key below.

_________________'s Reading Graph

Book: ___________________________________ Author: ____________________________

W O W G O O D O K ? ? ? ? ? — — — — — —

100																			
95																			
90																			
85																			
80																			
75																			
70																			
65																			
60																			
55																			
50																			
45																			
40																			
35																			
30																			
25																			
20																			
15																			
10																			
5																			

DATES :

WOW: I love it! GOOD: I like it! OK: Not bad! ????: No idea what is going on. ----: Yuck!

(Continued)

(Continued)

SOARING INTO READING

S can

O utline

A nalyze

R ead

Understanding Nonfiction

Reading nonfiction material requires different skills from those needed for reading fiction. Children need specific tools to help them extract pertinent details from textbooks, newspaper articles, magazines, online sources, and other nonfiction literature. Specific strategies such as *scanning, outlining,* and *analyzing* help students comprehend their *reading* (SOAR). Cooperatively working in groups based on common interests fosters further understanding. This SOARing technique helps students comprehend the information in subjects beyond English, such as social studies, science, or mathematics texts. This includes interpreting primary documents, scientific data, charts, graphs, digital activities, and more. *The more ways students read, the better their comprehension becomes.*

How SOARing Works With Stations

By scanning the material, students familiarize themselves with the layout of the textbook, noticing pictures, graphs, highlighted words, chapter divisions, table of contents, the glossary, the index, its length, and other dimensions of nonfiction reading material. Afterward, students form their outlines with the main idea, details, and personal reflections (M/D/Y Station), which are used as templates to help them organize and analyze their notes. After outlining the main idea, students soar into the material with stations. Learners choose stations for assigned textbook pages, specific articles, or other nonfiction material. Station choices include the following:

- Picture This Station (drawing more about main ideas)
- Word Station (creating a word search, pantomiming words, word acrostics)
- Teacher Station (designing a test based on textbook readings)
- Performance Station (creating a skit, poem, song, commercial, video game, or dance about the readings)
- Research Station (finding out more about specific topics using other resources such as texts, computers, encyclopedias, and the library)

Note for Teachers: SOARing Into Reading is designed to help all students become actively involved in their learning under the teacher's auspices. Specific classroom stations allow learners to choose their own way of understanding nonfiction. SOARing Into Reading pragmatically translates effective educational research about good teaching practices while motivating learners through differentiated instruction. Any of these stations can be modified according to students' needs and levels. Each group consists of four to six students who independently rotate around the classroom to cooperatively complete tasks outlined in written station directions. Even though students work together, all students are responsible for the finished product. Some students may find the assignments too difficult, for example, requiring fewer words for the word search. Others may need more challenges, in which case a teacher could modify the Word Station or just assign the acrostic to students who need greater challenges. Teacher discretion is then required for modifying the grading rubric. Teachers can encourage students to work with different classmates or may even randomly assign children to stations. The objective is to soar into reading, changing children's perspectives of reading textual material; some may even say, "More, please!"

SOARing Directions for Students

Scan

Look at all of the titles, pictures, bold letters, highlighted words, charts, graphs, and other cool things in print that you see in your textbook.

Outline

Read only the title headings of each section or chapter to determine what the main ideas are. Place the main idea inside the M section of your M/D/Y chart.

Analyze

You are not ready to read quite yet. Think about what you wrote as the main idea and how the pictures, charts, vocabulary, and other things you saw on the pages relate to that main idea. Get a general understanding of your topic.

Read

Now you are finally ready to read because you have previewed your topic. After you finish reading, fill in the D (Details) and Y (You) sections on your M/D/Y chart. The readings will now make a lot more sense.

After you have filled out the M/D/Y Station sheet, you will further explore the textbook pages by stopping at one or two of the following stations:

- Research Station
- Performance Station
- Word Station
- Picture This Station
- Teacher Station

Cooperatively work together to complete assigned tasks, following each station's directions. Plan your train ride carefully as you read more about your itinerary. Try to continually work with different classmates.

All Aboard for More Station Directions

The Main Idea (M) and Details (D) sections can be completed cooperatively. The You (Y) section on your M/D/Y chart is all about your reaction to the reading. It is to be completed individually. Share if you have ever heard of words or ideas in this text before. Did you like what you read? Do you want to learn more about this topic? Again, Y means you. At the bottom, there's a spot for vocabulary words and their definitions.

After you have cooperatively completed and shared the M/D/Y Station, everyone will *continue making more station stops,* as if traveling on a train. Each student must pick another station. If this is your second time doing this activity, pick a different train stop from the last time. *Follow all directions for individual stations and work cooperatively with other passengers.* Prepare your *oral presentation,* using note cards, following *presentation page directions.* Using the *peer-rating page,* let peers rate your helpfulness. *Study the rubric* to make sure all work is completed. Your teacher will then check all of your work. After your teacher reviews your completed oral and written assignments, a grade will be recorded on a *SOARing Reading Report.*

Most important, have fun on your textbook journey. Remember the book *The Little Engine That Could!*

Sound the whistle. All aboard!

M/D/Y STATION

for pages ______________________________

in my ______________________________ textbook

Name: ______________________________

Directions: Use the bolded titles or section headings in the textbook to help outline the main ideas. Read the words under these headings to discover and list important details. The last section, You, should be completed individually. It is a chance to tell your thoughts about the reading. Write neatly in small but readable handwriting.

Main Idea	Details	You
Look at the headings and titles of each chapter and section. Scan the pictures, charts, vocabulary, and other elements on the pages to understand the main idea of assigned pages.	Read the selection to discover details about the main idea. Concentrate on particulars that answer the questions who, what, when, where, why, and how.	Did you like the reading? Can you connect it to anything you have learned before? Did it remind you of a TV show, movie, book, or magazine, newspaper, or online article you read on the same topic? Do you think this information will be helpful?

Vocabulary	Write new words and their definitions.

Available for download at **www.corwin.com/inclusionstrategies**

PICTURE THIS STATION

Directions: Illustrate concepts from your reading that show more related details about the main ideas in the given boxes below. Refer to your M/D/Y sheet for the main ideas and include a caption for each picture. The group should cooperatively divide the textbook pages so each person illustrates different details about the main idea. Then, the illustrators should share pictures with each other by cutting them out and pasting them onto larger construction paper to create a group scrapbook. Sign your pictures.

Illustrator: ______________________________

Brief sentence explaining the picture: ______________________________

____

Illustrator: ______________________________

Brief sentence explaining the picture: ______________________________

____

WORD STATION

Directions: Choose *ten vocabulary words* from the reading selection. Using graph paper, create a *word search* for another classmate. Write your words in the box below. Then try to *pantomime one of the words* to see if members of your cooperative group can guess which vocabulary word you are demonstrating through your gestures and actions. Create *two-word acrostics* that further explain the vocabulary words.

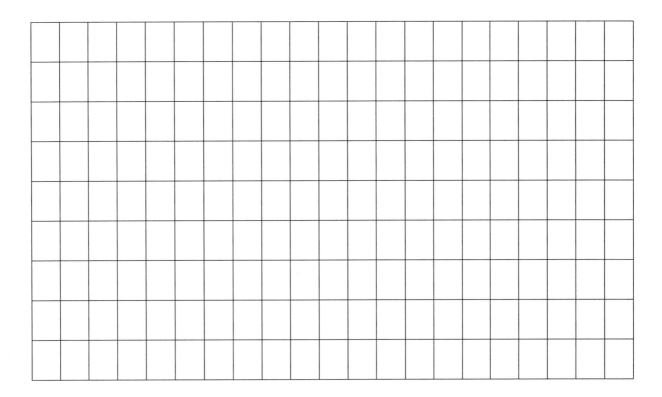

Look for these vocabulary words:

1. ______________________ 2. ______________________

3. ______________________ 4. ______________________

5. ______________________ 6. ______________________

7. ______________________ 8. ______________________

9. ______________________ 10. ______________________

Word Search Creators: ____

(Continued)

(Continued)

Directions: Work together in pairs, trios, and quartets.

Word Acrostic sentence examples:

Seeing data is what a scientist does. **C**omparing information is important. **I**nquiry can lead to discoveries. **E**xperiments help us learn about the world around us. **N**ow I understand more about the procedures involved. **C**ollecting data for research aids the process. **E**valuating the hypothesis is part of the scientific method.	**P**eople are part of the community. **E**xisting together is not an easy task. **O**rganizing a government requires a political process. **P**lanning together to reach agreements is necessary. **L**iving with diverse cultures will help this nation grow. **E**nvironmental differences affect how people live.

Choose two vocabulary words from the word search to create your sentence acrostics.

Acrostic created by ______________________________

TEACHER STATION

Directions: It's your chance to be the teacher. Your group will design a test based on the textbook readings. You can use the following question starters to help you begin. Remember to *vary the types of questions* and *use both big and little thought questions*. A little question can be answered with one word, while a big question requires more thought and details. All questions need an answer, either next to the question or on a separate answer key. The group must also decide the value (points given for correct answers) for each question, with the total possible test grade of 100 percent.

Sample Questions

Little thought question example: What is your name?

Big thought question example: Why do you attend school?

Sample Question Starters:

What is ______________________________?

A: ______________________________

Where is ______________________________?

A: ______________________________

How is ______________________________?

A: ______________________________

Why did ______________________________?

A: ______________________________

Which one of the following describes a ______________________________?

A: ______________________________

When did______________________________?

A: ______________________________

Which is *not* an example of ______________________________?

A: ______________________________

Tell the difference between ______________ and ______________

A: ______________________________

Vary your questions by including the following text-based question types:

True/False	Multiple choice	Fill-in
Essay	Matching	Short answers
Open ended		

Examiners: ______________________________

PERFORMANCE STATION

Directions: The group chooses one of the following cooperatively, and works to bring to life concepts or stories they have read.

1. Write a script for a *short skit, television commercial,* or *YouTube video* (check out www.showme.com) to demonstrate what you read. Remember that your characters must relate to the reading. It's your chance to make words come alive! Be creative!
2. Create a *poem, song, video game, advertisement,* or *dance* about the reading. Again, concentrate on stories or textbook concepts that you read.

Available classroom resources can be used (e.g., digital cameras, recorders, dictionaries, computers, thesauruses, rhyming lists, and CDs).

Performers:

RESEARCH STATION

Directions: Using classroom and library resources such as texts, computers, tablets, iPads, e-readers, and other reference materials, your group will find out more facts and details about the textbook material or story you have read. Be certain that you highlight important facts that you will orally share with the class. Consult your teacher for approved online sites.

Researchers learned the following:

____

Materials used: ____

Sources must be correctly cited using the format shown in the bibliography guidelines that follow.

Research conducted by ______________________________________

BIBLIOGRAPHY GUIDELINES FOR CITING SOURCES FROM RESEARCH STATION

Book—One Author

Author's last name, initial of first name. (year of book's publication). *Title of the book.* Place of publication: name of publisher.

Example:

Hoopmann, K. (2009). *All dogs have ADHD.* London, England: Jessica Kingsley Publishers.

Book—Multiple Authors

First author's last name, initial of first name, & next author's last name, initial of first name. (year of book's publication). *Title of the book.* Place of publication: name of publisher.

Example:

Winkler, H., & Oliver, L. (2003). *Niagara falls, or does it?* New York: Grosset & Dunlap.

Book—Editor Instead of Author

Name or names of editors—last name first, then first initial. (Ed.). (year of publication). *Title of book.* Place of publication: name of publisher.

Example:

Evans, J. (Ed.). (2006). *Ultimate visual dictionary.* New York: DK Publishing.

Magazine Article

Author's last name, first initial. (year, month and day of publication). Title of article. *Title of magazine,* page range.

Example:

Fischer, D. (2001, November 12). Feel good sports stories. *Sports Illustrated for Kids,* 47.

Online Information

Author's last name, first initial (if known). (Year, or n.d. if no date is listed). *Title of work.* Retrieved (retrieval date), from (Web address)

Example:

Chan, J. (2013, December 5). Nelson Mandela: 1918-2013.
Retrieved May 1, 2014 from http://www.timeforkids.com/node/97361/print

Depending on the available technology, these digital options can be explored to connect to the stations:

Research Station: Fact Monster, Zunal

Performance Station: Go Animate, Flocabulary, Digital Storytelling

Word Station: VisuWords, Discovery Education, Wordle, Tagxedo, MindMaps

Picture This Station: Glogster, Popplet, Pics4Learning, Scribblitt, Inspiration, Comic Creator, Online Visual Dictionary, Dipity

Teacher Station: Quizlet, ShowMe

PEER-RATING FORM

Directions: Place your name above the line where it says *your name,* and ask two peers (classmates) to evaluate your helpfulness at different stations. Your peer must indicate at which station you cooperatively worked, how you were helpful, and sign the statement. The peer can give you a rating from 1 to 5, with 5 being the most helpful and highest rating, 3 describing someone who was of average help, and 1 being for someone who offered little assistance. Add the two scores for your total.

First Peer Rating

______________________ helped me ______________________________
(your name)

____

______________________________________ at the __________________

Station by ____

____

Number Rating (1–5): ______ Peer's Signature ______________________

Second Peer Rating

______________________ helped me ______________________________
(your name)

____

______________________________________ at the __________________

Station by ____

____

Number Rating (1–5): ______ Peer's Signature ______________________

First Peer Rating Score: ____

Second Peer Rating Score: _______________________________________

Total Peer Score: ____

ORAL PRESENTATIONS

Presentation Page Directions

Speaking Hints

1. Look at the audience.
2. Glance at your notes, but do not read from them.
3. Use appropriate hand gestures to help your presentation.
4. Share relevant information with teachers and classmates.
5. Be prepared for your speech by using the following note card guidelines.

Note Card for Speech Explaining Station Chosen

Name of station: ______________________________

People you worked with: ______________________________

____

What Did You Learn?

Main idea: ______________________________

Supporting details: ______________________________

____

____

Procedure Followed in Correct Sequence

First ______________________________

Next ______________________________

After ______________________________

Finally ______________________________

Briefly Summarize What You Learned at the Station

____

____

____

____

TEACHER'S SOARING READING RECORD FOR STATION GRADES

Student	M/D/Y	Picture This	Word	Performance	Research	Teacher

Textbook: ______________________________ Pages: ______________________________

RUBRIC FOR SOARING STATIONS

	Beginning 1	Developing 2	Accomplished 3	Exemplary 4	Score
 All verbal and written station 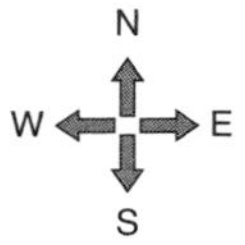 directions were completed.	Missing more than three station requirements. Unorganized. Illegible writing.	Legible but disorganized. Missing two station requirements.	Presentable work. Evidence of organization. Missing one station requirement.	Finished product is well organized and neat, with all station requirements met. Completed and followed all written directions.	
 Worked effectively with cooperative group  at stations.	Few positive statements from peers, with a peer rating total of 1 or less. Teacher does not observe any social interaction.	Some positive statements from peers, with a peer rating total of 2–4. Teacher observes some instances of working well with peers.	More positive statements from peers. Peer rating total of 5–7. Teacher observes frequent positive social interaction.	Positive statements from both peers, with rating total of 8–10. Teacher observes constant cooperative work with peers.	
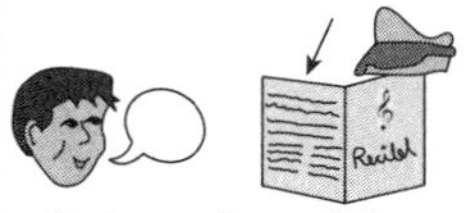 Oral Presentation	Incoherent speech. Little acknowledgment of audience. Did not stick to topic. Could not explain station work.	Difficulty retrieving information. Read from written work with little audience contact. Able to speak about work but lacked continuity. Concentrated more on details than the main idea.	Could answer most questions asked by peers and teacher. Good eye contact and gestures. Evidence of recall and good sequencing of station work in speech. Acknowledgment of audience. Focused on main idea and supporting details.	Able to explain work performed at each station, by sharing relevant information with teachers and classmates in speech. Excellent eye contact and gestures. Logical order of main idea with supporting details. Maintained audience interest.	

SOURCE: Created using rubistar.4teachers.org. Copyright © 2000–2008, ALTEC at the University of Kansas.

Rebus was created with Picture It, Copyright © 2012, SunCastle Technology.

Available for download at **www.corwin.com/inclusionstrategies**

BASIC WRITING RULES

1. Think about what you are going to write.
2. Use an outline, list, web, or template to help organize your thoughts.
3. Begin writing your rough/sloppy draft. It doesn't need to be smooth! Always skip lines; it leaves space for revisions.
4. Writing means rewriting, which means you need to repeatedly look at what you have written to make it better. Learn about Ed's Car! (A process for revising writing.)
5. Remember, writing is like talking on paper, since you can tell others what you are thinking through a short story, play, poem, newspaper article, tall tale, and more. Writing is a connection and gateway to all subjects!

=

Translation: **Writing** = **speaking on paper.**

Available for download at **www.corwin.com/inclusionstrategies**

Ways to Think Before Writing

Suppose your topic is successful classrooms. Think of relevant words and list them by the appropriate letter. Using the alphabet as your guide helps to organize thoughts across the curriculum. Writing can be as easy as the ABCs!

SUCCESSFUL CLASSROOMS

A	accommodations, assessments
B	
C	
D	
E	
F	
G	
H	
I	
J	
K	
L	
M	
N	
O	
P	
Q	
R	
S	
T	
U	
V	
W	
X	
Y	
Z	zero-reject

A–Z lists are used to introduce or review vocabulary across various curricula.

A–Z LISTING FOR SOCIAL STUDIES

A	
B	
C	
D	
E	
F	
G	
H	
I	
J	
K	
L	
M	
N	
O	
P	
Q	
R	
S	
T	
U	
V	
W	
X	
Y	
Z	

A–Z LISTING FOR SCIENCE

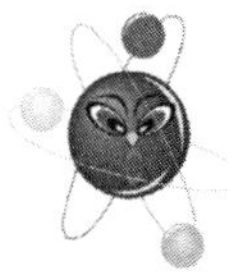

A	
B	
C	
D	
E	
F	
G	
H	
I	
J	
K	
L	
M	
N	
O	
P	
Q	
R	
S	
T	
U	
V	
W	
X	
Y	
Z	

Available for download at **www.corwin.com/inclusionstrategies**

APPLICATION OF ED'S CAR (REVISING WRITING)

What's Ed's Car?

Expand, Delete, Substitute, Combine And Rearrange

Expand—Write a simple sentence. Then, make it longer by asking *who, what, when, where, why,* or *how* questions.

For example,

The dog ran.

What kind of dog?

The cute dog ran.

Where did the dog run?

The cute dog ran around the block.

Why did the dog run around the block?

The cute dog ran around the block because the cat was chasing it.

When did the dog run?

The cute dog ran around the block yesterday because the cat was chasing it.

How did the dog run?

The cute dog quickly ran around the block yesterday because the cat was chasing it.

Delete—Take away unnecessary words that repeat the same thought. *The big canine dog ran* can be changed to *The big dog ran.* Writing less is better if the same thought is conveyed. Adding the word *canine* is unnecessary since it means the same as dog.

Substitute—Change words if another word can be more exact, or put in substitutes for overused words. *It was a good dog because it did good things.* That's quite a vague sentence. Here's the new one: *The loyal dog obeyed commands.* By substituting more descriptive words for *good* and *things,* the sentence's meaning becomes clearer.

Combine—

And

Rearrange—Combine similar thoughts expressed by subjects and verbs, and change the placement of words.

The playful dog ran today. The playful dog listened today.

New sentence: Today, the playful dog ran and listened.

If these strategies are too difficult, then some students in Grades K–1 or beginning writers could just focus on the expansion.

The following sign can be posted as a reminder to write with *Ed's Car* strategies.

SOURCE: Mnemonic designed by Adam J. Karten.

Ed's **Car**

E XPAND

D' ELETE

S UBSTITUTE

C OMBINE

A nd

R EARRANGE

APPLICATION OF ED'S CAR (REVISING WRITING)

Inclusion can help students. Inclusion is a way of teaching students. It can benefit students a lot. They can prepare for their future. Inclusion meets social, academic, and cognitive needs.

Revision Questions

- What word is often repeated?
- What phrase needs to be deleted?

Revised Writing

Helping diverse students achieve positive outcomes can be accomplished through inclusion. Using a variety of accommodations and planning strategies addresses social, academic, and cognitive needs. Inclusion, a way of approaching teaching, prepares students for future success.

Writing Tips Explaining Revisions

1. The first sentence says that inclusion helps students, but the revised version expands the sentence by telling what *kind* of student (a diverse one). It also varies the beginning of each sentence by starting with a verb (helping), instead of repeating the same word (inclusion).
2. The second sentence expands the original thought by telling *how* those needs are met. It also substitutes the word *met* with a more exact word, *addressed.* The original sentence was deleted because the writer had already stated that students are helped by inclusion. Even though the word *help* was changed to *benefit,* the thought was the same. There is no need to say it twice.
3. The last sentence combines and rearranges two separate sentences by using an *apposition*, which tells more about the noun by using a qualifying phrase. *Inclusion* (a noun), *a way of approaching teaching* (telling more about the noun), *prepares students for future success* (verb phrase).
4. Proofread, and then read it again. That's when you'll catch that repeated word or perhaps decide that you want to write the paragraph differently. Also, walking away from your writing helps, since you'll return with fresh eyes.

Collecting Writing Thoughts

Quite often, students need help to get started with their writing. Writing templates, easily accessible in writing folders, circumvent that "Where do I begin?" dilemma by neatly organizing thoughts. As students develop more confidence and familiarity with the writing process, they are weaned off the templates. It's comparable to using a special holiday cake tin for the batter. The ingredients make the taste, not the container. It's the students' writing, but it is organized by the template.

WRITING PLANNER (K–2)

Cars are important. First of all, ______________________________

In addition, ______________________________

Finally, ______________________________

After the words are filled in, the entire passage must be rewritten so that students gain a coherent writing experience.

OUR EARTH

Directions: Use the word box and outline below to help write a persuasive essay. Then, rewrite all sentences on another piece of paper.

pollution	water
ecology	air
environment	help
recycle	world
planet	future

First Paragraph: Introduction

Here are some reasons we should care about the Earth.

First, ____

In addition, ____________________________________

Also, ____

Second Paragraph (expand upon the first reason) ____________________

Third Paragraph (expand upon the second reason) ____________________

Fourth Paragraph (expand upon the third reason) ____________________

Fifth Paragraph (sum up all three reasons) In summary, ____________________

SENSORY WRITING PLANNER

This planner helps add sensory elements to set the scene. First, think of a place, and then put sensory words in columns to describe that place. The planner is then turned into a three-paragraph story about somewhere the student visited or read about. As an adaptation, some students might begin by choosing sentences that describe only one sense and location (e.g., hearing a parade or seeing a museum). Later on, the paragraph can be expanded to include other senses.

When I am at the _______________, I can __________________________.

Hear	See	Smell	Touch	Taste

First Paragraph (introduction) The _______________ is a place where ___________________ ____. People ____________________________ and ____ there.

The most interesting thing about ___________________________ is that _________________ ___ ____.

Second Paragraph (sensory details from chart) There are many different sights, sounds, smells, tastes, and things to touch at the _________________. Some include ____________________ and ________________. It sounds like ________________ and looks like ___________________. My favorite things there are ______________________ and ___________________________.

Third Paragraph (conclusion) Overall, ______________________________________ is a place that _________________________. It can best be described as ______________________________, and ________________________ and ___________________________ are the most exciting things there. To sum up, I think _________________ about ______________________________________.

PERSONAL NARRATIVE: WRITING PLANNER FOR GRADES 4–12

Directions: Collect your thoughts, and place them in the corresponding boxes as a planner for your narrative (the story about yourself). List words, not sentences.

Past—Yesterday, what already happened

What did you do when you were younger? Where were you born? What is your favorite memory? Remember past events.

Present—Today, what's happening now

What is your life like? Tell about your favorite things. Include information about family and friends. Concentrate on the present by adding specific life details.

Future—Tomorrow, what will happen in the time ahead

What are your plans? Have you picked a career?

What are your goals? Focus on thinking ahead.

(Continued)

(Continued)

Directions: After you have filled in the past, present, and future boxes on your planner, follow these steps for writing your personal narrative:

Paragraph 1: Tell about your present life. Include one to two sentences that refer to the past and one to two sentences about the future. Do not include any details, only main ideas.

I am presently a ________________________________ who ______________________, ______________________, and ______________________________. In the past, I did some fun things like __________________________, ____________________, and ____. In the future, I hope to ____.

Paragraph 2: Tell about past events only. Use minimum of three to five sentences.

When I was younger, I ____. I once ______________________. I remember ________________________________ ______________________________. I also______________________________.

Paragraph 3: Tell about present events only. What are you currently doing?

Today, I ____ ______________. I like ________________________________. My friends and I ____ __________________________. Sometimes, I ________________________ _____. My family members include ____________________________. We like to ______________ together. One of my favorite hobbies is ____________________.

Paragraph 4: Tell about the future only. Where do you see yourself five or ten years from now?

In the future, I want to ________________________________. Some of my dreams include ____ ________________. One day I will ______________________________________ ______________. Ultimately, ____ ____.

Paragraph 5: This is your conclusion.

To sum it up, my life has been ______________________________________ so far. I presently think my life is ____________________. Eventually, I hope to ______________ ______________. In conclusion, ________________ __________________________ ____.

Available for download at **www.corwin.com/inclusionstrategies**

WELL-PLANNED WRITING: A BALANCED MEAL

First Paragraph

Introduce your topic or story. Tell what it is about, without giving specific details. This paragraph should briefly explain to the reader what you will be writing more about and should answer questions such as the following:

Appetizer

Who? ______________________	Where? ______________________
What? ______________________	Why? ______________________
When? ______________________	How? ______________________

You can use sentences like

It all began when ______________________________________.

In the beginning, ______________________________________.

First, ______________________________________.

Early on, ______________________________________.

Second Paragraph

Tell the reader what happened next. Think about the main idea of the paragraph, and then add more details about that main idea with additional sentences.

Main Idea: ______________________________________

____

Soup

Details:

1. ______________________________________
2. ______________________________________
3. ______________________________________

You can use sentences like these in your following paragraphs:

Next, ______________________________________.

Immediately following, ______________________________________.

Shortly after, ______________________________________.

Then, ______________________________________.

SALAD	ENTREE	DESSERT
Third Paragraph: **Main Idea:**____________ ____________ **Details:** **1.** ____________ **2.** ____________ **3.** ____________ **Words like** Afterward, ________. Suddenly, ________. Later, ________.	**Fourth Paragraph:** **Main Idea:**____________ ____________ **Details:** **1.**____________ **2.**____________ **3.**____________ **Words like** After a while, ________. Some time later, ________. Eventually, ________.	**Fifth Paragraph:** **CONCLUSION** **Words like** All in all,________. Finally,________. Ultimately,________. On the whole,________. To summarize,________. Looking back,________.

DEVELOPING MY WRITING WITH A ROUGH DRAFT

Use this planner to start the rough draft.

First Paragraph: Introduction (Appetizer)
Questions to answer: Who? What? When? Where? Why? How?

First,

Second Paragraph (Soup)
Main Idea:

Next,

Third Paragraph (Salad)
Main Idea:

Then,

Fourth Paragraph (Entrée)
Main Idea:

After that,

Fifth Paragraph (Dessert)
Conclusion:

Finally,

HOW TO EXPAND WRITING WITH FIGURATIVE LANGUAGE

Language Locator

Find similes or metaphors in the story or textbook, or create your own based on what you read.

Examples:

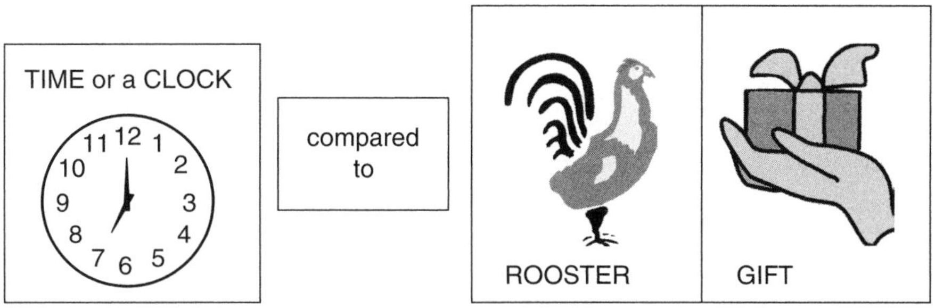

Concept/Noun | **A Totally Different Noun or Concept**

Simile: A clock is like a rooster that jolts us from our sleep.

Metaphor: A clock is a rooster, jolting us from our sleep.

Simile: Time is as precious as a birthday gift, given with love each year.

Metaphor: Time is each year's cherished birthday gift.

Now find or create your own similes or metaphors:

word/picture | compared to | word/picture

Concept/Noun | **A Totally Different Noun or Concept**

Simile: ______________________________

____

Metaphor: ______________________________

____

WRITING REFLECTIONS

Cooperative Writing Idea

All of these suggestions add a social component to writing, making it a less isolated activity.

Students can pool thoughts together to cooperatively write stories. Even though children's ideas are shared and brainstormed, each child must physically write the same story on paper or digitally. Of course, remind them to skip lines if they are using paper and pencil for revisions. They can indicate digital revisions with tracking tools or another color font. Encourage students to implement the strategies offered in Ed's Car. Some cooperative ideas include the following:

- Selecting a class topic, groups can cooperatively write different stories, fill in A–Z lists, and think about the who, what, where, when, why, and how questions. For example, everyone can write about Halloween, early colonies, endangered species, football, dancing, imperialism, *Animal Farm*, Shakespeare, or a favorite book with several versions, twists, or in a different genre.
- Two students can interview each other and record differences in a graphic organizer, such as a Venn diagram, which can later become a four-paragraph story:

  1st Paragraph: Introduction (telling about both students)

  2nd Paragraph: Similarities

  3rd Paragraph: Differences

  4th Paragraph: Conclusion
- The teacher can read a picture book to the class and then model how to retell that story using a different genre such as a tall tale, poem, or news report. Students will then choose their own picture book and retell the story with their chosen genre in groups of three or four.
- Using any curriculum topic, students can first answer the questions below as their planner, and then organize those thoughts into paragraphs, with a separate main idea and appropriate details for each one.

Who?	Where?
What?	Why?
When?	How?
- Shown a picture prompt, students can cooperatively and creatively write a story, giving their picture a past, present, and future.

What already happened?	What might happen later?
What's happening now?	

Writing Sources to Explore

Berninger, V., & Wolf, B. (2009). *Helping students with dyslexia and dysgraphia make connections: Differentiated instruction lesson plans in reading and writing.* Baltimore: Paul H. Brookes.

Gess, D., & Livingston, J. (2006). *Teaching writing: Strategies for improving literacy across the curriculum.* New York: Write Track.

Literacy for Life: www.fisherandfrey.com

Read, Write, and Think: www.readwritethink.org

Students can also create their own books. Check out these sources:

Book Writer: goodeffect.com

CAST Universal Design for Learning Bookbuilder: bookbuilder.cast.org

Treetop Publishers: www.barebooks.com

GENRE MENU: KEEPING TRACK OF WHAT I'VE READ AND WRITTEN

Name: ______________________________

Genre	Date	Title
Advertisement		
Biography or Autobiography		
Comic Strip		
Dystopia		
Fairy Tale or Fable		
Fantasy		
Graphic Novel		
Historical Fiction		
Letter		
Mystery		
Myth		
News Article		
Nonfiction		
Play		
Poem		
Realistic Fiction		
Science Fiction		
Song Lyrics		
Speech/Debate		
Tall Tale/Legend		
Travel Brochure		
Other		

Remember, the idea is to try different types of reading and writing!

WRITER'S NOTEBOOK IDEAS

Decorate your notebook with pictures from magazines, comic strips, something you drew, or whatever design you like best. This notebook could be a place for a favorite poem, a shopping list, an award you were given, ticket stubs, or a picture of your pet. Maybe one day you will choose to write about one of these things. It is your unique collection of thoughts and a home for your ideas.

Include items such as the following:

- Observations
- Lists
- Pictures
- Drawings
- Recipes
- Birthday cards
- Something special
- A flower you found
- Thoughts about . . . anything else you desire!

USING GUIDED QUESTIONS TO ASSESS AND REFLECT UPON WRITING

Date	a. Self b. Peers c. Teacher	Title of Work	Comments/Suggestions/Reflections (Write number of each question used)

Questions to Ponder

1. Were thoughts clearly stated?
2. Is the writing well organized?
3. Were words repeated? Were there instances where other words should be substituted? Was the same thought or concept repeated, using different words?
4. Did the writing flow with transitional words such as *first, in addition, later,* and *to sum up,* helping the reader know that a new thought is coming?
5. Did each paragraph have a separate thought with its own main idea and supporting details? Were sentences choppy? Could some sentences be combined?
6. Were there spelling errors?
7. Were the capitalization and punctuation reviewed?
8. Did you like reading/writing the piece? Why?
9. Do you understand what you just read/wrote?

THIRD R: 'RITHMETIC

Why Math?

Math was not one of my favorite subjects until I began to teach it. I hated those ridiculous word problems that only gave you a headache. Basically, who cares if so and so only had 4 boxes that fit 5 cookies each and had 25 friends who needed to eat those cookies? Does your head hurt yet? Math can be so much more than that!

It's about classifying, organizing, estimating, and understanding the world around you. Yes, you sometimes must add, subtract, multiply, and divide, but it need not be boring. Students need to know that different approaches can solve the same math problem. Math is a way of logically thinking and reasoning that carries over into all subject areas as a cognitive process. Verbalizing steps along the way helps, as does visualizing numbers in problems. Teachers need to assess whether students understand the problem itself or if the reading vocabulary in a word problem is the obstacle. Students can also learn more about numbers in a fun way, practicing basic skills while developing and applying critical thinking skills. Scaffolding may be needed to advance student levels as they make sense of problems or find entry points. The goal is for students to think abstractly and quantitatively, but educators must provide the structured and appropriate mathematical framework that will fulfill the rigor of the CCSS mathematical practices and grade-level standards. This includes greater focus on fewer topics for each grade, such as teaching problem solving with addition and subtraction skills in Grades K–2, but then delving into problem solving with multiplication and division of whole numbers and fractions in Grades 3–5. There is also more coherence with the linking of topics and thinking across grades, application of technology, using tools strategically, modeling, and attending to precision. Read on for more ways to do the math!

> Math is a complex subject requiring a variety of computational skills involving pictures, shapes, whole numbers, fractions, decimals, and words. Mathematical concepts and computational skills can be taught by applying sound educational strategies, such as establishing prior knowledge, proceeding from the simple to the complex, breaking the learning into its parts, using concrete examples, modeling the procedures, and varying instruction. Repeated practice, along with much praise for successes, *multiplies the learning*. Most important, math can be fun! No more headaches, please!

A Cornucopia of Skills

Ways to Approach Math, From the Simple to the Complex

Computational and conceptual skills such as these can be taught. These problems are paired with the student explanation of an answer/solution.

READINESS SKILLS: NEVER ASSUME

How many apples and books are shown?

______ apples

______ books

Can you write and solve a word problem that tells about this picture?

If I had 3 apples and 4 oranges and someone took 1 of the apples, what amount of fruit would be left? Circle the number sentence that would help solve this problem.

3 + 3 = 6   4 − 3 = 1   7 − 1 = 6   3 + 1 = 4

Draw as many happy faces as should be in the third box below.

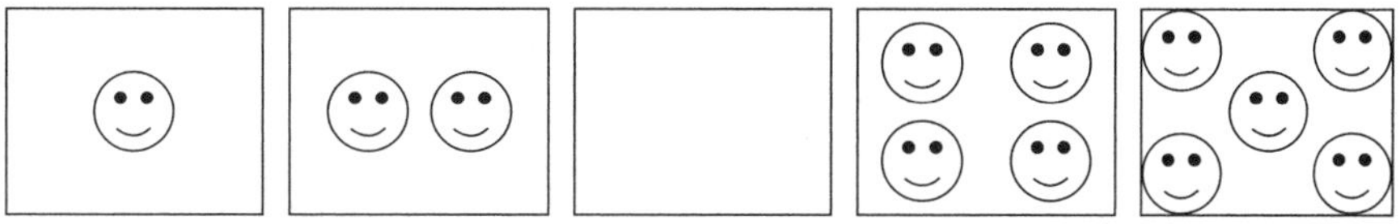

What numbers come just before and after the one below?

_____ 15 _____

How many more things does the largest group of objects have than the smallest one below?

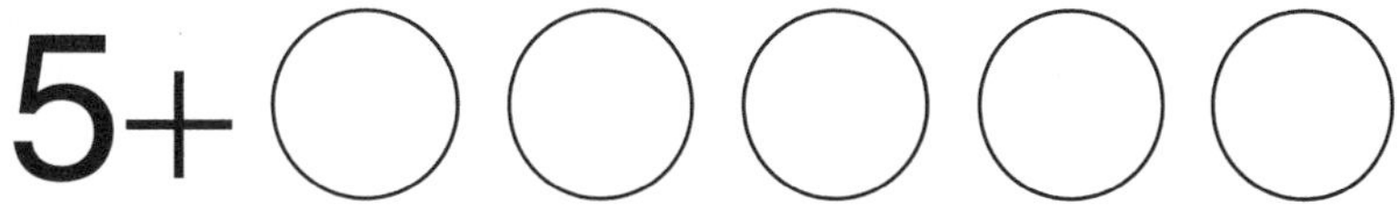

What time is shown on this clock?

Draw a 6-inch line.

(Continued)

(Continued)

Explain why 500 is the larger number by writing each number with words.

55.3 500

Round these numbers to the places named:

56	______	tens place
156	______	tens place
156	______	hundreds place
2,156	______	hundreds place
2,156	______	thousands place
21.45	______	tenths place
21.456	______	hundredths place

How many parts are in the circle below? ______

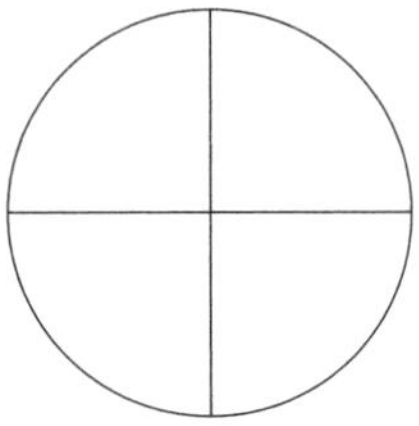

Which number sentence below would best describe this circle?

$\frac{1}{4} + \frac{1}{4} = \frac{2}{8}$ $2 + 2 = 4$ $\frac{4}{4} = 1$

What shape would fit into this space?

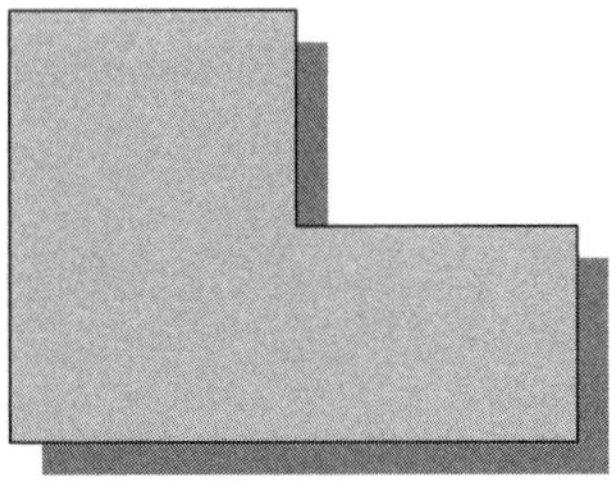

Can you name these shapes?

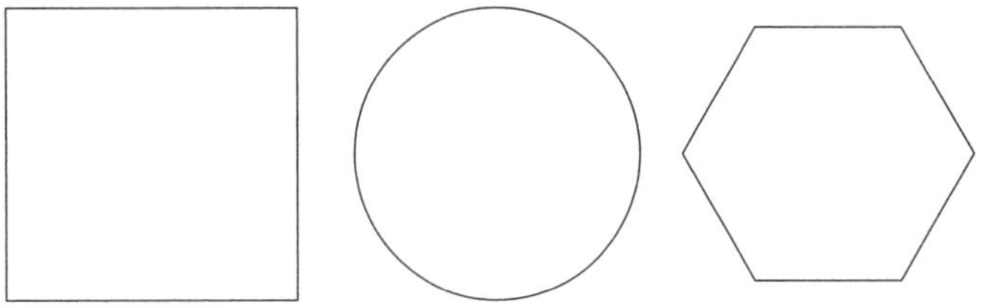

____________ ____________ ____________

What's the value of this number?

$4^2 =$ _______

EQUATIONS AND MORE

Can you solve this equation?

$$5 + (2 + 3)^2 - 6 \div 2 - 7 \times 2 - 1 = \_\_\_\_\_\_$$

Solve using the mnemonic **P**lease **E**xcuse **M**y **D**ear **A**unt **S**ally. Even though mnemonics and rules do not offer conceptual insights, they help students plunge into correct processes. Model a solution step-by-step:

Do what's inside the **P**arentheses first: $(2 + 3) = 5$

Next, solve the **E**xponents if they are in the equation: $5^2 = 25$

Then, **M**ultiply or **D**ivide, whichever one comes next. In this case, it's

division.

Division: $6 \div 2 = 3$

Multiplication follows: $7 \times 2 = 14$

Now we have: $5 + 25 - 3 - 14 - 1 = \_\_\_\_\_\_$

Adding is next: $5 + 25 = 30$

Last comes **S**ubtraction: $30 - 3 - 14 - 1 = 12$

Whew! The final answer is 12. Yes, that's my final answer!

Write 25% as a decimal: ______

as a fraction: ______

Can you identify what these signs mean?

$\cong$	$\neq$	$\approx$	$\geq$	Π
______	______	______	______	______

Solve this equation: $2x + 7 = 19$

Solution: First, subtract 7 from both sides, leaving $2x = 12$. Next, divide each side by 2, with a solution of $12 \div 2 = 6$.

Answer: $x = 6$

Remember to always check by substituting your answer for the variable.

Algebra hints: Students need to know that when solving equations, they must perform the same operations or procedures on both sides of the = sign. This can be compared to balancing weight on a seesaw. Manipulatives such as algebra tiles or hands-on equations offer concrete balancing representations.

MAKING MATH EASIER

Step by step, math becomes a lot easier.

Picture operations:

A
D
D
+
I
N
G

———

ADDING

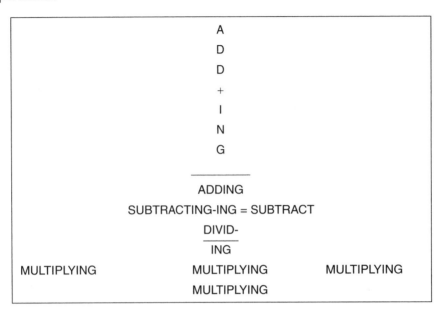

SUBTRACTING-ING = SUBTRACT

DIVID-
———
ING

MULTIPLYING MULTIPLYING MULTIPLYING
MULTIPLYING

Mathematics helps to develop thinking skills across the curriculum. Math is part of life!

Math Resources to Explore

Everyday Mathematics: everydaymath.uchicago.edu

AplusMath: www.aplusmath.com

Inside Mathematics: www.insidemathematics.org/common-core-resources/mathematical-practice-standards

Key Math Diagnostic Inventory of Essential Mathematics: www.keymath.com

Khan Academy: www.khanacademy.org/math/arithmetic, www.khanacademy.org/math/algebra, www.khanacademy.org/math/geometry

Mathematics Standards: www.corestandards.org/Math/

National Council for the Teachers of Mathematics (NCTM): www.nctm.org

Purplemath: www.purplemath.com

Singapore Math: www.singaporemath.com

Ten Marks: www.tenmarks.com

The Math Forum at Drexel Math Library: www.mathforum.org/library

Touchmath: www.touchmath.com

Math Tools That Help

REINFORCING COMPUTATIONAL SKILLS: USING A WHEEL

Practicing basic computational skills is important. Color-coding the related spokes might be a way to revisit the facts once they have been written.

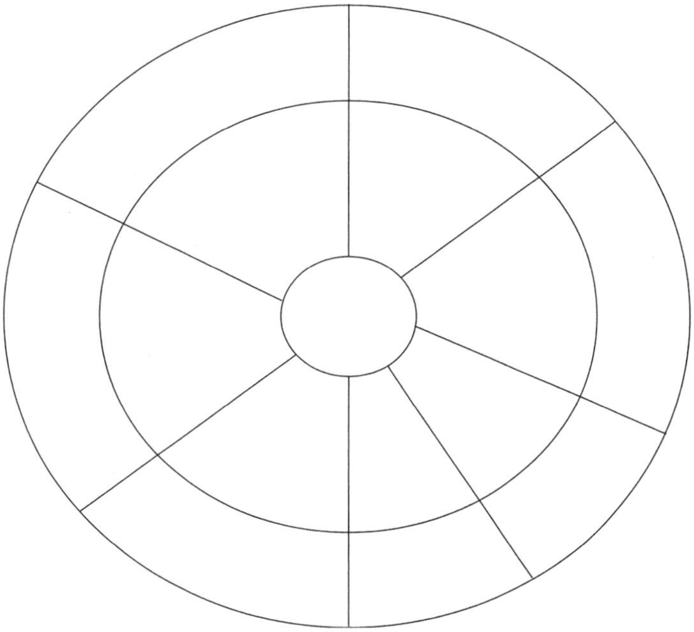

Directions: Place one of the operational signs in the middle circle with a given number, as in the following examples:

$$+6, -3, \times 9, \div 4$$

Then, fill in the inner circle with other numbers. The outer circle is where the answer is placed. Repeated computational practice can be used with circles such as these, store-bought flashcards, or even index cards.

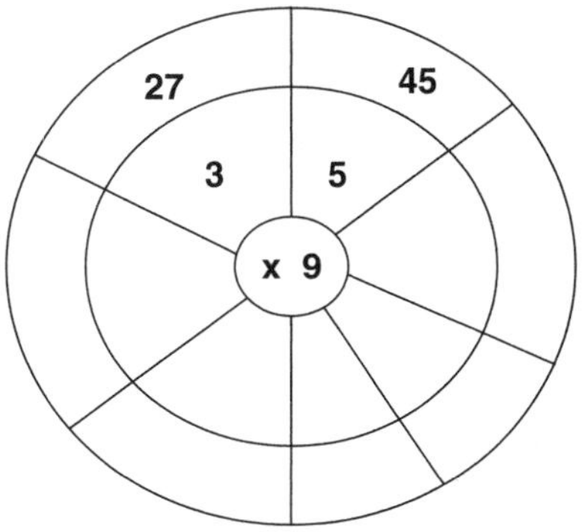

Many websites in the technology chapter of this book (Chapter 11) also reinforce computational skills in a fun way for students in Grades K–12.

Available for download at **www.corwin.com/inclusionstrategies**

ADDITION CHART

+	0	1	2	3	4	5	6	7	8	9
0										
1										
2										
3										
4										
5										
6										
7										
8										
9										

Choose the correct words from the box below to fill in the blanks.

1. Addition makes things ____________________.
2. The answer in an addition problem is called a ____________________.
3. Subtraction makes things ____________________.
4. The answer in a subtraction problem is called a ____________________.

bigger	smaller
sum	difference

MULTIPLICATION CHART

Notice that shaded areas of multiples can also be used to teach equivalent fractions.

×	0	1	2	3	4	5	6	7	8	9
0										
1	0	1	2	3	4	5	6	7	8	9
2	0	2	4	6	8	10	12	14	16	18
3	0	3	6	9	12	15	18	21	24	27
4	0	4	8	12	16	20	24	28	32	36
5										
6										
7										
8										
9										

Choose the correct words from the box below to fill in the blanks.

1. Multiplication makes things __________________________________.
2. The answer in a multiplication problem is called a __________________________________.
3. Division makes things __________________________________.
4. The answer in a division problem is called a __________________________________.

bigger	smaller
product	quotient

HUNDREDS CHART

Use this chart to skip count by 2s, 3s, 4s, 5s, 6s, 7s, 8s, 9s, or 10s by moving your fingers across the boxes and rows or by highlighting numbers in boxes to follow given patterns. Multiples of each number can be colored with different selections as multiples are found. Notice patterns going across (horizontally) and down (vertically). Circle only the odd or even numbers. Go backward to subtract; color multiples to multiply or divide. Have fun with the numbers!

1	2	3	4	5	6	7	8	9	10
11	12	13	14	15	16	17	18	19	20
21	22	23	24	25	26	27	28	29	30
31	32	33	34	35	36	37	38	39	40
41	42	43	44	45	46	47	48	49	50
51	52	53	54	55	56	57	58	59	60
61	62	63	64	65	66	67	68	69	70
71	72	73	74	75	76	77	78	79	80
81	82	83	84	85	86	87	88	89	90
91	92	93	94	95	96	97	98	99	100

MEANINGFUL CONNECTIONS

Math relates to life, but if children and teachers do not view it that way, then everyone is shortchanged. Students will only study for the test and not learn any lessons connected to life, while teachers record a meaningless grade. Concepts taught in lessons that actively involve students in real-life situations are better remembered. Below are examples of real-life applications that enhance math lessons much more than complete reliance on textbook instruction.

Teacher Questions	Real-Life Applications
How can I teach about averages?	Weather reports (e.g., weekly or monthly temperature readings compared to prior years or locations or tracking average daily precipitation during a month)
	Batting averages
	Report card grades
How can I teach geometry?	Looking around at objects, noticing different shapes
	Studying the architecture of past civilizations
	Analyzing famous paintings, noting the shapes, lines, and perspectives artists used
How can I teach about graphs?	Children cooperatively conduct a classroom or schoolwide survey on any topic, such as favorite food, subject, sport, book, movie, or television show. Then they construct a graph that visually records data. Vary graphs using a picture, pie, bar, or line.

How can I teach about ________________________________?

Real-life applications are infinite . . . . !

Available for download at **www.corwin.com/inclusionstrategies**

Explore These Sites for Additional Ideas, Tools, Lesson Ideas, and Resources

National Library of Virtual Manipulatives: nlvm.usu.edu/en/nav/vlibrary.html

NCTM's Illuminations: illuminations.nctm.org

MEANINGFUL CONNECTIONS: HOW DO YOU SPEND YOUR DAY?

Name: ____

Day chosen: ____

	Fraction	Decimal	Percent
School			
Eating			
Sleeping			
TV			
Video games			
Computer			
Music			
Telephone			
Reading			
Sports			
Studying/homework			
Friends			
Family			
Exercise			
Working/chores			
Other activities			
Totals			
	No more than 24 hours	No more than 1.00	No more than 100%

THINKING SKILLS

Word Problem Strategies: A Penny for Your Thoughts

1. Read the word problem once.
2. Now read the word problem again for more understanding.
3. Write down necessary information in the data box.
4. Write the question you need to answer in the question box.
5. Place a penny or an X in the strategy box you have chosen.
6. Using a step-by-step approach, figure out the answer to the question.
7. Go back to the question box. Does your answer make sense?

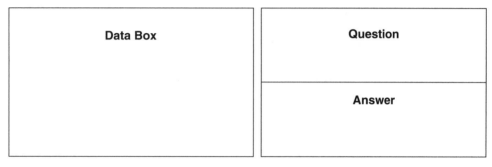

Data Box	Question
	Answer

Choose a Strategy

Estimate

It's about ______.
(28 is almost 30)

Guess and Check

Draw a Picture

Make a List
1.
2.
3.

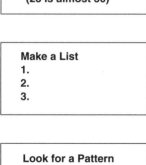

Break It Into Parts

Create a Chart or Table

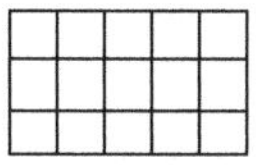

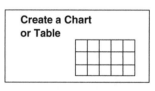

Look for a Pattern

2, 4, 6, 8, 10 ...

Work Backward

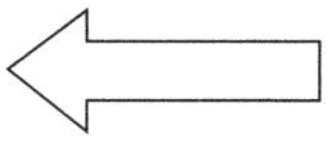

Act It Out

Use Logical Reasoning

Solve a Simpler Problem
How can I make this easier?

Set Up an Equation

A + B = C
C – B = A

USING ESTIMATION

What is a reasonable answer? Do students know how to estimate addition, subtraction, multiplication, or division problems to help them see if their answers make sense? Quite often, math becomes a rote process, and students fail to acquire clearly developed thinking skills. Sometimes, it's a race to see who can finish the worksheet or test first. However, in that race to the finish line, logical thinking is not used. Using estimation leads to more conceptualizations.

Estimations are simple to implement. Ask students to fold their papers into two columns, with one side for the estimated answer, and the other side for the actual or exact answer. Holding horizontally lined paper vertically helps students who have fine-motor or eye-hand coordination difficulties to keep columns straight.

(E) ESTIMATE (A) ACTUAL ANSWER

				9	0	0			9	4	5		
			×		3	0		×		2	8		
		2	7,	0	0	0	2	6,	4	6	0		

Then ask students to compare the sums, differences, products, and quotients in the E and A columns. Final questions include the following:

- Does my answer make sense?
- Are the estimated and actual answers close?

Obviously, the estimated answer of 27,000 is fairly close to 26,460. This kind of exercise helps students to think more about the numbers rather than performing operations by rote, without internalizing number sense.

Step-by-Step Rounding Tips

1. Ask students to circle the place they are rounding (hundreds).

5,⑦5 2

2. Then, tell them to underline the next place to the immediate right.

5,⑦<u>5</u> 2

3. If the number to the right is *5 or more,* change the circled number to one number higher.

⑦ becomes an 8

4. Everything to the right of the 8 becomes zeros. **5, 8 0 0**

5. Students can round numbers to the nearest place values (e.g., tens, hundreds, thousands) as long as they are consistent with their rounding choices within the same problem. Teachers should use their discretion and accept reasonable ranges of estimation.

ESTIMATE	ACTUAL ANSWER
200 + 40 = 240; 220 + 40 = 260	217 + 38 = 255
25, 000 + 68, 000 = 93, 000	24, 581 + 68, 356 = 92, 937
900 × 80 = 72,000	895 × 84: 3580 + 71600 = 75,180
42,000 ÷ 60 = 700	42,846 ÷ 56 = 765 R.6

Division estimates require finding the nearest basic division fact. In this example, it is 42 ÷ 6 = 7. Before doing division problems, some students may need to write the multiples of the divisor. For example, in this problem, 6, 12, 18, 24, 30, 36, 42, 48, 54, and 60 are the multiples of 6; students can count that 42 is the seventh multiple of 6. Multiples can also be highlighted on hundreds charts. When doing longer division, students then refer to the multiples each time they bring down a number.

> When initially teaching this concept, using differently colored pencils helps.

Available for download at **www.corwin.com/inclusionstrategies**

AN EDIBLE ESTIMATION

How many jellybeans, M&M's, or Cheerios would fit inside these different-sized circles?

Directions: Write your guesstimate on the chart below. Then, write the actual answer and calculate the difference.

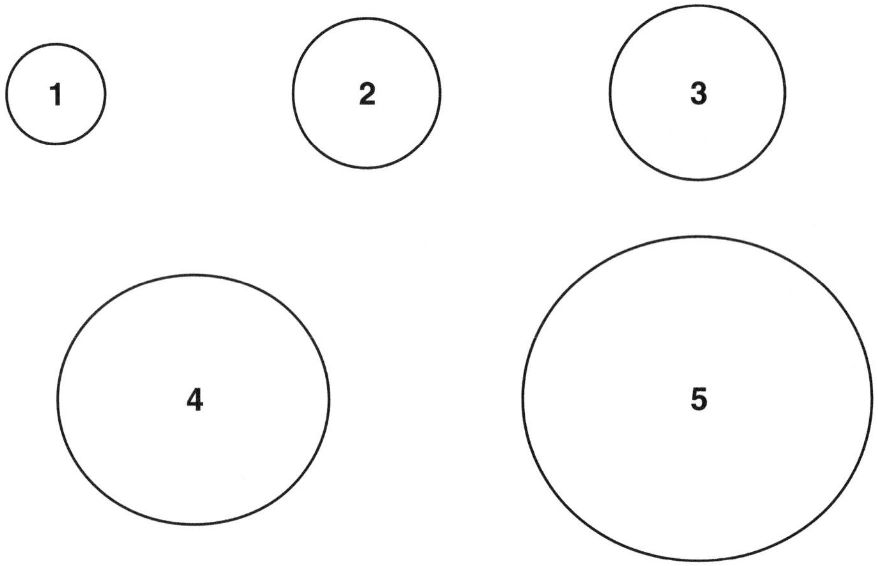

	Guesstimate	Actual Answer	Difference Between G and A
Circle 1			
Circle 2			
Circle 3			
Circle 4			
Circle 5			

Jellybeans, M&M's, and fruity Cheerios can also be sorted by colors and then graphed. As a precaution, always check individual children's health records with the school nurse to be certain food allergies or dietary restrictions do not interfere with children ingesting edible manipulatives. As a more healthful option, estimate carrot slices instead!

TOOTHPICKS AND MORE

Developing thinking skills can be accomplished through various mediums. Math manipulatives include toothpick designs, tangram shapes, fraction pizzas, abacuses, flashcards, Cuisenaire rods, algebra tiles, and more. The objective of the following lessons is to have students think about what they are doing, using logical sequencing while kinesthetically imprinting learning. Skills like these are then transferred to inferential reading comprehension and all kinds of cognitive thought across the curriculum. Aside from that, using toothpicks and more makes learning more appetizing!

Toothpick* Exercises

Follow directions to meet written toothpick requirements, always returning to this original position, using 12 toothpicks.

Note: There's a difference between the words *move* and *remove*.

Starting Position

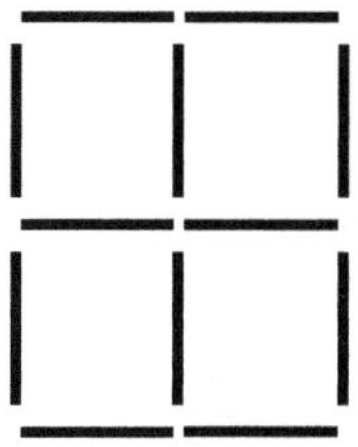

1. Move 2 toothpicks to make 7 squares.

2. Move 4 toothpicks to make 10 squares.

3. Remove 2 toothpicks to make 2 squares.

4. Move 3 toothpicks to make 3 squares.

*Flat toothpicks can be purchased in local supermarkets.

(Continued)

(Continued)

Toothpick Answers

1. Move 2 toothpicks to make 7 squares.

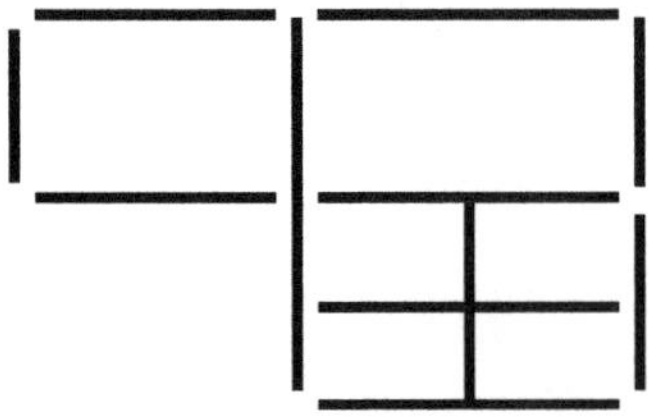

2. Move 4 toothpicks to make 10 squares.

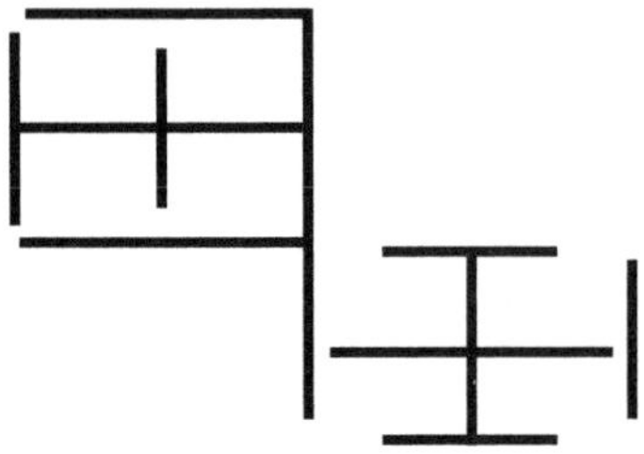

3. Remove 2 toothpicks to make 2 squares.

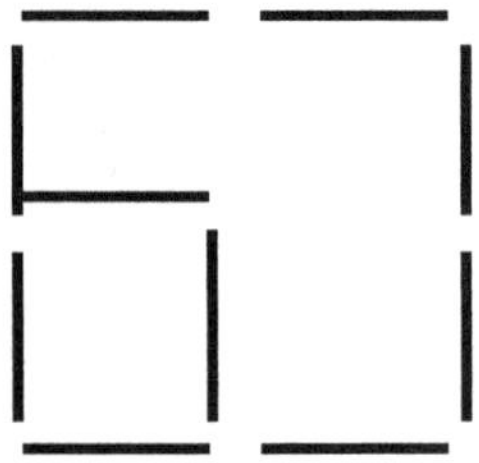

4. Move 3 toothpicks to make 3 squares.

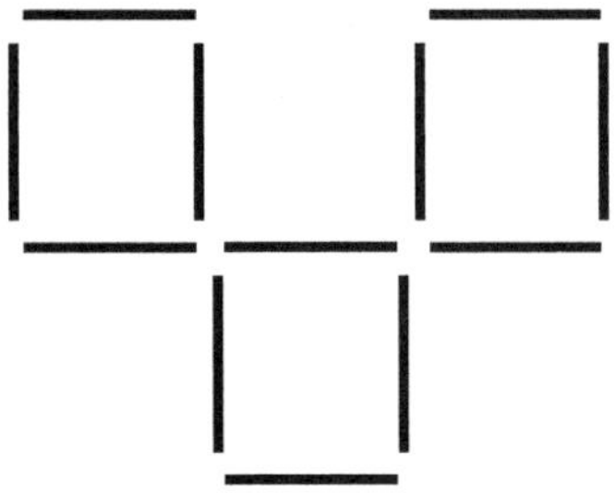

Check out this site for more ideas: www.education.com/activity/Toothpick_Math.

TANGRAMS

Directions: Form a perfect square using all of these seven geometric shapes: 5 triangles (2 big, 1 medium, and 2 small), 1 parallelogram, and 1 square.

Try to make these shapes, too!

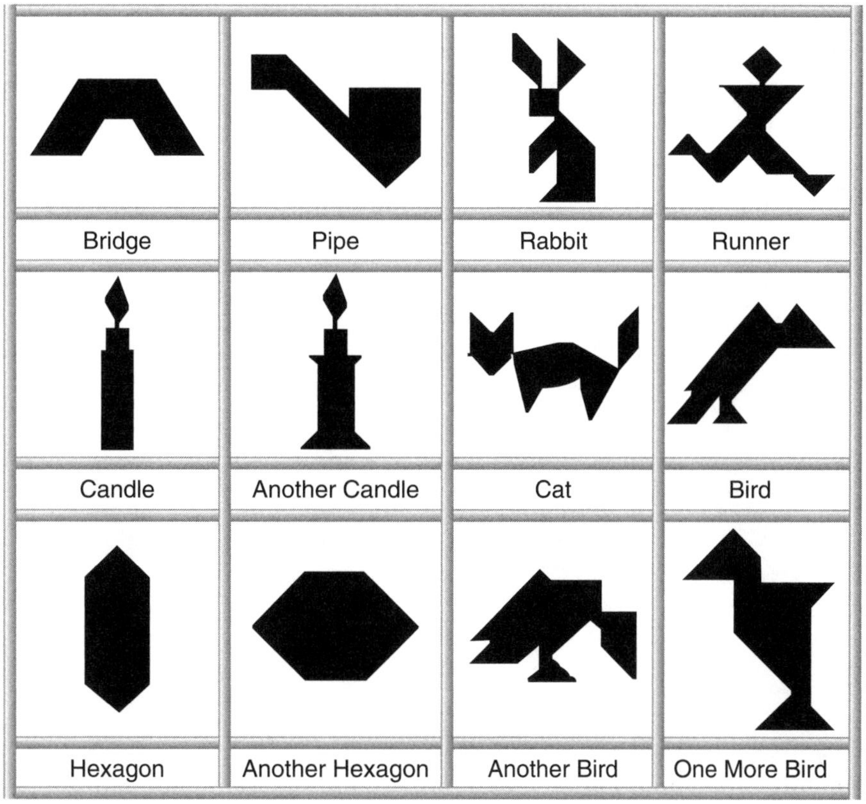

SOURCE: Images courtesy of Lee Stemkowski.

> The website www.curiouser.co.uk/tangram/template.htm gives you a printable tangram to cut out and manipulate.

Tangram Answer

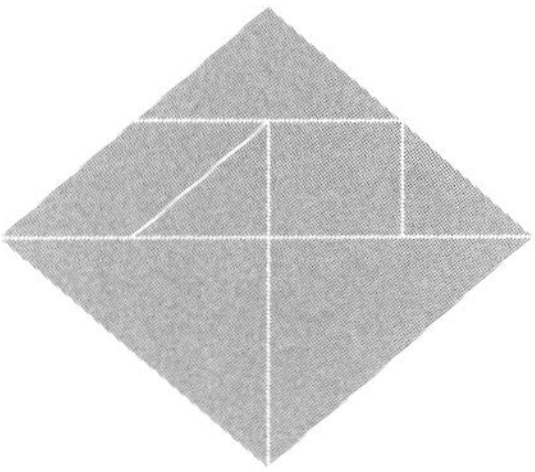

Available for download at **www.corwin.com/inclusionstrategies**

LOGIC BOXES

Directions: Solve a word problem together using a logic box, filling in yes or no answers.

	______	______	______	______
______				
______				
______				
______				
______				

Math Problem

Just before the Major League Baseball All-Star Game, the luggage got mixed up for players Albert Pujols, Paul Goldschmidt, Mike Trout, and Miguel Cabrera. One suitcase contained a pair of size 11½ shoes. Another had a pair of size 12. One had a pair of size 13, and the last suitcase had size 15 shoes.*

Clues

Albert's size is not an integer.

Paul's size is a multiple of 4.

Miguel's size is a prime number.

Who wears size 11½? ______________________

Who wears size 12? ______________________

Who wears size 13? ______________________

Who wears size 15? ______________________

*Shoe sizes for players are fictitious.

Learning needs to hold students' interest; for example, this word problem was about baseball. Even students who do not like math might be encouraged to attend to the task at hand since the subject matter, baseball, may have relevance and be of interest to them.

COMPLEMENTING THE BASICS

Investigative Learning

Reading, writing, and arithmetic are essential curriculum areas that are the basics of all education, but they do not exist in a vacuum. Teaching number sense, vocabulary, and how to express thoughts on paper can be accomplished while students are doing science experiments, researching historical events, listening to music, and being artistic. Lifelong learners emerge when thinking skills are developed across the curriculum.

In this age of information explosion, it is sometimes difficult to shop at all stores, yet exposure to the world opens up avenues of learning that can yield worthwhile returns. Emphasize the basics in conjunction with life!

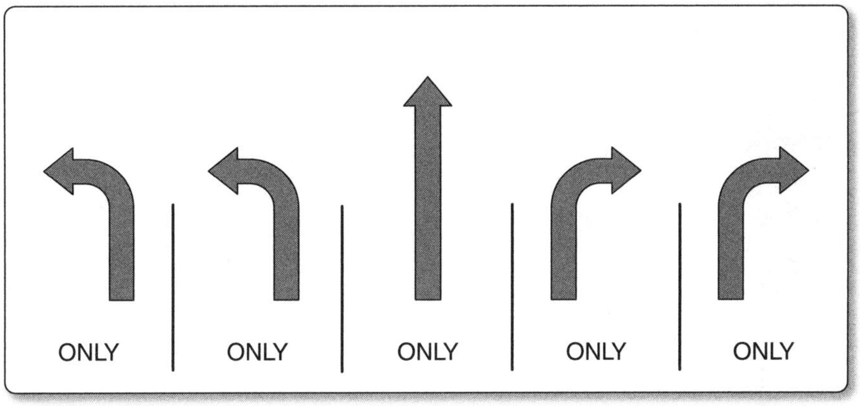

Basics + Knowledge + Delivery = Effective learning on life's many roads

BIOGRAPHIES ACROSS SUBJECT AREAS

Directions: Tell more about one of the people listed below. There are four required documents as well as other document choices from which you must pick two. Originality, accuracy of information, and proper language mechanics are required. Tell how this person was or is a citizen who contributes to our society and world.

Required Research Documents

1. Birth certificate
2. Résumé
3. Journal entry
4. Advertisement of contributions

Other Document Choices (Pick 2)

- Biographical song
- Visual of setting where the person lived
- Dance portraying a life event
- Newspaper article
- Commemorative poem
- Cartoon, portrait, caricature, or bubble dialogue
- Diagram or model of work
- Obituary from the newspaper
- Letter of reference written by a contemporary
- PowerPoint presentation
- Time line of important events

Choices Across the Curriculum

Math: Archimedes, M. C. Escher, Euclid, John Nash, Emmy Noether, Blaise Pascal, Pythagoras

Science/Technology: Elizabeth Blackwell, Copernicus, Jacques Cousteau, Marie Curie, Charles Darwin, Thomas Edison, Albert Einstein, Daniel Gabriel Fahrenheit, Galileo, Bill Gates, Jane Goodall, Stephen Hawking, Hippocrates, Steve Jobs, Antonie van Leeuwenhoek, Isaac Newton, Louis Pasteur, Carl Sagan, Jonas Salk, B. F. Skinner, Nikola Tesla, Steve Wozniak

Art: Mary Cassatt, Leonardo da Vinci, Edgar Degas, El Greco, M. C. Escher, Edward Hopper, Frida Kahlo, Jacob Lawrence, Michelangelo, Claude Monet, Georgia O'Keeffe, Pablo Picasso, Jackson Pollock, Raphael, Rembrandt, Henri de Toulouse-Lautrec

Literature: Maya Angelou, Geoffrey Chaucer, Charles Dickens, Theodore Geisel (Dr. Seuss), Ernest Hemingway, Toni Morrison, Edgar Allan Poe, J. K. Rowling, William Shakespeare, Shel Silverstein, Alice Walker

Music: Louis Armstrong, Bach, The Beatles, Beethoven, Beyoncé, Michele Branch, Miles Davis, Eminem, José Feliciano, George Gershwin, Richie Havens, Billie Holiday, Michael Jackson, Jay-Z, Billy Joel, Jonas Brothers, Lady Gaga, Liberace, Madonna, Bob Marley, Mozart, One Direction, Itzhak Perlman, Phillip Phillips, Elvis Presley, Rihanna, The Rolling Stones, Shakira, Frank Sinatra, Britney Spears, Bruce Springsteen, Barbra Streisand, Stevie Wonder, Xian Xinghai

Sports: Muhammad Ali, David Beckham, Joe DiMaggio, Wayne Gretzky, Michael Jordan, Nancy Lopez, Mickey Mantle, Willie Mays, Jesse Owens, Pelé, Michael Phelps, Jackie Robinson, Wilma Rudolph, Babe Ruth, Jim Thorpe, Venus Williams, Babe Didrikson Zaharias

Social Studies: Alexander the Great, Simón Bolivar, Julius Caesar, George Washington Carver, Winston Churchill, The 14th Dalai Lama, Benjamin Franklin, Indira Gandhi, King Hussein of Jordan, Thomas Jefferson, Joan of Arc, Lyndon B. Johnson, John F. Kennedy, Martin Luther King Jr., Abraham Lincoln, Malcolm X, Montezuma, Barack Obama, Saladin, Haile Selassie, Mao Zedong

As an option, students can use online sites to research, organize, and share their information. The following one for the singer Rihanna was created with an application called Trading Card Creator, from the International Reading Association and the National Council of Teachers of English, available at www.readwritethink.org/files/resources/interactives/trading_cards_2/.

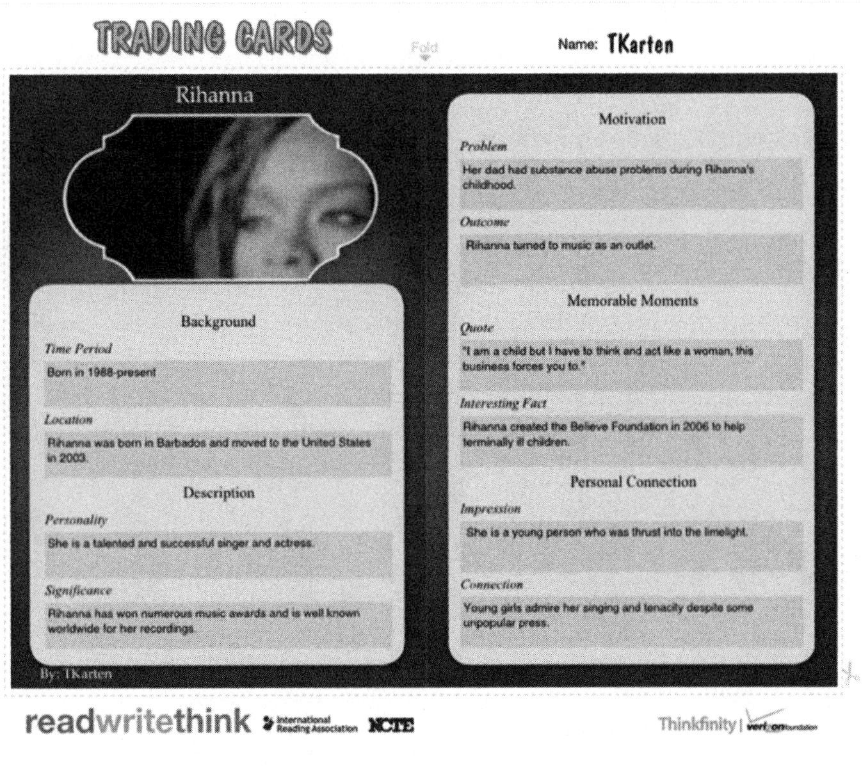

Available for download at **www.corwin.com/inclusionstrategies**

Children Around the World: Pen Pals

Growing up, I distinctly remember my elementary school principal returning from a trip to a faraway place called Europe, with a bag filled with letters from a school in a country called Greece. My fourth-grade teacher distributed these letters to the class, and that was the beginning of my correspondence with Georgia Dermati, who lived in a town right outside of Athens. We exchanged music (I gave her a recording from Peter, Paul, and Mary), sandals, and many letters about politics, food, and fun things for about five years, making our two worlds seem a lot closer. Another time, our class wrote letters to a different neighborhood school in the same city, but about an hour away. Since I grew up in Brooklyn, New York, such a school was like a totally different country. Again, the world became a smaller but less narrow place.

Introducing students to other children their own age is a wonderful way for students to learn how peers in another neighborhood, city, state, or country live. Learning about different cultures exposes children to a broader view of the world, instead of the same sights and familiar perspectives. The best part is that they explore these avenues by sharpening their writing skills through purposeful writing.

Online Ways to Find Class Pen Pals (With Adult Supervision Only)

www.surfnetkids.com/penpals.htm

www.friendshipthrougheducation.org

Including Content Areas

Music to My Ears

Music has powerful effects, helping you to drift, relax, lift up your spirits, or focus better. Optimum learning occurs when there is an unthreatening atmosphere of relaxation. Music can motivate you to be more creative as well as awaken active thinking skills in a brain more primed for receptive learning. Music and rhythm make up one of the intelligences recognized by Howard Gardner in his work on multiple intelligences. Some children with exceptionalities can better express themselves through music. Varied activities are not limited to these but can include the following:

- Rhythmic movement
- Transitioning to auditory cues
- Singing
- Playing an instrument
- Discriminating among sounds
- Sensing moods in music
- Attending to sounds
- Learning how music is a form of communication with its own written language
- Developing music appreciation

- Improving self-concept through musical creativity
- Relating music to curriculum areas with jingles, raps, and more!

Curriculum Connections

Math: Rhythmic patterns with subdivisions of time into fractions

Physical Education: Coordinating fingers, hands, arms, lips, cheeks, facial movement, throat, lungs, stomach, and chest muscles with sounds sent into the ears and then interpreted by the brain; marching bands

Social Studies: Teaching about other cultures around the world, telling about their identities, histories, and environments

Science: Acoustics and the science of hearing sounds; charting frequencies and intensities; adjusting volumes, pitches, melodies, and harmonies; learning how instruments are made

Languages: Universal language with global symbols that have no borders

Psychology: It's an individual choice that makes you feel good!

The National Core Music Standards of 2014 focus on developing music literacy and conceptual understandings through the artistic processes of creation, performance, and response. Increased grade-by-grade specificity with assessments is also valued. The National Association for Music Education's "Broader Minded" Campaign shares the impact of music beyond academics, encompassing how students understand themselves and the world around them. Additional information can be accessed at musiced.nafme.org/news/the-new-national-core-music-standards-are-out-and-heres-nafme-wants-you-to-know/.

Resources to Explore

Adamek, M., & Darrow, A. (2005). *Music in special education.* Silver Spring, MD: American Music Therapy Association.

American Music Therapy Association: www.musictherapy.org

Anderson, O., Marsh, M., & Harvey, A. (1999). *Learn with the classics: Using music to study smart at any age.* San Francisco, CA: Lind Institute.

Flocabulary: www.flocabulary.com

MusicFriends: www.musicfriends.org

National Association for Music Education: nafme.org

Songs for Teaching, Using Music to Promote Learning: www.songsforteaching.com

Vogt, J. (2006). *The amazing music activities book: Ideas and exercises for exploring music basics, ear training, music styles, and famous composers.* Dayton, OH: Heritage Music Press.

ARTFUL EDUCATION

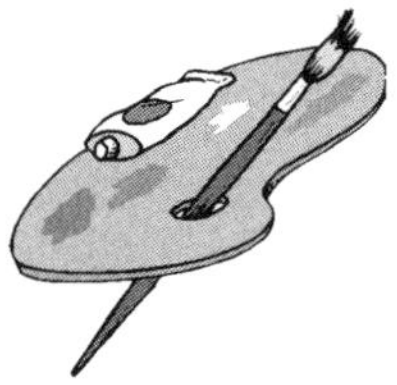

Art is a nonverbal form of expression that uses both sides of the brain. Creativity is channeled through the right side, while the mechanics of writing itself stem from the left-brain language centers. Art, like music and many other disciplines, is more than the finished product; it is the process itself. It can also be used as a way for children to express themselves while learning many classroom concepts. Most important, art is about seeing.

Seeing the world around you while paying attention to details is not an easy task. Betty Edwards (1989), in her book *Drawing on the Right Side of the Brain*, tells how art is not a talent but is more about learning how to see, processing visual information in a different way. Being aware of just how the brain handles that visual information helps us to draw our perceptions.

After almost a decade as an avid amateur artist, I have finally realized that I need not frame everything I create but can just enjoy the process of creation. The therapeutic advantages of art have helped many children with emotional issues deal with the sometimes-unfair world around them. Art therapy allows children of all ages a cathartic form of expression, with a healthy output (See www.arttherapy.org).

Cognitive, physical, emotional, social, behavioral, and sensory elements must be considered in art programs that disseminate the knowledge at different levels while honoring high expectations for all students. Art programs that allow everyone to have access to information accomplish this through a variety of sensory modes that incorporate not only visual modalities but auditory and kinesthetic-tactile ones as well. This may involve verbal descriptions, talking books, other accompanying writings, or opportunities to touch the art through raised experiences (See www.artbeyondsight.org/sidebar/yellowpages.shtml).

Institutions such as the Museum of Modern Art (MoMA) in New York (www.moma.org/learn/programs/access) allow students access to the art with programs that foster higher thinking skills. MoMA advocates teacher training that looks to build students' self-confidence. The goal is to offer all students, regardless of classification, the opportunity to both learn about the art and grow from their experiences. This includes resources for students who are blind, visually impaired, hard of hearing, or deaf, or have autism, Down syndrome, or other physical and cognitive potentials. The idea is to capitalize on students' strengths and interests. Participation in educational art programs is an option open to people of all abilities. This includes both art appreciation and art creation with school, family, and community collaboration, which can be set up with a museum, whether students are visiting interactive programs online (e.g., www.virtualfreesites.com/museums.museums.html) or in person on a class field trip. Just as in all other disciplines, art educators plan lessons that reflect students' differing needs to build strengths within art and across the disciplines. Multiage stations can relate to the curriculum with themes ranging from water or dinosaurs to Ancient Egypt, the Battle of Bunker Hill, or Escher's tessellations (See www.mcescher.com). When GE and SE teachers share their lessons with art teachers or specialists, then the student benefits are truly masterpieces!

Art Relates to Curriculum

Social Studies: Learning how other cultures, regions, and people creatively express themselves and think about their environment, politics, and history through art

Science: Seeing how different mediums react and combine with each other, mixing and separating colors, learning how pigments and dyes come from nature

Math: Being aware of the perspectives and geometric shapes that are artistic elements, the Golden Ratio, and fractals, measuring and using proportions to reduce and enlarge pictures or create rotations, creating transformations and reflections

Reading: Reading connections range from the observational skills involved in reading picture books to learning about the aesthetic value of different art and how the artists themselves developed

Perceptual Skills: The practice and slow movement required to make art helps students concentrate better and improve their visual-motor integration and laterality, which then aids reading.

Some artistic mediums include pencils, charcoal, watercolor, oil paint, clay, string, beads, felt, crayons, photography, digital platforms, and so on. Forms of expression can be displayed across curriculum areas with the creation of charts, posters, graphs, dioramas, picture books, models, scrapbooks, greeting cards, collages, picture e-books, and more!

PERCEPTUAL FUN WITH CONFIGURATION

Students can learn more about letters by placing them in the appropriate boxes and isolating them from the whole word. Concentrating on individual letters helps those with handwriting difficulties realize that letters have different sizes and shapes. These boxes stop those dancing letters. Students then transfer this skill to lined paper, now knowing that there's a reason for those lines!

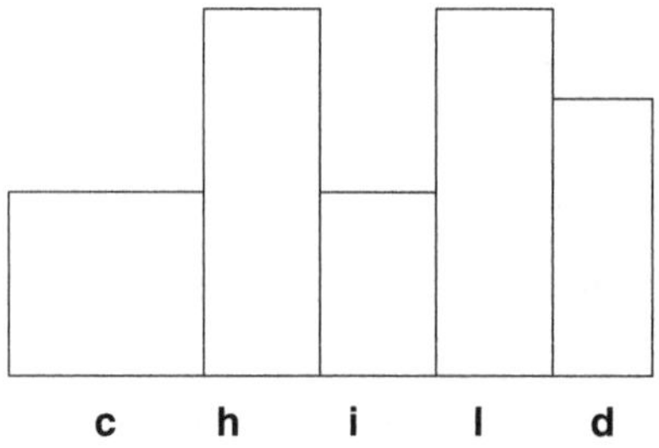

Write your own words in the box below. Then, try to configure their makeup by drawing correctly sized boxes that match the direction and size of each letter's lines.

GRAPHING A PICTURE

This graphing activity encourages students to create a drawing by enlarging a picture, box by box, on graph paper. The objective is to demonstrate a way that students with perceptual difficulties can be taught to pay attention to details by concentrating on individual elements. Using graph paper, a simple picture, scissors, tape, and rulers, students can cut, tape, and then alphabetically and numerically grid and copy a chosen picture by properly scaling proportions to enlarge the original picture. Perceptual proportions involved in this activity require a great deal of concentration, yet the exercise helps alleviate the fears of some that they can't draw. Step by step is quite easy when you are just concentrating on lines, instead of the whole picture. Graph paper and some pictures follow.

Students with learning difficulties need to slow down and pay closer attention to details. Sometimes they want to complete projects or assignments without accurately following each step. They might have neurological/ perceptual needs that can cause letter reversals and therefore must be taught to look carefully at details such as lines and shapes. The goal is not to draw the picture but to examine the intricacies it is composed of box by box. (A-1, B-2 . . .) In the picture above, the ratio of smaller picture to larger one is 1:3, since one box in the smaller horse is equivalent to three boxes in the larger one.

(Continued)

(Continued)

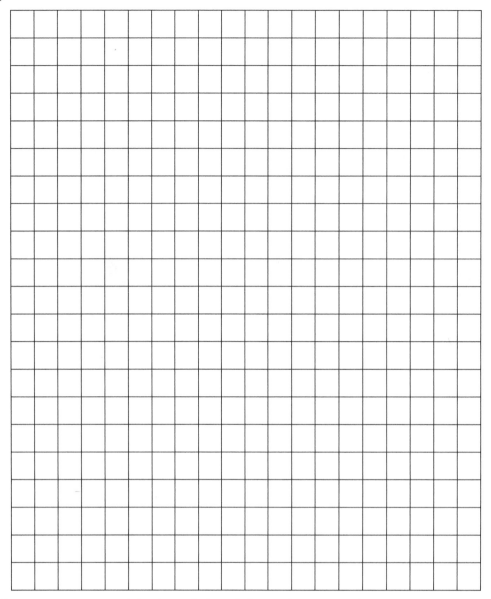

Directions: Choose, cut, paste, grid (with a ruler), and then enlarge one of these pictures or a choice of your own on graph paper.

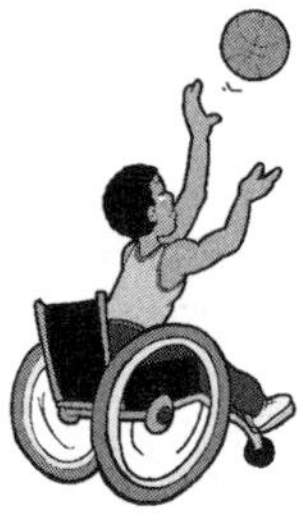

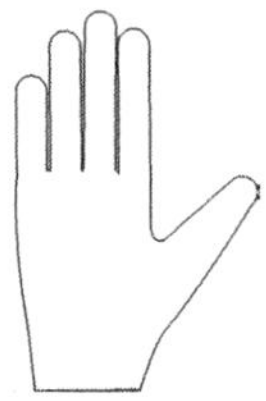

FOCUSING ON SHAPES

Directions: Look around your school, house, or community. Notice how everything is made up of shapes.

A circle 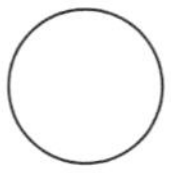 can become a 

A triangle  can become a 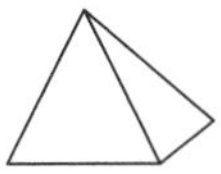

A square  can become a 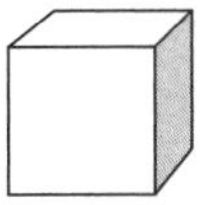

Create your own picture, using as many shapes as possible.

Artists to Investigate

Paul Cezanne, Paul Gauguin, Frida Kahlo, Piet Mondrian, Pablo Picasso

SOURCE: Yenawine (2006).

Resources with raised, textured images help people who are blind to *see* pictures of masters. The book *Art & the Alphabet* (2003) was produced with TechnoPrint and TechnoBraille with assistance from Rebecca McGinnis from Access Programs for the Blind at the Metropolitan Museum of Art and Ileana Sánchez Santiago, along with a grant from Sappi, Ideas That Matter. Its raised medium helps all students and art lovers understand more about the essential elements and shapes in pictures, giving *insight* to all! Also explore *Art Beyond Sight: A Resource Guide to Art, Creativity, and Visual Impairment* by Art Education for the Blind at www.afb.org/info/art-beyond-sight/5.

SCIENCE BY OBSERVING, DOING, AND THINKING

Students need to understand the following:

Science is about their life.
Scientists study our world.
Science has changed the way we live.
Science will change the way we live.
Science explains everyday occurrences, from seeds to space flight and everything in between.

The Next Generation Science Standards (NGSS) have three dimensions: practices, crosscutting concepts, and disciplinary core ideas. Practices include the behaviors of scientists that involve investigation and specific knowledge. Crosscutting concepts include organizing schema into a coherent and scientific view of the world. Disciplines include physical sciences, life sciences, the earth and space sciences, engineering, technology, and the applications of science, which are teachable and learnable over multiple grades. Science helps students understand and investigate complex ideas and solve problems. The NGSS proposes that scientific and technological knowledge relate to student experiences and interests.

Inquiry-based learning strategies and critical thinking skills in science can be presented, from the simple to the complex. Only having students list or define scientific terminology is okay for increasing their knowledge, but it does nothing to develop higher-level thinking skills or the possibly *dormant scientist* within. Inquiry in the standards is extended to a range of cognitive, social, and physical practices. Teachers can incorporate Bloom's taxonomy in their lessons across the curriculum to develop *inquiring minds.*

Hierarchy of Bloom's Taxonomy for Scientific Classrooms

This resource transcends all time. However, the former descriptive nouns from Bloom's taxonomy are now verbs! The original levels as nouns, in order, included the following:

Knowledge, Comprehension, Application, Analysis, Synthesis, Evaluation

Bloom's Taxonomy is now revised to use the following verbs:

Remembering: Memorizing or repeating general information such as vocabulary definitions, along with basic recall

Understanding: Explaining and/or relating information to other examples, paraphrasing information, describing data, drawing a diagram, or researching

Applying: Role-playing, constructing, demonstrating, distinguishing, experimenting, discovering, interviewing, collecting and organizing data

Analyzing: Comparing and contrasting, differentiating, deducing, determining, inferring, choosing, outlining, surveying, discovering, drawing conclusions

Evaluating: Summarizing in a position paper, evaluating data, judging, ranking, pretending, developing logical arguments, supporting choices

Creating: Constructing or designing products (written or concrete), inventing, writing an imaginary story, combining different facts

The next curriculum example offers what I call a "GAME plan" where students Gather, Apply, Manipulate, and Evaluate the learning in *astronomical* ways!

Topic: The Earth in the Solar System

G = Students identify the eight planets in order from the sun, making clay models and gathering factual information. Students realize that the Earth's movements affect our daily lives. They physically role-play how the Earth spins, or rotates, on its axis.

A = This group understands the specific effects of the Earth's movements (e.g., a revolution is the amount of time it takes for each planet to revolve around the sun; the Earth revolves around the sun in 365 days, or one year; and how a rotation translates to days and nights around the world).

M = Students conduct research and decide whether or not it is possible for plants, animals, and people to live on other planets.

E = These students learn how space exploration has affected life here on Earth (e.g., medical advances, environmental concerns, and everyday products).

This type of "GAME plan" allows teachers to differentiate objectives and assignments in a content area, with all students investigating more on their independent or instructional levels.

SOURCE: Adapted from Karten (2008a).

HOW TO DO AN EXPERIMENT

The following outlines more about Bloom's Taxonomy, giving classroom applications to develop better critical-thinking skills. It supports prior chapters on learning to analyze a process and also includes an interpersonal follow-up.

Remembering

1. Identify your topic.
2. List the materials in your experiment.
3. Define the vocabulary.

Understanding

1. What are you doing?
2. List the steps:

   First, ______________________________

   Next, ______________________________

   Later, ______________________________

   After that, __________________________

   Finally, _____________________________

Applying

1. Conduct the experiment.
2. Record data:
   What did you do?
   What did you see?

Analyzing

1. Think about what your results mean.
2. What are your conclusions?

Evaluating

1. Were you satisfied with the results?
2. What did you learn?
3. Criticize or defend the experiment.

Creating

1. Create a picture, graph, model, chart, diagram, poem, song, dance, news article, or PowerPoint presentation about the topic.
2. List some predictions about what would happen if you changed the procedure or any of the variables.

Interpersonal Follow-Up

Pastabilities: Mining Experiment. Place four types of pasta on the floor, such as bow tie, elbow, rigatoni, and shells. Divide the class into cooperative groups of four, and assign each group a pasta type. Then allow one person from each group some time (approximately two minutes) to excavate or grab his or her group's pasta. As each member excavates the pasta, the amount mined is counted and recorded. Each group's results are then graphed and shared. Individual members should be taking less and less pasta as the natural resources are depleted with each excavation. The knowledge, comprehension, application, analysis, synthesis, and evaluation are then addressed. Perhaps as a follow-up, pasta primavera can be served!

SOURCE: Used with permission. This activity is adapted from the Special Science Teams program developed at Rutgers, The State University of New Jersey, and funded by the National Science Foundation and Research for Better Schools.

Science Resources

Bloom, B. S. (Ed.). (1956). *Taxonomy of educational objectives*. Cognitive domain. New York, NY: David McKay.

Forte, I., & Schurr, S. (1995). *The all-new science mind stretchers: Interdisciplinary units to teach science concepts and strengthen thinking skills.* Nashville, TN: Incentive Publications.

Havasy, R. A. D. (2001). Getting a clue. *Education Week, 21*(10), 49.

Karten, T. (2007). *More inclusion strategies that work! Aligning student strengths with standards.* Thousand Oaks, CA: Corwin.

The Next Generation Science Standards: www.nextgenscience.org/next-generation-science-standards

Science DayBooks: www.greatsource.com

Tachell, P. (2010). *Science encyclopedia: Usborne Internet-linked discovery program*. London: Usborne Books.

SOCIAL STUDIES: CONNECTING STUDENTS TO THEIR WORLD

Social studies is more than a subject; it teaches students about life and how to better connect with each other to become global learners. Acquiring wisdom from past generations does not mean that students memorize facts in the texts. It is more important that the students learn to link those facts to themselves as they engage with their communities and the world. Topics such as history, economics, civics, government, and geography come alive when teachers infuse the social studies curriculum into students' everyday lives.

TIME LINES IN SOCIAL STUDIES AND LIFE, FROM THEN TO NOW

Question: How old is the United States?

Frightening Student Answer: 1,000 years old

Directions: Using time lines can help everyone learn more about sequencing. Start with a time line related to your life, listing specific years and details about the events below under the "Me" column. Then think of events related to our country, and list the specific years and brief details under the "Country" column.

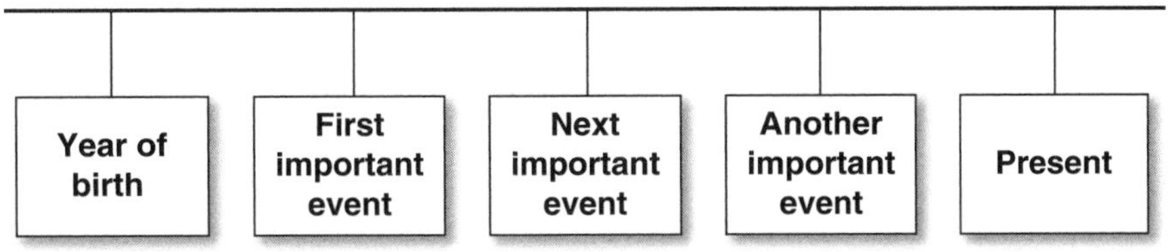

Illustrate sequential events on another paper.

Dates		**Details**	
Me	**Country**	**Me**	**Country**

As an option, students can create their own online interactive time line with multimedia components using a site such as Dipity, accessed at www.dipity.com.

WHERE IN THE WORLD IS . . . ?

Can you identify countries at these locations? Use an atlas if you need extra help.

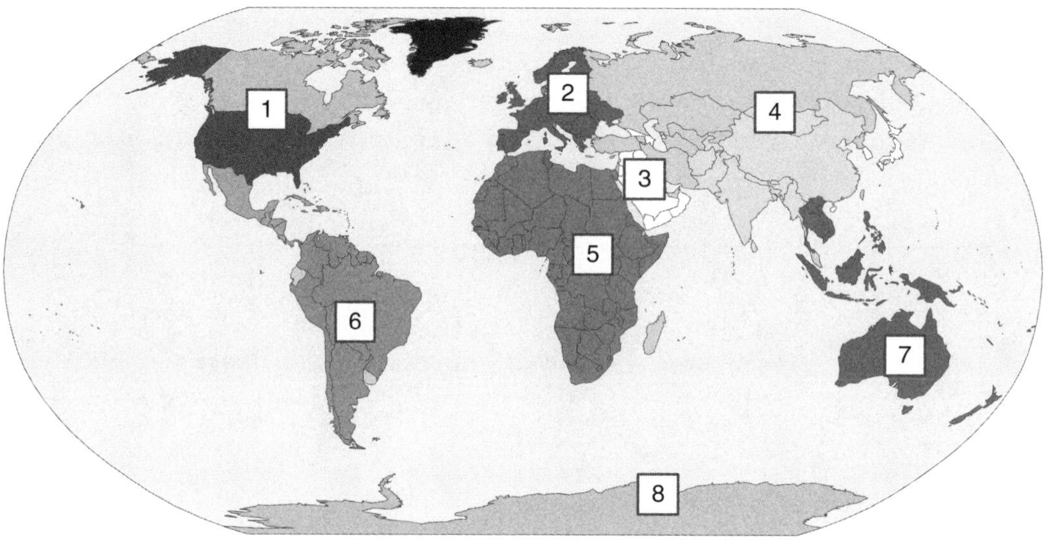

Label oceans in proper locations.

1. North America
2. Europe
3. Middle East
4. Asia
5. Africa
6. South America
7. Australia
8. Antarctica

Further investigation: Compare and contrast the governments and cultures of two countries.

CAN YOU IDENTIFY THESE U.S. STATES?

Directions: Place numbers inside locations of states you can identify, and name them in columns below.

Numbers	States	Numbers	States

NOTE: Alaska and Hawaii are not in their proper locations. Find a world map to locate these two states.

Possible Accommodations

Some students can refer to a map of the United States to identify the abbreviations. Other students may need a map of the United States cut up as a jigsaw puzzle with a color-coded template, so they can place the states in certain regions (e.g., Northeast, Southwest) rather than write the abbreviations of each state. For them, knowing the locations of regions would be a more meaningful task. Having a raised relief map is an excellent tactile approach to differentiate the way students locate landforms. Other students may require an even more advanced task, since this one may be too easy and result in bored and disinterested learners. Teachers might have them research how the geography affects how people make a living there.

VALUING PHYSICAL EDUCATION

Just as children have differing cognitive levels, they have various physical levels. A well-designed physical education program promotes each student's individual growth. Some children might hate to think while stationary in a classroom chair but be delighted to make decisions while actively moving about. Why not consider a physical education program that age-appropriately values each child's needs, strengths, and abilities?

Physical education teachers assess current levels, use basic learning principles, and build upon prior skills. It's no different from teaching fractions or conversational Spanish. Three simple questions are asked:

1. What are you going to teach?
2. How are you going to do it?
3. Are the students learning?

Preschool–Grade 3 Skills

- Locomotor activities such as jumping, running, hopping, and skipping
- Manipulating by bouncing, kicking, catching, throwing, and more
- Movement to increase body awareness, rhythm, and balance
- Simple games to promote interaction and following basic rules
- Exhibiting safety and respect for others

Grades 4–12

- Gymnastics, dance, physical fitness, and team sports
- Muscular strength
- Reaching goals and solutions with increased endurance and flexibility
- Attaching cognitive, emotional, behavioral, and social skills to physical activities, creativity, and healthy mind-sets

Modifying Physical Education

- Vary time requirements by slowing down an activity or reducing the number of repetitions.
- Use different equipment, for example, a ball with a bell for someone who is blind, or one with flashing lights for someone with auditory needs. Use lighter bats, or maybe lower basketball or volleyball nets.
- Provide structure, but eliminate distracters. Use signals with children.
- Increase rest time.
- Vary limits and expectations with outlined directions modeled.
- Remember that fair does not always mean equal.
- Concentrate on safety by specifically teaching rules.
- Communicate with special and general education teachers and case managers.
- Challenge children. Don't make more skilled students do easy activities, since the flavor of a game or exercise can be preserved without being diluted for all.

Ultimate Goal

Children feel good about themselves while being included with peers. Very often, when you ask children to name their favorite subject, the response is gym! Try integrating more movement activities into the classroom. Brain research confirms the fact that movement facilitates cognition.

> Exercise strengthens brain power!

Resources/Contacts

Jensen, E. (2005). *Teaching with the brain in mind* (2nd ed.). Alexandria, VA: Association for Supervision and Curriculum Development.

Kasser, S. (1995). *Inclusive games.* Champaign, IL: Human Kinetics.

Lengel, T. & Kuczala, M. (2010). *The kinesthetic classroom: Teaching and learning through movement*. Thousand Oaks, CA: Corwin.

The Leonard Gordon Institute for Human Development Through Play of Temple University: www.pecentral.org/websites/playsites.html

Lieberman, L., & Houston-Wilson, C. (2002). *Strategies for inclusion: A handbook for physical education.* Champaign, IL: Human Kinetics.

Positive Living for Active Youth: www.playfoundation.net/

Rouse, P. (2010). *Inclusion in physical education: Fitness, motor and social skills for students of all abilities.* Champaign, IL: Human Kinetics.

SHAPE America: Society of Health and Physical Educators: www.shapeamerica.org

Sports and Recreational Activities for Children with Physical Disabilities: www.cureourchildren.org/sports.htm

■ INTERDISCIPLINARY APPROACH: EDUCATIONAL SALADS

THEMATIC TEACHING

EDUCATIONAL SALADS:
Learning can be tossed together. Think of how a topic can be connected to different subjects.

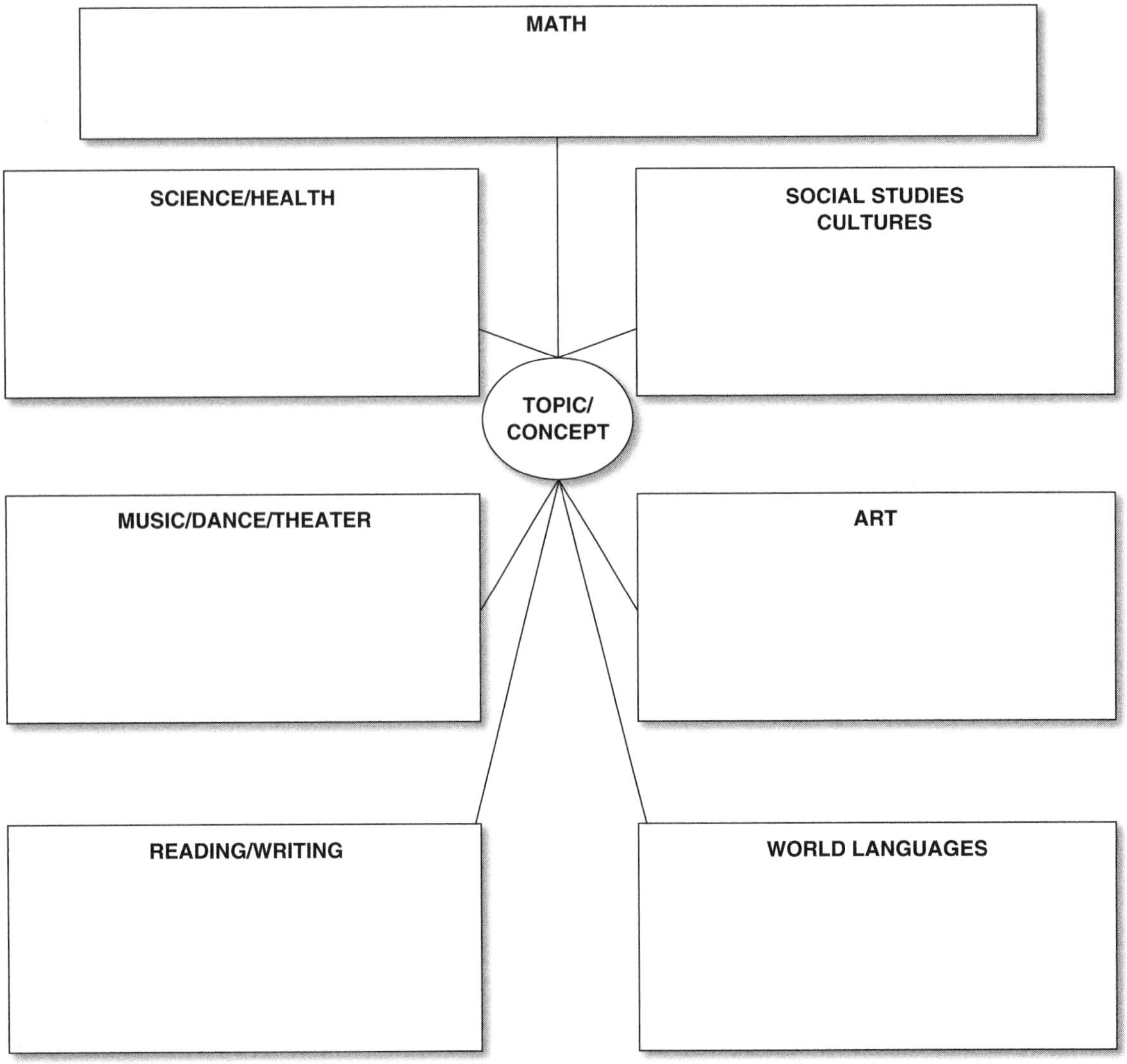

The following unit takes the famous painting *Starry Night*, by Vincent van Gogh, and offers some interdisciplinary connections across the curriculum.

- Science/Technology: Examine the sky, analyze the cloud depictions, explain what causes nighttime, tell what a star is composed of, investigate epilepsy, or create a PowerPoint or Glogster that dissects and elaborates on the individual elements of the painting.
- Math: Isolate and replicate the geometric shapes you see; figure out the circumference and area of the circles depicted; or calculate how much money Van Gogh would have today, if he were still alive, from the sale of five selected paintings.
- Music: Listen to Don McLean's song, "Vincent" (a.k.a. "Starry, Starry Night"). Then, change it into a rap or a strictly instrumental version.
- Language Arts/Writing: Create a biography of Van Gogh's life; choose ten adjectives that best describe the painting; write a haiku about his art; send a friendly letter from Van Gogh to Gauguin, Monet, or Pissarro; read a biography about Van Gogh; or write a persuasive essay telling him why he should not have committed suicide.
- Social Studies: Investigate the setting of the painting (e.g., the Netherlands in the mid-nineteenth century), describe what the culture in Europe was like then, or locate the village of Saint-Rémy-de-Provence, telling its latitude and longitude.
- Art: Obviously, there are innumerable connections!

The next interdisciplinary example depicts a thematic, *nutritious,* and inclusive primary lesson plan across many disciplines, ranging from language to social skills and many others *sandwiched* in between. The two codes, AA and FP, honor the PLOP (present level of performance) or as many states call them PLAAFP (present level of academic achievement and functional performance) requirement of IEPs:

AA: Academic Achievements

FP: Functional Performances

The next three codes honor the basic ingredients of lesson plans, telling what you plan to teach—*content,* how you will do it—*process,* and if it worked—*assessments.*

OMG: Objectives, materials, goals

PS: Procedures/strategies

CBA: Curriculum-based assessments

The CBAs can include but are not limited to work samples, portfolios, quizzes, tests, observations, cooperative group work, written essays, discussions, and center/station work.

Please note that the lesson plan includes interdisciplinary themes, and it is also differentiating in that it has baseline, more advanced, and knowing-beyond objectives that proactively prepare for a classroom of diverse learners.

The sentence BE WISE translates to the following:

*B*y the *E*nd of the *W*eek, *I*nclusion *S*trategies will *E*ducate learners to

BE WISE Primary Lesson Plan Theme: Nutrition* Week beginning: 9/22/14 Revisitation date: 11/24/14**
AA: Outline nutrition knowledge and healthy exercise habits through mathematics, reading, writing, social studies, and science. **FP:** Acknowledge and apply sound nutrition and exercise choices to daily lives and the curriculum.
More Advanced: Students will calculate how different ingredients are grown, prepared in recipes, and distributed to other locations.
Reading **OMG:** Establish prior knowledge with discussion and vocabulary about food origins, diet, and exercise while improving fluency, sight word recognition, knowledge of initial and final consonants, and written and oral reading comprehension with sequencing, context clues, main idea, details, and inferential skills. The books to be read as a class and in small groups are: Fiction: *Cloudy With a Chance of Meatballs* by Judi Barrett Nonfiction: *Food, Nutrition, and the Young Child* by Jeannette B. Endres, Robert E. Rockwell, and Cynthia G. Mense
PS: Have a whole-group discussion about nutrition and orally read books. Then, sort concrete food items with labels and ingredients listed on index cards according to phonetic and dietary guidelines (e.g., initial/final consonants, consonant blends, milk and dairy products, bread, vegetables). Give sequencing cards to each group to put story details in order. Students can work with digital books and talking websites, using headphones.
CBA: Have cooperative groups respond to questions distributed on index cards, looking for the answers in their books. The teacher should circulate about, listening to and recording fluency and responses. Some students will circle or draw pictures as answers, while others will write sentences or paragraphs.
Language Arts & Writing **OMG:** Identifying parts of speech and writing poems. Students will use rhyming and electronic dictionaries. The goal is to share poems with peers in a class-created book that includes use of vocabulary words: grains, vegetables, fruits, milk, meat/beans, fats, oils, and sweets, as well as goods, services, calories, balanced diets, and exercise.
PS: Students will sort words into their parts of speech (e.g., *meatball*—noun, *healthy*—adjective, *exercise*—noun and verb, *smartly*—adverb). Students will create diamantes about their favorite foods, exercise, or sound nutritional ideas with pictures that are either hand drawn or from clip art.

*This is a LOL: Lifelong ongoing lesson!

**Talking about nutrition before Thanksgiving is truly capitalizing on an opportune time!

CBA: Individual work samples and presentations of illustrated poems.

Mathematics

OMG: Understanding concepts of ordering, fractions, capacities, and applying computations. Materials include measuring cups, spoons, calculators, math texts, and a recipe book.

PS: Students double and halve their favorite recipes and cooperatively create, share, and solve word problems while learning diet, nutrition, and exercise facts.

CBA: Quiz with student- and teacher-created word problems.

Science & Technology

OMG: Identification and classification of foods along with accessing knowledge online.

PS: Students sort foods according to their ingredients, classifying different food types. The United States Department of Agriculture will be accessed for its games, activities, and healthy eating tips. Visit www.choosemyplate.gov/kids/. This site will be used to read more online books: www.enchantedlearning.com/books/food.

CBA: Finding clip art, drawing pictures, or collecting food labels and sorting the food representations into categories, and writing captions, which students will hand in to the teacher in individually signed envelopes or as collages and food charts.

Social Studies/Global Studies

OMG: To explore map skills (e.g., directions, latitude and longitude). Identify climates and landforms in countries in different hemispheres, and understand how similarities and differences affect economies, occupations, food choices, and daily living.

PS: Cooperative groups will outline where different products are found and locate countries at given coordinates and hemispheres.

CBA: Map test on latitude, longitude, cardinal and intermediate directions, and continents.

Perceptual/Sensory/Physical

OMG: To increase auditory and visual-perceptual skills, fine-motor skills, and laterality.

PS: Students follow the teacher's directions to cut out and trace the shapes of continents and place them on world maps to locate where foods are found. A visual tracking exercise asks students to circle nutrition and exercise vocabulary words broken up into syllables in alphabetical order from left to right (e.g., bal-ance, con-trol, di-et, ex-er-cise, nu-tri-tion, por-tion). Coordinate this lesson with the physical education teacher, PT, and OT.

CBA: Student worksheet mirrors classroom instruction to follow oral and written tracking directions. PE teachers offer classroom movements that students safely imitate and expand upon. Exercise logs are kept.

(Continued)

(Continued)

Communication/World Languages
OMG: Learn names of common foods in the language each student is studying. The goal is for each student to give a brief presentation in front of the class.
PS: Illustrated, student-created dictionaries with visuals and language translations of food terms are cooperatively completed.
CBA: Observation and student-completed work samples.
Study Skills
OMG: Keeping track of weekly work to increase self-monitoring with food and exercise diaries.
PS: Students fill in dated learning journals or diaries and check off tasks as completed.
CBA: Teacher–student conferencing about nutrition and exercise learning logs.
Social Skills
OMG: Improve social reciprocity and review food etiquette.
PS: Take daily pictures of students' table manners during lunch and snack time and share them. Model and reinforce proper etiquette.
CBA: Teacher observation, digital photos, and self-rating scale (e.g., "I was great!" or "Need to improve").

SOURCE: Karten (2010). Used with permission.

8

Emphasizing Comprehension and Study Skills

In order to succeed and navigate in this world, critical-thinking skills and being aware of ways to increase understanding are essential. Rote memorization shortchanges many students with disabilities from developing higher levels of cognitive thought, which then translates to fewer postsecondary options. Yes, students might score a decent grade on Tuesday's test, but then the following week that knowledge is lost, or shall we say, never really gained. Without effective study skills, even the basics are hard. When students with disabilities are educated in inclusive classrooms, the specially designed instruction they receive does not replace student accountability to achieve higher outcomes. As the learning demands become more complex, upper elementary, middle school and high school students need to learn how to successfully process information and organize their time to manage increased workloads. Younger students must also be encouraged to develop self-regulatory skills. Students need to discover how to read to learn and how to learn to be learners, whether the subject is English, music, art, social studies, physics, health education, family and consumer science, Spanish, or trigonometry. This chapter provides ways that teachers can help students develop these lifelong skills, emphasizing comprehension of content, rather than rote memorization. Teacher/student templates are included.

LEARNING MORE ABOUT LEARNING

It is essential that students learn to understand how they learn and how to use different metacognitive strategies to plan, monitor, and reflect on their learning, as well as being cognizant of motivation and emotion, which are volitional strategies (Gonzalez, 2013). An organized academic environment with personalized learning goals connects to life experiences. This next chart invites learners to reflect on their study skills, while it offers teachers a baseline level for students, with increased communication about learner attitudes and behaviors.

Inventory of Skills

This chart could be posted on a classroom wall to be periodically reviewed with students. Older students could self-monitor and cultivate these life skills, while younger or more concrete learners could focus on the pictures that accompany the dialogue and work on one skill at a time.

Explore Faces of Learning at www.facesoflearning.net to create your learner profile.

STUDY SKILLS—LEARNING VOWELS/VOWS

	AEIOUs	My Comments
Attitude	• Am I primed (ready) to learn? • Do I care about what's going on in the classroom? • Why am I here?	
Effort	• Am I trying my best? • Whom can I ask for extra help? • Will I review this after class?	
Involvement	• Will I ask questions if I don't understand something? • Am I just watching the others, or am I really listening to the teacher? • Do I review the learning outside of class—reading over my notes and/or reviewing text or online sources?	
Organization	• Am I *consistently* prepared for class with a pen/pencil, binder, or notebook with daily dated neat notes, books, homework, and anything else that is required for class?	
Understanding	• Do I understand that improvements will not happen overnight? • Do I know how to access more information and apply the concepts? • Am I patient and kind to others—family, teachers, classmates, bus drivers, lunchroom aides, classroom assistants, and most of all myself?	

Available for download at **www.corwin.com/inclusionstrategies**

HOW WELL DO YOU STUDY?

Name: ____

Check all appropriate answers:

1. When do you look at/read your textbook or class notes?

___ at night before a test

___ in class only

___ daily, at home and in class

___ occasionally

___ never

2. Where do you do your homework?

___ in a quiet place

___ in the kitchen

___ at a desk or table

___ on the bus ride home from school

___ other ______________________________________

3. Why do you study?

___ to get good grades

___ because parents give rewards or prizes for good grades

___ it makes me feel good about myself to do well in school

___ my parents force me to

___ I don't think I have to study

___ other reason ______________________________________

4. How do you study for a test?

___ juggle books

___ study while watching television

___ review notes

___ reread textbook

___ rewrite notes

___ use a study guide

___ another way ______________________________________

5. What do you think about school?

___ it can help me later on in life

___ it's a waste of time

___ it's boring

___ I love learning

___ other thoughts ______________________________________

TIMED EXERCISE: WHAT DO YOU KNOW?

Directions: Read all questions before you begin. This is a five-minute, timed exercise on different school topics.

1. Write your first and last name in the upper right-hand corner.
2. Underline the word *directions*.
3. Write the odd numbers from one to fifty.
4. List the continents in alphabetical order.
5. Write the lowercase alphabet in cursive or manuscript.
6. Draw a picture of something that is recyclable.

7. Whistle a patriotic tune.
8. List five words that rhyme with *school.*
9. Stand up and shout, "I love school!"
10. Now that you have read everything, do numbers one and two *only,* and patiently wait and watch classmates complete the worksheet.

Available for download at **www.corwin.com/inclusionstrategies**

Moral: Always read all directions carefully!

MNEMONICS, ACRONYMS, AND MASSIVE INITIALIZATIONS

MI Theory—Not Multiple Intelligences, but Massive Initializations

Acronyms are a wonderful way to remember information and use abbreviations or monograms to represent specific titles. Since the beginning of special education (BOSE), there has been a colossal tendency to abbreviate, shorten, or rename jargon-ish terms in the special education (SPED) field as the following indicates.

ED	Emotionally Disturbed
SLD	Specific Learning Disability
OHI	Other Health Impairment
CP	Cerebral Palsy
MS	Multiple Sclerosis, or Master of Science
MD	Muscular Dystrophy, or Medical Doctor
AT	Academically Talented or Assistive Technology
RR	Road Rage
FOED*	False Optimism Elevator Disorder (continually punching a lit elevator button to reach one's floor faster)
ISD*	Intentional Shame Disorder (using the supermarket express lanes, even though you have more than fifteen items)
Dyslyrica	Singing the wrong lyrics to songs
Dysnomia	Inability to remember names
IR&S	Interventions, Referrals, and Strategies, *not* Internal Revenue Service
RTI	Response to interventions, but more important, remembering to include!
CSI	Common sense inclusion

*SOURCE: Zirkel and Richards (1998, May/June).

Compile your own list of missed abbreviations:

1.
2.
3.
4.
5.
6.
7.
8.
9.
10.

(Continued)

(Continued)

Sound Familiar?

Using words or short phrases to recall unrelated facts, rules, concepts, or information is a valuable study tool. Do any of these ring *memory bells?*

1. My very educated mother just served us noodles!
2. FOIL
3. Every good boy does fine.
4. HOMES
5. Please excuse my dear Aunt Sally.
6. Daddy, mommy, sister, cousin, brother
7. All very determined students deserve infinitely more opportunities than school has ever offered.
8. TGIF
9. BFF
10. LOL

Answers:

1. Order of the eight planets that orbit the sun: Mercury, Venus, Earth, Mars, Jupiter, Saturn, Uranus, Neptune
2. Order of factoring to create a trinomial expression (first, outer, inner, last)—for example, $(2x + 7)(x - 2) = (2x)(x) + (2x)(-2) + (7)(x) + (+7)(-2)$, when like terms are combined, results in $2x^2 + 3x - 14$
3. Notes on a treble musical staff: E, G, B, D, F
4. Five Great Lakes: Huron, Ontario, Michigan, Erie, and Superior
5. Order of operations for solving mathematical expressions: parentheses, exponents, multiplication, division, addition, and subtraction, depending on which of these is present. For example, $3 \times 8^2 + 6 \div (2 + 1) = 194$.
6. Steps in long division: divide, multiply, subtract, compare, and bring down next number. Can also be remembered as *Does McDonald's serve cheeseburgers?*
7. Types of disabilities serviced by IDEA: autism, visual impairment, deafness, speech/language, deaf-ness/blindness, intellectual disabilities, multiple disabilities, other health impaired, traumatic brain injury, specific learning disability, hearing impaired, emotional disturbance, orthopedic impairment
8. Thank God it's Friday, or Thank God inclusion's feasible.
9. Best friends forever
10. Laughing out loud!

List some of your favorite acronyms or mnemonics:

1.
2.
3.
4.
5.

DEVELOPING BETTER PRACTICES ■

These suggestions are helpful for both teachers and students.

Following Directions

a. *Written instructions*, such as those on reading worksheets, tests, texts, how-to kits, science experiments, math word problems, and so forth, *must be read and reread.*

b. *Spoken words* need to be carefully *listened to and understood* before doing anything, with undivided attention given to *the person talking.*

Highlighting Important Information

a. Sticky notes with different colors, shapes, and sizes can be used to flag important facts and details, formulate questions about what was just read, or jot down any information to revisit. Digitally highlight information using text and commenting tools.

b. Certain notations, such as the ones in the box below, can be made for key information on worksheets, books, or duplicated text pages.

Interesting fact—will probably be on the test.
H U H ?
What was the cause and effect of this event?

? CONFUSING	♥ EMOTIONAL	↑ POSITIVE
! SURPRISING	* IMPORTANT	↓ NEGATIVE

c. *Different-colored pencils, pens, or highlighters* help facts and details stand out from the rest of the words on the page.

d. *Columned or boxed learnings* are graphically friendly presentations that help learning become more digestible.

Study Guides With Matching Q&As

Questions

Answers

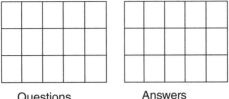

Word	Category	Details

Main Idea	Details	You

Available for download at **www.corwin.com/inclusionstrategies**

Memorization vs. Understanding

Parents and students often think that memorized facts prove that learning is taking place. Learning is more than rote memorization. Here are some memory factors to consider:

- Memory is a process that can be strengthened.
- Different memory spots in the brain are responsible for learning retrieval.
- Students can be great at remembering select things but weaker at remembering others, such as having good recall of television shows or names of dinosaurs but only fair recall of multiplication facts.
- Sometimes what we remember is influenced by the following factors:
    - Importance
    - Our age
    - Time elapsed (long-/short-term memory)
    - Attention
    - Association
    - Sensory elements
    - Concrete experiences (remembering what we do)
    - Traumatic experiences (either very happy or sad)

Everyone tends to forget things!

MEMORY TEST

1. What did you have for dinner two nights ago?
2. On what day of the week were you born?
3. What did you have for lunch yesterday?
4. Name your second-grade teacher.
5. Who was your first best friend?
6. Can you remember his or her phone number or address?
7. What is the zip code of the place you were born?
8. What was the first movie you saw in a theater?
9. Pick one of these three events and tell your age and location at the time of the event:
   a. John F. Kennedy's assassination
   b. Space shuttle *Challenger* accident
   c. 9/11

   (If you weren't alive during the event chosen, use negative numbers for your age.)
10. What time did you go to sleep last Saturday night?
11. Name the 19th president of the United States.
12. Who shot J. R. the first time?

Quite often, students can do well on tests but do not have a true grasp of the learning material. Students with ADHD often have difficulties when the memory demands increase beyond rote memorization, during which working memory is necessary (Vakil, Blachstein, Wertman-Elad, & Greenstein, 2012). Some students are excellent short-term memorizers, but when asked the same questions five days later, their responses do not match prior assessments. Students will understand more about any given subject area if there is repeated exposure to what they deem to be relevant or enjoyable learning. When they memorize by rote unrelated facts, there is a low level of understanding. Learning is more than memorizing! In addition, research supports that students learn best when material is repeated and practiced to lock it into their long-term memory (Willingham, 2004).

(*Answers:* 9. President Kennedy was assassinated in 1963; *Challenger* accident was in 1986; 9/11 happened in 2001. 11. Rutherford B. Hayes; 12. Sue Ellen's sister [original Dallas episode; http://www.today.com/entertainment/everyone-hated-him-do-you-remember-who-shot-j-r-822907])

Available for download at **www.corwin.com/inclusionstrategies**

CONCEPTUAL ORGANIZATION

Directions: Concept maps such as these can outline and connect facts, giving the learner a chance to view and study information at a quick glance.

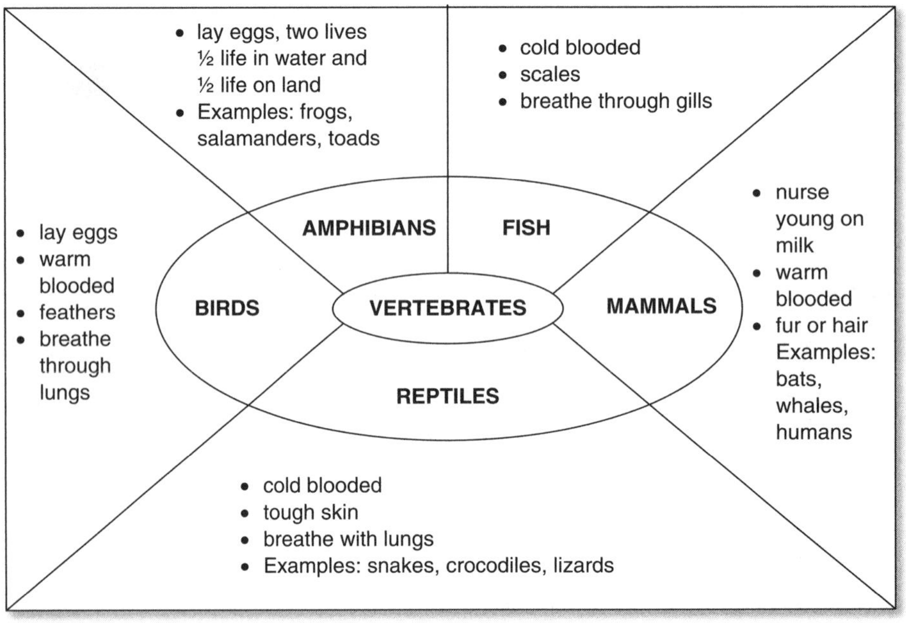

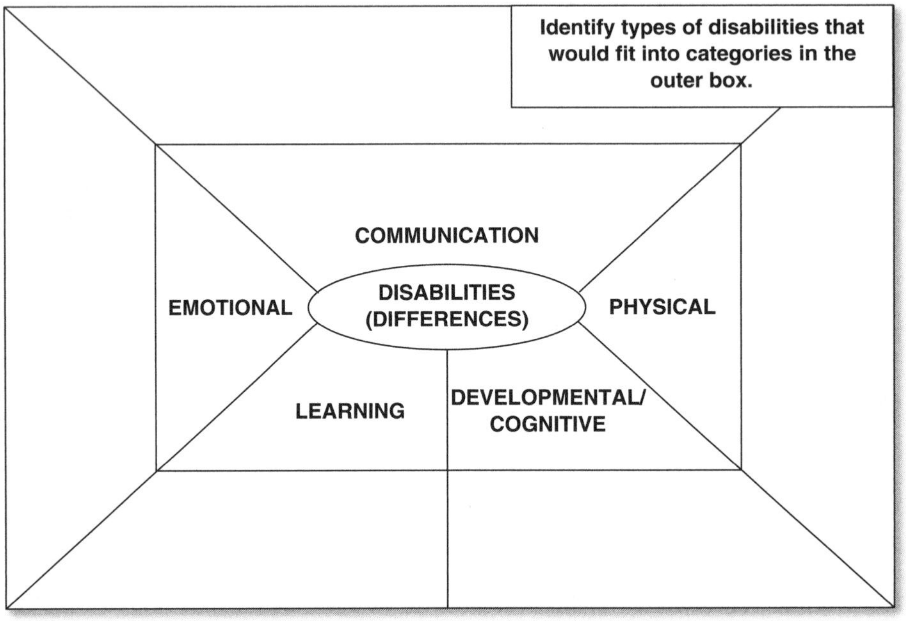

CALLIGRAM

Available for download at **www.corwin.com/inclusionstrategies**

Words can form pictures to help students organize and retain information. Visual learning accompanied by kinesthetic-tactile methods is an effective way to imprint information for learners whose strengths might be this type of learning presentation. Think of your own word to *draw.* Check out this website for primary learners to see words come alive: pbskids.org/wordworld.

GRAPHICALLY SPEAKING: TRACKING PROGRESS

Study Tip: Have students place a progress chart like the one below in an individual folder for periodic review. It circumvents conveniently forgetting that last test grade. Different dated sheets can be used for each subject and marking period. By graphing their test grades, students can see the *ups and downs* of their own learning. They can notice patterns and try to improve their next test score. This type of graphic visual concretizes the meaning of metacognition. Even if a student does not do well on a particular test, that does not mean he or she is a failure. It's just a *learning dip*.

My Spelling Grades

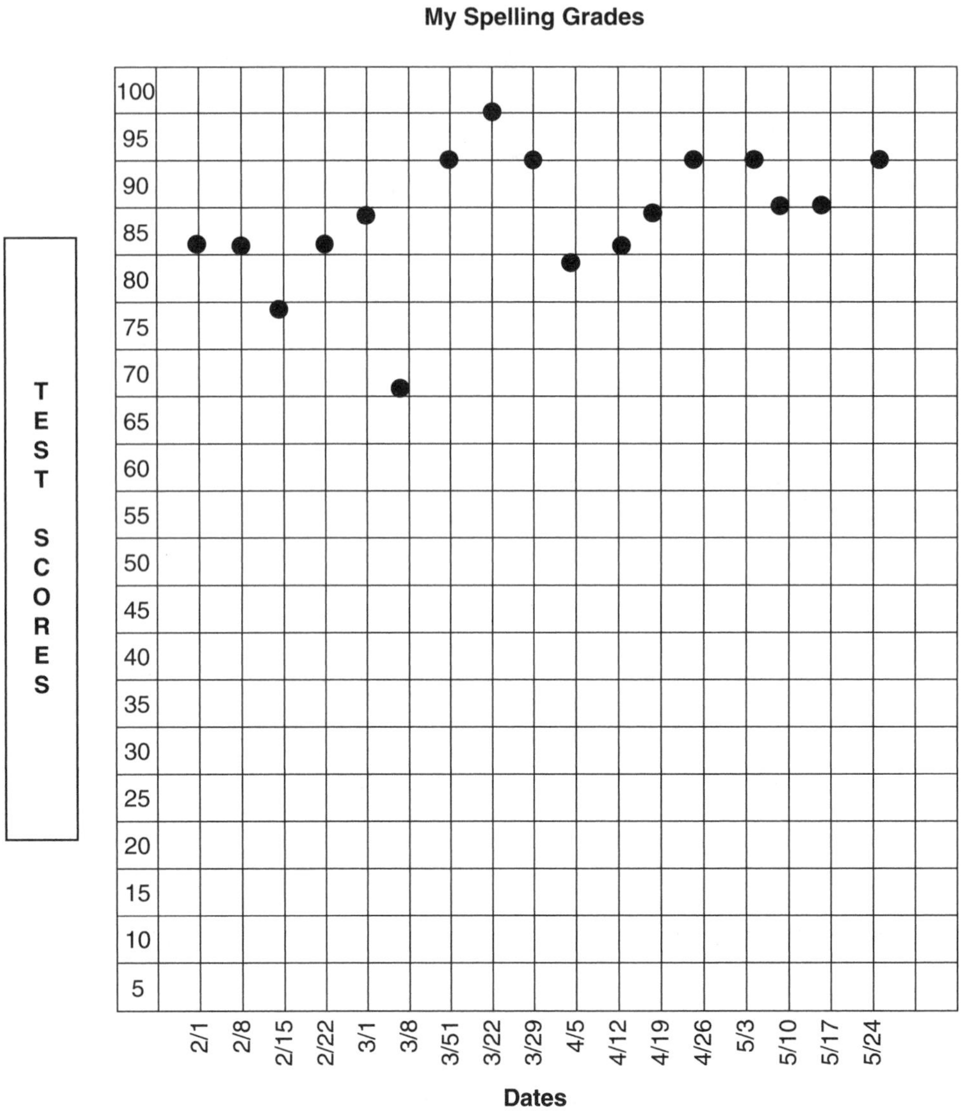

MY PROGRESS: LEARNING GRAPH

Setting Goals: Grades for Yesterday, Today, and Tomorrow

When? Now

How? Plot scores

Where? In class

Why? Important to see progress

Who? Me

What? Grades

Subject: ____________________________

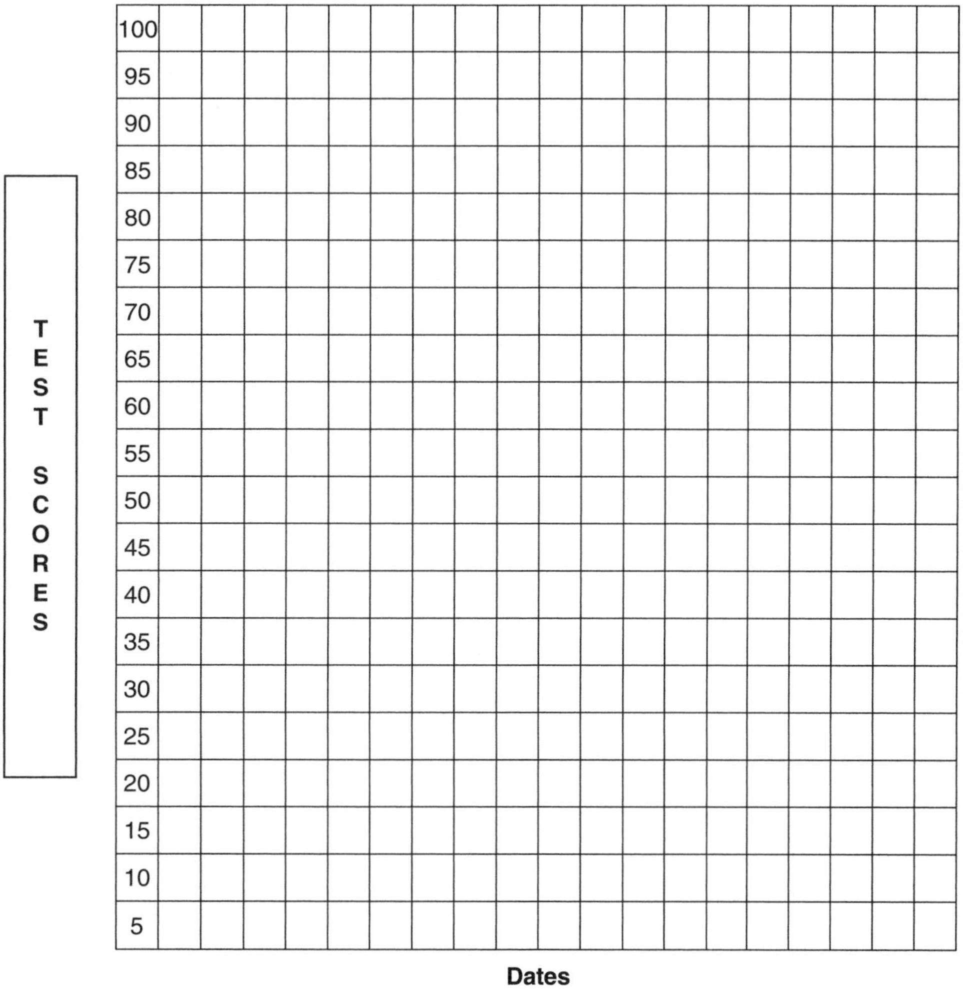

My Personal Goal Statement (about grades):

I plan to ____

TEACHING FOR MORE UNDERSTANDING

Compartmentalization

Learning needs its own compartments in which to store and fit bits or "bites" of information. *Neatly packaged learning is a better sell to students.* Teachers' presentations often matter a great deal in aiding students' retention. Just as filing cabinets externally help organize paperwork, *compartmentalization helps students organize learning material for better absorption.* Individual worksheets that make use of *boxing thoughts* help students realize how facts are related to each other within the bigger learning picture.

Even though a bakery might sell muffins, donuts, rolls, cakes, and cookies, before you leave the store, these items are placed in different-sized boxes or bags. You would probably not be pleased if the cheesecake was placed in a paper bag or too many rolls were squashed into a Ziploc bag. Just as a tie isn't really the right size for a shoebox, learning also has its own distinctive placement. Teachers need to separate the facts and help students to develop their own system of organization.

Curriculum Connection for World History

Compartmentalizing thoughts helps students when they take notes or review for tests. Without this external organization, content is not processed. Eventually, these *learning boxes* become internalized, as the brain no longer needs to see these concrete separations.

LEARNING BOXES—A WAY TO PAIR VISUALS WITH WRITTEN WORDS

1. Lived near Mediterranean Sea; Carthage was a great city of theirs
2. Were traders with other civilizations in the region
3. Greatest contribution was the alphabet

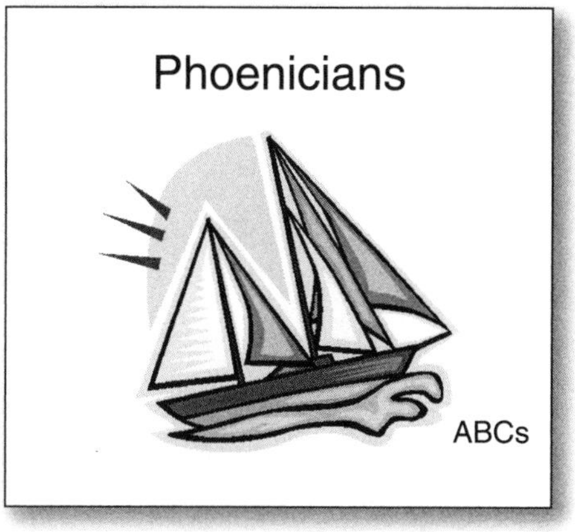

1. Cyrus the Great founded the Persian Empire around the 5th century B.C.
2. Darius I divided the Persian Empire into twenty provinces
3. Royal road improved communication

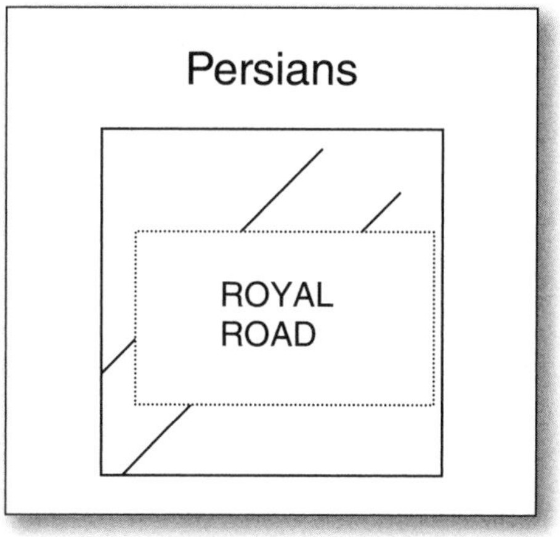

1. Iron weapons were used
2. Cavalry on mounted horses
3. Strong military power

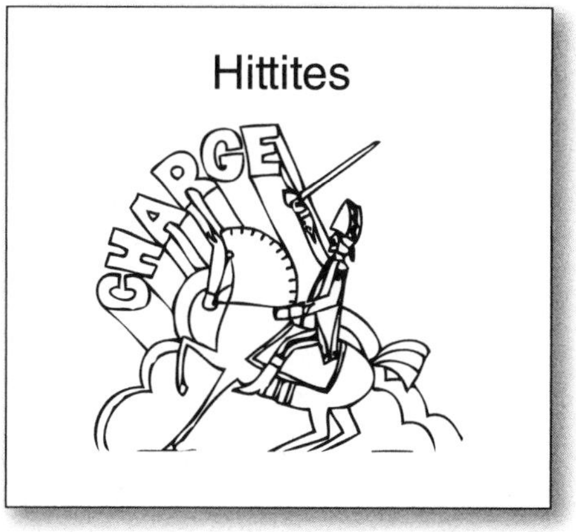

Fill in your own Learning Boxes below:

1. ______________________________

2. ______________________________

3. ______________________________

1. ______________________________

2. ______________________________

3. ______________________________

1. ______________________________

2. ______________________________

3. ______________________________

Curriculum Connection for Science

This chart delineates the difference between just memorizing and actually understanding definitions of science vocabulary. Words are defined in the chart, yet at the same time, relationships between words are seen at a quick glance, using the chart as a visual tool. Vocabulary words can be related to the same general topic yet differ in meaning. In addition, students can create their own models of atoms by using Legos or clay as concrete examples, act out the terms through short science skits, or teach and review with a partner for more retention. This allows kinesthetic and visual learners a chance to form better memory connections, with active learning taking place. Just divide some lined paper into three sections for columned note taking.

MY NOTES: TELLING MORE ABOUT ATOMS AND MOLECULES

Remember, all things in the universe are made of atoms, which are tiny particles. When two or more atoms are joined together, they make up a molecule (atom + atom = molecule). An electric charge means that atoms carry electricity with a positive or negative charge.

electrons	subatomic particle	(–) negatively charged whiz around nucleus # of electrons = # of protons
protons	subatomic particle	(+) positively charged found in nucleus
neutrons	subatomic particle	no electric charge found in nucleus

Remember, *matter is any physical thing that takes up space*. Matter is made up of atoms and molecules. Everything you see around you is either solid, liquid, gas, or plasma.

solids	state of matter	always keep their shape with molecules packed closely together
liquids	state of matter	do not keep the same shape; molecules are loosely packed and take the shape of whatever container they occupy
gases	state of matter	molecules are the furthest apart have no shape most are invisible
plasma	state of matter	gaseous material electrons (e.g., stars, comets)

TELL ABOUT . . . PLANNER

The following charts help learners to visually understand concepts. Just fold a paper into three columns like this to delineate relationships.

levers	simple machine	fulcrum, load arm, force arm (seesaw)
inclined plane	simple machine	slope
friction	force	resistance when things rub together in air or water
gravity	force	the pulling force of the Earth
heat	form of energy	measured in joules, vibrate, kinetic energy
sound	form of energy	molecules in air vibrate frequencies resonance

These charts allow learners to understand information in a simply presented, compartmentalized visual. More concrete learners will require more pictures and fewer words to solidify concepts.

TELL ABOUT . . .

Better Study Guides

The next template is used to help students study. With the following format, students can focus on individual questions rather than being overwhelmed by too much information. Guides like these visually separate questions into individual boxes, making them more manageable for students.

Students or teachers can write up to twenty-five questions on one grid sheet, while the corresponding twenty-five answers are placed on another matching grid. These grids can be differentiated to offer more or fewer challenges. The second sheet can just include the page number that the students can reference or a blank space for students to discover where the answers are on their own or in cooperative groups. Grids can be cooperatively completed in class if students divide each row of questions and then share and record responses. Class groups can then collectively review answers. By using these grids, students can also study independently, testing themselves.

Although students may use textbooks and class notes to locate information, they are not inundated with many pages of materials. This technique of reviewing and studying information allows them to transfer their knowledge to two user-friendly sheets. Different-colored sheets can be used to further distinguish question grids from answer grids.

Packaging makes a big difference in marketing, since people tend to gravitate toward more eye-catching items. Students also need visually appealing items to whet their appetites for learning. The simple conclusion is that items of learning need improved methods of ingestion!

BOXED MUSICAL CURRICULUM CONNECTIONS

Directions: Test your musical knowledge by trying to answer these questions before glancing at the answers on the grid that follows.

Which German composer who lived in the late 18th and early 19th century was best known for his famous symphonies?	Which 20th century American songwriter wrote "God Bless America"?	Name the American patriotic hymn from the 19th century that begins, "My country, 'tis of thee."	Who composed the music to the opera *Porgy and Bess?*	What lawyer and poet wrote "The Star-Spangled Banner"?
What stringed musical instrument is widely used in folk music?	Name a percussion instrument that is a large, round, metal plate.	Name all four instrument families.	What music piece is an introduction to a longer work?	What is a musical drama that is totally or mostly sung?
Name a high-pitched woodwind instrument, held horizontally, which is played by blowing across a hole.	What name is sometimes given to the violin when it is used in folk music or bluegrass?	What musical group do the French horn, trumpet, trombone, and tuba belong to?	What is a song of thanksgiving or praise called?	What's a quintet?
Name three musical elements.	What's a melody?	What term describes the simultaneous sounding of two pleasing musical notes?	Define jazz.	What word describes an extended musical composition for an orchestra that has several movements?
What name is given to a group of related sequenced musical movements?	Name a musical group that includes two violins, a viola, and a cello.	What's the highest range of the female voice called?	Define a chord.	Name your favorite musician.

MUSICAL ANSWERS

Ludwig van Beethoven	Irving Berlin	"America"	George Gershwin	Francis Scott Key
guitar	cymbal	• brass • percussion • strings • woodwind	overture	opera
flute	fiddle	brass	hymn	A group of five musicians or a piece of music for five instruments or voices
• harmony • melody • rhythm	songlike sequence of tones	harmony	Musical art form and expression with African American cultural roots	symphony
suite	string quartet	soprano	Sound of three or more notes in the same musical key, played together	Answers will vary

TEMPLATE

Concentration

"I Ate Cereal for Breakfast"

Once during small-group instruction, while I was explaining how to divide decimals by a divisor with a decimal, a student proceeded to tell me about a funny thing his dog did over the weekend. Okay, it's nice to share, but . . . I inexplicably turned to him and said, "I ate cereal for breakfast." He looked puzzled, started to ask a question, and then stopped. The message was received loudly and clearly. For the rest of the year, when someone else went off on an unrelated tangent, he would say, "I ate cereal for breakfast." Listening is an art. Sometimes the teacher really does say something, but it may never be heard by some students due to internal or external distractions. Share the suggestions below with students.

How Students Can Be Better Listeners

1. Concentrate on words being said in the classroom, without predicting or connecting everything to your own life; otherwise you might miss the lesson.
2. Listen to the actual words, but think about the meaning at the same time. Try to silently paraphrase what is said.
3. Focus, looking at the teacher or person speaking. Don't get involved in the extra stuff, such as playing at your desk or looking at silly faces someone might be making, which distracts your attention.
4. You can write notes about important facts or maybe things said that you are not sure about, but wait to ask questions, since they may be answered by the person speaking.
5. Be interested in what you are learning, even if you think it is boring!

Listening and Moving

Icebreakers increase student engagement and motivation with positive emotional connections that translate to more focus in academics (Johnson, 2012). This next activity, "Cruise or Dock," is a sample icebreaker.

CRUISE OR DOCK

Two signs (see above) are placed on opposite sides of the room. Decide on ports of call for a cruise. Perhaps the boat is headed to the Caribbean, Mediterranean, or South Seas (great catharsis!). Directions below are given with one instruction and demonstration at a time, repeating the prior steps before adding a new one (similar to "I'm Going on a Picnic"). The objective of this activity is to reinforce listening skills. Classroom benefits include the release of excess motor energy after a tedious reading assignment. It's a mind-body connection and an excellent *refueler*. It's bodily-kinesthetic, interpersonal, intrapersonal, musical-rhythmic, and verbal-linguistic (listening and reading). It's also great for concentration, memory, spatial awareness, and following directions. Besides all of that, it's fun! Students respond to prompts that are written on signs.

Prompt	Response
Large Waves	Students join hands and bob up and down
Shark	Frenzied, quick movement
Party Time	Students mingle
Land Sighted	Hands are placed over forehead while looking toward the dock
Dinghy	Pretend to be rowing
Bridge Open	Everyone freezes to allow ships to pass
Food Served	Rub belly in circular motion with your hand

Check out these sources:

Adapted Games & Activities: From Tag to Team Building by Pattie Rouse

Adapted Physical Education and Sport by Joseph Winnick (Ed.)

Inclusive Games by Susan Kasser

JumpBunch Sports & Fitness for Kids: www.jumpbunch.com/kidsfitness games.html

Kick-Start Your Class: Academic Icebreakers to Engage Students by Lou Anne Johnson

Silly Sports & Goofy Games by Spencer Kagan

Young Children & Movement: www.naeyc.org/tyc/files/tyc/file/V6N1/Dow2010.pdf

ORGANIZED ENVIRONMENTS

Student-Friendly Signs

Teachers post these signs on a classroom wall to highlight homework in different subjects. Each day, the work next to the sign changes, but students know where to consistently look for assignments. Signs can be laminated and magnetized. Activity/study centers in the classroom can be labeled as well, for a visually structured environment.

TRACKING MY ASSIGNMENTS

Subject	Date Due	Books/Materials	Check When Done

Available for download at **www.corwin.com/inclusionstrategies**

Organization With Calendars

Filling in dates and events for each month on calendars like this one helps students follow classroom routines. For example, students can make notations of assemblies, holidays, tests scheduled, when reports are due, birthdays, parent nights, spirit days, and much more. These monthly planners can be kept on students' desks. Small numbers in the right-hand corner of each box allow room for monthly activities. Keeping a calendar is particularly helpful for nonreaders, emergent readers, and English learners. Pictorial calendar concepts can be used with a large classroom calendar and magnet-backed icons to designate various school events, or even daily routines. In addition, many schools distribute or encourage the use of daily student planners to record homework assignments, long-range projects, and upcoming events.

CALENDAR TEMPLATE

Month: ______________________						
Sunday	Monday	Tuesday	Wednesday	Thursday	Friday	Saturday

Available for download at **www.corwin.com/inclusionstrategies**

Model how to break down larger long-term projects with mini due dates for project parts. It is also often quite helpful if student planners and homework assignment books are signed and reviewed by teachers and staff in school and parents or adults at home. Assigned study buddies can also check their peers' planners and calendars for preparation and accuracy.

You are invited to review these study skill and accessibility sites:

http://windows.microsoft.com/en-US/windows7/products/features/accessibility

http://www.washington.edu/doit

http://aim.cast.org/learn/practice/palm

http://www.superteachertools.com

http://quizhub.com/quiz/quizhub.cfm

http://www.learn4good.com/games/index.htm

http://tinyurl.com

http://www.easybib.com

http://www.quia.com

http://www.pocketmod.com

http://quizlet.com

http://www.studyisland.com

9

Assessing, Testing, and Grading Your Students

How do teachers assess what students know? Students with disabilities are no longer out of the accountability loop but expected to achieve the same curriculum standards as their peers without disabilities. The vast majority of students with individualized education programs (IEPs) are legislatively mandated to take the same standardized tests as their classmates, unless it can be shown that even with accommodations and modifications, the test is not appropriate. Tests need to be both reliable (giving stable and consistent results when repeated) and valid (meaningfully assessing what they claim to measure). Tests are also just one type of assessment, with many other curriculum-based assessments also yielding valuable instructional knowledge. Grading is the hardest thing for both teachers and students. Grades today may reflect or include letters such as A, B, C, D, or F, or percentage of mastery, pass-fail, comments, narratives, and more. Overall, grades need to be a fair, accurate, and meaningful communication of student performance minus bias (Guskey & Jung, 2009; Mastergeorge & Martínez, 2010). All staff needs to investigate and embrace positive attitudes. Data collection, along with research-based interventions, differentiated lessons, collaborative practices, ongoing assessments, interventions, and documentation are essential ingredients that reveal levels, gaps, and the necessary instructional bridges. Included in this chapter is a discussion of assessment dilemmas, along with creative options teachers can explore to help students gain skills beyond a numerical grade.

PURPOSEFUL ASSESSMENT REPRESENTATIONS ■

Appropriate assessment can be used to guide instruction, particularly for students who have disabilities. When teachers study error patterns, this information can be used for future lesson planning. It's more than just the grade; it's knowing what a student needs help with! Purposeful testing involves looking at error patterns, since these are indicators for teachers to help them to better teach students on their appropriate levels. Grades students receive are not gifts but should be earned by students. I once offered my math students a test, but I didn't call it by that name. I instructed students to head their papers with the following question: What do I know? It's critical for students at all ages to be aware of their levels and exactly what they need more help with. Both teachers and students need to evaluate just what learning has taken place since this information guides the next steps.

In addition, when teachers develop tests, they need to think about universal design for learning (UDL) with multiple representations of the content embedded in assessment. This goes beyond offering text-to-speech for a student who is blind or activating the closed captioning feature on a video for a student who is deaf. Embedded and varied assessment incorporates a variety of options and supports that are available to all students. These can include but are not limited to providing links that define vocabulary and offering pictures and models with additional background information to assist students to complete a book report, science lab, or research paper. Technology offers the option to monitor responses with embedded assessment that tracks and saves student responses. The Center for Applied Special Technology (CAST) offers a *Thinking Reader*, which contains rubrics and opportunities for self-reflection to practice comprehension strategies. The assessment then becomes a meaningful experience for the learner beyond the grade level. Allowing students to complete assessments in different formats with the necessary supports offer more accurate representations of learning achievement. CAST also has UDL guidelines for multiple means of representation, action and expression, and engagement at www.udlcenter.org/aboutudl/udlguidelines. The CCSS assessments offer accountability that is designed to improve both instruction and student performance. However, students are also offered accommodations that are based on personal needs profiles (PNP) as delineated by PARCC.

Understanding by design invites teachers to think about the outcomes desired at the outset and then plan the learning activities to match those objectives. This approach differs from proceeding with a lesson and then picking facts out of the text to be tested that were not emphasized or explored in class lessons. Test construction is just as important as the lessons themselves, with parallel concepts delivered and assessed. If general education (GE) and special education (SE) teachers are co-teachers, then both can share input in the test design, type of questions offered, embedded supports, and formats for the class. Maybe some students will need tests digitally read so as not to let reading difficulties interfere with content knowledge, if it is not a test of reading knowledge. Overall, accommodations and modifications need to match students' IEP requirements and 504 plans. Tests help gauge what students know and what educators may still have to teach to help students learn more. Response to interventions (RTI), as discussed in prior chapters, values assessments as ways of determining where to proceed next in the learning. The following offers an analogy that shows how to "sandwich in" assessments.

RTI SANDWICH

- The "crust" of the matter includes assessment of student's needs, sandwiching in the next two layers.
- "Lettuce" means let us figure out, identify, and problem-solve which interventions will best suit this student's current needs.
- The "meaty" parts of the RTI sandwich are the implementation of scientific, research-based strategies; appropriate instructional approaches; and plans.
- Now, let's go back to the "crust" of the matter: There are more assessments to determine if the interventions have produced acceptable results and see if the interventions were appropriate ones.

Otherwise, change concerning intervention methods is warranted. New "sandwich meat" is required!

SOURCE: Karten (2009).

Grading Options

The following are EPAS that need to be considered when grading students:

Effort	Working at optimum level
Progress	Growth over time
Achievement*	Mastery of standards and lesson's objectives
Self-awareness	Being cognizant of strengths and weaknesses, with a plan for improvement of skills

*Be cognizant of goals, accommodations, and types of testing procedures listed in IEPs, PNPs, and 504 plans.

Types of Assessment

1. *Norm-Referenced:* Students' grades are compared to those of peers, with same standards for all students.
2. *Criterion-Referenced:* Evaluation is based on mastery of standards, without comparison to others.
3. *Self-Referenced:* Grading is based on noted improvement of skills, with the individual needs, abilities, and efforts the student shows taken into consideration.

Don't forget about ABOWA (Assessment By Observation and Walking Around). Teachers who watch students will informally learn to assess their understanding quite accurately. Equally vital is sharing realistic, supportive, and timely feedback with students to improve levels of awareness, motivation, and achievements. Error analysis often reveals areas that require remediation before marching onward. It is through assessments that more instructional knowledge is gained.

Accountability Issues: What Do Tests Measure?

Sometimes tests can be a measure of students' *dis*abilities, not their competencies. In those cases, the test is disabled, not the student. In the past, some school districts even omitted the scores of classified students from their databases or allowed students to take an assessment on a lower grade level. Those scenarios deleted the student with special needs from accountability. Assessments can be vital tools that determine if all students are learning, but a child with a disability often faces the difficult task of being given the same assessment as a student who does not have a disability. Accommodating those differences does not necessarily devalue the entire assessment. Students are asked to meet standards of learning, and all students are expected to attain a given knowledge set. The intention of education is for students to show academic improvement in order to become productive, independent adults. The college and career readiness standards (CCR) of the Common Core State Standards (CCSS) are applicable to all students. Since many schools do not want to be labeled as "needing improvement," the law is being challenged in different ways to address concerns about the population of special education or non–English-speaking children in the school. A question sometimes asked is whether the students who have not had similar learning experiences are misidentified as having a learning disability, since their lack of educational exposures impacts their performance. It is then claimed that these students may unjustly influence and penalize that school or teacher's performance. Students with and without learning disabilities who are more affluent usually perform better on standardized tests. If that's the case, how can schools level the playing fields to account for the fact that many schools have students from families with lower socioeconomic status? There is also a question of how alternate assessments based on common core standards relate to college and career readiness (Kleinert, Kearns, Quenemoen, & Thurlow, 2013). These types of situational state allowances are debated and tested by families, administrators, educators, and the federal government.

Students with disabilities must participate in districts' assessments. A small percentage of students with disabilities who have significant cognitive disabilities may take an alternate CCSS assessment such as ones offered by Dynamic Learning Maps and the National Center and State Collaborative that states have adopted. This occurs when the grade-level test would be much too difficult for students with significant disabilities and would not provide helpful information.

IEP teams should collectively discuss these challenging questions:

- Does fair mean equal?
- Should students be compared to one another?

- How can a written test accurately measure a child's knowledge if he or she has learning and language difficulties?
- When does effort count?
- Should teachers or schools be held accountable for a child's lack of progress?
- What specific presentation, response, and time and scheduling accommodations will assist but not enable students?

Serving Knowledge

Food critics can enhance or demote a restaurant's status by the mighty pen that either raves about or deplores the meal served. As the review reaches vast audiences, restaurants may experience an increase in business or a devastating shutdown. However, consider how the following questions can affect the accuracy and value of a food critic's review:

1. Did the critic catch the chef on his or her best day?
2. How was the food prepared?
3. Did the critic ever eat that kind of food before?
4. Did the reviewer like the waiter or waitress who served the food?
5. What type of rating scale did the reviewer use?

Now consider the following educational concerns:

1. Did the teacher catch the child on his or her best day?
2. How were the students prepared for the test?
3. Had the student learned about that subject before?
4. Does the student like the teacher or have an interest in the subject matter?
5. What type of assessment format was used?

CLASSROOM SCENARIOS

1. Can't/Won't

There's a fine line between can't and won't. Teachers must help, not enable.

2. Filewild

If the word *wildlife* appears to the student as *filewild*, imagine how difficult written language is for such a student.

Written testing accompanied by orally read questions would definitely be appropriate, since a test needs to measure a child's understanding of a concept, not his or her reading disability.

3. Bed

A student with a hearing impairment responded that *bed* was the past tense for *be.* The student was applying his best effort but lacked an understanding of the spoken language.

Tests should not penalize students if they truly do not understand concepts. Teachers are here to help, not punish, students who are differently abled.

4. AMW

A worksheet asks for the abbreviation for *a married woman.* The student responds with AMW, instead of Mrs.

Some students are concrete learners who need direct skill instruction to compensate for varying background knowledge.

5. Half Credit

Given a multiple-choice question with three choices, a student circles two of the lettered choices. It turns out that one of the choices is correct, and the student argues for partial credit. No way!

Rules need to be enforced. The assessment is a valuable learning tool and teaches the meaning of accountability, not how to beat the system.

LEARNING CHOICES: ALTERNATE METHODS OF ASSESSMENT

The following table and contract expands assessments beyond paper and pencil to also infuse appropriate supports. It is important that staff explore meaningful student data for academic, social, emotional, and behavioral domains.

knowledge surveys	digital tools and online assessments	daily or weekly point charts	dated portfolios with work samples	multiple-choice responses
concept and mind maps	open-ended questions	observation	student-teacher conferences	Socratic discussions
rubrics	cooperative activities	bubbled responses	standardized tests	peer critiques
preassessments	chapter/unit tests	self-assessments	study guides	exit cards
multiple intelligences	formative assessments	essays	game-based learning	process vs. content skills
family contact and collaboration	student and/or teacher checklists	self-regulation	progress monitoring	differentiated feedback
positive reinforcement	repetition	interviews	student surveys	prompts, cues, models
learner profiles	visual, auditory, kinesthetic, and tactile (VAKT) approaches	sharing learning objectives	error analysis; valuing *mistakes*	nonexamples
performance-based assessments	homework and/or flipped learning	true-false questions	sentence-completion	one-to-one-small group instruction
anecdotal records	notebook checks	direct questioning	functional behavioral assessments	____________

Educational Contract Options

To prove that I understand about ______________________[topic], I will

_____ create a play

_____ compose a song

_____ make a cartoon

_____ write jokes on the topic

_____ paraphrase a speech

_____ create a PowerPoint presentation

_____ perform a dance

_____ keep a learning log

_____ complete a take-home test

_____ work on a group project

_____ teach it to another student

_____ do a written report

_____ host a debate

_____ research websites for more information

_____ teach a class lesson

_____ interview people about the topic

_____ write a newspaper article

_____ compose a graph or chart

_____ create a hand-drawn or digital poster

_____ create a sculpture

_____ design a game

_____ invent a product

_____ create a time line of important events or details

_____ other idea

Mutually agreed upon on _______________ (date) by ____________________ (student's name) and _______________________ (teacher's name). Will be completed by ________________ (date).

Student's initials ______ Teacher's initials ______

Home/Parent signature ____

NOTE: Paper is to be placed in student's portfolio as evidence of intended performance.

Available for download at **www.corwin.com/inclusionstrategies**

> Portfolios offer organized and concrete time lines of children's growth that can be reviewed by teachers, families, and students themselves as a reflection of progress achieved throughout the year.

USER-FRIENDLY TESTING FORMATS

> Sometimes it's not a student's disability that causes poor performance but the test itself that disables. Assessment should be visually appealing, with clear and precise directions.

COLONIAL KNOWLEDGE

Directions: Read the twelve statements below and place the correct numbers in the labeled colonial squares.

Roanoke	Both colonies	Jamestown

Colonial Statements

1. First settlement in English North American colonies
2. Second settlement in English North American colonies
3. Colonists traded with Native Americans
4. Located off the coast of Virginia
5. Located off the coast of North Carolina
6. Leader was John Smith
7. Leader was John White
8. Settled by the English
9. Colony failed with colonists disappearing
10. Colonists faced hardships before they were successful
11. Africans worked on tobacco farms
12. Located on the East Coast of the present-day United States

Now write a paragraph, poem, or song from the point of view of a colonist, Native American, or African American living at this time.

Rationale: Varying testing formats helps students to demonstrate their knowledge in a nonintimidating, jargon-free manner, with clear directions. This information was originally in multiple-choice format, but now the same knowledge is being tested using an approach that neatly boxes and numbers the information, helping students who have perceptual and writing difficulties. The option to produce a poem, song, or written paragraph allows the CCSS.ELA to connect to social studies and empowers students with three differentiated open-ended assessments.

LOGICAL MATCHING

Directions: Draw a line from the definition in the left column to the correct word in the right column. Next, with a partner, create and solve a word problem with at least two of these vocabulary words. Explain how you arrived at your solution.

bottom number of a fraction	multiplication ×
top number of a fraction	denominator $\frac{4}{5}$
mathematical operation that is repeated addition	numerator $\frac{3}{4}$
expressing a number out of 100	quadrilateral ▭
a polygon with four sides	percent %

Rationale: An uncluttered format such as this one deviates from the usual matching design, by switching the definition to the left column and the word choice to the right one. It may seem inconsequential to most students, but those with reading difficulties appreciate this type of matching layout, since they are not required to laboriously read every definition before choosing the right answer. This way, students can focus on one definition at a time, minimizing frustration. Accompanying visuals further explain the written words. In addition, the word problem allows students to apply the domain specific vocabulary with a connection to the CCSS for Mathematical Practice.

DRAMATIC ASSESSMENT

Drama can be an alternative assessment to written tests as a way for students to demonstrate their knowledge. For example, when studying the Roman Empire, students can set up a performance center and role-play the actions of the emperor, patricians, plebeians, artisans, and slaves, including appropriate historical facts through dialogue and actions. Students can role-play or pantomime Newton's Three Laws of Motion or reenact a scene from a written work, such as *Tales of a Fourth Grade Nothing*, *Where the Red Fern Grows*, *Macbeth*, and more!

Directions: Think of some topics students can dramatize.

ASSESSMENT TRENDS

Unfortunately, many students visualize themselves failing the test before it is even given. The tension is usually self-induced and leads to many disappointing assessments, since this type of negative thinking is a self-fulfilling prophecy. If possible, try not to schedule tests on a day that you know you will be absent. Often, students stare at a teacher during the test because they are reenacting the learning situation, perhaps a lecture or a review. Seeing the teacher (and not a substitute) may help trigger the learning.

Teacher Tips

Teachers can help ease testing tensions by:

1. Familiarizing students with the testing layout, whether that is a paper or digital format, explaining the type of questions that will be asked (e.g., essays, short answers, multiple choice, fill-ins, open-ended, true or false, matching, word boxes) and how to use the digital tools (e.g., embedded supports available, when to press continue or save for later)
2. Telling students the material to be tested ahead of time. Some children need at least a week to prepare for larger unit exams. Give exact textbook page numbers, study guides, or outlines as well as copies of PowerPoints, notes, outlines from programs such as Inspiration or Kidspiration software, and podcasts.
3. Testing frequently to alleviate the pressure of one test being the whole grade
4. Using his or her discretion on when to give extra-credit assignments for children who want to improve their grades
5. Giving students various ways to demonstrate their knowledge through other multiple intelligences besides verbal-linguistic and logical-mathematical ones
6. Having students consistently keep track of their grades, charting progress
7. Encouraging good note taking and organizational skills by consistently checking notebooks, loose-leaf folders, binders, desk, and work areas
8. Communicating frequently with parents and families, making them aware of their child's needs and progress so learning can be supported and bridged in both school and home environments.
9. Teaching the philosophy "Big Deal, So What!" to a student who thinks the world is over because he or she did poorly on one test. Encourage that child to use it as a learning experience by examining the problem: Was the material too difficult? Or was it a lack of effort?
10. Reexamining the test: Was it a fair assessment of material taught?

Examples of testing accommodations for students with disabilities may vary in terms of the following:

- *Presentation*—how the lesson is delivered (e.g., large print, directions read aloud, Braille edition, descriptive video, ASL video of test directions for a student who is deaf or hard of hearing, additional assistive technology, tactile graphics, text-to-speech, number of questions on a page)
- *Response*—avenues for answering (e.g., written, dictated to a scribe, calculator, computer/tablet, pointing to correct answers)
- *Scheduling*—time issues (e.g., frequent breaks, more time, mornings or afternoons, spread out over sessions or days)
- *Location/Setting*—where the test is given (e.g., small group, general education classroom, separate or quieter setting, take-home test, specialized equipment or furniture)

Consult these sources for additional research-based recommendations:

www.achieve.org/assessments

www.cehd.umn.edu/nceo/topicareas/UnivDesign/UnivDesignResources.htm

allthingsassessment.info

www.performanceassessment.org

digitales.us/evaluating-projects/scoring-guides

www2.ed.gov/teachers/assess/resources/edpicks.jhtml?src=ln

www.edudemic.com/digital-classroom-note-taking/

scale.stanford.edu/system/files/performance-assessment-era-standards-based-educational-accountability.pdf

wiki.ncscpartners.org/index.php/Main_Page

CCSS AND ASSESSMENTS

The Smarter Balanced Assessment Consortium (SBAC) and the Partnership for Assessment of Readiness for College and Careers (PARCC) developed assessments aligned to the CCSS. The majority of states across the country have adopted one of these CCSS assessments. These assessments are intended to present evidence of student mastery. Many accommodations are already built into the assessments for students with and without IEPs or 504 plans and English learners.

Accommodations for students with disabilities include but are not limited to dictation to a scribe; presentations such as Braille, sign language, closed captioning, or descriptive video; frequent breaks; extended time; alternate scheduling; and changes in location to a smaller classroom. Embedded supports for students include but are not limited to universal designs such as audio amplification, highlighting, and popup glossaries, with student and/or staff activated features. Personal Needs Profiles (PNPs), as required by PARCC, are intended to individualize the testing experience and delineate the needs of students with and without disabilities in advance. Observations, stated preferences, and input from the student and parent or guardian are valued. However, as stated by PARCC, reducing student expectations is not an option.

The CCSS Application to Students with Disabilities is available online at www.corestandards.org/assets/application-to-students-with-disabilities.pdf.

In addition, the National Center and State Collaborative (NCSC) and Dynamic Learning Maps (DLM) offer alternative formative and summative assessments for students with significant cognitive disabilities. These assessments offer a way for students with significant cognitive disabilities to demonstrate their learning. Their diagnostic nature allows school staff to plan instructional units based on individual student needs.

Additional resources about accommodations can be accessed from SBAC, PARCC, DLM, and NCSC at these online links:

www.smarterbalanced.org/wordpress/wp-content/uploads/2014/03/SmarterBalanced_Guidelines_091113.pdf

www.parcconline.org/parcc-accessibility-features-and-accommodations-manual

dynamiclearningmaps.org/content/assessments

www.ncscpartners.org/resources

All consortiums intend that honoring the goals and objectives in each student's IEP or 504 Plan be imperative to ensure that mastery levels are achieved. In addition, high expectations and meaningful outcomes are valued for students of all ability levels.

RUBRICS

To eliminate vague, subjective assessments, teachers can design an authentic assessment tool for grading in reading, writing, math, speech, and more.

Sample Writing Rubric

Category	4—Excellent	3—Good	2—Fair	1—Needs Improvement
Introduction	The introduction is inviting, states the main topic, and previews the structure of the paper.	The introduction clearly states the main topic and previews the structure of the paper but is not particularly inviting to the reader.	The introduction states the main topic but does not adequately preview the structure of the paper, nor is it particularly inviting to the reader.	There is no clear introduction of the main topic or structure of the paper.
Transitions (Organization)	A variety of thoughtful transitions is used. They clearly show how ideas are connected.	Transitions clearly show how ideas are connected, but there is little variety.	Some transitions work well, but connections between other ideas are fuzzy.	The transitions between ideas are unclear or nonexistent.
Support for Topic (Content)	Relevant, telling, quality details give the reader important information that goes beyond the obvious or predictable.	Supporting details and information are relevant, but one key issue or portion of the storyline is unsupported.	Supporting details and information are relevant, but several key issues or portions of the storyline are unsupported.	Supporting details and information are typically unclear or not related to the topic.
Focus on Topic (Content)	There is one clear, well-focused topic. Main idea stands out and is supported by detailed information.	Main idea is clear, but the supporting information is general.	Main idea is somewhat clear, but there is a need for more supporting information.	The main idea is not clear. There is a seemingly random collection of information.

(Continued)

(Continued)

Category	4—Excellent	3—Good	2—Fair	1—Needs Improvement
Sentence Length (Sentence Fluency)	Every paragraph has sentences that vary in length.	Almost all paragraphs have sentences that vary in length.	Some sentences vary in length.	Sentences rarely vary in length.
Grammar, Punctuation, & Spelling (Conventions)	Writer makes no errors in grammar, punctuation, or spelling that distract the reader from the content.	Writer makes one or two errors in grammar, punctuation, or spelling that distract the reader from the content.	Writer makes three or four errors in grammar, punctuation, or spelling that distract the reader from the content.	Writer makes more than four errors in grammar, punctuation, or spelling that distract the reader from the content.
Word Choice	Writer uses vivid words and phrases that linger or draw pictures in the reader's mind, and the choice and placement of the words seem accurate, natural, and unforced.	Writer uses vivid words and phrases that linger or draw pictures in the reader's mind, but occasionally the words are used inaccurately or seem overdone.	Writer uses words that communicate clearly, but the writing lacks variety, punch, or flair.	Writer uses a limited vocabulary that does not communicate strongly or capture the reader's interest. Jargon or clichés may be present and detract from the meaning.
Conclusion (Organization)	The conclusion is strong and leaves the reader with a feeling that he or she understands what the writer is "getting at."	The conclusion is recognizable and ties up almost all the loose ends.	The conclusion is recognizable but does not tie up several loose ends.	There is no clear conclusion; the paper just ends.

SOURCE: Created by author using rubistar.4teachers.org/index.php.

The next rubric offers a simpler report rubric, accompanied by pictures, which some students may require.

Sample Report Rubric

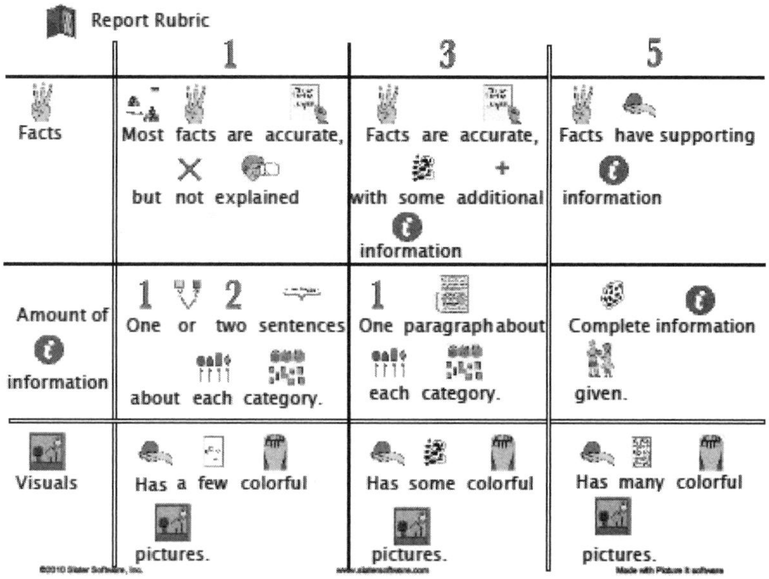

Report Rubric

	1	3	5
Facts	Most facts are accurate, but not explained	Facts are accurate, with some additional information	Facts have supporting information
Amount of information	One or two sentences about each category.	One paragraph about each category.	Complete information given.
Visuals	Has a few colorful pictures.	Has some colorful pictures.	Has many colorful pictures.

SOURCE: Used with permission. Made with Picture It Software © 1994–Present James E. and Jean M. Slater.

Available for download at **www.corwin.com/inclusionstrategies**

10

Working With Parents and Families of Students With Disabilities

Teachers must recognize the important role parents and families play in the learning process. While some families embrace inclusion because it challenges their children with more exposure to grade-level curriculum, opportunities for role modeling, and increased social interaction, some families fear that when their child with special needs is placed in an inclusive, general education classroom, he or she will lose individualized services (Salend, 2006). Parents of students without disabilities may embrace the inclusive classroom as an opportunity to increase the acceptance and tolerance of diverse abilities, while other parents may think that their son or daughter will receive less teacher attention or learn a diluted curriculum. However, when parents, families, and teachers act as allies and work together, this bond helps all children succeed. Coordination between home and school environments benefits learners. This chapter stresses that teachers cannot understand the student with special needs without effectively including parents and caregivers, appreciating their diverse struggles, perspectives, and celebrations.

■ VALUING PARENTS AND FAMILIES

Understanding Parental Emotions

> After parent conferences, teachers have often been heard to say, "*So and so* is exactly like her parent, whom I just met. The apple doesn't fall far from the tree." Unless you have experienced what it is like to have a *special* child of your own, you cannot begin to understand the intricate dynamics. The complexities involve more than apples.

The various emotive behaviors parents experience when raising a *special* child can be comparable to the grief or mourning process. Parental emotions can include the following:

Shock	plans, dreams, expectations, and lives are changed
Denial	feeling of frustration, can't be happening, not true!
Guilt	whatever went wrong was my fault, helplessness
Shopping Behavior	looking toward experts for different diagnoses and strategies
Depression	sadness and withdrawal, I don't want to face the world!
Hostility	state of anger, despair, being overwhelmed, exhaustion, pain, fear
(and finally) *Acceptance*	courageous, stronger, optimistic

Parental and Familial Understandings and Reflections

In addition to experiencing these emotions, parents and guardians must often deal with experts who complicate the process. Educators, doctors, friends, family, and others with good intentions express a range of emotions as well. It is difficult enough for parents to trust or even know their own instincts at this time, let alone deal with how others feel. This adjustment process encompasses a broad spectrum, with parents and family members often being the recipients of contrasting emotions, ranging from pity to support.

Sometimes parents and guardians are not the ones in denial; it is the interventions of educators or experts that *deny parents* as being the experts, the ones who are the most knowledgeable about their own child's strengths and needs. Parents and guardians are quite often experts on their own children and need accepting ears and advice on how to best meet their children's challenging needs. Other parents, guardians, or teachers sometimes let prior unsuccessful school experiences interfere with impartiality and objectivity in the planning process. Parents of students with disabilities who were interviewed by researchers offered advice that included acknowledging grief, making strong family bonds, seeking experienced yet professional and collaborative professionals, being proactive, developing creative funding, being spiritual, allocating time, and finding ways to include their child within the larger community (Schumacher Dyke & Bauer, 2010). Even though parents may know that their child is not on par with his or her peers in academic, perceptual, sensory, communication, physical, behavioral, emotional, or social areas, it becomes even more traumatic when vast differences are concretely shown and sometimes magnified with harsh-sounding written evaluations that do not outline or offer collaborative plans to move forward. Overall, caution needs to be exercised, since labeling people can put them in a holding pattern, actually cutting off possibilities for future collaborative planning. Most important is to listen to each other's views.

Parents rarely forget that first disability diagnosis, whether it is at birth or in the school years. The toll on families is enormous. Marriages are strained as expectations for children become altered, while siblings are also impacted as attention is drawn away from them. Stress levels of parents have an effect on students' overall performance (Lessenberry & Rehdfeldt, 2004). Which stage parents and families are in when the teacher meets them will influence the relationship.

Teachers also need to reflect on their own reactions, even with things that are not said, since actions or body language can sometimes speak louder than words. The children need to be the common ground for educators, parents, families, and support systems. Understanding and reflection are imperative for all.

PARENTS, FAMILIES, AND TEACHERS AS ALLIES

School-Home Communication

Parenting a child with special needs requires inner strength and much support from family and friends. Many support groups out there can help parents deal with difficulties that arise. Just knowing that others have gone through similar experiences helps parents and guardians a great deal. Other understanding parents and supportive family members can offer each other assistance, guidance, and comfort.

Mutual respect is first and foremost. It is understandable that the whole special education process, along with its associated jargon, can be overwhelming. Parents are often outnumbered by professionals at IEP meetings and can feel both threatened and anxious at the same time, trying to get the best program for their child. Families should be well informed on changing special education laws, looking at the safeguards and knowing how to best use them to help their children. Educators should be well informed about the individuality of each student in their classrooms, using strategies adapted to ensure not only that the content they teach is understood but also that the familial impact is appropriately respected.

Parental voices need empowerment to collaborate with teachers to make educational decisions based on jointly decided, appropriate services for children. Teachers, parents, and families are integral parts of this planning process, offering input to address the unique educational needs of each child with a disability. Even offering suggestions to parents and guardians such as which books to read with their children or describing some home activities to increase literacy or mathematical skills values the parents' and families' role. Always remember to also validate families' concerns and to point out the *good stuff,* too (e.g., through positive phone calls or showing improved student work samples). Many schools use a computerized grading system, and it takes two well-spent seconds to send an e-mail message to parents through these systems.

Empowerment and Communication for All

Teachers	Administration
Related staff	Parents/Families
Children	Guardians
Community	Siblings

Frequent Parent-Home Communication

- Averts problematic situations
- Sends a message of worth to the parents and guardians
- Tells students that there's a connection between the school and home environments
- Occurs not only at parent-teacher conferences or scheduled IEP meetings but throughout the school year if necessary
- Can be verbal or written such as informal notes or letters, report cards, e-mails, phone contacts, interim grade reports, checklists, behavioral charts, or signatures on tests and homework assignments

How Parents and Families Can Understand More

- Ask questions.
- Explain how you feel.
- Seek information.
- Maintain realistic expectations.
- Be patient with yourself, your child, and others.
- Learn to express your emotions.
- Take care of yourself.
- Keep daily routines.
- Recognize that you are not alone.
- Be involved with your child's day.
- Maintain positive attitudes.

PARENTAL/FAMILY INPUT

Child's Name: ____

Parent's/Guardian's Name: ______________________________________

1. What does my child think about school?

2. What do I visualize my daughter or son doing in ten or fifteen years?

3. What are my child's needs?

4. Some words I would use to describe my child are ______________, ______________________, and ______________________________.

5. What are my child's favorite things to do?

6. What are my pet peeves about my child's school?

7. What do I like about my child's class?

8. My areas of expertise are ______________________________ ______________ ______________________, and I am available to talk to my child's class on ______________ ______________________________.

9. I'd like to volunteer to help ______________________________ ______________ ______________________________________.

10. Contact me at

    E-mail: ____

    Telephone: Home ______________ Work ______________ Cell phone ______________

    Home Address: ____

    ____

    ____

WE'RE ALL ON THE SAME SIDE

Parents and Families

+

Teachers

+

Administrators

+

Students

+

Community

=

Learning

RESOURCES AND ORGANIZATIONS FOR PARENTS, GUARDIANS, AND FAMILIES

The Council for Exceptional Children (CEC): www.cec.sped.org

Exceptional Parent: www.eparent.com

All Kids Count: www.osepideasthatwork.org/ParentKit/allkidscount1.asp

Center for Parent Information and Resources: www.parentcenterhub.org

Common Core Information for Parents: commoncore.org/parents

Dictionary for Parents of Children with Disabilities: thespecialparent.com/wp-content/resources/dictionary.pdf

Directory of Parent Training and Information Centers (PTI) and Community Parent Resource Centers (CPRC): www.yellowpagesforkids.com/help/ptis.htm

Klein, S., & Schive, K. (2001). *You will dream new dreams.* New York, NY: Kensington Books. (Inspirational parental resource)

National Center for Families Learning: www.familieslearning.org

National Parent Teacher Association: www.pta.org

Parent Advocacy Coalition for Educational Rights (PACER): www.pacer.org

Shore, K. (2009). *A teacher's guide to working with parents.* Port Chester, NY: Dude Publishing.

11

Infusing Technology Into the Inclusive Classroom

This is an important topic, given the society in which we live and the increase in available tools to help our population of students with disabilities. Schools have undergone incredible changes throughout the years. Scientific discoveries have yielded benefits that have trickled down to educational forums to evaluate, assess, and instruct students. The one-room schoolhouse certainly did not offer today's classroom's range of technological options available to help all learners with varying abilities succeed. Technology today offers ways to increase the cognitive, physical, behavioral, social, emotional, communicative, and perceptual skills of students with varying dis*abilities* who in the past were not able to access the curriculum, nor the same opportunities to advance. Technology is an invaluable tool to differentiate classrooms with presentations, engagements, and assessments. Online tutorials such as those offered by Khan Academy allow students to access content lessons at home to repeat previously taught concepts, move ahead with enrichment on the next lesson, complete homework, and/or access a lesson if they were not physically present during class time because they were either pulled out for related services or absent. However, never think that technology such as these tutorials or a SMART Board is smarter than student-teacher interactions! The technological possibilities for students with and without disabilities are enormous, but the digital tools offered cannot replace the interactions of human beings, nor can the technology itself be the lesson. Technology may accompany and enhance lessons, with students responding to the animations, deliveries, and access they offer, but it is the teachers and school media and computer specialists themselves who operate, choose, and decide on which systems to use, how often, and to what degree. In addition, educators need ongoing support to appropriately access and use the technology tools. Included in this chapter are technological activities and resources that teachers can implement in their lessons. Technology, when used effectively, complements good teaching strategies.

BENEFITS AND PROMISING FUTURES

The Technology-Related Assistance for Individuals with Disabilities Act of 1988 and the Individuals with Disabilities Education Act (IDEA) Amendments of 1997 are two federal laws that mandate that schools provide students with disabilities with instructional and assistive technology services. When IDEA was reauthorized in 2004, the National Instructional Materials Access Center (NIMAC), a repository connected with the National Instructional Materials Accessibility Standard (NIMAS), was set up to provide instructional materials in a timely manner to students who require them. This requires the educational textbook industry, other publishers, state educational agencies, and local educational agencies follow NIMAS's mandates to provide textbooks and other curricular materials in accessible media, free of charge, to students in elementary and secondary schools who are blind or may have print disabilities. This includes specialized formats such as Braille, audio versions, digital text, and large print.

The intent of these laws is for technology to maximize accessibility and increase relevance for children with disabilities. The Technology-Related Assistance Act (1988) defines *assistive technology device* as any item or product, whether acquired commercially, off the shelf, modified, or customized, that is used to increase, maintain, or improve the functional capabilities of individuals with disabilities. The Assistive Technology Act of 2004, Public Law 108-364, can be accessed at www.resnaprojects.org/statewide/essentialdocs/pl108-364.pdf.

The International Society for Technology in Education (ISTE) Standards offers student standards, which are applicable for students with and without disabilities. This includes skills in basic operations and concepts, with social, ethical, and cultural issues addressed to increase productivity, communication, collaboration, research, creativity, problem solving, and decision making. Consult ISTE for additional information at www.iste.org/standards.

Many technological advances have been achieved because of the personal dedication and commitment of caring individuals. Necessity is the parent of many inventions. For example, Louis Braille, who was blind, invented the raised tactile system of dots for writing and reading. His vision enabled others to see. An engineer, John W. Holter, who was also the father of a boy with hydrocephalus, invented the shunt, which is used to drain extra fluid from the brain. Alexander Graham Bell invented the telephone by accident while he was seeking to create an amplification system for those with hearing impairments, like his mother. Christopher Reeve's book, *Nothing Is Impossible: Reflections on a New Life* (2002), documented his progress as he tried to find a way for himself and others with spinal cord injuries to walk. He poignantly reiterated how the heart, mind, and spirit are not diminished by a body's limitations. Mr. Reeve didn't have the word *limitations* in his vocabulary. Technology and increased medical knowledge are also limitless.

Future technological advances offer endless possibilities for those with physical disabilities.

- The breaking of the genetic code offers hope in detecting predisposed conditions such as Alzheimer's and Down syndrome.
- Students with dyslexia, dysgraphia, and those who are blind use digitized texts, word prediction programs, and text-to-speech applications. Students without disabilities often prefer this technology as well (e.g., Kindle, audiobooks, Smartpens, and macro tools).
- Podcasts offer options for replay of lectures and better understanding of concepts in other environments (e.g., quieter setting, home review).
- PET scanning enables doctors to see inside the human body.
- Technologies such as the MRI and CAT scans have been developed that evaluate differences in our brains, making it possible to identify some emotional illnesses, such as schizophrenia, and increasing the likelihood of better treatments for such conditions.
- Scientists build smart wheelchairs, robotic limbs, and other devices that help people manipulate objects and walk again. For example, Honda is working on Robolegs to help people walk, while Japan has a battery-powered suit that can assist people with disabilities in climbing stairs. The innate universal design for learning (UDL) also helps people lift heavy loads. Toyota and Honda are in the midst of researching ways for a wheelchair to be controlled by a computerized cap that analyzes a person's brainwaves with the goal of helping people who are paralyzed walk by controlling impulses with their minds with brain machine interface (BMI).
- Screen readers help people who are blind to navigate sites online.
- Screen magnifiers assist those with visual impairments.
- Digital pens read written text.
- People who are deaf or have hearing impairments are helped with tools and technology such as computers, TTYs (teletypewriters), cochlear implants, hair cell regeneration, assistive listening devices, closed captioning, phone texting, instant messaging, webcams, and VoIP (Voice Over Internet Protocol, which changes analog phone signals into digital signals that are then transmitted over the Internet). VoIP allows for clearer communication. For more information, consult www.disabilityresources.org/AT-DEAF.html.
- Students with physical disabilities can use a desk that enables them to work alongside peers within an inclusive classroom since it has accessible features. This includes its ability to tilt at appropriate angles and portability features that allow it to be carried to multiple classroom settings. For more information, consult www.desktopdesk.com.

The following table offers both lower and higher technology for students. The school staff, families, and students need to conduct a technology analysis and use practices that enhance current ones. If current tools used are sufficient, then there is no need to replace those practices.

Lower and Higher Technology for Students

Technology for a Student With . . .	Enhancing the Now	Perhaps . . . and Learning More (determined on a student-by-student basis with ongoing technology task analysis)
ADHD	schedule taped to the desk, verbal reminders, private signals, visuals, fidget toys	PocketMod, Remind 101, Google Calendar, Waze, BreadCrumbs, Guided Access, Zoom (picture-in-picture), Dropbox, Podcasts, Diigo, MyMedSchedule, Livescribe Pens, WordQ
Auditory Processing	Listening skill activities, overhead projector, visuals, and models	Sound Note, Audio Note, PowerPoint notes, Kidspiration-Inspiration, Popplet, Pics4Learning, Posit Science-Brain Fitness, Animoto, Glogster, sound amplification systems
Autism Spectrum	social stories; behavior improvement plans (BIPs); augmentative and alternative communication (AAC); pivotal response treatment (PRT); social communication, emotional regulation, and transactional support (SCERTS); prompting; verbal behavior therapy (VBT); discrete trial training (DTT); Floortime; increased visuals; three-ring binders; manila file folders	iPads, ABAFlashcards, Avatars, AutismHelp, eBooks, Aurasma, Vis. Sched. Planner, NL Autism Concepts: Sort & Categorize, ChoiceBoard-Creator, Comic Creator, Bitsboard, Proloquo2Go, Pictello, Able AAC, Data Collecting, Video Modeling, Glogster, ConnectABILITY, Picto Selector, Picture Scheduler, Model Me Kids, video cameras, complex voice output systems, scanners
Deafness/Hearing Impairment	Ringed pictures, communication boards, American Sign Language, FM Systems, cochlear implants, total comm.	Sign Language, Pics4Learning, ClaroRead, iCommunicate, customized communication boards, MonoAudio, Video Remote Interpreters (VRI), closed captioned iMovies, Dragon Dictation, TapTap, listening devices, video phones, www.signedstories.com, VOIP
Dyscalculia	abacus, graph paper, number lines, calculators, cue cards, time/organizational management systems, manipulatives	Virtual manipulatives, NCTM Illuminations, Khan Academy, Chime, WhenInTime, SpinCalc, Wolfram Alpha, CoolMath, www.aplusmath.com, Math Playground, Grapher, talking clocks, online stopwatch, ThinkAnalogy, Sudoku, OkiDoKu, KENKEN, Hands on Equations, text-to-speech, PageOnce, Money Counter Calculator, Equals, Digits, time wheel, talking tape measures, graphing calculators

Technology for a Student With . . .	Enhancing the Now	Perhaps . . . and Learning More (determined on a student-by-student basis with ongoing technology task analysis)
Dysgraphia	pencil grips, larger pencils, lined paper, scribe, graphic organizers, writing templates, keyboarding	Livescribe, freeology.org, Google Docs, Scribblit, Quizlet, Abilipad, Trading Cards, Inspiration, StickyKeys, Dragon Dictation, Draw With Stars, Co-Writer, Abby Pal, bookbuilder.cast.og, SpeechQ, VoiceOver (double-tap Function key for microphone and dictate), AudioNote,Voice Pad, Popplet, Kidspiration, Croak.it!, iWriteRead, Livescribe-Smartpens, MacSpeech Dictate, ClaroRead, Kurzweil 3000, Texthelp Read & Write, Englishtype Junior & Englishtype Senior
Dyslexia	tape recorders, auditory and kinesthetic presentations, scribe, alternate texts, Orton-Gillingham	iBooks, StoryKit, ReadIt, Project Gutenberg, Google Docs, Speech-to-Text, Podcasts, pics4learning, Fast ForWord, Flocabulary, VisuWords, Wordle, Tagxedo, Texthelp Read & Write, WordQ, VocabAhead, WordHippo, BrowseAloud, ABCPocket Phonics, Blio, AudioNotes, Learning Ally, Phonics Genius, Shakespeare, SpeakIt!, ClaroPDF, Ginger, Phonics Genius, iWordQ, WebReader, grammar/spell check, www.naturalreaders.com, www.bookshare.org
Emotional-Social-Behavioral Difference	behavioral charts, stickers, praise, BIPs, cues, prompting, mentors	Dojo, iReward, Working4, Behavior Tracker Pro, Draw Emotions, RxmindMe, Breathe2Relax, collaborative projects, ePals, Edmodo, Animoto, Podcasts, Comic Life, iZen Garden, Tallymander, Chore Pad HD, iPrompts, Pictello, www.socialthinking.com
Executive Processing	highlighters, verbal reminders, signals, graphic organizers	AutoSummarize, Inspiration, Kidspiration, Popplet, freeology.org, Remind 101, iHomework, Dropbox, ThinkAnalogy, Glogster, Google Calendar, Notability, myHomework Student Planner, 4KidShare, The HW App, hands-on organization

(Continued)

(Continued)

Technology for a Student With . . .	Enhancing the Now	Perhaps . . . and Learning More (determined on a student-by-student basis with ongoing technology task analysis)
Intellectual Dis*ability*	visuals, alternate texts, functional curriculum, alternate academic requirements, pictures, speech and language pathologists, occupational therapists	StoriestoLearn, VB-MAPP, First Then Visual Schedule, AAC-Proloquo2Go, Talking eBooks, interactive websites, eBooks, adaptive tools, word prediction programs, Voice Over, Inspiration, News2You, GoogleCalendar, VizWhiz
Other Health Impairments	manipulatives, schedules, scaffolding as needed, related service providers, assistive technology	accessibility features activated and customized for students, adaptive tools, learningdisabilities.about.com/od/mo/g/other_health_im.htm, built-in accessibility tools, www.washington.edu/doit/
Perceptual Differences	pegboards, visual trackers, visual/auditory activities, board games	EyeCanLearn.com, pics4learning, Zoom features, PuzzleMaster, Smart Kids Software, Artdoku, Auditory Workout, Earobics, AutoSummarize
Physical Dis*ability*	fine and gross motor adaptations, OT, physical therapy, assistive technology adapted classrooms	IntelliKeys, keyboard short cuts, word prediction program, alternate oversized trackball mouse, customized adaptive software, VoiceOver, accessibility tools, virtual keyboard, Desktop Desk, slow keys, head wands, sip and puff switch
Selective Mutism	handheld or handmade communication boards, memos, written notes	Text Edit, Croak.it!, Sock Puppets (app), Poll Everywhere, Comic Life, electronic notes, e-mail, Edmodo, social networking, ePals, AudiNote, Blabberize
Specific Learning Dis*ability*	classroom library stocked with differently leveled texts, visuals	iBooks, EverNote, iCardSort, Skitch, Diigo, Idea Sketch, e-books, iMovies, Learning Ally, AutoSummarize, BrainPop, Kidspiration, Inspiration, Abilipad Review other categories for comorbidity.

(Continued)

Technology for a Student With . . .	Enhancing the Now	Perhaps . . . and Learning More (determined on a student-by-student basis with ongoing technology task analysis)
Speech/Language Communication Impairment	laminated cards/folders, SLP, key rings with vocabulary, tape recorder, written schedule	Phrase Board, Small Talk Aphasia, Proloquo2Go, Voice Output Device, Talk Assist, Speak Pad, ArtikPix, Let's Predict, Small Talk Oral Motor Exercises, iChat, Skype, GoAnimate, Comic Life, Remind 101, Sock Puppets, Boardmaker Studio
Traumatic Brain Injury	verbal-written cues, Post-its, peer mentors, frequent breaks	Google Calendar, Diigo, interactive websites, BrainHQ (Posit Science), Memory Challenge (Parrot Software), WatchKnowLearn.org
Visual Impairment and Blindness	magnification pages, enlarged worksheets, Braille, auditory cues, kinesthetic-tactile opportunities, peer mentors	Zoom, Large text, VisionSim, Google Glasses, VoiceOver features, Learning Ally, iSpeech, Braille Keyboard, large cursor, LookTel Money Reader, Color ID Free, Voice Brief, Light Detector, VMAlert (video motion detector), Awareness! The Headphone App, Alarmed-Reminders, Timers, Alarm Clock, BARD Mobile, Firefly, VoiceReader

Available for download at **www.corwin.com/inclusionstrategies**

CLASSROOM AND COMMUNITY IMPLICATIONS AND RESOURCES

Technology can be as simple as using larger writing implements and pencil grips or taping paper to a desk to help those with fine motor difficulties. It might mean one child uses an eyedropper, while another uses a turkey baster. Technology augments the curriculum in a range of topics from the Brothers Grimm to Malcolm X. Students can be involved in an Iditarod virtual field trip (see www.field-guides.com/trips.htm) or even watch the virtual dissection of a frog (see froggy.lbl.gov/virtual). E-books with digital texts, e-mail, instant messaging, voice-operated computers, video conferencing, and multimedia presentations are all examples of how technology enhances communications and learning. Technology can help students with disabilities increase their mobility and independence despite learning, sensory, communication, or physical issues.

Students can gain academic information through both commercial and homemade products to achieve greater independence in schools and the community. Teachers can use technology to motivate and instruct students while increasing their own classroom productivity. Most important, teachers in inclusive classrooms can use technology to augment the curriculum, guiding and monitoring student usage for effective instructional gains. Written work improves as students gain more information and understanding of topics under the teacher's guidance.

> Everyone benefits when technological advances help those with disabilities become active participants in society. The level of disability acceptance a person with a disability has affects whether he or she might embrace or reject many of the technological changes, but just the mere existence of the technology offers increasing possibilities for the future.

SAMPLE HIGH SCHOOL IN-CLASS LESSON—COMBINING LITERATURE AND TECHNOLOGY

Requirements for Literature Assignment: Read one of the four books, then complete the assignment as follows:

1. Conduct research using the websites provided to detail information about the characters (at least three), setting, plot, resolution, themes, concepts, and symbolism. Web sources and paraphrased notes will be submitted with the final project.

   Reminder to students: Correctly cite all sources.

   Review these sites for advice about plagiarism and other writing essentials.

   Purdue University Online Writing Lab: owl.english.purdue.edu/owl/resource/677/01/

   EasyBib: www.easybib.com

2. Then, write an eight-paragraph essay as detailed below:

   Para. 1 Introduction—Reason you chose this book, brief overview of what will follow

   Para. 2 Analysis of characters—Tell about character traits, actions, and thoughts

   Para. 3 Setting—Where and when the story takes place

   Para. 4 Synopsis of plot, sequence of events

   Para. 5 Climax and ending, how story was resolved

   Para. 6 Themes/concepts/symbolism presented in book

   Para. 7 Compare book with online research about characters, settings, themes, authors

   Para. 8 Conclusion—State your opinion and overall impression of book and what further insights you gained from research.

(Continued)

(Continued)

	Book Choices			
	***To Kill a Mockingbird*, by Harper Lee**	***The Crucible*, by Arthur Miller**	***Of Mice and Men*, by John Steinbeck**	***The Catcher in the Rye*, by J. D. Salinger**
Characters	Scout, Jem, Dill, Tom Robinson, Atticus Finch, Arthur (Boo) Radley	Reverend Parris, Abigail Williams, Tituba, Betty Parris, Reverend Hale, John Proctor, Elizabeth, Sarah Good, Mrs. Putnam	George Milton, Lennie Small, Curly, Slim, Lulu, Candy, migrant workers	Holden Caulfield, Phoebe, Stradlater, Ackley, Sally Hayes, Mr. Antolini
Setting	Alabama, Great Depression, 1930s	Salem, Massachusetts, 17th century	California ranch, Salinas Valley, 1930s	New York City, Central Park, Penn Station, Rockefeller Center, 1950s
Plot/ Resolution	Lawyer's conflicts with court, community, and family while defending a falsely accused black man in the poor South	Paranoia about witchcraft in Puritan society	Relationship between a man and his friend as he tries to help him with his cognitive disabilities	Monologue told by 16-year-old boy, Holden Caulfield, who left a private school and went through some difficult times
Themes/ Concepts/ Symbolism	Race relations in the South Criminal justice Prejudice	Adversity Justice Compare to 20th-century Second Red Scare (communism), McCarthy era	Migrant workers Friendship Innocence Cognitive/physical disabilities	Childhood vs. adulthood Teenage depression
Sites for Research	www.novelguide.com/tokillamockingbird www.adl.org www.litcharts.com/lit/to-kill-a-mockingbird/themes www.tolerance.org	www.novelguide.com/thecrucible www.gradesaver.com/the-crucible/study-guide/ www.brighthubeducation.com/homework-help-literature/52748-mccarthyism-and-the-crucible/	www.novelguide.com/ofmiceandmen www.thearc.org aaidd.org www.gradesaver.com/of-mice-and-men/study-guide/	www.novelguide.com/thecatcherintherye www.nmha.org

Available for download at **www.corwin.com/inclusionstrategies**

USING COMPUTERS AS REFERENCE TOOLS

Disability Curriculum Web Search: Answer these questions by using the sites below.

Focus Questions	Websites
1. What is the DSM-5 definition of autism spectrum disorder? 2. What are the best strategies families and teachers can use to help students with autism spectrum disorder?	www.autism-society.org www.autismspeaks.org/dsm-5/faq www.autismspeaks.org teenautism.com
3. What types of modifications can be made in a classroom for children with hearing loss? 4. How do cochlear implants work?	listeningandspokenlanguage.org www.nidcd.nih.gov/health/hearing/coch.asp www.hearingloss.org
5. Name some areas that can be affected by a learning disability. 6. Identify some strategies that help children with auditory processing difficulties.	www.ldinfo.com www.ncld.org ldaamerica.org www.ldonline.org
7. What are the most common types of anxiety disorders in children?	www.mentalhealthamerica.net/go/get-info www.nimh.nih.gov/health/topics/index.shtml
8. Name some multimodal treatments for students with ADHD.	www.chadd.org www.webmd.com/add-adhd/childhood-adhd/multimodal-treatment-for-adhd
9. What are the educational/employment implications for a child with Down syndrome?	www.ndss.org www.ndsccenter.org www.downsyndrome.com gigisplayhouse.org
10. Name some sensitivities that need to be exhibited toward children with Tourette syndrome.	www.tsa-usa.org www.tourettesyndrome.net
11. Why is self-determination an important outcome for people with intellectual disabilities?	www.thearc.org aaidd.org
12. What are some sports programs available to people with cerebral palsy?	ucp.org/resources/health-and-wellness/wellness/physical-activity/ www.pecentral.org/adapted/adaptedmenu.html

Directions: Now choose a topic and design your own curriculum Web search. A good way to design one is to first find appropriate sites and then work backward and write questions.

These sites offer excellent ones for students and educators to either access or create WebQuests across the curriculum.

Zunal WebQuest Maker: zunal.com

QuestGarden: questgarden.com

COMPUTER CERTIFICATES

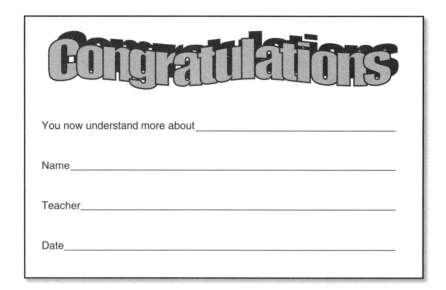

Congratulations

You now understand more about ________________________

Name ________________________

Teacher ________________________

Date ________________________

Teachers can create certificates of praise on the computer as recognition for students' achievements. Simple phrases such as these validate learning strides and offer specific feedback:

Appropriate usage of math tools to solve problems!

Excellent reading work when you cited text-based evidence!

Able to work well with peers in the cooperative writing project!

Perfect science project, since you analyzed your results!

Once students collect a certain number of these certificates, they can trade them in for an agreed-upon reward, such as lunch with the teacher, extra computer time, no-homework pass, teaching a lesson . . . or maybe just the attention itself is tangible enough!

WORD PROCESSING PROGRAMS AND COMPUTER TOOLS

Directions: Type the following paragraph on a word processing program, and then use the language tools of the thesaurus and spell check to revise your writing. The words with (sp) are *spelled incorrectly*, while the underlined words need to be replaced with a different or more exact word, *using the thesaurus* or your own replacement words to expand the thoughts. Check the Tools menu for other spelling and word options. Next, add another paragraph to this story, with specific details about your future plans. Afterward, use the language tools to revise that paragraph as well. After your story is completed, find and insert an appropriate graphic that tells about your future.

Skool (sp) is a good place for good students. Classrooms give many things that will help you in lif (sp). Practis (sp) good habuts (sp) now and you will benafit (sp) when you leave skool (sp) and pick a fewchure (sp). Prepair (sp) for laytor (sp).

Available for download at **www.corwin.com/inclusionstrategies**

EDUCATIONAL IDEAS, WEBSITES, AND RESOURCES

Microsoft has downloads and many templates for teachers at www.microsoft.com/education.

If students have dysgraphia, then Keyboarding Without Tears may help. Visit www.hwtears.com/kwt. Dance Mat Typing (primarygamesarena.com/Dance-Mat-Typing2012) along with Englishtype Junior & Englishtype Senior at (www.englishtype.com) offer options as well.

Students can create graphic novels with software (e.g., Comic Life by Plasq).

This Quick Response (QR) Code of my website was created online at www.qrstuff.com.

A QR generator stores URLs, text, and other information, which is then scanned and read by devices such as a tablet with a camera or a SmartPhone with apps such as QR Reader or QuickScan. Staff can offer students differentiated activities with QR codes that link to research on websites, kinesthetic QR math problem solving stations, or text. QR codes can be placed in books to activate prior knowledge or as enrichment. For example, I attached a QR code in the inner flap of *Black Beauty* that connected readers to facts about horses, while I placed QR codes inside the flap of *Bud, Not Buddy* to allow the readers to see a YouTube video about jazz and a link that offered a time line of the events that led to the Great Depression. QR code possibilities are endless, since learners are asked to perform tasks that are connected to the CCSS with everyday technology tools. Scan this QR code to cooperatively investigate ideas with a colleague.

Alliance for Technology Access: www.ataccess.org

Assistive Technology Industry Association: www.ATIA.org

Center for Applied Technology (CAST, offers excellent UDL options): www.cast.org

Deaf Blind Education: deafblindinfo.org

Educator's Reference Desk: www.eduref.org

Family Center on Technology and Disability: www.fctd.info

Internet4Classrooms: www.internet4classrooms.com

IntelliTools: www.intellitools.com

International Society for Technology in Education (ISTE) Standards: www.iste.org/standards

National Early Childhood Technical Assistance Center: www.nectac.org

National Center on Accessible Instructional Materials: aim.cast.org/learn

Quality Indicators for Assistive Technology: indicators.knowbility.org/indicators.html

Working Together: People With Disabilities and Computer Technology: www.washington.edu/doit/Video/wt_dis.html

U.S. Department of Education: www.ed.gov

Web AIM: Web Accessibility in Mind: webaim.org/articles/motor/assistive

SITES TO INVESTIGATE FOR STUDENTS AND STAFF ACROSS THE CURRICULUM

Literacy Skills

Audio Books-Learning Ally: www.learningally.org

CAST UDL Book Builder: bookbuilder.cast.org

Comic Life: comiclife.com

Creative Writing Prompts: www.creativewritingprompts.com

EdHelper Cloze Activities: www.edhelper.com/cloze.htm

Flocabulary: www.flocabulary.com

Grammar Bytes: www.chompchomp.com/menu.htm

Internet Field Trip: Essential Children's Literature Sites: www.scholastic.com/teachers/article/internet-field-trip-essential-childrenx2019s-literature-sites

National Council of Teachers of English: www.ncte.org

Online Graphic Dictionary: www.visuwords.com

Online Visual Dictionary: www.snappywords.com

PBS Reading Games: pbskids.org/games/reading.html

Poetry 180: www.loc.gov/poetry/180/

Popplet: popplet.com

Protocols for Accommodations in Reading: donjohnston.com/par

Purdue Online Writing Lab-OWL: owl.english.purdue.edu

Read, Write, Think: Comic Creator: www.readwritethink.org/classroom-resources/student-interactives/comic-creator-30021.html

SAT Vocabulary: VocabAhead.com

Story Starter for Kids: www.thestorystarter.com/jr.htm

Trading Cards: www.readwritethink.org/files/resources/interactives/trading_cards_2/

Visual Processing Skills: www.eyecanlearn.com

Vocabulary: www.vocabulary.com

Word Hippo: www.wordhippo.com

Science

Chemistry for Kids: www.chem4kids.com

Environmental Games: www.makeuseof.com/tag/10-environmental-games-teach-kids-earth-ecology-conservation/

How Stuff Works: science.howstuffworks.com

Interactive Labs: www.learner.org/courses/envsci/interactives/index.php

Interactive Science Simulations: phet.colorado.edu

Khan Academy: Biology: www.khanacademy.org/science/biology

Next Generation Science Standards: www.nextgenscience.org/next-generation-science-standards

Nitrogen Cycle: www.classzone.com/books/ml_science_share/vis_sim/em05_pg20_nitrogen/em05_pg20_nitrogen.html

Science Kids: www.sciencekids.co.nz

Science News for Kids: www.sciencenewsforkids.org

The Science Spot: sciencespot.net/Pages/kdztech.html

Zula: www.zula.com

Math

AplusMath (worksheets, games, flashcards): www.aplusmath.com

Bridging Art & Math: bridgesmathart.org

Cool Math: www.coolmath.com

Khan Academy: www.khanacademy.org/math

Math Forum (Drexel University): www.mathforum.org

Math Manipulatives: www.mathplayground.com/math_manipulatives.html

Math Practice (PreK–12): www.ixl.com/

Math Visual Dictionary: www.mathsisfun.com/definitions/index.html

National Council of Teachers of Mathematics: www.nctm.org

National Library of Virtual Manipulatives: nlvm.usu.edu/en/nav/vlibrary.html

NCTM: illuminations.nctm.org

Purplemath: www.purplemath.com

WolframAlpha: www.wolframalpha.com/examples/Math.html

Social Studies

300 Social Studies Games & Websites for Kids: www.learningreviews.com/Social-Studies-Websites-Games-for-Kids-Online.html

Facing History: www.facinghistory.org

Independence Hall Association in Philadelphia: www.ushistory.org

National Geographic for Kids: kids.nationalgeographic.com/kids

News-2-You: www.n2y.com/products/news2you/

Presidential Campaign Commercials (1952–2012): www.livingroomcandidate.org

Social Studies for Kids: www.socialstudiesforkids.com

Teaching Tolerance: www.tolerance.org

Technology in Inclusive Social Studies Classroom: www.youtube.com/watch?v=L3yes7RsvwQ

We the Jury: www.icivics.org

Videos, Multimedia Art, and Music

Animated Videos: goanimate.com

Artpad Digital Canvas: artpad.art.com/artpad/painter/

Brain Pop: www.brainpop.com, www.brainpopesl.com, www.brainpopjr.com

Dance Mat Typing: primarygamesarena.com/Dance-Mat-Typing2012

Drawing in One Point Perspective: www.olejarz.com/arted/perspective

Flocabulary—The Week in Rap: www.flocabulary.com/topics/week-in-rap

Glogster (Multimedia—text, images, music, video): edu.glogster.com

Inspiration: www.inspiration.com, www.inspiration.com/Kidspiration

National Association for Music Education: www.nafme.org

National Visual Arts Standards: www.arteducators.org/research/national-standards

Pics4Learning: www.pics4learning.com

Prezi: prezi.com/learn

Show Me: www.showme.com

Songs for Teaching: www.songsforteaching.com

Tagxedo: www.tagxedo.com

Toondoo: www.toondoo.com

Virtual Field Trips for Kids: www.meetmeatthecorner.org

Virtual Museums: http://www.museumlink.com/virtual.htm

Watch Know Learn: watchknowlearn.org

Wordle: www.wordle.net

The following link offers Pinterest inclusion resources:

www.pinterest.com/tkarten

12

Reflecting as Classroom Practice

Without reflection, teaching is an impossible and stagnant endeavor. When teachers look back on their lessons, as educators they take many steps forward to assist their students and themselves to grow as learners. Quite often, more is learned from the lesson that did *not* go so well to ensure that the next go-around will be better. Teaching itself is forever changing with new research stepping forward. Although students themselves are perpetual variables, they must be seen as individual learners. Students with dis*abilities* are just that—individual students. Educators need to reflect on the ways that these students are included with appropriate strategies. Included in this chapter are ways that the students must also be reflective partners in their education to become self-regulated learners. The purpose of this chapter is to connect the learning by revisiting major points from prior chapters. Many activities, templates, resources, strategies, and reflections about students with special needs have been discussed. But what do they mean to teachers in inclusive settings? This chapter serves as a textual conclusion to all that has been presented and a jumping-off point for all that will follow.

REVIEWING AND MAINTAINING SKILLS

How Much Do Students Remember?

Education requires the implementation of a maintenance plan to guarantee that learning actually occurred, not just that isolated facts were memorized or regurgitated. Teachers teach and then move on to the next topic. *Oops!* Many students forget those wonderfully designed but unmemorable lessons. Most educators can testify that what they thought they taught was only temporary learning. The learning needs to be extended to lifelong experiences with skills that prepare students for college and careers.

Some Questions to Ponder

- What about including the prior topic in the next one that is taught, or using project-based learning that allows students to demonstrate many related skills across interdisciplinary and thematic lessons?
- What about proactively including the outcomes as you design the objectives using an understanding by design (UbD) approach that expects accountability and outlines just what will be assessed from the lesson's outset?
- Can teachers check to see if students apply and generalize learning to a different situation or problem?
- Why does learning require periodic checkups?
- Can the CCSS encourage teachers to narrow down topics, picking and choosing those that let students build on and connect prior knowledge with new content?
- Can there be such a thing as learning weigh-ins?
- When is it appropriate to revisit information?
- Are basic skills being sacrificed in this age of knowledge explosion?
- How can we periodically weigh learning gains?

Even if learning is taught with a step-by-step method, establishing prior knowledge on a level that does not frustrate students, some students still do not retain information. Repetition means, "Say it again!" It is important that all learning be *overlearned.* Teachers too often make remarks such as, "I know I taught this," while students frequently retort, "The teacher never said it." Who's right? For the sake of diplomacy, the jury is permanently out. Review is essential!

■ PRETEACH, TEACH, RETEACH

VENI, VIDI, VICI—TEACHER PLANNER

Yesterday I taught

Today I'll review

Today I'll introduce

Homework practice:

Tomorrow I'll remind them

Next week I'll refresh memories about

Next month's learning will review

Future plans include

SELF-ASSESSMENT FORM

Directions: Answer the following two questions to reflect on your learning.

1. Before I learned about ______________________, I thought ______________________.
2. Now, I know ____

____.

Available for download at **www.corwin.com/inclusionstrategies**

REVIEWING WORK*

"Play it again, Sam," is a famous line; no need to repeat what it means!

Directions: List five points about any two special education, dis*ability,* or inclusion topics previously reviewed.

Topic:	**Topic:**
1.	1.
2.	2.
3.	3.
4.	4.
5.	5.

*Review the "TBC (To Be Continued)" column on page 86, filling in answers to the original questions that you now know more about.

Available for download at **www.corwin.com/inclusionstrategies**

SHAPELY REVIEW FOR CLASSROOM STUDY

Directions: This template is used as a classroom review. Each column represents a different topic with accompanying questions. Students are divided into teams and earn points for correctly answered questions on *shapely* topics. As an alternative, cooperative classroom groups can think of their own topics and questions on any curriculum area, making their own game. The next page has questions about inclusion and disabilities. Disability tables and text can be reviewed for answers. Create your own curriculum-related games at www.superteachertools.net/jeopardyx.

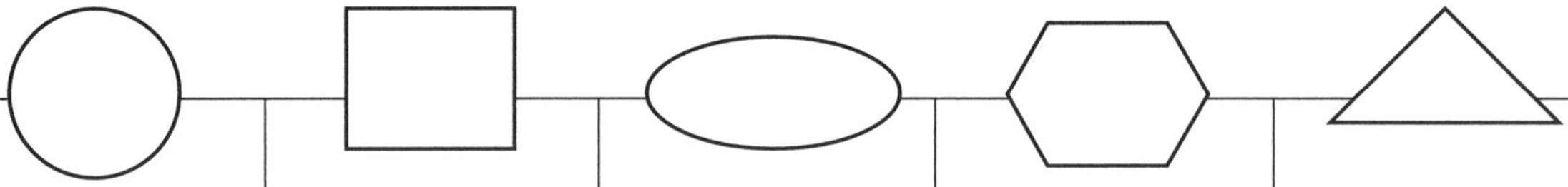

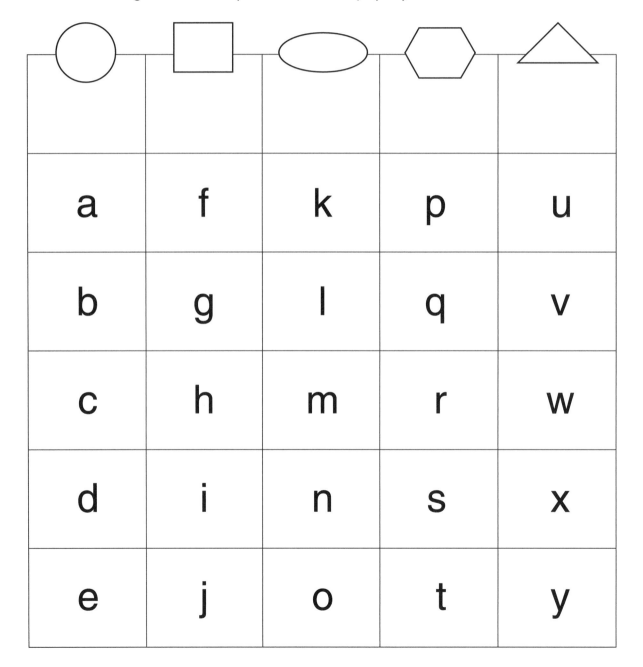

a	f	k	p	u
b	g	l	q	v
c	h	m	r	w
d	i	n	s	x
e	j	o	t	y

HOW MUCH DO YOU REMEMBER?

Questions

Directions: Try to answer as many questions as possible, and then check the answers to see how much learning has occurred. Work cooperatively, collectively, in game format, or solo.

Name the Strategy

a. Name for moving, feeling, or manipulating learning

b. Main tools you use to learn about the environment

c. Strategy that asks students to close their eyes and think about learning concepts

d. Term for visually separating information into boxes

e. These can be used to personalize learning

The Three Rs

f. Vowel patterns, syllabication, context clues, structural analysis, dictionary

g. Reading comprehension technique that deletes key words, asking students to fill in the appropriate words

h. Words the acronym "Ed's Car" stands for

i. Name of a program that makes students more aware of how to pronounce words they read

j. Mathematical term for a way to help students understand if computational answers make sense

Syndromes and Disorders

k. Characterized by varying degrees of difficulty with social interaction, verbal and nonverbal communication, along with repetitive patterns of behavior

l. Neurological disorder that can include involuntary tics and vocalizations

m. Congenital defect with failure of the spine to completely close, resulting in possible muscle weaknesses or paralysis

n. Acquired and developmental injury to the brain caused by an external force

o. Symptoms of this may be similar to ADHD, but it is not the result of a hearing loss

(Continued)

(Continued)

⬡ Disability Trivia

p. College where the huddle was invented

q. *Top Gun* actor who is an advocate, helping others develop literacy skills after his own struggle with dyslexia

r. Created by accident while trying to develop an amplification device for people who have a hearing impairment

s. Poverty rate for people ages twenty-five to sixty-four with a severe disability

t. Early 1900s baseball team that was the first to use hand signals

△ Legislative Issues

u. The 2001 revised version of 1965 Elementary and Secondary Education Act

v. Civil rights law from 1973 that stops discrimination against people with disabilities in public and private programs or activities that receive financial assistance

w. The 1990 civil rights law that guarantees rights for people with disabilities in public accommodations, employment, transportation, and telecommunications

x. The disability categories protected under IDEA

y. Abbreviation for written plan for a child who is eligible for special education services

HOW DID YOU DO?

Answer Key for *Shapely* Review

Name the Strategy—Answers

a. Kinesthetic learning

b. Modalities or senses

c. Visualization or imagining

d. Compartmentalization

e. Interest inventories

The Three Rs—Answers

f. These are ways to help students identify unfamiliar words

g. The cloze technique

h. Expand, delete, substitute, combine, and rearrange

i. Readacognition

j. Estimation

Syndromes and Disorders—Answers

k. Autism Spectrum Disorder (ASD)

l. Tourette syndrome

m. Spina bifida

n. Traumatic brain injury

o. Auditory processing difficulties, or CAPD

Disability Trivia—Answers

p. Gallaudet University in Washington, DC. Football plays, which were being signed, could be hidden from the opposing team.

q. Tom Cruise

(Continued)

(Continued)

r. The telephone. Discovery was made by Alexander Graham Bell.

s. 26 percent (Source: www.disabledinaction.org/census_stats_print.html)

t. The New York Giants. There was a pitcher named Luther H. Taylor who was deaf and unable to communicate with his teammates. The manager of the Giants, John McGraw, required the entire Giants team to learn American Sign Language. William Ellsworth Hoy, who was also deaf, used hand signals when he played for the Cincinnati Reds. That's the origin of baseball hand signals today.

Legislative Issues—Answers

u. No Child Left Behind

v. Section 504 of the Vocational and Rehabilitation Act

w. ADA, the Americans with Disabilities Act

x. Autism, visual impairment, deafness, speech/language, deafness/blindness, intellectual disability, multiple disabilities, other health impaired, traumatic brain injury, specific learning disability, hearing impaired, emotional disturbance, orthopedic impairment

y. An IEP, individualized education program, or "It's Educationally Prudent!"

Available for download at **www.corwin.com/inclusionstrategies**

ROUNDTABLE DISCUSSION

Directions: This activity uses a cooperative learning strategy—the roundtable. It allows for the simultaneous sharing of knowledge or opinions on varying topics and content areas by using prompts. The group gets together and divides the given prompts. Each person writes the letter of a different prompt from the list below at the top of his or her own paper. The student writes a brief response, and then the student exchanges papers with someone and writes comments on another prompt. The papers are passed around the table. Written comments on the prompts can then be collected for review or orally shared in class discussion.

Sample Roundtable Prompts

a. Children can benefit from inclusion.

b. Children with disabilities have difficulties with assignments.

c. Attitudes about disabilities vary.

d. Parental/family involvement can help.

e. Teachers need more support.

Available for download at **www.corwin.com/inclusionstrategies**

REVIEWING CONCEPTS WITH A WORD SEARCH

Directions: Use clues below to fill in missing words in sentences. Then locate the words in the word search. Students and teachers can design their own word searches and cloze exercises on a variety of topics, using the computer or even graph paper. It's a great way to study spelling words or review any subject!

S	Y	S	J	C	K	X	K	H	R	H	K	F	W	I	G	C	J	Q	Q	W	F	X	T	E
Q	E	W	P	Q	J	N	G	E	W	C	I	D	B	U	N	R	P	I	D	L	D	O	F	B
B	T	C	Y	J	C	Y	P	Z	T	P	N	Y	O	I	I	D	R	I	G	H	T	H	S	W
X	F	I	N	J	U	E	R	T	W	B	E	U	S	D	N	Z	I	D	R	Q	S	N	D	O
F	G	I	C	E	T	P	L	Y	W	L	S	R	I	V	R	N	W	V	R	E	U	O	S	Q
Q	N	A	F	I	G	B	Y	E	W	A	T	Q	J	Q	A	B	V	L	I	Y	R	G	E	G
J	D	Y	T	F	Q	I	A	Q	I	Z	H	I	Y	B	E	V	R	M	Y	D	B	M	I	Y
E	O	I	H	Y	H	I	L	Y	J	B	E	W	A	H	L	C	T	R	X	L	U	R	T	G
T	O	A	R	H	Y	W	G	L	N	N	T	N	H	T	E	E	A	W	Q	O	D	A	I	W
N	B	G	R	Q	W	X	Q	M	E	M	I	U	D	T	V	N	P	B	V	I	Z	P	L	E
S	T	S	E	R	E	T	N	I	U	T	C	O	E	W	I	R	J	V	X	V	F	M	I	S
N	K	H	X	O	U	E	T	Z	T	W	N	C	U	L	T	C	O	W	B	M	A	Z	B	I
E	U	H	Z	R	E	B	J	W	V	O	Q	I	P	B	A	M	A	E	X	V	T	E	A	Q
R	L	M	O	N	A	P	Z	F	H	B	B	I	E	V	R	F	B	B	B	G	F	Z	J	C
P	I	Z	K	E	F	A	T	D	L	Q	C	G	R	L	E	X	D	J	U	O	L	X	G	B
K	Q	D	H	J	E	L	E	C	H	S	S	J	P	U	P	F	W	I	D	W	F	W	J	A
N	R	W	Z	K	D	V	L	H	I	N	R	Z	I	B	O	I	K	T	C	T	Q	R	S	V
R	U	Z	P	E	I	A	I	D	C	G	R	H	L	U	O	L	T	U	H	F	M	D	M	H
L	U	B	H	Q	I	V	R	T	J	K	P	J	P	H	C	I	J	L	N	C	L	P	I	N
Y	Y	W	F	C	Y	E	Y	F	I	L	S	M	F	Y	D	W	M	B	U	C	B	R	G	N
G	X	M	E	I	T	N	J	K	S	S	Z	L	I	X	W	S	Q	T	I	M	Q	K	B	W
B	J	P	R	N	O	H	A	I	I	E	O	Y	D	K	R	O	Z	Z	P	X	S	M	J	Z
Q	S	Q	I	K	V	O	Z	M	K	P	U	P	M	K	T	X	I	K	K	E	E	H	B	V
V	T	M	H	P	K	B	F	A	C	O	L	L	A	B	O	R	A	T	I	O	N	J	S	I
N	Z	Y	R	Q	N	V	X	T	B	Z	O	N	O	D	C	A	Y	P	G	J	X	Y	T	P

ABILITIES
COLLABORATION
COOPERATIVE LEARNING
INDIVIDUALS
INTERDISCIPLINARY
INTERESTS
KINESTHETIC
MULTIPLE INTELLIGENCES
POSITIVE
REPETITION
RIGHT
SPECIAL

1. _____ education for all
2. _____ with Dis*abilities* Education Act
3. Essential ingredient for the retention of all learning matter
4. Noncompetitive teaching strategy
5. Type of reinforcement
6. "Touching" learning
7. More than one way of being smart
8. What a student likes
9. Two teachers working together
10. _____ angles of learning
11. Involving all subject areas when teaching
12. What people *can* do

■ SUMMING UP THE LEARNING

Simulations vs. Actualities

When students have problems with brain confusion, things do not make sense. In the activity below, the right part of the brain tries to say the shape, but the left brain wants to read the word. Remember that these are simulated problems, but some students face these types of difficulties on a daily basis. They do not always see things as they appear to others. Students with disabilities must solve problems that they did not create, whether social, cognitive, academic, or physical. Quite often, we do not pick our battles, nor do we always face the same choices in school. The *ins* and *outs* of life's daily occurrences can be filled with surprises and distortions.

What Do You See?

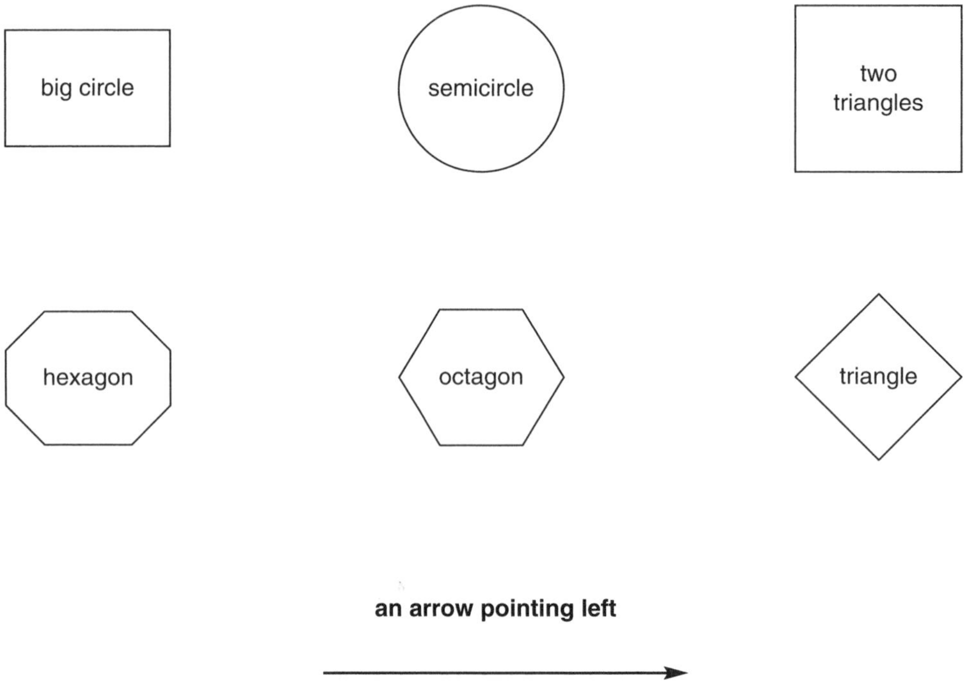

COMBINING ELEMENTS ■

Closure/Periodic Table

The periodic table reminds us that students of all ages have different abilities in varying combinations. These include special strengths and intelligences. The elements of a periodic table are properly combined to create uniqueness, differences, and similarities with proportional bonding. For example, sodium and chlorine separately are both poisonous, yet people can safely place a combination of the two on their food (NaCl = table salt). Children can also be combined in *tasteful* ways. Given proper opportunities and interventions, today's classmates will be tomorrow's productive members of the community and the world.

Inclusion has its own set of formulas that work!

Periodic Table of the Elements

	IA	IIA	IIIB	IVB	VB	VIB	VIIB	—— VIII		——	IB	IIB	IIIA	IVA	VA	VIA	VIIA	0
1	1 H																	2 He
2	3 Li	4 Be											5 B	6 C	7 N	8 O	9 F	10 Ne
3	11 Na	12 Mg											13 Al	14 Si	15 P	16 S	17 Cl	18 Ar
4	19 K	20 Ca	21 Sc	22 Ti	23 V	24 Cr	25 Mn	26 Fn	27 Co	28 Ni	29 Cu	30 Zn	31 Ga	32 Ge	33 As	34 Se	35 Br	36 Kr
5	37 Rb	38 Sr	39 Y	40 Zr	41 Nb	42 Mo	43 Tc	44 Ru	45 Rh	46 Pd	47 Ag	48 Cd	49 In	50 Sn	51 Sb	52 Te	53 I	54 Xe
6	55 Cs	56 Ba	57 +La	72 Hr	73 Ta	74 W	75 Re	76 Os	77 Ir	78 Pt	79 Au	80 Hg	81 Tl	82 Pb	83 Bi	84 Po	85 At	86 Rn
7	87 Fr	88 Ra	89 +Ac	104 Rf	105 Ha	106 Sg	107 Ns	108 Hs	109 Mt	110 110	111 111	112 112	113 113					

*Lanthanide Series	58 Ce	59 Pr	60 Nd	61 Pm	62 Sm	63 Eu	64 Gd	65 Tb	66 Dy	67 Ho	68 Er	69 Tm	70 Yb	71 Lu
+Actinide Series	90 Th	91 Pa	92 U	93 Np	94 Pu	95 Am	96 Cm	97 Bk	98 Cf	99 Es	100 Fm	101 Md	102 No	103 Lr

SOURCE: © 2014 by Los Alamos National Laboratory. Periodic table of elements: A resource for elementary, middle school, and high school students. Retrieved from http://periodic.lanl.gov/index.shtml

INCLUSIVE INGREDIENTS

Planning
Establishing Prior Knowledge
Learning About Abilities
Understanding Home Components
Awareness of Cultural Factors
Constructive Student Empowerment
Structured Classrooms
Repetition
Sensory Elements
Concrete Learning
Appropriate Accommodations and Modifications
Same Content but Less Complex
Size
Amount
Student-Friendly Format
Authentic Assessments
UbD, Understanding by Design
UDL, Universal Design for Learning
Working With Parents, Guardians, and Families
Measuring Learning Ingredients
Cooperative Learning
Multiple Intelligences
Creating Self-Regulated Learners
Increasing Self-Awareness
Emphasizing the Three Rs
Using Technology
Interdisciplinary Approach
Step-by-Step Learning
Repetition
Positive Attitude!
Inclusive Environments

____

____

____

Bottom Line: Successful Outcomes!

____

Resource A

Disability Tables

The dis*ability* tables list possible causes of certain common disabilities/ syndromes/disorders, characteristics of people who have these syndromes, educational strategies to use with students, and resources. As with all groups, please note that disabilities are heterogeneous and that each of these tables describes a syndrome, not a specific child. In addition, some characteristics and strategies may be shared and overlap with others, with comorbidity existing. The purpose of the information in the tables is to broaden knowledge, and it does not make anyone informed enough to diagnose. Remember that clinicians make diagnoses. Diagnoses and labels are serious things! Information for the tables in Resource A was obtained from field experts, the individual disability organizations listed, professional conferences, journals, the Center for Parent Information and Resources, and diagnostic criteria from the fifth edition of the *Diagnostic and Statistical Manual of Mental Disorders* (DSM-5) of the American Psychiatric Association. DSM-5 has changes from the prior version (DSM-IV) that replace a multiaxial system of disorders with relatedness of disorders aligned with practices by the World Health Organization's (WHO) International Classification of Disease (ICD-11). As examples, DSM-5 folded the diagnosis of Asperger syndrome into autism spectrum disorder (ASD) and added a childhood disorder known as disruptive mood dysregulation disorder (DMDD) to account for too many children being diagnosed as bipolar who are prescribed medications. Like the Individuals With Disabilities Education Act (IDEA), DSM-5 changed the term mental retardation to intellectual disability. DSM-5 uses a dimensional system, with many diagnoses given a level of functioning (LOF) rating of mild, moderate, and severe (e.g., types of anxiety or depression). Additional differences from the prior edition can be reviewed in the DSM-5. Disorder sections include neurodevelopmental, psychotic, bipolar and related, depressive, anxiety, obsessive-compulsive disorder (OCD) and related, trauma and stressor-related, dissociative, somatic symptom and related, feeding and eating, elimination, sleep-wake, gender dysphoria, disruptive, impulse control and conduct, substance-related and addiction, neurocognitive, personality, and paraphilic. The following tables list information, resources, strategies, and more knowledge about specific dis*abilities.*

FEEDING AND EATING DISORDERS

Anorexia Nervosa

Severely restricting food intake even if a person's body weight is way below normal

Causes

- Low self-confidence
- Feeling of inadequacy
- Possible genetic and environmental influences
- Hormone imbalances or incorrect neurotransmitter levels
- Fear of gaining weight

Possible Characteristics

- Usually appears in early to mid-adolescence
- Restriction of food intake to the extreme, such that the person fears any weight gain and has a constant obsession with thinness
- Mild, moderate, severe, or extreme—coded by body mass index (BMI) ranges
- May even use excessive exercise, diuretics, and laxatives to prevent any weight gain
- Muscle loss and weaknesses
- Unrealistic body image
- Can fatally affect other body systems

Bulimia Nervosa

Disorder in which the person purges food consumed in order to not gain any weight

Causes

- May be unable to deal with emotional situations and uses food as a vehicle for control
- Genetic and environmental influences

Possible Characteristics

- A person with bulimia can eat large quantities of food within a short time frame and will then purge
- May use exercise, laxatives, diuretics, or extreme diets to vigorously control weight
- Mild, moderate, severe, or extreme—coded by purging/compensatory episodes each week
- Purging is usually done secretively
- Calluses on hands and fingers from sticking fingers down their throat
- Fixation on body weight
- May be depressed but not necessarily
- Can also have fatal results

Binge Eating

Bulimia without purging/compensation

Eating more than usual for a time period with a feeling of not being able to stop or control the amount of food intake, leading to excessive food consumption

Avoidant/Restrictive Food Intake

Those who exhibit some symptoms of anorexia but do not meet all criteria (e.g., low weight, distorted body image)

- Lack of interest in eating or food
- Nutritional deficiency
- Excludes anorexia/bulimia

Compulsive Overeating

Causes

- Poor body image
- General feelings of unhappiness
- Environmental/genetic influences
- May have conflicting and unsettling emotions in response to stress, using food as a panacea to pacify those negative feelings, rather than eating from hunger

Possible Characteristics

- Will usually be a *closet eater*
- Binge eating is sometimes followed by guilt and depression for dietary overindulgences
- Health complications may fatally spiral

Obesity among children today is of overriding concern. Children need to be encouraged to exercise more and learn about proper nutrition.

Pica

Ingestion of nonnutritive substances over a period of at least one month that is severe enough for clinical attention and developmentally inappropriate

May present comorbidity with ASD and intellectual disability

Rumination Disorder

Repeated regurgitation of food that may be rechewed, reswallowed, or spit out

Contacts/Resources

Bulimia: www.bulimia.com

Kirberger, K. (2003). *No body's perfect.* New York: Scholastic.

National Association of Anorexia Nervosa and Associated Disorders (ANAD): www.anad.org

National Eating Disorder Association (NEDA): www.nationaleatingdisorders.org

> If left untreated, eating disorders may be fatal.
>
> Treatments must involve proactive coordination among school, home, and the community while valuing opportunities for individual growth with realistic plans that include positive body image, diet, and proper amount of exercise. Replace fast foods and sedentary activities with better diets and more movement.
>
> Private or group counseling sessions, including counseling from a nutritionist for balanced, healthy diets, can help students deal with the underlying reasons for eating disorders. School psychologists and guidance counselors can establish personal and trusting relationships with students, providing a safe haven for open communication of both positive and negative emotions.
>
> Educational programs must allow students to experience feelings of self-worth. Teachers can diminish academic pressures while health issues are of concern, establishing individual plans with students that would increase their frequency of positive reflections to combat inadequacies. Encourage journal keeping for more introspection.
>
> Regardless of their physique, students must feel that they belong to a nonjudgmental classroom environment that values them as contributing and successful individuals who have promising futures.

EMOTIONAL DISTURBANCES

General Overview

Causes

- Not determined
- Contributing factors include the following:
  - Heredity
  - Brain disorder
  - Diet
  - Stress
  - Family functioning
  - Neurological impairment
  - Brain injury
  - Chemical imbalance
  - Nutritional deficiency
  - Alcohol or drugs used by the parents
  - External factors, such as divorce, the death of a loved one, moving, and trauma, are situational and do not cause the actual disturbance. Environment may contribute to diagnosis but does not justify the classification

Contacts/Resources

Dr. Mac's Behavior Management Site: www.behavioradvisor.com

National Alliance on Mental Illness: www.nami.org

National Federation of Families for Children's Mental Health: www.ffcmh.org

Possible Characteristics

- These behaviors are evidenced *over long periods of time* and adversely affect a child's performance. According to IDEA, intellectual, sensory, or health factors cannot explain these behaviors. Review IDEA Sec. 300.8, *Child with a disability*, for exact language. Examples of emotional disturbance include the following:

- *Hyperactivity*—impulsiveness, short attention span
- *Aggression or self-injurious behavior*—acting out, fighting
- *Withdrawal*—excessive anxiety, failure to initiate interaction with others, intimidated by social interaction
- *Unsatisfactory interactions*—inability to maintain satisfactory interpersonal relationships with peers and teachers
- *Immaturity*—poor coping skills, inappropriate crying, temper tantrums
- *Learning difficulties*—academically performing below grade level due to behavior issues
- *More severe emotional disturbance*—distorted thinking, excessive anxiety, bizarre motor acts, abnormal mood swings; can include schizophrenia

Educational Strategies

- Behavior modification, charting frequency of desired behavior
- Establish a reason for the behavior (a functional behavior assessment, or FBA) to extinguish the motive and inappropriate desired result and to help develop a behavior intervention plan (BIP)
- Conflict resolution
- Psychological or counseling services
- Coordination of services among home, school, family, and therapeutic community with consistent communication
- Help student develop academic as well as social skills
- Establish rapport and trust with the student by disliking the behavior, not the child
- Let the student know that you are listening to him or her
- Smile, praise, trust
- Eye contact
- Structure with limits and consequences
- Yoga, breathing exercises
- Constructive outlets such as art or music
- Find ways for students to feel good about themselves
- Promote more self-awareness and self-evaluation with immediate positive reinforcement

Bipolar

Unusual and extreme shifts in mood disturbance with increased activity/energy and behavior that interfere with normal, healthy functioning

Separated from depressive disorders in DSM-5

Manic episode may be sandwiched between hypomanic or major depressive episodes

Causes

- Possible genetic predisposition or chemical imbalance
- Not caused by drugs, medication, or bereavement

Possible Characteristics

- Children can have highly volatile, short swings of mood; adults can have mood fluctuations that may last for days or weeks.
    - Inflated self-esteem
    - More talkative, changes topics frequently, cannot be interrupted
    - Racing thoughts
    - Distractibility
    - Decreased need for sleep
    - Psychomotor agitation
    - Increase in activities that could be harmful
    - Excessive pleasurable activities (e.g., buying spree)
    - School impairments in academics and social functioning with peers, along with home and family difficulties
    - Increased energy with little sleep
    - Physical complaints such as stomachaches, tiredness, headaches, or muscle pains

- Disruptive outbursts with sensitivity to failure or rejection, or may be overly silly or elated, talking excessively
- May evidence risk-taking behavior with alcohol, drugs, or by being sexually active
- If depressed, may show more sadness, with low tolerance for failure
- May also exhibit extremes with sleeping or eating

Educational Strategies

- Psychiatrists, individual/group counseling with supportive nonjudgmental adults who demonstrate concern by listening to child
- Behavior intervention plans
- Increase self-awareness
- Awareness of prescribed medication
- Individual educational support (tutoring)
- Positive attention or rewards for appropriate behavior with programs to increase self-esteem and guided peer relationships

Depressive Disorders (may be mild, moderate, or severe)

Disruptive Mood Dysregulation (DMDD)—with symptoms of outbursts and negative mood, diagnosed between ages six and eighteen, with outbursts and negative moods evidenced before age ten; can coexist with ADHD and CD (conduct disorder)

Persistent Depression (Dysthymia)—depression is severe but not episodic

Major Depression—depressed mood or anhedonia (lack of pleasure)

Anxiety Disorders—includes separation, selective mutism, specific phobia, panic, agoraphobia, social anxiety, generalized, substance/medication-induced, other medical conditions-psychotic

Selective Mutism—child does not speak in select social settings, not because the child is unable but because of internal feelings

Causes

- Possibly a psychiatric disorder related to anxiety
- Noncommunication is not caused by any other disorder, including a communication disorder
- Definitive cause unknown; can start at a young age, usually before age five
- Rare; fewer than 1 percent of children have selective mutism
- Slightly more common in girls than boys

Contacts/Resources

Anxiety and Depression Association of America: www.adaa.org

The Balanced Mind and Parent Network: www.thebalancedmind.org

Bipolar Child Support: www.bipolarchildsupport.com

Mental Health America: www.mentalhealthamerica.net

Selective Mutism Foundation: www.selectivemutismfoundation.org

Selective Mutism Group: www.selectivemutism.org

Social Anxiety: www.social-anxiety.com

Possible Characteristics

- No language or speech difficulties
- Consistent failure to speak in some social situations, such as school, but willingness to speak in other situations, such as home environment
- Language impairment with duration lasting more than a month
- Difficulty with relationships
- Problem may be related to anxiety or a social phobia since the children have the ability to both speak and understand language but fail to use this ability
- Social isolation/withdrawal
- Clinging behavior, compulsiveness, negativism, or temper tantrums with controlling or oppositional behavior, especially at home
- Can become peer scapegoat
- Usually lasts for only months but can continue for years

Educational Strategies

- Offer supportive, nonthreatening environment
- Enlist more outgoing peer to be buddy
- Seat student off center
- Use discrete task analysis to encourage speaking (e.g., reward small steps whenever the child makes sounds or words)
- Offer appropriate channels for communication and expression (e.g., tactile, visual, technology)
- Speech and language therapy with encouragement for family and child
- Be patient and calm
- Do not speak for the child!
- Do not try to force student to speak
- Include the child socially as an integral part of the classroom, regardless of lack of vocalizations
- Introduce other forms of communication (e.g., gestures, signs, written expression, communication board)
- Include more nonspeaking activities such as writing, using the computer, drawing, or silent reading
- Digitally record and note when child speaks to gain more understanding of speech patterns
- Have child speak in smaller setting (e.g., one to one, with a speaking buddy, or into a digital recorder) and then gradually add more people to conversations
- Keep a chart of gains that can be coordinated with a reward system in home and school environment, involving parents and families. Gradually phase out rewards as child speaks more.

Obsessive-Compulsive Disorder (OCD)

Causes

- OCD has multiple types and causes:
    - o Research is investigating neurobiological factors and environmental influences that contribute to this anxiety disorder.
    - o OCD is not due to a substance disorder (medicine, alcohol, or drug) or other medical condition.
    - o Genetic studies are being conducted to discover the molecular basis of OCD.
    - o Sometimes linked with Tourette syndrome and ADHD.
    - o Positron emission tomography (PET) scanning involving brain imaging suggests different patterns of neurochemical activity in the brain.
    - o National Institute of Health and other researchers believe strep throat and bacterial infections to be triggers of some types of obsessive-compulsive disorder as well as symptoms of Tourette syndrome (e.g., nervous tics).

Contacts/Resources

International OCD Foundation: http://iocdf.org

Possible Characteristics

- Repetitive, excessive, and unreasonable behavior (e.g., hand washing/fear of contamination, counting, rechecking, rearranging, repeated doubts)
- Obsessions and compulsions cause marked distress and significantly impact functioning
- Anxiety evidenced
- Inability to control thoughts, worries, panic, and compulsiveness
- Difficulty concentrating
- Cannot effectively follow school schedules and transitions
- Fear of contamination or a serious illness
- Sometimes behavior is hidden in front of classmates due to embarrassment
- May repeatedly erase and redo assignments, which can result in incomplete work

Educational Strategies

- Communicate consistently with parents
- Watch for side effects from some medication or drug combinations, such as nervousness or fatigue from insomnia

- Use behavioral plans and progress reports to control impulsivity
- Use cognitive behavioral therapy (CBT) to challenge and extinguish faulty compulsions
- Increase self-awareness, frequent and consistent self-monitoring
- Cue students for key points and signal classroom changes
- Establish an assignment book with a long-range calendar; use checklists to keep student organized
- Provide a model of desired outcome
- Have student repeat directions for understanding
- Establish trusting relationship
- Use cooperative learning
- Educate other school personnel and help develop positive social interactions

OCD and Related Disorders

In DSM-5 this chapter includes obsessive-compulsive disorder, trichotillomania (hair pulling), body dysmorphic, hoarding, and excoriation (skin picking) and substance/medication-induced obsessive-compulsive and other related disorders.

DISRUPTIVE, IMPULSE-CONTROL, AND CONDUCT DISORDERS

Oppositional-Defiant Disorder (ODD)

In DSM-5, ODD is included in the section, "Disruptive, Impulse-Control and Conduct Disorders," along with the categories of angry/irritable, argumentative/defiant, and vindictive. The number of settings in which symptoms are present indicates the range of mild, moderate, and severe. Intermittent explosive disorder (IED) involves verbal or physical explosions and can coexist with other disorders at age six or older. Conduct disorder needs to specify a childhood, adolescent, or unspecified onset and whether there are limited prosocial emotions, such as lack of remorse or guilt, callous lack of empathy, unconcerned about performance, shallow and deficient affect. Antisocial personality disorder is acknowledged, but criteria are listed in the "Personality Disorders" section. Kleptomania, pyromania, and others are also included in this section of DSM-5. Caution should be exhibited in the ODD diagnosis since oppositional behavior is frequently evidenced in preschool and adolescent children.

Causes

- Uncertain
- ODD is usually evident before age eight and not later than early adolescence
- Appears to be more common in families in which at least one parent has a history of mood, oppositional defiant, attention, or a substance-related disorder
- Criteria for the diagnosis of this conduct disorder are met if behaviors cause significant impairment in social, academic, or occupational functioning

Contacts/Resources

American Academy of Child & Adolescent Psychiatry: www.aacap.org

Mental Health America: www.mentalhealthamerica.net

Possible Characteristics

- Pattern of angry/irritable mood, argumentative/defiant behavior, or vindictiveness lasting at least six months
- Negative behavior toward authority figures or adults
- Deliberately doing things to annoy others
- Blaming others for his or her mistakes
- Often touchy or easily annoyed by others
- Resentment toward authority
- Refusal to do school assignments or chores at home
- Underachievement at school
- Pouting, stubbornness, obstructive behavior (interfering with the plans and activities of others)
- Easily frustrated
- Loses temper frequently

Educational Strategies

- Communication and consistency between home and school with parent management training (PMT) that advocates brief, nonaversive punishments
- Listen to the student before giving a reaction
- Avoid punitive patterns or negative attention for defiance; allow choices/ options under teacher's auspices (e.g., "pick three out of five") to diminish power struggles and to build on positives
- Give child meaningful responsibility in the classroom
- Offer frequent praise and rewards for compliance and improvements, which can also be nonverbal or even quietly whispered to the student
- Develop individual goal chart or behavioral plan to decrease defiant behavior and increase self-awareness
- School counseling or group therapy
- Private discussions to predetermine rules and consequences
- Opportunities for positive social interaction
- Emphasis on problem-solving skills
- Be aware of child's interests to increase the student's desire to learn
- Establish an atmosphere of trust and calmness
- Dislike the behavior, not the student

■ INTELLECTUAL DISABILITIES

Intellectual Disability (ID)

IDEA definition: Significantly subaverage general intellectual functioning, existing concurrently with deficits in adaptive behavior (adjustment to everyday life), which are manifested during the developmental period, and adversely affecting a child's educational performance.

DSM-5 has ID listed in the section, "Neurodevelopmental Disorders," with an IQ score no longer required. Diagnosis is made with level of functioning (LOF) in three domains: conceptual, social, and practical.

Causes

- Chromosome abnormalities
- Birth asphyxia (lack of oxygen when born or soon afterward)
- Blood incompatibilities between the mother and the fetus or maternal infections, such as rubella or herpes
- Problems during pregnancy such as not eating right with extreme malnutrition, using certain drugs, alcohol, or smoking (e.g., fetal alcohol syndrome [FAS]), exposure to poisons and environmental toxins such as lead or mercury
- Down syndrome and Fragile X (with severe mutations) are known genetic causes
- Malnutrition or inadequate medical care
- Disease after birth, such as meningitis or encephalitis, that leads to brain damage
- More than half of ID cases are caused by environmental factors
- Not a mental illness; cannot be cured

Contacts/Resources

American Association on Intellectual and Developmental Disabilities (AAIDD): www.aaidd.org

The Arc: www.thearc.org

Best Buddies: www.bestbuddies.org

Division on Autism and Developmental Disabilities, Council for Exceptional Children: www.daddcec.org

Special Olympics: www.specialolympics.org

> The word *retarded* developed such a negative connotation that the federal law now uses the term *intellectual disabilities* instead. This might cause some confusion with other learning disabilities. However, it is not the label but the criteria and services rendered that matter.

Possible Characteristics

- Low intellectual functioning or IQ and poor adaptive behavior or skills to live independently (e.g., daily living skills, communication, social, self-help)
- Different academic, social, and vocational skills, depending on impairment level
- Difficulties with the following areas:
    - Learning in school (e.g., remembering things)
    - Communication (e.g., receptive and expressive language)
    - Social skills (e.g, consequences, rules)
    - Academic issues (e.g., thinking logically or solving problems)
    - Vocational concerns
    - Personal needs (e.g., hygiene, dressing, eating)
    - Learning occurs but at a slower rate
    - Short-term memory impairment
    - Unable to form generalizations

Educational Strategies

- Set realistic and functional goals with family support and coordination
- Use concrete, age-appropriate materials, avoiding totally abstract levels of presentation but capitalizing on student's interests and strengths
- Early infant stimulation, preschool intervention, neighborhood school programs, transitional services, opportunities for schoolwork with emphasis on independent living skills
- Sensory educational considerations—more visuals, audios, hands-on (e.g., communication boards), interdisciplinary activities, and real-life situations (e.g., restaurant class, shopping in a store, community trips)
- Break down learning into smaller sequential steps with frequent review, going from simple to complex; honor each student's instructional level
- Use consistent, age-appropriate rewards
- Help students generalize and apply learning from one situation to the next through teacher modeling with immediate realistic feedback
- Alternate means of assessment, more verbal and less written
- Teach memory strategies (e.g., chunking, association)
- Offer lessons with functional and independent-living skills infused (e.g., manners, conversation rules, safety, health, reading street signs, ordering from a menu)
- Outline transitional goals with preparatory academic and career-oriented courses

Traumatic Brain Injury (TBI)

Acquired injury to the brain caused by an external force; does not include congenital or degenerative brain injuries

Causes

- Frequent causes of TBI are related to motor vehicle crashes, falls, sports accidents, physical abuse, assault, and other head injuries
- Other causes include chemical (insecticides, carbon monoxide, lead poisoning), hypoxia (lack of oxygen), and tumors
- Types of injuries vary and can range from mild to severe
- Sudden unexpected onset makes TBI differ from other disabilities since parents and children have not had time to emotionally deal with the disability and must suddenly learn how to manage and accept the changes

Contacts/Resources

Brain Injury Association of America: www.biausa.org

Brain Injury Survivor's Guide: braininjuryguide.org

Traumatic Brain Injury Resources: www.traumaticbraininjury.com

Possible Characteristics

- Symptoms vary depending on the location and extent of the brain injury. Impairments can be

  - *Physical*—speech, vision, hearing, sensory impairments, headaches, difficulty with fine and/or gross motor skills, balance, and coordination
  - *Cognitive*—short- and long-term memory deficits, concentration problems, slowness of thinking/judgment, perceptual issues, and disorganization, with academic difficulties such as trouble learning new information
  - *Psychosocial, Behavioral, or Emotional*—fatigue, mood swings, denial, self-centeredness, depression, inability to self-monitor, agitation, excessive laughing or crying, difficulty relating to others, poor impulse control

Educational Strategies

- Schools need to have appropriate neurological, psychological, speech/language, and educational evaluations to determine accurate classification
- Careful planning for school reentry
- Teach compensatory memory strategies
- Repeated practice
- Explain figurative language
- Provide concrete examples to illustrate new concepts
- Keep the environment as free of distractions as possible
- Provide student with rest breaks if stamina is low
- Family support and sharing of educational strategies for reinforcement at home

LEARNING/ATTENTION DISORDERS

ADHD (Attention Deficit Hyperactivity Disorder)

Causes

- Exact cause is unknown; can be linked to a chemical imbalance in neurotransmitters (chemicals in the brain that help brain cells communicate with each other)
- Differences in brain activity and structure that help control behavior and attention
- Might be genetically transmitted (tends to run in families, but this could also be environmental)
- Evidenced by both sexes; females are sometimes more inattentive than hyperactive
- Theories exist about poor nutrition or diet

Contacts/Resources

ADDitude: Strategies and Support for ADHD & LD: www.additudemag.com

Attention Deficit Disorder Association (ADDA): www.add.org

Centers for Disease Control and Prevention, Attention Deficit Hyperactivity Disorders Homepage: www.cdc.gov/ncbddd/adhd

Children and Adults with Attention-Deficit/Hyperactivity Disorder (CHADD): www.chadd.org

Possible Characteristics

- Persistent pattern of inattention and/or hyperactivity-impulsivity that interferes with functioning and development
- Inattention
  - Daydreaming
  - Inattentive to details
  - Careless in schoolwork (e.g., sloppy handwriting, crumpled homework), forgetful, disorganized, may lose things
  - Memory difficulties
  - Distracted by extraneous stimuli
  - Concentration and listening problems, such as in attending to a teacher while trying to take notes
  - Attention difficulties when initiating actions requiring foresight, sustaining concentration, inhibiting distractions and impulsive reactions, and shifting gears or transitioning to other tasks
  - Difficulties following multistep directions

- May be predominantly hyperactive-impulsive, which may be characterized by:

    - Frequent motion
    - Fidgeting with hands or feet (rocking in chair, twirling pencils)
    - Missing social cues; getting into fights
    - Difficulty in waiting turn—interrupts others
    - Impulsivity, such as blurting out answers
    - More accidents due to hyperactivity

- Students diagnosed with ADHD may have combined symptoms of both inattention and hyperactivity–impulsivity, which need to be present for past six months. Students with ADHD may also display a predominantly inattentive or predominantly hyperactive-impulsive behavior. According to DSM-5, symptoms need to be documented prior to age twelve. In addition, there could be a diagnosis of ADHD along with ASD.

Educational Strategies

- Structured, predictable environment
- Daily schedules and assignment pads
- Clear, concise directions with routines announced and posted; remove all extraneous materials
- Be aware of any medications as prescribed by child's physician, due to possible side effects
- Establish eye contact
- Have student rephrase or repeat directions
- Teach organization such as using crates for extra texts from desks or accordion files to hold notes and papers
- Color-code notebooks, folders, and text covers for different subjects
- Reinforce study skills
- Give frequent breaks combined with stretching activities to channel motor excess
- Write specific, formal behavioral plans with clear expectations, immediate feedback, and rewards
- Teach problem-solving, conflict-resolution, and peer-mediation skills
- To increase self-awareness and self-discipline, have student keep a log of impulsive and quieter behaviors
- Model with guided practice and application and share strategies with home environment
- Establish a nonthreatening classroom environment, using subtle cues for transitions
- Be aware of *quiet noises* in the room. For example, a low humming from the heater or the sounds coming from a nearby classroom may be ignored by most but distracting to a child with ADHD.
- Dislike the behavior, not the child, using positives before negatives

Specific Learning Disabilities (SLD)

Causes

- As stated by IDEA, SLD is not primarily the result of visual, hearing, or motor disabilities; intellectual disability; or emotional, economic, environmental, or cultural factors
- Varied spectrum of causes that may be linked to neurological or genetic factors
- Learning disability (LD) is a real disability, not laziness!

Contacts/Resources

Council for Exceptional Children Division of Learning Disabilities: teachingld.org

LD OnLine: www.ldonline.org

Learning Disabilities Association of America: ldaamerica.org

National Center for Learning Disabilities (NCLD): www.ncld.org

Possible Characteristics

- Wide range that can include difficulties with the following:

    - Reading comprehension or word decoding

- Arithmetic calculations or concepts
- Spoken language
- Writing (spelling, creative expression, language mechanics, or fine motor)
- Social skills
- Reasoning (getting thoughts together)

- May also exhibit the following traits:
  - Perceptual impairments
  - Inattention
  - Impulsiveness
  - Low tolerance for frustration
  - Poor organizational skills
  - Dyslexia (reading difficulties)
  - Dysgraphia (writing difficulties)
  - Dyscalculia (math difficulties) (These are discussed further on.)

> Former criteria classification required a severe discrepancy model (SDM) between measured achievement (which can include school performance) and ability (tested intelligence). The discrepancy criteria are not the sole criteria for placement under an SLD definition. Response to intervention (RTI) is used to help students who have learning difficulties receive services in whole classrooms, smaller groups, or 1:1 without regard to tested intelligence. The evaluation procedure now allows states to review whether students are responding to the scientific, research-based interventions, instead of exclusively using the severe discrepancy model.
>
> Stress to students that intelligence is separate from achievement. They are not less intelligent just because they might read differently. Everyone is stronger or weaker in one thing or another.

Educational Strategies

- Collaboratively design individualized education program (IEP) to address child's needs, with general education (GE) staff, special education (SE) staff, parents, families, and transitional services for children age sixteen and older, or younger, if appropriate
- Use concrete, kinesthetic materials that students can see and touch
- Break up learning into small bites and step-by-step lessons
- Capitalize on student strengths using multiple intelligences
- Use redundancy—repeat, restate, reiterate, and relate
- Vary instruction and assessment with more active involvement and fewer lectures, allowing appropriate motoric releases
- Offer immediate positive feedback without embarrassment
- Emphasize consistent expectations with accountability
- Use computers and digital tools to help with reading, writing, and math issues
- Shorten assignments based on level of mastery
- Instructional level should encourage independence with empowerment under teacher's auspices
- Secure appropriate accommodations based on individual needs, but have weaning plans in place as well
- Frequent home communication helps prevent misinformation
- DSM-5 has specifiers to note the impairment
  - *Reading* (word reading, reading rate or fluency, reading comprehension)
  - *Written Expression* (spelling, grammar/punctuation, clarity/organization)
  - *Mathematics* (number sense, calculation, reasoning, memorization)
- SLD also has a range of mild, moderate, and severe.

Dyslexia

Causes

- Genetic or neurological factors
- Lack of cerebral dominance
- Differences in brain function
- Auditory language deficit

Contacts/Resources

Academy of Orton-Gillingham Practitioners and Educators: www.ortonacademy.org

Davis Dyslexia Association International: www.dyslexia.com

The International Dyslexia Association: www.interdys.org

Jolly Learning: jollylearning.co.uk

Learning Ally: www.learningally.org

Wilson Language Training: www.wilsonlanguage.com

The Yale Center for Dyslexia & Creativity: dyslexia.yale.edu

Possible Characteristics

- Language-based learning disability
- May experience difficulties with sound-symbol association, fluency, reading comprehension, vocabulary, spelling, written expression, and auditory processing skills
- May show difficulties in reading and written and spoken language. Some need more help with spelling, grammar, textbooks, and writing essays.
- Sometimes have difficulties in use of numeric symbols in mathematics such as reversals of numbers or signs (+, –)
- Visual problems (e.g., eye tracking, eye movements)
- Lack of organization
- Reversals of letters or mirror writing may or may not be present
- Confusing vowels or substituting one consonant for another
- Clumsiness and awkwardness with hands
- Often gifted in other areas that do not require strong language skills, such as art, computer science, math, music, sports, and electronics

Educational Strategies

- Early diagnosis and interventions to improve phonemic awareness
- Use multisensory channels to teach with a structured language approach that involves hearing, seeing, and touching (e.g., more manipulatives and kinesthetic approaches, visuals, and sounds to break words into phonemes and syllables)
- Use colored overlays on texts
- Capitalize on student strengths and interests to improve weaker areas
- Activate word processing programs and learning activities with sound animation
- Allow access to digital tools (e.g., iBooks, LiveScribe, Dragon Naturally Speaking, speech-to-text)
- Use alternate/embedded assessments as needed with frequent progress monitoring
- *Orton-Gillingham approach,* which is language-based, multisensory, sequential, structured, and cumulative. Students start by learning sounds in isolation, then blend sounds into syllables and words with all the elements of language, from consonants and vowels to digraphs, blends, and diphthongs, and then syllable types.
- Teach structural analysis by breaking longer words into their parts, using index cards to separate syllables, root words, prefixes, and suffixes
- Use graded, color-coded sight words or flashcards with student, maintaining, adding, and reviewing alphabetical lists
- Use structured reading, spelling, and phonics programs with controlled text that build on a hierarchy of skills, avoiding small print
- Make modifications such as helping with note taking or allowing extra time to complete tests
- Build self-esteem with more positive reflections, including dated portfolios of completed work
- Allow older or adolescent students to use high-interest, controlled texts and age-appropriate words to practice reading, thereby honoring their dignity in the reading process rather than belittling them!
- Choral or echo reading for more difficult words within text not yet learned

Hyperlexia is a disorder where students may have high word recognition levels and read at an early age but have limited comprehension and difficulty with verbal language, verbal issues, and social skills (see ww2.hyperlexia.org).

Dysgraphia

Combination of fine-motor and eye–hand coordination problems, which can include improper pencil grip, confused hand dominance, poor wrist control, and illegible handwriting along with general difficulties putting thoughts into writings

Causes

- May involve a brain dysfunction that includes translating mental thoughts into written language
- Lack of hand strength developed early in infancy that, along with incorrect kinesthetic memory, led to incorrect motor routines and habits
- Difficulties arising from dysgraphia are compounded by emotional factors if a child is pushed into using handwriting at an early age or overly criticized

Contacts/Resources

Handwriting Without Tears: www.hwtears.com

Keyboarding Without Tears: www.hwtears.com/kwt

LDInfo: www.ldinfo.com

Learning Disabilities Association of America: ldaamerica.org/types-of-learning-disabilities/dysgraphia

Possible Characteristics

- Can include memory and attention difficulties or an inability to visualize letters and shapes
- Written work may be illegible, with related difficulties in spelling, drawing, spontaneous expression, or simply copying letters
- Writing hand may shake or cramp because of an awkward pencil grip or slower fine-motor speed
- Student may struggle with writing tasks, spending more time on how he or she forms the letters rather than the writing content
- Student dislikes writing tasks, showing tension when taking class notes or during other written assignments
- May be a creative writer but just dislikes the mechanics involved
- Motor movements are unsequenced and not automatically learned
- May complain of hand hurting or fatigue
- Slowness in completing assignments involving writing due to difficulties forming letters, collecting thoughts, and organizing ideas
- May omit words in sentences and display poor syntax
- Sometimes the student can't proofread own written work since he or she is unable to read it

Educational Strategies

- Multisensory approaches; value VAKT elements (visual, auditory, and kinesthetic/tactile)
- Strengthen fine motor skills using various media (e.g., crayons, clay, tactile glue, games, toys, felt boards, sky writing, sorting objects, sponges, pipe cleaners, Legos, stringing beads, scissors, stencils, salt, pencil grips, tracing paper, yarn)
- Verbalize letter formation steps using configuration strategies, noticing the size, shape, and—later, when ready—the slant of letters
- Provide student with a sheet that matches and compares manuscript to cursive writing
- Use purposeful writing such as labeling folders and other items in the classroom; making signs; writing letters, birthday cards, and thank-you notes; and designing bulletin boards
- Establish rubrics with acceptable writing samples and encourage self-evaluation
- Check how student is seated with emphasis on good posture, with paper correctly positioned and taped or Velcroed to desk
- Have students use graphic organizers and computer templates to collect thoughts and minimize writing; use writing strategies that compartmentalize thoughts

- Assign students a copying buddy to share more legible notes
- Make use of technology: digital recording pens and devices, electronic spell-checkers, keyboarding programs, laptop computers, distribute electronic copies of notes, allow student to record lessons to then play back at a slower pace
- Teach step-by-step ways to expand writing thoughts

Dyscalculia

Learning disability that affects ability to do math. Students may be *math phobic,* fearful of activities involving numbers, such as computations requiring addition, subtraction, multiplication, or division. In addition, learning new mathematical concepts or problem solving may be stressful.

Causes

- Can be based on prior negative experiences, poor self-confidence, or instructional synapses, along with genetic or neurological factors
- Brain imaging studies show different brain pulses in areas dealing with interpretation of numbers and spatial images

Contacts/Resources

Abeel, S. (2003). *My thirteenth winter.* New York: Scholastic. (Memoir about dyscalculia)

Dyscalculia.org: www.dyscalculia.org

LDInfo: www.ldinfo.com

Molko, M., Cachia, A., Rivière, D., Mangin, J., Bruandet, M., Le Bihan, et al. (2003). Functional and structural alterations of the intraparietal sulcus in a developmental dyscalculia of genetic origin. *Neuron, 40,* 847–858.

TouchMath: www.touchmath.com

Possible Characteristics

- Weakness with visual processing and memory
- Learning difficulties may be present in other content areas such as recalling important dates in social studies, or specific science and math formulas
- May not spell well
- May have poor fine-motor skills regarding size, spacing, organization, and alignment of letters and numbers
- Sequencing difficulties
- Limited organizational skills
- Difficulty extracting information to solve word problems
- Math test anxiety; may freeze or forget what is taught and learned, evidencing a flawed test performance
- If visual processing difficulties are the cause, reading comprehension and writing skills may be strengths, while spelling, applying phonetic rules, and sight-word development may be weaknesses

Educational Strategies

- Students need guided and systematic instruction to help them develop compensatory strategies to work with numbers
- Use specific, step-by-step examples to both explain and review concepts
- Teach new material, then review prior learning, consistently backtracking to maintain skills
- Encourage students to peruse and develop helpful visual information such as graphs, charts, tables, and pictures to simplify word problems or computations
- Allow students an opportunity to use an auditory approach by listening to their own voices, music, computer programs, peers, or teachers as they work
- Have students immediately apply skills; use less straightforward lecturing and more *student doing*
- Interview and conference with students to ensure math understandings and to develop math profiles
- Use a variety of concrete and online tools to allow students to internalize what they are learning (e.g., TouchMath, algebra tiles, hands-on equations, virtual

manipulatives, Cool Math Games, Khan Academy, Purplemath)

- Try to make math fun by incorporating students' interests (e.g., batting averages, weather) while meaningfully connecting mathematical skills and concepts to daily life (e.g., food products to learn about metrics, store circulars to teach comparison shopping, eating out in a restaurant)
- Develop user-friendly, uncluttered worksheets
- Allow students to hold lined paper horizontally to help keep the place value of numbers in columns
- Deliver consistent praise and realistic, timely math feedback on levels and progress
- Incorporate CCSS Standards for Mathematical Practices

AUTISM SPECTRUM DISORDERS (ASD)

General Overview

Diagnosis made from DSM-5 identifies ASD as a broad disorder with severity based on levels of functioning as 1 (lowest), 2, or 3, based on social communication and interactions in multiple contexts along with repetitive behaviors, interests, and activities. DSM-5 folded pervasive development disorders (PDD) and Asperger syndrome under an ASD category. Some individuals who have deficits in social communication but do not meet the criteria for ASD may be evaluated for social (pragmatic) communication disorder (SCD). Specifiers include *with or without intellectual impairment*, language impairment, association with another medical or genetic condition or environmental factors, association with another neurodevelopmental, mental, or behavior disorder, and catatonia.

Causes

- Exact etiology unknown. Some possibilities include the following:
  - Genetic and environmental factors
  - Biochemical imbalance in the brain
  - Metabolic and neurological factors
  - Theories about environmental/toxic influences
  - Not caused by psychological factors
  - Seems to be more prevalent in males
  - Familial heritability—increased frequency in families with members who have ASD

Contacts/Resources

Autism Research Institute: www.autism.com

Autism Society: www.autism-society.org

Autism Speaks: http://www.autismspeaks.org/what-autism/diagnosis/dsm-5-diagnostic-criteria

Centers for Disease Control and Prevention: http://www.cdc.gov/ncbddd/autism/index.html

Global Autism Collaboration: www.globalautismcollaboration.com

Possible Characteristics

- Depends on severity along with developmental level and chronological age
- Social impairment with communications and interactions (e.g., social reciprocity—can be unaware of how their behaviors might affect others)
- Difficulty relating to people; unusual play; appear unaware of others, negatively affecting peer interactions
- Restrictive, repetitive patterns of behaviors, interests, or activities that limit everyday functioning may be indicated by fascinations with own desires or idiosyncrasies as well as possible preoccupation with parts of objects
- Varying verbal and nonverbal deficits depending on age, intellectual level, language ability, and supports
- IQ can range from lower cognitive level to high intelligence
- Difficulties sharing interests or enjoyment with others
- Poor nonverbal behaviors, eye contact, facial expression; inappropriate body language

- Inflexible attachment to schedules and routines
- Possible motor delays or clumsiness
- Ineffective sensory processing with unusual responses to lights, noises, textures
- Communication difficulty—hard time using and understanding language; may use repetitive speech (echolalia), nonspeech vocalization; receptive language is usually better than expressive language, but both verbal and nonverbal behavior can be impacted
- Difficulty with abstract and/or unfamiliar concepts and routines

Educational Strategies

- Social behavior needs to be modeled, encouraged, practiced, and documented in school and at home with role-playing.
- Students can keep a social skills notebook or log and read guided social stories
- Increase self-awareness with concrete rewards, verbal praise, and much patience
- Adult and peer support needed to emphasize social appropriateness in academic settings, at first in smaller group or setting. Then add positive role models to increase interactions.
- Direct social skill instruction and prompting with peers
- Educate other students and adults about ASD
- Emphasis on routine and structure to reduce stress, using outlines, planners, and monthly calendars to help students deal with transitions and daily happenings
- If possible, give advance notice of changes in daily schedule (e.g., half day, assembly)
- Avoid sensory overstimulation
- Provide visual cues, sound signals, tactile learning, and handouts
- Use of pictures to outline day's schedule
- Allow embedded academic opportunities for motoric movement
- Be aware of students' likes and dislikes
- Teach compensatory strategies
- Use behavior modification program to reward desired behavior (e.g., more eye contact)
- Have instructional assistant shadow student if necessary, but encourage independence
- Provide a nurturing and accepting classroom and other quiet settings to channel behavior
- Reward social reciprocity
- Collaborate with related service providers (e.g. speech and language services with classroom and home coordination, occupational therapists, behavioral interventionists) and family
- Teach and value other ways to communicate if appropriate (e.g., communication boards, gestures, and music)
- Match visual and verbal presentation with concrete experiences (e.g., field trips, animations)
- Offer functional academics to enhance daily living if appropriate for level of severity
- Tactile stimulation such as gentle pats or arm strokes; water therapy can also be soothing
- Teach academics and socialization with step-by-step methods, focusing on strengths
- Use behavioral analysis to improve and reward targeted behaviors and verbal behavior (see the Association for Behavior Analysis International at www.abainternational.org)

PHYSICAL IMPAIRMENTS

General Overview

Physical disabilities can affect a lot of different areas. Physical relates to the body, and disability means not being able to do something. A child with a physical disability has a body that does not work in some way. A child's fine-motor skills can be affected, which means that he or she might not be able to hold things such as a spoon, fork, or pencil. Gross-motor skills can also be affected when a child uses his or her feet for things such as walking or riding a bicycle. Communicating with others by moving the lips to talk can be difficult for a child with a physical disability.

Contacts/Resources

Bright Hub Education: www.brighthubeducation.com/special-ed-physical-disabilities/

Disabled Sports USA: www.disabledsportsusa.org

National Council on Independent Living: www.ncil.org

Disabled World—Physical and Mobility Impairments: Facts, News, and Information: www.disabled-world.com/disability/types/mobility

Equal Access: Universal Design for Physical Access, University of Washington: www.washington.edu/doit/Brochures/Programs/equal_access_spaces.html

Special Olympics: www.specialolympics.org

Possible Characteristics

- Can be present at birth (e.g., spina bifida, cerebral palsy)
- May be caused by accidents (e.g., skiing, car injury, sports, spinal cord injury)
- Diseases can cause a physical impairment (e.g., polio, multiple sclerosis)
- Physical disabilities may increase with age as bone structure changes, and mobility can become limited
- Remember that sensitivities and common sense always apply. Don't freeze up!
- Attitudes toward those with a physical impairment are still archaic, since some people inaccurately or subconsciously assume that someone who can't walk properly cannot have total usage of his or her brain. For example, a person with cerebral palsy can be just as intelligent as an able-bodied individual.
- Awareness about others is most important; educate peers and staff.
- Collaborate with families.

Educational Strategies

- The environment needs to be physically arranged for optimum usage by those with physical dis*abilities,* not for the convenience of others (e.g., the use of parking spots, dressing rooms, and bathrooms designed for those with disabilities). Some school arrangements and accommodations include the following:
    - Bathroom accessibility to maneuver a wheelchair to turn
    - Lowered sinks, mirrors, and towel holders
    - Wider classroom aisles
    - Elevators for buildings with more than one floor, equipped with lights and bell signals, or tactile Braille for those with hearing and visual needs
    - Structural accommodations to allow access to all facilities, from water fountains to meeting rooms
    - Lowered windows that allow someone who uses a wheelchair to see outside
    - Positioning (e.g., raising or lowering) necessary adaptive equipment to facilitate student's independence
    - Use of a Velcro mat on a student's desk to prevent books, papers, pencils, and other materials from slipping, or securing papers to the desk with tape
    - Bean bag for student to sit on during floor activities to be on eye level with peers
    - Occupational therapy can be a related school service, targeting specific physical needs

- Enlist help of peers
    - A classmate can make copies of notes
    - Learning buddies can help students gather materials and assist with school or homework
    - Remember to try to be on eye level with someone in a wheelchair so he or she does not strain his or her neck by looking up at you
    - Encourage students to exchange cell phone numbers or e-mail addresses to

extend peer support and friendship outside of the school environment
- Set tone in class by example; treat student the same, socially and emotionally, as you would a student without physical impairments, seeing the student as a child first, not only as a child with a disability

Cerebral Palsy (CP)

Cerebral refers to the brain. *Palsy* refers to muscle movement that may be stiff, uncontrolled, or unbalanced, depending upon type of CP.

Causes

- Rarely associated with heredity since the damage to the brain usually occurs before, during, or shortly after birth
- Neurological in nature
- Mother's illness during pregnancy
- Premature delivery
- Lack of oxygen supply to the baby or poor blood flow reaching the fetal or newborn brain
- Can be a result of accident, lead poisoning, viral infection, or child abuse
- Might involve separation of the placenta, an awkward birth position, long labor, or interference from the umbilical cord
- Rh or ABO blood type incompatibility between parents may exist
- Mother infected with German measles during pregnancy
- Brain injury at birth

Contacts/Resources

My Child at CerebralPalsy.org: cerebralpalsy.org/about-cerebral-palsy/types-and-forms/

United Cerebral Palsy: www.ucp.org

Possible Characteristics

- Inability to fully control motor functions, ranging from mild to severe (e.g., student moving without assistance to using braces or a wheelchair)
- *Not a disease;* it is a nonprogressive condition that is not contagious
- Impairment may involve sight, hearing, and speech
- There are different types of cerebral palsy classifications
- Can be classified based on severity, a topographical distribution (which body parts affected—how and where), motor function (spastic-nonspastic), muscle tone-pyramidal (spastic) and extrapyramidal (nonspastic)
    - *Spastic*—stiff and difficult movement
    - *Athetoid Dyskinetic*—involuntary and uncontrolled movement (e.g., facial grimaces, drooling)
    - *Dystonia*—affects trunk muscles with twisted posture
    - *Ataxic*—coordinated movements, fine motor, sense of balance, and depth perception affected
    - Gross motor function classification system (GMFCS) refers to extent of ability and impairment limitation
- Depending on which part of the brain has been damaged and the degree of central nervous system (CNS) damage, characteristics can include the following:
    - Spasms
    - Tonal problems
    - Involuntary movements
    - Seizures
    - Disturbances in gait and mobility
    - Abnormal sensation and perception
    - Impairment of sight, hearing, or speech
    - Individuals may have mixed symptoms
    - Range of intelligence levels from high to lower

Educational Strategies

- General or special education with equal academic opportunities
- Technology with assistive equipment (e.g., electronic communication board, book holder, pencil grip, word processor, tether ball)
- Community integration opportunities

- Recreation
- Consult with occupational therapists (OT) and physical therapists (PT)
- Educate other students about misconceptions
- Classroom assistance
- Involvement and peer support in social and academic activities
- Teach self-advocacy
- Life-skills instructions with appropriate activities for daily living
- Focus on strengths and interests
- Provide opportunities for success
- Allow more rest periods
- Transitional services

Epilepsy

Causes

- Physical condition with sudden, brief change in how the brain works that in some cases happens for inexplicable reasons
- Consciousness, movement, or actions are altered for a short time (epileptic seizure)
- Repeated seizures can be caused by illness, brain damage, birth trauma, brain infection, head injury, metabolic imbalance in the body, drug intoxication, brain tumor, or disruption of blood to the brain
- Environmental factors that might bring on a seizure include sudden lighting changes, flashing lights (e.g., photosensitivity), or loud noises
- Some forms of epilepsy may be inherited
- A single seizure does not mean that a person has epilepsy; seizures can be caused by fevers, imbalance of body fluids, or alcohol or drug withdrawal.

Contacts/Resources

Epilepsy Foundation: www.epilepsy.com

Possible Characteristics

- Types of seizures—depends on which part of the brain is affected; types include primary generalized, partial, nonepileptic, and status epilepticus.
    - *Primary Generalized*—all brain cells are involved; might involve a convulsion with a complete loss of consciousness or might look like a brief period of fixed staring
    - *Partial*—occurs when brain cells are not working properly and is limited to one part of the brain; may cause periods of automatic behavior and altered consciousness with repetitive behavior that is usually not remembered
    - *Nonepileptic*—not caused by epilepsy
    - *Status epilepticus*—persistent seizures
- Other possible symptoms:
    - Involuntary movements of arms and legs
    - Blackouts or periods of confused memory, with episodes of staring or unexplained periods of unresponsiveness. Teachers should keep an eye out for this inattentive behavior as being a possible sign of a seizure if the child is known to have epilepsy.
    - Fainting spells with excessive fatigue following
    - Odd sounds, distorted perceptions, and episodic feelings of inexplicable fear

Educational Strategies

- Provide staff and students with information on seizure recognition and first aid with specific directions written into IEP (e.g., clear away dangerous objects, do not restrain the student, make the student comfortable by loosening clothing, never put anything in mouth—may bite hard)
- Be aware of effects of antiseizure or antianxiety medications
- Ensure good communication between school and home to gain more understanding for staff and parents
- Teacher should observe and keep accurate anecdotal logs
- Encourage other students/adults to treat someone with epilepsy with respect by educating peers about possible behaviors

- Provide student with downtime; he or she might be exhausted after a seizure
- Help students lead independent lives by teaching transitional skills

Multiple Sclerosis (MS)

Causes

- Neurological disorder
- *Multiple* means many, while *sclerosis* means a thickening or hardening of tissue
- The majority of people are diagnosed between the ages of twenty and fifty, but MS can also be found in the school-age population. Although no definitive cause is known, evidence suggests MS results from an autoimmune process in which immune cells (T cells) mistake *myelin,* the fatty coating around nerve cell fibers in the brain and spinal cord, for a foreign invader and attack it. Other theories of causation consider environment, infection, viruses, and genetics.

Contacts/Resources

Friends with MS: www.friendswithms.com

National Multiple Sclerosis Society: www.nationalmssociety.org

Multiple Sclerosis International Federation: www.msif.org

Possible Characteristics

- Can impair movement, vision, coordination, and other functions
- Depending on type and severity, MS is categorized in the following ways:
    - *Benign MS*—Condition does not worsen over time, and there is little or no permanent disability. This type cannot be identified until ten to fifteen years after onset; otherwise it falls under relapsing–remitting type. Approximately 5 percent of the 20 percent initially diagnosed stay with this type.
    - *Relapsing–Remitting*—Episodes followed by remissions (accounts for about 25 percent of patients with MS). Disappearing and reappearing of neurological functioning.
    - *Primary–Progressive*—Continuous worsening with some variations in rate and progression, but no remissions (affects about 15 percent).
    - *Secondary–Progressive*—Type that half of people with relapsing–remitting experience within ten years of initial diagnosis. Steady worsening with occasional flare-ups and minor remissions or plateaus. About 40 percent occurrence out of total diagnosed with MS.
- Many MS patients experience unpredictable day-to-day symptoms. Advances in treatment offer hope for future success in managing MS, especially when caught at an early stage.

Educational Strategies

- Occupational therapy to help with daily living activities
- Physical therapy to help patients with MS stand, walk, and maintain a range of motion with appropriate exercise
- Educational support and awareness to give people with MS an opportunity to learn more about how to help themselves and how to gain support from others
- Community–school connections and experiences
- Individual educational programs to address present and future academic and social needs

Muscular Dystrophy

Neuromuscular disease that involves both the nerves and muscles

Causes

- Can be X-linked recessive gene (female carriers) or autosomal dominant (defective gene is inherited from one parent's chromosomes in nonsex pairs 1 through 22)

- Flaws in muscle protein genes
- In general, genetic diseases can be related to these factors:
  - *Types of Chromosomes*—(a) autosomal (nonsex pairs 1–22) and (b) sex-linked (X-chromosome)
  - *Traits*—(a) dominant (caused by genes from one parent) and (b) recessive (caused by genes from both parents)

Contacts/Resources

National Library of Medicine National Institutes of Health: www.nlm.nih.gov/medlineplus/multiple sclerosis.html

Muscular Dystrophy Association: mda.org

Possible Characteristics

- Onset can be from early childhood to adulthood
- Severity and types vary from weakening and wasting of muscles in the hands, forearms, or lower legs to muscle cramps, twitches, or stiffness
- Some progression is slow with periods of rapid deterioration
- Can affect throat muscles or swallowing
- May include weaknesses in leg, hip, shoulder, or respiratory muscles
- Brain is sometimes involved with seizures, deafness, loss of balance and vision, and loss of lower cognitive abilities
- May need a wheelchair at any time
- May show signs of fatigue
- May be frustrated by immobility

Educational Strategies

- Emphasis on mobility and independent daily living
- Accessibility to and inclusion in all school facilities and functions
- Structured exercise program, with avoidance of intense physical demands
- Be alert for any physical changes
- Eliminate obstacles such as long note taking
- Assign peer buddy to help with arduous physical tasks such as lifting heavy books or maneuvering about in crowded halls
- Modified physical education program
- Technology to augment educational strategies might include the following:
  - Eye tracking to help those who lack physical power or dexterity to manually operate a keyboard or mouse (camera is employed to focus on the user's eye movement)
  - Voice-recognition technology for word processing
  - Cyberlink—band strapped around the forehead, offering a hands-free, alternative, augmentative type of communication that can detect both muscle and brain impulses to operate a computer mouse, video games, and more
- Staff should not lift or pull a student by the arms, since it could cause dislocation of limbs
- Peer support system for academic help and social inclusion
- Teach self-help skills
- Transitional planning

Spina Bifida

Causes

- Failure of the spinal cord to completely close up into one piece during early months of mother's pregnancy
- Congenital defect
- Affects newborns

Contact/Resources

Spina Bifida Resource Network: www.thesbrn.org

Possible Characteristics

- People born with spina bifida are not all alike
- Types of spina bifida include the following:
  - *Closed Neural Tube Defects* (with malformation of fat, bone, or membranes)—symptoms vary from

few or none to incomplete paralysis with urinary and bowel dysfunction
  - *Spina Bifida Manifesta*—includes the following two types:
    1. *Meningocele*—meninges (protective covering around the spinal cord) pushed out through an opening in the vertebrae in a sac called the meningocele, but the spinal cord is intact and can be repaired with little or no damage to the nerve pathways
    2. *Myelomeningocele*—severe form in which the spinal cord itself is damaged

- Nervous system (brain and spine) can be affected
- Muscle weakness or paralysis below the area of the spine where the cleft (incomplete closure) occurs with weak bones and joints
- Difficulty with bowel and bladder control in excretory system
- May have buildup of fluid in the brain (hydrocephalus), which can be surgically drained with a shunt; without a shunt implanted, the extra fluid can cause brain damage, seizures, or blindness
- Attention difficulties
- Need help with eye–hand coordination (e.g., perceptual activities)
- Language expression deficits
- Varying academic, physical, and social needs, with characteristics dependent on type and severity

Educational Strategies

- Placement in the least restrictive environment with nondisabled peers
- Adaptations in location and structure of the learning environment to meet physical needs, including fine- and gross-motor ones
- Early intervention for school preparation
- Communication with teachers concerning catheterization needs (tube inserted to allow passage of urine), with development of a school bladder management program if necessary
- Related services such as speech, physical, and occupational therapy
- Address emotional and social development by involving student in positive peer relationships (e.g., cooperative learning, community integration)
- Focus on positives and student's strengths
- Transitional services

SENSORY INVOLVEMENTS

Communication disorders: Speech is the production of sound; language is the form-and-function message in speech. Communication disorders (including speech, language, and hearing disorders) affect an estimated one of every ten people in the United States (see www.psychologytoday.com/conditions/communication-disorders). Communication involves both verbal and nonverbal behavior. Communication is delayed when the child is noticeably behind peers in the acquisition of speech or language:

DSM-5 includes the following communication disorder categories:

- Language Disorder. This involves reduced vocabulary, difficulties with the recall of words and sentences, and impairments in discourse.
- Speech Sound Disorder. Verbal communication of messages is affected by persistent difficulties with speech motor sound production, which interferes with social participation, academic achievement, or occupational performance. This includes articulation; phonological knowledge of speech sounds; movements of jaw, tongue, and lips; breathing; and vocalization. It is not attributable to congenital, medical, neurological, or acquired conditions.
- Childhood Onset Fluency Disorder (stuttering). A child's fluency and patterning of speech is inappropriate. He or she frequently repeats sounds and syllables, prolongs the sounds of consonants and vowels, breaks up words, and pauses. Onset is in the

early developmental period (two to seven years old)

- Social (Pragmatic) Communication Disorder. A child has deficits in verbal and nonverbal communication related to social contexts (e.g., greetings, conversation) and ambiguous language meanings—idioms, sarcasm, humor, and metaphors. According to DSM-5, these symptoms are not explained by ASD, ID, global developmental delay, or another mental disorder.
- Unspecified Communication Disorders. DSM-5 has this category for an individual who presents symptoms that do not meet full criteria for other communication disorders.

Communication Disorders

Causes

- Acquired or developmental:
  - Hearing loss
  - Brain injury
  - Drug abuse
  - Physical impairments such as cleft lip or palate
  - Vocal abuse or misuse
  - Hearing loss
  - Neurological disorder
- Cause is frequently unknown
- Some disorders are common in families
- *Apraxia* is a motor-speech disorder in which child has difficulties saying sounds, syllables, and words, along with difficulties transmitting brain messages to body parts (e.g., lips, jaw, tongue)
- Language disorders can be related to or overlap with other disabilities (e.g., developmental, intellectual, autism spectrum disorder, cerebral palsy)

Contacts/Resources

American Speech-Language-Hearing Association (ASHA): www.asha.org

Division for Communicative Disabilities and Deafness (DCDD) of the Council for Exceptional Children (CEC): community.cec.sped.org/DCDD/home/

Possible Characteristics

- Articulation
  - Distortions (e.g. "bud in yard" for bird)
  - Additions (e.g, "brook I read" for book)
  - Omissions (e.g., "we are see you" instead of seeing—can be ending sounds of words)
  - Substitutions (e.g., "wabbit wunning" for rabbit running)
- Voice quality
  - Intensity—softness or loudness
  - Resonance—nasality
  - Pitch—high or low tone
  - Onset fluency disorder (formerly called stuttering)—rhythm and flow
  - Interjections—repeats, hesitates, prolongs, or blocks sounds (e.g., well, um, you know)
  - Language disorders include reduced vocabulary and or sentence structure, limitations in social communication and conversations, and overall discourse
  - Impairment in understanding (receptive) and using/speaking (expressive) words in context
  - Difficulties with word retrieval, expressing ideas, grammar, reduced vocabulary, following directions, understanding a word's meaning; improper usage of words

Educational Strategies

- Timely intervention, since language and communication skills are easier to learn by age five
- Speech counseling and coordination with classroom teacher to develop communication goals for class and home, with consistent practice
- Communication boards with pictures (e.g., PECS—Picture Exchange Communication System)
- Technology for nonspeaking or severely disabled students
- Computer programs to link speech with writing
- Digital recorders

- Let speech relate to children's experiences, with instruction through conversation as well
- Mirrors
- More visuals
- Categorization of words
- Modeling, since children learn from others
- Patience (wait time)—do not talk for the child
- Praise for approximations

Deafness and Hearing Loss

Causes

- Hereditary and environmental factors
- Total deafness can be congenital
- Partial deafness may be attributed to loud noises, rubella, ear injury, or illness during pregnancy
- Types of hearing loss:
  - *Conductive*—caused by diseases or obstructions in the ear canal, eardrum, or middle ear
  - *Sensorineural*—results from damage to delicate sensory hair cells of the inner ear or the nerves
  - *Mixed*—combination of conductive and sensorineural loss (in both the outer or middle and the inner ear—cochlea or auditory nerve)

Contacts/Resources

American Society for Deaf Children (ASDC): www.deafchildren.org

Hearing Loss Association of America: www.hearingloss.org

Listening and Spoken Language Knowledge Center: listeningandspokenlanguage.org

Possible Characteristics

- Slight, mild, moderate, severe, or profound hearing loss
- *Conductive hearing loss* is usually not severe and can be helped medically, surgically, or with a hearing aid.
- *Sensorineural losses* range from mild to severe and can affect a person's ability to hear certain frequencies. Amplification does not help since a person might still hear distorted sounds. Hearing aids are also sometimes ineffectual.
- Frustration from not hearing can lead to behavioral outbursts.

Educational Strategies

- Sensitivity training for classroom peers with emphasis on social inclusion of students with hearing loss or deafness
- Appropriate speech services by trained professionals
- Amplification systems
- Note takers, sticky notes, communication boards, and interactive whiteboards
- Favorable seating
- Finger spelling or cued speech where hand signals and lip movements represent sounds
- Captioned films, videos
- Text telephones (TTY), CapTel (captioned telephone)
- More visuals, handouts, and outlines
- Interpreters to bridge communication between people who do not share same language (e.g., using sign language for a person who is deaf, then voicing it to a hearing person, such as with ASL) or transliterators to change one form of language to a different form of that same language (e.g., Cued Speech, see www.cuedspeech.org) with phonemes associated with language or Conceptually Accurate Signed English (CASE), which uses ASL concepts to sign words in proper English language order
- Oral transliteration has spoken words silently mouthed to the person with hearing loss or deafness, along with hand gestures and facial expressions. People should communicate with each other, not with the oral interpreter or transliterator, establishing eye contact and body language between parties having a conversation.
- C-print, a translation of classroom lecture in which instructional assistant, aide, or even an assigned classmate types the

lecture/notes on a computer in the back of the room that is then immediately sent to and read by the student at his or her own desk/laptop computer, can be a way to see the words. See www.rit.edu/ntid/cprint.
- Language development (help with idiomatic expressions, vocabulary, and grammar) with frequent monitoring
- Face the student when reading and giving directions, speaking slowly and clearly in conversational voice, not overemphasizing lip reading
- Eliminate background noises

Processing Disorders: Auditory

Causes

- *Not* a result of hearing loss

Contacts/Resources

American Speech-Language-Hearing Association: www.asha.org/public/hearing/Understanding-Auditory-Processing-Disorders-in-Children/

Bellis, T. J. (2002). *When the brain can't hear: Unraveling the mystery of auditory processing disorder.* New York: Atria.

National Coalition on Auditory Processing Disorders: www.ncapd.org

Possible Characteristics

- Symptoms similar to ADHD; must distinguish between the two
- Trouble hearing similarities and differences in sounds
- Blending word parts/decoding/phonics
- Expressive and receptive language difficulties
- Difficulties with any or all of the following:
    - Listening to lectures
    - Grammatical structure
    - Oral directions
    - Understanding music and lyrics
    - Spelling
- May involve the following:
    - Auditory discrimination—hearing whether sounds of letters are the same or different
    - Auditory memory—repeating a clapped sequence, following a band's rhythm, remembering sounds of familiar objects, following more than one direction
    - Auditory localization—determining the source or direction of a sound
    - Auditory figure-ground—paying attention in a noisy room

Educational Strategies

- Give brief, concise directions at a student's level of comprehension
- Accompany verbal directions with written ones
- Use more gestures when speaking
- Intermittently check student's understanding by asking simple questions, or request him or her to repeat or paraphrase what was said; use appropriate grade-level vocabulary
- Reduce the amount of background noises—place old cut-up tennis balls on bottom of desk and chair legs
- Ask school nurse to check student's hearing to rule out any medical concerns
- Increase student's self-awareness of type of mistakes made with words
- Make more eye contact with student before speaking
- Teach the student how to take notes while listening for main ideas presented; give the student a graphic organizer to follow
- Use more technology that offers audible learning, such as word processing programs with speech capabilities
- Have student connect with a partner or peer who can model and consult
- Utilize speech/language therapy and audiological services as necessary
- Teach phonetic rules vs. just sight-word programs or strict memorization to develop automaticity with linguistic skills

Central auditory processing disorder (CAPD) occurs when a child has normal hearing, but an area of the brain where auditory analysis occurs is not obtaining meaning from sounds and stimuli. It can affect memory, speech, language, and reading. Students have difficulties discriminating phonemes that are the basic building blocks of language and specific consonants, such as *b, d,* and *p.* They can confuse these sounds while reading. More strategies are also listed under the auditory processing heading: More visuals, repetition of directions, teaching configuration of words, strengthening expressive and receptive language skills, encouraging more self-awareness, and continual praise is crucial.

Source: Shprintzen (2000).

Processing Disorders: Visual Impairments

Can include disorders that lead to vision impairments such as retinal degeneration, albinism, cataracts, glaucoma, corneal disorders, diabetic retinopathy, infections, muscular problems that result in visual disturbances, and other congenital disorders

Causes

- Environmental or genetic
- Birth injuries, heredity, illness with fever, muscle problems

Contacts/Resources

AccessWorld Magazine: www.afb.org/aw/main.asp

American Foundation for the Blind: www.afb.org

Concordia Learning Center at St. Joseph's School for the Blind: www.clcnj.org

Learning Ally: www.learningally.org

National Center on Accessible Instructional Materials: aim.cast.org/learn/student_learning/ASR/forBVI#.VCIBZ0uPlH0

Possible Characteristics

- Vary with the age of onset, severity, type of loss, and overall functioning of the child
- May not explore things in the environment and may miss opportunities to imitate social behavior or understand nonverbal skills
- May involve difficulties with the following:
    - Easily understanding and remembering what is seen
    - Picturing words or concepts in their heads
    - Matching like shapes
    - Doing art activities
    - Reproducing patterns
    - Working on puzzles
    - Noticing the differences between objects, words, numbers
    - Spelling accurately
    - Poor handwriting
    - Organizational or neatness issues
- Accurate proofreading of writing, checking accuracy of computational problems, aligning columns in math, writing words and letters on lines
    - Dislikes learning when seeing it alone as the only method of presentation; students need kinesthetic (body) and tactile (touch) connections along with auditory input
- May involve the following:
    - Visual motor—may work close to a paper or desk, rotate papers and books
    - Visual figure-ground—completing work on crowded pages
    - Visual discrimination—matching shapes or forms, or distinguishing similar words, such as *hundreds* and *hundredths*
    - Visual closure—doing simple puzzles, not able to see objects or their functions in their entirety
    - Visual memory—for example, retelling three visual acts in sequence: close a door, sharpen a pencil, sit down
- Terminology:
    - *Hyperopia* (farsightedness)—when a person sees faraway objects better than objects that are nearby

  - *Myopia* (nearsightedness)—when objects close by can be seen, but there is difficulty seeing objects at a distance
  - *Strabismus*—eyes are not straight; each eye sends a different message to the brain
  - *Astigmatism*—blurred or distorted images
  - *Ocular motor*—muscles of the eye working together (e.g., fixate, follow, converge)
  - *Partially Sighted (Visually Impaired)*—some type of vision problem with sight ranging from 20/70 to 20/200 after correction with glasses. Signs of eye trouble include blinking a lot; rubbing eyes; squinting, shutting or covering one eye; red or swollen, watery eyes; and headaches
  - *Low Vision*—severe visual impairment
  - *Legally Blind*—less than 20/200 vision in better eye or limited field of vision
  - *Totally Blind*—complete darkness

Educational Strategies

- Support visual information with verbal instructions
- Reduce amount of work on pages, or block off part of the work
- Use stronger modalities (auditory or kinesthetic-tactile paired with auditory)
- Strengthen memory by associating how and where students originally saw learning material
- Use highlighters on worksheets and colored overlays on texts
- Compartmentalize information in student-friendly graphic organizers that visually separate information
- Provide more manipulatives, such as puzzles, tangrams, and geoboards; and sorting activities, such as categorizing words on index cards into syllable types
- Reduce clutter in the room, including extra materials by student's desk
- Use copiers to enlarge print
- Gradually increase time and difficulties of visual tasks
- Praise accomplishments
- Early intervention programs
- Technology—using computers with talking text programs
- Low-vision and optical aids for the partially sighted
- Magnification pages
- Audiobooks
- Large-print materials; Braille books
- Interdisciplinary approach, with learning through all subjects taught using more auditory and kinesthetic-tactile presentations
- Emphasize independent daily living and self-care skills (e.g., hygiene, mobility training, using kitchen tools, and following routines)
- Participation in regular classroom activities with appropriate support, understanding, and encouragement
- Adaptations in lighting
- Encourage positive peer social interactions

> **Processing speed** can affect memory, writing, reading, speaking, word retrieval, any type of timed activity, focusing while working independently, and staying on task for any reasonable time period.

SYNDROMES

Angelman Syndrome (AS)

Causes

- Genetic disorder with a deleted region of genes on chromosome 15
- Children with AS were formerly called *puppet children,* named after an oil painting *(Boy With a Puppet)* seen by Dr. Harry Angelman, which depicted a boy with similar characteristics as his patients. The name was later changed to Angelman syndrome
- Estimate of 1 in 15,000 to 1 in 30,000 are affected; exact numbers are unknown
- AS appears equally among all races and in both sexes

Contact/Resources

Angelman Syndrome Foundation:
www.angelman.org

Possible Characteristics

- Not usually detected at birth or in infancy, since there are nonspecific developmental delays
- Usual age of diagnosis is when features and characteristic behaviors become most evident (ages three to seven)
- Range of gait disorders with uncoordinated movements that affect walking, feeding, and reaching for objects
- Hypermotoric activity with short attention span
- Difficulty attending to social cues
- Excessive, often contagious laughter, with lots of smiling and a happy disposition
- Difficulty with conversational speech along with varying nonverbal skills
- Skin and eye *hypopigmentation*—no pigment in the retina
- *Strabismus*—eye coordination problem in which eyes do not concurrently focus on the same point, but may look in different directions
- Sleep disturbances

Educational Strategies

- Early training and enrichment programs
- Physical therapy for gross-motor difficulties
- Occupational therapy for oral-motor and fine-motor control
- Structured classroom design and environment to accommodate hypermotoric needs
- Speech and communication therapy including augmentative aids such as communication boards and more visuals
- Individualization with flexibility
- Behavior modification
- Peer support and awareness of syndrome
- Training of all staff working with children
- Home-to-school communication with coordination of physical, academic, and behavioral programs

Down Syndrome

Causes

- A chromosomal disorder that occurs from an accident in cell development that leaves 47, instead of the usual 46, chromosomes. It is determined by a *karyotype* (visual chromosome study).
- Most people with Down syndrome have an extra No. 21 chromosome
- Uncertain what causes this extra genetic material that happens at conception
- One of the leading clinical causes of intellectual disability
- Does not correlate to race, nationality, or socioeconomic status
- Higher incidence for mothers who give birth over age thirty-five

Contacts/Resources

American Association on Intellectual and Developmental Disabilities: aaidd.org

The Arc: www.thearc.org

Down Syndrome.com: www.downsyndrome.com

GiGi's Playhouse: Down Syndrome Achievement Centers: gigisplayhouse.org

National Down Syndrome Congress: www.ndsccenter.org

National Down Syndrome Society: www.ndss.org

Possible Characteristics

- Slower physical and intellectual growth
- Health-related problems could include heart defects, gastrointestinal tract problems, visual and hearing impairments (crossed eyes, farsightedness or nearsightedness, mild to moderate hearing loss), speech difficulties, atlantoaxial instability (misalignment of top two vertebrae of the neck), and respiratory difficulties, since they might have a lower resistance to infection. A cardiogram is needed at birth to identify heart concerns and appropriate medical care.
- Physical signs can include a smaller head; slanting eyes (epicanthal folds); short, broad hands, feet, and toes; flat bridge of the nose; short neck; low-set ears; and poor muscle tone (hypotonia). There is a wide range of mental abilities, from mild to severe cognitive impairments.

- Difficulties understanding directions and abstract concepts
- Receptive language better than expressive language (understanding more than communicating through speech)
- Memory affected

Educational Strategies

- Early educational and developmental services and therapies beginning in infancy
- Speech therapy
- Nutritional/hygiene counseling
- Peer education and sensitivity to reinforce acceptance, since children all have certain social/emotional needs in common; necessary whether or not children are placed in inclusive classrooms
- Increase usage of visuals, manipulatives, and concrete learning experiences
- Physical exercise program, including more wrist- and finger-strengthening activities such as cutting and sorting as well as activities to strengthen individual stamina
- Teach in a step-by-step manner with consistent, positive feedback, drill, and repetition
- Encourage independence under teacher's auspices with realistic but high expectations
- Concentrate on potentials, not limitations
- Consistent family communication of progress with home reinforcement of learned academic/social skills
- Transitional plans with planned community involvement and functional training for daily living skills with participation in supported employment with job shadowing and mentoring
- Relate new content to previously learned subjects and real-life situations

Prader-Willi Syndrome (PWS)

Complex rare genetic disorder that can cause cognitive disabilities, behavior problems, short stature, poor muscle tone, incomplete sexual development, and a chronic hungry feeling that if uncontrolled may lead to excessive eating and life-threatening obesity.

Causes

- Genetic cause is loss of unidentified genes (defect of chromosome 15) contributed by the father that occurs at or near time of conception for unknown reasons
- DNA analysis confirms PWS diagnosis
- Prevalence: 1 in 12,000 to 15,000 (both sexes, all races); one of the most common conditions seen in genetic clinics and leading genetic cause of obesity
- PWS-like disorder can occur after birth if the hypothalamus portion of the brain is damaged during surgery or injured

Contacts/Resources

Prader-Willi Syndrome Association USA: www.pwsausa.org

Possible Characteristics

- Excessive or rapid weight gain between ages one and six with possibility of obesity if not vigilantly monitored and nutritionally controlled
- Short stature by age fifteen
- Range of IQ from 40 to 105, with learning problems evident in those with average IQ
- May have short-term auditory memory problems, attention difficulties, and weak abstract thinking
- Good visual perception skills, long-term memory, reading ability, and receptive language
- Deficits in speech articulation, motor coordination, strength, and balance
- Habit of skin-picking
- Younger children usually do not exhibit behavioral problems, but most older children and adults with PWS have difficulties regulating behavior and dealing with transitions and unexpected changes
- May have outbursts of stubbornness; may steal money or items to buy/trade food; may be prone to lying
- Sleep disorders/fatigue

Educational Strategies

- Behavior plans that emphasize positive rewards, clear rules, limits, structure, and daily routines

- Physical and occupational therapies
- Exercise and sports-related activities that are less competitive (to accommodate poor muscle tone and fatigue)
- Social skills training
- Speech therapy
- Early infant stimulation
- Full range of appropriate services in least restrictive environment
- Peer support system
- Communicate with family to coordinate behavioral plans
- Food restriction plan in school and home; structured diet plan and lifelong diet supervision
- Transitional plans with preparation for adult living and maximum community involvement based on varying cognitive levels

Tourette Syndrome (TS)

Causes

- Genetic predisposition
- Neurological disorder
- Abnormal metabolism of neurotransmitters (chemicals in the brain), which might cause the tics
- Early diagnosis and treatment, since some children require medication

Contacts/Resources

Tourette Syndrome Association: www.tsa-usa.org, ts-stories.org

Tourette Syndrome "Plus" the Associated Disorders: www.tourettesyndrome.net

tic = sudden, rapid, recurrent, nonrhythmic, stereotyped motor movement or vocalization

Possible Characteristics

- Symptoms include involuntary tics and rapid motor or vocal movements that can range from simple to complex
- Onset is before the age of eighteen with most cases being mild
- Symptoms can decrease as children mature (late teens, early twenties) with possible remission of tic symptoms
- There are two types of Tourette syndrome:
  - *Simple*—motor: eye blinking, facial grimaces, shoulder shrugs, head jerking; vocal: noises such as tongue clicking, and other throat sounds
  - *Complex*—motor: twirling, jumping, touching possessions of others, and—rarely—self-injurious behavior; vocal: coprolalia (use of obscene language, e.g., derogatory remarks, swearing), which is present in less than 15 percent of the TS population
- Associated with impulsivity, attention problems (ADHD), and learning or perceptual difficulties
- Easily frustrated
- Misbehavior due to neurobiological disturbances

Educational Strategies

- Give the student more opportunities for movement, with frequent breaks outside of the classroom setting
- Involve school psychologist
- Educate peers and other staff (e.g., bus drivers, lunch aides, special subjects teachers)
- Reduce—break down, sequence, and color-code assignments
- Avoid front seating since tics can be embarrassing; even allow student a place to work outside of the classroom
- Try to seat student away from visual distractions
- Encourage use of a word processor, or allow alternatives to written assignments
- Allow extra time for class work or shorten assignments based on level of mastery
- Provide outlines and study guides
- Cue student about learning expectations before a new lesson; have student repeat directions for a task, and signal student for transitional activities
- Watch for side effects from medication

Resource B

Organizations

Academy of Orton-Gillingham Practitioners and Educators—www.ortonacademy.org
AccessWorld Magazine—www.afb.org/aw/main.asp
Achieve the Core—achievethecore.org
ADDitude: Strategies and Support for ADHD & LD—www.additudemag.com
American Academy of Child & Adolescent Psychiatry—www.aacap.org
American Association on Intellectual and Developmental Disabilities (AAIDD)—www.aaidd.org
American Foundation for the Blind—www.afb.org
The American Occupational Therapy Association—www.aota.org/About-Occupational-Therapy.aspx
American Physical Therapy Association—www.apta.org
American Society for Deaf Children—www.deafchildren.org
American Speech-Language-Hearing Association—www.asha.org
Angelman Syndrome Foundation—www.angelman.org
Anxiety and Depression Association of America—www.adaa.org
Anti-Defamation League—www.adl.org
The Arc—www.thearc.org
Association for Behavior Analysis International—www.abainternational.org
The Association for the Gifted (TAG), Division of the Council for Exceptional Children—www.cectag.org
Association on Higher Education and Disability (AHEAD)—www.ahead.org
Attention Deficit Disorder Association (ADDA)—www.add.org
Autism Research Institute—www.autism.com
Autism Society—www.autism-society.org
Autism Speaks—www.autismspeaks.org
The Balanced Mind Parent Network—www.thebalancedmind.org
Best Buddies—www.bestbuddies.org
Brain Injury Association of America—www.biausa.org
Brain Injury Survivor's Guide—braininjuryguide.org
Bright Hub Education—www.brighthubeducation.com/special-ed-physical-disabilities
Bulimia—www.bulimia.com
CAST: Center for Applied Technology—www.cast.org
Center for Applied Linguistics—www.cal.org
The Center for Effective Collaboration and Practice—cecp.air.org
Center for Parent Information and Resources—www.parentcenterhub.org
Centers for Disease Control and Prevention, Attention Deficit Hyperactivity Disorders—www.cdc.gov/ncbddd/adhd
Children and Adults with Attention-Deficit/Hyperactivity Disorder (CHADD)—www.chadd.org
The Children's Museum Kits Program—www.bostonchildrensmuseum.org/exhibits-programs/museum-professionals/exhibit-kits

The Collaborative for Academic, Social and Emotional Learning (CASEL)—www.casel.org
College Board Services for Students with Disabilities—www.collegeboard.org/students-with-disabilities
Common Core State Standards Initiative—www.corestandards.org
Concordia Learning Center at St. Joseph's School for the Blind—www.clcnj.org
The Council for Exceptional Children (CEC)—www.cec.sped.org
Council for Exceptional Children Division of Learning Disabilities—teachingld.org
Davis Dyslexia Association International—www.dyslexia.com
Developmental Delay Resources—devdelay.org
Disabled Sports USA—www.disabledsportsusa.org
Disabled World—Physical and Mobility Impairments: Facts, News, and Information—www.disabled-world.com/disability/types/mobility
Division for Communicative Disabilities and Deafness (DCD), for Council for Exceptional Children—community.cec.sped.org/DCDD/home/
Division on Autism and Developmental Disabilities, Council for Exceptional Children—www.daddcec.org
Down Syndrome on the Internet, Social Networking—www.downsyndrome.com
Dr. Mac's Behavior Management Site—www.behavioradvisor.com
Dyscalculia.org—www.dyscalculia.org
Dynamic Learning Maps—secure.dynamiclearningmaps.org/unc/modules.html
The Early Childhood Research Institute on Culturally and Linguistically Appropriate Services (CLAS)—clas.uiuc.edu
The Educator's Reference Desk—www.eduref.org
Elementary and Secondary Education Act—www.ed.gov/esea
Epilepsy Foundation—www.epilepsy.com
Equal Access: Universal Design for Physical Access: University of Washington—www.washington.edu/doit/Brochures/Programs/equal_access_spaces.html
Facing History—www.facinghistory.org
Friends with MS—www.friendswithms.com
GiGi's Playhouse, Down Syndrome Achievement Centers—gigisplayhouse.org
Global Autism Collaboration—www.globalautismcollaboration.com
Handwriting Without Tears—www.hwtears.com
Hearing Loss Association of America—www.hearingloss.org
HEATH Resource Center at George Washington University, National Youth Transitions Center—www.heath.gwu.edu
High Scope Curriculum—www.highscope.org/Content.asp?ContentId=1
The International Dyslexia Association—www.interdys.org
International OCD Foundation—www.ocfoundation.org
International Reading Association—www.reading.org
The International Society for Technology in Education (ISTE)—www.iste.org/standards
Intervention Central—www.interventioncentral.org
Jolly Phonics-Jolly Learning Ltd—www.jollylearning.co.uk
Keyboarding Without Tears—www.hwtears.com/kwt
The Kids on the Block, Inc.—www.kotb.com
LD OnLine—www.ldonline.org
Learning Ally—www.learningally.org
Learning Disabilities Association of America (LDA)—ldaamerica.org
Listening and Spoken Language Center—listeningandspokenlanguage.org
MAAP Services for Autism and Asperger Syndrome—www.aspergersyndrome.org
The Math Forum at Drexel Math Library—www.mathforum.org

Mayer-Johnson LLC—www.mayer-johnson.com
Mental Health America—www.mentalhealthamerica.net
Multiple Sclerosis International Foundation—www.msif.org, www.friendswithms.com
Muscular Dystrophy Association—www.mdausa.org
My Child at CerebralPalsy.org—cerebralpalsy.org/about-cerebral-palsy/types-and-forms
National Alliance on Mental Illness (NAMI)—www.nami.org
National Association of Anorexia Nervosa and Associated Disorders (ANAD)— www.anad.org
National Association for Bilingual Education—www.nabe.org
National Association for Down Syndrome (NADS)—www.nads.org
National Association for Gifted Children (NAGC)—www.nagc.org
National Association for Music Education—www.nafme.org
National Association for the Education of Young Children (NAEYC)—www.naeyc.org
National Business and Disability Council—www.viscardicenter.org/services/nbdc
National Center and State Collaborative—www.ncscpartners.org
National Center for Educational Statistics, Institute of Education Sciences, U.S. Dept. of Education—www.nces.ed.gov
National Center for Families Learning—www.familieslearning.org
National Center for Learning Disabilities (NCLD)—www.ncld.org
National Center on Accessible Instructional Materials—aim.cast.org
National Center on Disability and Journalism (NCDJ), ASU Walter Cronkite School of Journalism and Mass Communication—www.ncdj.org
National Center on Time and Learning—www.timeandlearning.org/time-innovation-matters-education-act
National Coalition on Auditory Processing Disorders—www.ncapd.org
National Council of Learning Disabilities—www.ncld.org
National Council of Teachers of English (NCTE)—www.ncte.org
National Council of Teachers of Mathematics (NCTM)—www.nctm.org
The National Council on Independent Living—www.ncil.org
National Cued Speech Association—www.cuedspeech.org
National Down Syndrome Congress—www.ndsccenter.org
National Down Syndrome Society—ndss.org
National Eating Disorder Association (NEDA)—www.nationaleatingdisorders.org
National Federation of Families for Children's Mental Health—www.ffcmh.org
National Institute on Deafness and Other Communication Disorders—www.nidcd.nih.gov/Pages/default.aspx
National Institutes of Mental Health—www.nimh.nih.gov/index.shtml
National Library of Medicine National Institutes of Health— www.nlm.nih.gov/medlineplus/multiplesclerosis.html
National Multiple Sclerosis Society—www.nationalmssociety.org
National Rehabilitation Information Center (NARIC)—www.naric.com
Newsela—newsela.com
The Next Generation Science Standards—www.nextgenscience.org/next-generation-science-standards
Obsessive-Compulsive Foundation (OCF)—www.ocfoundation.org
Office of Special Education and Rehabilitative Services (OSERS)—www.ed.gov/about/offices/list/osers/osep/index.html
Online Asperger Syndrome Information and Support (OASIS)—www.aspergersyndrome.org
Parent Advocacy Coalition for Educational Rights (PACER)—www.pacer.org; Technical Assistance ALLIANCE for Parent Centers at PACER Center—www.pacer.org/alliance/

The Partnership for 21st Century Skills—www.p21.org
The Partnership for Assessment of Readiness for College and Careers (PARCC)—www.parcconline.org/parcc-accessibility-features-and-accommodations-manual, parcconline.org
People Living Through Cancer—www.pltc.org
Pinterest by Toby Karten—www.pinterest.com/tkarten
The Prader-Willi Syndrome Association—www.pwsausa.org
Project Zero at the Harvard Graduate School of Education—www.pzweb.harvard.edu
PTA National Headquarters—www.pta.org, www.ptacentral.org
Respect Diversity Foundation—www.respectdiversity.org
Response to Intervention and Literacy Collaborative—www.lcosu.org/documents/PDFs/RtI_in_Literacy_Collaborative_Schools.pdf
Selective Mutism Foundation—www.selectivemutismfoundation.org
Selective Mutism Group—www.selectivemutism.org, www.social-anxiety.com
Sensory Resources at Future Horizons—fhautism.com/sensory-resources/
Services for Students With Disabilities (SAT)—www.collegeboard.org/students-with-disabilities
Smarter Balanced Assessment Consortium (SBAC)—www.smarterbalanced.org
Social Anxiety—www.social-anxiety.com
Social Studies for Kids—www.socialstudiesforkids.com
Southern Poverty Law Center, Teaching Tolerance—www.tolerance.org
Special Olympics—www.specialolympics.com
Spina Bifida Association of America—www.spinabifidaassociation.org
Spina Bifida Resource Network—www.thesbrn.org
Sports and Recreational Activities for Children With Physical Disabilities, The Cure Our Children Foundation—www.cureourchildren.org/sports.htm
Study Guides and Strategies—www.studygs.net
SunCastle Technology—www.suncastletech.com
Tangrams—www.curiouser.co.uk/tangram/template.htm
TASH, for Students With Significant Disabilities—www.tash.org
Teaching LD, Division of Learning Disabilities (DLD) of the Council for Exceptional Children—www.teachingld.org
Think College, College Options for Students With Intellectual Disabilities—www.thinkcollege.net
Thinking Cap Quiz Bowl—www.thinkingcapquizbowl.com/thinkingcap
TouchMath, Innovative Learning Concepts—www.touchmath.com
Tourette Syndrome Association—www.tsa-usa.org
Tourette Syndrome Information—www.tourettesyndrome.org
Traumatic Brain Injury Resources—www.traumaticbraininjury.com
Twice-Exceptional Online Newsletter—www.2enewsletter.com
United Cerebral Palsy—www.ucp.org
U.S. Department of Education, Building the Legacy: IDEA 2004—idea.ed.gov
What Works Clearinghouse, U.S. Dept. of Education, Institute of Education Sciences—ies.ed.gov/ncee/wwc
Wilson Language Training—www.wilsonlanguage.com
World Health Organization—www.who.int
Wrightslaw—www.wrightslaw.com
The Yale Center for Dyslexia & Creativity—dyslexia.yale.edu

Resource C

Alphabetized Acronyms

AA-AAS—alternate assessment based upon alternate academic achievement standards

AAIDD—American Association on Intellectual and Developmental Disabilities

ABA—applied behavior analysis

ABC—antecedent, behavior, consequence

ABOWA—assessment by observation and walking around

ADA—Americans with Disabilities Act

ADAAA—Americans with Disabilities Act Amendments Act

ADHD—attention deficit hyperactivity disorder

ADL—activities of daily living

AEIOU's of Study Skills—attitude, effort, involvement, organization, understanding

AIM—accessible instructional materials

APA—American Psychiatric Association

APD—auditory processing disorders

APE—adaptive physical education

ARC—The ARC

ARRA—American Recovery and Reinvestment Act of 2009

ASD—autism spectrum disorder

ASL—American Sign Language

AT—assistive technology

AYP—adequate yearly progress

BD—behavioral disorder

BIP—behavior intervention plan

BOE—Board of Education

BOSE—beginning of special education

BP—bipolar or "Be positive!"

CA—chronological age

CAPD—central auditory processing disorder

CAST—Center for Applied Special Technology

CBA—curriculum-based assessments

CBT—cognitive behavioral therapy

CC—closed captioning

CCR—college and career readiness

CCSS—Common Core State Standards

CCSSO—Council of Chief State School Officers

CD—conduct disorder

CEC—Council for Exceptional Children

CHADD—Children and Adults with Attention Deficit Disorder

CI—communication impaired

CNS—central nervous system

CP—cerebral palsy

CRAFT—communication, resourcefulness, accommodations, flexibility, training

CSI—common sense inclusion

CST—child study team

DA—dis*ability* awareness

DD—developmental dis*ability*

DI—differentiated instruction

DIBELS—Dynamic Indicators of Basic Early Literacy Skills

DMDD—disruptive mood dysregulation disorder

DOE—Department of Education

DRA—developmental reading assessment

DS—Down syndrome

DSM—Diagnostic and Statistical Manual of Mental Disorders

DVRS—Division of Vocational and Rehabilitation Services

EBP—evidence-based practice

ED—emotional disturbance

ED'S CAR—expand, delete, substitute, combine, and rearrange

EHA—Education of All Handicapped Children Act

EIS—early intervention services

EL—English learners

ELA—English language arts

ELC—early learning center

ELT—extra learning time

EPA'S of Grading—effort, progress, achievement, self-awareness

ESEA—Elementary and Secondary Education Act

ESL—English as a second language

ESY—extended school year

FAPE—free, appropriate public education

FAS—fetal alcohol syndrome

FBA—functional behavioral assessment

FERPA—Family Education Rights and Privacy Act

FSA—Family Support Act

GE—general education

GT—gifted and talented

HEATH—Higher Education and Training for People with Disabilities

HI—hearing impaired

HQT—highly qualified teacher

IAES—interim alternative educational setting

ID—intellectual disability

IDEA—Individuals with Disabilities Education Act

IDEIA—Individuals with Disabilities Education Improvement Act

IED—intermittent explosive disorder

IEP—individualized education program (or "It's educationally prudent!")

IES—Institute of Education Sciences

IFSP—individualized family service plan

IHE—Institutes of Higher Education

ILP—independent living plan

ILT—increased learning time

ISTE—International Society for Technology in Education

ITIP—instructional theory into practice

ITP—individualized transition plan

LD—learning dis*ability* or learning differences

LDA—Learning Disabilities Association of America

LEA—Local Education Agency

LOF—level of functioning

LRE—least restrictive environment

MAAP—more advanced individuals with autism, Asperger syndrome, and pervasive developmental disorder

MDR—manifestation determination review

MDT—multidisciplinary team

MI—multiple intelligences, or massive initializations

MS—multiple sclerosis, or master of science, or both!

NAEP—National Assessment of Educational Programs

NBDC—National Business & Disability Council

NCEO—National Center on Educational Outcomes

NCES—National Center for Education Statistics

NCLB—No Child Left Behind Act

NCLD—National Center for Learning Disabilities

NCTL—National Center for Technology Literacy

NGA—National Governors Association Center for Best Practices

NIH—National Institutes of Health

NIMAS—National Instructional Materials Accessibility Standard

NIMH—National Institute of Mental Health

OCD—obsessive–compulsive disorder

OCR—Office of Civil Rights

ODD—oppositional defiant disorder

OHI—other health impairment

OI—orthopedic impairment

O & M—orientation and mobility

OSEP—Office of Special Education Programs

OSERS—Office of Special Education and Rehabilitative Services

OT—occupational therapy

PACER—Parent Advocacy Coalition for Educational Rights

PALS—peer-assisted learning strategies

PANDAS—pediatric autoimmune neuropsychiatric disorders associated with streptococcal infections

PARCC—Partnership for Assessment of Readiness for College and Careers

PBL—problem-based learning, project-based learning

PBS—positive behavioral supports

PECS—picture exchange communication system

PET—positron emission tomography, or pupil evaluation team

PL—Public Law

PLAAFP—present level of academic achievement and functional performance

PLEP—present level of educational performance

PLOP—present level of performance

PNP—personal needs profile

PMT—parent management training

PS—preschool

PT—physical therapy

PWS—Prader-Willi Syndrome

RF—reading: foundational skills

RI—reading: informational text

RL—reading: literature

RS—related services

RTI—response to intervention (or "Remember to include!")

SAS—supplemental aids and services

SAT—Scholastic Aptitude Test

SB—spina bifida

SBAC—Smarter Balanced Assessment Consortium

SCD—social communication disorder

SDI—specially designed instruction

SDM—severe discrepancy model

SE—special education

SEA—State Education Agency

SEL—social and emotional learning

SES—supplemental educational services

SGO—student growth objective

SI or SID—sensory integration dysfunction

SIG—School Improvement Grant

SLD—specific learning disability

SLO—student learning objectives

SLP—speech-language pathologists

SOARing—scanning, outlining, analyzing, reading

SPED—special education

SPP—state performance plan

SST—student study team

TAG—talented and gifted

TBI—traumatic brain injury

TDD—telecommunication devices for the deaf, and test-driven development

TGIF—"Thank goodness inclusion's feasible!"

TIME—Time for Innovation Matters in Education Act

TIPS—topic, individuals, planning, setting

TLC—tender, loving care (What students in every classroom need!)

TPP—transition planning process

TS—Tourette syndrome, or transitional services

TTY—text telephone

UbD—understanding by design

UDL—universal design for learning

VAKT—visual, auditory, kinesthetic, tactile

VI—visual impairment

VoIP—voice over the Internet protocol

VR—vocational rehabilitation

VRI—video remote interpreting

WHO—World Health Organization

WHST—writing, history, science, and technical subjects

WWC—What Works Clearinghouse

WWCI—"Ways we can include!"

Available for download at **www.corwin.com/inclusionstrategies**

References and Further Readings

Abeel, S. (2003). *My thirteenth winter.* New York: Scholastic.

ADA Amendments Act of 2008, Pub. L. No. 110-325, 122 Stat. 3553, 3554 (2008).

Adamek, M., & Darrow, A. (2005). *Music in special education.* Silver Spring, MD: American Music Therapy Association.

Agassi, M. (2002). *Hands are not for hitting.* Minneapolis, MN: Free Spirit Publishing.

Allsopp, D., Kyger, M., Lovin, L., Gerretson, H., Carson, K., & Ray, S. (2008). Mathematics dynamic assessment: Informal assessment that responds to the needs of struggling learners in mathematics. *Teaching Exceptional Children, 40*(3), 6–16.

American Psychiatric Association. (2013). *Diagnostic and statistical manual of mental disorders* (5th ed.). Arlington, VA: American Psychiatric Publishing.

Americans With Disabilities Act, Pub. L. No. 101-336, 104 Stat. 327 (1990).

Anderson, O., Marsh, M., & Harvey, A. (1999). *Learn with the classics: Using music to study smart at any age.* San Francisco, CA: Lind Institute.

Armstrong, T. (2003b). *You're smarter than you think: A kid's guide to multiple intelligences.* Minneapolis, MN: Free Spirit.

Armstrong, T. (2009). *Multiple intelligences in the classroom.* Alexandria, VA: Association for Supervision and Curriculum Development.

Association for Supervision and Curriculum Development. (2002). *ASCD education update.* Alexandria, VA: Author.

Auer, C., & Blumberg, S. (2006). *Parenting a child with sensory processing disorder: A family guide to understanding and supporting your sensory-sensitive child.* Oakland, CA: Harbinger Publications.

Baker, J. (2001). *The social skills picture book: Teaching play, emotion, and communication to children with autism.* Arlington: TX: Future Horizons.

Baker, J. (2005). *Preparing for life: The complete guide for transitioning to adulthood for those with autism and Asperger's syndrome.* Arlington, TX: Future Horizons.

Beattie, J., Jordan, L., & Algozzine, B. (2006). *Making inclusion work: Effective practices for ALL teachers.* Thousand Oaks, CA: Corwin.

Belland, B.R., Glazewski, K.D., & Ertmer, P.A. (2009). Inclusion and problem-based learning: Roles of students in a mixed-ability group. *RMLE Online, 32*(9), 1–19.

Bellis, T. J. (2002). *When the brain can't hear: Unraveling the mystery of auditory processing disorder.* New York, NY: Atria.

Berninger, V., & Wolf, B. (2009). *Helping students with dyslexia and dysgraphia make connections: Differentiated instruction lesson plans in reading and writing.* Baltimore, MD: Paul H. Brookes.

Bloom, B. S. (Ed.). (1956). *Taxonomy of educational objectives: Cognitive domain.* New York, NY: David McKay.

Browder, D. (2006, March). *General curriculum: How to access the content and assess achievement for students with disabilities.* Paper presented at the meeting of the American Council on Rural Special Education, Lexington, KY.

Bulgren, J., Graner, P., & Deshler, D. (2013). Literacy challenges and opportunities for students with learning disabilities in social studies and history. *Learning Disabilities Research & Practice, 28*(1), 17–27.

Burke, K., & Sutherland, C. (2004). Attitudes toward inclusion: Knowledge vs. experience. *Education, 125*(2), 163–172.

Canfield, J., Hansen, M. V., & Kirberger, K. (2012). *Chicken soup for the teenage soul on tough stuff: Stories of tough times and lessons learned.* Pikesville, MD: BackList.

Carlson, E., Brauen, M., Klein, S., Schroll, K., & Willig Westat, S. (2002). *SPeNSE: Study of personnel needs in special education.* Retrieved from http://education.ufl.edu/spense/files/2013/06/Key-Findings-_Final_.pdf

Cassidy, J. (1994). *Earthsearch: A kid's geography museum in a book.* Palo Alto, CA: Klutz Press.

Center for Effective Collaboration and Practice. (2001). Functional behavioral assessment. Retrieved from http://cecp.air.org/fba

Center for Parent Information and Resources. (2012). Categories of disability under IDEA. Retrieved from http://www.parentcenterhub.org/repository/categories/

Chambers, C. (2008). Trends in special education. *District Administrator, 44*(4), 3.

Chorzempa, B., & Lapidua, L. (2009). To find yourself, think for yourself: Using Socratic discussions in inclusive classrooms. *Teaching Exceptional Children, 41*(3), 54–59.

Cisneros, S. (1984). *The house on Mango street.* New York, NY: Vintage.

Connolly, A. J., Nachtman, W., & Pritchett, E.M. (1976). *KeyMath diagnostic arithmetic test.* Circle Pines, MN: American Guidance Service.

Consortium for Citizens With Disabilities. (2010). Principles for the reauthorization of Elementary and Secondary Education Act. Retrieved from http://www.council-for-learning-disabilities.org/wp-content/uploads/2013/11/Final-CCD-ESEA-principles.pdf

Costley, K. (2013). Ongoing professional development: The prerequisite for and continuation of successful Inclusion meeting the academic needs of special students in public schools. Retrieved from http://eric.ed.gov/?id=ED541075

Cramer, S. (2006). *The special educator's guide to collaboration: Improving relationships with co-teachers, teams, and families.* Thousand Oaks, CA: Corwin.

Cross, L., Salazar, M. J., Dopson-Campuzano, N., & Batchelder, H. W. (2009). Best practices and considerations: Including young children with disabilities in early childhood settings. *Focus on Exceptional Children, 41*(8), 1–8.

Crowson, H., & Brandes, J. (2010). Predicting community opposition to inclusion in schools: The role of social dominance, contact, intergroup, anxiety, and economic conservatism. *The Journal of Psychology, 144*(2), 121–144.

Damasio, A. (2003). *Looking for Spinoza: Joy, sorrow, and the feeling brain.* New York, NY: Harcourt.

Dawkins, H. S. (2010). The impact of inclusion on the academic achievement of high school special education students. (Doctoral dissertation). Available from ProQuest Dissertations and Theses database. (UMI No. 3419120)

Discovery Education. (2014). Puzzlemaker. Retrieved from http://www.puzzlemaker.com

Dray, B. & Wisneski, D. (2011). Mindful reflection as a process for developing culturally responsive practices. *Teaching Exceptional Children, 44*(1) 28–36.

Duncan, A., & Ali, R. (2010). Student placement in elementary and secondary schools and Section 504 of the *Rehabilitation* Act and Title II of the *Americans with Disabilities* Act. Retrieved from http://www2.ed.gov/about/offices/list/ocr/docs/placpub.html#ftn1

Durlak, J. A., Weissberg, R. P., Dymnicki, A. B., Taylor, R. D., & Schellinger, K. B. (2011). The impact of enhancing students' social and emotional learning: A meta-analysis of school-based universal interventions. *Child Development, 82*(1), 405–432.

Easter Seals. (2009). *Friends who care: A disability awareness program for elementary students* [Video]. Available from http://www.easterseals.com/friendswhocare

Edwards, B. (1989). *Drawing on the right side of the brain* (Rev. ed.). New York, NY: Tarcher.

Edwards, B. (1999). *The new drawing on the right side of the brain.* New York, NY: Putnam.

Erikson, E. (1968). *Identity, youth, and crisis.* New York, NY: Norton.

Ertmer, P.A., & Simons, K. D. (2005). Scaffolding teachers' efforts to implement problem-based learning. *International Journal of Learning, 12*(4), 319–328.

Ferguson-Patrick, K. (2012, December). Developing an inclusive democratic classroom "in action" through cooperative learning. Paper presented at the Joint Australian Association for Research in Education and Asia-Pacific Educational Research Association Conference World Education Research Association Focal Meeting, Sydney, Australia.

Forte, I., & Schurr, S. (1995). *The all-new science mind stretchers: Interdisciplinary units to teach science concepts and strengthen thinking skills.* Nashville, TN: Incentive Publications.

Foss, B. (2013). *The dyslexia empowerment plan: A blueprint for renewing your child's confidence and love of learning*. New York, NY: Random House.

Friend, M., & Cook, L. (2003). *Interactions: Collaborative skills for school professionals* (4th ed.). New York, NY: Longman.

Gal, E., Schreur, N., & Engel-Yeger, B. (2010). Inclusion of children with disabilities: Teachers' attitudes and requirements for environmental accommodations. *International Journal of Special Education, 25*(2), 89–99.

Gardner, H. (2006). *Multiple intelligences: New horizons.* New York, NY: Basic Books.

Gehret, J. (1991). *Eagle eyes: A child's guide to paying attention.* New York, NY: Verbal Images Press.

Gess, D., & Livingston, J. (2006). *Teaching writing: Strategies for improving literacy across the curriculum.* New York, NY: Write Track.

Gill, V. (2007). *The ten students you'll meet in your classroom: Classroom management tips for middle and high school teachers*. Thousand Oaks, CA: Corwin.

Gonzalez, G. (2013). Learning goals and strategies in the self-regulation of learning. *US-China Education Review, 3*(1), 46–50.

Graham, S., & Harris, K. (2005). *Writing better: Effective strategies for teaching students with learning difficulties.* Baltimore, MD: Paul H. Brookes.

Gray, C., & Atwood, T. (2010). *The new social story book, revised and expanded 10th edition: Over 150 social stories that teach everyday social skills to children with autism, or Asperger's syndrome, and their peers.* Arlington, TX: Future Horizons.

Greenspan, S. (1998). *The child with special needs.* Boulder, CO: Perseus.

Guskey, T. & Jung, L. (2009). Grading and reporting in a standards-based environment: Implications for students with special needs. *Theory Into Practice, 48*(1), 5–62.

Hallahan, D., Kauffman, J., & Pullen, P. (2012). *Exceptional learners: An introduction to special education*. Upper Saddle River, NJ: Pearson Education.

Hallowell, E., & Ratey, J. (1994). *Driven to distraction.* New York, NY: Touchstone.

Hammeken, P. (2007). *The teacher's guide to inclusive education: 750 strategies for success.* Thousand Oaks, CA: Corwin.

Havasy, R. A. D. (2001). Getting a clue. *Education Week, 21*(10), 49.

Heasley, S. (2009, June 30). Wheelchairs of the future to be controlled by thought. *Disability Scoop*. Retrieved from http://www.disabilityscoop.com/2009/06/30/wheelchair-thought/3908/

Holler, R., & Zirkel, P. (2008). Section 504 and Public Schools: A national survey concerning "Section 504-only" students. *NASSP Bulletin, 92*(1), 19–43.

Hyde, A. (2007). Mathematics and cognition. *Educational Leadership, 65*(3), 43–47.

Irlen, H. (2008). Home and school tips: Irlen on Irlen syndrome. Retrieved from http://latitudes.org/home-and-school-tips-from-helen-irlen-on-dealing-with-irlen-syndrome/

Jenkins, J., Antil, L., Wayne, S., & Vadasy, P. (2003). How cooperative learning works for special education and remedial students. *Exceptional Children, 69*(3), 279–292.
Jensen, E. (2000). *Learning with the body in mind.* San Diego, CA: The Brain Store.
Jensen, E. (2005). *Teaching with the brain in mind* (2nd ed.). Alexandria, VA: Association for Supervision and Curriculum Development.
Jitendra, A., Burgess, C., & Gajria, M. (2011). Cognitive strategy instruction for improving expository text comprehension of students with learning disabilities: The quality of evidence. *Exceptional Children,* 77(2), 135–159.
Johnson, D., & Johnson, R. (1975). *Learning together and alone.* Englewood Cliffs, NJ: Prentice Hall.
Johnson, D. R., & Thurlow, M. L. (2003). *A national study on graduation requirements and diploma options for youth with disabilities* (Technical Report 36). Minneapolis: University of Minnesota, National Center on Educational Outcomes.
Johnson, J. (2003). What does the public say about accountability? *Educational Leadership, 61*(3), 39.
Johnson, L. (2012). *Kick-start your class: Academic ice-breakers to engage students.* Indianapolis, IN: Jossey-Bass.
Jolivette, K., Stichter, J., & McCormick, K. (2002). Making choices—improving behavior—engaging in learning. *Teaching Exceptional Children, 34*(3), 24–30.
Jung, A. (2011). Individualized education programs (IEPs) and barriers for parents from culturally and linguistically diverse backgrounds. *Multicultural Education, 19*(3), 21–25.
Justesen, T.R. (2005, June 27). Obligations of states and local educational agencies to parentally-placed private school children with disabilities [Memo]. Retrieved from http://www.k12.wa.us/specialEd/pubdocs/wac/federal/OSEP%2005-09%20private%20schools.pdf
Kagan, S. (1994). *Kagan cooperative learning.* San Juan Capistrano, CA: Kagan Cooperative Learning.
Kagan, S. (2000). *Silly sports & goofy games.* Bellevue, WA: Kagan.
Karten, T. (2007a). *Inclusion activities that work! Grades K–2.* Thousand Oaks, CA: Corwin.
Karten, T. (2007b). *Inclusion activities that work! Grades 3–5.* Thousand Oaks, CA: Corwin.
Karten, T. (2007c). *Inclusion activities that work! Grades 6–8.* Thousand Oaks, CA: Corwin.
Karten, T. (2007d). *More inclusion strategies that work! Aligning student strengths with standards.* Thousand Oaks, CA: Corwin.
Karten, T. (2008a). *Embracing disABILITIES in the classroom: Strategies to maximize students' assets.* Thousand Oaks, CA: Corwin.
Karten, T. (2008b). *Facilitator's guide to more inclusion strategies that work!* Thousand Oaks, CA: Corwin.
Karten, T. (2008c). *Inclusion succeeds with effective strategies (Grades K–5)* [Laminated reference guides]. Port Chester, NY: Dude Publishing.
Karten, T. (2008d). *Inclusion succeeds with effective strategies (Grades 6–12)* [Laminated reference guides]. Port Chester, NY: Dude Publishing.
Karten, T. (2009). *Inclusion strategies that work for adolescent learners!* Thousand Oaks, CA: Corwin.
Karten, T. (2010). *The inclusion lesson plan book for the 21st century.* Port Chester, NY: Dude Publishing.
Karten, T. (2013). *Inclusion coaching for collaborative schools.* Thousand Oaks, CA: Corwin.
Karten, T. (2014a). *Common Core Standards & English language arts: Strategies for student success: Grades 6–12.* Port Chester, NY: National Professional Resources.
Karten, T. (2014b). *Common Core Standards & mathematics: Strategies for student success: Grades 6–12.* Port Chester, NY: National Professional Resources.

Karten, T. (2014c). *IEPs & CCSS: Specially designed instructional strategies*. Port Chester, NY: National Professional Resources.

Kasser, S. (1995). *Inclusive games.* Champaign, IL: Human Kinetics.

Kent, D., & Quinlan, K. (1996). *Extraordinary people with disabilities.* New York, NY: Children's Press.

Kirberger, K. (2003). *No body's perfect.* New York: Scholastic.

Klein, S., & Schive, K. (2001). *You will dream new dreams.* New York, NY: Kensington Books.

Kleinert, H., Kearns, J., Quenemoen, R., & Thurlow, M. (2013). *NCSC GSEG policy paper: Alternate assessments based on Common Core State Standards: How do they relate to college and career readiness?* Minneapolis: University of Minnesota, National Center and State Collaborative.

Kniveton, B. (2004). A study of perceptions that significant others hold of the inclusion of children with difficulties in mainstream classes. *Educational Studies, 30*(3), 331–343.

Kranowitz, C. (1998). *The out-of-sync child: Recognizing and coping with sensory integration dysfunction.* New York, NY: Perigee.

LeDoux, J. (2002). *Synaptic self: How our brains become who we are.* New York, NY: Viking.

Lengel, T. & Kuczala, M. (2010). *The kinesthetic classroom: Teaching and learning through movement*. Thousand Oaks, CA: Corwin.

Lessenberry, B., & Rehdfeldt, R. (2004). Evaluating stress levels of parents of children with disabilities. *Exceptional Children, 70*(2), 231–244.

Levy, S., & Chard, D. J. (2001). Research on reading instruction for students with emotional and behavioral disorders. *International Journal of Disability, Development and Education, 48,* 429–444.

Liasidou, A. (2013). Bilingual and special educational needs in inclusive classrooms: Some critical and pedagogical considerations. *Support for Learning, 28*(1), 11–16.

Lieberman, L., & Houston-Wilson, C. (2002). *Strategies for inclusion: A handbook for physical education.* Champaign, IL: Human Kinetics.

Littky, D. (2004). *The big picture: Education is everyone's business.* Alexandria, VA: Association for Supervision and Curriculum Development.

Madrigal, S., & Winner, M.G. (2008). *Superflex: A superhero social thinking curriculum*. San Jose, CA: Think Social Publishing.

Marzano, R. (2007). *The art and science of teaching.* Alexandria, VA: Association for Supervision and Curriculum Development.

Mastergeorge, A. M., & Martínez, J. F. (2010). Rating performance assessments of students with disabilities: A study of reliability and bias. *Journal of Psychoeducational Assessment, 28*(6), 536–550.

Mauro, T. (n.d.). 504 plans for students with disabilities. Retrieved from http://specialchildren.about.com/od/504s/qt/%20sample504.htm

McCarney, S. B., Wunderlich, K. C., & Bauer, A. M. (2006). *The teacher's resource guide* (2nd ed.). Columbia, MO: Hawthorne Educational Services.

McCloud, C. (2006). *Have you filled a bucket today? A guide to daily happiness for kids.* Northville: MI: Nelson Publishing.

McFarlane, D. A. (2011). Multiple intelligences: The most effective platform for global 21st century educational and instructional methodologies. *College Quarterly, 14*(2). Retrieved from http://www.eric.ed.gov/contentdelivery/servlet/ERICServlet?accno=EJ962362

McIntyre, T. (n.d.). Teaching social skills. Retrieved from http://www.behavioradvisor.com/SocialSkills.html

McKinley, L., & Stormont, M. (2008). The school supports checklist: Identifying support needs and barriers for children with ADHD. *Teaching Exceptional Children, 41*(2), 14–19.

McNary, S., Glasgow, N., & Hicks, C. (2005). *What successful teachers do in inclusive classrooms: 60 research-based strategies that help special learners succeed.* Thousand Oaks, CA: Corwin.

Mitchell, M. (2009, March 31). Physical activity may strengthen children's ability to pay attention. University of Illinois News Bureau. Retrieved from http://news.illinois.edu/news/09/0331activity.html

Molko, M., Cachia, A., Rivière, D., Mangin, J., Bruandet, M., Le Bihan, D., et al. (2003). Functional and structural alterations of the intraparietal sulcus in a developmental dyscalculia of genetic origin. *Neuron, 40,* 847–858.

Mooney, J., & Cole, D. (2000). *Learning outside the lines: Two Ivy League students with learning disabilities and ADHD give you the tools.* New York, NY: Fireside.

Mostert, M. P., & Crockett, J. B. (2000). Reclaiming the history of special education for more effective practice. *Exceptionality, 8*(2), 133–143.

National Center for Education Statistics. (2013). Percentage distribution of students 6 to 21 years old served under Individuals with Disabilities Education Act (IDEA), Part B, by educational environment and type of disability: Selected years, fall 1989 through fall 2011. Retrieved from https://nces.ed.gov/programs/digest/d13/tables/dt13_204.60.asp

National Institute on Deafness and Other Communication Disorders. (2011). How loud is too loud? Retrieved from http://www.nidcd.nih.gov/health/hearing/ruler.asp

Nevin, A. I., Cramer, E., Voigt, J., & Salazar, L. (2008). Instructional modifications, adaptations, and accommodations of coteachers who loop: A descriptive case study. *Teacher Education and Special Education, 31*(4), 283–297.

Norris, D., & Schumacker, R. E. (1998, January). *Texas special education effectiveness study.* Paper presented at the Southwest Educational Research Association Conference, Houston, TX. Retrieved from http://eric.ed.gov/?id=ED427012

O'Brien, J., & Forest, M. (1989). *Action for inclusion: How to improve schools by welcoming children with special needs into regular classrooms.* Toronto, Canada: Inclusion Press.

Ozuru, Y., Dempsey, K., & McNamara, D. (2009). Prior knowledge, reading skill, and text cohesion in the comprehension of science texts. *Learning and Instruction, 19*(3), 228–242.

Palmer, S., Heyne, L., Montie, J., & Abery, B. (Eds.) (2011). Feature issue on supporting the social well-being of children and youth with disabilities [Special issue]. *Impact,* 24(1).

Piaget, J. (1952). *The origins of intelligence in children.* New York, NY: International University Press.

Pierangelo, R., & Giuliani, G. (2010, July 20). Prevalence of learning disabilities. Retrieved from http://www.education.com/reference/article/prevalence-learning-disabilities/

Pisha, B., & Stahl, S. (2005). The promise of new learning environments for students with disabilities. *Intervention in School & Clinic, 41*(2), 67–75.

Powell, S. & Stecker, S. (2014). Using data-based individualization to intensify mathematics intervention for students with disabilities. *Teaching Exceptional Children, 46*(4), 31–37.

Ratey, J. (2008). *SPARK: The revolutionary new science of exercise and the brain.* New York, NY: Little, Brown.

Raver, C. C. (2003). *Young children's emotional development and school readiness.* Champaign, IL: ERIC Clearinghouse on Elementary and Early Childhood Education.

Reeve, C. (2002). *Nothing is impossible: Reflections on a new life.* New York, NY: Random House.

Rosa's Law, Pub. L. No. 111-256, 124 Stat. 2643, 2644, & 2645 (2010).

Rothstein-Fisch, C., & Trumbull, E. (2008). *Managing diverse classrooms: How to build on students' cultural strengths.* Alexandria, VA: Association for Supervision and Curriculum Development.

Rouse, P. (2004). *Adapted games & activities: From tag to team building*. Champaign, IL: Human Kinetics.

Rouse, P. (2010). *Inclusion in physical education: Fitness, motor, and social skills for students of all abilities*. Champaign, IL: Human Kinetics.

Russo, C., Tiegerman, E., & Radziewicz, C. K. (2008). *RTI guide: Making it work, strategies = solutions*. Port Chester, NY: National Professional Resources.

Salend, S. (2005). *Creating inclusive classrooms: Effective and reflective practices for ALL students* (5th ed.). Columbus, OH: Pearson.

Salend, S. (2006). Explaining your inclusion program to families. *Teaching Exceptional Children, 38*(1), 6–11.

Sánchez Santiago, I., & McGinnis, R. (2003). *Art & the alphabet: A tactile experience*. Humacao, Puerto Rico: Creative Creativo.

Savard, J. (n.d.). *Braille alphabet*. Available at http://www.quadibloc.com/crypto/intro.htm

Schumacher Dyke, K., & Bauer, L. S. (2010). Lessons learned: Parents of children with disabilities offer recommendations for strategies that work. *Exceptional Parent, 40*(12), 21–22.

Shore, K. (2009). *A teacher's guide to working with parents*. Port Chester, NY: Dude Publishing.

Shprintzen, R. (2000). *Syndrome identification for speech-language pathology: An illustrated pocket guide*. New York: Singular.

Siperstein, G. N., Parker, R. C., Bardon, J. N., & Widaman, K. F. (2007). A national study of youth attitudes toward the inclusion of students with intellectual disabilities. *Exceptional Children, 73*(4), 435–455.

Skiba, R., Simmons, A., Ritter, S., Gibb, A., Rausch, M. K., Cuadrado, J., et al. (2008). Achieving equity in special education: History, status, and current challenges. *Exceptional Children, 74*(3), 264–288.

Slavin, R. E. (1990). *Cooperative learning: Theory, research, and practice*. Englewood Cliffs, NJ: Prentice Hall.

Smith, J. D. (2003). *Stories of disability in the human family: In search of better angels*. Thousand Oaks, CA: Corwin.

Snowman, J., McCown, R., & Biehler, R. (2009). *Applying psychology to teaching* (12th ed.). Boston, MA: Houghton Mifflin.

Sobsey, D. (1978). The ballad of special Eddie. Retrieved from http://www.our-kids.org/Archives/Spec_eddie.html

Sousa, D. A. (2007). *How the special needs brain learns*. Thousand Oaks, CA: Corwin.

Steen, L. (2007). How mathematics counts. *Educational Leadership, 65*(3), 8–14.

Stemkowski, L. (n.d.). *Tangrams*. Available from http://www.dartmouth.edu

Stockall, N., Dennis, L. R., & Rueter J. A. (2014). Developing a progress monitoring portfolio for children in early childhood special education programs. *Teaching Exceptional Children, 46*(3), 32–40.

Storey, K. (2007). Combating ableism in schools. *Preventing School Failure, 53*(1), 56–58.

Symeonidou, S., & Phtiaka, H. (2009). Using teachers' prior knowledge, attitudes and beliefs to develop in-service teacher education courses for inclusion. *Teaching and Teacher Education: An International Journal of Research and Studies, 25*(4), 543–550.

Tachell, P. (2003). *Science encyclopedia: Usborne Internet-linked discovery program*. London, England: Usborne Books.

Technology-Related Assistance for Individuals With Disabilities Act of 1988. Pub. L. No. 100-407, 102 Stat. 1044 (1988).

Thurlow, M. L. (2003, February). *Linking standards, assessments, and instructional practices*. Paper presented at the Pacific Rim International Conference on Disability and Diversity, Waikiki, HI. Retrieved from http://www.cehd.umn.edu/nceo/presentations/PACRIM.ppt

Tomlinson, C. A. (2008). The goals of differentiation. *Educational Leadership, 66*(3), 26–30.

Tomlinson, C., & McTighe, J. (2006). *Integrating differentiated instruction and understanding by design: Connecting content and kids.* Alexandria, VA: Association for Supervision and Curriculum Development.

Torbert, M. (1994). *Follow me: A handbook of movement activities for children* (Rev. ed.). Philadelphia, PA: Leonard Gordon Institute for Human Development Through Play of Temple University.

Tramer, H. (2007). Awareness of disability law up among lawyers, families. *Cleveland Business, 28*(15), 15.

Trout, A. L., Epstein, M. H., Nelson, R., Synhorst, L., & Hurley, K. D. (2006). Profiles of children served in early intervention programs for behavioral disorders: Early literacy and behavioral characteristics. *Topics in Early Childhood Special Education, 26*(4), 206–218.

Vakil, E., Blachstein, H., Wertman-Elad, R., & Greenstein, Y. (2012). Verbal learning and memory as measured by the Rey-Auditory Verbal Learning Test: ADHD with and without learning disabilities. *Child Neuropsychology, 18*(5), 449–466.

Vaughn, S., Bos, C., & Schumm, J. (2002). *Teaching exceptional, diverse, and at-risk students in the general classroom* (3rd ed.). Boston, MA: Allyn & Bacon.

Vega, V. (2012, November 7). Social and emotional learning research review. Retrieved from http://www.edutopia.org/sel-research-learning-outcomes

Verdick, E. (2010). *Don't behave like you live in a cave.* Minneapolis, MN: Free Spirit Publishing.

Vision Management Consulting. (n.d.). *IEP Planner: A compendium of educational and behavior goals and objectives.* Retrieved November 11, 2003, from http://www.visionplanet.com

Vogt, J. (2006). *The amazing music activities book: Ideas and exercises for exploring: Music basics, ear training, music styles, and famous composers.* Dayton, OH: Heritage Music Press.

Watson, A., & McCathren, R. (2009, March). Including children with special needs: Are you and your early childhood program ready? *Beyond the Journal:* Young Children *on the Web.* Retrieved from https://www.naeyc.org/files/yc/file/200903/BTJWatson.pdf

Wiener, D. (2005). *One state's story: Access and alignment to the GRADE-LEVEL content for students with significant cognitive disabilities* (Synthesis Report 57). Minneapolis: University of Minnesota, National Center on Educational Outcomes. Retrieved from http://education.umn.edu/NCEO/OnlinePubs/Synthesis57.html

Wiggins, G., & McTighe, J. (2005). *Understanding by design* (2nd ed.). Alexandria, VA: Association for Supervision and Curriculum Development.

Willingham, D. T. (2004, Spring). Practice makes perfect—but only if you practice beyond the point of perfection. *American Educator,* 31–33; 38–39.

Willis, C. (2009). *Creating inclusive learning environments for young children: What to do on Monday mornings.* Thousand Oaks, CA: Corwin.

Winnick, J. (Ed.) (2010). *Adapted physical education and sport* (5th ed.). Champaign, IL: Human Kinetics.

Yell, M., Katsiyannis, A., Collins, J. (2012). Exit exams, high-stakes testing, and students with disabilities: A persistent challenge. *Intervention in School and Clinic, 48*(1), 60–64.

Yenawine, P. (2006). *Shapes* (2nd ed.). New York, NY: Delacorte.

Zipprich, M., Grace, M., & Grote-Garcia, S. (2009). Building story schema: Using patterned books as a means of instruction for students with disabilities. *Intervention in School and Clinic, 44*(5), 294–299.

Zirkel, P., & Richards, D. (1998). The new disorder maze. *Teaching Exceptional Children, 30*(5), 2.

Index

CORWIN
A SAGE Company

Corwin is committed to improving education for all learners by publishing books and other professional development resources for those serving the field of PreK–12 education. By providing practical, hands-on materials, Corwin continues to carry out the promise of its motto: **"Helping Educators Do Their Work Better."**

TWELFTH EDITION

Current Issues and Enduring Questions

A Guide to Critical Thinking and Argument, with Readings

SYLVAN BARNET
Professor of English, Late of Tufts University

HUGO BEDAU
Professor of Philosophy, Late of Tufts University

JOHN O'HARA
Associate Professor of Critical Thinking, Reading, and Writing, Stockton University

bedford/st.martin's
Macmillan Learning
Boston | New York

For Bedford/St. Martin's
Vice President, Editorial, Macmillan Learning Humanities: Leasa Burton
Senior Program Manager: John E. Sullivan III
Executive Marketing Manager: Joy Fisher Williams
Director of Content Development, Humanities: Jane Knetzger
Senior Developmental Editor: Leah Rang
Assistant Editor: Cari Goldfine
Editorial Assistant: Alex Markle
Senior Content Project Manager: Peter Jacoby
Senior Workflow Project Supervisor: Joe Ford
Senior Workflow Project Manager: Paul Rohloff
Production Supervisor: Robin Besofsky
Media Product Manager: Rand Thomas
Media Editor: Julia Domenicucci
Editorial Services: Lumina Datamatics, Inc.
Composition: Lumina Datamatics, Inc.
Text Permissions Manager: Kalina Ingham
Senior Text Permissions Researcher: Elaine Kosta, Lumina Datamatics, Inc.
Photo Permissions Editor: Angela Boehler
Photo Researcher: Brittani Morgan Grimes, Lumina Datamatics, Inc.
Director of Design, Content Management: Diana Blume
Text Design: Lumina Datamatics, Inc.
Design Motif Opener Pattern: Irtsya/Shutterstock
Cover Design: William Boardman
Cover Image: Torben Giehler, German, born in 1973, *BOOGIE WOOGIE*, 1999, Acrylic on canvas, 205.7 × 195.6 cm (81 × 77 in.), Museum of Fine Arts, Boston, The Living New England Artist Purchase Fund, created by The Stephen and Sybil Stone Foundation 1999.499. Photo ©2020 Museum of Fine Arts, Boston.
Printing and Binding: LSC Communications

Manufactured in the United States of America.

1 2 3 4 5 6 24 23 22 21 20 19

For information, write: Bedford/St. Martin's, 75 Arlington Street, Boston, MA 02116

ISBN 978-1-319-19818-3

Acknowledgments
Text acknowledgments and copyrights appear at the back of the book on pages 733–38, which constitute an extension of the copyright page. Art acknowledgments and copyrights appear on the same page as the art selections they cover.

Preface

He who knows only his own side of the cause knows little. — JOHN STUART MILL

Current Issues and Enduring Questions: A Guide to Critical Thinking and Argument, with Readings is a text — a book about reading other people's arguments and writing your own arguments — and it is also an anthology — a collection of more than a hundred selections, ranging from Plato to the present, with a strong emphasis on critical thinking, reading, and writing about current issues.

Since the first edition, the quotation above has reflected the view of argument that underlies this book: In writing an essay, an author engages in a serious effort to discover his or her own ideas and, having found them, to contribute to a multisided conversation. The writer is not setting out to trounce an opponent. That is partly why we avoid expressions such as "marshaling evidence," "attacking an opponent," and "defending a thesis." Edmund Burke once wrote, "Our antagonist is our helper," and we agree that views and perspectives contrary to our own can help us sharpen our own thinking and writing. True, on television and social media we see pundits on the right and left who have made up their minds and who are indifferent or hostile to others' analysis and opinions. But in an academic community, and indeed in our daily lives, we learn by listening to others and by questioning our own ideas.

Two other foundational assumptions of this book are that arguments occur in a variety of forms, including but not limited to words on a page, and that arguments are shaped by the contexts in which they are made. In this edition, we reaffirm these beliefs with an expanded focus on visual rhetoric and information literacy, with heightened sensitivity to the interplay between argument and persuasion. We also recognize that academic and cultural discourses may make different arguments — asking different kinds of questions, making different kinds of claims, and using different kinds of evidence to support their views. Part Three, which focuses on approaches to argument, examines how philosophers, psychologists, literary critics, and debaters formulate arguments according to their unique purposes.

Just as arguments are instruments of inquiry and learning as well as expression, *Current Issues and Enduring Questions* aims to help students learn to think, read, and write in more effective ways. As *critical thinkers and readers,* students in courses that use this book should develop their abilities to

- ask good questions about the reasoning processes that shape arguments;
- understand why information is selected and how it is presented persuasively by producers of arguments;
- account for variation and discrepancy in diverse perspectives on issues;
- understand how various contexts inform the production and reception of ideas;
- analyze and evaluate the strength of the evidence, reasoning, and assumptions undergirding arguments; and
- reflect upon, interrogate, and judge the (stated and unstated) consequences of arguments.

As *critical writers*, students develop their abilities to

- summarize an argument accurately, identifying the thesis, support, and conclusion;
- analyze an argument by reasoning logically and convincingly about it;
- produce a clear and purposeful argument of their own appropriate to a situation or discourse;
- communicate effectively for a specific audience (using appropriate language, tone, style, depth, and detail);
- explore sources of information and incorporate them selectively and skillfully, with proper documentation; and
- synthesize all information, ideas, terms, and concepts in an orderly and coherent way.

We think about and draft a response to something we have read, and in the very act of drafting, we may find—if we think critically about the words we are putting down on paper—that we are changing (perhaps slightly, perhaps radically) our own position. In short, one reason we write is so that we can improve our ideas. And even if we do not drastically change our views, we and our readers at least come to a better understanding of why we hold the views we do.

Enduring Features

ANALYZING AND CRAFTING ARGUMENTS

Part One, Critical Thinking and Reading (Chapters 1–4), and Part Two, Critical Writing (Chapters 5–7), together offer a short course in methods of thinking about and writing arguments. By "thinking," we mean *critical* thinking—serious analytic thought, including analysis of one's own perspectives, assumptions, and predispositions as one encounters (and produces) arguments; by "writing," we mean *critical* writing—the use of effective, respectable techniques for reasoned, convincing analysis, not merely gut feelings and persuasive gimmicks. (We are reminded of the notorious note scribbled in the margin of a politician's speech: "Argument weak; shout here").

We offer lots of advice about how to set forth an argument, but we do not offer instruction in dissembling, deceiving, or practicing one-upmanship; rather, we discuss responsible ways of arguing persuasively. We know that before one can write a persuasive argument, one must learn about an issue and clarify one's own ideas — a process that includes thinking critically about others' positions (even when they are agreeable) and being critical about one's own positions before setting them forth responsibly. Therefore, we devote Chapter 1 to critical thinking; Chapters 2, 3, and 4 to critical reading (including reading images in Chapter 4); and Chapters 5, 6, and 7 to critical writing.

Parts One and Two, then, offer a preliminary (but we hope substantial) discussion of such topics as

- identifying assumptions;
- getting ideas by means of invention strategies;
- finding, evaluating, and citing printed and electronic sources;
- interpreting visual sources;
- evaluating kinds of evidence; and
- organizing material as well as an introduction to some ways of thinking.

Parts One and Two together contain thirty selections (eight are student essays) for analysis and discussion.

INQUIRY AND INVENTION

In the first chapter, we emphasize how the process of critical thinking is a generative process. We focus on identifying the purpose, fairness, and consequences of arguments to various stakeholders and on analyzing ideas and concepts by asking questions — and then asking still further questions — to inspire fair-minded learning.

Our instruction throughout the book is accompanied by essays and images that embody and challenge concepts in critical thinking and argument. Each essay is accompanied by a list of Topics for Critical Thinking and Writing, which is not surprising given the emphasis we place on evaluating arguments, asking questions, and investigating further so as to generate new ideas. Among the chief questions writers should ask, we suggest, are "What is *X*?" and "What is the value of *X*?" By asking such questions — for instance (to look only at these two types of questions), "Is the fetus a person?" or "Is Arthur Miller a better playwright than Tennessee Williams?" — a writer probably will find pathways for discovering new sources, new questions, and new ideas, at least after a few moments of head scratching. Developing an argument by identifying issues is nothing new. Indeed, it goes back to an ancient method of argument used by classical rhetoricians, who identified a stasis (an issue) and then asked questions about it: Did *X* do such and such? If so, was the action bad? If bad, how bad? (Finding an issue or stasis — a position where one stands — by asking questions is discussed in Chapter 6.)

STYLES OF ARGUMENTATION

In keeping with our emphasis on writing as well as reading, we raise issues not only of what can roughly be called the "content" of the essays, but also of what can (equally roughly) be called the "style" — that is, the *ways* in which the arguments are set forth. Content and style, of course, cannot finally be kept apart. As Cardinal Newman said, "Thought and meaning are inseparable from each other. . . . *Style is thinking out into language.*" In our Topics for Critical Thinking and Writing, we sometimes ask the student

- to evaluate the effectiveness of an essay's opening paragraph,
- to explain a shift in tone from one paragraph to the next, or
- to characterize the persona of the author as revealed in the whole essay.

In short, this book is not designed as an introduction to some powerful ideas (although in fact it is that, too); rather, it is designed as an aid to thinking about and *writing* well-reasoned, effective arguments on important political, social, scientific, ethical, legal, and religious issues.

The selections reprinted in this book also illustrate different styles of argument that arise, at least in part, from the different disciplinary backgrounds of the various authors. Essays by journalists, lawyers, social scientists, policy analysts, philosophers, critics, activists, and other writers — including first-year undergraduates — will be found in these pages. These authors develop and present their views in arguments that have distinctive features reflecting their special training and concerns. The differences in argumentative styles found in these essays foreshadow the differences students will encounter in the readings assigned in many of their other courses.

In Part Three, Further Views on Argument (Chapters 8–12), we acknowledge and detail some of the different approaches to argument and emphasize their potential usefulness to a particular writing situation — or as a means of framing an argument course or unit.

- Chapter 8, A Philosopher's View: The Toulmin Model, is a summary of the philosopher Stephen Toulmin's method for analyzing arguments, covering claims, grounds, warrants, backing, modal qualifiers, and rebuttals. This summary will assist those who wish to apply Toulmin's methods to the readings in this book.
- Chapter 9, A Logician's View: Deduction, Induction, and Fallacies, offers a more rigorous analysis of these topics than is usually found in composition courses and reexamines from a logician's point of view material introduced in Chapter 3.
- Chapter 10, A Psychologist's View: Rogerian Argument, with an essay by psychotherapist Carl R. Rogers, complements the discussion of audience, organization, and tone in Chapter 6.
- Chapter 11, A Literary Critic's View: Arguing about Literature, should help students see the things literary critics argue about and *how* they argue. Students can apply what they learn not only to the literary readings that appear in the chapter (poems by Robert Frost and Richard Blanco and a story by Kate Chopin)

but also to the readings that appear in Part Six, Enduring Questions: Essays, Poems, and Stories.

- Chapter 12, A Debater's View: Individual Oral Presentations and Debate, introduces students to standard presentation strategies and debate format.

THE ANTHOLOGY

Part Four, Current Issues: Occasions for Debate (Chapters 13–18) begins with some comments on binary, or pro-con, thinking. It then gives a Checklist for Analyzing a Debate and reprints six pairs of arguments — on student loan debt (should it be forgiven?), the pervasiveness of algorithms (do they promote or reduce bias?), free speech on campus (should speakers be permitted to share intolerant views?), childhood and parenting (what's best for kids?), genetic modification of human beings (it is ethical?), and military service (should it be required?). Here, as elsewhere in the book, students can easily study the *methods* the writers use, as well as the issues themselves.

Part Five, Current Issues: Casebooks (Chapters 19–25) presents seven chapters on issues discussed by several writers. For example, the first casebook concerns the nature and purpose of a college education: Should students focus their studies in STEM fields in the hopes of securing a more stable future and contributing to the economy, or should college be a place where students learn empathy, citizenship, and critical thinking — attributes often instilled by the humanities? Subsequent chapters focus on issues in the public discourse and relevant to students' lives now: race and the criminal justice system, the ethics of cultural appropriation, the impact of social networking on our relationships, immigration, the effects of #MeToo, and the state of the nation's democracy.

Part Six, Enduring Questions: Essays, Poems, and Stories (Chapters 26–28) provides a philosophical and theoretical context for the contemporary arguments. These chapters are also useful by themselves as a means of thinking and writing about important concepts: Chapter 26, What Is the Ideal Society? (the voices here range from Thomas More, Thomas Jefferson, and Martin Luther King Jr. to literary figures W. H. Auden, Walt Whitman, and Ursula K. Le Guin); Chapter 27, How and Why Do We Construct the "Other"? (authors in this chapter include Jean-Paul Sartre, W. E. B. Du Bois, and Simone de Beauvoir); and Chapter 28, What Is Happiness? (among the nine selections in this chapter are writings by Epictetus, the Dalai Lama, and C. S. Lewis).

What's New in the Twelfth Edition

This twelfth edition brings significant changes. The authors of the first ten editions established a firm foundation for the book: Hugo Bedau, professor of philosophy, brought analytical rigor to the instruction in argumentation, and Sylvan Barnet, professor of English, contributed expertise in writing instruction. They have since turned the project over to John O'Hara, professor of critical thinking, to contribute a third dimension, augmenting and enriching the material on critical thinking throughout, especially in the early chapters. Other changes have been made to ensure practical instruction and current topics.

Fresh and Timely New Readings, Debates, and Casebooks. More than a third of the total featured essays are new, as are topics such as free speech and fake news, confirmation and algorithm biases, student loan forgiveness, the sentience of animals, and video games as sports. Existing topics such as immigration have been carefully considered and updated to reflect our contemporary discourse and perspectives.

The topics in readings chapters were developed based on feedback from users of the text. New debates include Are Algorithms Biased (Or Are We)? and (Un)safe Spaces: Can We Tolerate Intolerant Speech on Campus? New casebook issues include Race and Criminal Justice: Is the System Broken?; The Ethics of Appropriation: Is It OK to Copy?; #MeToo: (How) Has Society Changed for Women?; and American Democracy: Is the Nation in Danger? To serve as philosophical context for several of these current issues, a new collection of essays and literature — both classic and contemporary — asks students to wrestle with the question, How and Why Do We Construct the "Other"?

A Sharper Focus on Fostering Critical Thinking and Information Literacy. Early chapters in Part One on critical reading and writing are updated to include an explanation of confirmation bias, a survey-analyze-evaluate process for working through an issue, an understanding of obstacles to critical thinking, and strategies for approaching an issue (or an assignment). Chapter 7, Using Sources, has been extensively updated to help students interrogate their sources for reliability, relevance, and accuracy. Given that today's digital natives seek and find information online, new sections on finding reliable sources online provide instruction and visual examples of sponsored content, fake news sites, and scholarly databases so that students can evaluate and use research effectively.

More Visual Guidance. In response to reviewer feedback, we have revised and updated some of the instruction to design new Visual Guides and create additional entry points to critical thinking. Colorful graphics and flowcharts aid students in designing their own paths through common argument tasks such as writing a critical summary and organizing an analysis.

In addition to the student essays that are marked to show the writers' strategies, this edition features annotated essays that make argument moves visible. Several selections by professional writers provide support for understanding argument during the reading process and highlight writers' rhetorical moves and persuasive strategies.

Writing Prompts That Support Major Course Assignments. Each chapter on critical thinking, reading, and writing now features a capstone writing prompt that allows students to practice argument in common assignment genres: examining assumptions and exploring an issue, critical summary, rhetorical analysis, visual analysis, argument analysis, argument, research paper, and literary criticism.

Acknowledgments

The authors would like to thank those who have strengthened this book by their comments and advice on the twelfth edition: Steven Acree, College of the Desert; Heidi E. Ajrami, Victoria College; Dan Baldwin, Scott Community College; Amber Barnes, Trinity Valley Community College; Larry Beason, University of South Alabama; Evelyn Beck, Harrisburg Area Community College; Ted Brown, Murray State University; Syble S. Davis, Houston

Community College – Central Campus; Gerri Dobbins, Gaston College; Michele Domenech, Gaston College; Tamara Fritzchle, Fresno City College; Rachael Groner, Temple University; Dara Liling, University of Maryland, College Park; Bridgette Sutton Marshall, Victoria College; Monica McFerrin, Tidewater Community College; John McKinnis, SUNY at Buffalo State; Jason Molloy, Ocean County College; Michelle Paulsen, Victoria College; Liam Quirk, Rider University; Jennifer Rideout, Tennessee Tech University; Reid T. Sagara, College of the Desert; Matthew Stenson, Tennessee Tech University; Casandra Sweeney, Cuyahoga Community College; Jayanti Tamm, Ocean County College; Christopher VanNostrand, Trinity Valley Community College; and Linda J. Webster, Sam Houston State University.

We are also deeply indebted to the people at Bedford/St. Martin's, especially to our thoughtful and supportive editor, Leah Rang, whose input, review, and feedback helped shape both the written chapters and the reading selections in this edition. Maura Shea, John Sullivan, and Adam Whitehurst, our editors for preceding editions, have also left a lasting impression on the book; without their work on the first eleven editions, there probably would not be a twelfth. Others at Bedford/St. Martin's to whom we are deeply indebted include Edwin Hill, Leasa Burton, Joy Fisher Williams, Peter Jacoby, Cari Goldfine, and Theresa Carcaldi, all of whom have offered countless valuable (and invaluable) suggestions. Special thanks go to Lexi DeConti and Alex Markle who were there for every step of the twelfth edition to provide insight and commentary, particularly so in the selection and layout of visual elements new to this edition. We would also like to thank Hilary Newman, Kalina Ingham, Arthur Johnson, Elaine Kosta, Angela Boehler, and Brittani Morgan Grimes, who adeptly managed art research and text permissions. Intelligent, informed, firm yet courteous, persuasive, and persistent—all these folks know how to think and argue.

Bedford/St. Martin's Puts You First

From day one, our goal has been simple: to provide inspiring resources that are grounded in best practices for teaching reading and writing. For more than thirty-five years, Bedford/St. Martin's has partnered with the field, listening to teachers, scholars, and students about the support writers need. We are committed to helping every writing instructor make the most of our resources.

How can we help *you*?

- Our editors can align our resources to your outcomes through correlation and transition guides for your syllabus. Just ask us.
- Our sales representatives specialize in helping you find the right materials to support your course goals.
- Our *Bits* blog on the Bedford/St. Martin's English Community (**community.macmillan.com**) publishes fresh teaching ideas weekly. You'll also find easily downloadable professional resources and links to author webinars on our community site.

Contact your Bedford/St. Martin's sales representative or visit **macmillanlearning.com** to learn more.

PRINT AND DIGITAL OPTIONS FOR *CURRENT ISSUES AND ENDURING QUESTIONS*

Choose the format that works best for your course and ask about our packaging options that offer savings for students.

Print

- *Paperback edition.* To order the paperback edition, use ISBN 978-1-319-19818-3.
- *Loose-leaf edition.* This format does not have a traditional binding; its pages are loose and hole punched to provide flexibility and a lower price to students. It can be packaged with our digital space for additional savings. To order the loose-leaf packaged with Achieve, use ISBN 978-1-319-33626-4.

Digital

- *Innovative digital learning space.* Bedford/St. Martin's suite of digital tools makes it easy to get everyone on the same page by putting student writers at the center. For details, visit **macmillanlearning.com/college/us/englishdigital**.
- *Popular e-book formats.* For details about our e-book partners, visit **macmillanlearning.com/ebooks**.
- *Inclusive Access.* Enable every student to receive their course materials through your LMS on the first day of class. Macmillan Learning's Inclusive Access program is the easiest, most affordable way to ensure that all students have access to quality educational resources. Find out more at **macmillanlearning.com/inclusiveaccess**.

YOUR COURSE, YOUR WAY

No two writing programs or classrooms are exactly alike. Our Curriculum Solutions team works with you to design custom options that provide the resources your students need. (Options below require enrollment minimums.)

- *ForeWords for English.* Customize any print resource to fit the focus of your course or program by choosing from a range of prepared topics, such as Sentence Guides for Academic Writers.
- *Macmillan Author Program (MAP).* Add excerpts or package acclaimed works from Macmillan's trade imprints to connect students with prominent authors and public conversations. A list of popular examples or academic themes is available upon request.
- *Bedford Select.* Build your own print handbook or anthology from a database of more than 900 selections, and add your own materials to create your ideal text. Package with any Bedford/St. Martin's text for additional savings. Visit **macmillanlearning.com/bedfordselect**.

INSTRUCTOR RESOURCES

You have a lot to do in your course. We want to make it easy for you to find the support you need — and to get it quickly.

Resources for Teaching Current Issues and Enduring Questions is available as a PDF that can be downloaded from **macmillanlearning.com**. The instructor's manual includes sample syllabi, notes for every selection and chapter, and additional topics for classroom discussion and student writing assignments.

How *Current Issues and Enduring Questions* Supports WPA Outcomes for First-Year Composition

The following chart provides information on how *Current Issues and Enduring Questions* helps students build proficiency and achieve the learning outcomes set by the Council of Writing Program Administrators, which writing programs across the country use to assess their students' work.

Rhetorical Knowledge	
Learn and use key rhetorical concepts through analyzing and composing a variety of texts	**Part One, Critical Thinking and Reading**, moves students from analyzing and evaluating an issue to analyzing specific written and visual arguments. • **Chapter 3, Critical Reading: Getting Deeper into Arguments**, gives students a vocabulary for key concepts of Aristotelian rhetoric — *ethos, logos, pathos* — and distinguishes between rational strategies (e.g., induction, deduction) and nonrational appeals (e.g., satire, irony, emotional appeals). • **Chapter 4, Visual Rhetoric: Thinking about Images as Arguments**, shows students how these strategies can be applied to visual arguments such as photographs, political cartoons, advertisements, and graphs. **Part Two, Critical Writing**, guides students from analysis to composing their own arguments. • **Chapter 5, Writing an Analysis of an Argument**, guides students through examining thesis, purpose, methods, persona, and the intended audience. An argument and a student's analysis, annotated to highlight the students' rhetorical strategies (pp. 188–90), explicate the process of assessing and evaluating an argument. • **Chapter 6, Developing an Argument of Your Own**, asks students to imagine and compose for their own audience (Imagining an Audience, pp. 216–18). **Select student essays are direct responses** to the professional selections and therefore model analysis and evaluation of a text.

Gain experience reading and composing in several genres to understand how genre conventions shape and are shaped by readers' and writers' practices and purposes	***Current Issues and Enduring Questions*** boasts 119 readings (including ten student essays) from a variety of sources, genres, and times. Selections for analysis and discussion include source-based arguments from professionals in different disciplines — journalists, lawyers, social scientists, policy analysts, philosophers, critics, activists, literary figures, and students. **Part Three, Further Views on Argument**, covers five different approaches to argument, providing students with multiple perspectives on how to both examine and craft arguments in different argument genres: Chapter 8, A Philosopher's View: The Toulmin Model; Chapter 9, A Logician's View: Deduction, Induction, and Fallacies; Chapter 10, A Psychologist's View: Rogerian Argument; Chapter 11, A Literary Critic's View: Arguing about Literature; and Chapter 12, A Debater's View: Individual Oral Presentations and Debate. The **Topics for Critical Thinking and Writing** that follow every reading in the text point to stylistic choices, heightening students' awareness of writing conventions. In Chapter 7, Using Sources, helpful tables detail the genre conventions of scholarly, popular, and trade sources (p. 258), as well as types of fake news (p. 267).
Develop facility in responding to a variety of situations and contexts calling for purposeful shifts in voice, tone, level of formality, design, medium, and/or structure	Each chapter on critical thinking, reading, and writing features a capstone writing prompt that allows students to practice argument in common assignment genres: examining assumptions and exploring an issue, critical summary, rhetorical analysis, visual analysis, argument analysis, argument, research paper, and literary criticism. Thinking Critically activities help scaffold composing in different genres. See, for example, Thinking Critically: Identifying Ethos (p. 78) and Thinking Critically: Examining Language to Analyze an Author's Argument (p. 186).
Understand and use a variety of technologies to address a range of audiences	The authors of *Current Issues and Enduring Questions* assume students will be composing in different media; therefore, instruction throughout emphasizes the affordances and constraints of composing in analog and digital when taking notes, evaluating and citing sources, presenting, and more.

Match the capacities of different environments (e.g., print and electronic) to varying rhetorical situations	In addition to coverage noted above that helps students understand the rhetorical situation, specific guidance on composing in different environments includes using images in writing (Chapter 4) and delivering oral and electronic presentations (Chapter 12).
Critical Thinking, Reading, and Composing	
Use composing and reading for inquiry, learning, critical thinking, and communicating in various rhetorical contexts	**Chapter 1, Critical Thinking**, emphasizes how the process of critical thinking is a generative process through acts of inquiry, reading, and writing. See Generating Ideas: Writing as a Way of Thinking (pp. 12–17). **Chapter 6, Developing an Argument of Your Own**, includes further guidance on inquiry and invention as part of the composing process. See Getting Ideas: Argument as an Instrument of Inquiry (p. 206), Revision as Invention (p. 210), and Asking Questions with Stasis Theory (pp. 210–13).
Read a diverse range of texts, attending especially to relationships between assertion and evidence, to patterns of organization, to the interplay between verbal and nonverbal elements, and to how these features function for different audiences and situations	**The 119 reading selections are sourced from diverse authors, disciplines, and genres.** Many of the readings are organized into casebooks, which highlight the different patterns of organization and rhetorical strategies used by different authors writing on the same topic. **Topics for Critical Thinking and Writing** that follow every reading prompt students to analyze the organization of arguments, the reliability of sources and their responsible use, and the effectiveness of arguments for the audience and situation. Several sections highlight the importance of strong organization to deliver sound logic, reasoning, and support for claims. See, for example: • Types of Reasoning (pp. 80–85) • Evidence: Experimentation, Examples, Authoritative Testimony, and Numerical Data (pp. 92–102) • Drafting and Revising an Argument (pp. 220–34) **Part Three, Further Views on Argument**, covers how five different argument approaches — Toulmin, formal logic, Rogerian, literary criticism, and debate — organize and use claims and support according to their different purposes.

Locate and evaluate (for credibility, sufficiency, accuracy, timeliness, bias, and so on) primary and secondary research materials, including journal articles and essays, books, scholarly and professionally established and maintained databases or archives, and informal electronic networks and internet sources	**Chapter 7, Using Sources**, is a comprehensive resource for finding and evaluating primary and secondary sources. • Finding Sources (pp. 248–55) advises students on finding sources online, in databases, and in libraries. • Performing Your Own Primary Research (pp. 271–75) guides students in interviewing peers and local authorities as well as conducting surveys and observations. • Evaluating Sources (pp. 255–71) helps students analyze the credibility, accuracy, and timeliness of sources. In this edition, Chapter 7 has been heavily updated to correlate with the Framework for Information Literacy for Higher Education from the Association of College and Research Libraries. Notable new entries that serve students' current research challenges include • Entering a Discourse (pp. 243–45) • Why Finding Reliable Internet Sources Is So Challenging (pp. 262–64) • A Word on "Fake News" (pp. 264–66)
Use strategies — such as interpretation, synthesis, response, critique, and design/redesign — to compose texts that integrate the writer's ideas with those from appropriate sources	**Synthesizing Sources** (p. 275) emphasizes the importance of synthesis as a way of thinking. **Chapter 7, Using Sources**, covers best practices for paraphrasing, summarizing, and avoiding plagiarism. Two sample student papers — one following MLA guidelines (pp. 302–8) and one following APA (pp. 309–13) — model outcomes for the research and writing process.
Processes	
Develop a writing project through multiple drafts	**Chapter 6, Developing an Argument of Your Own**, guides students through the writing process: generating ideas, developing and supporting a convincing thesis, imagining an audience, using transitions, maintaining a consistent tone and persona, and peer review. A sample student essay shows one student's process from rough notes to a final draft (pp. 236–40).
Develop flexible strategies for reading, drafting, reviewing, collaborating, revising, rewriting, rereading, and editing	**Chapter 2, Critical Reading: Getting Started**, covers active reading strategies such as previewing, underlining, highlighting, annotating, and rereading. A sample essay and a Thinking Critically: Previewing activity give students practice.

Use composing processes and tools as a means to discover and reconsider ideas	**Chapter 1, Critical Thinking**, and **Chapter 6, Developing an Argument of Your Own**, offer ample means of using composing to discover ideas and interrogate assumptions. Notable sections include • Survey, Analyze, and Evaluate the Issue (pp. 6–7) • Prompting Yourself: Classical Topics and Invention (pp. 16–17) • Three Brainstorming Strategies: Freewriting, Listing, and Diagramming (pp. 206–10)
Experience the collaborative and social aspects of writing processes	A new section on understanding and entering discourse (pp. 243–45) emphasizes the social aspect of writing. **Exercises** throughout the text offer opportunities for practicing and apply critical thinking and argument concepts in small groups.
Learn to give and to act on productive feedback to works in progress	**Chapter 6, Developing an Argument of Your Own**, covers the importance of peer review (pp. 234–36) and includes a Checklist for Peer Review of a Draft of an Argument that walks students through questions to ask when reviewing peers' work and providing feedback.
Adapt composing processes for a variety of technologies and modalities	**Reading, Writing, and Researching Tip** boxes highlight strategies for adapting writing to specific contexts, such as slide presentations. Instruction throughout *Current Issues and Enduring Questions* emphasizes the affordances and constraints of composing in analog and digital when taking notes, evaluating and citing sources, presenting, and more.
Reflect on the development of composing practices and how those practices influence their work	**Checklists** in every chapter invite students to reflect on their reading and writing processes, and **Thinking Critically** boxes throughout the text prompt students to apply the concepts they've learned via interactive exercises.
Knowledge of Conventions	
Develop knowledge of linguistic structures, including grammar, punctuation, and spelling, through practice in composing and revising	**Part Two, Critical Writing**, shows students how to recognize the characteristics of writing and teaches how those qualities contribute to effective (or ineffective) writing (see first outcome for more information). **Chapter 6, Developing an Argument of Your Own**, discusses how to establish an appropriate tone and persona; eliminate *we*, *one*, and *I* in argumentative writing; and avoid sexist language. Thinking Critically: Eliminating *We*, *One*, and *I* (p. 233) gives students a chance to put these concepts into practice, and a Checklist for Establishing Tone and Persona (p. 234) allows students to self-review and revise.

Understand why genre conventions for structure, paragraphing, tone, and mechanics vary	**Chapter 5, Writing an Analysis of an Argument**, helps students examine how an author's methods differ in relation to their purpose and audience. **Part Three, Further Views on Argument**, delves into expectations for different kinds of arguments.
Gain experience negotiating variations in genre conventions	**Assignments** at the end of every critical thinking, reading, and writing chapter prompt students to write common argument genres such as a critical summary, rhetorical analysis, or analysis of an argument. Additional prompts include multimodal composing.
Learn common formats and/or design features for different kinds of texts	**Previewing** (pp. 33–36) introduces students to design and genre features such as headings, subheadings, and abstracts to aid in basic comprehension and source evaluation. **Chapter 4, Visual Rhetoric: Thinking about Images as Arguments**, includes dozens of examples of visual arguments in different genres and highlights their design features. **MLA and APA style formatting conventions** are covered in detail in Chapter 7, Using Sources. Sample student papers in each style provide models.
Explore the concepts of intellectual property (such as fair use and copyright) that motivate documentation conventions	**Chapter 2, Critical Reading: Getting Started**, teaches best practices for recognizing and avoiding plagiarism and offers guidance on ethical paraphrase and summary. See, for example, Patchwriting and Plagiarism (pp. 49–50). **Chapter 7, Using Sources**, includes robust coverage of MLA and APA documentation styles, which discuss formatting conventions and include annotated sample student papers. • Compiling an Annotated Bibliography (pp. 278–79) shows students how to properly document and summarize their sources. • Quoting from Sources (pp. 279–83) shows students how to responsibly quote and integrate sources into their writing. • Checklists for evaluating print sources, websites, and fake news, avoiding plagiarism, and general strategies for source-based papers reinforce these concepts.
Practice applying citation conventions systematically in their own work	**MLA and APA style**, conveniently identified by blue- and green-edged pages, offer guidance on citation conventions, including dozens of models for in-text citations and reference lists.

Contents

PART ONE

Critical Thinking and Reading

1

Critical Thinking

What is the hardest task in the world? To think. — RALPH WALDO EMERSON

In all affairs it's a healthy thing now and then to hang a question mark on the things you have long taken for granted. — BERTRAND RUSSELL

Although Emerson said the hardest task in the world is simply "to think," he was using the word *think* in the sense of *critical thinking*. By itself, *thinking* can mean almost any sort of cognitive activity, from idle daydreaming ("I'd like to go camping") to simple reasoning ("but if I go this week, I won't be able to study for my chemistry exam"). Thinking by itself may include forms of deliberation and decision-making that occur so automatically they hardly register in our consciousness ("What if I do go camping? I won't be likely to pass the exam. Then what? I better stay home and study").

When we add the adjective *critical* to the noun *thinking*, we begin to examine this thinking process consciously. When we do so, we see that even our simplest decisions involve a fairly elaborate series of calculations. Just in choosing to study and not to go camping, for instance, we weighed the relative importance of each activity (both are important in different ways); considered our goals, obligations, and commitments (to ourselves, our parents, peers, and professors); posed questions and predicted outcomes (using experience and observation as evidence); and resolved to take the most prudent course of action (i.e., made a decision).

Many people associate being critical with fault-finding and nit-picking. The word *critic* might conjure an image of a sneering art or food critic eager to gripe about everything that's wrong with a particular work of art or menu item. People's low estimation of the stereotypical critic comes to light humorously in Samuel Beckett's play *Waiting for Godot*, when the two vagabond heroes, Vladimir and Estragon, engage in a name-calling contest to see who can hurl the worst insult at the other. Estragon wins hands-down when he fires the ultimate invective:

V: Moron!

E: Vermin!

V: Abortion!

E: Morpion!

V: Sewer-rat!

E: Curate!

V: Cretin!

E: (*with finality*) Crritic!

V: Oh! (*He wilts, vanquished, and turns away*)

However, being a good *critical* thinker isn't the same as being a "critic" in the derogatory sense. Quite the reverse: Because critical thinkers approach difficult questions and seek intelligent answers, they must be open-minded and self-aware, and they must analyze *their own* thinking as rigorously as they analyze others'. They must be alert to *their own* limitations and biases, the quality of evidence *they themselves* offer, the logic *they* use, and the conclusions *they* draw. In college, we may not aspire to become critics, but we all should aspire to become better critical thinkers.

Becoming more aware of our thought processes is a first step in practicing critical thinking. The word *critical* comes from the Greek word *krinein*, meaning "to separate, to choose"; above all, it implies *conscious* inquiry. It suggests that by breaking apart, or examining, our reasoning we can understand better the basis of our judgments and decisions — ultimately, so that we can make better ones.

Thinking through an Issue

When thinking about an issue, no matter how simple or controversial, we want to do it in a way that's fair to all parties and not just a snap judgment. Critical thinking means questioning not only the beliefs and assumptions of others, but also *one's own* beliefs and assumptions. When developing an argument, you ought to be identifying important problems, exploring relevant issues, and evaluating available evidence fairly — not merely collecting information to support a preestablished conclusion.

ANALYZING AND EVALUATING FROM MULTIPLE PERSPECTIVES

Let's think critically about an issue related to religious freedom, equality, and the law — one that we hope brings some humor to the activity but also inspires careful thinking and debate. In 2005, in response to pressure from some religious groups, the Kansas Board of Education gave preliminary approval for teaching alternatives to evolution in public school science classes. New policies would require science teachers to present "intelligent design" — the idea that the universe was created by an intentional, conscious force such as God — as an equally plausible explanation for natural selection and human development.

In a quixotic challenge to the legislation, twenty-four-year-old physics graduate Bobby Henderson wrote an open letter to the Kansas school board that quickly became popular on the internet and then was published in the *New York Times*. Henderson appealed for recognition of another theory that he said was equally valid: that an all-powerful deity called the

Flying Spaghetti Monster created the world. While clearly writing satirically on behalf of science, Henderson nevertheless kept a straight face and argued that if creationism were to be taught as a theory in science classes, then "Pastafarianism" must also be taught as another legitimate possibility. "I think we can all look forward to the time," he wrote, "when these three theories are given equal time in our science classes. . . . One third time for Intelligent Design; one third time for Flying Spaghetti Monsterism (Pastafarianism); and one third time for logical conjecture based on overwhelming observable evidence."

Gary Nelson/Crossville Chronicle

Under the establishment clause of the First Amendment, members of the Church of the Flying Spaghetti Monster were permitted to install a monument on the lawn of a Crossville, Tennessee, courthouse in 2008.

Since that time, the Church of the Flying Spaghetti Monster has become a creative venue where secularists and atheists construct elaborate mythologies, religious texts, and rituals, most of which involve cartoonish pirates and various noodle-and-sauce images. ("R'amen," they say at the end of their prayers.) However, although tongue in cheek, many followers have also used the organization seriously as a means to champion the First Amendment's establishment clause, which prohibits government institutions from *establishing*, or preferring, any one religion over another. Pastafarians have challenged policies and laws in various states that appear to discriminate among religions or to provide exceptions or exemptions based on religion. In Tennessee, Virginia, and Wisconsin, church members have successfully petitioned for permission to display statues or signs of the Flying Spaghetti Monster in places where other religious icons are permitted, such as on state government properties. One petition in Oklahoma argued that because the state allows a marble and granite Ten Commandments monument on the state courthouse lawn, then a statue of the Flying Spaghetti Monster must also be permitted; this effort ultimately forced the state to remove the Ten Commandments monument in 2015. Since then, individuals in California, Georgia, Florida, Texas, and Utah have asserted their right to wear religious head coverings in their driver's license photos — a religious exemption afforded to Muslims in those states — and have had their pictures taken with colanders on their heads.

Let's stop for a moment. Take stock of your initial reactions to the Church of the Flying Spaghetti Monster. Some responses might be quite uncritical, quite unthinking: "That's outrageous!" or "What a funny idea!" Others might be the type of snap judgment we discussed earlier: "These people are making fun of real religions!" or "They're just causing trouble." Think about it: If your hometown approved placing a Christmas tree on the town square during the holiday season and the Church of the Flying Spaghetti Monster argued that it, too, should be allowed to set up its holiday symbol — perhaps a statue — as a matter of religious equality, should it be afforded equal space? Why, or why not?

Be careful to exercise critical thinking here. Can one simply say, "No, that belief is ridiculous," in response to a religious claim? What if members of a different religious group were asking for equal space? Should a menorah (a Jewish holiday symbol) be allowed? A mural celebrating Kwanzaa? A Native American symbol? Can some religious expressions be included in public spaces and not others? If so, why? If not, why not?

In thinking critically about a topic, we must try to see it from all sides before reaching a conclusion. Critical thinking requires us to understand our own position and also see the other side. One mainstay of critical thinking is a *willingness to identify and consider objections to our own beliefs*. We conduct an argument with ourselves, advancing and then questioning different opinions. If someone were proposing a Spaghetti Monster holiday display, we should ask

- **Who** is *for* and *against* the proposition?
- **Why** are they *for* or *against* it?
- **What** can be said *for* and *against* the proposition?

When thinking critically, it's important to ask key questions about various positions. It is also important to weigh competing interests and predict the outcomes of any decision or action we take. Remember that to be fair, we must adopt a skeptical attitude not only toward views opposed to our own but also toward our own views and our own common sense — that is, toward ideas that seem to us obviously right. If we assume that we have a monopoly on the truth and dismiss those who disagree with us as misguided fools or if we assume that opponents are acting out of self-interest (or a desire to harass the community) and we don't analyze their views, we're being critical, but we aren't engaging in critical thinking.

SURVEY, ANALYZE, AND EVALUATE THE ISSUE

Seeing an issue such as the Church of the Flying Spaghetti Monster from multiple perspectives will require you to gather information — to find out what people are saying and thinking. You'll likely want to gather perspectives and opinions from religious leaders, community members, and legal experts and analyze them alongside one another (after all, you wouldn't want the town to be sued for discrimination). You'll want to examine points on which people agree and disagree. Try to familiarize yourself with current debates — perhaps about religious equality, free speech, or the separation of church and state — and consider the responsibility of public institutions to accommodate different viewpoints and various constituencies. Ask yourself: What are the bigger issues at stake? Finally, you'll want to evaluate the evidence used by all sides to support their claims. Remember that the Church of the Flying Spaghetti Monster didn't gain so much traction by being easy to dismiss. You'll certainly have to think beyond a knee-jerk value judgment like, "No, a Spaghetti Monster statue would be ugly."

To summarize our process, consider doing the following to enhance your ability to consider multiple perspectives:

1. **Survey different viewpoints**, considering as many as possible and paying attention to who stands to gain and lose in any debate.
2. **Analyze the conflicts**, identifying and separating out the problems or points of debate and trying to see the bigger issues at stake.
3. **Evaluate the ideas**, judging the merit of various claims and arguments and measuring the weight of the evidence.

If you survey, analyze, and evaluate comprehensively, you'll have better and more informed ideas; you'll generate a wide variety of ideas, each triggered by your own responses and the ideas your research brings to light. In short — and this point is key — *argument is an instrument of learning, decision-making, and persuasion*. You will be able to find your position by thinking through the issue and developing your argument. As you do so, you should be as thorough as possible and sensitive to the ideas and rights of many different people. After all, you may have to present your argument to the town council or community. If you simply decided that a Spaghetti Monster statue was insulting to other religions and ignored the law in your argument, you could be setting up your town for a lawsuit.

Use the Visual Guide: Evaluating a Proposal below to pursue some lines of questioning for evaluating a proposed regulation, policy, or procedure. Apply this line of thinking to the Flying Spaghetti Monster issue.

What do you think? If you were on your hometown's city council and a petition came through from the Church of the Flying Spaghetti Monster to permit a Spaghetti Monster display alongside the traditional Christmas tree and menorah on the town square, how would you answer the questions presented in the Visual Guide? How would you vote? Why? How would you explain your vote to opponents of the Spaghetti Monster display?

Visual Guide: Evaluating a Proposal

OBSTACLES TO CRITICAL THINKING

Because critical thinking requires engaging seriously with potentially difficult topics, topics about which you may already have strong opinions, and topics that elicit powerful emotional responses, it's important to recognize the ways in which your thinking may be compromised or clouded. The following attitudes might impede or otherwise negatively affect critical thinking in real life:

1. The topic is too controversial. I do not want to take a position on it.
2. The topic hits "too close to home" (i.e., "I have had direct experience with this").
3. The topic disgusts/angers/bores me.
4. Everyone I know thinks roughly the same thing I do about this topic.
5. Others may judge me if I verbalize what I think.
6. My opinion on this topic is *X* because it benefits me, my family, or my kind the most.
7. My parents raised me to think *X* about this topic.
8. One of my favorite celebrities believes *X* about this topic, so I should agree.
9. I know what I think, but my solutions are probably unrealistic. You can't change the system.
10. The answer is just common sense. Anyone who thinks differently lacks common sense.

Think about how each attitude might be detrimental to engagement with the question of approving a Flying Spaghetti Monster statue or might work as an impediment to drawing sound conclusions and making decisions on any issue.

ANTICIPATING COUNTERARGUMENTS

As we have shown, we generate ideas not only by supporting our initial thoughts, but also imagining opposing responses to them — sometimes called *counterpoints* or *counterpositions,* which help us clarify our thoughts. When we draw conclusions, we may also find **counterarguments** to our own position (other positions and points collected logically together toward a different conclusion). Sometimes, we avoid counterarguments — or avoid taking them seriously — because we do not want to face them or we simply cannot see things from another perspective. But we should try to take counterarguments seriously because they ultimately strengthen our thinking. When we write, they demonstrate that we have taken the time to consider other perspectives. We mention counterarguments here because they're an important component in argument, as you've already seen in our illustrations; we also spend more time discussing them in the Rebuttals section in Chapter 8.

WRITING TIP
Early in the process of conceiving your ideas on a topic, stop to ask yourself, "What might someone reasonably offer as an *objection* to my view?"

Critical Thinking at Work: From a Cluster to a Short Essay

Clustering is a type of brainstorming and a way of generating ideas, so it is a good tool for the process of thinking through an issue. Here's an example showing a student developing ideas about an issue related to the Church of the Flying Spaghetti Monster. The student, Alexa Cabrera, was assigned to write approximately 500 words about a specific legal challenge made by a member of the Church of the Flying Spaghetti Monster. She selected the case of Stephen Cavanaugh, a prisoner who had made a complaint against the Nebraska State Penitentiary after being denied the right to practice Pastafarianism while incarcerated there. Because the Department of Corrections had denied him those privileges, Cavanaugh filed suit citing civil rights violations and asked for his rights to be accommodated.

Alexa began thinking through her argument with a cluster, offering an initial idea and then building on it. Notice the role of counterpoints in the beginning of her cluster. Notice, too, that her cluster is not as elaborate as our earlier one. Her cluster was a *first* step, not a road map of the final essay. Finally, notice that Alexa's cluster contains ideas that did *not* make it into the final essay and that her essay — the product of several revised drafts — introduces points she had *not* thought of while clustering. In other words, the thinking process does not end when you begin the writing stage. Instead, writing an argument is a *continuous* process of thinking and learning as well as a method of persuasion.

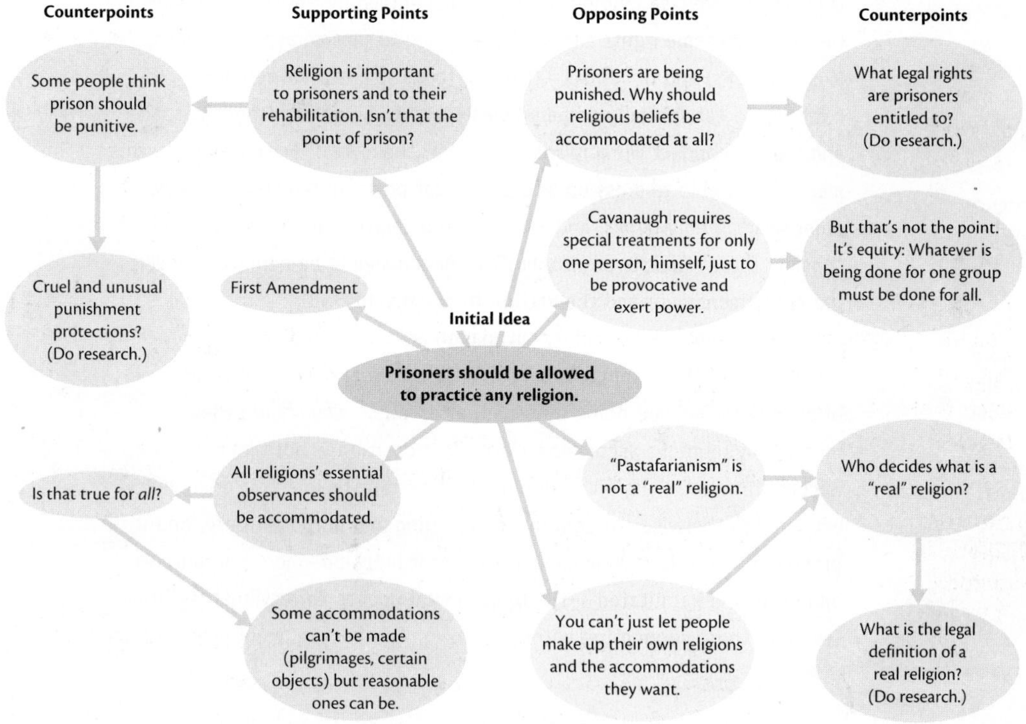

Cabrera 1

Alexa Cabrera

Professor Regina Dacus

English 112

8 October 2016

Title: Plays with words related to pasta and prison. The subtitle states the thesis.

Stirred and Strained: Pastafarians Should Be Allowed to Practice in Prison

Paragraph 1: Sets the stage. Nifty turn of phrase engages readers and sets the tone as playful but serious.

Stephen Cavanaugh is a member of the Church of the Flying Spaghetti Monster (FSM), a mostly web-based religious group notable for its members' demands that they be treated under the First Amendment like any other religion. The group strives to show that if Christians can place Nativity scenes on public grounds or if Muslims can wear head coverings in state driver's license photographs, then by god (or by pasta, as the case may be), they can too. Cavanaugh is in the Nebraska State Penitentiary, where inmates are permitted under the Religious Land Use and Institutionalized Persons Act (RLUIPA) to exercise religious freedoms guaranteed by the First Amendment. He wants the same rights and privileges given to incarcerated Christians, Muslims, Jews, and Buddhists—namely, to be able to wear religious clothing, to eat specially prepared meals, and to be given resources, space, and time to conduct worship with his fellow "believers." For Cavanaugh, this means being able to dress up as a pirate, eat pasta on selected holidays, order satirical holy books, and lead a weekly "prayer" group. Many people consider these requests absurd, but Cavanaugh should be permitted under the First Amendment and the RLUIPA to practice his faith.

Last sentence presents a clear thesis.

Paragraph 2: Counterarguments raised throughout.

Some arguments against Cavanaugh are easier to dismiss than others. One of these simply casts aside the spiritual needs and concerns of prisoners: They are being punished, after all, so why should they receive any religious accommodations? This position is both immoral and unconstitutional. Religion is an important sustaining force for prisoners who might otherwise struggle to find meaning and purpose in life, and it is protected by the First Amendment *because* it helps prisoners find purpose and become rehabilitated—the fundamental goal of correctional facilities (even for those serving life without parole). Another argument sees religion as important as long as it conforms to Judeo-Christian belief structures, which has for a long time been the only spiritual path available in American prisons. But today, in our diverse society, the RLUIPA *requires* prisons to provide religious accommodations for all faiths equally unless an undue administrative, financial, or security burden can be proven. Obviously, many religious observances cannot be accommodated. Prisons cannot permit inmates to carry crosses and staves, construct temples and sweat lodges, or make required religious pilgrimages. However, as long as *some* reasonable religious accommodations can be and are made for some groups—such as Catholics being offered fish on Fridays or Jewish and Muslim prisoners receiving kosher and halal meals—then all religious groups must be similarly accommodated.

The more challenging question about the Church of the Flying Spaghetti Monster is whether it is a religion at all, whether it deserves equal treatment among more established religions. When Cavanaugh was first denied his request, the prison claimed that FSM was not a religion but a "parody" of religion. The Nebraska State Penitentiary suggested it could not grant privileges to anyone who presents his whimsical desires as part of a religious philosophy. In dealing with a humorous and politically motivated "religion" without a strong tradition and whose founder may write a new gospel at any time, should the prison have to keep up with the possibility of constantly changing prisoner demands? Can anyone just make up a religion and then expect to be accommodated?

For better or worse, the answer is yes—as long as the accommodations represent valid forms of observance, are reasonable, and do not pose a substantial burden to the institution. Many religions have councils that at times alter the tenets of their faith. The state does not have the authority to determine what is or is not a "real" religion or religious practice. It does have an obligation under the RLUIPA to accommodate not just some but all forms of faith for incarcerated persons. As long as individuals sincerely hold certain beliefs, and as long as the accommodations requested meet the standards of reasonability and equity, state prisons, like all other government agencies and institutions, cannot discriminate. Some might argue that Cavanaugh's

Writer cites law's requirements.

Last sentence sustains the thesis and anticipates that readers may agree on this point but still not consider the FSM a religion.

Paragraph 3: Raises a possible counterposition and gives it due respect.

Responds to opposing position; writer is still discussing reasonable and fair treatment of inmates, not "anything goes."

Writer reminds readers that the state cannot determine a "real" or "unreal" religion, just as it cannot judge the depth, rigor, or literalness of an inmate's belief.

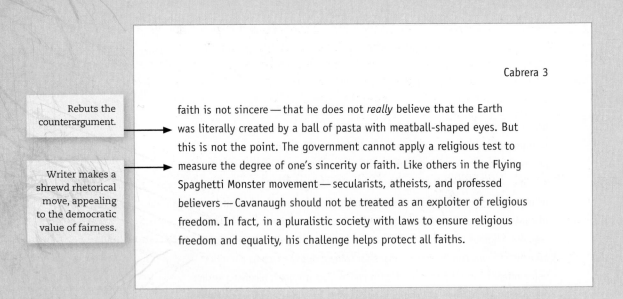

Rebuts the counterargument.

Writer makes a shrewd rhetorical move, appealing to the democratic value of fairness.

Cabrera 3

faith is not sincere — that he does not *really* believe that the Earth was literally created by a ball of pasta with meatball-shaped eyes. But this is not the point. The government cannot apply a religious test to measure the degree of one's sincerity or faith. Like others in the Flying Spaghetti Monster movement — secularists, atheists, and professed believers — Cavanaugh should not be treated as an exploiter of religious freedom. In fact, in a pluralistic society with laws to ensure religious freedom and equality, his challenge helps protect all faiths.

Topics for Critical Thinking and Writing

1. A paper begins with its title, not with its first paragraph. A good title makes readers curious and may let them know where the essay will take them. Does this title have that effect on you? Why, or why not? What other title would you suggest?
2. Are you convinced from this essay that it would be unfair to deny Cavanaugh and other Pastafarian inmates their demands? Why, or why not?
3. How would you define a "real" religion? Can it be any belief deeply and sincerely felt, or does it require something more? Explain your answer.

Generating Ideas: Writing as a Way of Thinking

"To learn to write," Robert Frost said, "is to learn to have ideas." But how does one "learn to have ideas"?

Sometimes, we discover ideas while talking with others. A friend shares an opinion about some issue, and we — who have never really thought much about the matter — find ourselves saying that we see their point but have a different opinion. We are, in a sense, offering a counterpoint, saying, "Well, yes, I see your point, but I'm not of that opinion. I see it differently — not as *X*, but as *Y*." For example, imagine someone is arguing against the US border wall proposal put forth by US President Donald Trump. Another person could say:

> *Yes*, I see your point that a wall will be expensive, *but* the fact is we do already have substantial border fences, and we spend a lot of money on enforcement. The wall proposal only strengthens what we already do and may even amount to long-term savings.

A third person might respond, "*Yes*, I see your point about money, *but* the wall will be destructive to the environment, which outweighs the financial savings." A fourth might add, "*Yes, and* a wall is also a symbol of division." Often, we get ideas when we add to others' observations. Maybe we find ourselves agreeing with someone and would like to extend the observation to include another position, too. We are essentially saying, "Yes, *X*, sure, and also *Y*, too."

Here's another example of how that might play out:

> *Yes*, a "soda tax" on high-sugar beverages would discourage unhealthy behaviors and generate much-needed revenue for the city, *and* come to think of it, it may encourage drink companies to lower the sugar content of their products.

Mere chance — a response a friend's comment — seems to have produced an idea. However, learning to have ideas is not usually a matter of chance. Or if chance *is* involved, well, as Louis Pasteur put it, "Chance favors the prepared mind." Lurking in the mind are bits of information, opinions that may arise in an unexpected circumstance — when talking, when listening to a lecture or a classroom discussion, or especially when reading.

Consider Archimedes, the ancient Greek mathematician who discovered a method to determine the volume of an irregularly shaped object. Here's how the story goes: A king gave a goldsmith a specific weight of gold and asked him to make a crown in the shape of laurel leaves. When the job was finished, the king weighed the crown and found that it matched the weight of the gold he had provided. Nevertheless, he suspected that the goldsmith might have substituted some silver for some of the gold. How could the king find out (without melting or otherwise damaging the crown) if the crown was pure gold?

For Archimedes, meditating on this problem produced no ideas at first, but when he entered a bathtub he noticed that the water level rose as he immersed his body. He suddenly realized that he could determine the purity of the crown by measuring the amount of water it displaced. Since silver is less dense than gold, it takes a greater volume of silver to equal a given weight of gold. In his excitement at his idea to measure equal weights and relative volumes by immersing the crown in water, Archimedes is said to have leaped out of the tub and run naked through the street, shouting "*Eureka*!" (Greek for "I have found [it]!").

Why do we tell this story? Partly because we like it, but chiefly because the word *eureka* captures that moment of unexpectedly finding an idea. Finding an idea can sometimes feel like reaching under the couch to retrieve a dog toy and finding a ten-dollar bill instead: "Hey, look what I found! *Eureka!*" But we rarely luck into ideas in this way. Actually, the word *eureka* comes from the same Greek word that has given us the word **heuristic** (pronounced hyoo-RIS-tik), which refers to a *method* or *process* of discovering ideas.

Gordon Marino/Alamy Stock Photo

Sculpture in Manchester, England, depicting Archimedes's bathtub "Eureka" moment.

When you're asked to think about something you've read in this book, if your first response is that you have no ideas, please do not just take a bath like Archimedes did. A better method is to immerse yourself not in water but in the issues at hand. You can do this by listening to what's being said in the world around you — both in and out of the classroom, as well as in the world of magazines, newspapers, books, and other media — and thinking about your responses to what you hear.

One of the most basic methods to discover ideas is the one we mention above — "Yes, *but* I see it differently" or "Yes, *and also*." This process can help you respond to a work and begin to develop ideas.

CONFRONTING UNFAMILIAR ISSUES

Generating ideas can be a challenge when you, as a student, are asked to read about and respond to new or unfamiliar issues. Sometimes, students wonder why they have to engage in particular topics and generate ideas about them. "I want to be a speech pathologist," one might say, "so why do I need to read essays and formulate ideas about capital punishment?"

One answer is that a college curriculum should spur students to think about pressing issues facing our society, so learning about capital punishment is important to all students. But this isn't the only answer. One could never study "all" the important social problems we face (and many of them change very rapidly). Instead, colleges seek to equip students with tools, methods, and habits of mind that enable them to confront arguments about *any* potential issue or problem. The primary goal of a college education (and of this book) is to help students develop an *intellectual apparatus* — a tool kit that can be applied to any subject matter, any issue.

The techniques presented in this book offer a practical framework for approaching issues, thinking about them carefully, asking good questions, identifying problems, and offering reasonable solutions — not necessarily because we want you to form opinions about the specific issues we have selected (although we hope you do), but because we want you to practice critical thinking, reading, and writing in ways that transfer to other aspects of your education as well as to your personal, professional, and civic life.

The Nigerian novelist Chinua Achebe said, "The writer must march up front." Rather than thinking that you must "agree or disagree" with the authors whose positions you'll read about in this book, imagine that you'll be practicing how to discover your own unique point of view by finding pathways into debates, negotiating different positions, and generating new ideas. So when you confront a new or unfamiliar issue in this book (or elsewhere), consider the strategies discussed in this chapter as practical methods — *heuristics* — for generating new ideas from the information at hand. That is what critical thinking (and writing) is all about.

USING CLUSTERING TO DISCOVER IDEAS

As you can see from the student cluster on the Pastafarian issue, we're big fans of clustering as a practical method for generating ideas and thinking through your argument. If you think with pencil and paper in hand and let your mind make associations by clustering, you'll find (perhaps to your surprise) that you have plenty of interesting ideas and that some can lead to satisfying conclusions. Doubtless you'll also have some ideas that represent gut reactions or poorly thought-out conclusions, but that's okay. When clustering, allow your thoughts to take shape without restriction; you can look over your ideas again and organize them later.

To start clustering, take a sheet of paper and jot down what you think is the most basic issue or the fundamental conflict. This will help shape the questions you ask and frame your initial idea. Write down your initial idea — your opinion on the issue or debate at hand — and then develop supporting ideas, explore counterpositions (and rebuttals), and jot down where you need to do some research, eventually leading you to a tighter argument. Review the cluster in this chapter on page 9 to help you work through an issue.

WRITING TIP
If you decide to generate ideas for your essay by clustering, don't worry that some ideas may be off the cuff or even nonsense. Just get ideas down on paper. You can evaluate them later.

APPROACHING AN ISSUE (OR AN ASSIGNMENT)

Anyone who has played baseball can tell you that one of the most challenging things to do is hit the ball. So, coaches often instruct their players to develop an *approach* to hitting. The hitter's approach begins in the dugout. First, you watch the pitcher. You make observations. What kind of pitches are being thrown? Are they largely inside pitches or outside pitches, high or low, fast or slow? Answering these questions can help determine what you do as you get ready to bat. You must also ask: What is the game situation? Are you attempting to hit long into the outfield or just get the ball in play, perhaps to advance your runners already on the bases? Once you step into the batter's box, where should you set your feet — farther away from the plate or close to it? In short, you are asking questions: *What am I facing? What is my goal?* and, quite literally, *Where do I stand?*

Not everyone plays baseball, but this metaphor is intended to get you thinking about how to prepare for an argument by asking some key questions:

- What should you look for in an issue or problem?
- What kinds of challenges will opponents likely throw at you?
- How will you position yourself?
- What do you want to achieve?

A critical thinker's approach, like a baseball batter's, is the preparation for the argument. It involves assessing issues, identifying key problems, and discovering your ideas.

In real life, and in this book, you may be given an assignment to think critically or make an argument. A professor (or a textbook author) assigning a prompt is much like a coach instructing you on your approach, and examining the assignment prompt carefully is like reading the pitcher. Ask: What is being thrown at you? How should you strategize to meet the challenges?

Perhaps the assignment prompts you to consider a certain aspect of an issue, compare two arguments, or take a side in a debate. Here is an example of an assignment that calls for a specific approach:

> At the time a county clerk in Kentucky named Kim Davis was refusing to sign marriage licenses for same-sex couples, some of her supporters compared her to civil

rights activists like Rosa Parks, who intentionally broke segregation laws in order to challenge them. Are Kim Davis's actions justifiable in the same way Rosa Parks's were? Are the two figures equivalent crusaders for justice?

A prompt like this doesn't tell you *what* to think, but *what to ask* and *how to argue*. It tells you to *compare*, *analyze*, and *evaluate*. In your comparison of Davis and Parks, you must judge whether or not their actions were morally or politically equivalent and then argue yes or no. You are being prompted to consider the motivations, purposes, and justifications for each figure's actions.

Many assignments call for these elements of comparison, analysis, and evaluation. They ask the questions and tell you how to argue. But by figuring out what to ask and how to argue yourself, you can develop arguments without prompts provided by your professors. When facing issues in your life, work, or society, you will sometimes have to prompt *yourself* to figure out what to think (and what to argue).

PROMPTING YOURSELF: CLASSICAL TOPICS AND INVENTION

One way of generating new ideas by prompting yourself is to consider what the ancient rhetoricians called **topics** — from the Greek *topoi*, meaning "places." (We see this word as a root in our word *topography*, a description of place.) Today, we often use the word *topic* to describe something very specific, as when a professor or committee leader says, "Today our topic for discussion is the proposed bike lane on our campus drive." But for the ancients, such as Aristotle in Greece and Cicero in Rome, the *topoi* (or topics) were more conceptual and were seen as the basic elements of arguments, debates, and conversations. Among the classical topics were *definition*, *comparison*, *relationship*, and *testimony*. When formulated as questions, they prompted thoughtful people to invent (from the Latin *invenire*, "to come upon, to find") ideas.

If you're at a loss for ideas when confronted with an issue — and an assignment to write about it — you might discover ideas by turning to the relevant classical topics, framing them as questions, and jotting down your responses. We'll use our campus bike lane as an example issue.

Definition: What are the elements in the debate?

What is a road? What is a bike lane? What is a college campus? How might these definitions help you think through the issues? If, for example, you define a *road* as a way people travel (especially students), a *bike lane* as a pathway for a certain means of safe transportation, and a *campus* as a place where students must be able to live and learn safely, then you may be able to discover a reasonable starting point for an argument: *Because many students use bikes and they need to get to class safely, a bike lane on campus is a reasonable accommodation.* Simply defining the basic elements within an issue may guide your thinking on a question.

Comparison: What are the elements like or unlike?

Comparing students to nonstudents, cars to bikes, or campuses to other public spaces may also help you discover your position. You may find that students have a special need for bikes that nonstudents do not have. Or you may find that bikes, compared to cars, are cheaper and more environmentally friendly. Maybe campus roads are not the same as some other public roads; they may be more like roads in parks, cutting through spaces of leisure, quietude, and study. Making comparisons like these can help you evaluate the various reasons bicycle lanes may be called for on campus. You may also compare other cases: Have other colleges built bike lanes? If so, to what effect?

Relationship: What are the causes and effects in play?

Think of relationships as "*if . . . then*" propositions. If we decided to build bike lanes, then we would likely increase safety and access on campus and help the environment. However, if we build bike lanes, then we would also spend a great deal of money, which may affect other budget priorities, some of which may also increase other kinds of access and safety. The point: Teasing out the relationships of actions to their consequences can help produce ideas. (You may also explore the consequences of nonactions: If we did not build bike lanes, then we would not be keeping up with institutions that are building them, making our school less attractive to new students.)

Testimony: What are the major opinions and forms of evidence?

All ideas need to be justified in consideration of opinions and evidence. What do drivers think? What do students think? What do experts and respected leaders say? What laws or rules are applicable? What evidence has been (or can be) gathered to testify to the need for bike lanes (or the lack of such a need)? Have there been accidents? Are students or drivers complaining about the risks? Gathering testimony — assessing data, trends, currents, opinions, and attitudes — can help inspire ideas.

The classical *topoi* are not solutions to any problems at hand, but a means of discovering solutions. They provide a set of categories that can work as guidelines to formulating an opinion or argument. In other words, they offer a way to organize the *process* of invention, of thinking through an issue to determine what you think and what position you want to take.

An Essay for Generating Ideas

Consider the following brief essay about the Food and Drug Administration's approval, in 2015, of a genetically engineered salmon. Although GMO (genetically modified organism) foods and medicines are common in the United States, this salmon will soon be the first genetically modified animal approved for food consumption in the United States. After you read the essay, refer to Thinking Critically: Generating Ideas with Topics (p. 19), which asks you to begin jotting down ideas on a sheet of paper along the lines of the classical topics. As an example of how to respond to the questions, we've included columns related to the Stephen Cavanaugh case. As you attempt to formulate ideas related to the essay about genetically engineered salmon, answer the questions related to the classical topics. There's no need to limit yourself to one answer per item as we did.

NINA FEDOROFF

Nina Fedoroff (b. 1942) is a molecular biologist and winner, in 2007, of the National Medal of Science. She served as science and technology advisor to the US secretary of state from 2007 to 2010 and is an emeritus Evan Pugh professor at Penn State University. The following essay originally appeared in the *New York Times* in December 2015.

The Genetically Engineered Salmon Is a Boon for Consumers and Sustainability

This is great news for consumers and the environment. Wild salmon populations have long been in deep trouble because of overfishing, and open-water cage farming of salmon pollutes coastal waters, propagates fish diseases, and sacrifices a lot of wild-caught fish to be consumed as salmon feed.

The fish is virtually identical to wild salmon, but it is a more sustainable food source, growing faster to maturity.

But just imagine, you'll soon be able to eat salmon guilt-free. AquaBounty has spent more than 20 years developing and testing this faster-growing salmon that will require less feed to bring it to a marketable size. It can be farmed economically in closed, on-land facilities that recirculate water and don't dump waste into the sea. Since the fish live in clean, managed water, they don't get diseases that are spread among caged fish in the sea. And the growing facilities could be closer to markets, cutting shipping costs.

All of these elements take pressure off wild salmon and make salmon farming more sustainable.

Much of the concern about AquaBounty's 5
salmon centers around several bits of added DNA, taken from another fish, that let the salmon grow continuously, not just seasonally. That does not make them "unnatural" or dangerous, it just makes them grow to market size on less feed.

We've been tinkering with our plants and animals to serve our food needs for somewhere between 10 and 20 thousand years. We created corn, for example. The seed-bearing structure of the original "wild" version, called teosinte, looked very different from the modern-day ear, packed with hundreds of soft, starch-and-protein-filled kernels. And it's people who developed the tomatoes we eat today. Mother Nature's are tiny: A pioneering breeder described them in an 1893 grower's guide as "small, hollow, tough, watery" fruits.

But there's money (and fame) in being anti-G.M.O. The organic food marketers want to sell their food, which is over-priced because organic farming is inefficient — not because the food's better — so they tell scare stories about the dangers of G.M.O.s.

There is also no reason to fear that these genetically engineered salmon will escape and destroy wild populations. Only sterile females will be grown for food. And since the fish will be grown in contained facilities on land, escapees can't survive either.

AquaBounty's salmon is salmon, plain and simple. I, for one, can't wait to taste it.

THINKING CRITICALLY *Generating Ideas with Topics*

Use the classical topics (pp. 16–17) to think through an issue. Provide the relevant information for a topic of your choice or for the topic of genetically engineered salmon explored in Fedoroff's essay. We have provided the issue of Steven Cavanaugh and the Church of the Flying Spaghetti Monster as an example.

TOPICS	QUESTIONS	EXAMPLE TOPIC: *PASTAFARIANISM*	YOUR TOPIC
Definition *Categories* *Descriptions* *Definitions* *Explanations*	What is it?	Define terms: *creationism* *religious freedom* *civil rights*	
Comparison *Similarities* *Differences* *Analogies* *Applications*	What is it like or unlike?	Civil disobedience Other struggles for religious rights	
Relationships *Antecedents* *Precedents* *Consequences* *Outcomes*	What are some causes and effects? (*If . . . , then*)	If Pastafarianism is permitted to continue, then . . . If prisoners cannot worship freely, then . . .	
Testimony *Statistics* *Maxims* *Laws* *Authorities/ Quotations*	What forms of evidence and opinion exist?	What have courts said in the past? What do supporters and/or detractors say? What laws exist to protect members of religions?	

THINKING CRITICALLY ABOUT THE ISSUE

What follows is an inner dialogue that you might engage in as you think critically about the question of genetically engineered salmon.

> The purpose of genetically engineered salmon is to protect against the ecological effects of overfishing — that seems to be a good thing.
>
> Another purpose is to protect consumers by ensuring that the price of salmon, one of the most commonly eaten fish, will not become so high that few people could afford it.
>
> But other issues are apparent. Should we turn to altering the genes of animals to protect the environment or consumer prices? Are there other solutions, like eating less salmon or regulating overfishing?
>
> Who gains and who loses, and what do they stand to gain or lose, by Federal Drug Administration (FDA) approval of genetically modified salmon?
>
> The author says no one should worry about "several bits of DNA added," but come to think of it, is this modification unethical or dangerous in any way? Is it okay to create a new type of animal by altering genes?
>
> The author attacks anti-GMO activists, saying they're just after money (and fame — why fame?). Isn't money (and fame?) also the goal of AquaBounty and other GMO food producers?

Part of the job is **analytic**, recognizing the elements or complexities of the whole, and part is **evaluative**, judging the adequacy of all the ideas, one by one. Both tasks require critical thinking in the form of analyzing and evaluating, and those processes themselves require a self-conscious and disciplined *approach*.

So far, we have jotted down a few thoughts and then immediately given some second thoughts contrary to the first. Be aware that your own counterpositions might not come to mind right away. They might not occur until you reread your notes or try to explain the issue to a friend, until you do some preliminary reading on the subject, or even until you begin drafting an essay aimed at supporting or undermining the FDA rules. Most likely, some good ideas won't occur until a second or third or fourth draft — or even until after you have published or turned in your work.

Here are some further thoughts on the issue of genetically modified salmon to show how different perspectives and questions lead to different approaches.

> According to one article, the FDA is not requiring companies to label the salmon as genetically engineered. Should this information at least be made available to consumers? Maybe their religious, ethical, or personal preferences would be not to eat modified fish species. If the fish were properly labeled and people knew of any risks associated with eating it, consumers could avoid it if they wished.
>
> - *Possible perspectives*: Social (consumer interest)

- *Questions*: How should consumers expect to be protected by the government in an era of new scientific developments such as GMOs and in relation to their right to know what goes into their food? How should the government respond to new scientific advances such as GMOs?
- *Approach*: Might I argue that the new regulations are okay, but strict labeling should be required?

It's actually pretty amazing that scientists have helped solve the problem of the dwindling salmon population from overfishing by making a genetic modification that allows fish to grow large and fast and sustainably. Like any new thing, people who are uncomfortable with technological change will resist the new processes but will soon become accustomed to them once their fears are allayed. I'll bet at one time, people were hesitant to accept the light bulb as an advancement. Like all new advances, once it is accepted, it will be a boost to consumers, the environment, and business.

- *Possible perspectives*: Scientific (technological change)
- *Questions*: What other technologies were resisted in the past and are now commonplace, and what lessons can we learn from them? Which technologies are now keystones for our economy? How has science contributed to solving food crises and environmental crises?
- *Approach*: Might I argue that people should be more open to technological innovation as a way to solve environmental, social, and economic issues related to the food supply?

Doubtless there is much that we haven't asked or thought about, but we hope you'll agree that the issue deserves careful thought. Some of these questions require you to do **research** on the topic. Some raise issues of fact, and relevant evidence probably is available. To reach a conclusion in which you have confidence, you'll likely have to do some research to find out what the facts — the objective data — are. Merely explaining your position without giving the evidence will not be convincing.

Even without doing any research, however, you might want to look over the pros and cons, perhaps adding some new thoughts or modifying or even rejecting (for reasons that you can specify) some of those already given. If you do think further about this issue (and we hope that you will), notice an interesting point about *your own* thinking: It probably isn't *linear* (moving in a straight line from *A* to *B* to *C*) but *recursive*, moving from *A* to *C* and back to *B* or starting over at *C* and then back to *A* and *B*. By zigging and zagging almost despite yourself, you'll reach a conclusion that may finally seem correct. In retrospect, it might seem obvious; *now* you can chart a nice line from *A* to *B* to *C* — but that probably wasn't at all evident at the start.

A CHECKLIST FOR CRITICAL THINKING

- ❒ Does my thinking show open-mindedness and intellectual curiosity?
- ❒ Am I approaching my subject from a particular perspective?
- ❒ Can I examine the assumptions that come with my approach?
- ❒ Am I willing to entertain different ideas, both those that I encounter while reading and those that come to mind while writing?
- ❒ Am I willing to exert myself — for instance, to do research — to acquire information, identify different viewpoints, and evaluate evidence?

A Short Essay Calling for Critical Thinking

When reading an essay, we expect the writer to have thought carefully about the topic. We don't want to read every false start, every fuzzy thought, and every ill-organized paragraph that the writer knocked off. Yes, writers make false starts, put down fuzzy thoughts, and write ill-organized paragraphs, but then they revise and revise yet again, ultimately producing a readable essay that seems effortlessly written. Still — and this is our main point — writers of argumentative essays need to show readers that they have made some effort; they need to show *how* they got to their views. It isn't enough for the writer to say, "I believe *X*"; rather, he or she must in effect say, "I believe *X* because I see things from this perspective. Others believe *Y* or *Z*, and although from their perspective, their answers might sound reasonable, my inquiry shows another way to think or act about the issue. There may be value in *Y* or *Z* (or maybe not), and on the surface they may be plausible (or maybe they are not plausible), but their beliefs do not take into account what I am arguing, that *X* is a better alternative because. . . ." Obviously you don't need to follow that exact pattern (although you could); the point is that writers often need to make their critical thinking explicit to convince their readers of the argument they make.

Notice in the following short essay — on employers using biometric devices to monitor employees' performance — that the author, Lynn Stuart Parramore, positions herself against new workplace technologies in a compelling way. As you read, think critically about how she presents her position and how she encourages readers to sympathize with her views. Ask questions about what she includes and excludes, whether she presents other perspectives amply or fairly, and what additional positions might be valid on these recent developments in the rapidly growing field of biometrics in business.

LYNN STUART PARRAMORE

Lynn Stuart Parramore is a senior research analyst at the Institute for New Economic Thinking and a senior editor of *AlterNet*, as well as a frequent contributor to *Reuters*, *HuffPost*, and other outlets. Reprinted here is an essay published by *Al Jazeera America* on September 18, 2015.

Provocative title leaves readers with a sense of Parramore's argument. →

Fitbits for Bosses

The writer throws in an ominous proposition, the "behavior-monitoring device," that could become routine. →

Imagine you've just arrived at your job with the Anywhere Bank call center. You switch on your computer and adjust the height of your chair. Then, you slide on the headset, positioning the mic in front of your lips. All that's left to do is to activate your behavior-monitoring device — the gadget hanging from your neck that tracks your tone of voice, your heart rate, and your physical movements throughout the day, sending real-time reports to your supervisor.

A scene from a dystopian movie? Nope. It's already happening in America. Welcome to the brave new world of workplace biosurveillance.

> Science-fiction language and references to a dystopian "brave new world" assist sense of foreboding.

It's obvious that wearable tracking technology has gone mainstream: Just look at the explosion of smart watches and activity monitors that allow people to count steps and check their calorie intake. But this technology has simultaneously been creeping into workplaces: The military uses sensors that scan for injuries, monitor heart rate, and check hydration. More and more, professional athletes are strapping on devices that track every conceivable dimension of performance. Smart ice skates that measure a skater's jump. Clothes that measure an athlete's breathing and collect muscle data. At this year's tryouts in Indianapolis, some NFL hopefuls wore the "Adidas miCoach," a device that sends data on speed and acceleration straight to trainers' iPads. Over the objection of many athletes, coaches and team owners are keen to track off-the-field activity, too, such as sleep patterns and diet. With million-dollar players at stake, big money seems poised to trump privacy.

> Presents as "obvious" the fact that biosurveillance technology has gone mainstream, "creeping" into the workplace. "So what?" Parramore is about to tell us.

Now employers from industries that don't even require much physical labor are getting in on the game.

> Single sentence turns the focus from two specialized fields to everyday jobs.

Finance is adopting sophisticated analytics to ensure business performance from 5
high-dollar employees. Cambridge neuroscientist and former Goldman Sachs trader John Coates works with companies to figure out how monitoring biological signals can lead to trading success; his research focuses on measuring hormones that increase confidence and other desirable states as well as those that produce negative, stressful states. In a report for Bloomberg, Coates explained that he is working with "three or four hedge funds" to apply an "early-warning system" that would alert supervisors when traders are getting into the hormonal danger zone. He calls this process "human optimization."

> Extends the dystopian theme and sci-fi language: Phrases like "alert supervisors" and "human optimization" hint at deeper control by managers.

People who do the most basic, underpaid work in our society are increasingly subject to physical monitoring, too—and it extends far beyond the ubiquitous urine test. Bank of America has started using smart badges that monitor the voice and behavior patterns of call-center workers, partnering with the creepily named Humanyze, a company specializing in "people analytics." Humanyze is the brainchild of the MIT Media Lab, the fancy research institute at the Massachusetts Institute of Technology dedicated to the "betterment of humanity," which, incidentally, receives a quarter of its funding from taxpayers. Humanyze concocted a computer dashboard complete with graphs and pie charts that can display the location of employees (Were you hanging out in the lounge today?) and their "social context" (Do you spend a lot of time alone?).

> Parramore enhances her argument through strong language and ironic, sardonic tone: "creepily named," "concocted."

Humanyze founder Ben Waber points out that companies already spend enormous resources collecting analytics on their customers. Why not their employees?

> Parramore quotes Humanyze's founder but presents his statement as anything but appealing.

A growing number of workers are being monitored by GPS, often installed on their smartphones. In the U.S. the Supreme Court ruled that law enforcement officials need a warrant to use GPS devices to track a suspect. But employers don't worry over such formalities in keeping tabs on employees, especially those who are mobile, such as truck drivers. A *Washington Post* report on GPS surveillance noted a 2012 study by the research firm Aberdeen Group, which showed that 62 percent of "field

> Supports claims with examples from a research study and a case study.

employees" — those who regularly perform duties away from the office — are tracked this way. In May, a California woman filed a lawsuit against her former employer, Intermex Wire Transfer, for forcing her to install a tracking app on her phone, which she was required to keep on 24/7. She described feeling like a prisoner wearing an ankle bracelet. After removing the app, the woman was fired.

> Provides a counterpoint offered by the industries that create these technologies.

Sensitive to Big Brother accusations, the biosurveillance industry is trying to keep testing and tool evaluations under the radar. Proponents of the technology point to its potential to improve health conditions in the workplace and enhance public safety. Wouldn't it be better, they argue, if nuclear power plant operators, airline pilots, and oil rig operatives had their physical state closely monitored on the job?

> Mentions "Young Americans" as a possible source of opposing argument. "What could go wrong?" Parramore asks.

Young Americans nurtured in a digital world where their behavior is relentlessly 10
collected and monitored by advertisers may shrug at an employer's demands for a biosurveillance badge. In a world of insecure employment, what choice do they have, anyway? Despite the revelations of alarming National Security Agency spying and increased government and corporate surveillance since 9/11, the young haven't had much experience yet with what's at stake for them personally. What could possibly go wrong?

> Parramore answers that question from previous paragraph, first with the word *dehumanizing*.

A lot: Surveillance has a way of dehumanizing workers. It prevents us from experimenting and exercising our creativity on the job because it tends to uphold the status quo and hold back change. Surveillance makes everyone seem suspicious, creating perceptions and expectations of dishonesty. It makes us feel manipulated. Some researchers have found that increased monitoring actually decreases productivity.

> Applies a well-known philosopher's theory of power to the new context of biosurveillance data.

Philosopher and social theorist Michel Foucault observed that the relationship between the watcher and the watched is mostly about power. The power of the observer is enhanced, while the person observed feels more powerless. When an employer or manager interprets our personal data, she gets to make categorical judgments about us and determine how to predict our behavior.

> Considers scenarios of possible discrimination or coercion with bio data and then questions the limits of oversight.

What if she uses the information to discriminate? Coerce? Selectively apply the rules? The data she uses to make her judgments may not even be telling the truth: Researchers have warned that big data can produce big errors. People looking at numbers tend to use them to confirm their own biases, cherry-picking the information that supports their beliefs and ditching the rest. And since algorithms are constructed by human beings, they are not immune to human biases, either. A consumer might be labeled "unlikely to pay a credit card bill" because of an ethnic name, thus promulgating a harmful stereotype.

> Reminds readers that measurements are prone to error and biases could lead to discriminatory uses of data.

As Americans, we like to tell ourselves that we value freedom and undue interference from authority. But when we are subjected to surveillance, we feel disempowered and disrespected. We may be more inclined to accept the government getting involved because of fears about terrorism — but when it comes to surveillance on the job, our tendency to object may be chilled by weakened worker protections and increased employment insecurity.

> Summarizes the potentially harmful outcomes of widespread implementation of biometric surveillance of employees.

Instead of producing an efficient and productive workplace, biosurveillance may 15
instead deliver troops of distracted, apathetic employees who feel loss of control and decreased job satisfaction. Instead of feeling like part of a team, surveilled workers

may develop an us-versus-them mentality and look for opportunities to thwart the monitoring schemes of Big Boss.

Perhaps what we really need is biosurveillance from the bottom up — members of Congress and CEOs could don devices that could, say, detect when they are lying or how their hormones are behaving. Colorful PowerPoints could display the results of data collection on public billboards for the masses to pore over. In the name of safety and efficiency, maybe we ought to ensure that those whose behavior can do society the most harm do not escape the panopticon.

Concludes by suggesting that those in power most need to be watched "in the name of safety and efficiency" — ostensibly the terms used to justify the practice as applied to workers.

Topics for Critical Thinking and Writing

1. Do you think biometric measurement by employers is ever justified, or do the privacy and security of one's own body always trump the concerns of employers? Why, or why not?
2. If your teachers or parents could monitor the time you spent, and how you felt, while doing homework and studying, what benefits and drawbacks might result? What types of personal monitoring of children are already in place (or possible) in schools and homes, and are these methods different from biometric surveillance?
3. Do you think Lynn Stuart Parramore fairly portrays the founder of Humanyze and others who see potential in the possibilities for biometric monitoring? Why, or why not? In what other ways might biometric measurements help employees and employers?
4. List some examples of Parramore's use of language, word choice, and phrasing that would influence readers to be suspicious of biometric monitoring. How does this language make the essay more or less effective or convincing?
5. In what way does Parramore's recommendation in the final paragraph support or contradict her argument about individuals' basic rights to privacy?

Examining Assumptions

In Chapter 3, we will discuss **assumptions** in some detail. Here we introduce the topic by emphasizing the importance of *identifying* and *examining* assumptions — those you'll encounter in the writings of others and those you'll rely on in your own essays.

With this in mind, let's again consider some of the assumptions suggested in this chapter's earlier readings. The student who wrote about Stephen Cavanaugh's case pointed out that Nebraska prison officials simply did not see the Church of the Flying Spaghetti Monster as a real religion. Their assumption was that some religions can be more or less "real" than others or can make more sense than others. Assumptions may be *explicit* or *implicit*, stated or unstated. In this case, the prison officials were forthright about their assumptions in their stated claim about the church, perhaps believing their point was obvious to anyone who thought seriously about the idea of a Flying Spaghetti Monster. It didn't occur to them to consider that even major and mainstream religions honor stories, claims, and rituals that seem absurd to others.

An implicit assumption is one that is not stated but, rather, is taken for granted. It works like an underlying belief that structures an argument. In Lynn Stuart Parramore's essay on workplace biometric devices, the unstated assumption is that these sorts of technological monitors in the workplace represent a kind of evil "big brother" intent on subduing and exploiting employees with newer and newer forms of invasion of privacy. Parramore's assumption, while not stated directly, is evident in her choice of language, as we've pointed out above with terms such as *dystopian* and *brave new world*.

Another way to discern her assumption is by looking at the scenarios and selections of examples she chooses. For example, in imagining a company that would seek to know how much time an employee spends in the lounge area or alone, Parramore sees only obsessive monitoring of employees for the purposes of regulating their time. But what if these technologies could enable a company to discover that productivity or worker satisfaction increases in proportion to the amount of time employees spend collaborating in the lounge? Maybe workplace conditions would improve instead of deteriorating (a bigger lounge, more comfortable chairs), and maybe more efforts would be made for team-building and improving interpersonal employee relations. From a position that is skeptical about how employers might use such technologies, biometric surveillance of employees appears to be a dramatic overreach on the part of industries that use them. Biometric devices are seen as an intrusion and perhaps a violation of workers' privacy rights. However, from a business or an organizational strategy perspective, these technologies could be seen as ways to improve workplace heath and productivity.

Assumptions can be powerful sources of ideas and opinions. Understanding our own and others' assumptions is a major part of critical thinking. Assumptions about race, class, disability, sex, and gender are among the most powerful sources of social inequality. The following essay by Helen Benedict was published in 2015, two years after the US Department of Defense lifted the ban on women in combat roles in the armed forces and shortly after Defense Secretary Ashton Carter further lifted exclusions pertaining to women by granting them access to serve in all capacities in combat, including in elite special forces units. One assumption we may make about these developments is that the changed regulations resulted in an equal-access military. However, as Benedict argues, women in the military continue to face obstacles to equality, many of which themselves are based on social assumptions about gender.

A CHECKLIST FOR EXAMINING ASSUMPTIONS

- ❒ Have I identified any of the assumptions presupposed in the writer's argument?
- ❒ Are these assumptions explicit or implicit?
- ❒ Are these assumptions important to the author's argument, or are they only incidental?
- ❒ Does the author give any evidence of being aware of the hidden assumptions in her or his argument?

(continues on next page)

A CHECKLIST FOR EXAMINING ASSUMPTIONS (CONTINUED)

- ❐ Would a critic be likely to share these assumptions, or are they exactly what a critic would challenge?
- ❐ What sort of evidence would be relevant to supporting or rejecting these assumptions?
- ❐ Am I willing to grant the author's assumptions? Would most readers grant them?

HELEN BENEDICT

Helen Benedict (b. 1952) is a professor at Columbia University's Graduate School of Journalism. She is best known for her journalism on social injustice and the Iraq War as well as her seven novels, most recently *Wolf Season*, which received *Publishers Weekly's* Best Contemporary War Novel award in 2018.

The Military Has a Man Problem

Army Specialist Laura Naylor, a Wisconsin native, spent a year in Baghdad with the 32nd Military Police Company in 2003 and 2004. During that time, she — like all of the more than quarter-million women deployed to Iraq and Afghanistan — was officially banned from ground combat. That technicality didn't slow down Naylor when an IED[1] hit her convoy and it began to take fire from a nearby building. "We had to search this house nearby, thinking they were the ones doing the shooting, and I was the lead person the whole way. I had a flashlight in one hand, a pistol in the other, and I'd kick the door open with my foot, look both ways, give the all clear, go to the next room, do the same thing," she recounted to me a few years later. "We were interchangeable with the infantry."

A friend in her unit, Specialist Caryle Garcia, was wounded when a roadside bomb went off beside her Humvee. Garcia was her team's gunner, her body exposed from the chest up above the Humvee's roof. Their close friend, 20-year-old Specialist Michelle Witmer, became the first National Guardswoman ever killed in action after being shot during another ambush. Witmer's death was a grim marker in a steady march that has seen one woman after another achieve milestones in military service since the September 11, 2001, attacks that would have been unimaginable just a generation ago. During the Vietnam War, female soldiers were not even allowed to carry guns.

In early 2013, outgoing Defense Secretary Leon Panetta, with the backing of the Joint Chiefs of Staff, finally lifted the ban on women serving in ground combat, belatedly admitting they had already been doing so. "Women have shown great courage and sacrifice on and off the battlefield," he said, "and proven their ability to serve in an expanding number of roles." President Barack Obama heralded the

[1]**IED** improvised explosive device; an unconventional bomb. [Editors' note]

move, which remains politically controversial on Capitol Hill, saying, "Valor knows no gender." Since Panetta's decree, the debate has centered on whether, now that women can serve in previously all-male combat units, they have the ability to actually do it. The Marine Corps, Army and Special Forces have all been busily, and publicly, putting women to the test, running them through training courses and assessments, and announcing gravely how many have passed or failed.

Yet to many female soldiers and the men who have witnessed their competence in battle over the past 13-plus years, this debate seems like closing the barn door after the horse has bolted — ignoring that the distinction between "rear echelon" and "front line" in these wars is obsolete. Of the roughly 300,000 American women who have deployed to the Afghanistan and Iraq wars since 2001, at least 800 have been wounded, and, as of last count, at least 144 have been killed. Two women have earned Silver Stars, the military's third-highest award.

5 For generations now, the debate over women in combat has put the onus on women to prove they can handle the infantry and other traditionally all-male units. Yet today's wars have made it clear that the military's problem lies not with its women, their ability or their courage. The military's problem, instead, is with some of its men — and a deeply ingrained macho culture that denigrates, insults and abuses women.

In eight years of covering women at war, I have noticed a pattern in attitudes toward women in the military: The men who have served with women are more than satisfied with their work, while the men who are most resistant to serving alongside women have never done it.

"Oh, it's too rough for women," such men tend to say. Others complain, "Women would ruin our camaraderie" or "We'd be competing for women instead of looking out for ourselves." As retired Gen. Gordon R. Sullivan, a former Army chief of staff, wrote, lifting the combat ban against women would be "confusing" and "detrimental to units."

These attitudes reveal deeply patriarchal, condescending and creaky stereotypes about women, as if they are capable of being nothing more than soft, sexy objects of romance — or sexual prey.

Some of the very same types of prejudiced objections were once raised against black and gay men entering the military, even though they had demonstrated their military prowess long before they were openly welcomed into the ranks. As former chairman of the Joint Chiefs Gen. John Shalikashvili wrote in 2007, many within the military were originally concerned that "letting people who were openly gay serve would lower morale, harm recruitment and undermine unit cohesion."

10 And yet, even after President Harry Truman forced the racial integration of the military in 1948 and even after the fall of "don't ask, don't tell" in 2011, the military is still standing. And nobody questions any longer whether black or gay people can serve as well as straight white men.

Canada, Denmark and Norway have allowed women to serve in combat since the 1980s. Canadian commanders found no "negative effect on operational performance or team cohesion," according to one report; neither did military leaders in Norway. Israel, which added women to combat units years ago, has found that they "exhibit superior skills" in discipline, shooting and weapons use.

Today's debate about women would be less antediluvian if, instead of questioning whether women can do the job they've already been doing for years, it focused on why so many men in all-male companies still don't want to work with women. To what sort of all-male camaraderie are they clinging, and why?

In some ways, it may seem hard to blame the men who feel this way. Military training inculcates these attitudes deep into their souls. Drill instructors dress down recruits by taunting them with suggestions that their girlfriends and wives are being unfaithful. Military cadences and songs can be astonishingly misogynist. One example from the Naval Academy: "*Who can take a chainsaw / Cut the bitch in two / F--- the bottom half / And give the upper half to you. . . .*"

Long after racist language was banned from training, drill instructors regularly insult male recruits by calling them "ladies," "pussies," "girls" and worse. As an Iraq veteran wrote about his time in Marine boot camp in 2008, "The Drill Instructor's nightly homiletic speeches, full of an unabashed hatred of women, were part of the second phase of boot camp: the process of rebuilding recruits into Marines."

In other words, stoking men's hatred and suspicion of women is a way of firing up those men to kill.

One of the most common objections put forth by men who don't want to work with women is that they would be so concerned with protecting the women in their units that it would risk the mission. That is, they would be too chivalrous to be good soldiers.

But as more data on the military's rampant sexual harassment and abuse come out, this chivalry argument becomes harder to believe. Given that half the women deployed to Iraq and Afghanistan reported being sexually harassed, and one in four reported being sexually assaulted, according to a Department of Veterans Affairs study, evidence of this gallantry is, to say the least, scant. Former Army Sgt. Rebekah Havrilla, who says she was raped while serving in Afghanistan, testified before the Senate Armed Services Committee: "I had no faith in my chain of command as my first sergeant previously had sexual harassment accusations against him and the unit climate was extremely sexist and hostile in nature towards women."

If the military wants to get serious about inviting female soldiers to play ever-larger roles in war, it will have to find ways to change the attitude of so many of its own soldiers, sailors, airmen and Marines.

Stories from recent years about the depths of the military's misogyny are legendary. In 2013, the head of the Air Force's sexual assault prevention office at the Pentagon, Jeffrey Krusinski, was himself arrested and charged with sexual battery by police in Arlington, Virginia, after allegedly accosting a woman in a parking lot. (He was later acquitted by a jury.) An Army sergeant at Fort Hood who worked as a sexual abuse educator was investigated for running a prostitution ring. The married Army general in charge of Fort Jackson, who oversaw training for many Army recruits, was suspended after allegedly physically attacking his girlfriend.

If these are examples of the people in charge of ensuring respectful treatment of women, is it any surprise that new recruits see women as less than equals? Not long after Krusinski's arrest, West Point's rugby team was disbanded after lewd emails about fellow female cadets surfaced that the school said suggested "a culture of disrespect towards women."

Until the military recognizes women as equal human beings, how can it recognize them as equal soldiers? As Colleen Bushnell, who was sexually assaulted while in the Air Force and now is an advocate for survivors, has said, "This is a predator problem, not a female problem."

Military culture may well be the last bastion of male protectionism in modern society, so it is no surprise that its arguments against admitting women fully are the same as those used whenever women first enter a previously all-male field — whether that is firefighting, policing, politics, sports or voting. Indeed, many of the objections macho military types make to women today mirror those their grandfathers and great-grandfathers made when women were trying to enter public life.

Yet there's precious little evidence that all-male cultures produce anything better than co-ed cultures, just as there is no evidence at all that the presence of women as voters, golfers, politicians, police officers, firefighters — or presidents — ruins anything other than male privilege.

War has changed. It is simply unfeasible to keep women off the front lines. "We're getting blown up right alongside the guys," as one female soldier who served in Iraq told me. "We're in combat! So there's no reason to keep us segregated anymore."

Admitting that the military's problem 25
with female soldiers is actually a man's problem, however, will necessitate stronger military and political leadership than we have yet seen. It will require a wholesale shift in how the military builds respect among its troops. And it means teaching the men who don't want to work with women that they must either respect their female comrades or leave. As Australia's Army chief, David Morrison, put it to his troops in 2013, "Female soldiers and officers have proven themselves worthy of the best traditions of the Australian army. . . . If that does not suit you, then get out. . . . There is no place for you amongst this band of brothers and sisters."

American military leaders, take note.

Topics for Critical Thinking and Writing

1. What purpose do the first two paragraphs of Helen Benedict's essay serve in her overall argument?
2. Identify Benedict's thesis. In your own words, what is she arguing?
3. In the past, what assumptions about women were the basis for excluding them from military combat service? How does Benedict see those assumptions still at work, despite formal recognition that women are capable of combat roles in the service?
4. What examples does Benedict use to make comparisons? How do her comparisons help advance her argument about the "man problem" in the military?
5. What changes or actions may be taken to reduce or eliminate the "man problem" in the military? If you were to make an argument about what can be done to solve the problem, what specific areas of military life could be addressed, and what new procedures might be instituted?
6. Construct an argument to defend your position on this question: Because women are now permitted to serve in all military combat positions, should all women, like all men, have to register for Selective Service and be subject to the military draft, if one were needed?

ASSIGNMENTS FOR CRITICAL THINKING

1. Choose one of the following topics and write down all the pro and con arguments you can think of in, say, ten minutes. Then, at least an hour or two later, return to your notes and see whether you can add to them. Finally, write a balanced dialogue between two imagined speakers who hold opposing views on the issue. You'll doubtless have to revise your dialogue several times, and in revising your drafts, you'll likely come up with further ideas. Present *both* sides as strongly as possible. (You may want to give the two speakers distinct characters, or personas.) After you have completed the exercise, write an exploratory essay in which you first identify the issue, then work through different perspectives, positions, ideas, and solutions related to your issue.

   If none of the suggested topics that follow interests you, ask your instructor about the possibility of choosing a topic of your own. Suggested topics:

   a. Colleges with large athletic programs should pay student athletes a salary or stipend.
   b. Bicyclists and motorcyclists should be required by law to wear helmets.
   c. High school teachers should have the right to carry concealed firearms in schools.
   d. Smoking should be prohibited on all college campuses, including in all buildings *and* outdoors.
   e. Honors students should have the privilege of registering for classes earlier than other students.
   f. Students should have the right to drop out of school at any age.
   g. Comfort animals — such as dogs, cats, ferrets, and snakes — that have been recommended to patients by doctors or therapists to ease anxiety should be allowed in college classrooms.

2. In April 2012, Williams College in Williamstown, Massachusetts, hosted a lecture and film screening of work by Jiz Lee, described in campus advertisements as a "genderqueer porn star." After inviting the adult entertainer to campus, the college came under fire by some students and members of the public (especially after the story was reported by national media). Opponents questioned the appropriateness and academic value of the event, which was brought to campus by the Mike Dively Committee, an endowment established to help "develop understanding of human sexuality and sexual orientation and their impact on culture." Proponents argued that (1) pornography is a subject that deserves critical analysis and commentary, (2) the Dively series is intended to create conversations about sexuality and sexual orientation in society and culture, and (3) treating any potential subject in an academic setting under the circumstances of the program is appropriate. What are your views? Should adult film stars ever be invited to college campuses? Should pornography constitute a subject of analysis on campus? Why, or why not?

   Now, imagine you're a student member of your campus programming board. Some faculty members from the Gender and Sexuality Program come to your committee seeking funds to invite a female former adult film star to campus to lecture on "The Reality of Pornography." Faculty and student sponsors have assured your committee that the visit by the actress in question is part of an effort to educate students and the public about the adult film industry and its impact on women. Graphic images and short film clips will be shown. Use the thinking strategies in this chapter to pose as many questions as you can about the potential benefits and risks of approving this invitation. How would you vote, and why? (If you can find a peer who has an opposing view, construct a debate on the issue.)

3. In 1984, the US Congress passed the National Minimum Drinking Age Act, mandating that all states implement and enforce raising the minimum drinking age from eighteen to twenty-one years. Through this legislation, the United States became one of a handful of developed countries to have such a high drinking age. In 2009, John McCardell, president emeritus of Middlebury College in Vermont, wrote a declaration signed by 136 college presidents supporting returning the drinking age to eighteen. McCardell's organization, Choose Responsibly, says that people age eighteen to twenty should be treated as the adults they are — for example, in terms of voting, serving on juries and in the military, or buying legal weapons. The organization encourages educational programs and awareness efforts that would introduce alcohol-related issues to young college students and demystify and discourage problem drinking. Lowering the drinking age is opposed by the organization Mothers Against Drunk Drivers, whose members argue that raising it to twenty-one has curbed traffic accidents and fatalities caused by drunk driving. How would you approach this question of returning the drinking age to eighteen? What perspectives should matter most? Apply the critical thinking questions from the section Survey, Analyze, and Evaluate the Issue (pp. 6–7) and decide: Should the drinking age be lowered to eighteen? Argue why or why not, trying to anticipate and address the counterarguments likely to be made against your position.

2

Critical Reading: Getting Started

Some books are to be tasted, others to be swallowed, and some few to be chewed and digested.
— FRANCIS BACON

Read parts of a newspaper quickly or an encyclopedia entry, or a fast-food thriller, but do not insult yourself or a book which has been created with its author's painstakingly acquired skill and effort, by seeing how fast you can dispose of it.
— SUSAN HILL

Active Reading

In the passages that we quote above, two good points are made. The first is that some types of reading do not need to be fully read at all — a taste of what they offer is enough. Some types of reading can be taken in completely and quickly, swallowed whole like a fast-food meal. But some types of reading call for much closer attention. Classical works of literature, for example, may require thoughtful consideration of their language, their meanings, and their relevancy to the present. Similarly, many arguments (usually essays, editorials, articles) require thoughtful deliberation, especially about the ideas they express.

But how do you know the difference between a book (or an essay) that may be read quickly and one that deserves to be read slowly? How can you judge the value of a piece of writing *before* deciding to read it carefully? And if you *do* decide a text is worth reading slowly and carefully, how do you prepare to think critically about it?

PREVIEWING

Even before reading a single word of a text, you may evaluate it to some degree. **Previewing** is a strategy for reading that allows you to use prior knowledge — such as the expectations of your teacher or your understanding of how certain kinds of texts generally work — to help guide your reading. Skilled readers rarely read a text "cold"; instead, they think about it in terms of what they already know. They first examine the text, **skimming** to identify and evaluate the following:

- the author
- the place of publication

- the **genre**, or type of writing
- the table of contents
- headnotes or an abstract (if available)
- the title and subtitle
- section headings
- other information that stands out at a glance (such as images, graphs, and tables)

By previewing and skimming effectively, you can quickly ascertain quite a bit of information about an article or essay. You can detect the author's claims and methods, see the evidence he or she uses (experience, statistics, quotations, etc.), examine the tone and difficulty level, and determine whether the piece of writing offers useful ideas for you. These strategies work well if you're researching a topic and need to review many essays — you can read efficiently to find those that are most important or relevant to you or those that offer different perspectives. Of course, if you do find an essay to be compelling during previewing and skimming, you can begin "chewing and digesting," as Francis Bacon put it — reading more closely and carefully (or else putting it aside for later when you can give it more time).

READING TIP
Instead of imagining previewing and slower, more careful reading as two separate stages, think of previewing as an activity that helps you decide — at any time — whether or not you should begin engaging in more careful reading.

One of the first things you can do to begin previewing a piece of writing is to identify the **author** — not just by name but also in terms of any other information you may know or can find out. You might already know, for example, that a work by Martin Luther King Jr. will probably deal with civil rights. You know that it will be serious and eloquent. You know that King's words will likely be related to the social conditions of the 1950s and 1960s and that he will be speaking in a somewhat different language than you are accustomed to. In contrast, if Stephen King is the author, you would change your expectations, probably anticipating the essay to be about fear, the craft of writing, or King's experiences as a horror novelist. You may also know that this King writes for a broad audience, so his essay won't be terribly difficult to understand. But even if you don't know the author, you can often discern something about him or her by looking at biographical information provided in the text or by doing a quick internet search. You can use this information to predict the subject of an essay and its style, as well as its author's possible assumptions and biases.

The **place of publication** may also reveal something about the essay in terms of its subject, style, and approach. For instance, the *National Review* is a conservative journal. If you notice that an essay on affirmative action was published in the *National Review*, you can tentatively assume that the essay will not endorse affirmative action. In contrast, knowing that *Ms.* magazine is a liberal publication, you can guess that an essay on affirmative action published there will probably be an endorsement. You often can learn a good deal about a magazine or journal simply by flipping through it and noticing the kinds of articles in it. The advertisements also tell you what kind of audience the magazine or journal likely has. If you don't know anything about a publication, you can quickly research it on the internet to find out more.

The **title** of an essay, too, may give an idea of what to expect. Of course, a title may announce only the subject and not the author's thesis or point of view ("On Gun Control"; "Should Drugs Be Legal?"). A title may also be opaque or mysterious ("The Chokehold"). Fairly often, though, a title will indicate the thesis (as in "Give Children the Vote" or "We Need Campaign Finance Reform Now"). If you can tell more or less what to expect from a title, you can probably take in some of the major points even on a quick reading. Glancing at subtitles, and any section headings and subheadings, too, can help you map the progression of an argument without fully reading the entire text.

THESIS Sometimes, you can find the **thesis** (the main point or major claim) of an essay by looking at the first paragraph. Other times, especially if the paragraphs are short, you can locate the thesis within the first several paragraphs. Depending on what you discover while skimming, you can speed up or slow down your reading as needed while you locate the thesis and get a sense of how the argument for it is structured. As we noted, if the essay has sections, pay attention to headings and subheadings to see how the thesis is supported by other minor claims.

CONTEXT When engaging with a text, you also consider the role of **context** — the situational conditions in which a piece was written. Context — literally, "with the text" — can refer to the time period, geographical location, cultural climate, political environment, or any other setting that helps you orient a piece of writing to the conditions surrounding it. Recognizing the context can reveal a lot about how an author treats a subject. For example, an essay about gun control written before the mass shootings of the past ten years might have a less urgent approach and advocate more lenient measures than one written today. An article about transgender identity or police brutality might convey different assumptions about those topics depending on whether it was written before or after the increased recognition of transgender rights or before or after the protests of the Black Lives Matter movement. Social conditions, in short, affect how writers and readers think.

Anything you read exists in at least two broad contexts: the context of its *production* (where and when it was written or published) and the context of its *consumption* (where and when it is encountered and read). One thing all good critical readers do when considering the validity of claims and arguments is to take *both* types of context into account. This means asking questions not only about the approaches, assumptions, and beliefs about certain subjects that were in place when an essay was written, but also about how current events and new trends in thinking that occurred after the original publication date may generate different issues and challenges related to the subject of the essay. The state of affairs in the time and place in which that argument is made *and received* matters to the questions you might ask, the evidence you might consider, and the responses you might produce.

Consider these words, spoken by Abraham Lincoln in his famous debates with Stephen Douglas, when the two campaigned against each other for a US Senate seat in 1858. Douglas had accused Lincoln of holding the then-unpopular view that the black race and white race were equal. Lincoln defended himself against these charges:

> I will say then that I am not, nor ever have been, in favor of bringing about in any way the social and political equality of the white and black races [Applause], that

> I am not nor ever have been in favor of making voters or jurors of negroes, nor of qualifying them to hold office, nor to intermarry with white people; and I will say in addition to this that there is a physical difference between the white and black races which I believe will forever forbid the two races living together on terms of social and political equality. And inasmuch as they cannot so live, while they do remain together there must be the position of superior and inferior, and I as much as any other man am in favor of having the superior position assigned to the white race.

Lincoln's ideas about race in this speech may surprise you. If you saw this quotation somewhere, it might make you think that Abraham Lincoln held racist views despite his reputation as "The Great Emancipator." However, it is crucial to put his words in context to develop a fuller, more mature understanding of them. Historians, for example, read these words in light of common and even "scientific" beliefs about race in the 1850s, informed by the situation at hand (a campaign speech, in which he might feel free to overstate or appeal to popular beliefs), and with knowledge of Lincoln's uncompromising efforts later to abolish slavery. How does consideration of these historical contexts help you understand Lincoln's words? How does consideration of the context in which you read it shape your understanding, given your expectations and your prior knowledge about Lincoln?

THE "FIRST AND LAST" RULE You may apply the "first and last" rule when skimming essays. This rule assumes that somewhere early and late in the writing you can locate the author's key points. Opening paragraphs are good places to seek out the author's central thesis, and final paragraphs are good places to seek out conclusive statements such as "Finally, then, *it is time that we* . . ." or "Given this evidence, *it is clear that* . . ." Final paragraphs are particularly important because they often summarize the argument and restate the thesis.

> **WRITING TIP**
> You can arrange elements in a sentence according to the "first and last" rule to control what points you want to emphasize most.

The first and last rule works because authors often place main points of emphasis at the beginnings and endings of essays, but they also do the same within individual paragraphs. Authors do not usually bury key ideas in the middle of long essays, and neither do they surround the key ideas of paragraphs with bulky text. Further, authors try not to hide their most important points in the middle of long sentences. Often, the main point of a sentence can be found by looking at the elements stated first and last. (Of course, there are always exceptions to the rule.) Consider the following sentences, each of which contains the same basic information arranged in different ways:

Here, the time period and the new smoking prohibitions get the most emphasis:

> Over the past fifteen years, the rate of smoking among New York City residents declined by more than 35% because of new health trends and new tobacco restrictions.

Here, the place and the percentage are most emphasized:

> In New York City, new tobacco restrictions and new health trends helped lower the smoking rate over fifteen years by more than 35%.

A SHORT ESSAY FOR PREVIEWING PRACTICE

Before skimming the following essay, apply the previewing techniques discussed on pages 33–36 and complete the Thinking Critically: Previewing activity below.

THINKING CRITICALLY *Previewing*

The following activity lists typical types of questions readers use while previewing. Provide the missing information for Sanjay Gupta and his essay "Why I Changed My Mind on Weed" (p. 38) or another essay of your choosing.

PREVIEWING STRATEGIES	TYPES OF QUESTIONS	ANSWERS
Author	Who is the author? What expertise and credibility does the author have? How difficult is the writing likely to be?	
Title	What does the title reveal about the essay's content? Does it give any clues about how the argument will take shape? Do headings or subheadings reveal any further information?	
Place of Publication	How does the place of publication help you understand the argument? What type of audiences will it be likely to target?	
Context	By placing the article in the context of its time — given trends in the conversations about or popular understandings of the subject — what can you expect about the author's position?	
Skimming	As you skim over the first several paragraphs, where do you first realize what the argument of the essay is? What major forms of evidence support the argument?	

SANJAY GUPTA

Dr. Sanjay Gupta (b. 1969) is a neurosurgeon and multiple Emmy Award–winning television personality. As a leading public health expert, he is most well known as CNN's chief medical correspondent. In 2011, *Forbes* magazine named him one of the ten most influential celebrities in the United States. The essay below originally appeared on CNN.com in August 2013.

Why I Changed My Mind on Weed

Over the last year, I have been working on a new documentary called "Weed." The title "Weed" may sound cavalier, but the content is not.

I traveled around the world to interview medical leaders, experts, growers and patients. I spoke candidly to them, asking tough questions. What I found was stunning.

Long before I began this project, I had steadily reviewed the scientific literature on medical marijuana from the United States and thought it was fairly unimpressive. Reading these papers five years ago, it was hard to make a case for medicinal marijuana. I even wrote about this in a *Time* magazine article, back in 2009, titled "Why I Would Vote No on Pot."

Well, I am here to apologize.

I apologize because I didn't look hard 5 enough, until now. I didn't look far enough. I didn't review papers from smaller labs in other countries doing some remarkable research, and I was too dismissive of the loud chorus of legitimate patients whose symptoms improved on cannabis.

Instead, I lumped them with the high-visibility malingerers, just looking to get high. I mistakenly believed the Drug Enforcement Agency listed marijuana as a Schedule 1 substance because of sound scientific proof. Surely, they must have quality reasoning as to why marijuana is in the category of the most dangerous drugs that have "no accepted medicinal use and a high potential for abuse."

They didn't have the science to support that claim, and I now know that when it comes to marijuana neither of those things are true. It doesn't have a high potential for abuse, and there are very legitimate medical applications. In fact, sometimes marijuana is the only thing that works. Take the case of Charlotte Figi, whom I met in Colorado. She started having seizures soon after birth. By age 3, she was having 300 a week, despite being on 7 different medications. Medical marijuana has calmed her brain, limiting her seizures to 2 or 3 per month.

I have seen more patients like Charlotte first hand, spent time with them and come to the realization that it is irresponsible not to provide the best care we can as a medical community, care that could involve marijuana.

We have been terribly and systematically misled for nearly 70 years in the United States, and I apologize for my own role in that.

I hope this article and upcoming docu- 10 mentary will help set the record straight.

On August 14, 1970, the Assistant Secretary of Health, Dr. Roger O. Egeberg, wrote a letter recommending the plant, marijuana, be classified as a Schedule 1 substance, and it has remained that way for nearly 45 years. My research started with a careful reading of that decades-old letter. What I found was unsettling. Egeberg had carefully chosen his words:

"Since there is still a considerable void in our knowledge of the plant and effects of the active drug contained in it, our recommendation is that marijuana be retained within Schedule 1 at least until the completion of certain studies now under way to resolve the issue."

Not because of sound science, but because of its absence, marijuana was classified as a Schedule 1 substance. Again, the year was 1970. Egeberg mentions studies that are under way, but many were never completed. As my investigation continued, however, I realized Egeberg did in fact have important research already available to him, some of it from more than 25 years earlier.

HIGH RISK OF ABUSE

In 1944, New York mayor Fiorello LaGuardia commissioned research to be performed by the New York Academy of Science. Among their conclusions: they found marijuana did not lead to significant addiction in the medical sense of the word. They also did not find any evidence marijuana led to morphine, heroin or cocaine addiction.

We now know that while estimates vary, marijuana leads to dependence in around 9 to 10% of its adult users. By comparison, cocaine, a Schedule 2 substance "with less abuse potential than Schedule 1 drugs," hooks 20% of those who use it. Around 25% of heroin users become addicted.

The worst is tobacco, where the number is closer to 30% of smokers, many of whom go on to die because of their addiction.

There is clear evidence that in some people marijuana use can lead to withdrawal symptoms, including insomnia, anxiety and nausea. Even considering this, it is hard to make a case that it has a high potential for abuse. The physical symptoms of marijuana addiction are nothing like those of the other drugs I've mentioned. I have seen the withdrawal from alcohol, and it can be life threatening.

I do want to mention a concern that I think about as a father. Young, developing brains are likely more susceptible to harm from marijuana than adult brains. Some recent studies suggest that regular use in teenage years leads to a permanent decrease in IQ. Other research hints at a possible heightened risk of developing psychosis.

Much in the same way I wouldn't let my own children drink alcohol, I wouldn't permit marijuana until they are adults. If they are adamant about trying marijuana, I will urge them to wait until they're in their mid-20s, when their brains are fully developed.

MEDICAL BENEFIT

While investigating, I realized something else quite important. Medical marijuana is not new, and the medical community has been writing about it for a long time. There were in fact hundreds of journal articles, mostly documenting the benefits. Most of those papers, however, were written between the years 1840 and 1930. The papers described the use of medical marijuana to treat "neuralgia, convulsive disorders, emaciation," among other things.

A search through the U.S. National Library of Medicine this past year pulled up nearly 20,000 more recent papers. But the majority were research into the harm of marijuana, such as "Bad trip due to anticholinergic effect of cannabis," or "Cannabis induced pancreatitis" and "Marijuana use and risk of lung cancer."

In my quick running of the numbers, I calculated about 6% of the current U.S. marijuana studies investigate the benefits of medical marijuana. The rest are designed to investigate harm. That imbalance paints a highly distorted picture.

THE CHALLENGES OF MARIJUANA RESEARCH

To do studies on marijuana in the United States today, you need two important things.

First of all, you need marijuana. And marijuana is illegal. You see the problem. Scientists can get research marijuana from a special farm in Mississippi, which is astonishingly located in the middle of the Ole Miss campus, but it is challenging. When I visited this year, there was no marijuana being grown.

The second thing you need is approval, and the scientists I interviewed kept reminding me how tedious that can be. While a cancer study may first be evaluated by the National Cancer Institute, or a pain study may go through the National Institute for Neurological Disorders, there is one more approval required for marijuana: NIDA, the National Institute on Drug Abuse. It is an organization that has a core mission of studying drug abuse, as opposed to benefit.

Stuck in the middle are the legitimate patients who depend on marijuana as a medicine, oftentimes as their only good option.

Keep in mind that up until 1943, marijuana was part of the United States drug pharmacopeia. One of the conditions for which it was prescribed was neuropathic pain. It is a miserable pain that's tough to treat. My own patients have described it as "lancinating, burning and a barrage of pins and needles." While marijuana has long been documented to be effective for this awful pain, the most common medications prescribed today come from the poppy plant, including morphine, oxycodone and dilaudid.

Here is the problem. Most of these medications don't work very well for this kind of pain, and tolerance is a real problem.

Most frightening to me is that someone dies in the United States every 19 minutes from a prescription drug overdose, mostly accidental. Every 19 minutes. It is a horrifying statistic. As much as I searched, I could not find a documented case of death from marijuana overdose.

It is perhaps no surprise then that 76% of physicians recently surveyed said they would approve the use of marijuana to help ease a woman's pain from breast cancer.

When marijuana became a Schedule 1 substance, there was a request to fill a "void in our knowledge." In the United States, that has been challenging because of the infrastructure surrounding the study of an illegal substance, with a drug abuse organization at the heart of the approval process. And yet, despite the hurdles, we have made considerable progress that continues today.

Looking forward, I am especially intrigued by studies like those in Spain and Israel looking at the anti-cancer effects of marijuana and its components. I'm intrigued by the neuroprotective study by Lev Meschoulam in Israel, and research in Israel and the United States on whether the drug might help alleviate symptoms of PTSD. I promise to do my part to help, genuinely and honestly, fill the remaining void in our knowledge.

Citizens in 20 states and the District of Columbia have now voted to approve marijuana for medical applications, and more states will be making that choice soon. As for Dr. Roger Egeberg, who wrote that letter in 1970, he passed away 16 years ago.

I wonder what he would think if he were alive today.

Exercise: The "First and Last" Rule

When writing, you can emphasize main points by using the first and last rule (see p. 36). Try it yourself by considering the following list of observations from Gupta's essay. Rearrange the statements any way you wish to write a single paragraph, using the first and last rule to emphasize the elements that you find most important. (You do not have to include all the details; you might want to add in some others, and feel free to rephrase them.) Next, compare your sentences to your classmates'. How do they compare in terms of emphasis?

- Gupta is one of the most respected voices in public health.
- Gupta argues for the legalization of medical marijuana.
- Gupta's letter was written for CNN News.
- Gupta rejects his previous position on medical marijuana and apologizes for his oversight.
- The article was important because it represented a shift in approach by a leading doctor.

READING WITH A CAREFUL EYE: UNDERLINING, HIGHLIGHTING, ANNOTATING

Once you have a general idea of the work — not only an idea of its topic and thesis but also a sense of the way in which the thesis is argued — you can go back and start reading it carefully.

As you read, **underline** or **highlight** key passages and make **annotations** in the margins. Because you're reading actively, or interacting with the text, you won't simply let your eye rove across the page.

- Highlight the chief points so that later when reviewing the essay you can easily locate the main passages.
- Don't overdo it. If you find yourself highlighting most of a page, you're probably not distinguishing the key points clearly enough.
- Make your marginal annotations brief and selective. They may consist of hints or clues, comments like "doesn't follow," "good," "compare with Jones," "check this," and "really?"
- Highlight key definitions. In the margin you might write "good," "in contrast," or "?" if you think the definition is correct, incorrect, or unclear.
- Use tools to highlight or annotate when using software to read a digital essay. Also consider copying and pasting passages that you would normally highlight into a new document file. Clearly identify these passages as direct quotations to avoid plagiarism, and type your annotations next to them using the review functions.

In all these ways, you interact with the text and lay the groundwork for eventually writing your own essay on what you have read.

What you annotate will depend largely on your **purpose**. If you're reading an essay to see how the writer organizes an argument, you'll annotate one sort of thing. If you're reading to challenge the thesis, you'll annotate other things. Here is a passage from an essay by Charles R. Lawrence titled "On Racist Speech," with a student's rather skeptical, even aggressive, annotations. But notice that the student apparently made at least one of the annotations — "Definition of 'fighting words'" — chiefly to remind herself to locate where the definition of an important term appears in the essay. The essay is presented in full on page 69.

Example of such a policy?	University officials who have formulated policies to respond to incidents of racial harassment have been characterized in the press as "thought police," but such policies generally do nothing more than
?	impose sanctions against intentional face-to-face insults. When racist
Example?	speech takes the form of face-to-face insults, catcalls, or other
What about sexist speech?	assaultive speech aimed at an individual or small group of persons, it falls directly within the "fighting words" exception to First Amendment
Definition of "fighting words"	protection. The Supreme Court has held that words "which 'by their very utterance inflict injury or tend to incite an immediate breach of the peace'" are not protected by the First Amendment.
	If the purpose of the First Amendment is to foster the greatest amount of speech, racial insults disserve that purpose.
Really? Probably depends on the individual.	Assaultive racist speech functions as a preemptive strike. The invective is experienced as a blow, not as a proffered idea, and once the blow is struck, it is unlikely that a dialogue will follow. Racial insults are
Why must speech always seek "to discover truth"?	particularly undeserving of First Amendment protection because the perpetrator's intention is not to discover truth or initiate dialogue
How does he know?	but to injure the victim. In most situations, members of minority groups realize that they are likely to lose if they respond to epithets by fighting and are forced to remain silent and submissive.

READING: FAST AND SLOW

Earlier, we recommended skimming as a quick previewing strategy to help you determine the author's purpose, general argument, and major forms of supporting evidence. Then we suggested a way to go a bit deeper, annotating as you read. However, once you determine that a particular text is worth digging into even further, you should alter your strategy so that you can engage with the argument in an even more analytical way. If critical thinking involves "taking apart" a specimen to help you understand it, then doing so with a text is akin to taking apart any complex system to understand better how it works (as with an automobile engine, for example). If you can see how all the parts of an argument work in relation to one another, you can see why they are convincing — or may *sound* convincing even when you disagree with them. But since your task is not just to understand arguments but also to evaluate, judge, and offer possible alternatives to them, you should be alert to areas where improvements can be made, where new questions may be asked, and where new parts can be added to support or challenge the conclusions. To do all this, you must *read more slowly*.

Reading slowly is sometimes called **close reading**, a technique that traces a text's details and patterns. Close reading means, for starters, paying attention to the *language* of an essay. By doing this, you can see how words and their meanings lend support to an argument — but perhaps also reveal assumptions on the part of an author. For example, an author who calls his city's crime problem a "monster" might argue for harsher law enforcement than another who refers to crime as a "sickness," who might argue for investigating the root causes of crime.

To develop new perspectives and solutions related to the issues presented in this book, you must interrogate the readings and test whether or not they hold up to your intellectual scrutiny. The issues raised in this book — and the arguments made about them — require more comment than President Calvin Coolidge supposedly provided when his wife, who hadn't been able to attend church one Sunday, asked him what the preacher talked about in his sermon. "Sin," Coolidge said. His wife persisted: "What did the preacher say about it?" Coolidge's response: "He was against it."

But, again, when we say that most of the arguments in this book require close reading, we don't mean that they are obscure or overly difficult; we mean, rather, that you have to approach them thoughtfully and deliberately, always examining their alternatives.

Some arguments appear convincing simply because all the parts work so well together. Such arguments may appear airtight and indisputable not because they offer the only reasonable or viable position, but just because they are so well constructed, because they appeal to common assumptions or rely on widely shared concepts. To close read effectively, you must employ **analysis**, another word from the Greek: *analusis*, "to loosen; to undo." We like this as a metaphor for close reading analysis because it suggests looking for the ways an argument has been put together and how it might be taken apart again.

When close reading, we often discover areas where an argument can be improved upon or challenged. The following patterns of thought may help you discover those spaces:

- The language in the article is characterized by . . .
- Although the argument is convincing, its assumptions are that . . .
- Although the argument is convincing, it fails to consider *X* alternative perspective . . .
- Although the argument does a good job offering . . . , it could be further improved by offering more of . . .
- The argument, rather than being convincing, instead proves or shows . . .
- Although the author looks at evidence showing . . . , he doesn't attend fully to other evidence showing . . .
- An audience might agree with this argument if they also believed . . .
- An audience might oppose this argument if they believed . . .
- The author's perspective is shaped by the values and interests of . . .
- An opponent's perspective might be shaped by the values and interests of . . .

As these sentence beginnings demonstrate, it takes close reading and analytical skill to decide whether to agree or disagree with an argument, or to draw a different conclusion, or to conceive of a new argument. You must practice disassembling arguments piece by piece, considering words, sentences, and paragraphs thoughtfully, one by one. Above all, go slow! In this vein, recall an episode from Lewis Carroll's *Through the Looking-Glass*:

> "Can you do Addition?" the White Queen asked. "What's one and one and one and one and one and one and one and one and one and one?"
>
> "I don't know," said Alice. "I lost count."
>
> "She can't do Addition," the Red Queen said.

Alice with the Red Queen and the White Queen.

It's easy enough to add one and one and one and so on, and of course Alice can do addition — but not at the pace that the White Queen sets. Similarly, you may find it difficult to perform thorough and thoughtful analysis if you read too quickly. Fortunately, you can set your own pace in reading the essays in this book. Skimming won't work, but slow and close reading — and thinking carefully about what you're reading — will.

When you first pick up an essay, you may indeed want to skim it, but if it is compelling enough, you will have to settle down to read it slowly, and perhaps you will read it more than one time. The effort could be worthwhile.

DEFINING TERMS AND CONCEPTS

Writers often attempt to provide a provisional definition of important terms and concepts to advance their arguments. They ask readers, in a way, to accept a definition for the purposes of the argument at hand. Readers may do so, but if they want to argue a different position, they must do so according to the definition offered by the author, or else they must offer their own definition.

Before going further, allow us to define the difference between a **term** and a **concept**. A rule of thumb is that a *term* is more concrete and fixed than a *concept*. You may be able to find an authoritative source (like a federal law or an official policy) to help define a word as a *term*. An author may write, for example, "According to the legal definition, the term 'exploitation' means *A*, *B*, and *C*" (a technical definition). It may be difficult to contend with an author who offers a definition of a term in a strict way such as this. Unless you can find a different standard, you may have to start out on the same basic ground: an agreed-upon definition.

A *concept* is more open-ended and may have a generally agreed-upon definition but rarely a strict or unchanging one. Writers may say, "For the purposes of this argument, let's define 'exploitation' as a moral concept that involves *A*, *B*, and *C*" (a broad definition). Concepts can be abstract but can also function powerfully in argumentation; love, justice, morality, psyche, health, freedom, bravery, masculinity — these are all concepts. You may look up such words in the dictionary, but it won't offer a strict definition and won't say much about how to apply the concept. Arguments that rely predominantly on concepts may be more easily added to or challenged, because concepts are so much more open-ended than terms.

To illustrate how terms and concepts work, suppose you're reading an argument about whether a certain set of images is pornography or art. For the present purpose, let's use a famous example from 1992, when American photographer Sally Mann published *Immediate Family*, a controversial book featuring numerous images of her three children (then ages twelve, ten, and seven) in various states of nakedness during their childhood on a rural Virginia farm. Mann is considered a great photographer and artist ("America's Best Photographer," according to *Time* magazine in 2001), and *Immediate Family* is very well regarded in the art community ("one of the great photograph books of our time," according to the *New Republic*). But some critics couldn't separate the images of Mann's own naked children from the label "child pornography."

WRITING TIP
When defining a term conceptually, you may cite an authoritative person, such as an expert in a field ("Stephen Hawking defines time as . . ."), or you might cite a respected leader or important text ("Mahatma Gandhi defines love as . . ."; "The bible says . . ."). Alternatively, you can combine several views and insert your own provisional definition.

If you wished to argue against this position, you might begin by asking, "What is *child pornography*? What is *art*?" If someone were to define child pornography to include *any* images of nude children, that definition would include photographs taken for any reason — medical, sociological, anthropological, scientific — and would include even the innocent photographs taken by proud parents of their children swimming, bathing, and so on. It would also apply to some of the world's great art. Most people do not seriously think the mere image of the naked body, child or adult, is pornography. If you wanted to argue that Mann's photographs are not child pornography, you could draw upon the legal term itself and apply it to the images. You could also offer your own conceptual definition of art and apply that to the images.

Sometimes whether a word is used as a term or a concept has major implications for certain groups and interests. In recent years, for example, the dairy industry has lobbied the Food and Drug Administration to force producers of soy- and almond-based drinks to stop using the word *milk* to describe them. The dairy industry claims that "milk" is a term with a technical definition: a high-fat, high-protein liquid secreted by female animals to nourish their young. It argues that calling soy- and almond-based products "milk" runs the risk of deceiving consumers by suggesting that these drinks are nutritionally equivalent to "real" milk. Obviously, for marketing purposes the producers of the drinks prefer avoiding the term "almond water" or "soy drink." They argue that the word "milk" is more conceptual, commonly used to describe different liquids, such as milk of magnesia, rose milk, and coconut milk. The two sides are fundamentally disagreeing about the definition of the word.

In 2018, the FDA signaled that a legal definition of milk might be on the horizon. It does make us wonder if we will be soon eating "legume paste" instead of peanut butter (given that peanuts are not technically "nuts" and mashed peanuts are not technically butter).

Summarizing and Paraphrasing

After previewing, skimming, and a first reading (maybe even a second one), perhaps the next best step, particularly with a fairly difficult essay, is to reread it (again). Simultaneously, take notes on a sheet of paper, summarizing each paragraph in a sentence or two, and then write an overall summary of the whole argument. Writing a **summary** will help you understand the contents and see the strengths and weaknesses of the piece. It will also help you prepare for writing by providing a snapshot of the argument in your notes.

Don't confuse a summary with a paraphrase. A **paraphrase** is a word-by-word or phrase-by-phrase rewording of a text, a sort of translation of the author's language into your own. A paraphrase is therefore as long as the original or even longer; a summary is much shorter. An entire essay, even a whole book, may be summarized in a page, in a paragraph, even in a sentence. Obviously, a summary will leave out most details, but it will accurately state the essential thesis or claim of the original.

Why would anyone summarize, and why would anyone paraphrase? Because, as we've already said, these two activities — in different ways — help you comprehend an author's ideas and offer ways to introduce those ideas into your arguments in a way that readers can follow. Summaries and paraphrases can help you

- **validate** the basis of your ideas by providing an instance in which someone else wrote about the same topic
- **support** your argument by showing readers where someone else "got it right" (corroborating your ideas) or "got it wrong" (countering your ideas, but giving you a chance to refute that position in favor of your own)
- **clarify** in short order the complex ideas contained in another author's work
- **lend authority** to your voice by showing readers that you have considered the topic carefully by consulting other sources
- **build new ideas** from existing ideas on the topic, enabling you to insert your voice into an ongoing debate made evident by the summary or paraphrase

When you *summarize*, you're standing back, saying briefly what the whole adds up to; you're seeing the forest, as the saying goes, not the individual trees. When you *paraphrase*, you're inching through the forest, scrutinizing each tree — finding a synonym for almost every word in the original in an effort to ensure that you know exactly what the original is saying. (Keep in mind that when you incorporate a summary or a paraphrase into your own essay, you should acknowledge the source and state that you are summarizing or paraphrasing.)

Let's examine the distinction between summary and paraphrase in connection with the first two paragraphs of Paul Goodman's essay "A Proposal to Abolish Grading," excerpted from his book *Compulsory Miseducation and the Community of Scholars* (1966):

> Let half a dozen of the prestigious universities — Chicago, Stanford, the Ivy League — abolish grading, and use testing only and entirely for pedagogic purposes as teachers see fit.

Anyone who knows the frantic temper of the present schools will understand the transvaluation of values that would be effected by this modest innovation. For most of the students, the competitive grade has come to be the essence. The naïve teacher points to the beauty of the subject and the ingenuity of the research; the shrewd student asks if he is responsible for that on the final exam.

A *summary* of these two paragraphs might read like this:

If some top universities used tests only to help students learn and not for grades, students would stop worrying about whether they got an A, B, or C and might begin to share the teacher's interest in the beauty of the subject.

Notice that the summary doesn't convey Goodman's style or voice (e.g., the wry tone in his pointed contrast between "the naïve teacher" and "the shrewd student"). That is not the purpose of summary.

Now for a *paraphrase*. Suppose you're not sure what Goodman is getting at, maybe because you're uncertain about the meanings of some words (e.g., *pedagogic* and *transvaluation*), or you just want to make sure you understand the point.

Suppose some of the top universities — such as Chicago, Stanford, Harvard, Yale, and others in the Ivy League — stopped using grades and instead used tests only to help students learn.

Everyone who is aware of the rat race in schools today will understand the enormous shift in values about learning that would come about by this small change. At present, idealistic instructors talk about how beautiful their subjects are, but smart students know that grades are what count. They only want to know if that subject will be on the exam.

In short, you may decide to paraphrase an important text if you want the reader to see the passage itself but you know that the full passage will be puzzling. In this situation, you offer help, *paraphrasing* before making your own point about the author's claim.

A second good reason to offer a paraphrase is if there is substantial disagreement about what the text says. The Second Amendment to the US Constitution is a good example of this sort of text:

A well regulated Militia being necessary to the security of a free State, the right of the people to keep and bear Arms shall not be infringed.

Exactly what, one might ask, is a "Militia"? What does it mean for a militia to be "well regulated"? And does "the

Bill Clark/Getty Images News/Getty Images

Gun control supporters marching in Washington, DC.

people" mean each individual or the citizenry as a unified group? After all, elsewhere in the document, where the Constitution speaks of individuals, it speaks of a "man" or a "person," not "the people." To speak of "the people" is to use a term (some argue) that sounds like a reference to a unified group — perhaps the citizens of each of the thirteen states — rather than a reference to individuals. However, if Congress did mean a unified group rather than individuals, why didn't it say, "Congress shall not prohibit the states from organizing militias"?

In fact, thousands of pages have been written about that sentence, and if you're going to write about it, you certainly have to let readers know exactly how you interpret each word. In short, you almost surely will paraphrase the sentence, going word by word, giving readers your own sense of what each word or phrase means. Here is one possible paraphrase:

> Because an independent society needs the protection of an armed force if it is to remain free, the government may not limit the right of the individuals (who may someday form the militia needed to keep the society free) to possess weapons.

In this interpretation, the Constitution grants individuals the right to possess weapons, and that is that.

Other students of the Constitution, however, offer very different paraphrases, usually along these lines:

> Because each state that is now part of the United States may need to protect its freedom (from the new national government), the national government may not infringe on the right of each state to form its own disciplined militia.

This paraphrase says that the federal government may not prevent each state from having a militia; it says nothing about every individual person having a right to possess weapons.

The first paraphrase might be offered by the National Rifle Association or any other group that interprets the Constitution as guaranteeing individuals the right to own guns. The second paraphrase might be offered by groups that seek to limit the ownership of guns.

Why paraphrase? Here are two reasons you might paraphrase a passage:

1. To help yourself understand it. In this case, the paraphrase does not appear in your essay.
2. To help your reader understand a passage that is especially important but

A CHECKLIST FOR A PARAPHRASE

- ❒ Do I have a good reason for offering a paraphrase rather than a summary?
- ❒ Is the paraphrase entirely in my own words — a word-by-word "translation" — rather than a patchwork of the source's words and my own, with some of my own rearrangement of phrases and clauses?
- ❒ Do I not only cite the source but also explicitly say that the entire passage is a paraphrase?

that is not immediately clear. In this case, you paraphrase to let the reader know exactly what the passage means. This paraphrase does appear in your essay.

Patchwriting and Plagiarism

We have indicated that only rarely will you have reason to paraphrase in your essays. In your notes, you might sometimes copy word for word (quote), paraphrase, or summarize, but if you produce a medley of borrowed words and original words in your essays, you are **patchwriting**, and it can be dangerous: If you submit such a medley, you risk the charge of **plagiarism** *even if you have rearranged the phrases and clauses, and even if you have cited your source.*

Here's an example. First, we give the source: a paragraph from Helen Benedict's essay on the "man problem" in the military reprinted in full beginning on page 27:

> For generations now, the debate over women in combat has put the onus on women to prove they can handle the infantry and other traditionally all-male units. Yet today's wars have made it clear that the military's problem lies not with its women, their ability or their courage. The military's problem, instead, is with some of its men — and a deeply ingrained macho culture that denigrates, insults and abuses women.

Here is a student's patchwriting version:

> Over the past two generations, debates about women's roles in the military have focused on whether or not they can handle the infantry duty. Yet everyday they do. Helen Benedict points out that women are not the problem in the military — the men are, especially those who hold ideas ingrained in a macho culture that is insulting and abusive to women.

As you can see, the student writer has used patchwriting because she followed the source almost phrase by phrase, making small verbal changes here and there, such as substituting new words and key phrases, while at other points using the same vocabulary slightly rearranged. That is, the sequence of ideas and their arrangement, as well as most of the language, are entirely or almost entirely derived from the source, even if some of the words are different. Thus, even if the student cites the source, it is plagiarism.

What the student should have done is either (1) *quote the passage exactly*, setting it off to indicate that it's a quotation and indicating the source, or (2) *summarize it briefly* and credit the source — maybe in a version such as this:

> Helen Benedict points out that arguments used in the past to keep women out of military combat roles were unfounded. Women have proved themselves time and time again since the ban on women in combat roles was lifted. However, Benedict argues, even though women now have the opportunity to serve, they are by no means "equal" in the military. Benedict details the sexist

culture in the military—what she calls the military's "man problem"—a problem that subjects women to a deeply hostile environment.

The above example frankly summarizes a source and attributes it to the author, Benedict. The reader knows these ideas are Benedict's, not the writer's. This allows the writer to build on her source's ideas to establish—and distinguish—her own argument.

Citing a source is not enough to protect you from the charge of plagiarism. Citing a source tells the reader that some fact or idea—or some groups of words enclosed within quotation marks or set off by indentation—comes from the named source; it does *not* tell the reader that almost everything in the paragraph is, in effect, someone else's writing with a few words changed, a few words added, and a few phrases moved.

The best way to avoid introducing patchwriting into your final essay is to make certain that when taking notes you indicate, *in the notes themselves,* what sort of notes they are. For example:

- When quoting word for word, put the passage within quotation marks and cite the page number(s) of the source.
- When paraphrasing—perhaps to ensure that you understand the writer's idea or because your readers won't understand the source's highly technical language unless you put it into simpler language—use some sign, perhaps (*par*), to remind yourself later that this passage is a paraphrase and thus is not really *your* writing.
- When summarizing, use a different key, such as (*sum*), and cite the page(s) or online location of the source.

If you have taken notes properly, with indications of the sort we've mentioned, when writing your paper you can say things like the following:

- *X*'s first reason is simple. *X* says, ". . ." (here you quote *X*'s words, putting them within quotation marks).
- *X*'s point can be summarized thus: . . . (here you cite the page).
- *X*, writing for lawyers, uses some technical language, but we can paraphrase her conclusion in this way: . . . (here you give the citation).

For additional information about plagiarism, see the section A Note on Plagiarizing on pages 276–78 in Chapter 7.

Strategies for Summarizing

As with paraphrases, summaries can help you establish your understanding of an essay or article. Summarizing each paragraph or each group of closely related paragraphs will enable you to follow the threads of the argument and will ultimately provide a useful map of the essay. Then, when rereading the essay, you may want to underline passages that you now realize are the author's key ideas — for instance, definitions, generalizations, and summaries. You may also want to jot notes in the margins, questioning the logic, expressing your uncertainty, or calling attention to other writers who see the matter differently.

How long should your summaries be? They can be as short as a single sentence or as long as an entire paragraph. Here's a one-sentence summary of Martin Luther King Jr.'s famous essay "Letter from Birmingham Jail," which King wrote after his arrest for marching against racial segregation and injustice in Birmingham, Alabama.

> In his letter, King argues that the time is ripe for nonviolent protest throughout the segregated South, dismissing claims by local clergymen who opposed him and arguing that unjust laws need to be challenged by black people who have been patient and silent for too long.

King's essay, however, is quite long. Obviously, our one-sentence summary cannot convey substantial portions of King's eloquent arguments, sacrificing almost all the nuance of his rationale, but it serves as an efficient summation and allows the writer to move on to his or her own analysis promptly.

WRITING TIP
Your essay is *likely to include brief summaries* of points of view with which you agree or disagree, but it will *rarely include a paraphrase* unless the original is obscure and you feel compelled to present a passage at length in words that are clearer than those of the original. If you do paraphrase, explicitly identify the material as a paraphrase. Never submit patchwriting.

A longer summary might try to capture more nuance, especially if, for the purposes of your essay, you need to capture more. How much you summarize depends largely on the *purpose* of your summary (see again our list of reasons to summarize on p. 46). Here is a longer summary of King's letter:

> In his letter, King argues that the time is ripe for nonviolent protest in the segregated South despite the criticism he and his fellow civil rights activists received from various authorities, especially the eight local clergymen who wrote a public statement against him. King addresses their criticism point by point, first claiming his essential right to be in Birmingham with his famous statement, "injustice anywhere is a threat to justice everywhere," and then saying that those who see the timing of his group's nonviolent direct action as inconvenient must recognize at least two things: one, that his "legitimate and unavoidable impatience" resulted from undelivered promises by authorities in the past; and two, that African Americans had long been told over and over again to wait for change with no change forthcoming. "This 'wait' has almost always meant 'never,'" King writes. For those who criticized his leadership, which encouraged people to break laws prohibiting their march, King says that breaking *unjust* laws may actually be construed as a *just* act. For those who called him an extremist, he revels in the definition ("was not Jesus an extremist in love?" he asks) and reminds them of the more extremist groups who call for violence in the face of blatant discrimination and brutality (and who will surely rise, King suggests, if no redress is forthcoming for the peaceful southern protestors he leads). Finally, King rails against "silence," saying that to hold one's tongue in the face of segregation is tantamount to supporting it — a blow to "white moderates" who believe in change but do nothing to help bring it about.

This summary, obviously much longer than the first, raises numerous points from King's argument and preserves through quotation some of King's original tone and substance. It sacrifices much, of course, but seeks to provide a thorough account of a long and complex document containing many primary and secondary claims.

If your instructor asks for a summary of an essay, most often he or she won't want you to include your own thoughts about the content. Of course, you'll be using your own words, but try to "put yourself in the original author's shoes" and provide a summary that reflects the approach taken by the source. It should *not* contain ideas that the original piece doesn't express. If you use exact words and phrases drawn from the source, enclose them in quotation marks.

Summaries may be written for exercises in reading comprehension, but the point of summarizing when writing an essay is to assist your own argument. A faithful summary — one without your own ideas interjected — can be effective when using a source as an example or showing another writer's concordance with your argument. Consider the following paragraph written by a student who wanted to use Henry David Thoreau's 1849 essay, "Resistance to Civil Government," to make a point in her paper on sweatshops and other poor labor conditions in the supply chains of our everyday products. Thoreau famously argued that many northerners who objected to slavery in the United States did not always realize how economically tied up in slavery they were. He argued that true opposition to slavery meant withdrawing fully from all economic activity related to it. The student was arguing that if a person today purchases goods manufactured in sweatshops or under other inadequate labor conditions, he or she is in a sense just as responsible for the abuses of labor as the companies who operate them. Thoreau provided a convenient precedent. Notice how the student offers a summary (underlined) along the way and how it assists her argument.

> Americans today are so disconnected from the source and origins of the products they buy that it is entirely possible for them one day to march against global warming and the next to collect a dividend in their 401k from companies that are the worst offenders. It is possible to weep over a news report on child labor in China and then post an emotional plea for justice on Facebook using a mobile device made by Chinese child laborers. In 1849, Henry David Thoreau wrote in "Resistance to Civil Government" how ironic it was to see his fellow citizens in Boston opposed to slavery in the South, yet who read the daily news and commodity prices and "fall asleep over them both," not recognizing their own investments in, or patronage of, the very thing that offends their consciences. To Thoreau, such "gross inconsistency" makes even well-intentioned people "agents of injustice." Similarly, today we do not see the connections between our consumer habits and the various kinds of oppression that underlie our purchases — forms of oppression we would never support directly and outright.

The embedded short summary addresses only one point of Thoreau's original essay, but it shows how summaries may serve in an integrative way — as analogy, example, or illustration — to support an argument even without adding the writer's own commentary or analysis.

CRITICAL SUMMARY

When writing a longer summary that you intend to integrate into your argument, you may interject your own ideas; the appropriate term for this writing is **critical summary**. It signifies that you're offering more than a thorough and accurate account of an original source, because you're adding your evaluation of it as well. Think of it as weaving together your neutral summary with your own argument so that the summary meshes seamlessly with your overall writing goal. Along the way, during the summary, you may appraise the original author's ideas, commenting on them as you go — even while being faithful to the original.

How can you faithfully account for an author's argument while commenting on its merits or shortcomings? One way is to offer examples from the original. In addition, you might assess the quality of those examples or present others that the author didn't consider. Remember, being critical doesn't necessarily mean refuting the author. Your summary can refute, support, or be more balanced, simply recognizing where the original author succeeds and fails.

> **WRITING TIP**
> When writing a critical summary, you can problematize by examining areas not considered by the author. Ask: What has the author missed? What evidence or examples have been misinterpreted?

A STRATEGY FOR WRITING A CRITICAL SUMMARY Follow these five steps when writing a critical summary:

1. **Introduce** the summary. You don't have to provide all these elements, but consider offering the *author's name* and *expertise*, the *title* of the source, the *place* of publication, the *year* of publication, or any other relevant information. You may also start to explain the author's main point that you are summarizing:

> Pioneering feminist Betty Friedan, in her landmark book *The Feminine Mystique* (1963), argued that . . .

Don't overdo it. Select the most important details carefully and work toward concision. Remember that this is a summary, so "get in and get out." That is, move quickly back to your analysis.

2. **Explain** the major point the source makes. Here you have a chance to tell your readers what the original author is saying, so be faithful to the original but also highlight the point you're summarizing:

> Pioneering feminist Betty Friedan, in her landmark book *The Feminine Mystique* (1963), argued that women of the early 1960s were falling victim to a media-created image of ideal femininity that pressured them to prioritize homemaking, beauty, and maternity above almost all other concerns.

Here you can control the readers' understanding through simple adjectives such as *pioneering* and *landmark*. (Compare how "*stalwart* feminist Betty Friedan, in her *provocative* book" might dispose the reader to interpret your material differently.)

3. **Exemplify** by offering one or more representative examples or evidence on which the original author draws. Feel free to quote if needed, although it is not required in a summary.

> Friedan examines post–World War II trends that included the lowering of the marriage age, the rise of the mass media, and what she calls "the problem that has no name" — that of feminine unfulfillment, or what we might today call "depression."

Feel free to use a short quotation or utilize signature terms, phrases, or concepts from the source.

4. **Problematize** by placing your assessment, analysis, or question into the summary.

> Although the word *depression* never comes up in Friedan's work, one could assume that terms like *malaise, suffering*, and *housewives' fatigue* signal an emerging understanding of the relationship between stereotypical media representations of social identity and mental health.

If you're working toward a balanced critique or rebuttal, here is a good place to insert your ideas or those of someone with a slightly different view. Consider utility phrases that help tie these elements of critical summary together. More adjectives and strong verbs can help indicate your critique and judgment. For example:

> In her *careful* analysis of contemporary horror films, Simpson looks at movies like *X, Y*, and *Z*, showing how *inadequately* women are represented as *weak, vulnerable* victims in need of rescue, mostly by men. Nevertheless, while her analysis is *convincing*, her examples *ignore* films such as *A, B*, and *C*, and this glaring omission shows . . .

5. **Extend** by tying the summary to your argument, helping transition out of the critical summary and back into your own analysis. Imagine your final task as saying (without saying) something like, *And this summary is important to my overall thesis because it shows . . .*

> Friedan's work should raise questions about how women are portrayed in the media today and about what mental health consequences are attributable to the ubiquitous and consistent messages given to women about their bodies, occupations, and social roles.

WRITING TIP
Use strong adjectives to establish your assessment or judgments on the value, worth, or quality of the writer's argument, thesis, presentation, or sources (e.g., *landmark* essay, *controversial* book, *blunt* critique).

It is possible to use this method — **Introduce**, **Explain**, **Exemplify**, **Problematize**, and **Extend** — in many ways, but essentially it is a way of providing a critical summary, any element of which can be enhanced or built upon as needed. When you're writing your own critical summary, refer to the Visual Guide (p. 55) for reference.

Visual Guide: Writing a Critical Summary

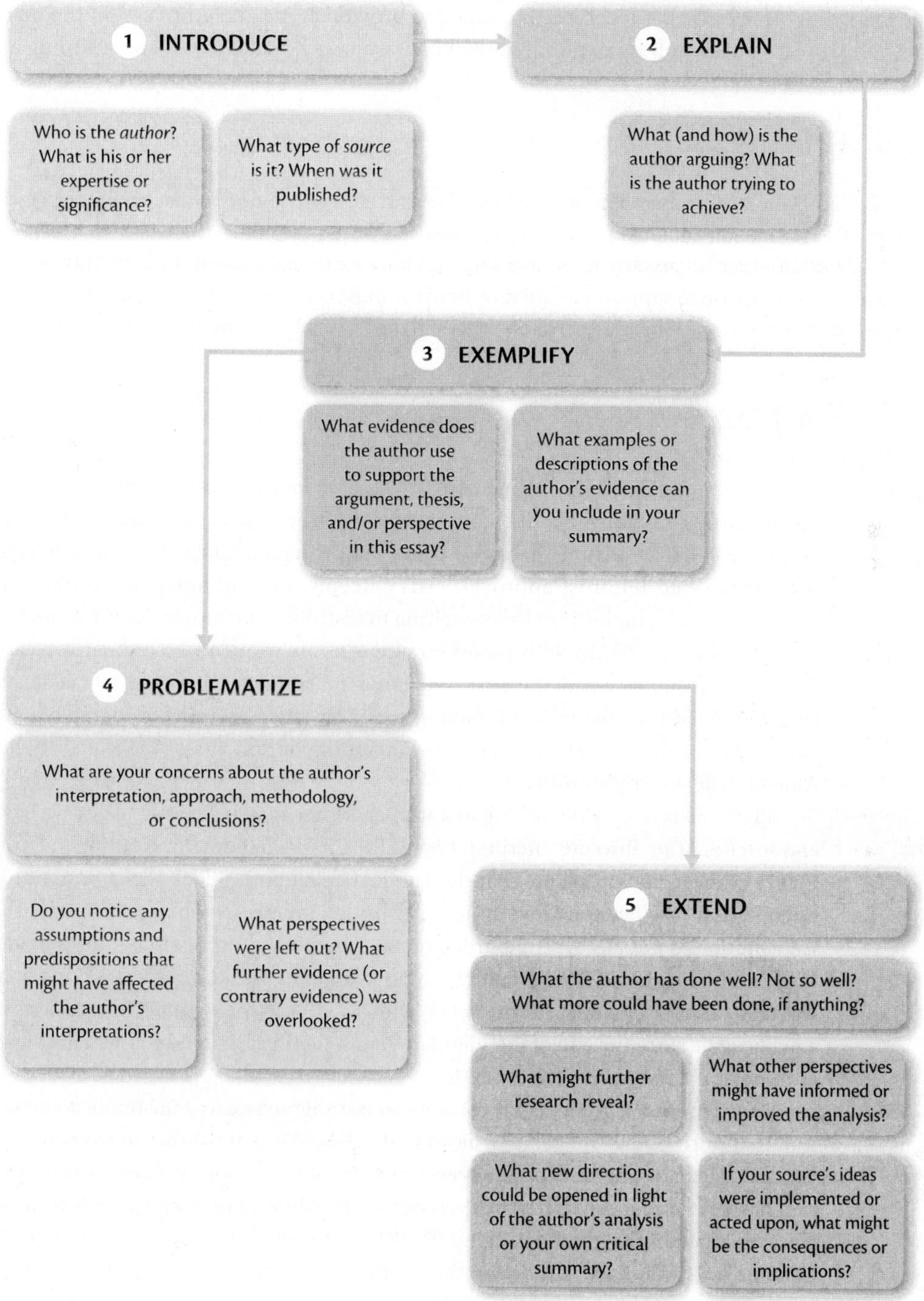
1 INTRODUCE
Who is the *author*? What is his or her expertise or significance?
What type of *source* is it? When was it published?
2 EXPLAIN
What (and how) is the author arguing? What is the author trying to achieve?
3 EXEMPLIFY
What evidence does the author use to support the argument, thesis, and/or perspective in this essay?
What examples or descriptions of the author's evidence can you include in your summary?
4 PROBLEMATIZE
What are your concerns about the author's interpretation, approach, methodology, or conclusions?
Do you notice any assumptions and predispositions that might have affected the author's interpretations?
What perspectives were left out? What further evidence (or contrary evidence) was overlooked?
5 EXTEND
What the author has done well? Not so well? What more could have been done, if anything?
What might further research reveal?
What other perspectives might have informed or improved the analysis?
What new directions could be opened in light of the author's analysis or your own critical summary?
If your source's ideas were implemented or acted upon, what might be the consequences or implications?

A SHORT ESSAY FOR SUMMARIZING PRACTICE

The following piece by Susan Jacoby is annotated to provide a "rough summary" in the margins, more or less paragraph by paragraph, the kind you might make if you are outlining an essay or argument.

SUSAN JACOBY

Susan Jacoby (b. 1946), a journalist since the age of seventeen, is well known for her feminist writings. "A First Amendment Junkie" (our title) appeared in the Hers column in the *New York Times* in 1978. Notice that her argument zigs and zags, not because Jacoby is careless but because in building a strong case to support her point of view, she must consider some widely held views that she does *not* accept; she must set these forth and then give her reasons for rejecting them.

A First Amendment Junkie

Paragraph 1: Although feminists usually support the First Amendment, when it comes to pornography many feminists take the position of opposing the Equal Rights Amendment, abortion, and other causes of the women's movement.

It is no news that many women are defecting from the ranks of civil libertarians on the issue of obscenity. The conviction of Larry Flynt, publisher of *Hustler* magazine — before his metamorphosis into a born-again Christian — was greeted with unabashed feminist approval. Harry Reems, the unknown actor who was convicted by a Memphis jury for conspiring to distribute the movie *Deep Throat*, has carried on his legal battles with almost no support from women who ordinarily regard themselves as supporters of the First Amendment. Feminist writers and scholars have even discussed the possibility of making common cause against pornography with adversaries of the women's movement — including opponents of the Equal Rights Amendment and "right-to-life" forces.

Paragraph 2: Larry Flynt produces garbage, but Jacoby thinks his conviction represents an unconstitutional limitation of freedom of speech.

All of this is deeply disturbing to a woman writer who believes, as I always have and still do, in an absolute interpretation of the First Amendment. Nothing in Larry Flynt's garbage convinces me that the late Justice Hugo L. Black was wrong in his opinion that "the Federal Government is without any power whatsoever under the Constitution to put any type of burden on free speech and expression of ideas of any kind (as distinguished from conduct)." Many women I like and respect tell me I am wrong; I cannot remember having become involved in so many heated discussions of a public issue since the end of the Vietnam War. A feminist writer described my views as those of a "First Amendment junkie."

Paragraphs 3, 4: Feminists who want to censor pornography argue that it poses a greater threat to women than similar repulsive speech poses to other groups. They can make this case, but it is absurd to say that pornography is a "greater threat" to women than "neo-Nazi . . . extermination camps."

Many feminist arguments for controls on pornography carry the implicit conviction that porn books, magazines, and movies pose a greater threat to women than similarly repulsive exercises of free speech pose to other offended groups. This conviction has, of course, been shared by everyone — regardless of race, creed, or sex — who has ever argued in favor of abridging the First Amendment. It is the argument used by some Jews who have withdrawn their support from the American Civil Liberties Union because it has defended the right of American Nazis to march through a community inhabited by survivors of Hitler's concentration camps.

If feminists want to argue that the protection of the Constitution should not be extended to *any* particularly odious or threatening form of speech, they have a reasonable argument (although I don't agree with it). But it is ridiculous to suggest that the porn shops on 42nd Street are more disgusting to women than a march of neo-Nazis is to survivors of the extermination camps.

5 The arguments over pornography also blur the vital distinction between expression of ideas and conduct. When I say I believe unreservedly in the First Amendment, someone always comes back at me with the issue of "kiddie porn." But kiddie porn is not a First Amendment issue. It is an issue of the abuse of power — the power adults have over children — and not of obscenity. Parents and promoters have no more right to use their children to make porn movies than they do to send them to work in coal mines. The responsible adults should be prosecuted, just as adults who use children for back-breaking farm labor should be prosecuted.

Paragraph 5: Trust in the First Amendment is not refuted by kiddie porn; kiddie porn is an issue of child abuse.

Susan Brownmiller, in *Against Our Will: Men, Women, and Rape*, has described pornography as "the undiluted essence of antifemale propaganda." I think this is a fair description of some types of pornography, especially of the brutish subspecies that equates sex with death and portrays women primarily as objects of violence.

The equation of sex and violence, personified by some glossy rock record album covers as well as by *Hustler*, has fed the illusion that censorship of pornography can be conducted on a more rational basis than other types of censorship. Are all pictures of naked women obscene? Clearly not, says a friend. A Renoir nude is art, she says, and *Hustler* is trash. "Any reasonable person" knows that.

But what about something between art and trash — something, say, along the lines of *Playboy* or *Penthouse* magazines? I asked five women for their reactions to one picture in *Penthouse* and got responses that ranged from "lovely" and "sensuous" to "revolting" and "demeaning." Feminists, like everyone else, seldom have rational reasons for their preferences in erotica. Like members of juries, they tend to disagree when confronted with something that falls short of 100 percent vulgarity.

Paragraphs 6, 7, 8: Some feminists think censorship of pornography can be more "rational" than other kinds of censorship, but a picture of a nude woman strikes some women as base and others as "lovely." There is no unanimity.

In any case, feminists will not be the arbiters of good taste if it becomes easier to harass, prosecute, and convict people on obscenity charges. Most of the people who want to censor girlie magazines are equally opposed to open discussion of issues that are of vital concern to women: rape, abortion, menstruation, contraception, lesbianism — in fact, the entire range of sexual experience from a woman's viewpoint.

10 Feminist writers and editors and filmmakers have limited financial resources: Confronted by a determined prosecutor, Hugh Hefner[1] will fare better than Susan Brownmiller. Would the Memphis jurors who convicted Harry Reems for his role in *Deep Throat* be inclined to take a more positive view of paintings of the female genitalia done by sensitive feminist artists? *Ms.* magazine has printed color reproductions of some of those art works; *Ms.* is already banned from a number of high school libraries because someone considers it threatening and/or obscene.

Paragraphs 9, 10: If feminists censor girlie magazines, they are unwittingly helping opponents of the women's movement censor discussions of rape, abortion, and so on.

[1] **Hugh Hefner** Founder and longtime publisher of *Playboy* magazine.

Paragraphs 11, 12: Like other would-be censors, feminists want to use the power of the state to achieve what they have not achieved in "the marketplace of ideas." They lack faith in "democratic persuasion."

Feminists who want to censor what they regard as harmful pornography have essentially the same motivation as other would-be censors: They want to use the power of the state to accomplish what they have been unable to achieve in the marketplace of ideas and images. The impulse to censor places no faith in the possibilities of democratic persuasion.

It isn't easy to persuade certain men that they have better uses for $1.95 each month than to spend it on a copy of *Hustler*. Well, then, give the men no choice in the matter.

Paragraphs 13, 14: This attempt at censorship reveals a "desire to shift responsibility from individuals to institutions." The responsibility is properly the parents'.

I believe there is also a connection between the impulse toward censorship on the part of people who used to consider themselves civil libertarians and a more general desire to shift responsibility from individuals to institutions. When I saw the movie *Looking for Mr. Goodbar*, I was stunned by its series of visual images equating sex and violence, coupled with what seems to me the mindless message (a distortion of the fine Judith Rossner novel) that casual sex equals death. When I came out of the movie, I was even more shocked to see parents standing in line with children between the ages of ten and fourteen.

I simply don't know why a parent would take a child to see such a movie, any more than I understand why people feel they can't turn off a television set their child is watching. Whenever I say that, my friends tell me I don't know how it is because I don't have children. True, but I do have parents. When I was a child, they did turn off the TV. They didn't expect the Federal Communications Commission to do their job for them.

Paragraph 15: We can't have too much of the First Amendment.

I am a First Amendment junkie. You can't OD on the First Amendment, because 15
free speech is its own best antidote.

SUMMARIZING JACOBY If we want to present a *brief summary* in the form of one coherent paragraph — perhaps as part of an essay arguing for or against — we might write something like the one shown in the paragraph below. (Of course, we would introduce it with a lead-in along these lines: "Susan Jacoby, writing in the *New York Times*, offers a forceful argument against censorship of pornography. Jacoby's view, briefly, is . . .")

> When it comes to censorship of pornography, some feminists take a position shared by opponents of the feminist movement. They argue that pornography poses a greater threat to women than other forms of offensive speech offer to other groups, but this interpretation is simply a mistake. Pointing to kiddie porn is also a mistake, for kiddie porn is an issue involving not the First Amendment but child abuse. Feminists who support censorship of pornography will inadvertently aid those who wish to censor discussions of abortion and rape or censor art that is published in magazines such as *Ms.* The solution is not for individuals to turn to institutions (i.e., for the government to limit the First Amendment) but for individuals to accept the responsibility for teaching young people not to equate sex with violence.

In contrast, a *critical summary* of Jacoby — an evaluative summary in which we introduce our own ideas and examples — might look like this:

Susan Jacoby, writing for the *New York Times* in 1978, offers a forceful argument against censorship of pornography, but one that does not have foresight of the internet age and the new availability of extreme and exploitative forms of pornography. While she dismisses claims by feminists that pornography should be censored because it constitutes violence against women, what would Jacoby think of such things as "revenge porn" and "voyeuristic porn" today or the array of elaborate sadistic fantasies readily available to anyone with access to a search engine? Jacoby says that censoring pornography is a step toward censoring art, and she proudly wears the tag "First Amendment junkie," ostensibly to protect what she finds artistic (such as images of female genitalia in *Ms.* magazine). However, her argument does not help us account for these new forms of exploitation and violence disguised as art or "free speech." Perhaps she would see revenge porn and voyeur porn in the same the way she sees kiddie porn — not so much as an issue of free speech but as an issue of other crimes. Perhaps she would hold her position that we can avoid pornography by just "turning off the TV," but the new internet pornography is intrusive, entering our lives and the lives of our children whether we like it or not. Education is part of the solution, Jacoby would agree, but we could also consider . . .

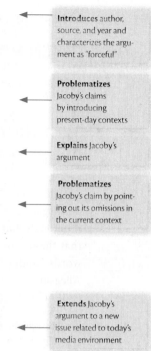

Introduces author, source, and year and characterizes the argument as "forceful"

Problematizes Jacoby's claims by introducing present-day contexts

Explains Jacoby's argument

Problematizes Jacoby's claim by pointing out its omissions in the current context

Extends Jacoby's argument to a new issue related to today's media environment

This example not only summarizes and applies the other techniques presented in this chapter (e.g., accounting for context and questioning definitions of terms and concepts) but also weaves them together with a central argument that offers a new response and a practicable solution.

A CHECKLIST FOR A SUMMARY

- ☐ Have I adequately previewed the work?
- ☐ Can I state the thesis?
- ☐ If I have written a summary, is it accurate?
- ☐ Does my summary mention all the chief points?
- ☐ If there are inconsistencies, are they in the summary or the original selection?
- ☐ Will my summary be clear and helpful?
- ☐ Have I considered the audience for whom the author is writing?

Essays for Analysis

GWEN WILDE

This essay was written for a composition course at Tufts University.

Why the Pledge of Allegiance Should Be Revised (Student Essay)

All Americans are familiar with the Pledge of Allegiance, even if they cannot always recite it perfectly, but probably relatively few know that the *original* Pledge did *not* include the words "under God." The original Pledge of Allegiance, published in the September 8, 1892, issue of the *Youth's Companion,* ran thus:

> I pledge allegiance to my flag, and to the Republic for which it stands: one Nation indivisible, with Liberty and justice for all. (Djupe 329)

In 1923, at the first National Flag Conference in Washington, DC, it was argued that immigrants might be confused by the words "my Flag," and it was proposed that the words be changed to "the Flag of the United States." The following year it was changed again, to "the Flag of the United States of America," and this wording became the official — or, rather, unofficial — wording, unofficial because no wording had ever been nationally adopted (Djupe 329).

In 1942, the United States Congress included the Pledge in the United States Flag Code (4 USC 4, 2006), thus for the first time officially sanctioning the Pledge. In 1954, President Dwight D. Eisenhower approved adding the words "under God." Thus, since 1954 the Pledge reads:

> I pledge allegiance to the flag of the United States of America, and to the Republic for which it stands: one nation under God, indivisible, with Liberty and Justice for all. (Djupe 329)

In my view, the addition of the words "under God" is inappropriate, and they are needlessly divisive — an odd addition indeed to a nation that is said to be "indivisible."

5 Very simply put, the Pledge in its latest form requires all Americans to say something that some Americans do not believe. I say "requires" because although the courts have ruled that students may not be compelled to recite the Pledge, in effect peer pressure does compel all but the bravest to join in the recitation. When President Eisenhower authorized the change, he said, "In this way we are reaffirming the transcendence of religious faith in America's heritage and future; in this way we shall constantly strengthen those spiritual weapons which forever will be our country's most powerful resource in peace and war" (Sterner).

Exactly what did Eisenhower mean when he spoke of "the transcendence of religious faith in America's heritage" and when he spoke of "spiritual weapons"? I am not sure what "the transcendence of religious faith in America's heritage" means. Of course, many Americans have been and are deeply religious — no one doubts it — but the phrase certainly goes far beyond saying that many Americans have been devout. In any case, many Americans have *not* been devout, and many Americans have *not* believed in "spiritual weapons," but they have nevertheless been patriotic Americans. Some of them have fought and died to keep America free.

In short, the words "under God" cannot be uttered in good faith by many Americans. True, something like 70 or even 80% of Americans say they are affiliated with some form of Christianity, and approximately another 3% say they are Jewish. I don't have the figures for persons of other faiths, but in any case we can surely all agree that although a majority of Americans say they have a religious affiliation, nevertheless several million Americans do *not* believe in God.

If one remains silent while others are reciting the Pledge, or even if one remains silent only while others are speaking the words "under God," one is open to the charge that one is unpatriotic, is "unwilling to recite the Pledge of Allegiance." In the Pledge, patriotism is connected with religious belief, and it is this connection that makes it divisive and (to be blunt) un-American. Admittedly, the belief is not very specific: one is not required to say that one believes in the divinity of Jesus, or in the power of Jehovah, but the fact remains, one is required to express belief in a divine power, and if one doesn't express this belief one is — according to the Pledge — somehow not fully an American, maybe even un-American.

Please notice that I am not arguing that the Pledge is unconstitutional. I understand that the First Amendment to the Constitution says that "Congress shall make no law respecting an establishment of religion, or prohibiting the free exercise thereof." I am not arguing that the words "under God" in the Pledge add up to the "establishment of religion," but they certainly do assert a religious doctrine. Like the words "In God We Trust," found on all American money, the words "under God" express an idea that many Americans do not hold, and there is no reason why these Americans — loyal people who may be called upon to defend the country with their lives — should be required to say that America is a nation "under God."

It has been argued, even by members of 10
the Supreme Court, that the words "under God" are not to be taken terribly seriously, not to be taken to say what they seem to say. For instance, Chief Justice Rehnquist wrote:

> To give the parent of such a child a sort of "heckler's veto" over a patriotic ceremony willingly participated in by other students, simply because the Pledge of Allegiance contains the descriptive phrase "under God," is an unwarranted extension of the establishment clause, an extension which would have the unfortunate effect of prohibiting a commendable patriotic observance. (qtd. in Stephens et al. 104)

Chief Justice Rehnquist here calls "under God" a "descriptive phrase," but descriptive of *what*? If a phrase is a "descriptive phrase," it describes something, real or imagined. For many Americans, this phrase does *not* describe a reality. These Americans may perhaps be mistaken — if so, they may learn of their error at Judgment Day — but the fact is, millions of intelligent Americans do not believe in God.

Notice, too, that Chief Justice Rehnquist goes on to say that reciting the Pledge is "a commendable patriotic observance." Exactly. That is my point. It is a *patriotic* observance, and it should not be connected with religion. When we announce that we respect the flag — that we are loyal Americans — we should not also have to announce that we hold a particular religious belief, in this case a belief in monotheism, a belief that there is a God and that God rules.

One other argument defending the words "under God" is often heard: The words "In God We Trust" appear on our money. It is claimed that these words on American money are analogous to the words "under God" in the Pledge. But the situation really is very different. When we hand some coins over, or some paper money, we are concentrating on the business transaction, and we are not making any affirmation about God or our country. But when we recite the Pledge — even if we remain silent at the point when we are supposed to say "under God" — we are very conscious that we are supposed to make this affirmation, an affirmation that many Americans cannot in good faith make, even though they certainly can unthinkingly hand over (or accept) money with the words "In God We Trust."

Because I believe that *reciting* the Pledge is to be taken seriously, with a full awareness of the words that is quite different from when we hand over some money, I cannot understand the recent comment of Supreme Court Justice Souter, who in a case said that the phrase "under God" is "so tepid, so diluted, so far from compulsory prayer, that it should, in effect, be beneath the constitutional radar" (qtd. in "Guide"). I don't follow his reasoning that the phrase should be "beneath the constitutional radar," but in any case I am willing to put aside the issue of constitutionality. I am willing to grant that this phrase does not in any significant sense signify the "establishment of religion" (prohibited by the First Amendment) in the United States. I insist, nevertheless, that the phrase is neither "tepid" nor "diluted." It means what it says — it *must* and *should* mean what it says, to everyone who utters it — and, since millions of loyal Americans cannot say it, it should not be included in a statement in which Americans affirm their loyalty to our great country.

15 In short, the Pledge, which ought to unite all of us, is divisive; it includes a phrase that many patriotic Americans cannot bring themselves to utter. Yes, they can remain silent when others recite these two words, but, again, why should they have to remain silent? The Pledge of Allegiance should be something that *everyone* can say, say out loud, and say with pride. We hear much talk of returning to the ideas of the Founding Fathers. The Founding Fathers did not create the Pledge of Allegiance, but we do know that they never mentioned God in the Constitution. Indeed, the only reference to religion, in the so-called establishment clause of the First Amendment, says, again, that "Congress shall make no law respecting an establishment of religion, or prohibiting the free exercise thereof." Those who wish to exercise religion are indeed free to do so, but the place to do so is not in a pledge that is required of all schoolchildren and of all new citizens.

WORKS CITED

Djupe, Paul A. "Pledge of Allegiance." *Encyclopedia of American Religion and Politics*. Edited by Paul A. Djupe and Laura R. Olson, Facts on File, 2003.

"Guide to Covering 'Under God' Pledge Decision." *ReligionLink*, 17 Sept. 2005, religionlink.com/database/guide-to-covering-under-god/.

Stephens, Otis H., et al., editors. *American Constitutional Law*. 6th ed., vol. 1, Cengage Learning, 2014.

Sterner, Doug. "The Pledge of Allegiance." *Home of Heroes*, homeofheroes.com/hallofheroes/1st_floor/flag/1bfc_pledge_print.html. Accessed 13 Apr. 2016.

Topics for Critical Thinking and Writing

1. Summarize the essay in a paragraph.
2. What words are defined in this essay? Are they defined more as terms or as concepts? Explain *how* the author, Gwen Wilde, defines one word or phrase.
3. Does Wilde give enough weight to the fact that no one is compelled to recite the Pledge of Allegiance? Explain your answer.
4. What arguments does Wilde offer in support of her position?
5. Does Wilde show an adequate awareness of counterarguments? Identify one place where she raises and refutes a counterargument.
6. What is Wilde's strongest argument? Are any of her arguments notably weak? If so, how could they be strengthened?
7. What assumptions — tacit or explicit — does Wilde make? Do you agree or disagree with them? Explain your response.
8. What do you take the words "under God" to mean? Do they mean "under God's special protection"? Or "acting in accordance with God's rules"? Or "accountable to God"? Or something else? Explain.
9. Chief Justice Rehnquist wrote that the words "under God" are a "descriptive phrase." What do you think he meant by this?
10. What is the purpose of the Pledge of Allegiance? Does the phrase "under God" promote or defeat that purpose? Explain your answer.
11. What do you think about substituting "with religious freedom" for "under God"? Set forth your response, supported by reasons, in about 250 words.
12. Wilde makes a distinction between the reference to God on US money and the reference to God in the Pledge of Allegiance. Do you agree with her that the two cases are not analogous? Explain.
13. What readers might *not* agree with Wilde's arguments? What values do they hold? How might you try to persuade an audience who disagrees with Wilde to consider her proposal?
14. Putting aside your own views on the issue, what grade would you give this essay as a work of argumentative writing? Support your evaluation with reasons.
15. Consider how you would summarize a photograph such as this one by following the steps of introducing, explaining, exemplifying, problematizing, and extending it (see pp. 53–55).

Spencer Platt/Getty Images News/Getty Images

ZACHARY SHEMTOB AND DAVID LAT

Zachary Shemtob, formerly editor in chief of the *Georgetown Law Review*, is a clerk in the US District Court for the Southern District of New York. David Lat is a former federal prosecutor. Their essay originally appeared in the *New York Times* in 2011.

Executions Should Be Televised

Earlier this month, Georgia conducted its third execution this year. This would have passed relatively unnoticed if not for a controversy surrounding its videotaping. Lawyers for the condemned inmate, Andrew Grant DeYoung, had persuaded a judge to allow the recording of his last moments as part of an effort to obtain evidence on whether lethal injection caused unnecessary suffering.

Though he argued for videotaping, one of Mr. DeYoung's defense lawyers, Brian Kammer, spoke out against releasing the footage to the public. "It's a horrible thing that Andrew DeYoung had to go through," Mr. Kammer said, "and it's not for the public to see that."

We respectfully disagree. Executions in the United States ought to be made public.

Right now, executions are generally open only to the press and a few select witnesses. For the rest of us, the vague contours are provided in the morning paper. Yet a functioning democracy demands maximum accountability and transparency. As long as executions remain behind closed doors, those are impossible. The people should have the right to see what is being done in their name and with their tax dollars.

5 This is particularly relevant given the current debate on whether specific methods of lethal injection constitute cruel and unusual punishment and therefore violate the Constitution.

There is a dramatic difference between reading or hearing of such an event and observing it through image and sound. (This is obvious to those who saw the footage of Saddam Hussein's hanging in 2006 or the death of Neda Agha-Soltan during the protests in Iran in 2009.) We are not calling for opening executions completely to the public — conducting them before a live crowd — but rather for broadcasting them live or recording them for future release, on the web or TV.

When another Georgia inmate, Roy Blankenship, was executed in June, the prisoner jerked his head, grimaced, gasped, and lurched, according to a medical expert's affidavit. The *Atlanta Journal-Constitution* reported that Mr. DeYoung, executed in the same manner, "showed no violent signs in death." Voters should not have to rely on media accounts to understand what takes place when a man is put to death.

Cameras record legislative sessions and presidential debates, and courtrooms are allowing greater television access. When he was an Illinois state senator, President Obama successfully pressed for the videotaping of homicide interrogations and confessions. The most serious penalty of all surely demands equal if not greater scrutiny.

Opponents of our proposal offer many objections. State lawyers argued that making Mr. DeYoung's execution public raised safety concerns. While rioting and pickpocketing occasionally marred executions in the public square in the eighteenth and nineteenth centuries, modern security and technology obviate this concern. Little would change in the death chamber; the faces of witnesses and executioners could be edited out, for privacy reasons, before a video was released.

10 Of greater concern is the possibility that broadcasting executions could have a numbing effect. Douglas A. Berman, a law professor, fears that people might come to equate human executions with putting pets to sleep. Yet this seems overstated. While public indifference might result over time, the initial broadcasts would undoubtedly get attention and stir debate.

Still others say that broadcasting an execution would offer an unbalanced picture — making the condemned seem helpless and sympathetic, while keeping the victims of the crime out of the picture. But this is beside the point: the defendant is being executed precisely because a jury found that his crimes were so heinous that he deserved to die.

Ultimately the main opposition to our idea seems to flow from an unthinking disgust — a sense that public executions are archaic, noxious, even barbarous. Albert Camus related in his essay "Reflections on the Guillotine" that viewing executions turned him against capital punishment. The legal scholar John D. Bessler suggests that public executions might have the same effect on the public today; Sister Helen Prejean, the death penalty abolitionist, has urged just such a strategy.

That is not our view. We leave open the possibility that making executions public could strengthen support for them; undecided viewers might find them less disturbing than anticipated.

Like many of our fellow citizens, we are deeply conflicted about the death penalty and how it has been administered. Our focus is on accountability and openness. As Justice John Paul Stevens wrote in *Baze v. Rees*, a 2008 case involving a challenge to lethal injection, capital punishment is too often "the product of habit and inattention rather than an acceptable deliberative process that weighs the costs and risks of administering that penalty against its identifiable benefits."

15 A democracy demands a citizenry as informed as possible about the costs and benefits of society's ultimate punishment.

Topics for Critical Thinking and Writing

1. In paragraphs 9–13, Zachary Shemtob and David Lat discuss objections to their position. Are you satisfied with their responses to the objections, or do you think they do not satisfactorily dispose of one or more of the objections? Explain.
2. In paragraph 4, the authors say that "[t]he people should have the right to see what is being done in their name and with their tax dollars." But in terms of *rights*, should the person being executed have a right to die in privacy? Articulate a position that weighs the public's right to see what is being done with its tax dollars against death row prisoners' rights to privacy.
3. In the concluding paragraph, the authors imply that their proposal, if enacted, will help inform citizens "about the costs and benefits of society's ultimate punishment." Do you agree? Why, or why not? What reasons do the authors offer to support their proposal?
4. In your view, what is the strongest argument the authors give on behalf of their proposal? What is the weakest? Explain why you made these choices.

A Casebook for Critical Reading: Should Some Kinds of Speech Be Censored?

In addition to the essays by Jacoby, Wilde, and Shemtob and Lat, we present two additional essays on the topic of free speech and censorship. We suggest you read each one through to get its gist and then read it a second time, writing down after each paragraph a sentence or two summarizing the paragraph. Consider the essays individually and also in relation to one another, keeping in mind the First Amendment to the Constitution, which reads, in its entirety, as follows:

> Congress shall make no law respecting an establishment of religion, or prohibiting the free exercise thereof; or abridging the freedom of speech, or of the press; or the right of the people peaceably to assemble, and to petition the government for a redress of grievances.

SUZANNE NOSSEL

Suzanne Nossel, a graduate of Harvard Law School, is a leading voice on issues related to freedom of expression. She has held executive roles in Amnesty International USA and Human Rights Watch and is currently the chief executive officer of PEN America, a leading human rights advocacy group. Nossel's writing has appeared in several prominent newspapers and in scholarly journals such as *Foreign Affairs*, *Dissent*, and *Democracy*. She is a feature columnist for *Foreign Policy* magazine, where this essay first appeared in October 2017.

The Pro–Free Speech Way to Fight Fake News

After the gunfire ended, false claims that the Las Vegas carnage was the work of Islamic State terrorists or left-leaning Donald Trump opponents flooded Facebook pages, YouTube searches, and news feeds. Again, we saw how so-called "fake news" can fuel chaos and stoke hatred. Like most fraudulent news, those deceptive articles are protected speech under the First Amendment and international free expression safeguards. Unless they cross specific legal red lines — such as those barring defamation or libel — fake news stories are not illegal, and our government does not have the power to prohibit or censor them.

But the fact that fake news is free speech does not nullify the danger it poses for open discourse, freedom of opinion, or democratic governance. The rise of fraudulent news and the related erosion of public trust in mainstream journalism pose a looming crisis for free expression. Usually, free expression advocacy centers on the defense of contested speech from efforts at suppression, but it also demands steps to fortify the open and reasoned debate that underpins the value of free speech in our society and our lives. The championing of free speech must not privilege any immutable notion of the truth to the exclusion of others. But this doesn't mean that free speech proponents should be indifferent to the quest for truth, or to attempts to deliberately undermine the public's ability to distinguish fact from falsehood.

Both the First Amendment and international law define free speech to include the right to receive and impart information. The power of free speech is inextricably tied to the opportunity to be heard and believed, and to persuade. Fake news undermines precisely these sources of power. If public discourse becomes so flooded with disinformation that listeners can no longer distinguish signal from noise, they will tune out. Autocrats know this well and thus tightly control the flow of information. They purvey falsehoods to mislead, confuse, and — ultimately — to instill a sense of the futility of speech that saps the will to cry foul, protest, or resist. On social media, the problem is not one of control, but of chaos. The ferocious pace with which false information can spread can make defending the truth or correcting the record seem like mission impossible, or an invitation to opponents to double down in spreading deceit.

The problem of fraudulent news right now is compounded by social and political divisions that undercut the traditional ways in which truth ordinarily prevails. Investigations, exposés, and studies fall short in a situation where a significant portion of the population distrusts a wide array of sources they perceive as politically or ideologically hostile — including sources that traditionally commanded broad if not universal respect.

The debate over solutions to fraudulent [5] news has centered on what the government, news outlets, social media platforms, and civil society actors like fact-checking groups can do. Each has an important role to play, but they also must respect sharp limits to their interventions. Of course, no president should routinely denigrate legitimate news that he dislikes — as Donald Trump continually does. But Trump's misuse of his authority merely reminds us that it's for good reasons that the Constitution forbids the government from adjudicating which news is true and which is false. Google and Facebook, as private platforms, should monitor their sites to make sure that dangerous conspiracy theories don't go viral — but if they over-police what appears on their pages, they'll create new impairments for edgy speech. Certainly, news outlets should strive to uphold professional and ethical standards, but they alone can't convince cynical readers to trust them. Similarly, those who believe fake news tend to distrust the fact-checking outlets that try to tell them the stories are bogus.

Ultimately, the power of fake news is in the minds of the beholders — namely, news consumers. We need a news consumers' equivalent of the venerable Consumers Union that, starting in the 1930s, mobilized millions behind taking an informed approach to purchases, or the more recent drive to empower individuals to take charge of their health by reading labels, counting steps, and getting tested for risk factors.

When there were only a few dishwashers to choose from, buyers didn't need *Consumer Reports* to sort through their features and flaws. But when the appliance shopper began to face information overload, trusted arbiters were established to help them sort out the good from the bad. In decades past, news consumption centered on newspapers, magazines, and network shows that had undergone layers of editing and fact-checking. Most consumers saw little necessity to educate themselves about the political leanings of media owners, modes of attribution for quotes, journalistic sourcing protocols, the meaning of datelines, or other indicators of veracity.

Now, with the proliferation of overtly partisan media, lower barriers to entry into public discourse, and information flooding across the web and cable news, consumers need new tools to sort through choices and make informed decisions about where to invest their attention and trust. The fight against fake news will hinge not on inculcating trust in specific sources of authority but on instilling skepticism, curiosity, and a sense of agency among consumers, who are the best bulwark against the merchants of deceit.

A news consumers' movement should include several prongs, building on PEN America's newly released "News Consumers Bill of Rights and Responsibilities" from its new report, "Faking News: Fraudulent News and the Fight for Truth." The movement should furnish credible information to help consumers weigh the reliability of varied news sources. It should include an advocacy arm to prod newsrooms, internet platforms, and social media giants into being transparent about their decisions as to what news is elevated and how it is marked. This movement should advance news literacy curricula in schools and equip the next generation to navigate the information ocean they were born into. It should conduct outreach to diverse constituencies and strive continually to avoid ideological bias. It should develop an investigative research arm to expose, name, and shame the purveyors of fraudulent news and their financial backers. And it might provide periodic ranking of, and reporting on, newsrooms and other outlets to hold them accountable to their audiences. The movement should also mobilize the public to become good news consumers by encouraging them to apply a critical eye to news sources, favor those that are trustworthy, validate reports before sharing them on social media, and report errors when they see them.

10 Recognizing fraudulent news as a threat to free expression cannot be grounds to justify a cure — in the form of new government or corporate restrictions on speech — that may end up being worse than the disease. Unscrupulous profiteers and political opportunists may never cease in their efforts to infect the global information flow of information to serve their purposes. The best prescription against the epidemic of fake news is to inoculate consumers by building up their ability to defend themselves.

Topics for Critical Thinking and Writing

1. What problem does Suzanne Nossel identify for free speech advocates in paragraph 2? Why do you think she believes that free speech advocates should defend fake news despite its potential to spread falsehoods?
2. In paragraph 3, Nossel writes, "The power of free speech is inextricably tied to the opportunity to be heard and believed, and to persuade." In 250 words or so, explain how critical thinking provides both the means to support fake news and fight against it.
3. Examine Nossel's argument in paragraph 6. Do you agree or disagree with the idea of an organization that would label information sources – a sort of *Consumer Reports* for fake news? Do you think it would work? Why or why not?
4. What news sources do you rely upon, and why do you see them as credible and trustworthy? Trace your news sources and evaluate each of them. What criteria do they have to meet for you to trust them?

5. Do you believe that social media platforms like Facebook and Twitter are good for free speech in an open society or bad for it? Explain your answer in about 350 words, using specific examples to support your ideas.

CHARLES R. LAWRENCE III

Charles R. Lawrence III (b. 1943), author of numerous articles in law journals and coauthor of *We Won't Go Back: Making the Case for Affirmative Action* (1997), teaches law at the William S. Richardson School of Law at the University of Hawai'i at Manoa. This essay originally appeared in the *Chronicle of Higher Education* (October 25, 1989), a publication read chiefly by faculty and administrators at colleges and universities. An amplified version of the essay appeared in the *Duke Law Journal* (February 1990).

On Racist Speech

I have spent the better part of my life as a dissenter. As a high school student, I was threatened with suspension for my refusal to participate in a civil defense drill, and I have been a conspicuous consumer of my First Amendment liberties ever since. There are very strong reasons for protecting even racist speech. Perhaps the most important of these is that such protection reinforces our society's commitment to tolerance as a value, and that by protecting bad speech from government regulation, we will be forced to combat it as a community.

But I also have a deeply felt apprehension about the resurgence of racial violence and the corresponding rise in the incidence of verbal and symbolic assault and harassment to which blacks and other traditionally subjugated and excluded groups are subjected. I am troubled by the way the debate has been framed in response to the recent surge of racist incidents on college and university campuses and in response to some universities' attempts to regulate harassing speech. The problem has been framed as one in which the liberty of free speech is in conflict with the elimination of racism. I believe this has placed the bigot on the moral high ground and fanned the rising flames of racism.

Above all, I am troubled that we have not listened to the real victims, that we have shown so little understanding of their injury, and that we have abandoned those whose race, gender, or sexual preference continues to make them second-class citizens. It seems to me a very sad irony that the first instinct of civil libertarians has been to challenge even the smallest, most narrowly framed efforts by universities to provide black and other minority students with the protection the Constitution guarantees them.

The landmark case of *Brown v. Board of Education* is not a case that we normally think of as a case about speech. But *Brown* can be broadly read as articulating the principle of equal citizenship. *Brown* held that segregated schools were inherently unequal because of the *message* that segregation conveyed — that black children were an untouchable caste, unfit to go to school with white children. If we understand the necessity of eliminating the system of signs and symbols that signal the inferiority of blacks, then we should hesitate before proclaiming that all racist speech that stops short of physical violence must be defended.

5 University officials who have formulated policies to respond to incidents of racial harassment have been characterized in the press as "thought police," but such policies generally do nothing more than impose sanctions against intentional face-to-face insults. When racist speech takes the form of face-to-face insults, catcalls, or other assaultive speech aimed at an individual or small group of persons, it falls directly within the "fighting words" exception to First Amendment protection. The Supreme Court has held that words which "by their very utterance inflict injury or tend to incite an immediate breach of the peace" are not protected by the First Amendment.

If the purpose of the First Amendment is to foster the greatest amount of speech, racial insults disserve that purpose. Assaultive racist speech functions as a preemptive strike. The invective is experienced as a blow, not as a proffered idea, and once the blow is struck, it is unlikely that a dialogue will follow. Racial insults are particularly undeserving of First Amendment protection because the perpetrator's intention is not to discover truth or initiate dialogue but to injure the victim. In most situations, members of minority groups realize that they are likely to lose if they respond to epithets by fighting and are forced to remain silent and submissive.

Courts have held that offensive speech may not be regulated in public forums such as streets where the listener may avoid the speech by moving on, but the regulation of otherwise protected speech has been permitted when the speech invades the privacy of the unwilling listener's home or when the unwilling listener cannot avoid the speech. Racist posters, fliers, and graffiti in dormitories, bathrooms, and other common living spaces would seem to clearly fall within the reasoning of these cases. Minority students should not be required to remain in their rooms in order to avoid racial assault. Minimally, they should find a safe haven in their dorms and in all other common rooms that are a part of their daily routine.

I would also argue that the university's responsibility for ensuring that these students receive an equal educational opportunity provides a compelling justification for regulations that ensure them safe passage in all common areas. A minority student should not have to risk becoming the target of racially assaulting speech every time he or she chooses to walk across campus. Regulating vilifying speech that cannot be anticipated or avoided would not preclude announced speeches and rallies — situations that would give minority-group members and their allies the chance to organize counterdemonstrations or avoid the speech altogether.

The most commonly advanced argument against the regulation of racist speech proceeds something like this: We recognize that minority groups suffer pain and injury as the result of racist speech, but we must allow this hate mongering for the benefit of society as a whole. Freedom of speech is the lifeblood of our democratic system. It is especially important for minorities because often it is their only vehicle for rallying support for the redress of their grievances. It will be impossible to formulate a prohibition so precise that it will prevent the racist speech you want to suppress without catching in the same net all kinds of speech that it would be unconscionable for a democratic society to suppress.

Whenever we make such arguments, we 10 are striking a balance on the one hand between our concern for the continued free flow of ideas and the democratic process dependent on that flow, and, on the other, our desire to further the cause of equality. There can be no meaningful discussion of how we should reconcile our commitment to equality and our commitment to free speech until it is acknowledged that there is real harm inflicted by racist speech and that this harm is far from trivial.

To engage in a debate about the First Amendment and racist speech without a full understanding of the nature and extent of that harm is to risk making the First Amendment an instrument of domination rather than a vehicle of liberation. We have not all known the experience of victimization by racist, misogynist, and homophobic speech, nor do we equally share the burden of the societal harm it inflicts. We are often quick to say that we have heard the cry of the victims when we have not.

The *Brown* case is again instructive because it speaks directly to the psychic injury inflicted by racist speech by noting that the symbolic message of segregation affected "the hearts and minds" of Negro children "in a way unlikely ever to be undone." Racial epithets and harassment often cause deep emotional scarring and feelings of anxiety and fear that pervade every aspect of a victim's life.

Brown also recognized that black children did not have an equal opportunity to learn and participate in the school community if they bore the additional burden of being subjected to the humiliation and psychic assault contained in the message of segregation. University students bear an analogous burden when they are forced to live and work in an environment where at any moment they may be subjected to denigrating verbal harassment and assault. The same injury was addressed by the Supreme Court when it held that sexual harassment that creates a hostile or abusive work environment violates the ban on sex discrimination in employment of Title VII of the Civil Rights Act of 1964.

Carefully drafted university regulations would bar the use of words as assault weapons and leave unregulated even the most heinous of ideas when those ideas are presented at times and places and in manners that provide an opportunity for reasoned rebuttal or escape from immediate injury. The history of the development of the right to free speech has been one of carefully evaluating the importance of free expression and its effects on other important societal interests. We have drawn the line between protected and unprotected speech before without dire results. (Courts have, for example, exempted from the protection of the First Amendment obscene speech and speech that disseminates official secrets, that defames or libels another person, or that is used to form a conspiracy or monopoly.)

15 Blacks and other people of color are skeptical about the argument that even the most injurious speech must remain unregulated because, in an unregulated marketplace of ideas, the best ones will rise to the top and gain acceptance. Our experience tells us quite the opposite. We have seen too many good liberal politicians shy away from the issues that might brand them as being too closely allied with us.

Whenever we decide that racist speech must be tolerated because of the importance of maintaining societal tolerance for all unpopular speech, we are asking blacks and other subordinated groups to bear the burden for the good of all. We must be careful that the ease with which we strike the balance against the regulation of racist speech is in no way influenced by the fact that the cost will be borne by others. We must be certain that those who will pay that price are fairly represented in our deliberations and that they are heard.

At the core of the argument that we should resist all government regulation of speech is the ideal that the best cure for bad speech is good, that ideas that affirm equality and the worth of all individuals will ultimately prevail. This is an empty ideal unless those of us who would fight racism are vigilant and unequivocal in that fight. We must look for ways to offer assistance and support to students whose speech and political participation are chilled in a climate of racial harassment.

Civil rights lawyers might consider suing on behalf of blacks whose right to an equal education is denied by a university's failure to ensure a nondiscriminatory educational climate or conditions of employment. We must embark upon the development of a First Amendment jurisprudence grounded in the reality of our history and our contemporary experience. We must think hard about how best to launch legal attacks against the most indefensible forms of hate speech. Good lawyers can create exceptions and narrow interpretations that limit the harm of hate speech without opening the floodgates of censorship.

Everyone concerned with these issues must find ways to engage actively in actions that resist and counter the racist ideas that we would have the First Amendment protect. If we fail in this, the victims of hate speech must rightly assume that we are on the oppressors' side.

Topics for Critical Thinking and Writing

1. Summarize Charles Lawrence's essay in a paragraph. (You may find it useful first to summarize each paragraph in a sentence and then to revise these summary sentences into a paragraph.)
2. In one sentence, state Lawrence's thesis (his main point).
3. Why do you suppose Lawrence included his first paragraph? What does it contribute to his argument?
4. In paragraph 8, Lawrence speaks of "racially assaulting speech" and of "vilifying speech." It's easy to think of words that fit these descriptions, but what about other words? Is *Uncle Tom,* used by an African American about another African American who is eager to please whites, an example of "racially assaulting speech"? Or consider the word *gay.* Surely this word is acceptable because it's widely used by homosexuals, but what about *queer* (used by some homosexuals but sometimes derogatory when used by heterosexuals)? What might make these words seem "assaulting" or "vilifying"?
5. Find out if your college or university has a code — perhaps online — governing hate speech. If it does, summarize and evaluate it in no more than 500 words, capturing its key provisions and requirements. If your college has no such code, make a case for why such a policy should be developed and made available to students and faculty.

ASSIGNMENTS FOR CRITICAL READING

Definition in Three Parts

1. Construct a definition (three to five sentences) of *cyberbullying*. If you use sources, cite them.
2. Find a technical definition of cyberbullying as defined by a law, rule, or code, and compare it to your definition in exercise 1 above. What limits and restrictions are included? (Be sure to cite your source.)
3. Given the admittedly scanty information that we have on the Evans case, do you think a suspension was reasonable in light of the definitions of cyberbullying above? If you think it was reasonable, explain why. If you think it was unreasonable, explain why. Indicate also whether you think a different punishment might have been appropriate. Your essay should be about 250 to 300 words in length.

Letter to the Editor

Your college newspaper has published a letter that links a hateful attribute to a group and that clearly displays hatred for the entire group. (For instance, the letter charges that interracial marriages should be made illegal because "African Americans carry a criminal gene" or that "Jews should not be elected to office because their loyalty is to Israel, not the United States" or that "Muslims should not be allowed to enter the country because they are intent on destroying America.") The letter generates many letters of response; some, supporting the editor's decision to publish the letter, make these points:

- The writer of the offending letter is a student in the college, and she has a right to express her views.
- The point of view expressed is probably held only by a few persons, but conceivably it expresses a view held by a significant number of students.
- Editors should not act as censors.
- The First Amendment guarantees freedom of speech.
- Freedom of expression is healthy — that is, society gains.

In contrast, among the letters opposing the editor's decision to publish, some make points along these lines:

- Not every view of every nutty student can be printed; editors must make responsible choices.
- The First Amendment, which prohibits the government from controlling the press, has nothing to do with a college newspaper.
- Letters of this sort do not foster healthy discussion; they merely heat things up.

Write a 250- to 500-word letter to the editor expressing your view of the decision to publish the first letter. (If you wish, you can assume that the letter addressed one of the topics we specify in the second sentence of this exercise. In any case, address the general issue of the editor's decision, not just the specific issue of the charge or charges made in the first letter.)

Critical Summary

Write a critical summary of an essay you have read in this book. In a critical summary, you are relating the argument, but along the way adding your opinion and perspective, commenting on the quality of evidence, pointing out where the argument succeeds and fails, and asking further questions.

Use the moves in the following list to guide your summary, and refer to the Visual Guide: Writing a Critical Summary on page 55. You can combine some of these moves into one sentence, reorder information, provide quotations, and begin problematizing at any point by inserting your position through careful use of words and phrases, adding an evaluative sentence of your own, or providing commentary on a quote or paraphrase from the essay.

- **Introduce:** Provide the author and title and contextualize the information.
- **Explain:** Identify and describe the thesis and argument.
- **Exemplify:** Provide some of the author's original evidence.
- **Problematize:** Pose critical questions or provide an evaluation of the argument.
- **Extend:** Ask further questions or apply, test, or consider the argument in ways that support your evaluation of it.

For more on writing a critical summary, see the following sections in Chapter 2: Summarizing and Paraphrasing (pp. 46–49), Patchwriting and Plagiarism (pp. 49–50), and A Checklist for a Summary (p. 59).

3

Critical Reading: Getting Deeper into Arguments

Not everything that is faced can be changed, but nothing can be changed until it is faced.
—JAMES BALDWIN

Persuasion, Argument, and Rhetorical Appeals

When we think seriously about an argument, not only do we encounter ideas that may be unfamiliar, but also we are forced to examine our own cherished opinions—and perhaps for the first time really see the strengths and weaknesses of what we believe. As the philosopher John Stuart Mill put it, "He who knows only his own side of the case knows little."

It is useful to distinguish between **persuasion** and **argument**. Persuasion has the broader meaning. To **persuade** is to convince someone else to accept or adopt your position. To be persuasive does not necessarily mean your argument is sound. Persuasion can be accomplished

- by giving reasons (i.e., by argument, by logic);
- by appealing to the emotions; or
- by bullying, lying to, or threatening someone.

Argument, we mean to say, represents only one form of persuasion, but a special one: one that elevates the cognitive or intellectual capacity for reason. Rhetoricians often use the Greek word ***logos***, which means "word" or "reason," to denote this aspect of persuasive writing. An appeal to reason may by conducted by using such things as

- physical evidence, data, and facts;
- the testimony of experts, authorities, or respected persons;
- common sense; or
- probability.

Visual Guide: Evaluating Persuasive Appeals

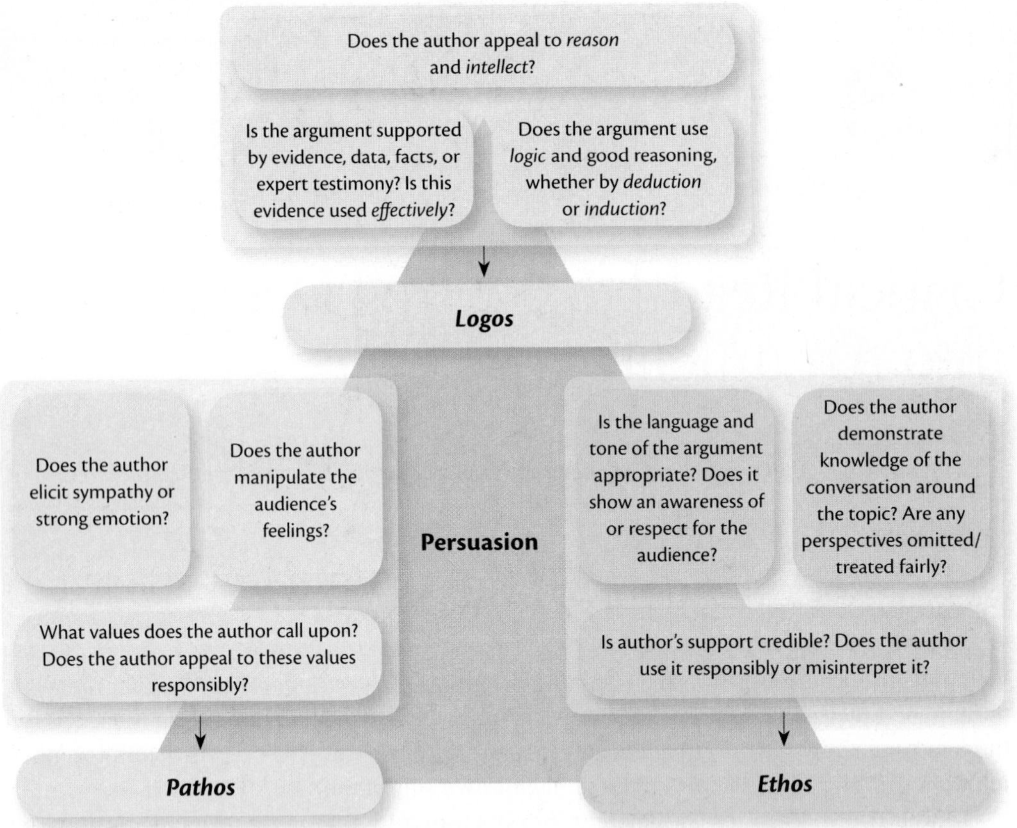

Put it this way: The goal of *argument* is to convince by demonstrating the truth (or probable truth) of an assertion, whereas the goal of *persuasion* is simply to convince by any means whatsoever. ***Logos***, the root word of *logic*, means appealing to the intellect to make rational claims and reasoned judgments.

An appeal to the emotions is known as ***pathos***, which is Greek for "feeling," and elicits the sym*path*ies (note the root word here) in one form or another. Appeals to the sympathies may call upon any number of emotions, such as anger, fear, pity, or envy, or they may call upon passionate feelings about honor, duty, family, or patriotism. In critical thinking, we may be tempted to privilege the mind (*logos*) over the heart (*pathos*), but we must note that emotions inform decision-making in important ways, too, and most arguments use *logos* and *pathos*, reason and passion, in different degrees. Most of this book is about argument in the sense of presenting reasonable support of claims, but reason is not the whole story.

If an argument is to be effective, it must be presented persuasively, and writers may convincingly call upon readers' feelings to make a sound argument. Consider two broad arguments that were made in 2018 about the Department of Homeland Security's policy of separating families of illegal immigrants at the US–Mexico border. Many conservatives argued by appealing to reason: The law requires all illegal immigrants to be detained and

John Moore/Getty Images News/Getty Images

Images of children held in detention centers, such as this one from 2014, appealed to the emotions of Americans in 2018. What aspects of this photograph make it particularly convincing as an appeal to emotions and values?

processed, and children need special accommodations and, therefore, separate detention centers. However, many liberals argued by appealing primarily to emotions, using heart-rending images and stories of incarcerated children separated from their parents to inspire public outcry. In response, just over a month after it started, President Donald Trump signed an executive order stopping the practice of separating families at the border.

In short, emotion won the day over reason — yet in no way can we say that feelings led us astray. Emotions can, in fact, guide us toward wise choices because emotions are often closely connected to values, ideals, morals, ethics, and principles. Feelings can impassion us to make rash decisions, sure, but they can also inspire bold ones. And reason, a powerful tool of the intellect, can just as soon lead us toward the dark rather than the light. As the poet Emily Dickinson wrote, "Much madness is divinest sense / To a discerning eye / Much sense the starkest madness." To conduct our lives strictly according to pure reason *or* pure feeling would lead, we think, to an intolerable existence in either case. We rely upon both of these faculties, and we need both kinds of appeals.

Because of this, most arguments do not divide easily along the lines of *logos* and *pathos*. Nor do arguments always imply two opposing speakers and positions. Of course, arguments *may* put reason and passion in opposition and present clearly opposing positions, but it is not a *requirement* that arguments do so, nor that they contain any special degree of *logos* or *pathos*. For example, the Declaration of Independence is an argument, one that sets forth the colonists' reasons for declaring their independence (*logos*) but also includes powerful language that condemns tyranny and appeals to "Life, Liberty, and the Pursuit of Happiness," words that evoke strong emotion (*pathos*). Even everyday arguments utilize both kinds of appeals. If you were explaining to your parents why you are changing your major, you might supply reasons and justifications for your decision (perhaps by comparing statistics about overall costs, future income potential, and job prospects), thus constructing a *rational* argument based on *logos*, but you may also be appealing to your family's passionate beliefs about happiness, using emotional persuasion to convince them you are making the right choice.

WRITING TIP

An argument doesn't require two opposing positions. Even when writing only for oneself, trying to clarify one's thinking by setting forth reasons and justifications for an idea, the result is an argument.

In addition to *logos* and *pathos*, the Greek philosopher Aristotle (384–322 BCE) defined a third type of rhetorical appeal. ***Ethos***, the Greek word for "character," involves the careful presentation of self, what Aristotle called "the speaker's personal character when the speech is so spoken as to make us think him credible" (*Rhetoric* 1.2.1356a.4-15). Aristotle emphasized the importance of impressing upon the audience that the speaker is a person of authority, good sense, and moral integrity. When writers convey their *ethos*, their trustworthiness or good character, they may

- establish authority and credibility (e.g., by demonstrating or stating expertise, credentials, or experience),
- use language appropriate to the setting (e.g., by avoiding vulgar language, slang, and colloquialism),
- demonstrate familiarity with their audience (e.g., by achieving the right tone and level of complexity),
- show fair-mindedness (e.g., by offering other points of view in goodwill and by recognizing that contrary points of view may have some merit), or
- show attention to detail (e.g., by citing relevant statistics and careful interpretation of evidence).

THINKING CRITICALLY *Identifying Ethos*

For each method listed, locate a sentence in one of the readings in this book. Provide a quotation that shows the author establishing *ethos*.

METHOD	EXAMPLES	YOUR TURN
Use personal experience or credentials to establish authority.	"As a student who works and attends school full-time, I can speak firsthand about . . ."	
Acknowledge weaknesses, exceptions, and complexities.	"Although I have shown that X is important, investigation into Y is also necessary to truly understand . . ." "Understandably, my solution may be seen as too simple or reductive, but it may work as a starting point for . . ."	
Mention the qualifications of any sources as a way to boost your own credibility.	"According to X, author and noted professor of Y at Z University, . . ."	

In short, writers who are concerned with *ethos* — and all writers should be — employ devices that persuade readers that they are reliable, intelligent persons in whom their readers can have confidence.

Reason, Rationalization, and Confirmation Bias

We know that if we set our minds to a problem, we can often find reasons (not always necessarily sound ones) for almost anything we want to justify. In an entertaining example from Benjamin Franklin's *Autobiography*, Franklin tells of being hungry and wrestling with his vegetarianism on a voyage from Boston while watching his fellow passengers hauling in cod from the sea:

> Hitherto I had stuck to my resolution of not eating animal food, and on this occasion, I considered with my master Tryon the taking of every fish as a kind of unprovoked murder, since none of them had or ever could do us any injury that might justify the slaughter. All this seemed very reasonable.

However, once the fish was fried,

> it smelt admirably well. I balanced some time between principle and inclination, till I recollected that when the fish were opened I saw smaller fish taken out of their stomachs. Then thought I, if you eat one another, I don't see why we mayn't eat you. So I dined upon cod very heartily and continued to eat with other people, returning only now and then occasionally to a vegetable diet. So convenient a thing it is to be a *reasonable creature*, since it enables one to find or make a reason for everything one has a mind to do.

Franklin is being playful in commenting on how rationalizations work, but he touches on a truth: If necessary, we can find reasons to justify whatever we want. That is, instead of reasoning, we may *rationalize* (a self-serving but dishonest form of reasoning), like the fox in Aesop's fables who, finding the grapes he desired were out of reach, consoled himself with the thought that they were probably sour.

Another aspect of rationalization is **confirmation bias**. Confirmation bias is a type of cognitive bias that describes the tendency to seek out, find, and employ evidence that reinforces our inclinations or preexisting beliefs. In this process, only *confirmatory* ideas, information, and data are accounted for and taken seriously while disconfirming data are ignored or treated with skepticism. In other words, whether consciously or unconsciously, we ignore the full picture, disregard other perspectives without first listening to them, and search only for support for our position, no matter how credible or representative it is. Cognitive bias occurs most when deeply ingrained beliefs or views impede our ability to interpret information fairly. It also occurs when students write papers and research only tidbits of sources — easy quotes or factoids — that support their thesis, rather than fully reading the source material to get the full picture of what the source's argument is. (Be careful of this in your own writing; cherry-picking evidence from sources often leads to misinterpretation, which will damage your own *ethos*.)

Perhaps we can never be certain that we aren't rationalizing or falling victim to confirmation bias, except when being playful like Franklin. But we can think critically about how our own reasoning process can be affected by our own self-interest, beliefs, and worldviews. The more we can be alert to the ways these shape our thinking, the more fairly we can reason.

Types of Reasoning

Reason may not be the only way of finding the truth, but it is a way on which we often rely when making arguments, whether we are making them to ourselves or others. Traditionally, arguments are often said to be **inductive** or **deductive**; that is, to proceed along two different pathways toward their conclusions. (We spend some time discussing logical reasoning here, but a more in depth discussion can also be found in Chapter 9, A Logician's View: Deduction, Induction, and Fallacies.)

INDUCTION

Inductive reasoning, or *induction,* is essentially a process of thinking in which patterns of evidence and examples accumulate until the thinker draws a reasonable conclusion from what has been observed. One might say, for example: "In my experience, the subway always arrives promptly at 6:00 a.m., so I infer from this evidence that it will also run promptly today at 6:00 a.m." Induction uses information about observed cases to reach a conclusion about unobserved cases.

The word *induction* comes from the Latin *in ducere,* "to lead into" or "to lead up to." In inductive reasoning, we draw from the specific to make generalizations about reality. We discern patterns and expand toward an explanation or a theory. If, on a fishing trip, a green-eyed horsefly bites you (specific incident), you may reasonably conclude that other flies like it in the area will also bite you (generalization). Although it seems obvious, you used induction to infer a conclusion. Your inferences might be even broader: You may be tempted to generalize that these green-eyed horseflies are native to the area and that other fishing streams in the area are likely to have them. Induction has taken your reasoning from a specific example to a general theory of reality.

WRITING TIP
By far the most common way to test the adequacy of an inductive argument is to consider one or more **counterexamples**. If the counterexamples are numerous, genuine, and reliable, the generalization can be challenged.

DEDUCTION

In Latin, the term *deduction* means "lead down from," the opposite of induction's tendency "to lead up to." *Deductive reasoning* is the mental process of moving down from one given, true statement through another true statement to produce a reasonable conclusion. That is to say, the generalizations come first, and the specific conclusion is, because of them, therefore proven true.

One of the best ways to think through an argument, especially a deductive argument, is to use a syllogism, so in the next section we examine more closely how syllogisms work.

PREMISES AND SYLLOGISMS

In classical argument, a **syllogism** — Latin for "a reckoning together" — is often used to show the truth or factuality of a conclusion. A syllogism shows two or more propositions called **premises** that are given, or assumed to be true. The word *premise* comes from a Latin word meaning "to set in front." A deductive argument is said to be **valid** if its internal logic is so strong that it makes it impossible for the premises to be true and the conclusion nevertheless to be false. A classical syllogism therefore joins the premises with a third statement presented as a logical conclusion. Thus, premises are set down before the argument begins.

The classic example of a syllogism is this:

Premise: All human beings are mortal.

Premise: Socrates is a human being.

Conclusion: Socrates is mortal.

The purpose of a syllogism is simply to present reasons that establish the truth of a conclusion. Truth can be demonstrated if the argument satisfies both of two independent criteria:

1. All of the premises *must be true*.
2. The syllogism *must be valid*.

If each premise is *true* and the syllogism is *valid*, then the argument is said to be **sound**.

SOUND ARGUMENTS: TRUE AND VALID But how do we tell in any given case if an argument is sound? We can perform two different tests, one for the *truth* of each of the premises and another for the overall *validity* of the conclusions drawn from the premises.

The basic test for the **truth** of a premise is to determine whether what it asserts corresponds with reality; if it does, then it is true, and if it doesn't, then it is false. The truth of a premise depends on its content — what it asserts — and the evidence provided for it.

The basic test for **validity** is different. A valid argument is one in which the conclusion *necessarily follows* from the premises, so that if all the premises are true, then the conclusion must be true, too. Consider this syllogism:

Extracting oil from the Arctic Wildlife Refuge would adversely affect the local ecology.

Adversely affecting the local ecology is undesirable unless there is no better alternative fuel source.

Alex Segre/Shutterstock.com

The great fictional detective Sherlock Holmes was credited with having unusual powers of deduction. Holmes could see the logical consequences of many and apparently disconnected premises.

Therefore, extracting oil from the Arctic Wildlife Refuge is undesirable unless there is no better alternative fuel source.

Here, if we grant the premises to be true and the conclusion necessarily follows from the premises, then the argument is valid.

VALID BUT NOT SOUND Part of being a good critical thinker is the ability to analyze the premises and determine the validity and soundness of an argument. The problem is that arguments can have many premises, or premises that are quite complex, making it difficult to ascertain their truth. Suppose that one or more of a syllogism's premises are false but the syllogism itself is valid. What does that indicate about the truth of the conclusion? Consider this example:

All Americans prefer vanilla ice cream to other flavors.

Jimmy Fallon is an American.

Therefore, Jimmy Fallon prefers vanilla ice cream to other flavors.

The first (or major) premise in this syllogism is false. Yet the argument passes our formal test for validity: If one grants both premises, then one must accept the conclusion. So we can say that the conclusion *follows from* its premises, even though the premises *do not prove* the conclusion. This is not as paradoxical as it may sound. For all we know, the argument's conclusion may in fact be true; Jimmy Fallon may indeed prefer vanilla ice cream, and the odds are that he does because consumption statistics show that a majority of Americans prefer vanilla. Nevertheless, if the conclusion in this syllogism is true, it's not because this argument proved it.

TRUE BUT NOT VALID Some arguments may have true premises yet nevertheless have false conclusions. This occurs when the premises are not related to one another, or when conclusions do not *necessarily* follow from the premises. Consider this syllogism:

X minority group is disadvantaged in schools.

John Doe is a member of *X* minority group.

Therefore, John Doe is disadvantaged in school.

Here, let's grant that the premises are true. Let's also grant that the conclusion may well be true: John Doe could indeed be disadvantaged. But it's also possible that the conclusion is false. Suppose you were to argue that minority groups aren't the only ones who are disadvantaged. Consider, for example, how a learning disability may affect a student's success. In short, the truth of the two premises is no guarantee that the conclusion is also true.

Chemists may use litmus paper to determine instantly whether the liquid in a test tube is an acid or a base; unfortunately, we cannot subject most arguments to a litmus test like this to determine their reasonability. Logicians beginning with Aristotle have developed techniques to test any given argument, no matter how complex or subtle, for centuries; we cannot hope to express the results of their labor in a few pages. Apart from advising you to consult Chapter 9, A Logician's View: Deduction, Induction, and Fallacies, all we can do here is reiterate the core questions you must always ask when evaluating any argument:

- Is it vulnerable to criticism on the grounds that one (or more) of its premises is false?
- Does one of the premises not necessarily relate to another premise?
- Even if all the premises were true, would the conclusion still not necessarily follow?

ENTHYMEMES Much reasoning that occurs in writing happens in a form of a special form called an **enthymeme**, an incomplete or abbreviated syllogism in which a conclusion is drawn without stating one or more of the premises. To use the classical example, we might say

> Socrates is mortal because he is human.

Here, the unstated premise is that all humans are mortal; the premise is missing but remains operative.

We can reason better about what we read and write by thinking about the things that "go without saying." The rhetoric of advertisers and politicians, for example, can sometimes be dismantled by thinking about how enthymemes work to hide the implicit premises. Consider the following claim:

> You will improve your complexion by using Clear-Away.

The premises and conclusion here might be presented as a syllogism:

Unstated premise:	All people who use Clear-Away improve their complexion.
Premise:	You use Clear-Away.
Conclusion:	You will improve your complexion.

Or consider this example:

> Jim Hartman doesn't know accurate statistics on crime in his state; therefore, he is unqualified to be governor.

Bob Mankoff/Cartoon Stock

This might be stated as this syllogism:

> People who do not know accurate statistics about crime in their states are unqualified to be governor.
>
> Jim Hartman doesn't know accurate statistics.
>
> Jim Hartman is unqualified to be governor.

Occasionally, it is not the premises that are unstated in an enthymeme, but the conclusions that are left out. Consider this example:

> Lucky Charms breakfast cereal is fortified with vitamins!

The premises and conclusion might be stated this way:

> All food fortified with vitamins is healthy.
>
> Lucky Charms cereal is a food fortified with vitamins.
>
> Lucky Charms cereal is healthy.

Just these few examples should indicate that our alertness to the unstated premises or conclusions of an enthymeme can be valuable.

A WORD ON WEAK AND INVALID ARGUMENTS Inductive and deductive arguments can both be critically examined and challenged by searching for weaknesses in their premises or weaknesses in the inferences that lead to their conclusions. Below, for example, you will see an inductive argument presented as a syllogism. (Inductive arguments are not typically presented as such; when they are, they are called "statistical" or "nondeductive" syllogisms.) Working inductively, however, we can present two premises based on observations and draw a generalization:

> Every fish we have taken from the harbor has a fungus.
>
> Every fish we observed with the fungus has died.
>
> All the fish in the harbor are dying of a fungus.

Now, examine the probability of this conclusion. It may well be true that all the fish in the harbor are dying, yet this is still not a *valid* conclusion. It is not valid because the conclusion does not *necessarily follow* from the premises. In fact, inductive arguments are not referred to as valid or invalid at all, or sound or unsound, but as *strong* or *weak* depending on the probability of the conclusion. The example above has *weak induction* because we do not have information about *how many or what types of fish were sampled* or further *what other factors might have contributed to the deaths of the sampled fish.*

When we reason inductively, weaknesses frequently lie in the size and the quality of the **sample**. If we're offering an argument concerning the political leanings of sorority and fraternity members at our campus, we cannot interview *every* member, so instead we select a sample. But we must ask if the sample is a fair one: Is it representative of the larger group? We may interview five members of Alpha Tau Omega and find that all five are Republicans, yet we cannot conclude

WRITING TIP
An argument that uses samples ought to tell the reader how the samples were chosen. If it doesn't provide this information, the reader should treat the argument with suspicion.

that all members of fraternities at our school are Republicans. To get a more *representative sample*, we would measure opinions from across the various sororities and fraternities.

A larger sample doesn't necessarily mean a *representative* one, however. A poll of the political leanings of college students would tell us very little if it included only students at small private colleges. We could not use that data to extrapolate about *all* college students. Ask yourself: Why not?

Inductive arguments are susceptible to challenges because they tend to generalize, or "lead up" from observations to a conclusion. They are always contingent upon new observations and new data and are susceptible to overgeneralization (which occurs when we extend the application or relevancy of the observed cases too far). Deductive arguments, on the other hand, which "lead down" from their premises toward a conclusion, often posit facts or principles as their premises. Therefore, because deduction can (although it does not always) produce incontrovertible truths, deductive arguments tend to be more reliable than inductive arguments, which can be very strong but never attain 100 percent certainty. When they are sound, deductive arguments based on incontrovertibly true premises provide an *absolutely* necessary conclusion.

Some Procedures in Argument

DEFINITIONS

In our current discussion, we are primarily analyzing the logic of arguments — the *logos* — and prioritizing the procedures of thinking and argument that emphasize reason. Another important element to this kind of thought is *definition*. Earlier, in the section Defining Terms and Concepts in Chapter 2 (pp. 44–45), we discussed how definitions of key terms and concepts underpin arguments. As to whether or not a local stream is "polluted," for example, you may use a strict (terminological) or loose (conceptual) definition of the word *pollution* to argue either way. You might define the word *pollution* as a term set forth by your state's environmental protection agency, which perhaps requires that water contains a minimum threshold of toxins, or you might describe *pollution* according to your own concept of having a lot of garbage lying alongside of it. Either definition may help you argue for a state cleanup effort. When we define key words, we're answering the question "What is it?" and setting out our definition for the purposes of the argument at hand. In answering this question as precisely as we can, we can then find, clarify, and develop ideas accordingly.

Trying to decide the best way to define key terms and concepts is often difficult — and sometimes controversial. Consider one of the most contentious debates in our society: abortion rights. Many arguments about abortion depend on a definition of "life." Traditionally, human life has been seen as beginning at birth. Nowadays, most people see "life" as something that begins at least at viability (the capacity of a fetus to live independently of the uterine environment). But modern science has made it possible to see the beginning of "life" in different ways. Some who want abortion to be prohibited by law define life as beginning with *brain birth*, the point at which "integrated brain functioning begins to emerge." Still others see life beginning as early as fertilization. Whatever the merits of these definitions, the debate itself is convincing evidence of just how important it can be to define your important terms and concepts when making arguments.

STIPULATION When you are writing, you may define your terms and concepts by **stipulating** definitions. The word *stipulate* comes from the Latin verb *stipulari*, meaning "to bargain" or "to secure a guarantee." When you stipulate, you ask the reader to agree with a certain definition for the sake of the argument at hand (although, of course, a reader may not want to make that bargain). For example, you may write one of the following:

- If we can agree the definition of *X* is *Y*, then . . .
- If we can agree the strict definition of *X* does not include *Y*, then . . .

Establishing your definition then allows the reader to consider and evaluate your argument according to your definition.

In contracts, you can often find stipulated definitions made very explicitly because, in a legal context, key terms need to be precisely defined and agreed upon by all parties to avoid disputes. For example, consider this language from a portion of a California home insurance policy covering damage caused by an earthquake:

> For the purposes of this policy . . . the term Earthquake shall mean seismic activity, including earth movement, landslide, mudslide, sinkhole, subsidence, volcanic eruption, or Tsunami, as defined herein. . . . The term Tsunami shall mean a wave or series of waves caused by underwater earthquakes and/or seismic activity, including, but not limited to, volcanic eruptions, landslides, earth movement, mudslide, sinkhole, or subsidence. In no event shall this Company be liable for any loss caused directly or indirectly by fire, explosion or other excluded perils as defined herein.

Parties mutually agree to certain definitions by signing the contract itself. Other forms of writing also require comprehensive definitions. For instance, if you were a legislator writing a law to limit "internet gambling" in your state, you must have a very precise definition of what that means. (The actual legal definition of internet gambling in the US legal code is more than 1,000 words!)

You do not have to be writing a contract or a law to make stipulative definitions. In your arguments, you may stipulate a definition in the following cases:

- when you are seeking to secure a shared understanding of the meaning of a term or concept
- when no fixed or standard definition is available

If you are call something *undemocratic*, you must define what you mean by *democratic*. If you call a painting or a poem a *masterpiece*, you may want to try to define that word, perhaps by offering criteria art must meet to be called a masterpiece. What is your definition of what it means for a nation to *advance*? What definition of *cruel and unusual punishment* will you use in your argument about solitary confinement? How are you defining *food insecurity* in your call to end hunger on campus? Not everyone may accept your stipulative definitions, and there will likely be defensible alternatives. However, when you stipulate a definition, your audience knows what *you* mean by the term.

Consider the opening paragraph of a 1975 essay by Richard B. Brandt titled "The Morality and Rationality of Suicide." Notice that the author does two things:

- He first stipulates a definition.
- Then, aware that the definition may strike some readers as too broad and therefore unreasonable or odd, he offers a reason on behalf of his definition.

> "Suicide" is conveniently defined, for our purposes, as doing something which results in one's death, either from the intention of ending one's life or the intention to bring about some other state of affairs (such as relief from pain) which one thinks it certain or highly probable can be achieved only by means of death or will produce death. It may seem odd to classify an act of heroic self-sacrifice on the part of a soldier as suicide. It is simpler, however, not to try to define "suicide" so that an act of suicide is always irrational or immoral in some way; if we adopt a neutral definition like the above we can still proceed to ask when an act of suicide in that sense is rational, morally justifiable, and so on, so that all evaluations anyone might wish to make can still be made. (61)

Sometimes, a definition that at first seems extremely odd can be made acceptable by offering strong reasons in its support. Sometimes, in fact, an odd definition marks a great intellectual leap forward. For instance, in 1990 the US Supreme Court recognized that *speech* includes symbolic nonverbal expressions such as protesting against a war by wearing armbands or by flying the American flag upside down. Such actions — although they are nonverbal — are considered speech because they express ideas or emotions. More controversially, in 2010 the Supreme Court ruled in *Citizens United vs. Federal Election Commission* that corporate spending in the form of campaign contributions constitutes speech and cannot be limited under the First Amendment. This decision spurred unprecedented spending on elections by corporations and today remains a divisive definition of speech.

Our object with these examples is to make one overall point clear: An argument will be most fruitful if the participants first share an understanding of the concepts they are talking about.

SYNONYM One way to define a term or concept is through **synonym**. For example, *pornography* can be defined, at least roughly, as "obscenity" (something indecent). But definition by synonym is usually only a start; you then have to define or explain the synonym, too, because, in fact, *pornography* and *obscenity* are not exact synonyms. Imagine writing, "This company's strategy is essentially a *con game*" or "Spanking children is *child abuse*." In each case, synonyms were provided to help define the terms of the argument, but now the synonyms need to be explained.

EXAMPLE Another way to define a word is to point to an example (sometimes called an **ostensive definition**, from the Latin *ostendere*, "to show"). This method can be very helpful, ensuring that both writer and reader are talking about the same thing — and adding not only clarity but vivid detail. If you are reviewing a movie and you want to define "tween movies," you could point to specific examples of the kinds of films you mean. You could say that "tween movies" are those films marketed to a certain age demographic — young people between eight and sixteen years old — but the definition may be made concrete and visible by quickly surveying such films: "Tween movies include films that feature plots developed around preteen or teenage characters, such as *The Sandlot* (1993) and *High School Musical* (2006)." Or imagine you are attempting to define American folk heroes as those characters, whether based on real people or wholly invented, whose stories have been exaggerated and transformed in various genres, such as *Johnny Appleseed*, *John Henry*, and *Casey Jones*.

Definitions by example also have their limitations, so choosing the right examples, ones that have all the central or typical characteristics and that will best avoid misinterpretation, is important to using this method of definition effectively. A few decades ago, many people pointed to James Joyce's *Ulysses* and D. H. Lawrence's *Lady Chatterley's Lover* as examples of obscene novels. Today these books are regarded as literary masterpieces. It's possible that they can be obscene and also be literary masterpieces. (Joyce's wife is reported to have said of her husband, "He may have been a great writer, but . . . he had a very dirty mind.")

ESTABLISHING SUFFICIENT AND NECESSARY CONDITIONS A final way to define a term or concept is by establishing its *sufficient and necessary conditions*. For writers, this just means controlling definitions by offering certain preconditions. For example, if you say a "sport" is defined as any activity meeting *sufficient* conditions of competition and

Tom Cheney, The New Yorker Collection/The Cartoon Bank

"It all depends on how you define 'chop.'"

physical endurance, you can also argue that video gaming, which meets those criteria, may be called a sport. (See Matthew Walther's essay, "Sorry Nerds: Video Games Are Not a Sport," on p. 194 on this very subject.) If you were to argue vaping should not be subject to the same rules on your campus as smoking, you could define "smoking" as an activity requiring the *necessary* conditions of combustion and smoke, neither of which is a feature of a vaporizer.

One common way in formal logic to distinguish between sufficient and necessary conditions is to imagine them phrased as conditional propositions. Sufficient conditions are usually presented as "if, then" propositions, whereas necessary conditions are usually presented as "*if and only if*, then . . ." propositions. Suppose we want to define the word *circle* and are conscious of the need to keep circles distinct from other geometric figures such as rectangles and spheres. We might express our definition by citing sufficient and necessary conditions as follows: "Anything is a circle *if and only if* it is a closed plane figure and all points on the circumference are equidistant from the center." Using the connective "if and only if" between the definition and the term being defined helps make the definition neither too exclusive (too narrow) nor too inclusive (too broad). Of course, for most ordinary purposes we don't require such a formally precise definition.

Exercise: Definitions

Read the selections below and (a) identify the term or concept being defined; (b) explain which type of definition it is (stipulation, synonym, example); and (c) use details from the examples to support your answer.

> Marriage is primarily an economic arrangement, an insurance pact. It differs from the ordinary life insurance agreement only in that it is more binding, more exacting. Its returns are insignificantly small compared with the investments. In taking out an insurance policy one pays for it in dollars and cents, always at liberty to discontinue payments. If, however, woman's premium is a husband, she pays for it with her name, her privacy, her self-respect, her very life, "until death doth part."
>
> —Emma Goldman, *Marriage and Love* (1911)

> Pentagon spending is reaching into areas of American life previously neglected: entertainment, popular consumer brands, sports. Rick and Donna's home is full of this incursion. As they putter around the kitchen, getting ready for the day ahead, they move from the wall cabinets (purchased at DoD contractor Lowe's Home Center) to the refrigerator (from defense contractor Maytag), choosing their breakfast from a cavalcade of products made by Pentagon contractors. These companies that, quite literally, feed the Pentagon's war machine, are the same firms that fill the shelves of America's kitchens. . . . No part of the hours of the day will be lacking in products produced by Pentagon contractors . . . 3M Post-It notes, Microsoft Windows software, Lexmark printers, Canon Photocopiers, AT&T telephones, Maxwell House coffee from Altria.
>
> —Nicholas Turse, *The Complex* (2008)

A slander is a spoken defamation, whether that act of speech is public and one-time or recorded and redistributed. Slander also includes defamation by gesture, which could include making a gesture that suggests professional incompetence or mental illness. Slander carries the additional burden for a plaintiff of having to prove that they suffered actual loss due to the false statement.

—Mitch Ratcliffe, *How to Prevent Against Online Libel and Defamation* (2009)

When considering a subject as abstract and intangible as peace, it is important to define the term itself. In the context of this discussion, peace may be defined as it is in Webster's dictionary as a community's "freedom from civil disturbance, or a state of security or order provided for by law or custom."

—Kincaid Fitzgerald, *Peace in the Global Neighborhood* [student paper at Leiden University] (2018)

ASSUMPTIONS

Even the longest and most complex chains of reasoning or proof, and even most carefully constructed definitions, are fastened to assumptions—one or more *unexamined beliefs*. These taken-for-granted, hidden, or neglected beliefs affect how writers and readers make inferences and draw conclusions. If you attend a birthday party, you might *assume* that cake will be served. If the ceiling is wet, you may *assume* that the roof is leaking.

However, false assumptions can be dangerous. If you assume that a person of a certain race, class, or gender will behave in predictable ways, you may be stereotyping that individual and making guesses about that person's actions without evidence. If you assume that traffic will stop at a red light and you proceed through an intersection without looking, you could end up in a car crash. Suppose a business executive assumes that sales are down because of poor marketing and not the quality of her company's product; she could end up ignoring the real problem and wasting time and money on a new advertising campaign instead of improving the product.

Assumptions are sometimes deeply embedded in our value systems and therefore hard to recognize. Consider this case: When education researchers questioned race and class disparities on the SAT exam in the early 2000s, they found it odd that minorities and other economically disadvantaged students performed worse than their white, middle-class counterparts on the *easier* verbal and math questions, *not* the more difficult ones. That is, some basic vocabulary words like *horse* and *canoe* were likely to be misidentified by minority and lower-income students than more challenging words like *anathema* and *intractable*. (Colloquially, *horse* could be a verb, as in "play around," or it could refer to heroin. *Canoe*, meanwhile, describes what happens to a cigar when one side burns faster than another.) Researchers found that the problem was the assumptions made by the test designers, not the student test-takers. The more "difficult" words typically learned in school or in textbooks were understood more uniformly among all students. The test designers had assumed that persons of all socioeconomic groups hear language the same way and therefore that their proficiency could be measured using the same linguistic standards. By challenging the assumptions of the exam, researchers were able to challenge the disparities in exam results. As a result, college admissions boards began to regard the SAT as a weaker indicator of academic potential for some groups, while test designers began to address other deeply embedded assumptions in the exam.

Sometimes assumptions may be stated explicitly, especially when writers feel confident that readers share their values. Benjamin Franklin, for example, argued against paying salaries to the holders of executive offices in the federal government on the grounds that men are moved by ambition (love of power) and by avarice (love of money) and that powerful positions conferring wealth incite men to do their worst. These assumptions he stated, although he felt no need to argue them at length because he also guessed that his readers shared them.

Matthew Diffee/The New Yorker Collection/The Cartoon Bank

"Let me guess. You want French and you want ranch?"

Assumptions may also be unstated. Writers, painstakingly arguing specific points, may choose to keep one or more of their argument's assumptions tacit, or unspoken. Or they may be completely unaware of an underlying assumption they hold. For example, Franklin didn't even bother to state two other assumptions:

- Persons of wealth who accept an unpaying job (after all, only persons of wealth could afford to hold unpaid government jobs) will have at heart the interests of all classes of people, not only the interests of their own class.
- Those wealthy government servants will be male.

Probably Franklin didn't state these assumptions because he thought they were perfectly obvious. But if you think critically about the first assumption listed above, you may find reasons to doubt that people who attain wealth will no longer be motivated by self-interest. The second assumption runs even more deeply: Although women could not vote in Franklin's time, there were no legal restrictions on women running for office, yet the assumption Franklin shared with his audience was that politics was a male domain. Both of these assumptions have now shifted to a great extent: We now assume that paying legislators ensures that the government does not consist only of people whose incomes may give them an inadequate view of the needs of others, and our society now assumes that people who are not (or who do not identify as) male can also hold government positions. After the midterm elections of 2018, more than 100 women occupied seats in the US House of Representatives for the first time in history.

Good critical thinking involves sharpening your ability to identify assumptions, especially those that seem so self-evident, or commonsensical, that they hardly need to be stated. When you are evaluating arguments or writing your own, you should question the basic ideas upon which a writer's claims rest and ask yourself if there are other, contradictory, or opposed ideas that could be considered. If there are, you can explore the alternative forms of understanding — alternative assumptions — to test or to critique an argument and perhaps offer a different analysis or a different possibility for action. When you are hunting for assumptions (your own and others'), try the following:

- **Identify** the ideas, claims, or values that are presented as obvious, natural, or given (so much so that they are sometimes not even stated).
- **Examine** those ideas to test for their commonality, universality, and necessity. Are other ways of thinking possible?
- **Determine** whether or not contradictory ideas, claims, or values provide a fruitful new way of interpreting or understanding the information at hand.

Exercise: Assumptions

Read the following sentences and identify the assumptions that are embedded in them. State the assumptions and then challenge the claims of each sentence.

- Jamaican Blue Mountain coffee is expensive; therefore, it must be high-quality coffee.
- All students were given a syllabus detailing the policies and procedures for this course, so they all know the absence policy.
- If you do not vote, you have no right to complain about politicians.
- Someday Joseph will ask Jill to marry him.
- It's hard to believe the president is wasting time golfing when there is an economic crisis at hand.
- After decades of increasing divorce rates in the United States, the divorce rate has dropped by 18 percent in the past ten years; clearly, staying married is more popular now than it was in the past.
- Although my downtown apartment is close to my workplace, crime has been on the rise in the city, so I am moving to the suburbs where I am safer.

EVIDENCE: EXPERIMENTATION, EXAMPLES, AUTHORITATIVE TESTIMONY, AND NUMERICAL DATA

In a courtroom, evidence bearing on the guilt of the accused is introduced by the prosecution, and evidence to the contrary is introduced by the defense. Not all evidence is admissible (e.g., hearsay is not, even if it's true), and the law of evidence is a highly developed subject in jurisprudence. In daily life, the sources of evidence are less disciplined. Daily experience, a memorable observation, or an unusual event — any or all of these may serve as evidence for (or against) some belief, theory, hypothesis, or explanation a person develops.

In making arguments, people in different disciplines use different kinds of evidence to support their claims. For example:

- In literary studies, texts (works of literature, letters, journals, notes, and other kinds of writing) are the chief forms of evidence.
- In the social sciences, field research (interviews, observations, surveys, data) usually provides the evidence.
- In the hard sciences, reports of experiments are the usual evidence; if an assertion cannot be tested — if one cannot show it to be false — it is an *opinion*, not a scientific hypothesis.

When you are offering evidence to support your arguments, you are drawing on the specific information that makes your claims visible, concrete, *evident*. For example, in arguing that the entertainment industry needs to address the problem of sexual harassment among powerful male celebrities, you could point to the many men who have been accused of these behaviors. Each instance constitutes **evidence** for the problem. If you are arguing that bump stocks (devices that allow semiautomatic guns to operate like automatic ones) should be banned, you will point to specific cases in which bump stocks were used to commit crimes in order to show the need for regulation. Evidence can take many forms. Here, we discuss three broad categories of evidence.

EXPERIMENTATION Often, the forms of evidence that scientists use, whether in the natural and mathematical sciences or in the social sciences, is the result of **experimentation**. Experiments are deliberately contrived situations, often complex in their methodology or the technologies they use, that are designed to yield particular observations. What the ordinary person does with unaided eye and ear, the scientist does much more carefully and thoroughly, often in controlled situations and with the help of laboratory instruments. For example, a natural scientist studying the biological effects of a certain chemical might expose specially bred rodents to carefully monitored doses of the chemical and then measure the effects. A health scientist might design a study in which people who exercise regularly are compared to people who do not in order to argue the beneficial effects of consistent exercise on heart health. A psychologist might introduce a certain type of therapy to a group of people and then compare the results to other treatment methods.

It's no surprise that society attaches much more weight to the findings of scientists than to the corroborative (much less the contrary) experiences of ordinary people. No one today would seriously argue that the sun really does go around the earth just because it looks that way, nor would we argue that the introduction of carcinogens to the human body through smoking does not increase the risk for cancers. Yet because some kinds of scientific validation (such as repeatability) produce unarguable fact, we sometimes assume that all forms of experimentation are equal in their ability to point to truth. However, we should also be skeptical, since experiment designs can also be flawed — by bad design, bad samples, measurement error, or a host of other problems. Moreover, the results of experimentation can also be used to make different kinds of arguments. Consider that the same scientific data are used by people who argue that humans are the primary cause of climate change as well as by people who deny that humans play a significant role in climate change.

EXAMPLES Unlike the hard sciences, the variety, extent, and reliability of the evidence obtained in the humanities — and in daily life — are quite different from those obtained in the laboratory. In all forms of writing, examples constitute the primary evidence. We follow here with an explanation of examples and a description of several common forms of examples.

Nearly all arguments use examples. Suppose we argue that a candidate is untrustworthy and shouldn't be elected to public office. We may point to episodes in his career — his misuse of funds in 2008 and the false charges he made against an opponent in 2016 — as examples of his untrustworthiness. Or if we're arguing that President Harry Truman ordered the atom bomb dropped to save American (and, for that matter, Japanese) lives that otherwise would have been lost in a hard-fought invasion of Japan, we could point to the fierce resistance of the Japanese defenders in battles on the islands of Saipan, Iwo Jima, and Okinawa, where Japanese soldiers fought to the death rather than surrender. These examples indicate that the Japanese defenders of the main islands would have fought to their deaths without surrendering, even though they knew defeat was certain.

An *example* is a type of *sample*. These two words come from the same Old French word, *essample*, from the Latin *exemplum*, which means "something taken out" — that is, a selection from the group, something held up as indicative. A Yiddish proverb shrewdly says, "'For example' is no proof," but the evidence of well-chosen examples can go a long way toward helping a writer convince an audience.

In arguments, three sorts of examples are especially common:

- real events
- invented instances (artificial or hypothetical cases)
- analogies

We will treat each of these briefly.

Real Events In referring to Truman's decision to drop the atom bomb, we touched upon examples drawn from real events — the various named battles — to demonstrate our claim that it was ultimately the best option. Yet an example drawn from reality may not be as clear-cut as we would like. We used the Japanese army's behavior on Saipan and on Iwo Jima as evidence for our claim that the Japanese later would have fought to the death in an American invasion of Japan. This, we argued, would therefore have inflicted terrible losses on the Japanese and on the Americans. Our examples could be countered by evidence that in June and July 1945 certain Japanese diplomats sent out secret peace feelers to Switzerland and offered to surrender if the Emperor Hirohito could retain power so that in August 1945, when Truman authorized dropping the bomb, the situation was very different. If we were to argue that Truman should *not* have dropped the bomb, we could cite those peace feelers specifically, indicating a Japanese willingness to end the war without such destruction.

But most arguments using real events require further support. Some may argue that we are not currently under threat of a nuclear war, and they may offer examples of various agreements made among nuclear-armed nations as evidence. But such an argument needs more support because of the weight of counterexamples. As much as nations have sought to reduce the nuclear threat, arguing that the threat does not exist ignores many examples showing that nuclear war remains a possibility: The continuation of some nuclear programs, the development of new nuclear weapons systems, and documented attempts by terrorists to acquire nuclear material on the black market — all these real events provide counterexamples that could challenge the claim that nuclear war is no longer a possibility.

In short, *real* events are often so entangled in historical circumstances that they might not be adequate or fully relevant evidence in the case being argued. When using real events as examples (a perfectly valid strategy), the writer must

- demonstrate that they are representative,
- anticipate counterexamples, and
- argue against counterexamples, showing that one's own examples can be considered outside of other contexts.

Thus, in our earlier argument against Truman's use of the atomic bomb, we might raise the facts of the fierceness of Japanese resistance in specific earlier battles but then argue that they are not relevant because our examples show that the Japanese were seeking peace. Similarly, if others were arguing that Truman did the right thing, they could mention the peace feelers, but argue that it would not have desirable to permit the emperor to retain power.

Invented Instances An **invented instance** is an **artificial** or **hypothetical** example. Take this case: A writer poses a dilemma in his argument that "Stand Your Ground" laws are morally indefensible. (These laws allow individuals the right to protect themselves against threats of bodily harm, to the point of using lethal force in self-defense.) In his discussion, he raises the most famous of these cases, involving the death of unarmed Florida teenager Trayvon Martin, who was killed in 2012 by a self-appointed neighborhood watchman named George Zimmerman, who mistook the African American youth as a threat. He writes: "If Trayvon Martin had been of age and legally armed, in fact, he would have had the right to kill Zimmerman when Zimmerman approached him in a hostile way." By imagining this scenario, the writer asks readers to apply the principles of justice underlying the law to the reverse scenario: What happens when neither party is clear about which of them is standing his ground? Even though the example isn't "real" — although it alters the details of a real event — it sets forth the problem in a clear way.

Offering an invented instance is something like a drawing of the parts of an atom in a physics textbook. It is admittedly false, but by virtue of its simplification it sets forth the relevant details very clearly. Thus, in a discussion of legal rights and moral obligation, the philosopher Charles Frankel says:

> It would be nonsense to say, for example, that a nonswimmer has a moral duty to swim to the help of a drowning man.

If Frankel were talking about a real event and a real person, he could get bogged down in details about the actual person and the circumstances of the event, losing his power to put the moral dilemma forward in its clearest terms.

When an example is invented, it is almost certain to support the writer's point — after all, the writer is making it up, so it is bound to be the ideal example. That said, invented instances have drawbacks. First and foremost, they cannot serve as the highest quality of evidence. A purely hypothetical example can illustrate a point, but it cannot substitute for actual events. Sometimes, hypothetical examples are so fanciful that they fail to convince the reader. Here is — what else? — an example of what we mean: The philosopher Judith Jarvis Thomson, in the course of an argument entitled "A Defense of Abortion," asks you to imagine waking up one day and finding that against your will a celebrated violinist has been hooked up to your body for life support. She then asks: Do you have the right to unplug the violinist? Whatever you answer, you have to agree that such a scenario is not exactly the same as asking whether or not a woman has a right to an abortion.

But we add one point: Even a highly fanciful invented case can have the valuable effect of forcing us to see where we stand. A person may say that she is, in all circumstances, against torture — but what would she say if a writer proposed a scenario in which the location of a ticking bomb were known only by one person and extracting that information through torture could save hundreds or thousands of lives? Artificial cases of this sort can help us examine our beliefs; nevertheless, they often create exceptional scenarios that may not be generalized convincingly to support an argument.

Analogies The third sort of example, **analogy**, is a kind of comparison. Here's an example:

> Before the Roman Empire declined as a world power, it exhibited a decline in morals and in physical stamina; our society today shows a decline in both morals (consider the high divorce rate and the crime rate) and physical culture (consider obesity in children). America, like Rome, will decline as a world power.

Strictly speaking, an analogy is an extended comparison in which different things are shown to be similar in several ways. Thus, if one wants to argue that a head of state should have extraordinary power during wartime, one can offer an analogy that, during wartime, the state is like a ship in a storm: The crew is needed to lend its help, but the major decisions are best left to the captain. Notice that an analogy like this compares things that are relatively *un*like, similar to metaphor and simile. Simply comparing the plight of one state to another is not an analogy; it's merely an inductive inference from one case of the same sort to another such case.

"Do you mind if I use yet another sports analogy?"

Let's consider another analogy. We have already glanced at Judith Thomson's hypothetical case in which the reader wakes up to find herself hooked up to a violinist in need of life support. Thomson uses this situation as an analogy in an argument about abortion. The reader stands for the mother; the violinist, for the unwanted fetus. You may want to think about whether this analogy holds up: Is a pregnant woman really like a person hooked up to such a machine? Is an embryo or fetus really equivalent to a celebrated violin player?

The problem with argument by analogy is this: Because different things are similar in some ways does not mean they are similar in all ways. Thomson's argument is basically developed on the premise that being the reader hooked up to a violinist is like being the pregnant mother hooked up to a fetus. But those two things are obviously quite different. Similarly, a state is not a ship in a storm. The government is not a business. As Bishop Butler is said to have remarked in the early eighteenth century, "Everything is what it is, and not another thing."

Analogies can be convincing, however, when they simplify complex issues. "Don't change horses in midstream" isn't a statement about riding horses across a river but, rather, about changing a course of action in critical times. Still, in the end, analogies don't necessarily prove anything. What may be true about riding horses across a stream may not be true about, say, choosing a new leader in troubled times. What is true for one need not be true for the other.

Analogies can be helpful in developing our thoughts and in helping listeners or readers understand a point we're trying to make. It is sometimes argued, for instance, that newspaper and television reporters and their confidential sources should share the right to confidential privilege, like the doctor–patient, attorney–client, or priest–confessor relationship. The analogy is worth thinking about: Do the similarities run deep enough, or are there fundamental differences in the types of confidentiality we should expect between journalists and their sources and between people and their doctors, lawyers, or priests?

AUTHORITATIVE TESTIMONY Another form of evidence is **testimony**, the citation or quotation of authorities. In daily life, we rely heavily on authorities of all sorts: We get a doctor's opinion about our health, we read a book because an intelligent friend recommends it, we see a movie because a critic gave it a good review, and we pay at least a little attention to the weather forecaster.

In setting forth an argument, one often tries to show that one's view is supported by notable figures — perhaps Jefferson, Lincoln, Martin Luther King Jr., or scientists who won a Nobel Prize — but authorities do not have to be figures of such a high stature. You may recall that when talking about medical marijuana legalization in Chapter 2, we presented an open letter by Sanjay Gupta. To make certain that you were impressed by his ideas, we described him as CNN's chief medical correspondent and a leading public health expert. In our Chapter 2 discussion of Sally Mann, we qualified our description of her controversial photographs by noting that *Time* magazine called her "America's Best Photographer" and the *New Republic* called her book "one of the great photograph books of our time." But heed some words of caution:

- Be sure that the authority, however notable, is *an authority on the topic in question.* (A well-known biologist might be an authority on vitamins but not on the justice of war.)
- Be sure that the authority is *unbiased.* (A chemist employed by the tobacco industry isn't likely to admit that smoking may be harmful, and a producer of violent video games isn't likely to admit that playing those games stimulates violence.)

- Beware of *nameless* authorities: "a thousand doctors," "leading educators," "researchers at a major medical school." (If possible, offer at least one specific name.)
- Be careful when using authorities who indeed were great authorities in their day but *who now may be out of date.* (Examples include Adam Smith on economics, Julius Caesar on the art of war, Louis Pasteur on medicine.)
- Cite authorities *whose opinions your readers will value.* (William F. Buckley Jr.'s conservative/libertarian opinions mean a good deal to readers of the magazine that he founded, the *National Review,* but probably not to most liberal thinkers. Gloria Steinem's liberal/feminist opinions carry weight with readers of the magazines that she cofounded, *New York* and *Ms.* magazine, but probably not with most conservative thinkers.)

THINKING CRITICALLY *Authoritative Testimony*

Locate one authority on each issue and use the table to examine whether or not that person is an adequate authority. In the last box, explain why this is a reliable testimony.

ISSUE	EXPERT NAME AND QUALIFICATIONS	TIME PERIOD	PLACE OF PUBLICATION	YOUR EXPLANATION
Recreational marijuana				
Spanking children				
How to manage test anxiety				
Restoring voting rights to felons				
The quality of the latest Academy Award–winning Best Picture				

One other point: *You* may be an authority. You probably aren't nationally known, but on some topics you might have the authority of personal experience. You may have been injured on a motorcycle while riding without wearing a helmet, or you may have escaped injury because you wore a helmet. You may have dropped out of school and then returned. You may have tutored a student whose native language isn't English, you may be such a student who has received tutoring, or you may have attended a school with a bilingual education program. In short, your personal testimony on topics relating to these issues may be invaluable, and a reader will probably consider it seriously.

NUMERICAL DATA The last sort of evidence we discuss here is data based on math or collections of numbers, also referred to as **quantitative** or **statistical** evidence. Sometimes quantitative evidence offers firm answers. Suppose the awarding of honors at graduation from college is determined based on a student's cumulative grade-point average (GPA). The undisputed assumption is that the nearer a student's GPA is to a perfect record (4.0), the more deserving he or she is of highest honors. Consequently, a student with a GPA of 3.9 at the end of her senior year is a stronger candidate for honors than another student with a GPA of 3.6. When faculty members determine the academic merits of graduating seniors, they know that these quantitative, statistical differences in student GPAs will be the basic (if not the only) kind of evidence under discussion.

Here, numbers prove to be reliable evidence, used to justify the argument that one student deserves honors more than another. However, in many cases, numbers do not simply speak for themselves. Numerical information can be presented in many forms. Graphs, tables, and pie charts are familiar ways of presenting quantitative data in an eye-catching manner, but how the numbers are organized, interpreted, and presented can make a difference in how well they support an argument's claims. (See the section Visuals as Aids to Clarity: Maps, Graphs, and Pie Charts on pp. 159–63 in Chapter 4 for more on graphs.)

Let's look how some different kinds of numbers are commonly used as evidence.

Presenting Numbers In an argument, you may need to evaluate whether it is more persuasive to present numbers in percentages or real numbers. For example, arguing that the murder rate increased by 30 percent in one city sounds more compelling than saying there were thirteen murders this year compared to ten last year (only three more, but a technical increase of 30 percent). Should an argument examining the federal budget say that it (1) underwent a *twofold increase* over the decade, (2) increased by *100 percent*, (3) *doubled*, or (4) was *one-half of its current amount ten years ago*? As you can see, these are equivalent ways of saying the same thing, but by making a choice among them, a writer can play up or play down the increase to support different arguments in more or less dramatic ways.

Other kinds of choices may be made in interpreting numbers: Suppose in a given city in 2017, 1 percent of the victims in fatal automobile accidents were bicyclists. In the same city in 2018, the percentage of bicyclists killed in automobile accidents was 2 percent. Was the increase 1 percent (not an alarming figure), or was it 100 percent (a staggering figure)? The answer is both, depending on whether we're comparing (1) bicycle deaths in automobile accidents *with all deaths in automobile accidents* (that's an increase of 1 percent) or (2) bicycle deaths in automobile accidents *only with other bicycle deaths in automobile accidents* (an increase of 100 percent). An honest statement would say that bicycle deaths due to automobile accidents doubled in 2018, increasing from 1 to 2 percent. But here's another point: Although every such death is lamentable, if there was only one such death in 2017 and two in 2018, the increase from one death to two — an increase of 100 percent! — hardly suggests a growing problem that needs attention. No one would be surprised to learn that in the following years there were no deaths at all, or only one or two.

Consider how different calculations can impact the meaning of numerical data. Here are some statistics that pop up in conversations about wealth distribution in the United States. In 2017, the Census Bureau calculated that the **median** household income in the United States was $61,372, meaning that half of households earned less than this amount and half earned above it. However, the **average** — technically, the **mean** — household income in the same year was $86,220, or $24,848 (or 40 percent) higher. Which number more accurately represents the typical household income? Both are "correct," but both are calculated with different measures (median and mean). If a politician wanted to argue that the United States has a strong middle class, he might use the average (mean) income as evidence, a number calculated by dividing the total income of all households by the total number of households. If another politician wished to make a rebuttal, she could point out that the average income paints a rosy picture because the wealthiest households skew the average higher. The median income (representing the number above and below which two halves of all households fall) should be the measure we use, the rebutting politician could argue, because it helps reduce the effect of the limitless ceiling of higher incomes and the finite floor of lower incomes at zero.

Our point: This just shows how different methods of calculating — or how writers may use the results of those different methods — can produce different understandings of an issue.

Unreliable Statistical Evidence Because we know that 90 percent is greater than 75 percent, we're usually ready to grant that any claim supported by 90 percent of cases is more likely to be true than an alternative claim supported in only 75 percent of cases. The greater the difference, the greater our confidence. Yet statistics often get a bad name because it's so easy to misuse them (unintentionally or not) and so difficult to be sure that they were gathered correctly in the first place. (One old saying goes, "There are lies, damned lies, and statistics.") Every branch of social science and natural science needs statistical information, and countless decisions in public and private life are based on quantitative data in statistical form. It's therefore important to be sensitive to the sources and reliability of the statistics and to develop a healthy skepticism when you confront statistics whose parentage is not fully explained. Always ask: Who gathered the statistics? For what purpose?

Consider this example of statistics, from the self-described "culture jammer" Kalle Lasn, the founder of AdBusters, a group that commonly criticizes aspects of consumer society:

> Advertisements are the most prevalent and toxic of the mental pollutants. From the moment your radio alarm sounds in the morning to the wee hours of

late-night TV, microjolts of commercial pollution flood into your brain at the rate of about three thousand marketing messages per day. (Kalle Lasn, *Culture Jam* [1999], 18–19)

Lasn's book includes endnotes as documentation, so, being curious about the statistics, we turned to the appropriate page and found this information concerning the source of his data:

> "three thousand marketing messages per day." Mark Landler, Walecia Konrad, Zachary Schiller, and Lois Therrien, "What Happened to Advertising?" *BusinessWeek*, September 23, 1991, page 66. Leslie Savan in *The Sponsored Life* (Temple University Press, 1994), page 1, estimated that "16,000 ads flicker across an individual's consciousness daily." I did an informal survey in March 1995 and found the number to be closer to 1,500 (this included all marketing messages, corporate images, logos, ads, brand names, on TV, radio, billboards, buildings, signs, clothing, appliances, in cyberspace, etc., over a typical twenty-four hour period in my life). (219)

Well, this endnote is odd. In the earlier passage, the author asserted that about "three thousand marketing messages per day" flood into a person's brain. In the documentation, he cites a source for that statistic from *BusinessWeek* — although we haven't the faintest idea how the authors of the *BusinessWeek* article came up with that figure. Oddly, he goes on to offer a very different figure (16,000 ads) and then, to our confusion, offers yet a third figure (1,500) based on his own "informal survey."

Probably the one thing we can safely say about all three figures is that none of them means very much. Even if the compilers of the statistics explained exactly how they counted — let's say that among countless other criteria they assumed that the average person reads one magazine per day and that the average magazine contains 124 advertisements — it would be hard to take them seriously. After all, in leafing through a magazine, some people may read many ads and some may read none. Some people may read some ads carefully — but perhaps just to enjoy their absurdity. Our point: Although Lasn said, without implying any uncertainty, that "about three thousand marketing messages per day" reach an individual, it's evident from the endnote that even he is confused about the figure he gives.

WRITING TIP
When writing, consider presenting your numerical data in ways that have the most impact. A quarter, 25%, and 1 out of 4 are all the same but may resonate differently with your audience. But be ethical; don't try to manipulate your reader.

We'd like to make a final point about the unreliability of some statistical information — data that looks impressive but that is, in fact, insubstantial. Consider Marilyn Jager Adams's book *Beginning to Read: Thinking and Learning about Print* (1994), in which she pointed out that poor families read to their preschool children only 25 hours per year over a five-year period, whereas in the same period middle-income families read to their preschool children 1,000 to 1,700 hours. The figures were much quoted in newspapers and by children's advocacy groups. Adams could not, of course, interview every family in these two groups; she had to rely on samples. What were her samples? For poor families, she selected twenty-four children in twenty families, all in Southern California. (Ask yourself: Can families from only one geographic area provide an adequate sample for a topic such as this?) And how many families constituted Adams's sample of middle-class families? Exactly one — her own. We leave it to you to judge the validity of her findings.

Sometimes the definition of what is being counted can affect the statistical results. Sociologist Joel Best notes in his book *Stat Spotting* an interesting case: When research several years ago showed that "one-fifth [20 percent] of college students practice self-injury," the dramatic statistic attracted journalists and news media who published all kinds of worrying articles. But a closer look at the study revealed not only that the survey was limited to two Ivy League universities (a sampling problem), but also that it *defined* self-injury in a very broad way, to include minor acts that most psychologists would consider to be within the range of normal behavior — such as pinching, scratching, or hitting oneself. In actuality, as another analysis showed, only 1.6 percent of college students reported injuring themselves to the point of needing medical treatment — quite a lot fewer than 20 percent.

We are not suggesting that everyone who uses statistics is trying to deceive (or is unconsciously being deceived by them). We suggest only that statistics are open to widely different interpretations and that often those columns of numbers, which appear to be so precise with their decimal points and their complex formulas, may actually be imprecise and possibly worthless if they're based on insufficient samples, erroneous methodologies, or biased interpretation.

A CHECKLIST FOR EVALUATING STATISTICAL EVIDENCE

Regard statistical evidence (like all other evidence) cautiously and don't accept it until you have thought about these questions:

- ❒ Was the evidence compiled by a disinterested (impartial) source? The source's name doesn't always reveal its particular angle (e.g., People for the American Way), but sometimes it lets you know what to expect (e.g., National Rifle Association, American Civil Liberties Union).
- ❒ Is it based on an adequate sample?
- ❒ What is the definition of the thing being counted or measured?
- ❒ Is the statistical evidence recent enough to be relevant?
- ❒ How many of the factors likely to be relevant were identified and measured?
- ❒ Are the figures open to a different and equally plausible interpretation?
- ❒ If a percentage is cited, is it the average (or *mean*), or is it the median?

Nonrational Appeals

In talking about induction and deduction, definitions, and types of evidence, we've been talking about means of rational persuasion, things normally falling under the purview of *logos*. However, as mentioned earlier, there are also other means of persuasion. Force is an example. If Stacey kicks Janée, and threatens to destroy Janée's means of livelihood, and threatens Janée's life, Stacey may persuade Janée to cooperate or agree with her. Writers, of course, cannot use such kinds of force on their readers (nor would they want to, we hope). But they do have at their disposal forms of persuasion that are more associated with *pathos*. These types of appeals do not rely on rational logic or inference (*logos*), but predominantly on the feeling — the emotions — of readers.

SATIRE, IRONY, SARCASM

One form of irrational but sometimes highly effective persuasion is **satire** — that is, witty ridicule. A cartoonist may persuade viewers that a politician's views are unsound by caricaturing (thus ridiculing) her appearance or by presenting a grotesquely distorted (funny, but unfair) picture of the issue she supports.

Satiric artists often use caricature; satiric writers, also seeking to persuade by means of ridicule, often use **verbal irony**. This sort of irony contrasts what is said and what is meant. For instance, words of praise may actually imply blame (when Shakespeare's Cassius says,

Roger Cracknell 01/classic/Alamy Stock Photo

How does this mural by street artist Banksy use visual irony?

"Brutus is an honorable man," he wants those who hear him to think that Brutus is dishonorable). Occasionally, words of modesty may actually imply superiority ("Of course, I'm too dumb to understand this problem"). Such language, when heavy-handed, is **sarcasm** ("You're a great guy," someone who is actually criticizing you says). If it's witty and clever, we call it irony rather than sarcasm.

Although ridicule isn't a form of reasoning, passages of ridicule, especially verbal irony, sometimes appear in argument essays. These passages, like reasons or like appeals to the emotions, are efforts to persuade the reader to accept the writer's point of view. The key to using humor in an argument is, on the one hand, to avoid wisecracking like a smart aleck and, on the other hand, to avoid mere clownishness. In other words, if you get too silly, acerbic, or outright insulting, you may damage your *ethos* and alienate your audience.

EMOTIONAL APPEALS

It is sometimes said that good argumentative writing appeals only to reason, never to emotion, and that any emotional appeal is illegitimate and irrelevant. "Tears are not arguments," the Brazilian writer Machado de Assis said. Logic textbooks may even stigmatize with Latin labels the various sorts of emotional appeal — for instance, *argumentum ad populam* (appeal to the prejudices of the mob, as in "Come on, we all know that schools don't teach anything anymore") and *argumentum ad misericordiam* (appeal to pity, as in "No one ought to blame this poor kid for stabbing a classmate because his mother was often institutionalized").

LEARNING FROM SHAKESPEARE True, appeals to emotion may distract from the facts of the case; they may blind the audience by, in effect, throwing dust in its eyes or by provoking tears. A classic example occurs in Shakespeare's *Julius Caesar*, when Marc Antony addresses the Roman populace after Brutus, Cassius, and Casca have conspired to assassinate Caesar. The real issue is whether Caesar was becoming tyrannical (as the assassins claim). Antony turns from the evidence and stirs the crowd against the assassins by appealing to its emotions. Shakespeare drew from an ancient Roman biographical writing, Plutarch's *Lives of the Noble Grecians and Romans*. Plutarch says this about Antony:

> [P]erceiving that his words moved the common people to compassion, . . . [he] framed his eloquence to make their hearts yearn [i.e., grieve] the more, and, taking Caesar's gown all bloody in his hand, he laid it open to the sight of them all, showing what a number of cuts and holes it had upon it. Therewithal the people fell presently into such a rage and mutiny that there was no more order kept.

Here's how Shakespeare reinterpreted the event in his play:

> Friends, Romans, countrymen, lend me your ears;
> I come to bury Caesar, not to praise him.

After briefly offering insubstantial evidence that Caesar gave no signs of behaving tyrannically (e.g., "When that the poor have cried, Caesar hath wept"), Antony begins to play directly on his hearers' emotions. Descending from the platform so that he may be in closer contact with his audience (like a modern politician, he wants to work the crowd), he calls attention to Caesar's bloody toga:

> If you have tears, prepare to shed them now.
> You all do know this mantle; I remember
> The first time ever Caesar put it on:
> 'Twas on a summer's evening, in his tent,
> That day he overcame the Nervii.
> Look, in this place ran Cassius' dagger through;
> See what a rent the envious Casca made;
> Through this, the well-belovèd Brutus stabbed . . .

In these few lines, Antony accomplishes the following:

- He prepares the audience by suggesting to them how they should respond ("If you have tears, prepare to shed them now").
- He flatters them by implying that they, like Antony, were intimates of Caesar (he credits them with being familiar with Caesar's garment).
- He then evokes a personal memory of a specific time ("a summer's evening") — the day that Caesar won a battle against the Nervii, a particularly fierce tribe in what is now France. (In fact, Antony was not at the battle and did not join Caesar until three years later.)

Antony doesn't mind being free with the facts; his point here is not to set the record straight but to stir people against the assassins. He goes on, daringly but successfully, to identify one particular slit in the garment with Cassius's dagger, another with Casca's, and a third with Brutus's. Antony cannot know which dagger made which slit, but his rhetorical trick works.

Notice, too, that Antony arranges the three assassins in climactic order, since Brutus (Antony claims) was especially beloved by Caesar:

> Judge, O you gods, how dearly Caesar loved him!
> This was the most unkindest cut of all;
> For when the noble Caesar saw him stab,
> Ingratitude, more strong than traitor's arms,
> Quite vanquished him. Then burst his mighty heart.

Nice. According to Antony, the noble-minded Caesar — Antony's words have erased all thought of the tyrannical Caesar — died not from wounds inflicted by daggers but from the heartbreaking perception of Brutus's ingratitude. Doubtless there wasn't a dry eye in the crowd. Let's all hope that if we are ever put on trial, we'll have a lawyer as skilled in evoking sympathy as Antony.

ARE EMOTIONAL APPEALS FALLACIOUS? Antony's oration was obviously successful in the play and apparently was successful in real life, but it is the sort of speech that prompts logicians to write disapprovingly of attempts to stir feeling in an audience. (As mentioned earlier, the evocation of emotion in an audience is **pathos**, from the Greek word for "emotion" or "suffering.") There is nothing inherently wrong in stimulating an audience's emotions when attempting to establish a claim, but when an emotional appeal confuses the issue being argued or shifts attention away from the facts, we can reasonably speak of the emotional appeal as a fallacy.

No fallacy is involved, however, when an emotional appeal heightens the facts, bringing them home to the audience rather than masking them. In talking about legislation that would govern police actions, for example, it's legitimate to show a photograph of the battered, bloodied face of an alleged victim of police brutality. True, such a photograph cannot tell the whole truth; it cannot tell if the subject threatened the officer with a gun or repeatedly resisted an order to surrender. But it can demonstrate that the victim was severely beaten and (like a comparable description in words) evoke emotions that may properly affect the audience's decision about the permissible use of police violence. Similarly, an animal rights activist who argues that calves are cruelly confined might reasonably talk about the inhumanely small size of their pens, in which they cannot turn around or even lie down. Others may argue that calves don't care about turning around or have no right to turn around, but the evocative verbal description of their pens, which makes an emotional appeal, cannot be called fallacious or irrelevant.

THINKING CRITICALLY *Nonrational Appeals*

Identify the emotion summoned by the following nonrational appeals and explain how the claim may be countered by logic or reason.

NONRATIONAL APPEAL	EMOTION	LOGICAL COUNTER
Football players and other athletes should not be allowed to kneel for the National Anthem to protest police violence because it disrespects the American flag and all those people who died defending it.		
Nowadays, it seems anything goes on television, and even primetime shows feature foul language, sex, and violence. Don't they realize children are watching?		
The Powerball jackpot this week is more than $500 million. Even if you don't normally play the lottery, it's time to buy a ticket!		

In appealing to emotions, then, keep in mind these strategies:

- Do not falsify (especially by oversimplifying) the issue.
- Do not distract attention from the facts of the case.
- Do think ethically about how emotional appeals may affect the audience.

You should focus on the facts and offer reasons (essentially, statements linked with "because"), but you may also legitimately bring the facts home to your readers by seeking to provoke appropriate emotions. Your words will be fallacious only if you stimulate emotions that aren't connected with the facts of the case.

Does All Writing Contain Arguments?

Our answer to the question in the heading is no — however, *most* writing probably *does* contain an argument of sorts. The writer wants to persuade the reader to see things the way the writer sees them — at least until the end of the essay. After all, even a recipe for a cherry pie in a food magazine — a piece of writing that's primarily expository (how to do it) rather than argumentative (how a reasonable person ought to think about this topic) — probably starts out with a hint of an argument, such as "*Because* [a sign that a *reason* will be offered] this pie can be made quickly and with ingredients (canned cherries) that are always available, give it a try. It will surely become one of your favorites." Clearly, such a statement cannot stand as a formal argument — a discussion that addresses counterarguments, relies chiefly on logic and little if any emotional appeal, and draws a conclusion that seems irrefutable.

Still, the statement is technically an argument on behalf of making a pie with canned cherries. In this case, we can identify a claim (the pie will become a favorite) and two *reasons* in support of the claim:

- It can be made quickly.
- The chief ingredient — because it is canned — can always be at hand.

There are two underlying *assumptions*:

- Readers don't have a great deal of time to waste in the kitchen.
- Canned cherries are just as tasty as fresh cherries — and even if they aren't, no one who eats the pie will know the difference.

When we read a lead-in to a recipe, then, we won't find a formal argument, but we'll probably see a few words that seek to persuade us to keep reading. And most writing does contain such material — sentences that engage our interest and give us a reason to keep reading. If the recipe is difficult and time consuming, the lead-in may say this:

> Although this recipe for a cherry pie, using fresh cherries that you will have to pit, is a bit more time consuming than the usual recipes that call for canned cherries, once you have tasted it you will never go back to canned cherries.

Again, although the logic is scarcely compelling, the persuasive element is evident. The assumption is that readers have a discriminating palate; once they've tasted a pie made with fresh cherries, they'll never again enjoy the canned stuff. The writer isn't making a formal argument with abundant evidence and detailed refutation of counterarguments, but we know where he stands and how he wishes us to respond.

In short, almost all writers are trying to persuade readers to see things *their* way. As you read the essays in this chapter, keep in mind the questions in the checklist for analyzing an argument. They can help you take apart an argument and discover where strengths and weakness lie and perhaps find new points to make (and things to say) in important discussions and debates.

A CHECKLIST FOR ANALYZING AN ARGUMENT

Thesis and Claims

- ❒ Is the author's claim or thesis clear?
- ❒ Are any parts of the argument based on *logos*, *pathos*, or *ethos*?
- ❒ Are any premises false or questionable?
- ❒ Is the logic — deductive or inductive — valid?
- ❒ Are important terms and concepts defined satisfactorily?
- ❒ Does the writer make assumptions that are problematic for his or her argument?

Support and Evidence

- ❒ Does the writer use evidence to support his or her claims?
- ❒ Are the examples — imagined, invented, or hypothetical — relevant and convincing?
- ❒ Are the statistics (if any) relevant, accurate, and complete?
- ❒ Are other interpretations of evidence possible?
- ❒ Can authorities who offer evidence be considered impartial?

Fairness

- ❒ Are alternative viewpoints and counterexamples adequately considered?
- ❒ Is there any evidence of dishonesty or of a discreditable attempt to manipulate the reader?
- ❒ Is the writer's tone and use of language appropriate to the subject and the audience?

An Example: An Argument and a Look at the Writer's Strategies

The following essay, "The Reign of Recycling" by John Tierney, concerns the efficacy of recycling — whether or not it is helping the environment in significant ways or if it has gone beyond its originally good intentions to become an unsustainable or even counterproductive measure. We follow Tierney's essay with some comments about the ways in which he constructs his argument.

JOHN TIERNEY

John Tierney (b. 1953) is an award-winning journalist for the *New York Times* who publishes frequently on issues related to science, environmentalism, and politics. He has also published extensively in magazines such as the *Atlantic, Rolling Stone, Newsweek, Discover,* and *Esquire.* Known for his skepticism toward climate science and big government, Tierney is regarded as a conservative critic. This essay appeared in the *New York Times* in 2015.

The Reign of Recycling

Reign in the title suggests that recycling is a powerful, perhaps even tyrannical, trend.

If you live in the United States, you probably do some form of recycling. It's likely that you separate paper from plastic and glass and metal. You rinse the bottles and cans, and you might put food scraps in a container destined for a composting facility. As you sort everything into the right bins, you probably assume that recycling is helping your community and protecting the environment. But is it? Are you in fact wasting your time?

Tierney presents a common assumption — recycling is helping — but questions it.

In 1996, I wrote a long article[1] for *The New York Times Magazine* arguing that the recycling process as we carried it out was wasteful. I presented plenty of evidence that recycling was costly and ineffectual, but its defenders said that it was unfair to rush to judgment. Noting that the modern recycling movement had really just begun just a few years earlier, they predicted it would flourish as the industry matured and the public learned how to recycle properly.

Establishes *ethos*: he has long been familiar with (and right about) the central issues and questions.

So, what's happened since then? While it's true that the recycling message has reached more people than ever, when it comes to the bottom line, both economically and environmentally, not much has changed at all.

Tierney's thesis:
Premise: Recycling was costly and ineffectual in 1996.
Premise: Not much has changed since 1996.
Conclusion: Recycling remains costly and ineffectual.

Despite decades of exhortations and mandates, it's still typically more expensive for municipalities to recycle household waste than to send it to a landfill. Prices for recyclable materials have plummeted because of lower oil prices and reduced demand for them overseas. The slump has forced some recycling companies to shut plants and cancel plans for new technologies. The mood is so gloomy that one industry

Tierney gestures toward evidence, but he does not present concrete examples.

[1]John Tierney, "Recycling Is Garbage," *New York Times*, June 30, 1996, nyti.ms/2kqksIS. [All citations in this selection are the editors'; they appeared as hyperlinks in the original publication.]

veteran tried to cheer up her colleagues this summer with an article in a trade journal titled, "Recycling Is Not Dead!"[2]

5 While politicians set higher and higher goals, the national rate of recycling has stagnated in recent years. Yes, it's popular in affluent neighborhoods like Park Slope in Brooklyn and in cities like San Francisco, but residents of the Bronx and Houston don't have the same fervor for sorting garbage in their spare time.

> Notice Tierney quotes an expert authority for corroborating evidence. Why would a Waste Management executive agree with Tierney?

The future for recycling looks even worse. As cities move beyond recycling paper and metals, and into glass, food scraps and assorted plastics, the costs rise sharply while the environmental benefits decline and sometimes vanish. "If you believe recycling is good for the planet and that we need to do more of it, then there's a crisis to confront," says David P. Steiner, the chief executive officer of Waste Management, the largest recycler of household trash in the United States. "Trying to turn garbage into gold costs a lot more than expected. We need to ask ourselves: What is the goal here?"

Recycling has been relentlessly promoted as a goal in and of itself: an unalloyed public good and private virtue that is indoctrinated in students from kindergarten through college. As a result, otherwise well-informed and educated people have no idea of the relative costs and benefits.

> Tierney suggests the EPA itself may not be trustworthy. Note that the EPA is commonly a target of pro-business conservatives.

They probably don't know, for instance, that to reduce carbon emissions, you'll accomplish a lot more by sorting paper and aluminum cans than by worrying about yogurt containers and half-eaten slices of pizza. Most people also assume that recycling plastic bottles must be doing lots for the planet. They've been encouraged by the Environmental Protection Agency, which assures the public that recycling plastic results in less carbon being released into the atmosphere.

But how much difference does it make? Here's some perspective: To offset the greenhouse impact of one passenger's round-trip flight between New York and London, you'd have to recycle roughly 40,000 plastic bottles, assuming you fly coach. If you sit in business- or first-class, where each passenger takes up more space, it could be more like 100,000.

> Proposes that people who think they are doing good for the environment are actually doing worse. How ironic!

10 Even those statistics might be misleading. New York and other cities instruct people to rinse the bottles before putting them in the recycling bin, but the E.P.A.'s life-cycle calculation doesn't take that water into account. That single omission can make a big difference, according to Chris Goodall, the author of "How to Live a Low-Carbon Life." Mr. Goodall calculates that if you wash plastic in water that was heated by coal-derived electricity, then the net effect of your recycling could be *more* carbon in the atmosphere.

> Begins to address "zero waste" proposals, implicitly criticizing New York's decision to pursue such a goal.

To many public officials, recycling is a question of morality, not cost-benefit analysis. Mayor Bill de Blasio of New York declared that by 2030 the city would no longer send any garbage to landfills. "This is the way of the future if we're going to save our earth," he explained[3] while announcing that New York would join San Francisco,

[2]Patty Moore, "Recycling Is Not Dead," *Resource Recycling*, July 1, 2015, resource-recycling.com/node/6130.

[3] Jill Jorgensen, "Bill de Blasio Calls for the End of Garbage by 2030," *Observer*, April 22, 2015, observer.com/2015/04/bill-de-blasio-calls-for-the-end-of-garbage-by-2030/.

Seattle and other cities in moving toward a "zero waste" policy, which would require an unprecedented level of recycling.

The national rate of recycling rose during the 1990s to 25 percent, meeting the goal set by an E.P.A. official, J. Winston Porter. He advised state officials that no more than about 35 percent of the nation's trash was worth recycling, but some ignored him and set goals of 50 percent and higher. Most of those goals were never met and the national rate has been stuck around 34 percent in recent years.

"It makes sense to recycle commercial cardboard and some paper, as well as selected metals and plastics," he says. "But other materials rarely make sense, including food waste and other compostables. The zero-waste goal makes no sense at all — it's very expensive with almost no real environmental benefit."

Tierney cites another authority, J. Winston Porter, but he may be shifting the issue; Porter actually says some forms of recycling are good.

One of the original goals of the recycling movement was to avert a supposed crisis because there was no room left in the nation's landfills. But that media-inspired fear was never realistic in a country with so much open space. In reporting the 1996 article I found that all the trash generated by Americans for the next 1,000 years[4] would fit on one-tenth of 1 percent of the land available for grazing. And that tiny amount of land wouldn't be lost forever, because landfills are typically covered with grass and converted to parkland, like the Freshkills Park being created on Staten Island. The United States Open tennis tournament is played on the site of an old landfill — and one that never had the linings and other environmental safeguards required today.

Tierney undermines assumptions that landfills are bad.

Though most cities shun landfills, they have been welcomed in rural communities 15
that reap large economic benefits (and have plenty of greenery to buffer residents from the sights and smells). Consequently, the great landfill shortage has not arrived, and neither have the shortages of raw materials that were supposed to make recycling profitable.

With the economic rationale gone, advocates for recycling have switched to environmental arguments. Researchers have calculated that there are indeed such benefits to recycling, but not in the way that many people imagine.

Counterarguments are raised, but Tierney uses them to defend landfills.

Most of these benefits do not come from reducing the need for landfills and incinerators. A modern well-lined landfill in a rural area can have relatively little environmental impact. Decomposing garbage releases methane, a potent greenhouse gas, but landfill operators have started capturing it and using it to generate electricity. Modern incinerators, while politically unpopular in the United States, release so few pollutants that they've been widely accepted in the eco-conscious countries of Northern Europe and Japan for generating clean energy.

Moreover, recycling operations have their own environmental costs, like extra trucks on the road and pollution from recycling operations. Composting facilities around the country have inspired complaints about nauseating odors, swarming rats, and defecating sea gulls. After New York City started sending food waste to be composted in Delaware, the unhappy neighbors of the composting plant successfully campaigned to shut it down last year.

Pathos: In arguing against composting facilities, Tierney turns stomachs.

[4] A. Clark Wiseman. *U.S. Wastepaper Recycling Policies: Issues and Ethics* (1990; *Google Books*), books.google.com/books/about/U_S_Wastepaper_Recycling_Policies.html?id=m9YsAQAAMAAJ.

The environmental benefits of recycling come chiefly from reducing the need to manufacture new products — less mining, drilling and logging. But that's not so appealing to the workers in those industries and to the communities that have accepted the environmental trade-offs that come with those jobs.

Tierney establishes common ground.

Nearly everyone, though, approves of one potential benefit of recycling: reduced 20
emissions of greenhouse gases. Its advocates often cite an estimate by the E.P.A. that recycling municipal solid waste in the United States saves the equivalent of 186 million metric tons of carbon dioxide, comparable to removing the emissions of 39 million cars.

According to the E.P.A.'s estimates, virtually all the greenhouse benefits — more than 90 percent — come from just a few materials: paper, cardboard and metals like the aluminum in soda cans. That's because recycling one ton of metal or paper saves about three tons of carbon dioxide, a much bigger payoff than the other materials analyzed by the E.P.A. Recycling one ton of plastic saves only slightly more than one ton of carbon dioxide. A ton of food saves a little less than a ton. For glass, you have to recycle three tons in order to get about one ton of greenhouse benefits. Worst of all is yard waste: it takes 20 tons of it to save a single ton of carbon dioxide.

Tierney mixes a fraction and a percentage to present his numerical data. But America still has a huge carbon footprint. Is Tierney downplaying the impact of recycling here?

Once you exclude paper products and metals, the total annual savings in the United States from recycling everything else in municipal trash — plastics, glass, food, yard trimmings, textiles, rubber, leather — is only two-tenths of 1 percent of America's carbon footprint.

As a business, recycling is on the wrong side of two long-term global economic trends. For centuries, the real cost of labor has been increasing while the real cost of raw materials has been declining. That's why we can afford to buy so much more stuff than our ancestors could. As a labor-intensive activity, recycling is an increasingly expensive way to produce materials that are less and less valuable.

Recyclers have tried to improve the economics by automating the sorting process, but they've been frustrated by politicians eager to increase recycling rates by adding new materials of little value. The more types of trash that are recycled, the more difficult it becomes to sort the valuable from the worthless.

In New York City, the net cost of recycling a ton of trash is now $300 more than 25
it would cost to bury the trash instead. That adds up to millions of extra dollars per year — about half the budget of the parks department — that New Yorkers are spending for the privilege of recycling. That money could buy far more valuable benefits, including more significant reductions in greenhouse emissions.

So what is a socially conscious, sensible person to do?

Tierney claims his source is "the most thorough" study without defining his criteria. The source title indicates that it is a study of Japan. Does this use of evidence effectively support Tierney's claim?

It would be much simpler and more effective to impose the equivalent of a carbon tax on garbage, as Thomas C. Kinnaman has proposed after conducting what is probably the most thorough comparison of the social costs[5] of recycling, landfilling and incineration. Dr. Kinnaman, an economist at Bucknell University, considered everything from environmental damage to the pleasure that some people take in recycling (the "warm glow" that makes them willing to pay extra to do it).

[5] Thomas C. Kinnaman et al., "The Socially Optimal Recycling Rate: Evidence from Japan," *Journal of Environmental Economics and Management*, vol. 68, no. 1 (2014): 54–70, digitalcommons.bucknell.edu/fac_journ/774/.

He concludes that the social good would be optimized by subsidizing the recycling of some metals, and by imposing a $15 tax on each ton of trash that goes to the landfill. That tax would offset the environmental costs, chiefly the greenhouse impact, and allow each municipality to make a guilt-free choice based on local economics and its citizens' wishes. The result, Dr. Kinnaman predicts, would be a lot less recycling than there is today.

Then why do so many public officials keep vowing to do more of it? Special-interest politics is one reason — pressure from green groups — but it's also because recycling intuitively appeals to many voters: It makes people feel virtuous, especially affluent people who feel guilty about their enormous environmental footprint. It is less an ethical activity than a religious ritual, like the ones performed by Catholics to obtain indulgences for their sins.

Religious rituals don't need any practical justification for the believers who per- 30
form them voluntarily. But many recyclers want more than just the freedom to practice their religion. They want to make these rituals mandatory for everyone else, too, with stiff fines for sinners who don't sort properly. Seattle has become so aggressive that the city is being sued by residents who maintain that the inspectors rooting through their trash are violating their constitutional right to privacy.

Definition by synonym: recycling is a religion.

It would take legions of garbage police to enforce a zero-waste society, but true believers insist that's the future. When Mayor de Blasio promised to eliminate garbage in New York, he said it was "ludicrous" and "outdated" to keep sending garbage to landfills. Recycling, he declared, was the only way for New York to become "a truly sustainable city."

But cities have been burying garbage for thousands of years, and it's still the easiest and cheapest solution for trash. The recycling movement is floundering, and its survival depends on continual subsidies, sermons and policing. How can you build a sustainable city with a strategy that can't even sustain itself?

Tierney ends by proposing a solution: the status quo.

Topics for Critical Thinking and Writing

1. What kinds of claims make John Tierney's essay persuasive? How might he be more convincing?
2. What assumptions are at work in Tierney's essay? For example, what are some of the assumptions about environmentalism that he challenges?
3. In paragraph 29, Tierney defines environmentally conscious behaviors as a "religious ritual." What kind of definition is this? How do you know? (For a refresher, see pp. 44–45.)
4. What does Tierney identify as the main problem, and what solution is he proposing? Provide a summary of his solution, tracing his line of reasoning.
5. Find at least three places where Tierney offers examples to support his claims. What kind of examples are they? Do they stand up to scrutiny?
6. Does Tierney rely more on *logos*, *pathos*, or *ethos*? How and where? In your opinion, should he have relied on one (or more) of these appeals more heavily than he did? Explain your answer.

Arguments for Analysis

KWAME ANTHONY APPIAH

Kwame Anthony Appiah (b. 1954) established his reputation as a philosopher at Cornell, Yale, Harvard, Princeton, and New York University. He is a noted cultural theorist, African historian, and novelist decorated with awards and recognitions for more than a dozen books, most recently *As If: Idealization and Ideals* (2017) and *The Lies that Bind: Rethinking Identity* (2018).

Go Ahead, Speak for Yourself

"As a white man," Joe begins, prefacing an insight, revelation, objection or confirmation he's eager to share — but let's stop him right there. Aside from the fact that he's white, and a man, what's his point? What does it signify when people use this now ubiquitous formula ("As a such-and-such, I . . .") to affix an identity to an observation?

Typically, it's an assertion of authority: As a member of this or that social group, I have experiences that lend my remarks special weight. The experiences, being representative of that group, might even qualify me to represent that group. Occasionally, the formula is an avowal of humility. It can be both at once. ("As a working-class woman, I'm struggling to understand Virginia Woolf's blithe assumptions of privilege.") The incantation seems indispensable. But it can also be — to use another much-loved formula — problematic.

The "as a" concept is an inherent feature of identities. For a group label like "white men" to qualify as a social identity, there must be times when the people to whom it applies act as members of that group, and are treated as members of that group. We make lives *as* men and women, *as* blacks and whites, *as* teachers and musicians. Yet the very word "identity" points toward the trouble: It comes from the Latin *idem*, meaning "the same." Because members of a given identity group have experiences that depend on a host of other social factors, they're *not* the same.

Being a black lesbian, for instance, isn't a matter of simply combining African-American, female and homosexual ways of being in the world; identities interact in complex ways. That's why Kimberle Crenshaw, a feminist legal theorist and civil-rights activist, introduced the notion of intersectionality, which stresses the complexity with which different forms of subordination relate to one another. Racism can make white men shrink from black men and abuse black women. Homophobia can lead men in South Africa to rape gay women but murder gay men. Sexism in the United States in the 1950s kept middle-class white women at home and sent working-class black women to work for them.

Let's go back to Joe, with his NPR mug and 5
his man bun. (Or are you picturing a "Make America Great Again" tank top and a high-and-tight?) Having an identity doesn't, by itself, authorize you to speak on behalf of everyone of that identity. So it can't really be that he's speaking for all white men. But he can at least speak to what it's like to live as a white man, right?

Not if we take the point about intersectionality. If Joe had grown up in Northern Ireland as a gay white Catholic man, his experiences might be rather different from those of his gay white *Protestant* male friends there — let alone those of his childhood pen pal, a straight, Cincinnati-raised reform Jew. While identity affects your experiences, there's no guarantee that what you've learned from them is going to be the same as what other people of the same identity have learned.

We've been here before. In the academy during the identity-conscious 1980s, many humanists thought that we'd reached peak "as a." Some worried that the locution had devolved into mere prepositional posturing. The literary theorist Barbara Johnson wrote, "If I tried to 'speak as a lesbian,' wouldn't I be processing my understanding of myself through media-induced images of what a lesbian is or through my own idealizations of what a lesbian *should* be?" In the effort to be "real," she saw something fake. Another prominent theorist, Gayatri Chakravorty Spivak, thought that the "as a" move was "a distancing from oneself," whereby the speaker became a self-appointed representative of an abstraction, some generalized perspective, and suppressed the actual multiplicity of her identities. "One is not just one thing," she observed.

It's because we're not just one thing that, in everyday conversation, "as a" can be useful as a way to spotlight some specific feature of who we are. Comedians do a lot of this sort of identity-cuing. In W. Kamau Bell's recent Netflix special, "Private School Negro," the "as a" cue, explicit or implicit, singles out various of his identities over the course of an hour. Sometimes he's speaking as a parent, who has to go camping because his kids enjoy camping. Sometimes he's speaking as an African-American, who, for ancestral reasons, doesn't see the appeal of camping ("sleeping outdoors *on purpose*?"). Sometimes — as in a story about having been asked his weight before boarding a small aircraft — he's speaking as "a man, a heterosexual, cisgender *Dad* man." (Hence: "I have no idea how much I weigh.")

The switch in identities can be the whole point of the joke. Here's Chris Rock, talking about his life in an affluent New Jersey suburb: "As a black man, I'm against the cops, but as a man with property, well, I need the cops. If someone steals something, I can't call the Crips!" Drawing attention to certain identities you have is often a natural way of drawing attention to the contours of your beliefs, values or concerns.

But *caveat auditor:* Let the listener beware. 10
Representing an identity is usually volunteer work, but sometimes the representative is conjured into being. Years ago, a slightly dotty countess I knew in the Hampstead area of London used to point out a leather-jacketed man on a park bench and inform her companions, with a knowing look, "He's the *head gay.*" She was convinced that gays had the equivalent of a pontiff or prime minister who could speak on behalf of all his people.

Because people's experiences vary so much, the "as a" move is always in peril of presumption. When I was a student at the University of Cambridge in the 1970s, gay men were *très chic*: You couldn't have a serious party without some of us scattered around like throw pillows. Do my experiences entitle me to speak for a queer farmworker who is coming of age in Emmett, Idaho? Nobody appointed me head gay.

If someone is advocating policies for gay men to adopt, or for others to adopt toward gay men, what matters, surely, isn't whether the person is gay but whether the policies are sensible. As a gay man, you could oppose same-sex marriage (it's just submitting to our culture's heteronormativity, and anyway monogamy is a patriarchal invention) or advocate same-sex marriage (it's an affirmation of equal dignity and a way to sustain gay couples). Because members of an identity group won't be identical, your "as a" doesn't settle anything. The same holds for religious, vocational and national identities.

And, of course, for racial identities. In the 1990s the black novelist Trey Ellis wrote a screenplay, "The Inkwell," which drew on his childhood in the milieu of the black bourgeoisie. A white studio head (for whom race presumably eclipsed class) gave it to Matty Rich, a young black director who'd grown up in a New York City housing project. Mr. Rich apparently worried that the script wasn't "black enough" and proposed turning the protagonist's father, a schoolteacher, into a garbage man. Suffice to say, it didn't end well. Are we really going to settle these perennial debates over authenticity with a flurry of "as a" arrowheads?

Somehow, we can't stop trying. Ever since Donald Trump eked out his surprising electoral victory, political analysts have been looking for people to speak for the supposedly disgruntled white working-class voters who, switching from their former Democratic allegiances, gave Mr. Trump the edge.

15 But about a third of working-class whites voted for Hillary Clinton. Nobody explaining why white working-class voters went for Mr. Trump would be speaking for the millions of white working-class voters who didn't. One person could say that she spoke *as* a white working-class woman in explaining why she voted for Mrs. Clinton just as truthfully as her sister could make the claim in explaining her support for Mr. Trump — each teeing us up to think about how her class and race might figure into the story. No harm in that. Neither one, however, could accurately claim to speak *for* the white working class. Neither has an exclusive on being representative.

So we might do well to ease up on "as a" — on the urge to underwrite our observations with our identities. "For me," Professor Spivak once tartly remarked, "the question 'Who should speak' is less crucial than 'Who will listen?'"

But tell that to Joe, as he takes a sip of kombucha — or is it Pabst Blue Ribbon? All right, Joe, let's hear what you've got to say. The speaking-as-a convention isn't going anywhere; in truth, it often serves a purpose. But here's another phrase you might try on for size: "Speaking for myself . . ."

Topics for Critical Thinking and Writing

1. In paragraph 2, Kwame Anthony Appiah says that speaking through the lens of an identity group is usually "an assertion of authority." How is this so? In your opinion, are there experiences that are unique to one's identity that allow them to speak with more or less authority on certain topics? If so, identify the topics and give an example.
2. How does Appiah define the term *intersectionality* in this essay? Is it adequately defined? Paraphrase the definition of *intersectionality* in this essay and then look up the term in a reputable resource and provide another definition. Does the new definition clarify or contradict Appiah's definition? How so?
3. Where does Appiah use humor or sarcasm in this essay? Explain how his humor serves to support the argument. Is it the most effective choice for the argument? Why or why not?
4. Appiah writes at length about how speaking "as a" certain identity is inadequate for establishing authority and therefore not legitimate. Explain how Appiah's concerns are really concerns about inductive reasoning and sampling. (See Types of Reasoning, pp. 80–85.)

5. Does Appiah's essay appeal more to *logos, ethos,* or *pathos*? How do you know? Was this an effective choice for his audience?
6. Examine your own identity categories and write about whether you feel you have the authority to speak "as" one of those categories. Why do you think you do? Are there identity categories in which you fit that you would not feel authoritative in speaking for the larger group? Why not?

NAUSICAA RENNER

Nausicaa Renner is digital editor of the *Columbia Journalism Review* and senior editor of *n+1*, a digital and print magazine on literature, culture, and politics. Renner's writerly interests include current events, psychoanalysis, and social media. Her essays have appeared numerously in these publications and others, including the *New York Times Magazine, Bookforum*, the *Nation*, and *National Review.*

How Do You Explain the "Obvious"?

There's nothing more persuasive than the obvious. To appeal to it is to ask people to be bigger, better, more noble — to take a sweeping look at the facts, admit what is plain and do the right thing. Tell me with a fixed gaze and an air of confidence that something is obvious. I will be tempted to believe you, if only to join in the clarity and sense of purpose that comes with accepting what is staring me in the face.

In July 2018, after President Trump's meeting with Vladimir Putin in Helsinki, David Remnick, the editor of *The New Yorker,* called on congressional Republicans to recognize the obvious. Trump, he wrote, had spent his trip working "to humiliate the leaders of Western Europe and declare them 'foes'; to fracture longstanding military, economic and political alliances; and to absolve Russia of its attempts to undermine the 2016 election. He did so clearly, repeatedly and with conviction." *Use your heads,* Remnick seemed to say, inviting G.O.P. leadership out of the darkness and into the light, asking which of them would "stand up not to applaud the Great Leader but to find the capacity to say what is obvious and what is true." *New York* magazine went further, using the blunt instrument of obviousness to impugn the Republican Party: "G.O.P. Senators: Trump's Obvious Russia Lie Is Good Enough for Us," read one headline, soon after the president claimed that he had, during a news conference with Putin, accidentally said "would" when he meant "wouldn't." ("It should have been obvious," he said, defending himself. "I thought it would be obvious.")

The obvious is a common tool in political arguments; there is something about calling on voters' "common sense" that makes the opposition look like sophists and weasels, waffling and equivocating. The obvious cuts through nonsense. It asks why we have hundreds of pages of tax law instead of one; it insists on straightforward fixes for immigration policy. And part of the appeal of universal health care is simply that it's universal: no compromises, no complex incentive systems, no loopholes, less a policy than a statement of rights. In a recent *Vox* article, Tim Higginbotham and Chris Middleman wrote that Medicare-for-all plans present a "resolute vision, one in which our common well-being and dignity take obvious precedence over the profits of a few." The stance is sure of itself; it has the certitude to weigh health care against profit and reach a decisive answer, while others remain lost in a mental fog.

But we also appeal to the obvious as a last-ditch effort when, after decades of conflict, we're further than ever from clarity. After the 2012 shooting at Sandy Hook Elementary School, President Obama gave an emotional speech at a vigil for the 20 children and six adults who were killed, asking the nation to look at itself: "Are we really prepared to say that we're powerless in the face of such carnage, that the politics are too hard?" A few years later, in a speech calling for bipartisan agreement on gun laws, he noted that after Sandy Hook, 90 percent of Americans supported a "common-sense compromise" bill. But Republicans had voted that bill down. The speech had a ring of desperation and defeat: If we can't agree on something this obvious, the president seemed to ask, what can we agree on?

5 In Edgar Allan Poe's "The Purloined Letter," the detective Auguste Dupin is able to find a stolen letter in the apartment of an unscrupulous government minister — a letter no one else could find, because everyone else assumed it would be treated as if it were valuable and hidden. Instead, the letter was hiding in plain sight, not carefully preserved but crumpled and torn like trash. It escapes detection "by dint of being extremely obvious." We prefer our politicians to be like Dupin: able to rise above the mire of small details and see the whole.

This is harder than it sounds. The letter either pops out or it doesn't. The obvious can be like a Magic Eye poster, one of those novelties whose hidden 3-D image only leaps out at you when you look at it just right: You can't really help someone else see it. It has been a signature move of the Trump administration to disrupt the obvious, beginning with a debate over the size of the crowd at the moment the president was sworn in. The mind is great at coming up with viable alternatives to ideas it doesn't want to accept, and those unwilling to accept invocations of the obvious, like Remnick's, find themselves safely tangled in a web of possibilities. With Trump, "rather than acknowledge the obvious, the supporters spin theories of 'Art of the Deal,'" wrote Jim Schutze in a column in the *Dallas Observer*, "imputing all kinds of cleverness and guile, saying he pretends to be an idiot as part of a wily strategy." At its least extreme, this entails a belief that there is some cunning in Trump's most transparent lies and clumsiest public statements; at its most extreme, it puts him at the center of an elaborate plot to destroy the "deep state." What is "obvious" is taken as false because it's *too* obvious.

This is because the obvious is, essentially, a shortcut: It appeals to a set of values we'd formed some consensus around, a set of ideas we once agreed no serious person would question. To call something "obvious" or "common sense" is to call it settled and refuse to relitigate it or revisit all the work that went into determining it was so inarguable in the first place. In a recent book, "At War with the Obvious," the psychoanalyst Donald Moss writes that "the obvious is adaptive. It mutates under pressure, like cells." If you need evidence of this, he writes, consider the status of gay, queer and trans people over the past few decades. In the 1990s, the American mainstream found it obvious that gay people should have no right to marry; today, it's regarded by many as broadly obvious that they should. An idea that was once marginal enough to require laborious defense gradually became so self-evident that it was hardly worth explaining; like the crumpled letter, its presence was taken for granted.

The difficulty is that, later, when such propositions are threatened, people may find themselves shocked, out of practice, struggling to defend their values with the passion or eloquence that first brought them into existence. Last month, for instance, Michael Anton, a former national-security official in the Trump administration, published a *Washington Post* op-ed arguing that, contrary to the understanding of most readers, birthright citizenship was based in a misreading of the law and should be ended by executive order. The fury that met this suggestion was sputtering: For anyone not already immersed in constitutional law, being horrified by Anton's claims meant arguing in favor of something that had long been so obvious that it was easy to forget what made it obvious in the first place. Justin Fox, a columnist for *Bloomberg Opinion*, allowed that a majority of the world's nations didn't offer birthright citizenship. But the claim that the authors of the 14th Amendment intended anything else, he wrote, "is, to anyone who takes the time to read a few pages of congressional debate, obviously false."

America is built on an appeal to the obvious. The Declaration of Independence holds its truths to be "self-evident" — axiomatic, irreducible, not needing justification because they justify themselves. (It was not obvious to the authors that those truths applied to all Americans, though this seems obvious to most of us now.)

10 What Americans have confronted lately is a state of affairs in which many of our most basic paradigms are no longer obvious to everyone. Appeals to obviousness seem to wilt as soon as they appear. "Are we prepared to say that such violence visited on our children, year after year after year, is somehow the price of our freedom?" asked Obama in his Sandy Hook speech. This was a rhetorical question; the obvious answer is supposed to be "no." But what if some Americans answer with "yes"?

Politicians and the press still invoke obviousness in the hope of summoning some conviction we all still share, some bedrock of group belief we can agree on. To see them fail, repeatedly, is unsettling; it makes our deepest values seem impotent. It had seemed obvious to some that a modern presidential administration would not defend white nationalists or that the United States government would seek to avoid taking babies from their parents' arms — or that a man who bragged about harassing women wouldn't be elected in the first place. In the summer of 2017, NPR celebrated the Fourth of July by tweeting, line by line, the text of the Declaration of Independence; its account was immediately attacked by angry Americans accusing the organization of spreading seditious anti-Trump propaganda. The nation's founding values have come to seem, somehow, unfamiliar and contentious; we can't recognize the Declaration of Independence when we see it. Let the obvious sit too long and it becomes like an animal in a zoo: pointed at, but never exercised, and idly wandered past by people who have forgotten how powerful it is in action.

Topics for Critical Thinking and Writing

1. In her first paragraph, Nausicaa Renner refers to an "appeal" to the obvious. What kind of appeal is this? Is it more of an appeal to reason (*logos*) or an appeal to emotion (*pathos*)? Or is it something else? Explain your answer.
2. Does Renner use an inductive or deductive means in describing the "obvious"? (See Types of Reasoning, pp. 80–85.) Explain.
3. What other strategies does Renner use to define the "obvious"?
4. What does Renner's central argument compel readers to *do*, if anything? Does she recommend any specific course of action? If so, how do you think it could benefit you?
5. Make a short list of things — three or four ideas, customs, or beliefs — that seemed obvious at one time in history but are no longer taken as obvious. What do you think will be the major changes in the obvious over the next generation?

ANNA LISA RAYA

Daughter of a second-generation Mexican American father and a Puerto Rican mother, Anna Lisa Raya grew up in Los Angeles. In 1994, while she was an undergraduate at Columbia University in New York, she wrote and published this essay on identity.

It's Hard Enough Being Me (Student Essay)

When I entered college, I *discovered* I was Latina. Until then, I had never questioned who I was or where I was from: My father is a second-generation Mexican American, born and raised in Los Angeles, and my mother was born in Puerto Rico and raised in Compton, California. My home is El Sereno, a predominantly Mexican neighborhood in L.A. Every close friend I have back home is Mexican. So I was always just Mexican. Though sometimes I was just Puerto Rican — like when we would visit Mamo (my grandma) or hang out with my Aunt Titi.

Upon arriving in New York as a first-year student, 3,000 miles from home, I not only experienced extreme culture shock, but for the first time I had to define myself according to the broad term "Latina." Although culture shock and identity crisis are common for the newly minted collegian who goes away to school, my experience as a newly minted Latina was, and still is, even more complicating. In El Sereno, I felt like I was part of a majority, whereas at the College I am a minority.

I've discovered that many Latinos like myself have undergone similar experiences. We face discrimination for being a minority in this country while also facing criticism for being "whitewashed" or "sellouts" in the countries of our heritage. But as an ethnic group in college, we are forced to define ourselves according to some vague, generalized Latino experience. This requires us to know our history, our language, our music, and our religion. I can't even be a content "Puerto Mexican" because I have to be a politically-and-socially-aware-Latina-with-a-chip-on-my-shoulder-because-of-how-repressed-I-am-in-this-country.

I am none of the above. I am the quintessential imperfect Latina. I can't dance salsa to save my life, I learned about Montezuma and the Aztecs in sixth grade, and I haven't prayed to the *Virgen de Guadalupe* in years.

5 Apparently I don't even look Latina. I can't count how many times people have just assumed that I'm white or asked me if I'm Asian. True, my friends back home call me *güera* ("whitey") because I have green eyes and pale skin, but that was as bad as it got. I never thought I would wish my skin were a darker shade or my hair a curlier texture, but since I've been in college, I have — many times.

Another thing: My Spanish is terrible. Every time I call home, I berate my mama for not teaching me Spanish when I was a child. In fact, not knowing how to speak the language of my home countries is the biggest problem that I have encountered, as have many Latinos. In Mexico there is a term, *pocha*, which is used by native Mexicans to ridicule Mexican Americans. It expresses a deep-rooted antagonism and dislike for those of us who were raised on the other side of the border. Our failed attempts to speak pure, Mexican Spanish are largely responsible for the dislike. Other Latin American natives have this same attitude. No matter how well a Latino speaks Spanish, it can never be good enough.

Yet Latinos can't even speak Spanish in the U.S. without running the risk of being called "spic" or "wetback." That is precisely why my mother refused to teach me Spanish when I was a child. The fact that she spoke Spanish was constantly used against her: It prevented her from getting good jobs, and it would have placed me in bilingual education — a construct of the Los Angeles public school system that has proved to be more of a hindrance to intellectual development than a help.

To be fully Latina in college, however, I *must* know Spanish. I must satisfy the equation: Latina [equals] Spanish-speaking.

So I'm stuck in this black hole of an identity crisis, and college isn't making my life any easier, as I thought it would. In high school, I was being prepared for an adulthood in which I would be an individual, in which I wouldn't have to wear a Catholic school uniform anymore. But though I led an anonymous adolescence, I knew who I was. I knew I was different from white, black, or Asian people. I knew there was a language other than English that I could call my own if I only knew how to speak it better. I knew there were historical reasons why I was in this country, distinct reasons that make my existence here easier or more difficult than other people's existence. Ultimately, I was content.

10 Now I feel pushed into a corner, always defining, defending, and proving myself to classmates, professors, or employers. Trying to understand who and why I am, while understanding Plato or Homer, is a lot to ask of myself.

A month ago, I heard three Nuyorican (Puerto Ricans born and raised in New York) writers discuss how New York City has influenced their writing. One problem I have faced as a young writer is finding a voice that is true to my community. I was surprised and reassured to discover that as Latinos, these writers had faced similar pressures and conflicts as myself; some weren't even taught Spanish in childhood. I will never forget the advice that one of them gave me that evening: She said that I need to be true to myself. "Because people will always complain about what you are doing — you're a 'gringa' or a 'spic' no matter what," she explained. "So you might as well do things for yourself and not for them."

I don't know why it has taken 20 years to hear this advice, but I'm going to give it a try. *Soy yo* and no one else. *Punto.*[1]

[1] **Soy yo . . . Punto.** I'm me . . . Period (Spanish). [Editors' note]

Topics for Critical Thinking and Writing

1. When Anna Lisa Raya says she "*discovered*" she was Latina (para. 1), to what kind of event is she referring? Was she coerced or persuaded to declare herself as Latina, or did it come about in some other way? Explain.
2. Is Raya glad or sorry she didn't learn Spanish as a child? What evidence in her essay indicates one way or the other?
3. What is an "identity crisis" (para. 9)? Does everyone go through such a crisis upon entering college? Did you? Or is this an experience that only racial minorities in predominantly white American colleges undergo? Explain your responses.

RONALD TAKAKI

Ronald Takaki (1939–2009), the grandson of agricultural laborers who emigrated from Japan, was a professor of ethnic studies at the University of California–Berkeley. He edited *From Different Shores: Perspectives on Race and Ethnicity in America* (1987) and wrote (among other works) *Strangers from a Different Shore: A History of Asian-Americans* (1989). The essay reprinted here appeared originally in the *New York Times* on June 16, 1990.

The Harmful Myth of Asian Superiority

Asian Americans have increasingly come to be viewed as a "model minority." But are they as successful as claimed? And for whom are they supposed to be a model?

Asian Americans have been described in the media as "excessively, even provocatively" successful in gaining admission to universities. Asian American shopkeepers have been congratulated, as well as criticized, for their ubiquity and entrepreneurial effectiveness.

If Asian Americans can make it, many politicians and pundits ask, why can't African Americans? Such comparisons pit minorities against each other and generate African American resentment toward Asian Americans. The victims are blamed for their plight, rather than racism and an economy that has made many young African American workers superfluous.

The celebration of Asian Americans has obscured reality. For example, figures on the high earnings of Asian Americans relative to Caucasians are misleading. Most Asian Americans live in California, Hawaii, and New York — states with higher incomes and higher costs of living than the national average.

Even Japanese Americans, often touted for 5
their upward mobility, have not reached equality. While Japanese American men in California earned an average income comparable to Caucasian men in 1980, they did so only by acquiring more education and working more hours.

Comparing family incomes is even more deceptive. Some Asian American groups do have higher family incomes than Caucasians. But they have more workers per family.

The "model minority" image homogenizes Asian Americans and hides their differences. For example, while thousands of Vietnamese American young people attend universities, others are on the streets. They live in motels and hang out in pool halls in places like East Los Angeles; some join gangs.

Twenty-five percent of the people in New York City's Chinatown lived below the poverty level in 1980, compared with 17 percent of the city's population. Some 60 percent of the workers in the Chinatowns of Los Angeles and San Francisco are crowded into low-paying jobs in garment factories and restaurants.

"Most immigrants coming into Chinatown with a language barrier cannot go outside this confined area into the mainstream of American industry," a Chinese immigrant said. "Before, I was a painter in Hong Kong, but I can't do it here. I got no license, no education. I want a living; so it's dishwasher, janitor, or cook."

10 Hmong and Mien refugees from Laos have unemployment rates that reach as high as 80 percent. A 1987 California study showed that three out of ten Southeast Asian refugee families had been on welfare for four to ten years.

Although college-educated Asian Americans are entering the professions and earning good salaries, many hit the "glass ceiling" — the barrier through which high management positions can be seen but not reached. In 1988, only 8 percent of Asian Americans were "officials" and "managers," compared with 12 percent for all groups.

Finally, the triumph of Korean immigrants has been exaggerated. In 1988, Koreans in the New York metropolitan area earned only 68 percent of the median income of non-Asians. More than three-quarters of Korean greengrocers, those so-called paragons of bootstrap entrepreneurialism, came to America with a college education. Engineers, teachers, or administrators while in Korea, they became shopkeepers after their arrival. For many of them, the greengrocery represents dashed dreams, a step downward in status.

For all their hard work and long hours, most Korean shopkeepers do not actually earn very much: $17,000 to $35,000 a year, usually representing the income from the labor of an entire family.

But most Korean immigrants do not become shopkeepers. Instead, many find themselves trapped as clerks in grocery stores, service workers in restaurants, seamstresses in garment factories, and janitors in hotels.

15 Most Asian Americans know their "success" is largely a myth. They also see how the celebration of Asian Americans as a "model minority" perpetuates their inequality and exacerbates relations between them and African Americans.

Topics for Critical Thinking and Writing

1. What is the thesis of Ronald Takaki's essay? What evidence does he offer for its truth? Do you find his argument convincing? Explain your answers to these questions.
2. Takaki several times uses statistics to make a point. What effect do the statistics have on the reader? Do some of the statistics seem more convincing than others? Explain your responses.
3. Consider the title of Takaki's essay. To what group(s) is the myth of Asian superiority harmful?
4. Suppose you believed that Asian Americans are economically more successful in America today, relative to white Americans, than African Americans are. Does Takaki agree or disagree with you? Why, or why not? What evidence, if any, does he cite to support or reject the belief?
5. Takaki attacks the "myth" of Asian American success and thus rejects the idea that Asian Americans are a "model minority" (recall the opening and closing paragraphs). Do you think a model is possible to describe any minority group? Why, or why not?

JAMES Q. WILSON

James Q. Wilson (1931–2012) was Collins Professor of Management and Public Policy at the University of California–Los Angeles. Among his books are *Thinking about Crime* (1975), *Bureaucracy* (1989), *The Moral Sense* (1993), and *Moral Judgment* (1997). This essay appeared originally in the *New York Times Magazine* on March 20, 1994.

Just Take Away Their Guns

The president wants still tougher gun control legislation and thinks it will work. The public supports more gun control laws but suspects they won't work. The public is right.

Legal restraints on the lawful purchase of guns will have little effect on the illegal use of guns. There are some 200 million guns in private ownership, about one-third of them handguns. Only about 2 percent of the latter are employed to commit crimes. It would take a Draconian,[1] and politically impossible, confiscation of legally purchased guns to make much of a difference in the number used by criminals. Moreover, only about one-sixth of the handguns used by serious criminals are purchased from a gun shop or pawnshop. Most of these handguns are stolen, borrowed, or obtained through private purchases that wouldn't be affected by gun laws.

What is worse, any successful effort to shrink the stock of legally purchased guns (or of ammunition) would reduce the capacity of law-abiding people to defend themselves. Gun control advocates scoff at the importance of self-defense, but they are wrong to do so. Based on a household survey, Gary Kleck, a criminologist at Florida State University, has estimated that every year, guns are used — that is, displayed or fired — for defensive purposes more than a million times, not counting their use by the police. If his estimate is correct, this means that the number of people who defend themselves with a gun exceeds the number of arrests for violent crimes and burglaries.

Our goal should not be the disarming of law-abiding citizens. It should be to reduce the number of people who carry guns unlawfully, especially in places — on streets, in taverns — where the mere presence of a gun can increase the hazards we all face. The most effective way to reduce illegal gun-carrying is to encourage the police to take guns away from people who carry them without a permit. This means encouraging the police to make street frisks.

5 The Fourth Amendment to the Constitution bans "unreasonable searches and seizures." In 1968 the Supreme Court decided (*Terry v. Ohio*) that a frisk — patting down a person's outer clothing — is proper if the officer has a "reasonable suspicion" that the person is armed and dangerous. If a pat-down reveals an object that might be a gun, the officer can enter the suspect's pocket to remove it. If the gun is being carried illegally, the suspect can be arrested.

The reasonable-suspicion test is much less stringent than the probable-cause standard the police must meet in order to make an arrest. A reasonable suspicion, however, is more than just a hunch; it must be supported by specific facts. The courts have held, not always consistently, that these facts include

[1] **Draconian** Harsh or severe, often excessively so. [Editors' note]

someone acting in a way that leads an experienced officer to conclude criminal activity may be afoot; someone fleeing at the approach of an officer; a person who fits a drug courier profile; a motorist stopped for a traffic violation who has a suspicious bulge in his pocket; a suspect identified by a reliable informant as carrying a gun. The Supreme Court has also upheld frisking people on probation or parole.

Some police departments frisk a lot of people, but usually the police frisk rather few, at least for the purpose of detecting illegal guns. In 1992 the police arrested about 240,000 people for illegally possessing or carrying a weapon. This is only about one-fourth as many as were arrested for public drunkenness. The average police officer will make *no* weapons arrests and confiscate *no* guns during any given year. Mark Moore, a professor of public policy at Harvard University, found that most weapons arrests were made because a citizen complained, not because the police were out looking for guns.

It is easy to see why. Many cities suffer from a shortage of officers, and even those with ample law-enforcement personnel worry about having their cases thrown out for constitutional reasons or being accused of police harassment. But the risk of violating the Constitution or engaging in actual, as opposed to perceived, harassment can be substantially reduced.

Each patrol officer can be given a list of people on probation or parole who live on that officer's beat and be rewarded for making frequent stops to insure that they are not carrying guns. Officers can be trained to recognize the kinds of actions that the Court will accept as providing the "reasonable suspicion" necessary for a stop and frisk. Membership in a gang known for assaults and drug dealing could be made the basis, by statute or Court precedent, for gun frisks.

10 The available evidence supports the claim that self-defense is a legitimate form of deterrence. People who report to the National Crime Survey that they defended themselves with a weapon were less likely to lose property in a robbery or be injured in an assault than those who did not defend themselves. Statistics have shown that would-be burglars are threatened by gun-wielding victims about as many times a year as they are arrested (and much more often than they are sent to prison) and that the chances of a burglar being shot are about the same as his chances of going to jail. Criminals know these facts even if gun control advocates do not and so are less likely to burgle occupied homes in America than occupied ones in Europe, where the residents rarely have guns.

Some gun control advocates may concede these points but rejoin that the cost of self-defense is self-injury: Handgun owners are more likely to shoot themselves or their loved ones than a criminal. Not quite. Most gun accidents involve rifles and shotguns, not handguns. Moreover, the rate of fatal gun accidents has been declining while the level of gun ownership has been rising. There are fatal gun accidents just as there are fatal car accidents, but in fewer than 2 percent of the gun fatalities was the victim someone mistaken for an intruder.

Those who urge us to forbid or severely restrict the sale of guns ignore these facts. Worse, they adopt a position that is politically absurd. In effect, they say, "Your government, having failed to protect your person and your property from criminal assault, now intends to deprive you of the opportunity to protect yourself."

Opponents of gun control make a different mistake. The National Rifle Association and its allies tell us that "guns don't kill, people kill" and urge the Government to punish more severely people who use guns to commit crimes. Locking up criminals does protect society from future crimes, and the prospect of being locked up may deter criminals. But our experience with meting out tougher sentences is mixed. The tougher the prospective sentence the less likely it is to be imposed, or at least to be imposed swiftly. If the Legislature adds on time for crimes committed with a gun, prosecutors often bargain away the add-ons; even when they do not, the judges in many states are reluctant to impose add-ons.

Worse, the presence of a gun can contribute to the magnitude of the crime even on the part of those who worry about serving a long prison sentence. Many criminals carry guns not to rob stores but to protect themselves from other armed criminals. Gang violence has become more threatening to bystanders as gang members have begun to arm themselves. People may commit crimes, but guns make some crimes worse. Guns often convert spontaneous outbursts of anger into fatal encounters. When some people carry them on the streets, others will want to carry them to protect themselves, and an urban arms race will be under way.

15 And modern science can be enlisted to help. Metal detectors at airports have reduced the number of airplane bombings and skyjackings to nearly zero. But these detectors only work at very close range. What is needed is a device that will enable the police to detect the presence of a large lump of metal in someone's pocket from a distance of ten or fifteen feet. Receiving such a signal could supply the officer with reasonable grounds for a pat-down. Underemployed nuclear physicists and electronics engineers in the post-cold-war era surely have the talents for designing a better gun detector.

Even if we do all these things, there will still be complaints. Innocent people will be stopped. Young black and Hispanic men will probably be stopped more often than older white Anglo males or women of any race. But if we are serious about reducing drive-by shootings, fatal gang wars and lethal quarrels in public places, we must get illegal guns off the street. We cannot do this by multiplying the forms one fills out at gun shops or by pretending that guns are not a problem until a criminal uses one.

Topics for Critical Thinking and Writing

1. If you had to single out one sentence in James Wilson's essay that best states his thesis, what sentence would that be? Why do you think it states, better than any other sentence, the essay's thesis?
2. In paragraph 3, Wilson reviews research by a criminologist purporting to show that guns are important for self-defense in American households. Evaluate the evidence: Does the research as reported show that displaying or firing guns in self-defense actually prevented crimes? Or wounded aggressors? Suppose you were also told that in households where guns may be used defensively, thousands of innocent people are injured and hundreds are killed — for instance, children who find a loaded gun and play with it. Would you regard these injuries and deaths as a fair trade-off? Explain. What does the research presented by Wilson really show?
3. In a brief statement, explain the difference between the "reasonable suspicion" test (para. 5) and the "probable cause standard" (para. 6) that the courts use in deciding whether a street frisk is lawful. (You may want to organize your essay into two paragraphs, one on each topic, or perhaps into three if you include a brief introductory paragraph.)

4. Wilson reports in paragraph 7 that the police arrest four times as many drunks on the streets as they do people carrying unlicensed firearms. Does this strike you as absurd, reasonable, or mysterious? Does Wilson explain it to your satisfaction? Why, or why not?
5. In paragraph 12, Wilson says that people who want to severely restrict the ownership of guns are in effect saying, "'Your government, having failed to protect your person and your property from criminal assault, now intends to deprive you of the opportunity to protect yourself.'" What reply might an advocate of severe restrictions make? (Even if you strongly believe Wilson's summary is accurate, put yourself in the shoes of an advocate of gun control and come up with the best reply that you can.)
6. In his final paragraph, Wilson grants that his proposal entails a difficulty: "Innocent people will be stopped. Young black and Hispanic men will probably be stopped more often than older white Anglo males or women of any race." Assuming that his predictions are accurate, is his proposal therefore fatally flawed and worth no further thought, or (taking the other extreme view) will innocent people who fall into certain classifications just have to put up with frisking for the public good? Explain your response.

BERNIE SANDERS

Bernie Sanders (b. 1941), former mayor of Burlington, Vermont, was elected to the US Congress in 1990, becoming the first independent to win a seat since 1950. In 2006, he won election as US senator from Vermont and, in 2016, made an unsuccessful but widely popular bid to earn the nomination of the Democratic Party for the US presidency. A self-avowed "democratic socialist," Sanders has advocated throughout his life for civil rights and workers' rights.

We Must Make Public Colleges and Universities Tuition Free

Our nation needs the best-educated workforce in the world to succeed in the ever more competitive global economy. Sadly, we are moving further and further away from that goal. As recently as 1995, the United States led the world in college graduation rates, but today we have fallen to 11th place. We are now behind such countries as Japan, South Korea, Canada, England, Ireland, Australia, and Switzerland. Eleventh place is not the place for a great nation like the United States.

Why is this so important? Because fifty years ago, if you had a high school degree, odds were that you could get a decent job and make it into the middle class. But that is no longer the case. While not all middle-class jobs in today's economy require post-secondary education, an increasing number do. By 2020, two-thirds of all jobs in the United States will require some education beyond high school.

And these jobs tend to pay better, too. Nationally, a worker with an associate's degree will earn about $360,000 more over their career than a worker with a high school diploma. And a worker with a bachelor's degree will earn almost $1 million more.

If it makes sense to get a college degree, why aren't more high school students enrolling in and graduating from college? The main reason is because the ever-rising cost of higher education puts college out of reach for many families, or requires students to take on a mountain of debt.

5 It's time to change that dynamic. It's time to make public colleges and universities tuition-free for the working families of our country. It is time for every child to understand that if they study hard and take their school work seriously they will be able to get a higher education, regardless of their family's income. It's time to reduce the outrageous burden of student debt that is weighing down the lives of millions of college graduates.

Today, our system of higher education is in a state of crisis. As tuition and fees steadily rise and as states cut funding for colleges and universities year after year, American families are finding it increasingly difficult to afford college. Every year, hundreds of thousands of bright young people can't get a higher education because it is simply too expensive. Equally disgraceful, millions of college graduates have had to take on life-long debt for the "crime" of getting the education they need.

Some 44 million Americans already owe more than $1.3 trillion in student loans, and the vast majority of current college students will graduate deeply in debt. For most graduates, this debt will take many years to repay, which not only impacts their career choices, but also their ability to get married, have kids, or buy a home.

In the richest country in the history of the world, everyone who has the desire and the ability should be able to get a college education regardless of their background and ability to pay. That's why I introduced the *College for All Act,* to make public colleges and universities in America tuition-free for families earning $125,000 per year or less — which covers 86 percent of our population.

This is not a radical idea. Many other nations around the world invest in an educated workforce that isn't burdened with enormous student debt. In Germany, Finland, Denmark, Iceland, Norway, and Sweden public colleges and universities are free. In Germany, public colleges are free not only for Germans, but also for international students.

10 It wasn't that long ago that our own government understood the value of investing in higher education. In 1944, Congress passed the GI Bill, which provided a free college education to millions of World War II veterans. This was one of the most successful pieces of legislation in modern history, laying the groundwork for the extraordinary post-war economic boom and an unprecedented expansion of the middle class.

But it was not just the federal government that acted. In 1965, average tuition at a four-year state public university was just $256, and many excellent colleges — such as the City University of New York — did not charge any tuition at all. The University of California system, considered by many to be the crown jewel of public higher education in this country, did not charge tuition until the 1980s.

The good news is that governors, state legislators, and local officials around the country now understand the crisis and are acting. This year, the City College of San Francisco began offering tuition-free college, and its enrollment for residents is up by 51 percent compared to last year. In New York, tens of thousands will go to the city's public colleges and universities this year without paying tuition. Similar programs have popped up in Tennessee, Oregon, Detroit and Chicago.

We are making progress on this issue, but we still have a long way to go. Making America great is not spending tens of billions more on weapons systems or providing trillions in tax breaks for the very rich. Rather, it is having a well-educated population that can compete in the global economy, and making it possible that every American, regardless of income, has the opportunity to get the education they need to thrive.

Topics for Critical Thinking and Writing

1. Examine the first paragraph of Bernie Sanders's essay and describe Sanders's approach to his argument. How does he use rhetorical appeals? Assumptions? Definition?
2. Use the structure of the syllogism (see Premises and Syllogisms, pp. 81–85) to list a series of premises in Sanders's argument that lead to the conclusion, "Therefore, we must make US colleges and universities tuition free." (Keep in mind that you can list as many premises as you want.) Do you think the argument is *valid*? If you had to work to undermine it, where would you point in the premises to show areas that are challengeable?
3. How does Sanders's argument use emotional appeals (*pathos*)?
4. Do you think Sanders provides a thoughtful consideration of opposing viewpoints? What negative consequences can you think of that might result from passing the College for All Act?
5. Examine Sanders's use of numbers. How does he use numerical data to support his argument? Do you find his presentation of numbers effective or misleading? How might he have presented them differently?

ASSIGNMENTS FOR CRITICAL READING

1. Choose one of the essays in this book and write a rhetorical analysis. In other words, investigate *how* the author makes his or her argument in order to convince the intended audience. Here are some questions to consider as you plan your analysis:

   - What is the writer's claim or thesis?
   - Who is the writer's audience?
   - What is the writer's purpose? What outcome does the writer want to see?
   - In what ways is the argument based on *logos*, *pathos*, or *ethos*? What is the balance of these appeals?
   - What types of support (evidence) is offered on behalf of the claim?
   - What emotions are evoked by the argument and how?
   - How does the writer establish credibility?
   - Are the writer's strategies effective in convincing the intended audience? If not, what should the writer have done differently?

   Use A Checklist for Analyzing an Argument on page 108 to further guide your analysis.

2. Write your own definition for any term or concept you can imagine needing a definition — or *re*definition — and develop it into a paragraph or full essay using one (or more) of the definition types discussed in this chapter: stipulation, synonym, example, or establishing sufficient and necessary conditions. Here are some ideas to help you. You may also supply your own term or concept or apply this exercise to a current argument you are writing.

hipster culture	American-made car	capital punishment
apocalyptic anxiety	wasting time	alcoholism
the 1960s	being a good neighbor	stereotypes (or stereotypes of *X*)

4

Visual Rhetoric: Thinking about Images as Arguments

"What is the use of a book," thought Alice, "without pictures or conversations?"

— LEWIS CARROLL

All photographs are accurate. None of them is the truth.

— RICHARD AVEDON

Uses of Visual Images

Most visual materials that accompany written arguments serve one of several functions. One of the most common is to appeal to the reader's emotions (e.g., a photograph of a sad-eyed calf in a narrow pen assists an argument against eating veal by inspiring sympathy for the animal). Pictures can also serve as visual evidence, offering proof that something occurred or appeared in a certain way at a certain moment (e.g., a security photograph shows the face of a bank robber to a jury). Pictures can help clarify numerical data (e.g., a graph shows five decades of law school enrollment by males and females). They can also add humor or satire to an essay (a photograph of an executive wearing a blindfold made of dollar bills supports an argument that companies are blinded by their profit motives). In this chapter, we concentrate on thinking critically about visual images. This means reading images in the same way we read print (or electronic) texts: by looking closely at them and discerning not only *what* they show but also *how* and *why* they show what they do and how they convey a particular message or argument.

When we discussed the appeal to emotion, ***pathos***, in Chapter 3 (see Persuasion, Argument, and Rhetorical Appeals, pages 75–79), we explained how certain words and ideas can muster the emotions of an audience. Images can do the same without words or with minimal, carefully selected, and thoughtfully displayed words. In a very immediate way, they can make us laugh, cry, or gasp. Furthermore, when used as evidence, some images, graphs, and visuals have an additional advantage over words: They carry a high level of what communications scholars call *indexical value*, meaning that they seem to point to what is true and indisputable.

In courtrooms today, trial lawyers and prosecutors help stir the audience's emotions when they

- hold up a murder weapon for jurors to see,
- introduce victims of crime as witnesses, or
- exhibit images of a bloody corpse or a crime scene.

Whether presented sincerely or gratuitously, visuals can have a significantly persuasive effect. Visuals may be rationally connected to an argument: A gruesome image of a diseased lung in an anti-smoking ad makes a reasonable claim, as does a photograph of crime scene that establishes the veracity of the locations of evidence. But the immediate impact of a photograph is more often on the viewer's heart (*pathos*) rather than mind (*logos*). Speaking of those appeals, we can also say that images can help establish *ethos*: Think about how lawyers might present to the jury images of defendants portrayed in wholesome contexts — receiving an award, hugging a family member — in order to bolster their character or credibility (even if their defendants are actually lacking these qualities).

Like any kind of evidence, images make statements and support arguments. When the US Congress debated whether to allow drilling in the Arctic National Wildlife Refuge (ANWR), opponents and supporters both used images to support their verbal arguments:

- *Opponents* of drilling showed beautiful pictures of polar bears frolicking, wildflowers in bloom, and caribou on the move, arguing that such a landscape would be despoiled.
- *Proponents* of drilling showed bleak pictures of what they called "barren land" and "a frozen wasteland," pointing to a useless and barely habitable environment.

Both sides knew very well that images are powerfully persuasive, and they didn't hesitate to use them as supplements to words.

US Fish and Wildlife Service/Getty Images

David Howells/Corbis Historical/Getty Images

These two photographs, both of the Arctic National Wildlife Refuge, show different uses of images to argue about the value and use of land.

We invite you to reflect upon the appropriateness of using such images in arguments. Was either side manipulating the "reality" of the ANWR? Both images were *real*, after all. Each side selected a particular *kind* of image for a specific **purpose** — to support its position on drilling in the ANWR. Neither side was being dishonest, and both were showing true pictures, but both were also appealing to emotions.

Exercise: Responding to Images

In a paragraph, discuss how these images of the ANWR offer reasonable support (*logos*) and emotional support (*pathos*) for an argument. Go further: Examine the source of the photographs and also discuss how *ethos* is established.

TYPES OF EMOTIONAL APPEALS

After reading Chapter 3, you understand much about how arguments appeal to reason through induction and deduction, by definitions and examples, by drawing conclusions, and so forth. You also learned something about *persuasion*, which is a broad term that can include appeals to various kinds of emotions — for example, an **appeal to pity**, such as the image of a sad-eyed calf mentioned at the beginning of this chapter. You might be moved emotionally by such an image and say, "Well, I am never eating meat again because doing so implies the inhumane treatment of helpless animals," and regard the image as both *reasonable* and *emotionally powerful*. Or you might say, "Although it's emotionally powerful, this image doesn't describe the condition of every calf. Some are treated humanely, slaughtered humanely, and eaten ethically." In your argument, you might include an alternative image of a pasture-raised calf on an organic, locally owned farm (although you too would be appealing to emotions).

The point is that images can be persuasive even if they don't make good or complete arguments. The gangster Al Capone famously said, "You can get a lot more done with a kind word and a gun than with a kind word alone." A threat of violence — do this *or else* — is actually a *kind* of an argument, just one that appeals exclusively to the emotions — specifically, to fear.

Although they do not threaten violence, advertisers commonly use the **appeal to fear** as a persuasive technique. The appeal to fear is a threat of sorts. Showing a scary burglary, a visceral car crash, embarrassing age spots, or a nasty cockroach infestation can successfully convince consumers to buy a product — a home security system, a new car insurance policy, an age-defying skin cream, a pesticide. Such images generate fear and anxiety at the same time they offer the solution for it.

However, appeals to fear — like all the appeals we will discuss — are not confined to the world of advertising. Appeals to fear often drive political arguments, especially during a campaign season. Even arguments about art and culture can utilize fear to support an argument. In 1985, the Parents Music Resource Center (PMRC), founded by Tipper Gore (then wife of politician Al Gore), argued that some popular music was undermining society

What fears are evoked by this political video ad from Georgia, distributed during the 2018 midterm elections?

by promoting occult beliefs, precocious sexuality, and drug and alcohol use. After a US Senate hearing was convened, the PMRC successfully lobbied the recording industry to require "Parental Advisory" warnings on all music deemed inappropriate for children.

There are different kinds of fear to which writers can appeal. Appeals to fear are at work in a recently named phenomenon called FOMO, or Fear of Missing Out, which occurs when someone adopts the latest trends, attends events, or otherwise engages in some activity because they worry about not being part of it. FOMO occurs too when we are hurried to take advantage of a scarce or limited-time opportunity.

Violence and fear can also support arguments made to end acts of terror and cruelty. Images played a crucial role in the antislavery movement in the nineteenth century. The collection shown on page 135 offers three different types of visuals and three depictions of the slave experience. The first is a diagram showing how human cargo was packed into a slave ship; it was distributed with Thomas Clarkson's *Essay on the Slavery and Commerce of the Human Species* (1804), one of the first antislavery treatises. Following is Civil War surgeon Frederick W. Mercer's photograph (April 2, 1863) of Gordon, a "badly lacerated" runaway slave. Images such as the slave ship and the runaway slave worked against slave owners' claims that slavery was a humane institution—claims that also were supported by illustrations, such as the woodcut *Attention Paid to a Poor Sick Negro* from Josiah Priest's *In Defence of Slavery* (1843). Examine each picture closely and consider whether you think they make appeals to reason or emotion.

Appeal to self-interest is another persuasive tactic that speakers and writers can use. Consider these remarks, which use the word *interest* in the sense of "self-interest":

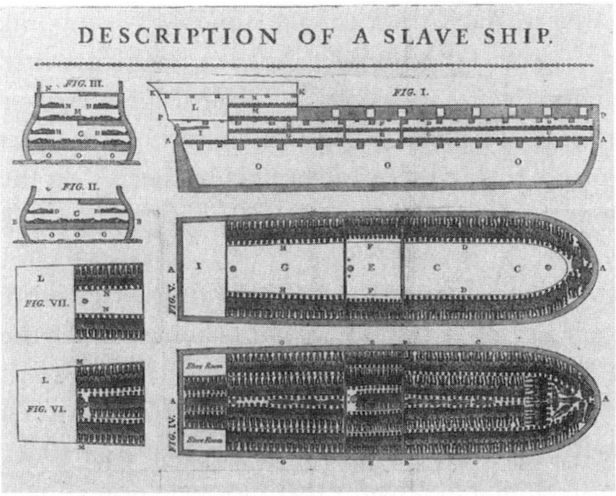

Description of a Slave Ship, 1789 (print)/English School (18th century)/Wilberforce House Museum/Wilberforce House, Hull City Museums and Art Galleries, UK/Bridgeman Images

Diagram "Description of a Slave Ship," distributed with Thomas Clarkson's *Essay on the Slavery and Commerce of the Human Species* (1804).

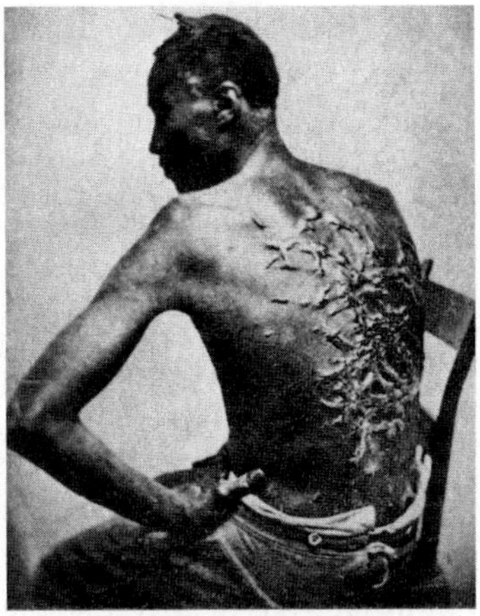

Bettmann/Getty Images

Frederick W. Mercer's photograph (April 2, 1863) of Gordon, a "badly lacerated" runaway slave.

Josiah Priest's In Defense of Slavery, Rare Books and Manuscripts Department, Boston Public Library

Attention Paid to a Poor Sick Negro, a woodcut from Josiah Priest's *In Defense of Slavery* (1843).

Would you persuade, speak of Interest, not Reason. — BENJAMIN FRANKLIN

There are two levers for moving men — interest and fear. — NAPOLEON BONAPARTE

Appeals to self-interest may be quite persuasive because they speak directly to what benefits *you* the most, not necessarily what benefits others in the community, society, or world. Such appeals are also common in advertising. "You can save bundles by shopping at Maxi-Mart," a commercial might claim, without making reference to third-world sweatshop labor conditions in the supply chain, the negative impact of global commerce, or other troublesome aspects of what you see only as a great savings for yourself. Maxi-Mart would never say, "Maxi-Mart offers low prices by buying products made cheaply on the other side of the world and shipping them to the United States on inefficient fuel-guzzling cargo ships."

You may be familiar with other types of advertising that speak to the senses more than reason. These kinds of appeals don't necessarily make *good* arguments for the products in question, but they can be highly persuasive — sometimes affecting us subconsciously — because they speak so much to our individual feelings and interests. Of course, as with all appeals, those made to self-interest can be seen in all kinds of arguments, but the appeals of advertisements are often so blunt and obvious that they help us highlight their effects. Thinking critically about appeals in advertisements can be helpful then in developing our ability to analyze other basic kinds of appeals in words and other kinds of images.

Here is a list of some other emotional appeals commonly used in advertising:

- sexual appeals (e.g., a bikini-clad model standing near a product)
- bandwagon appeals (e.g., crowds of people rushing to a sale)
- humor appeals (e.g., a cartoon animal drinking *X* brand of beverage)
- celebrity appeals (e.g., a famous person driving *X* brand of car)
- testimonial appeals (e.g., a doctor giving *X* brand of vitamins to her kids)
- identity appeals (e.g., a "good family" going to *X* restaurant)
- prejudice appeals (e.g., a "loser" drinking *X* brand of beer)
- lifestyle appeals (e.g., a jar of *X* brand of mustard on a silver platter)
- stereotype appeals (e.g., a Latinx person enjoying *X* brand of salsa)
- patriotic appeals (e.g., *X* brand of mattress alongside an American flag)

Exercise: Emotional Appeals in Visual Arguments

Select two of the appeals listed above and think of another real-life instance outside advertising in which the type of appeal occurs, either in words or images. For example, images of former pro football quarterback Colin Kaepernick have been used to appeal to the patriotism of audiences in arguments about the appropriateness of his dissent: kneeling on the football field during the national anthem to protest police violence against African Americans.

Seeing versus Looking: Reading Advertisements

Advertising is one of the most common forms of visual persuasion we encounter in everyday life. The influence of advertising in our culture is pervasive and subtle. Part of its power comes from our habit of internalizing the intended messages of words and images without thinking deeply about them. Once we begin decoding the ways in which advertisements are constructed — once we view them critically — we can understand how (or if) they work as arguments. We may then make better decisions about whether to buy particular products and what factors convinced us or failed to convince us. Further, by sharpening our critical skills, we can approach images in all their forms with a more careful and skeptical approach.

To read any image critically, it helps to consider some basic rules from the field of **semiotics**, the study of signs and symbols. Fundamental to semiotic analysis is the idea that visual signs have shared meanings in a culture. If you approach a sink and see a red faucet and a blue faucet, you can be pretty sure which one will produce hot water and which one will produce cold water. Thus, one of the first strategies we can use in reading advertisements critically is **deconstructing** them, taking them apart to see what makes them work.

For starters, it's helpful to remember that advertisements are enormously expensive to produce and disseminate, so nothing is left to chance. Teams of people typically scrutinize every part of an advertisement to ensure it communicates the intended message — although this doesn't imply that viewers must accept those messages. Taking apart an advertisement (or any image) means examining each visual element carefully in order to understand its purpose, its strategy, and effect.

Consider this 2007 advertisement for Nike shoes featuring basketball star LeBron James. Already, you should see the celebrity appeal — an implicit claim that Nike shoes

The text draws on language commonly used in religious settings to describe the second coming of Christ.
The Nike logo is the only reference to the brand being advertised. It is a powerful symbol and identity marker, much like a cross.
WE ARE ALL WITNESSES.
CLEVELAND
23
James's arms are outstretched, Christ-like, and seem to be illuminated by divine light from above.
The number 23 references basketball legend (and Nike spokesperson) Michael Jordan. James is, in a way, presented as a new incarnation of a sports "god."

A Nike advertisement featuring basketball star Lebron James, annotated to show a deconstruction of the image.

help make James a star player. The ad creates an association between the shoes and the sports champion. But look closer, paying attention to how the elements work together to make meaning.

Let's also consider this advertisement in the context of James's famous 2014 return to the Cleveland Cavaliers, his hometown team, after leaving the team abruptly to play four seasons with the Miami Heat. James's own second coming resonated with themes of forgiveness, redemption, and salvation among Cleveland sports fans. In 2018, James signed with the Los Angeles Lakers in free agency. In one of his first public statements about his decision, James said, "I believe the Lakers is a historical franchise, we all know that, but it's a championship franchise and that's what we're trying to get back to. And I'm happy to be part of the culture and be a part of us getting back to that point." Considering these comments, we wonder if this same image of James in a Lakers jersey would have the same resonance.

In the ad on p. 137, all these associations work together to elevate James, Jordan, and Nike to exalted status. Of course, our description here is tongue in cheek. We're not gullible enough to believe this literally, and the ad's producers don't expect us to be; but they do hope that such an impression will be powerful enough to make us think of Nike the next time we shop for athletic shoes. If sports gods wear Nike, why shouldn't we?

This kind of analysis is possible when we recognize a difference between *seeing* and *looking*. **Seeing** is a physiological process involving light, the eye, and the brain. **Looking**, however, is a social process involving the mind. It suggests apprehending an image in terms

Image Courtesy of The Advertising Archives

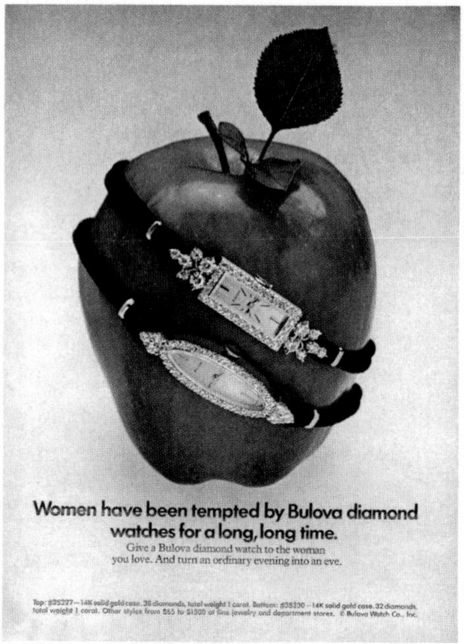

Image Courtesy of The Advertising Archives

How do the DKNY and Bulova advertisements use the symbolic, connotative meanings of the apple to make an argument about their products?

of symbolic, metaphorical, and other social and cultural meanings. To do this, we must think beyond the *literal* meaning of an image or image element and consider its *figurative* meanings. If you look up *apple* in the dictionary, you'll find its literal, **denotative** meaning — a round fruit with thin red or green skin and a crisp flesh. But an apple also communicates figurative, **connotative** meanings. Connotative meanings are the cultural or emotional associations that an image suggests.

The connotative meaning of an apple in Western culture dates back to the biblical story of the Garden of Eden, where Eve, tempted by a serpent, eats the fruit from the forbidden tree of knowledge and brings about the end of paradise on earth. Throughout Western culture, apples have come to represent knowledge and the pursuit of knowledge. Think of the ubiquitous Apple logo gracing so many mobile phones, tablets, and laptops: With its prominent bite, it symbolizes the way technology opens up new worlds of knowing. Sometimes, apples represent forbidden knowledge, temptation, or seduction — and biting into one suggests giving in to desires for new understandings and experiences. The story of Snow White offers just one example of an apple used as a symbol of temptation.

When you are looking — and not just seeing in the simplest sense — you are attempting to discern the ways in which symbolic meanings are used to communicate a message. Take, for example, the following advertisement for Play-Doh, one of the most enduring and popular toys of the past century. First developed in 1930s, Play-Doh has sold billions of canisters around the world. Today, Play-Doh competes with a wide array of technological toys for children, such as smartphones and video game systems.

An advertisement for the timeless toy, Play-Doh, that takes on its digital competitors.

The ad for Play-Doh featured here makes an argument with just a single line of text: "No In-App Purchases." These words are set below the image of a shopping cart with a plus sign made of Play-Doh, which has come to be an almost universally recognized symbol for an electronic shopping cart online. Both the words and the icon are textured and look a little rough at the edges, suggesting that they are also made of Play-Doh. In a blue open space suggesting three-dimensionality, the advertisement seems to make a case for the role of real-life,

A CHECKLIST FOR ANALYZING IMAGES

- ❒ What is the overall effect of the design (e.g., colorful and busy, quiet and understated, old-fashioned or cutting-edge)?
- ❒ Is color (or the lack of it) used for a particular purpose? Do colors signify any cultural meaning?
- ❒ Does the image evoke a particular emotional response? Which elements contribute to that response?
- ❒ Is the audience for the image apparent? Does the image successfully appeal to this audience?
- ❒ Is there an argument present? If so, does it appeal to reason (*logos*) — perhaps using statistics, charts, or graphs — or to feelings (*pathos*) — evoking emotional responses or deeply held values? Or is it both?
- ❒ If there is an appeal to character or credibility (*ethos*), suggesting good sense, trustworthiness, or prudence, is it effective?
- ❒ Is there any text? If so, what is its relation to the image?

non-digital play in the development of children. It presents Play-Doh as a traditional, value-based proposition without manipulative sales tactics, something trustworthy and honest. The way children play has changed dramatically since the 1930s, but by fashioning the electronic icon and text out of a nearly century-old product, the ad implies that just because a toy — or anything else — is new and high-tech, that does not make it inherently better than old-fashioned things. After all, the product being advertised has stood the test of time; how long will an app on a smartphone or tablet last until it is replaced with a newer version requiring a new update?

Levels of Images

One helpful way of deriving the meanings of images by *looking* at them is to use *seeing* first as a way to define what is plainly or literally present in them. You can begin by *seeing* — identifying the elements that are indisputably "there" in an image (the denotative level). In a sense, you are merely taking an inventory of what is visible and evident. Then you move on to *looking* — interpreting the meanings suggested by the elements that are present (the connotative level). Arguably, when we *see*, we pay attention only to the denotative level — that is, we observe just the explicit elements of the image. We aren't concerned with the meaning of the image's elements yet, just with the fact that they're present.

When we *look*, we move to the connotative level — that is, we speculate on the elements' deeper meanings: what they suggest figuratively, symbolically, or metaphorically in our cultural system. We may also consider the relationship of different elements to one another.

Seeing	**Looking**
Denotation	Connotation
Literal	Figurative
What is present	What it means
Understanding/Textual	Interpreting/Subtextual/Contextual

Further questions we can ask have to do with the contexts in which they are created, disseminated, and received. Within each of those, other questions arise.

Visual Guide: Analyzing Images

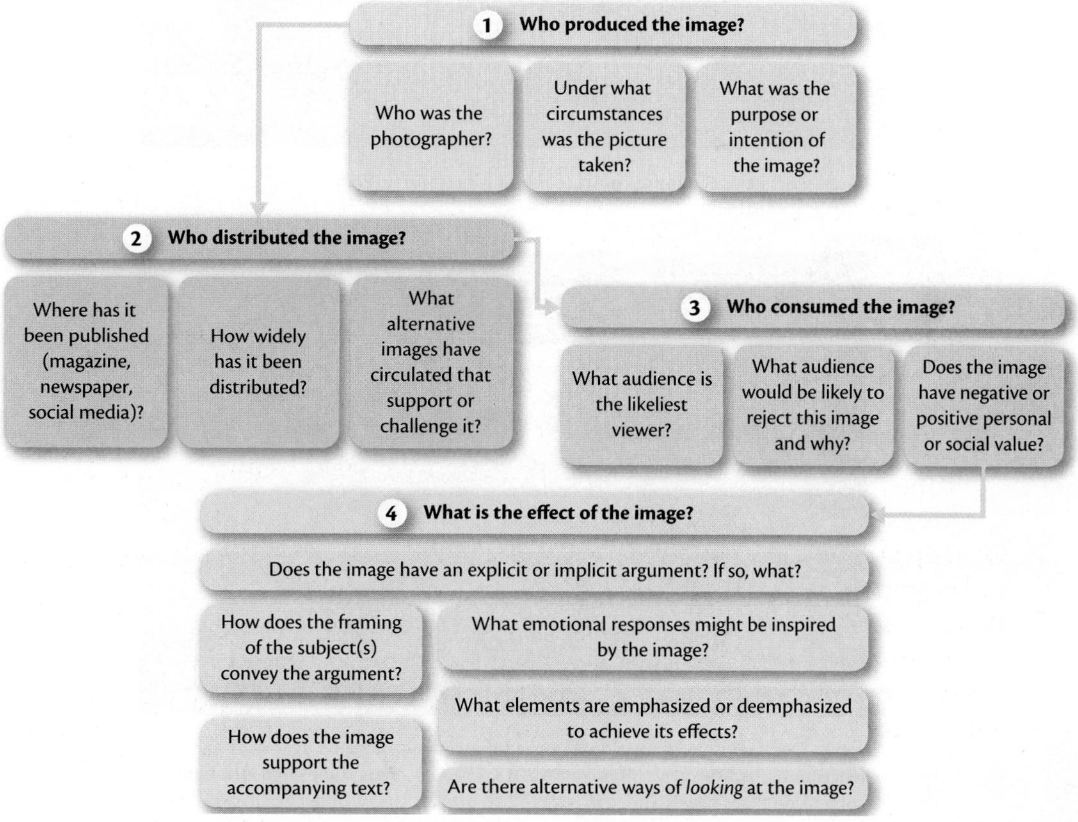
1 Who produced the image?
Who was the photographer?
Under what circumstances was the picture taken?
What was the purpose or intention of the image?
2 Who distributed the image?
Where has it been published (magazine, newspaper, social media)?
How widely has it been distributed?
What alternative images have circulated that support or challenge it?
3 Who consumed the image?
What audience is the likeliest viewer?
What audience would be likely to reject this image and why?
Does the image have negative or positive personal or social value?
4 What is the effect of the image?
Does the image have an explicit or implicit argument? If so, what?
How does the framing of the subject(s) convey the argument?
What emotional responses might be inspired by the image?
What elements are emphasized or deemphasized to achieve its effects?
How does the image support the accompanying text?
Are there alternative ways of *looking* at the image?

Exercise: Seeing versus Looking

Examine the images below and do the following:

1. *See* the image. Thoroughly describe the image. Write down as many elements as possible that you see: colors, shapes, text, people, objects, lighting, framing, perspective, and so forth.
2. *Look* at the image. Take the elements you have observed and relate what they suggest by considering their figurative meanings, their meanings in relation to one another, and their meanings in the context of the images' production and consumption.

Ferdinando Scianna/Magnum Photos

Cattle grazing in a California pasture near a wind farm in 1996.

Moms Demand Action, a national public safety advocacy group against gun violence, published this advertisement in 2013. The text reads, "One child is holding something that's been banned in America to protect them. Guess which one."

Documenting Reality: Reading Photographs

As we learned with the uses of images relating to the Arctic National Wildlife Refuge (see p. 132), photographs can serve as evidence but have a peculiar relationship to the truth. We must never forget that images are constructed, selected, and used for specific purposes.

When advertisers use images, we know they're trying to convince consumers to purchase a product or service. But when images serve as documentary evidence, we often assume that they're showing the "truth" of the matter at hand. When we see an image in the newspaper or a magazine, we may assume that it captures a particular event or moment in time *as it really happened*. Our level of skepticism may be lower than when we are looking at images designed to persuade us.

But these kind of images — historical images, images of events, news photographs, and the like — are not free from the potential for manipulation or for (conscious or unconscious) bias. Consider how liberal and conservative media sources portray the nation's president in images: One source may show him proud and smiling in bright light with the American flag behind him, whereas another might show him scowling in a darkened image suggestive of evil intent. Both are "real" images, but the framing, tinting, setting, and background can inspire significantly different responses in viewers.

As we saw with the image of LeBron James, certain postures, facial expressions, and settings can contribute to a photograph's interpretation. Martin Luther King Jr.'s great speech of August 28, 1963, "I Have a Dream," still reads very well on the page, but part of its immense appeal derives from its setting: King spoke to some 200,000 people in Washington, DC, as he stood on the steps of the Lincoln Memorial. That setting, rich with associations of slavery and freedom, strongly assists King's argument. In fact, images of King delivering his speech are nearly inseparable from the very argument he was making. The visual aspects — the setting (the Lincoln Memorial with the Washington Monument and the Capitol in the distance) and King's gestures — are part of the speech's persuasive rhetoric.

Bettmann/Getty Images

Martin Luther King Jr. delivering his "I Have a Dream" speech on August 28, 1963, from the steps of the Lincoln Memorial.

Derrick Alridge, a historian, examined dozens of accounts of Martin Luther King Jr. in history books, and he found that images of King present him overwhelmingly as a messianic figure — standing before crowds, leading them, addressing them in postures reminiscent of a prophet. Although King is an admirable figure, Alridge asserts, history books err by presenting him as more than human. Doing so ignores his personal struggles and failures and makes a myth out of the real man. This myth suggests he was the epicenter of the civil rights movement, an effort that was actually conducted in different ways via different strategies on the part of many other figures whom King eclipsed. We may even get the idea that the entire civil rights movement began and ended with

John W. Mosley Photograph Collection, Charles L. Blockson Afro-American Collection, Temple University Libraries

Martin Luther King Jr. on "Chicken Bone Beach" in Atlantic City.

King alone. When history books present King as a holy prophet, Alridge argues, it becomes easier to focus on his gospel of love, equality, and justice and not on the specific policies and politics he advocated — his avowed socialist stances, for instance. In short, while photographs of King seek to help us remember, they may actually portray him in a way that causes us to forget other things — for example, that his approval rating among whites at the time of his death was lower than 30 percent and among blacks lower than 50 percent.

A WORD ON "ALTERNATIVE FACTS"

All this discussion of "seeing and looking" is intended to underscore how much photographs that seem to provide a clear window into reality are not absolute guarantors of truth. How images are selected, created, and circulated has much to do with their meaning and value. Furthermore, in the digital age, it's remarkably easy to alter photographs. Because of this, we have become more suspicious of photographs as direct evidence of reality. We retain our skepticism when we encounter images of celebrities on the internet who have been obviously "Photoshopped." However, we sometimes do not anticipate the degree to which all kinds of published images may be altered for persuasive purposes. When those purposes are the result of political or ideological bias, we are particularly vulnerable to misinformation because of our assumptions about the reality or truth-value of images.

One memorable moment brings to light how disputes over the truth of images matter. During the inauguration of President Donald Trump, some media outlets were accused by the president of deliberately downplaying the crowd size by comparing images of that day to images of larger crowds at the 2009 Obama inaugural. "[W]e caught them [the media] in a real beauty," the president said. Probably referring to a tweet by the *New York Times* showing side-by-side images of the two inaugurals, White House Press Secretary Sean Spicer said that the photographs "were intentionally framed . . . to minimize the enormous support that had gathered on the National Mall."

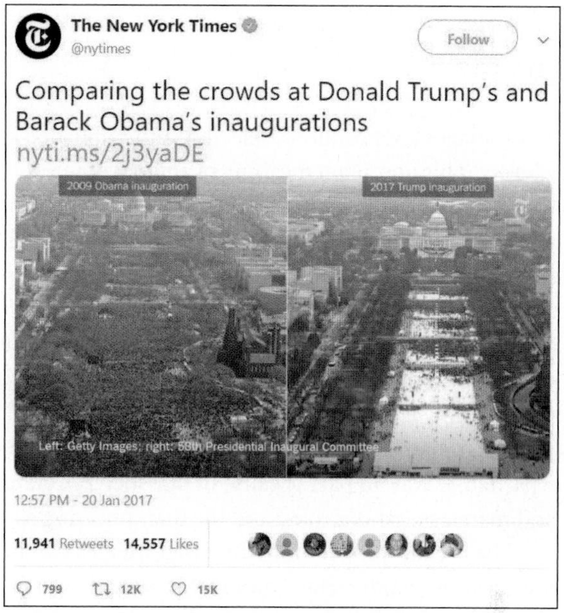

A *New York Times* tweet comparing the crowd sizes at the Obama and Trump inaugurals in 2009 and 2017 drew the ire of the White House, which accused the media of bias.

Spicer's claim may or may not have been true, but he insisted that "this was the largest audience ever to witness an inauguration, period." He referred to what his colleague Kellyanne Conway now famously called "alternative facts": his calculations of the crowd size, the ridership levels on the DC Metro system, and images of the inauguration ceremony produced by the National Park Service, which had been cropped in such a way as to depict a larger crowd size.

AP Photo/Patrick Semansky

Empty spaces were cropped out of this image produced by the National Park Service at the White House's request for more flattering images of the crowd size at the 2017 inauguration. These images were subsequently released to media outlets.

We think this story gets us to the heart of what is meant by alternative facts. To be blunt, the phrase simply means alternative *beliefs* or alternative *forms of evidence* that people present as facts. Although two contradictory facts can't be true, two depictions of the same event may be presented, and therefore seen and interpreted, as factual. To counteract our own tendency to think that "seeing is believing," we can be more critical about images by approaching them through three broad frameworks: accommodation, resistance, and negotiation.

Accommodating, Resisting, and Negotiating the Meaning of Images

Most images are produced, selected, and published so as to have a specific effect on readers and viewers. This dominant meaning of an image supposes that the audience will react in a predictable way or take away a specific message, usually based on the widespread **cultural codes** that operate within a society. Images of elegant women in designer dresses, rugged men driving pickup trucks, stodgy teachers, cutthroat CEOs, hipster computer programmers, and so on speak to generally accepted notions of what certain types of people are like. An image of a suburban couple in an automobile advertisement washing their new car subconsciously confirms and perpetuates a certain ideal of middle-class suburban life (a heterosexual couple, a well-trimmed lawn, a neatly painted house and picket fence — and a brand-new midsize sedan). An image of a teary-eyed young woman accepting a diamond ring from a handsome man will likely touch the viewer in a particular way, in part because of our society's cultural codes about the rituals of romantic love and marriage, gender roles, and the diamond ring as a sign of love and commitment.

These examples demonstrate that images can be constructed according to dominant connotations of gender, class, and racial, sexual, and political identity. When analyzing an image, ask yourself what cultural codes it endorses, what ideals it establishes as natural, and what social norms or modes of everyday life it idealizes or assumes.

As image consumers, we often **accommodate** (i.e., passively accept) those messages and cultural codes promoted by media images. For example, in the hypothetical advertisement featuring a marriage proposal — a man kneeling, a woman crying sentimentally — you might not decide to buy a diamond, but you might accept the messages that diamond rings are the appropriate objects to represent love and commitment. Further, you might accept the cultural codes about the rituals of romantic love, marriage, and gender roles, sharing the assumption that men should propose to women and that women are more emotional than men.

When you *accommodate* cultural codes without understanding them critically, you allow the media that perpetuate these codes to interpret the world for you. That is, you accept their interpretations without questioning the social and cultural values implicit in their assumptions, many of which may actually run counter to your own or others' social and cultural values. When analyzing an image, ask yourself what cultural codes it endorses, what ideals it establishes as natural, and what social norms it assumes or idealizes.

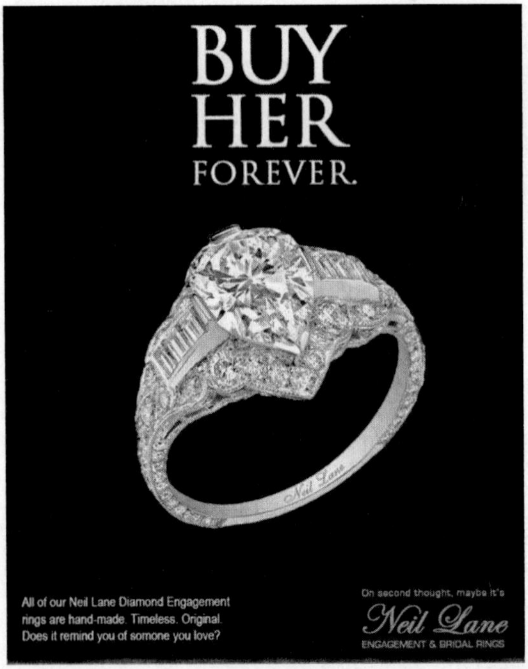

BUY
HER
FOREVER.
All of our Neil Lane Diamond Engagement rings are hand-made. Timeless. Original. Does it remind you of somone you love?
On second thought, maybe it's
Neil Lane
ENGAGEMENT & BRIDAL RINGS

What cultural codes does this ad accommodate?

If you **resist** the cultural codes of an image, you actively criticize its message and meaning. Suppose you (1) question how the ad presents gender roles and marriage, (2) claim that it idealizes heterosexual marriage, and (3) point out that it confirms and extends traditional gender roles in which men are active and bold and women are passive and emotional. Moreover, you (4) argue that the diamond ring represents a misguided commodification of love because diamonds are kept deliberately scarce by large companies and, as such, are overvalued and overpriced; meanwhile, you say, the ad prompts young couples to spend precious money at a time when their joint assets might be better saved, and because many diamonds come from third-world countries under essentially slave labor conditions, the diamond is more a symbol of oppression than of love. If your analysis follows such paths, you *resist* the dominant message of the image in question. Sometimes, this is called an *oppositional reading.*

Negotiation, or a *negotiated reading*, the most useful mode of reading and viewing, involves a middle path — a process of revision that seeks to recognize and change the conditions that give rise to certain negative aspects of cultural codes. Negotiation implies a practical intervention into common viewing processes that help construct and maintain social conditions and relations. A negotiated reading enables you to emphasize the ways in which individuals, social groups, and others relate to images and their dominant meanings and how different personal and cultural perspectives can challenge those meanings. This intervention can be important when inequalities or stereotypes are perpetuated by cultural codes. Without intervention, there can be no revision, no positive social or cultural change. You *negotiate* cultural codes when:

- you understand the underlying messages of images and accept the general cultural implications of these codes, *but*
- you acknowledge that in some circumstances the general codes do not apply.

snsif/Shutterstock.com

Memes often use humor to present oppositional ideas. However, in doing so, they sometimes reaffirm other cultural codes and assumptions.

The Saturday Evening Post
LEGO...the most creative adventure you can give to a child
Colorful, durable, snap-together tiles that can build almost anything. Snap...and build. Snap apart...and build again. New fun every day!
Lego is Imagination. Expression. Experiment. Creating. It's the most doing-making-building-thinking way to play that's ever been devised. Put magical Lego into the hands of a five-year-old and she will make you a camel. A little boy will turn his Lego into an airplane on Monday...snap apart and it's a train on Tuesday, a skyscraper on Wednesday. A twelve-year-old might even build a whole city! There's great adventure in each box of these smooth, shiny, plastic tiles. For Christmas stockings $1.95, $2.95, $4.95 sets. Lots more pieces in the $7.95, $10.95, $16.95 sets. Enough Lego to build a town in the big $25.00 set. Supplemental kits with choice of all Lego parts including extra trees, gas pumps, etc., available at 50¢.
LEGO System
BY Samsonite

Image Courtesy of The Advertising Archives

Exercise: Accommodating, Resisting, and Negotiating Images

Examine the image shown here of an advertisement for Lego building blocks or choose your own ad, PSA, or other image. Provide brief examples of how a viewer could accommodate, resist, or negotiate the images in the ad.

Are Some Images Not Fit to Be Shown?: Politics and Pictures

Images of suffering — either human or animal — can be immensely persuasive. In the nineteenth century, for instance, the antislavery movement made extremely effective use of images in its campaign. We reproduced two antislavery images earlier in this chapter, as well as a counterimage that sought to assure viewers that slavery was a beneficent system (p. 135). But are there some images not fit to print?

Until recently, many newspapers did not print pictures of lynched African Americans, hanged and burned and maimed. The reasons for not printing such images probably differed between South and North: Southern papers may have considered the images to be discreditable to whites, and northern papers may have deemed the images too revolting. Even today, when it's commonplace for newspapers and television news to show pictures of dead victims of war, famine, or traffic accidents, one rarely sees bodies that are horribly maimed. (For traffic accidents, the body is usually covered, and we see only the smashed car.) The US government refused to release photographs showing the bodies of American soldiers killed in the war in Iraq, and it was most reluctant to show pictures of dead Iraqi soldiers and civilians. Only after many Iraqis refused to believe that former Iraqi president Saddam Hussein's two sons had been killed did the US government reluctantly release pictures showing the two men's blood-spattered faces — and some American newspapers and television programs refused to use the images.

There have been notable exceptions to this practice, such as Huynh Cong (Nick) Ut's 1972 photograph of children fleeing a napalm attack in Vietnam (p. 149), which was widely reproduced in the United States and won the photographer a Pulitzer Prize in 1973. It's impossible to measure the influence of this particular photograph, but many people believe that it played a substantial role in increasing public pressure to end the Vietnam War. Another widely reproduced picture of horrifying violence is Eddie Adams's 1968 picture (p. 150) of a South Vietnamese chief of police allied with the United States firing a pistol into the head of a Viet Cong prisoner.

Huynh Cong (Nick) Ut, *The Terror of War: Children on Route 1 near Trang Bang*, 1972.

The issue remains: Are some images unacceptable? For instance, although capital punishment — by methods including lethal injection, hanging, shooting, and electrocution — is legal in parts of the United States, every state prohibits the publication of pictures showing the execution.

AN ARGUMENT ON PUBLISHING IMAGES

A twenty-first-century example concerning the appropriateness of showing certain images arose early in 2006. In September 2005, a Danish newspaper, accused of being afraid to show political cartoons that were hostile to Muslim terrorists, responded by publishing twelve cartoons. One cartoon showed the prophet Muhammad wearing a turban that looked like a bomb. The images at first didn't arouse much attention, but when they were reprinted in Norway in January 2006, they attracted worldwide attention and outraged Muslims, most of whom regard any depiction of Muhammad as blasphemous. Some Muslims in various Islamic nations burned Danish embassies and engaged in other acts of violence. Most non-Muslims agreed that the images were in bad taste, and, apparently in deference to Islamic sensibilities (but possibly also out of fear of reprisals), very few Western newspapers reprinted the cartoons when they covered the news events. Most newspapers (including the *New York Times*) merely described the images. The editors of these papers believed that readers should be told the news, but that because the drawings were so offensive to some persons, they should be described rather than reprinted. A controversy then arose: Do readers of a newspaper deserve to *see* the evidence for themselves, or can a newspaper adequately fulfill its mission by offering only a verbal description? These questions arose again after the 2007 bombing of

AP Photo/Eddie Adams

Eddie Adams, *Execution of Viet Cong Prisoner, Saigon*, 1968.

the French satirical newspaper *Charlie Hebdo* and then after another mass shooting at the same newspaper in 2015 that claimed the lives of twelve editors and staff members.

Persons who argued that the images should be reproduced in the media generally made these points:

- Newspapers should yield neither to the delicate sensibilities of some readers nor to threats of violence.
- Jews for the most part do not believe that God should be depicted (the prohibition against "graven images" appears in Exodus 20.3), but they raise no objections to such Christian images as the ceiling of the Sistine Chapel. Further, when Andres Serrano (a Christian) in 1989 exhibited a photograph of a small plastic crucifix submerged in urine, it outraged a wider public (several US senators condemned it because the artist had received federal funds), but virtually all newspapers showed the image, and many even printed its title, *Piss Christ*. The subject was judged to be newsworthy, and the fact that some viewers would regard the image as blasphemous was not considered highly relevant.
- Our society values freedom of speech, and newspapers should not be intimidated. When certain pictures are a matter of news, readers should be able to see them.

In contrast, opposing voices made these points:

- Newspapers must recognize deep-seated religious beliefs. They should indeed report the news, but there is no reason to *show* images that some people regard as blasphemous. The images can be adequately *described* in words.

- The Jewish response to Christian images of God, and even the tolerant Christians' response to Serrano's image of the crucifix immersed in urine, are irrelevant to the issue of whether a Western newspaper should represent images of the prophet Muhammad. Virtually all Muslims regard depictions of Muhammad as blasphemous, and that's what counts.
- Despite all the Western talk about freedom of the press, the press does *not* reproduce all images that become matters of news. For instance, news items about the sale of child pornography do not include images of the pornographic photos.

Exercises: Thinking about Images

1. In June 2006, two American soldiers were captured in Iraq. Later their bodies were found, dismembered and beheaded. Should newspapers have shown photographs of the mutilated bodies? Why, or why not? (In July 2006, insurgents in Iraq posted images on the internet showing a soldier's severed head beside his body.)
2. Hugh Hewitt, an Evangelical Christian, offered a comparison to the cartoon of Muhammad wearing a bomb-like turban. Suppose, he asked, an abortion clinic were bombed by someone claiming to be an Evangelical Christian. Would newspapers publish "a cartoon of Christ's crown of thorns transformed into sticks of TNT"? Do you think they would? If you were the editor of a newspaper, would you? Why, or why not?
3. A week after the 2015 attack on *Charlie Hebdo*, and in response to media hesitancy to republish the offending images of Muhammad, the Index on Censorship and several other journalistic organizations called for all newspapers to publish them simultaneously and globally on January 8, 2015. "This unspeakable act of violence has challenged and assailed the entire press," said Lucie Morillon of Reporters Without Borders. "Journalism as a whole is in mourning. In the name of all those who have fallen in the defense of these fundamental values, we must continue *Charlie Hebdo*'s fight for the right to freedom of information." Evaluate this position.
4. Examine the image shown here by photojournalist Paul Fusco of the November 22, 2003, funeral for Sgt. Scott C. Rose, who was killed in Iraq. In an argumentative essay of about 500 words, argue your view on this photograph. Is such a photograph so intimately personal that it should not be made public? What possible uses of this photograph can you imagine?

Writing about Political Cartoons

Most editorial pages print political cartoons as well as editorials. Like the writers of editorials, cartoonists seek to persuade, but they rarely use words to *argue* a point. True, they may use a few words in speech balloons or in captions, but generally the drawing does most of the work. Because their aim usually is to convince the viewer that some person's action or proposal is ridiculous, cartoonists almost always **caricature** their subjects: They exaggerate the subject's distinctive features to the point at which the subject becomes grotesque and ridiculous — absurd, laughable, contemptible.

We agree that it's unfair to suggest that because, say, a politician who proposes a new law dresses in outdated clothes and has a distinctive jawline, his proposal is ridiculous, but that's the way cartoonists work. Further, cartoonists are concerned with producing a striking image, not with exploring an issue, so they almost always oversimplify, implying that there really is no other sane view.

In the course of saying that (1) the figures in a cartoon are ridiculous and *therefore* their ideas are contemptible and (2) there is only one side to the issue, cartoonists often use **symbolism**. Here's a list of common symbols:

- symbolic figures (e.g., the US government as Uncle Sam)
- animals (e.g., the Democratic Party as donkey and the Republican Party as elephant)
- buildings (e.g., the White House as representing the nation's president)
- things (e.g., a bag with a dollar sign on it as representing a bribe)

For anyone brought up in American culture, these symbols (like the human figures they represent) are obvious, and cartoonists assume that viewers will instantly recognize the symbols and figures, will get the joke, and will see the absurdity of whatever issue the cartoonist is seeking to demolish.

In writing about the argument presented in a cartoon, normally you will discuss the ways in which the cartoon makes its point. Caricature usually implies, "This is ridiculous, as you can plainly see by the absurdity of the figures depicted" or "What *X*'s proposal adds up to, despite its apparent complexity, is nothing more than . . ." As we have said, this sort of persuasion, chiefly by ridicule, probably is unfair: Almost always the issue is more complicated than the cartoonist indicates. But cartoons work largely by ridicule and the omission of counterarguments, and we shouldn't reject the possibility that the cartoonist has indeed highlighted the absurdity of the issue.

In analyzing the cartoon and determining the cartoonist's attitude, consider the following elements:

- the relative size of the figures in the image
- the quality of the lines (e.g., thin and spidery, thick and seemingly aggressive)

- the amount of empty space in comparison with the amount of heavily inked space (a drawing with lots of inky areas conveys a more oppressive tone than a drawing that's largely open)
- the degree to which text is important, as well as its content and tone (e.g., witty, heavy-handed)

Your essay will likely include an *evaluation* of the cartoon. Indeed, the *thesis* underlying your analytic/argumentative essay may be that the cartoon is effective (persuasive) for such-and-such reasons but unfair for such-and-such other reasons.

The cartoon by Pulitzer Prize–winning cartoonist Walt Handelsman responds to recent breaches of political decorum. It depicts a group of Washington, DC, tourists being driven past what the guide calls "The Museum of Modern American Political Discourse," a building in the shape of a giant toilet. The toilet as a symbol of the level of political discussion dominates the cartoon, effectively driving home the point that Americans are watching our leaders sink to new lows as they debate the future of our nation. By drawing the toilet on a scale similar to that of familiar monuments in Washington, Handelsman may be pointing out that today's politicians, rather than being remembered for great achievements like those of George Washington or Abraham Lincoln, will instead be remembered for their rudeness and aggression. If you were accommodating the meaning of this cartoon, you might agree with Handelsman, but if you were resisting its message, you could point out that it blames politicians solely for the state of political discourse and portrays the "people" as separate from it (or subject to it); however, as we must recognize, political discourse is also in bad shape among the people themselves, too.

Walt Handelsman/Chicago Tribune/TNS

THINKING CRITICALLY *Analysis of a Political Cartoon*

Find a recent political cartoon to analyze, pulled from a print or online news publication. For each Type of Analysis section in the chart below, provide your own answer based on the cartoon.

TYPE OF ANALYSIS	QUESTIONS TO ASK	YOUR ANSWER
Context	Who is the artist? Where and when was the cartoon published? What situations, issues, or political conditions does it respond to?	
Description	What do you see in the cartoon? What elements does it include?	
Analysis	Looking more closely at the images and considering their meanings, how does the cartoon make its point? Is it effective? How could you accommodate, resist, or negotiate the meanings of this image?	

A CHECKLIST FOR ANALYZING POLITICAL CARTOONS

- ❒ Is there a lead-in?
- ❒ Is there a brief but accurate description of the drawing?
- ❒ Is the source of the cartoon cited (perhaps with a comment by the cartoonist)?
- ❒ Is there a brief report of the event or issue that the cartoon is targeting, as well as an explanation of all the symbols?
- ❒ Is there a statement of the cartoonist's claim (thesis)?
- ❒ Is there an analysis of the evidence, if any, that the image offers in support of the claim?
- ❒ Is there an analysis of the ways in which the drawing's content and style help convey the message?
- ❒ Is there adequate evaluation of the drawing's effectiveness?
- ❒ Is there adequate evaluation of the effectiveness of the text (caption or speech balloons) and of the fairness of the cartoon?

Kwon 1

Ryan Kwon

Professor Carter

English 101

17 September 2018

The American Pipe Dream?

Visual arguments are powerful tools used by photographers, advertisers, and artists to persuade an audience. Two powerful examples of visual arguments about a shared subject, the so-called American Dream, occur in two different types of images, yet they both point to important questions about the attainability of the dream in two different contexts. The first is Margaret Bourke-White's 1937 photograph of flood victims, and the second is Mike Keefe's 2012 political cartoon from InToon.com. Both images, although seventy-five years apart, aim to persuade the audience that the ideology of the American Dream is unattainable in reality. While Bourke-White does so through the use of appeals to irony, juxtaposition, and color contrast, Keefe does so through heavy symbolism and carefully selected text. By comparing these two images, we can see how the American dream is—and always was—elusive.

Thesis: Two visual arguments from different contexts reveal the irony of the American Dream.

Bourke-White's photo of flood victims waiting in a bread line in 1937 (Fig. 1) is not a staged photo like an advertisement, but on closer inspection, it utilizes visual framing to undermine the ideology of the American Dream through appeals to irony, juxtaposition, and color contrast. The billboard is loaded with emotive, powerful phrases like, "World's Highest Standard of Living" and "There's no way like the American Way." The family in the billboard image is nicely dressed, smiling, and driving a shiny, new car. This billboard presents the good life that the American Dream is known to give its citizens.

Makes use of an "inventory" of elements in the photograph—billboard, words, clothing, smiles, car, dog, empty baskets.

However, the juxtaposition of this billboard with the line of flood victims beneath it creates an appeal to irony. The American good life is

Margaret Bourke-White/Time & Life Pictures/Getty Images

Fig. 1. Margaret Bourke-White, *Kentucky Flood* (1937).

Kwon recognizes visual metaphor: Being stuck in line is a symbol for social immobility.

Placing the photograph in historical context helps interpret meaning.

More on how the form and visual details of the photograph add meaning.

physically above the heads of the people in line, as if it were nothing more than a dream. The family on the billboard is "free" in the sense that they are on the open road. Even the dog appears to be smiling. Meanwhile, the flood victims, stuck in line, are not moving at all. Unlike the family, they do not appear to be enjoying the privileges of ownership: their baskets are (literally and figuratively) empty. The billboard creates the illusion that all American citizens can live the good life simply by being a citizen, but the realities of the flood victims in this photograph say otherwise.

The audience must also take into account that in 1937, racism and segregation of blacks from whites was heavily prominent. Since the billboard pictures a white family, it excludes minorities from the American Dream. Therefore, this photograph demonstrates specifically that minorities are unable to attain the American Dream. The color contrast in this photo further emphasizes the division between light and dark, black people and white people. The billboard is bright, white, and promising, in a

Mike Keefe/Cagle Cartoons

Fig. 2. Mike Keefe, "The American Pipe Dream with Attached Mirage . . ." (2012).

dreamlike world above the heads the real individuals who are shadowed and dark, demonstrating that the American Dream is nothing more than an unattainable dream for some.

Keefe's more recent political cartoon (Fig. 2) also demolishes the attainability of the American Dream, but adds a more modern perspective through the use of symbolism and carefully selected text. The description of the cartoon reads, "The American Pipe Dream with Attached Mirage . . ." Since political cartoons are meant to be read in a matter of seconds by the audience, it is important for the cartoonist to get his or her message across quickly. Keefe manages to do so by setting the tone with this description. A white family, like the one in Bourke-White's photo, is drawn struggling to climb up a desert mountain, demonstrated by their wide eyes, their open mouths, and the beads of sweat surrounding the man's head. They are struggling because they are weighed down by four objects: a prison ball named "Underemployment"; a treasure chest of "Credit Card Debt"; a big bag of "Student Loans"; and a wide-eyed infant. The prison ball weighs the man

Again, author shows how visual details can be interpreted as metaphors.

down because without steady income from a secure job, he cannot support his family. Credit card debt is represented as a treasure chest because a credit card can buy lots of material items, but one must pay off the bill. Leaving the bill unpaid means all of the so-called treasures are taken away. The woman is literally carrying baggage, and that baggage is the amount of student loans that add into the credit card debt. Finally, having a child without a job and with heavy debt is an extra expense. With all of these items weighing the family down, it is no surprise they are struggling to achieve the American Dream, represented by the floating mirage of a suburban home.

Author uses evidence from the image to establish the American Dream as something unreachable—always an ideal, but not a reality for all.

The American Dream is floating above the struggling family in Keefe's image, much like the billboard in Bourke-White's photo. This time, however, it is a white family who is struggling to achieve the American Dream, the same kind of family who, ironically, were once the face of it. Thus, Keefe's cartoon manages to express the modern unattainability of the American Dream for all to its audience in a matter of moments, in a way that is just as effective as Bourke-White's photograph.

Clearly, visuals are powerful tools that can persuade an audience to take a stance on a certain political ideology, such as the American Dream. Both Bourke-White and Keefe make their stances about the unattainability of the American Dream clear, and even build off of each other to make the message stronger, despite their works being created in two different contexts. While textual arguments are certainly accredited more for their persuasion, visual arguments play a powerful role with the ability to persuade an audience.

Works Cited

Bourke-White, Margaret. *Kentucky Flood. Life*, Time Inc., 1937, images.google.com/hosted/life/bdb4f71a5f11cf96.html.

Keefe, Mike. "American Pipe Dream." *InToon.com,* The Association of American Editorial Cartoonists, 13 Apr. 2012, editorialcartoonists .com/cartoon/display.cfm/110032/. Accessed 20 Sep. 2018.

Visuals as Aids to Clarity: Maps, Graphs, and Pie Charts

Often, writers use visual aids that are not images but still present information or data graphically in order to support a point. Maps were part of the argument in the debate over drilling in the Arctic National Wildlife Refuge we discussed at the beginning of this chapter.

- Advocates of drilling argued that it would take place only in a tiny area. Their drawn map showed the entire state of Alaska, with a smaller inset showing a much smaller part of the state that was the refuge. The map points out the drilling area with an arrow, implying it is too insignificant of an area to matter because it is too miniscule to show.
- Opponents utilized a close-up image to show the extent of industrial sprawl and roads that would have to be constructed across the refuge for drilling to take place. The map uses many icons to show how intrusive the drilling would be to this green natural area. The inset Alaska map is much smaller, deemphasizing the size of the refuge relative to the state.

By changing the scale and orienting viewers to the information in different ways, maps of the same area support different arguments.

Graphs, tables, and pie charts usually present quantitative data in visual form, helping writers clarify dry, statistical assertions. For instance, a line graph may illustrate how many immigrants came to the United States in each decade of the twentieth century.

A bar graph (with bars running either horizontally or vertically) offers similar information. In the Coming to America graph on page 160, we can see at a glance that, say, the second bar on the lower left is almost double the height of the first, indicating that the number of immigrants almost doubled between 1850 and 1860.

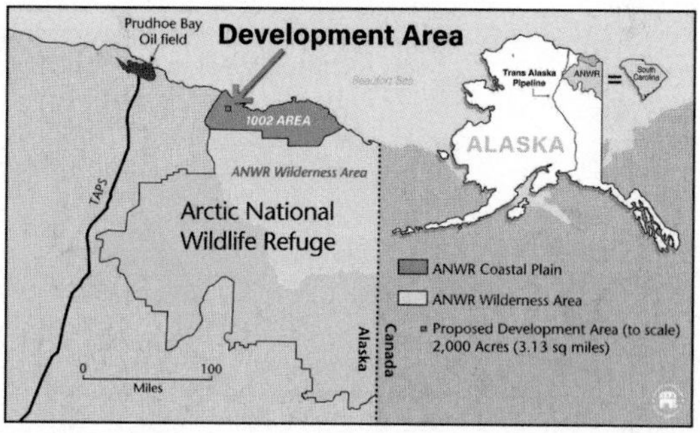

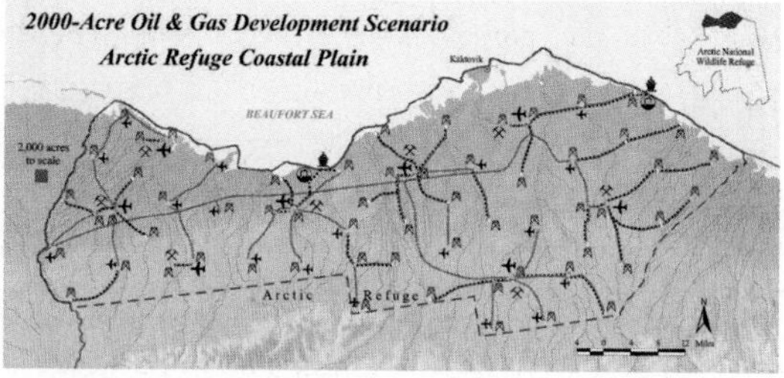

Maps showing the refuge in different ways for different purposes: advocates of drilling used the map on the top to emphasize size, and opponents used the map on the bottom to emphasize industrial transformation.

A pie chart is a circle divided into wedges so that we can see, literally, how a whole comprises its parts. We can see, for instance, in the From Near and Far chart on page 160, an entire pie representing the regions of foreign-born US immigrants: 32 percent were born in Central America and Mexico, 40 percent in Asia, 9 percent in Europe, and so on.

COMING TO AMERICA . . .

Both the percentage and number of foreign-born people in the United States dropped during much of the twentieth century, but after 1970, the tide was turning again.

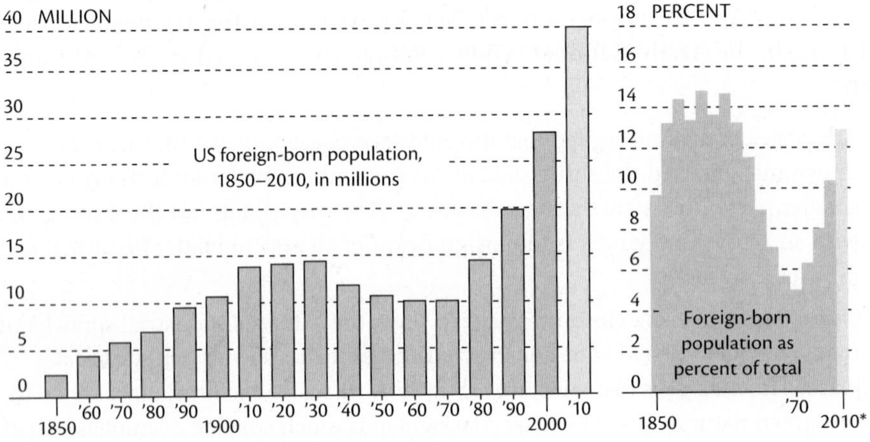

. . . FROM NEAR AND FAR

Central America, Mexico, and Asia contribute most to the foreign-born population.

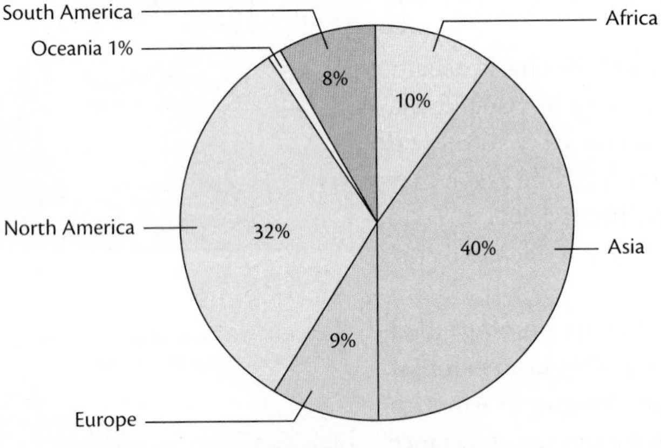

Foreign-born population by region of birth, 2010

*Most recent estimate

Data from U.S. Department of Homeland Security

A WORD ON MISLEADING OR MANIPULATIVE VISUAL DATA

Because maps, charts, tables, and graphs offer empirical data to support arguments, they communicate a high degree of reliability and tend to be convincing. "Numbers don't lie," it is sometimes said, and to some extent this is true. It's difficult to spin a fact like 1 + 1 = 2. However, as author Charles Seife notes in his book *Proofiness*, numbers are cold facts, but the measurements that numbers actually chart aren't always so clear or free from bias and manipulation. Consider two examples of advertising claims that Seife cites — one for a L'Oréal mascara offering "twelve times more impact" and another for a new and improved Vaseline product that "delivers 70% more moisture in every drop." Such measurements *sound* good but remain relatively meaningless. (How was eyelash "impact" measured? What is a percentage value of moisture?)

Another way data can be relatively meaningless is when it addresses only part of the question at stake. In 2013, a Mayo Clinic study found that drinking coffee regularly lowered participants' risk of the liver disease known as primary sclerosing cholangitis (PSC). But PSC is already listed as a "rare disease" by the Centers for Disease Control and Prevention, affecting fewer than 1 in 2,000 people. So even if drinking coffee lowered the risk of PSC by 25 percent, a person's chances would improve only slightly from 0.0005 percent chance to 0.0004 percent chance — hardly a change at all, and hardly a rationale for drinking more coffee. Yet statistical information showing a 25 percent reduction in PSC sounds significant, even more so when provided under a headline proclaiming "Drinking coffee helps prevent liver disease."

A CHECKLIST FOR CHARTS AND GRAPHS

- ❐ Is the source authoritative?
- ❐ Is the source cited?
- ❐ Will the chart or graph be intelligible to the intended audience?
- ❐ Is the caption, if any, clear and helpful?

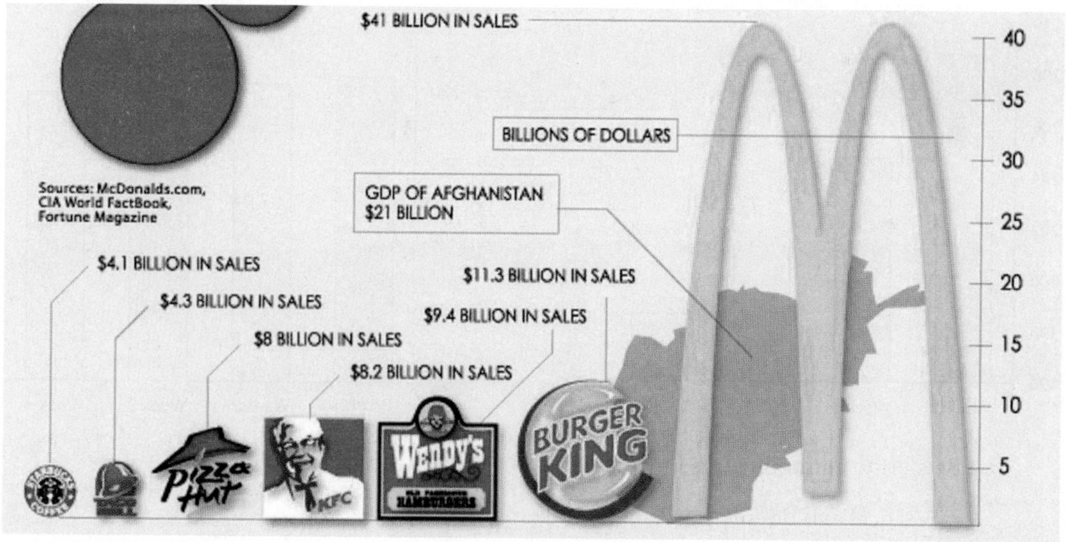

2003 INA - www.princeton.edu/~INA

In this graph, McDonald's $41 billion in sales are shown to be about 3.5 times higher than the revenues of its next closest competitor, Burger King (at $11.3 billion), but the McDonald's logo graphic is about 13 times larger than Burger King's.

Consider other uses of numbers that Seife shows in his book to constitute "proofiness" (his title and word to describe the misuse of numbers as evidence):

- In his 2006 State of the Union Address, George W. Bush declared No Child Left Behind (NCLB) a success: "[B]ecause we acted," he said, "students are performing better in reading and math." (True, fourth to eighth graders showed improved scores, but other grade levels declined. In addition, fourth- to eighth-grade reading and math scores had been improving at an unchanged rate both before and after the NCLB legislation.)
- In 2000, the *New York Times* reported "Researchers Link Bad Debt to Bad Health" (the "dark side of the economic boom"). The researchers claimed that debt causes more illness, but in doing so they committed the correlation-causation fallacy: Just because two phenomena are correlated does not mean they are causally related. (Example: More people wear shorts in the summer and more people eat ice cream in the summer than during other seasons, but wearing shorts does not *cause* higher ice cream consumption.)

Finally, consider the following graph showing that eating Quaker Oats decreases cholesterol levels after just four weeks of daily servings. The bar graph suggests that cholesterol levels will plummet. But a careful look at the graph reveals that the vertical axis doesn't begin at zero. In this case, a relatively small change has been (mis)represented as much bigger than it actually is.

A more accurate representation of cholesterol levels after four weeks of eating Quaker Oats, using a graph that starts at zero, would look more like the second graph — showing essentially unchanged levels.

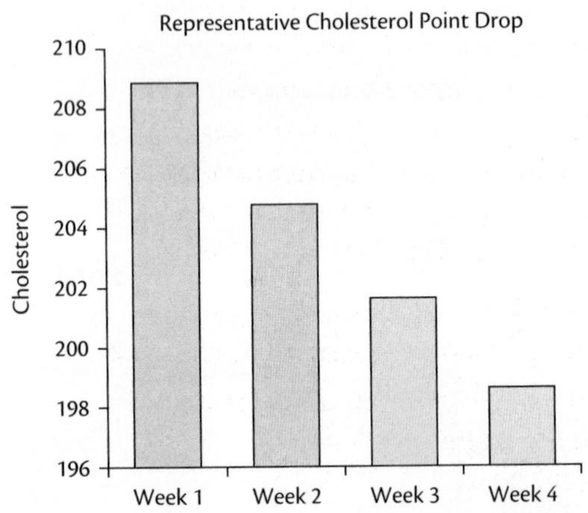

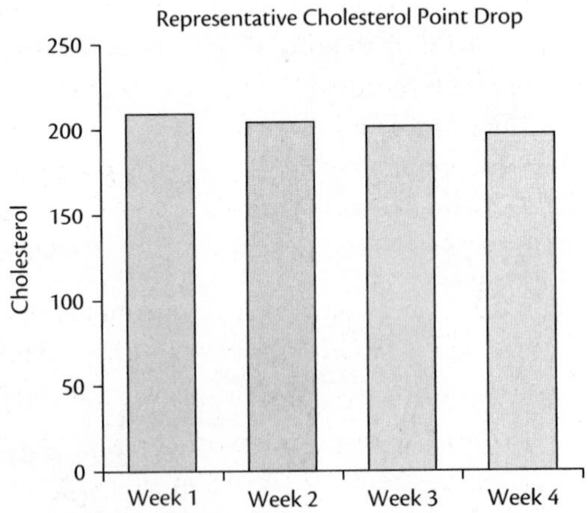

Be alert to common ways in which graphs can be misleading:

- Vertical axis doesn't start at zero or skips numbers.
- Scale is given in very small units to make changes look big.
- Pie charts don't accurately divide on scale with percentages shown.
- Oversized graphics don't match the numbers they represent.

Exercise: Misleading Visuals

Examine these two graphs and describe how the way data from the Bureau of Labor Statistics is visualized presents two different stories about the declining unemployment rate in the United States.

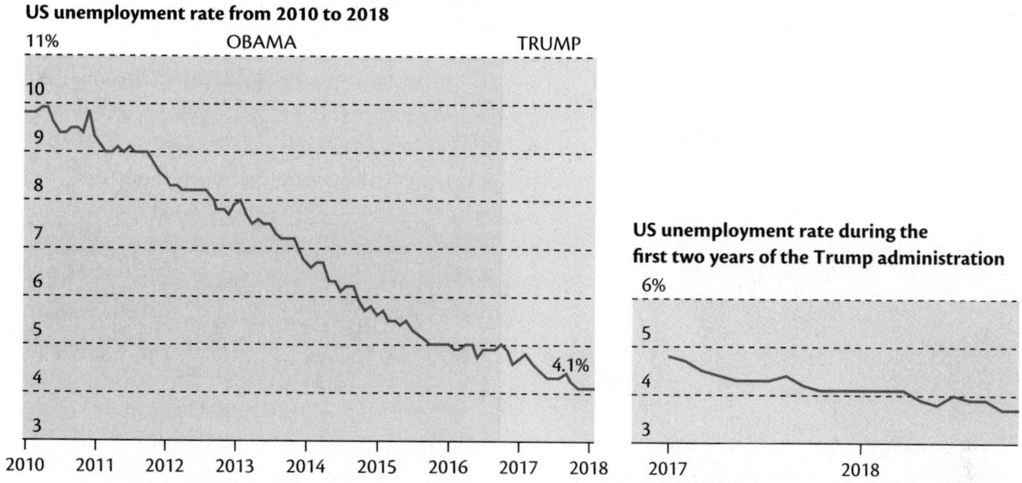

Using Visuals in Your Own Paper

Every paper uses some degree of visual persuasion, merely in its appearance. Consider these elements of a paper's "look": title page; margins (ample, but not so wide that they indicate the writer's inability to produce a paper of the assigned length); double-spaced text for the reader's convenience; headings and subheadings that indicate the progression of the argument; paragraphing; and so on. But you may also want to use visuals such as pictures, graphs, tables, or pie charts to provide examples, help readers digest statistical data more quickly, or simply liven up your essay or presentation. Keep a few guidelines in mind as you work with visuals, "writing" them into your own argument with as much care as you would read them in others' arguments:

- Consider your audience's needs and attitudes and select the type of visuals — graphs, drawings, photographs — likely to be most persuasive to that audience.
- Consider the effect of color, composition, and placement within your document. Because images are most effective when they appear near the text that they supplement, do not group all images at the end of the paper.

Remember especially that images are almost never self-supporting or self-explanatory. They may be evidence for your argument (e.g., Ut's photograph of napalm victims is *very* compelling evidence of suffering), but they aren't arguments themselves.

- Be sure to explain each visual that you use, integrating it into the verbal text that provides the logic and principal support behind your thesis.
- Be sure to cite the source of any visual that you paste into your argument.

Additional Images for Analysis

DOROTHEA LANGE

In 1936, photographer Dorothea Lange (1895–1965) took a series of a migrant mother and her children. Widely reprinted in the nation's newspapers, these photographs helped dramatize for the American public the poverty of displaced workers during the Great Depression.

Migrant Mother

Art Resource, NY

Library of Congress, Prints & Photographs Division, Reproduction number LC-DIG-fsa-8b29516.

Topics for Critical Thinking and Writing

1. Dorothea Lange drew increasingly near to her subject as she took a series of pictures. Make a list of details gained and lost by framing the mother and children more closely. The final shot in the series (right) became the most famous and most widely reprinted. Do you find it more effective than the other? Why, or why not?
2. Notice the expression on the mother's face, the position of her body, and the way she interacts with her children. What sorts of relationships are implied? Why is it significant that she doesn't look at her children or at the camera? How do the photographs' effects change according to how much you can see of the children's faces?
3. These photographs constitute a sort of persuasive "speech." Of what, exactly, might the photographer be trying to persuade her viewers? Write a brief essay (about 250 words) explaining Lange's purpose for her photographs and how she achieves that purpose. What assumptions does she make about her original audience? What sorts of evidence does she use to reach them?

During World War II, the US government produced a series of recruitment posters bearing the legend "This is the enemy." These posters depicted racially stereotyped images of both German and Japanese soldiers, typically engaged in acts of savage violence or clandestine surveillance.

World War II Recruitment Poster

Produced by the General Motors Corporation, 1942/NARA Still Picture Branch/(NWDNS-44-PA-2314)

Topics for Critical Thinking and Writing

1. It has been claimed that one role of propaganda is to dehumanize the enemy so that (1) soldiers will feel less remorse about killing opposing soldiers and (2) civilians will continue to support the war effort. What specific features of this poster contribute to this propaganda function?
2. Some would claim that such a racially provocative image of a Japanese person should never have been used because of the potential harm to all Asians, including patriotic Asian Americans. (Did you know that the 442nd Regimental Combat Team, consisting solely of Japanese American volunteers, was by war's end the most decorated unit in US military history for its size and length of service?) Others believe that the ordinary rules do not apply in times of national crisis and that, as an old saying has it, "All's fair in love and war." In an essay of about 500 words, argue for one or the other of these propositions. Refer to this poster as one piece of your evidence.

NORA EPHRON

Nora Ephron (1941–2012) attended Wellesley College and then worked as a reporter for the *New York Post* and as a columnist and senior editor for *Esquire*. Ephron wrote screenplays and directed films, including *Sleepless in Seattle* (1993) and *You've Got Mail* (1998), and continued to write essays on a wide variety of topics. "The Boston Photographs" is from her collection *Scribble, Scribble: Notes on the Media* (1978).

The Boston Photographs

"I made all kinds of pictures because I thought it would be a good rescue shot over the ladder . . . never dreamed it would be anything else. . . . I kept having to move around because of the light set. The sky was bright and they were in deep shadow. I was making pictures with a motor drive and he, the fire fighter, was reaching up and, I don't know, everything started falling. I followed the girl down taking pictures. . . . I made three or four frames. I realized what was going on and I completely turned around, because I didn't want to see her hit."

You probably saw the photographs. In most newspapers, there were three of them. The first showed some people on a fire escape — a fireman, a woman, and a child. The fireman had a nice strong jaw and looked very brave. The woman was holding the child. Smoke was pouring from the building behind them. A rescue ladder was approaching, just a few feet away, and the fireman had one arm around the woman and one arm reaching out toward the ladder. The second picture showed the fire escape slipping off the building. The child had fallen on the escape and seemed about to slide off the edge. The woman was grasping desperately at the legs of the fireman, who had managed to grab the ladder. The third picture showed the woman and child in midair, falling to the ground. Their arms and legs were outstretched, horribly distended. A potted plant was falling too. The caption said that the woman, Diana Bryant, nineteen, died in the fall. The child landed on the woman's body and lived.

The pictures were taken by Stanley Forman, thirty, of the *Boston Herald American*. He used a motor-driven Nikon F set at 1/250, f5.6-S. Because of the motor, the camera can click off three frames a second. More than four hundred newspapers in the United States alone carried the photographs: The tear sheets from overseas are still coming in. The *New York Times* ran them on the first page of its second section; a paper in south Georgia gave them nineteen columns; the *Chicago Tribune*, the *Washington Post*, and the *Washington Star* filled almost half their front pages, the *Star* under a somewhat redundant headline that read: SENSATIONAL PHOTOS OF RESCUE ATTEMPT THAT FAILED.

The photographs are indeed sensational. They are pictures of death in action, of that split second when luck runs out, and it is impossible to look at them without feeling their extraordinary impact and remembering, in an almost subconscious way, the morbid fantasy of falling, falling off a building, falling to one's death. Beyond that, the pictures are classics, old-fashioned but perfect examples of photojournalism at its most spectacular. They're throwbacks, really, fire pictures, 1930s tabloid shots; at the same time they're technically superb and thoroughly modern — the sequence could not have been taken at all until the development of the motor-driven camera some sixteen years ago.

5 Most newspaper editors anticipate some reader reaction to photographs like Forman's; even so, the response around the country was enormous, and almost all of it was negative. I have read hundreds of the letters that were printed in letters-to-the-editor sections, and they repeat the same points. "Invading the privacy of death." "Cheap sensationalism." "I thought I was reading the *National Enquirer*." "Assigning the agony of a human being in terror of imminent death to the status of a side-show act." "A tawdry way to sell newspapers." The *Seattle Times* received sixty letters and calls; its managing editor even got a couple of them at home. A reader wrote the *Philadelphia Inquirer*: "*Jaws* and *Towering Inferno* are playing downtown; don't take business away from people who pay good money to advertise in your own paper." Another reader wrote the *Chicago Sun-Times*: "I shall try to hide my disappointment that Miss Bryant wasn't wearing a skirt when she fell to her death. You could have had some award-winning photographs of her underpants as her skirt billowed over her head, you voyeurs." Several newspaper editors wrote columns defending the pictures: Thomas Keevil of the *Costa Mesa* (California) *Daily Pilot* printed a ballot for readers to vote on whether they would have printed the pictures; Marshall L. Stone of Maine's *Bangor Daily News*, which refused to print the famous assassination picture of the Vietcong prisoner in Saigon, claimed that the Boston pictures showed the dangers of fire escapes and raised questions about slumlords. (The burning building was a five-story brick apartment house on Marlborough Street in the Back Bay section of Boston.)

For the last five years, the *Washington Post* has employed various journalists as ombudsmen, whose job is to monitor the paper on behalf of the public. The *Post*'s current ombudsman is Charles Seib, former managing editor of the *Washington Star*; the day the Boston photographs appeared, the paper received over seventy calls in protest. As Seib later wrote in a column about the pictures, it was "the largest reaction to a published item that I have experienced in eight months as the *Post*'s ombudsman. . . .

"In the *Post*'s newsroom, on the other hand, I found no doubts, no second thoughts . . . the question was not whether they should be printed but how they should be displayed. When I talked to editors . . . they used words like 'interesting' and 'riveting' and 'gripping' to describe them. The pictures told of something about life in the ghetto, they said (although the neighborhood where the tragedy occurred is not a ghetto, I am told). They dramatized the need to check on the safety of fire escapes. They dramatically conveyed something that had happened, and that is the business we're in. They were news. . . .

"Was publication of that [third] picture a bow to the same taste for the morbidly sensational that makes gold mines of disaster movies? Most papers will not print the picture of a dead body except in the most unusual circumstances. Does the fact that the final picture was taken a millisecond before the young woman died make a difference? Most papers will not print a picture of a bare female breast. Is that a more inappropriate subject for display than the picture of a human being's last agonized instant of life?" Seib offered no answers to the questions he raised, but he went on to say that although as an editor he would probably have run the pictures, as a reader he was revolted by them.

In conclusion, Seib wrote: "Any editor who decided to print those pictures without giving at least a moment's thought to what purpose they served and what their effect was likely to be on the reader should ask another question: Have I become so preoccupied with manufacturing a product according to professional traditions and standards that I have forgotten about the consumer, the reader?"

It should be clear that the phone calls 10
and letters and Seib's own reaction were

Stanley Forman

Stanley Forman

occasioned by one factor alone: the death of the woman. Obviously, had she survived the fall, no one would have protested; the pictures would have had a completely different impact. Equally obviously, had the child died as well — or instead — Seib would undoubtedly have received ten times the phone calls he did. In each case, the pictures would have been exactly the same — only the captions, and thus the responses, would have been different.

But the questions Seib raises are worth discussing — though not exactly for the reasons he mentions. For it may be that the real lesson of the Boston photographs is not the danger that editors will be forgetful of reader reaction, but that they will continue to censor pictures of death precisely because of that reaction. The protests Seib fielded were really a variation on an old theme — and we saw plenty of it during the Nixon-Agnew years — the "Why doesn't the press print the good news?" argument. In this case, of course, the objections were all dressed up and cleverly disguised as righteous indignation about the privacy of death. This is a form of puritanism that is often justifiable; just as often it is merely puritanical.

Seib takes it for granted that the widespread though fairly recent newspaper policy against printing pictures of dead bodies is a sound one; I don't know that it makes any sense at all. I recognize that printing pictures of corpses raises all sorts of problems about taste and titillation and sensationalism; the fact is, however, that people die. Death happens to be one of life's main events. And it is irresponsible — and more than that, inaccurate — for newspapers to fail to show it, or to show it only when an astonishing set of photos comes in over the Associated Press wire. Most papers covering fatal automobile accidents will print pictures

Stanley Forman

Stanley Forman

of mangled cars. But the significance of fatal automobile accidents is not that a great deal of steel is twisted but that people die. Why not show it? That's what accidents are about. Throughout the Vietnam War, editors were reluctant to print atrocity pictures. Why *not* print them? That's what that was about. Murder victims are almost never photographed; they are granted their privacy. But their relatives are relentlessly pictured on their way in and out of hospitals and morgues and funerals.

I'm not advocating that newspapers print these things in order to teach their readers a lesson. The *Post* editors justified their printing of the Boston pictures with several arguments in that direction; every one of them is irrelevant. The pictures don't show anything about slum life; the incident could have happened anywhere, and it did. It is extremely unlikely that anyone who saw them rushed out and had his fire escape strengthened. And the pictures were not news — at least they were not national news. It is not news in Washington, or New York, or Los Angeles that a woman was killed in a Boston fire. The only newsworthy thing about the pictures is that they were taken. They deserve to be printed because they are great pictures, breathtaking pictures of something that happened. That they disturb readers is exactly as it should be: that's why photojournalism is often more powerful than written journalism.

Topics for Critical Thinking and Writing

1. In paragraph 5, Nora Ephron refers to "the famous assassination picture of the Vietcong prisoner in Saigon" (see p. 150). The photo shows the face of a prisoner who is about to be shot in the head at close range. Jot down the reasons you would or would not approve of printing this photo in a newspaper. Think, too, about this: If the photo on page 150 weren't about a war — if it didn't include the soldiers and the burning village in the rear but instead showed children fleeing from an abusive parent or an abusive sibling — would you approve of printing it in a newspaper?
2. In paragraph 9, Ephron quotes a newspaperman as saying that before printing Forman's pictures of the woman and the child falling from the fire escape, editors should have asked themselves "what purpose they served and what their effect was likely to be on the reader." If you were an editor, what would your answers be? By the way, the pictures were *not* taken in a poor neighborhood, and they did *not* expose slum conditions.
3. In fifty words or so, write a precise description of what you see in the third of the Boston photographs. Do you think readers of your description would be "revolted" by the picture (para. 8), as were many viewers, the *Washington Post*'s ombudsman among them? Why, or why not?
4. Ephron thinks it would be good for newspapers to publish more photographs of death and dying (paras. 11–13). In an essay of approximately 500 words, state her reasons and your evaluation of them. In the context of the internet age, when gruesome and grisly photographs and videos showing death are widely available, do you think Ephron's ideas still hold up? Why, or why not?

ASSIGNMENTS IN VISUAL RHETORIC

1. Choose a visual text and analyze its argument. Then evaluate whether the argument is effective or not. Support your analysis and evaluation with strong evidence and detail from the visual. (Advertisements, public service announcements, and political cartoons work particularly well for this assignment, although photographs and other visuals can also be rich resources.)
   - Identify the author(s) of the image. Who was the photographer/artist/designer? Who produced or sponsored the image?
   - Identify the intended audience for the image. Consumers? Art lovers? Newspaper reader of a particular political leaning? A particular demographic (age, gender, race, nationality, etc.)? Explain how you know that is the intended audience (context of publication, producer of the image, etc.).
   - Identify and describe the central argument of the image. If you cannot identify the argument, explain why you cannot really describe what the argument is.
   - Does the image appeal primarily to reason (*logos*), perhaps even using statistics, charts, graphs, tables, or illustrations? Does it appeal to feelings (*pathos*), evoking emotional responses or deeply held values? Or does it appeal to credibility and character (*ethos*), suggesting good sense, trustworthiness, or prudence? Use details from the image to explain how you know.
   - Are there any assumptions you can identify in the argument, either assumptions held by the creator or by the audience?
   - Are there any visual symbols present that contribute to the argument?
   - What single aspect of the image immediately captures your attention? Why exactly does it stand out? Its size? Position on the page? Beauty? Grotesqueness? Humor? How does the visceral impact of this element contribute to the visual's overall argument?
   - What is the relation of any text to the image? Does the visual part do most of the work, or does it serve to attract us and lead us on to read the text?
   - What elements at first go unnoticed or seem to be superfluous to the image? Are they important? If so, how? If not, why are they present?
2. Watch the commercials that air during a television show or examine the print advertisements in a popular magazine. Identify as many examples as possible of the types of appeals mentioned in Types of Emotional Appeals on pages 133–36. Select two good examples and explain what you think is the intended (or unintended) effect of the appeals. Is there a rational basis for the appeals you selected? Or are the appeals irrational even if they are effective? Or are they a little of both? Are the advertisements' appeals effective for the intended audience? Explain.

NicoElNino/Shutterstock.com

Kaspars Grinvalds/Shutterstock.com

3. Imagine that you work for a business and are asked to advertise one of the products above in a campaign that will be placed in a publication such as *Time* or *Newsweek*. Design the advertisement according to your purpose and in consideration of your audience. In addition, write a 250- to 500-word analysis of your advertisement, identifying your target audience (college students? young couples about to buy their first home? retired persons? environmental activists?) and your message and explaining the strategy you employ to persuade this audience and sell your product.

4. Gather some of the graphic materials used to promote and reflect your college or university — including a screen shot of its website, the college catalog, and the brochures and other materials sent to prospective students — and choose one of the following options:

   - What is the dominant image that your college or university administration seems to be promoting? Are there different, even competing, images of your school at work? How accurate is the story that these materials tell about your campus? Write an essay (approximately 500 words) in which you explain to prospective students the ways in which the promotional materials capture, or fail to capture, the true spirit of your campus.

   - Compare the website of your institution to one or two from very different institutions — perhaps a community college, a large state university, or an elite private college. How do you account for the similarities and differences among the images shown on the two different sites?

PART TWO

Critical Writing

5

Writing an Analysis of an Argument

To expect truth to come from thinking signifies that we mistake the need to think with the urge to know. Thinking can and must be employed in the attempt to know, but in the exercise of this function it is never itself; it is but the handmaiden of an altogether different enterprise.

— HANNAH ARENDT

I don't wait for moods. You accomplish nothing if you do that. Your mind must know it has got to get down to work.

— PEARL S. BUCK

Fear not those who argue but those who dodge.

— MARIE VON EBNER-ESCHENBACH

Analyzing an Argument

Most of your writing in other courses will require you to write an analysis of someone else's writing. In a political science course, you may have to analyze, say, an essay first published in *Foreign Affairs*, perhaps reprinted in your textbook, that argues against raising tariffs on foreign goods. A course in sociology may require you to analyze a report on the correlation between fatal accidents and drunk drivers under the age of twenty-one. In much of your college writing, you will be asked to set forth reasoned responses to your reading as preparation for making arguments of your own.

EXAMINING THE AUTHOR'S THESIS

Obviously, you must understand an essay before you can analyze it thoughtfully. You must read it several times — not just skim it — and (the hard part) you must think critically about it. You'll find that your thinking is stimulated if you take notes and if you ask yourself questions about the material. Are there any websites or organizations dedicated to the material you are analyzing? If there are, visit some to see what others are saying about the material you are reviewing. Notes will help you keep track of the writer's thoughts and also of your own responses to the writer's thesis. The writer probably *does* have a **thesis**—a main claim or point—and if so, you must try to locate it. Perhaps the thesis is explicitly stated in the title, in a sentence or two near the beginning of the essay, or in a concluding paragraph, or perhaps it is not directly stated and you will have to infer it from the essay as a whole.

Notice that we said the writer *probably* has a thesis, stated or unstated. Much of what you read will indeed be primarily an **argument**: a writer explicitly or implicitly trying to support some thesis and to convince readers to agree with it. But some of what you read will be relatively neutral, with the argument just faintly discernible—or even with no argument at all. A work may, for instance, chiefly be a report: Here is the data, or here is what *X*, *Y*, and *Z* said; make of it what you will. A report might simply state how various ethnic groups voted in an election, for example. In a report of this sort, of course, the writer hopes to persuade readers that the facts are correct, but no thesis is advanced—at least not consciously; the writer is not evidently arguing a point and trying to change readers' minds. Such a document differs greatly from an essay by a political analyst who presents those same findings to persuade a candidate to sacrifice the votes of one ethnic bloc to get more votes from other blocs.

If you are looking for evidence that what you are reading is an argument, look for the presence of two elements:

- Transitions implying the drawing of a conclusion (such as *therefore*, *because*, *for the reason that*, and *consequently*) and
- Verbs implying proof (such as *confirms*, *verifies*, *accounts for*, *implies*, *proves*, *disproves*, *is (in)consistent with*, *refutes*, and *it follows that*).

Keep your eye out for such terms and examine their role whenever they appear. If the essay does not seem to be advancing a clear thesis, think of one it might support or some conventional belief it might undermine. That could be the implicit thesis. (See also Thinking Critically: Examining Language to Analyze an Author's Argument on p. 186.)

EXAMINING THE AUTHOR'S PURPOSE

While reading an argument, try to form a clear idea of the author's **purpose**. A first question is this: Judging from the essay or the book, is the purpose to persuade, or is it to report? An analysis of a persuasive argument requires more investment in the analysis of language and rhetoric, whereas an analysis of a pure report (a work apparently without a thesis or argumentative angle) calls for dealing chiefly with the accuracy of the report. (The analysis must also consider whether the report really has an argument built into it, consciously or unconsciously.)

Purpose can mean many things because people write for many reasons. We write notes and emails sometimes with a purpose to persuade:

> Dear Professor, please forgive my absence from class this morning. I hit a deer on the way to class. Thankfully, only my car got damaged. I do hope I can make up the exam.

Such an email seems simple enough, but this note is a pretty carefully constructed argument. It establishes *ethos* (in a polite and formal tone) and appeals to *pathos* (by pointing to a sympathetic circumstance). It reasons, without really stating it, that the unforeseeable nature of the event is a good excuse to allow a make-up exam. If necessary, it could feasibly be underwritten by evidence (such as an accident report or an image of the damaged car).

In formal writing, purposes may vary. Sometimes, writers are trying to change an opinion, arguing that a certain perspective or interpretation of events is the correct one. A historian may assemble evidence from the past to argue that something occurred a certain way or that one event bore a relationship to some other events. A literary scholar might examine a novel and argue that some constellation of details amounts to something significant. In the sciences, the interpretation of data could be an effort to persuade. In opinion columns, blogs, and newspapers, people routinely write editorials sharing their perspectives and interpretations of the world. Whether the purpose is to change minds, challenge common assumptions, criticize institutionalized ideas, or argue that people should take some specific action, all arguments have a purpose.

When you are analyzing arguments, you will have a specific purpose. Perhaps you want simply to inform, attempting to convey someone else's argument as accurately as you can as if it were a report. Or perhaps you want to affirm (or challenge) the argument, making another argument (or counterargument) or your own. You might also satirize the argument, the writer, or the kind of thinking it represents. Whenever you analyze an argument, you are paying special attention to the author, context, language, medium — everything about the setting of an argument — and how those details and choices help the author achieve his or her purpose.

EXAMINING THE AUTHOR'S METHODS

If the essay advances a thesis to achieve a clear purpose, you will want to analyze the strategies or **methods** of argument that allegedly support the thesis.

- Is the argument aimed at a particular audience? Do the author's chosen methods work for that particular audience?
- Does the writer quote authorities? What publications does the writer draw from? Are these authorities competent in this field? Does the writer consider equally competent authorities who take a different view?
- Does the writer use statistics? If so, who compiled them, and are they appropriate to the point being argued? Can they be interpreted differently?
- Does the writer build the argument by using examples or analogies? Are they satisfactory?
- Does the writer include images (photos, graphs, charts, screenshots)? Are the image sources reliable? Do they support the writer's argument well, perhaps by an appeal to *logos* or *pathos*?
- Are the writer's assumptions acceptable?
- Does the writer consider all relevant factors? Has he or she omitted some points that you think should be discussed? For instance, should the author recognize certain opposing positions and perhaps concede something to them?
- Does the writer seek to persuade by means of humor or ridicule? If so, is the humor or ridicule fair? Is it supported also by rational argument?

EXAMINING THE AUTHOR'S PERSONA

You will probably also want to analyze something a bit more elusive than the author's explicit arguments: the author's self-presentation. Does the author seek to persuade readers partly by presenting himself or herself as conscientious, friendly, self-effacing, authoritative, or in some other light? Most writers, while they present evidence, also present themselves (or, more precisely, they present the image of themselves that they wish us to behold). In persuasive writing, this **persona** — this presentation of self, which can often be discerned from *language*, *voice*, and *tone* of the author — may be no less important than the presentation of evidence. In some cases, the persona may not much matter, but the point is that you should look at the author's self-presentation to consider if it's significant.

In establishing a persona, writers adopt various rhetorical strategies, ranging from the level of vocabulary they use, to their specific word choices, to the way they approach or organize their argument. The author of an essay may be polite, for example, and show fair-mindedness and open-mindedness, treating the opposition with great courtesy and expressing interest in hearing other views. Such a tactic is itself a persuasive device. Another author may use a technical vocabulary and rely on a range of hard evidence such as statistics. This reliance on a scientific tone and seemingly objective truths is itself a way of seeking to persuade — a rational way, to be sure, but a mode of persuasion nonetheless.

Consider these further examples:

- A writer who speaks of an opponent's "gimmicks" instead of "strategy" probably is trying to downgrade the opponent and also to convey the self-image of a street-wise person.
- A writer who uses legalistic language and cites numerous court cases is seeking to reveal her fluency in the law and her research capabilities to convince readers she is authoritative.
- A writer who seems professorial or pedantic, referencing a lot of classical figures and citing intellectual sources, is hoping to present himself as a person of deep knowledge and wisdom.
- A writer who draws a lot of examples from daily life in their ordinary neighborhood is wanting to be seen as a regular, commonsense person.

On a larger scale, then, consider not only the language, voice, and tone of the author, but also the *kind* of evidence that is used and the *ways* in which it is organized and presented. One writer may first bombard the reader with facts and then spend relatively little time drawing conclusions. Another may rely chiefly on generalizations, waiting until the end of the essay to bring the thesis home with a few details. Another may begin with a few facts and spend most of the space reflecting on these. All such devices deserve comment in your analysis.

The writer's persona may color the thesis and help it develop in a distinctive way. If we accept the thesis, it is no doubt partly because the writer has won our goodwill by persuading us of his or her good character or *ethos*. Good writers present themselves not as know-it-alls, wise guys, or bullies, but as decent people whom the reader presumably would like to invite to dinner.

In short, the author's self-presentation usually matters. A full analysis of an argument must recognize its effect, whether positive or negative.

EXAMINING THE AUTHOR'S AUDIENCE

Another key element in understanding an argument lies in thinking about the intended audience — how the author perceives the audience and what strategies the author uses to connect to it. We have already said something about the creation of the author's persona. An author with a loyal following is, almost by definition, someone who in earlier writings has presented an engaging persona, a persona with a trustworthy *ethos*. A trusted author can sometimes cut corners and can perhaps adopt a colloquial tone that would be unacceptable in the writing of an unknown author. The acclaimed mythologian Joseph Campbell once said, "You can always tell an author who is still working under the authorities by the number of footnotes he provides in his text."

Authors who want to convince their audiences need to think about how they present information and how they present themselves. Consider how you prefer people to talk to you. What sorts of language do you find engaging? Much, of course, depends on the circumstances, notably the topic, the audience, and the place. A joke may be useful in an argument about whether the government should regulate junk food, but almost surely a joke will be inappropriate — will backfire, will alienate the audience — in an argument about abortion. The *way* an author addresses the reader (through an invented persona) can have a significant impact on the reader's perception of the author, which is to say perception of the author's *views* and *argument*. A slip in tone or an error of fact, however small, may be enough for the audience to dismiss the author's argument. When you write your own arguments, understanding audience means thinking about all the possible audiences who may come into contact with your writing or your message and thinking about the consequences of what you write and where it is published.

Consider the impact of President Donald Trump's frequent use of Twitter to share his opinions and ideas. In that venue, he commonly castigates his political opponents (and sometimes his friends) and rails against policies and people he disagrees with. For many people, including some Republicans, not only does he generalize and oversimplify — after all, he is limited to a special number of characters — but his curious uses of capitalization and common misspellings are seen to detract from his *ethos*. For others, who may argue that Twitter is only one limited channel of communication where misspellings and solecisms are common, Trump's *ethos* is not damaged. Regardless of whether you think Trump strengthens or weakens his *ethos* through his tweets, they are on public record and will doubtlessly be analyzed long into the future; as the ancient Roman poet Horace said, *"Nescit vox missa reverti"* ("The word once spoken can never be recalled"), or, in plain proverbial English, "Think twice before you speak."

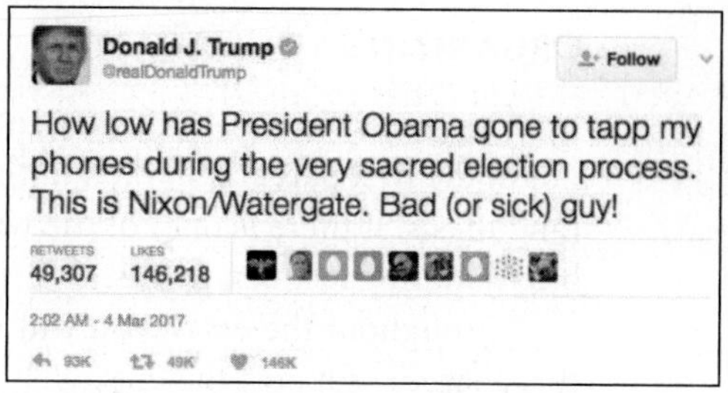

A tweet from Donald Trump claiming that Barack Obama ordered surveillance in Trump Tower during the 2016 US presidential campaign.

Our point is that we must consider the author's persona in conjunction with the publication type or venue in which an argument occurs in order to fully analyze the argument — whether it is occurring in a tweet, an editorial, a magazine article, a review, or a scholarly essay — because each publication context has a specific intended audience to whom the author is appealing.

Consider your own social media usage. Have you ever seen something posted by a friend or influencer on Facebook, Instagram, or Twitter and then swiftly taken down again? Have you ever received a text message or email not intended for you? Just as you must consider the purposes of the authors in those cases, when you are reading more formal essays it is equally important to think about who wrote them (author and author's persona) and for whom they were intended (audience). These factors can help you better discern the perspective and intentions of the author, which can significantly inform the ways evidence was gathered, interpreted, and represented.

A CHECKLIST FOR ANALYZING AN AUTHOR'S INTENDED AUDIENCE

- ❐ Where did the piece appear? Who published it? Why, in your view, might someone have found it worth publishing?
- ❐ In what technological format does this piece appear? Print journal? Online magazine? Blog? What does the technological format say about the piece, the author, or the audience?
- ❐ Is the writing relatively informal — for instance, a tweet or a Facebook status update? Why is this medium good or bad for the message?
- ❐ Who is the intended audience? Are there other audiences who may also have an interest but whom the author has failed to consider?
- ❐ If *you* are the intended audience, what shared values do you have with the author?
- ❐ What strategies does the writer use to create a connection with the audience?

ORGANIZING YOUR ANALYSIS

In writing an analysis of an argument, it is usually a good idea at the start of your analysis — if not in the first paragraph, then in the second or third — to let the reader know the purpose (and thesis, if there is one) of the work you are analyzing and then to summarize the work briefly, noting its main points.

Throughout the essay, you will want to analyze the strategies or methods of argument that allegedly support the thesis. Thus, you will probably find it useful (and your readers will certainly find it helpful) to write out *your* thesis (your evaluation or judgment). You might say, for instance, that the essay is impressive but not conclusive, or is undermined by convincing contrary evidence, or relies too much on unsupported generalizations, or is wholly admirable. It all depends on what you conclude as you go through the process of analyzing the argument at hand.

And then, of course, comes the job of setting forth your analysis and the support for your thesis. There is no one way of going about this work, and the organization of your analysis may or may not follow the organization of the work you are analyzing. (The Visual Guide: Organizing Your Analysis graphic shows some options, but there are, of course, others that may better suit your argument.)

Especially in analyzing a work in which the author's persona, ideas, and methods are blended, you will want to spend some time commenting on the persona. Whether you discuss it near the beginning of your analysis or near the end will depend on how you want to construct your essay, and this decision will partly depend on the work you are analyzing. For example, if the author's persona is kept in the background and is thus relatively invisible, you may want to make that point fairly early to get it out of the way and then concentrate on more interesting matters. If, however, the persona is interesting — and perhaps seductive, whether because it seems so scrupulously objective or so engagingly subjective — you may want to hint at this quality early in your essay and then develop the point while you consider the arguments.

Visual Guide: Organizing Your Analysis

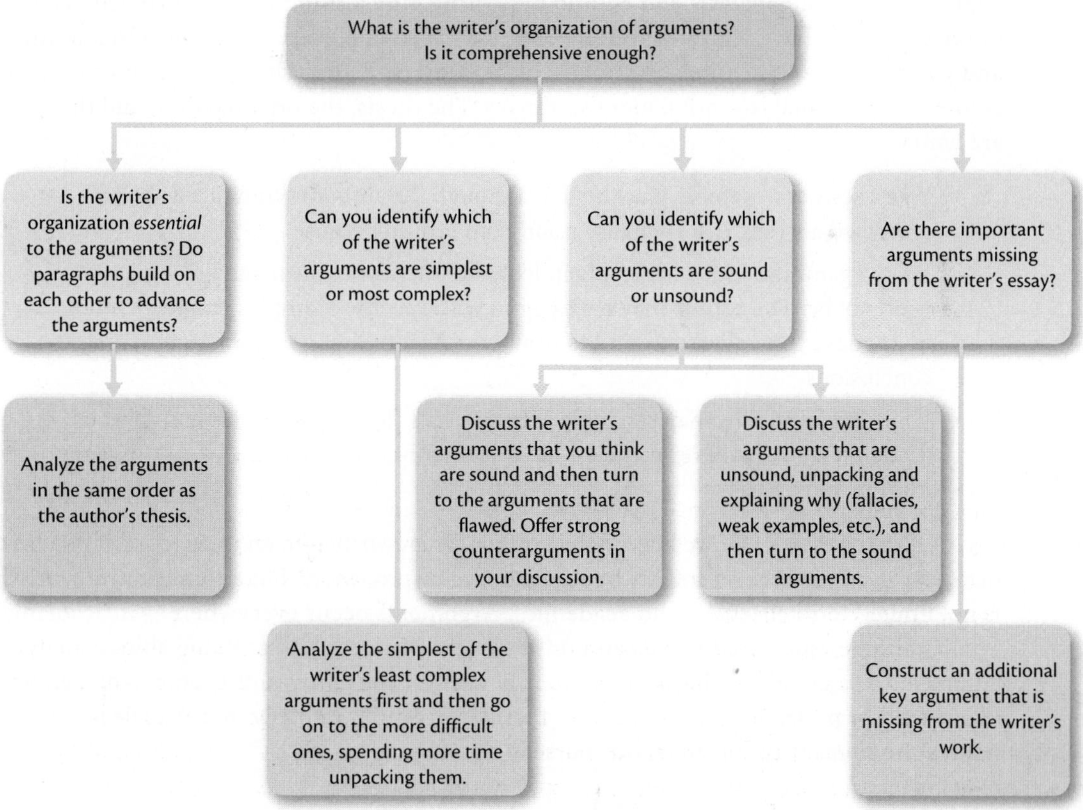

A good conclusion for an analysis of an argument might offer a reassessment of the major points made by the author and a final statement about the validity or viability of the argument. You also have a chance in the conclusion to test the author's argument further, perhaps applying it to new or different situations that highlight its effectiveness or show where it falls short. If readers were to accept or reject the argument, what would be the implications? What other arguments would gain or lose currency by accepting or rejecting this one? Does the argument represent a new kind of potential or a new kind of threat — in a general sense, does it disrupt or attempt to disrupt current thinking, and, if so, is that a good or bad thing?

SUMMARY VERSUS ANALYSIS

In the last few pages, we have tried to persuade you that, in writing an analysis of a reading:

- Most of the nonliterary material that you will read is designed to argue, to report, or to do both. Read and reread thoughtfully, and take careful notes.
- Most of this material also presents the writer's personality, or voice, and this voice usually merits attention in an analysis.

There is yet another point, equally obvious but often neglected by students who begin by writing an analysis and end up by writing only a summary, a shortened version of the work they have read: Although your essay is an analysis of someone else's writing and you may have to include a summary of the work you are writing about, your essay is *your* essay, your analysis, not a mere summary. The thesis, the organization, and the tone are yours.

- Your thesis, for example, may be that although the author is convinced she has presented a strong case, her case is far from proved because . . .
- Your organization may be deeply indebted to the work you are analyzing, but it need not be. The author may have begun with specific examples and then gone on to make generalizations and to draw conclusions, but you may begin with the conclusions.
- Your tone, similarly, may resemble your subject's (let's say the voice is courteous academic), but it will nevertheless have its own ring, its own tone of, say, urgency, caution, or coolness.

Most of the essays that we have included thus far are written in an intellectual if not academic style, and indeed several are by students and by professors. But argumentative writing is not limited to intellectuals and academics. Arguments occur everywhere — in academic articles and newspaper editorials and on the backs of cereal boxes. Being able to analyze arguments is essential to being a wise citizen, a skeptical consumer, and a competent member of any field or profession. If it weren't all these things (and probably more), colleges would not require so many people to take a course in the subject.

A CHECKLIST FOR ANALYZING A TEXT

Have I considered all the following matters?

- ❒ Does the author have a self-interest in writing this piece?
- ❒ Is there evidence in the author's tone and style that enables me to identify anything about the intended audience? Is the tone appropriate?
- ❒ Given the publication venue (or any other contexts), can I tell if the audience is likely to be neutral, sympathetic, or hostile to the argument?
- ❒ Does the author have a thesis? Does the argument ask the audience to accept or to do anything?
- ❒ Does the author make assumptions? Does the audience share those assumptions? Do I?
- ❒ Is there a clear line between what is factual information and what is interpretation, belief, or opinion?
- ❒ Does the author appeal to reason (*logos*), to the emotions (*pathos*), or to our sense that the speaker is trustworthy (*ethos*)?
- ❒ Is the evidence provided convincing? If visual materials such as graphs, pie charts, or pictures are used, are they persuasive?
- ❒ Are significant objections and counterevidence adequately discussed?
- ❒ Is the organization of the text effective? Are the title, the opening paragraphs, and the concluding paragraphs effective?
- ❒ Is the overall argument correct in its conclusions? Or is there anything missing that I could use to add to or challenge the argument?
- ❒ Has the author convinced me?

An Argument, Its Elements, and a Student's Analysis of the Argument

In many types of media, we are exposed to the opinions and judgments of others, often capable writers, who argue their positions clearly, reasonably, and convincingly. We want to think carefully before we accept an argument, so we encourage skepticism but not entrenchment in your own position. You must be willing to hear and seriously consider different positions. Consider the following argument by columnist Nicholas Kristof, published in the *New York Times* in 2005. Analyze the essay and, after you do, examine our analysis of Kristof's argument, as well as the analysis provided by student Theresa Carcaldi, to see how it matches your own.

NICHOLAS D. KRISTOF

Nicholas D. Kristof (b. 1959), a two-time Pulitzer Prize winner, grew up on a farm in Oregon. After graduating from Harvard, he was awarded a Rhodes scholarship to Oxford, where he studied law. In 1984, he joined the *New York Times* as a correspondent, and since 2001 he has written as a columnist. The editorial that follows first appeared in the *New York Times* in 2005.

For Environmental Balance, Pick Up a Rifle

Here's a quick quiz: Which large American mammal kills the most humans each year?

It's not the bear, which kills about two people a year in North America. Nor is it the wolf, which in modern times hasn't killed anyone in this country. It's not the cougar, which kills one person every year or two.

Rather, it's the deer. Unchecked by predators, deer populations are exploding in a way that is profoundly unnatural and that is destroying the ecosystem in many parts of the country. In a wilderness, there might be ten deer per square mile; in parts of New Jersey, there are up to 200 per square mile.

One result is ticks and Lyme disease, but deer also kill people more directly. A study for the insurance industry estimated that deer kill about 150 people a year in car crashes nationwide and cause $1 billion in damage. Granted, deer aren't stalking us, and they come out worse in these collisions — but it's still true that in a typical year, an American is less likely to be killed by Osama bin Laden[1] than by Bambi.

5 If the symbol of the environment's being out of whack in the 1960s was the Cuyahoga River in Cleveland catching fire, one such symbol today is deer congregating around what they think of as salad bars and what we think of as suburbs.

So what do we do? Let's bring back hunting.

Now, you've probably just spilled your coffee. These days, among the university-educated crowd in the cities, hunting is viewed as barbaric.

The upshot is that towns in New York and New Jersey are talking about using birth control to keep deer populations down. (Liberals presumably support free condoms, while conservatives back abstinence education.) Deer contraception hasn't been very successful, though.

Meanwhile, the same population bomb has spread to bears. A bear hunt has been scheduled for this week in New Jersey — prompting outrage from some animal rights groups (there's also talk of bear contraception: make love, not cubs).

10 As for deer, partly because hunting is perceived as brutal and vaguely psychopathic, towns are taking out contracts on deer through discreet private companies. Greenwich, Connecticut, budgeted $47,000 this year to pay a company to shoot eighty deer from raised platforms over four nights — as well as $8,000 for deer birth control.

Look, this is ridiculous.

[1] The Al-Qaeda leader and mastermind of the 9/11 attack who was still at large at Kristof's writing. [Editors' note]

We have an environmental imbalance caused in part by the decline of hunting. Humans first wiped out certain predators — like wolves and cougars — but then expanded their own role as predators to sustain a rough ecological balance. These days, though, hunters are on the decline.

According to "Families Afield: An Initiative for the Future of Hunting," a report by an alliance of shooting organizations, for every hundred hunters who die or stop hunting, only sixty-nine hunters take their place.

I was raised on *Bambi* — but also, as an Oregon farm boy, on venison and elk meat. But deer are not pets, and dead deer are as natural as live deer. To wring one's hands over them, perhaps after polishing off a hamburger, is soggy sentimentality.

15 What's the alternative to hunting? Is it preferable that deer die of disease and hunger? Or, as the editor of *Adirondack Explorer* magazine suggested, do we introduce wolves into the burbs?

To their credit, many environmentalists agree that hunting can be green. The New Jersey Audubon Society this year advocated deer hunting as an ecological necessity.

There's another reason to encourage hunting: it connects people with the outdoors and creates a broader constituency for wilderness preservation. At a time when America's wilderness is being gobbled away for logging, mining, or oil drilling, that's a huge boon.

Granted, hunting isn't advisable in suburban backyards, and I don't expect many soccer moms to install gun racks in their minivans. But it's an abdication of environmental responsibility to eliminate other predators and then refuse to assume the job ourselves. In that case, the collisions with humans will simply get worse.

In October, for example, Wayne Goldsberry was sitting in a home in northwestern Arkansas when he heard glass breaking in the next room. It was a home invasion — by a buck.

20 Mr. Goldsberry, who is six feet one inch and weighs two hundred pounds, wrestled with the intruder for forty minutes. Blood spattered the walls before he managed to break the buck's neck.

So it's time to reestablish a balance in the natural world — by accepting the idea that hunting is as natural as bird-watching.

Topics for Critical Thinking and Writing

1. What is Nicholas Kristof's chief thesis? (State it in one sentence.)
2. Does Kristof make any assumptions — tacit or explicit — with which you agree or disagree? Why?
3. Is the slightly humorous tone of Kristof's essay inappropriate for a discussion of deliberately killing wild animals? Why, or why not?
4. What kind of evidence does Kristof offer to justify his claim that more hunting is needed? What interpretations of Kristof's evidence could be made if you were trying to challenge him?
5. Do you agree that "hunting is as natural as bird-watching" (para. 21)? In any case, do you think that an appeal to what is "natural" is a good argument for expanding the use of hunting? Why, or why not?
6. To whom is Kristof talking? How do you know?

THINKING CRITICALLY *Examining Language to Analyze an Author's Argument*

Look at Nicholas D. Kristof's essay on page 184. Provide two examples of sentences from Kristof's essay that use each type of conclusion or proof.

LANGUAGE	EXAMPLES	TWO EXAMPLES FROM KRISTOF'S ESSAY
Transitions that imply the drawing of a conclusion	*therefore, because, for the reason that, consequently*	
Verbs that imply proof	*confirms, verifies, accounts for, implies, proves, disproves, is (in)consistent with, refutes, it follows that*	

THE ESSAY ANALYZED

By now you have read and begun to analyze Kristof's essay. Now let's examine his argument with an eye to identifying those elements we mentioned earlier in this chapter that deserve notice when examining *any* argument: the author's *thesis, purpose, methods, persona,* and *audience* (see Analyzing an Argument, pp. 175–83). It is important to point out that analysis does not always (or even usually) happen in a linear way.

When analyzing, we always consider the author, the publication type, and the context in which the argument was written. We knew that Kristof is a self-described progressive but is also known to take provocative positions somewhat out of step with typical liberal attitudes (for example, Kristof argued elsewhere in several *New York Times* editorials that sweatshops in foreign countries could be a good thing, a necessary stage on the way to progress). Thus, we could better interpret his argument about hunting deer: Although it involves guns and the killing of animals, it presents ethical and ecological reasons likely to be valued by liberals. We also knew that the essay appeared in a newspaper, the *New York Times*, where paragraphs are customarily very short, partly to allow for easy reading. Taking all this information together, we can assume that Kristof's intended audience was a commonsense, urban (or suburban) moderate who might hold typical liberal values about guns and hunting. This assumption allows us to read Kristof's tone — funny and acerbic but not cutting or insulting — as one suitable to the writer's purpose: to challenge a relatively sympathetic audience and at the same time gently ridicule their more "bleeding-heart" brethren.

Thesis Kristof does not *announce* the thesis in its full form until paragraph 6 ("Let's bring back hunting"); instead he begins with evidence that builds up to the thesis. (It's worth noting that his paragraphs are very short, and if the essay were published in a book instead of a newspaper, Kristof's first two paragraphs probably would be combined, as would the third and fourth.)

Purpose He wants to *persuade* readers to adopt his view. Kristof does not show that his essay is argumentative by using key terms that normally mark argumentative prose: *in conclusion, therefore,* or *because of this.* Almost the only traces of the language of argument are "Granted" (para. 18) and "So" (i.e., *therefore*) in his final paragraph. But the argument is clear — if unusual — and he wants readers to accept his argument as *true.* Possibly, part of his purpose is that he wants to make this argument specifically to a liberal audience unlikely to assume that hunting or guns could be a solution.

Methods Kristof offers evidence identifying the problem of deer overpopulation, pointing out the annual number of deaths, and comparing that number — with a reference to a global terrorist — to the number of deaths from terrorism. He also points out other hazards such as Lyme disease and the economic impact of deer overpopulation. Kristof's methods of presenting evidence include providing ***statistics*** (paras. 3, 4, 10, and 13), giving ***examples*** (paras. 10, 19–20), and citing ***authorities*** (paras. 13 and 16).

Persona Kristof presents himself as a confident, no-nonsense fellow, a newspaper columnist. A folksy tone ("Here's a quick quiz") and informal, humorous language establish a good relationship with readers. A well-known columnist, Kristof is a progressive who often takes nontypical views and presents a voice of "common sense." His readers probably know what to expect, and they read him with pleasure.

Audience Kristof is known to be progressive, and he knows his audience is, too ("Now you've probably just spilled your coffee," he says when he proposes hunting as a solution). But he also mocks the "the university-educated crowd in the cities, [for whom] hunting is viewed as barbaric" (para. 7). So he is mocking liberal dogmas even though his audience is presumable of the same ilk. But he is not conservative (in fact, he spoofs them, too). Ordinarily, it is a bad idea to make fun of persons, whether they're you're intended audience or not; impartial readers rarely want to align themselves with someone who mocks others. In the essay we are looking at, however, Kristof gets away with this smart-guy tone because he not only has loyal readers but also has written the entire essay in a highly informal or playful manner.

Let's now turn to a student's written analysis of Kristof's essay and then to our own analysis of the student's analysis.

Theresa Carcaldi

Professor Markle

ENG 120

13 July 2018

For Sound Argument, Drop the Jokes:
How Kristof Falls Short in Convincing His Audience

Carcaldi examines the paradox of the title—for a liberal goal, use a gun.

Note in Carcaldi's thesis her primary critique of Kristof's argument.

In recent years, the action of hunting wild animals has become controversial. However, the *New York Times* columnist Nicholas D. Kristof attempts to argue for the necessity of hunting deer in America in his piece, "For Environmental Balance, Pick up a Rifle." Kristof certainly engages his audience in this newspaper column, especially progressive-minded readers who might believe any expansion of guns or hunting is abhorrent. He presents evidence that at first seems convincing; however, it is clear that the soundness of his argument falls short as a result of replacing his arguments with jokes, failing to provide adequate evidence, and including lines that are both incapable of relating to a majority of the population as well as disbelieving.

Analyzes how Kristof establishes *ethos*.

Points out Kristof's persuasive strategy.

Before describing why Kristof's essay falls short of being sound, it is first important to concede the fact that Kristof's essay appeared in a newspaper column that is meant to be read in a quick manner, so the tone of his essay as well as its length and lack of evidence and full development of ideas is to be expected. His sarcastic, conversational tone is layered with occasional jokes and creates a friendly relationship with the audience that sets the stage for trust between author and reader. Therefore, some initial evidence sets out the problems of deer overpopulation in a way likely to be accepted, including dramatic statistics about human highway deaths caused by deer and the incident rates of Lyme disease spread by deer. By doing this, Kristof appeals to fear in the basic structure of his argument: the drastic rise in the deer population is wreaking havoc across America, and the solution to this problem is to hunt more deer.

Accounts for the fact that there is a problem, but takes issue with how that problem is overdramatized.

No doubt, deer do cause serious problems. As Kristof says, deer "kill people more directly" each year than any other mammal (para. 4). However, the evidence is mostly unconvincing. By showing the deer threat to be more significant than the threat of terrorism, Kristof intends to highlight the often irrationality of his audience's anxieties. However, his sample is too small: just because deaths caused by deer in a single year exceed that of terrorism in America, that does not mean that a major terrorist attack will not happen in the future.

Carcaldi reinterprets and challenges the evidence Kristof uses.

Even with the threats deer do pose, the idea of hunting being the best solution is unconvincing. While Kristof states in paragraph 16 that the New Jersey Audubon Society "advocated deer hunting as an ecological necessity," this is only convincing if the audience is aware of what the New Jersey Audubon Society advocates for — which Kristof fails to explain. To add, Kristof proposes that the present alternative to deer hunting is to let the deer perish from natural causes like "disease and hunger" (para. 15). While this appeal to the audience's sensitivities about animal cruelty is good evidence for supporting deer hunting, Kristof does not fully explain why other solutions, such as deer birth control, are inadequate; instead, he just jokes about it, poking fun at the oversensitive "make love, not cubs" crowd. Rather than giving an argument, in other words, he makes a joke, then adds a further one that "Liberals presumably support free condoms, while conservatives back abstinence education" (para. 8). While this may make the audience laugh, it also suggests that people's political attitudes often prevent them from using common sense. This is an appeal to humor and to common sense, but is certainly not a fully stated reason for why deer contraception is not a solution. Kristof once states, "Deer contraception hasn't been very successful" (para. 8), yet does not explain why — he merely makes a statement without evidence, which does not contribute to a sound argument.

Suggests that the argument Kristof makes is presented as one (although not the only or best) solution.

Acknowledges other types of appeals Kristof makes.

In addition, Kristof ends his essay with unbelievable statements. First, he claims hunting "connects people with the outdoors and creates a broader constituency for wilderness preservation" (para. 17). This statement contradicts his previous statement that "Humans first wiped out certain predators — like wolves and cougars" (para. 12). After stating the negative effects hunting has had on wildlife preservation, it is difficult to

Carcaldi 3

claim that hunting nowadays would be any different. Finally, Kristof ends with "hunting is as natural as bird-watching" (para. 21). While hunting in the wild is certainly natural, it goes without saying that hunting with manmade weapons is far from being natural. Thus, with these two statements, not only does Kristof contradict himself, but he jeopardizes his audience's trust. While Kristof may use transitions of argumentation, such as "Granted" (para. 3), "Meanwhile" (para. 9), and "To their credit" (para. 16), his writing is primarily based on unsupported statements and jokes rather than sound reasoning. Ultimately, his essay is left labeled as an unsound argument.

Carcaldi concludes by reiterating her own thesis and main points.

Clearly, Kristof has written an engaging article about a controversial topic and has written it well for the medium in which it was produced and for the audience he sought. However, this does not mean his argument is logical and sound. As a result of his lack of evidence, his often overconfident statements, and the logical fallacies ridden throughout the piece, his argument is left unsound, and his audience is left utterly unconvinced that the only solution to the deer issue across America is to hunt them.

AN ANALYSIS OF THE STUDENT'S ANALYSIS

Carcaldi's essay seems to us to be excellent, doubtless the product of a good deal of thoughtful revision. She does not cover every possible aspect of Kristof's essay — she concentrates on Kristof's reasoning and says very little about his style — but we think Carcaldi does a good job in a short space. What makes her essay effective?

- She has a strong title ("For Sound Argument, Drop the Jokes: How Kristof Falls Short in Convincing His Audience") that is of at least a little interest; it picks up Kristof's method of using humor, and it gives a hint of what is to come.
- She promptly identifies Kristof's subject and gives us a hint of where she will be going, telling us outright that it is "clear that the soundness of his essay falls short."
- She recognizes Kristof's audience at the start and analyzes his use of language and his assumptions with that knowledge in mind.

- She uses a few brief quotations to give us a feel for Kristof's essay and to let us hear the evidence for itself, but she does not pad her essay with long quotations.
- She considers all Kristof's main points.
- She organizes her essay reasonably, letting us hear Kristof's thesis, letting us know the degree to which she accepts it, and finally letting us know her specific reservations about Kristof's essay.
- She concludes without the formality of "in conclusion" but structures her analysis in such a way as to account for the charm or effectiveness of Kristof's essay but not agree with his solutions.
- Notice, finally, that she sticks closely to Kristof's essay. She does not go off on a tangent about the virtues of vegetarianism or the dreadful politics of the *New York Times*, the newspaper that published Kristof's essay. She was asked to analyze the essay, and she has done so.

A CHECKLIST FOR WRITING AN ANALYSIS OF AN ARGUMENT

- ❒ Have I accurately stated the writer's thesis (claim) and summarized his or her supporting reasons?
- ❒ Have I indicated early in the essay where I will be taking my reader (i.e., have I indicated my general response to the essay I am analyzing)?
- ❒ Have I called attention to the strengths, if any, and the weaknesses, if any, of the essay?
- ❒ Have I commented on the ways *logos* (logic, reasoning), *pathos* (emotion), and *ethos* (character of the writer) are presented in the essay?
- ❒ Have I explained any disagreements I might have about definitions of important terms and concepts?
- ❒ Have I examined the chief uses of evidence in the essay and offered supporting or refuting evidence or interpretation?
- ❒ Have I used occasional brief quotations to let my reader hear the author's tone and to ensure fairness and accuracy?
- ❒ Is my analysis effectively organized?
- ❒ Have I taken account of the author's audience(s)?
- ❒ Does my essay, perhaps in the concluding paragraphs, indicate my agreement or disagreement with the writer but also my view of the essay as a piece of argumentative writing?
- ❒ Is my tone appropriate?

Arguments for Analysis

JEFF JACOBY

Jeff Jacoby (b. 1959) is a columnist for the *Boston Globe*, where this essay was originally published on the op-ed page on February 20, 1997. As an opinion columnist, Jacoby is known for his conservative slant: In 1999, he won the Breindal Prize for opinion journalism from Rupert Murdoch's News Corporation, and in 2004, he won the Thomas Paine Award from the Institute for Justice, a libertarian law firm.

Bring Back Flogging

Boston's Puritan forefathers did not indulge miscreants lightly.

For selling arms and gunpowder to Indians in 1632, Richard Hopkins was sentenced to be "whipt, & branded with a hott iron on one of his cheekes." Joseph Gatchell, convicted of blasphemy in 1684, was ordered "to stand in pillory, have his head and hand put in & have his toung drawne forth out of his mouth, & peirct through with a hott iron." When Hannah Newell pleaded guilty to adultery in 1694, the court ordered "fifteen stripes Severally to be laid on upon her naked back at the Common Whipping post." Her consort, the aptly named Lambert Despair, fared worse: He was sentenced to twenty-five lashes "and that on the next Thursday Immediately after Lecture he stand upon the Pillory for . . . a full hower with Adultery in Capitall letters written upon his brest."

Corporal punishment for criminals did not vanish with the Puritans — Delaware didn't get around to repealing it until 1972 — but for all relevant purposes, it has been out of fashion for at least 150 years. The day is long past when the stocks had an honored place on the Boston Common, or when offenders were publicly flogged. Now we practice a more enlightened, more humane way of disciplining wrongdoers: We lock them up in cages.

Imprisonment has become our penalty of choice for almost every offense in the criminal code. Commit murder; go to prison. Sell cocaine; go to prison. Kite checks; go to prison. It is an all-purpose punishment, suitable — or so it would seem — for crimes violent and nonviolent, motivated by hate or by greed, plotted coldly or committed in a fit of passion. If anything, our preference for incarceration is deepening — behold the slew of mandatory minimum sentences for drug crimes and "three-strikes-you're-out" life terms for recidivists. Some 1.6 million Americans are behind bars today. That represents a 250 percent increase since 1980, and the number is climbing.

5 We cage criminals at a rate unsurpassed in the free world, yet few of us believe that the criminal justice system is a success. Crime is out of control, despite the deluded happy talk by some politicians about how "safe" cities have become. For most wrongdoers, the odds of being arrested, prosecuted, convicted, and incarcerated are reassuringly long. Fifty-eight percent of all murders do *not* result in a prison term. Likewise 98 percent of all burglaries.

Many states have gone on prison-building sprees, yet the penal system is choked to bursting. To ease the pressure, nearly all convicted felons are released early — or not locked up at all. "About three of every four convicted criminals," says John DiIulio, a noted Princeton criminologist, "are on the streets without meaningful probation or parole supervision." And while everyone knows that amateur thugs should be deterred before they become career criminals, it is almost unheard of for judges to send first- or second-time offenders to prison.

Meanwhile, the price of keeping criminals in cages is appalling — a common estimate is $30,000 per inmate per year. (To be sure, the cost to society of turning many inmates loose would be even higher.) For tens of thousands of convicts, prison is a graduate school of criminal studies: They emerge more ruthless and savvy than when they entered. And for many offenders, there is even a certain cachet to doing time — a stint in prison becomes a sign of manhood, a status symbol.

But there would be no cachet in chaining a criminal to an outdoor post and flogging him. If young punks were horsewhipped in public after their first conviction, fewer of them would harden into lifelong felons. A humiliating and painful paddling can be applied to the rear end of a crook for a lot less than $30,000 — and prove a lot more educational than ten years' worth of prison meals and lockdowns.

Are we quite certain the Puritans have nothing to teach us about dealing with criminals?

10 Of course, their crimes are not our crimes: We do not arrest blasphemers or adulterers, and only gun control fanatics would criminalize the sale of weapons to Indians. (They would criminalize the sale of weapons to anybody.) Nor would the ordeal suffered by poor Joseph Gatchell — the tongue "peirct through" with a hot poker — be regarded today as anything less than torture.

But what is the objection to corporal punishment that doesn't maim or mutilate? Instead of a prison term, why not sentence at least some criminals — say, thieves and drunk drivers — to a public whipping?

"Too degrading," some will say. "Too brutal." But where is it written that being whipped is more degrading than being caged? Why is it more brutal to flog a wrongdoer than to throw him in prison — where the risk of being beaten, raped, or murdered is terrifyingly high?

The *Globe* reported in 1994 that more than two hundred thousand prison inmates are raped each year, usually to the indifference of the guards. "The horrors experienced by many young inmates, particularly those who . . . are convicted of nonviolent offenses," former Supreme Court Justice Harry Blackmun has written, "border on the unimaginable." Are those horrors preferable to the short, sharp shame of corporal punishment?

Perhaps the Puritans were more enlightened than we think, at least on the subject of punishment. Their sanctions were humiliating and painful, but quick and cheap. Maybe we should readopt a few.

Topics for Critical Thinking and Writing

1. When Jeff Jacoby says (para. 3) that today we are more "enlightened" than our Puritan forefathers because where they used flogging, "We lock them up in cages," is he being ironic? Explain.
2. Suppose you agree with Jacoby. Explain precisely (1) what you mean by *flogging* (does Jacoby explain what he means?) and (2) how much flogging is appropriate for different crimes such as housebreaking, rape, robbery, and murder.

3. In an essay of about 250 words, explain why you think that flogging would be more (or less) degrading and brutal than imprisonment.
4. At the end of his essay Jacoby draws to our attention the terrible risk of being raped in prison as an argument in favor of replacing imprisonment with flogging. Do you think this is sound reasoning? Why, or why not?
5. Jacoby draws the line (para. 11) at punishment that would "maim or mutilate." Why draw the line here? Some societies punish thieves by amputating a hand. Suppose we knew that this practice really did seriously reduce theft. Should we adopt it? How about adopting castration (surgical or chemical) for rapists? For child molesters? Explain your response.

MATTHEW WALTHER

Matthew Walther is a national correspondent at the *Week*, a widely circulated online and print magazine of news, opinion, and commentary published in both UK and US editions. Walther also contributes to the *Spectator of London*, the *Catholic Herald*, and the *National Review*. This piece was first published in May 2018.

Sorry, Nerds: Video Games Are Not a Sport

As a columnist you hate to get a reputation for having anything negative to say about a large group of people. Which is why I am often at great pains to admit that nerd culture has given the world lots of wonderful things and not just wizard erotica, minarchism, and all the anti-anti arguments about racism and misogyny you can find on Reddit. I just don't know what they are yet.

My biggest problem with nerd culture, though, is not that it exists but that it has territorial ambitions. Two decades ago, comic books were still a fringe phenomenon; now they are the only things directors are allowed to make films about, notwithstanding mumblecore and Oscar bait. Oh well. Movie tickets are too expensive anyway. But at sports I feel like it is necessary to draw a line in the sand and, unlike President Obama, to act when my opponents cross it.

In 2016 something called the National Association of Collegiate Esports was established in order to regulate competitions between young adult gamers, taking over a role that had previously belonged to their mothers who needed the garbage taken out. Two years earlier, a private university in Illinois created the nation's first varsity gaming team and began awarding "athletic" scholarships to skilled players. Imagine being that kid's parents. "Oh, yes, Dylan just got accepted with an athletic scholarship." "That's wonderful. Cross country, right?" "No, *Wario's Woods*."

Video games are not a sport. On the loosest imaginable definition a sport involves not only skill and competition but physical exertion and at least the possibility of injury. Even darts and pool and ping pong are, in the broadest sense, sports. Sitting on a couch interacting with your television set is not a sport, otherwise watching CNN with your grandfather would be one. So would self-abuse.

5 It's actually not difficult to understand why universities are getting into this business.

Even for those not lucky enough to make first string on U.C. Berkeley's traveling *Overwatch* team — which has an actual coach — there are plenty of opportunities on our nation's college campuses for people who want to pretend that there is no difference between *FIFA* and FIFA. At Western Michigan University in Kalamazoo, a mid-tier state school, it was recently announced that the administration is spending half a million dollars on "a new facility" for "multiplayer video games."

This is just a continuation of what these colleges have done for decades now when they advertised wave pools and cool dining facilities and hip-looking plate-glass dorms. Undergraduate education is actually a four-year-long debt-financed summer camp for lazy overgrown teenagers. It has nothing to do with the life of the mind, and even less to do with old-fashioned vocational training. One worthless piece of paper is as good as any other, which means that the directional state former polytechnics have to find some non-academic means of competing with each other for the loan dollars that will one day crush their underemployed 20-something graduates.

Which is not to say that no opportunities await the Doug Fluties of *Mario Kart*. As I write this, hundreds of millions of dollars are being made streaming video games on the internet by people with few or any other marketable skills. The amount of revenue generated by advertising and sponsorships from "esports" is soon expected to reach $1 billion annually.

Treating video games as sports is a civilizational rather than a semantic problem. Enjoyed in moderation, they are probably a harmless pastime like anything else. But increasingly the reality is not 10-year-olds leveling up their Pikachus on the school bus or even high-school kids unwinding with a little *Goldeneye* but adults — almost all of them men — in their 20s, 30s, and even 40s playing games for hours every day. Gaming is not only a compulsion, but something far more sinister — what one game designer has called "a simulation of being an expert." In a country without meaningful or well-paying opportunities for work young people disappear into their fantasies of competence in which they fly airplanes and score touchdowns and perform daring commando raids without having to go further than the refrigerator.

Video games are, in other words, another of those illusions we peddle to convince people that the world's problems do not exist. Sports, by comparison, are very much of this world. Compared with what's going on inside a PlayStation the most insignificant Saturday afternoon baseball game between two clubs with losing records is a thing of epochal significance, brimming with meaningful human drama.

Topics for Critical Thinking and Writing

1. In his first paragraph, does Matthew Walther define his key terms, *nerds* and *sports*? If so, where? If not, provide the definitions you think Walther assumes.
2. In paragraph 2, why do you think that Walther takes a dig at President Obama? How do you think this affects his relationship with the audience (*ethos*)?
3. Overall, how would you characterize Walther's tone and language? What about it makes it effective and persuasive — or not?
4. What kinds of evidence does Walther provide to support his position that video games are not a sport? Is the evidence adequate enough to be convincing?

5. What assumptions does Walther make about the motivations for people playing video games? Are his assumptions fair? Why, or why not?
6. How does Walther compare "real sports" to video games? Do you think he is right or wrong that video games do not offer the same types of "meaningful human drama" that sports do? Why?

JUSTIN CRONIN

Justin Cronin (b. 1962) is an award-winning writer of five best-selling novels and a winner of the Hemingway Foundation/PEN Award. Educated at Harvard and the Iowa Writer's Workshop, Cronin taught at La Salle University in Philadelphia, Pennsylvania, and at Rice University in Houston, Texas. The following selection was published in the *New York Times* in 2013.

Confessions of a Liberal Gun Owner

I am a New England liberal, born and bred. I have lived most of my life in the Northeast—Boston, New York, and Philadelphia—and my politics are devoutly Democratic. In three decades, I have voted for a Republican exactly once, holding my nose, in a mayoral election in which the Democratic candidate seemed mentally unbalanced.

I am also a Texas resident and a gun owner. I have half a dozen pistols in my safe, all semiautomatics, the largest capable of holding twenty rounds. I go to the range at least once a week, have applied for a concealed carry license, and am planning to take a tactical training course in the spring. I'm currently shopping for a shotgun, either a Remington 870 Express Tactical or a Mossberg 500 Flex with a pistol grip and adjustable stock.

Except for shotguns (firing one feels like being punched by a prizefighter), I enjoy shooting. At the range where I practice, most of the staff knows me by sight if not by name. I'm the guy in the metrosexual eyeglasses and Ralph Lauren polo, and I ask a lot of questions: What's the best way to maintain my sight picture with both eyes open? How do I clear a stove-piped round?

There is pleasure to be had in exercising one's rights, learning something new in midlife, and mastering the operation of a complex tool, which is one thing a gun is. But I won't deny the seductive psychological power that firearms possess. I grew up playing shooting games, pretending to be Starsky or Hutch or one of the patrolmen on *Adam-12*, the two most boring TV cops in history.

A prevailing theory holds that boys are 5
simultaneously aware of their own physical powerlessness and society's mandate that they serve as protectors of the innocent. Pretending to shoot a bad guy assuages this anxiety, which never goes away completely. This explanation makes sense to me. Another word for it is catharsis, and you could say that, as a novelist, I've made my living from it.

There are a lot of reasons that a gun feels right in my hand, but I also own firearms to protect my family. I hope I never have to use one for this purpose, and I doubt I ever will. But I am my family's last line of defense. I have chosen to meet this responsibility, in part, by being armed. It wasn't a choice I made lightly. I am aware that, statistically speaking, a gun in the home represents a far greater danger to its inhabitants than to an intruder. But not every choice we make is data-driven. A lot comes from the gut.

Apart from the ones in policemen's holsters, I don't think I saw a working firearm until the year after college, when a friend's girlfriend, after four cosmopolitans, decided to show off the .38 revolver she kept in her purse. (Half the party guests dived for cover, including me.)

It wasn't until my mid-forties that my education in guns began, in the course of writing a novel in which pistols, shotguns, and rifles, but also heavy weaponry like the AR-15 and its military analogue, the M-16, were widely used. I suspected that much of the gunplay I'd witnessed in movies and television was completely wrong (it is) and hired an instructor for a daylong private lesson "to shoot everything in the store." The gentleman who met me at the range was someone whom I would have called "a gun nut." A former New Yorker, he had relocated to Texas because of its lax gun laws and claimed to keep a pistol within arm's reach even when he showered. He was perfect, in other words, for my purpose.

My relationship to firearms might have ended there, if not for a coincidence of weather. Everybody remembers Hurricane Katrina; fewer recall Hurricane Rita, an even more intense storm that headed straight for Houston less than a month later. My wife and I arranged to stay at a friend's house in Austin, packed up the kids and dog, and headed out of town — or tried to. As many as 3.7 million people had the same idea, making Rita one of the largest evacuations in history, with predictable results.

By two in the morning, after six hours on 10
the road, we had made it all of fifty miles. The scene was like a snapshot from the Apocalypse: crowds milling restlessly, gas stations and minimarts picked clean and heaped with trash, families sleeping by the side of the road. The situation had the hopped-up feel of barely bottled chaos. After Katrina, nobody had any illusions that help was on its way. It also occurred to me that there were probably a lot of guns out there — this was Texas, after all. Here I was with two tiny children, a couple of thousand dollars in cash, a late-model S.U.V. with half a tank of gas and not so much as a heavy book to throw. When my wife wouldn't let me get out of the car so the dog could do his business, that was it for me. We jumped the median, turned around, and were home in under an hour.

As it happened, Rita made a last-minute turn away from Houston. But what if it hadn't? I believe people are basically good, but not all of them and not all the time. Like most citizens of our modern, technological world, I am wholly reliant upon a fragile web of services to meet my most basic needs. What would happen if those services collapsed? Chaos, that's what.

It didn't happen overnight, but before too long my Northeastern liberal sensibilities, while intact on other issues, had shifted on the question of gun ownership. For my first pistol I selected a little Walther .380. I shot it enough to decide it was junk, upgraded to a full-size Springfield 9-millimeter, liked it but wanted something with a thumb safety, found a nice Smith & Wesson subcompact that fit the bill, but along the way got a little bit of a gun-crush on the Beretta M-9 — and so on.

Lots of people on both sides of the aisle own firearms, or don't, for reasons that supersede their broader political and cultural affiliations. Let me be clear: my personal armory notwithstanding, I think guns are woefully under-regulated. It's far too easy to buy a gun — I once bought one in a parking lot — and I loathe the National Rifle Association. Some of the Obama administration's proposals strike me as more symbolic than effective, with some 300 million firearms on the loose. But the White House's recommendations seem like a good starting point and nothing that would prevent me from protecting my family in a crisis. The AR-15 is a fascinating weapon, and, frankly, a gas to shoot. So is a tank, and I don't need to own a tank.

Alas, the days of à la carte politics like mine seem over, if they ever even existed. The bigger culprit is the far right and the lunatic pronouncements of those like Rush Limbaugh. But in the weeks since Newtown, I've watched my Facebook feed, which is dominated by my coastal friends, fill up with antigun dispatches that seemed divorced from reality. I agree it would be nice if the world had exactly zero guns in it. But I don't see that happening, and calling gun owners "a bunch of inbred rednecks" doesn't do much to advance rational discussion.

15 Thus, my secret life — though I guess it's not such a secret anymore. My wife is afraid of my guns (though she also says she's glad I have them). My sixteen-year-old daughter is a different story. The week before her fall semester exams, we allowed her to skip school for a day, a tradition in our house. The rule is, she gets to do whatever she wants. This time, she asked to take a pistol lesson. She's an NPR listener like me, but she's also grown up in Texas, and the fact that one in five American women is a victim of sexual assault is not lost on her. In the windowless classroom off the range, the instructor ran her through the basics, demonstrating with a Glock 9-millimeter: how to hold it, load it, pull back the slide.

"You'll probably have trouble with that part," he said. "A lot of the women do."

"Oh really?" my daughter replied, and with a cagey smile proceeded to rack her weapon with such authority you could have heard it in the parking lot.

A proud-papa moment? I confess it was.

Topics for Critical Thinking and Writing

1. This essay could with equal accuracy be called "Confessions of a Texas Gun Owner." Why do you suppose Justin Cronin chose the title he did rather than our imagined title?
2. Why does Cronin devote so many sentences to autobiographical matters since, in fact, none of the autobiography actually involves using a gun to protect himself or his family against an intruder?
3. How would you characterize Cronin's persona as he presents it in this essay? Do you feel that his persona effectively connects with you as a reader? Why, or why not?
4. What *arguments* does Cronin offer on behalf of gun ownership? Do you think his thesis might have been strengthened if he had cited statistics or authorities, or do you think that such evidence probably would have been inappropriate in a highly personal essay? Explain your response.
5. In paragraph 12, Cronin writes, "It didn't happen overnight, but before too long my Northeastern liberal sensibilities . . . had shifted on the question of gun ownership." Why did his attitude shift?
6. In paragraph 13, Cronin says that he believes "guns are woefully under-regulated" and that he "loathe[s] the National Rifle Association," but he doesn't go into any detail about what

sorts of regulations he favors. Do you think his essay might have been more convincing if he had given us details along these lines? Explain.

7. Each of Cronin's last three paragraphs is very short. We have discussed how, in general, a short paragraph is usually an underdeveloped paragraph. Do you think these paragraphs are underdeveloped, or do you think Cronin knows exactly what he is doing? Explain.

CARL SAFINA

Carl Safina (b. 1955) is a marine biologist and author whose work on animal and ocean conservation has been recognized in McArthur, Pew, and Guggenheim Fellowships and whose books have earned him awards ranging from a National Academies literary award to John Burroughs, James Beard, and George Rabb medals. He holds the Endowed Chair for Nature and Humanity at Stony Brook University and is the founding director of the not-for-profit foundation The Safina Center. He has published widely in the *New York Times*, *Orion*, and *Audubon* magazines and was host of the ten-part PBS series *Saving the Ocean with Carl Safina* in 2013. The selection below is from his book *Beyond Words: What Animals Think and Feel* (2015).

Never Mind Theory

Experiments showed at first that wolves could not follow human hand pointing to find hidden food. Dogs often can. But the wolves had been tested with a fence separating them from the human who was pointing. Dog tests were of course barrier-free, and dogs usually had their most familiar human companions with them. When experimenters finally leveled the playing field, wolves did as well as dogs — with no training.

Experiments can be powerful for learning about behavior. But sometimes, experimental situations are so pinched and artificial — as with wolves behind fences — that they hide capabilities they're trying to investigate. Real-life behaviors and decisions can't always be stuffed into an experiment.

Any ecologist who watches free-living animals feels humbled by the depth and nuance of how they negotiate the world and how easily they slip the noose of human observation as they go about their business of working to keep themselves and their babies alive.

On the other hand, laboratory studies seem preoccupied with "testing" academically generated concepts such as "self-awareness" and — my pet peeve — "theory of mind." It's not that these *ideas* aren't helpful. They are. It's that animals don't care about academic classifications and testing setups. They have no interest in arguments over wafer-thin slices of categories, such as whether an otter smashing a clam with a stone is using a tool but a gull dropping a clam on a stone is not using a tool. They care about survival. Some academic researchers, meanwhile, chop concepts into so many pieces, you'd think behavior was shish kebab. So in this section I want to have a little fun with some muddles that behavioral scientists have created. We'll be blowing away some smoke and breaking some mirrors. And as for the kebab, the first skewer goes to "theory of mind."

5 “Theory of mind” — such an awkward phrase — is an idea. Exactly what the idea is depends on whom you ask. Naomi Angoff Chedd, who works with autistic children, tells me it is “knowing that another can have thoughts that differ from yours.” I like that definition; it’s helpful. Dolphin researcher Diana Reiss says it’s the ability to feel that “I have an idea of what’s on your mind.” That’s different. Still others assert — oddly, I think — that it’s the ability “to read the minds of others.” The “mind-reading” camp gets the most press, and its adherents get the most carried away with themselves. Italian neuroscientist and philosopher Vittorio Gallese writes of “our sophisticated mind-reading abilities.”

I don’t know about you (I guess that’s my point), but I cannot read anyone’s mind. Informed guessing based on experience and body language is just about all we can really do. If a sketchy-looking stranger crosses the street to come toward us, our first problem is that we *can’t* know what they’re thinking. If “theory of mind” is defined as understanding that another can hold thoughts different from yours, then fine, there’s that. But claims about humans’ “sophisticated mind-reading abilities” are nonsense. That’s why we say, “How are you?”

“Theory of mind” was coined in 1978 by researchers who tested chimpanzees. With an impressive lack of human insight into what could be an appropriate context or meaningful to a chimp, they showed chimpanzees videotapes of human actors trying to access out-of-reach bananas, or trying to play music while the record player was unplugged, or shivering because a heater wasn’t working, and so on. A chimpanzee was supposed to prove that it understood the human’s problem by choosing a photo of the solution to the problem. It was supposed to choose, for instance, “a lit wick for the malfunctioning heater.” No, the researchers *weren’t* kidding. If the chimps didn’t select the correct photo, the researchers declared that chimpanzees didn’t understand the videotaped human actor’s problem and, thus, had no “theory of mind.” (Now, imagine you’re a chimp, led into a room, shown a video of a man shivering next to a heater, and without anyone being able to explain the problem, the experiment, or the uses of fire, you’re supposed to choose a lit wick. Imagine, for that matter, that you’re Thomas Jefferson being shown a video of a man trying to play a phonograph that is unplugged. You’d have no idea what you were looking at.) In the decades since, and many studies later, scientists in the field have finally suggested that those results might have been affected by the test’s setup. Science marches on. Well, hello.

So far, some scientists grant theory-of-mind ability — basically, understanding that another can have thoughts and motives that differ from yours — to apes and dolphins. A few allow elephants and crows. Occasional researchers have admitted dogs. But many continue to insist that theory of mind is “uniquely human.” Even while I was writing this, science journalist Katherine Harmon wrote, “In most animal species, scientists have failed to see even a glimmer of evidence.”

Not a glimmer? It’s *blinding*. People who don’t see the evidence aren’t paying attention. Frans de Waal pays attention. The shenanigans of chimps who like to spray water on unsuspecting zoo visitors, he says, reflects, “a complex, and familiar, inner life.”

Whether researchers do or don’t think that chimpanzees, dogs, and other animals “have theory of mind” hardly matters. What matters: What do they have, and how do they have it? What do dogs do? And what motivates them? Rather than asking whether a dog or chimp follows a human gaze, let’s ask how dogs and chimps direct one another’s attention.

Humans are better at reading humans than we are at reading dogs. Dolphins are better at reading dolphins. Chimps at chimp reading. We judge the sketchy stranger's friendly or evil intent by their body language. But so do our dogs. Other animals are highly skilled body-language readers. The stakes can be life or death, and they can't ask questions. Our orphaned raccoon, Maddox (whom we bottle-raised but never caged; she lived free-range), could sometimes read my intent almost as fast as the thought occurred to me, though I couldn't understand what cue I was giving. She'd suddenly bristle and put her back up, for instance, if I'd just decided that it was time to stop playing in the kitchen and usher her outdoors. I used to joke that I had a mind-reading raccoon. (It must have been something in the way I looked at her, but, wow, was she sharp. And so were her teeth.)

Watching free-living animals negotiate the world on their terms shows you their rich mental abilities. And you can start by looking at who's scampering around your house, gazing up at you imploringly, awaiting your response.

In the morning I'm making coffee, and because it's chilly I raise the screens and lower the storm windows; the phone rings, and I answer it. Chula follows all my movements, looking me in the eyes for any clues that I might wish to interact — or perhaps move toward the jar of treats. She does not understand coffee, screens, or phones. A human from most of our history or a Native American from an intact tribe in 1880 or a hunter-gatherer today would also not understand anything I am doing. The difference between my crazy dog and Crazy Horse is that Crazy Horse could have learned everything I am doing (and perhaps vice versa). But, again, the point is not whether dogs are just like us. The point is that they are like themselves. The interesting question is: What are they like?

Our daughter, Alexandra, aged twenty, sees our other dog, Jude, appear at the screen door and indicate his desire to come in. Usually the doggies are both either in or out together, but Chula happens to be inside when Jude comes to the screen. Alex sees the whole thing and describes it like this: "Jude whined to be let in. Chula went to the screen and stared at Jude like, 'Ha,' as if teasing him like she does before they start playing; then she put her paw to the door, but just lightly, just like a person would open the door, and just opened the door and turned and went back to the bone she'd been chewing. She knew what she was doing. She had already turned around by the time Jude entered. She just got up to open the door, like, 'Okay, fine, come in.' The specific thing that was so interesting," Alex wants to emphasize, "was how she opened the door for him and then turned away and went back to what she'd been doing, just as I myself would have let Jude in."

We grab our jackets, and Chula and Jude get excited. They hope — it's safe to say — that we're taking them for a run. I open the door and say, "Car," and they run for the car's back hatch.

At the river, we let them out. They love this, of course. A swan sees them running along the shore. He steps gingerly into the water, paddling just out of easy reach. The dogs go into the water up to their bellies and bark at the swan a few times. The swan is actually stemming the current in place, not paddling away, not even drifting away. Either he doesn't want to move from this point along the shore, or he's taunting them, or he feels some conflict between challenging them and fleeing. But it's not nesting season, and the swans are not being territorial with one another. It seems he's taunting the dogs, but why would he? I don't know why he's holding right there — but he must know. Is this his idea of fun?

Chula weighs her option of swimming to the swan. You can see her trying to figure out what to do next. She wades deep enough to almost float but seems to understand that this won't work for her. The swan clearly understands that this won't work for Chula, because he is staring directly at her from just a few strokes away, but not moving one feather farther. In a minute the dogs realize that this is not going to get any more fun for them, and they splash to shore and gambol off.

The swan just showed that he understood that he needed to avoid the dogs *and* that he understood the limitations of their movement in water. He understands how to use the water to stay completely safe while holding himself so close that, were he on land, the dogs could cover the distance in two bounds, requiring perhaps half a second. The swan demonstrated theory of mind and mastery of medium.

Farther down the shore, Chula bounds into the water near where some mallard ducks are floating. They, too, paddle to deeper water but do not fly. A few hundred yards farther along the shore, the river enters Long Island Sound. The river's mouth is perhaps a hundred yards across. Out in mid-river, several hundred scaup — another kind of duck — are diving for mussels. They ignore the dogs. But when four humans appear on the far shore, all the ducks fly up in alarm, leaving the vicinity of the river and flying out into the Sound. As they pass over other sitting groups of scaup and long-tailed ducks, those ducks also take flight and head out over the Sound, in a wide-spreading panic.

Why would the ducks merely paddle away from their age-old enemy the wolf (in domesticated form) yet become panicked by the mere appearance of humans on a farther shore? Because the ducks understand a dog's limits and have learned that humans can kill at great distance — that's why. They know that causing harm can be on a human's mind, and they have some concept either of death or attack or great danger. And because for millions of years of evolution they had no experience of guns, their accurate judgment about what constitutes differing safe distances from dogs and humans is learned and recent. Do they "have" a theory of mind? The question gets less interesting as the richness of behaviors and perceptions become more apparent. What the birds do and why; that's what's so interesting.

20 When we get home, I towel off Chula, whose fur is full of sand and damp with brackish water. She endures it but doesn't love it. Yet as soon as I unfurl the towel, Jude dives headlong into it, tail wagging widely as he snaps his jaws randomly while prancing like a terry-cloth ghost. Jude loves playing blindman's buff. The game is to grab and release his muzzle while he's blindly snapping. Take the towel off, he stops snapping and tries to get into the towel again. Chula has no interest in this game, or in Jude when he's being so silly.

Later, in the yard surrounding our house, the dogs chase each other in totally unnecessary play. They fake each other out when racing around the shed or cottage. Chula will try to double back to intercept Jude, but Jude will stop to see from which way Chula is coming. They know what is going on, and they seem to understand that the other is trying to fool them. That's "theory of mind," too. One is evaluating what the other is thinking, each showing clear understanding that the other might be faked into a false belief about which direction they'll be charging from. Because they're playing, there's both cleverness and humor in this. (Unless they're just two unconscious machines interacting without sensation or perception. Some people still insist that "we can't be sure." That's what I mean by denial.)

A dog who has never before seen a ball would not bring it to a person and lay it at their feet. But a dog experienced with balls comes to invite play. They envision the game, plan a way to start it, and execute the plan with a human partner who they understand is knowing. Theory of mind.

Any dog who goes into a play bow is inviting you, understanding that you might engage. (The play bow isn't strictly canine; Maddox the raccoon frequently invited play this way.) Dogs and others don't play-bow to trees, chairs, or other inanimate objects. Our puppy Emi play-bowed to the first ball she ever saw when I rolled it her way. She assumed anything moving so purposefully along the floor had to be alive — but she did that only once. In moments she realized that this was a wonderful new thing but that it was inanimate, not capable of an aware response or voluntary play. It therefore needed no further invitation, nor consideration, nor restraint in being chewed, flung, and pounced on.

Chula once barked at a life-sized concrete dog, but only once — a sniff told her that its shape had lied. A dog — or an elephant, say — often validates the authenticity of things by scent. A dog that loves chasing rabbits will give one perfunctory sniff to a porcelain rabbit. It obviously recognizes rabbits on sight but is too clever to be fooled by a fake. To a dog, if it looks like a duck and quacks like a duck, it's not a duck unless it *smells* like a duck.

25 These little stories reveal dogs' shrewd ability to discern what has a mind — and what doesn't. Theory thereof. You can't bring swimming swans and flocks of diving ducks into a lab. Sometimes, rather than "testing" animals in contraptions and contrived setups where they can't be who they are, we might simply define the concept we're interested in, then watch the animals in free-living situations appropriate to their lives. Do they show an understanding that others hold different thoughts and agendas and can even be fooled? Yes. It's happening all around us, twenty-four/seven, blindingly obvious. But you have to have your eyes open. Lab psychologists and philosophers of behavior often don't seem to know about how perceptions function in the real world. I wish they'd go outside, watch, and have some fun.

Topics for Critical Thinking and Writing

1. Does the reader have to infer Carl Safina's thesis, or does he state it directly? What, in your opinion, is the closest thing to a thesis statement Safina offers?
2. What assumptions does Safina propose are among the shortcomings of scientific research into animal intelligence?
3. What is Safina's persona in this essay? Is his presentation of himself effective? How do you think it contributes to his argument overall?
4. What is Safina's fundamental dispute with the ways researchers have tested animals with the theory of mind? How does he establish his form of evidence as a vital alternative to scientific understandings?
5. Define the terms *anthropomorphism* and *anthropocentrism*. Think of an example of each, and argue whether or not either concept helps or hurts Safina's argument.

6. Safina's language and voice might appeal to a specific audience. What do you think are some potential characteristics of Safina's likeliest readers? Who do you think might disagree with him, and what do you think would be their primary criticism? Are those criticisms valid?
7. Write down your own thoughts on the intelligence of your own or a friend's pet. Closely examine your own assumptions about what the pet is thinking — or what the pet is thinking about you — and then share your thoughts with classmates. Do their experiences with their own pets support or undermine your assumptions? Could any of these experiences be used to support or refute Safina? How so?

ASSIGNMENT FOR WRITING AN ANALYSIS OF AN ARGUMENT

Choose a selection not yet discussed in class or an essay assigned by your instructor. In an essay of 500 words, analyze and evaluate the essay. In writing an analysis of a reading, do the following:

- Read and reread thoughtfully the essay you are analyzing. Composing and keeping notes in the margins or in new documents will help you think about what you are reading.
- Be sure to examine the author's thesis, purpose, methods, persona, intended audience, and tone.
- Examine closely the *organization* of an argument. Is the thesis explicitly or implicitly stated, at the very beginning or somewhere later in the essay? What is the author's strongest piece of evidence? Is it presented right off the bat and then supported by further evidence, or does the essay build up to the key evidence? Is the organization effective?
- Remember that although your essay is an analysis of someone else's writing and you may have to include a summary of the work you are writing about, your essay is *your* essay, your analysis, not a mere summary; the thesis, the organization, and the tone are yours.

6

Developing an Argument of Your Own

The difficult part in an argument is not to defend one's opinion but to know what it is.
— ANDRÉ MAUROIS

No greater misfortune could happen to anyone than that of developing a dislike for argument.
— PLATO

Planning an Argument

First, hear the wisdom of Mark Twain: "When the Lord finished the world, He pronounced it good. That is what I said about my first work, too. But Time, I tell you, Time takes the confidence out of these incautious early opinions."

All of us, teachers and students, have our moments of confidence, when we feel certain that our thoughts and judgments are settled. However, for the most part we know too that new information and new experiences can always change our early opinions on matters. To execute a well-informed, well-reasoned argument takes time and effort, and most of all a willingness to revise: to revise our thinking as we learn, and our writing as we produce it. Clear, thoughtful, seemingly effortless prose is not common on the first try. Good writing requires rethinking and revision. In a live conversation we can always claim ignorance and cover ourselves with such expressions as "Well, I don't know, but I sort of think . . . ," and we can always revise our words instantly ("Oh, well, I didn't mean it that way"). However, once we have had the chance to learn about and reason through an issue, and are committed to writing down our thoughts — and once we have handed in the final version of our writing — we are helpless. We are (putting it strongly) naked to our enemies.

Producing the strongest arguments requires good planning — but that can be difficult when you do not yet know what to think about something. Thus, planning your argument starts with developing it.

GETTING IDEAS: ARGUMENT AS AN INSTRUMENT OF INQUIRY

In Chapter 1, we quoted Robert Frost, "To learn to write is to learn to have ideas," and we offered strategies about generating ideas, a process traditionally called **invention**. A moment ago we said that we often improve our ideas when explaining them to someone else. Partly, of course, we're responding to questions or objections raised by our companion in the conversation. But in writing we must respond to other writers and also to ourselves: Almost as soon as we think we know what we have to say, we may find that it won't do. If we're lucky, we may find a better idea surfacing. One of the best ways of getting ideas is to talk things over.

When it comes to writing, the process of "talking things over" usually begins with a dialogue between yourself and a text that you're reading: Your notes, your summary, and your annotations are a kind of dialogue between you and the author. You can also have a dialogue with classmates and friends about your topic to try out and develop ideas. You may be arguing, but not chiefly to persuade; rather, you're using argument to find the truth — testing ideas, playing the devil's advocate, speaking hypothetically. Through reading, taking notes, and talking, you may find that you have developed some clear ideas that can be put into writing. So you take up a sheet of blank paper, but then a paralyzing thought suddenly strikes: "I have ideas but just can't put them into words." The blank white page (or screen) stares back at you.

All writers, even professional ones, are familiar with this experience. Good writers know that waiting for inspiration is usually not the best strategy. You may be waiting a long time. The best thing to do is begin. Recall some of what we said in Chapter 1: *Writing is a way of thinking.* It's a way of *getting and developing ideas. Argument* is an instrument of inquiry as well as persuasion. It is an important *method* of *critical thinking.* It helps us clarify what we think. One reason we have trouble writing is our fear of putting ourselves on record, but another reason is our fear that we have no ideas worth putting down. However, by writing notes — or even free associations — and by writing a draft, no matter how weak, we can begin to think our way toward good ideas.

When you are planning an argument, talking with others can help, but sometimes there isn't time to chat live. Take advantage of the tools at your disposal. Use the internet, including your email, social media, search engines, blogs, and wikis, to involve yourself in the conversation. Posting on social media or writing a blog entry in a public space about your topic can foster conversations about the topic and help you discover what others think — and your own opinions. Using the internet to uncover and refine a topic is common practice, especially early in the brainstorming process.

THREE BRAINSTORMING STRATEGIES: FREEWRITING, LISTING, AND DIAGRAMMING

If you are facing an issue, debate, or topic and don't know what to write, it is likely because you don't yet know what you think. If, after talking about the topic with yourself (via your reading notes) and others (via any means), you are still unclear on what you think, try one of three strategies: freewriting, listing, or diagramming.

FREEWRITING Write for five or six minutes, nonstop, without censoring what you produce. You may use what you write to improve your thinking. You may even dim your computer screen so you won't be tempted to look up and fiddle too soon with what you've just written. Once you have spent the time writing out your ideas, you can use what you've written to look further into the subject at hand.

Freewriting should be totally free. As a topic, let's imagine the writer below is thinking about how children's toys are constructed for different genders. The student is reflecting on the release of the Nerf Rebelle, a type of toy gun made specifically for girls. A good freewrite might look like this:

> FREEWRITING: Nerf released a new toy made for girls, the Nerf Rebelle gun. It was an attempt the company made to offer toys for girls that have been traditionally made for boys. This seems good — showing an effort toward equality between the sexes. Or is Nerf just trying to broaden its market and sell more toys (after all, boys are only half the population)? Or is it both? That could be my central question. But it is not like the gun is gender-neutral. It is pink and purple and has feminine-looking designs on it. And with its "elle" ending the gun sounds small, cute, and girly. Does this toy represent true equality between the sexes, or does it just offer more in the way of feminine stereotypes? It shoots foam arrows, unlike the boys' version of the gun, which shoots bullets. This suggests Cupid, maybe — a figure whose arrows inspire love. A stereotype that girls aren't saving the world with their weapons but seeking love and marriage. What kind of messages does this send to young girls? Is it the same message suggested by the gun? How does this work in other areas of life, like business and politics?

Notice that the writer here is jumping around, generating and exploring ideas while writing. Later she can return to the freewriting and begin organizing her ideas and observations. Notice that right in the middle of the freewriting she made a connection between the toy and Cupid, and by extension to the larger culture in which forms of contemporary femininity can be found. This connection seems significant, and it may help the student to broaden her argument from a critique of the company's motives early on, to a more evidence-based piece about assumptions underlying certain trends in consumer and media culture. The point is that freewriting in this case led to new paths of inquiry and may have inspired further research into different kinds of toys and media.

LISTING Writing down keywords, just as you do when making a shopping list, is another way of generating ideas. When you make a shopping list, you write *ketchup*, and the act of writing it reminds you that you also need hamburger rolls — and *that* in turn reminds you that you also need tuna fish. Similarly, when preparing a list of ideas for a paper, just writing down one item will often generate another. Of course, when you look over the list, you'll probably drop some of these ideas — the dinner menu will change — but you'll be making progress. If you have a smartphone or tablet, use it to write down your thoughts. You can even email these notes to yourself so you can access them later, or you can store them digitally in the cloud.

Here's an example of a student listing questions and making associations that could help him focus on a specific argument within a larger debate. The subject here is whether prostitution should be legalized. Key terms are underlined.

LIST: Prostitutes & Law

- What types of prostitutes exist?
- How has the law traditionally policed sex in history and in different places?
- How many prostitutes are arrested every year?
- Individual rights vs. public good?
- Why shouldn't people be allowed to sell sex?
- Could prostitution be taxed?
- Who gains or suffers most from enforcement? From legalization?
- If it were legal, could its negative effects be better controlled?
- Aren't "escort services" really prostitution rings for people with more money?
- Who goes into the "oldest business" and why?

Notice that the student doesn't really know the answers yet but is asking questions by free-associating and seeing what turns up as a productive line of analysis. The questions range from the definition of prostitution to its effects, and they might inspire the student to do some basic internet research or even deeper research. Once you make a list, see if you can observe patterns or similarities among the items you listed or if you invented a question worthy of its own thesis statement (e.g., "The enforcement of prostitution laws hurts *X* group unequally, and it uses a lot of public money that could better be used in other areas or toward regulating the trade rather than jailing people").

DIAGRAMMING Sketching a visual representation of an essay is a kind of listing. Three methods of diagramming are especially common.

Clustering As we discuss on page 9, you can make an effective cluster by writing, in the middle of a sheet of paper, a word or phrase summarizing your topic (e.g., *fracking*, the process of forcing high pressure into rock to extract natural resources; see diagram), circling it, and then writing down and circling a related word or idea (e.g., *energy independence*). You then circle these phrases and continue jotting down ideas, making connections, and indicating relationships. Here, the economic and environmental impacts of fracking seem to be the focus. Whether you realize it or not, an argument is taking shape.

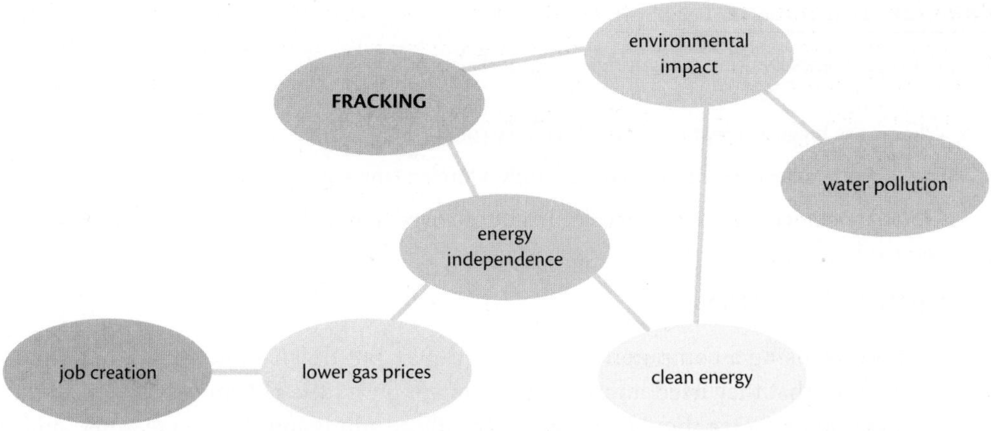

Branching Some writers find it useful to draw a tree, moving from the central topic to the main branches (chief ideas) and then to the twigs (aspects of the chief ideas).

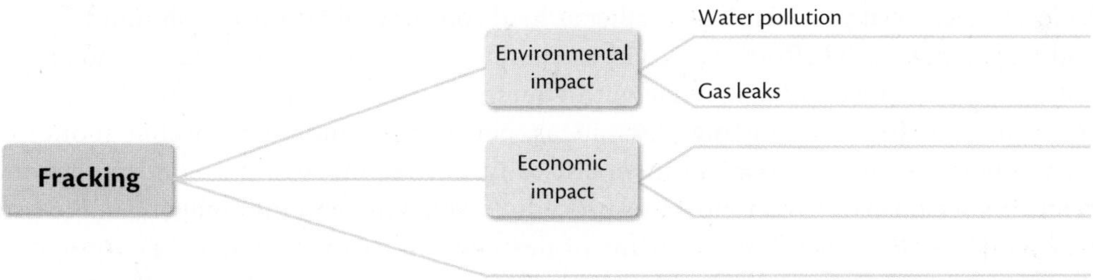

Comparing in columns Draw a line down the middle of the page and then set up two columns showing oppositions. For instance, if you are concerned with the environmental and economic impacts of fracking, you might produce columns that look something like this:

Environmental	**Economic**
water pollution	employment
chemicals used	independence from unstable oil-producing countries
gas leaks	cheaper fuel
toxic waste	cheaper electricity

All these methods can, of course, be executed with pen and paper, but you may also be able to use them on your computer, depending on the capabilities of your software. You might also find templates from a good website helpful.

Exercise: Brainstorming

Consider these topics by using freewriting, listing, or diagramming:

- What is the biggest threat to national security today?
- Should your college require students to study a foreign language?
- Should monuments to Confederate leaders be removed from public spaces?

REVISION AS INVENTION

Whether you're using a computer or a pen, you may put down some words and almost immediately see that they need improvement, not simply a little polishing but a substantial overhaul. You write, "Race should be counted in college admissions for two reasons," and as soon as you write those words, a third reason comes to mind. Or perhaps one of those "two reasons" no longer seems very good. As E. M. Forster said, "How can I know what I think till I see what I say?" We have to see what we say — we have to get something down on the page — before we realize that we need to make it better.

Writing, then, is really **rewriting** — that is, **revising** — and a revision is a *re-vision*, a second look. The essay that you submit — whether as hard copy or as digital file — should be clear and may appear to be effortlessly composed, but in all likelihood the clarity and apparent ease are the result of a struggle with yourself during which you refined your first thoughts. You begin by putting down ideas, perhaps in random order, but sooner or later comes the job of looking at them critically, developing what's useful in them and removing what isn't. If you follow this procedure, you will be in the company of Picasso, who said that he "advanced by means of destruction." Any passages that you cut or destroy can be kept in another file in case you want to revisit those deletions later. Sometimes, you end up restoring them and developing what you discarded into a new essay with a new direction.

Whether you advance bit by bit (writing a sentence, revising it, writing the next, etc.) or whether you write an entire first draft and then revise it and revise it again and again is chiefly a matter of temperament. Probably most people combine both approaches, backing up occasionally but trying to get to the end fairly soon so that they can see rather quickly what they know, or think they know, and can then start the real work of thinking, of converting their initial ideas into something substantial.

ASKING QUESTIONS WITH STASIS THEORY

Generating ideas, we said when talking about **topics** and invention strategies in Chapter 1 (p. 16), is mostly a matter of asking (and then thinking about) questions. In this book, we include questions at the end of each argumentative essay not to torment you, but to help you think about the arguments — for instance, to turn your attention to especially important matters. If your instructor asks you to write an answer to one of these questions, you are lucky: Examining the question will stimulate your mind to work in a specific direction.

Another method of using your own questions is to use **stasis theory**, an invention process used by ancient rhetoricians like Aristotle and Cicero to work through a topic and find what facts and judgments "hold." (*Stasis* means something like "stability," so you can image the process as leading you to what is true about a topic or issue.) If your instructor doesn't assign a topic for an argumentative essay, you'll find that some ideas may be generated by applying the four key questions of stasis theory. These four questions, for the ancients, sought to establish the facts, the meaning, the importance, and the action needed in a given situation. We present an example of using stasis theory below.

First, consider these questions in general:

1. What is *X*? (*definition*)
2. What is the value or seriousness of *X*? (*quality*)
3. What are the causes (or the consequences) of *X*? (*fact*)
4. What should (or could or must) we do about *X*? (*policy*)

Let's spend a moment looking at each of these questions.

1. *What is X?* Suppose your topic was capital punishment; *defining* what that is could be its own argument, although you would certainly want to go beyond saying simply, "Capital punishment is the legally authorized killing of a person." That does not need to be argued. Similarly, we can hardly argue about which states utilize capital punishment and which do not, or about how many people have been sentenced to death in the United States in the past ten years — a glance at the appropriate reports will answer those questions. You might instead define the uses, limits, evolution, or means of capital punishment as administered in the United States. Which uses might constitute cruel and unusual punishment? How has the death penalty changed over time, and what does that say about a changing society? Is the death penalty discriminatory? Your definition does not necessarily have to argue that it should or should not be abolished, or that it should or should not be applied fairly. You might be doing enough just by establishing a clear definition of the topic and its problems. An argument about abortion, for example, might concentrate strictly on the definition of a "person" or of the "viability" of a fetus, or even the definition of "when life begins." Arguments of this sort may make a claim — and may take a stand — but they do not also have to argue for an action. You may establish a clear definition of the problem and leave it to others for possible responses.

2. *What is the value or seriousness of X?* Assessing the value of a topic or issue is thinking about its meaning and how it reflects or relates to a larger significance, whether personal, social, political, religious, and so on. Why should a general audience of American readers care about your examination of the death penalty? Why should your target audience — lawyers, Catholics, general voters, or whomever — care? What is the *seriousness* of discrimination in the criminal

> **WRITING TIP**
> College courses often call for arguments about art and literature. In writing an evaluation, you have to rely on criteria particular to literature. For instance, in comparing the artistic merit of plays by Tennessee Williams and Arthur Miller, you may want to talk about the quality of the characterization, the importance of the theme, and so on.

justice system? What morals, values, or principles are at stake? An essay offering this kind of evaluation normally has two purposes:

- to set forth an assessment
- to convince readers that the assessment is reasonable

In writing an evaluation, you have to rely on criteria, and these will vary depending on your topic. What criteria serve best in making an evaluation? Probably some or all of the following:

- testimony of authorities
- inductive evidence
- appeals to logic ("it follows, therefore, that . . .")
- appeals to emotion

3. *What are the causes (or the consequences) of X?* When you ask about the causes and consequences of an issue, you are assessing the real or conjectured facts of the matter. Think about this in relation to the topic of capital punishment: You might look at what the actual or probable effects are (or would be) for various groups of people either personally affected or professionally interested in this aspect of our justice system.

Consider also this example concerning the academic performance of girls in single-sex schools. It is pretty much agreed (based on statistical evidence) that the graduates of these schools do better, as a group, than girls who graduate from coeducational schools. But why? What is the *cause*? Administrators of girls' schools usually attribute the success to the fact that their classrooms offer an atmosphere free from male intimidation: Girls allegedly gain confidence and become more expressive without the presence of boys. This may be the answer, but skeptics have attributed the graduates' success to two other causes:

- Most single-sex schools require parents to pay tuition, and it is a documented fact that the children of well-to-do parents do better, academically, than the children of poorer parents.
- Most single-sex schools are selective private schools whose students are chosen based upon academic promise — that is, students who have *already done well academically.*

The lesson? Be cautious in attributing a cause. There may be multiple causes and factors.

The kinds of support that usually accompany claims of consequence and cause include the following:

- factual data, especially statistics
- analogies ("The Roman Empire declined because of *X* and *Y*"; "Our society exhibits *X* and *Y*; therefore . . .")
- inductive evidence

4. What should (or could or must) we do about X? Whether you end up arguing that a problem exists to identify it, diagnose its larger importance, or demonstrate its unfortunate consequences, you may find yourself in a position to recommend a partial or full solution to the problem. What action should be taken, and by whom? Continuing our example, should the death penalty be abolished? Should parents change the ways they discipline their children? Should the law allow eighteen-year-olds to drink alcohol? Should eighteen-year-old women be required to register for Selective Service? Should steroid use by athletes be banned? These questions involve conduct and policy; how you answer them will reveal your values and principles.

(See the Visual Guide: Organizing Your Argument on p. 225 for an example of how an argument of policy might be structured.)

Support for claims of policy usually include the following:

- statistics
- testimony of authorities
- appeals to common sense and to the reader's moral sense

Again, an argument may be entirely based on one, two, three, or all of the four basic questions discussed in this section. Someone interested in analyzing the debate over censorship of fake news may construct the argument exclusively about what fake news *is* (a question of definition); about the *seriousness* of fake news in a democratic society (a question of quality); about how efforts to curb fake news limit free speech (a question of fact); or that some entity or institution, such as the US government or Facebook, should act to limit fake news (a question of policy). Of course, all of these questions could also be combined in a more comprehensive argument.

As you work through various questions and discover your argument, keep in mind that other elements of critical thinking and argument we have discussed up to this point are still relevant. You should still address different perspectives and possible objections to your ideas — counterarguments — and refute them if possible. Most of all, you should be careful to support your ideas with carefully selected evidence and examples.

WRITING TIP
If a question seems relevant or a piece of evidence inspires new questions and answers in your mind, it's a good idea to start writing — even just fragmentary sentences if necessary. You'll probably find that one idea leads to another and that new questions and issues begin to appear. Even if your ideas seem weak as you write them, don't be discouraged; you will have put something on paper, and returning to these words, perhaps in five minutes or even the next day, you'll probably find that some ideas aren't at all bad and may stimulate even better ones.

THE THESIS OR MAIN POINT

Let's assume that you are writing an argumentative essay — perhaps an evaluation of an argument in this book — and you have what seems to be a pretty good draft or at least a collection of notes that are the result of hard thinking. You really do have ideas now, and you want to present them effectively. How will you organize your essay? No one formula works best for every essayist and for every essay, but it is usually advisable to formulate a basic **thesis** (a claim, a central point, a chief position) and to state it early. Every essay that is any good, even a book-length one, has a thesis (a main point), which can be stated briefly, usually in one sentence. Remember Calvin Coolidge's alleged remark to his wife on the preacher's sermon on sin: "He was against it." Don't confuse the **topic** (sin) with the thesis (sin is bad). The thesis is the argumentative theme, the author's primary claim or contention, the proposition that the rest of the essay will explain and defend. Of course, the thesis may sound commonplace, but the book or essay or sermon ought to develop it in an interesting and convincing way.

When you formulate a thesis and ask questions about it — such as who the readers are, what they believe, what they know, and what they need to know — you also begin to get ideas about how to organize the material (or, at least, you realize that you'll have to work out some sort of organization). The thesis may be clear and simple, but the reasons (the argument) may take many pages. The thesis is the point; the argument sets forth the evidence that supports the thesis.

RAISING THE STAKES OF YOUR THESIS Imagine walking across campus and coming upon a person ready to perform on a tightrope suspended between two buildings. He is wearing a glittering leotard and is eyeing up his challenge very seriously. Here's the thing, though: His tightrope is only *one foot off the ground*. Would you stop and watch him walk across it? Maybe, maybe not. Most people are likely to take a look and move on. If you did spend a few minutes watching, you wouldn't be very worried about the performer falling. If he lost his balance momentarily, you wouldn't gasp in horror. And if he walked across the tightrope masterfully, you might be somewhat impressed but not enraptured.

Now imagine the rope being *a hundred feet off the ground*. You and many others would almost certainly stop and witness the feat. The audience would likely be captivated, nervous about the performer potentially falling, "oohing" if he momentarily lost his balance, and cheering if he crossed the rope successfully.

Consider the tightrope as your thesis statement, the performer as writer, and the act of crossing as the argument. What we call "low-stakes" thesis statements are comparable to low tightropes: A low-stakes thesis statement itself may be interesting, but not much about it is vital to any particular audience. Low-stakes thesis statements lack a sense of importance or

Kay Nietfeld/DPA/Getty Images

Edu Silva 2ev/Shutterstock.com

Considering thesis statements as tightropes strung at different heights can help you consider the stakes of your argument.

relevance. They may restate what is already widely known and accepted, or they may make a good point but not discuss any consequences. Some examples:

Good nutrition and exercise can lead to a healthy life.

Our education system focuses too much on standardized tests.

Children's beauty pageants are exploitative.

Students can write well-organized, clear, and direct papers on these topics, but if the thesis is "low stakes" like these, the performance would be similar to that of an expert walking across a tightrope that is only one foot off the ground. The argument may be well executed, but few in the audience will be inspired by it.

However, if you raise the stakes by "raising the tightrope," you can compel readers to *want* to read and keep reading. There are several ways to raise the tightrope. First, *think about what is socially, culturally, or politically important* about your thesis statement and argument. Some writing instructors tell students to ask themselves "So what?" about the thesis, but this can be a vague directive. Here are some better questions:

- Why is your thesis important?
- What is the impact of your thesis on a particular group or demographic?
- What are the consequences of what you claim?
- What could happen if your position were *not* recognized?
- How can your argument benefit readers or compel them to action (by doing something or adopting a new belief)?
- What will readers *gain* by accepting your argument as convincing?

In formulating your thesis, keep in mind the following points.

- *Different thesis statements may speak to different target audiences.* An argument about changes in estate tax laws may not thrill all audiences, but for a defined group — accountants, lawyers, or the elderly, for instance — it may be quite controversial and highly relevant.
- *Not all audiences are equal — or equally interested in your thesis or argument.* In this book, we generally select topics of broad importance. However, in a literature course, a film history course, or a political science course, you'll calibrate your thesis statements and arguments to an audience that is invested in those fields.

A CHECKLIST FOR A THESIS STATEMENT

- ❒ Does the statement make an arguable assertion rather than (1) merely assert an unarguable fact, (2) merely announce a topic, or (3) declare an unarguable opinion or belief?
- ❒ Is the statement broad enough to cover the entire argument that I will be presenting, and is it narrow enough for me to cover the topic in the space allotted?
- ❒ Does the thesis have consequences beneficial to some audience or consequences that would be detrimental if it were not accepted? (In other words, are there stakes?)

THINKING CRITICALLY *"Walking the Tightrope"*

Examine the low-stakes thesis statements provided below and expand each one into a high-stakes thesis by including the importance of asserting it and by proposing a possible response. The first one has been done as an example.

LOW-STAKES THESIS	HIGH-STAKES THESIS
Good nutrition and exercise can lead to a healthy life.	One way to help solve the epidemic obesity problem in the United States is to remind consumers of a basic fact accepted by nearly all reputable health experts: Good nutrition and exercise can lead to a healthy life.
Every qualified American should vote.	
Spanking children is good/bad.	
Electric cars will reduce air pollution.	

In writing about the steep decline in bee populations, your argument might look quite different if you're speaking to ecologists as opposed to gardeners. (We will discuss audience more in the following section.)

- *Be wary of compare-and-contrast arguments.* One of the most basic approaches to writing is to compare and contrast, a maneuver that produces a low-tightrope thesis. It normally looks like this: "*X* and *Y* are similar in some ways and different in others." But if you think about it, *anything* can be compared and contrasted in this way, and doing so doesn't necessarily *tell* anything important. So, if you're writing a compare-and-contrast paper, make sure to include the reasons why it is important to compare and contrast these things. What benefit does the comparison yield? What significance does it have to some audience or some issue?

IMAGINING AN AUDIENCE

Raising the tightrope of your thesis will also require you to imagine the *audience* you're addressing. The questions that you ask yourself in generating thoughts on a topic will primarily relate to the topic, but additional questions that consider the audience are always relevant:

- Who are my readers?
- What do they believe?

- What common ground do we share?
- What do I want my readers to believe?
- What do they need to know?
- Why should they care?

Let's think about these questions. The literal answer to the first probably is "my teacher," but (unless you receive instructions to the contrary) you should not write specifically for your teacher. Instead, you should write for an audience that is, generally speaking, like your classmates. In short, your imagined audience is literate, intelligent, and moderately well informed, but its members don't know everything that you know, and they don't know your response to the problem being addressed. Your audience needs more information along those lines to make an intelligent decision about the issue.

For example, in writing about how children's toys shape the minds of young boys and girls differently, it may not be enough to simply say, "Toys are part of the gender socialization process." ("Sure they are," the audience might already agree.) However, if you raise the stakes based on who your intended audience is and the audience's level of intelligence, you have an opportunity to direct a more complex argument that results from this observation: You frame the questions, lay out the issues, identify the problems, and note the complications that arise because of your basic thesis. You could point out that toys have a significant impact on the interests, identities, skills, and capabilities that children develop and carry into adulthood. Because toys are so significant, is it important to ask questions about whether they perpetuate gender-based stereotypes? Do toys help perpetuate social inequalities between the sexes? Most children think toys are "just fun," but they may be teaching kids to conform unthinkingly to the social expectations of their sex, to accept designated sex-based social roles, and to cultivate talents differently based on sex. What we want you to see is that asking broader questions about the implications of your argument extends it further and gives it social importance to make it relevant to your audience.

WRITING TIP
If you wish to persuade, finding premises that you share with your audience can help establish common ground, a function of *ethos*.

What audiences should be concerned with your topic? Maybe you're addressing the general public who buys toys for children at least some of the time. Maybe you're addressing parents who are raising young children. Maybe you're addressing consumer advocates, encouraging them to pressure toy manufacturers and retailers to produce more gender-neutral offerings. The point is that your essay should contain (and sustain) an assessment of the impact of your high-stakes thesis, and it should set out a clear course of action for a particular audience.

That said, if you know your audience well, you can argue for different courses of action that are most likely to be persuasive. You may not be very convincing if you argue to parents in general that they should avoid all Disney-themed toys. Perhaps you should argue simply that parents should be conscious of the gender messages that toys convey, offer their kids diverse toys, and talk to their children while playing with them about alternatives to the stereotypical messages that the toys convey. However, if you're writing for a magazine called *Radical Parenting* and your essay is titled "Buying Toys the Gender-Neutral Way," your audience and its expectations — therefore, your thesis and argument — may look far different. The bottom line is not just to know your audience but to define it.

The essays in this book are from many different sources with many different audiences. An essay from the *New York Times* addresses educated general readers; an essay from *Ms.* magazine targets readers sympathetic to feminism. An essay from *Commonweal*, a Roman Catholic publication for nonspecialists, is likely to differ in point of view or tone from one in *Time*, even though both articles may advance approximately the same position. The *Commonweal* article may, for example, effectively cite church fathers and distinguished Roman Catholic writers as authorities, whereas the *Time* article would probably cite few or none of these figures because a non-Catholic audience might be unfamiliar with them or, even if familiar, might be unimpressed by their views.

The tone as well as the gist of the argument is in some degree shaped by the audience. For instance, popular journals, such as *National Review* and *Ms.* magazine, are more likely to use ridicule than are journals chiefly addressed to, say, an academic audience.

Instructors sometimes tell students to imagine their audience as their classmates. What they probably mean is that your argument should be addressed to people invested in the world of ideas, not just your literal classmates. Again, ask yourself the following questions:

- "What do my readers need to know?"
- "What do I want them to believe?"

Exercise: Imagining Your Audience

Consider one of the four topics below and write your responses to each question for your chosen topic.

Animal intelligence | Free college tuition | Screen time | Minimum wage

1. Who are my readers?
2. What do they believe?
3. What common ground do we share?
4. What do I want my readers to believe?
5. What do they need to know?
6. Why should they care?

ADDRESSING OPPOSITION AND ESTABLISHING COMMON GROUND

Presumably, your imagined audience does not share all your views. But why? By putting yourself into your readers' shoes — and your essay will almost surely summarize the views that you're going to speak against — and by thinking about what your audience knows or thinks it knows, you will also generate ideas. Ask yourself:

- Why does your audience not share your views? What views do they hold?
- How can these readers hold a position that to you seems unreasonable?

You may also spend time online reviewing websites dedicated to your topic to discover facts and assess common views and opinions.

Let's assume that you believe the minimum wage should be raised, but you know that some people hold a different view. Why do they hold it? Try to state their view *in a way that would be satisfactory to them*. Having done so, you may perceive that your conclusions and theirs differ because they're based on different premises — perhaps different ideas about how the economy works — or different definitions, concepts, or assumptions about fairness or employment. Examine the opposition's premises carefully and explain, first to yourself (and ultimately to your readers) why you see things differently.

Perhaps some facts are in dispute, such as whether or not an oil pipeline poses a serious threat to the local ecology. The thing to do, then, is to check the facts. If you search online on a reputable website or in a database and find that environmental harms have not been common in cases of other pipelines, yet you are still against one in your own area, you can't premise your argument on the harm the pipeline is likely to cause. You'll have to develop an argument that takes account of the facts and interprets them reasonably.

Among the relevant facts there surely are some that your audience or your opponent will not dispute. The same is true of the values relevant to the discussion; both sides very likely believe in some of the same values. These areas of shared agreement are crucial to effective persuasion in argument.

There are two good reasons for identifying and isolating the areas of agreement:

- There is no point in disputing facts or values on which you and your readers already agree.
- It usually helps establish goodwill between yourself and your opponent when you can point to shared beliefs, assumptions, facts, and values.

Recall that in composing college papers it's usually best to write for a general audience, an audience rather like your classmates but without the specific knowledge that they all share as students enrolled in one course. If the topic is raising the minimum wage, the audience presumably consists of supporters and nonsupporters, as well as people who hold no opinion at all (*yet*, perhaps, until they read your ideas). Thinking "What do readers need to know?" may prompt you to give statistics about the rising cost of living and the number of people who make just the minimum wage. Or if you're arguing against raising the minimum wage, it may prompt you to cite studies showing how doing so increases the cost of goods and

A protest for a higher minimum wage.

Cem Ozdel/Anadolu Agency/Getty Images

the rate of unemployment. If you are writing for a general audience, asking "What does the audience believe?" is important because many people will not be familiar with the basic facts about the minimum wage and the implications of raising it. You will likely be painting with broad strokes, arguing from the widest possible perspectives. But if the audience is specialized, such as a group of economists, a union group, or a sector of small business owners who fear that rate hikes will interfere with their business, an effective essay will have to address their special beliefs.

In addressing the beliefs of your likely opponents, you must try to establish some common ground. If you advocate for the minimum wage hike, you should recognize the possibility that this represents a threat to some proprietors of small businesses. But perhaps you can argue that increases in the minimum wage typically result in more spending at small businesses, which would be good for small business owners in the long run. This is how your thoughts in imagining an audience can prompt you to think of other kinds of evidence — perhaps testimony or statistics on this issue, for example.

A CHECKLIST FOR IMAGINING AN AUDIENCE

- ❒ Have I identified my readers as a general or more specific audience?
- ❒ Do I understand how much my readers need to be told based on what I believe they already know?
- ❒ Have I provided necessary background (including definitions of special terms) if the imagined readers probably are not especially familiar with the topic?
- ❒ Am I able to identify whether or not my readers are likely to be neutral, sympathetic, or hostile to my views?
    - ❒ For neutral audience members, have I offered good reasons to persuade them?
    - ❒ If they're sympathetic, have I done more than merely reaffirm their present beliefs? That is, have I perhaps enriched their views or encouraged them to act?
    - ❒ If they're hostile, will they nevertheless feel respected and informed by my position? Have I taken account of their positions and recognized their strengths but also called attention to their limitations? Have I offered a position that might persuade them to modify their position?

Drafting and Revising an Argument

There is no one way to begin writing. As we have suggested earlier in this chapter, sometimes the best way to get started writing is just to start writing, building ideas, and seeing where your pen (or keyboard) takes you. But, alas, at a certain point, you will want to begin organizing your essay more deliberately, considering your purpose, audience, language, and the organization of your ideas.

THE TITLE

One of the first things you might do in planning an argument is invent a **title**, where you can announce the thesis or topic explicitly, or simply attract the attention of readers in a unique or imaginative way. If you examine the titles of essays in this book, you can see titles that announce their positions and topics both more and less explicitly than others:

"We Must Make Public Colleges and Universities Tuition-Free" (announces thesis)

"The Boston Photographs" (announces topic)

"A First Amendment Junkie" (invites readers' curiosity)

Be prepared to rethink your title *after* completing the last draft of your paper. A working title can help guide your inquiry, but do not hesitate to rethink your title after you have written your argument to ensure it accurately represents your position and analysis.

WRITING TIP
It's better to invent a simple, direct, informative title than a strained, puzzling, or overly cute one. You want to engage readers, not turn them off.

THE OPENING PARAGRAPHS

Opening paragraphs are difficult to write, so don't worry about writing an effective opening when you're drafting. Just get some words down on paper and keep going. But when you revise your first draft, you should begin to think seriously about the effect of your opening.

A good introduction arouses readers' interest and prepares them for the rest of the paper. How? One convenient method of writing an introduction is to offer a "hook" first — something to simultaneously attract the reader and set the stage for the essay. The following table lists some strategies for opening paragraphs.

Hook	Description	Example
Anecdote	A brief story or vignette	I was having lunch recently in the newly built food court, and I noticed the word *organic* on my package of carrots, and I began to wonder . . .
Statistic	A relevant (sobering, shocking, attention-grabbing) number	According to a 2017 Common Sense Media report, American children between the ages of 0 and 8 spend an average of 2.25 hours per day of "screen time" . . .

(Continued)

Hook	Description	Example
Noteworthy event	A recent news story, real-life account, or interesting illustration of the current situation	When the president said this year in his State of the Union address that more must be done for the nation's infrastructure, he touched on an issue that . . .
Analogy	A case similar in structure but different in detail from the point being established	When a leopard stalks its prey, it can spend a full day establishing a prime ambush position, then all at once dart at over 35 miles per hour and jump over 20 feet to close the deal. This is something like . . .
Quotation	Wise, poignant, or landmark words framing your discussion	In 1903, W. E. B. Du Bois said in *The Souls of Black Folk* that "the problem of the twentieth century is the problem of the color line." In the twenty-first century, . . .
Historical account	A brief account of the background or evolution of the topic	The evolution of the monster movie extends from early films such as *Nosferatu* (1922) and *The Hunchback of Notre Dame* (1923) to today's renditions such as *The Babadook* (2014) and *Slenderman* (2018). In that evolution, we can see . . .

You may set your hook quickly, provide a more elaborate version, or even combine the strategies listed in the table. In addition to grabbing readers' attention, opening paragraphs also usually do at least one (and often all) of the following:

- prepare readers for the topic (naming the topic, giving some idea of its importance, noting conventional beliefs about it, or relaying in brief what people are saying about it)
- provide readers with definitions of key terms and concepts (stipulating, quoting an authority, etc.)
- establish a context for your argument by linking your subject, topic, and views to relevant social issues, debates, and trends
- reveal the thesis
- provide readers a map of the argument (giving a sense of how the essay will be organized)

You may not wish to announce your thesis in the title, but if you don't announce it there, you should set it forth early in the argument, in the introductory paragraph or paragraphs. Although it is possible for the thesis to be blurted out in the first line, usually writers spend some time preparing the argument before providing the thesis. And although it is possible never to state the thesis directly but only imply it throughout the argument, thesis statements may also be bold and daring.

Another thing you can do in an introduction is spend some time outlining the general subject into which your topic fits. The subject is the general area in which your questions and research reside, whereas your specific topic might be narrower. For example, the subject of your paper may be workers' rights, or immigration, or national security, but your topic will usually be something that falls within that subject — the minimum wage, or the border wall, or WikiLeaks, for example. You may go to great lengths to frame your topic within a subject, or you may just mention it, but it usually helps to position your discussion in a larger framework.

After announcing the topic, giving the necessary background and context, and stating your position in as engaging a manner as possible, you will do well to give the reader an idea of *how* you will proceed — that is, how the essay will be organized. It is not a requirement that all writers must state exactly what they will be doing in each part of their essay — and in fact, it may not be an effective strategy for certain audiences and purposes. Nevertheless, at any point in your introduction, you may announce that there are, say, four common objections to your thesis and that you will take them up one by one. You could add that you will move from the weakest (or most widely held) to the strongest (or least familiar), after which you will advance your own view in greater detail. Or you might announce that three primary views of an issue exist, and you will spell them out before moving on.

WRITING TIP
If your argument will be written or published online, you might establish a context for your argument by linking to a news video that outlines the topic, or you might offer your thesis and then link to a news story that supports your claim. (Remember that using any videos, images, or links also requires a citation of some kind.)

Not every writer states plans like this outright. But if your analysis is methodical and perhaps complex, you can tell readers where you will be taking them and by what route. In effect, you are giving them a look at your own outline. How far you go to clue the reader in to your method of analysis is up to you, just as it is up to you to decide how much background, context, definition, and so on you include. Ultimately, these decisions will impact the length and style of your introduction and set the foundations for the rest of your argument.

It is important to note that all the elements of introductions we have laid out so far do not have to be included categorically or in a formulaic way. You might do more background work, you might provide a very detailed account of competing perspectives in order to position yourself within a debate, you might offer both an anecdote and a statistic, or you might combine some elements and leave out others. The following introduction has been annotated to show the writer's choices.

According to a 2017 Common Sense Media report, American children between the ages of 0 and 8 spend an average of 2.25 hours per day involved in "screen time," a term used to denote the total time a child

Hooks reader with a dramatic statistic.

Defines a key term.

Author inserts her own voice to express concern.

Contextualizes the debate about screen time.

Provides a "map" of how the analysis will proceed.

Concedes to possible counterpoints, but enters into the conversation with a relevant, impactful thesis.

spends in front of any visual electronic media, whether television, video game, or internet. If that is correct, then children are spending a whopping 34 days — a full month and then some — each year on "screens." The debate over how much screen time is appropriate for children, and what its ultimate effects are on children's development, has been lively in the fully connected digital world. But since the advent of the iPhone in 2007, the debate has heated up even more. One group of investors, JANA Partners, recently worried about the "toxic" effects of the current levels of screen time on children, and others have correlated increasing levels of anxiety and depression in children with high levels of internet usage. To understand the potential impact of screen time on children, and what may be done about it, it is important first to examine what kinds of screen time might be positive or negative. As I will show, some kinds of screen time act as positive influences in children's life, increasing children's creativity and in some instances sociability. While there may be negative impacts to some kinds of "screen time" or too much "screen time" (even with positive or educational media), if parents and educators understand more about how to select and control children's media usage, we can work toward a practical solution in a society where these kinds of technologies are not likely to disappear.

ORGANIZING THE BODY OF THE ESSAY

We begin with a wise remark by a newspaper columnist, Robert Cromier: "The beautiful part of writing is that you don't have to get it right the first time — unlike, say, a brain surgeon."

In drafting an essay, you will, of course, begin with an organization that seems appropriate, but you may find, in rereading the draft, that some other organization is better. For a start, in the Visual Guide: Organizing Your Argument, we offer three types of organization that are common in argumentative essays. Please note, however, that we do not mean to suggest that essays should be formulaic. These general structures need to be considered alongside your argument's needs to present counterpoints at the appropriate times, to relate an anecdote in the middle of things, or to introduce shorter summaries of others' arguments. Occasionally, these items warrant new paragraphs. The best writers know how to manage structure and how to go down little rabbit holes to explore a point further (perhaps with an analogy, anecdote, or example) but without being *digressive*, departing too far from the main point.

Even if you were to adhere closely to the patterns, you have a lot of room for variation. But let's assume that in the introductory paragraphs you have sketched the topic (and have shown, or implied, that the reader doubtless is interested in it) and have fairly and courteously set forth the opposition's view, recognizing its merits ("I grant that," "admittedly," "it is true that") and indicating the degree to which you can share part of that view. You now want to set forth arguments explaining why you differ on some essentials.

Visual Guide: Organizing Your Argument

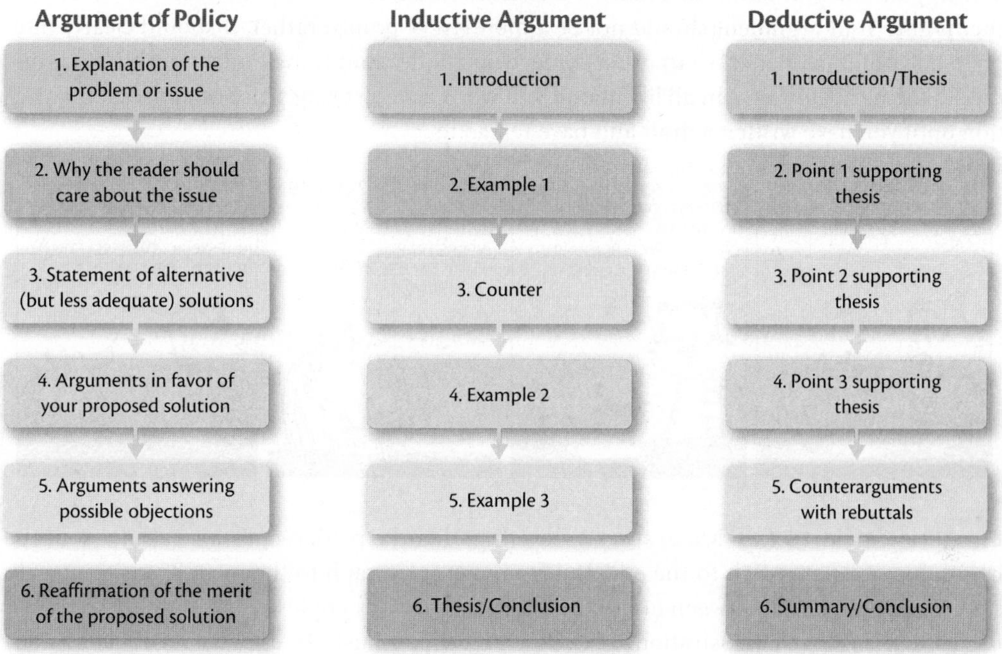
Argument of Policy
1. Explanation of the problem or issue
2. Why the reader should care about the issue
3. Statement of alternative (but less adequate) solutions
4. Arguments in favor of your proposed solution
5. Arguments answering possible objections
6. Reaffirmation of the merit of the proposed solution
Inductive Argument
1. Introduction
2. Example 1
3. Counter
4. Example 2
5. Example 3
6. Thesis/Conclusion
Deductive Argument
1. Introduction/Thesis
2. Point 1 supporting thesis
3. Point 2 supporting thesis
4. Point 3 supporting thesis
5. Counterarguments with rebuttals
6. Summary/Conclusion

In presenting your own position, you can begin with either your strongest or your weakest reasons. Each method of organization has advantages and disadvantages.

- If you begin with your strongest examples or reasons, your essay could impress your readers and then peter out, leaving them asking, "Is that all?"
- If you begin with your weakest material, you build to a climax, but readers may not still be with you because they may have felt that the beginning of the essay was frivolous or irrelevant.

The obvious solution is to ensure that even your weakest argument demonstrates strength. Yet because we are not always so fortunate to have equally strong reasons, you can always assure your readers explicitly how you are going to proceed. For example, you may go ahead and say that stronger points will soon follow and you offer this point first to show that you are aware of it and that, slight though it is, it deserves some attention. The body of the essay, then, is devoted to arguing a position in whatever ways you need to explain yourself best.

> **WRITING TIP**
> By acknowledging arguments other than your own — and possible objections to your points — you let readers know that you've done your homework and build their trust. You also have a chance to preempt critiques of your ideas, which helps you be more persuasive.

Doubtless you'll sometimes be uncertain, while drafting an essay, whether to present a given point before or after another point, or when you should explain why you are proceeding the way you are.

When you write, and certainly when you revise, try to put yourself into the reader's shoes: Which point do you think the reader needs to know first? Which point *leads to* which further point? Your argument should not be a mere list of points; rather, it should clearly integrate one point with another in order to develop an idea and transition smoothly from one idea to the next. However, in all likelihood you won't have a strong sense of the best organization until you have written a draft and have reread it.

CHECKING TRANSITIONS Make sure, in revising, that the reader can move easily from the beginning of a paragraph to the end and from one paragraph to the next. Transitions help signal the connections between units of the argument. For example ("For example" is a transition, indicating that an illustration will follow), they may illustrate, establish a sequence, connect logically, amplify, compare, contrast, summarize, or concede (see Thinking Critically: Using Transitions in Argument). Transitions serve as guideposts that enable the reader to move easily through your essay.

When writers revise an early draft, they chiefly do these tasks:

- They **unify** the essay by eliminating irrelevancies.
- They **organize** the essay by keeping in mind the imagined audience.
- They **clarify** the essay by fleshing out thin paragraphs, by ensuring that the transitions are adequate, and by making certain that generalizations are adequately supported by concrete details and examples.

We are not talking here about polish or elegance; we are talking about fundamental matters. Be especially careful not to abuse the logical connectives (*thus, as a result*, and so on). If you write several sentences followed by *therefore* or a similar word or phrase, be sure that what you write after the *therefore* really *does follow* from what has gone before. Logical connectives are not mere transitional devices that link disconnected bits of prose. They are supposed to mark a real movement of thought, which is the essence of an argument.

THE ENDING

What about concluding paragraphs, in which you summarize the main points and reaffirm your position? A conclusion — the word comes from the Latin *claudere*, "to shut" — ought to provide a sense of closure, but it can be much more than a restatement of the writer's thesis.

THINKING CRITICALLY *Using Transitions in Argument*

Fill in examples of the types of transitions listed below, using topics of your choice. The first one has been done as an example.

TYPE OF TRANSITION	TYPE OF LANGUAGE USED	EXAMPLE OF TRANSITION
Illustrate	*for example, for instance, consider this case*	"Many television crime dramas contain scenes of graphic violence. For example, in an episode of *Law and Order . . .*"
Establish a sequence	*a more important objection, a stronger example, the best reason*	
Connect logically	*thus, as a result, therefore, so, it follows*	
Amplify	*further, in addition to, moreover*	
Compare	*similarly, in a like manner, just as, analogously*	
Contrast	*on the one hand . . . on the other hand, but, in contrast, however*	
Summarize	*in short, briefly*	
Concede	*admittedly, granted, to be sure*	

It can, for instance, make a quiet, emotional appeal by suggesting that the issue is important and that the ball is now in the reader's court.

If you can look back over your essay and add something that both enriches it and wraps it up, fine; but don't feel compelled to say, "Thus, in conclusion, I have argued *X*, *Y*, and *Z*, and I have refuted Jones." After all, *conclusion* can have two meanings: (1) ending, or finish, as the ending of a joke or a novel; or (2) judgment or decision reached after deliberation. Your essay should finish effectively (the first sense), but it need not announce a judgment (the second).

If the essay is fairly short, so that a reader can keep its general gist in mind, you may not need to restate your view. Just make sure that you have covered the ground and that your last sentence is a good one. Notice that the student essay presented later in this chapter (p. 239) doesn't end with a formal conclusion, although it ends conclusively, with a note of finality.

By "a note of finality" we do *not* mean a triumphant crowing. It's far better to end with the suggestion that you hope you have by now indicated why those who hold a different view may want to modify it and accept yours.

If you study the essays in this book or the editorials and op-ed pieces in a newspaper, you will notice that writers often provide a sense of closure by using one of the following devices:

- a return to something stated in the introduction
- a glance at the wider implications of the issue (i.e., what would happen if your solution were implemented or not)
- a hint toward unasked or answered questions that the audience might consider in light of the writer's argument (i.e., predict new questions or issues, and let them ring out at the end as guides to further thinking)
- a suggestion that the reader can take some specific action or do some further research (i.e., the ball is now in the reader's court)
- an anecdote that illustrates the thesis in an engaging way (i.e., a brief account, real or imagined, that brings your ideas into a visible form)
- a brief summary (i.e., a recap. But note that this sort of ending may seem unnecessary and tedious if the paper is short and the summary merely repeats what the writer has already said.)

USES OF AN OUTLINE

Outlines may seem rigid to many writers, especially to those who compose online, where we're accustomed to cutting, copying, moving, and deleting as we draft. You're probably familiar with the structure known as a **formal outline**. Major points are indicated by I, II, III; points within major points are indicated by A, B, C; divisions within A, B, C are indicated by 1, 2, 3; and so on. Thus:

I. Arguments for opening all Olympic sports to professionals

  A. Fairness

    1. Some Olympic sports are already open to professionals.

    2. Some athletes who really are not professionals are classified as professionals.

  B. Quality (achievements would be higher)

However, an outline — whether you write it before drafting or use it to evaluate the organization of something you've already written — is meant to be a guide rather than a straitjacket.

THE OUTLINE AS A PRELIMINARY GUIDE Some writers sketch an outline as soon as they think they know what they want to say, even before writing a first draft. This procedure can be helpful in planning a tentative organization, but remember that in revising a draft you'll likely generate some new ideas and have to modify the outline accordingly. A preliminary outline is chiefly useful as a means of getting going, not as a guide to the final essay.

THE OUTLINE AS A WAY OF CHECKING A DRAFT Whether or not you use a preliminary outline, we strongly suggest that after writing what you hope is your last draft, you make an outline of it; there is no better way of finding out whether the essay is well organized.

Go through the draft and write down the chief points in the order in which you make them. That is, prepare a table of contents — perhaps a phrase for each paragraph. Next, examine your notes to see what kind of sequence they reveal in your paper:

- Is the sequence reasonable? Can it be improved?
- Are any passages irrelevant?
- Does something important seem to be missing?

If no coherent structure or reasonable sequence clearly appears in the outline, the full prose version of your argument probably doesn't have any either. Therefore, produce another draft by moving things around, adding or subtracting paragraphs — cutting and pasting them into a new sequence, with transitions as needed — and then make another outline to see if the sequence now is satisfactory.

A CHECKLIST FOR ORGANIZING AN ARGUMENT

- ❒ Does the introduction let the readers know where the author is taking them?
  - ❒ Does the introduction state the problem or issue?
  - ❒ Does it state the claim (the thesis)?
  - ❒ Does it suggest the organization of the essay, thereby helping the reader follow the argument?
- ❒ Do subsequent paragraphs support the claim?
  - ❒ Do they offer evidence?
  - ❒ Do they face objections to the claim and offer reasonable responses?
  - ❒ Do they indicate why the author's claim is preferable?
  - ❒ Do transitions (signposts such as *Furthermore*, *In contrast*, and *Consider as an example*) guide the reader through the argument?
- ❒ Does the essay end effectively, with a paragraph (at most, two paragraphs) bringing a note of closure?

TONE AND THE WRITER'S PERSONA

Although this book is chiefly about argument in the sense of rational discourse — the presentation of reasons in support of a thesis or conclusion — the appeal to reason (*logos*) is only one form of persuasion, as we have shown in earlier chapters. Another form is the appeal to emotion (*pathos*) — to pity, for example — and a third form of persuasion is the appeal to the speaker's character (*ethos*). What Aristotle called the **ethical appeal** is the idea that effective speakers convey the suggestion that they are

- informed,
- intelligent,
- fair minded (persons of goodwill), and
- honest

Because they are perceived as trustworthy, their words inspire confidence in their listeners. It is a fact that when reading an argument we're often aware of the *person* or *voice* behind the words, and our assent to the argument depends partly on the extent to which we share the speaker's assumptions and see the matter from his or her point of view — in short, the extent to which we can *identify* with the speaker.

How can a writer inspire the confidence that lets readers identify with him or her? First, the writer should possess the virtues Aristotle specified: intelligence or good sense, honesty, and benevolence or goodwill. As a Roman proverb puts it, "No one gives what he does not have." Still, possession of these qualities is not a guarantee that you will convey them in your writing. Like all other writers, you'll have to revise your drafts so that these qualities become apparent; stated more moderately, you'll have to revise so that nothing in the essay causes a reader to doubt your intelligence, honesty, and goodwill. A blunder in logic, a misleading quotation, a snide remark, even an error in spelling — all such slips can cause readers to withdraw their sympathy from the writer.

Of course, all good argumentative essays do not sound exactly alike; they do not all reveal the same speaker. Each writer develops his or her own voice, or (as literary critics and instructors call it) **persona**. (We discussed persona in more detail in Chapter 5, Examining the Author's Persona, pp. 178–79.) In fact, one writer may have several voices or personae, depending on the topic and the audience. The president of the United States delivering an address on the State of the Union has one persona; when chatting with a reporter at his summer home, he has another. This change is not a matter of hypocrisy. Different circumstances call for different language. As a French writer put it, there is a time to speak of "Paris" and a time to speak of "the capital of the nation." When Abraham Lincoln spoke at Gettysburg, he didn't say "Eighty-seven years ago"; instead, he intoned "Four score and seven years ago." We might say that just as some occasions required him to be the folksy Honest Abe during election campaigns, the occasion of the dedication of hallowed ground at Gettysburg, where so many Civil War soldiers lost their lives, required him to be formal and solemn — thus, as president of the United States he appropriately used biblical language.

When we talk about a writer's persona, we mean the way in which the writer presents his or her attitudes

- toward *the self,*
- toward *the audience*, and
- toward *the subject.*

Thus, if a writer says:

I have thought long and hard about this subject, and I can say with assurance that . . .

we may feel that he is a self-satisfied egotist who probably is mouthing other people's opinions. Certainly he's mouthing clichés: "long and hard," "say with assurance."

Let's look at a subtler example of an utterance that reveals certain attitudes:

President Nixon was hounded out of office by journalists.

The statement above conveys a respectful attitude toward Nixon ("President Nixon") and a hostile attitude toward the press (they are beasts, curs who "hounded" our elected leader). If the writer's attitudes were reversed, she might have said something like this:

The press turned the searchlight on Tricky Dick's criminal shenanigans.

"Tricky Dick" and "criminal" are obvious enough, but notice that "shenanigans" also implies the writer's contempt for Nixon, and "turned the searchlight" suggests that the press is a source of illumination, a source of truth. The original version and the opposite version both say that the press was responsible for Nixon's resignation, but the original version ("President Nixon was hounded") conveys indignation toward journalists, whereas the revision conveys contempt for Nixon.

These two versions suggest two speakers who differ not only in their view of Nixon but also in their manner, including the seriousness with which they take themselves. Although the passage is very short, it seems to us that the first speaker conveys righteous indignation ("hounded"), whereas the second conveys amused contempt ("shenanigans"). To our ears, the tone, as well as the point, differs in the two versions.

WRITING TIP
Present yourself so that readers see you as knowledgeable, honest, open-minded, and interested in helping them to think about the significance of an issue.

LOADED WORDS We are talking now about **loaded words**, which convey the writer's attitude and, through their connotations, seek to win the reader to the writer's side. Compare the words in the left-hand column with those in the right:

freedom fighter	terrorist
pro-choice	pro-abortion
pro-life	antichoice
economic refugee	illegal alien
terrorist surveillance	domestic spying

The words in the left-hand column sound like good things; speakers who use them seek to establish themselves as virtuous people supporting worthy causes. The **connotations** (associations, overtones) of these pairs of words differ, even though the **denotations** (explicit meanings, dictionary definitions) are the same — just as the connotations of *mother* and *female parent* differ, although the denotations are the same. Similarly, although Lincoln's "four score and seven" and "eighty-seven" both denote "thirteen less than one hundred," they differ in connotation.

Tone is not only a matter of connotation (*hounded out of office* versus, let's say, *compelled to resign*, or *pro-choice* versus *pro-abortion*); it is also a matter of such things as the selection and type of examples. A writer who offers many examples, especially ones drawn from ordinary life, conveys a persona different from that of a writer who offers no examples or only an occasional invented instance. The first writer seems friendlier, more honest, more down-to-earth.

USING TONE TO ADDRESS OPPOSITION On the whole, when writing an argument, it's advisable to be courteous and respectful of your topic, your audience, and people who hold views opposite to yours. It is rarely good for one's own intellectual development to regard as villains or fools persons who hold views different from one's own, especially if some of them are in the audience. Keep in mind the story of two strangers on a train who, striking up a conversation, found that both were clergymen, although of different faiths. Then one said to the other, "Well, why shouldn't we be friends? After all, we both serve God, you in your way and I in His."

Complacency is all right when telling a joke, but not when offering an argument:

- Recognize opposing views.
- Assume that they are held in good faith.
- State them fairly. If you don't, you do a disservice not only to the opposition but also to your own position because the perceptive reader won't take you seriously.
- Be temperate in arguing your own position: "If I understand their view correctly . . ."; "It seems reasonable to conclude that . . ."; "Perhaps, then, we can agree that . . ."
- Write calmly. If you become overly emotional, readers may interpret you as biased or unreasonable, and they may lose their confidence in you.

WE, ONE, OR I?

The use of *we* in the last paragraph brings us to another point: Is it correct to use the first-person pronouns *I* and *we*? In this book, because three of us are writing, we often use *we* to mean the three authors. Sometimes we use *we* to mean the authors and the readers, or *we* the people in general. This shifting use of one word can be troublesome, but we hope (clearly, the *we* here refers only to the authors) that we have avoided ambiguity. But can, or should, or must an individual use *we* instead of *I*? The short answer is no.

If you're simply speaking for yourself, use *I*. Attempts to avoid the first-person singular by saying things like "This writer thinks . . ." and "It is thought that . . ." and "One thinks that . . ." are far more irritating (and wordy) than the use of *I*. The so-called editorial *we* sounds as odd in a student's argument as the royal *we* does. (Mark Twain said that the only ones who can appropriately say *we* are kings, editors, and people with a tapeworm.) It's advisable to use *we* only when you are sure you're writing or speaking directly to an audience who holds membership in the same group, as in "We *students of this university should* . . ." or "We *the members of Theta Chi fraternity need to. . . .*" If the *we* you refer to has a referent, simply refer to what it means: Say "Americans are" rather than "We are," or "College students should" rather than "We should," or "Republicans need to" rather than "We need to."

Many students assume that using *one* will solve the problem of pronouns. But because one *one* leads to another, the sentence may end up sounding, as James Thurber once said, "like a trombone solo." It's best to admit that you are the author and to use *I*. However, there is no need to preface every sentence with "I think." The reader knows that the essay is yours and that the opinions are yours; so use *I* when you must, but not needlessly. Do not write, "I think *X* movie is terrible"; simply say, "*X* movie is terrible." And do not add extra words that say more obvious things, like "*It is my idea that* the company needs a new mission statement." Just write, "*The company needs a new mission statement.*"

Often you'll see *I* in journalistic writing and autobiographical writing — and in some argumentative writing, too — but in most argumentative writing, it's best to state the facts and (when drawing reasonable conclusions from them) to keep yourself in the background. Why? The more you use *I* in an essay, the more your readers will attach *you* directly to the argument and may regard your position as personal rather than as relevant to themselves.

THINKING CRITICALLY *Eliminating* We, One, *and* I

Rewrite the following sentences to eliminate unnecessary uses of *we, one, I,* and other gratuitous statements of opinion. (The first row has been completed as an example.)

ORIGINAL SENTENCE	REWRITTEN SENTENCE
I think fracking is the best way to achieve energy independence and to create jobs.	Fracking is the best way to achieve energy independence and to create jobs.
In our country, we believe in equality and freedom.	
One should consider one's manners at formal dinner parties.	
In my opinion, the government should not regulate the sizes of sodas we can order.	
It is clearly the case that the new policy treats employees unfairly.	

A CHECKLIST FOR ESTABLISHING TONE AND PERSONA

- ❒ Do I have a sense of what the audience probably knows or thinks about the issue to best present myself to them?
- ❒ Have I tried to establish common ground and then moved on to advance my position?
- ❒ Have I used appropriate language (e.g., defined terms that are likely to be unfamiliar)?
- ❒ Have I indicated why readers should care about the issue and should accept my views, or at least give them serious consideration?
- ❒ Have I presented myself as a person who is fair, informed, and worth listening to? In short, have I conveyed a strong *ethos*?

AVOIDING SEXIST LANGUAGE

Courtesy — as well as common sense — requires that you respect your readers' feelings. Many people today find offensive the implicit gender bias in the use of male pronouns ("As the reader follows the argument, he will find . . .") to denote not only men but also women or people who use nonbinary gender pronouns such as *ze* or *they*. And sometimes the use of the male pronoun to denote all people is ridiculous ("An individual, no matter what his sex, . . .").

In most contexts, there is no need to use gender-specific nouns or pronouns. One way to avoid using *he* when you mean any person is to use *he or she* (or *she or he*), but the result is sometimes cumbersome — although superior to the overly conspicuous *he/she* and *s/he*. Some people will accept *they*, even when the syntax of a sentence calls for a singular pronoun, to avoid this issue ("When a person enters the exhibit, they will see . . ."), but not everyone accepts this usage in formal writing yet.

Here are two simple ways to solve the problem:

- *Use the plural* ("As readers follow the argument, they will find . . .").
- *Recast the sentence* so that no pronoun is required ("Readers following the argument will find . . .").

Because *man* and *mankind* strike many readers as sexist when used in such expressions as "Man is a rational animal" and "Mankind has not yet solved this problem," consider using such words as *human being, person, people, humanity,* and *we* (e.g., "Human beings are rational animals"; "We have not yet solved this problem").

Peer Review

Your instructor may suggest — or require — that you submit an early draft of your essay to a fellow student or small group of students for comment. Such a procedure benefits both author and readers: You get the responses of a reader, and the student-reader gets experience

A CHECKLIST FOR PEER REVIEW

Read through the draft quickly. Then read it again, with the following questions in mind. Remember: You are reading a draft, a work in progress. You're expected to offer suggestions, and you're expected to offer them courteously.

In a sentence, indicate the degree to which the draft shows promise of fulfilling the assignment.

- ❒ Is the writer's tone appropriate? Who is the audience?
- ❒ Looking at the essay as a whole, what thesis (main idea) is advanced?
- ❒ Are the needs of the audience kept in mind? For instance, do some words need to be defined?
- ❒ Is the evidence (e.g., the examples and the testimony of authorities) clear and effective?
- ❒ Can I accept the assumptions? If not, why not?
- ❒ Is any obvious evidence (or counterevidence) overlooked?
- ❒ Is the writer proposing a solution? If so,
  - ❒ Are other equally attractive solutions adequately examined?
  - ❒ Has the writer overlooked some unattractive effects of the proposed solution?

Look at each paragraph separately.

- ❒ What is the basic point?
- ❒ How does each paragraph relate to the essay's main idea or to the previous paragraph?
- ❒ Should some paragraphs be deleted? Be divided into two or more paragraphs? Be combined? Be moved elsewhere? (If you outline the essay by writing down the gist of each paragraph, you'll get help in answering these questions.)
- ❒ Is each sentence clearly related to the sentence that precedes and to the sentence that follows? If not, in a sentence or two indicate examples of good and bad transitions.
- ❒ Is each paragraph adequately developed? Are there sufficient details, perhaps brief supporting quotations from the text?
- ❒ Are the introductory and concluding paragraphs effective?

Look at the paper as a whole.

- ❒ What are the paper's chief strengths?
- ❒ Make at least two specific suggestions that you think will help the author improve the paper.

in thinking about the problems of developing an argument, especially such matters as the degree of detail that a writer needs to offer to a reader and the importance of keeping the organization evident to a reader.

Oral peer reviews allow for the give and take of discussion, but probably most students and most instructors find written peer reviews more helpful because reviewers think more carefully about their responses to the draft, and they help essayists to get beyond a knee-jerk response to criticism. Online reviews on a class website, through email, or via another platform such as a file-sharing service or internet-based document tool are especially helpful precisely because they are not face to face; the peer reviewer gets practice *writing*, and the essayist is not directly challenged.

A Student's Essay, from Rough Notes to Final Version

While we were revising this textbook, we asked the students in one of our classes to write a short essay (500–750 words) on some ethical problem that concerned them. Because this assignment was the first writing assignment in the course, we explained that a good way to generate ideas is to ask oneself some questions, write down responses, question those responses, and write freely for ten minutes or so, not worrying about contradictions. We invited our students to hand in their initial notes along with the finished essay so that we could get a sense of how they proceeded as writers. Not all of them chose to hand in their notes, but we were greatly encouraged by those who did. What encouraged us was the confirmation of an old belief — we call it a fact — that students will hand in a thoughtful essay if before preparing a final version they ask themselves *why* they think this or that, write down their responses, and are not afraid to change their minds as they proceed.

Here are the first notes of a student, Emily Andrews, who elected to write about whether to give money to street beggars. She simply put down ideas, one after the other.

> Help the poor? Why do I (sometimes) do it?
>
> I feel guilty, and think I should help them: poor, cold, hungry (but also some of them are thirsty for liquor, and will spend the money on liquor, not on food).
>
> I also feel annoyed by them — most of them.
>
> Where does the expression "the deserving poor" come from?
>
> And "poor but honest"? Actually, that sounds odd. Wouldn't "rich but honest" make more sense?
>
> Why don't they work? Fellow with red beard, always by bus stop in front of florist's shop, always wants a handout. He is a regular, there all day every day, so I guess he is in a way "reliable," so why doesn't he put the same time in on a job?
>
> Or why don't they get help? Don't they know they need it? They *must* know they need it.
>
> Maybe that guy with the beard is just a con artist. Maybe he makes more money by panhandling than he would by working, and it's a lot easier!

Kinds of poor — how to classify??

drunks, druggies, etc.
mentally ill (maybe drunks belong here, too)
decent people who have had terrible luck

Why private charity?

Doesn't it make sense to say we (fortunate individuals) should give something — an occasional handout — to people who have had terrible luck? (I suppose some people might say there's no need for any of us to give anything — the government takes care of the truly needy — but I *do* believe in giving charity. A month ago a friend of the family passed away, and the woman's children suggested that people might want to make a donation in her name to a shelter for battered women. I know my parents made a donation.)

BUT how can I tell who is who, which are which? Which of these people asking for "spare change" really need (deserve???) help, and which are phonies? Impossible to tell.

Possibilities:

Give to no one.
Give to no one but make an annual donation, maybe to United Way.
Give a dollar to each person who asks. This would probably not cost me even a dollar a day.
Occasionally do without something — maybe a new album or a meal in a restaurant — and give the money I save to people who seem worthy.

WORTHY? What am I saying? How can I, or anyone, tell? The neat-looking guy who says he just lost his job may be a phony, and the dirty bum — probably a drunk — may desperately need food. (OK, so what if he spends the money on liquor instead of food? At least he'll get a little pleasure in life. No! It's not all right if he spends it on drink.)

Other possibilities:

Do some volunteer work?
To tell the truth, I don't want to put in the time. I don't feel *that* guilty.

So what's the problem?

Is it, How I can help the very poor (handouts, or through an organization)? or

How I can feel less guilty about being lucky enough to be able to go to college and to have a supportive family?

I can't quite bring myself to believe I should help every beggar who approaches, but I also can't bring myself to believe that I should do nothing, on the grounds that:

a. it's probably their fault
b. if they are deserving, they can get gov't help. No, I just can't believe that. Maybe some are too proud to look for government help, or don't know that they're entitled to it.

What to do?

On balance, it seems best to:

a. give to United Way
b. maybe also give to an occasional individual, if I happen to be moved, without worrying about whether he or she is "deserving" (since it's probably impossible to know)

A day after making these notes Emily reviewed them, added a few points, and then made a very brief selection from them to serve as an outline for her first draft:

Opening para.: "poor but honest"? Deserve "spare change"?

Charity: private or through organizations?

pros and cons
guy at bus
it wouldn't cost me much, but . . . better to give through organizations

Concluding para.: still feel guilty?

maybe mention guy at bus again?

After writing and revising a draft, Emily submitted her essay to a fellow student for review. She then revised her work in light of the peer's suggestions and her own further thinking.

Emily's final essay appears below. If after reading the final version you reread Emily's early notes, you'll notice that some of her notes never made it into the final version. But without the notes, the essay probably wouldn't have been as interesting as it is. When Emily made the notes, she wasn't so much putting down her ideas as *finding* ideas through the process of writing. (By the way, Emily told us that in her next-to-last draft, the title was "Is It Right to Spare 'Spare Change'?" This title, unlike the revision, introduces the topic but not the author's position.)

Andrews 1

Emily Andrews
Professor Barnet
English 102
January 15, 2019

Why I Don't Spare "Spare Change"

"Poor but honest." "The deserving poor." I don't know the origin of these quotations, but they always come to mind when I walk through my city, Boston, and encounter "the poor" on the streets asking for money. When I do, I have to face an ethical dilemma — not as to whether or not I *can* spare my spare change, but whether or not I *should*. Panhandlers by definition are people who solicit money for their personal use without providing goods or services. This forces me to consider the behavior I am enabling by giving away money on the street. Many of these people, perhaps through alcohol or drugs, have ruined not only their own lives but also the lives of others in order to indulge in their own habits. Perhaps alcoholism and drug addiction really are "diseases," as many people say, but my own feeling — based, of course, not on any serious study — is that most alcoholics and drug addicts can be classified with the "undeserving poor." And that is largely why I don't distribute spare change to panhandlers.

Surely among street people there are also some who can rightly be called "deserving." Deserving of what? A fair shake in life, or government assistance? Perhaps. But my spare change? It happens that I have been brought up to believe that it is appropriate to make contributions to charity — let's say a shelter for battered women — but if I give some change to a panhandler, I may be helping someone, or, on the contrary, I could just as easily be encouraging someone to continue their alcohol or drug abuse, and not to get help. Maybe even worse: maybe I am supporting a criminal, or con artist, or someone who could use my money to get high and take advantage of someone else. The fact is, I don't know.

If one believes in the value of private charity, one can give either to needy individuals or to charitable organizations. Money given to panhandlers may indeed help a person badly in need, but it could just as easily be misused and cause greater harm. In giving to an organization

Title is informative, alerting the reader to the topic and the author's position.

Opening paragraph holds readers' interest by alluding to familiar phrases and an anecdote.

Defines a key term: *panhandler*.

Author presents general outline of argument and thesis.

Voices the reader's probably uneasy response to the opening, showing audience awareness.

Supports her argument with reason.

Clearly sets forth the alternatives. A reader may disagree with them, but they are stated fairly.

such as the United Way, in contrast, one can feel that one's money is likely to be used wisely. True, confronted by a panhandler one may feel that *this* particular unfortunate individual needs help at *this* moment — a cup of coffee or a sandwich — and the need will not be met unless I put my hand in my pocket right now. But I have come to think that the beggars whom I encounter can get along without my spare change. If they choose, they can go to shelters where charitable contributions can be collected and spent wisely. Indeed, panhandlers may actually be better off if people did not give them spare change which they can subsequently use on alcohol or drugs.

Paragraphs 4 and 5 are more personal than the earlier paragraphs. The writer, more or less having stated what she takes to be the facts, now is entitled to offer a highly personal response to them.

It happens that in my neighborhood I encounter a few panhandlers regularly. There is one fellow who is always by the bus stop where I catch the bus to the college, and I never give him anything precisely because he is always there. He is such a regular that, I think, he ought to be able to hold a regular job. Putting him aside, I routinely encounter about three or four beggars in an average week. (I'm not counting street musicians. These people seem quite able to work for a living. If they see their "work" as playing or singing, let persons who enjoy their performances pay them. I do not consider myself among their audience.) The truth of the matter is that since I meet so few beggars, I could give each one a dollar and hardly feel the loss. At most, I might go without seeing a movie some week. But I know nothing about these people, and it's my impression — based on what I see — that they simply prefer begging to working.

The final paragraph nicely concludes with a reference to the title, giving the reader a sense of completeness.

That's why I usually do not give "spare change," and I don't think I will in the future. These people will get along without me, and may get along better without me if their needs eventually lead them to a shelter or a food bank. Someone else will have to come up with money for their coffee or their liquor, or, at worst, they will just have to do without. I will continue to contribute occasionally to a charitable organization, not simply (I hope) to salve my conscience but because I believe that these organizations actually do good work. But I will not attempt to be a mini-charitable organization, distributing spare change likely to go to an unworthy cause.

Topics for Critical Thinking and Writing

1. Does the writer establish a good sense of *ethos* in this essay? Explain what works best and what works least in terms of establishing credibility or goodwill.
2. Do you think this essay has a strong thesis? A strong argument? Explain.
3. What assumptions are made about panhandlers in this essay? If you wanted to challenge these assumptions, what kinds of questions could you ask and what evidence could you seek?
4. What are some alternative solutions or counterarguments that the writer did not address?
5. Who is the writer's intended audience? Do you think the writer's language and tone are appropriate?

ASSIGNMENT FOR DEVELOPING AN ARGUMENT OF YOUR OWN

In a brief essay, state a claim and support it with evidence. Choose an issue in which you are genuinely interested and about which you already know something. You may want to interview a few experts and do some reading, but don't try to write a highly researched paper. Be sure to organize your argument thoughtfully, with consideration of your audience, the context of the argument, and alternative viewpoints. Sample topics:

1. Students in laboratory courses should not be required to participate in the dissection of animals.
2. Washington, DC, should be granted statehood.
3. In wartime, women should be subject to the military draft.
4. The annual Miss America contest was right to eliminate the swimsuit competition.
5. The government should not offer financial support to the arts.
6. The chief fault of the curriculum in high school was . . .
7. No specific courses should be required in colleges or universities.

7

Using Sources

Research is formalized curiosity. It is poking and prying with a purpose.
— ZORA NEALE HURSTON

There is no way of exchanging information that does not involve an act of judgment.
— JACOB BRONOWSKI

I have yet to see any problem, however complicated, which, when you looked at it in the right way, did not become still more complicated.
— POUL ANDERSON

A university is just a group of buildings gathered around a library.
— SHELBY FOOTE

Why Use Sources?

We have pointed out that one gets ideas by writing. While prewriting and drafting, ideas form and stimulate further ideas, especially when you question and *think critically* about what you are writing. Of course, when writing about complex, serious questions, nobody is expected to invent all the answers out of thin air. On the contrary, a writer is expected to be familiar with the chief answers already produced by others and to make use of them through selective incorporation and criticism. When you write about an issue, you are not expected to reinvent the wheel; sometimes, simply adding a spoke is enough.

You may be familiar with some directives about research from previous courses. Your instructors may have asked you to locate three sources, or four sources, or six sources, and to use those sources in support of an argument (perhaps with some added requirement that one or more of these be scholarly sources). However, your teachers generally do not want you simply to go out and find a fixed number of sources to plug in to your essay for the sake of it. The goal of research is more idealistic. The point is not that a minimum number of sources is right for every argument, nor is it to send you off on a scavenger hunt for types of sources. Instead, research is intended to encourage learning, thoughtful engagement with a topic, and the production of an informed view.

ENTERING A DISCOURSE

Kenneth Burke (1887–1993), one of America's most important theorists of rhetoric, wrote:

> Imagine that you enter a parlor. You come late. When you arrive, others have long preceded you, and they are engaged in a heated discussion, a discussion too heated for them to pause and tell you exactly what it is about. In fact, the discussion had already begun long before any of them got there, so that no one present is qualified to retrace for you all the steps that had gone before. You listen for a while, until you decide that you have caught the tenor of the argument; then you put in your oar. Someone answers; you answer him; another comes to your defense; another aligns himself against you, to either the embarrassment or gratification of your opponent, depending upon the quality of your ally's assistance. However, the discussion is interminable. The hour grows late, you must depart. And you do depart, with the discussion still vigorously in progress.[1]

When you are writing, imagine you are entering a discussion, but not a live one as in Burke's analogy. Imagine instead you are entering into a **discourse**. A discourse is a type of discussion, surely. But unlike a live conversation, a discourse takes place over a longer period of time among many participants in various types of writing and public venues. A discourse is a conversation writ large, one that has gone on before you enter the fray, and one that will likely continue after you leave.

So why are sources important in discourse?

- The first answer is practical: You use sources because they are where conversations about important topics occur.
- The second is more idealistic: It is your responsibility as an intelligent citizen to participate meaningfully in discourses.

From sources, you learn what the facts are, what issues are current, and what positions certain people or groups are taking on the issues. Through sources, you discover new ideas, questions, and answers. When you perform research on a topic, you are *finding*, *evaluating*, and *synthesizing* sources so as to position yourself to speak within that kind of conversation known as a discourse.

Two caveats are important. First, although we will discuss finding, evaluating, and synthesizing sources separately, once you begin researching you will see that these activities are not entirely separable. As you find sources, you will simultaneously be assessing their relevancy and value (evaluating) and placing sources into conversation with one another (synthesizing) while considering ways to integrate them into your own writing.

Second, the boundaries of discourse are not clear-cut. Obviously, many conversations about many different topics occur constantly in a variety of places. We may speak generally of political discourse, scientific discourse, or economic discourse, and we may speak more particularly of discourses on women's rights, environmentalism, or taxation. Any subject at all may be thought

[1] *The Philosophy of Literary Form* (Baton Rouge: Louisiana State University Press, 1941), 110–11.

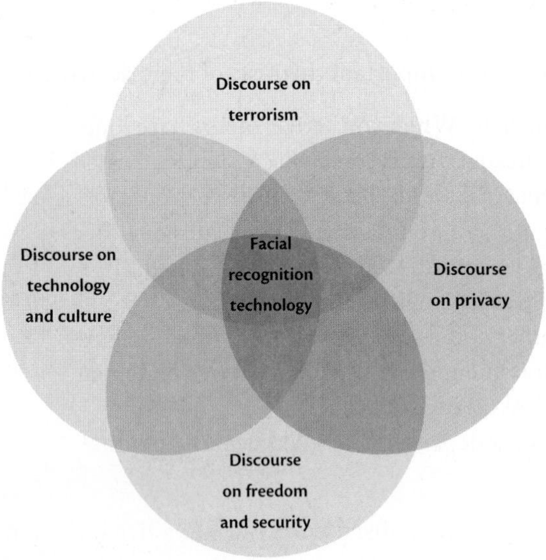

Intersecting discourses

of in terms of the discourses (or conversations) that take place about it. Consider, for example, the conversation about security and freedom in the United States. This conversation — this *discourse* — has been ongoing since the nation was founded, and it continues today. In articles, essays, speeches, legal reviews, court opinions, congressional debates, and elsewhere, people continue to weigh the appropriate balance between security and freedom: The country needs to be kept safe, and so law enforcement agencies are granted many powers to investigate, detect, and prevent lawbreaking, yet American citizens are also protected by the US Constitution from unwarranted harassment, search and seizure, and other invasions of privacy. Today, terrorism, illegal immigration, stop-and-frisk practices, and cybersecurity are just a few areas of focus in this conversation-writ-large. Within each of those categories, even narrower conversations occur. Airport security, border security, cell phone searches, facial recognition technology — the list goes on and on. Many combined, overlapping conversations (some very general, some quite specific) may all be said to be part of this *discourse* about freedom and security. Even fictional novels, plays, films, and television shows contribute to the discourse. A television series like *House of Cards* (2013–2018) or a blockbuster superhero movie like *Captain America: Winter Soldier* (2014) can represent and spur discussion about topical issues related to freedom and security — and potentially be a rich source for research and analysis to support your own argument and entry into the conversation.

A **discourse community** is any group of people who share general interests, assumptions, and values and who communicate with one another in some form of media, usually adhering to a set of conventions for that communication. For example, imagine a professor of physics who is active in the scientific discourse on thermodynamics, publishing his theories in academic books and articles. In those, he is addressing one discourse community of scientists and experts in a particular type of writing style or genre. But maybe he is also an environmentalist in his hometown who publishes on the Sierra Club blog and posts videos about local ecology. And maybe he is also a fan of X-Men and writes passionately about the Marvel mutants on a listserv dedicated to that series. In those cases, he is addressing narrower discourse communities.

Now, this hypothetical professor would be likely to research and write differently depending on which discourse community he is engaging. Understanding discourse communities is important because it can help you

- focus your own research by determining which types of sources you need to seek,
- evaluate the sources you find,

- define your audience and purpose in writing, and
- write more persuasively.

UNDERSTANDING INFORMATION LITERACY

During your college courses — and in work and daily life — you will be reading and listening to ongoing conversations within and among discourse communities. Sometimes, you will want (or need) to participate yourself. You will have to interject, responding to issues by speaking and writing. Thus, when you set out to learn about and contribute to a discourse, how you discover, evaluate, and use your sources is crucial. Together, these are integrated skills known as **information literacy**. According to the Association of College and Research Libraries, these skills encompass

- the thoughtful and reflective discovery of information,
- the understanding of how information is produced and valued, and
- the ethical use of information in creating new ideas by participating in various academic or civic discourses.

Information literacy involves being able to survey what and how knowledge circulates about a topic, thinking critically while you learn. It allows you to see what kinds of questions have been raised and what answers have been provided. As you poke and pry into a topic, you can distinguish between strong and weak sources and separate the wheat from the chaff.

Information literacy skills are necessary to be able to navigate the vast fields of information to which we are exposed constantly in the digital media environment. Even when we are trying to be diligent in our efforts to find quality sources, we face obstacles. Search engines, for example, simply cannot index, curate, and return results from the billions of websites on the ever-expanding internet. This means we need to develop skills on *how* to search: how to use search operators and phrases to limit the results we get and how to search for only certain kinds of websites or file types. But even the best search strategies will not return full-length published books or password-protected content such as subscription-only magazines, newspapers, and journals, many of which are carefully edited and vetted for quality (and are often the best possible sources).

Further, we should also be aware that search engines are not neutral. They commonly return results that are most popular (or most highly paid for), not necessarily those that are most thorough, interesting, or reliable. Some search engines tailor the top results to your previous searches and online activity through "personalized" search results, leading to an information ecosystem susceptible to "filter bubble" and "echo chamber" effects in which people are led to information limited by a single perspective or ideology. If you are searching for a political topic and your search engine knows your political leanings, it will likely return in your top results webpages that reflect your political views. This practice seriously raises the potential for confirmation bias (discussed on p. 79).

Once you narrow in on a topic and adopt a central idea or position on an issue — a thesis — your ability to persuade an audience will depend on the sources you provide, evaluate, and cite. Even one citation of a fraudulent website or one uncritical reference to a highly partisan or narrowly ideological source can undermine your credibility. On the other hand, well-researched and thoughtfully discussed sources show that you are an educated participant in a discourse — or even one small area of it — who is equipped with foundational facts and evidence drawn from reputable sources; you have an argument worth listening to.

Choosing a Topic

Because of the complexity of discourses — the plurality of topics, issues, ideas, and opinions (in so many different forms and from so many different groups) — the research process isn't straightforward and neat. Research is a form of inquiry that can range from finding answers to simple questions to exploring complex topics, problems, or issues discussed within or among discourse communities. Part of conducting a successful, fruitful research effort is first selecting an area of focus and narrowing the scope of your research to suit the needs of your assignments or interests.

If a topic is not assigned, choose one that

- interests you, and
- can be researched with reasonable thoroughness in the allotted time.

Topics such as censorship, the environment, and sexual harassment obviously impinge on our lives, and it may well be that one such topic is of special interest to you. But the breadth of these topics (like with freedom vs. security, discussed earlier) makes researching them potentially overwhelming. Type the word *censorship* into an internet search engine, and you will be referred to millions of information sources.

This brings us to our second point: getting a manageable topic. Any of the previous topics would need to be refined substantially before you could begin researching in earnest. Similarly, even more specific topics such as "the effects of the Holocaust" can hardly be mastered in a few weeks or argued in a ten-page paper. They are simply too big. (The questions that immediately come to mind are, What kind of effects do you mean? Political effects? Psychological effects? For whom? Where? When? Where will you find the evidence?) Getting a manageable topic often means working on one area of a larger puzzle, pinpointing the places where you can add your piece. You can do that by

- seeking gaps or areas of conflict within or among discourses (places where you can weigh in) or
- breaking down complex topics, issues, or debates into simpler questions (perhaps focusing on one question informing the larger issue).

WRITING TIP
You may think you have little to contribute to conversations whose participants are illustrious authorities and experts. However, by dint of being a student, you have a unique perspective: You are on the edge of the future, able to apply new questions and issues in the present to those old primary and secondary resources. Or maybe you may have a purpose for writing that is fundamentally different from anyone else's.

By focusing your research on one area within a broader discourse, you can limit the range and types of resources you consult based on your circumstances and goals. As you research, you may find yourself drawn toward even more specific questions. If you were writing about the psychological effects of the Holocaust, for instance, you could focus on an affected ethnic group like Jewish people or focus further on German, French, Russian, or American Jews; you could define a time frame; or you could deal with a specific postwar generation, or consider a group within that generation, such as women, men, children, or second-generation survivors (those born after the war). If you chose to develop your analysis around specific traumatic events, places, or even practices, such as the use of gas chambers, you might seek evidence in psychological studies, memoirs, and testimony or in the arts.

One strategy for narrowing your topic is, first, to find your general topic and then apply some basic questions to discover how you might find an entry point into the conversations about it.

Find Relevance

- What are some of the ways people have been discussing this topic recently?
- To whom — that is, to what groups or audiences — is this topic especially important now?
- Is there any data, any evidence, or an example that arguments on this topic have not yet accounted for?

Develop a New Approach

- What is most important or interesting to *me* about this topic?
- Is there a perspective or an application that has been underreported in the discourses on this topic?
- Can I ask new questions by thinking politically, historically, religiously, scientifically, psychologically, philosophically, culturally — or in some combination of these?

Determine Your Research Goals and Writing Context

- Where do I stand?
- What type of audience do I want to reach most?
- How do I want to position myself in the discourse on this topic (i.e., in what genre, in what format will I make myself heard, including considerations of length and depth)?

Exercise: Exploring Your Topic

Once you've narrowed your focus, spend a little time exploring your topic to see if you can locate interesting conversations and manageable topics or issues by taking one or more of these approaches:

- ***Do a web search on the topic.*** You can quickly put your finger on the pulse of popular approaches to a topic by scanning the first page or two of results to see who is talking about it (individuals, groups, etc.) and in what forms (articles, news, blogs, etc.).
- ***Plug the topic into one of the library's article databases.*** Just by scanning the titles in a general database, you can get a sense of what questions have been and are currently being raised about your topic.
- ***Browse the library shelves where books on the topic are kept.*** A quick check of the tables of contents of recently published books may give you ideas of how to narrow your topic.
- ***Ask a librarian to show you where specialized reference books on your topic are found.*** Instead of general encyclopedias, try sources like *CQ Researcher* or *Encyclopedia of Science, Technology, and Ethics.*
- ***Talk to an expert.*** Members of the faculty who specialize in the area of your topic might be able to point you to key sources and discourses.

Finding Sources

Your sources' quality and integrity are crucial to your own credibility and to the strength of your argument. In Chapters 5 and 6, we discussed *ethos* as an appeal that establishes credibility with readers. When you do competent research, you let your audience see that you have done your homework, which thereby increases your *ethos*. Sources, we mean to say, provide evidence in support of your argument, but they also collectively serve as evidence that you are familiar with the discourses on your topic, that you know what you're talking about, and that your interpretation is sound.

To find good sources, you must have a strategy for searching. What strategy you use will depend on your topic. Researching a social problem or a new economic policy may involve reading recent newspaper articles, scanning information on government websites, and locating current statistics. On the other hand, researching the meaning of a pop culture trend, for example, may be best tackled by seeking out books and scholarly journal articles on the sociological nature of fashion and also some popular style magazines or videos to use as evidence. In all your research, you will be attempting to identify the places where conversations on your topic are taking place — in specific academic journals, magazines, websites, annual conferences, and so on. By noting what is common among your sources, what data and evidence are shared, you may find other authoritative sources and get leads on further research.

If your topic warrants it, you may also want to supplement your library or internet research with your own fieldwork. You could conduct surveys or interviews, design an experiment, or visit a museum. You could perform research in an archive or other repository to analyze original documents or artifacts. This kind of research is called **primary research** because you are the one gathering the basic evidence and data. **Secondary research** is the term given to the kind of inquiry that involves your study of research done by others.

Visual Guide: Finding Discourse on Your Topic

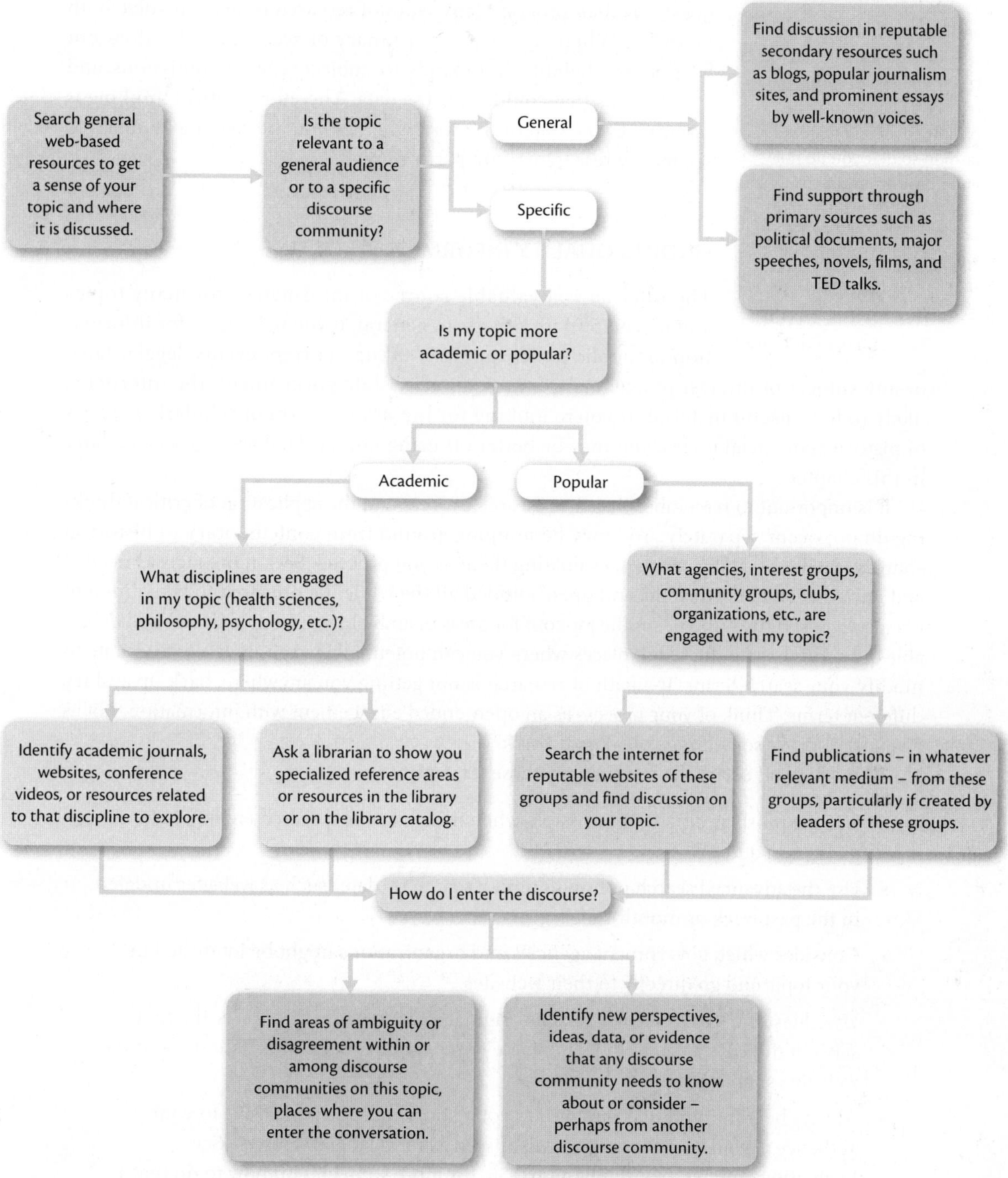
Search general web-based resources to get a sense of your topic and where it is discussed.
Is the topic relevant to a general audience or to a specific discourse community?
General
Specific
Find discussion in reputable secondary resources such as blogs, popular journalism sites, and prominent essays by well-known voices.
Find support through primary sources such as political documents, major speeches, novels, films, and TED talks.
Is my topic more academic or popular?
Academic
Popular
What disciplines are engaged in my topic (health sciences, philosophy, psychology, etc.)?
What agencies, interest groups, community groups, clubs, organizations, etc., are engaged with my topic?
Identify academic journals, websites, conference videos, or resources related to that discipline to explore.
Ask a librarian to show you specialized reference areas or resources in the library or on the library catalog.
Search the internet for reputable websites of these groups and find discussion on your topic.
Find publications – in whatever relevant medium – from these groups, particularly if created by leaders of these groups.
How do I enter the discourse?
Find areas of ambiguity or disagreement within or among discourse communities on this topic, places where you can enter the conversation.
Identify new perspectives, ideas, data, or evidence that any discourse community needs to know about or consider – perhaps from another discourse community.

RESEARCH TIP
Practice the prewriting and invention strategies we discuss in earlier chapters to help guide your research. Keep your notes on sources in an organized fashion so that you do not end up with a lot of links, digital files, printouts, and books, with no record of what you thought about them.

One form of research is not necessarily better than the other, although some may be better suited to certain topics or research questions than others. Many types of research projects involve both methods. Whether research is primary or secondary also does not bear on its reliability. Both kinds are subject to biases, omissions, and assumptions that could color the data. Therefore, critical thinking is essential every step of the way, whether you are seeking primary or secondary research or are performing it.

FINDING QUALITY INFORMATION ONLINE

The internet is a valuable source of information for many topics and less helpful for others. In general, if you're looking for information on public policy, popular culture, current events, legal affairs, or any subject of interest to agencies of the federal or state government, the internet is likely to have useful material. If you're looking for literary criticism or scholarly analysis of historical or social issues, you may be better off using library databases, described later in this chapter.

It is important to remember that the research process and the application of critical thinking do not occur separately: You may be jumping around from contemporary to historical sources, databases, and webpages, evaluating them as you proceed. Seek more facts as needed and remain adaptable, flexible, and open-minded all the while. Be prepared to take different perspectives seriously and be on the lookout for areas of ambiguity, unsettled issues, and debatable questions. Again, these are places where you can potentially weigh in. Do not hesitate to modify your search terms. If a path of research is not getting you anywhere, back up and try different terms. Think of your process as an open-ended engagement with information, not as an effort to prove something you already think.

To make good use of the internet, try these strategies:

- Use the most specific terms possible when using a general search engine; put phrases in quotes.
- Use the advanced search option to limit a search by date (such as websites updated in the past week or month).
- Consider which government agencies and organizations might be interested in your topic and go directly to their websites.
- Use clues in URLs to see where sites originate. Delete everything after the first slash in the URL to go to the parent site to see if it provides information about the website's source, origin, or purpose.
- Always bear in mind that the sources you choose must be persuasive to your audience. Avoid sites that may be dismissed as unreliable or biased. (See Evaluating Sources, beginning on p. 255, for more strategies on how to do that.)

A WORD ABOUT *WIKIPEDIA* Links to *Wikipedia* often rise to the top of search results. This vast and decentralized site provides nearly six million articles on a wide variety of topics. However, anyone can contribute to the online encyclopedia, so the accuracy of articles varies, and in some cases, the coverage of a controversial issue is one-sided or disputed. In other cases, businesses, political campaigns, and public relations firms patrol *Wikipedia* and manage their own or their clients' "online reputation" by adding and subtracting information from the website. Nevertheless, many articles are accurate, particularly when they are noncontroversial; however, like any encyclopedia, they provide only basic information. *Wikipedia*'s founder, Jimmy Wales, cautions students against using it as a source, except for obtaining general background knowledge: "You're in college; don't cite the encyclopedia."[2] *Wikipedia* is most valuable when you use it for basic undisputed facts or to locate bibliographies that will help you conduct further independent research.

FINDING ARTICLES USING LIBRARY DATABASES

Your library has a wide range of general and specialized databases available through its website. When you search through a database, you are searching within an electronic index of citations from published sources, both popular and scholarly. Some databases provide references to articles (and perhaps abstracts or summaries), and some provide direct links to the full text of entire articles.

Through your school library, you may have access to general and interdisciplinary databases such as Academic Search Premier (produced by the EBSCOhost company) and Expanded Academic Index (from InfoTrac), which provide access to thousands of publications, including both scholarly and popular sources. LexisNexis or ProQuest Newsstand are particularly useful for newspaper articles that are not available for free online. More specialized databases include PsycINFO (for psychology research) and ERIC (focused on topics in education). Others, such as JSTOR, are full-text digital archives of scholarly journals. Some databases offer the archives of a single publication, like the *New York Times*, *Wall Street Journal*, or *JAMA* (the *Journal of the American Medical Association*). Others offer scientific, medical, or economic data exclusively (such as Web of Science, MEDLINE, EconLit), and still others are virtual archives (such as African American Newspapers of the Nineteenth Century or The Sixties, a searchable database of independent newspapers and ephemera of that age). Some databases offer art (ArtStor), video (Films on Demand), music (Database of Recorded American Music [DRAM]), or photography (Associated Press Images Collection). Others may offer excellent resources for highly specific material: The Burns Archive, for example, offers one million historic photographs and is recognized by

> **RESEARCH TIP**
> Beware of trying to find the "perfect source." Students often get frustrated with the research process because they have an excellent original idea but cannot find analysis, commentary, or opinion that directly supports it. Although it may not feel like it, not being able to find sources may actually be a *good* thing: It may indicate you have an original perspective or argument, a perfect place to add your voice.

[2] "Wikipedia Founder Discourages Academic Use of His Creation," *Chronicle of Higher Education Wired Campus*, June 12, 2006, http://www.chronicle.com/wiredcampus/article/1328/wikipedia-founder-discourages-academic-use-of-his-creation.

scholars as a primary resource for early medical photography. Look at your library's website and find out where you can browse the databases.

As you can see, databases abound. To navigate them and find the right one for your topic and project, look at your library's offerings and roll your cursor over database titles to get some information about the scope and holdings of each one. Never hesitate to ask a librarian at the reference desk for a quick tutorial on how to use your university databases — after all, you technically pay for these subscriptions through your tuition.

When using databases for research, first choose a topic, then narrow your topic using the strategies outlined earlier in this chapter. List synonyms for your key search terms. As you search, look at words used in titles and descriptors for alternative ideas and make use of the "advanced search" option so that you can easily combine multiple terms. Rarely will you find exactly what you're looking for right away. Try different search terms and different ways to narrow your topic. Consider limiting the date range of your search to find historical sources on your topic or narrowing results to show scholarly journal articles only.

Most databases have an advanced search option that offers fillable forms for combining multiple terms. In Figure 7.1, we show a search field using Boolean operators (AND, OR, and NOT) to seek targeted information on the use of anabolic steroids. Because a simple search of "anabolic steroids" retrieved far too many results, we used this advanced search to combine three concepts: anabolic steroids, legal aspects of their use, and use of them by athletes. Related terms are combined with the word "or": *law* or *legal*. The last letters of a word have been replaced with an asterisk so that any ending will be included in the search. *Athlet** will search for *athlete, athletes,* or *athletics.* Options on both sides of the list of articles retrieved offer opportunities to refine a search by date of publication or to restrict the results

Figure 7.1 A Database Search

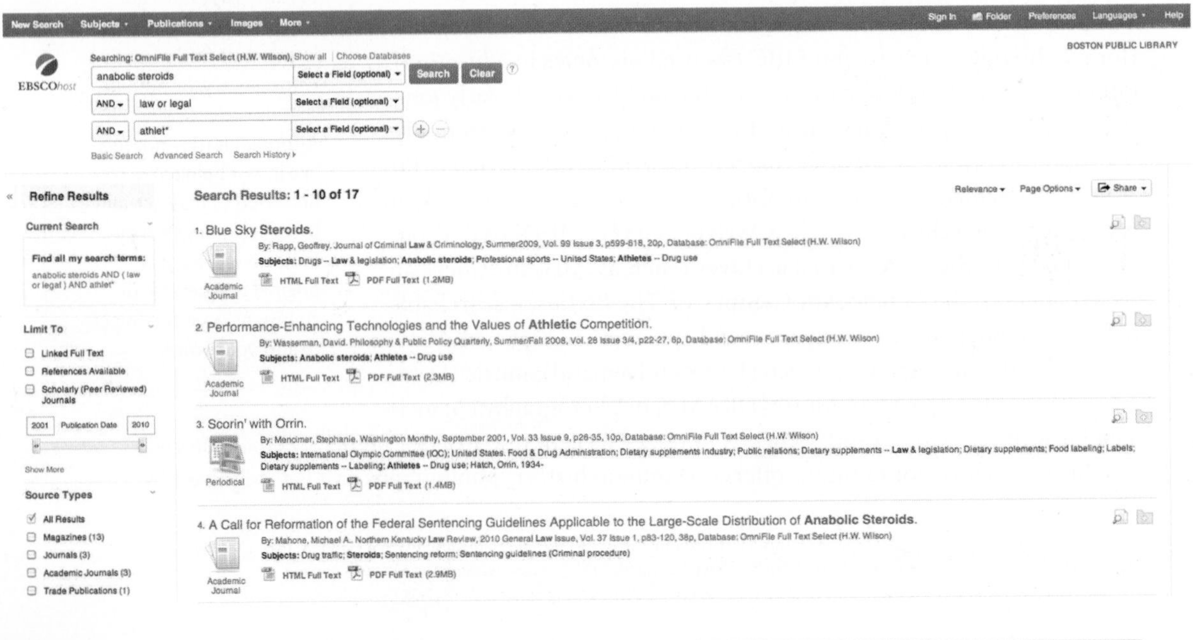

to only academic journals, magazines, or newspapers. Notice in Figure 7.2 some further ways to limit your searches.

As with an internet search, when you search through databases, you'll need to make critical choices about which articles are worth pursuing. Some results may not be useful. A title might tell you right away that a source is not exactly about your topic, or you might notice that the publication date is not relevant to your questions. The subject lines may contain some keywords associated with your topic (or not), and if you open the source, you may find an abstract that tells you more about the contents and findings of the source. All these leads can let you know how much further to look into your source.

Don't forget that your sources need not have links to the full text for you to retrieve them easily. It is the role of a library to get you the information you need. If you cannot link to the full text of an article you want to read, find your library's Interlibrary Loan (ILL) system, which you can use to request books and copies of articles to be sent to your library for you. Often, ILL materials take less than a day for electronic delivery and anywhere from two days to two weeks for physical books.

> **RESEARCH TIP**
> Sources that at first appear to be unrelated to your topic may actually be *relatable* to your topic. If you are writing about poor labor conditions in US clothing companies' supply chains in Asia, and you find an article about the working conditions of agricultural laborers in South America, don't just cast that article aside. Rather, explore the possible overlaps. Determine whether or not you can apply one situation to the other.

As you choose and use sources, keep track of them. You can save them in a folder, or you can use your library's system for selecting and saving resources. You can save, email, or print the references you have selected. You may also have an option to export references to a citation management program such as RefWorks or EndNote. These programs allow you to create your own personal database of sources in which you can store your references and take notes. Later, when you're ready to create a bibliography, these programs will automatically format your references in MLA, APA, or another style. Ask a librarian if one of these programs is available to students on your campus.

Figure 7.2 Advanced Search Options

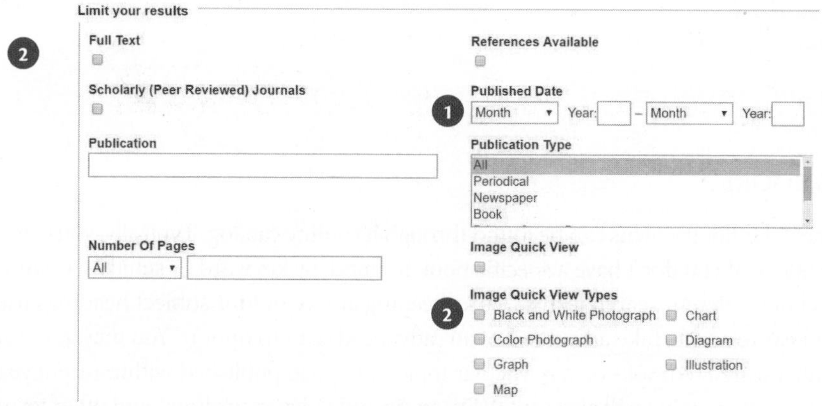

1 Drop-down menus specify types of documents, types of publications, languages, and dates.

2 Check boxes specify full text, references, cover stories, image types, and file types.

THINKING CRITICALLY *Using Search Terms*

Imagine that your research question is this: Should first-year college students be required to live on campus? Identify useful key issues, terms, and related terms that you can use to search. (The first row has been completed as an example.)

QUESTION	KEY TERMS	RELATED TERMS	SEARCH TERMS
Should first-year college students be required to live on campus?	first-year students required to live on campus	freshmen freshman year residency policies residence hall requirement dorm dormitory	freshman OR first-year student* Residency rules OR residence requirement dorm*
Which schools have a first-year residency requirement, and which do not?			
What are the benefits and drawbacks of living on campus?			
How do alternative on- or off-campus living situations compare?			

LOCATING BOOKS

The books that your library owns can be found through its online catalog. Typically, you can search by author or title or, if you don't have a specific book in mind, by keyword or subject. As with databases, think about different search terms to use, keeping an eye out for subject headings used for books that appear relevant. Take advantage of an "advanced search" option. You may, for example, be able to limit a search to books on a particular topic in English published within recent years. In addition to books, the catalog will also list DVDs, audio and video recordings, and other formats.

Unlike articles, books tend to cover broad topics, so be prepared to broaden your search terms. It may be that a book has a chapter or ten pages that are precisely what you need, but the catalog typically doesn't index the contents of books in detail. Think instead of what kind of book might contain the information you need.

Once you've found some promising books in the catalog, note down the call numbers, find them on the shelves, and then browse. Because books on the same topic are shelved together, you can quickly see what additional books are available by scanning the shelves. As you browse, be sure to look for books that have been published recently enough for your purposes. You do not have to read a book from cover to cover to use it in your research. Instead, skim the introduction to see if it will be useful and then use its table of contents and index to pinpoint the sections of the book that are the most relevant.

If you are searching for a very specific name or phrase, you might try typing it into Google Book Search (books.google.com), which searches the contents of more than twenty-five million scanned books. Although it tends to retrieve too many results for most topics and you may only be able to see a snippet of content, it can help you locate a particular quote or identify which books might include an unusual name or phrase. There is a "find in a library" link that will help you determine whether the books are available in your library.

Exercise: Practicing Research

Select one of the research questions below or use one you're currently working on. Using the Visual Guide: Finding Discourse on Your Topic as well as the instruction in this chapter, determine the best research strategy: General internet searching? Library databases? Books? Narrow it down: Which websites will you visit? Which databases will you use? What books can you peruse by searching your library's catalog?

Research Question 1: How do children's toys impact the development of gender?

Research Question 2: What are the dangers and benefits of nationalism?

Research Question 3: Should big college sports programs pay athletes?

Then, find your sources online, in the database, or in your library's catalog. Use words or phrases from the research question and combine them with your own words to search for related information to answer it. Practice maneuvers like limiting results by date range, looking for scholarly and popular sources, searching for images, or seeking only certain kinds of documents.

Evaluating Sources

Each step of the way in your research process, you will be making choices about your sources. As you proceed, from selecting promising items in a database search to browsing the book collection, you will want to use the techniques for previewing and skimming detailed on pages 33–36 in order to make your selections and develop your argument as you research. Begin by asking yourself some basic questions:

- Is this source relevant?
- Is it current enough?

- Does the title or abstract suggest it will address an important aspect of my topic?
- Am I choosing sources that represent a range of ideas, not simply ones that support my opinion?
- Do I have a reason to believe that these sources are trustworthy?

Once you have collected a number of likely sources, you will want to do further filtering. Examine each one with these questions in mind:

- ***Is this source credible? Does it include information about the author and his or her credentials that can help me decide whether to rely on it?*** In the case of books, you might check a database for book reviews for a second opinion. In the case of websites, find out where the site came from and why it has been posted online. Don't use a source if you can't determine its authorship or purpose.
- ***Will my audience find this source credible and persuasive?*** A story about US politics from the *Washington Post*, whose writers conduct firsthand reporting in the nation's capital, carries more clout than a story from a small-circulation newspaper that is drawing its information from a wire service.
- ***Am I using the best evidence available?*** Quoting directly from a government report may be more effective than quoting a news story that summarizes the report. Finding evidence that supports your claims in a president's speeches or letters is more persuasive than drawing your conclusions from a page or two of a history textbook.
- ***Am I being fair to all sides?*** Make sure you are prepared to address alternate perspectives, even if you ultimately take a position. Avoid sources that clearly promote an agenda in favor of ones that your audience will consider balanced and reliable.
- ***Can I corroborate my key claims in more than one source?*** Compare your sources to ensure that you aren't relying on facts that can't be confirmed. If you're having trouble confirming a source, check with a librarian.
- ***Do I really need this source?*** It's tempting to use all the books and articles you have found, but if two sources say essentially the same thing, choose the one that is likely to carry the most weight with your audience.

RESEARCH TIP
During your research, write down observations and questions. This way, you won't find yourself with a pile of printouts and books and no idea what to say about them. What you have to say will flow naturally out of the prewriting you've already done — and that prewriting will help guide your further research.

SCHOLARLY, POPULAR, AND TRADE SOURCES

An important part of finding and evaluating the reliability of your sources is determining whether they are **scholarly** or **popular** sources. In the table shown on p. 258, we cover some of the basic elements that distinguish these two types of publications. We also examine a third category called **trade** publications.

Scholarly publications are generally considered the gold standard of reliability in the production of knowledge and the circulation of discourse. This is primarily because scholarly publications are generally

- nonprofit;
- built on a mission to advance knowledge in a specific area;
- organized according to disciplinary methodologies, standards, and ethics; and
- peer-reviewed or refereed (meaning that before publication, the articles are reviewed and accepted by a group of experts in that field and in that specific area).

Popular publications — newspapers, magazines, newsletters, websites, blogs — may be more or less reliable sources, but they generally do not carry the academic weight of scholarly ones. Popular sources have relative value: Some have high journalistic and editorial standards — think of the *Los Angeles Times* or the *Economist* magazine — and may contain articles and essays by respected journalists and experts — even scholars. But even intellectual magazines like *Science* or the *New Yorker* are popular publications in the same sense that *Cosmopolitan, Game Informer, Better Homes and Gardens*, or *Car and Driver* are: They are written for a general audience, and they are driven by profit.

Consider the implications. Magazines and newspapers must publish articles that sell to broad audiences; indeed, the goal of any commercial media enterprise is to make money from sales, subscriptions, and sponsors. Therefore, they are not as likely as academic sources to offer the widest range of subjects or perspectives, the same level of complexity, or the deepest, most thorough, and thoughtful forms of analysis.

Trade publications, the third category of sources, are more related to publications in the popular category; however, trade sources are designed for people in particular industries and professional associations. They sometimes appear to be very complex because they assume that readers are familiar with an insider's vocabulary. However, they are not popular because they are not for a general audience, and they are not scholarly because they do not involve a peer review process. Nevertheless, trade publications often utilize the latest field-specific research and expert voices and may be considered reliable resources in many cases. That said, we must remember that industry groups are likely to interpret issues through the lens of their interests — so, for example, *Coal Age* magazine (published by Mining Media International) and *SNLEnergy* (published by the American Coal Council) are much more likely to view coal production and use favorably as compared to *Solar Today Magazine* (published by the American Solar Energy Society).

Remember that just because something is published in a scholarly journal doesn't mean it is peer reviewed. In some journals, a peer-reviewed article may sit side by side with a book review or an editorial. Popular magazines will almost never contain scholarly articles; a respected scholar might contribute an original essay to a popular magazine, but again that doesn't mean the article is "scholarly."

Types of Sources

	Scholarly	Popular	Trade
Publisher	Universities, government agencies, research foundations, and institutions	Media companies, for-profit groups, internet website owners, interest groups	Professional associations, trade groups, unions, business groups, consortiums
Purpose	To report on research, experiments, and theories to expand human knowledge	To inform, entertain, and engage; to expand influence or profit or both	To inform, entertain, and engage; to expand influence in a specific field or industry
Audience	Academics, intellectuals, specialists, researchers	General public	People who have interests in a specific trade or industry
Language	Complex, technical, authoritative	Accessible, conversational	Accessible but with insider-speak such as jargon and acronyms
Sources cited	Always	Sometimes, usually through in-text reference or hyperlinks	Sometimes, usually through in-text reference or hyperlinks
Features and characteristics	Plain style; lots of footnotes or endnotes, long articles; few advertisements (if any); often charts and graphs; longer paragraphs and titles; peer reviewed	Glossy, attractive style; shorter and easier-to-digest articles; many advertisements; simple charts and graphs; shorter paragraphs and titles (if any); not peer reviewed	Various styles ranging from newsprint to glossy styles; technical but easier-to-digest articles, titles indicating industry-specific issues, advertising related to field; not peer reviewed
Frequency	Usually quarterly, semiannually	Usually daily, weekly, biweekly, monthly	Sometimes quarterly or semiannually; most often daily, weekly, monthly, bimonthly
Examples	*American Journal of Sociology, Harvard Asia Pacific Review, Foreign Affairs,* government reports	*Time, New York Times, Vogue, Popular Mechanics, HuffPost, Business Insider*	*AdWeek, Publishers Weekly, Columbia Journalism Review, Chronicle of Higher Education, Comics and Games Retailer*

EVALUATING ONLINE SOURCES

Unlike the information found in a library or published and circulated widely in print, much information online does not go through an evaluative process, as when librarians curate their collections or an editor reviews and selects material for a publication. Thus, one of the first things you must do to determine the quality and reliability of information online is consider the pathway of its publication on the internet. Did the information pass through any review process? Who was doing the reviewing? If the comments section in the *New York Times* shows someone claiming to be a doctor giving advice on some health issue, should you believe it? After all, you too could claim to be a doctor and publish your comments somewhere. At the same time, it may be that the commentator *is* a doctor and *is* reliable — but how would you know? In this hypothetical case, we would recommend corroborating the alleged doctor's claim using a respectable, reviewed medical publication (even if it happens to be openly available online).

Today, most print publications offer their content online in a digital format. However, there are also reliable online resources that are not duplicated in print, from high-quality citizen journalism to TED talks to university lectures online. There may be thoughtful blogs or other publication formats (video, podcast, indexes) created or curated by people who have a high degree of credibility, but you must be cautious. The popularity of a website, blog, or podcast does not automatically confer expertise upon the creators or producers. Neither does the way a website *looks*. Given the ease of entry into the marketplace of ideas via the internet and the relative ease of designing a professional-looking webpage, the popularity and design of a website cannot be considered key criteria in evaluating reliability.

A further problem is caused by the surge in disreputable publication venues that offer open-access publishing in journals that appear to be peer reviewed but really have dramatically lower standards — or none at all. These venues are usually predatory: They project the veneer of a scholarly journal, often with academic-sounding titles to match. For a fee, or sometimes for free (if they are ad revenue–based), these "journals" will publish material with little or no quality control. They are primary locations for fraudulent and hoax papers. Be wary of online journals discovered on the open internet and review them very carefully. It is always safer to use your university databases for scholarly sources.

Nevertheless, it is likely most of us will seek sources on the internet. The best steps you can take to remain a skeptical but open-minded researcher is to apply critical thinking skills. The first thing to do is consider all the contexts that inform your online sources:

- How did they get onto the internet?
- What organizations or individuals are behind their publication?
- Were they originally published elsewhere?
- What are the limitations of this particular kind of online resource?

- Why is this type of source a legitimate form of evidence in the context of your analysis?
- What special authority does the individual or group cited have for speaking on an issue?

WRITING TIP
You can use (and cite) the information you find on websites, in blogs, in comments, and on social media posts; just make sure you frame that information with a fair accounting of the source. ("One user on YouTube with the handle *SportsTVFan* commented that the latest Super Bowl commercials are 'X.'" or "Twitter user @DavidScottRedpath, an amateur astronomer with over a million followers, posted a tweet that claimed *X* about black holes.")

With so much information online, you don't always get the basic indicators of authority, such as author credentials or an indication of editorial review. Remember that anyone can publish online with no review process. All that is needed is access to the internet.

You need not discount information available online, though; the internet provides a stunning array of unique perspectives and analyses. It has made it possible for people everywhere to contribute their arguments, opinions, and comments to public discourses.

Many students have been told to examine the domains of websites to judge the reliability of a source; however, whether a website is a *.com*, *.org*, or *.edu* is a weak marker of a source's reliability. All domain types can host reliable or unreliable information. Similarly, tweets and comments, even when written by experts, may or may not carry much weight depending on the subject and occasion of their tweets or comments.

The information you will look for as you evaluate internet sources is often the same as what you need to record in any citation. Use clues in URLs to see where sites originate. For example, URLs containing *.k12* are hosted at elementary and secondary schools, so they may be intended for a young audience; those ending in *.gov* are government agencies, so they tend to provide official information, but if a *.gov* website is followed by a country code, you must also consider the context of place revealed by that origin. A website with a domain such as *.gov.ca* (Canada) may be more trustworthy than one from a country where freedoms of speech are curtailed, such as *.gov.kp* (North Korea). You can streamline the process of creating a list of works cited by identifying these elements as you find and begin to evaluate a source. (See Documentation later in this chapter for more on how to properly cite sources.)

In Figure 7.3, the URL includes the ending *.gov*, meaning it is a government website, an official document that has been vetted. There is an "about" link that will explain the government agency's mission. This appears to be a high-quality source of basic information on the issue. The information you need to cite this report is also on the page; make sure you keep track of where you found the source and when, since websites can change. One way to keep track is by creating an account at a social bookmarking site such as Diigo (diigo.com) where you can store and annotate websites.

Figure 7.3 A Page from a Government Website

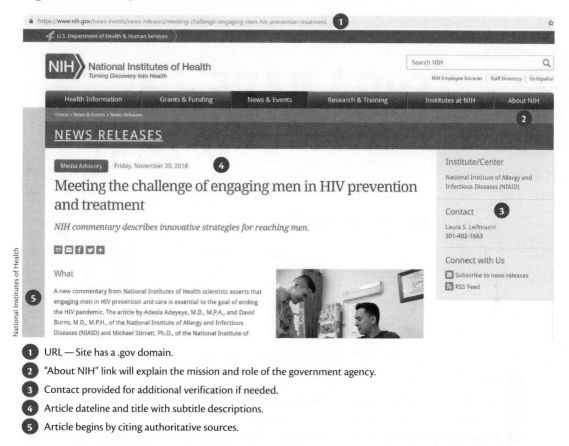

National Institutes of Health

1. URL — Site has a .gov domain.
2. "About NIH" link will explain the mission and role of the government agency.
3. Contact provided for additional verification if needed.
4. Article dateline and title with subtitle descriptions.
5. Article begins by citing authoritative sources.

Figure 7.4 on page 262 shows how the information on a web page might lead you to reject it as a source. Clearly, although this site purports to provide educational information in a well-meaning way, its primary purpose is to sell services and products. The focus on marketing should send up a red flag.

Exercise: Finding Reliable Websites

Perform an internet search on a topic and find a more reliable and less reliable website, using the questions below (and continued on the next page) to help you determine the factors that indicate reliability. *Hint*: To get past the most popular results from major news organizations, go deeper in the search results.

- What kind of domain does the website have? Does it impact its reliability? How so?
- Can you follow an "about" link (or delete everything after the first slash in the URL to go to the parent site)? If so, who is behind the website?
- What is the purpose or mission of the individual or organization operating the website?

Figure 7.4 A Page from a Commercial Website

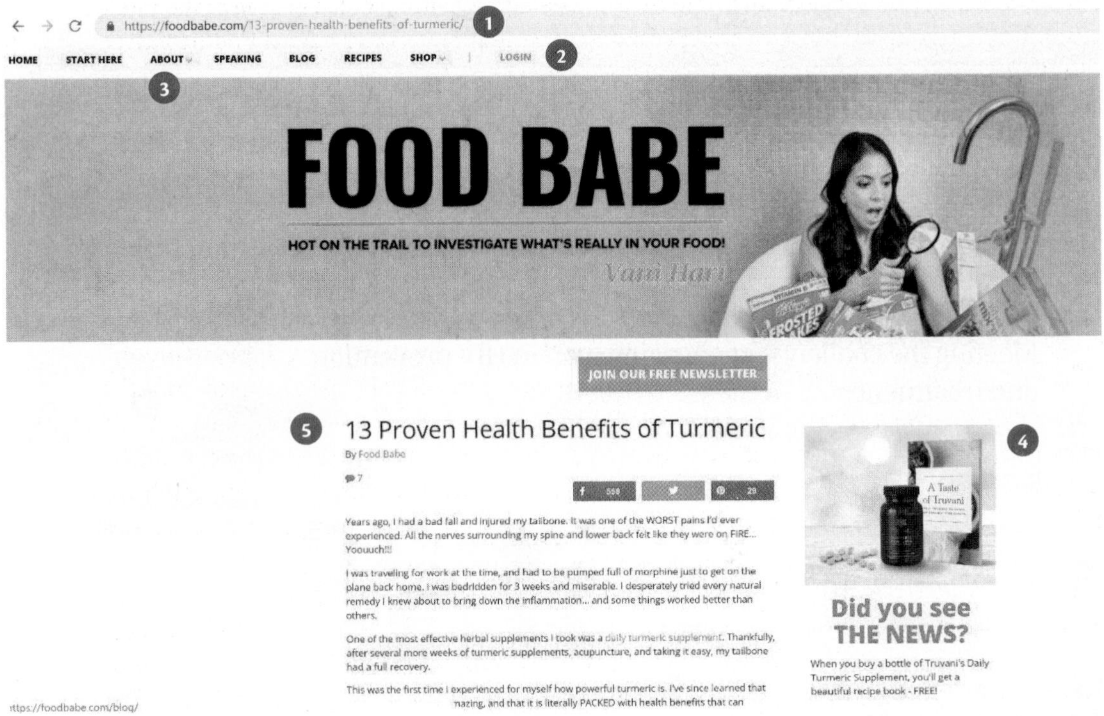

1. URL shows that the site is a .com (commercial) site.
2. Menu bar offers speaking services, recipes that use sponsored products, and shopping for sponsored products.
3. "About" link tells us that author's qualifications do not include formal education in health science.
4. Additional link to the "news" is actually an advertisement. (We suspect the "free newsletter" will also be ad-driven.)
5. Article on "proven" benefits of turmeric is list-based and anecdotal, and it supports the ad nearby.

- Are there advertisements visible on the page? If so, what kind of products are they? Is the content of the website related to the products being advertised? How?
- Is the information on the website reviewed by anyone before it is selected and posted? Who is selecting and reviewing? Is that person (or body) reputable and reliable? Why or why not?

WHY FINDING RELIABLE INTERNET SOURCES IS SO CHALLENGING

With our instant access to so much knowledge, and in the midst of an online cacophony of perspectives and voices, finding dependable, trustworthy sources of information can be difficult. Today, individuals can articulate their views publicly in a variety of online venues. With just a few clicks, individuals can expose poor customer service at a restaurant or abuses of power by police. They can report on news events as they happen, rally like-minded people to causes and activism, and share their opinions about almost anything in videos, blogs, tweets, and comments. This suggests an unprecedented democratic potential: The role of the internet in facilitating Arab Spring, a series of antigovernment protests across the Middle East in 2010–2011, or the #occupy, #blacklivesmatter, and #metoo movements in the United States, is inspiring. The internet's structure gives voice to the voiceless, allowing underrepresented and systematically marginalized people to share experiences and form discourse communities across the globe.

At the same time, this democratic potential is accompanied by serious perils. Hate groups and narrowly ideological activist organizations, for example, sometimes deliberately spread propaganda, promoting shallow conspiracy theories and outright lies. Consider a couple of claims popularized by such groups in recent years: that the Sandy Hook Elementary School shooting was staged by gun-control activists seeking to push through new firearms controls; that Barack Obama was not born in the United States; that the September 11, 2001, attacks on the World Trade Center were an "inside job"; that a secret society called the Illuminati controls the world. These false stories were created and perpetuated by highly partisan, conspiracy-driven, or fraudulent websites and were amplified by individual social media users vulnerable to such misinformation who shared the stories with networks of friends and followers.

Critical thinking can help mitigate the dangers of the media environment, which includes the possibility that lies, hysteria, and even violence can result from the unsafe, uncritical acceptance of information available on the internet. The proliferation of "fake news" stories and websites, viral misinformation campaigns, clickbait articles, and fraudulent websites all complicate our efforts to find quality information online. But not all fake news is created by political operatives, foreign agents, malicious bots, or entrepreneurs seeking to make money from advertising on bogus websites. Some fake news stories are created by everyday individuals. In 2016, Tim Tucker, a Twitter user who photographed a line of buses near a Donald Trump election rally in Austin, Texas, claimed that his photographs were evidence of Democratic Party busing in paid anti-Trump protesters. By his own admission, this claim was false, invented out of thin air, yet although he started with only 40 followers on Twitter, his post was shared 16,000 times on that site and 350,000 times on Facebook in a single day and subsequently was covered by a variety of conservative news outlets. Soon, it was referenced by Trump himself on his Twitter account. In just a few days, one user's incautious post created a national firestorm. ("Anytime

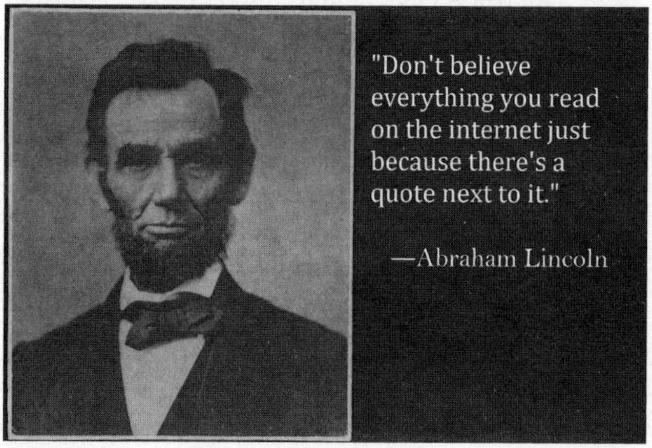
"Don't believe everything you read on the internet just because there's a quote next to it."
—Abraham Lincoln
Sometimes "authority" can be misleading.

you see me in the future," Tucker later said, "I can assure you I am going to try my best to be balanced with the facts and very clear about what is opinion and what is not.")

In sum, the internet gives us unprecedented access to information and to our own assertions of authority, but this empowerment also requires us to examine information carefully and proffer it responsibly. It is important to respect accuracy and reliability when sharing our ideas on the internet, to track the sources of viral stories, and to fact-check as much as possible the claims and details they offer.

A WORD ON "FAKE NEWS"

It has become somewhat fashionable to label as "fake news" any kind of information that does not accord with one's own worldview. For example, politicians often call into question the objectivity and reliability of news outlets that have been the standard-bearers of ethical journalism in the United States for decades — in some cases, more than a century (the *New York Times*, for example). Here we must be emphatic: The mainstream news media, such as the *New York Times*, CNN, FOX, MSNBC, and others, are *not* fake news outlets. These organizations may or may not exhibit political biases and may or may not privilege information likely to attract certain kinds of readers and viewers, but they also carefully demarcate what they consider to be news programs and opinion programs, and they follow the most rigorous standards of verifiable reporting. (Also remember that taking a thoughtful position is not the same as having a bias. In fact, taking a thoughtful position means *overcoming* biases, integrating a range of perspectives, meeting challenges to your own views, and adhering strictly to the goals of fairness and accuracy.)

Whether today's fake news stories are created by nefarious individuals or antagonistic intelligence agencies, their purpose is to sow confusion, doubt, and disorder by promoting falsehoods on the internet. Often these stories play upon base prejudices and superstitions. Their creators are not shy about telling wholesale lies, inventing quotations, and manipulating charts, graphs, and images, for example. They are indiscriminate in their attacks on truth: Liberals and conservatives, celebrities and everyday people have been targeted. Sometimes, fake news stories are built around issues: unscientific claims denying climate change, the efficacy of vaccinations, and the integrity of elections are just a few instances. Other types of fake news stories are created to further the agendas of activist organizations. Still others are designed merely to be eye-catching, their sole purpose to generate traffic to a website.

Unreliable or misleading news sources also include popular tabloids such as the *National Enquirer*, which blurs the lines between fiction and reality with salacious, screaming headlines like "Muslim Spies in Obama's CIA" and "Ted Cruz's Father Linked to JFK Assassination." Consider, too, satirical publications and programs like *The Onion*, *The Daily Show* (Comedy Central), or *Last Week Tonight* (HBO). Although such programs offer sometimes sharp commentary and analysis, their purpose is largely to entertain, not to inform. As such, they should not be considered quality sources of information.

ANATOMY OF A FAKE NEWS STORY NewsPunch is a fake news website posing as a legitimate news outlet, which you can see in Figure 7.5. It has a respectable title and a "punchy" tagline ("Where Mainstream Fears to Tread"), as well as a clean design and layout characteristic of respectable news websites (a navigation menu of relevant topics and lists of recent and popular articles). There is even a headline ticker bar that scrolls between titles as if they were breaking news stories. When we visited the site, clickbait titles appeared such as "Under Obama, US Became World's #1 Hotspot for Pedophilia." Thus, although the site projects some signs of journalistic legitimacy, we knew we needed to look more closely to determine if it was actually reliable.

We looked at the first story on the page and searched for author Sean Adl-Tabatabai to verify his credentials as a writer. We discovered through a quick internet search that

Figure 7.5 A Fake News Website

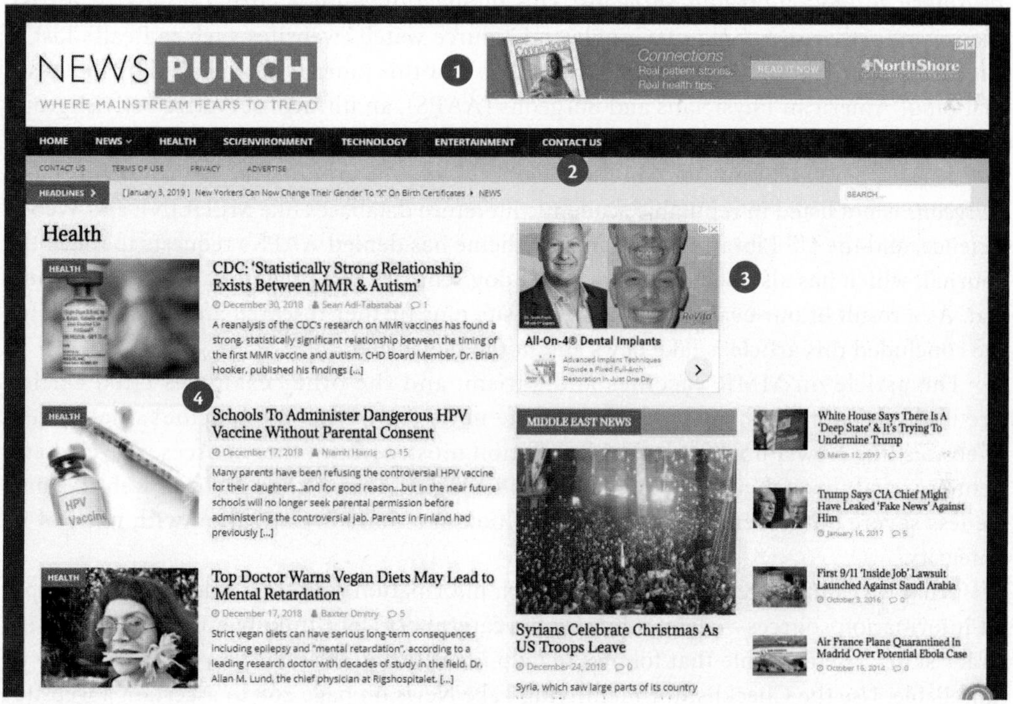

1. The title bar features an ad, which is uncommon on most reputable news sites and signals a page that is revenue-driven.
2. The navigation menu looks standard, but "Contact Us" is repeated on both lines, and there is an option for "Advertise," another warning sign.
3. Another ad, higher and more prominent on the page than most articles.
4. The stories mimic the layout of news sites: a photo with a category label ("Health") and a title, publication date, author, and first lines of the article.

the former television producer is the founder of this fake news site, and the site has been flagged by a European Union task force charged with investigating Russian efforts to destabilize Western democracies. We found no information about the second author listed, Niamh Harris.

The first headline, "CDC: 'Statistically Strong Relationship Exists Between MMR and Autism,'" suggests that the Centers for Disease Control and Prevention (CDC), the US government's national health protection agency, makes this claim. In fact, the CDC is *very* clear that MMR vaccines do NOT cause autism — the CDC uses huge letters on its website to emphasize its position — and it has devoted significant resources to debunking dangerous theories that they do. The quotation in the headline is actually attributed to Dr. Brian Hooker of the Children's Health Defense organization, an activist group widely discredited in the medical community for its antivaccine stance and not associated at all with the CDC.

Hooker's findings were first published (the NewsPunch article tells us) in the *Journal of American Physicians and Surgeons*. This publication sounds fairly impressive at first. However, further searching on Google and "source watch" websites such as Beall's List of Predatory Journals and Publications showed us that this journal is published by the Association of American Physicians and Surgeons (AAPS), an ultraconservative activist group advocating a range of scientifically discredited theories, including that HIV does not cause AIDS and that abortion leads to breast cancer. The *Journal of American Physicians and Surgeons* is not listed in reputable academic literature databases like MEDLINE and Web of Science, and the US Library of National Medicine has denied AAPS's requests to index the journal, which has also been listed by watchdog scholars as a predatory open-access journal. As a result of our evaluation of the website plus further research and cross-checking, we concluded this article is fake news and not to be trusted.

The article on MMR vaccines and autism, and the other examples cited earlier, are undoubtedly the strictest forms of fake news (spurious, mendacious, malicious). Websites like NewsPunch contain information mostly from other sources, recycled and reinterpreted through a sensationalistic or ideological lens. Other partisan websites may be less severe but nevertheless project the look of a news organization with none of its integrity.

What we cannot stress enough is that such information sources — and, in fact, *all* types of information sources — demand our most careful critical thinking and information literacy skills. Use the table that follows to help identify and evaluate resources that may be unreliable. Use the Checklist for Identifying Fake News on page 268 to ascertain a website's origins, legitimacy, and value and to dig further into the online sources you find to measure their validity.

NATIVE ADVERTISING AND BRANDED CONTENT

Some magazines, you probably have noticed, contain nearly as many (or even more) pages of advertisements than original content — a sign that the publication's content may be driven by the sponsors. In some publications, content itself can be part of an overall marketing scheme.

Types of "Fake News" and Unreliable Content

Type	Creator(s)	Purpose(s)	Features	Example(s)
Propaganda	Government agencies, activist groups, political organizations, corporations	To affect social and political beliefs, attitudes, and behaviors to further an agenda	Widespread, often misleading or biased; one-sided (not objective or neutral)	Advertising, issue-based political messages, public service announcements, recruitment or indoctrination materials
Clickbait	Companies and paid content creators	To entice viewers to navigate to websites designed to generate ad revenue based on traffic volume	Sensational "teaser" headlines with links	"Amazing" health news, discoveries, celebrity gossip, lists, inspirational or revolting personal stories
Sponsored content	Companies and marketing firms	To present advertisements as news or interest stories so as to drive revenue	Designed to look like news, will reference products or services in main text	Articles worked into major news sources and webpages directing users to third-party content; often labeled
Partisan news	Media companies and special-interest groups	To provide perspective-based information to like-minded viewers/readers	Ideological; not impartial (although may claim to be); facts may be present but selective; biased interpretations of facts	Self-identified liberal or conservative information outlets, news personalities; some mainstream networks
Conspiracy theory	Special-interest groups, individuals	To subvert, fool, or entertain (for political or other purposes)	Dismisses experts and authorities; provides simplistic or sensationalistic answers to complex questions; spreads beliefs rooted in paranoia, fear, uncertainty	Material claiming to provide the "real" truth contrary to accepted knowledge or beliefs; claims to expose "hoaxes" perpetuated by powerful persons or interests

In the magazine industry, this type of content is known as "ad-friendly copy" or "advertorial," with articles deliberately written to puff up a person, product, or service. On the internet, you have probably seen links to "sponsored content," which is like a digital version of advertorial (see Fig. 7.6, p. 268). Even reputable news agencies will include links to sponsored content (and will usually indicate as much). These are not good sources because they are not neutral: They are less interested in providing quality information and more interested in selling a product or service.

Figure 7.6 Sponsored Content

https://www.nytimes.com/paidpost/aetna/dreams-and-reality-why-sleep-matters.html

SECTIONS

The New York Times

LOG IN

PAID FOR AND POSTED BY

aetna

Dreams and Reality

WHY SLEEP MATTERS

DID YOU GET ENOUGH SLEEP LAST NIGHT?

For many Americans, the answer is no, sadly. Almost a quarter of Americans said they didn't get enough shut-eye because they were busy "concentrating on things," according to the Center For Disease Control and Prevention.

1. Website is the *New York Times*, but content is clearly marked "Paid for and posted by Aetna."
2. No author listed (the company Aetna is the author and sponsor).
3. Features of actual news articles imitated (title, citations of sources, a pull quote).

A CHECKLIST FOR IDENTIFYING FAKE NEWS

Website

- ❐ Does my source appear to be on a reputable website? Is it a .com, .edu, .org, or .net?
- ❐ Is there an "About" link (or a "Who We Are" or "Mission" link)? What individual or organization is behind the website?
- ❐ Is the content edited, or can users post anything?
- ❐ Does the website respect intellectual property? What website policies ensure (or compromise) source integrity?
- ❐ Do errors or misspellings on the website signal a lack of quality or reputability?
- ❐ How is the website supported (ads, donations, sponsorships)? What kinds of products and services are being sold, directly or indirectly, on the website? Are ads and sponsored content clearly marked as such?

(continues on next page)

A CHECKLIST FOR IDENTIFYING FAKE NEWS (CONTINUED)

- ❒ Are there a lot of pop-ups, surveys, or other distractions? Are visitors being asked for personal information or to sign up for something?

Authors

- ❒ Are authors or contributors named? Are they identifiable people with first and last names, or are they known just by "handles"?
- ❒ Are they real people? Can I find additional information about them?
- ❒ What authority do they have? What biases or other ideological predispositions might they have, if any?

Accuracy

- ❒ Does the information in my source check against other reputable sources?
- ❒ Are there links or citations in the articles (and do they point to other reputable, timely sources)? What kind of sources are being quoted and cited?
- ❒ Can I verify or cross-reference images to ensure that they have not been manipulated?

Comments

- ❒ What kind of audience seems to be involved in the debate?
- ❒ Do comments agreeing with the source tend to reflect reasonable ideas and common values? What about dissenting comments?
- ❒ If the site does not allow commenting, why?

CONSIDERING HOW CURRENT SOURCES ARE

Popular sources do have one major advantage in that they are very current. Newspapers and magazines publish frequently enough — daily, weekly, monthly — that they can respond to events as they occur. Although this schedule makes them prone to errors of fact and misreadings of developing situations, they have an indispensable immediacy. Academic journals, on the other hand, usually publish quarterly or semiannually because the peer-review process is so elaborate and the content so rich: Although it takes a longer time to write, review, and publish issues of an academic journal, the content tends not to age as fast. Because academic journals are so deeply researched, analyzed, and reviewed, their findings generally have staying power.

So far, we have been discussing the difference between scholarly, popular, and trade **periodicals** — that is, publications that appear on a regular basis. Whether they are scholarly, popular, or trade publications, or appear frequently or not, reputable publications have strong editorial review processes and abide by the codes of journalistic ethics. Full-length books, too, may be popular or scholarly, published by a university press or a respected organization. Although scholarly books are not always peer reviewed, many academic publishers are overseen by editorial boards who solicit feedback from expert reviewers. Academic books are also subject to a secondary review process in scholarly journals after they are published, so you can always examine how a source has been regarded by other experts if you wanted to verify its credibility. Like with popular and scholarly periodicals, full-length books may also have different levels of continuing relevance. Some books are published quickly and are intended to speak to current events; others take years to write, vet, and publish and may stick around as authoritative sources for a long time, even decades.

Remember, however, that academic books *do* age. Those you find on the library shelves may be much older than the relevant results from an internet or database search. Such books published long ago may be of historical interest, but they are rarely the strongest sources speaking directly to current issues, and they must be regarded in context. A book about juvenile delinquency published by a sociologist in 1955 cannot be used as evidence for a theory of adolescence nowadays, and even a landmark work, like Sigmund Freud's *The Interpretation of Dreams* (1899), may be an interesting book to study in and of itself or may prove to be an excellent background reference in your work, but it would not serve as evidence in an argument that the Oedipal complex — Freud's famous theory of psychosexual development — should inform how parents interact with their children today.

A CHECKLIST FOR EVALUATING SOURCES

- ❒ Can I identify the person or organization who produced the source?
- ❒ Can I identify the source's purpose?
- ❒ Are the authors real, reliable, and credentialed?
- ❒ Do sources cited represent a range of ideas, not simply ones that support one viewpoint?
- ❒ Are images verifiable from other sources?
- ❒ Is the source recent? If not, is the information I will be using from it likely or unlikely to change over time?
- ❒ Does the source treat the topic superficially or in depth?
- ❒ Does the article speak directly (or relevantly) to my topic and tentative thesis?
- ❒ If the article is from a scholarly journal, am I sure I understand it?
- ❒ Is the source titled and marketed as entertainment? If so, have I considered the author's commercial biases?

(continues on next page)

A CHECKLIST FOR EVALUATING SOURCES (CONTINUED)

- ❒ Is the source targeted at a specific audience likely to be sympathetic to its claims?
- ❒ Do the arguments in the source seem sound, based on what I have learned about skillful critical reading and writing?

Performing Your Own Primary Research

Research isn't limited to the world of professors and scientists. In one way or another, everyone does research at some point. If you decided to open your own business, you would want to do market research to persuade the bank that you are likely to be profitable enough to repay a loan. If you wanted to find out how and why a campus monument was erected, you could visit the university library's institutional archives and seek out information on it. If you were reviewing a film or book, you would probably go to the cinema or read in a comfortable place. Doing any of these things is performing primary research. In college, you might find yourself working on primary research alongside faculty members or participating in a class project to collect data. In other circumstances, you may wish to supplement your arguments with primary sources. Here, we touch on several kinds of primary research commonly performed by students.

INTERVIEWING PEERS AND LOCAL AUTHORITIES

For many topics, consider that you are surrounded by experts at your college. You ought to try to consult them — for instance, members of the faculty or other authorities on art, business, law, university administration, and so forth. You can also consult interested laypersons. Remember that experts may have their biases and "ordinary" people may have knowledge that experts lack. When interviewing experts, keep in mind Pablo Picasso's comment: "You mustn't always believe what I say. Questions tempt you to tell lies, particularly when there is no answer."

If you are interviewing your peers, you will probably want to make an effort to get a representative sample. Of course, even within a group not all members share a single view — for example, many African Americans favor affirmative action, but not all do; some lawmakers support capital punishment, but again, many do not. Make an effort to talk to a range of people who might offer varied opinions. You may learn some unexpected things.

You may also collect **testimonial** evidence from professors, students, community members, or family members. If you are writing about the women's rights movement of the 1970s, you might interview a professor or family member who lived through the era or participated in civil rights activities. You may know veterans who can speak to issues surrounding US wars or the experience of military service. Or perhaps an expert on a particular subject is visiting your campus for a lecture or talk, and you can find a way to put some questions of interest to her.

Visual Guide: Conducting Interviews

1 Find subjects for interviews

If you are looking for expert opinions, you may want to start with a faculty member on your campus. Search department and college websites for information about the special interests of the faculty and also about lecturers who will be visiting the campus.

2 Request the interview

Request the interview, preferably in writing, a week in advance.

- Ask for ample time, but respect the interviewee's schedule.
- Indicate whether the material will be confidential and (if relevant) ask if you may record the interview.

If the person accepts the invitation:

- Ask if he or she recommends any reading.
- Establish a suitable time and place.

3 Prepare thoroughly

- Read any recommended or background material.
- Formulate some questions, keeping in mind that you want detailed answers. Questions beginning with *Why* and *How* will usually require the interviewee to go beyond yes and no answers.

4 Conduct the interview

- Begin by engaging in brief conversation, without taking notes.
- Come prepared with an opening question or two, but as the interview proceeds, don't hesitate to ask questions that you hadn't anticipated asking.
- Even if your subject has consented to let you record the interview, be prepared to take notes on points that strike you as especially significant.
- Near the end, ask the subject if he or she wishes to add anything, perhaps by way of clarifying some earlier comment.
- Conclude by thanking the interviewee and by offering to provide a copy of the final version of your paper.

5 Write up the interview

- As soon as possible, type up your notes and observations and clarify them, filling in any abbreviations or shorthand you used while you still remember.
- If you recorded the interview, transcribe it or use a transcription program such as Transcribe. (You can also upload the audio to YouTube and then click on the transcribe button as it plays.)
- Scan the transcription and mark the parts that now strike you as especially significant.
- Be especially careful to indicate which words are direct quotations from your interview and which are your own observations. If in doubt, check with the interviewee.

CONDUCTING OBSERVATIONS

Observational research is the process of collecting information by situating yourself in a real-life context and making observations of what is present or what occurs. It may be *structured*, which means that you spend time designing your observation in a systematic way so as to get consistent results. For example, perhaps you want to see if male and female children are more likely to select gender-specific toys from a toy chest if they are with peers of the same sex; to prepare, you might code each toy according to its gendered properties and then watch and record while same-sex and mixed-sex groups of children are at play in the toy chest. To aim for consistent results, you might conduct the observation in multiple sittings, but always at the same time with the same number of children in each group.

Observational research may also be *unstructured*, meaning that you simply immerse yourself in a situation and carefully note what you see or experience. If you visited a toy store to gather impressions about how children's toys are segregated according to gender, you would be performing unstructured observational research. The same goes for attending a political convention as an observer (as opposed to a participant) or riding along with a police officer.

However, when you conduct observations, you must be careful to abide by ethical standards; you should not record people without their consent, for example. You must also be aware of observer biases — the notion that people's behavior changes when they know they are being watched, for one thing, and also that you yourself as a researcher may get swept up in what you are observing to a degree that you are not able to be neutral or objective in your observations.

CONDUCTING SURVEYS

Surveys are excellent ways to ascertain the opinions and beliefs of a certain population. Whether you distribute your surveys via paper or set up an online survey through an online service like Doodle or SurveyMonkey, your college's in-house software such as Qualtrics, or even a Facebook poll, be sure to distribute your survey to the target population. Whether you are trying to collect opinions, values, behaviors, or facts, your survey questions should be constructed carefully to get the data that you want. Here are some other pitfalls of collecting surveys:

- ***Not enough respondents/bad sample size:*** If only five women responded to your survey on attitudes about fraternities on campus, you shouldn't use just five responses to say "80% of women on campus have a favorable view of fraternities."
- ***Leading questions:*** Leading questions use language likely to influence respondents' answers, such as "How fast should drivers be allowed to go on our serene campus roads?" As you can see, the language "leads" the respondent: For these questions, respondents are likely to answer lower speeds for "serene" roads. A more appropriate version of this question would be "What in your opinion is a safe driving speed for campus roads?"
- ***Loaded questions:*** Loaded questions push respondents to answer questions that don't fully or accurately represent their actual opinions. "On a scale of 1 to 5," a loaded question might ask, "how awful do you think it is that our

administration is raising tuition?" Such a question forces all respondents to answer in the "awful" range, even if they are somewhat satisfied with the tuition amount overall.

RESEARCH IN ARCHIVES AND SPECIAL COLLECTIONS

Archives are collections of material maintained and preserved by organizations such as college and university libraries, public libraries, corporations, governments, churches, museums, and historical societies. Archives generally contain records that are important to an institution's own history and that may be relevant to others. The National Archives in Washington, DC, for example, curates a vast number of resources, including America's founding documents and military service records. Coca-Cola's company archives and the Walt Disney archives are examples of corporate archives that hold a vast array of materials related to those companies' pasts. Your college or university probably keeps its own institutional archives in its library.

Special collections are bodies of original material — including photographs, films, letters, memos, manuscripts of unique interests, and often material artifacts — usually gathered around a specialized topic, theme, or individual. Special collections often include original, rare, and valuable artifacts that may require permission for access or examination. Many libraries and museums offer at least limited access to digital archives and special collections via their websites, and some databases offer access to primary research sources, too (letters, original newspapers, early manuscripts, and so on).

Some special collections are broad and deep: The Library of Congress, the Smithsonian, and other national museums, for example, hold special collections on a variety of subjects in American political, social, and natural history. Other special collections can be quite specific, ranging from collections of science fiction pulp novels of the 1950s; to letters from combat veterans of World War II; to photograph, film, art, and music collections, antique and contemporary. The Blues Archive at the University of Mississippi contains — among other treasures — the musician B.B. King's personal record collection. The popular culture collection at Bowling Green State University holds 10,000 comic books and graphic novels, among other curiosities like a complete Pokémon set and *Star Trek* memorabilia.

Exercises: Conducting Primary Research

1. ***Observation***: Visit a location on campus or a local event and report on the subjects or interactions you find there. Try to formulate a question you want answered: Do people tend to eat lunch outside more often when the cafeteria is busy? Do more people dress in school colors on days when the football team or basketball team is competing?
2. ***Survey***: Design three to five survey questions that will help you aggregate data about attitudes, beliefs, opinions, or behaviors of students on your campus. Your survey might be about a specific campus issue or political or social opinions, or you could imagine a demographic you are trying to reach, such as in-state or out-of-state or international students, African American or Latinx students, or students of a particular religion. Reflect on how you might distribute this survey — electronically or using paper — and why.

3. ***Archives***: Visit the website of your own school, or another local college or museum, and examine its special collections. Identify the special collections available and choose one that sounds especially interesting. Look further into it: What kinds of materials are in the collection? Is digital access available? If so, select an example of an original artifact (document, image, etc.) and save it or print it out for closer inspection. For what kind of research topics might it be an important or relevant item? If digital access is unavailable, identify an item you would like to get access to and outline the process of doing so.

Synthesizing Sources

When you are evaluating sources, consider the words of Francis Bacon, Shakespeare's contemporary:

> Some books are to be tasted, others to be swallowed, and some few to be chewed and digested.

Your instructor will expect you not just to find but to digest your sources. This doesn't mean you need to accept them but only that you need to read them thoughtfully. Your readers will expect you to tell them *what you make of your sources*, which means that you will go beyond writing a summary and will synthesize the material into your own contribution to the discourse. *Your* view is what is wanted, and readers expect this view to be thoughtful — not mere summary and not mere tweeting.

Let's pause for a moment and consider the word ***synthesis***. You probably are familiar with *photosynthesis*, the chemical process in green plants that produces carbohydrates from carbon dioxide and hydrogen. Synthesis combines preexisting elements and produces something new. In your writing, you will *synthesize* sources, combining existing material into something new, drawing nourishment from what has already been said (giving credit, of course), and converting it into something new — a view that you think is worth considering. In our use of the word *synthesis*, even a view that you utterly reject becomes a part of your new creation *because it helped stimulate you to formulate your view*; without the idea that you reject, you might not have developed the view that you now hold.

During the process of reading and evaluating sources, and afterward, you will want to listen, think, and say to yourself something like the following:

- "No, no, I see things very differently; it seems to me that . . ."
- "Yes, of course, but on one large issue I think I differ."
- "Yes, sure, I agree, but I would go further and add . . ."
- "Yes, I agree with the conclusion, but I hold this conclusion for reasons different from the ones offered."

WRITING TIP
In your final draft, *you must give credit to all your sources*. Let the reader know whether you are quoting (in this case, you will use quotation marks around all material directly quoted), whether you are summarizing (you will explicitly say so), or whether you are paraphrasing (again, you will explicitly say so).

Taking Notes

Whether you are performing primary or secondary research, using library special collections or online resources, you should be keeping notes along the way. When it comes to taking notes, all researchers have their own habits that they swear by: We still prefer to take notes on four-by-six-inch index cards; others use a notebook or a computer for note taking. If you use a citation management program such as RefWorks or EndNote, you can store your personal notes and commentary with the citations you have saved. By using the program's search function, you can easily pull together related notes and citations, or you can create project folders for your references so that you can easily review what you've collected.

Whatever method you use, the following techniques should help you maintain consistency and keep organized during the research process:

1. If you use a notebook or index cards, organize them carefully, write in ink (pencil gets smudgy), and write on only one side of the paper or card to avoid losing track of your material. If you keep notes electronically, consider an online tool such as Microsoft OneNote, a Google Doc, or another cloud-based service so that you will not lose your research in the event of a computer crash or a lost laptop.
2. Summarize, for the most part, rather than quote at length. Quote only passages in which the writing is especially effective or passages that are in some way crucial. Make sure that all quotations are exact.
3. Indicate the source. The author's last name is enough if you have consulted only one work by the author, but if you consult more than one work by an author, you need further identification, such as both the author's name and a short title.
4. Add your own comments about the substance of what you are recording. Such comments as "but contrast with Sherwin" or "seems illogical" or "evidence?" will ensure that you are thinking as well as reading and writing.
5. In a separate computer file, or on a separate card or page, write a bibliographic entry for each source. The information in each entry will vary, depending on whether the source is a book, a periodical, an electronic document, and so forth. The kind of information (e.g., author and title) needed for each type of source can be found in the sections MLA Format: The List of Works Cited (p. 287) and APA Format: The List of References (p. 297).

A Note on Plagiarizing

Plagiarism is the unacknowledged use of someone else's work. The word comes from a Latin word for "kidnapping," and plagiarism is indeed the stealing of something engendered by someone else. Your college or your class instructor probably has issued a statement concerning plagiarism. If there is such a statement, be sure to read it carefully.

We won't deliver a sermon on the dishonesty (and folly) of plagiarism; we intend only to help you understand exactly what plagiarism is. The first thing to say is that plagiarism is not limited to the unacknowledged quotation of words.

PARAPHRASING A *paraphrase* is a sort of word-by-word or phrase-by-phrase translation of the author's language into your own language. Unlike a summary, then, a paraphrase is approximately as long as the original.

Paraphrase thus has its uses, but writers often use it unnecessarily, and students who overuse it may find themselves crossing the border into plagiarism. True, if you paraphrase you are using your own words, but you are also using someone else's ideas, and, equally important, you are using this other person's sequence of thoughts.

Even if you change every third word in your source, you are plagiarizing. Here is an example of this sort of plagiarism, based on the previous sentence:

> Even if you alter every second or third word that your source gives, you still are plagiarizing.

Further, even if the writer of this paraphrase had cited a source after the paraphrase, he or she would still have been guilty of plagiarism. How, you may ask, can a writer who cites a source be guilty of plagiarism? Easy. Readers assume that only the gist of the idea is the source's and that the development of the idea — the way it is set forth — is the present writer's work. A paraphrase that runs to several sentences is in no significant way the writer's work: The writer is borrowing not only the idea but also the shape of the presentation, the sentence structure. What the writer needs to do is to write something like this:

> Changing an occasional word does not free the writer from the obligation to cite a source.

And, if the central idea were not a commonplace one, the source would still need to be cited.

Now consider this question: *Why* paraphrase? As we explained in Summarizing and Paraphrasing in Chapter 2 (pp. 46–49), the chief reason to paraphrase a passage is to clarify it — that is, to ensure that you and your readers understand a passage that — perhaps because it is badly written — is obscure. Often there is no good answer for why you should paraphrase. Since a paraphrase is as long as the original, you might as well quote the original, if you think that a passage of that length is worth quoting. Probably it is *not* worth quoting in full; probably you should *not* paraphrase but rather should drastically *summarize* most of it, and perhaps quote a particularly effective phrase or two.

A CHECKLIST FOR AVOIDING PLAGIARISM

Ask yourself these questions, first about your notes:

- ❑ Did I *always* put quoted material within quotation marks?
- ❑ Did I summarize *in my own words* and give credit to the source for the idea?
- ❑ Did I avoid paraphrasing? That is, did I avoid copying, keeping the structure of the source's sentences but using some of my own words?

And then about your paper:

- ❑ If I set forth a borrowed idea, do I give credit, even though the words and the structure of the sentences are entirely my own?
- ❑ If I quote directly, do I put the words within quotation marks and cite the source?
- ❑ Do I *not* cite material that can be considered common knowledge?
- ❑ If I have the slightest doubt about whether I should or should not cite a source, have I taken the safe course and cited the source?

Compiling an Annotated Bibliography

When several sources have been identified and gathered, many researchers prepare an annotated bibliography. That's a list providing all relevant bibliographic information (just as it will appear in your Works Cited list or References list), as well as a brief descriptive and evaluative summary of each source — perhaps one to three sentences. Your instructor may ask you to provide an annotated bibliography for your research project.

An annotated bibliography serves four main purposes:

1. It helps you master the material contained in any given source. To find the heart of the argument presented in an article or book, to phrase it briefly, and to comment on it, you must understand it fully.
2. It helps you think about how each portion of your research fits into the whole of your project, how you will use it, and how it relates to your topic and thesis.
3. It allows your readers to see quickly which items may be especially helpful in their own research.
4. It gives you hands-on practice at bibliographic format, thereby easing the job of creating your final bibliography (the Works Cited list or References list of your paper).

Following is an example entry for an annotated bibliography in MLA (Modern Language Association) format for a project on the effect of violence in the media. Notice that the entry does three things:

1. It begins with a bibliographic entry — author (last name first), title, and so forth.
2. Then it provides information about the content of the work under consideration.
3. Then it suggests how the source might work to support your argument in the final research paper you are writing.

Clover, Carol J. *Men, Women, and Chain Saws: Gender in the Modern Horror Film*. Princeton UP, 1992. The author focuses on Hollywood horror movies of the 1970s and 1980s. She studies representations of women and girls in these movies and the responses of male viewers to female characters, suggesting that this relationship is more complex and less exploitative than the common wisdom claims. Could use this source to establish a counterpoint to the idea that all women are represented stereotypically in horror films.

CITATION GENERATORS There are many citation generators available online. These generators allow you to enter the information about your source, and, with a click, they will create Works Cited entries in APA or MLA format. But just as you cannot trust spell- and grammar-checkers in Microsoft Word, you cannot trust these generators completely. If you use them, be sure to double-check what they produce before submitting your essay. Always remember that responsible writers take care to cite their sources properly and that failure to do so puts you at risk for accusations of plagiarism.

Quoting from Sources

When is it necessary, or appropriate, to quote? Using your notes, consider where the reader would benefit by seeing the exact words of your source. If you are arguing that *Z*'s definition of *rights* is too inclusive, your readers have to know exactly how *Z* defined *rights*, word for word. If your source material is so pithy and well worded that summarizing it would weaken its force, give your readers the pleasure of reading the original. Of course, readers won't give you credit for writing these words, but they will appreciate your taste and your effort to make their reading experience pleasant. In short, use (but don't overuse) quotations. Don't quote *too often* and don't quote *too much* of the original source (and never use quotations to achieve more length!). Speaking roughly,

- quotations should occupy no more than 10 to 15 percent of your paper;
- they may occupy much less; and
- most of your paper should set forth your ideas, not other people's ideas.

LONG AND SHORT QUOTATIONS **Long quotations** (more than four lines of typed prose or three or more lines of poetry) are set off from the text. To set off material, start on a new line, indent one-half inch from the left margin, and type the quotation double-spaced. Do not enclose quotations within quotation marks if you are setting them off.

Short quotations are treated differently. They are embedded within the text; they are enclosed within quotation marks, but otherwise they do not stand out.

All quotations, whether set off or embedded, must be exact. If you omit any words, you must indicate the ellipsis by substituting three spaced periods for the omission; if you insert any words or punctuation, you must indicate the addition by enclosing it within square brackets, not to be confused with parentheses.

Original	The Montgomery bus boycott not only brought national attention to the discriminatory practices of the South, but elevated a twenty-six-year-old preacher to exalted status in the civil rights movement.
Quotation in student paper	"The Montgomery bus boycott . . . elevated [King] to exalted status in the civil rights movement."

LEADING INTO A QUOTATION Now for a less mechanical matter: The way in which a quotation is introduced. To say that it is "introduced" implies that one leads into it, although on rare occasions a quotation appears without an introduction, perhaps immediately after the title. Normally one leads into a quotation by giving any one or more of the following (but be aware that using them all at once can get unwieldy and produce awkward sentences):

- the *name of the author* and (no less important) the author's expertise or authority
- an indication of *the source of the quotation*, by title and/or year
- *clues signaling the content of the quotation and the purpose* it serves in the present essay

For example:

William James provides a clear answer to Huxley when he says that ". . ."

In *The Will to Believe* (1897), psychologist William James provides a clear answer to Huxley when he says that ". . ."

Either of these lead-ins work, especially because William James is quite well known. When you're quoting from a lesser-known author, it becomes more important to identify his or her expertise and perhaps the source, as in

Biographer Theodora Bosanquet, author of *Henry James at Work* (1982), subtly criticized Huxley's vague ideas on religion by writing, "...."

Notice that in all these samples, the writer uses the lead-in to signal to readers the general tone of the quotation to follow. The writer uses the phrase "a clear answer" to signal that what's coming is, in fact, clear, uses the terms "subtly criticized" and "vague" to indicate that the following words by Bosanquet will be critical and will point out a shortcoming in Huxley's ideas. In this way, the writer anticipates and controls the meaning of the quotation for the reader. If the writer believed otherwise, the lead-ins might have run thus:

> William James's weak response to Huxley does not really meet the difficulty Huxley calls attention to. James writes, ". . . ."

> Biographer Theodora Bosanquet, author of *Henry James at Work* (1982), unjustly criticized Huxley's complex notion of religion by writing ". . . ."

In these examples, clearly the words "weak" and "unjustly criticized" imply how the essayist wants the reader to interpret the quotation. In the second one, Huxley's idea is presented as "complex," not vague.

SIGNAL PHRASES Think of your writing as a conversation between you and your sources. As in conversation, you want to be able to move smoothly between different, sometimes contrary, points of view. You also want to be able to set your thoughts apart from those of your sources. Signal phrases make it easy for readers to know where your information came from and why it's trustworthy by pointing to key facts about the source:

> *According to* psychologist Stephen Ceci . . .

> A report published by the US Bureau of Justice Statistics *concludes* . . .

> Feminist philosopher Sandra Harding *argues* . . .

To avoid repetitiveness, vary your sentence structure:

> . . . *claims* Stephen Ceci.

> . . . *according to* a report published by the US Bureau of Statistics.

Some useful verbs to introduce sources include the following:

acknowledges	contends	points out
argues	denies	recommends
believes	disputes	reports
claims	observes	suggests

Note that papers written using MLA style refer to sources in the present tense (*acknowledge, argue, believe*). Papers written in APA style use the past tense (*acknowledged, argued, believed*).

LEADING OUT OF A QUOTATION You might think of providing quotations as a three-stage process that includes the **lead-in**, the **quotation** itself, and the **lead-out**. The lead-out gives you a chance to interpret the quoted material, further controlling the intended meaning and telling the reader what is most important.

Visual Guide: Integrating Quotations

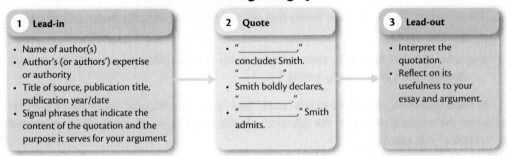

1 Lead-in

- Name of author(s)
- Author's (or authors') expertise or authority
- Title of source, publication title, publication year/date
- Signal phrases that indicate the content of the quotation and the purpose it serves for your argument

2 Quote

- "__________," concludes Smith. "________."
- Smith boldly declares, "__________."
- "__________," Smith admits.

3 Lead-out

- Interpret the quotation.
- Reflect on its usefulness to your essay and argument.

In the lead-out, you have a chance to reflect on the quotation and to shift back toward your own ideas and analysis. Consider this three-stage process applied in the following two ways:

> In his first book, *A World Restored* (1954), future Secretary of Defense Henry Kissinger wrote the famous axiom "History is the memory of states." It is the collective story of an entire people, displayed in public museums and libraries, taught in schools, and passed on from generation to generation.

> In his first book, *A World Restored* (1954), Nixon's former Secretary of Defense Henry Kissinger wrote glibly, "History is the memory of states." By asserting that history is largely the product of self-interested propaganda, Kissinger's words suggest that the past is maintained and controlled by whatever groups happen to hold power.

Notice the three-step process, and notice especially how the two examples convey different meanings of Kissinger's famous phrase. In the lead-in to the first sample, Kissinger's "future" role suggests hope. It signals a figure whose influence is growing. By using "famous" and "axiom," the author presents the quotation as true or even timeless. In the lead-out, the role of the state in preserving history is optimistic and idealistic.

In the second sample, "former" is used in the lead-in, suggesting Kissinger's later association with the ousted president he served, Richard Nixon. Readers are told that Kissinger "wrote glibly" even before they are told what he wrote, so readers may tend to read the quoted words that way. In the lead-out, the state becomes a more nefarious source of history keeping, one not interested in accommodating marginal voices or alternative perspectives, or remembering events inconvenient to its authority or righteousness.

WRITING TIP
In introducing a quotation, it is usually advisable to signal the reader *why* you are using the quotation by means of a lead-in consisting of a verb or a verb and adverb, such as *admits* or *convincingly shows*.

Again, we hope you can see in these examples how the three-step process facilitates a writer's control over the meanings of quotations. Returning to our earlier example, if after reading something by Huxley the writer

THINKING CRITICALLY *Using Signal Phrases*

In the space provided, rewrite each signal phrase using a different structure. The first has been done as an example. Use different verbs to introduce each source.

ORIGINAL SIGNAL PHRASE	REVISED SIGNAL PHRASE
According to political economist Robert Reich . . .	. . . claims Robert Reich.
The National Health Council reports . . .	
The *Harvard Law Review* claims . . .	
As science essayist Jennifer Ackerman suggests . . .	

had merely stated that "William James says . . . ," readers wouldn't know whether they were getting confirmation, refutation, or something else. The essayist would have put a needless burden on the readers. Generally speaking, the more difficult the quotation, the more important is the introductory or explanatory lead-in, but even the simplest quotation profits from some sort of brief lead-in, such as "James reaffirms this point when he says . . ."

Documentation

In the course of your essay, you will probably quote or summarize material derived from a source. You must give credit, and although there is no one form of documentation to which all scholarly fields subscribe, you will probably be asked to use one of two. One, established by the Modern Language Association (MLA), is used chiefly in the humanities; the other, established by the American Psychological Association (APA), is used chiefly in the social sciences.

We include two papers that use sources. "An Argument for Corporate Responsibility" (p. 303) uses the MLA format. "Does Ability Determine Expertise?" (p. 309) follows the APA format. (You may notice that various styles are illustrated in other selections we have included.)

In some online venues, you can link directly to your sources. If your assignment is to write a blog or some other online text, linking helps the reader look at a note or citation or the direct source quickly and easily. For example, in describing or referencing a scene in a movie, you can link to reviews of the movie, to a YouTube video of the trailer, or to the exact scene you're discussing. These kinds of links can help your audience get a clearer sense of your point. When formatting such a link in your text, make sure the link opens in a new window so that readers won't lose their place in your original text. In a blog, linking to sources usually is easy and helpful.

A NOTE ON FOOTNOTES (AND ENDNOTES)

Before we discuss these two formats, a few words about footnotes are in order. Before the MLA and the APA developed their rules of style, citations commonly appeared in footnotes. Although today footnotes are not so frequently used to give citations, they still may be useful for another purpose. (The MLA suggests endnotes rather than footnotes, but most readers seem to think that, in fact, footnotes are preferable to endnotes. After all, who wants to keep shifting from a page of text to a page of notes at the end?) If you want to include some material that may seem intrusive in the body of the paper, you may relegate it to a footnote. For example, you might translate a quotation given in a foreign language, or you might demote from text to footnote a paragraph explaining why you aren't taking account of such-and-such a point. By putting the matter in a footnote, you signal to the reader that it is dispensable — that it's relevant but not essential, something extra that you are, so to speak, tossing in. Don't make a habit of writing this sort of note, but there are times when it is appropriate to do so.

MLA Format: Citations within the Text

Brief citations within the body of the essay give credit, in a highly abbreviated way, to the sources for material you quote, summarize, or make use of in any other way. These *in-text citations* are made clear by a list of sources, titled Works Cited, appended to the essay. Thus, in your essay you may say something like this:

> Commenting on the relative costs of capital punishment and life imprisonment, Ernest van den Haag says that he doubts "that capital punishment really is more expensive" (33).

The **citation,** the number 33 in parentheses, means that the quoted words come from page 33 of a source (listed in the Works Cited) written by van den Haag. Without a Works Cited list, a reader would have no way of knowing that you are quoting from page 33 of an article that appeared in the February 8, 1985, issue of the *National Review.*

Usually, the parenthetic citation appears at the end of a sentence, as in the example just given, but it can appear elsewhere; its position will depend chiefly on your ear, your eye, and the context. You might, for example, write the sentence thus:

> Ernest van den Haag doubts "that capital punishment really is more expensive" than life imprisonment (33), but other writers have presented figures that contradict him.

Five points must be made about these examples:

1. *Quotation marks* The closing quotation mark appears after the last word of the quotation, not after the parenthetic citation. Because the citation is not part of the quotation, the citation is not included within the quotation marks.

2. *Omission of words (ellipsis)* If you are quoting a complete sentence or only a phrase, as in the examples given, you do not need to indicate (by three spaced periods) that you are omitting material before or after the quotation. But if for some reason you want to omit an interior part of the quotation, you must indicate the omission by inserting an ellipsis, the three spaced dots. To take a simple example, if you omit the word "really" from van den Haag's phrase, you must alert the reader to the omission:

> Ernest van den Haag doubts that "capital punishment . . . is more expensive" than life imprisonment (33).

3. *Punctuation with parenthetic citations* In the preceding examples, the punctuation (a period or a comma in the examples) follows the citation. If, however, the quotation ends with a question mark, include the question mark within the quotation, since it is part of the quotation, and put a period after the citation:

> Van den Haag asks, "Isn't it better — more just and more useful — that criminals, if they do not have the certainty of punishment, at least run the risk of suffering it?" (33).

But if the question mark is your own and not in the source, put it after the citation, thus:

> What answer can be given to van den Haag's doubt that "capital punishment really is more expensive" (33)?

4. *Two or more works by an author* If your list of Works Cited includes two or more works by an author, you cannot, in your essay, simply cite a page number — the reader will not know which of the works you are referring to. You must give additional information. You can give it in your lead-in; thus:

> In "New Arguments against Capital Punishment," van den Haag expresses doubt that "capital punishment really is more expensive" than life imprisonment (33).

Or you can give the title, in a shortened form, within the citation:

> Van den Haag expresses doubt that "capital punishment really is more expensive" than life imprisonment ("New Arguments" 33).

5. *Citing even when you do not quote* Even if you don't quote a source directly but instead use its point in a paraphrase or a summary, you will give a citation:

> Van den Haag thinks that life imprisonment costs more than capital punishment (33).

Notice that in all the previous examples, the author's name is given in the text (rather than within the parenthetic citation). But there are several other ways of giving the citation, and we shall look at them now.

AUTHOR AND PAGE NUMBER IN PARENTHESES

> It has been argued that life imprisonment is more costly than capital punishment (van den Haag 33).

AUTHOR, TITLE, AND PAGE NUMBER IN PARENTHESES

Doubt has been expressed that capital punishment is as costly as life imprisonment (van den Haag, "New Arguments" 33).

A GOVERNMENT DOCUMENT OR A WORK OF CORPORATE AUTHORSHIP

The Commission on Food Control, in *Food Resources Today*, concludes that there is no danger (37–38).

A WORK BY TWO AUTHORS

There is not a single example of the phenomenon (Christakis and Fowler 293).

Christakis and Fowler insist there is not a single example of the phenomenon (293).

A WORK BY MORE THAN TWO AUTHORS

If there are *more than two authors*, give the last name of the first author, followed by *et al.* (an abbreviation for *et alia*, Latin for "and others")

Gittleman et al. argue (43) that . . .

On average, the cost is even higher (Gittleman et al. 43).

PARENTHETICAL CITATION OF AN INDIRECT SOURCE (CITATION OF MATERIAL THAT ITSELF WAS QUOTED OR SUMMARIZED IN YOUR SOURCE)

Suppose you're reading a book by Jones in which she quotes Smith and you wish to use Smith's material. Your citation must refer the reader to Jones—the source you're using—but of course, you cannot attribute the words to Jones. You will have to make it clear that you are quoting Smith, so after a lead-in phrase like "Smith says," followed by the quotation, you will give a parenthetic citation along these lines:

(qtd. in Jones 324-25).

PARENTHETICAL CITATION OF TWO OR MORE WORKS

The costs are simply too high (Smith 301; Jones 28).

AN ANONYMOUS WORK

For an anonymous work, or for a work where the author is unknown, give the title in your lead-in or give it in a shortened form in your parenthetic citation:

A Prisoner's View of Killing includes a poll taken of the inmates on death row (32).

According to the website for the American Civil Liberties Union . . .

AN INTERVIEW

Vivian Berger, in an interview, said . . .

If you don't mention the source's name in the lead-in, you'll have to give it in the parentheses:

Contrary to popular belief, the death penalty is not reserved for serial killers and depraved murderers (Berger).

AN ONLINE SOURCE

Generally, you can use the same formatting of the entries we've discussed so far for an online source. If the source uses pages or breaks down further into paragraphs or screens, insert the appropriate identifier or abbreviation (*p.* or *pp.* for page or pages; *par.* or *pars.* for paragraph or paragraphs; *screen* or *screens*) before the relevant number:

The growth of day care has been called "a crime against posterity" by a spokesman for the Institute for the American Family (Terwilliger, screens 1-2).

MLA Format: The List of Works Cited

As the previous pages explain, parenthetic documentation consists of references that become clear when the reader consults the list titled Works Cited at the end of an essay. Here are some general guidelines.

FORM ON THE PAGE

The list of Works Cited begins on its own page.

- Continue the pagination of the essay: If the last page of text is 10, then the Works Cited begins on page 11.
- Type the heading Works Cited, centered, one inch from the top, and then double-space and type the first entry.
- Double-space the page; that is, double-space each entry, and double-space between entries.
- Begin each entry flush with the left margin, and indent a half inch for each succeeding line of the entry. This is known as a hanging indent, and you can set most word processing programs to achieve this formatting easily.
- Italicize titles of works published independently (which the MLA also calls *containers*; see page 288), such as books, pamphlets, and journals.
- Enclose within quotation marks a work not published independently — for instance, an article in a journal or a short story.

- Arrange the list of sources alphabetically by author, with the author's last name first. For anonymous works, use the title, and slot in your list alphabetically. For works with more than one author, and two or more works by one author, see sample entries that follow. If your list includes two or more works by one author, do not repeat the author's name for the second title; instead represent it by three hyphens followed by a period (---.).
- Anonymous works are listed under the first word of the title or the second word if the first is *A*, *An*, or *The* or a foreign equivalent. We discuss books by more than one author, government documents, and works of corporate authorship in the sample entries in this section.

CONTAINERS AND PUBLICATION INFORMATION

When a source being documented comes from a larger source, the larger source is considered a *container* because it contains the smaller source you are citing. For example, a container might be an anthology, a periodical, a website, a television program, a database, or an online archive. The context of a source will help you determine what counts as a container.

In Works Cited lists, the title of a container is listed after the period following the author's name. The container title is generally italicized and followed by a comma, since the information that follows describes the container. Here are some guidelines:

- Capitalize the first word and the last word of the title.
- Capitalize all nouns, pronouns, verbs, adjectives, adverbs, and subordinating conjunctions (e.g., *although, if, because*).
- Do not capitalize articles (e.g., *a, an, the*), prepositions (e.g., *in, on, toward, under*), coordinating conjunctions (e.g., *and, but, or, for*), or the *to* in infinitives, unless it's the first or last word of the title or the first word of the subtitle.
- Disregard any unusual typography, such as the use of all capital letters or the use of an ampersand (&) for *and*.
- Italicize the container title (and subtitle, if applicable; separate them by a colon), but do not italicize the period that concludes this part of the entry.

When citing a source within a container, the title of the source should be the first element following the author's name. The source title should be set within quotation marks with a period inside the closing quotation mark. The title of the container is then listed, followed by a comma, with additional information — including publication information, dates, and page ranges — about the container set off by commas.

The following example cites a story, "Achates McNeil," from an anthology — or container — called *After the Plague: Stories*. The anthology was published by Viking Penguin in 2001, and the story appears on pages 82 through 101.

Boyle, T. C. "Achates McNeil." *After the Plague: Stories*, Viking Penguin, 2001, pp. 82-101.

Notice that the full name of the publisher is listed. Always include the full names of publishers except for terms such as "Inc." and "Company"; retain terms such as "Books" and "Publisher." The only exception is university presses, which are abbreviated thus: *Yale UP, U of Chicago P, State U of New York P.*

On the following pages, you will find more specific information for listing different kinds of sources. Although we have covered many kinds of sources, it's entirely possible that you will come across a source that doesn't fit any of the categories that we have discussed. For greater explanations of these matters, covering the proper way to cite all sorts of troublesome and unbelievable (but real) sources, see the *MLA Handbook*, Eighth Edition (Modern Language Association of America, 2016).

BOOKS

A BOOK BY MORE THAN ONE AUTHOR

The book is alphabetized under the last name of the first author named on the title page. If there are *two authors*, the name of the second author is given in the normal order, *first name first, after the first author's name.*

Gilbert, Sandra M., and Susan Gubar. *The Madwoman in the Attic: The Woman Writer and the Nineteenth-Century Literary Imagination*. Yale UP, 1979.

If there are *more than two authors*, give the name only of the first, followed by a comma, and then add *et al.* (Latin for "and others").

Zumeta, William, et al. *Financing American Higher Education in the Era of Globalization*. Harvard Education Press, 2012.

WORKS OF CORPORATE AUTHORSHIP

Begin the citation with the corporate author, even if the same body is also the publisher.

American Psychiatric Association. *Psychiatric Glossary*. American Psychiatric Association, 1984.

Human Rights Watch. *World Report of 2018: Events of 2017*. Seven Stories Press, 2018.

A REPRINT

After the title, give the date of original publication (it can usually be found on the reverse of the title page of the reprint you are using), then a period, and then the publisher and date of the edition you are using.

de Mille, Agnes. *Dance to the Piper*. 1951. Introduction by Joan Acocella, New York Review Books, 2015.

A BOOK WITH AN AUTHOR AND AN EDITOR

Kant, Immanuel. *The Philosophy of Kant: Immanuel Kant's Moral and Political Writings*. Edited by Carl J. Friedrich, Modern Library, 1949.

A TRANSLATED BOOK

Ullmann, Regina. *The Country Road: Stories*. Translated by Kurt Beals, New Directions Publishing, 2015.

AN INTRODUCTION, FOREWORD, OR AFTERWORD

Usually, an introduction or comparable material is listed under the name of the author of the book (here Karr) rather than under the name of the writer of the foreword (here Dunham), but if you are referring to the apparatus rather than to the book itself, use the form given.

Dunham, Lena. Foreword. *The Liars' Club*, by Mary Karr, Penguin Classics, 2015, pp. xi-xiii.

A BOOK WITH AN EDITOR BUT NO AUTHOR

Horner, Avril, and Anne Rowe, editors. *Living on Paper: Letters from Iris Murdoch*. Princeton UP, 2016.

A WORK WITHIN A VOLUME OF WORKS BY ONE AUTHOR

The following entry indicates that a short work by Susan Sontag, an essay called "The Aesthetics of Silence," appears in a book by Sontag titled *Styles of Radical Will.* Notice that the inclusive page numbers of the short work are cited — not merely page numbers that you may happen to refer to, but the page numbers of the entire piece.

Sontag, Susan. "The Aesthetics of Silence." *Styles of Radical Will*, Farrar, Straus, and Giroux, 1969, pp. 3-34.

A BOOK REVIEW

Walton, James. "Noble, Embattled Souls." Review of *The Bone Clocks and Slade House*, by David Mitchell. *The New York Review of Books*, 3 Dec. 2015, pp. 55-58.

If a review is anonymous, list it under the first word of the title or under the second word if the first is *A*, *An*, or *The.* If an anonymous review has no title, begin the entry with *Review of* and then give the title of the work reviewed; alphabetize the entry under the title of the work reviewed.

AN ARTICLE OR ESSAY IN A COLLECTION

A book may consist of a collection (edited by one or more persons) of new essays by several authors. Here, the essay by Sayrafiezadeh occupies pages 3 to 29 in a collection edited by Marcus.

Sayrafiezadeh, Saïd. "Paranoia." *New American Stories*, edited by Ben Marcus, Vintage Books, 2015, pp. 3-29.

MULTIPLE WORKS FROM THE SAME COLLECTION

You may find that you need to cite multiple sources from within a single container, such as several essays from the same edited anthology. In these cases, provide an entry for the entire anthology (the entry for Marcus below) and a shortened entry for each selection. Alphabetize the entries by authors' or editors' last names.

Eisenberg, Deborah. "Some Other, Better Otto." Marcus, pp. 94-136.

Marcus, Ben, editor. *New American Stories*. Vintage Books, 2015.

Sayrafiezadeh, Saïd. "Paranoia." Marcus, pp. 3-29.

ARTICLES IN PERIODICALS

AN ARTICLE IN A REFERENCE WORK (INCLUDING A WIKI)

For a *signed* article, begin with the author's last name. Provide the name of the article, the publication title, edition number (if applicable), the publisher, and the copyright year. For an unsigned article, begin with the title of the article:

Robinson, Lisa Clayton. "Harlem Writers Guild." *Africana: The Encyclopedia of the African and African American Experience*. 2nd ed., Oxford UP, 2005.

"The Ball's in Your Court." *The American Heritage Dictionary of Idioms*. 2nd ed., Houghton Mifflin Harcourt, 2013.

For an online reference work, such as a wiki, include the author name and article name followed by the name of the website, the date of publication or the most recent update, and the URL (without *http://* before it).

Durante, Amy M. "Finn Mac Cumhail." *Encyclopedia Mythica*, 17 Apr. 2011, www.pantheon.org/articles/f/finn_mac_cumhail.html.

"House Music." *Wikipedia*, 16 Nov. 2015, en.wikipedia.org/wiki/House_music.

AN ARTICLE IN A SCHOLARLY JOURNAL

The title of the article is enclosed within quotation marks, and the title of the journal is italicized.

Matchie, Thomas. "Law versus Love in the Round House." *Midwest Quarterly*, vol. 56, no. 4, Summer 2015, pp. 353-64.

Matchie's article occupies pages 353 to 364 in volume 56, which was published in 2015. When available, give the issue number as well.

AN ARTICLE IN A MAGAZINE

Do not include volume or issue numbers, even if given.

Thompson, Mark. "Sending Women to War: The Pentagon Nears a Historic Decision on Equality at the Front Lines." *Time*, 14 Dec. 2015, pp. 53-55.

AN ARTICLE IN A NEWSPAPER

Because a newspaper usually consists of several sections, a section number or a capital letter may precede the page number. The example indicates that an article appears on page 1 of section C.

Bray, Hiawatha. "As Toys Get Smarter, Privacy Issues Emerge." *The Boston Globe*, 10 Dec. 2015, p. C1.

AN ARTICLE IN AN ONLINE PERIODICAL

Give the same information as you would for a print article, plus the URL. (See Fig. 7.7.)

Acocella, Joan. "In the Blood: Why Do Vampires Still Thrill?" *New Yorker*, 16 March 2009. www.newyorker.com/magazine/2009/03/16/in-the-blood.

Figure 7.7 Citing an Online Magazine

1. URL
2. Title of periodical
3. Title of article
4. Subtitle of article
5. Author
6. Publication date (If the article doesn't have a publication date, include the date you accessed it.)

AN UNSIGNED EDITORIAL OR LETTER TO THE EDITOR

Include the label "Editorial" or "Letter" at the end of the entry (and before any database information).

"The Religious Tyranny Amendment." *New York Times*, 15 Mar. 1998, p. 16. Editorial.

Adrouny, Salpi. "Our Shockingly Low Local Voter Turnout." *AJC.com*, 8 Nov. 2015, www.ajc.com/news/news/opinion/readers-write-nov-8/npHrS/. Letter.

A DATABASE SOURCE

Treat material obtained from a database like other printed material, but at the end of the entry add (if available) the title of the database (italicized) and a permalink or DOI (digital object identifier) if the source has one. If a source does not have that information, include a URL (without the protocol, such as *http://*).

Coles, Kimberly Anne. "The Matter of Belief in John Donne's Holy Sonnets." *Renaissance Quarterly*, vol. 68, no. 3, Fall 2015, pp. 899-931. JSTOR, doi:10.1086/683855.

Macari, Anne Marie. "Lyric Impulse in a Time of Extinction." *American Poetry Review*, vol. 44, no. 4, July/Aug. 2015, pp. 11-14. *General OneFile*, go.galegroup.com/.

GOVERNMENT DOCUMENTS

If the writer is not known, treat the government and the agency as the author.

United States, Department of Agriculture, Food and Nutrition Service, Child Nutrition Programs. *Eligibility Manual for School Meals: Determining and Verifying Eligibility*. July 2015, www.fns.usda.gov/sites/default/files/cn/SP40_CACFP18_SFSP20-2015a1.pdf.

INTERVIEWS

A PUBLISHED OR BROADCAST INTERVIEW

Give the name of the interview subject and the interviewer, followed by the relevant publication or broadcast information, in the following format:

Weddington, Sarah. "Sarah Weddington: Still Arguing for *Roe*." Interview by Michele Kort, *Ms.*, Winter 2013, pp. 32-35.

Tempkin, Ann, and Anne Umland. Interview by Charlie Rose. *Charlie Rose: The Week*, PBS, 9 Oct. 2015.

AN INTERVIEW YOU CONDUCT

Akufo, Dautey. Personal interview, 11 Apr. 2016.

ONLINE SOURCES

A WEBSITE AND PARTS OF WEBSITES

Include the following elements: the name of the person who created the site or authored the page (omit if not given, as in Figure 7.8); page title (in quotation marks), if applicable, and

Figure 7.8 Citing a Blog

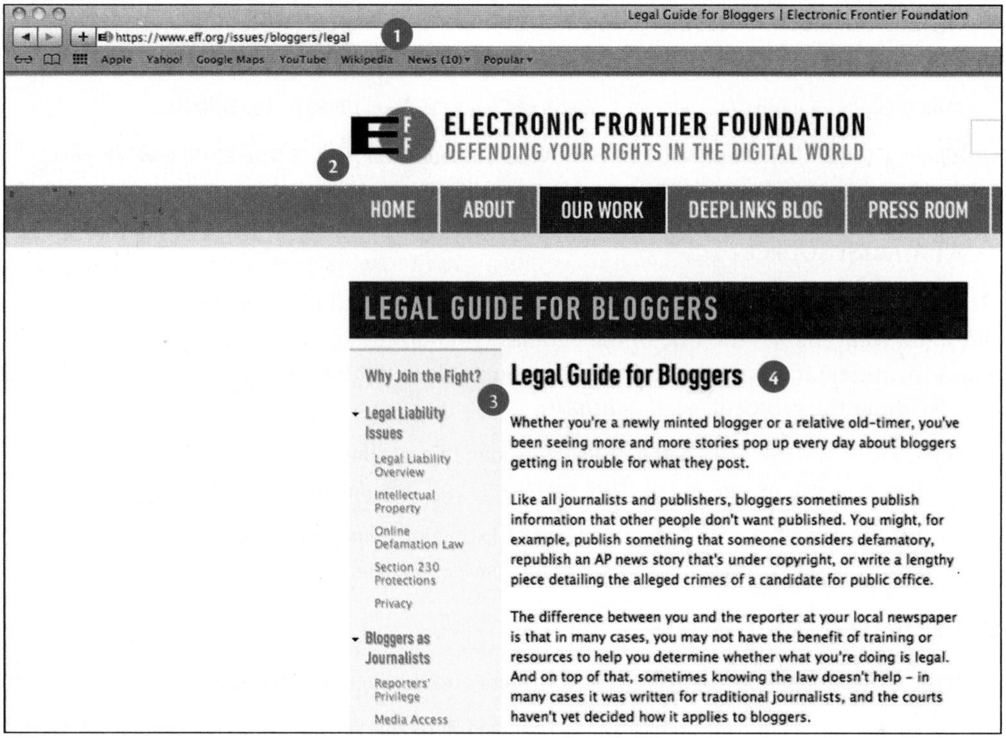

1. URL
2. Sponsor of website
3. No author given; start citation with the title.
4. No date of publication given; include date of access in citation.

site title (italicized); any sponsoring institution or organization (if the title of the site and the sponsor are the same or similar, use the title of the site but omit the sponsor); date of electronic publication or of the latest update (if given; if not, provide the date you accessed the site at the end of the citation); and the URL (without *http://*).

Legal Guide for Bloggers. Electronic Frontier Foundation, www.eff.org/issues/bloggers/legal. Accessed 5 Apr. 2016.

Bae, Rebecca. Home page. Iowa State U, 2015, www.engl.iastate.edu/rebecca-bae-directory-page.

Enzinna, Wes. "Syria's Unknown Revolution." *Pulitzer Center on Crisis Reporting*, 24 Nov. 2015, pulitzercenter.org/projects/middle-east-syria-enzinna-war-rojava.

ENTIRE BLOG

Kiuchi, Tatsuro. Tatsuro Kiuchi: *News & Blog*. tatsurokiuchi.com. Accessed 3 Mar. 2016.

Ng, Amy. Pikaland. Pikaland Media, 2015, www.pikaland.com.

A SOCIAL MEDIA POST OR COMMENT

Include the name of the social media page (e.g., Facebook, Instagram) on which the post appeared, the name of the post (or the post on which the comment appears), the name of the site, the date, and the URL of the post or comment.

Bedford English. "Stacey Cochran Explores Reflective Writing in the Classroom and as a Writer: http://ow.ly/YkjVB." *Facebook*, 15 Feb. 2016, www.facebook.com/BedfordEnglish/posts/10153415001259607.

For Twitter, include the handle of the poster, the content of the tweet (enclosed in quotation marks), the name of the site, the date and time of the post, and the URL.

Curiosity Rover. "Can you see me waving? How to spot #Mars in the night sky: https://youtu.be/hv8hVvJlcJQ." *Twitter*, 5 Nov. 2015, 11:00 a.m., twitter.com/marscuriosity/status/672859022911889408.

@grammarphobia (Patricia T. O'Conner and Steward Kellerman). "When Dickens don't use 'doesn't' #English #grammar #usage." *Twitter*, 11 June 2018, 8:10 a.m., twitter.com/grammarphobia.

MULTIMEDIA SOURCES

WORK OF ART (INCLUDING PHOTOGRAPHS)

Bradford, Mark. *Let's Walk to the Middle of the Ocean*. 2015, Museum of Modern Art, New York.

Hura, Sohrab. *Old Man Lighting a Fire*. 2015. *Magnum Photos*, pro.magnumphotos.com/CS.aspx?VP3=SearchResult&VBID=2K1HZO4JVP42X8&SMLS=1&RW=1280&RH=692.

CARTOON OR COMIC

Zyglis, Adam. "City of Light." *Buffalo News*, 8 Nov. 2015, buffalonews.com/2015/11/08/city-of-light/. Cartoon.

ADVERTISEMENT

AT&T. *National Geographic*, Dec. 2015, p. 14. Advertisement.

Toyota. *The Root*. Slate Group, 28 Nov. 2015, www.theroot.com. Advertisement.

VISUALS (TABLES, CHARTS, GRAPHICS, ETC.)

Add the type of visual at the end, if it's not obvious from the title or website. This is optional, but good for clarity.

"Number of Measles Cases by Year." *Centers for Disease Control and Prevention*, 6 June 2019, www.cdc.gov/measles/cases-outbreaks.html. Table.

Brown, Evan. "15 Golden Principles of Visual Hierarchy." *DesignMantic*, 15 Oct. 2014, www.designmantic.com/blog/infographics/15-golden-principles-of-visual-hierarchy. Infographic.

A TELEVISION OR RADIO PROGRAM

Be sure to include the title of the episode or segment (in quotation marks), the title of the show (italicized), the producer or director of the show, the network, and the date of the airing. Other information, such as performers, narrator, and so forth, may be included if pertinent.

"Fast Times at West Philly High." *Frontline*, produced by Debbie Morton, PBS, 17 July 2012.

"Federal Role in Support of Autism." *Washington Journal*, narrated by Robb Harleston, C-SPAN, 1 Dec. 2012.

PODCAST

Include the podcast host(s) and the title of the episode. Then list the title of the podcast, the network or service, the date, and the place where you access the episode. If you access the podcast through an app or a platform such as Spotify, treat the app or platform as a separate container, similar to a database.

McDougall, Christopher. "How Did Endurance Help Early Humans Survive?" *TED Radio Hour*, NPR, 20 Nov. 2015, www.npr.org/2015/11/20/455904655/how-did-endurance-help-early-humans-survive.

FILM

Begin with whatever you are emphasizing in your work: entire film (first model), director (second model), and so forth.

Birdman or (The Unexpected Virtue of Ignorance). Directed by Alejandro González Iñárritu, performances by Michael Keaton, Emma Stone, Zach Galifianakis, Edward Norton, and Naomi Watts, Fox Searchlight, 2014.

Scott, Ridley, director. *The Martian*. Performances by Matt Damon, Jessica Chastain, Kristen Wiig, and Kate Mara, Twentieth Century Fox, 2015.

VIDEO FROM AN ONLINE SOURCE (SUCH AS YOUTUBE)

Nayar, Vineet. "Employees First, Customers Second." *YouTube*, 9 June 2015, www.youtube.com/watch?v=cCdu67s_C5E.

APA Format: Citations within the Text

The APA style emphasizes the date of publication; the date appears not only in the list of references at the end of the paper but also in the paper itself, when you give a brief parenthetic citation of a source that you have quoted or summarized or in any other way used. Here is an example:

Statistics are readily available (Smith, 1989, p. 20).

The title of Smith's book or article will be given at the end of your paper in the list titled References. We discuss the form of the material listed in the References after we look at some typical citations within the text of a student's essay.

A SUMMARY OF AN ENTIRE WORK

Smith (1988) holds the same view.

Similar views are held widely (Smith, 1988; Jones & Metz, 1990).

A REFERENCE TO A PAGE OR TO PAGES

Lanier (2018) argues that "to free yourself, to be more authentic . . . delete your accounts" (p. 24).

A REFERENCE TO AN AUTHOR WHO HAS MORE THAN ONE WORK IN THE LIST OF REFERENCES

If in the References you list two or more works that an author published in the same year, the works are listed in alphabetical order, by the first letter of the title. The first work is labeled *a*, the second *b*, and so on. Here is a reference to a second work that Smith published in 1989:

Florida presents "a fair example" of how the death penalty is administered (Smith, 1989b, p. 18).

APA Format: The List of References

Your paper will conclude with a separate page headed References, on which you list all your sources. If the last page of your essay is numbered 10, number the first page of the References 11. Here are some general guidelines.

FORM ON THE PAGE

- Begin each entry flush with the left margin, but if an entry runs to more than one line, indent five spaces for each succeeding line of the entry.
- Double-space each entry and double-space between entries.

ALPHABETICAL ORDER

- Arrange the list alphabetically by author.
- Give the author's last name first and then the initial of the first name and of the middle name (if any).
- If there is more than one author, name all of the authors up to seven, again inverting the name (last name first) and giving only initials for first and middle names. (But do not invert the editor's name when the entry begins with the name

of an author who has written an article in an edited book.) When there are two or more authors, use an ampersand (&) before the name of the last author. For example (here, of an article in the tenth volume of a journal called *Developmental Psychology*):

Drabman, R. S., & Thomas, M. H. (1974). Does media violence increase children's tolerance of real-life aggression? *Developmental Psychology, 10,* 418-421.

- For eight or more authors, list the first six followed by three ellipsis dots (. . .) and then the last author.
- If you list more than one work by an author, do so in the order of publication, the earliest first. If two works by an author were published in the same year, give them in alphabetical order by the first letter of the title, disregarding *A*, *An*, or *The*, and a foreign equivalent. Designate the first work as *a*, the second as *b*, and so forth. Repeat the author's name at the start of each entry.

Donnerstein, E. (1980a). Aggressive erotica and violence against women. *Journal of Personality and Social Psychology, 39,* 269-277.

Donnerstein, E. (1980b). Pornography and violence against women. *Annals of the New York Academy of Sciences, 347,* 227-288.

Donnerstein, E. (1983). Erotica and human aggression. In R. Green & E. Donnerstein (Eds.), *Aggression: Theoretical and empirical reviews* (pp. 87-103). New York, NY: Academic Press.

FORM OF TITLE

- In references to books, capitalize only the first letter of the first word of the title (and of the subtitle, if any) and capitalize proper nouns. Italicize the complete title (but not the period at the end).
- In references to articles in periodicals or in edited books, capitalize only the first letter of the first word of the article's title (and subtitle, if any) and all proper nouns. Do not put the title within quotation marks or italicize it. Type a period after the title of the article.
- In references to periodicals, give the volume number in arabic numerals, and italicize it. Do not use *vol.* before the number and do not use *p.* or *pg.* before the page numbers.

SAMPLE REFERENCES

For a full account of the APA method of dealing with all sorts of unusual citations, see the sixth edition (2010) of the APA manual, *Publication Manual of the American Psychological Association.*

BOOKS

A BOOK BY ONE AUTHOR

Pavlov, I. P. (1927). *Conditioned reflexes* (G. V. Anrep, Trans.). London, England: Oxford University Press.

A BOOK BY MORE THAN ONE AUTHOR

Belenky, M. F., Clinchy, B. M., Goldberger, N. R., & Torule, J. M. (1986). *Women's ways of knowing: The development of self, voice, and mind*. New York, NY: Basic Books.

A COLLECTION OF ESSAYS

Christ, C. P., & Plaskow, J. (Eds.). (1979). *Woman-spirit rising: A feminist reader in religion*. New York, NY: Harper & Row.

A WORK IN A COLLECTION OF ESSAYS

Fiorenza, E. (1979). Women in the early Christian movement. In C. P. Christ & J. Plaskow (Eds.), *Woman-spirit rising: A feminist reader in religion* (pp. 84-92). New York, NY: Harper & Row.

ARTICLES IN PERIODICALS

AN ARTICLE IN A JOURNAL

Tversky, A., & Kahneman, D. (1981). The framing of decisions and the psychology of choice. *Science, 211*, 453-458.

Foot, R. J. (1988-89). Nuclear coercion and the ending of the Korean conflict. *International Security, 13*(4), 92-112.

The reference informs us that the article appeared in issue number 4 of volume 13.

AN ARTICLE FROM A MAGAZINE

Bensman, D. (2015, December 4). Security for a precarious workforce. *The American Prospect*. Retrieved from http://prospect.org/

Greenwald, J. (1989, February 27). Gimme shelter. *Time, 133*, 50-51.

AN ARTICLE IN A NEWSPAPER

Connell, R. (1989, February 6). Career concerns at heart of 1980s campus protests. *Los Angeles Times*, pp. 1, 3.

Roberson, K. (2015, May 3). Innovation helps address nurse shortage. *Des Moines Register*. Retrieved from http://www.desmoinesregister.com/

(*Note:* If no author is given, simply begin with the title followed by the date in parentheses.)

AN ARTICLE FROM A DATABASE

Lyons, M. (2015). Writing upwards: How the weak wrote to the powerful. *Journal of Social History, 49*(2), 317-330. https://doi.org/10.1093/jsh/shv038

A BOOK REVIEW

Daniels, N. (1984). Understanding physician power [Review of the book *The social transformation of American medicine*]. *Philosophy and Public Affairs, 13*, 347-356.

Daniels is the reviewer, not the author of the book. The book under review is called *The Social Transformation of American Medicine*, but the review, published in volume 13 of *Philosophy and Public Affairs*, had its own title, "Understanding Physician Power."

If the review does not have a title, retain the square brackets and use the material within as the title. Proceed as in the example just given.

GOVERNMENT PUBLICATIONS

If the writer is not known, treat the government and the agency as the author. If a document number has been assigned, insert that number in parentheses between the title and the following period.

U.S. Census Bureau, Bureau of Economic Analysis. (2015, December). *U.S. international trade in goods and services, October 2015* (Report No. CB15-197, BEA15-60, FT-900 [15-10]). Retrieved from http://www.census.gov/foreign-trade/Press-Release/current_press_release/ft900.pdf

ONLINE SOURCES

WEBSITES AND PARTS OF WEBSITES

Do not include an entire website in the reference list; instead, give the URL in parentheses within your paper.

Badrunnesha, M., & Kwauk, C. (2015, December). *Improving the quality of girls' education in madrasa in Bangladesh*. Retrieved from Brookings Institution website: http://www.brookings.edu/research/papers/2015/12/05-bangladesh-girls-education-madrasa-badrunnesha

BLOG POST

Costandi, M. (2015, April 9). Why brain scans aren't always what they seem [Blog post]. Retrieved from http://www.theguardian.com/science/neurophilosophy/2015/apr/09/bold-assumptions-fmri

COMMENT ON AN ONLINE ARTICLE

MintDragon. (2015, December 9). Re: The very real pain of exclusion [Comment]. *The Atlantic.* Retrieved from http://www.theatlantic.com/

A SOCIAL MEDIA POST

National Science Foundation. (2015, December 8). Simulation shows key to building powerful magnetic fields 1.usa.gov/1TZUiJ6 #supernovas #supercomputers [Tweet]. Retrieved from https://twitter.com/NSF/status/674352440582545413

MULTIMEDIA SOURCES

WORK OF ART (INCLUDING PHOTOGRAPHS)

Sabogal, J. (2015). *Los hijos of the Revolution* [Outdoor mural]. San Francisco, CA.

Whitten, J. (2015). *Soul map* [Painting]. Retrieved from http://www.walkerart.org/

TELEVISION OR RADIO PROGRAM

Oliver, J. (Host), & Leddy, B. (Director). (2015, October 4). Mental health [Television series episode]. In *Last week tonight with John Oliver.* New York, NY: HBO.

PODCAST

Abumrad, J., & Krulwich, R. (2015, August 30). *Remembering Oliver Sacks* [Audio podcast]. Retrieved from https://www.wnycstudios.org/shows/radiolab/

DATA SET OR GRAPHIC REPRESENTATION OF DATA (GRAPH, CHART, TABLE)

Gallup. (2015). *Gallup worldwide research data collected from 2005-2018* [Data set]. Retrieved from http://www.gallup.com/services/177797/country-data-set-details.aspx

U.S. Department of Agriculture, Economic Research Service. (2015). *USDA expenditures for food and nutrition assistance, FY 1980-2014* [Chart]. Retrieved from http://www.ers.usda.gov/data-products/chart-gallery/detail.aspx?chartId=40105&ref=collection&embed=True

A VIDEO FROM AN ONLINE SOURCE (SUCH AS YOUTUBE)

Renaud, B., & Renaud, C. (2015, October 8). *Between borders: America's migrant crisis* [Video file]. Retrieved from https://www.youtube.com/watch?v=rxF0t-SMEXA

A CHECKLIST FOR CRITICAL PAPERS USING SOURCES

- ❒ Are all borrowed words and ideas credited, including those from internet sources?
- ❒ Are all summaries and paraphrases acknowledged as such?
- ❒ Are quotations and summaries not too long?
- ❒ Are quotations accurate? Are omissions of words indicated by three spaced periods? Are additions of words enclosed within square brackets?
- ❒ Are quotations provided with helpful lead-ins?
- ❒ Is documentation in proper form?

Of course, you will also ask yourself the questions that you would ask of a paper that did not use sources, such as:

- ❒ Is the topic sufficiently narrowed?
- ❒ Is the thesis stated early and clearly, perhaps even in the title?
- ❒ Is the audience kept in mind? Are opposing views stated fairly and as sympathetically as possible? Are controversial terms defined?
- ❒ Is the purpose and focus clear (evaluation, recommendation of policy)?
- ❒ Is evidence (examples, testimony, statistics) adequate and sound?
- ❒ Is the organization clear (effective opening, coherent sequence of arguments, unpretentious ending)?
- ❒ Is the tone appropriate?
- ❒ Is the title effective?

An Annotated Student Research Paper in MLA Format

The following argument makes good use of sources. Early in the semester, students were asked to choose one topic from a list of ten and to write a documented argument of 750 to 1,250 words (three to five pages of double-spaced typing) as a prelude to working on a research paper of 2,500 to 3,000 words. Citations are given in the MLA form.

Timmerman 1

Lesley Timmerman

Professor Jennifer Wilson

English 102

15 August 2016

An Argument for Corporate Responsibility

Title is focused and announces the thesis.

Opponents of corporate social responsibility (CSR) argue that a company's sole duty is to generate profits. According to them, by acting for the public good, corporations are neglecting their primary obligation to make money. However, as people are becoming more and more conscious of corporate impacts on society and the environment, separating profits from company practices and ethics does not make sense. Employees want to work for institutions that share their values, and consumers want to buy products from companies that are making an impact and improving people's lives. Furthermore, businesses exist in an interdependent world where the health of the environment and the well-being of society really do matter. For these reasons, corporations have to take responsibility for their actions, beyond making money for shareholders. For their own benefit as well as the public's, companies must strive to be socially responsible.

Double-space between the title and first paragraph—and **all lines** throughout the essay.

Brief statement of one side of the issue.

In his article "The Case against Corporate Social Responsibility," *Wall Street Journal* writer Aneel Karnani argues that CSR will never be able to solve the world's problems. Thinking it can, Karnani says, is a dangerous illusion. He recommends that instead of expecting corporate managers to act in the public interest, we should rely on philanthropy and government regulation. Karnani maintains that "Managers who sacrifice profit for the common good [. . .] are in effect imposing a tax on their shareholders and arbitrarily deciding how that money should be spent." In other words, according to Karnani, corporations should not be determining what constitutes socially responsible behavior; individual donors and the government should. Certainly, individuals should continue to make charitable gifts, and governments should maintain laws and regulations to protect the public interest. However, Karnani's reasoning for why corporations should be exempt from social responsibility is flawed. With very few exceptions, corporations' socially responsible actions are not arbitrary and do not sacrifice long-term profits.

Summary of the opposing view.

Lead-in to quotation.

Essayist's response to the quotation.

1" margin on each side and at bottom.

Author concisely states her position.

In fact, corporations have already proven that they can contribute profitably and meaningfully to solving significant global problems by integrating CSR into their standard practices and long-term visions. Rather than focusing on shareholders' short-term profits, many companies have begun measuring their success by "profit, planet and people" — what is known as the "triple bottom line." Businesses operating under this principle consider their environmental and social impacts, as well as their financial impacts, and make responsible and compassionate decisions. For example, such businesses use resources efficiently, create healthy products, choose suppliers who share their ethics, and improve economic opportunities for people in the communities they serve. By doing so, companies often save money. They also contribute to the sustainability of life on earth and ensure the sustainability of their own businesses. In their book *The Triple Bottom Line: How Today's Best-Run Companies Are Achieving Economic, Social, and Environmental Success,* coauthors Savitz and Weber demonstrate that corporations need to become sustainable, in all ways. They argue that "the only way to succeed in today's interdependent world is to embrace sustainability" (xi). The authors go on to show that, for the vast majority of companies, a broad commitment to sustainability enhances profitability (Savitz and Weber 39).

Transitions ("For example," "also") alert readers to where the writer is taking them.

For example, PepsiCo has been able to meet the financial expectations of its shareholders while demonstrating its commitment to the triple bottom line. In addition to donating over $16 million to help victims of natural disasters, Pepsi has woven concerns for people and for the planet into its company practices and culture (Bejou 4). For instance, because of a recent water shortage in an area of India where Pepsi runs a plant, the company began a project to build community wells (Savitz and Weber 160). Though Pepsi did not cause the water shortage nor was its manufacturing threatened by it, "Pepsi realizes that the well-being of the community is part of the company's responsibility" (Savitz and Weber 161). Ultimately, Pepsi chose to look beyond the goal of maximizing short-term profits. By doing so, the company improved its relationship with this Indian community, improved people's daily lives and opportunities, and improved its own reputation. In other words, Pepsi embraced CSR and ensured a more sustainable future for everyone involved.

Another example of a wide-reaching company that is working toward greater sustainability on all fronts is Walmart. The corporation has issued a CSR policy that includes three ambitious goals: "to be fully supplied by renewable energy, to create zero waste and to sell products that sustain people and the environment" ("From Fringe to Mainstream"). As Dr. Doug Guthrie, dean of George Washington University's School of Business, noted in a recent lecture, if a company as powerful as Walmart were to succeed in these goals, the impact would be huge. To illustrate Walmart's potential influence, Dr. Guthrie pointed out that the corporation's exports from China to the United States are equal to Mexico's total exports to the United States. In committing to CSR, the company's leaders are acknowledging how much their power depends on the earth's natural resources, as well as the communities who produce, distribute, sell, and purchase Walmart's products. The company is also well aware that achieving its goals will "ultimately save the company a great deal of money" ("From Fringe to Mainstream"). For good reason, Walmart, like other companies around the world, is choosing to act in *everyone*'s best interest.

Author provides two examples of forward-thinking moves by major companies.

Recent research on employees' and consumers' social consciousness offers companies further reason to take corporate responsibility seriously. For example, studies show that workers care about making a difference (Meister). In many cases, workers would even take a pay cut to work for a more responsible, sustainable company. In fact, 45% of workers said they would take a 15% reduction in pay "for a job that makes a social or environmental impact" (Meister). Even more said they would take a 15% cut in pay to work for a company with values that match their own (Meister). The numbers are most significant among Millennials (those born between, approximately, 1980 and the early 2000s). Fully 80% of Millennials said they "wanted to work for a company that cares about how it impacts and contributes to society," and over half said they would not work for an "irresponsible company" (Meister). Given this more socially conscious generation, companies are going to find it harder and harder to ignore CSR.

Author now introduces statistical evidence that, if introduced earlier, might have turned the reader off.

To recruit and retain employees, employers will need to earn the admiration, respect, and loyalty of their workers by becoming "good corporate citizen[s]" (qtd. in "From Fringe to Mainstream").

Similarly, studies clearly show that CSR matters to today's consumers. According to an independent report, 80% of Americans say they would switch brands to support a social cause (Cone Communications 6). Fully 88% say they approve of companies' using social or environmental issues in their marketing (Cone Communications 5). And 83% say they "wish more of the products, services and retailers would support causes" (Cone Communications 5). Other independent surveys corroborate these results, confirming that today's customers, especially Millennials, care about more than just price ("From Fringe to Mainstream"). Furthermore, plenty of companies have seen what happens when they assume that consumers do not care about CSR. For example, in 1997, when Nike customers discovered that their shoes were manufactured by child laborers in Indonesia, the company took a huge financial hit (Guthrie). Today, Information Age customers are even more likely to educate themselves about companies' labor practices and environmental records. Smart corporations will listen to consumer preferences, provide transparency, and commit to integrating CSR into their long-term business plans.

Author argues that it is in the *companies'* interest to be socially responsible.

In this increasingly interdependent world, the case against CSR is becoming more and more difficult to defend. Exempting corporations and relying on government to be the world's conscience does not make good social, environmental, or economic sense. Contributors to a recent article in the online journal *Knowledge@Wharton*, published by the Wharton School of Business, agree. Professor Eric Orts maintains that "it is an outmoded view to say that one must rely only on the government and regulation to police business responsibilities. What we need is re-conception of what the purpose of business is" (qtd. in "From Fringe to Mainstream"). The question is, what should the purpose of a business be in today's world? Professor of Business Administration David Bejou of Elizabeth City State University has a thoughtful and sensible answer to that question. He writes,

Author's lead-in to the quotation guides the reader's response to the quotation.

> . . . it is clear that the sole purpose of a business is not merely that of generating profits for its owners. Instead, because compassion provides the necessary equilibrium between a company's purpose and the needs of its communities, it should be the new philosophy of business. (Bejou 1)

Author uses a block quotation for quotation longer than three lines in text.

As Bejou implies, the days of allowing corporations to act in their own financial self-interest with little or no regard for their effects on others are over. None of us can afford such a narrow view of business. The world is far too interconnected. A seemingly small corporate decision — to buy coffee beans directly from local growers or to install solar panels — can affect the lives and livelihoods of many people and determine the environmental health of whole regions. A business, just like a government or an individual, therefore has an ethical responsibility to act with compassion for the public good.

Fortunately, corporations have many incentives to act responsibly. Customer loyalty, employee satisfaction, overall cost-saving, and long-term viability are just some of the advantages businesses can expect to gain by embracing comprehensive CSR policies. Meanwhile, companies have very little to lose by embracing a socially conscious view. These days, compassion is profitable. Corporations would be wise to recognize the enormous power, opportunity, and responsibility they have to effect positive change.

Works Cited list begins on a new page.

Alphabetical by author's last name.

Hanging indent ½".

An article on a blog without a known author.

A clip from YouTube.

Works Cited

Bejou, David. "Compassion as the New Philosophy of Business." *Journal of Relationship Marketing,* vol. 10, no. 1, Apr. 2011, pp. 1-6. *Taylor and Francis*, doi:10.1080/15332667.2011.550098.

Cone Communications. 2010 *Cone Cause Evolution Study*. Cone, 2010, www.conecomm.com/research-blog/2010-cause-evolution-study.

"From Fringe to Mainstream: Companies Integrate CSR Initiatives into Everyday Business." *Knowledge@Wharton*, 23 May 2012, knowledge .wharton.upenn.edu/article/from-fringe-to-mainstream-companies -integrate-csr-initiatives-into-everyday-business/.

Guthrie, Doug. "Corporate Social Responsibility: A State Department Approach." *Promoting a Comprehensive Approach to Corporate Social Responsibility (CSR)*, George P. Shultz National Foreign Affairs Training Center, 22 May 2012. *YouTube*, 23 Aug. 2013, www.youtube.com /watch?v=99cJMe6wERc.

Karnani, Aneel. "The Case against Corporate Social Responsibility." *Wall Street Journal*, 14 June 2012, www.wsj.com/articles /SB10001424052748703338004575230112664504890.

Meister, Jeanne. "Corporate Social Responsibility: A Lever for Employee Attraction & Engagement." *Forbes*, 7 June 2012, www.forbes.com /sites/jeannemeister/2012/06/07/corporate-social-responsibility -a-lever-for-employee-attraction-engagement/#6125425a7511.

Savitz, Andrew W., with Karl Weber. *The Triple Bottom Line: How Today's Best-Run Companies Are Achieving Economic, Social, and Environmental Success*, Jossey-Bass, 2006.

An Annotated Student Research Paper in APA Format

The following paper is an example of a student paper that uses APA format.

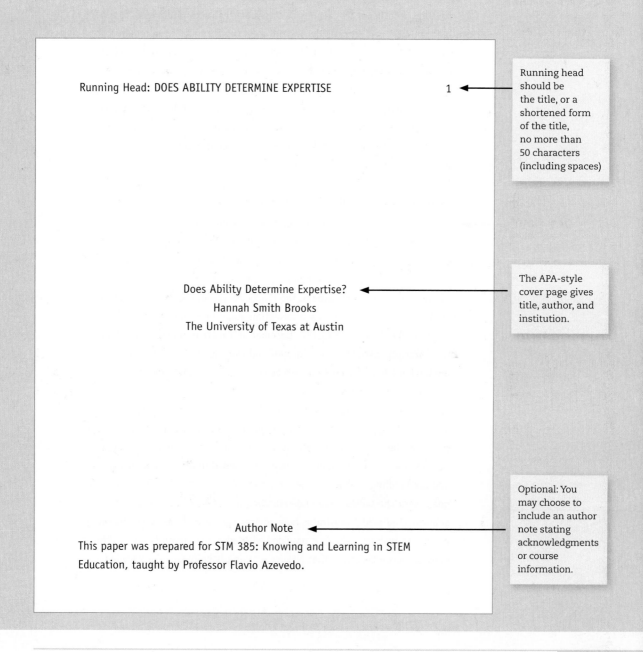

Running Head: DOES ABILITY DETERMINE EXPERTISE 1

Running head should be the title, or a shortened form of the title, no more than 50 characters (including spaces)

Does Ability Determine Expertise?

Hannah Smith Brooks

The University of Texas at Austin

The APA-style cover page gives title, author, and institution.

Author Note

This paper was prepared for STM 385: Knowing and Learning in STEM Education, taught by Professor Flavio Azevedo.

Optional: You may choose to include an author note stating acknowledgments or course information.

Short form of title and page number as running head.

Thesis explicitly introduced.

Headings aligned center and set in boldface to help readers navigate the essay.

DOES ABILITY DETERMINE EXPERTISE 2

Does Ability Determine Expertise?

To become an expert requires long-term commitment to the field of study, whether it be calculus or classroom instruction provided by a teacher. Thus, expertise is dependent upon the context of the required task or the domain specific information presented. Classifying individuals as novices means only that they have limited experience with a particular topic. If provided with an appropriate context, a novice may think deeply and demonstrate effective problem-solving strategies. An individual may be adept at managing student behavior, but he or she may have very little understanding of the biological brain development of adolescents. His or her expertise is defined by the required task of managing a classroom. Importantly, domain experts have extensive experience interacting with the content or skill throughout varied scenarios.

The Development of Expertise

Picture a classroom teacher who interacts with groups of students each day. That teacher develops a deep understanding of student behavior, instructional strategies, and building relationships with young people. During a year in the classroom, the teacher is presented with hundreds of students, each providing new information about how adolescence influences learning. Over time, the teacher becomes an expert in understanding how to effectively instruct student groups and manage student interactions, reinforcing the idea that expertise develops out of many different experiences within a domain.

Saxe (1992) suggests that cognitive development often follows along a pathway driven by goal-directed activities. These goals can shift based on the activity requirements and accumulation of new knowledge. Our classroom teacher might use goals embedded in lesson plan design and the building of diverse student groups. As the teacher completes each goal, he or she builds more understanding of the art of teaching. This goal-directed model illustrates how novices can move through the learning process to become experts if provided with adequate supports and scaffolds. Constructivism theorizes that all new learning is built on prior knowledge and conceptions. Smith, diSessa, and Roschelle (1993/1994) discuss the role of student conceptions in the development of expertise. They argue that more complex cognitive structures must build on existing structures, illustrating how expertise can be developed exclusive of any innate ability. There must be a basic understanding of the foundational concepts in order for knowledge and information to build towards expertise, but these foundational concepts are learned, not inherent.

Many argue that an individual's natural interests may dictate success across domains. However, interest and expertise may not be directly related. Some would argue that all understanding occurs when new information is fully integrated into one's existing cognitive structure (Carey, 1985). Using this definition, interest could be seen as driving an individual to understand and learn more about a particular topic or concept, but does not guarantee integration of information into the cognitive structure. Similarly, while an individual may move through the learning process at a unique speed, the rate of learning does not correlate to an underlying ability to become a "better expert." Individuals are not born with an inherent ability or pre-existing cognitive structure that allows immediate and deep understanding of domain specific concepts, whether interested or not. In order to become recognized as an expert, the individual must actively build the domain-specific cognitive structure. Expertise is based on area specificity, where novices are only novices based on the contextual environment.

Author and date cited for summary or paraphrase.

Author raises and refutes well-researched counterarguments.

An important factor in the development of expertise is the learning environment in which the individual interacts. Cultural practices, social experiences, and the physical world influence how an individual sees and understands the world. The goal directed activities mentioned previously are determined by the specific cultural norms and expectations acting in the environment of the individual. In addition, the early interactions of childhood can greatly impact the belief system of a developing student. These influences can shape academic outcomes, but are not based on the inherent ability an individual may or may not be born with.

When author's name appears in text, only the date is cited parenthetically.

Bracketed word not in quotation in the original source. Author, date, and page number are cited for a direct quotation.

Conclusion restates and strengthens thesis.

How Do Experts Differ From Novices?

There are some notable differences between experts and novices, and I would argue that each of the following skills or strategies is based on a repeated set of experiences and interactions with the domain specific content, not an inherent ability. Goldman and Petrosino (1999) conclude that experts are able to use acquired knowledge of their domain to improve the ability to notice subtle differences and characteristics of presented problems. They continue to suggest that expertise allows an individual to better develop problem-solving strategies and process information using complex creative mental representations. Each of these strategies is based on the continued experience and exposure to content-specific concepts and ideas, not an individual's inherent problem-solving ability. An expert is "not simply [a] 'general problem solver' who [has] learned a set of strategies that operate across all domains" (Bransford, Brown, & Cocking, 1999, p. 48). I consider myself a very creative problem solver inside the walls of a science classroom. If I was asked to solve for a derivative, I would be hopelessly lost and unable to draw upon my extensive problem-solving experience. As Goldman and Petrosino (1999) state, a deep domain-specific knowledge does not equate to an individual's general intelligence. Bransford, Brown and Cocking (1999) take this one step further and suggest that specialization within a specific domain actually reduces the amount of general knowledge an individual can hold at any given time.

Conclusion

If provided with the supports and scaffolds to learn the required mathematical processes and calculations, I could grow into an expert within that domain. Successful acquisition of skills or knowledge in either area is based on my desire to improve and learn, not an inherent ability. Expertise arises with extended and extensive study and exposure to a specific area of study or content. While a student may be more interested in science, they are not born with an inherent ability that precedes the learning process. Everyone must learn how to incorporate new ideas, strategies, and skills into a unique cognitive structure that promotes increased understanding of the world around us to become an expert.

References

References begin on new page.

Bransford, J., Brown A. L., & Cocking, R. R. (1999). How experts differ from novices. In *How people learn: Brain, mind, experience, and school.* Retrieved from https://www.nap.edu/read/9853/chapter/1

Carey, S. (1985). *Conceptual change in childhood*. Cambridge, MA: MIT Press.

A book.

Goldman, S., & Petrosino, A. (1999). Design principles for instruction in content domains: Lessons from research on expertise and learning. In F. T. Durso & R. S. Nickerson (Eds.), *Handbook of applied cognition* (pp. 595-627). Chichester, NY: Wiley.

An article or a chapter in a book.

Saxe, G. B. (1992). Studying children's learning in context: Problems and prospects. *Journal of the Learning Sciences, 2*, 215-234.

Smith, J. P., diSessa, A., & Roschelle, J. (1993/1994). Misconceptions reconceived: A constructivist analysis of knowledge in transition. *Journal of the Learning Sciences, 3*, 115-163. Retrieved from http://www.jstor.org/stable/1466679

An article in a journal, retrieved from a database.

ASSIGNMENTS FOR USING SOURCES

1. Write an essay in which you enter a discourse (an ongoing conversation) on a topic and make an argument. To research effectively, you'll need to do the following:

   - Narrow your topic sufficiently to make the research manageable.
   - Research your topic thoroughly. Find appropriate sources through library or online research (see Finding Sources, pp. 248–55) or conduct your own primary research (see Performing Your Own Primary Research, pp. 271–75).
   - Evaluate your sources to determine if they are credible, relevant, and appropriate to your argument. (See Evaluating Sources, pp. 255–71.)
   - Take good, thorough notes that you can organize later to form the outline of your paper. Be sure to mark which ideas are your sources' and which are yours during this process. (See Taking Notes, p. 276.)

   When writing your essay, build your argument according to the strategies discussed in Chapter 6. In using sources, be sure to adequately introduce and describe the discourse you're entering: What are people saying about your topic? What "sides" or approaches are there, and who takes them? How will you contribute to the conversation? Support your argument with evidence from your research, making sure to summarize, paraphrase, and quote effectively and ethically, citing your source in the appropriate format (see Documentation, pp. 283–302). Address counterpositions and counterarguments you find in your sources to show you are aware of the various strains in the discourse, but be sure to return to and support your own argument and claims to persuade your audience of your thesis.

2. Find what you take to be a "fake news" article from a news source on the internet. Apply the evaluation methods outlined in this chapter to argue that the site or the story is "fake." Be sure to identify and analyze the three or four major factors that caused you to judge it as such. What visual features warned you the web page was suspicious? What other sources did you use to check, verify, or invalidate the source?

PART THREE

Further Views on Argument

8

A Philosopher's View: The Toulmin Model

All my ideas hold together, but I cannot elaborate them all at once. — JEAN-JACQUES ROUSSEAU

[Philosophy is] a peculiarly stubborn effort to think clearly. — WILLIAM JAMES

Fight for the things you care about, but do it in a way that will lead others to join you. — RUTH BADER GINSBURG

In Chapter 3, we explained the contrast between making *deductive* and *inductive* arguments, the two main methods people use to reason. Either

- we make explicit something concealed in what we already accept (**deduction**), or
- we use what we have observed as a basis for asserting something new (**induction**).

These two types of reasoning share some structural features, as we also noticed. Both deductive and inductive reasoning seek to establish a thesis (or reach a conclusion) by offering *reasons*. Thus, every argument contains both a thesis and one or more supportive reasons.

After a little scrutiny, we can in fact point to several features shared by all arguments, whether deductive or inductive, good or bad. We use the vocabulary popularized by Stephen Toulmin, Richard Rieke, and Allan Janik in their book *An Introduction to Reasoning* (1979; second edition 1984) to explore the various elements of argument. Once these elements are understood, it is possible to analyze an argument using their approach and their vocabulary in what has come to be known as the Toulmin method.

The major components of arguments using this model are laid out in the Visual Guide to the Toulmin Method (p. 318), and we go into more detail about each of them throughout this chapter.

Visual Guide: The Toulmin Method

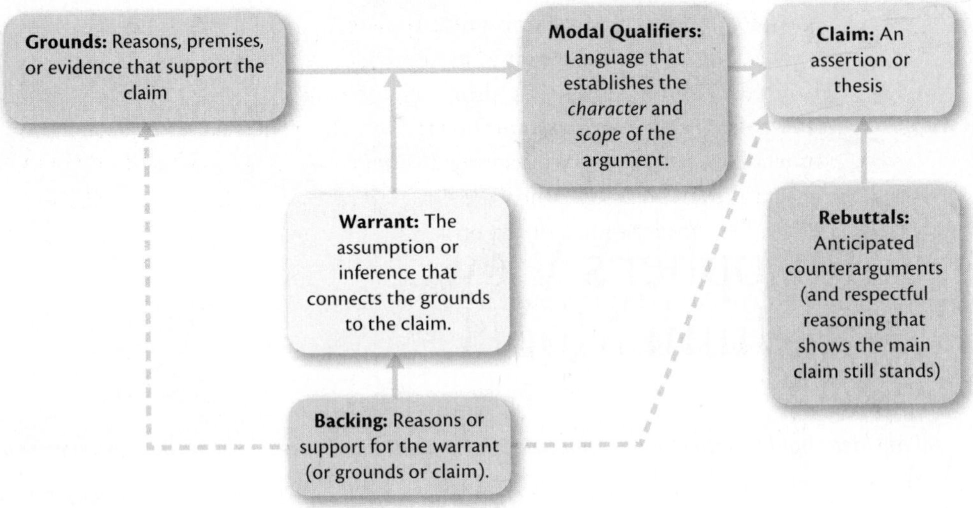

Components of the Toulmin Model

THE CLAIM

Every argument has a purpose, goal, or aim — namely, to establish a **claim** (*conclusion* or *thesis*). Claims may be general or specific. As we have noted in earlier chapters, arguments may attempt to persuade readers simply to change an opinion or adopt a belief, or they may advocate for some action or seek to convince people to take some action. In other words, the *claim* being made in an argument is the whole point of making the argument in the first place. Consequently, when you read or analyze an argument, the first questions you should ask are these:

1. What is the argument intending to prove or establish?
2. What claim is it making?

Different types of claims will lead to different types of grounds, warrants, and backing and to different types of qualifiers and rebuttals.

Suppose you are arguing in a very general sense that men and women should receive equal pay for equal work. You might state your thesis or claim as follows:

> Men and women ought to be paid equally for the same kinds of jobs.

A more specific and precise claim might be the following:

> The Equal Pay Act of 1963 should be strengthened in order to guarantee that men and women are paid equally for the same kinds of jobs.

Both formulations are arguments with strong claims. They make similar but still distinguishable arguments. One is general, and the other is solution-based. Thus, the components of each argument — their grounds, warrants, backing, and so on — will also be slightly different.

GROUNDS

If a claim is clearly formulated and unambiguously asserts what it advocates, it does not matter how general or specific it is. As long as the argument's chief purpose or point is present, we can look for the reasons — in short, the **grounds** — for that claim. You may think of the word *groundwork* to understand better the meaning of an argument's *grounds*. You may ask, On what *groundwork* — what *ground*, what firmament of fact — does the claim rest? In *deductive* arguments, the grounds are the premises; in *inductive* arguments, the grounds are the samples, observations, or experimental results that make the claim possible and plausible.

Consider the differences in the grounds for the two claims about equal pay.

Claim 1: Men and women ought to be paid equally for the same kinds of jobs.

Grounds: According to the US Census Bureau in 2018, women on average make 19.5 percent lower incomes than men for the same kinds of work.

Claim 2: The Equal Pay Act of 1963 should be strengthened in order to guarantee that men and women are paid equally for the same kinds of jobs.

Grounds: The Equal Pay Act was passed in 1963 to eliminate the gender pay gap. Because women still earn on average 19.5 percent lower incomes for the same kinds of work as men, the Equal Pay Act has not been effective.

But something is missing. We have provided the grounds and claim, but neither explains the reasoning or justifications that connects them. That women earn less money for similar work doesn't in and of itself justify the claim that pay should be equal among the sexes. One might simply counter that, no, women *should* make less money than men (and with only grounds and a claim you could not effectively argue back). Your opponent's argument might look like this:

Claim: Women and men get paid exactly what they deserve.

Grounds: According to the US Census Bureau in 2018, women on average currently make 19.5 percent lower incomes than men for the same kinds of work.

In this case, the grounds are the same as in the argument *against* pay inequity. Thus, good arguments exhibit — and require — another feature: the *warrant*.

WARRANTS

Once we have determined the claim of an argument and have isolated the grounds for its existence, the next question to ask is, What **warrants** it? That is, exactly what reasoning helps connect the claim and grounds, or why does the claim arise from the grounds?

The word *warrant* is related to the Old French word *gurant*, the root of our word *guarantee*. A warrant in this context is like the *warranty* you get when you buy something. It guarantees it. With an argument, you might ask what *guarantees* that a rational claim may arise given these grounds. What reasons could be proffered to justify the claim?

Warrants help establish the *connections* between the claim and the grounds. Imagine you establish your grounds (the existence of the pay gap). You claim women and men should be paid equally for similar work. Someone might ask you, What *warrants* your claim? *Why* should women and men get equivalent pay for the same kinds of jobs? You might offer something such as:

> Well, we live in a society where people are not to be discriminated against based on sex, and unequal pay based on sex is discriminatory.

In this case, your warrant is the legal (and perhaps moral) proposition about equality that connects the claim and grounds. (Part of your warrant, too, is that the US Census Bureau numbers are reliable.) Warrants are, in a sense, *interpretations* of how the data and the arguments stemming from them are inherently related.

In ordinary and straightforward *deductive* arguments, warrants may be quite simple. If John is six feet tall and Mary is five feet tall, you have the grounds to argue that John is taller than Mary. The warrant here is just a matter of language: "Taller than" means exceeding something in a measurement of height, so the warrant is "People are said to be taller than other people when they exceed them in measurements of height." The *warrant* here is the common understanding of what the phrase "taller than" means.

In ordinary *inductive* arguments, we are likely to point to the way in which observations or sets of data constitute a *representative sample*. When Anne McKee, a neuropathologist, examined the brains of 110 deceased professional football players and found that 99 percent of them showed signs of chronic traumatic encephalopathy (CTE), she claimed that playing professional football increases the likelihood of brain damage. Her warrant was the reasoning about such a high percentage of her sample showing signs of CTE — that one (football) caused the other (CTE); the warrant is the logic that connected her grounds and her claim.

Establishing the warrants for our reasoning can be a highly technical and exacting procedure when we are making more complex, ambiguous, or values-based claims — that is, when we are explaining why our grounds really do support our claims about why something is right or wrong, moral or immoral, just or unjust. Developing a "feel" for why grounds are or are not relevant to what they are alleged to support is important. "That's just my view" is *not* a convincing warrant for any argument.

Even without formal training, however, one can sense that something is wrong with many bad arguments. Here is one example. British professor C. E. M. Joad found himself standing on a station platform, annoyed because he had just missed his train. Then another train, making an unscheduled stop, pulled up to the platform in front of him. Joad decided to jump aboard, only to hear the conductor say, "I'm afraid you'll have to get off, Sir. This train doesn't stop here." "In that case," replied the professor, "don't worry. I'm not on it."

BACKING

Warrants, remember, explain why our *grounds* support our *claims*. The next task is to be able to show that we can back up what we have claimed by showing the reasons our warrants are good, reasonable, or rational. To establish that kind of further support for an argument is to provide **backing**.

What is appropriate backing for one kind of argument might be quite inappropriate for another kind of argument. For example, the kinds of reasons relevant to support the warrant that men and women should be paid equally may be completely different from the reason used to justify the claim that the Equal Pay Act should be amended. For the first argument, you might draw upon political documents, speeches, and other evidence showing that gender equality is a value and priority that necessitates action. In the second argument, you are claiming that the Equal Pay Act has been ineffective and needs strengthening, so your backing might consist of arguments about that piece of legislation specifically — theories and illustrations about what makes good, effective, and practical policy, for example. (Notice you are *not* arguing that women and men should be paid equally, per se; you are taking that for granted, making an assumption about shared beliefs.)

Another way of stating this point is to recognize that once you have given reasons for a claim, you are then likely to be challenged to explain why your reasons are good reasons — why, that is, anyone should believe your reasons rather than regard them skeptically. They have to be the right *kinds* of reasons given the field you are arguing about. A claim about the constitutionality of corporate personhood (in which corporations are regarded legally as sharing rights and responsibilities of natural persons) would have to be rationalized using backing quite different from the backing required to settle the question of what motivated Chinese people to immigrate to the United States in the nineteenth century. The *canons* (the established conventions, rules, laws, principles, and important texts) in two such dramatically different arguments have to do with the scholarly communities in law and history, respectively, that have developed over the years to justify, support, defend, challenge, and undermine ideas in those two areas of discourse.

Why (to give a simple example) should we accept the testimony of Dr. *X* when Dr. *Y*, equally renowned, supports the opposite side? What more do we need to know about "expert testimony" before it can be believably invoked? Consider a different kind of case: When and why is it safe to rest a prediction on a small — although admittedly carefully selected — sample? (McKee has been criticized for examining only the *donated* brains of professional football players, suggesting that those players or their families suspected CTE in the first place.) Why is it legitimate to argue that building a border wall, spanking children, or smoking cigarettes indoors is (or is not) appropriate? What evidence explains your thinking?

To answer questions of these sorts is to support one's reasons, to give them legitimate *backing*. No argument is any better than its backing.

MODAL QUALIFIERS

As we have seen, all arguments are made up of assertions or propositions that can be sorted into four categories:

- *claims* (theses to be established)
- *grounds* (explicit reasons advanced)
- *warrants* (guarantees, evidence, or principles that connect grounds and claims)
- *backing* (relevant support)

All the kinds of propositions that emerge when we assert something in an argument have what philosophers call a **modality**. In other words, propositions generally indicate — explicitly or tacitly — the *character* and *scope* of what is believed to be their likely truth.

CHARACTER **Character** has to do with the nature of the claim being made, the extent of an argument's presumed reach. Both making and evaluating arguments require being clear about whether they are

- *necessary,*
- *probable,*
- *plausible,* or
- *possible.*

Consider, for example, a claim that it is to the advantage of a college to have a racially diverse student body. Is that *necessarily* true or only *probably* true? What about an argument that a runner who easily wins a 100-meter race should also be able to win a 200-meter race? Is that *plausible*, or is it only *possible*? Indicating the *character* with which an assertion is advanced is crucial to any argument for or against it. Furthermore, if there is more than one reason for making a claim and all those reasons are *good*, it is still possible that one of those good reasons may be *better* than the others. If so, the better reason should be stressed.

SCOPE Indicating the **scope** of an assertion is equally crucial to how an argument plays out. *Scope* entails such considerations as whether the proposition is thought to be true *always* or just *sometimes*. Further, is the claim being made supposed to apply in *all* instances or just in *some*? Assertions are usually clearer, as well as more likely to be true, if they are explicitly *quantified* and *qualified*. Suppose, for example, you are arguing against smoking, and the ground for your claim is this:

Heavy smokers cut short their life span.

In this case, there are three obvious alternative quantifications to choose among: *All* smokers cut short their life span, *most* do, or only *some* do. Until the assertion is quantified in one of these ways, we really don't know what is being asserted, and so we don't know what degree and kind of evidence or counterevidence is relevant. Other quantifiers include *few, rarely, often, sometimes, perhaps, usually, more or less, regularly,* and *occasionally*.

Scope also reflects that empirical generalizations are typically **contingent** on various factors. Indicating such contingencies clearly is an important way to protect a generalization against obvious counterexamples. Thus, consider this empirical generalization:

Students do best on final examinations if they study hard for them.

Are we really to believe that students who cram ("study hard" in that concentrated sense) for an exam will do better than those who do the work diligently throughout the whole course ("study hard" in that broader sense) and therefore do not need to cram for the final? Probably not; what is really meant is that, *all other things being equal* (in Latin, *ceteris paribus*), concentrated study just before an exam will yield good results. Alluding in this way to the contingencies — the things that might derail the argument — shows that the writer is aware of possible exceptions and is conceding them from the start.

In sum, sensitivity to both character and (especially) scope — paying attention to the role played by quantifiers, qualifiers, and contingencies and making sure you use appropriate ones for each of your assertions — will strengthen your arguments enormously. Not least of the benefits is that you will reduce the peculiar vulnerabilities of an argument that is undermined by exaggeration and other misguided generalizations.

REBUTTALS

Very few arguments of any interest are beyond dispute, conclusively knockdown affairs. Only very rarely is the claim of an argument so rigidly tied to its grounds, warrants, and backing — and with its quantifiers and qualifiers argued in so precise a manner — that it proves its conclusion beyond any possibility of doubt. On the contrary, most arguments have many counterarguments, and sometimes one of these counterarguments is more convincing than the original argument. When writers raise counterarguments, they build their *ethos* and assure readers that other views are taken seriously; however, those counterarguments should not be raised simply to challenge your own position. If you indeed believe in your position, you can offer a **rebuttal** to the counterargument — telling your readers where it succeeds, perhaps, but also where it fails (thus implying or stating that *your* position is more convincing).

Suppose someone has taken a sample that appears to be random: An interviewer on your campus approaches the first ten students she encounters, and seven of them are fraternity or sorority members. She is now ready to argue that seven-tenths of enrolled students belong to Greek organizations.

You believe, however, that the Greeks are in the minority; you point out that she happens to have conducted her interview around the corner from the Panhellenic Society's office just off Sorority Row. Her random sample is anything but random. The ball is now back in her court as you await her response to your rebuttal.

As this example illustrates, it is safe to say that we do not understand our own arguments very well until we have tried to get a grip on the places in which they are vulnerable to criticism, counterattack, or refutation. As Edmund Burke astutely observed, "He that wrestles with us strengthens our nerves, and sharpens our skill. Our antagonist is our helper."

THINKING CRITICALLY *Constructing a Toulmin Argument*

Choose a topic or issue that interests you. In the spaces provided, supply a sentence or two for each step of a Toulmin argument about your topic.

STEP OF TOULMIN ARGUMENT	QUESTION THIS STEP ADDRESSES	YOUR SENTENCE(S)
Claim	*What is your argument?*	
Grounds	*What is your evidence?*	
Warrant	*What reasoning connects your evidence to your argument?*	
Backing	*What can you provide as support to convince the reader to agree with your grounds, claims, and warrants?*	
Qualifier	*What are the limits of your argument?*	
Rebuttal	*What are the objections to your argument — and can you reason that your argument still holds?*	

Putting the Toulmin Method to Work: Responding to an Argument

Let's take a look at another argument — on why buying directly from farmers near you won't save the planet — and see how the Toulmin method can be applied. The checklist on page 327 can help you focus your thoughts as you read.

JAMES E. McWILLIAMS

James E. McWilliams (b. 1968), the author of *Just Food: Where Locavores Get It Wrong and How We Can Truly Eat Responsibly* (2009), is a professor of history at Texas State University. This piece first appeared in *Forbes Magazine* on August 3, 2009.

The Locavore Myth: Why Buying from Nearby Farmers Won't Save the Planet

Buy local, shrink the distance food travels, save the planet. The locavore movement has captured a lot of fans. To their credit, they are highlighting the problems with industrialized food. But a lot of them are making a big mistake. By focusing on transportation, they overlook other energy-hogging factors in food production.

Take lamb. A 2006 academic study (funded by the New Zealand government) discovered that it made more environmental sense for a Londoner to buy lamb shipped from New Zealand than to buy lamb raised in the U.K. This finding is counterintuitive — if you're only counting food miles. But New Zealand lamb is raised on pastures with a small carbon footprint, whereas most English lamb is produced under intensive factory-like conditions with a big carbon footprint. This disparity overwhelms domestic lamb's advantage in transportation energy.

New Zealand lamb is not exceptional. Take a close look at water usage, fertilizer types, processing methods, and packaging techniques and you discover that factors other than shipping far outweigh the energy it takes to transport food. One analysis, by Rich Pirog of the Leopold Center for Sustainable Agriculture, showed that transportation accounts for only 11 percent of food's carbon footprint. A fourth of the energy required to produce food is expended in the consumer's kitchen. Still more energy is consumed per meal in a restaurant, since restaurants throw away most of their leftovers.

Locavores argue that buying local food supports an area's farmers and, in turn, strengthens the community. Fair enough. Left unacknowledged, however, is the fact that it also hurts farmers in other parts of the world. The U.K. buys most of its green beans from Kenya. While it's true that the beans almost always arrive in airplanes — the form of transportation that consumes the most energy — it's also true that a campaign to shame English consumers with small airplane stickers affixed to flown-in produce threatens the livelihood of 1.5 million sub-Saharan farmers.

Another chink in the locavores' armor 5
involves the way food miles are calculated. To choose a locally grown apple over an apple trucked in from across the country might seem easy. But this decision ignores economies of scale. To take an extreme example, a shipper sending a truck with 2,000 apples over 2,000 miles would consume the same amount of fuel per apple as a local farmer who takes a pickup 50 miles to sell 50 apples at his stall at the green market. The critical measure here is not food miles but apples per gallon.

The one big problem with thinking beyond food miles is that it's hard to get the information you need. Ethically concerned consumers know very little about processing practices, water availability, packaging waste, and fertilizer application. This is an opportunity for watchdog groups. They should make life-cycle carbon counts available to shoppers.

Until our food system becomes more transparent, there is one thing you can do to shrink the carbon footprint of your dinner: Take the meat off your plate. No matter how you slice it, it takes more energy to bring meat, as opposed to plants, to the table. It takes 6 pounds of grain to make a pound of chicken and 10 to 16 pounds to make a pound of beef. That difference translates into big differences in inputs. It requires 2,400 liters of water to make a burger and only 13 liters to grow a tomato. A majority of the water in the American West goes toward the production of pigs, chickens, and cattle.

The average American eats 273 pounds of meat a year. Give up red meat once a week and you'll save as much energy as if the only food miles in your diet were the distance to the nearest truck farmer.

If you want to make a statement, ride your bike to the farmer's market. If you want to reduce greenhouse gases, become a vegetarian.

Thinking with the Toulmin Method

Remember to make use of the Visual Guide on page 318 as you work to find the claim(s), grounds, and warrant(s) that McWilliams puts forward in this short essay.

1. What **claim** is the author making? Is it in the title? Is it in the opening sentence? Or is it buried in the first paragraph?

McWilliams really gives away his game in the title, even though he opens the essay itself in a way that might make the reader think he is about to launch into a defense of the locavore movement. He even goes out of his way to praise its members ("To their credit . . ."). The signal that his claim really appears already in the title and that he is *not* going to defend the locavore movement is the way he begins the fourth sentence. Notice that although you may have been told that starting a sentence with *But* isn't the best way to write, McWilliams here does so to good effect. Not only does he dramatically counter what he said just prior to that, but he also sets up the final sentence of the paragraph, which turns out to be crucial. In this way, he draws sharp attention to his *claim*. How would you state his claim?

2. What are the **grounds**, the evidence or reasons, that the author advances in support of his claim?

As it turns out, McWilliams spells out only one example as evidence for his claim. What is it? Is it convincing? Should he have provided more evidence or reasons at this point? It turns out that he does have other grounds to offer, but he mentions them only later. What are those other pieces of evidence?

3. What **warrants** does McWilliams offer to show why we should accept his grounds? What authority does he cite? How effective and convincing is this way of trying to get us to accept the grounds he offered in support of his claim?

The essence of the Toulmin method lies in these three elements: the claim(s), the grounds, and the warrant(s). If you have extracted these from McWilliams's essay, you are well on the way to being able to identify the argument he is putting forward. So far, so good. Further probing, however — looking for the other three elements of the Toulmin method (the backing, the modal qualifiers and quantifiers, and the rebuttal) — is essential before you are in a position to actually evaluate the argument. So let's go on.

4. What **backing** does McWilliams provide? What reasons does he give that might persuade us to accept his argument? Look for what he claimed came out of the analysis that was his basic warrant. He certainly seems to be using factual information — but what if you challenged him? Has he provided adequate reasons for us to believe him? What could he (or would he have to) be able to tell us if we challenged him with questions like "How do you know . . . ?" or "Why do you believe . . . ?" In other words, has he provided adequate backing? Or does he want us to just accept his statement of the facts?
5. Does McWilliams use **modal qualifiers**? Can you find phrases like "in most cases" or "generally it is true that . . ."? Or does he write so boldly — with little in the way of qualifiers or quantifiers — that readers are left uncertain about whether to accept his position? Where might he have effectively used qualifiers?
6. Does McWilliams prepare **rebuttals**, the reasons given in anticipation of someone rejecting the author's claim or conceding the claim but rejecting the grounds? Does he offer anything to forestall criticisms? If so, what is it that he does? If not, what could or should he have done?

Just how good an argument has McWilliams made? Is he convincing? If you identified weak points in his argument, what are they? Can you help strengthen the argument? If so, how?

A CHECKLIST FOR USING THE TOULMIN METHOD

- ❐ What claim does the argument make?
- ❐ What grounds are offered for the claim?
- ❐ What warrants connect the grounds to the claim?
- ❐ What backing supports the claim?
- ❐ With what modalities are the claim and grounds asserted?
- ❐ To what rebuttals are the claim, grounds, and backing vulnerable?

9

A Logician's View: Deduction, Induction, and Fallacies

Logic is the anatomy of thought.

— JOHN LOCKE

Logic takes care of itself; all we have to do is to look and see how it does it.

— LUDWIG WITTGENSTEIN

In Chapter 3, we introduced the terms *deduction*, *induction*, and *fallacy*. In this chapter, we discuss them in more detail and present some principles of *formal logic* to help you develop your ability to understand arguments.

Using Formal Logic for Critical Thinking

Formal logic is a discipline of philosophy that studies the *nature* and *structure* of arguments abstracted from their content. Formal logic emerged in the ancient world and was developed further during the Enlightenment (ca. 1685–1815), a time of great scientific ferment, as an attempt to understand truth according to *a priori* rules — that is, rules that exist before, or *prior* to, any specific content. Formal logic is closely related to mathematics. Each expresses reality using symbols and variables. In math, the phrase *two plus two equals four* is true no matter if apples or oranges are being counted. Consider the structure of an equation:

If $A + B = C$, then $C + D = (A + B) + D$.

This formula expresses logical truth no matter what numbers you plug into the letters. The variables can change, but not the truth of the matter: If the first proposition is true, the second must be, too.

Perhaps for obvious reasons, formal logic is quite important in computer science, which is based on binaries of 0 and 1. But even in our everyday lives, we still use methods of formal logic to demonstrate truth ("If I take a lower-paying job, there will be less household income overall; if there is lower household income, there will be less money to pay for *X*, *Y*, and *Z*; therefore, some cuts to one or more of *X*, *Y*, or *Z* are inevitable if I take the lower-paying job").

But as soon as we enter the world of values, language, principles, and morals — where we encounter questions of what words mean and what we *should* or *ought* to do, or have a *right* to do — we must recognize the limits of formal logic's ability to demonstrate absolute truth. For arguments to work, the components must have meaning. Therefore, arguments that make assertions of human value involve applied reasoning, empirical observation, speculation, and other ways of thinking. Nevertheless, formal logic can assist us in seeing the ways even these types of arguments are structured and ultimately help us judge such arguments and think more carefully about our own.

Visual Guide: Deduction and Induction

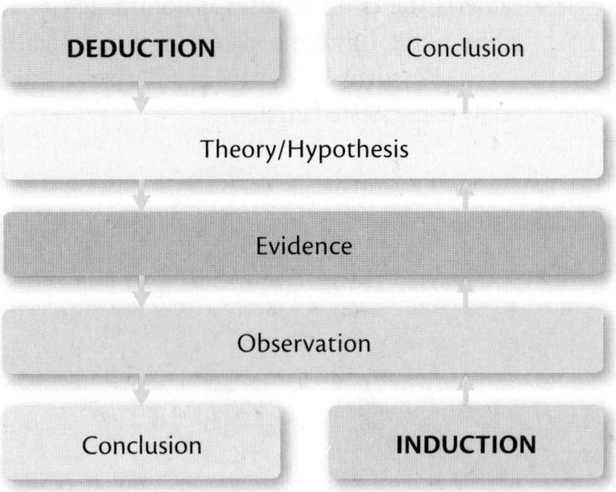

Deduction

The basic aim of deductive reasoning is to start with some given premise and extract from it a conclusion — a logical consequence — that is concealed but implicit in it. When we introduced the idea of deduction in Chapter 3, we gave as our primary example the *syllogism*, and we provided a classical syllogism to represent how one aspect of formal logic, deduction, can lead to true conclusions:

Premise: All human beings are mortal.

Premise: Socrates is a human being.

Conclusion: Socrates is mortal.

If the premises are absolutely true, and the conclusion necessarily follows from them, the syllogism is *valid* and the argument is *sound*.

Here is another example:

Texas is larger than California.

California is larger than Arizona.

Therefore, Texas is larger than Arizona.

The conclusion in this syllogism can be derived from the two premises; that is, anyone who asserts the two premises is committed to accepting the conclusion as well, whatever one thinks of it. It is not a matter of perspective, opinion, or dispute.

Using formal logic, we can derive an equation of sorts to represent the argument graphically using nested circles:

Premise:

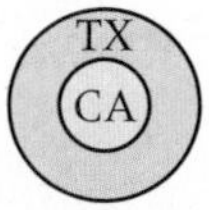

Premise:

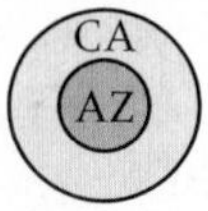

Conclusion:

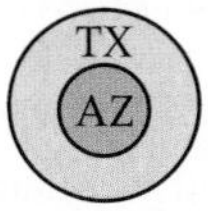

We can see that this conclusion follows from the premises because it amounts to nothing more than what one gets by superimposing the two premises on each other. Thus, the whole argument can be represented like this:

The so-called middle term in the argument — California — disappears from the conclusion; its role is confined to be the link between the other two terms, Texas and Arizona, in the premises. In a graphic depiction, as with an equation, one can literally *see* that the conclusion follows from the premises. (This technique is an adaptation of one used in elementary formal logic known as Venn diagrams.)

In formal logic, the validity of a deductive inference depends on being able to show how the concepts in the premises are related to the concepts in the conclusion. In this case, the validity of the inference depends on the meaning of a key concept, *being larger than*. This concept has the property of *transitivity*, a property that many concepts share (e.g., *is equal to*, *is to the right of*, *is smarter than*). Transitive concepts can be represented symbolically in equations. Consequently, regardless of what is represented by A, B, and C, we can say:

If $A > B$, and $B > C$, then $A > C$.

This is all intended to show that the validity of deductive inference is a purely *formal* property of argument. You can substitute any state for Texas, California, and Arizona — or anything at all for the variables *A*, *B*, and *C*—as long as they adhere to the meaning of the transitive concept *larger than*.

Understanding this technique can help you see how some arguments can appear to be valid, but may also be challenged. For example:

If *A* is to the right of *B* and *B* is to the right of *C*, then *A* is to the right of *C*.

or

If *A* is smarter than *B* and *B* is smarter than *C*, then *A* is smarter than *C*.

Let's dig into these examples. First, on the earth, if *A* is to the right of *B* and *B* is to the right of *C*, it is purely logical that *A* is to the right of *C*, too—until we circle the globe and place *A* directly to the left of *C*, in which case the syllogism may be refuted on the grounds that it assumes an infinite plane surface. The very meaning of the phrase *to the right of* has been challenged. In the second example, *smarter than* is a category that needs definition. To challenge this argument, you can contest the comparative meaning of the term *smarter than*: Does "smart" refer to IQ level, grades earned in school, street smarts, or something else? Here you have two examples of valid syllogism, neither of which is necessarily true.

Now let's look at an example of another syllogism that is **valid** but not true.

Rhode Island is larger than Texas.

Texas is larger than Canada.

Therefore, Rhode Island is larger than Canada.

How, you might ask, can this syllogism be valid? Again, remember this about the formal properties of arguments: If you grant that the premises are true and the conclusion is inherently related to the premises, it is valid *even if it not true*.

Why is all this important to your learning about arguments? Well, if all one can say about an argument is that it is valid—that is, its conclusion follows from the premises—one has not given a sufficient reason for accepting the argument's conclusion. It has been said that the devil can quote scripture; similarly, an argument can be deductively valid and of no value whatsoever because valid (but false) conclusions can be drawn from false, misleading, or meaningless premises.

In short, a valid deductive argument doesn't prove anything unless the premises and the conclusion are *true*, but they can't be true unless they *mean* something in the first place. Consider this nonsense syllogism:

If the slithy toves, then the gyres gimble. The slithy toves. Therefore, the gyres gimble.

This argument has the following form:

If *A*, then *B*; *A*; therefore *B*.

As a piece of deductive inference, it is every bit as good (valid) as the other arguments above. Unlike them, however, it is of no interest at all because its assertions make no sense (unless you're a reader of Lewis Carroll's "Jabberwocky," and even then it is doubtful).

This example shows that the form of an argument can be good but the argument itself bad. We work through these problems because understanding the structures of arguments helps us better think about, analyze, and construct arguments ourselves. Think about this one:

> If President Truman knew the Japanese were about to surrender, then it was immoral of him to order that atom bombs be dropped on Hiroshima and Nagasaki. Truman knew the Japanese were going to surrender. Therefore, it was immoral of him to order dropping those bombs.

Once again, anyone who assents to the *if . . . then* proposition in the premise and accepts that Truman knew the Japanese were about to surrender must assent to the conclusion. But do the premises *prove* the conclusion? That depends on whether both premises are true. Well, are they? The answer turns on a number of considerations, and it is worth pausing to examine how we might think critically about this argument.

Let's begin by examining the second premise, which proposes a fact: Did Truman really know the Japanese were about to surrender? This question is controversial even today. Autobiography, memoranda, other documentary evidence — all are needed to assemble the evidence to back up the grounds for the thesis or claim made in the conclusion of this argument. Evaluating this material effectively may involve further deductions (and perhaps inductive reasoning as well).

As to the first premise, its truth doesn't depend on facts about the past but, rather, on moral principles. The first premise contains a hypothetical ("if") and asserts a connection between two very different kinds of things (prior knowledge and morality). This premise as a whole can thus be seen as expressing *a principle of moral responsibility.* The principle is this: If we have knowledge that makes violence unnecessary, it is immoral to act violently anyway. Someone could compare Truman's decision to an argument that shares its form: If someone is surrendering, it is immoral to do violence to him. Such principles can, of course, be supported or contested.

EXAMPLES OF DEDUCTION

When we engage with and construct arguments, it is useful to keep in mind some of the basic structures (including but not limited to *syllogism*) because they help us see what is going on under the surface of an argument.

DISJUNCTION One common form of argument occurs through **disjunctive syllogism**, so called because its major premise is a **disjunction**, or a relationship between distinct alternatives. For example:

> Either censorship of fake news is overdue or our society is indifferent to hostile forces meddling in elections.
>
> Our society is not indifferent to propaganda on social media affecting our elections.
>
> Therefore, censorship of fake news is overdue.

Notice, by the way, that the validity of an argument, as in this case, does not turn on pedantic repetition of every word or phrase: Nonessential elements can be dropped or equivalent expressions substituted without adverse effect on the reasoning as long as those relationships are established. Thus, in conversation or in writing, this argument might actually be presented like this:

> Either censorship of fake news is overdue or our society is indifferent to the role fake news propaganda has in our elections. Of course, our political elections are susceptible to the effects of fake news, which is why some kind of censorship is overdue.

The key feature of disjunctive syllogism is that the conclusion is whichever of the alternatives remains after the others have been negated. We could easily have a very complex disjunctive syllogism with a dozen alternatives in the first premise and seven of them denied in the second, leaving a conclusion of the remaining five. Usually, however, a disjunctive argument is formulated in this manner: Assert a disjunction with two or more alternatives in the major premise, *deny all but one* in the minor premise, and then infer validly the remaining alternative(s) as the conclusion.

DILEMMA Another type of argument, especially favored by orators and rhetoricians, is the **dilemma**. Ordinarily, we use the term *dilemma* in the sense of an awkward predicament, as when we say, "His dilemma was that he didn't have enough money to pay the waiter." But when logicians refer to a dilemma, they mean a forced choice between two or more equally unattractive alternatives. For example, the predicament faced by the US government in fighting the Islamic State (ISIS) in Syria can be posed as a dilemma. The United States could ally itself with the Syrian government, a dictatorship under Bashar al-Assad, who is also trying to destroy ISIS influence in Syria. But al-Assad's government is hostile to the United States, has attempted to crush political reform movements in Syria, and actively supports groups the United States deems terrorist organizations. On the other hand, the United States could extend support to the Syrian Democratic Forces (SDF), a large militia inside Syria comprised mostly of Kurdish majority people who are fighting against ISIS and opposing al-Assad; however, in doing so, the United States risks expanding conflict in Syria, a Russian ally, and alienates its own ally, Turkey, which sees the SDF as a force of instability in its own country. The dilemma might be phrased as such:

> If the United States supports the Syrian government's fight against ISIS, it would be supporting a dictatorship linked to terrorism and crimes against humanity. If the United States supports the SDF, it risks further conflict with the Bashar al-Assad regime (and perhaps Russia) and also compromises its own relationship with Turkey. Thus, in fighting the Islamic State in Syria, either the United States supports a dictatorship or it supports a resistance group opposed to our own ally. In either case, unattractive consequences follow.

Notice first the structure of the argument: two conditional propositions asserted as premises followed by another premise that states a **necessary truth**. The premise, "Either we support the dictatorship or we support the SDF," is a disjunction; because the two alternatives are presented as exhaustive (the only options), one of the two alternatives must be true.

(Such a statement is often called analytically true, or a *tautology.*) No doubt the conclusion of this dilemma ("unattractive consequences") follows from its premises.

But does the argument *prove*, as it purports to do, that whatever the US government does, it will suffer "unattractive consequences"? It is customary to speak of "the horns of the dilemma," as though the challenge posed by the dilemma were like a bull ready to gore us no matter which direction we turn. But if the two conditional premises failed to exhaust the possibilities, we can escape from the dilemma by going "between the horns" — by finding a third alternative (or a fourth or fifth).

If alternatives are not possible, we can still ask whether both of the main premises are true. Neither of the main premises spells out all or even most of the consequences that could be foreseen, and perhaps backing the SDF would not result in compromising our relationship with Turkey. In cases where both of the conditional premises are true, then, it may be that the consequences of one alternative are not as bad as those of the other. If that is true, but our reasoning stops before evaluating that fact, we may be guilty of failing to distinguish between the greater and the lesser of two evils. The logic of the dilemma itself cannot decide this choice for us. Instead, we must bring to bear empirical inquiry and imagination to the evaluation of the grounds of the dilemma.

REDUCTIO AD ABSURDUM Finally, one of the most powerful and dramatic forms of argument is **reductio ad absurdum** (from the Latin, meaning "reduction to absurdity"). The idea of a reductio argument is to disprove a proposition by showing the absurdity of its inevitable conclusion. It is used, of course, to refute your opponent's position and prove your own. For example, in Plato's *Republic*, Socrates asks an old gentleman, Cephalus, to define *right conduct.* Cephalus says it consists of paying your debts and keeping your word. Socrates rejects this answer by showing that it leads to a contradiction. He argues that Cephalus cannot have given the correct answer because if we believe that he did, we will quickly encounter contradictions; in some cases, when you keep your word, you will nonetheless be doing the wrong thing. Suppose, says Socrates, you borrowed a weapon from a man, promising to return it when he asks for it. One day he comes to your door, demanding his weapon and swearing angrily that he intends to murder a neighbor. Keeping your word under those circumstances would be absurd, Socrates implies, and the reader of the dialogue is left to infer that Cephalus's definition, which led to this result, has been refuted.

A. Hyatt Mayor Purchase Fund, Marjorie Phelps Starr Bequest, 1982

Socrates Looking in a Mirror by Bernard Vaillant, c. 17th century.

Let's look at another example. Suppose you are opposed to any form of gun control, whereas we are in favor of gun control. We might try to refute your position by attacking it with a reductio argument. We start out by assuming the very opposite of what we believe or favor and try to establish a contradiction that results from following out the consequences of your initial assumption:

> Your position is that there ought to be no legal restrictions of any kind on the sale and ownership

of guns. That means that you'd permit having every neighborhood hardware store sell pistols and rifles to whoever walks in the door. But that's not all. You apparently also would permit selling machine guns to children, antitank weapons to lunatics, and small-bore cannons to the nearsighted, as well as guns and ammunition to anyone with a criminal record. But that is utterly preposterous; no one could favor such a dangerous policy. So the only question worth debating is what kind of gun control is necessary.

Now in this example, our reductio of your position on gun control is not based on claiming to show that you have strictly contradicted yourself, for there is no purely logical contradiction in opposing all forms of gun control. Instead, what we have tried to do is to show that there is a contradiction between what you profess — no gun controls at all — and what you probably really believe, if only you'll stop to think about it — which is that no lunatic should be allowed to buy a loaded machine gun. Our refutation of your position rests on whether we succeed in establishing an inconsistency among your own beliefs. If it turns out that you really believe lunatics should be free to purchase guns and ammunition, our attempted refutation fails.

CONTRADICTION, CONSISTENCY, AND CONJUNCTION In explaining reductio ad absurdum, we have had to rely on another idea fundamental to logic, that of **contradiction**, or inconsistency. The opposite of contradiction is **consistency**, a notion important to good reasoning. These concepts deserve a few words of further explanation and illustration. Consider this pair of assertions:

A. Abortion is homicide.

B. Racism is unfair.

No one would plausibly claim that we can infer or deduce *B* from *A* or, for that matter, *A* from *B*. There is no evident connection between these two assertions. They are unrelated assertions; logically speaking, they are *independent* of each other. The two assertions are potentially *consistent*; that is, both could be true — or both could be false. But now consider another proposition:

C. Euthanasia is not murder.

Could a person assert *A* (*Abortion is homicide*) and also assert *C* (*Euthanasia is not murder*) and be consistent? Could you assert these two propositions as a **conjunction**? Now consider:

D. Abortion is homicide, and euthanasia is not murder.

It's not so easy to say whether these are consistent or inconsistent. One person could assert one of these propositions and reject the other, leading to a conclusion of general inconsistency. Another could be convinced that there is no inconsistency in asserting that *Abortion is homicide* and that *Euthanasia is not murder.* (For instance, suppose you believe both that the unborn are persons who deserve a chance to live and that putting terminally ill persons to death in a painless manner and with their consent confers a benefit on them.)

Let us generalize: We can say of any set of propositions that they are consistent *if and only if* all could be true together. Remember that, once again, the truth of the assertions in question doesn't matter. Two propositions can be consistent or not, quite apart from whether they are true. That's not so with falsehood: It follows from our definition of consistency that an *inconsistent* proposition must be *false.* (We have relied on this idea in explaining how a reductio ad absurdum argument works.)

Assertions or claims that are not consistent can take either of two forms. Suppose you assert that abortion is homicide, early in an essay you are writing, but later you assert that abortion is harmless. You have now asserted a position on abortion that is strictly contrary to the one with which you began — both cannot be true. It is simply not true that if an abortion involves killing a human being (which is what *homicide* strictly means), it causes no one any harm (killing a person always causes harm — even if it is excusable, justifiable, not wrong, the best thing to do in the circumstances, and so on). Notice that while both cannot be true, they *can* both be false. In fact, many people who are perplexed about the morality of abortion believe precisely this. They concede that abortion does harm the fetus, but they also believe that abortion doesn't kill a person.

Let's consider another, simpler case. If you describe the glass as half empty and I describe it as half full, both of us can be right; the two assertions are consistent, even though they sound vaguely incompatible. (This is the reason that disputing over whether the glass is half full or half empty has become the popular paradigm of a futile, purely *verbal disagreement.*) But if I describe the glass as half empty whereas you insist that it is two-thirds empty, we have a real disagreement; your description and mine are strictly contrary, in that both cannot be true — although both *can* be false. (Both are false if the glass is only one-fourth full.)

This, by the way, enables us to define the difference between a pair of **contradictory** propositions and a pair of **contrary** propositions. Two propositions are contrary if and only if both cannot be true (though both can be false); two propositions are contradictory if and only if they are such that if one is true the other must be false, and vice versa. Thus, if Jack says that Alice Walker's *The Color Purple* is a better novel than Mark Twain's *Huckleberry Finn*, and Jill says, "No, *Huckleberry Finn* is better than *The Color Purple*," she is contradicting Jack. If what either one of them says is true, then what the other says must be false.

A more subtle case of contradiction arises when two or more of one's own beliefs implicitly contradict each other. We may find ourselves saying "Travel is broadening" and saying an hour later "People don't really change." Just beneath the surface of these two beliefs lies a self-contradiction: How can travel broaden us unless it influences — and changes — our beliefs, values, and outlook? But if we can't really change ourselves, traveling to new places won't change us, either. (Indeed, there is a Roman saying to the effect that travelers change the skies above them, not their hearts.) "Travel is broadening" and "People don't change" collide with each other; something has to give.

Our point, of course, is not that you must never say today something that contradicts something you said yesterday. Far from it; if you think you were mistaken yesterday, of course you will take a different position today. But what you want to avoid is what George Orwell called *doublethink* in his novel *1984*: "*Doublethink* means the power of holding two contradictory beliefs in one's mind simultaneously, and accepting them both."

PARADOX While we're speaking of inconsistency, let's spend a moment on **paradox**. The word refers to two different things:

- an assertion that is essentially self-contradictory and therefore cannot be true
- a seemingly contradictory assertion that nevertheless may be true

An example of the first might be "Evaluations concerning quality in literature are all a matter of personal judgment, but Shakespeare is the world's greatest writer." It is hard to make any sense out of this assertion. Contrast it with a paradox of the second sort, a *seeming* contradiction that may make sense, such as "The longest way around is the shortest way home," or "Work is more fun than fun," or "The best way to find happiness is not to look for it." Here we have assertions that are striking because as soon as we hear them we realize that although they seem inconsistent and self-defeating, they contain (or may contain) profound truths. If you use the word *paradox* in your own writing — for instance, to characterize an argument you're reading — be sure the reader will understand in which sense you're using the word. (And, of course, you won't want to write paradoxes of the first, self-contradictory sort.)

Induction

Deduction involves logical thinking that applies to absolutely any assertion or claim — because every possible statement, true or false, has deductive logical consequences. Induction, remember, is the type of thinking that begins with specific **empirical** or *factual* observations and leads to general conclusions. Induction is relevant to one kind of assertion only. Other kinds of assertions (such as definitions, mathematical equations, and moral or legal norms) simply are not the product of inductive reasoning and cannot serve as a basis for further inductive thinking.

So, in studying the methods of induction, we are exploring tactics and strategies useful in gathering and then using **evidence** — empirical, observational, experimental — in support of a belief as its ground. Modern scientific knowledge is the product of these methods, and they differ somewhat from one science to another because they depend on the theories and technology appropriate to each of the sciences. Here all we can do is discuss generally the more abstract features common to inductive inquiry. For fuller details, you must eventually consult a physicist, chemist, geologist, or their colleagues and counterparts in other scientific fields.

OBSERVATION AND INFERENCE

Let's begin with a simple example. Suppose we have evidence (actually we don't, but that won't matter for our purposes) in support of this claim:

> In a sample of 500 smokers, 230 persons observed have cardiovascular disease.

The basis — the evidence or grounds — for asserting this claim would be, presumably, straightforward physical examination of the 500 persons in the sample, one by one.

With this claim in hand, we can think of the purpose and methods of induction as pointing in two opposite directions: toward establishing the basis or ground of the very empirical proposition with which we start (in this example, the observation stated above) or toward understanding what that observation indicates or suggests as a more general, inclusive, or fundamental fact of nature.

In each case, we start from something we *do* know (or take for granted and treat as a sound starting point)—some fact of nature, perhaps a striking or commonplace event that we have observed and recorded—and then go on to something we do *not* fully know and perhaps cannot directly observe. In the smoking example above, only the second of these two orientations (the 230 persons with cardiovascular disease) is of any interest, so let's concentrate exclusively on it.

GENERALIZATION Anyone truly interested in the observed fact that *230 of 500 smokers have cardiovascular disease* is likely to start speculating about, and thus be interested in finding out, whether any or all of several other propositions are also true. For example, one might wonder whether the following claim is true:

> *All* smokers have cardiovascular disease or will develop it during their lifetimes.

This claim is a straightforward generalization of the original observation as reported in the first claim. When we think inductively, we are reasoning from an observed sample (some smokers—i.e., 230 of the 500 *observed*) to the entire membership of a more inclusive class (*all* smokers, whether observed or not). The fundamental question raised by reasoning from the narrower claim to the broader claim is whether we have any ground for believing that what is true of *some* members of a class is true of them *all*. So the difference between these claims is that of *quantity* or scope.

RELATION We can also think inductively about the *relation* between the factors mentioned in the original claim, *In a sample of 500 smokers, 230 persons observed have cardiovascular disease*. Having observed data, we may be tempted to assert a different and more profound kind of claim:

> Smoking *causes* cardiovascular disease.

Here our interest is not merely in generalizing from a sample to a whole class; it is the far more important one of *explaining* the observation with which we began. Certainly, the preferred, even if not the only, mode of explanation for a natural phenomenon is a *causal* explanation. In this claim, we propose to explain the presence of one phenomenon (cardiovascular disease) by the prior occurrence of an independent phenomenon (smoking). The original observation about the number of diseased smokers is now serving as evidence or support for this new conjecture.

But there is a third way to think inductively beyond our original claim. Instead of a straightforward generalization or a pronouncement on the cause of a phenomenon, we might have a more complex and cautious further claim in mind, such as this:

> Smoking is a factor in the causation of cardiovascular disease in some persons.

This proposition also advances a claim about causation, although it is obviously weaker than the claim *Smoking causes cardiovascular disease*. That is, other observations, theories, or evidence that would support the "factor" claim could easily fail to be enough to support the claim that smoking is the sole or main cause. Claiming that smoking is only one factor allows for other (unmentioned) factors in the causation of cardiovascular disease (e.g., genetic or dietary factors) that may not be found in all smokers.

INDUCTIVE INFERENCE (OR HYPOTHESIS) We began by assuming that our first proposition states an empirical fact based on direct observation but that the propositions that follow do not. Instead, they state empirical *hypotheses* or conjectures — tentative generalizations not fully confirmed — each of which goes beyond the observed facts. As such, they can be regarded as an *inductive inference* from the first proposition or observation.

PROBABILITY

Another way of thinking about inferences and hypotheses is to say that whereas a statement of observed fact (*230 out of 500 smokers have cardiovascular disease*) has a **probability** of 1.0 — that is, it is absolutely certain — the probability of each of the hypotheses that followed, *relative* to 1.0, is smaller than 1.0. (We need not worry here about how much smaller than 1.0 the probabilities are, nor about how to calculate these probabilities precisely.) But it takes only a moment's reflection to realize that no matter what the probability actually is, those probabilities in each case will be quite different relative to different information, such as this:

Ten persons observed in a sample of 500 smokers have cardiovascular disease.

The idea that *a given proposition can have different probabilities* relative to different bases is fundamental to all inductive reasoning. The following example makes a convincing illustration. Suppose we want to consider the probability of this proposition being true:

Susanne Smith will live to be eighty.

Taken as an abstract question of fact, we cannot even guess what the probability is with any assurance. But we can do better than guess; we can, in fact, even calculate the answer — if we get some further information. Thus, suppose we are told that Susanne Smith is seventy-nine. Our original question then becomes one of determining the probability that the proposition is true given this fact — that is, relative to the evidence. There's no doubt that if Susanne Smith really is seventy-nine, the probability that she will live to be eighty is greater than if we know only that Suzanne Smith is more than nine years old. Obviously, a lot can happen to Susanne in the seventy years between nine and seventy-nine that isn't very likely to happen in the one year between seventy-nine and eighty. So our proposition is more probable relative to the evidence of Susanne's age of seventy-nine than of "more than nine years old."

Let's suppose for the sake of the argument that the following is true:

Ninety percent of women alive at age seventy-nine live to be eighty.

Given this additional information and the information that Susanne is seventy-nine, we now have a basis for answering our original question about our proposition about Susanne's longevity with some precision. But suppose, in addition, we are also told that

Susanne Smith is suffering from inoperable cancer.

and also that

The survival rate for women suffering from inoperable cancer is 0.6 years (i.e., the average life span for women after a diagnosis of inoperable cancer is about seven months).

With this new information, the probability that Susanne will live to eighty drops significantly, all because we can now estimate the probability in relation to a new body of evidence.

The probability of an event, thus, is not a fixed number but one that varies because it is always relative to some evidence — and given different evidence, one and the same event can have different probabilities. In other words, the probability of any event is always relative to how much is known (assumed, believed), and because different persons may know different things about a given event or the same person may know different things at different times, one and the same event can have two or more probabilities. This conclusion is not a paradox but, rather, a logical consequence of the concept of what it is for an event to have (i.e., to be assigned) a probability.

S. Harris/Cartoonstock

MILL'S METHODS

Now let's return to our earlier discussion of smoking and cardiovascular disease and consider in greater detail the question of a causal connection between the two phenomena. We began thus:

In a sample of 500 smokers, 230 persons observed have cardiovascular disease.

We regarded this claim as an observed fact, although in truth, of course, it is mere supposition. Our question now is how we might augment this information so as to strengthen our confidence of our causal hypotheses that

Smoking *causes* cardiovascular disease.

or at least that

Smoking is a factor in the causation of cardiovascular disease in some persons.

Suppose further examination showed that

In the sample of 230 smokers with cardiovascular disease, no other suspected factor (such as genetic predisposition, lack of physical exercise, age over fifty) was also observed.

Such an observation would encourage us to believe that our hypotheses are true. Why? Because we're inclined to believe also that no matter what the cause of a phenomenon is, it must *always* be present when its effect is present. Thus, the inference from observed fact to our hypotheses is supported by this new evidence, using **Mill's Method of Agreement**, named after the British philosopher John Stuart Mill (1806–1873), who first formulated it. It's called a method of agreement because of the way in which the inference relies on *agreement* among the observed phenomena where a presumed cause is thought to be *present*.

Let's now suppose that in our search for evidence to support our hypotheses we conduct additional research and discover that

In a sample of 500 nonsmokers, selected to be representative of both sexes, different ages, dietary habits, exercise patterns, and so on, none is observed to have cardiovascular disease.

This observation would further encourage us to believe that we had obtained significant additional confirmation of our hypotheses. Why? Because we now know that factors present (such as male sex, lack of exercise, family history of cardiovascular disease) in cases where the effect is absent (no cardiovascular disease observed) cannot be the cause. This is an example of **Mill's Method of Difference**, so called because the cause or causal factor of an effect must be *different* from whatever factors are present when the effect is *absent*.

Suppose now that, increasingly confident we've found the cause of cardiovascular disease, we study our first sample of 230 smokers ill with the disease, and we discover this:

Those who smoke two or more packs of cigarettes daily for ten or more years have cardiovascular disease either much younger or much more severely than those who smoke less.

This is an application of **Mill's Method of Concomitant Variation**, perhaps the most convincing of the three methods. Here we deal not merely with the presence of the conjectured cause (smoking) or the absence of the effect we are studying (cardiovascular disease), as we were previously, but with the more interesting and subtler matter of the *degree and* *regularity of the correlation* of the supposed cause and effect. According to the observations reported here, it strongly appears that the more we have of the "cause" (smoking), the sooner or the more intense the onset of the "effect" (cardiovascular disease).

Notice, however, what happens to our confirmation if, instead, we had discovered this:

> In a representative sample of 500 nonsmokers, cardiovascular disease was observed in 34 cases.

(We won't pause here to explain what makes a sample more or less representative of a population, although the representativeness of samples is vital to all statistical reasoning.) Such an observation would lead us almost immediately to suspect some other or additional causal factor: Smoking might indeed be *a* factor in causing cardiovascular disease, but it can hardly be *the* cause because (using Mill's Method of Difference) we cannot have the effect, as we do in the observed sample of 34 cases reported above, unless we also have the cause.

An observation such as this is likely to lead us to think our hypothesis that *smoking causes cardiovascular disease* has been disconfirmed. But we have a fallback position ready — we can still defend our weaker hypothesis: *Smoking is a factor in the causation of cardiovascular disease in some persons.* It is still quite possible that smoking is a factor in causing this disease, even if it isn't the *only* factor.

Fallacies

The straight road on which sound reasoning proceeds gives little latitude for cruising about. Irrationality, carelessness, passionate attachment to one's unexamined beliefs, and the sheer complexity of some issues occasionally spoil the reasoning of even the best of us. An inventory of some common fallacies proves an instructive and potentially amusing exercise — instructive because the diagnosis and repair of error help us understand more principles of sound reasoning and amusing because we are so constituted that our perception of the nonsense of others can stimulate our minds, warm our hearts, and give us comforting feelings of superiority.

The discussion that follows, then, is a quick tour through the twisting paths, mudflats, and quicksands one sometimes encounters in reading arguments that stray from the way of clear thinking.

FALLACIES OF AMBIGUITY

AMBIGUITY Near the center of the town of Concord, Massachusetts, is an empty field with a sign reading "Old Calf Pasture." Hmm. A pasture in which calves grazed in former times? Or a pasture now in use for elderly calves? Or something that used to be a calf pasture but is now something else? These alternative readings arise because of **ambiguity**; brevity in the sign has produced a group of words that give rise to more than one possible interpretation, confusing the reader and (presumably) frustrating the sign writer's intentions.

Common Fallacies

	Fallacy	Definition	Example
Fallacies of Ambiguity	Ambiguity (p. 342)	Using a word, phrase, or claim that gives rise to more than one possible interpretation.	People have equal rights, and so everyone has a right to property.
	Division (p. 345)	Assuming all members of a set share characteristics of the set as a whole.	PETA is a radical organization; therefore, anyone who is a member of PETA is radical.
	Composition (p. 345)	Assuming that a set shares characteristics with a given member of a set (the reverse of division fallacy).	Kimberly is a freelance writer and makes a lot of money; freelance writers must make a lot of money.
	Equivocation (p. 345)	Making two words or phrases equivalent in meaning while ignoring contextual differences.	Evolution is a natural process, so this company's growth is natural and good.
	Non sequitur (p. 346)	Literally, "it does not follow." Drawing conclusions that are unrelated or do not follow logically from the premises.	Because Sammy is good at math, we should let him draw up our annual budget.
Fallacies of Presumption	Distorting the Facts (p. 346)	Misrepresenting information, data, or facts in an argument.	Video games have been shown to cause violence in one out of five kids; 20 percent of the next generation will be violent citizens.
	Post Hoc, Ergo Propter Hoc (p. 346)	Literally, "after this, therefore because of this." Assuming that sequence equals consequence.	After the invention of the birth control pill, the divorce rate increased; therefore, the "pill" contributed to the rising divorce rate.
	Many Questions (p. 347)	Presupposing facts that are assumed in the question itself.	Can selfish and self-interested politicians be trusted to do anything to bring about banking reform?
	Hasty Generalization (p. 347)	Jumping to conclusions based on insufficient evidence or biases.	I'm not moving to that neighborhood. When I visited it, there were two people fighting in the street.
	Slippery Slope (p. 347)	Arguing that an idea or action will lead inevitably to unrealistically steeper and steeper consequences.	If we allow legal recreational marijuana, other drugs will soon follow, and soon there will be addicts everywhere.
	False Analogy (p. 348)	Comparing two things that may be similar in some ways but remain different in other ways.	Building a border wall is just like fencing in our backyards; it is simply a safe and reasonable precaution.
	Straw Man (p. 348)	Misrepresenting an argument so that you can attack the misrepresentation rather than the actual argument.	If you want prison reform, you are basically saying you want to treat criminals like they're at a resort. We should not be rewarding criminals!
	Special Pleading (p. 348)	Making an unwarranted claim by misapplying or misusing rules and standards.	I should get an A because I worked really hard.
	Begging the Question (p. 348)	Making an argument in which the premises are based on the truth of the conclusion.	We have a free press because the Constitution guarantees it.

(*Continued*)

Common Fallacies (*Continued*)

	Fallacy	Definition	Example
Fallacies of Presumption	False Dichotomy (p. 349)	Establishing only two opposing positions or points when more might be available or when the opposing positions are not mutually exclusive.	Either we drill for natural gas, or we keep using carbon fuel.
	Oversimplification (p. 349)	Reducing a complex thing to a simple cause or consequence.	With all the bullying on the internet, it is no wonder school shootings are happening.
	Red Herring (p. 349)	Presenting a question or issue intended to divert and distract from the central or most relevant question or issue.	I recognize that the issue of race and police violence needs to be addressed, but the real question is whether or not athletes should kneel during the national anthem.
Fallacies of Irrelevance	Tu Quoque (p. 350)	Literally, "you also." Discrediting an argument by attacking the speaker's failure to adhere to his or her conclusion.	How can my professor say that electric vehicles are the future when he still drives a fuel-cell car?
	Genetic Fallacy (p. 350)	Arguing a position based on the real or imagined origin, history, or source of the idea.	In ancient times, men were hunters and women were gatherers — that's why women tend to be more domestic than men.
	Appeal to Ignorance (p. 350)	Saying that something is true because there is no evidence against it.	No one has complained about our new chili recipe, so it must be good.
	Poisoning the Well (p. 351)	Creating negative associations preemptively to discredit another person or position.	Now that I have highlighted the importance of keeping the controversial monument on campus, watch out because all the liberal snowflakes are going to argue that it "injures" them.
	Ad Hominem (p. 351)	Literally, "against the man [person]." Attacking the character of a person by providing irrelevant negative information.	How can this woman be the mayor when she can't even hold her own family together?
	Appeal to Authority (p. 351)	Asserting that a claim is true by citing someone thought to be an authority, regardless of the merits of the position or the relevance of the authority's expertise.	If the coach says throwing balls at the players makes them tougher, it must be true.
	Appeal to Fear (p. 352)	Supporting a position by instilling irrational fear of the alternatives.	If we don't strengthen our drug laws, drug dealers will see our community as a place to buy and sell openly on the streets.
Other	Death by a Thousand Qualifications (p. 352)	Justifying a weak idea or position by changing (or qualifying) it each time it is challenged.	Television is so bad for kids. (Well, not all television, and not all kids, and not in moderation, etc.)
	Protecting the Hypothesis (p. 352)	Distorting evidence to support a preexisting belief or idea.	According to the prophecy, the world was supposed to end. It didn't end. Therefore, the prophecy was not wrong, but we must have misinterpreted it.

Consider a more complex example. Suppose someone asserts *People have equal rights* and also *Everyone has a right to property.* Many people believe both these claims, but their combination involves an ambiguity. According to one interpretation, the two claims entail that everyone has an *equal right* to property. (That is, you and I each have an equal right to whatever property we have.) But the two claims can also be interpreted to mean that everyone has a *right to equal property.* (That is, whatever property you have a right to, I have a right to the same, or at least equivalent, property.) The latter interpretation is revolutionary, whereas the former is not. Arguments over equal rights often involve this ambiguity.

DIVISION In the Bible, we read that the apostles of Jesus were twelve and that Matthew was an apostle. Does it follow that Matthew was twelve years old? No. To argue in this way from a property of a group to a property of a member of that group is to commit the **fallacy of division**. The example of the apostles may not be a very tempting instance of this error. A classic version may be a bit more interesting: If it is true that the average American family has 1.8 children, does it follow that your brother and sister-in-law are likely to have 1.8 children? If you think it does, you have committed the fallacy of division.

COMPOSITION Could an all-star team of professional basketball players beat the Boston Celtics in their heyday — say, the team of 1985–1986? Perhaps it could in one game or two, but probably not in seven out of a dozen games in a row. As students of the game know, teamwork is an indispensable part of outstanding performance, and the 1985–1986 Celtics were famous for their self-sacrificing style of play.

The **fallacy of composition** can therefore be convincingly illustrated in this argument: *A team of five NBA all-stars is the best team in basketball if each of the five players is the best at his position.* The fallacy is called composition because the reasoning commits the error of arguing from the true premise that each member of a group has a certain property to the not necessarily true conclusion that the group (the composition) itself has the property (i.e., because *A* is the best player at forward, *B* is the best center, and so on; therefore, the team of *A*, *B*, . . . is the best team).

EQUIVOCATION In a delightful passage in Lewis Carroll's *Through the Looking-Glass*, the king asks his messenger, "Who did you pass on the road?" and the messenger replies, "Nobody." This prompts the king to observe, "Of course, Nobody walks slower than you," provoking the messenger's sullen response: "I do my best. I'm sure nobody walks much faster than I do." At this the king remarks with surprise, "He can't do that or else he'd have been here first!" (This, by the way, is the classic predecessor of the famous comic dialogue "Who's on First?" between the comedians Bud Abbott and Lou Costello.) The king and the messenger are equivocating on the term *nobody.* The messenger uses it in the normal way as an indefinite pronoun equivalent to "not anyone." But the king uses the word as though it were a proper noun, *Nobody*, the rather odd name of some person. It's no wonder the king and the messenger talk right past each other.

Equivocation (from the Latin for "equal voice" — i.e., giving utterance to two meanings at the same time in one word or phrase) can ruin otherwise good reasoning, as in this example: *Euthanasia is a good death; one dies a good death when one dies peacefully in old age; therefore, euthanasia is dying peacefully in old age.* The etymology of *euthanasia* is literally "a good death," so the first premise is true. And the second premise is certainly plausible. But the conclusion of this syllogism is false. Euthanasia cannot be defined as a peaceful death in one's old age for two reasons. First, euthanasia requires the intervention of another person who kills someone (or lets the person die); second, even a very young person can be euthanized. The problem arises because "a good death" works in the second premise in a manner that does not apply to euthanasia. Both meanings of "a good death" are legitimate, but when used together, they constitute an equivocation that spoils the argument.

NON SEQUITUR The fallacy of equivocation takes us from the discussion of confusions in individual claims or grounds to the more troublesome fallacies that infect the linkages between the claims we make and the grounds (or reasons) for them. These fallacies occur in statements that, following the vocabulary of the Toulmin method, are called the *warrant* of reasoning. Each fallacy is an example of reasoning that involves a **non sequitur** (Latin for "it does not follow"). That is, the *claim* (the conclusion) does not follow from the *grounds* (the premises).

For a start, here is an obvious non sequitur: "He went to the movies on three consecutive nights, so he must love movies." Why doesn't the claim ("He must love movies") follow from the grounds ("He went to the movies on three consecutive nights")? Perhaps the person was just fulfilling an assignment in a film course (maybe he even hated movies so much that he had postponed three assignments to see films and now had to see them all in quick succession), or maybe he went with a girlfriend who was a movie buff, or maybe . . . — there are any number of other possible reasons.

FALLACIES OF PRESUMPTION

DISTORTING THE FACTS Facts can be distorted either intentionally (to deceive or mislead) or unintentionally, and in either case usually (but not invariably) to the benefit of whoever is doing the distortion. Consider this case. In 1964, the US surgeon general reported that smoking cigarettes increased the likelihood that smokers would eventually suffer from lung cancer. The cigarette manufacturers vigorously protested that the surgeon general relied on inconclusive research and was badly misleading the public about the health risks of smoking. It later turned out that the tobacco companies knew that smoking increased the risk of lung cancer — a fact established by the company's own laboratories but concealed from the public. Today, thanks to public access to all the facts, it is commonplace knowledge that inhaled smoke — including secondhand smoke — is a risk factor for many illnesses.

POST HOC, ERGO PROPTER HOC One of the most tempting errors in reasoning is to ground a claim about causation on an observed temporal sequence — that is, to argue "after this, therefore because of this" (which is what **post hoc, ergo propter hoc** means in Latin). When the medical community first announced that smoking tobacco caused lung cancer, advocates for the tobacco industry replied that doctors were guilty of this fallacy.

These industry advocates argued that medical researchers had merely noticed that in some people, lung cancer developed *after* considerable smoking — indeed, years after — but (they insisted) that this correlation was not at all the same as a causal relation between smoking and lung cancer. True enough. The claim that *A causes B* is not the same as the claim that *B comes after A*. After all, it was possible that smokers as a group had some other common trait and that this factor was the true cause of their cancer.

As the long controversy over the truth about the causation of lung cancer shows, to avoid the appearance of fallacious post hoc reasoning one needs to find some way to link the observed phenomena (the correlation between smoking and the onset of lung cancer). This step requires some further theory and preferably some experimental evidence for the exact sequence or physical mechanism, in full detail, of how ingestion of tobacco smoke is a crucial factor — and is not merely an accidental or happenstance prior event — in the subsequent development of the cancer.

MANY QUESTIONS Some questions contain presuppositions that are presented as true and are built into the question itself. Loaded questions, leading questions, and trick questions are all part of the many questions fallacy. The old saw, "When did you stop beating your wife?" is sometimes used to illustrate the **fallacy of many questions**. This question, as one can readily see, is unanswerable unless all three of its implicit presuppositions are true. The questioner presupposes that (1) the addressee has or had a wife, (2) he or she has beaten her, and (3) he or she has stopped beating her. If any of these presuppositions is false, the question is pointless; it cannot be answered strictly and simply with a date or time.

HASTY GENERALIZATION From a logical point of view, **hasty generalization** is the precipitous move from true assertions about *one* or a *few* instances to dubious or even false assertions about *all*. For example, although it may be true that the only native Hungarians you personally know do not speak English very well, that is no basis for asserting that all Hungarians do not speak English very well. Likewise, if the clothes you recently ordered online turn out not to fit very well, it doesn't follow that *all* online clothes turn out to be too large or too small. A hasty generalization usually lies behind a **stereotype** — that is, a person or event treated as typical of a whole class.

SLIPPERY SLOPE One of the most familiar arguments against any type of government regulation is that if it is allowed, it will be just the first step down the path that leads to ruinous interference, overregulation, and totalitarian control. Fairly often we encounter this mode of argument in the public debates over handgun control, the censorship of pornography, and physician-assisted suicide. The argument is called the **slippery slope** (or the wedge argument, from the way people use the thin end of a wedge to split solid things apart; it is also called, rather colorfully, "letting the camel's nose under the tent"). The fallacy here is in implying that the first step necessarily leads to the second and so on down the slope to disaster, when in fact there is no necessary slide from the first step to the second. (Would handgun registration lead to a police state? Well, it hasn't in Switzerland.)

Closely related to the slippery slope is what lawyers call a **parade of horrors**, an array of examples of terrible consequences that will or might follow if we travel down a certain path.

A good example appears in Justice William Brennan's opinion for the US Supreme Court in *Texas v. Johnson* (1989) regarding a Texas law against burning the American flag in political protest. If this law is allowed to stand, Brennan suggests, we may next find laws against burning the presidential seal, state flags, and the Constitution.

FALSE ANALOGY Argument by analogy, as we point out in Chapter 3 and as many of the selections in this book show, is a familiar and even indispensable mode of argument. But it can be treacherous because it runs the risk of the **fallacy of false analogy**. Unfortunately, we have no simple or foolproof way of distinguishing between the useful, legitimate analogies and the others. The key question to ask yourself is, Do the two things put into analogy differ in any essential and relevant respect, or are they different only in unimportant and irrelevant aspects?

In a famous example from his discussion in support of suicide, philosopher David Hume rhetorically asked: "It would be no crime in me to divert the Nile or Danube from its course, were I able to effect such purposes. Where then is the crime of turning a few ounces of blood from their natural channel?" This is a striking analogy — except that it rests on a false assumption. No one has the right to divert the Nile or the Danube or any other major international watercourse; it would be a catastrophic crime to do so without the full consent of people living in the region, their government, and so forth. Therefore, arguing by analogy, one might well say that no one has the right to take his or her own life either. Thus, Hume's own analogy can be used to argue against his thesis that suicide is no crime. But let's ignore the way in which his example can be turned against him. The analogy is a terrible one in any case. Isn't it obvious that the Nile, regardless of its exact course, would continue to nourish Egypt and the Sudan, whereas the blood flowing out of someone's veins will soon leave that person dead? The fact that the blood is the same blood, whether in a person's body or in a pool on the floor (just as the water of the Nile is the same body of water no matter what path it follows to the sea) is, of course, irrelevant to the question of whether one has the right to commit suicide.

STRAW MAN It is often tempting to reframe or report your opponent's thesis to make it easier to attack and perhaps refute it. If you do so in the course of an argument, you are creating a straw man, a thing of no substance that's easily blown away. The straw man you've constructed is usually a radically conservative or extremely liberal thesis, which few if any would want to defend. That is why it is easier to refute the straw man than refute the view your opponent actually holds: "So you defend the death penalty — and all the horrible things done in its name." It's highly unlikely that your opponent supports *everything* that has been done in the name of capital punishment — crucifixion and beheading, for example, or execution of the children of the guilty offender.

SPECIAL PLEADING We all have our favorites — relatives, friends, and neighbors — and we're all too likely to show that favoritism in unacceptable ways. Here is an example: "I know my son punched another boy but he is not a bully, so there must have been a good reason."

BEGGING THE QUESTION The fallacy called "begging the question," *petitio principii* in Latin, is so named because the conclusion of the argument is hidden among its assumptions — and so the conclusion, not surprisingly, follows from the premises. The argument over whether the death penalty is a deterrent to crime illustrates this fallacy. From the facts that you live in a death-penalty state and were not murdered yesterday, we cannot infer that the death penalty was a deterrent. Yet it is tempting to make this inference, perhaps because — all unaware — we are relying on the **fallacy of begging the question**. If someone tacitly assumes from the start that the death penalty is an effective deterrent, the fact that you weren't murdered yesterday certainly looks like evidence for the truth of that assumption. But it isn't, as long as there are competing but unexamined alternative explanations, as in this case.

Of course, that you weren't murdered is *consistent* with the claim that the death penalty is an effective deterrent, just as someone else being murdered is also consistent with that claim (because an effective deterrent need not be a *perfect* deterrent). In general, from the fact that two propositions are consistent with each other, we cannot infer that either is evidence for the other.

Note: "Begging the question" is often wrongly used to mean "raises the question," as in "His action of burning the flag begs the question, What drove him to do such a thing?"

FALSE DICHOTOMY Sometimes, oversimplification takes a more complex form in which contrary possibilities are wrongly presented as though they were exhaustive and exclusive. "Either we get tough with drug users, or we must surrender and legalize all drugs." Really? What about doing neither and instead offering education and counseling, detoxification programs, and incentives to "Say no"? A favorite of debaters, **either/or reasoning** always runs the risk of ignoring a third (or fourth) possibility. Some disjunctions are indeed exhaustive: "Either we get tough with drug users, or we do not." This proposition, although vague (what does "get tough" really mean?), is a tautology; it cannot be false, and there is no third alternative. But most disjunctions do not express a pair of *contradictory* alternatives: They offer only a pair of *contrary* alternatives, and mere contraries do not exhaust the possibilities (recall our discussion of contraries versus contradictories on pp. 335–36).

OVERSIMPLIFICATION "Poverty causes crime," "Taxation is unfair," "Truth is stranger than fiction" — these are examples of generalizations that exaggerate and therefore oversimplify the truth. Poverty as such can't be the sole cause of crime because many poor people do not break the law. Some taxes may be unfairly high, others unfairly low — but there is no reason to believe that *every* tax is unfair to all those who have to pay it. Some true stories do amaze us as much or more than some fictional stories, but the reverse is true, too. (In the language of the Toulmin method, **oversimplification** is the result of a failure to use suitable modal qualifiers in formulating one's claims or grounds or backing.)

RED HERRING The fallacy of **red herring**, less colorfully named "irrelevant thesis," occurs when one tries to distract one's audience by invoking a consideration that is irrelevant to the topic under discussion. (This fallacy probably gets its name from the fact that a rotten herring, or a cured herring, which is reddish, will throw pursuing hounds off the right track.) Consider this case: Some critics, seeking to defend the US government's refusal to sign the Kyoto accords to reduce climate change, argue that signing is supported mainly by left-leaning scientists. This argument supposedly shows that climate change is not a serious, urgent issue. But claiming that the supporters of these accords are left-inclined is a red herring, an irrelevant thesis. By raising doubts about the political views of the advocates of signing, critics distract attention from the scientific question (Is there climate change?) and also from the separate political question (Ought the US government to sign the accords?). The refusal of a government to sign the accords doesn't show there is no such thing as climate change. And even if all the advocates of signing were left-leaning (they aren't), this fact (if it were a fact, but it isn't) would not show that worries about climate change are exaggerated.

FALLACIES OF IRRELEVANCE

TU QUOQUE The Romans called one particular type of fallacy *tu quoque*, for "you also." Consider this: "You're a fine one, trying to persuade me to give up smoking when you indulge yourself with a pipe and a cigar from time to time. Maybe I should quit, but then so should you. It's hypocritical of you to complain about my smoking when you persist in the same habit." The fallacy is this: The merit of a person's argument has nothing to do with the person's character or behavior. Here the assertion that smoking is bad for one's health is *not* weakened by the fact that a smoker offers the argument.

GENETIC FALLACY A member of the family of fallacies that includes poisoning the well and ad hominem (see below) is the **genetic fallacy**. Here the error takes the form of arguing against a claim by pointing out that its origin (genesis) is tainted or that it was invented by someone deserving our contempt. For example, an opponent of the death penalty might argue this:

> Capital punishment arose in barbarous times, but we claim to be civilized; therefore, we should discard this relic of the past.

Such reasoning shouldn't be persuasive because the question of the death penalty for our society must be decided by the degree to which it serves our purposes — justice and defense against crime, presumably — to which its historic origins are irrelevant. The practices of beer- and wine-making are as old as human civilization, but their origin in antiquity is no reason to outlaw them in our time. The curious circumstances in which something originates usually play no role in its validity. Anyone who would argue that nothing good could possibly come from molds and fungi is refuted by Sir Alexander Fleming's discovery of penicillin in 1928.

APPEAL TO IGNORANCE In the controversy over the death penalty, the issues of deterrence and executing the innocent are bound to be raised. Because no one knows how many innocent persons have been convicted for murder and wrongfully executed, it is tempting for abolitionists to argue that the death penalty is too risky. It is equally tempting for proponents of the death penalty to argue that since no one knows how many people have been deterred from murder by the threat of execution, we abolish it at society's peril.

Each of these arguments suffers from the same flaw: the **fallacy of appeal to ignorance**. Each argument invites the audience to draw an inference from a premise that is unquestionably true, but what is that premise? It asserts that there is something "we don't know." But what we *don't* know cannot be *evidence* for (or against) anything. Our ignorance is no reason for believing anything, except perhaps that we ought to undertake an appropriate investigation so as to replace our ignorance with reliable information.

POISONING THE WELL During the 1970s, some critics of the Equal Rights Amendment (ERA) argued against it by pointing out that Marx and Engels, in their *Communist Manifesto*, favored equality of women and men — and therefore the ERA was immoral, undesirable, and perhaps even a Communist plot. This kind of reasoning is an attempt to **poison the well**; that is, it is an attempt to shift attention from the merits of the argument — the validity of the reasoning, the truth of the claims — to the source or origin of the argument. Such criticism deflects attention from the real issue — namely, whether the view in question is true and what the quality of evidence is in its support. The mere fact that Marx (or Hitler, for that matter) believed something does not show that the belief is false or immoral; just because some scoundrel believes the world is round is no reason for you to believe it is flat.

AD HOMINEM Closely allied to poisoning the well is another fallacy, **ad hominem** argument (from the Latin for "against the person"). A critic can easily yield to the temptation to attack an argument or theory by trying to impeach or undercut the credentials of its advocates.

Consider this example: Jones is arguing that prayer should not be permitted in public schools, and Smith responds by pointing out that Jones has twice been convicted of assaulting members of the clergy. Jones's behavior doubtless is reprehensible, but the issue is not Jones, it is prayer in school, and what must be scrutinized is Jones's argument, not his police record or his character.

APPEAL TO AUTHORITY One might easily imagine someone from the South in 1860 defending the slave-owning society of that day by appealing to the fact that no less a person than Thomas Jefferson — a brilliant public figure, thinker, and leader by any measure — owned slaves. Or today one might defend capital punishment on the ground that Abraham Lincoln, surely one of the nation's greatest presidents, signed many death warrants during the Civil War, authorizing the execution of Union soldiers. No doubt the esteem in which such figures as Jefferson and Lincoln are deservedly held amounts to impressive endorsement for whatever acts and practices, policies, and institutions, they supported. But the **authority** of these figures in itself is not evidence for the truth of their views, so their authority cannot be a reason for anyone to agree with them.

Sometimes, the appeal to authority is fallacious because the authoritative person is not an expert on the issue in dispute. The fact that a high-energy physicist has won the Nobel Prize is no reason for attaching any special weight to her views on the causes of cancer, the reduction of traffic accidents, or the legalization of marijuana. We all depend heavily on the knowledge of various experts and authorities, so we tend to respect their views. Conversely, we should resist the temptation to accord their views on diverse subjects the same respect that we grant them in the area of their expertise.

APPEAL TO FEAR The Romans called the **appeal to fear** fallacy *ad baculum*, for "resorting to violence" (*baculum* means "stick" or "club"). Trying to persuade people to agree with you by threatening them with painful consequences is obviously an appeal that no rational person would contemplate. The violence need not be physical; if you threaten someone with the loss of a job, for instance, you are still using a stick. Violence or the threat of harmful consequences in the course of an argument is beyond reason and always shows the haste or impatience of those who appeal to it. It is also an indication that the argument on its merits would be unpersuasive, inconclusive, or worse. President Theodore Roosevelt's epigrammatic doctrine for the kind of foreign policy he favored — "Speak softly but carry a big stick" — illustrates an attempt to have it both ways; an appeal to reason for starters, but a recourse to coercion, or the threat of coercion, as a backup if needed.

ADDITIONAL FALLACIES

Finally, we add two fallacies, not easily embraced by Engels's three categories that have served us well thus far (ambiguity, erroneous presumption, and irrelevance): death by a thousand qualifications and protecting the hypothesis.

DEATH BY A THOUSAND QUALIFICATIONS **Death by a thousand qualifications** gets its name from the ancient torture of death by a thousand small cuts. Thus, a bold assertion can be virtually killed and its true content reduced to nothing, bit by bit, as all the appropriate or necessary qualifications are added to it. Consider an example. Suppose you hear a politician describing another country (let's call it Ruritania so as not to offend anyone) as a "democracy" — except it turns out that Ruritania doesn't have regular elections, lacks a written constitution, has no independent judiciary, prohibits religious worship except of the state-designated deity, and so forth. So what remains of the original claim that Ruritania is a democracy is little or nothing. The qualifications have taken all the content out of the original description.

PROTECTING THE HYPOTHESIS In Chapter 3, we contrasted *reasoning* and *rationalization* (or the finding of bad reasons for what one intends to believe anyway). Rationalization can take subtle forms, as the following example indicates. Suppose you're standing with a friend on the shore or on a pier and you watch as a ship heads out to sea. As it reaches the horizon, it slowly disappears — first the hull, then the upper decks, and finally the tip of the mast. Because the ship (you both assume) isn't sinking, it occurs to you that this sequence of observations provides evidence that the earth's surface is curved. Nonsense, says your companion. Light waves sag, or bend down, over distances of a few miles, and so a flat surface (such as the ocean) can intercept them. Therefore, the ship, which appears to be going "over" the horizon, really isn't: It's just moving steadily farther and farther away in a straight line. Your friend, you discover to your amazement, is a card-carrying member of the Flat Earth Society, a group who insists the earth is a plane surface. Now most of us would regard the idea that light rays bend down in the manner required by the Flat Earther's argument as a rationalization whose sole purpose is to protect the flat-earth doctrine against counterevidence. We would be convinced it was a rationalization, and not a very good one at that, if the Flat Earther held to it despite a patient and thorough explanation from a physicist that showed modern optical theory to be quite incompatible with the view that light waves sag.

This example illustrates two important points about the *backing* of arguments. First, it is always possible to **protect a hypothesis** by abandoning adjacent or connected hypotheses; this is the tactic our Flat Earth friend has used. This maneuver is possible, however, only because—and this is the second point—whenever we test a hypothesis, we do so by taking for granted (usually, quite unconsciously) many other hypotheses as well. So the evidence for the hypothesis we think we are confirming is impossible to separate entirely from the adequacy of the connected hypotheses. As long as we have no reason to doubt that light rays travel in straight lines (at least over distances of a few miles), our Flat Earth friend's argument is unconvincing. But once that hypothesis is itself put in doubt, the idea that seemed at first to be a pathetic rationalization takes on an even more troublesome character.

There are, then, not one but two fallacies exposed by this example. The first and perhaps graver one is in rigging your hypothesis so that *no matter what* observations are brought against it, you will count nothing as falsifying it. The second and subtler one is in thinking that as you test one hypothesis, all your other background beliefs are left safely to one side, immaculate and uninvolved. On the contrary, our beliefs form a corporate structure, intertwined and connected to one another with great complexity, and no one of them can ever be singled out for unique and isolated application, confirmation, or disconfirmation to the world around us.

A CHECKLIST FOR EVALUATING AN ARGUMENT WITH LOGIC

- ❐ Can I identify the premises and the conclusion of the argument?
- ❐ Given the premises, is the argument valid?
- ❐ If it is valid, are all its premises true?
- ❐ If all the premises are true, does the conclusion necessarily follow from them?
- ❐ Are there any claims that are inconsistent in the argument?
- ❐ Does the argument contain one or more fallacies?
- ❐ If the argument is inductive, on what observations is it based?
- ❐ Do the observations or data make the conclusion probable?
- ❐ Is there enough evidence to disconfirm the conclusion?

THINKING CRITICALLY *Identifying Fallacies*

Here are some fallacies in action. Using the explanations in this section, identify what type of fallacy the argument example commits and then explain your reasoning.

EXAMPLE	TYPE OF FALLACY	EXPLANATION
Senator Case was friends with a disgraced racketeer; he shouldn't be your selection in the upcoming election.		
These activists say they want justice, but is it really justice to clog up the streets with the protests?		
East Coast urban liberals are going to say that hunting is inhumane. They do not realize how narrow-minded they are.		
There have been few terrorist attacks since September 11, 2001; therefore, our national security efforts must be working.		
If you start out with a bottle of beer a day and then go on to a glass or two of wine on the weekends, you're well on your way to becoming a hopeless drunk.		
My marriage was a failure, which just proves my point: Don't ever get married in the first place.		
Not until astronauts sailed through space around the moon did we have adequate reason to believe that the moon even had a back side.		
Going to church on a regular basis is bad for your health. Instead of sitting in a pew for an hour each Sunday, you'd be better off taking an hour's brisk walk.		

EXAMPLE	TYPE OF FALLACY	EXPLANATION
A professional baseball player has a good-luck charm. When he wears it, the team wins.		
How come herbivores don't eat herbs?		

MAX SHULMAN

Max Shulman (1919–1988) began his career as a writer when he was a journalism student at the University of Minnesota. Later he wrote humorous novels, stories, and plays. One of his novels, *Barefoot Boy with Cheek* (1943), was made into a musical, and another, *Rally Round the Flag, Boys!* (1957), was made into a film starring Paul Newman and Joanne Woodward. *The Tender Trap* (1954), a play he wrote with Robert Paul Smith, still retains its popularity with theater groups.

"Love Is a Fallacy" was first published in 1951, when demeaning stereotypes about women and minorities were widely accepted in the marketplace, as well as the home. Thus, jokes about domineering mothers-in-law or about dumb blondes routinely met with no objection.

Love Is a Fallacy

Cool was I and logical. Keen, calculating, perspicacious, acute, and astute — I was all of these. My brain was as powerful as a dynamo, as precise as a chemist's scales, as penetrating as a scalpel. And — think of it! — I was only eighteen.

It is not often that one so young has such a giant intellect. Take, for example, Petey Bellows, my roommate at the university. Same age, same background, but dumb as an ox. A nice enough fellow, you understand, but nothing upstairs. Emotional type. Unstable. Impressionable. Worst of all, a faddist. Fads, I submit, are the very negation of reason. To be swept up in every new craze that comes along, to surrender yourself to idiocy just because everybody else is doing it — this, to me, is the acme of mindlessness. Not, however, to Petey.

One afternoon I found Petey lying on his bed with an expression of such distress on his face that I immediately diagnosed appendicitis. "Don't move," I said. "Don't take a laxative. I'll call a doctor."

"Raccoon," he mumbled thickly.

"Raccoon?" I said, pausing in my flight. 5

"I want a raccoon coat," he wailed.

I perceived that his trouble was not physical, but mental. "Why do you want a raccoon coat?"

"I should have known it," he cried, pounding his temples. "I should have known they'd come back when the Charleston came back.

Like a fool I spent all my money for textbooks, and now I can't get a raccoon coat."

"Can you mean," I said incredulously, "that people are actually wearing raccoon coats again?"

"All the Big Men on Campus are wearing them. Where've you been?"

"In the library," I said, naming a place not frequented by Big Men on Campus.

He leaped from the bed and paced the room. "I've got to have a raccoon coat," he said passionately. "I've got to!"

"Petey, why? Look at it rationally. Raccoon coats are unsanitary. They shed. They smell bad. They weigh too much. They're unsightly. They ——"

"You don't understand," he interrupted impatiently. "It's the thing to do. Don't you want to be in the swim?"

"No," I said truthfully.

"Well, I do," he declared. "I'd give anything for a raccoon coat. Anything!"

My brain, that precision instrument, slipped into high gear. "Anything?" I asked, looking at him narrowly.

"Anything," he affirmed in ringing tones.

I stroked my chin thoughtfully. It so happened that I knew where to get my hands on a raccoon coat. My father had had one in his undergraduate days; it lay now in a trunk in the attic back home. It also happened that Petey had something I wanted. He didn't *have* it exactly, but at least he had first rights on it. I refer to his girl, Polly Espy.

I had long coveted Polly Espy. Let me emphasize that my desire for this young woman was not emotional in nature. She was, to be sure, a girl who excited the emotions, but I was not one to let my heart rule my head. I wanted Polly for a shrewdly calculated, entirely cerebral reason.

I was a freshman in law school. In a few years I would be out in practice. I was well aware of the importance of the right kind of wife in furthering a lawyer's career. The successful lawyers I had observed were, almost without exception, married to beautiful, gracious, intelligent women. With one omission, Polly fitted these specifications perfectly.

Beautiful she was. She was not yet of pin-up proportions, but I felt sure that time would supply the lack. She already had the makings.

Gracious she was. By gracious I mean full of graces. She had an erectness of carriage, an ease of bearing, a poise that clearly indicated the best of breeding. At table her manners were exquisite. I had seen her at the Kozy Kampus Korner eating the specialty of the house — a sandwich that contained scraps of pot roast, gravy, chopped nuts, and a dipper of sauerkraut — without even getting her fingers moist.

Intelligent she was not. In fact, she veered in the opposite direction. But I believed that under my guidance she would smarten up. At any rate, it was worth a try. It is, after all, easier to make a beautiful dumb girl smart than to make an ugly smart girl beautiful.

"Petey," I said, "are you in love with Polly Espy?"

"I think she's a keen kid," he replied, "but I don't know if you'd call it love. Why?"

"Do you," I asked, "have any kind of formal arrangement with her? I mean are you going steady or anything like that?"

"No. We see each other quite a bit, but we both have other dates. Why?"

"Is there," I asked, "any other man for whom she has a particular fondness?"

"Not that I know of. Why?"

I nodded with satisfaction. "In other words, if you were out of the picture, the field would be open. Is that right?"

"I guess so. What are you getting at?"

"Nothing, nothing," I said innocently, and took my suitcase out of the closet.

"Where you going?" asked Petey.

"Home for the weekend." I threw a few things into the bag.

"Listen," he said, clutching my arm eagerly, "while you're home, you couldn't get some money from your old man, could you, and lend it to me so I can buy a raccoon coat?"

"I may do better than that," I said with a mysterious wink and closed my bag and left.

"Look," I said to Petey when I got back Monday morning. I threw open the suitcase and revealed the huge, hairy, gamy object that my father had worn in his Stutz Bearcat in 1925.

"Holy Toledo!" said Petey reverently. He plunged his hands into the raccoon coat and then his face. "Holy Toledo!" he repeated fifteen or twenty times.

"Would you like it?" I asked.

"Oh yes!" he cried, clutching the greasy pelt to him. Then a canny look came into his eyes. "What do you want for it?"

"Your girl," I said, mincing no words.

"Polly?" he said in a horrified whisper. "You want Polly?"

"That's right."

He flung the coat from him. "Never," he said stoutly.

I shrugged. "Okay. If you don't want to be in the swim, I guess it's your business."

I sat down in a chair and pretended to read a book, but out of the corner of my eye I kept watching Petey. He was a torn man. First he looked at the coat with the expression of a waif at a bakery window. Then he turned away and set his jaw resolutely. Then he looked back at the coat, with even more longing in his face. Then he turned away, but with not so much resolution this time. Back and forth his head swiveled, desire waxing, resolution waning. Finally he didn't turn away at all; he just stood and stared with mad lust at the coat.

"It isn't as though I was in love with Polly," he said thickly. "Or going steady or anything like that."

"That's right," I murmured.

"What's Polly to me, or me to Polly?"

"Not a thing," said I.

"It's just been a casual kick — just a few laughs, that's all."

"Try on the coat," said I.

He complied. The coat bunched high over his ears and dropped all the way down to his shoe tops. He looked like a mound of dead raccoons. "Fits fine," he said happily.

I rose from my chair. "Is it a deal?" I asked, extending my hand.

He swallowed. "It's a deal," he said and shook my hand.

I had my first date with Polly the following evening. This was in the nature of a survey; I wanted to find out just how much work I had to do to get her mind up to the standard I required. I took her first to dinner. "Gee, that was a delish dinner," she said as we left the restaurant. Then I took her to a movie. "Gee, that was a marvy movie," she said as we left the theater. And then I took her home. "Gee, I had a sensaysh time," she said as she bade me good night.

I went back to my room with a heavy heart. I had gravely underestimated the size of my task. This girl's lack of information was terrifying. Nor would it be enough merely to supply her with information. First she had to be taught to *think*. This loomed as a project of no small dimensions, and at first I was tempted to give her back to Petey. But then I got to thinking about her abundant physical charms and about the way she entered a room and the way she handled a knife and fork, and I decided to make an effort.

I went about it, as in all things, systematically. I gave her a course in logic. It happened that I, as a law student, was taking a course in logic myself, so I had all the facts at my fingertips. "Polly," I said to her when I picked her up on our next date, "tonight we are going over to the Knoll and talk."

"Oo, terrif," she replied. One thing I will say for this girl: You would go far to find another so agreeable.

We went to the Knoll, the campus trysting place, and we sat down under an old oak, and she looked at me expectantly: "What are we going to talk about?" she asked.

"Logic."

She thought this over for a minute and decided she liked it. "Magnif," she said.

"Logic," I said, clearing my throat, "is the science of thinking. Before we can think correctly, we must first learn to recognize the common fallacies of logic. These we will take up tonight."

"Wow-dow!" she cried, clapping her hands delightedly.

I winced, but went bravely on. "First let us examine the fallacy called Dicto Simpliciter."

"By all means," she urged, batting her lashes eagerly.

"Dicto Simpliciter means an argument based on an unqualified generalization. For example: Exercise is good. Therefore everybody should exercise."

"I agree," said Polly earnestly. "I mean exercise is wonderful. I mean it builds the body and everything."

"Polly," I said gently, "the argument is a fallacy. *Exercise is good* is an unqualified generalization. For instance, if you have heart disease, exercise is bad, not good. Many people are ordered by their doctors *not* to exercise. You must *qualify* the generalization. You must say exercise is *usually* good, or exercise is good *for most people.* Otherwise you have committed a Dicto Simpliciter. Do you see?"

"No," she confessed. "But this is marvy. Do more! Do more!"

"It will be better if you stop tugging at my sleeve," I told her, and when she desisted, I continued. "Next we take up a fallacy called Hasty Generalization. Listen carefully: You can't speak French. I can't speak French. Petey Bellows can't speak French. I must therefore conclude that nobody at the University of Minnesota can speak French."

"Really?" said Polly, amazed. "*Nobody?*"

I hid my exasperation. "Polly, it's a fallacy. The generalization is reached too hastily. There are too few instances to support such a conclusion."

"Know any more fallacies?" she asked breathlessly. "This is more fun than dancing even."

I fought off a wave of despair. I was getting nowhere with this girl, absolutely nowhere. Still, I am nothing if not persistent. I continued. "Next comes Post Hoc. Listen to this: Let's not take Bill on our picnic. Every time we take him out with us, it rains."

"I know somebody just like that," she exclaimed. "A girl back home — Eula Becker, her name is. It never fails. Every single time we take her on a picnic ——"

"Polly," I said sharply, "it's a fallacy. Eula Becker doesn't *cause* the rain. She has no connection with the rain. You are guilty of Post Hoc if you blame Eula Becker."

"I'll never do it again," she promised contritely. "Are you mad at me?"

I sighed. "No, Polly, I'm not mad."

"Then tell me some more fallacies."

"All right. Let's try Contradictory Premises."

"Yes, let's," she chirped, blinking her eyes happily.

I frowned, but plunged ahead. "Here's an example of Contradictory Premises: If God can do anything, can He make a stone so heavy that He won't be able to lift it?"

"Of course," she replied promptly.

"But if He can do anything, He can lift the stone," I pointed out.

"Yeah," she said thoughtfully. "Well, then I guess He can't make the stone."

"But He can do anything," I reminded her.

She scratched her pretty, empty head. "I'm all confused," she admitted.

"Of course you are. Because when the premises of an argument contradict each other, there can be no argument. If there is an irresistible force, there can be no immovable object. If there is an immovable object, there can be no irresistible force. Get it?"

"Tell me some more of this keen stuff," she said eagerly.

I consulted my watch. "I think we'd better call it a night. I'll take you home now, and you go over all the things you've learned. We'll have another session tomorrow night."

I deposited her at the girls' dormitory, where she assured me that she had had a perfectly terrif evening, and I went glumly home to my room. Petey lay snoring in his bed, the raccoon coat huddled like a great hairy beast at his feet. For a moment I considered waking him and telling him that he could have his girl back. It seemed clear that my project was doomed to failure. The girl simply had a logic-proof head.

But then I reconsidered. I had wasted one evening; I might as well waste another. Who knew? Maybe somewhere in the extinct crater of her mind a few embers still smoldered. Maybe somehow I could fan them into flame. Admittedly it was not a prospect fraught with hope, but I decided to give it one more try.

Seated under the oak the next evening I said, "Our first fallacy tonight is called Ad Misericordiam."

She quivered with delight.

"Listen closely," I said. "A man applies for a job. When the boss asks him what his qualifications are, he replies that he has a wife and six children at home, the wife is a helpless cripple, the children have nothing to eat, no clothes to wear, no shoes on their feet, there are no beds in the house, no coal in the cellar, and winter is coming."

A tear rolled down each of Polly's pink cheeks. "Oh, this is awful, awful," she sobbed.

"Yes, it's awful," I agreed, "but it's no argument. The man never answered the boss's question about his qualifications. Instead he appealed to the boss's sympathy. He committed the fallacy of Ad Misericordiam. Do you understand?"

"Have you got a handkerchief?" she blubbered.

I handed her a handkerchief and tried to keep from screaming while she wiped her eyes. "Next," I said in a carefully controlled tone, "we will discuss False Analogy. Here is an example: Students should be allowed to look at their textbooks during examinations. After all, surgeons have X rays to guide them during an operation, lawyers have briefs to guide them during a trial, carpenters have blueprints to guide them when they are building a house. Why, then, shouldn't students be allowed to look at their textbooks during an examination?"

"There now," she said enthusiastically, "is the most marvy idea I've heard in years."

"Polly," I said testily, "the argument is all wrong. Doctors, lawyers, and carpenters aren't taking a test to see how much they have learned, but students are. The situations are altogether different, and you can't make an analogy between them."

"I still think it's a good idea," said Polly.

"Nuts," I muttered. Doggedly I pressed on. "Next we'll try Hypothesis Contrary to Fact."

"Sounds yummy," was Polly's reaction.

"Listen: If Madame Curie had not happened to leave a photographic plate in a drawer with a chunk of pitchblende, the world today would not know about radium."

"True, true," said Polly, nodding her head. "Did you see the movie? Oh, it just knocked me out. That Walter Pidgeon is so dreamy. I mean he fractures me."

"If you can forget Mr. Pidgeon for a moment," I said coldly, "I would like to point out that the statement is a fallacy. Maybe Madame Curie would have discovered radium at some later date. Maybe somebody else would have discovered it. Maybe any number of things would have happened. You can't start with a hypothesis that is not true and then draw any supportable conclusions from it."

"They ought to put Walter Pidgeon in more pictures," said Polly. "I hardly ever see him anymore."

One more chance, I decided. But just one more. There is a limit to what flesh and blood can bear. "The next fallacy is called Poisoning the Well."

"How cute!" she gurgled.

"Two men are having a debate. The first one gets up and says, 'My opponent is a notorious liar. You can't believe a word that he is going to say.' . . . Now, Polly, think. Think hard. What's wrong?"

I watched her closely as she knit her creamy brow in concentration. Suddenly a glimmer of intelligence — the first I had seen — came into her eyes. "It's not fair," she said with indignation. "It's not a bit fair. What chance has the second man got if the first man calls him a liar before he even begins talking?"

"Right!" I cried exultantly. "One hundred percent right. It's not fair. The first man has *poisoned the well* before anybody could drink from it. He has hamstrung his opponent before he could even start. . . . Polly, I'm proud of you."

"Pshaw," she murmured, blushing with pleasure.

"You see, my dear, these things aren't so hard. All you have to do is concentrate. Think — examine — evaluate. Come now, let's review everything we have learned."

"Fire away," she said with an airy wave of her hand.

Heartened by the knowledge that Polly was not altogether a cretin, I began a long, patient review of all I had told her. Over and over and over again I cited instances, pointed out flaws, kept hammering away without letup. It was like digging a tunnel. At first everything was work, sweat, and darkness. I had no idea when I would reach the light, or even *if* I would. But I persisted. I pounded and clawed and scraped, and finally I was rewarded. I saw a chink of light. And then the chink got bigger and the sun came pouring in and all was bright.

Five grueling nights this took, but it was worth it. I had made a logician out of Polly; I had taught her to think. My job was done. She was worthy of me at last. She was a fit wife for me, a proper hostess for my many mansions, a suitable mother for my well-heeled children.

It must not be thought that I was without love for this girl. Quite the contrary. Just as Pygmalion loved the perfect woman he had fashioned, so I loved mine. I decided to acquaint her with my feelings at our very next meeting. The time had come to change our relationship from academic to romantic.

"Polly," I said when next we sat beneath our oak, "tonight we will not discuss fallacies."

"Aw, gee," she said, disappointed.

"My dear," I said, favoring her with a smile, "we have now spent five evenings together. We have gotten along splendidly. It is clear that we are well matched."

"Hasty Generalization," said Polly brightly.

"I beg your pardon," said I.

"Hasty Generalization," she repeated. "How can you say that we are well matched on the basis of only five dates?"

I chuckled with amusement. The dear child had learned her lessons well. "My dear," I said, patting her hand in a tolerant manner, "five dates is plenty. After all, you don't have to eat a whole cake to know that it's good."

"False Analogy," said Polly promptly. "I'm not a cake. I'm a girl."

I chuckled with somewhat less amusement. The dear child had learned her lesson perhaps too well. I decided to change tactics. Obviously the best approach was a simple, strong, direct declaration of love. I paused for a moment while my massive brain chose the proper words. Then I began:

"Polly, I love you. You are the whole world to me, and the moon and the stars and the constellations of outer space. Please, my darling, say that you will go steady with me, for if you will not, life will be meaningless. I will languish. I will refuse my meals. I will wander the face of the earth, a shambling, hollow-eyed hulk."

There, I thought, folding my arms, that ought to do it.

"Ad Misericordiam," said Polly.

I ground my teeth. I was not Pygmalion; I was Frankenstein, and my monster had me by the throat. Frantically I fought back the tide of panic surging through me. At all costs I had to keep cool.

"Well, Polly," I said, forcing a smile, "you certainly have learned your fallacies."

"You're darn right," she said with a vigorous nod.

"And who taught them to you, Polly?"

"You did."

"That's right. So you do owe me something, don't you, my dear? If I hadn't come along you never would have learned about fallacies."

"Hypothesis Contrary to Fact," she said instantly.

I dashed perspiration from my brow. "Polly," I croaked, "you mustn't take all these things so literally. I mean this is just classroom stuff. You know that the things you learn in school don't have anything to do with life."

"Dicto Simpliciter," she said, wagging her finger at me playfully.

That did it. I leaped to my feet, bellowing like a bull. "Will you or will you not go steady with me?"

"I will not," she replied.

"Why not?" I demanded.

"Because this afternoon I promised Petey Bellows that I would go steady with him."

I reeled back, overcome with the infamy of it. After he promised, after he made a deal, after he shook my hand! "That rat!" I shrieked, kicking up great chunks of turf. "You can't go with him, Polly. He's a liar. He's a cheat. He's a rat."

"Poisoning the Well," said Polly, "and stop shouting. I think shouting must be a fallacy too."

With an immense effort of will, I modulated my voice. "All right," I said. "You're a logician. Let's look at this thing logically. How could you choose Petey Bellows over me? Look at me — a brilliant student, a tremendous intellectual, a man with an assured future. Look at Petey — a knothead, a jitterbug, a guy who'll never know where his next meal is coming from. Can you give me one logical reason why you should go steady with Petey Bellows?"

"I certainly can," declared Polly. "He's got a raccoon coat."

Topic for Critical Thinking and Writing

After you have finished reading "Love Is a Fallacy," consider the following hypothetical conversation and then join the conversation: Write your own, final response that points out to these three peers how their arguments succeed or fail, using the elements of logic from this chapter (premises, conclusions, assumptions, fallacies, etc.). Finally, make your own argument about the nature of this story and how it bears on the question of sexism and publication.

CAITLYN: The story is condescending and even insulting to women. You could even call it sexist. Sexist stories should not be in college textbooks, and therefore this story should not have been published in this college textbook.

JOSHUA: This story may be sexist, but that is acceptable in the context of learning. Now if any story were racist, you would have a point about not including it in a textbook. But this story was written in 1951, and it wasn't considered sexist in its own time.

SAM: Max Shulman was a great humorist who worked in old-time television and invented the iconic character Dobie Gillis. The story is intended to be funny; therefore, it is not sexist. If anything, it should not be included in this textbook because it is not funny.

10

A Psychologist's View: Rogerian Argument

Real communication occurs . . . when we listen with understanding. — CARL ROGERS

The first duty of a wise advocate is to convince his opponents that he understands their arguments, and sympathizes with their just feelings. — SAMUEL TAYLOR COLERIDGE

Rogerian Argument: An Introduction

Carl R. Rogers (1902–1987), perhaps best known for his book entitled *On Becoming a Person* (1961), was a psychotherapist, not a teacher of writing. Nonetheless, Rogers's approach to argument (put forth in the short essay by Rogers beginning on p. 366) has exerted much influence on instructors who teach argument.

On the surface, many arguments seem to show *A* arguing with *B*, presumably seeking to change *B*'s mind, but *A*'s argument is really directed not to *B* but to *C*. This attempt to persuade a nonparticipant is evident in the courtroom, where neither the prosecutor (*A*) nor the defense lawyer (*B*) is really trying to convince the opponent. Rather, both are trying to convince a third party, the jury (*C*). Prosecutors don't care whether they convince defense lawyers; they don't even mind infuriating defense lawyers because their only real goal is to convince the jury. Similarly, the writer of a letter to a newspaper, taking issue with an editorial, doesn't expect to change the paper's policy. Rather, the writer hopes to convince a third party, the reader of the newspaper.

Michael Rougier/Getty Images

Carl R. Rogers (second from the right) leading a panel discussion in 1966.

But suppose *A* really does want to bring *B* around to *A*'s point of view and suppose *B* is also arguing with *A*, too, trying to persuade *A* that his or her way is best. Politicians often argue with one another in just such ways. In such instances, both parties may be reluctant to listen to the other. Rogers points out that when we engage in an argument, if we feel our integrity or our identity is threatened, we will stiffen our position. The sense of threat may be so great that we are unable to consider the alternative views being offered, and we therefore remain unpersuaded. Threatened, we may defend ourselves rather than our argument, and little communication will take place. Of course, a third party might say that we or our opponent presented the more convincing case, but we, and perhaps the opponent, have scarcely listened to each other, and so the two of us remain apart.

Rogers therefore suggests that a writer who wishes to communicate with someone (as opposed to convincing a third party) needs to reduce the threat. In a sense, the participants in the argument need to become partners rather than adversaries. Rogers, a therapist, was keen to highlight **empathy**, the understanding of someone else's perspective or experiences, as a fundamental part of effective communication. But writers, like therapists, also must work toward understanding their partners in communication. That is achieved partially through an honest attempt to inhabit the psyche of the other, to see and feel the issues through the other's perspectives, in light of their perceptions and feelings. Instead of point–counterpoint argument, the goal is to foster emotional and intellectual reciprocity. Listeners are more willing to be persuaded when they see their partner in communication as an honest collaborator instead of an opponent. Rogers wrote, "Mutual communication tends to be pointed toward solving a problem rather than toward attacking a person or group."

Visual Guide: Rogerian Argument

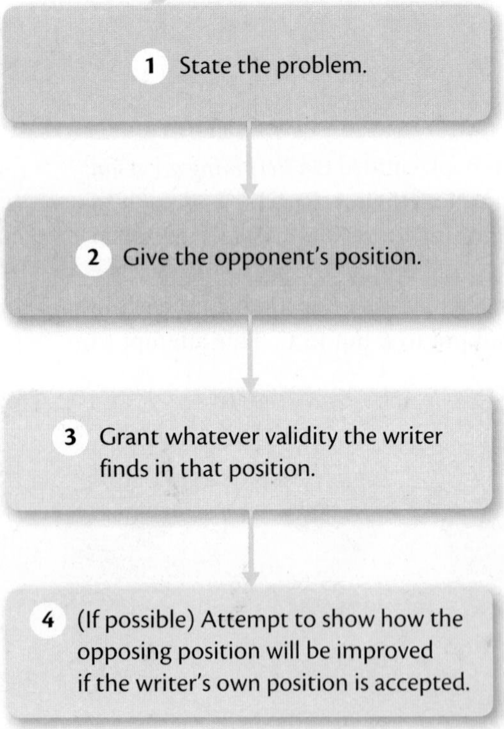
1 State the problem.
2 Give the opponent's position.
3 Grant whatever validity the writer finds in that position.
4 (If possible) Attempt to show how the opposing position will be improved if the writer's own position is accepted.

Thus, in an essay on standardized testing, for instance, the writer need not — and probably should not — see the issue as black or white, as *either/or*. Such an essay might indicate that testing is undesirable because it has negative effects on students or teaching, *but in some circumstances* it may be seen as reasonable and acceptable. This qualification does not mean that one must compromise. Thus, the essayist might argue that high-stakes testing increases student anxiety, constrains teachers, and devalues the arts, but may also recognize the value of the tests in ensuring educational consistency across public school systems.

A writer who wishes to reduce the psychological threat to the opposition and thus facilitate partnership in the study of some issue can do several things:

- show sympathetic understanding of the opposing argument
- recognize what is valid in it
- recognize and demonstrate that those who take the other side are nonetheless persons of goodwill

Advocates of Rogerian argument are likely to contrast it with Aristotelian argument, saying that the style of argument associated with Aristotle (384–322 BCE, Greek philosopher and rhetorician) has these two characteristics:

- It is adversarial, seeking to refute other views.
- It sees the listener as wrong, as someone who now must be overwhelmed by evidence.

A CHECKLIST FOR ANALYZING ROGERIAN ARGUMENT

- ❒ Have I stated the problem and indicated that a dialogue is possible?
- ❒ Have I stated at least one other point of view in a way that would satisfy its proponents?
- ❒ Have I been courteous to those who hold views other than mine?
- ❒ Have I enlarged my own understanding to the extent that I can grant validity, at least in some circumstances, to at least some aspects of other positions?
- ❒ Have I stated my position and indicated the contexts in which I believe it is valid?
- ❒ Have I pointed out the ground that we share?
- ❒ Have I shown how other positions will be strengthened by accepting some aspects of my position?

In contrast to the confrontational Aristotelian style, which allegedly seeks to present an airtight case that compels belief, Rogerian argument (it is said) has the following characteristics:

- It is nonconfrontational, collegial, and friendly.
- It respects other views and allows for multiple truths.
- It seeks to achieve some degree of assent and empathy rather than convince utterly.

Sometimes, of course, the differing positions may be so far apart that no reconciliation can be proposed, in which case the writer will probably seek to show how the problem can best be solved by adopting the writer's own position. These matters are discussed in Chapter 6, but not from the point of view of a psychotherapist, and so we reprint Rogers's essay here.

CARL R. ROGERS

Carl R. Rogers (1902–1987), perhaps best known for his book *On Becoming a Person* (1961), was a psychotherapist. The following essay was originally presented on October 11, 1951, at Northwestern University's Centennial Conference on Communications. In it, Rogers reflects the political climate of the cold war between the United States and the Soviet Union, which dominated headlines for more than forty years (1947–1989). Several of Rogers's examples of bias and frustrated communication allude to the tensions of that era.

Communication: Its Blocking and Its Facilitation

It may seem curious that a person whose whole professional effort is devoted to psychotherapy should be interested in problems of communication. What relationship is there between providing therapeutic help to individuals with emotional maladjustments and the concern of this conference with obstacles to communication? Actually the relationship is very close indeed. The whole task of psychotherapy is the task of dealing with a failure in communication. The emotionally maladjusted person, the "neurotic," is in difficulty first because communication within himself has broken down, and second because as a result of this his communication with others has been damaged. If this sounds somewhat strange, then let me put it in other terms. In the "neurotic" individual, parts of himself which have been termed unconscious, or repressed, or denied to awareness, become blocked off so that they no longer communicate themselves to the conscious or managing part of himself. As long as this is true, there are distortions in the way he communicates himself to others, and so he suffers both within himself, and in his interpersonal relations. The task of psychotherapy is to help the person achieve, through a special relationship with a therapist, good communication within himself. Once this is achieved he can communicate more freely and more effectively with others. We may say then that psychotherapy is good communication, within and between men. We may also turn that statement around and it will still be true. Good communication, free communication, within or between men, is always therapeutic.

It is, then, from a background of experience with communication in counseling and psychotherapy that I want to present here two ideas. I wish to state what I believe is one of the major factors in blocking or impeding communication, and then I wish to present what in our experience has proven to be a very important way to improving or facilitating communication.

I would like to propose, as an hypothesis for consideration, that the major barrier to mutual interpersonal communication is our very natural tendency to judge, to evaluate, to approve or disapprove, the statement of the person, or the other group. Let me illustrate my meaning with some very simple examples. As you leave the meeting tonight, one of the statements you are likely to hear is, "I didn't like that man's talk." Now what do you respond? Almost invariably your reply will be either approval or disapproval of the attitude expressed. Either you respond, "I didn't either. I thought it was terrible," or else you tend to reply, "Oh, I thought it was really good." In other words, your primary reaction is to evaluate what has just been said to you, to evaluate it from *your* point of view, your own frame of reference.

Or take another example. Suppose I say with some feeling, "I think the Republicans are behaving in ways that show a lot of good sound sense these days," what is the response that arises in your mind as you listen? The overwhelming likelihood is that it will be evaluative. You will find yourself agreeing, or disagreeing, or making some judgment about me such as "He must be a conservative," or "He seems solid in his thinking." Or let us take an illustration from the international scene. Russia says vehemently, "The treaty with Japan is a war plot on the part of the United States." We rise as one person to say "That's a lie!"

This last illustration brings in another 5
element connected with my hypothesis. Although the tendency to make evaluations is common in almost all interchange of language, it is very much heightened in those situations where feelings and emotions are deeply involved. So the stronger our feelings, the more likely it is that there will be no mutual element in the communication. There will be just two ideas, two feelings, two judgments, missing each other in psychological space. I'm sure you recognize this from your own experience. When you have not been emotionally involved yourself, and have listened to a heated discussion, you often go away thinking, "Well, they actually weren't talking about the same thing." And they were not. Each was making a judgment, an evaluation, from his own frame of reference. There was really nothing which could be called communication in any genuine sense. This tendency to react to any emotionally meaningful statement by forming an evaluation of it from our own point of view, is, I repeat, the major barrier to interpersonal communication.

But is there any way of solving this problem, of avoiding this barrier? I feel that we are making exciting progress toward this goal and I would like to present it as simply as I can. Real communication occurs, and this evaluative tendency is avoided, when we listen with understanding. What does that mean? It means *to see the expressed idea and attitude from the other person's point of view, to sense how it feels to him, to achieve his frame of reference in regard to the thing he is talking about.*

Stated so briefly, this may sound absurdly simple, but it is not. It is an approach which we have found extremely potent in the field of psychotherapy. It is the most effective agent we know for altering the basic personality structure of an individual, and improving his relationships and his communications with others. If I can listen to what he can tell me, if I can understand how it seems to him, if I can see its personal meaning for him, if I can sense the emotional flavor which it has for him, then I will be releasing potent forces of change in him. If I can really understand how he hates his father, or hates the university, or hates communists — if I can catch the flavor of his fear of insanity, or his fear of atom bombs, or of Russia — it will be of the greatest help to him in altering those very hatreds and fears, and in establishing realistic and harmonious relationships with the very people and situations toward which he has felt hatred and fear. We know from our research that such empathic understanding — understanding *with* a person, not *about* him — is such an effective approach that it can bring about major changes in personality.

Some of you may be feeling that you listen well to people, and that you have never seen such results. The chances are very great indeed that your listening has not been of the type I have described. Fortunately I can suggest a little laboratory experiment which you can try to test the quality of your understanding. The next time you get into an argument with your wife, or your friend, or with a small group of friends, just stop the discussion for a moment and for an experiment, institute this rule. "Each person can speak up for himself only *after* he has first restated the ideas and feelings of the previous speaker accurately, and to that speaker's satisfaction." You see what this would mean. It would simply mean that before presenting your own point of view, it would be necessary for you to really achieve the other speaker's frame of reference — to understand his thoughts and feelings so well that you could summarize them for him. Sounds simple, doesn't it? But if you try it you will discover it one of the most difficult things you have ever tried to do. However, once you have been able to see the other's point of view, your own comments will have to be drastically revised. You will also find the emotion going out of the discussion, the differences being reduced, and those differences which remain being of a rational and understandable sort.

Can you imagine what this kind of an approach would mean if it were projected into larger areas? What would happen to a labor-management dispute if it was conducted in such a way that labor, without necessarily agreeing, could accurately state management's point of view in a way that management could accept; and management, without approving labor's stand, could state labor's case in a way that labor agreed was accurate? It would mean that real communication was established, and one could practically guarantee that some reasonable solution would be reached.

10 If then this way of approach is an effective avenue to good communication and good relationships, as I am quite sure you will agree if you try the experiment I have mentioned, why is it not more widely tried and used? I will try to list the difficulties which keep it from being utilized.

In the first place it takes courage, a quality which is not too widespread. I am indebted to Dr. S. I. Hayakawa, the semanticist, for pointing out that to carry on psychotherapy in this fashion is to take a very real risk, and that courage is required. If you really understand another person in this way, if you are willing to enter his private world and see the way life appears to him, without any attempt to make evaluative judgments, you run the risk of being changed yourself. You might see it his way, you might find yourself influenced in your attitudes or your personality. This risk of being changed is one of the most frightening prospects most of us can face. If I enter, as fully as I am able, into the private world of a neurotic or psychotic individual, isn't there a risk that I might become lost in that world? Most of us are afraid to take that risk. Or if we had a Russian communist speaker here tonight, or Senator Joe McCarthy, how many of us would dare to try to see the world from each of these points of view? The great majority of us could not *listen*; we would find ourselves compelled to *evaluate*, because listening would seem too dangerous. So the first requirement is courage, and we do not always have it.

But there is a second obstacle. It is just when emotions are strongest that it is most difficult to achieve the frame of reference of the other person or group. Yet it is the time the attitude is most needed, if communication is to be established. We have not found this to be an insuperable obstacle in our experience in psychotherapy. A third party, who is able to lay aside his own feelings and evaluations, can assist greatly by listening with understanding to each person or group and clarifying the views and attitudes each holds. We have found this very effective in small groups in which contradictory or antagonistic attitudes exist. When the parties to a dispute realize that they are being understood, that someone sees how the situation seems to them, the statements grow less exaggerated and less defensive, and it is no longer necessary to maintain the attitude, "I am 100 percent right and you are 100 percent wrong." The influence of such an understanding catalyst in the group permits the members to come closer and closer to the objective truth involved in the relationship. In this way mutual communication is established and some type of agreement becomes much more possible. So we may say that though heightened emotions make it much more difficult to understand *with* an opponent, our experience makes it clear that a neutral, understanding, catalyst type of leader or therapist can overcome this obstacle in a small group.

This last phrase, however, suggests another obstacle to utilizing the approach I have described. Thus far all our experience has been with small face-to-face groups — groups exhibiting industrial tensions, religious tensions, racial tensions, and therapy groups in which many personal tensions are present. In these small groups our experience, confirmed by a limited amount of research, shows that this basic approach leads to improved communication, to greater acceptance of others and by others, and to attitudes which are more positive and more problem-solving in nature. There is a decrease in defensiveness, in exaggerated statements, in evaluative and critical behavior. But these findings are from small groups. What about trying to achieve understanding between larger groups that are geographically remote? Or between face-to-face groups who are not speaking for themselves, but simply as representatives of others, like the delegates at Kaesong?[1] Frankly we do not know the answers to these questions. I believe the situation might be put this way. As social scientists we have a tentative test-tube solution of the problem of breakdown in communication. But to confirm the validity of this test-tube solution, and to adapt it to the enormous problems of communication breakdown between classes, groups, and nations, would involve additional funds, much more research, and creative thinking of a high order.

Even with our present limited knowledge we can see some steps which might be taken, even in large groups, to increase the amount of listening *with*, and to decrease the amount of evaluation *about*. To be imaginative for a moment, let us suppose that a therapeutically oriented international group went to the Russian leaders and said, "We want to achieve a genuine understanding of your views and even more important, of your attitudes and feelings, toward the United States. We will summarize and resummarize the views and feelings if necessary, until you agree that our description represents the situation as it seems to you." Then suppose they did the same thing with the leaders in our own country. If they then gave the widest possible distribution to these two views, with the feelings clearly described but not expressed in name-calling, might not the effect be very great? It would not guarantee the type of understanding I have been describing, but it would make it much more possible. We can understand the feelings of a person who hates us much more readily when his attitudes are accurately described to us by a neutral third party, than we can when he is shaking his fist at us.

But even to describe such a first step is to suggest another obstacle to this approach of understanding. Our civilization does not yet have enough faith in the social sciences to utilize their findings. The opposite is true of the physical sciences. During the war[2] when a test-tube solution was found to the problem of synthetic rubber, millions of dollars and an army of talent was turned loose on the problem of using that finding. If synthetic rubber could be made in milligrams, it could and would be made in the thousands of tons. And it was. But in the social science realm, if a way is found of facilitating communication and mutual understanding in small groups, there is no guarantee that the

[1]**the delegates at Kaesong** Representatives of North Korea and South Korea met at the border town of Kaesong to arrange terms for an armistice to hostilities during the Korean War (1950–1953). [Editors' note]

[2]**the war** World War II. [Editors' note]

finding will be utilized. It may be a generation or more before the money and the brains will be turned loose to exploit that finding.

In closing, I would like to summarize this small-scale solution to the problem of barriers in communication, and to point out certain of its characteristics.

I have said that our research and experience to date would make it appear that breakdowns in communication, and the evaluative tendency which is the major barrier to communication, can be avoided. The solution is provided by creating a situation in which each of the different parties come to understand the other from the *other's* point of view. This has been achieved, in practice, even when feelings run high, by the influence of a person who is willing to understand each point of view empathically, and who thus acts as a catalyst to precipitate further understanding.

This procedure has important characteristics. It can be initiated by one party, without waiting for the other to be ready. It can even be initiated by a neutral third person, providing he can gain a minimum of cooperation from one of the parties.

This procedure can deal with the insincerities, the defensive exaggerations, the lies, the "false fronts" which characterize almost every failure in communication. These defensive distortions drop away with astonishing speed as people find that the only intent is to understand, not judge.

This approach leads steadily and rapidly 20
toward the discovery of the truth, toward a realistic appraisal of the objective barriers to communication. The dropping of some defensiveness by one party leads to further dropping of defensiveness by the other party, and truth is thus approached.

This procedure gradually achieves mutual communication. Mutual communication tends to be pointed toward solving a problem rather than toward attacking a person or group. It leads to a situation in which I see how the problem appears to you, as well as to me, and you see how it appears to me, as well as to you. Thus accurately and realistically defined, the problem is almost certain to yield to intelligent attack, or if it is in part insoluble, it will be comfortably accepted as such.

This then appears to be a test-tube solution to the breakdown of communication as it occurs in small groups. Can we take this small-scale answer, investigate it further, refine it; develop it and apply it to the tragic and well-nigh fatal failures of communication which threaten the very existence of our modern world? It seems to me that this is a possibility and a challenge which we should explore.

Topics for Critical Thinking and Writing

1. What obstacles to effective argument does Carl R. Rogers outline in his essay? Consider that it was written in the 1950s. Are there any additional obstacles we face today? How might they be overcome through critical thinking and effective argument?
2. Rogers writes in paragraph 12 that it is "when emotions are strongest that it is most difficult to achieve the frame of reference of the other person or group." Select a current debate in the news and explain how strong emotions — about issues or in relation to particular factors — inhibit effective communication in that debate. Is each side equally emotional, or do emotions inhibit one side more than the other? How can one or the other side argue more effectively not by discounting the emotions of the other but expressing understanding?

3. List three additional debate topics with two generally opposing positions. Then identify potentially shared goals or outcomes among the two positions. (Use the Visual Guide on p. 364 as a model.) Reflect on the exercise: What challenges did you face following the Rogerian framework for argument? What do you think may help and hinder empathy between the two positions?

EDWARD O. WILSON

Edward O. Wilson, born in Birmingham, Alabama, in 1929, is an emeritus professor of evolutionary biology at Harvard University. A distinguished writer as well as a researcher and teacher, Wilson has twice won the Pulitzer Prize for General Non-Fiction. We reprint a piece first published in 2006 in Wilson's book *The Creation: An Appeal to Save Life on Earth.*

Letter to a Southern Baptist Minister

Dear Pastor:

We have not met, yet I feel I know you well enough to call you friend. First of all, we grew up in the same faith. As a boy I too answered the altar call; I went under the water. Although I no longer belong to that faith, I am confident that if we met and spoke privately of our deepest beliefs, it would be in a spirit of mutual respect and good will. I know we share many precepts of moral behavior. Perhaps it also matters that we are both Americans and, insofar as it might still affect civility and good manners, we are both Southerners.

I write to you now for your counsel and help. Of course, in doing so, I see no way to avoid the fundamental differences in our respective worldviews. You are a literalist interpreter of Christian Holy Scripture. You reject the conclusion of science that mankind evolved from lower forms. You believe that each person's soul is immortal, making this planet a way station to a second, eternal life. Salvation is assured those who are redeemed in Christ.

I am a secular humanist. I think existence is what we make of it as individuals. There is no guarantee of life after death, and heaven and hell are what we create for ourselves, on this planet. There is no other home. Humanity originated here by evolution from lower forms over millions of years. And yes, I will speak plain, our ancestors were apelike animals. The human species has adapted physically and mentally to life on Earth and no place else. Ethics is the code of behavior we share on the basis of reason, law, honor, and an inborn sense of decency, even as some ascribe it to God's will.

For you, the glory of an unseen divinity; for me, the glory of the universe revealed at last. For you, the belief in God made flesh to save mankind; for me, the belief in Promethean[1] fire seized to set men free. You have found your final truth; I am still searching. I may be wrong, you may be wrong. We may both be partly right.

5 Does this difference in worldview separate us in all things? It does not. You and I and every other human being strive for the same

[1]**Promethean** In Greek mythology, Prometheus was a Titan who looked after mankind, going so far as to steal fire from Mount Olympus to give it to humans. [Editors' note]

imperatives of security, freedom of choice, personal dignity, and a cause to believe in that is larger than ourselves.

Let us see, then, if we can, and you are willing, to meet on the near side of metaphysics in order to deal with the real world we share. I put it this way because you have the power to help solve a great problem about which I care deeply. I hope you have the same concern. I suggest that we set aside our differences in order to save the Creation. The defense of living Nature is a universal value. It doesn't rise from, nor does it promote, any religious or ideological dogma. Rather, it serves without discrimination the interests of all humanity.

Pastor, we need your help. The Creation — living Nature — is in deep trouble. Scientists estimate that if habitat conversion and other destructive human activities continue at their present rates, half the species of plants and animals on Earth could be either gone or at least fated for early extinction by the end of the century. A full quarter will drop to this level during the next half century as a result of climate change alone. The ongoing extinction rate is calculated in the most conservative estimates to be about a hundred times above that prevailing before humans appeared on Earth, and it is expected to rise to at least a thousand times greater or more in the next few decades. If this rise continues unabated, the cost to humanity, in wealth, environmental security, and quality of life, will be catastrophic.

Surely we can agree that each species, however inconspicuous and humble it may seem to us at this moment, is a masterpiece of biology, and well worth saving. Each species possesses a unique combination of genetic traits that fits it more or less precisely to a particular part of the environment. Prudence alone dictates that we act quickly to prevent the extinction of species and, with it, the pauperization of Earth's ecosystems — hence of the Creation.

You may well ask at this point, Why me? Because religion and science are the two most powerful forces in the world today, including especially the United States. If religion and science could be united on the common ground of biological conservation, the problem would soon be solved. If there is any moral precept shared by people of all beliefs, it is that we owe ourselves and future generations a beautiful, rich, and healthful environment.

I am puzzled that so many religious 10
leaders, who spiritually represent a large majority of people around the world, have hesitated to make protection of the Creation an important part of their magisterium.[2] Do they believe that human-centered ethics and preparation for the afterlife are the only things that matter? Even more perplexing is the widespread conviction among Christians that the Second Coming is imminent, and that therefore the condition of the planet is of little consequence. Sixty percent of Americans, according to a 2004 poll, believe that the prophecies of the book of Revelation are accurate. Many of these, numbering in the millions, think the End of Time will occur within the life span of those now living. Jesus will return to Earth, and those redeemed by Christian faith will be transported bodily to heaven, while those left behind will struggle through severe hard times and, when they die, suffer eternal damnation. The condemned will remain in hell, like those already consigned in the generations before them, for a trillion trillion years, enough for the universe to expand to its own, entropic

[2]**magisterium** The official teaching of the Roman Catholic Church. [Editors' note]

death, time enough for countless universes like it afterward to be born, expand, and likewise die away. And that is just the beginning of how long condemned souls will suffer in hell — all for a mistake they made in choice of religion during the infinitesimally small time they inhabited Earth.

For those who believe this form of Christianity, the fate of 10 million other life forms indeed does not matter. This and other similar doctrines are not gospels of hope and compassion. They are gospels of cruelty and despair. They were not born of the heart of Christianity. Pastor, tell me I am wrong!

However you will respond, let me here venture an alternative ethic. The great challenge of the twenty-first century is to raise people everywhere to a decent standard of living while preserving as much of the rest of life as possible. Science has provided this part of the argument for the ethic: the more we learn about the biosphere, the more complex and beautiful it turns out to be. Knowledge of it is a magic well: the more you draw from it, the more there is to draw. Earth, and especially the razor-thin film of life enveloping it, is our home, our wellspring, our physical and much of our spiritual sustenance.

I know that science and environmentalism are linked in the minds of many with evolution, Darwin, and secularism. Let me postpone disentangling all this (I will come back to it later) and stress again: to protect the beauty of Earth and of its prodigious variety of life forms should be a common goal, regardless of differences in our metaphysical beliefs.

To make the point in good Gospel manner, let me tell the story of a young man, newly trained for the ministry, and so fixed in his Christian faith that he referred all questions of morality to readings from the Bible. When he visited the cathedral-like Atlantic rainforest of Brazil, he saw the manifest hand of God and in his notebook wrote, "It is not possible to give an adequate idea of the higher feelings of wonder, admiration, and devotion which fill and elevate the mind."

That was Charles Darwin in 1832, early into 15
the voyage of HMS *Beagle*, before he had given any thought to evolution.

And here is Darwin, concluding *On the Origin of Species* in 1859, having first abandoned Christian dogma and then, with his newfound intellectual freedom, formulated the theory of evolution by natural selection: "There is grandeur in this view of life, with its several powers, having been originally breathed into a few forms or into one; and that, whilst this planet has gone cycling on according to the fixed law of gravity, from so simple a beginning endless forms most beautiful and most wonderful have been, and are being, evolved."

Darwin's reverence for life remained the same as he crossed the seismic divide that divided his spiritual life. And so it can be for the divide that today separates scientific humanism from mainstream religion. And separates you and me.

You are well prepared to present the theological and moral arguments for saving the Creation. I am heartened by the movement growing within Christian denominations to support global conservation. The stream of thought has arisen from many sources, from evangelical to unitarian. Today it is but a rivulet. Tomorrow it will be a flood.

I already know much of the religious argument on behalf of the Creation, and would like to learn more. I will now lay before you and others who may wish to hear it the scientific argument. You will not agree with all that I say about the origins of life — science and religion do not easily mix in such matters — but I like to think that in this one life-and-death issue we have a common purpose.

Topics for Critical Thinking and Writing

1. Edward O. Wilson claims to be a "secular humanist" (para. 3). How would you define that term? Are you a secular humanist? Why, or why not?
2. What does Wilson mean by "metaphysics" (para. 6)? Which if any of his views qualify as metaphysical?
3. Wilson obviously seeks to present his views in a fashion that makes them as palatable as possible to his reader. Do you think he succeeds in this endeavor? Write an essay of about 500 words arguing for or against his achievement in this regard, pointing to instances in the text where he succeeds or fails.

11

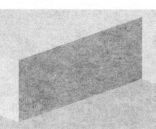

A Literary Critic's View: Arguing about Literature

Literary criticism [is] a reasoned account of the feeling produced upon the critic by the book he is reading.

— D. H. LAWRENCE

A true classic . . . is an author who has enriched the human mind, increased its treasure, and caused it to advance a step; who has discovered some moral and not equivocal truth, or revealed some eternal passion in that heart where all seemed known and discovered; who has expressed his thought, observation, or invention, in no matter what form, only provided it be broad and great, refined and sensible, sane and beautiful in itself; who has spoken to all in his own peculiar style, a style which is found to be also that of the whole world, a style new without neologism, new and old, easily contemporary with all time.

— CHARLES AUGUSTIN SAINTE-BEAUVE

Stories have been used to dispossess and to malign. But stories can also be used to empower, and to humanize. Stories can break the dignity of a people. But stories can also repair that broken dignity.

— CHIMAMANDA NGOZI ADICHIE

You might think that literature — fiction, poetry (including songs), drama — is meant only to be enjoyed, not to be argued about. Yet literature is constantly the subject of argumentative writing — not all of it by teachers of English. For instance, if you glance at the current issue of a local city newspaper or the *New Yorker*, you probably will find a review of a play suggesting that the play is worth seeing or is not worth seeing. In the same publication, you may find an article reporting that a senator or member of Congress argued that the National Endowment for the Arts insulted taxpayers by making an award to a writer who defamed the American family.

Probably most writing about literature, whether done by college students, professors, journalists, politicians, or whomever, is devoted to one or more of these goals: interpreting, judging (evaluating), or theorizing. Let's look at each of these, drawing our examples chiefly from comments about Shakespeare's *Macbeth*.

Interpreting

Interpreting literature in an argument is centrally a matter of setting forth the *meaning* (or meanings) of a work. However, the meaning of a work of literature is a complex question.

Take Shakespeare's tragedy *Macbeth* as an example of a work that has yielded many interpretations over time. Let's take two fairly simple and clearly opposed views:

> Macbeth is a villain who, by murdering his lawful king, offends God's rule, so he is overthrown by God's earthly instruments, Malcolm and Macduff. Macbeth is justly punished; the reader or spectator rejoices in his defeat.
>
> Macbeth is a hero-villain, a man who commits terrible crimes but who never completely loses the reader's sympathy; although he is justly punished, the reader believes that with the death of Macbeth the world has become a smaller place.

A writer *must* offer evidence in an essay that presents one of these theses or indeed presents any interpretation. For instance, to support the latter thesis, a writer might argue that although Macbeth's villainy is undeniable, his conscience never deserts him — here one would point to specific passages and would offer some brief quotations.

For many readers, a work of literature might appear to have meanings clearly intended by the writer. For others, the meanings might be latent in the text itself (whether or not intended by the author). So, we have two basic kinds of interpretation, one *author-centered* and one *text-centered*. Further, because individual readers experience texts in unique ways, we may add a third general category of interpretation, a *reader-centered* one.

Author-centered interpretation deals chiefly with the meanings intended by the author. Let's again take up our example of *Macbeth*, sometimes called "The Scottish Play." It is about a Scottish king, written by Shakespeare soon after a Scot — James VI of Scotland — had been installed as James I, King of England. One thing James did was announce that he would be the new sponsor of Shakespeare's Theater Company. If someone asked,

> Was Shakespeare paying homage to James I, his king and patron, in *Macbeth*?

he or she might seek evidence by exploring Shakespeare's relationship to James I and tracing allusions to the king apparent in *Macbeth*. For example, *Macbeth* is overflowing with biblical imagery, and King James was an avid reader and eventually the first translator of the Bible into English. Add to that the "two-fold balls and treble scepters" of James's double coronation, another allusion to the foiled Gunpowder Plot of 1607 to kill James, and the fact that the play was presented at James's court, and a convincing argument emerges that Shakespeare was indeed paying homage to James I in the play.

Author-centered arguments need not be strictly about the author's intentions. They may also be rooted in efforts to show the meaning of the work in the author's *milieu* — how it was read or how it impacted people (or a specific group of people) at the particular time of publication (or performance) regardless of the author's intentions. In such arguments, one might explore how specific themes of *Macbeth* — heredity, ambition, blood, power, and the supernatural — would have been interpreted by ordinary English audiences sharing with

Shakespeare the general worldview of the early seventeenth century and the particularities of life in England at the time. Or someone might ask,

> How would the portrayal of Banquo have been understood by members of James's court, where we know it was presented?

Author-centered arguments, in other words, may consider the author's intentions, or they may consider the time and place in which the author, text, and audience coexisted.

Text-centered interpretation usually focuses on "the text itself" as the primary source of meaning. For some critics, it is futile to attempt to discern an author's intentions and only marginally interesting to argue about what a text might have meant in its own time. What is more immediately important is how literature's formal elements — plot, characterization, language, symbols, setting, tension, ironies — combine to make its meanings. By performing **close reading**, one can discern and describe *how* literary texts produce powerful meanings. A text-centered interpretation of *Macbeth* might examine a certain set of metaphors to discover a theme in the play, asking questions such as:

> How do images of clothing (and nakedness) recur in the play to demonstrate the artificiality of social positions?
>
> How does blood appear in the play as a symbol of guilt?
>
> How are Macbeth, MacDuff, and Banquo similarly and differently characterized?

Arguments in this vein may be supported by prior interpretations, but in text-centered arguments, the text itself is often the primary source of evidence.

Reader-centered interpretations of literature concern the experience of reading itself, especially the ways in which a work becomes meaningful to an individual reader. From this perspective, the point of reading is not to discover biographical or historical meanings (author-centered) or to construct meanings thought to be inherent within the text itself (text-centered). Instead, the point is to pay attention to the reading experience as a means to discover the self — to understand oneself and one's own relationship to the world at large. In this view, literature can help people articulate their views on the world, clarify their own personal values, and connect to others. A reader-centered critic might ask,

> How does Macbeth relate to ambition in my own life and times?

Reader-centered interpretation does not always mean purely subjective interpretation; it may also concentrate on meanings that are relevant to particular groups of people. Thus, political interpretations, feminist readings, psychological approaches, and a range of cultural studies methodologies may be considered reader-focused. Such readings might focus on marginalized or oppressed groups evident (or absent) from texts or examine how ideologies are extended or suppressed through works of literature. One reader-centered argument might claim that Lady Macbeth — the devious schemer who convinces her husband to murder King Duncan and usurp the throne — presents a vision not of evil but of rebellion against gender norms. (At one point in the play, she asks the spirits to "unsex" her so she may gain the will to power.) Sometimes undermining or challenging previous interpretations with one's own idiosyncratic interpretation can be an empowering act. Reader-centered interpretation recognizes that meaning itself is not permanent or universal but changes according to reader, time, and place.

For most critics today, a work of literature has many meanings — the meaning it had for the writer and the audience, the meanings it has accumulated over time, and the meanings it has for today's diverse readers. In the end, the meaning of a work of literature involves readers, texts, and authors, all of which are important. Arguments about literature in this sense may be thought of as **intersectional**. Consider the reader-centered interpretation of Lady Macbeth above. To fully articulate the argument, it may be important to analyze the symbolic power of blood, motherhood, and heredity in the play (a text-centered approach) and also to attempt to understand Elizabethan values about the proper roles of women (an author-centered approach).

Judging (or Evaluating)

Evaluative arguments about literature are primarily concerned with the value of a work: Is *Macbeth* a great tragedy? Is *Macbeth* a greater tragedy than *Romeo and Juliet*? What is the importance of *Macbeth*? Does *Macbeth* contribute positively to our understanding of the nature and limits of ambition? As with any thesis statement, if a writer judges the worth of a play, the claim must be supported by an argument and expressed in sentences that offer supporting evidence.

Let's pause for a moment to think about evaluation in general. When we say "This is a great play," are we in effect saying only "I like this play"? That is, are we merely *expressing* our taste rather than *asserting* something independent of our tastes and feelings? On the other hand, a statement such as "I like the New York Yankees" is not an argument that requires justification — it is merely an opinion. However, statements such as "The New York Yankees are the best team in the league" or "The Yankees are the most important franchise in Major League Baseball" would require an argument and evidence.

Now consider another statement, "This is a really good book." It is entirely reasonable for someone to ask you *why* you say that. You might answer with any one of the following:

- "Well, the author really captured the tensions of a rapidly transforming society." (author-centered)
- "The characters are realistically portrayed, and the plot is dramatic with a gripping climax." (text-centered)
- "I really gained insights into the question of betrayal, which is important to me because I was once betrayed and now I can see how forgiveness is the only path." (reader-centered)

Even when we are *evaluating*, we are also often *interpreting* in various modes at the same time. The key in judging or evaluating the worth of a work of literature, then, is to state as clearly as possible what kind of **criteria** you are using, such as

- the skill or motivation of the author
- the innovation, uniqueness, or originality of the work
- the faithfulness of the work in its depiction of *X*
- the importance, status, or durability of the work
- the degree to which the work helps people understand themselves or another group better
- the artistic quality in terms of the work's structure, balance, coherence, unity, or use of other literary devices (characterizations, settings, dialogue, etc.)

At the very least, we should show *why* we evaluate the work as we do and suggest that if readers try to see it from our point of view, they may then accept our evaluation.

Evaluations are always based on assumptions, although these assumptions may be unstated; in fact, the writer may even be unaware of them. For instance, what does it mean to be a "skillful" author? Is "originality" a good thing in and of itself? Is the "faithfulness" of a literary depiction dependent upon a realistic description of a time and place, or can abstraction or impressionism also do the job? Can a work of literature be awful but important or be excellent but insignificant? As usual with arguments, the more you define your criteria (and the reasons you use those criteria), the more convincing you may be.

Some common ideas about art often play the role of criteria in literary judgments.

1. A good work of art, even when fictional, says something about real life. If you believe that art is a means by which people connect themselves to enduring human ideas and values, or to society at large, you bring to your evaluation of art an assumption that a good work of art reflects reality (or even impacts it) in some meaningful way. If you hold the view that human beings encounter fairly common experiences and behave in fairly consistent ways — that is, that each of us has an enduring "character" — you probably will judge as inferior a work in which the plot is implausible or one in which characters are inconsistent or inadequately motivated. The novelist Henry James said, "You will not write a good novel unless you possess the sense of reality."

However, there are plenty of arguments to be made for the worth of artworks that do not reflect reality in the usual or expected ways. Some kinds of literary expression are not intended to *say* anything at all (in and of themselves, at least). Consider the poetic form haiku or this imagistic piece by the Japanese poet Matsuo Bashō (1644–1694):

An old pond
Leap, splash
A frog.

This poem, like a haiku, presents an image only and tells us little to nothing about how to interpret it. Experimental fiction and poetry, absurdist drama, and other forms often challenge us to reconceive our ideas about the role and goal of literature. Can a story be successful or good if it offers two or more different endings? Should supernatural events occur in otherwise true-to-life plots? We do not have the answers, but we think the questions are worth pondering.

2. A good work of art is complex yet unified. One of the staples of literary criticism is the idea that a successful work of art exhibits a unified, complex whole constructed out of carefully arranged elements. In many ways, today's audiences continue to value those works in which structure, character, setting, irony, paradox, language, symbol, plot — indeed any of the imaginable literary devices — all work together in meaningful, interconnected ways. *Macbeth* is a good work of art, one might argue, partly because it shows us so many aspects of life (courage, fear, loyalty, treachery, for a start) through richly varied language (the diction ranges from a grand passage in which Macbeth says that his bloody hands will "incarnadine," or make red, "the multitudinous seas" to colloquial passages such as the drunken porter's "Knock, knock"). The play shows the heroic Macbeth tragically destroying his own life through villainy, and it shows the comic porter making coarse jokes about deceit and damnation, jokes that (although the porter doesn't know it) connect with Macbeth's crimes. A work may be considered complex yet unified when it contains a rich and multivalent symbolic structure in which all the parts contribute to the complexity of the whole.

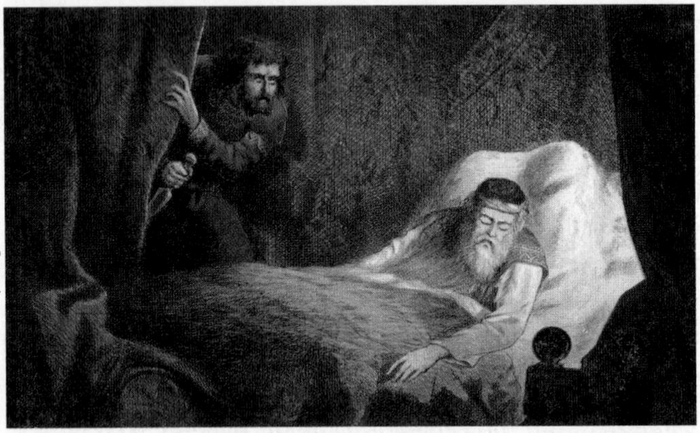

Print Collector/Getty Images

A seventeenth-century artist's interpretation of Macbeth's murder of King Duncan.

Of course, wholeness itself is also an aspect of successful art explicitly challenged by some artists and critics. In the twentieth century, "fragmented" texts were deliberately constructed by some authors to defy the principle of wholeness: James Joyce's *Finnegan's Wake*, for example, contains this indicative passage:

> The great fall of the offwall entailed at such short notice the pftjschute of Finnegan, erse solid man, that the humptyhillhead of humself prumptly sends an unquiring one well to the west in quest of his tumptytumtoes: and their upturapikepointandplace is at the knock out in the park where oranges have been laid to rust upon the green since dev-linsfirst loved livvy.

Joyce's language reflects the basically random, nonlinear, and episodic nature of experience — all mixed in with inner monologues, daydreams, puns, and breakdowns of language that defy any sense of coherence in the mind or art. Today, authors readily combine genres, mix historical fiction and nonfiction, create plots that go nowhere, or include other unaccustomed elements such as stream of consciousness, shifting narrators, or multiple endings that disrupt the ideal of unity in literature.

3. A good work of art sets forth a wholesome view of life. The general public widely believes that a work should be judged partly or largely on the moral view that it sets forth. (Esteemed philosophers, notably Plato, have felt the same way.) Thus, a story that demeans women — perhaps one that takes a casual view of sexual assault — would be held in low estimation, as would a play that treats a mass murderer as a hero.

Implicit in this approach is what is called an *instrumentalist* view — the idea that a work of art is an instrument, a means, to some higher value. Thus, many people hold that reading great works of literature makes us better — or at least does not make us worse. In this view, a work that is pornographic or in some other way considered immoral will be devalued.

Moral judgments, of course, must be considered very carefully in arguments about the quality of art or literature. Historically, platitudes about what is decent and good have led in some instances to censorship. Changing values have also transformed the ways artists have been regarded and how artworks have been interpreted. Edgar Allan Poe, a pioneer of the horror genre and now a celebrated American author, was castigated in his own time for moral shortcomings in his life and stories. Walt Whitman's landmark poem *Leaves of Grass* (1855), one of the most influential works of American literature, was accused by one critic in *Criterion* magazine as exhibiting "a degrading, beastly sensuality that is fast rotting the health core of all social virtues." Finally, Kate Chopin, a southern realist — whose short story "The Story of an Hour" appears in this chapter — had her career ruined by critics who deemed her 1899 novel *The Awakening* "immoral" for its depiction of a married woman's sexuality and her transgression of gender norms. Even today, arguments about the ways in which art may instruct or corrupt audiences remain at the heart of cultural debates. For instance, current law requires the National Endowment for the Arts to take into account standards of decency when making awards.

4. A good work of art is original. The assumption that a good work of art is original puts special value on new techniques and new subject matter in art. If a writer employs a new or innovative way to structure a novel, for instance, he or she might get a kind of critical extra credit. Nicholson Baker's novel *The Mezzanine* (1988), for example, takes place over the course of a character's single trip up an escalator — a digressive exploration of the spectacular array of thoughts that occur in the mind of a person in just a few short moments. New kinds of characters and story lines tend to be valued, as do new ways of representing reality in literature, such as techniques that help represent email, text messaging, and tweeting. Sometimes, the *first* text to introduce a new subject (say, AIDS) gets that critical extra credit, so to speak, for opening a needed conversation or debate. Or returning to Shakespeare, consider that one sign of his genius, it is held, is that he was so highly varied — none of his tragedies seems merely to duplicate another;

each is a world of its own, a new kind of achievement. (Compare, for instance, *Romeo and Juliet*, with its two youthful and innocent heroes, with *Macbeth*, with its deeply guilty hero.)

Of course, just because a work is new or innovative may not reflect qualitatively on it. A full-length novel written entirely through tweets might be a neat idea or a somewhat interesting concept, but it need not signal genius. Newness or originality, that is, is not necessarily synonymous with excellence.

5. *A good work of art is important.* When we consider if a piece of art deals with an important subject, we are often concerned with themes: Great works, in this view, must deal with great themes. Love, death, patriotism, and God, say, are great themes; a work that deals with these subjects may achieve a height, an excellence, that, say, a work describing a dog scratching for fleas may not achieve. (Of course, if the reader believes that the dog is a symbol of humanity plagued by invisible enemies, the poem about the dog may reach the heights; but then, too, it is *not* a poem about a dog and fleas: It is really a poem about humanity and the invisible.)

Another way to construe the importance of a work of literature is to regard it as a social or political object. Works of literature commonly derive their importance by being relevant to public beliefs and attitudes. Some may be important to specific communities. Some may help mark in public memory the meaning of historical events. In this sense, a work's importance is found in its ability to reflect (and reproduce) culture.

The point is that in writing an evaluation, you must let the reader know *why* you value the work as you do. Obviously, it is not enough just to keep saying that *this* work is great whereas *that* work is not so great; the reader wants to know *why* you offer the judgments you do, which means that you must

- set forth your criteria and then
- offer evidence that is in accord with them.

Theorizing

Another kind of argument about literature is more theoretical; as such, it is more of a metacognitive discourse, one that attempts to understand and define the very nature of literary expression and interpretation. Some literary criticism is concerned with such theoretical questions as these:

- What is tragedy? Can the hero be a villain? How does tragedy differ from melodrama?
- Why do tragedies — works showing good or at least interesting people destroyed — give us pleasure?
- How did the detective genre develop over time, and how is it different in different places and times?

Other kinds of criticism might explore theories about the value of literature and ask questions such as these:

- Are classic works of Western literature great because they contain great wisdom or beauty, or are they great because they have been privileged over time?
- Can a work of art really be said to offer anything that can be called "truth"?
- Does a work of art have meaning in itself, or is the meaning simply whatever anyone wishes to say it is?

Yet again, one hopes that anyone asserting a thesis concerned with any of these topics will offer evidence — will, indeed, *argue* rather than merely assert.

A CHECKLIST FOR ARGUING ABOUT LITERATURE

- ❒ Can I identify if my argument is primarily author-centered, text-centered, or reader-centered?
- ❒ Can I determine whether my thesis is based on interpreting, judging, or theorizing about the work of literature at hand (or whether it is some combination of the three)?
- ❒ Do I have a good reason to make my reader interested in hearing my point of view about a work?
- ❒ Is my essay supported with evidence from the text itself?
- ❒ If I am using sources such as interpretations written by others or other contextual material, am I integrating them well to support my argument?

Examples: Two Students Interpret Robert Frost's "Mending Wall"

Let's consider two competing interpretations of a poem, Robert Frost's "Mending Wall." We say "competing" because these interpretations clash head-on. Differing interpretations need not be incompatible, of course. For instance, a historical interpretation of *Macbeth*, arguing that an understanding of the context of English–Scottish politics around 1605 helps us appreciate the play, need not be incompatible with a psychoanalytic interpretation that tells us that Macbeth's murder of King Duncan is rooted in an Oedipus complex, the king being a father figure. Different approaches thus can illuminate different aspects of the work, just as they can emphasize or subordinate different elements in the plot or characters portrayed. But, again, in the next few pages we will deal with mutually incompatible interpretations of the meaning of Frost's poem.

After reading the poem and the two interpretations written by students, spend a few minutes thinking about the questions that we raise after the second interpretation.

ROBERT FROST

Robert Frost (1874–1963) studied for part of one term at Dartmouth College in New Hampshire, then did odd jobs (including teaching), and from 1897 to 1899 was enrolled as a special student at Harvard. He then farmed in New Hampshire, published a few poems in newspapers, did some more teaching, and in 1912 left for England, where he hoped to achieve success as a writer. By 1915, he was known in England, and he returned to the United States. By the time of his death, he was the nation's unofficial poet laureate. "Mending Wall" was first published in 1914.

Mending Wall

Something there is that doesn't love a wall,
That sends the frozen-ground-swell under it,
And spills the upper boulders in the sun;
And makes gaps even two can pass abreast.
The work of hunters is another thing:
I have come after them and made repair
Where they have left not one stone on a stone,
But they would have the rabbit out of hiding,
To please the yelping dogs. The gaps I mean,
No one has seen them made or heard them made,
But at spring mending-time we find them there.
I let my neighbor know beyond the hill;
And on a day we meet to walk the line
And set the wall between us once again.
We keep the wall between us as we go.
To each the boulders that have fallen to each.
And some are loaves and some so nearly balls
We have to use a spell to make them balance:
"Stay where you are until our backs are turned!"
We wear our fingers rough with handling them.
Oh, just another kind of outdoor game,
One on a side. It comes to little more:
There where it is we do not need the wall:
He is all pine and I am apple orchard.
My apple trees will never get across
And eat the cones under his pines, I tell him.
He only says, "Good fences make good neighbors."
Spring is the mischief in me, and I wonder
If I could put a notion in his head:
"*Why* do they make good neighbors? Isn't it
Where there are cows? But here there are no cows.
Before I built a wall I'd ask to know
What I was walling in or walling out,
And to whom I was like to give offense.
Something there is that doesn't love a wall,
That wants it down." I could say "Elves" to him,
But it's not elves exactly, and I'd rather
He said it for himself. I see him there
Bringing a stone grasped firmly by the top
In each hand, like an old-stone savage armed.
He moves in darkness as it seems to me,
Not of woods only and the shade of trees.
He will not go behind his father's saying,
And he likes having thought of it so well
He says again, "Good fences make good neighbors."

Deutsch 1

Jonathan Deutsch
Professor Walton
English 102
5 March 2016

The Deluded Speaker in Frost's "Mending Wall"

Our discussions of "Mending Wall" in high school showed that most people think Frost is saying that walls between people are a bad thing and that we should not try to separate ourselves from each other unnecessarily. Perhaps the wall, in this view, is a symbol for race prejudice or religious differences, and Frost is suggesting that these differences are minor and that they should not keep us apart. In this common view, the neighbor's words, "Good fences make good neighbors" (lines 27 and 45), show that the neighbor is shortsighted. I disagree with this view, but first I want to present the evidence that might be offered for it, so that we can then see whether it really is substantial.

Indication of an author-centered approach.

Thesis and preliminary map of essay.

First of all, someone might claim that in lines 23 to 26 Frost offers a good argument against walls:

Textual evidence presented as opposition to the writer's view.

> There where it is we do not need the wall:
> He is all pine and I am apple orchard.
> My apple trees will never get across
> And eat the cones under his pines, I tell him.

The neighbor does not offer a valid reply to this argument; in fact, he doesn't offer any argument at all but simply says, "Good fences make good neighbors."

Another piece of evidence supposedly showing that the neighbor is wrong, it is said, is found in Frost's description of him as "an old-stone savage" and someone who "moves in darkness" (40, 41). And a third piece of evidence is said to be that the neighbor "will not go behind his father's saying" (43), but he merely repeats the saying.

There is, however, another way of looking at the poem. As I see it, the speaker is a very snide and condescending person. He is confident that he

Writer examines language closely to criticize the speaker of the poem.

knows it all and that his neighbor is an ignorant savage; he is even willing to tease his supposedly ignorant neighbor. For instance, the speaker admits to "the mischief in me" (28), and he is confident that he could tell the truth to the neighbor but arrogantly thinks that it would be a more effective form of teaching if the neighbor "said it for himself" (38).

The speaker is not only unpleasantly mischievous and condescending toward his neighbor, but he is also shallow, for he does not see the great wisdom that there is in proverbs. The *American Heritage Dictionary of the English Language*, Third Edition, defines a proverb as "A short, pithy saying in frequent and widespread use that expresses a basic truth." Frost, or at least the man who speaks this poem, does not seem to realize that proverbs express truths. He just dismisses them, and he thinks the neighbor is wrong not to "go behind his father's saying" (43). But there is a great deal of wisdom in the sayings of our fathers. For instance, in the Bible (in the Old Testament) there is a whole book of proverbs, filled with wise sayings such as "Reprove not a scorner, lest he hate thee: rebuke a wise man, and he will love thee" (9:8); "He that trusteth in his riches shall fall" (11:28); "The way of a fool is right in his own eyes" (12:15; this might be said of the speaker of "Mending Wall"); "A soft answer turneth away wrath" (15:1); and (to cut short what could be a list many pages long), "Whoso diggeth a pit shall fall therein" (26:27).

Writer treads the line between author-centered and text-centered interpretation. It is not clear that the writer thinks Frost intended to characterize the speaker of the poem in this way.

The speaker is confident that walls are unnecessary and probably bad, but he doesn't realize that even where there are no cattle, walls serve the valuable purpose of clearly marking out our territory. They help us to preserve our independence and our individuality. Walls — manmade structures — are a sign of civilization. A wall more or less says, "*This* is mine, but I respect *that* as yours." Frost's speaker is so confident of his shallow view that he makes fun of his neighbor for repeating that "Good fences make good neighbors" (27, 45). But he himself repeats his own saying, "Something there is that doesn't love a wall" (1, 35). And at least the neighbor has age-old tradition on his side, since the proverb is the

Author reinterprets the phrases of the neighbor not as simple or archaic but as time-tested and the speaker's ideas as vague.

saying of his father. In contrast, the speaker has only his own opinion, and he can't even say what the "something" is.

It may be that Frost meant for us to laugh at the neighbor and to take the side of the speaker, but I think it is much more likely that he meant for us to see that the speaker is mean-spirited (or at least given to unpleasant teasing), too self-confident, foolishly dismissing the wisdom of the old times, and entirely unaware that he has these unpleasant characteristics.

Text-based approach.

Writer uses textual evidence to show irony: despite being against walls, the speaker is willing to play this outdoor game.

Writer continues to offer a positive reading of the speaker by associating him with nature.

Felicia Alonso

Professor Walton

English 102

5 March 2016

The Debate in Robert Frost's "Mending Wall"

I think the first thing to say about Frost's "Mending Wall" is this: The poem is not about a debate over whether good fences do or do not make good neighbors. It is about two debaters: one of the debaters is on the side of vitality, and the other is on the side of an unchanging, fixed — dead, we might say — tradition.

How can we characterize the speaker? For one thing, he is neighborly. Interestingly, it is *he*, and not the neighbor, who initiates the repairing of the wall: "I let my neighbor know beyond the hill" (line 12). This seems strange, since the speaker doesn't see any point in this wall, whereas the neighbor is all in favor of walls. Can we explain this apparent contradiction? Yes; the speaker is a good neighbor, willing to do his share of the work and willing (perhaps in order not to upset his neighbor) to maintain an old tradition even though he doesn't see its importance. It may not be important, he thinks, but it is really rather pleasant, "another kind of outdoor game" (21). In fact, sometimes he even repairs fences on his own, after hunters have destroyed them.

Second, we can say that the speaker is on the side of nature. "Something there is that doesn't love a wall," he says (1, 35), and of course, the "something" is nature itself. Nature "sends the frozen-ground-swell" under the wall and "spills the upper boulders in the sun; / And makes gaps even two can pass abreast" (2–4). Notice that nature itself makes the gaps and that "two can pass abreast" — that is, people can walk together in a companionable way. It is hard to imagine the neighbor walking side by side with anyone.

Third, we can say that the speaker has a sense of humor. When he thinks of trying to get his neighbor interested in the issue, he admits that "the mischief" is in him (28), and he amusingly attributes his playfulness to a natural force, the spring. He playfully toys with the obviously preposterous idea of suggesting to his neighbor that elves caused the stones to fall, but he stops short of making this amusing suggestion to his very serious neighbor. Still, the mere thought assures us that he has a playful, genial nature, and the idea also again implies that not only the speaker but also some sort of mysterious natural force dislikes walls.

Finally, though, of course, he thinks he is right and that his neighbor is mistaken, he at least is cautious in his view. He does not call his neighbor "an old-stone savage" (40); rather, he uses a simile ("like") and then adds that this is only his opinion, so the opinion is softened quite a bit. Here is the description of the neighbor, with italics added to clarify my point. The neighbor is . . .

> *like* an old-stone savage armed.
> He moves in darkness *as it seems to me* . . . (40–41)

Writer examines language very closely to derive the meaning of what might first be taken as insulting.

Of course, the only things we know about the neighbor are those things that the speaker chooses to tell us, so it is not surprising that the speaker comes out ahead. He comes out ahead not because he is right about walls (real or symbolic) and his neighbor is wrong — that's an issue that is not settled in the poem. He comes out ahead because he is a more interesting figure, someone who is neighborly, thoughtful, playful. Yes, maybe he seems to us to feel superior to his neighbor, but we can be certain that he doesn't cause his neighbor any embarrassment. Take the very end of the poem. The speaker tells us that the neighbor

> . . . will not go behind his father's saying,
> And he likes having thought of it so well
> He says again, "Good fences make good neighbors."

The speaker is telling *us* that the neighbor is utterly unoriginal and that the neighbor confuses *remembering* something with *thinking*. But the speaker doesn't get into an argument; he doesn't rudely challenge his neighbor and demand reasons, which might force the neighbor to see that he can't think for himself. And in fact we probably like the neighbor just as he is, and we don't want him to change his mind. The words that ring in our ears are not the speaker's but the neighbor's: "Good fences make good neighbors." The speaker of the poem is a good neighbor. After all, one can hardly be more neighborly than to let the neighbor have the last word.

Reading a Poem and a Story

RICHARD BLANCO

Richard Blanco (b. 1968) is a native-born Cuban who emigrated to the United States with his family as an infant. A 1991 graduate of Florida International University, Blanco worked as an engineer in Miami before returning to that university to pursue poetry, earning his MFA in 1997. His first collection of poems, *City of a Hundred Fires* (1998), won the Agnes Lynch Starret Poetry Prize from the University of Pittsburgh, and his later efforts, *Directions to the Beach of the Dead* (2005) and *Looking for the Gulf Motel* (2012), earned him international recognition. Blanco's recent work includes a critically acclaimed memoir, *The Prince of Los Cocuyos: A Miami Childhood* (2014), and his latest collection of poems, *How to Love a Country* (2019). In 2012, President Barack Obama invited Blanco to become the fifth presidential inaugural poet, the first Latino, immigrant, and openly gay person in that role. On January 21, 2013, Blanco read "One Today," a poem written for that inauguration and reprinted here.

One Today

One sun rose on us today, kindled over our shores,
peeking over the Smokies, greeting the faces
of the Great Lakes, spreading a simple truth
across the Great Plains, then charging across the Rockies.
One light, waking up rooftops, under each one, a story
told by our silent gestures moving behind windows.

My face, your face, millions of faces in morning's mirrors,
each one yawning to life, crescendoing into our day:
pencil-yellow school buses, the rhythm of traffic lights,
fruit stands: apples, limes, and oranges arrayed like rainbows
begging our praise. Silver trucks heavy with oil or paper — bricks or milk, teeming over highways alongside us,
on our way to clean tables, read ledgers, or save lives —
to teach geometry, or ring up groceries, as my mother did
for 20 years, so I could write this poem.

All of us as vital as the one light we move through,
the same light on blackboards with lessons for the day:
equations to solve, history to question, or atoms imagined,
the "I have a dream" we keep dreaming,
or the impossible vocabulary of sorrow that won't explain
the empty desks of 20 children marked absent°
today, and forever. Many prayers, but one light
breathing color into stained glass windows,
life into the faces of bronze statues, warmth

[21] **empty desks of 20 children** Reference to the December 14, 2012, Sandy Hook Elementary School massacre in Newtown, Connecticut.

onto the steps of our museums and park benches
as mothers watch children slide into the day.

One ground. Our ground, rooting us to every stalk
of corn, every head of wheat sown by sweat
and hands, hands gleaning coal or planting windmills
in deserts and hilltops that keep us warm, hands
digging trenches, routing pipes and cables, hands
as worn as my father's cutting sugarcane
so my brother and I could have books and shoes.

The dust of farms and deserts, cities and plains
mingled by one wind — our breath. Breathe. Hear it
through the day's gorgeous din of honking cabs,
buses launching down avenues, the symphony
of footsteps, guitars, and screeching subways,
the unexpected song bird on your clothes line.

Hear: squeaky playground swings, trains whistling,
or whispers across cafe tables, Hear: the doors we open
for each other all day, saying: hello, shalom,
buon giorno, howdy, namaste, or buenos días
in the language my mother taught me — in every language
spoken into one wind carrying our lives
without prejudice, as these words break from my lips.

One sky: since the Appalachians and Sierras claimed
their majesty, and the Mississippi and Colorado worked
their way to the sea. Thank the work of our hands:
weaving steel into bridges, finishing one more report
for the boss on time, stitching another wound
or uniform, the first brush stroke on a portrait,
or the last floor on the Freedom Tower°
jutting into a sky that yields to our resilience.

One sky, toward which we sometimes lift our eyes
tired from work: some days guessing at the weather
of our lives, some days giving thanks for a love
that loves you back, sometimes praising a mother
who knew how to give, or forgiving a father
who couldn't give what you wanted.

We head home: through the gloss of rain or weight
of snow, or the plum blush of dusk, but always — home,
always under one sky, our sky. And always one moon
like a silent drum tapping on every rooftop
and every window, of one country — all of us —
facing the stars
hope — a new constellation
waiting for us to map it,
waiting for us to name it — together

[53] **Freedom Tower** The main building of the rebuilt World Trade Center in New York City, completed in 2013.

Topics for Critical Thinking and Writing

1. The word *one* appears in the title and throughout the poem. What do you think Richard Blanco was trying to accomplish with repetition of this word? Explain your answer.
2. This poem was written on the occasion of Barack Obama's second inauguration; it was read aloud by Blanco and broadcast nationally during the ceremony. (Find the clip on YouTube and watch it if you can.) How do you think these facts affect the meaning of the poem? What do you think Blanco intended to convey?
3. How do colors and sounds work in the poem to support its meanings?
4. What does time signify, and how is it captured in the poem?
5. What twenty-first-century events are important to understanding this poem? Are there events outside the text (i.e., not mentioned directly) that inform the ways audiences would understand it at the time of its recitation and publication?
6. In your opinion, is the poem overly optimistic? Explain your answer in about 500 words.
7. Blanco identifies as a gay male Latino immigrant. Do you think these biographical facts assist in deciphering the meaning of the poem, or are they irrelevant?

KATE CHOPIN

Kate Chopin (1851–1904) was born in St. Louis and named Katherine O'Flaherty. At the age of nineteen she married a cotton broker in New Orleans, Oscar Chopin (the name is pronounced something like "show pan"), who was descended from the early French settlers in Louisiana. After her husband's death in 1883, Kate Chopin turned to writing fiction. The following story was first published in 1894.

The Story of an Hour

Knowing that Mrs. Mallard was afflicted with a heart trouble, great care was taken to break to her as gently as possible the news of her husband's death.

It was her sister Josephine who told her, in broken sentences, veiled hints that revealed in half concealing. Her husband's friend Richards was there, too, near her. It was he who had been in the newspaper office when intelligence of the railroad disaster was received, with Brently Mallard's name leading the list of "killed." He had only taken the time to assure himself of its truth by a second telegram, and had hastened to forestall any less careful, less tender friend in bearing the sad message.

She did not hear the story as many women have heard the same, with a paralyzed inability to accept its significance. She wept at once, with sudden, wild abandonment, in her sister's arms. When the storm of grief had spent itself she went away to her room alone. She would have no one follow her.

There stood, facing the open window, a comfortable, roomy armchair. Into this she sank, pressed down by a physical exhaustion that haunted her body and seemed to reach into her soul.

She could see in the open square before her house the tops of trees that were all aquiver with the new spring life. The delicious breath of rain was in the air. In the street below a peddler was crying his wares. The notes of a distant song which some one was singing reached her faintly, and countless sparrows were twittering in the eaves.

There were patches of blue sky showing here and there through the clouds that had met and piled one above the other in the west facing her window.

She sat with her head thrown back upon the cushion of the chair, quite motionless, except when a sob came up into her throat and shook her, as a child who has cried itself to sleep continues to sob in its dreams.

She was young, with a fair, calm face, whose lines bespoke repression and even a certain strength. But now there was a dull stare in her eyes, whose gaze was fixed away off yonder on one of those patches of blue sky. It was not a glance of reflection, but rather indicated a suspension of intelligent thought.

There was something coming to her and she was waiting for it, fearfully. What was it? She did not know; it was too subtle and elusive to name. But she felt it, creeping out of the sky, reaching toward her through the sounds, the scents, the color that filled the air.

Now her bosom rose and fell tumultuously. She was beginning to recognize this thing that was approaching to possess her, and she was striving to beat it back with her will — as powerless as her two white slender hands would have been.

When she abandoned herself a little whispered word escaped her slightly parted lips. She said it over and over under her breath: "Free, free, free!" The vacant stare and the look of terror that had followed it went from her eyes. They stayed keen and bright. Her pulses beat fast, and the coursing blood warmed and relaxed every inch of her body.

She did not stop to ask if it were not a monstrous joy that held her. A clear and exalted perception enabled her to dismiss the suggestion as trivial.

She knew that she would weep again when she saw the kind, tender hands folded in death; the face that had never looked save with love upon her, fixed and gray and dead. But she saw beyond that bitter moment a long procession of years to come that would belong to her absolutely. And she opened and spread her arms out to them in welcome.

There would be no one to live for her during those coming years; she would live for herself. There would be no powerful will bending her in that blind persistence with which men and women believe they have a right to impose a private will upon a fellow creature. A kind intention or a cruel intention made the act seem no less a crime as she looked upon it in that brief moment of illumination.

And yet she had loved him — sometimes. Often she had not. What did it matter! What could love, the unsolved mystery, count for in face of this possession of self-assertion which she suddenly recognized as the strongest impulse of her being.

"Free! Body and soul free!" she kept whispering.

Josephine was kneeling before the closed door with her lips to the keyhole, imploring for admission. "Louise, open the door! I beg; open the door — you will make yourself ill. What are you doing, Louise? For heaven's sake open the door."

"Go away. I am not making myself ill." No; she was drinking in a very elixir of life through that open window.

Her fancy was running riot along those days ahead of her. Spring days, and summer days, and all sorts of days that would be her own. She breathed a quick prayer that life might be long. It was only yesterday she had thought with a shudder that life might be long.

20 She arose at length and opened the door to her sister's importunities. There was a feverish triumph in her eyes, and she carried herself unwittingly like a goddess of Victory. She clasped her sister's waist, and together they descended the stairs. Richards stood waiting for them at the bottom.

Some one was opening the front door with a latchkey. It was Brently Mallard who entered, a little travel-stained, composedly carrying his gripsack and umbrella. He had been far from the scene of accident, and did not even know there had been one. He stood amazed at Josephine's piercing cry; at Richards' quick motion to screen him from the view of his wife.

But Richards was too late.

When the doctors came they said she had died of heart disease — of joy that kills.

Topics for Critical Thinking and Writing

Read the following assertions and consider whether you agree or disagree, and why. For each assertion, draft a paragraph with your arguments.

1. The railroad accident is a symbol of the destructiveness of the Industrial Revolution.
2. The story accurately captures how trapped many women felt by marriage in the nineteenth century.
3. This story's setting is unclear, which makes the story less effective than if the setting had been specified.
4. Mrs. Mallard's death at the end is a just punishment for the joy she takes in her husband's death.
5. The story is rich in irony. Some examples: (1) The other characters think Mrs. Mallard is grieving, but she is rejoicing; (2) she prays for a long life, but she dies almost immediately; (3) the doctors say she died of the "joy that kills," but they think her joy was seeing her husband alive.
6. The story is excellent because it has a surprise ending.

Thinking about the Effects of Literature

What about the *consequences* of literature? Does literature shape our character and therefore influence our behavior? It is generally believed that it does have an effect. One hears, for example, that literature (like travel) is broadening, that it makes us aware of, and tolerant of, kinds of behavior that differ from our own and from what we see around us. One of the chief arguments against pornography, for instance, is that it desensitizes us, makes us too tolerant of abusive relationships, relationships in which people (usually men) use other people (usually women) as mere things or instruments for pleasure.

(A contrary view: Some people argue that pornography provides a relatively harmless outlet for fantasies that otherwise might be given release in the real world. In this view, pornography acts as a sort of safety valve.)

Other topics are also the subjects of controversy. For instance, in recent decades, parents and educators have been much concerned with fairy tales. Does the violence in some fairy tales ("Little Red Riding Hood," "The Three Little Pigs") have a negative effect on children? Do some of the stories teach the wrong lessons, implying that women should be passive and men active ("Sleeping Beauty," for instance, in which the sleeping woman is brought to life by the action of the handsome prince)? The Greek philosopher Plato (427–347 BC) strongly believed that the literature we hear or read shapes our later behavior, and since most of the ancient Greek traditional stories (notably Homer's *Odyssey* and *Iliad*) celebrate acts of love and war rather than of justice, he prohibited the reading of such material in his ideal society. (We reprint a relevant passage from Plato on p. 397.)

Exercise: Thinking about the Effects of Literature

1. If you have responded strongly (favorably or unfavorably) to some aspect of the social content of a literary work — for instance, its depiction of women, a particular minority group, or a political perspective —analyze the response in a 250- to 500-word essay and try to determine whether you are talking chiefly about yourself or the work. Can we really see literary value — *really* see it — in a work that deeply offends us?
2. Read the following brief claims about literature; then choose one and write a 250-word essay offering support or taking issue with it.

   The pen is mightier than the sword. — EDWARD BULWER-LYTTON

   [The arts] supply our best data for deciding which experiences are more valuable than others. — I. A. RICHARDS

   I believe as the Victorian novelists did that a novel isn't simply a vehicle for private expression, but that it also exists for social examination. — MARGARET ATWOOD

   Poetry makes nothing happen. — W. H. AUDEN

   Literature is *without proofs*. By which it must be understood that it cannot prove, not only *what* it says, but even that it is worth the trouble of saying it.

   — ROLAND BARTHES

   Of course the illusion of art is to make one believe that great literature is very close to life, but exactly the opposite is true. Life is amorphous, literature is formal.

   — FRANÇOISE SAGAN

   Of course I'm a black writer. . . . I'm not just a black writer, but categories like black writer, woman writer and Latin American writer aren't marginal anymore. We have to acknowledge that the thing we call "literature" is more pluralistic now, just as society ought to be. — TONI MORRISON

3. Do you think authors control the meaning of their poems and stories? Is the author's intention the correct meaning of a work of literature? Explain your answer in approximately 500 words.
4. What possible public benefit can come from supporting the arts? Can one argue that we should support the arts for the same reasons that we support public schools — that is, to have a civilized society? Explain your response.

PLATO

Plato (427–347 BC), an Athenian aristocrat by birth, was the student of one great philosopher (Socrates) and the teacher of another (Aristotle). His legacy of more than two dozen dialogues — imaginary discussions between Socrates and one or more other speakers, usually young Athenians — has been of such influence that the whole of Western philosophy can be characterized, A. N. Whitehead wrote, as "a series of footnotes to Plato." Plato's interests encompassed the full range of topics in philosophy: ethics, politics, logic, metaphysics, epistemology, aesthetics, psychology, and education.

This selection from Plato's *Republic*, one of his best-known and longest dialogues, is about the education suitable for the rulers of an ideal society. *The Republic* begins, typically, with an investigation into the nature of justice. Socrates (who speaks for Plato) convincingly explains to Glaucon that we cannot reasonably expect to achieve a just society unless we devote careful attention to the moral education of the young men who are scheduled in later life to become the rulers. (Here as elsewhere, Plato's elitism and aristocratic bias shows itself; as readers of *The Republic* soon learn, Plato is no admirer of democracy or of a classless society.) Plato cares as much about what the educational curriculum should exclude as what it should include. His special target was the common practice in his day of using for pedagogy the Homeric tales and other stories about the gods. He readily embraces the principle of censorship, as the excerpt explains, because he thinks it is a necessary means to achieve the ideal society.

The Greater Part of the Stories Current Today We Shall Have to Reject

"What kind of education shall we give them then? We shall find it difficult to improve on the time-honored distinction between the physical training we give to the body and the education we give to the mind and character."

"True."

"And we shall begin by educating mind and character, shall we not?"

"Of course."

"In this education you would include stories, 5
would you not?"

"Yes."

"These are of two kinds, true stories and fiction.[1] Our education must use both, and start with fiction."

"I don't know what you mean."

"But you know that we begin by telling children stories. These are, in general, fiction,

[1]The Greek word *pseudos* and its corresponding verb meant not only "fiction" — stories, tales — but also "what is not true" and so, in suitable contexts, "lies": and this ambiguity should be borne in mind. [Editors' note: All footnotes are by the translator, but some have been omitted.]

though they contain some truth. And we tell children stories before we start them on physical training."

"That is so."

"That is what I meant by saying that we must start to educate the mind before training the body."

"You are right," he said.

"And the first step, as you know, is always what matters most, particularly when we are dealing with those who are young and tender. That is the time when they are easily molded and when any impression we choose to make leaves a permanent mark."

"That is certainly true."

"Shall we therefore readily allow our children to listen to any stories made up by anyone, and to form opinions that are for the most part the opposite of those we think they should have when they grow up?"

"We certainly shall not."

"Then it seems that our first business is to supervise the production of stories, and choose only those we think suitable, and reject the rest. We shall persuade mothers and nurses to tell our chosen stories to their children, and by means of them to mold their minds and characters which are more important than their bodies. The greater part of the stories current today we shall have to reject."

"Which are you thinking of?"

"We can take some of the major legends as typical. For all, whether major or minor, should be cast in the same mold and have the same effect. Do you agree?"

"Yes: but I'm not sure which you refer to as major."

"The stories in Homer and Hesiod and the poets. For it is the poets who have always made up fictions and stories to tell to men."

"What sort of stories do you mean and what fault do you find in them?"

"The worst fault possible," I replied, "especially if the fiction is an ugly one."

"And what is that?"

"Misrepresenting the nature of gods and heroes, like a portrait painter whose portraits bear no resemblance to their originals."

"That is a fault which certainly deserves censure. But give me more details."

"Well, on the most important of subjects, there is first and foremost the foul story about Ouranos[2] and the things Hesiod says he did, and the revenge Cronos took on him. While the story of what Cronos did, and what he suffered at the hands of his son, is not fit as it is to be lightly repeated to the young and foolish, even if it were true; it would be best to say nothing about it, or if it must be told, tell it to a select few under oath of secrecy, at a rite which required, to restrict it still further, the sacrifice not of a mere pig but of something large and difficult to get."

"These certainly are awkward stories."

"And they shall not be repeated in our state, Adeimantus," I said. "Nor shall any young audience be told that anyone who commits horrible crimes, or punishes his father unmercifully, is doing nothing out of the ordinary but merely what the first and greatest of the gods have done before."

"I entirely agree," said Adeimantus, "that these stories are unsuitable."

"Nor can we permit stories of wars and plots and battles among the gods; they are quite untrue, and if we want our prospective guardians to believe that quarrelsomeness is one of the worst of evils, we must certainly not let them be told the story of the Battle of the Giants or embroider it on robes, or tell them other tales about many and various

[2]**Ouranos** The sky, the original supreme god. Ouranos was castrated by his son Cronos to separate him from Gaia (mother earth). Cronos was in turn deposed by Zeus in a struggle in which Zeus was helped by the Titans.

quarrels between gods and heroes and their friends and relations. On the contrary, if we are to persuade them that no citizen has ever quarreled with any other, because it is sinful, our old men and women must tell children stories with this end in view from the first, and we must compel our poets to tell them similar stories when they grow up. But we can admit to our state no stories about Hera being tied up by her son, or Hephaestus being flung out of Heaven by his father for trying to help his mother when she was getting a beating, nor any of Homer's Battles of the Gods, whether their intention is allegorical or not. Children cannot distinguish between what is allegory and what isn't, and opinions formed at that age are usually difficult to eradicate or change; we should therefore surely regard it as of the utmost importance that the first stories they hear shall aim at encouraging the highest excellence of character."

"Your case is a good one," he agreed, "but if someone wanted details, and asked what stories we were thinking of, what should we say?"

To which I replied, "My dear Adeimantus, you and I are not engaged on writing stories but on founding a state. And the founders of a state, though they must know the type of story the poet must produce, and reject any that do not conform to that type, need not write them themselves."

"True: but what are the lines on which our poets must work when they deal with the gods?"

"Roughly as follows," I said. "God must surely always be represented as he really is, whether the poet is writing epic, lyric, or tragedy."

"He must."

"And in reality of course god is good, and he must be so described."

"Certainly."

"But nothing good is harmful, is it?"[3]

"I think not."

"Then can anything that is not harmful do harm?"

"No."

"And can what does no harm do evil?"

"No again."

"And can what does no evil be the cause of any evil?"

"How could it?"

"Well then; is the good beneficial?"

"Yes."

"So it must be the cause of well-being."

"Yes."

"So the good is not the cause of everything, but only of states of well-being and not of evil."

"Most certainly," he agreed.

"Then god, being good, cannot be responsible for everything, as is commonly said, but only for a small part of human life, for the greater part of which he has no responsibility. For we have a far smaller share of good than of evil, and while god must be held to be the sole cause of good, we must look for some factors other than god as cause of the evil."

"I think that's very true," he said.

"So we cannot allow Homer or any other poet to make such a stupid mistake about the gods, as when he says that

> Zeus has two jars standing on the floor
> of his palace, full of fates, good in one and
> evil in the other

[3]The reader of the following passage should bear the following ambiguities in mind: (1) the Greek word for good (*agathos*) can mean (a) morally good, (b) beneficial or advantageous; (2) the Greek word for evil (*kakos*) can also mean harm or injury; (3) the adverb of *agathos* (*eu* — the well) can imply either morally right or prosperous. The word translated "cause of" could equally well be rendered "responsible for."

and that the man to whom Zeus allots a mixture of both has "varying fortunes sometimes good and sometimes bad," while the man to whom he allots unmixed evil is "hased by ravening despair over the face of the earth."[4] Nor can we allow references to Zeus as "dispenser of good and evil." And we cannot approve if it is said that Athene and Zeus prompted the breach of solemn treaty and oath by Pandarus, or that the strife and contentions of the gods were due to Themis and Zeus. Nor again can we let our children hear from Aeschylus that

> God implants a fault in man, when he
> wishes to destroy a house utterly.

No: We must forbid anyone who writes a play about the sufferings of Niobe (the subject of the play from which these last lines are quoted), or the house of Pelops, or the Trojan war, or any similar topic, to say they are acts of god; or if he does he must produce the sort of interpretation we are now demanding, and say that god's acts were good and just, and that the sufferers were benefited by being punished. What the poet must not be allowed to say is that those who were punished were made wretched through god's action. He may refer to the wicked as wretched because they needed punishment, provided he makes it clear that in punishing them god did them good. But if a state is to be run on the right lines, every possible step must be taken to prevent anyone, young or old, either saying or being told, whether in poetry or prose, that god, being good, can cause harm or evil to any man. To say so would be sinful, inexpedient, and inconsistent."

"I should approve of a law for this purpose and you have my vote for it," he said.

"Then of our laws laying down the principles which those who write or speak about the gods must follow, one would be this: *God is the cause, not of all things, but only of good.*"

"I am quite content with that," he said.

[4]Quotations from Homer are generally taken from the translations by Dr. Rieu in the Penguin series. At times (as here) the version quoted by Plato differs slightly from the accepted text.

Topics for Critical Thinking and Writing

1. In the beginning of the dialogue, Plato says that adults recite fictions to very young children and that these fictions help mold character. Think of some story that you heard or read when young, such as "Snow White and the Seven Dwarfs" or "Ali Baba and the Forty Thieves." Try to think of a story that, in the final analysis, is not in accord with what you consider to be proper morality, such as a story in which a person triumphs through trickery or a story in which evil actions — perhaps murders — are set forth without unfavorable comment. (Was it naughty of Jack to kill the giant?) On reflection, do you think children should not be told such stories? Why, or why not? Or think of the early film westerns in which, on the whole, the Indians (except for an occasional Uncle Tonto) are depicted as bad guys and the white cowboys (except for an occasional coward or rustler) are depicted as good guys. Many people who now have gray hair enjoyed such films in their childhood. Are you prepared to say that such films are not damaging? Or, in contrast, are you prepared to say they are damaging and should be prohibited?

2. It is often objected that censorship of reading matter and of television programs available to children underrates children's ability to think for themselves and to discount the dangerous, obscene, and tawdry. Do you agree with this objection? Does Plato? Explain your response.
3. Plato says that allowing poets to say what they please about the gods in his ideal state would be "inconsistent." Explain what he means by this criticism and then explain why you agree or disagree with it.
4. Do you believe that parents should censor the "fiction" their children encounter (literature, films, pictures, music) but that the community should not censor the "fiction" of adults? Write an essay of about 500 words on one of these topics: "Censorship and Hip-Hop Lyrics," "X-Rated Films," or "Ethnic Jokes." (These topics are broadly worded; you can narrow one and offer any thesis you wish.)
5. Were you taught that any of the founders of the United States ever acted disreputably or that any American hero had any serious moral flaw? Or that the United States ever acted immorally in its dealings with other nations? Do you think it appropriate for children to hear such things? Explain your responses.

12

A Debater's View: Oral Presentations and Debate

He who knows only his own side of the case knows little of that. — JOHN STUART MILL

A philosopher who is not taking part in discussions is like a boxer who never goes into the ring. — LUDWIG WITTGENSTEIN

Freedom is hammered out on the anvil of dissension, dissent, and debate. — HUBERT HUMPHREY

Oral Presentations

Forensic comes from the Latin word *foris*, meaning "out of doors," which also produced the word *forum*, an open space in front of a public building. In the language of rhetoricians, the place where one delivers a speech to an audience is the forum — whether it is a classroom, a court of law, or the steps of the Lincoln Memorial. In fact, the earliest meaning of *forensics* in English was related to public discussion and debate.

Your instructor may ask you to make an oral presentation (in which case, the forum would be the classroom), and if he or she doesn't make such a demand, later life almost certainly will. For example, you'll find that at a job interview, you will be expected to talk persuasively (perhaps to a group) about what good qualities or experience you can bring to the place of employment. Similarly, when you have a job, you'll sometimes have to summarize a report orally or argue your case out loud, perhaps so that your colleagues might do something they are hesitant to do.

The goal of your classroom talk is to persuade the audience to share your view or, if you can't get them to agree completely, to get them to see that at least there is something to be said for this view — that it is a position a reasonable person can hold.

Elsewhere in this book we have said that the subjects of persuasive writing are usually

- matters of fact (e.g., statistics show that the death penalty does — or does not — deter crime),
- matters of value (e.g., separating families is — or is not — immoral), or
- matters of policy (e.g., government should — or should not — make college "free").

Similarly, many kinds of public speaking involve just such matters, and the habits of critical thinking, argument, and persuasion we have discussed to this point now need to be personified and articulated.

No matter what your subject is, when you draft and revise your talk, make certain that a thesis statement underlies the whole (e.g., "Proposition 2 is a bad idea because . . .").

The text of an oral presentation ought not to be identical with the text of a written presentation. Both must have a clear organization, but oral presentations usually require making the organization a bit more obvious, with abundant **signposts**. Signposts help audiences listen to your key points. For example, audiences benefit from knowing how long they are expected to listen. (Think about it: Who hasn't checked the time remaining in a movie or television show to help anticipate where they are in the plot?) It sometimes helps to inform your audience: "In *the next ten minutes*, I will be speaking to you about *X*"; "Before I talk about *X*, I am going *to spend a minute or two* on background"; or "Now, *with just few minutes remaining*, I would like to make my key point." Skilled speakers know how to raise their audience's perceptions at key moments. Following are some more signpost words and phrases that can help an audience hear what you them to hear most.

SPEAKING TIPS

- *In preparing your oral presentation, keep your thesis in mind.* You may be giving counterarguments, examples, definitions, and so forth, but make sure that your thesis is evident to the audience and return to it occasionally as a reminder.
- *Keep your audience in mind.* Inevitably, you will have to make assumptions about what the audience does and does not know about your topic. Do not overestimate their knowledge and do not underestimate their intelligence.

Transitioning to a new topic or another point

Up to this point we have been discussing *X*. *Turning now to Y*, we can see something different.

Now *let me pause for a second* before moving on. My first point was *X*. This supports my argument. But so does *Y*, a different kind of case.

Exploring something further

Now, *for just a minute*, let's look at this more deeply.

X is worth *elaborating on for a couple minutes* before I continue.

Digressing

Let's *take a detour* for a second.

I am going *to stop for a minute and tell a brief story* to show a perfect example.

Summarizing or returning to the beginning

To recap everything I have said here, *let me walk through the key points* . . .

Going back to my previous points, A, B, and *C*, we can safely conclude . . .

In general, when speaking, you will have to repeat a bit more than you would in a written presentation. An old rule of thumb suggests that to make your audience remember something, you may need only to write it only once but say it three times. After all, a reader can turn back to check a sentence or a statistic, but a listener cannot. Thus, you may find yourself saying things out loud that you would scarcely or ever write, such as "The authorities were wrong. So that's my first conclusion. The authorities were wrong," or "The reason Jones was arrested was unjust. *I repeat*: The reasons were unjust."

You will want to think carefully about the **organization** of your talk. We've already stressed the need to develop essays with clear thesis statements and logical supporting points. Oral presentations are no different, but remember that when you are speaking in public, a clear organization will always help alleviate anxiety and reassure you. Thus, you can deliver a powerful message without getting tripped up yourself. We suggest you try the following:

- Outline your draft in advance to ensure it has clear organization.
- Inform the audience at the start about the organization of your presentation. Early in the talk, you probably should say something along these lines, although not in as abbreviated a form:

  In talking about *A*, I'll have to define a few terms, *B* and *C*, and I will also have to talk about two positions that differ from mine, *D* and *E*. I'll then try to show why *A* is the best policy to pursue, clearly better than *D* and *E*.

- So that the listeners can easily follow your train of thought, be sure to use transitions such as "Furthermore," "Therefore," "Although it is often said," and "Some may object that." Sometimes, you may even remind the listeners what the previous stages were, with a comment such as "We have now seen three approaches to the problem of . . ."

METHODS OF DELIVERY

After thinking about helping the audience follow your speech, consider how much help you'll need delivering it. Depending on your comfort level with the topic and your argument, you might decide to

- deliver a memorized talk without notes,
- read the talk from a written text, or

- speak from an outline, perhaps with quotations and statistics written down.

Each of these methods has strengths and weaknesses. A memorized talk allows for plenty of eye contact with the audience, but unless you are a superb actor, it is almost surely going to seem a bit mechanical. A talk that you read from a text will indeed let you say to an audience exactly what you intend (with the best possible wording), but reading a text inevitably establishes some distance between you and the audience, even if you occasionally glance up from your pages. If you talk from a mere outline, almost surely some of your sentences will turn out to be a bit awkward — although a little awkwardness may help convey sincerity and therefore be a plus.

No matter what form of delivery you choose, try to convey the impression that you're conversing with the audience, not talking down to them (even though if you're standing on a platform you will be literally talking down).

You may want to use **multimedia aids** in your presentation. These can range from such low-tech materials as handouts, blackboards, and whiteboards to high-tech PowerPoint presentations, Prezis, or videos and recordings. Each has advantages and disadvantages. For instance, if you distribute handouts when the talk begins, the audience may start thumbing through them during your opening comments. And although software like PowerPoint can provide highly useful aids, some speakers make too much use of it simply because it's available. Any software you use, or any supplementary materials you introduce, should be essential to communicating your message effectively, not superfluous or merely decorative. And these materials should be legible: If you do use visuals, make certain that your words and images are large enough to be seen by all given the size of the room and the expectation that not everyone can see equally clearly. A graph with tiny words won't impress your audience, nor will words that cannot be read by everyone. Also, to accommodate as many people as possible, it helps to describe your slides even when you have created them to be extremely clear.

SPEAKING TIP

Some common errors in using PowerPoint include providing too much information on slides or providing too many words. You do not want your audience to read your presentation; rather, you want the audience to see the key points you are making, supported perhaps by images, charts, and graphs. (These too should not be too complex. Also, be prepared to help your audience interpret your images, charts, and graphs.)

AUDIENCE

It is not merely because topics are complicated that we cannot agree that one side is reasonable and correct and the other side irrational and wrong. The truth is that we are swayed not only by reason (*logos*) but also by appeals to the emotions (*pathos*) and by the speaker's character (*ethos*). (For more on these appeals, see Persuasion, Argument, and Rhetorical Appeals on pp. 75–79 in Chapter 3.) We can combine these last two factors and put it this way: Sometimes we are inclined to agree with *X* rather than with *Y* because *X* strikes us as a more appealing person (perhaps more open-minded, more intelligent, better informed, more humane, and less cold). *X* is the sort of person we want to have as a friend. We disagree with *Y*— or at least we're unwilling to associate ourselves with *Y*— because *Y* is, well, *Y* just isn't the sort of person we want to agree with. *Y*'s statistics don't sound right, or *Y* seems like a bully;

A CHECKLIST FOR AN ORAL PRESENTATION

Keep the following in mind, whether you are evaluating someone else's talk or preparing your own.

Delivery

- ❒ Voice loud enough but not too loud.
- ❒ Appropriate degree of speed — neither hurried nor drawn out.
- ❒ Dress and attitude toward audience appropriate.
- ❒ Gestures and eye contact appropriate.
- ❒ Language clear (e.g., technical words adequately explained).
- ❒ Audiovisual aids, if any, appropriate and effectively used.

Content

- ❒ Thesis clear and kept in view.
- ❒ Argument steadily advanced, with helpful transitions.
- ❒ Thesis supported by evidence.
- ❒ Lightweight material (e.g., bits of humor, relevant and genuinely engaging).

for some reason, we just don't have confidence in *Y*. Confidence is easily lost: Alas, even a mispronunciation will diminish the audience's confidence in *Y*. As Peter de Vries said, "You can't be happy with someone who pronounces both *d*'s in Wednesday."

Earlier in the book, we talked about the importance of **tone** and of the writer's **persona**. We have also made the point that the writer's tone will depend partly on the audience. A person writing for a conservative journal whose readership is almost entirely conservatives can adopt a highly satiric manner in talking about liberals and will win much approval. But if this conservative writer is writing in a liberal journal and hopes to get a sympathetic hearing, he or she will have to avoid satire and wisecracks and, instead, present himself or herself as a person of goodwill who is open-minded and eager to address the issue seriously.

The **language** you use — the degree to which it is formal as opposed to colloquial and the degree to which it is technical as opposed to general — will also depend on the audience. Speaking broadly, in oral argument you should speak politely but not formally. You do not want to be one of those people who "talk like a book." But you also don't want to be overly colloquial. Choose a middle course, probably a notch below the style you would use in a written paper. For instance, in an oral presentation you might say, "We'll consider this point in a minute or two," whereas in a written paper you probably would write, "We will consider this point shortly."

Technical language is entirely appropriate if your audience is familiar with it. If you are arguing before members of Amnesty International about the use of torture, you can assume certain kinds of specialized knowledge. You can, for instance, breezily speak of the DRC and of KPCS, and your listeners will know what you're talking about because Amnesty International has been active with issues concerning the Democratic Republic of Congo and the Kimberley Process Certification Scheme. In contrast, if you are arguing the same case before a general public, you'll have to explain these abbreviations, and you may even have to explain what Amnesty International is. If you are arguing before an audience of classmates, you probably have a good idea of what they know and don't know.

DELIVERY

Your audience will in some measure determine not only your tone but also the way you appear when giving the speech. Part of the delivery is the speaker's appearance. The medium is part of the message. The president can appear in golf clothes when he chats about his reelection plans, but he wears a suit and a tie when he delivers the State of the Union address. Just as we wear one kind of clothing when playing tennis, another when attending classes, and yet another when going for a job interview, an effective speaker dresses appropriately. A lawyer arguing before the Supreme Court wears a dark suit or dress. The same lawyer, arguing at a local meeting, speaking as a community resident, may well dress informally — maybe in jeans — to show that he or she is not stuffy or overly formal but, rather, a regular member of the community.

Your appearance when you speak is not merely a matter of clothing; it includes your **facial expressions**, your **posture**, your **gestures**, and your general demeanor. In general, you should avoid bodily motions — swaying, thumping the table, craning your neck, smirking — that are so distracting that they cause the audience to concentrate on the distraction rather than on the argument. ("That's the third time he straightened his necktie. I wonder how many more times he will — oops, that's the fourth!") Most of us are unaware of our annoying habits; if you're lucky, a friend, when urged, will tell you about them. In preparation, you may also film yourself speaking to observe your physical gestures from a third-person perspective.

You probably can't do much about your **voice** and its unique character — it may be high-pitched, or it may be gravelly — but you can make sure to speak loudly enough for the audience members to hear you and slowly and clearly enough for them to understand you.

We have some advice about quotations, too. First, if possible, use an effective quotation or two, partly because — we'll be frank here — the quotations may be more impressively worded than anything you come up with on your own. A quotation may be the chief thing your audience comes away with: "Hey, yes, I liked that: 'War is too important to be left to the generals' "; "When it comes down to it, I agree with that Frenchman who said 'If we are to abolish the death penalty, I should like to see the first step taken by the murderers' "; or "You know, I think it was all summed up in that line by Margaret Mead, something like, 'No one would remember the Good Samaritan if he'd had only good intentions. He had money as well.' Yes, that's pretty convincing. Morality isn't enough. You need money." You didn't invent the words that you quote, but you did bring them to your listeners' attention, and they will be grateful to you.

Our second piece of advice concerning quotations is this: If the quotation is only a phrase or a brief sentence, you can memorize it and be confident that you'll remember it, but if it's longer than a sentence, write it on a sheet in your notes or on a four-by-six-inch card in print large enough for you to read easily. You have chosen these words because they are effectively put, so you don't want to misquote them or hesitate in delivering them.

CONTENT

As for the talk itself, well, we have been touching on it in our discussion of such matters as the speaker's relation to the audience, the need to provide signposts, and the use of quotations. All our comments in earlier chapters about developing a written argument are also relevant to oral arguments, but here we should merely emphasize that because the talk is oral and the audience cannot look back to an earlier page to remind itself of some point, the speaker may have to repeat and summarize a bit more than is usual in a written essay.

Remember, too, that a reader can see when the essay ends — there is blank space at the end of the page — but a listener depends on aural cues. Nothing is more embarrassing — and less effective as argument — than a speaker who seems (to the audience) to suddenly stop and sit down. In short, give your hearers ample clues that you are ending (post such signs as "Finally," "Last," or "Let me end by saying"), and be sure to end with a strong sentence. It may not be as good as the end of the Gettysburg Address ("government of the people, by the people, for the people, shall not perish from the earth"), nor will it be as good as the end of Martin Luther King Jr.'s "I Have a Dream" speech ("Free at last! Free at last! Thank God Almighty, we are free at last!"), but those are the models to emulate.

Formal Debates

It would be nice if all arguments ended with everyone, participants and spectators, agreeing that the facts are clear, that one presentation is more reasonable than the other, and therefore that one side is right and the other side is wrong. But in life, most issues are complicated. High school students may earnestly debate — this is a real topic in a national debate —

> Resolved: That education has failed its mission in the United States but it takes only a moment of reflection to see that neither the affirmative nor the negative can be true. Yes, education has failed its mission in many ways, but, no, it has succeeded in many ways. Its job now is (in the words of Samuel Beckett) to try again: "Fail. Fail again. Fail better."

Debates of this sort, conducted before a judge and guided by strict rules concerning "Constructive Speeches," "Rebuttal Speeches," and "Cross-Examinations," are not attempts to get at the truth; like lawsuits, they are attempts to win a case. Each speaker seeks not to persuade the opponent but only to convince the judge. Although most of this section is devoted not to forensics in the strictest sense but more generally to the presentation of oral arguments, we begin with the standard format.

STANDARD DEBATE FORMAT

Formal debates occur within a structure that governs the number of speeches, their order, and the maximum time for each one. The format may vary from place to place, but there is always a structure. In most debates, a formal resolution states the reason for the debate ("Resolved: That capital punishment be abolished in juvenile cases"). The affirmative team supports the resolution; the negative team denies its legitimacy. The basic structure has three parts:

- *The constructive phase*, in which the debaters construct their cases and develop their arguments (usually for ten minutes).
- *The rebuttal*, in which debaters present their responses and also present their final summary (usually for five minutes).
- *The preparation*, in which the debater prepares for presenting the next speech. (During the preparation — a sort of time-out — the debater is not addressing the opponent or audience. The total time allotted to a team is usually six or eight minutes, which the individual debaters divide as they wish.)

We give, very briefly, the usual structure of each part, although we should mention that another common format calls for a cross-examination of the First Affirmative Constructive by the Second Negative, a cross-examination of the First Negative Constructive by the First Affirmative, a cross-examination of the Second Affirmative by the First Negative, and a cross-examination of the Second Negative by the Second Affirmative:

First Affirmative Constructive Speech: Serves as introduction, giving summary overview, definitions, criteria for resolution, major claims and evidence, statement, and intention to support the resolution.

First Negative Constructive Speech: Responds by introducing the basic position, challenges the definitions and criteria, suggests the line of attack, emphasizes that the burden of proof lies with the affirmative, rejects the resolution as unnecessary or dangerous, and supports the status quo.

Jewel Samad/Getty Images

US Democratic presidential candidates Hillary Clinton and Bernie Sanders during a debate at the University of New Hampshire in Durham on February 4, 2016. A successful debate can help change the tide of a candidate's campaign.

A CHECKLIST FOR PREPARING FOR A DEBATE

- ❒ Have I done adequate preparation in my research?
- ❒ Are my notes legible, with accurate quotations and credible sources?
- ❒ Am I prepared to take good notes during the debate?
- ❒ Is my proposition clearly stated?
- ❒ Do I have adequate evidence to support the thesis (main point)?
- ❒ Do I have backup points in mind?
- ❒ Have I given thought to issues my opponents might raise?
- ❒ Does the opening properly address the instructor, the audience, the opponents? (Remember, you are addressing an audience, not merely the opponents.)
- ❒ Are my visual aids focused on major points?
- ❒ Is my demeanor professional and is my dress appropriate?

Second Affirmative Constructive: Rebuilds the affirmative case; refutes chief attacks, especially concerning definitions, criteria, and rationale (philosophic framework); and further develops the affirmative case.

Second Negative Constructive: Completes the negative case, if possible advances it by rebuilding portions of the first negative construction, and contrasts the entire negative case with the entire affirmative case.

First Negative Rebuttal: Attacks the opponents' arguments and defends the negative constructive arguments (but a rebuttal may not introduce new constructive arguments).

First Affirmative Rebuttal: Usually responds first to the second negative construction and then to the first negative rebuttal.

Second Negative Rebuttal: Constitutes final speech for the negative, summarizing the case and explaining to the judge why the negative should be declared the winner.

Second Affirmative Rebuttal: Summarizes the debate, responds to issues pressed by the second negative rebuttal, and suggests to the judge that the affirmative team should win.

PART FOUR

Current Issues

Occasions for Debate

Debates as an Aid to Thinking

Throughout this book, we emphasize critical thinking, which — to put the matter briefly — means thinking analytically not only about the ideas of others but also about your *own* ideas. As we often say in these pages, *you* are your first reader, and you should be a demanding one. You have ideas, but you want to think further about them, to improve them — partly so that you can share them with others, but also so that they can help you build a thoughtful, useful, satisfying life.

To do so, as we say elsewhere in the book, you must have (or at least try to have) an open mind, one that welcomes comments on your own ideas. You are, we hope, ready to grant that someone with differing views may indeed have something to teach you. When you hear other views, of course you won't always embrace them; at times, though, you may find merit in some aspects of them, and you will to some degree reshape your own views. (We discuss the importance of trying to find shared ground and moving onward and upward from there in Chapter 10, A Psychologist's View: Rogerian Argument.)

Much of the difficulty in improving our ideas lies in our tendency to think in an either/or pattern. To put the point in academic terms, we incline toward *binary* (Latin, "two by two") or *dichotomous* (Greek, "divided into two") thinking. We often think in terms of contrasts: life and death, good and evil, right and left, up and down, on and off, white and black, boys and girls, men and women, yes and no, freedom and tyranny. We understand what something is partly by thinking of what it is not: "He is liberal; she is conservative." In Gilbert and Sullivan's *Iolanthe*, one of the characters sees things this way:

I am an intellectual chap,
And think of things that would astonish you.
I often think it is comical
How nature always does contrive
That every boy and every gal,
That's born into the world alive,
Is either a little Liberal,
Or else a little Conservative.

We have our liberals and conservatives too, our Democrats and Republicans, and we talk about fate and free will, day and night, and so on. But we also know that there are imperceptible gradations. We know everything is not binary. We know that there are conservative Democrats and liberal Republicans, and although we may refer to red states and blue states, we can see there are, in fact, many types of people along a spectrum of political belief in all states. True, there are times when gradations are irrelevant: In the polling booth, when voting for a political candidate, people must decide between *X* and *Y*. At that stage, it is either/or, not both/and, or "Well, let's think further about this." But in much of life we are not so set in our ways. We may act decisively at a moment, yes, but often we do so through weighing and balancing our priorities and making a decision that may not be the perfect solution, but represents our best effort in the face of deciding. In writing about complex issues, Virginia Woolf said the following:

> When a subject is highly controversial . . . one cannot hope to tell the truth. One can only show how one came to hold whatever opinion one does hold. One can only give one's audience the chance of drawing their own conclusions as they observe the limitations, the prejudices, the idiosyncrasies of the speaker.

What we're getting at is this: The debates in the next five chapters present opposed views, usually based on an either/or perspectives. Each essay sets forth a point of view, often with the implication that on this particular issue there are only two points of view, the writer's view and the wrong view. Some of the writers in these debates, convinced that only one view makes sense, evidently are not interested in hearing other opinions; they are out to convince — indeed, to conquer.

The very word *debate* (from Latin *battere*, "to fight," "to battle") implies a combative atmosphere, a contest in which there will be a winner and a loser. And, indeed, the language used to describe a debate is often militant. Debaters *aim* their arguments, *destroy* the arguments of their *opponents* by *rebutting* (from Old French, *boter*, "to butt") and *refuting* (from Latin *futare*, "to beat") them.

We urge you, however, to read these arguments not to decide who is right and who is wrong but, rather, to think about the issues. In short, although the debates may be reductive, stating only two sides and supporting only one, you should think critically about both sides of any given argument and allow the essays to enrich your own ideas about the topics. Above all, use the cut and thrust of debate as a device to explore the controversy, not as a weapon to force the other side into submission.

See, too, what you can learn about *writing* from these essays — about ways of organizing thoughts, about ways of presenting evidence, and especially about ways of establishing a voice, a *tone* that the reader takes as a representation of the sort of person you are. Remember, as E. B. White said, "No author long remains incognito." Authors reveal their personalities, be they belligerent, witty, thoughtful, courteous, or whatever. If an author here turns you off, let's say by using heavy sarcasm or by being unwilling to face contrary evidence, well, there is a lesson for you as a writer.

In reading essays debating a given issue, keep in mind the questions given in A Checklist for Analyzing a Debate. These questions are very similar to those you should ask when analyzing any argument, with a few additional points of special relevance to debates.

A CHECKLIST FOR ANALYZING A DEBATE

- ❒ Is the writer's thesis clear?
  - ❒ Have I identified the writer's claim?
  - ❒ Has the writer made any assumptions?
  - ❒ Are key terms defined satisfactorily?
- ❒ Does the writer offer adequate support for the claim?
  - ❒ Are examples relevant and convincing?
  - ❒ Are statistics relevant, accurate, and convincing?
  - ❒ Are the authorities appropriate?
  - ❒ Is the logic — deductive and inductive — valid?
  - ❒ If there is an appeal to emotion, is this appeal acceptable?
- ❒ Does the writer seem fair?
  - ❒ Are counterarguments considered?
  - ❒ Is there any evidence of dishonesty?
- ❒ Do the disputants differ in
  - ❒ assumptions?
  - ❒ interpretations of relevant facts?
  - ❒ selection of and emphasis on these facts?
  - ❒ definitions of key terms?
  - ❒ values and norms?
  - ❒ goals?
- ❒ Do the disputants share any common ground?
- ❒ Does one argument stand out to me as better than the other?

13

Student Loans: Should Some Indebtedness Be Forgiven?

ROBERT APPLEBAUM

In 2012, Congressman Hansen Clarke (D-MI) introduced (with seventeen cosponsors) the Student Loan Forgiveness Act of 2012 (HR 4170). This proposal included the 10/10 Loan Repayment Plan, which forgave loan debts of up to $45,000 after payments of 10 percent of the debtor's income per year for ten years. Robert Applebaum (b. 1952), a graduate of Fordham University School of Law, started a petition of support that argued relieving student loan debt would help the economy. Applebaum wrote:

> Student loan debt has become the latest financial crisis in America and, if we do absolutely nothing, the entire economy will eventually come crashing down again, just as it did when the housing bubble popped. . . . Those buried under the weight of their student loan debt are not buying homes or cars, not starting businesses or families, and they're not investing, inventing, innovating, or otherwise engaged in any of the economically stimulative activities that we need all Americans to be engaged in if we're ever to dig ourselves out of the giant hole created by the greed of those at the very top.

The bill did not pass that year, but it was followed up by President Barack Obama's Student Loan Forgiveness Act of 2016, which set out different relief parameters based on a number of factors, and President Donald Trump's later proposals, such as one calling for the elimination of the Public Service Loan Forgiveness program. Here is a short essay Applebaum later published, in 2012, in the *Hill*, a Washington, DC, publication, laying out the basic principles underlying of student loan debt forgiveness.

Debate on Student Loan Debt Doesn't Go Far Enough

As Congress debates the extremely narrow issue of whether to extend the current 3.4 percent interest rate on Federal Student Loans, or to let that rate expire and, thus, double to its previous level of 6.8 percent, both sides of the aisle are missing an opportunity to do something unique, decisive, and bold: adopt legislation that forgives excessive student loan debt after a reasonable repayment period.

Representative Hansen Clarke (D-MI) introduced an unprecedented piece of legislation in March — HR 4170, The Student Loan Forgiveness Act of 2012, in response to over 660,000 people who signed a petition I started in favor of student loan forgiveness. Yet, despite the public outcry, only one member initially stepped up to put his name and reputation on the line in order to draw attention to the ever-growing crisis of student loan debt. Rep. Clarke has taken on the role of Champion for the educated poor — the 36 million Americans who are drowning under the weight of their student loan debts. A new petition I started in favor of HR 4170 currently has over 939,000 signatures.

The Student Loan Forgiveness Act of 2012 is not a free ride, nor is it a bailout. It's a recognition that millions of Americans have grossly overpaid for their educations, due in part to governmental interference in the marketplace. With the availability of so much seemingly "free money" available to anyone with a pulse who wants to take out a student loan, colleges and universities have had no incentive to keep costs down — and they haven't. The outrageous costs of obtaining a college education or beyond today have very little to do with the inherent value of the degrees sought; rather, it has much more to do with brand new stadiums and six-figure administrative salaries. After all, if the degrees obtained today were worth the increased cost to obtain them, compared with thirty to forty years ago, then shouldn't those degrees also yield greater salaries upon graduation?

Tuition rates continue to soar and students are required to go further and further into debt each year, merely to obtain an education. Every other country in the industrialized world has figured out how to pay for higher education for its citizens, but here in America, we continue to treat education as a commodity that benefits only the individual obtaining the education, rather than what it truly is: a public good and an investment in our collective future as a country.

Education should be a right, not a commodity reserved only for the rich or those willing to hock their futures for the chance (not a guarantee) to get a job. Gone are the days when tuition rates had any kind of rational connection to the salaries one could expect upon graduating. With each passing year, students are left with no choice but to borrow more and more through both Federal and private student loans to finance their educations, as if the degrees obtained today are worth any more than they were a generation or two ago. In fact, they're worth far, far less than in years past, precisely because of the high cost of tuition combined with the decimated job market where middle-class wages have gone down, not up, over the last decade.

We've long ago passed the point where we have become what my friend, Aaron Calafato, writer, director, and star of the play *For Profit*, would call a "borrow to work" society. Far worse than "pay to play," borrow to work is a modern form of indentured servitude, where millions of Americans are told since birth that in order to get ahead, they must obtain a higher education.

What they aren't being told, however, is that in order to obtain that education, students must necessarily mortgage their futures and spend the rest of their lives paying back the loans that gave them the "privilege" of working at jobs they hate for salaries that simply do not allow them to make ends meet.

How do we ever expect the housing market to improve when the very people we rely upon to purchase homes — college grads and professionals — are graduating with mortgage-sized debts that they can neither live in, nor use as intended in today's job market?

Are we content to live in a society where only the privileged few are able to obtain an education without sacrificing their future? Do we really want to price the middle and working classes out of public service? And who's going to be buying cars, starting businesses, and making investments in our future if not the middle class? We're not yet an oligarchy, but we're fast on our way toward becoming one if we knowingly fail to address this ever-growing crisis, before it's too late.

10 Unfortunately, the $1 trillion in student loan debt outstanding in America is not a ceiling, merely a disturbing milestone along the national path to poverty. If Congress does nothing, it'll only get worse.

Topics for Critical Thinking and Writing

1. In paragraph 1, Robert Applebaum speaks of "excessive" student debt. Whom does he blame for this debt — students, colleges, lenders, government, or someone else?
2. In paragraph 5, Applebaum says that education — meaning higher education — should be a right. In the United States, education through high school is free — it is a right (and actually an obligation) — although one can argue that there really is no such thing as "free" education (or "free" medical care, etc.); technically, taxpayers foot the bill for K–12 education. Should all citizens have a right to some form of *free* post–high school education? If not, why not? If so, should that include any kind of study — vocational, arts, humanities, sciences, and so on? Explain your reasoning.
3. In about 250 words, discuss how Applebaum uses language as a persuasive tool throughout his argument. How would you characterize the emotional tone of the essay?

Analyzing a Visual: Student Loan Debt

Anadolu Agency/Getty Images

Topic for Critical Thinking and Writing

Briefly, what arguments are on display in this photo? What particular aspects of college education are these protesters critical of? Do you agree or disagree with them? Why?

JUSTIN WOLFERS

Justin Wolfers (b. 1972), a professor of economics and public policy at the University of Michigan, was invited by the economics blog *Freakonomics* to comment on Robert Applebaum's idea in his petition for support that forgiving student loan indebtedness would stimulate the nation's economy: Freed from debt, Applebaum argued, consumers would spend thousands of additional dollars, which would then encourage businesses to hire more workers to meet the increased demand for goods. (The argument that forgiveness of loans will stimulate job growth is offered also in Congressman Hansen Clarke's Student Loan Forgiveness Act of 2012 [HR 4170].) We reprint Wolfers's contribution to *Freakonomics*, September 19, 2011. When he wrote this short piece in 2011, Applebaum's petition had 300,000 signatures.

Forgive Student Loans? Worst Idea Ever

Let's look at this through five separate lenses:

Distribution: If we are going to give money away, why on earth would we give it to college grads? This is the one group who we know typically have high incomes, and who have enjoyed income growth over the past four decades. The group who has been hurt over the past few decades is high school dropouts.

Macroeconomics: This is the worst macro policy I've ever heard of. If you want stimulus, you get more bang-for-your-buck if you give extra dollars to folks who are most likely to spend each dollar. Imagine what would happen if you forgave $50,000 in debt. How much of that would get spent in the next month or year? Probably just a couple of grand (if that). Much of it would go into the bank. But give $1,000 to each of fifty poor people, and nearly all of it will get spent, yielding a larger stimulus. Moreover, it's not likely that college grads are the ones who are liquidity-constrained. Most of 'em could spend more if they wanted to; after all, they are the folks who could get a credit card or a car loan fairly easily. It's the hand-to-mouth consumers — those who can't get easy access to credit — who are most likely to raise their spending if they get the extra dollars.

Education Policy: Perhaps folks think that forgiving educational loans will lead more people to get an education. No, it won't. This is a proposal to forgive the debt of folks who already have an education. Want to increase access to education? Make loans more widely available, or subsidize those who are yet to choose whether to go to school. But this proposal is just a lump-sum transfer that won't increase education attainment. So why transfer to these folks?

Political Economy: This is a bunch of 5
kids who don't want to pay their loans back. And worse: Do this once, and what will happen in the next recession? More lobbying for free money, rather than doing something socially constructive. Moreover, if these guys succeed, others will try, too. And we'll just get more spending in the least socially productive part of our economy — the lobbying industry.

Politics: Notice the political rhetoric? Give free money to us, rather than "corporations, millionaires, and billionaires." Opportunity cost is one of the key principles of economics. And that principle says to compare your choice with the next best alternative. Instead, they're comparing it with the worst alternative.

So my question for the proponents: Why give money to college grads rather than the 15 percent of the population in poverty?

Conclusion: Worst. Idea. Ever.

And I bet that the proponents can't find a single economist to support this idiotic idea.

Topics for Critical Thinking and Writing

1. What do you make of Justin Wolfers's first "lens" about distribution, that the last people to whom we should "give money away" are college graduates? Is this idea fair? Why, or why not?
2. Is Wolfers's second point about giving money to people who will most readily spend it the fastest way to stimulate the economy? Why, or why not?
3. Is Wolfers's argument a good refutation of Applebaum's? Why, or why not?
4. Examine Wolfers's last two paragraphs. Would the essay be more effective if he omitted the final paragraph? What if he reversed the sequence of the last two paragraphs? Explain.
5. Imagine that you are Applebaum. Write a response to Wolfers.

14

Are Algorithms Biased (Or Are We)?

SAFIYA UMOJA NOBLE

Safiya Umoja Noble, an associate professor at the University of California, Los Angeles, and a visiting faculty member at the Annenberg School of Communication at the University of Southern California, researches and teaches about the impact of digital media on contemporary society and culture. Her most recent book, *Algorithms of Oppression: How Search Engines Reinforce Racism* (2018), focuses on racial biases in search engines, social media, and other algorithm-based platforms. Noble is also a co-editor of two other volumes, *The Intersectional Internet: Race, Sex, Class and Culture Online* (2016), and *Emotions, Technology and Design* (2016). In 2019, she became a senior research fellow with the Oxford Internet Institute at Oxford University, United Kingdom.

Missed Connections: What Search Engines Say about Women

On occasion, I ask my university students to follow me through a day in the life of an African-American aunt, mother, mentor, or friend who is trying to help young women learn to use the Internet. In this exercise, I ask what kind of things they think young black girls might be interested in learning about: music, hair, friendship, fashion, popular culture?

I ask them if they could imagine how my nieces' multicultural group of friends who are curious to learn about black culture and contributions (beyond watching rap music videos or Tyler Perry movies) might go to Google to find information about black accomplishments, identities, and intellectual traditions. I ask them to think about the book report they might write, or the speech they might give about famous black girls involved in human and civil rights movements in the United States and across the world. I remind my students that to be black is to encompass more than an African-American identity, but to embrace an affinity with black people in the diaspora, that it is our identification with others of African descent in Africa, the Caribbean, Latin America, Europe, and all parts of the globe. I remind them of the reclamation of the word "black" that my parents' and their grandparents' generations fought for, as in "Black Is Beautiful." I ask them to imagine a 16-year-old, or even an 8-year-old, opening up Google in her browser and searching for herself and her friends by typing in the words "black girls."

Someone inevitably volunteers to come forward and open a blank Google search page—a portal to the seemingly bottomless array of information online—intending to find accurate and timely information that can't easily be found without a library card or a thoughtful and well-informed teacher.

Last semester, SugaryBlackP---y.com was the top hit. No matter which year or class the students are in, they always look at me in disbelief when their search yields this result. They wonder if they did something wrong. They double-check. They try using quotation marks around the search terms. They make sure the computer isn't logged in to Gmail, as if past searches for pornography might be affecting the results. They don't understand.

5 I consider myself far from prudish. I don't care if someone types "porn" into a search engine and porn is what they get. I do care about porn turning up in the results when people are searching for support, knowledge, or answers about identity. I care that someone might type in "black girls," "Latinas," or other terms associated with women of color and instantly find porn all over their first-page results. I care that women are automatically considered "girls," and that actual girls find their identities so readily compromised by porn.

At the moment, U.S. commercial search engines like Google, Yahoo!, and Bing wield tremendous power in defining how information is indexed and prioritized. Cuts to public education, public libraries, and community resources only exacerbate our reliance on technology, rather than information and education professionals, for learning. But what's missing in the search engine is awareness about stereotypes, inequity, and identity. These results are deeply problematic and are often presented without any way for us to change them.

Last year when I conducted these exercises in class, the now-defunct HotBlackP---y.com outranked SugaryBlackP---y.com, indicating that the market for black women and girls' identities online is also in flux, and changes as businesses and organizations can afford to position and sustain themselves at the top of the search pile. These search engine results, for women whose identities are already maligned in the media, only further debase and erode efforts for social, political, and economic recognition and justice.

While preparing to write this article, I did a search for "women's magazines," having a hunch that feminist periodicals would not rise to the top of the search pile. After looking through the websites provided by Google, I gave up by page 11, never to find *Bitch* magazine. This search raises questions about why "women's magazines" are automatically linked to unfeminist periodicals like *Cosmopolitan* and *Women's Day.* (Not coincidentally, these titles are all owned by the Hearst Corporation, which has the funds to purchase its way to the top of the search pile, and which benefits from owning multiple media properties that can be used for cross-promotional hyperlinks that mutually push each other higher in the rankings.) These titles are the default for representations of women's magazines, while alternative women's media — say, those with a feminist perspective — can be found only via searching by name or including purposeful search terms like "feminist."

Try Google searches on every variation you can think of for women's and girls' identities and you will see many of the ways in which commercial interests have subverted a diverse (or realistic) range of representations. Try "women athletes" and do your best not to cringe at the lists of "Top 25 Sexiest Female Athletes" that surface. Based on these search results, constructions of women's identities and interests seem to be based on traditional, limited sexist norms, just as they are in the traditional media. What does it mean that feminism — or, barring a specific identification with that term, progressivism — has been divorced from the definitions or representations of "women" in a commercial search engine? That antifeminist or even pornographic representations of women show up on the first page of results in search engines by default?

10 Google's search process is based on identifying and assigning value to various types of information through web indexing. Many search engines, not just Google, use the artificial intelligence of computers to determine what kinds of information should be retrieved and displayed, and in what order. Complex mathematical formulations are developed into algorithms that are part of the automation process. But these calculations do not take social context into account.

If you were to try my classroom experiments for yourself (which I imagine you may do in the middle of reading this article), you may get a variation on my students' results. The truth is, search engine results are impacted by myriad factors. Google applications like Gmail and social media sites like Facebook track your identity and previous searches to unearth something slightly different. Search engines increasingly remember where you've been and what links you've clicked in order to provide more customized content. Search results will also vary depending on whether filters to screen out porn are enabled on your browser. In some cases, there may be more media and interest in non-pornographic information about black girls in your locale that push such sites higher up to the first page, like a strong nonprofit, blog, or media source that gets a lot of clicks in your region (I teach in the Midwest, which may have something to do with the results we get when we do Google searches in class). Information that rises to the top of the search pile is not the same for every user in every location, and a variety of commercial advertising and political, social, and economic factors are linked to the way search results are coded and displayed.

Recently, the Federal Trade Commission started looking into Google's near-monopoly status and market dominance and the harm this could cause consumers. Consumer Watchdog.org's report "Traffic Report: How Google Is Squeezing Out Competitors and Muscling into New Markets," from June 2010, details how Google effectively blocks sites that it competes with and prioritizes its own properties to the top of the search pile (YouTube over other video sites, Google Maps over MapQuest, and Google Images over Photobucket and Flickr). The report highlights how Universal Search is not a neutral search process, but rather a commercial one that moves sites that buy paid advertising (as well as Google's own investments) to the top of the pile. But many analysts watching the antitrust debates around Google argue that in the free market economy, market share dominance and control over search results isn't a crime. In a September 2011 Businessweek.com article, reporter Mathew Ingram suggested that "it would be hard for anyone to prove that the company's free services have injured consumers."

But Ingram is arguably defining "injury" a little too narrowly. Try searching for "Latinas," or "Asian women," and the results focus on porn, dating, and fetishization. "Black women" will give you sites on "angry black women," and articles on "why black women are less attractive." The largest commercial search engines fail to provide relevant and culturally situated knowledge on how women of color have traditionally been discriminated against, denied rights, or been violated in society and the media even though we have organized and resisted this on many levels. Search engine results don't only mask the unequal access to social, political, and economic life in the United States as broken down by race, gender, and sexuality — they also maintain it.

You might think that Google would want to do something about problematic search results, especially those that appear racist or sexist. Veronica Arreola wondered as much on the *Ms.* blog in 2010, when Google Instant, a search-enhancement tool, initially did not include the words "Latinas," "lesbian," and "bisexual," because of their X-rated front-page results: "You're Google. I think you could figure out how to put porn and violence-related results, say, on the second page?" But they don't — except where it's illegal (Google will not surface certain neo-Nazi websites in France and Germany, where Holocaust denial is against the law). Siva Vaidhyanathan's 2011 book reminds us why this is an important matter to trace. He chronicles recent attempts by the Jewish community and the Anti-Defamation League to challenge Google's priority ranking of anti-Semitic, Holocaust-denial websites. So troublesome were these search results that in 2011 Google issued a statement about its search process, encouraging people to use "Jews" and "Jewish people" in their searches, rather than the pejorative term "Jew" — which they claim they can do nothing about white supremacist groups co-opting. The need for accurate information about Jewish culture and the Holocaust should be enough evidence to start a national discussion about consumer harm, to which we can add a whole host of cultural and gender-based identities that are misrepresented in search engine results.

Google's assertion that its search results, 15
though problematic, were computer-generated (and thus not the company's fault) was apparently a good enough answer for the ADL, which was "extremely pleased that Google has heard our concerns and those of its users about the offensive nature of some search results and the unusually high ranking of peddlers of bigotry and anti-Semitism." A search for the word "Jew" today will surface a beige box from Google linking to its lengthy disclaimer about your results — which remain a mix of both anti-Semitic and informative sites.

These kinds of disclaimers about search results are not enough, and though our collective (and at times tormented) love affair with Google continues, it should not be given a pass just because it issues apologies under the guise of its motto, "Don't be evil." Just because search engines are shrouded in high-tech processes that may be difficult for the average Internet user to grasp doesn't mean that the search methods of all the market leaders shouldn't be examined. In addition, it is important that those who feel harmed by what goes to the top of a page-ranking system be heard in these processes. The question that the Federal Trade Commission might ask is whether search engines like Google should be probed about the values they assign to keyword combinations like "black girls," "Latinas," and other racial, gendered, and sexual-identity combinations, and whether saying they are not responsible for what happens through disclaimers should suffice.

The rapid shift over the past decade from public-interest journalism to the corporate takeover of U.S. news media — which has made highlighting any kind of alternative news increasingly difficult — has occurred simultaneously with the erosion of professional standards applied to information provision on the web. As the search arena is consolidated to a handful of corporations, it's even more crucial to pay close attention to the types of biases that are shaping the information prioritized in search engines. The higher a web page is ranked, the more it's trusted. And unlike the vetting of journalists and librarians, who have been entrusted to fact-check and curate information for the public, the legitimacy of websites is taken for granted. When it comes to commercial search engines, it is no longer enough to simply share news and education on the web — we must ask ourselves how the things we want to share are found, and how the things we find have surfaced.

These shifts are similar to the ways that certain kinds of information are prioritized to the top of the search pile: information, products, and ideas promoted by businesses and sold to industries that can afford to purchase keywords at a premium, or URLS and advertising space online that drive their results and links to the top of the near-infinite pile of information available on the web. All of these dynamics are important for communities and organizations that want to make reliable information, education, culture, and resources available to each other — and not on page 23 of a Google search.

The Pew Internet & American Life consumer-behavior tracking surveys are conducted on a regular basis to understand the ways that Americans use the Internet and technology. An August 9, 2011, report found that 92 percent of adults who use the Internet — about half of all Americans — use search engines to find information online, and 59 percent do so on a typical day. These results indicate searching is the most popular online activity among U.S. adults. An earlier Pew report from 2005, "Search Engine Users," specifically studied trust and credibility, finding that for the most part, people are satisfied with the results they find in search engines, with 64 percent of respondents believing search engines are a fair and unbiased source of information.

But in the case of a search on the words 20
"black girls," the results that come up are certainly not fair or unbiased representations of actual black girls. In a centuries-old struggle for self-determination and a decades-long effort to have control over our media misrepresentations — from mammies to sapphires, prostitutes to vixens — black women and girls have long been subject to exploitation in the media. Since we are so reliant on search engines for providing trusted information, shouldn't we question the ways in which "information" about women is offered up to the highest bidder, advertiser, or

company that can buy search terms and portray them any way they want?

When I conducted my classroom exercise this semester, Black Girls Rock!, a nonprofit dedicated to empowering young women of color, was ranked high on the first-page results, showing that there are, indeed, alternatives to the usual search results. This coincided with a national campaign the organization was doing for an upcoming TV special, meaning a lot of people visited their site, helping move them up to the front page. But not all organizations have the ability to promote their URL via other media. One of the myths of our digital democracy is that what rises to the top of the pile is what is most popular. By this logic, sexism and pornography are the most popular values on the Internet when it comes to women. There is more to result ranking than simply "voting" with our clicks.

Search engines have the potential to display information and counternarratives that don't prioritize the most explicit, racist, or sexist formulations around identity. We could experience freedom from such contrived and stereotypical representations by not supporting companies that foster a lack of social, political, and economic context in search engine results, especially as search engines are being given so much power in schools, libraries, and in the public domain. We could read more for knowledge and understanding and search less for decontextualized snippets of information. We could support more funding for public resources like schools and libraries, rather than outsourcing knowledge to big corporations. We need more sophisticated and thoughtful rankings of results that account for historical discrimination and misrepresentation. Otherwise, it appears that identity-based search results could be nothing more than old bigotry packaged in new media.

Topics for Critical Thinking and Writing

1. Identify the problem Safiya Umoja Noble proposes at the beginning of her article. As thoroughly as you can, describe the problem. Is it a problem particular to African American girls? Explain.
2. Do you think Noble singles out Google unfairly? Why, or why not?
3. What is Noble's purpose (or purposes) in writing this essay? Does she argue that anything should be done to correct biases she discusses in her article? If so, what? What might you add to the list of things that can be done to lessen the impact of racial, gender, and class biases in search engines?
4. Analyze the statistics Noble cites in paragraph 19. How do these statistics contribute to her argument? What do you think she is trying to say in offering these statistics?

Analyzing a Visual: Predictive Search

Topics for Critical Thinking and Writing

1. In her essay, Safiya Umoja Noble imagines that readers will try searching on their own to see what kinds of results are returned (para. 11). Examine the results in this image. Do they confirm or refute Noble's claims? Since her article was published, search engine companies have attempted to rectify clear instances of racial and other biases in search results. Do you think the problem is solved? Why, or why not?
2. In approximately 500 words, write about a time when you believed that your searches for information were affected by predictive algorithms that suggested results based on popularity or your own previous usage. Consider questions such as the following: Did you feel like the technologies made undue assumptions about what results would be best for you? Were you led to advertising sites? Were the best results obscured by paying or popular companies that rose to the top of the list? Refer to the visual — or provide your own for analysis — in your answer.

ALEX P. MILLER

Alex P. Miller, a researcher in digital experimentation and machine learning, is completing his doctoral degree in Information Systems and Technology at the Wharton School, University of Pennsylvania. This article appeared on Towards Data Science, a platform on Medium.com, on January 11, 2018.

Why Do We Care So Much about Explainable Algorithms? In Defense of the Black Box

Algorithms are starting to be used in applications with high-stakes consequences across a variety of domains. These include sentencing criminals, making medical prescriptions, and hiring employees. In response to this shift towards AI-driven decision making, much ink has been spilled and many brows furled in consternation about the problem of "black box" machine learning algorithms.[1] Many journalists and critics have thoughtfully pointed to the potential of algorithms discriminating against minorities, loading on spurious variables that shouldn't affect consequential decisions, and using inscrutably complicated logic that can't be rationalized by any human being.

In many situations, these concerns are well-founded and algorithms should be implemented with a great deal of caution. However, as we continue to find new applications for machine learning algorithms, we should not let this focus on algorithmic explainability blind us from a harsh truth about the world: human decisions are often capricious, irrational, and not any more explainable than the most opaque algorithm out there.

CONTEXT MATTERS

For purposes of this discussion, it's useful to break down applications of algorithms into two categories: one category is for when algorithms are being used to automate a decision that is currently made by humans; the other category is for applications in which algorithms are being used to replace rule-based processes. Rule-based processes are those in which a simple set of easily-measured criteria are used to make a decision. Rule-based processes are great precisely because they are so scrutable. Of course, the rules themselves might not be great (as in many mandatory sentencing statutes), but at least rules-based processes have clearly articulated criteria that can be debated and evaluated against other proposals.

The value of "explainability" in this second category of applications is quite apparent. Moving from a rules-based world to the black box world of random forests and neural nets[2] can understandably be disorienting for policymakers. If a university used to use simple SAT and GPA cutoffs for admissions decisions, replacing this process with a deep neural net trained on dozens of features would clearly raise some specific questions about how SAT

[1]**"black box" machine learning algorithms** Refers to artificial intelligence systems that solve problems without being programmed to do so. [Editors' note]

[2]**random forests and neural nets** Complex algorithmic decision-making programs modeled on randomized decision trees and the structure of neurons, respectively. [Editors' note]

scores and GPAs factor into the algorithm's admissions decisions.

However, I do not think the same standards of explainability should be required for applications from the first category — when algorithms are being used to replace purely human decisions. As I've mentioned elsewhere (and other researchers have emphasized as well), it is important to evaluate the utility of algorithms against the system that they are replacing. This is why the distinction between the two types of applications — those replacing humans and those replacing rules — is important. And when we focus specifically on applications in which algorithms are replacing humans, it becomes clear that explainability is an indefensible double standard.

HUMANS ARE PREDICTABLY IRRATIONAL

While the latest advancements in machine learning and algorithmic decision making have taken place fairly recently, human brains have been around for a long time. There is plenty of new research emerging about how algorithms make decisions, but researchers have had decades (if not millennia!) to investigate how the human brain makes decisions. And one of the most replicable and consistent findings from this research is that extraneous factors affect human decisions in almost every context imaginable.

A simple example of this is what psychologists call the "anchoring effect." To demonstrate just how easily humans are influenced by irrelevant information, consider this classic study by Ariely, Lowenstein, & Prelec (2003): The researchers asked students to write down the last two digits of their social security numbers and indicate whether they would be willing to pay that amount for a box of chocolates. To elicit the students' true valuation of the chocolates, they then had the students bid on the box in an enforced auction. While it should be clear to you and me that the last two digits of your SSN (essentially a random number) should have no bearing on how much you value a box of chocolates, the researchers found a significant correlation between the SSN digits and the students' actual willingness-to-pay. Furthermore, despite statistical evidence to the contrary, the vast majority of students insisted that their SSN digits had zero impact on their bids.

Another widely publicized example of irrelevant factors influencing human decisions is the "hungry judges" study. The study's results suggest that judges are more likely to grant favorable parole decisions to defendants just after their lunch break (when their stomachs are full) than just before their lunch break (when their blood sugar is low).

Maybe you have some misgivings about these particular examples: they feel too contrived, the stakes aren't high enough, the sample sizes weren't big enough, or the confounding variables weren't sufficiently controlled for. (Valid criticisms do exist; for example, see Fudenberg et al., "On the Robustness of Anchoring Effects in WTP and WTA Experiments," from *American Economic Journal*; and Lakens, "Impossibly Hungry Judges," *Nautilus*.) You are more than welcome to ignore these studies, but there are hundreds of well-researched examples of major cognitive biases. Indeed, the behavioral economist Richard Thaler recently won the Nobel Prize, largely for his career's worth of work demonstrating that these cognitive biases persist even in high-stakes situations with significant consequences. What you can't ignore is the overwhelming conclusion from this vast body of research on judgment and decision making: humans consistently let extraneous factors affect their decisions.

AT LEAST WE CAN EXPLAIN OURSELVES . . . RIGHT?

While cognitive biases are pernicious themselves, what's worse is that when you ask people to explain their decisions, they often have no idea why they acted the way they did. Just as Ariely's students insisted that their social security numbers did not affect how they perceived the box of chocolates, we often aren't even aware of how biases enter into our thought processes. Furthermore, even when we do provide plausible reasons for a particular decision, there is ample evidence that these are often mere confabulations.

A classic paper that demonstrates these effects is "Telling more than we can know" by Nisbett and Wilson (1977). I highly recommend reading the entire paper to fully appreciate just how absurdly common it is for humans to pull plausible rationalizations out of thin air, but I will let a simple summary from their abstract illustrate the point:

> Evidence is reviewed which suggests that there may be little or no direct introspective access to higher order cognitive processes. Subjects are sometimes (a) unaware of the existence of a stimulus that importantly influenced a response, (b) unaware of the existence of the response, and (c) unaware that the stimulus has affected the response.

This is all a fancy academic way of saying that people often have no idea why they made a particular decision, even when researchers can statistically prove that extraneous factors are involved.

ALGORITHMS AREN'T SO BAD AFTER ALL

When we properly evaluate the use of algorithms to automate human decisions — by keeping in mind the prevalence and predictability of our own cognitive biases — they actually start to look quite favorable in comparison. At least an algorithm will give you the same answer at both the beginning and end of its shift. Algorithms also don't have any social reputations or egos to maintain. So when we start peeking under the hood and investigating how they arrived at a particular decision, they can't defend themselves with seemingly plausible, post hoc, just-so rationalizations.

Don't get me wrong: I am all for a better understanding of how opaque algorithms make their decisions. But it's time we stop fooling ourselves into believing that human beings are any less opaque when it comes to rationalizing their decisions. In fact, it is only with the determinism and consistency of algorithms — not the unpredictability and capriciousness of humans — that we can even begin to rigorously interrogate their logic and measure their improvement over time.

WE LOSE UNDERSTANDING, BUT WE GAIN RESULTS

To a social scientist or economist, explainability is absolutely paramount: the primary goal in most scientific research is to arrive a *theory* that explains how and why things work the way they do. However, to a consequentialist — i.e., someone who's principal concern is about what is actually happening in the world — explainability must take a back seat. If we care about reducing the amount of racial injustice and increasing equitable access for all classes of people, then this is the metric by which we should compare human and algorithmic decision makers.

So long as algorithms actually do reduce bias and discrimination — as they have been shown to do in existing studies on the topic — we should sideline explainability as a secondary priority. Ensuring that algorithms be explainable is no doubt a valuable goal — but those who insist on explainability must ask whether this goal is more valuable than actual outcomes in the systems we are seeking to improve.

WORKS CITED

Dan Ariely, George Loewenstein, Drazen Prelec. 2003. "Coherent Arbitrariness": Stable Demand Curves Without Stable Preferences. *The Quarterly Journal of Economics*, 118 (1): 73–106.

Richard E. Nisbett and Timothy DeCamp Wilson. 1977. Telling More Than We Can Know: Verbal Reports on Mental Processes. *Psychological Review*, 84 (3): 231–259.

Topics for Critical Thinking and Writing

1. In comparing algorithmic and human decision making in paragraph 5, Alex P. Miller writes, "explainability is an indefensible double standard." What does he mean?
2. Examine *ethos* as it pertains to both Noble's essay and Miller's essay. How does each author establish *ethos* similarly and differently?
3. In paragraph 9, Miller remarks that "humans consistently let extraneous factors affect their decisions." In 500 to 750 words, discuss an instance (or more than one) in which human beings — people in general, you, or someone you know — make poor or irrational decisions or judgments contrary to reason. Why are the decisions wrong or unreasonable? What might people do to make better decisions?
4. Describe in about 500 words a recent important or significant decision you made, one that had consequences for yourself or others. What thinking processes did you use when considering your decision? Do you think you were influenced by any biases or extraneous factors in making your decision?
5. Do you think that "an algorithm will give you the same answer at both the beginning and end of its shift" (para. 12) proves that algorithms are better or fairer than humans in making decisions? Can you think of circumstances in which you would rather have a computer make an important decision and times when you would rather have a human? Why?
6. Many online dating apps use algorithms to match potential couples based on their usage patterns and habits, such as whether or not they log in during the early morning or late night hours or how frequently they interact with people with tattoos or with people with certain physical features. Do you think algorithms can help people find love successfully? Or do you think love should remain something that is pursued in "real life"? What are the advantages and disadvantages of each?

15

(Un)safe Spaces: Can We Tolerate Intolerant Speech on Campus?

JULIA SERANO

Julia Serano (b. 1967) is an author, activist, and biologist based in Oakland, California. She has written three books, and her work has appeared in numerous publications, including *Time*, the *Guardian*, and *Ms*. This selection was originally posted on Medium.com on February 6, 2017.

Free Speech and the Paradox of Tolerance

Any time activists (regardless of affiliation) protest a public speaking event, or the publication of a particular book or article, there will inevitably be claims that such actions threaten "free speech" or constitute "censorship." Lately, these sorts of claims have been heard following the presidential-inauguration-day silencing (via punching) of white nationalist leader Richard Spencer while he was being interviewed, and after protesters attempted to force the cancellation of Brietbart editor Milo Yiannopoulos's speaking engagements at University of Washington and UC Berkeley. Some people who take such a stance do so for purely political reasons — they share Spencer's and Yiannopoulos's views, and invoke "free speech" to make their ideologies appear unassailable. Many others who do not share these views may instead adhere to *free speech absolutism*, and their reasoning might be summarized as follows:

1. The First Amendment to the Constitution (or analogous statutes in other countries) ensures our right to "freedom of speech."
2. Therefore, even if we detest Spencer's and Yiannopoulos's extreme racist, misogynistic, and xenophobic beliefs, we must nevertheless defend their right to freely express them.
3. Any attempt to suppress or silence Spencer or Yiannopoulos (or their views) is essentially an attack on freedom of speech itself. And once we start down that slippery slope, it is only a matter of time before we find that our own freedom of speech is in jeopardy as well.

While the free speech absolutist position may sound compelling on the surface —

indeed, it is what most of us were taught in school, and what most intellectuals espouse — the reality is not nearly so clear-cut. For instance, the courts have ruled that false statements of fact, defamation, obscenity, fighting words, and incitement (e.g., shouting "fire" in a crowded theater) do not qualify as protected speech. There are also occasions where our right to free speech bumps up against (and therefore, may be restricted by) other rights (e.g., privacy) and laws (e.g., copyright protection).

Aforementioned exceptions aside, while the First Amendment prohibits the government from passing laws that prohibit our freedom of speech (plus freedom of press, the right to peaceably assemble, and so on), this by no means guarantees us the right to speak our minds however and wherever we want. I obviously do not have the right to give a speech in your living room, or to force you to publish my article in your newspaper. And of course, free speech does not shield us from criticism: If you don't like what I have to say, then you have every right (via your freedom of speech) to criticize me, sign a petition condemning me, and/or protest my next public appearance. An organization is free to invite me to give a talk in their space, but they are also free to rescind that invitation upon further consideration (e.g., if they think that I might offend or injure members of their community, or if they simply want to avoid "bad press" — yet another manifestation of freedom of expression).

In other words, we have the right to free speech, but that right is somewhat limited. We are by no means entitled to "free speech without criticism or consequences," nor are we entitled to an audience.

5 While it is important to keep these well-established limitations on free speech in mind, what I really want to focus on in this essay — especially given the steep rise in openly expressed white nationalist rhetoric over the last year — is the *paradox* of free speech. Here is what I mean: Spencer has used his right to free speech to call for "peaceful ethnic cleansing" — presumably this entails scaring people into fleeing and/or using the legal system to forcibly purge all people of color and indigenous peoples from the United States. Wouldn't that be tantamount to silencing these groups, thereby violating their freedom of speech (not to mention countless other rights)? Or take what happened to actor/comedian Leslie Jones last summer: She was forced to leave the social media platform Twitter and had to shut down her personal website after Yiannopoulos incited a fierce campaign of doxxing[1] and harassment against her. In other words, he used his free speech to suppress her free speech. (And for the record, he has done this to many other people.)

Hate speech, and other speech acts designed to harass and intimidate (rather than merely express criticism or dissent), are routinely used to thwart other people's freedom of expression. Free speech absolutists tend not to consider or fully appreciate this, probably because most of them have never felt silenced by pervasive or systemic hatred and intolerance before. Others of us, however, have experienced this firsthand.

I grew up during the 1970s and '80s, during a time when transgender people were extremely stigmatized and not tolerated by society at large. As a child, I saw how gender-variant people were openly and relentlessly mocked, so I decided not to tell anyone about what I was experiencing. As a young adult, I continued to remain quiet about my identity.

[1]**doxxing** From *dox*, an abbreviation for documents. Doxxing refers to researching and posting private information about an individual on the internet. [Editors' note.]

Colloquially, we call this being "in the closet," but that's just a fancy way of saying "hiding from hate speech and harassment." Of course, I *technically* had free speech, but that doesn't count for much if speaking your mind is likely to result in you being bombarded with epithets, losing your job, being ostracized by your community, and possibly other forms of retribution. When I attended my first transgender support group in the early '90s, we held our meetings in a secret location because, despite our First Amendment right to peaceably assemble, it was simply not safe for us to meet in public or be discovered by others.

Free speech absolutists love to cite George Orwell's *1984* as harbinger of what might come to pass if we fail to adhere to complete unadulterated free speech. I find this ironic, as it was my favorite book growing up. This was not because I was fascinated with its futuristic dystopian setting, but because the world it described very much reflected my own personal circumstances. I identified with the main character Winston — the panic he felt as he wrote in his journal, his fear of what might happen if he were ever found out. Years later, I would name myself Julia after the female protagonist of the book — like me, she was a passionate person who kept that part of herself hidden from an inhospitable world; she was a survivor who took pride in her ability to conceal what she was really thinking.

I think that "freedom of speech" is a lovely aphorism. And aphorisms are useful. But I am not gullible enough to believe that "free speech" (as free speech absolutists envision it) actually exists, or that it is something that I have ever truly possessed. The truth of the matter is that there are two types of speech or expression: those that we (either as individuals, or as a society) are willing to tolerate, and those that we do not. You may cherish a particular word, idea, expression, or identity. But if enough people collectively refuse to tolerate it, well . . . you can shout "free speech!" at the top of your lungs all you want, but it isn't going to protect you.

10 Believing that freedom of speech is generally a good thing — an ideal worth striving for — but also knowing that speech can be (and often is) used to suppress other people's freedom of expression, the question becomes: How do we best strike a balance between these two competing forces? I remember expressing a potential solution to this problem in a conversation that I had with a friend in the late '90s. I told him that I tolerate all forms of expression, except for expressions that convey intolerance toward others. My friend was a free speech absolutist, and found my pronouncement to be hypocritical. He argued that being intolerant of intolerance was itself a form of intolerance. I argued the reverse: If I tolerated intolerance, that would *not* make me a tolerant person; it would merely make me an enabler of, or accomplice to, intolerance.

Years later, thanks to the invention of Internet search engines, I discovered that the line of reasoning that I had forwarded had been previously (and more eloquently) expressed by someone who had considered this problem far longer and in more depth than most of the rest of us have. In *The Open Society and Its Enemies*, philosopher Karl Popper described this as "the paradox of tolerance." Here is how he put it:

> Unlimited tolerance must lead to the disappearance of tolerance. If we extend unlimited tolerance even to those who are intolerant, if we are not prepared to defend a tolerant society against the onslaught of the intolerant, then the tolerant will be destroyed, and tolerance with them.

Popper's words are (unfortunately) highly relevant to our current situation. (Much of *The*

Open Society and Its Enemies is concerned with how societies can avoid plummeting into totalitarianism.) There is a reason why expressions of white nationalism are suddenly cropping up everywhere — in our high schools and colleges, on social media and in the mainstream press, and worst of all, in our federal government. Until recently, we (as a society) viewed such expressions as reprehensible, and we absolutely refused to tolerate them. But Trumpism has pushed the envelope — shifted the Overton Window,[2] as they say — such that now increasing numbers of people perceive white nationalistic rhetoric to be merely "radical" rather than "unthinkable." These people (most of whom are not personally threatened by white nationalism and/or have not seriously considered the paradox of tolerance) now seem to view extreme expressions of racism and xenophobia, and the misogyny that often goes hand-in-hand with them, as merely unsavory rather than anathema. Increasingly, people are mistaking this blatant hate rhetoric for simply another form of "free speech" that we must reflexively defend.

Those of us who are passionate about free speech, and who want to live in a truly open society, cannot afford to be bystanders anymore. We must absolutely refuse to tolerate intolerant speech and the people who promote intolerant ideologies. The First Amendment may prohibit Congress from passing laws censoring white nationalist beliefs, but the rest of us are well within our rights to wholly refuse to accept, and to refuse to provide a platform for, anyone who espouses or enables such intolerant ideologies.

Skeptics might ask, "Well, how do we precisely define intolerance, and who gets to make that determination?" This is admittedly a potential point of contention (one that I plan to write about soon), but it is not formally any different from current debates we may have over what counts as protected free speech (e.g., does a particular statement constitute libel or fighting words?). While we may each have somewhat different opinions on precise definitions, I believe that we can (and should) easily come to a consensus that people who explicitly advocate ethnic cleansing (as Spencer has), or who incite campaigns of hate speech and harassment targeting women, people of color, transgender people, immigrants, and other minorities (as Yiannopoulos has), are clearly attempting to suppress other people's right to free expression, and as such, they are promoting intolerance. And we should not tolerate them!

The strategy of free speech absolutism has 15
seemed to suffice over the last fifty years, but that is not because it works per se. Rather, in a post–World War II, post–civil rights world, most (albeit not all) Americans collectively decided not to tolerate blatant unabashed bigotry — that is what kept nefarious ideologies like white nationalism at bay. But cracks are now showing in this shared public commitment. And free speech absolutism will not save us from this — if anything, it will only make matters worse by allowing intolerance to fester, to proliferate, and to garner momentum. In this sense, free speech absolutism is akin to laissez-faire approaches to economic policy: Both seem to promote unadulterated freedom (after all, what could possibly be more free than a completely hands-off approach?). But any system that entirely forgoes standards or regulations will ultimately result in atrocities, infringements on other people's rights, and the consolidation of power in the hands-off a few.

This is what we face now. And the only way to stop this from happening, to reverse this trend, is to absolutely refuse to tolerate intolerance.

[2]**Overton Window** A set of political ideas broadly acceptable to the public, named after political scientist Joseph P. Overton. [Editors' note]

Topics for Critical Thinking and Writing

1. Examine the reasoning behind free speech absolutism (enumerated in para. 1). Do you agree or disagree that we *must* defend people's rights to express racist, misogynistic, or xenophobic beliefs? Why, or why not?
2. Would you call Julia Serano's argument a *valid* argument? (See pp. 81–85 for a reminder on validity.) Why, or why not?
3. Serano points to Richard Spencer and Milo Yiannopoulos as examples of people who seek to harass and intimidate under the protection of free speech. Do you think it is reasonable to cite their intentions as a good reason to prohibit further speeches on college campuses?
4. What are the implications of Serano's thesis — that is, if we were to accept her argument, what paradox does it lead to? Do you think Serano resolves the paradox? If so, how?
5. Characterize Serano's overall argument. If you agree with her, discuss in about 500 words the *weakest* points in the argument. If you disagree with her, discuss the *strengths* of the argument.
6. Do you agree or disagree with Karl Popper's statement in paragraph 11 that "we should consider incitement to intolerance and persecution as criminal"? Why?

Analyzing a Visual: Student Views on Speech

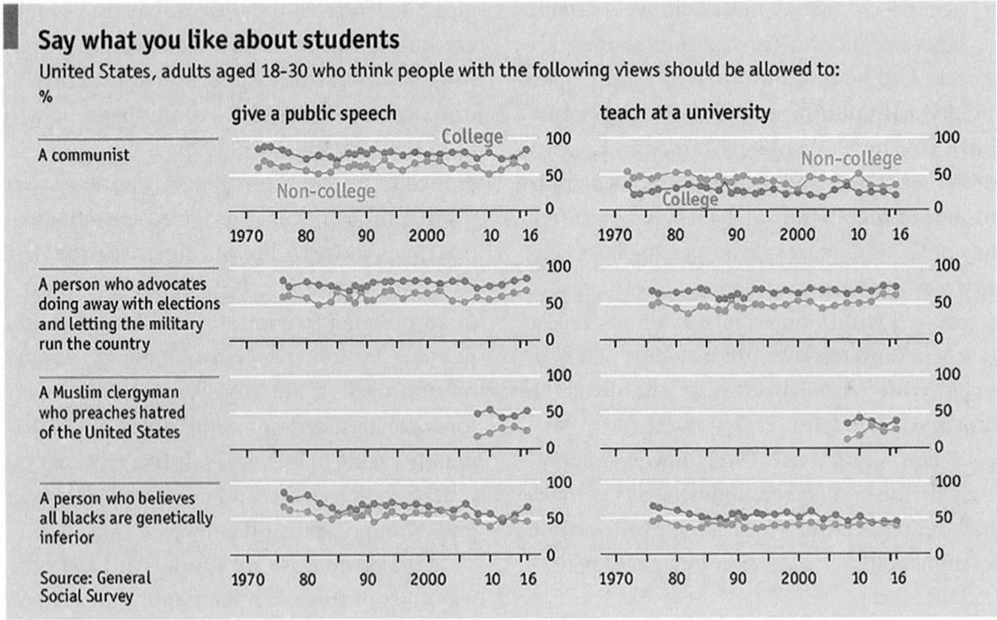

Topics for Critical Thinking and Writing

1. Between 2014 and 2017, college graduates and nongraduates went from about the same views on "communists giving a public speech" to a divergence in attitudes on this subject. What do you think explains this divergence? Compare your answers to your peers' answers and discuss how different people might interpret data differently.
2. Consider the data on "a Muslim clergyman who preaches hatred of the United States." In your view, should someone who preaches hatred of the United States be permitted to teach at a university? If you think yes, tell why and then explain any exceptions. If you think no, tell why and then explain under what circumstances such an appointment would be acceptable, if any.

   Now consider the data on "a person who believes all blacks are genetically inferior" and apply the same questions: Do you think someone who believes this should teach at a university?

   Are your answers consistent or inconsistent for the two beliefs? Explain.
3. Do you think this graph offers useful information? If so, what do you think is most useful? If not, what do you think is not useful? Does any of the information in the graph surprise you?

DEREK BOK

Derek Bok was born in 1930 in Bryn Mawr, Pennsylvania, and educated at Stanford University and Harvard University, where he received a law degree. From 1971 to 1991, he served as president of Harvard University. The following essay, first published in the *Boston Globe* in 1991, was prompted by the display of Confederate flags hung from a window of a Harvard dormitory.

Protecting Freedom of Expression on the Campus

For several years, universities have been struggling with the problem of trying to reconcile the rights of free speech with the desire to avoid racial tension. In recent weeks, such a controversy has sprung up at Harvard. Two students hung Confederate flags in public view, upsetting students who equate the Confederacy with slavery. A third student tried to protest the flags by displaying a swastika.

These incidents have provoked much discussion and disagreement. Some students have urged that Harvard require the removal of symbols that offend many members of the community. Others reply that such symbols are a form of free speech and should be protected.

Different universities have resolved similar conflicts in different ways. Some have enacted codes to protect their communities from forms of speech that are deemed to be insensitive to the feelings of other groups. Some have refused to impose such restrictions.

It is important to distinguish between the appropriateness of such communications and their status under the First Amendment. The fact that speech is protected by the First Amendment does not necessarily mean that it is right, proper, or civil. I am sure that the vast majority of Harvard students believe that hanging a Confederate flag in public view — or displaying a swastika in response — is insensitive and unwise because any satisfaction it gives to the students who display these symbols is far outweighed by the discomfort it causes to many others.

I share this view and regret that the students involved saw fit to behave in this fashion. Whether or not they merely wished to manifest their pride in the South — or to demonstrate the insensitivity of hanging Confederate flags, by mounting another offensive symbol in return — they must have known that they would upset many fellow students and ignore the decent regard for the feelings of others so essential to building and preserving a strong and harmonious community.

To disapprove of a particular form of communication, however, is not enough to justify prohibiting it. We are faced with a clear example of the conflict between our commitment to free speech and our desire to foster a community founded on mutual respect. Our society has wrestled with this problem for many years. Interpreting the First Amendment, the Supreme Court has clearly struck the balance in favor of free speech.

While communities do have the right to regulate speech in order to uphold aesthetic standards (avoiding defacement of buildings) or to protect the public from disturbing noise, rules of this kind must be applied across the board and cannot be enforced selectively to prohibit certain kinds of messages but not others.

Under the Supreme Court's rulings, as I read them, the display of swastikas or Confederate flags clearly falls within the protection of the free-speech clause of the First Amendment and cannot be forbidden simply because it offends the feelings of many members of the community. These rulings apply to all agencies of government, including public universities.

Although it is unclear to what extent the First Amendment is enforceable against private institutions, I have difficulty understanding why a university such as Harvard should have less free speech than the surrounding society — or than a public university.

One reason why the power of censorship is so dangerous is that it is extremely difficult to decide when a particular communication is offensive enough to warrant prohibition or to weigh the degree of offensiveness against the potential value of the communication. If we begin to forbid flags, it is only a short step to prohibiting offensive speakers.

I suspect that no community will become humane and caring by restricting what its members can say. The worst offenders will simply find other ways to irritate and insult.

In addition, once we start to declare certain things "offensive," with all the excitement and attention that will follow, I fear that much ingenuity will be exerted trying to test the limits, much time will be expended trying to draw tenuous distinctions, and the resulting publicity will eventually attract more attention to the offensive material than would ever have occurred otherwise.

Rather than prohibit such communications, with all the resulting risks, it would be better to ignore them, since students would then have little reason to create such displays and would soon abandon them. If this response is not possible — and one can understand why — the wisest course is to speak with those who perform insensitive acts and try to help them understand the effects of their actions on others.

Appropriate officials and faculty members should take the lead, as the Harvard House Masters have already done in this case. In talking with students, they should seek to educate and persuade, rather than resort to ridicule or intimidation, recognizing that only persuasion is likely to produce a lasting, beneficial effect. Through such efforts, I believe that we act in the manner most consistent with our ideals as an educational institution and most calculated to help us create a truly understanding, supportive community.

Topics for Critical Thinking and Writing

1. Derek Bok sketches the following argument (paras. 8 and 9): The First Amendment protects free speech in public universities and colleges; Harvard is not a public university; therefore, Harvard does not enjoy the protection of the First Amendment. Bok finds this argument invalid. He clearly rejects the conclusion, stating in paragraph 9, "I have difficulty understanding why . . . Harvard should have less free speech . . . than a public university." What would need to be revised in the premises to make that argument valid? Do you think Bok would accept or reject such a revision? Why, or why not?
2. Bok objects to censorship that simply prevents students from being "offended." He would not object to the campus police preventing students from being harmed. In about 200 words, explain the difference between conduct that is *harmful* and conduct that is *offensive*. (If you think such a distinction cannot be made, explain why.)
3. Bok advises campus officials (and students) to "ignore" offensive words, flags, and so forth (para. 13). Do you agree with this advice? In about 500 words, tell why, or why not.
4. Do you think Bok's argument is applicable to schools today? In what ways might new conditions in the present — as discussed by Serano, for example — challenge or complicate Bok's argument? What issues must a college president today consider when facing intolerant symbols or speech on campus? Do these issues justify limitations or curtailments of speech?
5. Visit the website of FIRE, the Foundation for Individual Rights in Education, a nonprofit group dedicated to protecting free speech on college campuses. On the homepage, you will see a button for "cases," leading you to news items involving conflicts over freedom of speech on campus. Select a case and profile it in about 500 words. What kind of speech is under scrutiny? What groups are involved? What does each side say? How have officials responded? If possible, seek additional sources to learn as much as you can about the case.

16

The Current State of Childhood: Is "Helicopter Parenting" the "Problem" with Millennials?

NICK GILLESPIE

Nick Gillespie (b. 1963) is a journalist and political commentator who served as the editor in chief for the libertarian magazine *Reason* from 2001 to 2008 and then for Reason.com and Reason TV until 2017, where he is currently an editor at large. Gillespie, who holds a doctorate in literature from the State University of New York at Buffalo, is also a co-author of *The Declaration of Independents: How Libertarian Politics Can Fix What's Wrong with America* (2011). This article was originally published in *Time* as an opinion piece on parenting on August 21, 2014.

Millennials Are Selfish and Entitled, and Helicopter Parents Are to Blame

It's natural to resent younger Americans — *they're younger!* — but we're on the verge of a new generation gap that may make the nasty old fights between baby boomers and *their* "Greatest Generation" parents look like something out of a Norman Rockwell painting.

Seventy-one percent of American adults think of 18-to-29-year-olds — millennials, basically — as "selfish," and 65% of us think of them as "entitled." That's according to the latest Reason-Rupe Poll, a quarterly survey of 1,000 representative adult Americans.

If millennials are self-absorbed little monsters who expect the world to come to them and for their parents to clean up their rooms well into their 20s, we've got no one to blame but ourselves — especially the moms and dads among us.

Indeed, the same poll documents the ridiculous level of kid-coddling that has now become the new normal. More than two-thirds of us think there ought to be a law that kids as old as 9 should be supervised while playing at a public park, which helps explain (though not justify) the arrest of a South Carolina mother who let her phone-enabled daughter play in a busy park while she worked at a nearby McDonald's. We think on average that kids should be 10 years old before they "are allowed to play in the front yard unsupervised." Unless you live on a traffic island or a war zone, that's just nuts.

5 It gets worse: We think that our precious bundles of joy should be 12 before they can wait alone in a car for five minutes on a cool day or walk to school without an adult, and that they should be 13 before they can be trusted to stay home alone. You'd think that kids raised on *Baby Einstein* DVDs should be a little more advanced than that.

Curiously, this sort of ridiculous hyperprotectiveness is playing out against a backdrop in which children are safer than ever. Students reporting bullying is one-third of what it was 20 years ago, and according to a study in *JAMA Pediatrics*, the past decade has seen massive declines in exposure to violence for kids. Out of 50 trends studied, summarize the authors, "there were 27 significant declines and no significant increases between 2003 and 2011. Declines were particularly large for assault victimization, bullying, and sexual victimization. There were also significant declines in the perpetration of violence and property crime."

There are surely many causes for the mainstreaming of helicopter parenting. Kids cost a hell of a lot to raise. The U.S. Department of Agriculture figures a child born in 2013 will set back middle-income parents about $245,000 up to age 17 (and that's before college bills kick in). We're having fewer children, so we're putting fewer eggs in a smaller basket, so to speak. According to the Reason-Rupe poll, only 27% of adults thought the media were overestimating threats to the day-to-day safety of children, suggesting that 73% of us are suckers for sensationalistic news coverage that distorts reality (62% of us erroneously think that today's youth face greater dangers than previous generations). More kids are in institutional settings — whether preschool or school itself — at earlier ages, so maybe parents just assume someone will always be on call.

But whatever the reasons for our insistence that we childproof the world around us, this way madness lies. From *King Lear* to *Mildred Pierce*, classic literature (and basic common sense) suggests that coddling kids is no way to raise thriving, much less grateful, offspring. Indeed, quite the opposite. And with 58% of millennials calling *themselves* "entitled" and more than 70% saying they are "selfish," older Americans may soon be learning that lesson the hard way.

Topics for Critical Thinking and Writing

1. In paragraphs 4 and 5, Nick Gillespie cites a number of statistics indicating support for restrictions on when and where children can be on their own. He ends paragraph 4 with the statement, "Unless you live on a traffic island or a war zone, that's just nuts." Does the dismissive tone of that statement undercut Gillespie's argument? In your opinion, what would have been a more convincing response to parental concerns about their children's safety?
2. Gillespie states in paragraph 6 that contrary to popular belief, "children are safer than ever." He cites a study that shows the decline in violence against children between 2003 and 2011. What does Gillespie suggest are the reasons that popular perceptions of danger toward children have increased? Do you agree with his argument? Why, or why not?

3. Gillespie's final paragraph ends with an implied threat: Children who have been coddled will grow up to be selfish adults who will ignore the needs of their parents when they reach their senior years. Do you agree with Gillespie's assessment? Why, or why not?

Analyzing a Visual: Overparenting

Kansas City Star/Getty Images

Topics for Critical Thinking and Writing

1. Explain the visual metaphor presented in this image as extensively as you can. What does the image suggest about parents? What does it suggest about children? Is the image effective? How?
2. Provide a reading of the image above that negotiates the meaning of the intended message (see Chapter 4, pp. 146–48). To do so, account for some of the ways the image shown overstates the problem or ignores aspects of parenting that may be important to children's development.

3. Make a list (on your own or collaboratively) of as many things you can think of that parents "do" for their children's benefit, protection, or well-being. Which items on your list might be considered reasonable, and which might be considered too much parenting? Discuss, or pick one you think is "overparenting" and tell why.

ALFIE KOHN

Alfie Kohn (b. 1957) has made a career of being a critic of conventional wisdom regarding education, parenting, and human behavior. In his many books, Kohn has argued against the use of grades, standardized testing, homework, values education, conventional parenting and discipline practices, and even workplace incentives. This excerpt is from his 2014 book published by Beacon Press, *The Myth of the Spoiled Child: Challenging the Conventional Wisdom about Children and Parenting.*

The One-Sided Culture War against Children

Have a look at the unsigned editorials in left-of-center newspapers, or essays by columnists whose politics are mostly progressive. Listen to speeches by liberal public officials. On any of the controversial issues of our day, from tax policy to civil rights, you'll find approximately what you'd expect.

But when it comes to schooling and education, almost all of them take a hard-line position very much like what we hear from conservatives. In education, they endorse a top-down, corporate-style version of school reform that includes prescriptive, one-size-fits-all teaching standards and curriculum mandates; weakened job protection for teachers; frequent standardized testing; and a reliance on rewards and punishments to raise scores on those tests and compel compliance on the part of teachers and students.

Admittedly, there is some disagreement about the proper role of the federal government in all of this — and also about the extent to which public schooling should be privatized — but otherwise, liberal Democrats and conservative Republicans, the *New York Times* and the *Daily Oklahoman*, sound the identical themes of "accountability," "raising the bar" and "global competitiveness" (meaning that education is conceived primarily in economic terms). President Barack Obama didn't just continue George W. Bush's education policies; he intensified them, piling the harsh test-driven mandates of a program called "Race to the Top" on the harsh test-driven mandates of "No Child Left Behind."

Applause for this agenda has come not only from corporate America but also from both sides of the aisle in Congress and every major media outlet in the United States. Indeed, the generic phrase "school reform" has come to be equated with these specific get-tough policies. To object to them is to risk being labeled a defender of the "status quo," even though they have defined the status quo for some time now.

Many of the people who have objected are 5 teachers and other education experts who see firsthand just how damaging this approach has been, particularly to low-income students and the schools that serve them. But a key element of "reform" is to define educators as part of the problem, so their viewpoint has mostly been dismissed.

What's true of attitudes about education is also largely true of the way we think about children in general — what they're like and how they should be raised. Of course, politicians are far less likely to speak (or newspapers to editorialize) about parenting. But columnists do weigh in from time to time and, when they do, those who are generally liberal — like the *New York Times*' Frank Bruni, the *Boston Globe*'s Scot Lehigh and the late William Raspberry of the *Washington Post* — once again do a remarkable imitation of conservatives. Articles about parenting in general-interest periodicals, meanwhile, reflect the same trend. The range of viewpoints on other topics gives way to a stunningly consistent perspective where children are concerned.

That perspective sounds something like this:

- We live in an age of indulgence in which permissive parents refuse to set limits for, or say no to, their children.
- Parents overprotect their kids rather than let them suffer the natural consequences of their own mistakes. Children would benefit from experiencing failure, but their parents are afraid to let that happen.
- Adults are so focused on making kids feel special that we're raising a generation of entitled narcissists. They get trophies even when their team didn't win; they're praised even when they didn't do anything impressive; and they receive A's for whatever they turn in at school. Alas, they'll be in for a rude awakening once they get out into the unforgiving real world.
- What young people need — and lack — is not self-esteem but self-discipline: the ability to defer gratification, control their impulses and persevere at tasks over long periods of time.

These "traditionalist" convictions (for lack of a better word) are heard everywhere and repeated endlessly. Taken together, they have become our society's conventional wisdom about children, to the point that whenever a newspaper or magazine addresses any of these topics, it will almost always be from this direction. If the subject is self-esteem, the thesis will be that children have an oversupply. If the subject is discipline (and limits imposed by parents), the writer will insist that kids today get too little. And perseverance or "grit" is always portrayed positively, never examined skeptically.

This widespread adoption of a traditionalist perspective helps us to make sense of the fact that, on topics related to children, even liberals tend to hold positions whose premises are deeply conservative. Perhaps it works the other way around as well: The fact that people on the left and center find themselves largely in agreement with those on the right explains how the traditionalist viewpoint has become the conventional wisdom. Child rearing might be described as a hidden front in the culture wars, except that no one is fighting on the other side.

Writing a book about the conventional 10
wisdom on childrearing, I've had to track down research studies on the relevant issues so as to be able to distinguish truth from myth. But I've also come across dozens of articles in the popular press, articles with titles like "Spoiled Rotten: Why Do Kids Rule the Roost?" (*New Yorker*, 7/2/12), "How to Land Your Kid in Therapy" (*Atlantic*, 6/7/11), "Just Say No: Why Parents Must Set Limits for Kids

Who Want It All" (*Newsweek*, 9/12/04), "Parents and Children: Who's in Charge Here?" (*Time*, 8/6/01), "The Child Trap: The Rise of Overparenting" (*New Yorker* again, 11/17/08), "The Abuse of Overparenting" (*Psychology Today*, 4/2/12), "The Trouble with Self-Esteem" (*New York Times Magazine*, 2/3/12) and "Millennials: The Me Me Me Generation" (*Time* again, 5/9/13), to name just a few.

If you've read one of these articles, you've pretty much read all of them. The same goes for newspaper columns, blog posts and books on the same themes. Pick any one of them at random and the first thing you'll notice is that it treats a diverse assortment of complaints as if they're interchangeable. Parents are criticized for hovering and also for being too lax (with no acknowledgment that these are two very different things). In one sentence, kids are said to have too many toys; in the next, they're accused of being disrespectful. Or unmotivated. Or self-centered.

Anything that happens to annoy the writer may be tossed into the mix. Kids are exposed to too many ads! Involved in too many extra-curricular activities! Distracted by too much technology! They're too materialistic and individualistic and narcissistic — probably because they were raised by parents who are pushy, permissive, progressive. (If the writer is an academic, a single label may be used to organize the indictment — "intensive parenting" or "nurturance overload," for example — but a bewildering variety of phenomena are offered as examples.)

In fact, the generalizations offered in these books and articles sometimes seem not merely varied but contradictory. We're told that parents push their children too hard to excel (by ghostwriting their homework and hiring tutors, and demanding that they triumph over their peers), but also that parents try to protect kids from competition (by giving trophies to everyone), that expectations have declined, that too much attention is paid to making children happy.

Similarly, young adults are described as self-satisfied twits — more pleased with themselves than their accomplishments merit — but also as being so miserable that they're in therapy. Or there's an epidemic of helicopter parenting, even though parents are so focused on their gadgets that they ignore their children. The assumption seems to be that readers will just nod right along, failing to note any inconsistencies, as long as the tone is derogatory and the perspective is traditionalist.

Rarely are any real data cited — either 15
about the prevalence of what's being described or the catastrophic effects being alleged. Instead, writers tend to rely primarily on snarky anecdotes, belaboring them to give the impression that these carefully chosen examples are representative of the general population, along with quotes from authors who accept and restate the writer's thesis about permissive parents and entitled kids who have never experienced failure.

Oddly, though, even as these writers repeat what everyone else is saying, they present themselves as courageous contrarians who are boldly challenging the conventional wisdom.

Perhaps the experience of reading all those articles — sloppy, contradictory or unpersuasive though they may be — wouldn't have been so irritating if it were also possible to find essays that questioned the dominant assumptions, essays that might have been titled "The New Puritanism: Who Really Benefits When Children Are Trained to Put Work before Play?" or "Why Parents Are So Controlling . . . and How It Harms Their Kids" or "The Invention of 'Helicopter Parenting': Creating a Crisis out of Thin Air." If anything along these lines has appeared in a mainstream publication, I've been unable to locate it.

The numbing uniformity of writings on children and parenting, and the lack of critical inspection on which the consensus rests, is troubling in itself. When countless publications offer exactly the same indictment of spoiled children and entitled Millennials — and accuse their parents of being lax or indulgent — this has a very real impact on the popular consciousness, just as a barrage of attack ads, no matter how misleading, can succeed in defining a political candidate in the minds of voters. But of course what matters more than whether a consensus exists is whether it makes sense, whether there's any merit to the charges.

Consider the accusation that parents involve themselves too closely in their children's lives and don't allow them to fail. It's common to come across — in fact, it's hard to avoid — hyperbolic references in the media to "kids who leave for college without ever having crossed the street by themselves" (*New York Times*, 2/9/09) and "'Lawnmower Parents' [who] have 'mowed down' so many obstacles (including interfering at their children's workplaces, regarding salaries and promotions) that these kids have actually never faced failure" (*Business Insider*, 8/17/12). Just in the few years before my book went to press in 2013, articles about overparenting appeared in the *Atlantic* (1/29/13), the *New Yorker* (11/17/08), *Time* (11/30/09), *Psychology Today* (4/2/12), *Boston Magazine* (12/11) and countless newspapers and blogs.

In each case, just as with condemnations 20
of permissiveness, the phenomenon being attacked is simply assumed to be pervasive; there's no need to prove what everyone knows. The spread of overparenting is vigorously condemned by journalists and social critics, but mostly on the basis of anecdotes and quotations from other journalists and social critics. On the relatively rare occasions when a writer invokes research in support of the claim that overparenting is widespread (or damaging), it's instructive to track down the study itself to see what it actually says.

A case in point: In 2013, several prominent American blogs, including those sponsored by the *Atlantic* (1/29/13) and the *New York Times* (1/25/13), reported an Australian study purportedly showing that parents were excessively involved in their children's schooling. But anyone who took the time to actually read the study realized that the authors had just asked a handpicked group of local educators to tell stories about parents whom they personally believed were doing too much for their children. There were no data about what impact, if any, this practice had on the kids, nor was there any way to draw conclusions about how common the practice was — at least beyond this small, presumably unrepresentative sample.

More remarkably, only 27 percent of the educators in the sample report having seen "many" examples of this sort of overinvolved parenting. (This low number somehow did not make it into any of the press coverage.) If anything, the effect of the study was to raise doubts about the assumption that overparenting is a widespread problem. But the study's very existence allowed bloggers to recycle a few anecdotes, giving the appearance that fresh evidence supported what they (and many of their readers) already believed.

Another example: In 2010, Lisa Belkin, a writer for the *New York Times Magazine*, devoted a blog post (7/19/10) to an article in a California law review (*UC Davis Law Review*, 4/12/10) that declared a tilt toward excess "has dominated parenting in the last two decades." But how did the authors of the law review article substantiate this remarkable assertion? They included a footnote that referenced a 2009 *New York Times Magazine* column (5/29/09) written by . . . Lisa Belkin.

It's striking that evidence on this topic is so scarce that academic journals must rely on opinion pieces in the popular press. But in this case, the popular press was actually claiming that the trend had already peaked. That was true not only of Belkin's column ("Could the era of overparenting be over?") but of a *Time* cover story ("The Growing Backlash against Overparenting," 11/20/09) that was cited by an essay in another academic journal. The latter essay began with the sweeping (and rather tautological[1]) statement that an "epidemic" of overparenting was "running rampant" — which is exactly what its sources claimed was no longer true.

So who's right? There are, as far as I can 25
tell, no good data to show that most parents do too much for their children. It's all impressionistic, anecdotal and, like most announcements of trends, partly self-fulfilling.

[1]**tautological** Needlessly repetitive. [Editors' note]

Topics for Critical Thinking and Writing

1. In the opening paragraphs of this excerpt, Alfie Kohn argues that otherwise liberal writers and public officials have taken conservative or "traditionalist" positions when it comes to the subject of raising children. Why does the fact that many liberals and conservatives are in agreement on this issue bother Kohn? What alternatives, if any, does he propose?
2. In paragraph 7, Kohn presents a bullet-point list of common observations that older Americans make about children and young adults today. Do you agree with the statements in the list? Why, or why not?
3. In paragraph 8, Kohn argues that values such as "perseverance or 'grit'" have not been examined skeptically. In what ways might "grit" be bad? Be specific in your response.
4. In paragraph 15, Kohn comments that most of the conclusions about children these days are not based on data but on "snarky anecdotes." What is the problem with anecdotal information? In contrast, what problems could there be with data-based research about attitudes and values? How can the limitations of either approach be solved, if indeed they can?
5. In what ways are the reports about how today's children are raised contradictory? What can account for the apparent contradictions? In particular, to what does Kohn ascribe these contradictions?

17

Genetic Modification of Human Beings: Is It Acceptable?

RONALD M. GREEN

Ronald M. Green (b. 1942) is the Eunice and Julian Cohen Professor Emeritus for the Study of Human Ethics and Human Values in the Department of Religion at Dartmouth College and a professor in the Department of Community and Family Medicine at Dartmouth's Geisel School of Medicine. He is the author of nine books, including *Babies by Design: The Ethics of Genetic Choice* (2007). This *Washington Post* article was posted online on April 13, 2008.

Building Baby from the Genes Up

The two British couples no doubt thought that their appeal for medical help in conceiving a child was entirely reasonable. Over several generations, many female members of their families had died of breast cancer. One or both spouses in each couple had probably inherited the genetic mutations for the disease, and they wanted to use in-vitro fertilization and preimplantation genetic diagnosis (PGD) to select only the healthy embryos for implantation. Their goal was to eradicate breast cancer from their family lines once and for all.

In the United States, this combination of reproductive and genetic medicine — what one scientist has dubbed "reprogenetics" — remains largely unregulated, but Britain has a formal agency, the Human Fertilization and Embryology Authority (HFEA), that must approve all requests for PGD. In July 2007, after considerable deliberation, the HFEA approved the procedure for both families. The concern was not about the use of PGD to avoid genetic disease, since embryo screening for serious disorders is commonplace now on both sides of the Atlantic. What troubled the HFEA was the fact that an embryo carrying the cancer mutation could go on to live for forty or fifty years before ever developing cancer, and there was a chance it might never develop. Did this warrant selecting and discarding embryos? To its critics, the HFEA, in approving this request, crossed a bright line separating legitimate medical genetics from the quest for "the perfect baby."

Like it or not, that decision is a sign of things to come — and not necessarily a bad sign. Since the completion of the Human Genome Project in 2003, our understanding of the genetic bases of human disease and non-disease traits has been growing almost exponentially. The National Institutes of Health has initiated a quest for the "$1,000 genome," a ten-year program to develop machines that could identify all the genetic letters in anyone's genome at low cost (it took more than $3 billion to sequence the first human genome). With this technology, which some believe may be just four or five years away, we could not only scan an individual's — or embryo's — genome, we could also rapidly compare thousands of people and pinpoint those DNA sequences or combinations that underlie the variations that contribute to our biological differences.

With knowledge comes power. If we understand the genetic causes of obesity, for example, we can intervene by means of embryo selection to produce a child with a reduced genetic likelihood of getting fat. Eventually, without discarding embryos at all, we could use gene-targeting techniques to tweak fetal DNA sequences. No child would have to face a lifetime of dieting or experience the health and cosmetic problems associated with obesity. The same is true for cognitive problems such as dyslexia. Geneticists have already identified some of the mutations that contribute to this disorder. Why should a child struggle with reading difficulties when we could alter the genes responsible for the problem?

5 Many people are horrified at the thought of such uses of genetics, seeing echoes of the 1997 science-fiction film *Gattaca*, which depicted a world where parents choose their children's traits. Human weakness has been eliminated through genetic engineering, and the few parents who opt for a "natural" conception run the risk of producing offspring — "invalids" or "degenerates" — who become members of a despised underclass. Gattaca's world is clean and efficient, but its eugenic obsessions have all but extinguished human love and compassion.

These fears aren't limited to fiction. Over the past few years, many bioethicists have spoken out against genetic manipulations. The critics tend to voice at least four major concerns. First, they worry about the effect of genetic selection on parenting. Will our ability to choose our children's biological inheritance lead parents to replace unconditional love with a consumerist mentality that seeks perfection?

Second, they ask whether gene manipulations will diminish our freedom by making us creatures of our genes or our parents' whims. In his book *Enough*, the techno-critic Bill McKibben asks: If I am a world-class runner, but my parents inserted the "Sweatworks2010 GenePack" in my genome, can I really feel pride in my accomplishments? Worse, if I refuse to use my costly genetic endowments, will I face relentless pressure to live up to my parents' expectations?

Third, many critics fear that reproductive genetics will widen our social divisions as the affluent "buy" more competitive abilities for their offspring. Will we eventually see "speciation," the emergence of two or more human populations so different that they no longer even breed with one another? Will we recreate the horrors of eugenics that led, in Europe, Asia, and the United States, to the sterilization of tens of thousands of people declared to be "unfit" and that in Nazi Germany paved the way for the Holocaust?

Finally, some worry about the religious implications of this technology. Does it amount to a forbidden and prideful "playing God"?

To many, the answers to these questions 10
are clear. Not long ago, when I asked a large class at Dartmouth Medical School whether they thought that we should move in the direction of human genetic engineering, more than 80 percent said no. This squares with public opinion polls that show a similar degree of opposition. Nevertheless, "babies by design" are probably in our future — but I think that the critics' concerns may be less troublesome than they first appear.

Will critical scrutiny replace parental love? Not likely. Even today, parents who hope for a healthy child but have one born with disabilities tend to love that child ferociously. The very intensity of parental love is the best protection against its erosion by genetic technologies. Will a child somehow feel less free because parents have helped select his or her traits? The fact is that a child is already remarkably influenced by the genes she inherits. The difference is that we haven't taken control of the process. Yet.

Knowing more about our genes may actually increase our freedom by helping us understand the biological obstacles — and opportunities — we have to work with. Take the case of Tiger Woods. His father, Earl, is said to have handed him a golf club when he was still in the playpen. Earl probably also gave Tiger the genes for some of the traits that help make him a champion golfer. Genes and upbringing worked together to inspire excellence. Does Tiger feel less free because of his inherited abilities? Did he feel pressured by his parents? I doubt it. Of course, his story could have gone the other way, with overbearing parents forcing a child into their mold. But the problem in that case wouldn't be genetics, but bad parenting.

Granted, the social effects of reproductive genetics are worrisome. The risks of producing a "genobility," genetic overlords ruling a vast genetic underclass, are real. But genetics could also become a tool for reducing the class divide. Will we see the day when perhaps all youngsters are genetically vaccinated against dyslexia? And how might this contribute to everyone's social betterment?

As for the question of intruding on God's domain, the answer is less clear than the critics believe. The use of genetic medicine to cure or prevent disease is widely accepted by religious traditions, even those that oppose discarding embryos. Speaking in 1982 at the Pontifical Academy of Sciences, Pope John Paul II observed that modern biological research "can ameliorate the condition of those who are affected by chromosomic diseases," and he lauded this as helping to cure "the smallest and weakest of human beings . . . during their intrauterine life or in the period immediately after birth." For Catholicism and some other traditions, it is one thing to cure disease, but another to create children who are faster runners, longer-lived, or smarter.

But why should we think that the human 15
genome is a once-and-for-all-finished, untamperable product? All of the biblically derived faiths permit human beings to improve on nature using technology, from agriculture to aviation. Why not improve our genome? I have no doubt that most people considering these questions for the first time are certain that human genetic improvement is a bad idea, but I'd like to shake up that certainty.

Genomic science is racing toward a future in which foreseeable improvements include reduced susceptibility to a host of diseases, increased life span, better cognitive functioning, and maybe even cosmetic enhancements such as whiter, straighter teeth. Yes, genetic orthodontics may be in our future. The challenge is to see that we don't also unleash the demons of discrimination and oppression. Although I acknowledge the risks, I believe that we can and will incorporate gene technology into the ongoing human adventure.

Topics for Critical Thinking and Writing

1. By the end of paragraph 2, did you think the British are probably right to be cautious, to require approval for all requests for PGD? Explain your position.
2. Paragraph 4 talks, by way of example, about avoiding obesity and "cognitive problems." At this stage in your reading of the essay, did you find yourself saying "Great, let's go for it," or were you thinking "Wait a minute"? Why, or why not?
3. Do paragraphs 5 and 6 pretty much set forth your own response? If not, what *is* your response?
4. Does Bill McKibben's view, mentioned in paragraph 7, represent your view? If not, what would you say to McKibben?
5. If you are a believer in any of "the biblically derived faiths," does the comment in paragraph 15 allay whatever doubts you may have had about the acceptability of human genetic improvement? Explain.
6. In his final paragraph, Ronald Green says that he acknowledges the risks of gene technology. Are you satisfied that he does acknowledge them adequately? Explain.

Analyzing a Visual: Genetic Modification of Human Beings

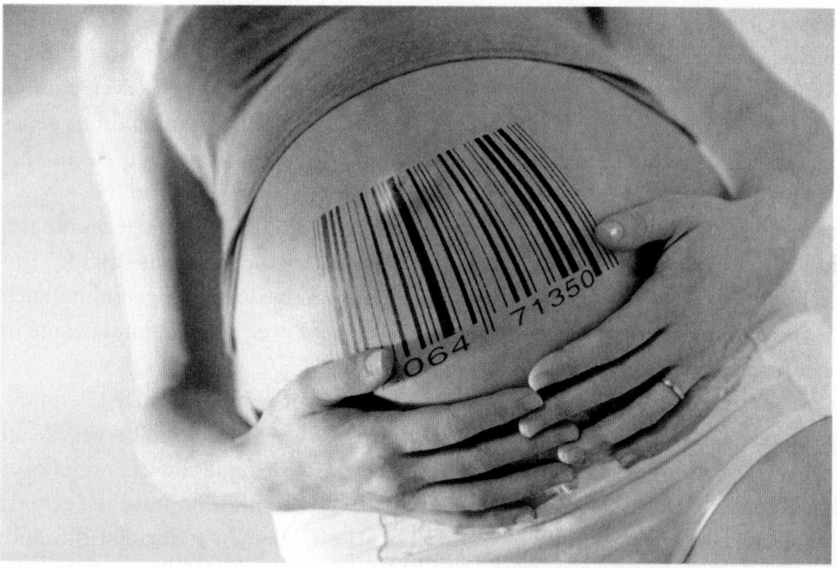

Caroline Purser/Getty Images

Topics for Critical Thinking and Writing

1. What does this photograph seem to say about human genetic modification? Why do you think the photographer included a bar code in the image? In a couple of paragraphs, analyze the ways the photo makes an argument and evaluate the photo's effectiveness.
2. Do you agree with the point of view expressed in the photograph? In 250 words, write a description of a photograph that might work as a rebuttal to this one.

RICHARD HAYES

Richard Hayes (b. 1945) is executive director of the California-based Center for Genetics and Society, an organization that describes itself as "working to encourage responsible uses and effective society governance of the new human genetic and reproductive technologies. . . . The Center supports benign and beneficent medical applications of the new human genetic and reproductive technologies, and opposes those applications that objectify and commodify human life and threaten to divide human society." Hayes is also a visiting scholar at the University of California at Berkeley College of Natural Resources. This essay originally appeared in the *Washington Post* on April 15, 2008.

Genetically Modified Humans? No Thanks

In an essay in Sunday's Outlook section, Dartmouth ethics professor Ronald Green asks us to consider a neoeugenic future of "designer babies," with parents assembling their children quite literally from genes selected from a catalogue. Distancing himself from the compulsory, state-sponsored eugenics that darkened the first half of the last century, Green instead celebrates the advent of a libertarian, consumer-driven eugenics motivated by the free play of human desire, technology, and markets. He argues that this vision of the human future is desirable and very likely inevitable.

To put it mildly: I disagree. Granted, new human genetic technologies have real potential to help prevent or cure many terrible diseases, and I support research directed towards that end. But these same technologies also have the potential for real harm. If misapplied, they would exacerbate existing inequalities and reinforce existing modes of discrimination. If more widely abused, they could undermine the foundations of civil and human rights. In the worst case, they could undermine our experience of being part of a single human community with a common human future.

Once we begin genetically modifying our children, where do we stop? If it's acceptable to modify one gene, why not two, or twenty or two hundred? At what point do children become artifacts designed to someone's specifications rather than members of a family to be nurtured?

Given what we know about human nature, the development and commercial marketing of human genetic modification would likely spark a techno-eugenic rat-race. Even parents opposed to manipulating their children's genes would feel compelled to participate in this race, lest their offspring be left behind.

Green proposes that eugenic technologies 5
could be used to reduce "the class divide." But nowhere in his essay does he suggest how such a proposal might ever be made practicable in the real world.

The danger of genetic misuse is equally threatening at the international level. What happens when some rogue country announces an ambitious program to "improve the genetic stock" of its citizens? In a world still barely able to contain the forces of nationalism, ethnocentrism, and militarism, the last thing we need to worry about is a high-tech eugenic arms race.

In his essay, Green doesn't distinguish clearly between different uses of genetic technology — and the distinctions are critical.

It's one thing to enable a couple to avoid passing on a devastating genetic condition, such as Tay-Sachs.[1] But it's a different thing altogether to create children with a host of "enhanced" athletic, cosmetic, and cognitive traits that could be passed to their own children, who in turn could further genetically modify their children, who in turn . . . you get the picture. It's this second use of gene technology (the technical term is "heritable genetic enhancement") that Green most fervently wants us to embrace.

In this position, Green is well outside the growing national and international consensus on the proper use of human genetic science and technology. To his credit, he acknowledges that 80 percent of the medical school students he surveyed said they were against such forms of human genetic engineering, and that public opinion polls show equally dramatic opposition. He could have noted, as well, that nearly forty countries — including Brazil, Canada, France, Germany, India, Japan, and South Africa — have adopted socially responsible policies regulating the new human genetic technologies. They allow genetic research (including stem cell research) for medical applications, but prohibit its use for heritable genetic modification and reproductive human cloning.

In the face of this consensus, Green blithely announces his confidence that humanity "can and will" incorporate heritable genetic enhancement into the "ongoing human adventure."

Well, it's certainly possible. Our desires for 10
good looks, good brains, wealth and long lives, for ourselves and for our children, are strong and enduring. If the gene-tech entrepreneurs are able to convince us that we can satisfy these desires by buying into genetic modification, perhaps we'll bite. Green certainly seems eager to encourage us to do so.

But he would be wise to listen to what medical students, the great majority of Americans, and the international community appear to be saying: We want all these things, yes, and genetic technology might help us attain them, but we don't want to run the huge risks to the human community and the human future that would come with altering the genetic basis of our common human nature.

[1]**Tay-Sachs** A progressive disorder that destroys nerve neurons in the brain and spinal cord. [Editors' note]

Topics for Critical Thinking and Writing

1. Do you believe that in his first paragraph, Richard Hayes fairly summarizes Green's essay? Explain your reasoning.
2. Does the prospect raised in paragraph 6 frighten you? Why, or why not?
3. In his final paragraph, Hayes speaks of "huge risks." What are these risks? Are you willing to take them? Why, or why not?

18

Military Service: Should It Be Required?

CHARLES RANGEL

Charles Rangel (b. 1930), from the Harlem neighborhood of New York City, is a Korean War veteran who served in the House of Representatives for more than four decades (1971–2017). A Democrat, Rangel has been an outspoken voice for civil rights and social justice. This article, in which he argues in favor of a universal national service requirement, initially appeared in the January/February 2013 issue of the *Saturday Evening Post*.

The Draft Would Compel Us to Share the Sacrifice

On a freezing night in November of 1950, I found myself and dozens of fellow soldiers marching along the icy banks of the Ch'ongch'on River amid the cracks of mortar fire and the glints of Chinese bayonets. The war in Korea was in full force, and my battalion was retreating because our vehicle column had sustained an attack. After a three-day nightmarish trek through enemy territory, 40 of us escaped. In the battles around Kunu-ri, more than 5,000 American soldiers were killed, wounded, or captured. Ninety percent of my unit was killed.

When we returned home, many of my comrades were haunted by memories of their combat experience. They were consumed with guilt, couldn't sleep or function in their jobs, and became severely depressed. In short, they developed "shell shock," or what today we call post-traumatic stress disorder or PTSD. Following the lead of generations of soldiers, most of them suffered in silence, did not seek treatment, and never got better.

Today, we have the awareness and the resources to protect our troops from PTSD. We now know that prolonged exposure to combat is a primary cause of this affliction. A 2008 Army Surgeon General's study confirmed that more tours of duty mean a greater risk of PTSD for soldiers. Twelve percent of soldiers on their first deployment suffer mental health problems, compared to 27 percent of those on their third and fourth tours.

Moreover, suicide rates among veterans of the Iraq and Afghanistan Wars are approximately three times higher than in the general population. Yet we subject our troops to more cumulative months of combat than ever before, with shorter rest periods in between.

During Vietnam, almost no Americans were required to serve more than a single tour of duty overseas, although some volunteered for more. In Iraq and Afghanistan, however, nearly half of all soldiers are sent on multiple combat tours — sometimes as many as four. These are separated by reprieves that constantly shift in length, but are always too short to allow for substantive mental health treatment.

This is the inevitable result of having less 5
than 1 percent of our population carry the burden of war for the remaining 99 percent. More than 15 million registered for the Selective Service System; only 1.4 million are on active duty. This explains why 300,000 veterans of the Iraq and Afghanistan wars — nearly 20 percent of the returning forces — suffer from PTSD or major depression. It is not fair or morally defensible to saddle the brave Americans who volunteer for the Armed Forces with tours of duty that expand in length and frequency as our conflicts intensify.

As a nation we should ask ourselves how we can protect our troops' mental health while maintaining our national defense. Two years of civil service from all U.S. residents would allow us to meet both of these goals. Our military ranks would swell and there would be no need to demand repeated service from our troops. That is why I continue to call for Universal National Service, which would mandate a two-year service requirement for Americans ages 18 to 25. While my "draft" bill is unlikely to become law, it is important that we open a national conversation about how we can all share in the sacrifice for our country.

Requiring two years of service from everyone would compel us to rethink how and why we send young Americans into harm's way. Too few of the country's leaders have a personal stake in the well-being of the Armed Forces, and the outcome is predictable. Since the end of the draft in 1973, every president, Democrat and Republican alike, has approached warfare with the mind-set of invading, occupying, and expanding our nation's influence. It was this attitude that got us into the unnecessary and costly wars in Iraq and Afghanistan and that threatens to mire us in deadly wars in the future. We make decisions about war without worry over who fights them. Those who do the fighting have no choice; when the flag goes up, they salute and follow orders.

A universal service mandate would do more than deter future military entanglements. As shown in a report by the Congressional Budget Office, most of our volunteer troops come from economically depressed urban and rural areas. We have developed, in effect, a mercenary army. In New York City, an overwhelming majority of volunteers are black or Hispanic, recruited from lower income communities such as the South Bronx, East New York, and Long Island City. These enlistees are enticed by bonuses up to $40,000 and thousands in educational benefits.

Military service is a privilege, and it should not be shouldered only by those for whom the economic benefits justify great personal risk. If young men and women of all races and socioeconomic statuses served together, our citizens would come to share or at least understand one another's values, points of view, and beliefs. Empathy and mutual respect would provide a much-needed antidote to the cynicism that today's youth feel because of the extreme partisanship in Washington.

10 A universal national service requirement, even if it does not mandate enlistment in the Armed Forces, is the one mechanism we know will truly protect our troops, unify the nation, and bring fairness to our military. Furthermore, it will season our future leaders with the harrowing realities of war, ensuring that they will never commit our troops to the battlefield unless they are willing to send their own children.

Topics for Critical Thinking and Writing

1. What is the effect of Charles Rangel starting his argument about national service with a recounting of a harrowing experience during the Korean War? How does recounting the incident serve as a way to introduce his overall argument?
2. How is the comparison to the experiences of Vietnam veterans appropriate for a discussion of the experiences of veterans of the conflicts in Iraq and Afghanistan? What conclusion does Rangel draw from the difference?
3. In paragraph 6, Rangel proposes that all US residents should be required to give two years of civil service. What points does he use to specifically support such a proposal? Do you agree with his proposal? Why, or why not?
4. In paragraph 6, Rangel concedes that his proposal "is unlikely to become law," yet he doesn't specifically address the reasons why or offer rebuttal arguments to those who oppose a draft. What does that say about the strength, or weakness, of Rangel's own arguments? How might you have approached supporting his argument differently?

LC-USZC4-595 Library of Congress Prints and Photographs Division Washington, D.C. 20540 USA

Analyzing a Visual: Military Recruiting

Topics for Critical Thinking and Writing

1. If you had to guess at the approximate date this poster was created, what year would you guess? What elements in the image helped you estimate? What knowledge of your own did you bring to your guess?
2. To whom is this image speaking (who is the "you" in the context of this image's production)? Who exactly does Uncle Sam want in the US Army (and who does he not want)?
3. Find one or two current images or advertisements that address "you" as the viewer and consider who is included and excluded by the usage of the pronoun "you."
4. Compare an Army recruitment poster or print advertisement from today with the Uncle Sam image. How is it different? What appeals does it make to encourage enlistment?

JAMES LACEY

James Lacey (b. 1958) is a professor and course director of War, Policy, and Strategy at the Marine Corps War College and a US Army veteran serving as an officer in the 82nd and 101st Airborne Divisions. He holds a degree in history from the Citadel and a PhD in military history from Leeds University. This article, in which he argues against a universal national service requirement, initially appeared with Charles Rangel's piece in the January/February 2013 issue of the *Saturday Evening Post.*

We Need Trained Soldiers, Not a Horde of Draftees

Thanks to Rep. Charles B. Rangel, the recurring question of whether to reinstate the draft has been thrust to the front of the public-policy debate. Those calling for a renewed draft have a variety of arguments at their disposal. These range from the high cost of payrolls and recruiting to building a common experience in our youth that will bind us together as a nation. Under close examination, none of them holds a lot of water.

The best reason for not calling for a draft is that no member of the combined Joint Chiefs of Staff is asking for one. These are the men responsible for protecting our country and ensuring that our armed forces are fully prepared to meet any potential enemy. It is a trust that these men take very seriously. After 10 years of war they are intimately acquainted with the kind of army the nation needs to meet the uncertainties of the future. All of these senior officers came of age in the wreckage of the post-Vietnam military. They saw firsthand the ruinous effects a large draft force can have when there is no national emergency to justify the call to arms. These men built from the bottom up the professional military that has not lost a single engagement in a generation. If they prefer a highly trained professional force over a large influx of half-trained, short-serving draftees the nation would do well to heed their advice.

If the Joint Chiefs do not want a draft, there had better be a good reason to force one on them. The congressman claims that we need a draft to ensure that the burden of any future conflict is shared by all and does not fall primarily on the poor and on minorities. This is an old canard that he trots out from time to time to make his fellow legislators feel guilty about voting to commit military force. Disproportionate military losses among minorities is a myth that began in the Vietnam era and is a total fabrication. Minorities did not die in Vietnam or in any conflict thereafter in any greater numbers than they are represented in the population. And, with the exception of 1966, the exact opposite has been the case. Blacks made up 12 percent of the deaths in Vietnam, 13.1 percent of the U.S. population, and almost 11 percent of our troops in Vietnam. Whites (including Hispanics) made up 86.4 percent of those who served in Vietnam and 88 percent of those who died there. The highest rate of black deaths in Vietnam was 16.3 percent (in 1966) — and almost all of those killed that year were volunteers for elite units, not reluctant draftees.

That still leaves open the question of whether our military is composed mostly of economic refugees. The evidence says no. Virtually every member of the armed forces has a high-school diploma, in contrast to 79 percent of the comparable youth population. Practically all new recruits place in the top three intellect categories (as measured by the Armed Forces Qualification Test), versus 69 percent of their civilian counterparts. New soldiers also read at a higher level than their civilian counterparts. Overall, the U.S. military closely reflects the makeup of our large middle class.

5 The real moral danger of a draft is that it will provide so many troops that there might be a temptation to waste them in useless engagements. This is what history has demonstrated over and over again. The bloody charges into massed rifles during the Civil War could not have been sustained without a draft to replace those slaughtered. In World War I, British Prime Minister David Lloyd George actually began holding back reinforcements so that his generals could not waste their lives in another big-push offensive. Finally, does anyone think the useless carnage of Vietnam could have continued year after year if we had a volunteer force?

Furthermore, those who are calling for a draft fail to recognize that war has changed dramatically in the past three decades. A high-technology force conducting incredibly rapid operations requires well-trained professionals, not short-term draftees. An army of draftees would be little more than cannon fodder for any advanced force to chew up. Moreover, in the complex counterinsurgency environments of Afghanistan and Iraq, success depends on sending long-serving professionals repeatedly back into situations in which they are intimately familiar. Sending a new crop of annual draftees into these countries would have translated into skyrocketing casualty lists and failure on the battlefield. The thoroughly trained and professional U.S. military is the most dominant battlefield force in the world, capable of winning a stand-up fight against any opponent. Our national policy makers may misuse this force from time to time, but why would we ever put our military preeminence at risk in favor of a mass of half-trained grumbling draftees?

Then there is the cost. If we require every able-bodied male to serve 18 months to two years after he turns 18, then we are talking about inducting more than 1.5 million draftees a year. Equipping and training that force to even a reasonable standard would cost in the area of $3 trillion — and another $1 trillion a year to maintain it. Of course, no one is going to bankrupt the nation to build a military 10 times larger than what we currently need. This means that less than one in five of the eligible draftees would be needed or called.

Given that only a proportion of the eligible males would be called, anyone who thinks that the draft will remain a fair cross section of our society is living in a dream world. More likely the military would become even less representative of society as the rich and middle class would do whatever they had to in order to avoid contact with the "undesirable elements" who would be caught up in a draft. At present, recruiters seeking the highest-quality volunteers turn these undesirables away. As a former recruiting commander, I often lamented how many people we had to interview, physically examine, and test just to get one qualified applicant. Throughout my tenure, the ratio never fell below 14-to-1, though some other districts did a bit better. If the services lowered their standards even minimally, they could enlist their yearly goals by March and close their recruiting offices.

Some, including Rangel, make the argument that if the military cannot use all of the draftees, then they should be enlisted into some other form of national service. Has anyone thought about the size of the bureaucracy that would have to be created to mobilize, train, deploy, feed, house, and monitor several million 18 year olds every year? You would need a second army dedicated to doing nothing but keeping track of teenagers. Besides, what rational being believes that the federal government is the best organization for putting our youth to useful work? In no time at all our children will become pawns for whatever is the political flavor of the day.

10 As Doug Bandow states in his Cato Institute study of the draft, "A return to conscription would yield a less experienced, less stable, and less efficient military. Inducement, not coercion, is the answer to sagging retention. Studies have consistently indicated that the most effective remedy is improved compensation." By taking care of our soldiers, using them only for critical missions, and ensuring that they have the best equipment and training available, we maintain a quality force, capable of defeating any enemies we may face in coming decades.

Topics for Critical Thinking and Writing

1. James Lacey appeals to the authority of the Joint Chiefs of Staff, the highest-level officers of the different military services, when he says that because they don't want a draft, there should be no draft. Lacey states in paragraph 2 that senior officers' experiences showed them "the ruinous effects a large draft force can have when there is no national emergency to justify the call to arms." In what ways does the experience of the Vietnam War argue against the use of the draft? If necessary, research that period of American military history to form your own conclusions.
2. Also in paragraph 2, Lacey uses the term "half-trained" to describe draftees called into service. What is the effect of using that term? How justified is Lacey in referring to draftees as half-trained? If necessary, do research to determine the training and effectiveness of a military built on the draft versus an all-volunteer force.
3. In paragraph 3, Lacey asserts that in 1966, "almost all [of black soldiers] killed that year were volunteers for elite units, not reluctant draftees." Research the truth of this claim. What does that say about the nature of deaths in the Vietnam War in 1966 based on race?
4. In paragraph 5, Lacey argues that having a draft might encourage military leaders to "waste" lives in "useless engagements." He cites evidence from the Civil War and the British use of forces during World War I. In your opinion, is this still a likely scenario? Why, or why not?
5. A prime aspect of Lacey's argument is that the military needs to rely on experienced professionals to fight today's battles, not "half-trained grumbling draftees" as he states in paragraph 6. Given that Charles Rangel argues that rates of PTSD increase as soldiers go on more and more tours, what sort of balance can be struck between the need for experience and the desire not to subject fighting men and women to unbearable wartime stress?

PART FIVE

Current Issues

Casebooks

19

A College Education: What Is Its Purpose?

ANDREW DELBANCO

Andrew Delbanco (b. 1952) is a widely published author who teaches at Columbia University, where he is the Alexander Hamilton Professor of American Studies. The following essay first appeared in *Parade*, a magazine-like supplement that is part of the Sunday edition of many newspapers, and was later included in Delbanco's book *College: What It Was, Is, and Should Be* (2012). In 2012, Delbanco was awarded the National Humanities Medal by President Barack Obama.

3 Reasons College Still Matters

The American college is going through a period of wrenching change, buffeted by forces — globalization, economic instability, the information technology revolution, the increasingly evident inadequacy of K–12 education, and, perhaps most important, the collapse of consensus about what students should know — that make its task more difficult and contentious than ever before.

For a relatively few students, college remains the sort of place that Anthony Kronman, former dean of Yale Law School, recalls from his days at Williams, where his favorite class took place at the home of a philosophy professor whose two golden retrievers slept on either side of the fireplace "like bookends beside the hearth" while the sunset lit the Berkshire Hills "in scarlet and gold." For many more students, college means the anxious pursuit of marketable skills in overcrowded, underresourced institutions. For still others, it means traveling by night to a fluorescent office building or to a "virtual classroom" that only exists in cyberspace.

It is a pipe dream to imagine that every student can have the sort of experience that our richest colleges, at their best, provide. But it is a nightmare society that affords the chance to learn and grow only to the wealthy, brilliant, or lucky few. Many remarkable teachers in America's community colleges, unsung private colleges, and underfunded public colleges live this truth every day, working to keep the ideal of democratic education alive. And so it is my unabashed aim to articulate in my forthcoming book, *College: What It Was, Is, and Should Be*, what a college — any college — should seek to do for its students.

What, then, are today's prevailing answers to the question, what is college for? The most common answer is an economic one. It's clear that a college degree long ago supplanted the high school diploma as the minimum qualification for entry into the skilled labor market, and there is abundant evidence that people with a college degree earn more money over the course of their lives than people without one. Some estimates put the worth of a bachelor of arts degree at about a million dollars in incremental lifetime earnings.

5 For such economic reasons alone, it is alarming that for the first time in history, we face the prospect that the coming generation of Americans will be less educated than its elders.

Within this gloomy general picture are some especially disturbing particulars. For one thing, flat or declining college attainment rates (relative to other nations) apply disproportionately to minorities, who are a growing portion of the American population. And financial means have a shockingly large bearing on educational opportunity, which, according to one authority, looks like this in today's America: If you are the child of a family making more than $90,000 per year, your odds of getting a BA by age twenty-four are roughly one in two; if your parents make less than $35,000, your odds are one in seventy.

Moreover, among those who do get to college, high-achieving students from affluent families are four times more likely to attend a selective college than students from poor families with comparable grades and test scores. Since prestigious colleges serve as funnels into leadership positions in business, law, and government, this means that our "best" colleges are doing more to foster than to retard the growth of inequality in our society. Yet colleges are still looked to as engines of social mobility in American life, and it would be shameful if they became, even more than they already are, a system for replicating inherited wealth.

Not surprisingly, as in any discussion of economic matters, one finds dissenters from the predominant view. Some on the right say that pouring more public investment into higher education, in the form of enhanced subsidies for individuals or institutions, is a bad idea. They argue against the goal of universal college education as a fond fantasy and, instead, for a sorting system such as one finds in European countries: vocational training for the low scorers, who will be the semiskilled laborers and functionaries; advanced education for the high scorers, who will be the diplomats and doctors.

Other thinkers, on the left, question whether the aspiration to go to college really makes sense for "low-income students who can least afford to spend money and years" on such a risky venture, given their low graduation rates and high debt. From this point of view, the "education gospel" seems a cruel distraction from "what really provides security to families and children: good jobs at fair wages, robust unions, affordable access to health care and transportation."

10 One can be on either side of these questions, or somewhere in the middle, and still believe in the goal of achieving universal college education. Consider an analogy from another sphere of public debate: health care. One sometimes hears that eliminating smoking would save untold billions because of

the immense cost of caring for patients who develop lung cancer, emphysema, heart disease, or diabetes. It turns out, however, that reducing the incidence of disease by curtailing smoking may actually end up costing us more, since people who don't smoke live longer and eventually require expensive therapies for chronic diseases and the inevitable infirmities of old age.

In other words, measuring the benefit as a social cost or gain does not quite get the point — or at least not the whole point. The best reason to end smoking is that people who don't smoke have a better chance to lead better lives. The best reason to care about college — who goes, and what happens to them when they get there — is not what it does for society in economic terms but what it can do for individuals, in both calculable and incalculable ways.

The second argument for the importance of college is a political one, though one rarely hears it from politicians. This is the argument on behalf of democracy. "The basis of our government," as Thomas Jefferson put the matter near the end of the eighteenth century, is "the opinion of the people." If the new republic was to flourish and endure, it required, above all, an educated citizenry.

This is more true than ever. All of us are bombarded every day with pleadings and persuasions — advertisements, political appeals, punditry of all sorts — designed to capture our loyalty, money, or, more narrowly, our vote. Some say health care reform will bankrupt the country, others that it is an overdue act of justice; some believe that abortion is the work of Satan, others think that to deny a woman the right to terminate an unwanted pregnancy is a form of abuse. The best chance we have to maintain a functioning democracy is a citizenry that can tell the difference between demagoguery and responsible arguments.

Education for democracy also implies something about what kind of education democratic citizens need. A very good case for college in this sense has been made recently by Kronman, the former Yale dean who now teaches in a Great Books program for Yale undergraduates. In his book *Education's End*, Kronman argues for a course of study that introduces students to the constitutive ideas of Western culture, including, among many others, "the ideals of individual freedom and toleration," "a reliance on markets as a mechanism for the organization of economic life," and "an acceptance of the truths of modern science."

Anyone who earns a BA from a reputable 15
college ought to understand something about the genealogy of these ideas and practices, about the historical processes from which they have emerged, the tragic cost when societies fail to defend them, and about alternative ideas both within the Western tradition and outside it. That's a tall order for anyone to satisfy on his or her own — and one of the marks of an educated person is the recognition that it can never be adequately done and is therefore all the more worth doing.

There is a third case for college, seldom heard, perhaps because it is harder to articulate without sounding platitudinous and vague. I first heard it stated in a plain and passionate way after I had spoken to an alumni group from Columbia, where I teach. The emphasis in my talk was on the Jeffersonian argument — education for citizenship. When I had finished, an elderly alumnus stood up and said more or less the following: "That's all very nice, professor, but you've missed the main point." With some trepidation, I asked him what that point might be. "Columbia," he said, "taught me how to enjoy life."

What he meant was that college had opened his senses as well as his mind to experiences that would otherwise be foreclosed to him. Not only had it enriched his capacity to read demanding works of literature and to grasp fundamental political ideas, it had also heightened and deepened his alertness to color and form, melody and harmony. And now, in the late years of his life, he was grateful. Such an education is a hedge against utilitarian values. It slakes the human craving for contact with works of art that somehow register one's own longings and yet exceed what one has been able to articulate by and for oneself.

If all that seems too pious, I think of a comparably personal comment I once heard my colleague Judith Shapiro, former provost of Bryn Mawr and then president of Barnard, make to a group of young people about what they should expect from college: "You want the inside of your head to be an interesting place to spend the rest of your life."

What both Shapiro and the Columbia alum were talking about is sometimes called "liberal education" — a hazardous term today, since it has nothing necessarily to do with liberal politics in the modern sense of the word. The phrase "liberal education" derives from the classical tradition of *artes liberales*, which was reserved in Greece and Rome — where women were considered inferior and slavery was an accepted feature of civilized society — for "those free men or gentlemen possessed of the requisite leisure for study." The tradition of liberal learning survived and thrived throughout European history but remained largely the possession of ruling elites. The distinctive American contribution has been the attempt to democratize it, to deploy it on behalf of the cardinal American principle that all persons, regardless of origin, have the right to pursue happiness — and that "getting to know," in poet and critic Matthew Arnold's much-quoted phrase, "the best which has been thought and said in the world" is helpful to that pursuit.

20 This view of what it means to be educated is often caricatured as snobbish and narrow, beholden to the old and wary of the new; but in fact it is neither, as Arnold makes clear by the (seldom quoted) phrase with which he completes his point: "and through this knowledge, turning a stream of fresh and free thought upon our stock notions and habits."

In today's America, at every kind of institution — from underfunded community colleges to the wealthiest Ivies — this kind of education is at risk. Students are pressured and programmed, trained to live from task to task, relentlessly rehearsed and tested until winners are culled from the rest. Too many colleges do too little to save them from the debilitating frenzy that makes liberal education marginal — if it is offered at all.

In this respect, notwithstanding the bigotries and prejudices of earlier generations, we might not be so quick to say that today's colleges mark an advance over those of the past.

Consider a once-popular college novel written a hundred years ago, *Stover at Yale*, in which a young Yalie declares, "I'm going to do the best thing a fellow can do at our age, I'm going to loaf." The character speaks from the immemorial past, and what he says is likely to sound to us today like a sneering boast from the idle rich. But there is a more dignified sense in which "loaf" is the colloquial equivalent of contemplation and has always been part of the promise of American life. "I loaf and invite my soul," says Walt Whitman in that great democratic poem "Song of Myself."

Surely, every American college ought to defend this waning possibility, whatever we call it. And an American college is only true to itself when it opens its doors to all — the rich, the middle, and the poor — who have the capacity to embrace the precious chance to think and reflect before life engulfs them. If we are serious about democracy, that means everyone.

Topics for Critical Thinking and Writing

1. In two or three sentences, describe what Andrew Delbanco is arguing for. Then, in another two or three sentences, describe what he is he arguing against.
2. What do you think Delbanco considers to be the most important outcomes of a college education? What outcomes are less important to him?
3. In 300 to 500 words, explain whether you think the higher education system perpetuates inequalities or whether it helps resolve inequalities in the United States. Or is it a little of both? Explain.
4. Why is higher education good for freedom and democracy? What evidence can you cite from Delbanco as support for your answer? What evidence can you cite on your own?
5. In paragraph 10, Delbanco introduces, as an analogy, the cost of lung cancer and other life-threatening diseases (although he goes on to reject this comparison). Do you think his use of this analogy is effective? Why, or why not?
6. Using Delbanco's own formulation of a "liberal education" in paragraph 19, assess your own university's liberal education requirements and explain whether you think it is a valuable part of your education. Would you prefer an education that trained you only in your chosen career field or one that spreads learning across disciplines and experiences? If possible, talk to a humanities professor at your institution about the importance of a liberal education and include his or her thoughts, agreeing or countering them as you see fit, in your assessment.

CARLO ROTELLA

Carlo Rotella (b. 1964) is a professor in the English Department at Boston College and a writer for the *New York Times Magazine*. A former columnist for the *Boston Globe*, his work has also appeared in magazines such as the *New Yorker*, *Harper's*, and *Slate* and in academic journals such as *Critical Inquiry*, *American Quarterly*, and the *American Scholar*. This piece appeared in the *Boston Globe* on December 24, 2011.

No, It Doesn't Matter What You Majored In

I woke up on Wednesday morning with two routine but pressing jobs to accomplish: I had a column to write, and I had a stack of twenty-page papers to grade. The two duties wouldn't seem to have anything to do with each other. But they do, and what they have in common says something about the value of higher education.

Almost everybody agrees that college costs too much. If a relative handful of relatively rich people want to pay a lot to go to the most exclusive schools, that's up to them; it's a victimless crime. But if a good college education costs too much across the board, that's a major social problem, especially because a college degree has increasingly become a minimum qualification for the kind of job that puts you in the middle class — which is where most Americans, wishfully or not, still imagine themselves to belong. And this all looks worse because the economic crisis has hit many public institutions especially hard.

Some have called this situation a higher-education bubble. Some have begun to investigate what students are really getting out of college for their money. They're asking necessary questions about curriculum and teaching, and about institutions' and students' commitment to academic excellence.

But this vitally important discussion is often hamstrung by a tendency to reduce college to vocational education in the crudest, most unrealistic ways. This kind of reduction often zeroes in on the humanities and parts of the social sciences — together often mislabeled as "the liberal arts" (when, in fact, math and science are also part of the liberal arts) — as the most overvalued, least practical aspect of higher education. If you study engineering you can become an engineer, if you study biology or physics you can be a scientist, and if you're pre-med or pre-law then you can go on to be a doctor or a lawyer. But what kind of job can you get if you study Renaissance art, or Indonesian history, or any kind of literature at all?

5 It's a fair question, even when asked unfairly. If Deval Patrick,[1] an English major, was available, I'd let him answer. But he's busy being governor, so I'll take a shot at it.

Let's first defenestrate a mistaken assumption that many students and their parents cling to. Prospective employers frequently don't really care what you majored in. They might look at where you went to school and how you did, and they will definitely consider whether you wrote a decent cover letter, but they don't sit there and think, "Anthropology?! We don't need an anthropologist."

They do care that you're a college graduate. What that means, if you worked hard and did your job properly and your teachers did theirs, is that you have spent four years developing a set of skills that will serve you in good stead in the postindustrial job market. You can assimilate and organize large, complex bodies of information; you can analyze that information to create outcomes that have value to others; and you can express your ideas in clear, purposeful language. Whether you honed these skills in the study of foreign policy or Russian novels is secondary, even trivial. What matters is that you pursued training in the craft of mastering complexity, which you can apply in fields from advertising to zoo management.

The papers on my desk are from a course on the city in literature and film. They're about, among other things, 9/11 stories, inner-city documentaries, and the literary tradition of Washington, D.C. Instead of worrying about whether you can get paid to know about these topics, consider this: You can't fake a twenty-page paper. Either you've done the work this semester and know what you're talking about, or you don't. Either you can deliver a sustained reasoned argument, or you can't. It's a craft, like cabinet making.

I make my living building such figurative cabinets — like this column, a miniature one I assembled using skills I learned first in school and then honed doing various jobs in the private and public sectors: policy analyst, teacher, reporter, writer, very small businessman. Whatever else happens at college, higher education is about learning to drive the postindustrial nails straight.

[1] **Deval Patrick** Governor of Massachusetts when Rotella's article was published. [Editors' note]

Topics for Critical Thinking and Writing

1. Carlo Rotella's thesis appears in his title. Do you think he presents a convincing argument in the essay? Why, or why not?
2. Rotella references a course he teaches about the role of the city in literature and film. Do you think such a course would be a valuable addition to your own higher education?
3. Do you think students deciding what major to select would benefit from reading Rotella's essay? Explain your reasoning.
4. On what points do you think Delbanco would agree with Rotella's argument? On what points might Delbanco differ? Explain.

EDWARD CONARD

Edward Conard (b. 1956), who has an MBA from Harvard, is best known for his controversial book on the US economy, *Unintended Consequences: Why Everything You've Been Told about the Economy Is Wrong* (2012). He has made more than one hundred television appearances, debating luminaries such as Paul Krugman and Jon Stewart. This article appeared as part of a Pro/Con debate in the *Washington Post* on July 30, 2013.

We Don't Need More Humanities Majors

It's no secret that innovation grows America's economy. But that growth is constrained in two ways. It is constrained by the amount of properly trained talent, which is needed to produce innovation. And it is constrained by this talent's willingness to take the entrepreneurial risks critical to commercializing innovation. Given those constraints, it is hard to believe humanities degree programs are the best way to train America's most talented students.

According to the Bureau of Labor Statistics (BLS), U.S. employment has grown roughly 45 percent since the early 1980s. Over the same period, Germany's employment grew roughly 20 percent, while France's employment grew less than 20 percent and Japan's only 13 percent. U.S. employment growth put roughly 10 million immigrants to work since the BLS started keeping track in 1996 and it has employed tens of millions of people offshore. The share of people in the world living on less than $1.25-a-day has fallen from over 50 percent to nearly 20 percent today, according to The World Bank. Name another high-wage economy that has done more than the United States for the employment of the world's poor and middle class during this time period.

Contrary to popular belief, U.S. employment growth isn't outpacing other high-wage economies because of growing employment in small businesses. Europe has plenty of small family-owned businesses. U.S. growth is predominately driven by successful high-tech startups, such as Google, Microsoft, and Apple, which have spawned large industries around them.

A Kauffman Institute survey of over 500 engineering and tech companies established between 1995 and 2005 reveals that 55 percent of the U.S.-born founders held degrees in the science, engineering, technology or mathematics, so called STEM-related fields, and over 90 percent held terminal degrees in STEM, business, economics, law and health care. Only 7 percent held terminal degrees in other areas — only 3 percent in the arts, humanities or social sciences. It's true some advanced degree holders may have earned undergraduate degrees in humanities, but they quickly learned humanities degrees alone offered inadequate training, and they returned to school for more technical degrees.

Other studies reach similar conclusions. 5
A seminal study by Stanford economics professor Charles Jones estimates that 50 percent of the growth since the 1950s comes from increasing the number of scientific researchers relative to the population.

Another recent study from UC–Davis economics professor Giovanni Peri and Colgate economics associate professor Chad Sparber finds the small number of "foreign scientists and engineers brought into this country under the H-1B visa program have contributed to 10%–20% of the yearly productivity growth in the U.S. during the period 1990–2010." Despite the outsized importance of business and technology to America's economic growth, nearly half of all recent bachelor's degrees in the 2010–2011 academic year were awarded in fields outside these areas of study. Critical thinking is valuable in all forms, but it is more valuable when applied directly to the most pressing demands of society.

At the same time, U.S. universities expect to graduate a third of the computer scientists our society demands, according to a study released by Microsoft. The talent gap in the information technology sector has been bridged by non-computer science majors, according to a report by Daniel Costa, the Economic Policy Institute's director of immigration law and policy research. Costa finds that the sector has recruited two-thirds of its talent from other disciplines — predominately workers with other technical degrees. But with the share of U.S. students with top quintile SAT/ACT scores and GPAs earning STEM-related degrees declining sharply over the last two decades, the industry has turned to foreign-born workers and increasingly offshore workers to fill its talent needs. While American consumers will benefit from discoveries made in other countries, discoveries made and commercialized here have driven and will continue to drive demand for U.S. employment — both skilled and unskilled.

UC–Berkeley economics professor Enrico Moretti estimates each additional high-tech job creates nearly five jobs in the local economy, more than any other industry. Unlike a restaurant, for example, high-tech employment tends to increase demand overall rather than merely shifting employment from one competing establishment to another. If talented workers opt out of valuable training and end up underemployed, not only have they failed to create employment for other less talented workers, they have taken jobs those workers likely could have filled.

Thirty years ago, America could afford to misallocate a large share of its talent and still grow faster than the rest of the world. Not anymore; much of the world has caught up. My analysis of data collected by economics professors Robert Barro of Harvard University and Jong-Wha Lee of Korea University reveals that over the last decade America only supplied 10 percent of the increase in the world's college graduates, much less than the roughly 30 percent it supplied thirty years ago. Fully harnessing America's talent and putting it to work addressing the needs of mankind directly would have a greater impact on raising standards of living in both the United States and the rest of the world than other alternatives available today.

Topics for Critical Thinking and Writing

1. In paragraph 1, Edward Conard makes clear his thesis: "It is hard to believe humanities degree programs are the best way to train America's most talented students." What assumption is Conard making about college degrees and the economy? Do you agree? Why, or why not?
2. Conard argues in paragraph 2 that the rate of employment in the United States has outpaced that of other advanced nations. To what does he attribute this growth? How does the US economy in turn provide worldwide prosperity?
3. Conard argues that economic growth is not generated by small businesses, as many people believe, but by start-up companies that become huge, such as Google, Microsoft, and Apple (para. 3). What other companies, if any, have started up in recent decades outside of the technological fields that have had a major impact on the economy, including job growth?
4. In paragraph 7, Conard points out that the United States is graduating only about one-third of the number of graduates needed in the fields of science, technology, engineering, and mathematics (STEM). Why is that? Do some research to support your answer.
5. Conard's arguments are driven almost entirely by economic concerns, not issues of personal happiness or career satisfaction. In your opinion, to what extent should those factors, as opposed to economic concerns, play a role in one's choice of a major? Explain your answer.

CHRISTIAN MADSBJERG AND MIKKEL B. RASMUSSEN

Christian Madsbjerg and Mikkel B. Rasmussen are senior partners at ReD Associates, a consulting firm that, in the words of its website, uses "social science tools to understand how people experience their reality" so that businesses can better reach customers. Together, Madsbjerg and Rasmussen wrote *The Moment of Clarity: Using Human Sciences to Solve Your Toughest Business Problems* (2014). This article appeared as part of a Pro/Con debate in the *Washington Post* on July 30, 2013.

We Need More Humanities Majors

It has become oddly fashionable to look down on the humanities over the last few decades. Today's students are being told that studying the classics of English literature, the history of the twentieth century, or the ethics of privacy are a fun but useless luxury. To best prioritize our scarce education resources, we ought instead to focus on technical subjects such as math and engineering.

This short-term market logic doesn't work across the thirty-or-so-year horizon of a full career. A generation ago, lawyers made more money than investment bankers. Today, we have too many law graduates (though there appears to be data to support it's still worth the money) and the investment banks complain about a lack of talent. It is basically impossible to project that sort of thing into the far future.

We are also told that a degree in the humanities is unlikely to make you successful. Take North Carolina Governor Pat McCrory (R), who, while making the case for subsidizing state community colleges and universities based on how well they do in terms of placing students in the workforce, said this in January:

> " . . . frankly, if you want to take gender studies, that's fine. Go to a private school and take it, but I don't want to subsidize that if that's not going to get someone a job. . . . It's the tech jobs that we need right now."

But quite a few people with humanities degrees have had successful careers and, in the process, created numerous jobs. According to a report from *Business Insider*, the list includes A.G. Lafley of Procter & Gamble (French and History), former Massachusetts Governor and Republican presidential nominee Mitt Romney (English), George Soros (Philosophy), Michael Eisner of Disney (English and Theater), Peter Thiel of Paypal (Philosophy), Ken Chenault of American Express (History), Carl Icahn (Philosophy), former Secretary of the Treasury Hank Paulson (English), Supreme Court Justice Clarence Thomas (English), Ted Turner of CNN (History), and former IBM CEO Sam Palmisano (History). *Business Insider* has a list of 30 business heavyweights in total.

5 One might think that most people starting out or running tech companies in the heart of Silicon Valley would be from the science, technology, engineering and mathematics (STEM) fields. Not so. Vivek Wadhwa, a columnist for *The Washington Post*'s Innovations section and a fellow at the Rock Center for Corporate Governance at Stanford University, found that 47 percent of the 652 technology and engineering company founders surveyed held terminal degrees in the STEM fields, with 37 percent of those degrees being in either engineering or computer technology and 2 percent in mathematics. The rest graduated with a healthy combination of liberal arts, healthcare and business degrees.

This leads us to a very important question: What good is a degree in the humanities in the real world of products and customers? Here's the answer: Far more than most people think. It all comes down to this: Is it helpful to know your customers? Deeply understanding their world, seeing what they see and understanding why they do the things they do, is not an easy task. Some people have otherworldly intuitions. But for most of us, getting under the skin of the people we are trying to serve takes hard analytical work.

By analytical work we mean getting and analyzing data that can help us understand the bigger picture of people's lives. The real issue with understanding people, as opposed to bacteria, or numbers, is that we change when we are studied. Birds or geological sediments do not suddenly turn self-conscious, and change their behavior just because someone is looking. Studying a moving target like this requires a completely different approach than the one needed to study nature. If you want to understand the kinds of beings we are, you need to use your own humanity and your own experience.

Such an approach can be found in the humanities. When you study the writings of, say, David Foster Wallace, you learn how to step into and feel empathy for a different world than your own. His world of intricate, neurotic detail and societal critique says more about living as a young man in the 1990s than most market research graphs. But more importantly: The same skills involved in being a subtle reader of a text are involved in deeply understanding Chinese or Argentinian consumers of cars, soap or computers. They are hard skills of understanding other people, their practices and context.

The market is naturally on to this: In a recent study, Debra Humphreys from the Association of American College & Universities concludes that 95 percent of employers say that "a candidate's demonstrated capacity to think critically, communicate clearly, and solve complex problems is more important than their undergraduate major." These all are skills taught at the highest level in the humanities.

10 Companies — with the most sophisticated ones such as Intel, Microsoft and Johnson & Johnson leading the charge — are starting to launch major initiatives with names such as "customer-centric marketing" and "deep customer understanding." The goal of these programs is to help companies better understand the people they're selling to.

The issue is that engineers and most designers, by and large, create products for people whose tastes resemble their own. They simply don't have the skill set of a humanities major — one that allows a researcher or executive to deeply understand what it is like to be an Indonesian teenager living in Jakarta and getting a new phone, or what kind of infused beverages a Brazilian 25-year-old likes and needs.

The humanities are not in crisis. We need humanities majors more now than before to strengthen competitiveness and improve products and services. We have a veritable goldmine on our hands. But, in order for that to happen, we need the two cultures of business and the humanities to meet. The best place to start is collaboration between companies and universities on a research level — something that ought to be at the top of the minds of both research institutions and R&D departments in the coming decade.

Topics for Critical Thinking and Writing

1. Christian Madsbjerg and Mikkel B. Rasmussen note at the beginning of their article that there has been a significant trend of pushing students to major in the fields of science, technology, engineering, and mathematics (STEM). Why has that trend occurred? What do they say is the problem with doing so? Why?
2. In paragraph 4, the authors list several big-name businesspeople, politicians, and others who have degrees in the humanities. Are they merely cherry-picking examples (i.e., finding the few examples that support your position while ignoring the vast majority that do not), or do those examples accurately reflect the broader whole? Do research to support your answer.
3. What argument do the authors make about the abilities of humanities majors being superior to the abilities of those who major in technical fields? Do you find the authors' argument credible? Why, or why not?
4. In paragraph 9, the authors use the example of studying literature as a way to better understand human nature. Is that a fair claim? Why, or why not?
5. The authors point out that employers want to see employment candidates who can "think critically, communicate clearly, and solve complex problems" (para. 9). The authors argue that humanities graduates best fit that description. In your opinion, is that true or not? Be specific in your response.

6. In paragraph 11, the authors state, "The issue is that engineers and most designers, by and large, create products for people whose tastes resemble their own." Consider a specific recent product or invention and argue whether its design is reflective of what a customer wants or what an engineer or designer wants. Why?
7. In their conclusion, the authors argue that the "two cultures of business and the humanities" need to come together (para. 12). What does that statement assume about the purpose of higher education? What objections to it can you think of? Why?

CAROLINE HARPER

Caroline Harper holds a PhD in political science with concentrations in black politics and international relations from Howard University, where she is a lecturer. Located in Washington, DC, Howard is the most prominent historically black university in the United States. This essay was first published in May 14, 2018, on the blog *Higher Education Today*, operated by the American Council on Education.

HBCUs, Black Women, and STEM Success

The demand for professionals in science, technology, engineering, and math, or STEM, has been on the rise since 2000 — and projections indicate that the need for qualified candidates will not slow down any time soon. As new technology has driven market growth around the world, the United States has struggled to develop a workforce capable of maintaining a competitive edge in the global market. The ability to compete in the global market is contingent upon our ability to maximize resources that educate and prepare a diverse pipeline of students who understand the necessity of global citizenship.

During the White House College Opportunity Summit in 2014, President Obama reiterated the need to develop long-term strategies that expose students to STEM disciplines in elementary and middle school, increase college access, and maintain postsecondary affordability. These goals become increasingly important as projections indicate that more students from low-income and underrepresented minorities will pursue college degrees by 2025. According to the Bureau of Labor Statistics, women will make up 47.2 percent of the total labor force by 2024. It has become clear that postsecondary education is the gateway to obtaining professional opportunities in STEM occupations. In 2015, the Bureau of Labor Statistics confirmed that more than 99 percent of jobs in STEM required postsecondary education, compared to 36 percent of occupations overall.

The ability to create a pathway from degree attainment to gainful employment ensures that the STEM workforce reflects the diversity of our country. In recognizing this, the White House Council on Women and Girls and the Office of Science and Technology Policy have worked to encourage more women and girls to earn college degrees and pursue careers in STEM fields. But do existing strategies ensure a diverse STEM pipeline? Do these strategies reduce disparities between degree attainment and labor force outcomes among women and minorities?

CONDITIONS OF THE STEM PIPELINE

Although policy efforts to encourage STEM degree attainment are laudable, the STEM pipeline is leaky when it comes to underrepresented minorities. At the high school level, it is difficult to maintain a campus culture that encourages equity in the pursuit of STEM degrees when calculus and physics courses are available in only 33 percent and 48 percent of high schools with high black and Latino student enrollment, respectively.

5 Beyond access to courses that serve as the foundation to STEM careers, many black and Latino students have limited access to college and career readiness counselors. According to a national survey of school counselors, in high schools in which the student body is primarily low-income and/or underrepresented minority, the average caseload is at least 1,000 students per counselor — at least twice the national average. As a consequence of factors beyond their control, it is especially difficult for these students to successfully navigate a career trajectory that incorporates course selection, experiential learning opportunities, extracurricular activities, and college admission requirements.

Although many of the students aspire to attend college, black students are struggling to meet mathematics (13 percent), science (11 percent) and general STEM (4 percent) ACT test benchmarks, which are often seen as a measure of college readiness. What is the alternative for students who are interested in pursuing STEM careers but need additional resources to overcome limitations in their K–12 education?

CAMPUS CULTURE AND COLLEGE SUCCESS

Despite limited access to resources during high school, students who choose to pursue their undergraduate degrees at Historically Black Colleges and Universities (HBCUs) are welcomed by a nurturing environment that provides critical resources to overcome academic, social, and financial hurdles. For more than 150 years, HBCUs have continued to serve first-generation, low-income, and underprepared students.

According to the U.S. Census Bureau, the number of traditional college-aged Americans is projected to grow to 13.3 million by 2025. The largest growth is expected to occur among students who identify as black, Hispanic, or Asian/Pacific Islander. In an analysis of black student graduation rates, about half of all four-year HBCUs enrolled freshmen classes where 75 percent of students were from low-income backgrounds, compared to 1 percent of the 676 non-HBCUs in the study. Among the institutions where 40–75 percent of the freshman class was low-income, the graduation rate for black students who attended HBCUs was 37.8 percent — five percentage points higher than their counterparts at non-HBCUs.

HBCUs produced 46 percent of black women who earned degrees in STEM disciplines between 1995 and 2004. HBCUs produced 25 percent of all bachelor's degrees in STEM fields earned by African Americans in 2012. In 2014, black women represented the highest percentage of minority women who earned bachelor's degrees in computer sciences. HBCUs such as North Carolina A&T State University, Howard University, Florida A&M University, and Xavier University of Louisiana continue producing undergraduate STEM degree earners who pursue graduate degrees in their field.

Beyond producing bachelor's degrees,[10] research confirms that HBCUs are the institution of origin among almost 30 percent of blacks who earned doctorates in science and engineering. According to the National Science Foundation, within STEM fields such as mathematics, biological sciences, physical sciences, agricultural sciences, and earth, atmospheric, and ocean sciences, a large percentage of doctorate degree holders earned their bachelor's degrees at HBCUs.

CAREER OUTCOMES

While the campus culture at HBCUs provides black students with a sense of community, self-confidence, and efficacy, the workforce provides a stark contrast. Relative to their share of degree attainment, blacks are underrepresented in the overall context of the workforce and earnings.

Research has shown that compared to their Hispanic and Asian counterparts, blacks have the highest rate of unemployment. Among minorities currently employed in a STEM occupation, 41.4 percent are Asian, 18.4 percent are Hispanic or Latino, and only 17.4 percent are black. Moreover, blacks who work full time, year-round in STEM occupations are paid less than their Asian and Hispanic counterparts.

Despite disparities in employment rates and income, there are still important achievements that should be considered as the STEM workforce continues to grow. Within mathematical occupations, there were more black operations research analysts than any other minority group in 2011. In engineering occupations, black engineers outnumbered other minorities in the petroleum engineering field and rivaled Asians in roles related to environmental engineering, surveyors, cartographers, and photogrammetrists. Black scientists outnumbered other minorities in chemical technician and nuclear scientist roles. Compared to their Hispanic counterparts, there was a higher percentage of black professionals in conservation sciences and forestry occupations and geological and petroleum technician roles.

NEXT STEPS

While HBCUs do their share of producing black graduates with STEM degrees, there is a greater need for equity throughout the education pipeline and in workforce hiring practices. Suggestions to fill gaps in the STEM pipeline and ensure a diverse workforce that increases our ability to compete internationally include:

- Ensure that high schools serving low-income and minority students are provided with adequate resources to hire additional school counselors proportional to the student body and with the capacity to help students develop strategies to achieve college and career readiness.
- Provide funding to support collaborations with organizations that encourage academic rigor in STEM disciplines, including calculus and physics, in addition to advanced placement and honors courses. Specifically, funds should be designated to increase access to STEM foundation courses, advanced placement, and honors courses.
- Encourage private corporations to actively engage in the process of creating a diverse workforce

by developing partnerships that encourage diversity in recruitment, hiring, and development of African American college students pursuing degrees in STEM disciplines.

- Develop internship opportunities in collaboration with HBCU campuses to provide students with opportunities to put their coursework into practice while developing skills that can be transferred into the workforce.

HBCUs have maintained their legacies of 15
producing African American professionals in critical professions. Staying true to their mission, HBCUs continue to provide a nurturing environment where students gain academic and professional training to drive innovation in STEM fields and make valuable contributions in communities around the world.

Topics for Critical Thinking and Writing

1. What is Caroline Harper's argument? Describe how she lays out the problem and solution over the course of the essay. Use details and examples from her essay in your description.
2. What does Harper mean by the STEM pipeline? In 250 words or so, define the STEM pipeline in your own words, using your own examples.
3. In approximately 250 words, explain why Harper thinks HBCUs are the ideal places for correcting the inequities between different economic, racial, and gender groups.
4. Does Harper's argument imply that the kind of humanities-based, liberal arts education advocated by Delbanco and by Madsbjerg and Rasmussen is not as important for underrepresented minorities as advancement in STEM skills and fields? In 300 to 500 words, supplement Harper's argument with your own ideas on why it might be important for underrepresented minorities to take courses in history, art, or other humanities fields.

20

Race and Criminal Justice: Is the System Broken?

ADAM GOPNIK

Adam Gopnik (b. 1956) has written on a wide variety of subjects for the *New Yorker* magazine since 1986 and has published his essays as the magazine's Paris correspondent in the award-winning collection *Paris to the Moon* (2000). In addition to children's books, music, and published lectures on music, food, sports, art, and culture, his works include *Through the Children's Gate: A Home in New York* (2006); *Angels and Ages: A Short Book about Lincoln, Darwin, and Modern Life* (2009); and *The Table Comes First: Family, France, and the Meaning of Food* (2011). His writings have been anthologized widely. The essay reprinted here was published in the *New Yorker* in 2012.

The Caging of America

How did we get here? How is it that our civilization, which rejects hanging and flogging and disemboweling, came to believe that caging vast numbers of people for decades is an acceptably humane sanction? There's a fairly large recent scholarly literature on the history and sociology of crime and punishment, and it tends to trace the American zeal for punishment back to the nineteenth century, apportioning blame in two directions. There's an essentially Northern explanation, focusing on the inheritance of the notorious Eastern State Penitentiary, in Philadelphia, and its "reformist" tradition; and a Southern explanation, which sees the prison system as essentially a slave plantation continued by other means. Robert Perkinson, the author of the Southern revisionist tract "Texas Tough: The Rise of America's Prison Empire," traces two ancestral lines, "from the North, the birthplace of rehabilitative penology, to the South, the fountainhead of subjugationist discipline." In other words, there's the scientific taste for reducing men to numbers and the slave owners' urge to reduce blacks to brutes.

William J. Stuntz, a professor at Harvard Law School who died shortly before his masterwork, "The Collapse of American Criminal

Justice," was published, last fall, is the most forceful advocate for the view that the scandal of our prisons derives from the Enlightenment-era, "procedural" nature of American justice. He runs through the immediate causes of the incarceration epidemic: the growth of post-Rockefeller drug laws, which punished minor drug offenses with major prison time; "zero tolerance" policing, which added to the group; mandatory-sentencing laws, which prevented judges from exercising judgment. But his search for the ultimate cause leads deeper, all the way to the Bill of Rights. In a society where Constitution worship is still a requisite on right and left alike, Stuntz startlingly suggests that the Bill of Rights is a terrible document with which to start a justice system — much inferior to the exactly contemporary French Declaration of the Rights of Man, which Jefferson, he points out, may have helped shape while his protégé Madison was writing ours.

The trouble with the Bill of Rights, he argues, is that it emphasizes process and procedure rather than principles. The Declaration of the Rights of Man says, Be just! The Bill of Rights says, Be fair![1] Instead of announcing general principles — no one should be accused of something that wasn't a crime when he did it; cruel punishments are always wrong; the goal of justice is, above all, that justice be done — it talks procedurally. You can't search someone without a reason; you can't accuse him without allowing him to see the evidence; and so on. This emphasis, Stuntz thinks, has led to the current mess, where accused criminals get laboriously articulated protection against procedural errors and no protection at all against outrageous and obvious violations of simple justice. You can get off if the cops looked in the wrong car with the wrong warrant when they found your joint, but you have no recourse if owning the joint gets you locked up for life. You may be spared the death penalty if you can show a problem with your appointed defender, but it is much harder if there is merely enormous accumulated evidence that you weren't guilty in the first place and the jury got it wrong. Even clauses that Americans are taught to revere are, Stuntz maintains, unworthy of reverence: the ban on "cruel and unusual punishment" was designed to *protect* cruel punishments — flogging and branding — that were not at that time unusual.

The obsession with due process and the cult of brutal prisons, the argument goes, share an essential impersonality. The more professionalized and procedural a system is, the more insulated we become from its real effects on real people. That's why America is famous both for its process-driven judicial system ("The bastard got off on a technicality," the cop-show detective fumes) and for the harshness and inhumanity of its prisons. Though all industrialized societies started sending more people to prison and fewer to the gallows in the eighteenth century, it was in Enlightenment-inspired America that the taste for long-term, profoundly depersonalized punishment became most aggravated. The inhumanity of American prisons was as much a theme for Dickens, visiting America in 1842, as the cynicism of American lawyers. His shock when he saw the Eastern State Penitentiary, in Philadelphia — a "model" prison, at the time the most expensive public building ever constructed in the country, where

[1]The Bill of Rights is the first ten amendments to the US Constitution, approved by Congress in 1789. The Declaration of the Rights of Man and of the Citizen, written in consultation with Thomas Jefferson, was adopted in 1789 by France's National Constituent Assembly during the French Revolution. [Editors' note]

every prisoner was kept in silent, separate confinement — still resonates:

> I believe that very few men are capable of estimating the immense amount of torture and agony which this dreadful punishment, prolonged for years, inflicts upon the sufferers. . . . I hold this slow and daily tampering with the mysteries of the brain, to be immeasurably worse than any torture of the body: and because its ghastly signs and tokens are not so palpable to the eye and sense of touch as scars upon the flesh; because its wounds are not upon the surface, and it extorts few cries that human ears can hear; therefore I the more denounce it, as a secret punishment which slumbering humanity is not roused up to stay.

Not roused up to stay — that was the point. 5 Once the procedure ends, the penalty begins, and, as long as the cruelty is routine, our civil responsibility toward the punished is over. We lock men up and forget about their existence. For Dickens, even the corrupt but communal debtors' prisons of old London were better than *this*. "Don't take it personally!" — that remains the slogan above the gate to the American prison Inferno. Nor is this merely a historian's vision. Conrad Black, at the high end, has a scary and persuasive picture of how his counsel, the judge, and the prosecutors all merrily congratulated each other on their combined professional excellence just before sending him off to the hoosegow for several years. If a millionaire feels that way, imagine how the ordinary culprit must feel.

In place of abstraction, Stuntz argues for the saving grace of humane discretion. Basically, he thinks, we should go into court with an understanding of what a crime is and what justice is like, and then let common sense and compassion and specific circumstance take over. There's a lovely scene in "The Castle," the Australian movie about a family fighting eminent-domain eviction, where its hapless lawyer, asked in court to point to the specific part of the Australian constitution that the eviction violates, says desperately, "It's . . . just the *vibe* of the thing." For Stuntz, justice ought to be just the vibe of the thing — not one procedural error caught or one fact worked around. The criminal law should once again be more like the common law, with judges and juries not merely finding fact but making law on the basis of universal principles of fairness, circumstance, and seriousness, and crafting penalties to the exigencies of the crime.

The other argument — the Southern argument — is that this story puts too bright a face on the truth. The reality of American prisons, this argument runs, has nothing to do with the knots of procedural justice or the perversions of Enlightenment-era ideals. Prisons today operate less in the rehabilitative mode of the Northern reformers "than in a retributive mode that has long been practiced and promoted in the South," Perkinson, an American Studies professor, writes. "American prisons trace their lineage not only back to Pennsylvania penitentiaries but to Texas slave plantations." White supremacy is the real principle, this thesis holds, and racial domination the real end. In response to the apparent triumphs of the sixties, mass imprisonment became a way of reimposing Jim Crow. Blacks are now incarcerated seven times as often as whites. "The system of mass incarceration works to trap African Americans in a virtual (and literal) cage," the legal scholar Michelle Alexander writes. Young black men pass quickly from a period of police harassment into a period of "formal control" (i.e., actual imprisonment) and then are doomed for life to a system of "invisible control." Prevented from voting, legally discriminated against for the rest of their lives, most will cycle back through the prison system. The system, in this view, is not really broken; it is doing what it was designed to do. Alexander's grim conclusion: "If mass incarceration is considered as a system of social control — specifically, racial control — then the system is a fantastic success."

Northern impersonality and Southern revenge converge on a common American theme: a growing number of American prisons are now contracted out as for-profit businesses to for-profit companies. The companies are paid by the state, and their profit depends on spending as little as possible on the prisoners and the prisons. It's hard to imagine any greater disconnect between public good and private profit: the interest of private prisons lies not in the obvious social good of having the minimum necessary number of inmates but in having as many as possible, housed as cheaply as possible. No more chilling document exists in recent American life than the 2005 annual report of the biggest of these firms, the Corrections Corporation of America. Here the company (which spends millions lobbying legislators) is obliged to caution its investors about the risk that somehow, somewhere, someone might turn off the spigot of convicted men:

> Our growth is generally dependent upon our ability to obtain new contracts to develop and manage new correctional and detention facilities. . . . The demand for our facilities and services could be adversely affected by the relaxation of enforcement efforts, leniency in conviction and sentencing practices or through the decriminalization of certain activities that are currently proscribed by our criminal laws. For instance, any changes with respect to drugs and controlled substances or illegal immigration could affect the number of persons arrested, convicted, and sentenced, thereby potentially reducing demand for correctional facilities to house them.

Brecht could hardly have imagined such a document: a capitalist enterprise that feeds on the misery of man trying as hard as it can to be sure that nothing is done to decrease that misery.

10 Yet a spectre haunts all these accounts, North and South, whether process gone mad or penal colony writ large. It is that the epidemic of imprisonment seems to track the dramatic decline in crime over the same period. The more bad guys there are in prison, it appears, the less crime there has been in the streets. The real background to the prison boom, which shows up only sporadically in the prison literature, is the crime wave that preceded and overlapped it.

For those too young to recall the big-city crime wave of the sixties and seventies, it may seem like mere bogeyman history. For those whose entire childhood and adolescence were set against it, it is the crucial trauma in recent American life and explains much else that happened in the same period. It was the condition of the Upper West Side of Manhattan under liberal rule, far more than what had happened to Eastern Europe under socialism, that made neo-con polemics look persuasive. There really was, as Stuntz himself says, a liberal consensus on crime ("Wherever the line is between a merciful justice system and one that abandons all serious effort at crime control, the nation had crossed it"), and it really did have bad effects.

Yet if, in 1980, someone had predicted that by 2012 New York City would have a crime rate so low that violent crime would have largely disappeared as a subject of conversation, he would have seemed not so much hopeful as crazy. Thirty years ago, crime was supposed to be a permanent feature of the city, produced by an alienated underclass of super-predators; now it isn't. Something good happened to change it, and you might have supposed that the change would be an opportunity for celebration and optimism. Instead, we mostly content ourselves with grudging and sardonic references to the silly side of gentrification, along with a few all-purpose explanations, like broken-window policing. This is a general human truth: things that work interest us less than things that don't.

So what *is* the relation between mass incarceration and the decrease in crime? Certainly, in the 1970s and 1980s, many experts became persuaded that there was no way to make bad people better; all you could do was warehouse them, for longer or shorter periods. The best research seemed to show, depressingly, that nothing works — that rehabilitation was a ruse. Then, in 1983, inmates at the maximum-security federal prison in Marion, Illinois, murdered two guards. Inmates had been (very occasionally) killing guards for a long time, but the timing of the murders, and the fact that they took place in a climate already prepared to believe that even ordinary humanity was wasted on the criminal classes, meant that the entire prison was put on permanent lockdown. A century and a half after absolute solitary first appeared in American prisons, it was reintroduced. Those terrible numbers began to grow.

And then, a decade later, crime started falling: across the country by a standard measure of about forty per cent; in New York City by as much as eighty per cent. By 2010, the crime rate in New York had seen its greatest decline since the Second World War; in 2002, there were fewer murders in Manhattan than there had been in any year since 1900. In social science, a cause sought is usually a muddle found; in life as we experience it, a crisis resolved is causality established. If a pill cures a headache, we do not ask too often if the headache might have gone away by itself.

15 All this ought to make the publication of Franklin E. Zimring's new book, "The City That Became Safe," a very big event. Zimring, a criminologist at Berkeley Law, has spent years crunching the numbers of what happened in New York in the context of what happened in the rest of America. One thing he teaches us is how little we know. The forty per cent drop across the continent — indeed, there was a decline throughout the Western world — took place for reasons that are as mysterious in suburban Ottawa as they are in the South Bronx. Zimring shows that the usual explanations — including demographic shifts — simply can't account for what must be accounted for. This makes the international decline look slightly eerie: blackbirds drop from the sky, plagues slacken and end, and there seems no absolute reason that societies leap from one state to another over time. Trends and fashions and fads and pure contingencies happen in other parts of our social existence; it may be that there are fashions and cycles in criminal behavior, too, for reasons that are just as arbitrary.

But the additional forty per cent drop in crime that seems peculiar to New York finally succumbs to Zimring's analysis. The change didn't come from resolving the deep pathologies that the right fixated on — from jailing super-predators, driving down the number of unwed mothers, altering welfare culture. Nor were there cures for the underlying causes pointed to by the left: injustice, discrimination, poverty. Nor were there any "Presto!" effects arising from secret patterns of increased abortions or the like. The city didn't get much richer; it didn't get much poorer. There was no significant change in the ethnic makeup or the average wealth or educational levels of New Yorkers as violent crime more or less vanished. "Broken windows" or "turnstile jumping" policing, that is, cracking down on small visible offenses in order to create an atmosphere that refused to license crime, seems to have had a negligible effect; there was, Zimring writes, a great difference between the slogans and the substance of the time. (Arrests for "visible" nonviolent crime — e.g., street prostitution and public gambling — mostly went *down* through the period.)

Instead, small acts of social engineering, designed simply to stop crimes from happening, helped stop crime. In the nineties, the N.Y.P.D. began to control crime not by fighting minor crimes in safe places but by putting lots of cops in places where lots of crimes happened — "hot-spot policing." The cops also began an aggressive, controversial program of "stop and frisk" — "designed to catch the sharks, not the dolphins," as Jack Maple, one of its originators, described it — that involved what's called pejoratively "profiling." This was not so much racial, since in any given neighborhood all the suspects were likely to be of the same race or color, as social, involving the thousand small clues that policemen recognized already. Minority communities, Zimring emphasizes, paid a disproportionate price in kids stopped and frisked, and detained, but they also earned a disproportionate gain in crime reduced. "The poor pay more and get more" is Zimring's way of putting it. He believes that a "light" program of stop-and-frisk could be less alienating and just as effective, and that by bringing down urban crime stop-and-frisk had the net effect of greatly reducing the number of poor minority kids in prison for long stretches.

Zimring insists, plausibly, that he is offering a radical and optimistic rewriting of theories of what crime is and where criminals are, not least because it disconnects crime and minorities. "In 1961, twenty six percent of New York City's population was minority African American or Hispanic. Now, half of New York's population is — and what that does in an enormously hopeful way is to destroy the rude assumptions of supply side criminology," he says. By "supply side criminology," he means the conservative theory of crime that claimed that social circumstances produced a certain net amount of crime waiting to be expressed; if you stopped it here, it broke out there. The only way to stop crime was to lock up all the potential criminals. In truth, criminal activity seems like most other human choices — a question of contingent occasions and opportunity. Crime is not the consequence of a set number of criminals; criminals are the consequence of a set number of opportunities to commit crimes. Close down the open drug market in Washington Square, and it does not automatically migrate to Tompkins Square Park. It just stops, or the dealers go indoors, where dealing goes on but violent crime does not.

And, in a virtuous cycle, the decreased prevalence of crime fuels a decrease in the prevalence of crime. When your friends are no longer doing street robberies, you're less likely to do them. Zimring said, in a recent interview, "Remember, nobody ever made a living mugging. There's no minimum wage in violent crime." In a sense, he argues, it's recreational, part of a life style: "Crime is a routine behavior; it's a thing people do when they get used to doing it." And therein lies its essential fragility. Crime ends as a result of "cyclical forces operating on situational and contingent things rather than from finding deeply motivated essential linkages." Conservatives don't like this view because it shows that being tough doesn't help; liberals don't like it because apparently being nice doesn't help, either. Curbing crime does not depend on reversing social pathologies or alleviating social grievances; it depends on erecting small, annoying barriers to entry.

20 One fact stands out. While the rest of the country, over the same twenty-year period, saw the growth in incarceration that led to our current astonishing numbers, New York, despite the Rockefeller drug laws, saw a marked decrease in its number of inmates. "New York City, in the midst of a dramatic reduction in crime, is locking up a much smaller number of people, and particularly of young people, than it was at the height of the crime wave," Zimring observes. Whatever happened to make street crime fall, it had nothing to do with putting more men in prison. The logic is self-evident if we just transfer it to the realm of white-collar crime: we easily accept that there is no net sum of white-collar crime waiting to happen, no inscrutable generation of super-predators produced by Dewar's-guzzling dads and scaly M.B.A. profs; if you stop an embezzlement scheme here on Third Avenue, another doesn't naturally start in the next office building. White-collar crime happens through an intersection of pathology and opportunity; getting the S.E.C. busy ending the opportunity is a good way to limit the range of the pathology.

Social trends deeper and less visible to us may appear as future historians analyze what went on. Something other than policing may explain things — just as the coming of cheap credit cards and state lotteries probably did as much to weaken the Mafia's Five Families in New York, who had depended on loan sharking and numbers running, as the F.B.I. could. It is at least possible, for instance, that the coming of the mobile phone helped drive drug dealing indoors, in ways that helped drive down crime. It may be that the real value of hot spot and stop-and-frisk was that it provided a single game plan that the police believed in; as military history reveals, a bad plan is often better than no plan, especially if the people on the other side think it's a good plan. But one thing is sure: social epidemics, of crime or of punishment, can be cured more quickly than we might hope with simpler and more superficial mechanisms than we imagine. Throwing a Band-Aid over a bad wound is actually a decent strategy, if the Band-Aid helps the wound to heal itself.

Which leads, further, to one piece of radical common sense: since prison plays at best a small role in stopping even violent crime, very few people, rich or poor, should be in prison for a nonviolent crime. Neither the streets nor the society is made safer by having marijuana users or peddlers locked up, let alone with the horrific sentences now dispensed so easily. For that matter, no social good is served by having the embezzler or the Ponzi schemer locked in a cage for the rest of his life, rather than having him bankrupt and doing community service in the South Bronx for the next decade or two. Would we actually have more fraud and looting of shareholder value if the perpetrators knew that they would lose their bank accounts and their reputation, and have to do community service seven days a week for five years? It seems likely that anyone for whom those sanctions aren't sufficient is someone for whom no sanctions are ever going to be sufficient. Zimring's research shows clearly that if crime drops on the street, criminals coming out of prison stop committing crimes. What matters is the incidence of crime in the world, and the continuity of a culture of crime, not some "lesson learned" in prison.

At the same time, the ugly side of stop-and-frisk can be alleviated. To catch sharks and not dolphins, Zimring's work suggests, we need to adjust the size of the holes in the nets — to make crimes that are the occasion for stop-and-frisks *real* crimes, not crimes like marijuana possession. When the New York City police stopped and frisked kids, the main goal was not to jail them for having pot but to get their fingerprints, so that they could be identified if they committed a more serious crime. But all over America the opposite happens: marijuana possession becomes the serious crime. The cost is so enormous, though, in lives ruined and money spent, that the obvious thing to do is not to enforce the law less but to change it now. Dr. Johnson said once that manners make law, and that when manners alter, the law must, too. It's obvious that marijuana is now an almost universally accepted drug in America: it is not only used casually (which has been true for decades) but also talked about casually on television and in the movies (which has not). One need only watch any stoner movie to see that the perceived risks of smoking dope are not that you'll get arrested but that you'll get in trouble with a rival frat or look like an idiot to women. The decriminalization of marijuana would help end the epidemic of imprisonment.

The rate of incarceration in most other rich, free countries, whatever the differences in their histories, is remarkably steady. In countries with Napoleonic justice or common law or some mixture of the two, in countries with adversarial systems and in those with magisterial ones, whether the country once had brutal plantation-style penal colonies, as France did, or was once itself a brutal plantation-style penal colony, like Australia, the natural rate of incarceration seems to hover right around a hundred men per hundred thousand people. (That doesn't mean it doesn't get lower in rich, homogeneous countries — just that it never gets much higher in countries otherwise like our own.) It seems that one man in every thousand once in a while does a truly bad thing. All other things being equal, the point of a justice system should be to identify that thousandth guy, find a way to keep him from harming other people, and give everyone else a break.

Epidemics seldom end with miracle cures. 25
Most of the time in the history of medicine, the best way to end disease was to build a better sewer and get people to wash their hands. "Merely chipping away at the problem around the edges" is usually the very best thing to do with a problem; keep chipping away patiently and, eventually, you get to its heart. To read the literature on crime before it dropped is to see the same kind of dystopian despair we find in the new literature of punishment: we'd have to end poverty, or eradicate the ghettos, or declare war on the broken family, or the like, in order to end the crime wave. The truth is, a series of small actions and events ended up eliminating a problem that seemed to hang over everything. There was no miracle cure, just the intercession of a thousand smaller sanities. Ending sentencing for drug misdemeanors, decriminalizing marijuana, leaving judges free to use common sense (and, where possible, getting judges who are judges rather than politicians) — many small acts are possible that will help end the epidemic of imprisonment as they helped end the plague of crime.

"Oh, I have taken too little care of this!" King Lear cries out on the heath in his moment of vision. "Take physic, pomp; expose thyself to feel what wretches feel." "This" changes; in Shakespeare's time, it was flat-out peasant poverty that starved some and drove others as mad as poor Tom. In Dickens's and Hugo's time, it was the industrial revolution that drove kids to mines. But every society has a poor storm that wretches suffer in, and the attitude is always the same: either that the wretches, already dehumanized by their suffering, deserve no pity or that the oppressed, overwhelmed by injustice, will have to wait for a better world. At every moment, the injustice seems inseparable from the community's life, and in every case the arguments for keeping the system in place were that you would have to revolutionize the entire social order to change it — which then became the argument for revolutionizing the entire social order. In every case, humanity and common sense made the insoluble problem just get up and go away. Prisons are our this. We need take more care.

Topics for Critical Thinking and Writing

1. How does Adam Gopnik establish a lineage from today's prison system to the prison systems of the past? Do you find his connections convincing?
2. According to William Stuntz (para. 6), criminal law should not be determined by "one procedural error caught or one fact worked around," but instead "on the basis of universal principles of fairness, circumstance, and seriousness." Describe the differences between these two approaches in your own words, using real or imagined cases as an example.
3. In paragraph 4, Gopnik states, "The more professionalized and procedural a system is, the more insulated we become from its real effects on real people." What does Gopnik mean by that? Is it not true that a professionalized and procedural system ensures fairness and consistency? Explain your answer in 250 to 500 words.
4. Gopnik recalls the rise of inner-city crime in the 1960s and 1970s and the trauma it caused. Yet now, crime rates in major cities are significantly lower than they were in those decades. To what does Gopnik attribute the drop in crime? What does that mean for approaches to fighting crime in the future?
5. In paragraph 22, Gopnik asserts as "common sense" that "very few people, rich or poor, should be in prison for a nonviolent crime." Do you agree? Explain your answer.
6. One police technique that Gopnik argues has been highly successful is "profiling" — a controversial practice that many civil rights activists claim unfairly focuses on minority men. Research the issue of profiling as a police tactic and argue either for or against its validity in safeguarding public safety.

MARIAN WRIGHT EDELMAN

Marian Wright Edelman (b. 1939), educated at Spelman College and Yale University, is the founder of the Children's Defense Fund, a group that, according to its website, is dedicated to "the needs of poor children, children of color and those with disabilities." She has received numerous awards, including a MacArthur Fellowship (1985), the Albert Schweitzer Prize for Humanitarianism (1988), and the Presidential Medal of Freedom (2000). This article appeared as an editorial in *Preventing Chronic Disease: Public Health Research, Practice, and Policy* in July 2007.

The Cradle to Prison Pipeline

Suppose that during the next decade, a quarter of all the children born in New York, North Carolina, Texas, Colorado, Ohio, and Pennsylvania were infected by a virulent new strain of polio or tuberculosis sometime during their youth. Clearly, our response to a health crisis affecting that many children would be to mobilize the nation's vast public health resources. Medical laboratories would operate around the clock to develop new vaccines.

Unfortunately, an infection akin to this hypothetical tragedy is actually coursing through African American and Latino communities across the nation. I'm not referring to a virus such as HIV/AIDS or a hazardous bacterium. I'm talking about the criminalization of poor children and children from minority races who enter what the Children's Defense Fund (CDF) identified as America's Cradle to Prison Pipeline. Together, African Americans and Latinos comprise a segment of the U.S. population equal to that of the six states I mentioned earlier. Like the victims of a crippling or wasting disease, once drawn into the prison pipeline, massive numbers of young people lose their opportunity to live happy, productive lives, not because of festering microbes but because of years spent behind bars.

Through its Cradle to Prison Pipeline initiative, the Children's Defense Fund has studied the grim effects of being trapped in a criminalizing environment from which the obstacles to escape are formidable. The Cradle to Prison Pipeline consists of a complex array of social and economic factors as well as political choices that converge to reduce the odds that poor children — especially poor black and Latino children — will grow up to become productive adults. These factors include limited access to health care (including mental health care), underperforming schools, broken child welfare and juvenile justice systems, and a toxic youth culture that praises pimps and glorifies violence.

Hardened by long terms of incarceration, released criminalized youngsters return to communities that are ill equipped to reintegrate them positively. Outcast and unemployed, they become the teachers and role models for a new crop of youngsters pushed onto the streets of America's most depressed neighborhoods. This cycle of infection makes the Cradle to Prison Pipeline one of the most damaging health problems in America today.

A major factor in determining whether 5
a child enters the prison pipeline is access to health care. Currently, nine million children in America are without health insurance (1). Among low-income communities, there is a high incidence of teen pregnancy and low-birthweight babies (1). Physical and mental developmental delays among young children are commonly left undiagnosed and often go untreated (2,3). Unlike the children from affluent families, children from low-income families rarely have access to institutions that can intervene and address their health problems (2,3).

Few public schools in economically depressed neighborhoods have the resources to recognize health issues such as dyslexia, attention deficit disorder, hyperactivity disorder, or post-traumatic stress disorder and then to provide counseling and therapy for children with these disorders (1). Instead, their behavior is more often perceived as insubordinate or disruptive than it is recognized as symptomatic of a disorder or of the environment in which these children live (1,4). In these cases, zero-tolerance disciplinary standards are frequently applied, and thousands of students are expelled and even arrested for subjectively defined behaviors such as "disorderly conduct" and "malicious mischief" (5).

We must dismantle the Cradle to Prison Pipeline now because all children are sacred. What is required are collaborative efforts at the community, municipal, and state levels. To start with, we should demand the passage of legislation that would guarantee health care, including mental health care, to all children.

We need new investment to support proven community health delivery programs such as the National Campaign to Prevent Teen Pregnancy, which promotes community and school programs focused on delaying sexual activity (6), and the Nurse-Family Partnership, which supplies nurses for home visits to low-income, first-time mothers through their pregnancies and for two years after they give birth (7). Other valuable programs provide early intervention in cases of family violence (8). A healthy child is an empowered child. Communities should strive to replicate model umbrella programs that mentor and empower children such as the Harlem Children's Zone (9), the Boston TenPoint Coalition (10), and the CDF Freedom Schools program (11).

The effects of the Cradle to Prison Pipeline constitute a scourge of epidemic proportions. We must act to dismantle the prison pipeline now. We fail at our peril. The future of our nation is at stake.

REFERENCES

1. The state of America's children 2005. Washington (DC): Children's Defense Fund; 2005. Available from: http://www.childrensdefense.org/site/DocServer/Greenbook_2005.pdf?docID=1741
2. Manderscheid RW, Berry JT. Mental health, United States, 2004. Rockville (MD): U.S. Department of Health and Human Services, Substance Abuse and Mental Health Services Administration; 2004. Available from: http://download.ncadi.samhsa.gov/ken/pdf/SMA06-4195/CMHS_MHUS_2004.pdf
3. Burns BJ, Phillips SD, Wagner HR, Barth RP, Kolko DJ, Campbell Y, et al. Mental health need and access to mental health services by youths involved with child welfare: a national survey. *J Am Acad Child Adolesc Psychiatry* 2004;43(8):960-70.
4. Cocozza JJ, Skowyra KR. Youth with mental health disorders: issues and emerging responses. *Juvenile Justice* 2000;7(1):3-13.
5. Advancement Project, Civil Rights Project of Harvard University. Opportunities suspended: the devastating consequences of zero tolerance and school discipline. Proceeding from the National Summit on Zero Tolerance. 2000 Jun 15-16; Washington, DC. Available from: http://www.civilrightsproject.harvard.edu/research/discipline/cover_tableofcontents.pdf
6. Kirby D. No easy answers: research findings on programs to reduce teen pregnancy (summary). Washington (DC): The National Campaign to Prevent Teen Pregnancy; 1997.
7. Nurse-Family Partnership overview. Denver (CO): NFP National Service Office; [cited 2007 Feb 15]. Available from: http://www.nursefamilypartnership.org/resources/files/PDF/Fact_Sheets/NFPOverview.pdf

8. Fisher BS, editor. Violence against women and family violence: developments in research, practice, and policy. Rockville (MD): National Criminal Justice Reference Service; 2004. Available from: http://www.ncjrs.gov/pdffiles1/nij/199701.pdf

9. Harlem children's zone [homepage]. New York (NY): Harlem Children's Zone; [cited 2007 Feb 15]. Available from: http://www.hcz.org/index.html

10. Boston TenPoint Coalition [homepage]. Boston (MA): Boston TenPoint Coalition; [cited 2007 Feb 15]. Available from: http://www.bostontenpoint.org/index.html

11. Children's Defense Fund freedom schools. Washington (DC): Children's Defense Fund; [cited 2007 Feb 15]. Available from: http://www.childrensdefense.org/site/PageServer?pagename=Freedom_Schools

Topics for Critical Thinking and Writing

1. In your opinion, how effective is the opening to Marian Wright Edelman's article? Did drawing a comparison between physical diseases like tuberculosis and polio to the "criminalization of poor children" (para. 2) strike you as appropriate, or did you find it overstated? Why, or why not?
2. In paragraph 3, Edelman states that many children grow up in a "criminalizing environment." What do you think she means by that? How do children facing the obstacles she lists in this paragraph become "criminalized"?
3. Edelman also speaks of a "toxic youth culture that praises pimps and glorifies violence" (para. 3). Do you agree or disagree that youth culture contributes to the prison pipeline? Be specific in your answer.
4. In paragraph 6, Edelman discusses the problems with "zero-tolerance disciplinary standards." Research the zero-tolerance standards, particularly in schools. Investigate why they were created and what effects they have had. Then argue either for or against the use of zero-tolerance standards.
5. Consider Butler's essay on "The Chokehold" on page 496 and Edelman's notion of the cradle to prison pipeline. In 300 to 500 words, write a brief argument defining the concept of the chokehold as it is used by Butler, using Edelman's ideas as supporting evidence.
6. Research the terms *systemic racism* and *institutionalized racism* and find some examples, noting facts, statistics, and opinions about each term. In what specific ways does this kind of racism work to disempower or oppress certain groups of people? What are some of the problems that impede change in these kinds of systems?
7. The overarching idea of the "Cradle to Prison Pipeline" slogan suggests that some children in our society are virtually doomed from birth to wind up in prison. Opponents might argue that individual choices and responsibilities are at the root of crime, not environment. Do you agree with Edelman or her opponents? Support your answer.

PRISON POLICY INITIATIVE

The Prison Policy Initiative (PPI) is a nonprofit think tank whose mission is to produce research and analysis about the carceral system in the United States and to advocate for justice and equality in the system. The graphic shown here was created in 2018 and attempts to capture the variations among types of prisoners in the United States and the crimes that led to their incarceration.

Mass Incarceration: The Whole Pie

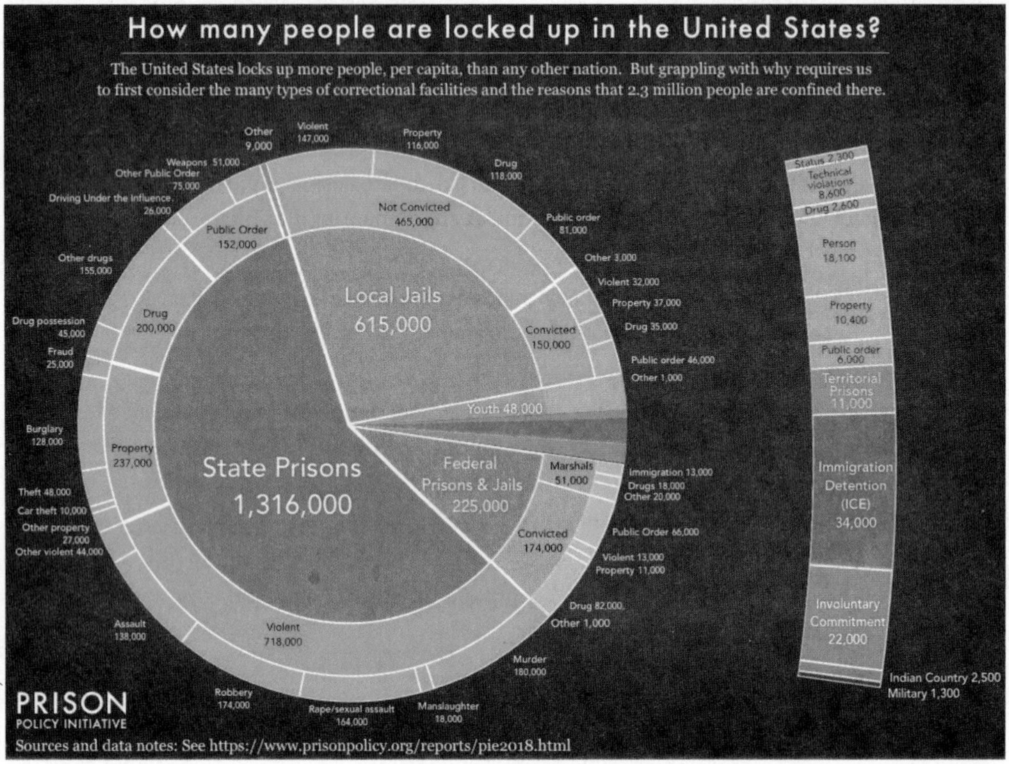

Prison Policy Initiative

Topics for Critical Thinking and Writing

1. At a glance, what does this graphic tell you to be mindful about when you talk about "the prison population"?
2. What statistic revealed in the graph surprises you most or challenges any assumptions you might have had about the prison population?
3. Examine the close-up on the right side of the graphic, where Immigration Detention is listed. Is the number of incarcerated immigrants today higher or lower than the number given there? What factors explain any change you find?
4. Is information that might be relevant to understanding incarceration in the United States missing from the graph? If so, what kind?

HEATHER MAC DONALD

Heather Mac Donald (b. 1956), educated at Stanford, Yale, and Cambridge, is a conservative columnist and Thomas W. Smith fellow at the Manhattan Institute. She is the author of *The Burden of Bad Ideas: How Modern Intellectuals Misshape Our Society* (2000), *Are Cops Racist?* (2003), and, more recently, *The War on Cops: How the New Attack on Law and Order Makes Everyone Less Safe* (2016) and *The Diversity Delusion: How Race and Gender Pandering Corrupt the University and Undermine Our Culture* (2018). Presented here is Mac Donald's 2015 written testimony before the United States Senate Judiciary Committee hearings on criminal justice reform legislation that would release some prisoners previously convicted of drug offenses on the basis of unfair sentencing guidelines and requirements.

The Myth of Criminal-Justice Racism

Chairman Grassley, Ranking Member Leahy, and members of the Committee, my name is Heather Mac Donald. I am honored to address you today regarding the Sentencing Reform and Corrections Act of 2015. I am the Thomas W. Smith fellow at the Manhattan Institute for Policy Research, a public policy think tank in New York City. I have written extensively on law enforcement and criminal justice.

Today I want to examine the broader political context of the Sentencing Reform and Corrections Act. We are in the midst of a national movement for deincarceration and decriminalization. That movement rests on the following narrative: America's criminal justice system, it is said, has become irrationally draconian, ushering in an era of so-called "mass incarceration." The driving force behind "mass incarceration," the story goes, is a misconceived war on drugs. As President Barack Obama said in July in Philadelphia: "The real reason our prison population is so high" is that we have "locked up more and more nonviolent drug offenders than ever before, for longer than ever before." In popular understanding, prisons and jails are filled with harmless pot smokers.

The most poisonous claim in the dominant narrative is that our criminal justice system is a product and a source of racial inequity. The drug war in particular is said to be infected by racial bias. "Mass incarceration" is allegedly destroying black communities by taking fathers away from their families and imposing crippling criminal records on released convicts. Finally, prison is condemned as a huge waste of resources.

Nothing in this dominant narrative is true. Prison remains a lifetime achievement award for persistence in criminal offending. Drug enforcement is not the driving factor in the prison system, violent crime is. Even during the most rapid period of prison growth from 1980 to 1990, increased sentences for violent crime played a larger role than drug sentences in the incarceration build up. Since 1999, violent offenders have accounted for all of the increase in the national prison census.

Today, only 16 percent of state prisoners 5
are serving time for drug offenses — nearly all of them for trafficking. Drug possession accounts for only 3.6 percent of state prisoners. Drug offenders make up a larger portion of the federal prison caseload — about 50 percent — but only 13 percent of the nation's prisoners are under federal control. In 2014, less than 1 percent of sentenced drug offenders in federal court were convicted of simple

drug possession; the rest were convicted of trafficking. The size of America's prison population is a function of our violent crime rate. The U.S. homicide rate is seven times higher than the combined rate of 21 Western nations plus Japan, according to a 2011 study by researchers of the Harvard School of Public Health and UCLA School of Public Health.

The most dangerous misconception about our criminal justice system is that it is pervaded by racial bias. For decades, criminologists have tried to find evidence proving that the overrepresentation of blacks in prison is due to systemic racial inequity. That effort has always come up short. In fact, racial differences in offending account for the disproportionate representation of blacks in prison. A 1994 Justice Department survey of felony cases from the country's 75 largest urban areas found that blacks actually had a lower chance of prosecution following a felony than whites. Following conviction, blacks were more likely to be sentenced to prison, however, due to their more extensive criminal histories and the gravity of their current offense.

The drug war was not a war on blacks. It was the Congressional Black Caucus that demanded a federal response to the 1980s crack epidemic, including more severe penalties for crack trafficking. The Rockefeller drug laws in New York State were also an outgrowth of black political pressure to eradicate open-air drug markets. This local demand for suppression of the drug trade continues today. Go to any police-community meeting in Harlem, South-Central Los Angeles, or Anacostia in Washington, D.C., and you will hear some variant of the following plea: "We want the dealers off the streets, you arrest them and they are back the next day." Such voices are rarely heard in the media.

Incarceration is not destroying the black family. Family breakdown is in fact the country's most serious social problem, and it is most acute in black communities. But the black marriage rate was collapsing long before incarceration started rising at the end of the 1970s, as my colleague Kay Hymowitz has shown. Indeed, the late Senator Daniel Patrick Moynihan issued his prescient call for attention to black out-of-wedlock child-rearing in 1965, just as that era's deincarceration and decriminalization movement was gaining speed.

It is crime, not incarceration, that squelches freedom and enterprise in urban areas. And there have been no more successful government programs for liberating inner-city residents from fear and disorder than proactive policing and the incapacitation of criminals.

10 Compared with the costs of crime, prison is a bargain. The federal system spends about $6 billion on incarceration; the state system spent $37 billion in 2010 on institutional corrections. The economic, social, and psychological costs of uncontrolled crime and drug trafficking dwarf such outlays. And prison spending is a minute fraction of the $1.3 trillion in taxpayer dollars devoted to means-tested federal welfare programs, as Senator Sessions has documented.

To be sure, the federal drug penalties are not sacrosanct. But though all sentencing schemes are ultimately arbitrary, our current penalty structure arguably has been arrived at empirically through trial and error. Sentences were increased incrementally in response to the rising crime rates of the 1960s and 1970s. Those rising crime rates were themselves the product of an earlier era of deincarceration and decriminalization. Sentences lengthened until they took a serious bite out of crime, in conjunction with the policing revolution of the 1990s.

Violent crime is currently shooting up again in cities across the country. Police officers are backing away from proactive enforcement in response to the yearlong campaign that holds that police are the greatest threat facing young black men today. Officers encounter increasing hostility and resistance when they make a lawful arrest. With pedestrian stops, criminal summons, and arrests falling precipitously in urban areas, criminals are becoming emboldened. While I do not think that the current crime increase is a result of previous changes in federal sentencing policy, it behooves the government to tread cautiously in making further changes. However, I unequivocally support the "productive activities" component of Section 202 of the Act, to the extent that it aims to engage all prisoners in work.

In closing, let me say that the committee would provide an enormous public service if it could rebut the myth that the criminal justice system is racist. Thank you for your attention.

Topics for Critical Thinking and Writing

1. Examine the features of Heather Mac Donald's whole testimony. In what ways is it similar to a written argumentative essay? How does it differ?
2. After opening with an account of a "dominant narrative" about the criminal justice system, Mac Donald begins paragraph 4 by saying, "Nothing in this dominant narrative is true." What are her primary arguments against that dominant narrative?
3. In paragraph 6, Mac Donald writes, "The most dangerous misconception about our criminal justice system is that it is pervaded by racial bias." Using your own research or evidence from other essays in this chapter, verify Mac Donald's claim or provide a rebuttal in at least 500 words.
4. In paragraph 8, Mac Donald says, "Incarceration is not destroying the black family." Do some research on your own to discover facts and opinions on the effect of incarceration on black families and communities and use your findings to support or refute Mac Donald's claim (or take a middle ground).
5. Examine the graph on page 490, "Mass Incarceration: The Whole Pie," and consider Mac Donald's claims. Does the image support or refute Mac Donald's claims?

STEVE CHAPMAN

Steve Chapman (b. 1954) is a columnist and editorial writer for the *Chicago Tribune*. Chapman has contributed work to numerous other publications as well, including *Slate*, the *Weekly Standard*, *American Spectator*, and *National Review*. This article was published on December 5, 2014.

Are Blacks to Blame for Cops' Actions?

When a white cop kills an unarmed black man, many blacks see a pattern of prejudice that generates official suspicion, hostility and abuse based on skin color. Many whites, however, say it's the fault of blacks. If they weren't committing so much crime, they wouldn't get so much attention from police.

This is not just a favorite theme of overt bigots and Internet trolls. It's the view of Rudy Giuliani, the former New York mayor and Republican presidential candidate, and many other whites.

Black-on-black crime "is the reason for the heavy police presence in the black community," he asserted on NBC's *Meet the Press.* "So why don't (they) cut it down so so many white police officers don't have to be in black areas?"

In this view, African-Americans have only themselves to blame for the presence and behavior of cops in their neighborhoods. If they would get serious about cleaning up the problems in their own communities, police would not be arresting or killing so many black people.

5 There's an element of truth to this line of argument. Violent crime rates are far higher among blacks than among whites and other groups. One reason cops have a disproportionate number of interactions with African-American males is that these men commit a disproportionate number of offenses.

Where the argument fails is in its assumption that blacks are complacent about these realities and that whites are blameless. The gist of the message is that blacks created the problem and blacks need to solve it.

But the problem didn't originate recently. In 1958 — a time of lynchings, universal discrimination and legal segregation — *Time* magazine reported that in big cities, the "biggest and most worrisome problem is the crime rate among Negroes" and said Negro leaders and civil rights groups should start "accepting responsibility in an area where they habitually look the other way."

The common impulse of whites, then and now, was to blame blacks for pathologies that whites played a central role in creating. Criminologist Charles Silberman wrote in 1978 that "it would be hard to imagine an environment better calculated to evoke violence than the one in which black Americans have lived." Pretending black crime is a black-created problem is like pretending New Orleans never got hit by a hurricane.

The Giuliani view omits some vital facts. The epidemic of unarmed blacks being killed by police comes not when black crime is high but when it is low.

10 Homicides committed by African-Americans declined by half between 1991 and 2008.

Since the early 1990s, arrests of black juveniles have plunged by more than half.

In New York City, where Eric Garner was killed by police, the rate of homicides by blacks is down by 80 percent. In Chicago, where most murders are committed by African-Americans, the number last year was the lowest since 1965 — and this year's could be lower yet.

What is also easy to forget in the denunciation of black crime is that the vast majority of blacks are not criminals. In any given year, less than 5 percent of African-Americans are involved in violent crime as perpetrators or victims. The fact that blacks make up a large share of the violent criminal population gives many whites the impression that violent criminals make up a large share of the black population. They don't.

Why don't more blacks living in bad neighborhoods learn to behave like sober middle-class suburbanites, some people ask? One reason is the shortage of stable families, steady incomes, good schools and safe streets. If you grow up with those advantages, it's relatively easy to do the right thing. If you don't, it's a lot harder.

15 People trapped in a poor and dangerous slum can't depend on the authorities to keep them safe. They face serious threats every time they leave home. But a young black man who packs or uses a weapon to protect himself against gangs is committing a crime. Even motivated, well-intended kids can wind up in jail.

Crime and poverty create a vicious cycle: A child raised in a chaotic environment is not likely to learn the habits that foster success. Black children afflicted with these disadvantages often take the wrong path as teens or adults. And when they turn out badly, people like Giuliani act as though whites bear no responsibility.

Conservatives are right to say that many of the problems afflicting black communities grow out of lamentable conditions in black communities. Their mistake is thinking that's the end of the discussion. It's only the beginning.

Topics for Critical Thinking and Writing

1. In paragraph 1, Steve Chapman begins by discussing how some black people and white people see the killing of unarmed black men by white police officers differently. What explains these different attitudes?
2. In paragraph 4, Chapman writes that many whites have the belief that "if they [blacks] would get serious about cleaning up the problems in their own communities, police would not be arresting or killing so many black people." He follows that in the next paragraph with this comment: "There's an element of truth to this line of argument." What truth is he referring to? In what ways is the statement true, and in what ways is it not?
3. In paragraph 7, Chapman points out that whites blaming blacks for crime has a long past. He cites a *Time* magazine article blaming blacks for crime in 1958, which was "a time of lynchings, universal discrimination and legal segregation" — conditions that whites themselves created. Can the white community be said to have contributed to crimes by blacks? Defend your answer.
4. Beginning in paragraph 9, Chapman points out data showing that crime has been trending downward across the board, including crimes by blacks. Thus, the "epidemic" of police shooting unarmed black men doesn't appear to be caused by police responding to rampant crime. What, then, might be the cause of the increase in police shootings? Do research to support your answer.
5. In paragraph 14, Chapman argues that blacks living in bad neighborhoods cannot be expected to act like "sober middle-class suburbanites." Do you find his argument convincing? Why, or why not?
6. Chapman states, "Crime and poverty create a vicious cycle" (para. 16). Research whether rates of crime are connected to the presence of poverty or other economic problems. Argue whether poverty is a major cause of crime. Defend your answer.

PAUL BUTLER

Paul Butler (b. 1961) is an author, a former criminal prosecutor, and the Albert Brick Professor in Law at Georgetown University. His book, *Chokehold: Policing Black Men* (2017), was a finalist for both the 2018 National Council on Crime and Delinquency's Media for a Just Society Award and the 49th NAACP Image Award for outstanding nonfiction. *Chokehold* became a ubiquitous word in discourses on race and police violence in 2014, when an African American man, Eric Garner, was suffocated to death in a chokehold by New York City police after being detained for selling individual cigarettes on the street. Garner's last words, "I can't breathe," were recorded by onlookers, and the phrase became a rallying cry for reformers. This selection was adapted from *Chokehold*.

The Chokehold

Chokehold: a maneuver in which a person's neck is tightly gripped in a way that restrains breathing. A person left in a chokehold for more than a few seconds can die.

The former police chief of Los Angeles Daryl Gates once suggested that there is something about the anatomy of African Americans that makes them especially susceptible to serious injury from chokeholds, because their arteries do not open as fast as arteries do on "normal people."

The truth is any human being will suffer distress when pressure on the carotid arteries interrupts the supply of blood from the heart to the brain. Many police departments in the United States have banned chokeholds, but this does not stop some officers from using them when they perceive a threat.

The United States supreme court decided a case about chokeholds that tells you everything you need to know about how criminal "justice" works for African American men.

5 In 1976, Adolph Lyons, a 24-year-old black man, was pulled over by four Los Angeles police officers for driving with a broken taillight. The cops exited their squad cars with their guns drawn, ordering Lyons to spread his legs and put his hands on top of his head.

After Lyons was frisked, he put his hands down, causing one cop to grab Lyons's hands and slam them against his head. Lyons had been holding his keys and he complained that he was in pain. The police officer tackled Lyons and placed him in a chokehold until he blacked out. When Lyons regained consciousness, he was lying facedown on the ground, had soiled his pants, and was spitting up blood and dirt. The cops gave him a traffic citation and sent him on his way.

Lyons sued to make the LAPD stop putting people in chokeholds. He presented evidence that in recent years 16 people — including 12 black men — had died in LAPD custody after being placed in chokeholds. In City of Los Angeles v Lyons, the US supreme court denied his claim, holding that because Lyons could not prove that he would be subject to a chokehold in the future, he had no "personal stake in the outcome." Dissenting from the court's opinion, Thurgood Marshall, the first African American on the supreme court, wrote:

> It is undisputed that chokeholds pose a high and unpredictable risk of serious injury or death. Chokeholds are intended to bring a subject under control by causing pain and rendering him

> unconscious. Depending on the position of the officer's arm and the force applied, the victim's voluntary or involuntary reaction, and his state of health, an officer may inadvertently crush the victim's larynx, trachea, or hyoid. The result may be death caused by either cardiac arrest or asphyxiation. An LAPD officer described the reaction of a person to being choked as "do[ing] the chicken," in reference apparently to the reactions of a chicken when its neck is wrung.

The work of police is to preserve law and order, including the racial order. Hillary Clinton once asked a room full of white people to imagine how they would feel if police and judges treated them the way African Americans are treated. If the police patrolled white communities with the same violence that they patrol poor black neighborhoods, there would be a revolution.

A chokehold is a process of coercing submission that is self-reinforcing. A chokehold justifies additional pressure on the body because the body does not come into compliance, but the body cannot come into compliance because of the vise grip that is on it.

This is the black experience in the United 10
States. This is how the process of law and order pushes African American men into the criminal system. This is how the system is broke on purpose.

There has never, not for one minute in American history, been peace between black people and the police. And nothing since slavery — not Jim Crow segregation, not lynching, not restrictive covenants in housing, not being shut out of New Deal programs like social security and the GI bill, not massive white resistance to school desegregation, not the ceaseless efforts to prevent blacks from voting — nothing has sparked the level of outrage among African Americans as when they have felt under violent attack by the police.

Most of the times that African Americans have set aside traditional civil rights strategies like bringing court cases and marching peacefully and instead have rioted in the streets and attacked symbols of the state have been because of something the police have done. Watts in 1965, Newark in 1967, Miami in 1980, Los Angeles in 1992, Ferguson in 2015, Baltimore in 2016, Charlotte in 2016 — each of these cities went up in flames sparked by the police killing a black man.

The problem is the criminal process itself.

Cops routinely hurt and humiliate black people because that is what they are paid to do. Virtually every objective investigation of a US law enforcement agency finds that the police, *as policy*, treat African Americans with contempt.

In New York, Baltimore, Ferguson, 15
Chicago, Los Angeles, Cleveland, San Francisco, and many other cities, the US justice department and federal courts have stated that the *official* practices of police departments include violating the rights of African Americans. The police kill, wound, pepper spray, beat up, detain, frisk, handcuff, and use dogs against blacks in circumstances in which they do not do the same to white people.

It is the moral responsibility of every American, when armed agents of the state are harming people in our names, to ask why.

Every black man in America faces a symbolic chokehold every time he leaves his home. The sight of an unknown black man scares people, and the law responds with a set of harsh practices of surveillance, control and punishment designed to put down the threat.

The people who carry out the chokehold include cops, judges, and politicians. But it's not just about the government. It's also about you. People of all races and ethnicities make the most consequential and the most mundane decisions based on the chokehold. It impacts everything from the neighborhood you choose to live in and who you marry to where you look when you get on an elevator.

I like hoodies, but I won't wear one, and it's not mainly because of the police. It's because when I put on a hoodie everybody turns into a neighborhood watch person. When the sight of a black man makes you walk quicker or check to see if your car door is locked, you are enforcing the chokehold.

You are not alone. As an African American man, I'm not only the target of the chokehold. I've also been one of its perpetrators. I've done so officially — as a prosecutor who sent a lot of black men to prison. I represented the government in criminal court and defended cops who had racially profiled or used excessive force. Many of those prosecutions I now regret. I can't turn back time, but I can expose a morally bankrupt system.

But before I get too high and mighty, you should know that I've also enforced the chokehold outside my work as a prosecutor. I am a black man who at times is afraid of other black men. And then I get mad when people act afraid of me.

Other times I have been more disgusted or angry with some of my brothers than scared. I read the news articles about "black-on-black" homicide in places like Chicago and Los Angeles. I listen to some hip-hop music that seems to celebrate thug life. And as a kid I got bullied by other black males. Sometimes I think if brothers would just do right, we would not have to worry about people being afraid of us. I have wondered if we have brought the chokehold on ourselves.

In my years as a prosecutor, I learned some inside information that I am now willing to share. Some of it will blow your mind, but I don't feel bad for telling tales out of school. I was on the front lines in carrying out the chokehold. Now I want to be on the front lines in helping to crush it.

My creds to write this don't come just from my experience as a law enforcement officer, my legal training at Harvard, or the more than 20 years I have spent researching criminal justice. I learned as much as an African American man who got arrested for a crime I did not commit — during the time that I served as a federal prosecutor. I didn't beat my case because I was innocent, even though I was. I beat my case because I knew how to work the system.

The chokehold does not stem from hate of African Americans. Its anti-blackness is instrumental rather than emotional. As slaves built the White House, the chokehold builds the wealth of white elites. Discriminatory law enforcement practices such as stop and frisk, mass incarceration, and the war on drugs are key components of the political economy of the United States. After the civil rights movement of the 1960s stigmatized overt racism, the national economy, which from the founding has been premised on a racialized form of capitalism, still required black bodies to exploit. The chokehold evolved as a "color-blind" method of keeping African Americans down, and then blaming them for their own degradation. The rap group Public Enemy said: "It takes a nation of millions to hold us back."

Actually all it takes is the chokehold. It is the invisible fist of the law.

The chokehold means that what happens in places like Ferguson, Missouri, and

Baltimore, Maryland — where the police routinely harass and discriminate against African Americans — is not a flaw in the criminal justice system. Ferguson and Baltimore are examples of how the system is *supposed* to work. The problem is not bad-apple cops. The problem is police work itself. American cops are the enforcers of a criminal justice regime that targets black men and sets them up to fail.

The chokehold is how the police get away with shooting unarmed black people. Cops are rarely prosecuted because they are, literally, doing their jobs. This is why efforts to fix "problems" such as excessive force and racial profiling are doomed to fail. If it's not broke, you can't fix it. Police violence and selective enforcement are not so much flaws in American criminal justice as they are integral features of it. The chokehold is why, legally speaking, black lives don't matter as much as white lives.

The whole world knows that the United States faces a crisis in racial justice, but the focus on police and mass incarceration is too narrow. We might be able to fix those problems the way that we "fixed" slavery and segregation, but the chokehold's genius is its mutability. Throughout the existence of America, there have always been legal ways to keep black people down. Slavery bled into the old Jim Crow; the old Jim Crow bled into the new Jim Crow. In order to halt this wretched cycle we must not think of reform — we must think of transformation. The United States of America must be disrupted, and made anew.

30 One of the consequences of the chokehold is mass incarceration, famously described by Michelle Alexander as "the new Jim Crow." The chokehold also brings us police tactics such as stop and frisk, which are designed to humiliate African American males — to bring them into submission. The chokehold demands a certain kind of performance from a black man every time he leaves his home. He must affirmatively demonstrate — to the police and the public at large — that he is not a threat. Most African American men follow the script. Black men who are noncompliant suffer the consequences.

The chokehold is perfectly legal. Like all law, it promotes the interests of the rich and powerful. In any system marked by inequality, there are winners and losers. Because the chokehold imposes racial order, who wins and who loses is based on race.

White people are the winners. What they win is not only material, like the cash money that arresting African Americans brings to cities all over the country in fines and court costs. The criminalizing of blackness also brings psychic rewards. American criminal justice enhances the property value of whiteness.

As the chokehold subordinates black men, it improves the status of white people. It works as an enforcement mechanism for keeping the black man in his place literally as well as figuratively. Oh the places African American men don't go because of the chokehold. It frees up urban space for coffeehouses and beer gardens.

But it's not just the five-dollar latte crowd that wins. The chokehold is something like an employment stimulus plan for working-class white people, who don't have to compete for jobs with all the black men who are locked up, or who are underground because they have outstanding arrest warrants, or who have criminal records that make obtaining legal employment exceedingly difficult. Poor white people are simply not locked up at rates similar to African Americans. These benefits make crushing the chokehold more difficult because if it ends, white people lose — at least in the short term.

35 Progressives often lambast poor white people for voting for conservative Republicans like Donald Trump, suggesting that those votes are not in their best interests. But low-income white folks might have better sense than pundits give them credit for. A vote for a conservative is an investment in the property value of one's whiteness. The criminal process makes white privilege more than just a status symbol, and more than just a partial shield from the criminal process (as compared to African Americans). Black men are locked up at five times the rate of white men. There are more African Americans in the US criminal justice system than there were slaves in 1850.

By reducing competition for jobs, and by generating employment in law enforcement and corrections, especially in the mainly white rural areas where prisons are often located, the chokehold delivers cash money to many working-class white people.

The chokehold relegates black men to an inferior status of citizenship. We might care about that as a moral issue, or as an issue of racial justice. But honestly, many people will not give a damn for those reasons. African Americans have been second-class citizens since we were allowed — after the bloodiest war in US history and an amendment to the constitution — to become citizens at all.

The political scientist Lisa Miller has described the United States as a "failed state" for African Americans. Indeed some activists involved in the movement for black lives speak of their work as creating a "Black Spring," similar to the Arab Spring movements that attempted to bring democracy to some Middle Eastern countries.

We face a crucial choice. Do we allow the chokehold to continue to strangle our democracy and risk the rebellion that always comes to police states? Or do we transform the United States of America into the true multiracial democracy that, at our best, we aspire to be? It is about the urgency of transformation. All of the people will be free, or none of them will. "All the way down, this time."

Topics for Critical Thinking and Writing

1. What is the effect of telling the story of what happened to Adolph Lyons in 1976 at the beginning of the essay? How does it contribute to Paul Butler's argument?
2. In paragraph 8, Butler writes, "If the police patrolled white communities with the same violence that they patrol poor black neighborhoods, there would be a revolution." What does this claim suggest about crime and justice in the United States?
3. In about 250 words, explain how Butler uses the chokehold as a literal and metaphorical form of strangulation.
4. Describe Butler's tone in this essay. Do you find his style effective or ineffective? Why, or why not?
5. Examine Butler's appeals in this essay: does he effectively use *ethos*, *pathos*, and *logos* to advance his argument? Support your answer with examples from the selection.
6. Butler focuses primarily on the chokehold as an issue affecting black men. Consider black women: do you think the chokehold as Butler describes it affects black women as

powerfully as it does men? Answer in about 500 words, supporting your claim with evidence from Butler or elsewhere.

7. Butler's last line is borrowed from feminist Robin Morgan's 1970 essay, "Goodbye to All That," which has become a classic in women's liberation movements: "We are rising with a fury older and potentially greater than any force in history, and this time we will be free or no one will survive. Power to the people or to none. All the way down, this time." Do you think Butler's use of that phrase out of context is appropriate? Why, or why not? Do you find these words threatening and radical, or reasonable and justifiable?
8. In about 500 words, address the concept of responsibility in Butler's essay. According to Butler, who is responsible for the chokehold, and what might be done to release people from it?

21

The Ethics of Appropriation: Is It OK to Copy?

KENAN MALIK

Kenan Malik (b. 1960) is an India-born British writer, lecturer, and broadcaster whose work on the history of thought has appeared in the *Guardian*, the *Financial Times*, the *Independent*, the *Sunday Times*, and the *New York Times*. Malik's writing on topics related to diversity, equality, and freedom of expression has been published in several books, including *The Meaning of Race: Race, History and Culture in Western Society* (1996), *Strange Fruit: Why Both Sides Are Wrong in the Race Debate* (2008), and *Multiculturalism and Its Discontents: Rethinking Diversity after 9/11* (2013). His most recent book is *The Quest for a Moral Compass: A Global History of Ethics* (2014). The following selection was published by *Al Jazeera* on April 14, 2016.

The Bane of Cultural Appropriation

Another week, another controversy about "cultural appropriation." The latest has been the furor over Justin Bieber's dreadlocks. The Bieber furor followed similar controversies over Beyonce's Bollywood outfit, Kylie Jenner's cornrows, Canadians practicing yoga, English students wearing sombreros and American students donning Native American Halloween costumes.

Many of these controversies may seem as laughable as Bieber's locks. What they reveal, however, is how degraded have become contemporary campaigns for social justice.

Cultural appropriation is, in the words of Susan Scafidi, professor of law at Fordham University, and author of *Who Owns Culture? Appropriation and Authenticity in American Law*, "Taking intellectual property, traditional knowledge, cultural expressions, or artifacts from someone else's culture without permission." This can include the "unauthorized use of another culture's dance, dress, music, language, folklore, cuisine, traditional medicine, religious symbols, etc."

A COLONIAL PAST?

But what is it for knowledge or an object to "belong" to a culture? And who gives permission for someone from another culture to use such knowledge or forms?

The idea that the world could be divided into distinct cultures, and that every culture belonged to a particular people, has its roots in late 18th-century Europe.

The Romantic movement, which developed in part in opposition to the rationalism of the Enlightenment, celebrated cultural differences and insisted on the importance of "authentic" ways of being.

For Johann Gottfried Herder, the German philosopher who best articulated the Romantic notion of culture, what made each people — or "volk" — unique was its particular language, history and modes of living. The unique nature of each volk was expressed through its "volksgeist" — the unchanging spirit of a people refined through history.

Herder was no reactionary — he was an important champion of equality — but his ideas about culture were adopted by reactionary thinkers. Those ideas became central to racial thinking — the notion of the volksgeist was transformed into the concept of racial make-up — and fueled the belief that non-Western societies were "backward" because of their "backward" cultures.

Radicals challenging racism and colonialism rejected the Romantic view of culture, adopting instead a universalist perspective. From the struggle against slavery to the anticolonial movements, the aim was not to protect one's own special culture but to create a more universal culture in which all could participate on equal terms.

ENTER IDENTITY POLITICS

In recent decades, however, the universalist viewpoint has eroded, largely as many of the social movements that embodied that viewpoint have disintegrated. The social space vacated by that disintegration became filled by identity politics.

As the broader struggles for social transformation have faded, people have tended to retreat into their particular faiths or cultures, and to embrace more parochial forms of identity. In this process, the old cultural arguments of the racists have returned, but now rebranded as "antiracist."

But how does creating gated cultures, and preventing others from trespassing upon one's culture without permission, challenge racism or promote social justice?

Campaigners against cultural appropriation argue that when "privileged" cultures adopt the styles of "less privileged" ones they help create stereotypes of what such cultures are like, and assert racial power.

"By dressing up as a fake Indian," one Native American told white students, "you are asserting your power over us, and continuing to oppress us."

The trouble is that in making the case against cultural appropriation, campaigners equally perpetuate stereotypes.

After all, to suggest that it is "authentic" for blacks to wear locks, or for Native Americans to wear a headdress, but not for whites to do so, is itself to stereotype those cultures.

Cultures do not, and cannot, work through notions of "ownership." The history of culture is the history of cultural appropriation — of cultures borrowing, stealing, changing, transforming.

Nor does preventing whites from wearing locks or practicing yoga challenge racism in any meaningful way.

What the campaigns against cultural appropriation reveal is the disintegration of the meaning of "anti-racism." Once it meant to struggle for equal treatment for all.

20 Now it means defining the correct etiquette for a plural society. The campaign against cultural appropriation is about policing manners rather than transforming society.

WHO IS THE AUTHORITY?

This takes us to the second question: who does the policing? Who gives permission for people of other cultures to use particular cultural forms? Who acts as the gatekeepers to gated cultures?

Most black people could probably not care less what Justin Beiber does to his hair. Inevitably, the gatekeepers are those who are outraged by Bieber's locks.

The very fact of being outraged makes one the arbiter of what is outrageous. The gatekeepers, in other words, define themselves, because they are ones who want to put up the gates.

The debates around Justin Bieber's hair or Beyonce's Bollywood outfit are relatively trivial. But, in other contexts, the creation of gatekeepers has proved highly problematic.

25 In many European nations, minority groups have come to be seen as distinct communities, each with their own interests, needs and desires, and each with certain so-called "community leaders" acting as their representatives.

Such leaders are frequently religious, often conservative, and rarely representative of their communities. But they wield great power as mediators between their communities and wider society. In effect, they act as gatekeepers to those communities.

Their role as gatekeepers is particularly problematic when it comes to policing not fashion styles or cuisine but ideas. Community leaders often help define what is acceptable to say about particular communities, and what is "offensive."

And notions of "offense" are often used to police not just what outsiders may say about a particular community, but to shut down debate within those communities — think of the fatwa against Salman Rushdie or the shutting down by Sikh activists of Sikh playwright Gurpreet Kaur Bhatti's play *Behzti*, which explored the role of women within Sikh communities.

The campaign against cultural appropriation is, in other words, part of the broader attempt to police communities and cultures. Those who most suffer from such policing are minority communities themselves, and in particular progressive voices within those communities.

30 The real fight against injustice begins with ridding ourselves of our self-appointed gatekeepers.

Topics for Critical Thinking and Writing

1. Apply Susan Scafidi's definition of cultural appropriation (para. 3) to the examples offered by Kenan Malik of recent instances of it (e.g., Justin Bieber's dreadlocks, Beyonce's Bollywood garb). Are such fashion choices acceptable? Are some more acceptable than others? Why, or why not?

2. What factors should inform people's choices to adopt forms of dress or decoration whose origins lie in other cultures? What benefits or drawbacks, potentialities or pitfalls, are suggested by such attire? (Feel free to add your own examples.)
3. Examine Malik's account of the tensions between a Romantic view of culture and a universalist view of culture (paras. 4–9). In 250 words or so, discuss some reasons each view could be celebrated or condemned.
4. Explain Malik's thinking in paragraph 11 that "the old cultural arguments of the racists have returned, but now rebranded as 'anti-racist.' " Do you agree or disagree with Malik that people arguing against cultural appropriation can be considered "racist"? Explain your reasoning.
5. Do you agree with Malik (para. 20) that "the campaign against cultural appropriation is about policing manners rather than transforming society"? Explain in about 250 words.
6. In the last section of Malik's argument, he explores the negative effects of holding too firmly to the idea that communities and cultures need to be protected from offense. What does he mean? Do you think this part of his argument follows from his arguments about appropriation? Why, or why not?
7. Consider your own cultural background. Are there forms of dress, decoration, language, or rituals that you see as acceptable for others to "borrow" and others you see as unacceptable? Explain in about 250 words, using examples as you respond.

YO ZUSHI

Yo Zushi (b. 1981) is a British Japanese songwriter and performer who contributes essays on culture and politics to the *New Statesman*. The selection below was published in October 2015. Zushi's most recent albums are *It Never Entered My Mind* (2015) and *King of the Road* (2018).

What's Mine Is Yours

The policing of appearance is nothing new. In the mid-1920s, the then Mexican president, Plutarco Elías Calles, forbade Catholic priests from wearing clerical collars outdoors; more recently, on 14 September 2010, the French Senate passed the *Loi interdisant la dissimulation du visage dans l'espace public*, better known in the English-speaking world as "the burqa ban." What is curious, however, is that the latest round of strictures on how individuals can present themselves comes not from repressive, dictatorial regimes or panicked politicians but from those who consider themselves progressives: liberals united against the menace of "cultural appropriation."

In August, a student committee at Western University in Canada announced a ban on the wearing of cultural symbols such as turbans, dreadlock wigs and ethnic headdresses by white volunteers during orientation week. The sale of Native American headdresses has also been proscribed at Glastonbury Festival, after an online petition that garnered just 65 signatures persuaded organizers that offering them as a "costume" was insensitive. (The Canadian festival Bass Coast has similarly issued a prohibition on guests wearing the war bonnets.) Pharrell Williams came under fire on Twitter when he posed in a feather headdress for an *Elle* cover in 2014 — a striking image that the magazine initially boasted was the singer's "best-ever shoot" — and was forced to apologize. "I respect and honor every kind of race, background and culture," he said. "I am genuinely sorry."

From Katy Perry's adoption of geisha garb at the 2013 American Music Awards to Lena Dunham's cornrows and their supposed flaunting of racial identity theft, all cultural cross-pollination now seems to be fair game for a drubbing at the hands of the new race activists. Recently in the *Guardian*, Julianne Escobedo Shepherd denounced the adoption of the Mexican-American *chola* style — dark-outlined lips, crucifixes, elaborate fringes, teardrop tattoos — by fashion labels and the pop star Rihanna as a "fashion crime" that amounted to an "ignorant harvesting" of the self-expression of others; she then mocked Sandra Bullock's admission that she would "do anything to become more Latina." Back off, whitey.

At a time of heightened racial tensions across the world, with police shootings of black men in the United States and Islamophobia (and phobias of all kinds) seemingly on the rise, this rage against cultural appropriation is understandable: no right-minded liberal wants to cause unnecessary offense, least of all to minorities. Yet simply to point out instances of appropriation in the assumption that the process is by its nature corrosive seems to me a counterproductive, even reactionary pursuit; it serves no end but to essentialize race as the ultimate component of human identity.

5 I'm Japanese but I felt no anger when I read that the Museum of Fine Arts in Boston was holding kimono try-on sessions to accompany its recent exhibition "Looking East: Western Artists and the Allure of Japan" — after all, it was a show that specifically set out to examine the orientalist gaze. However, some protesters (carrying signs that read "Try on the kimono, learn what it's like to be a racist imperialist today!" and "This is orientalism") evidently did. Their complaints against the show, which was organized in collaboration with NHK, Japan's national broadcaster, swiftly led to the cancellation of the "Kimono Wednesday" sessions. "We thought it would be an educational opportunity for people to have direct encounters with works of art and understand different cultures and times better," said Katie Getchell, the justifiably surprised deputy director of the museum.

"Stand against yellowface!" the protesters declaimed on blogs and on Facebook. Elsewhere, the white rapper Iggy Azalea — like Elvis and Mick Jagger before her — was accused of "blackfacing" her way to stardom, after she became the fourth solo female hip-hop artist ever to reach the top of the *Billboard* Hot 100 with her 2014 single "Fancy." At the end of that year, the African-American rapper Azealia Banks suggested that Azalea's "cultural smudging" was yet another careless instance of cross-racial stealing; that white adoption of a historically black genre had an "undercurrent of kinda like, 'F--k you.' There's always a 'f--k y'all, n----s. Y'all don't really own shit . . . not even the shit you created for yourself.' "

Many of those calling out cultural appropriation of all kinds — from clothing and hair to musical genres — seem to share this proprietorial attitude, which insists that culture, by its nature a communally forged and ever-changing project, should belong to specific peoples and not to all. Banks is doubtless correct to feel this "undercurrent" of racial persecution by an industry that prefers its stars to be white and what they sell to be black, yet there is also truth in the second part of that undercurrent: "Y'all don't really own shit." When it comes to great movements in culture, the racial interloper is not wrong. None of us can, or should, "own" hip-hop, cornrows, or the right to wear a kimono.

Speaking to the website Jezebel, the law professor Susan Scafidi of Fordham University in New York explained that appropriation involves "taking intellectual property, traditional knowledge, cultural expressions or artifacts from someone else's culture without permission." Yet such a definition seems to assume the existence of mythical central organizations with absolute mandates to represent minority groups — a black HQ, an Asian bureau, a Jewish head office — from which permissions and authorizations can be sought. More troubling is that it herds culture and tradition into the pen of a moral ownership not dissimilar to copyright, which may suit a legalistic outlook but jars with our human impulse to like what we like and create new things out of it.

Elvis liked black music. While other kids dashed around at school picnics, the juvenile Presley would sit off by himself, "plunking softly at that guitar," as one teacher later recalled. He shared with the Sun Records founder, Sam Phillips, the opinion that African-American music was of that magic kind in which "the soul of man never dies," and when he launched into a hopped-up version of Arthur Crudup's blues "That's All Right" at the tail end of a recording session in 1954, it was a natural, uncalculated act of cultural appropriation. "Elvis just started singing this song, jumping around and acting the fool," remembered the guitarist Scotty Moore, who played on the single that many credit as the foundation stone of rock'n'roll.

10 It wasn't the first of its kind. Rock'n'roll grew organically out of the miscegenation of rhythm'n'blues and hillbilly music, and other contenders for that title include Goree Carter's "Rock Awhile" (1949) and Jackie Brenston's "Rocket '88' " (1951). Both Carter and Brenston were black — but they are now largely forgotten. The smoking gun in the periodically revived argument that Elvis should be condemned for having participated in interracial plundering is Phillips's often quoted remark: "If I could find a white man who had the Negro feel, I could make a billion dollars." Yet the studio owner's remark was, if anything, more a groan of exasperation than the blueprint for a robbery. He had tried to make a billion dollars before he recorded Elvis, with B B King, Howling Wolf and other black musicians; indeed, it was Phillips who recorded Brenston's song. The racism wasn't in the studio or cut into the record grooves. It was out there, woven into American life in the 1950s.

That tainted life was altered for the better by the emergence of rock'n'roll, whose enormous popularity forced many previously white-oriented labels to sign African-American artists and changed for ever the social interactions of black and white teenagers. It gave them a common culture based less on skin color than on the spirit of youth, frightening reactionaries who were perturbed precisely by what they viewed as an unnatural cultural appropriation. After Elvis performed the "Big Mama" Thornton song "Hound Dog" on national television on 5 June 1956, Congressman Emanuel Celler stated disapprovingly, "Rock'n'roll has its place: among the colored people." Many white fans of the music, appropriators all, could not help but realize that their place and that of "colored" fans were one and the same.

What was so with rock'n'roll goes also for rap, fashion and even that packet of tortilla chips you ate at the movies or the shish kebab you had on the way home. Appropriation tests imaginary boundaries. It questions them and exposes, just as Judith Butler did in relation to gender, the performative aspects of our racial and cultural identity: much of our yellowness, brownness, blackness or whiteness is acted out and not intrinsic to our being. It shows that we can select who we are and who we want to be. By opposing it unilaterally under the banner of racial justice, activists often end up placing themselves on the side of those who insist on terrifying ideals of "purity": white and black should never mix and the Australian-born Iggy Azalea should leave rap alone. She should stick to performing . . . what, exactly? Perhaps she should consult a family tree. But how far back is she expected to go? And should we impose some sort of one-drop rule?

It is true that cultural appropriation can hurt those whose traditions, religions and ways of life have been lifted, taken out of context and repackaged as a new aesthetic trend or exotic bauble. The feather headdress, for instance, has deep symbolic value to many Native Americans and to see it balancing on the wobbly head of a drunk, white festivalgoer might feel like an insult. Yet is it a theft at all, when that original value is still felt by the Native American tribe? Little of substance has been taken away. To the white reveller, those feathers probably signify something as simple as: "I am trying my best to have fun." There is no offense intended. If it channels anything of the headdress's origins, it is no doubt a distant echo of some ancient myth that placed "Indians" as the other, the sworn enemies of the "cowboys."

Appropriations of this sort can, if unchallenged, entrench negative racial mythologies. But such myths are part of the language of human culture and their potential for harm can only truly be diffused by putting forward stronger, newer narratives about ourselves and by tackling the systemic injustices that oppress us: in law, in government, in the workplace. I can live in the knowledge that the *Mikado* myth continues to have some currency and that films, songs and books still toy with the orientalist fantasy of Japan. That is partly because their sting has been dulled by an ever-increasing understanding in the west of what real life in east Asia is like. I accept that our culture can be transformed and absorbed into the folklore of another people — and when this happens, we have only a limited claim on that folklore. Like it or not, it becomes theirs as much as ours. Sometimes, we have to let culture do its thing.

Topics for Critical Thinking and Writing

1. Select one of the examples Yo Zushi refers to in his essay and do some further research to assess general opinions on the instance or incident. What issues were at stake? Whose view do you think was most convincing, and why?
2. In about 250 words, examine the critique of Iggy Azalea as "'blackfacing' her way to stardom" and being guilty of "cultural smudging" (para. 6). Should Azalea be faulted? Why, or why not?
3. Zushi compares the cultural appropriations of rock and roll, rap, and fashion with "that packet of tortilla chips you ate at the movies or the shish kebab you had on the way home" (para. 12). Is this comparison a form of equivocation (see p. 345)? Tell why or why not in 250 words or so.

4. Zushi writes that as a Japanese man he had little trouble accepting people trying on kimonos, a traditional Japanese fashion, at the Museum of Fine Arts in Boston, even while protestors condemned the activity, with one person's sign reading, "This is orientalism" (para. 10). In your opinion, do Zushi's race and ethnicity help or hurt his overall argument, or do they have no effect at all? Why?
5. On the whole, whose argument did you find to be more fair-minded, Malik's or Zushi's? Explain in 100 to 200 words.
6. Do some research into the historical and cultural roots of a musical genre or style (e.g., rock, punk, rap, jazz, blues, country, or folk). In about 300 words, address questions related to the themes of Zushi's and Malik's essays: Were these forms based on cultural appropriation? Who, if anyone, can claim "authenticity"? Could any artists or performers be said to have stolen or misused another culture's expressions? Why, or why not?

K. TEMPEST BRADFORD

K. Tempest Bradford (b. 1978) is an African American science fiction and fantasy writer whose stories have appeared in literary magazines such as *Strange Horizons* and *Electric Velocipede* and whose essays, op-eds, and reviews appear in various online and print media sources. This piece was published online at National Public Radio's Code Switch, which covers race and culture. In it, she responds to a piece written for the *New York Times* by Kenan Malik, "In Defense of Cultural Appropriation." Malik's essay "The Bane of Cultural Appropriation" appears earlier in this chapter.

Cultural Appropriation Is, in Fact, Indefensible

In June 2017, the *New York Times* published an op-ed titled "In Defense of Cultural Appropriation" in which writer Kenan Malik attempted to extol the virtues of artistic appropriation and chastise those who would stand in the way of necessary "cultural engagement." What would have happened, he argues, had Elvis Presley not been able to swipe the sounds of black musicians?

Malik is not the first person to defend cultural appropriation. He joins a long list that, most recently, has included prominent members of the Canadian literary community and author Lionel Shriver.

But the truth is that cultural appropriation is indefensible. Those who defend it either don't understand what it is, misrepresent it to muddy the conversation, or ignore its complexity — discarding any nuances and making it easy to dismiss both appropriation and those who object to it.

At the start of the most recent debate, Canadian author Hal Niedzviecki called on the readers of *Write* magazine to "Write what you don't know . . . Relentlessly explore the lives of people who aren't like you. . . . Win the Appropriation Prize." Amid the outcry over this editorial, there were those who wondered why this statement would be objectionable. Shouldn't authors "write the Other"? Shouldn't there be more representative fiction?

5 Yes, of course. The issue here is that Niedzviecki conflated cultural appropriation and the practice of writing characters with

very different identities from yourself — and they're not the same thing. Writing inclusive fiction might involve appropriation if it's done badly, but that's not a given.

Cultural appropriation can feel hard to get a handle on, because boiling it down to a two-sentence dictionary definition does no one any favors. Writer Maisha Z. Johnson offers an excellent starting point by describing it not only as the act of an individual, but an individual working within a "*power dynamic* in which members of a dominant culture take elements from a culture of people who have been systematically oppressed *by that dominant group*."

That's why appropriation and exchange are two different things, Johnson says — there's no power imbalance involved in an exchange. And when artists appropriate, they can profit from what they take, while the oppressed group gets nothing.

I teach classes and seminars alongside author and editor Nisi Shawl on Writing the Other, and the foundation of our work is that authors *should* create characters from many different races, cultures, class backgrounds, physical abilities, and genders, even if — especially if — these don't match their own. We are not alone in this. You won't find many people advising authors to only create characters similar to themselves. You will find many who say: Don't write characters from minority or marginalized identities if you are not going to put in the hard work to do it well and avoid cultural appropriation and other harmful outcomes. These are different messages. But writers often see or hear the latter and imagine that it means the former. And editorials like Niedzviecki's don't help the matter.

Complicating things even further, those who tend to see appropriation as exchange are often the ones who profit from it.

Even Malik's example involving rock and roll isn't as simple as Elvis "stealing" from black artists. Before he even came along, systematic oppression and segregation in America meant black musicians didn't have access to the same opportunities for mainstream exposure, income, or success as white ones. Elvis and other rock and roll musicians were undoubtedly influenced by black innovators, but over time the genre came to be regarded as a cultural product created, perfected by, and only accessible to whites.

This is the "messy interaction" Malik breezes over in dismissing the idea of appropriation as theft: A repeating pattern that's recognizable across many different cultural spheres, from fashion and the arts to literature and food.

And this pattern is why cultures and people who've suffered the most from appropriation sometimes insist on their traditions being treated like intellectual property — it can seem like the only way to protect themselves and to force members of dominant or oppressive cultures to consider the impact of their actions.

This has lead to accusations of gatekeeping by Malik and others: Who has the right to decide what is appropriation and what isn't? What does true cultural exchange look like? There's no one easy answer to either question.

But there are some helpful guidelines: The Australian Council for the Arts developed a set of protocols for working with Indigenous artists that lays out how to approach Aboriginal culture as a respectful guest, who to contact for guidance and permission, and how to proceed with your art if that permission is not granted. Some of these protocols are specific to Australia, but the key to all of them is finding ways for creativity to flourish while also reducing harm.

All of this lies at the root of why cultural appropriation is indefensible. It is, without question, harmful. It is not inherent to writing representational and inclusive fiction, it is not a process of equal and mutually beneficial exchange, and it is not a way for one culture to honor another. Cultural appropriation does damage, and it should be something writers and other artists work hard to avoid, not compete with each other to achieve.

For those who are willing to do that hard work, there are resources out there. When I lecture about this, I ask writers to consider whether they are acting as Invaders, Tourists, or Guests, according to the excellent framework Nisi Shawl lays out in her essay "Appropriate Cultural Appropriation." And then I point them towards "The Cultural Appropriation Primer" and all the articles and blog posts I've collected over time on the subject of cultural appropriation, to give them as full a background in understanding, identifying, and avoiding it as I possibly can.

Because I believe that, instead of giving people excuses for why appropriation can't be avoided (it can), or allowing them to think it's no big deal (it is), it's more important to help them become better artists whose creations contribute to cultural understanding and growth that benefits us all.

Topics for Critical Thinking and Writing

1. In paragraph 3, K. Tempest Bradford states her argument boldly. Do you find this approach to be a strong rhetorical move? Why, or why not? What might an effective alternative approach look like?
2. Why might it be objectionable for an author to write a story or novel from the perspective of a different racial or cultural group? Is it similarly objectionable for musicians to utilize the instruments, forms, or expressions of a different culture's music? Why, or why not?
3. Reread Maisha Z. Johnson's definition of appropriation in paragraph 6. Do you agree that appropriation is particularly wrong when the group appropriating from another culture is the dominant group? Does this definition establish a double standard? Why, or why not?
4. Write an essay in which you explore an example of appropriation that is exploitative and an example of appropriation that constitutes "exchange" (see para. 7). Do you think this standard of evaluation established by Bradford is a fair one?
5. Do you think it is reasonable to define intellectual property rights for certain cultural groups' myths, traditions, and symbols?
6. Describe the similarities and differences between the kinds of appropriation Bradford discusses and those Zushi deals with. Are all kinds of appropriation equal? What kinds do you find acceptable, and why? What kinds do you not find acceptable, and why?

CONOR FRIEDERSDORF

Conor Friedersdorf is a graduate of Pomona College and New York University and a regular contributor to the *Atlantic*, where he writes about politics and international affairs. This piece was published in the *Atlantic* on December 21, 2015.

A Food Fight at Oberlin College

In the winter of 2015, students at Oberlin made national headlines for casting complaints about bad dining-hall food — a perennial lament of collegians — as a problematic social-justice failure. Word spread via people who saw their behavior as political correctness run amok. *The New York Post* gleefully mocked the students "at Lena Dunham's college." On social media, many wondered if the controversy was a parody.

In fact, it is quite real.

The core student grievance, as reported by Clover Lihn Tran at *The Oberlin Review*: Bon Appétit, the food service vendor, "has a history of blurring the line between culinary diversity and cultural appropriation by modifying the recipes without respect for certain Asian countries' cuisines. This uninformed representation of cultural dishes has been noted by a multitude of students, many of who have expressed concern over the gross manipulation of traditional recipes."

One international student suffered a *sando-aggression*:

> Diep Nguyen, a College first-year from Vietnam, jumped with excitement at the sight of Vietnamese food on Stevenson Dining Hall's menu at Orientation this year. Craving Vietnamese comfort food, Nguyen rushed to the food station with high hopes. What she got, however, was a total disappointment. The traditional Banh Mi Vietnamese sandwich that Stevenson Dining Hall promised turned out to be a cheap imitation of the East Asian dish. Instead of a crispy baguette with grilled pork, pate, pickled vegetables and fresh herbs, the sandwich used ciabatta bread, pulled pork and coleslaw. "It was ridiculous," Nguyen said. "How could they just throw out something completely different and label it as another country's traditional food?"

Multiple students were dissatisfied with 5
their landlocked, Midwestern institution's take on the cuisine of an island nation with Earth's most sophisticated fishing culture:

> Perhaps the pinnacle of what many students believe to be a culturally appropriative sustenance system is Dascomb Dining Hall's sushi bar. The sushi is anything but authentic for Tomoyo Joshi, a College junior from Japan, who said that the undercooked rice and lack of fresh fish is disrespectful. She added that in Japan, sushi is regarded so highly that people sometimes take years of apprenticeship before learning how to appropriately serve it.
>
> "When you're cooking a country's dish for other people, including ones who have never tried the original dish before, you're also representing the meaning of the dish as well as its culture," Joshi said. "So if people not from that heritage take food, modify it and serve it as 'authentic,' it is appropriative."

Another student, Yasmine Ramachandra, offered a distinct complaint, saying she was compelled to join the protest "after arriving at

Stevenson Dining Hall with other South Asian students on Diwali, a Hindu holiday, and finding the traditional Indian tandoori made with beef, which many Hindi people do not eat for religious reasons."

Even *Red State* grants that her grievance is legitimate.

Her grievance aside, the typical response to the controversy from observers across the ideological spectrum is weary, bemused disagreement with the students.

What exactly are they thinking?

10 In the ongoing debate about the state of academia, Oberlin is properly seen as an outlier, not a reflection of what most campuses are like. This story is hardly all there is to Oberlin — it's an outlying story about a small number of students plucked by the tabloid most adept at trolling its readers from the stream of campus news. There are dissenters at the school. And students at many campuses often complain about food in overwrought ways.

Still, it's possible to glean insights from the most absurd events at Oberlin as surely as it's possible to learn something about America by observing the biggest Black Friday sales, the most over-the-top displays of militarism at professional sporting events, or the most extreme reality televisions show. Every subculture and ideology has its excesses. And Oberlin, where the subculture is unusually influenced by "social justice" activism, can starkly illuminate the particular character of that ideology's excesses.

One caveat: Although it's easy to minimize college student complaints about the dining halls — especially since they're likely *much* better than what older college graduates ate in the era before sushi bars — the transition from a Japanese or Vietnamese diet to dining-hall food in Ohio would be challenging for a lot of people. At that basic level, I feel empathy for the international students, as well as for American students whose only food options leave them not wanting to eat anything. If I were an Oberlin professor, I'd be quietly amassing spices and recipes to have a few of the homesick students over for whatever they consider comfort food. And a lot of people mocking the students would have a hard time adjusting to the dining-hall cuisine of an Asian country if forced to live abroad there for a year.

But there's a flip side to my empathy. Many people relate to the complaint, "Gosh, this food is awful — can't you dining hall people make it better." Yet Oberlin culture — I feel certain that the international students did not import these modes of expression — re-framed a banal, sympathetic complaint in a way that alienated millions.

Can Oberlin insiders help explain why?

15 Some find the approach of the Oberlin students off-putting because it strikes them as ultimately cynical. One reader of Rod Dreher's blog at *The American Conservative* explained that reaction this way:

> Are all college students like this? Of course not. If they were, one shudders to think what they'd make of the Ramen noodle industry. Still. Better, more authentic, more flavorful foods aren't necessarily bad.
>
> It's a cause you might support!
>
> But there are no longer complaints or gripes or suggestions. Only outrage. "Hey, putting ketchup on the linguini isn't really Italian night," becomes, "You are oppressing me with your white privilege." Why? Because it works. Saying that to a college administrator is like telling a self conscious girl that she looks fat in her jeans, or telling a young fella that size really does matter and, sorry pal, you don't measure up.
>
> And threatening to do these things publicly.

If this *is* a cynical power play on some level, its effectiveness cannot be denied. While being mocked in the national press, the students are getting results at Oberlin:

> Following claims of Campus Dining Services appropriating traditional Asian dishes, representatives from the South Asian, Vietnamese and Chinese student associations met with CDS to discuss students' concerns . . .
>
> "They took us very seriously and were taking notes the whole time," said Clover Linh Tran, College sophomore and Vietnamese Student Association co-chair . . . "They seemed very willing to learn and fix what was offending people." Tran organized the meeting after coordinating with CDS representatives and inviting fellow students through a Facebook event.
>
> Michele Gross, director of CDS; Eric Pecherkiewicz, campus registered dietitian; and John Klancar, Bon Appétit director of operations, were all in attendance.

The less-cynical explanation is that these students really do feel culturally disrespected by low-wage dining hall staff making do with sub-optimal ingredients.

Even observers who presume the earnestness of the students have taken aim at the substance of their beliefs, pointing out that there is nothing wrong with radically tweaking dishes from different culinary traditions — and it's particularly incoherent to complain about "appropriative" treatments of items like the bánh mi sandwich (one half expects them to protest the colonialism of the baguette rather than its absence) or General Tsao's Chicken that are themselves inseparable from cultural collisions. The dining hall is serving cheap imitations of East Asian dishes because all college campuses serve cheap imitations of *all dishes* — they're trying to feed students as cheaply as possible, and authentic bánh mis, never mind sushi, would cost much more. And, of course, East Asian students are hardly alone in being served inauthentic versions of foods they grew up eating. As the grandson of two French Cajuns, I can assure aggrieved Oberlin students that the "gumbo" and "jambalaya" I was sometimes served for campus meals was in no way authentic! (Nor was the spaghetti carbonara, nor the Danishes, nor the beef goulash.)

The avowed position of these students strikes some observers as so wrongheaded that they prefer to believe that the young people don't *really* believe what they're saying.

20 "I am more sympathetic to campus activists' concerns than most people here, but the 'cultural appropriation' business fills me with blind fury," another reader at Rod Dreher's blog wrote. "Mixing and matching and intermingling and borrowing and stealing and creating new traditions out of whole cloth is what America does, and in my view, it is the encapsulation of what is best about this country . . . to crap on the one thing that makes America one of the few successful multicultural countries in the world on the basis of half-understood theories is beyond infuriating. The best spin I could put on this is that these people are basically using the language of appropriation to push for better food service, but I am afraid they are serious."

So how about it, Oberlin insiders?

The majority of you aren't participating in this activist effort. Help outsiders to understand what's really going on. Should these students be understood as having an understandable desire for higher-quality food — who can blame them for urging the powers that be to feed them better? — and opportunistically co-opting the language of social justice to get their way? Or are they framing their complaints in terms of cultural appropriation and "problematic" affronts to enlightened behavior because they really believe that's what is going on?

Neither option seems quite right to me. Maybe there's another that I'm missing. Oberlin is full of intelligent people.

If there is, in fact, some opportunism to the way these students are framing their complaints, does it suggest that Oberlin would do well to better guard against the exploitation of its frequently admirable efforts to be inclusive? Or if students really believe that they are the victims of "problematic" behavior, is social-justice ideology causing them to conclude that they face more antagonism than is in fact the case?

25 I suppose my questions telegraph my perspective. At the very least, these students would be well served by more exposure to different ways of thinking, if only so that they can understand why so many outsiders perceive *them* to be the privileged jerks of this particular story. As an Oberlin alum commented in the student newspaper, "I worked in multiple dining halls and was friendly with many of the staff there, and out of everyone I met, maybe two of them had been out of the country before. One of them even told me that she had never seen or heard of a chickpea before she started working there. Before students start labeling the lack of authenticity of their food as 'cultural appropriation,' maybe they should take a step back and think about the likely differences between themselves and the people who are preparing it."

Freddie de Boer put it more pointedly:

> an undergrad at a $50K/year liberal arts college berating cafe workers making $12/hour in the name of social justice on a human face forever[1]
>
> — Fredrik deBoer (@freddiedeboer)
> December 19, 2015

These critiques may be harsh, but are not grounded in antagonism toward the students. Were I an Oberlin administrator, I'd diligently inquire into any complaints about poor food quality and negotiate for the best fare possible, given cost constraints, even if students expressed their dissatisfaction in an off-putting manner.

But I like to think I'd call them on their nonsense, too.

It seems to me that staff and administrators at Oberlin ill-serve these students insofar as they accommodate behavior of this sort without offering any critique in response. After all, beyond allowing them to persist in their highly dubious and wildly unpopular beliefs, they're training students to air grievances in a way that will be counterproductive — and thus serve them ill — *everywhere except college campuses*. As de Boer wrote, "I'm a college educator. It's the only job I ever wanted. It's my job to take college activists seriously. And this reflects bigger problems . . . life is full of political injustice, but also full of just sucky and disappointing shit, and you need to know the difference . . . I have this crazy hang up: I care about student activists so much, I pay attention to whether their tactics can actually win or not."

30 I understand why some observers are inclined to defend young people when they become objects of ridicule in the *New York Post*. I certainly oppose demonizing these students. But constructive criticism is not only legitimate, it is salutary. It confronts students who've been acculturated into a seductive ideology with the diversity of thought they need to refine their ideas. From the outside, Oberlin seems unable to provide dissent in anything like the quality and quantity needed to prepare these young people for the enormous complexity of life in a diverse society, where few defer to claims just because they are expressed in the language of social justice.

Is that how it looks from the inside, too?

[1]Reference to George Orwell's novel *1984*, in which the dystopian future is pictured as "a boot stamping on a human face forever." [Editors' note]

Topics for Critical Thinking and Writing

1. Examine the argument made by Clover Lihn Tran in paragraph 3. Is it a reasonable request that culture-specific foods be served in accordance with a standard of authenticity? Is it reasonable to argue that failing to establish such a standard constitutes appropriation and is therefore offensive? Think of some other grounds upon which an argument for food quality standards could be made.
2. Do you think there is a difference in the critique made by Tomoyo Joshi related to sushi and the critique made by Yasmine Ramachandra about the tandoori? Explain.
3. How does Conor Friedersdorf characterize the students at Oberlin who argued for more authentic food and charged the college and the cafeteria with appropriation and cultural insensitivity? Tell why you agree or disagree with Friedersdorf's characterization.
4. Do you agree with Friedersdorf that the Oberlin students working for improved food need to be "call[ed] out" (para. 28)? Do you think the author does so successfully? Explain your answers.

KENNETH GOLDSMITH

Kenneth Goldsmith (b. 1961) is an American poet, writer, musician, DJ, and performance artist. In 2007, a documentary feature on his art, *Sucking on Words*, premiered at the British Library, and in 2013, he became the Museum of Modern Art's first poet laureate. Goldsmith teaches in the English department at the University of Pennsylvania, where he is senior editor of PennSound, an online poetry archive. The selection below was published in the *Chronicle of Higher Education* in the lead-up to the release of his book, *Uncreative Writing: Managing Language in the Digital Age* (2012).

Uncreative Writing

In 1969 the conceptual artist Douglas Huebler wrote, "The world is full of objects, more or less interesting; I do not wish to add any more." I've come to embrace Huebler's idea, though it might be retooled as: "The world is full of texts, more or less interesting; I do not wish to add any more."

It seems an appropriate response to a new condition in writing: With an unprecedented amount of available text, our problem is not needing to write more of it; instead, we must learn to negotiate the vast quantity that exists. How I make my way through this thicket of information — how I manage it, parse it, organize and distribute it — is what distinguishes my writing from yours.

The prominent literary critic Marjorie Perloff has recently begun using the term "unoriginal genius" to describe this tendency emerging in literature. Her idea is that, because of changes brought on by technology and the Internet, our notion of the genius — a romantic, isolated figure — is outdated. An updated notion of genius would have to center around one's mastery of information and its dissemination. Perloff has coined another term, "moving information," to signify both the act of pushing language around as well as the act of being emotionally moved by that process. She posits that today's writer resembles more a programmer than a tortured genius, brilliantly conceptualizing, constructing, executing, and maintaining a writing machine.

Perloff's notion of unoriginal genius should not be seen merely as a theoretical conceit but rather as a realized writing practice, one that dates back to the early part of the 20th century, embodying an ethos in which the construction or conception of a text is as important as what the text says or does. Think, for example, of the collated, note-taking practice of Walter Benjamin's *Arcades Project*[1] or the mathematically driven constraint-based works by Oulipo[2], a group of writers and mathematicians.

5 Today technology has exacerbated these mechanistic tendencies in writing (there are, for instance, several Web-based versions of Raymond Queneau's 1961 laboriously hand-constructed *Hundred Thousand Billion Poems*), inciting younger writers to take their cues from the workings of technology and the Web as ways of constructing literature. As a result, writers are exploring ways of writing that have been thought, traditionally, to be outside the scope of literary practice: word processing, databasing, recycling, appropriation, intentional plagiarism, identity ciphering, and intensive programming, to name just a few.

In 2007 Jonathan Lethem published a pro-plagiarism, plagiarized essay in *Harper's* titled, "The Ecstasy of Influence: A Plagiarism." It's a lengthy defense and history of how ideas in literature have been shared, riffed, culled, reused, recycled, swiped, stolen, quoted, lifted, duplicated, gifted, appropriated, mimicked, and pirated for as long as literature has existed. Lethem reminds us of how gift economies, open-source cultures, and public commons have been vital for the creation of new works, with themes from older works forming the basis for new ones. Echoing the cries of free-culture advocates such as Lawrence Lessig and Cory Doctorow, he eloquently rails against copyright law as a threat to the lifeblood of creativity. From Martin Luther King Jr.'s sermons to Muddy Waters's blues tunes, he showcases the rich fruits of shared culture. He even cites examples of what he had assumed were his own "original" thoughts, only later to realize — usually by Googling — that he had unconsciously absorbed someone else's ideas that he then claimed as his own.

It's a great essay. Too bad he didn't "write" it. The punchline? Nearly every word and idea was borrowed from somewhere else — either appropriated in its entirety or rewritten by Lethem. His essay is an example of "patchwriting," a way of weaving together various shards of other people's words into a tonally cohesive whole. It's a trick that students use all the time, rephrasing, say, a Wikipedia entry into their own words. And if they're caught, it's trouble: In academia, patchwriting is considered an offense equal to that of plagiarism. If Lethem had submitted this as a senior thesis or dissertation chapter, he'd be shown the door. Yet few would argue that he didn't construct a brilliant work of art — as well as writing a pointed essay — entirely in the words of others. It's the way in which he conceptualized and executed his writing machine — surgically choosing what to borrow, arranging those words in a skillful way — that wins us over. Lethem's piece is a self-reflexive, demonstrative work of unoriginal genius.

[1] ***Arcades Project*** Walter Benjamin's (1892–1940) collected notes and observations of the Parisian arcades, published posthumously in 1999. [All notes are the editors'.]

[2] **Oulipo** A group of French experimental writers and mathematicians founded in 1960 who created innovative writing forms (e.g., poems with only one vowel).

Lethem's provocation belies a trend among younger writers who take his exercise one step further by boldly appropriating the work of others without citation, disposing of the artful and seamless integration of Lethem's patchwriting. For them, the act of writing is literally moving language from one place to another, proclaiming that context is the new content. While pastiche and collage have long been part and parcel of writing, with the rise of the Internet plagiaristic intensity has been raised to extreme levels.

Over the past five years, we have seen a retyping of Jack Kerouac's *On the Road* in its entirety, a page a day, every day, on a blog for a year; an appropriation of the complete text of a day's copy of *The New York Times* published as a 900-page book; a list poem that is nothing more than reframing a listing of stores from a shopping-mall directory into a poetic form; an impoverished writer who has taken every credit-card application sent to him and bound them into an 800-page print-on-demand book so costly that he can't afford a copy; a poet who has parsed the text of an entire 19th-century book on grammar according to its own methods, even down to the book's index; a lawyer who re-presents the legal briefs of her day job as poetry in their entirety without changing a word; another writer who spends her days at the British Library copying down the first verse of Dante's *Inferno* from every English translation that the library possesses, one after another, page after page, until she exhausts the library's supply; a writing team that scoops status updates off social-networking sites and assigns them to the names of deceased writers ("Jonathan Swift has got tix to the Wranglers game tonight"), creating an epic, never-ending work of poetry that rewrites itself as frequently as Facebook pages are updated; and an entire movement of writing, called Flarf, that is based on grabbing the worst of Google search results: the more offensive, the more ridiculous, the more outrageous, the better.

10 These writers are language hoarders; their projects are epic, mirroring the gargantuan scale of textuality on the Internet. While the works often take an electronic form, paper versions circulate in journals and zines, purchased by libraries, and received by, written about, and studied by readers of literature. While this new writing has an electronic gleam in its eye, its results are distinctly analog, taking inspiration from radical modernist ideas and juicing them with 21st-century technology.

Far from this "uncreative" literature being a nihilistic, begrudging acceptance — or even an outright rejection — of a presumed "technological enslavement," it is a writing imbued with celebration, ablaze with enthusiasm for the future, embracing this moment as one pregnant with possibility. This joy is evident in the writing itself, in which there are moments of unanticipated beauty — some grammatical, others structural, many philosophical: the wonderful rhythms of repetition, the spectacle of the mundane reframed as literature, a reorientation to the poetics of time, and fresh perspectives on readerliness, to name just a few. And then there's emotion: yes, emotion. But far from being coercive or persuasive, this writing delivers emotion obliquely and unpredictably, with sentiments expressed as a result of the writing process rather than by authorial intention. . . .

While home computers have been around for about two decades, and people have been cutting and pasting all that time, it's the sheer penetration and saturation of broadband that makes the harvesting of masses of language easy and tempting. On a dial-up, although it was possible to copy and paste words, in the beginning texts were doled out one screen at a time. And even though it was text, the load time was still considerable. With broadband, the spigot runs 24/7.

By comparison, there was nothing native to typewriting that encouraged the replication of texts. It was slow and laborious to do so. Later, *after* you had finished writing, you could make all the copies you wanted on a Xerox machine. As a result, there was a tremendous amount of 20th-century postwriting print-based *detournement:*[3] William S. Burroughs's cutups and fold-ins and Bob Cobbing's distressed mimeographed poems are prominent examples. The previous forms of borrowing in literature, collage, and pastiche — taking a word from here, a sentence from there — were developed based on the amount of labor involved. Having to manually retype or hand-copy an entire book on a typewriter is one thing; cutting and pasting an entire book with three keystrokes — select all/copy/paste — is another.

Clearly this is setting the stage for a literary revolution.

15 Or is it? From the looks of it, most writing proceeds as if the Internet had never happened. The literary world still gets regularly scandalized by age-old bouts of fraudulence, plagiarism, and hoaxes in ways that would make, say, the art, music, computing, or science worlds chuckle with disbelief. It's hard to imagine the James Frey or J.T. Leroy scandals[4] upsetting anybody familiar with the sophisticated, purposely fraudulent provocations of Jeff Koons or the rephotographing of advertisements by Richard Prince, who was awarded a Guggenheim retrospective for his plagiaristic tendencies. Koons and Prince began their careers by stating upfront that they were appropriating and being intentionally "unoriginal," whereas Frey and Leroy — even after they were caught — were still passing off their works as authentic, sincere, and personal statements to an audience clearly craving such qualities in literature. The ensuing dance was comical. In Frey's case, Random House was sued and had to pay hundreds of thousands of dollars in legal fees and thousands to readers who felt deceived. Subsequent printings of the book now include a disclaimer informing readers that what they are about to read is, in fact, a work of fiction.

Imagine all the pains that could have been avoided had Frey or Leroy taken a Koonsian tack from the outset and admitted that their strategy was one of embellishment, with dashes of inauthenticity, falseness, and unoriginality thrown in. But no.

Nearly a century ago, the art world put to rest conventional notions of originality and replication with the gestures of Marcel Duchamp's ready-mades, Francis Picabia's mechanical drawings, and Walter Benjamin's oft-quoted essay "The Work of Art in the Age of Mechanical Reproduction." Since then, a parade of blue-chip artists from Andy Warhol to Matthew Barney have taken these ideas to new levels, resulting in terribly complex notions of identity, media, and culture. These, of course, have become part of mainstream art-world discourse, to the point where counterreactions based on sincerity and representation have emerged.

Similarly, in music, sampling — entire tracks constructed from other tracks — has become commonplace. From Napster to gaming, from karaoke to torrent files, the culture appears to be embracing the digital and all the complexity it entails — with the exception of writing, which is still mostly wedded to promoting an authentic and stable identity at all costs.

I'm not saying that such writing should be discarded: Who hasn't been moved by a great memoir? But I'm sensing that literature — infinite in its potential of ranges and expressions — is in a rut, tending to hit the same note again and again, confining itself to the narrowest

---

[3]***Detournement*** (Fr., "hijacking; rerouting") A critical concept and technique of performing a variation on an existing text or artwork to resist its original meanings.

[4]**James Frey or J.T. Leroy scandals** Frey (b. 1961) was disgraced by plagiarism and falsification charges for his 2001 memoir, *A Million Little Pieces*. J.T. Leroy, after three autobiographical books, was discovered to be a persona invented by the American writer Laura Albert (b. 1965).

of spectrums, resulting in a practice that has fallen out of step and is unable to take part in arguably the most vital and exciting cultural discourses of our time. I find this to be a profoundly sad moment — and a great lost opportunity for literary creativity to revitalize itself in ways it hasn't imagined. . . .

20 For the past several years, I've taught a class at the University of Pennsylvania called "Uncreative Writing." In it, students are penalized for showing any shred of originality and creativity. Instead they are rewarded for plagiarism, identity theft, repurposing papers, patchwriting, sampling, plundering, and stealing. Not surprisingly, they thrive. Suddenly what they've surreptitiously become expert at is brought out into the open and explored in a safe environment, reframed in terms of responsibility instead of recklessness.

We retype documents and transcribe audio clips. We make small changes to Wikipedia pages (changing an "a" to "an" or inserting an extra space between words). We hold classes in chat rooms, and entire semesters are spent exclusively in Second Life.[5] Each semester, for their final paper, I have them purchase a term paper from an online paper mill and sign their name to it, surely the most forbidden action in all of academia. Students then must get up and present the paper to the class as if they wrote it themselves, defending it from attacks by the other students. What paper did they choose? Is it possible to defend something you didn't write? Something, perhaps, you don't agree with? Convince us.

All this, of course, is technology-driven. When the students arrive in class, they are told that they must have their laptops open and connected. And so we have a glimpse into the future. And after seeing what the spectacular results of this are, how completely engaged and democratic the classroom is, I am more convinced that I can never go back to a traditional classroom pedagogy. I learn more from the students than they can ever learn from me. The role of the professor now is part party host, part traffic cop, full-time enabler.

The secret: the suppression of self-expression is impossible. Even when we do something as seemingly "uncreative" as retyping a few pages, we express ourselves in a variety of ways. The act of choosing and reframing tells us as much about ourselves as our story about our mother's cancer operation. It's just that we've never been taught to value such choices.

After a semester of my forcibly suppressing a student's "creativity" by making her plagiarize and transcribe, she will tell me how disappointed she was because, in fact, what we had accomplished was not uncreative at all; by not being "creative," she had produced the most creative body of work in her life. By taking an opposite approach to creativity — the most trite, overused, and ill-defined concept in a writer's training — she had emerged renewed and rejuvenated, on fire and in love again with writing.

25 Having worked in advertising for many years as a "creative director," I can tell you that, despite what cultural pundits might say, creativity — as it's been defined by our culture, with its endless parade of formulaic novels, memoirs, and films — is the thing to flee from, not only as a member of the "creative class" but also as a member of the "artistic class." At a time when technology is changing the rules of the game in every aspect of our lives, it's time for us to question and tear down such clichés and reconstruct them into something new, something contemporary, something — finally — relevant.

Clearly, not everyone agrees. Recently, after I finished giving a lecture at an Ivy League

[5]**Second Life** An online multiuser virtual world launched in 2003.

university, an elderly, well-known poet, steeped in the modernist tradition, stood up in the back of the auditorium and, wagging his finger at me, accused me of nihilism and of robbing poetry of its joy. He upbraided me for knocking the foundation out from under the most hallowed of grounds, then tore into me with a line of questioning I've heard many times before: If everything can be transcribed and then presented as literature, then what makes one work better than another? If it's a matter of simply cutting and pasting the entire Internet into a Microsoft Word document, where does it end? Once we begin to accept all language as poetry by mere reframing, don't we risk throwing any semblance of judgment and quality out the window? What happens to notions of authorship? How are careers and canons established, and, subsequently, how are they to be evaluated? Are we simply re-enacting the death of the author, a figure that such theories failed to kill the first time around? Will all texts in the future be authorless and nameless, written by machines for machines? Is the future of literature reducible to mere code?

Valid concerns, I think, for a man who emerged from the literary battles of the 20th century victorious. The challenges to his generation were just as formidable. How did they convince traditionalists that disjunctive uses of language, conveyed by exploded syntax and compound words, could be equally expressive of human emotion as time-tested methods? Or that a story need not be told as strict narrative in order to convey its own logic and sense? And yet, against all odds, they persevered.

The 21st century, with its queries so different from those of the last, finds me responding from another angle. If it's a matter of simply cutting and pasting the entire Internet into a Microsoft Word document, then what becomes important is what you — the author — decide to choose. Success lies in knowing what to include and — more important — what to leave out. If all language can be transformed into poetry by merely reframing — an exciting possibility — then she who reframes words in the most charged and convincing way will be judged the best. . . .

In 1959 the poet and artist Brion Gysin claimed that writing was 50 years behind painting. He might still be right: In the art world, since Impressionism, the avant-garde has been the mainstream. Innovation and risk taking have been consistently rewarded. But, in spite of the successes of modernism, literature has remained on two parallel tracks, the mainstream and the avant-garde, with the two rarely intersecting. Now the conditions of digital culture have unexpectedly forced a collision, scrambling the once-sure footing of both camps. Suddenly we all find ourselves in the same boat, grappling with new questions concerning authorship, originality, and the way meaning is forged.

Topics for Critical Thinking and Writing

1. Does the concept of "cultural appropriation" undermine Kenneth Goldsmith's endorsement of a shared information economy open for "sampling, plundering, and stealing" (para. 20)? Why, or why not?
2. Is there a difference between creative, literary, or artistic forms of "theft" (borrowing, sampling, appropriating) and forms of plagiarism in argumentative writing? If so, characterize the difference(s), and tell why one form is "worse" than another. If you think there are no substantial differences, explain why.

3. Is it fair that the novelist Jonathan Lethem published an entirely plagiarized essay in a national magazine (para. 7), while a student who might write the same essay for a literature course would likely be charged with plagiarism? Explain your answer.
4. Reread the descriptions of conceptual art projects Goldsmith lists in paragraph 9. Do you think these projects rise to the level of art? Explain why or why not.
5. In 300 to 500 words, experiment with a type of writing Goldsmith would describe as "uncreative writing": that is, adopt, appropriate, reuse, or steal another type of writing and reframe it in such a way that "the construction or conception of [the] text is as important as what the text says or does" (para. 4). Then, reflect on your project, explaining your writing choices and experience and how effective you think the outcome is.

ANDREA PITZER

Andrea Pitzer graduated from Georgetown University's School of Foreign Service in 1994 and went on to study journalism at MIT and Harvard University. Her writing has appeared in publications such as the *Washington Post*, the *Daily Beast*, *Vox*, *USA Today*, *McSweeney's*, and *Lapham's Quarterly*, and she has published two books, *The Secret History of Vladimir Nabokov* (2013) and *One Long Night: A Global History of Concentration Camps* (2017). This essay on the iconic singer and songwriter Bob Dylan appeared in *Slate* in June 2013.

Bob Dylan is one of America's most celebrated singers and songwriters. His songs include "Blowin' in the Wind" (1963), "The Times They Are a-Changin' " (1963), and "Like a Rolling Stone" (1965), which was designated the number one rock and roll song of all time by *Rolling Stone* magazine in 2011. Dylan has won numerous prestigious musical awards, including three Grammys for Album of the Year (1973, 1998, and 2002) and the prestigious Grammy for Lifetime Achievement in 1992. He was inducted in the Rock and Roll Hall Fame in 1988; won the National Book Award for his autobiography, *Chronicles: Volume One*, in 2004; and was awarded the Nobel Prize in Literature in 2016.

The Freewheelin' Bob Dylan

If a songwriter can win the Nobel Prize for literature, can ClifsNotes be art? During his official lecture recorded on June 4, 2017, laureate Bob Dylan described the influence on him of three literary works from his childhood: *The Odyssey*, *All Quiet on the Western Front*, and *Moby-Dick*. Soon after, writer Ben Greenman noted that in his lecture Dylan seemed to have invented a quote from *Moby-Dick*.

Those familiar with Dylan's music might recall that he winkingly attributed fabricated quotes to Abraham Lincoln in his "Talkin' World War III Blues." So Dylan making up an imaginary quote is nothing new. However, I soon discovered that the *Moby-Dick* line Dylan dreamed up last week seems to be cobbled together out of phrases on the website SparkNotes, the online equivalent of CliffsNotes.

In Dylan's recounting, a "Quaker pacifist priest" tells Flask, the third mate, "Some men who receive injuries are **led to God, others are led to bitterness**" (my emphasis). No such line appears anywhere in Herman Melville's novel. However, SparkNotes' character list describes the preacher using similar phrasing, as "someone whose trials have **led him toward God rather than bitterness**" (again, emphasis mine).

Following up on this strange echo, I began delving into the two texts side by side and found that many lines Dylan used throughout his Nobel discussion of *Moby-Dick* appear to have been cribbed even more directly from the site. The SparkNotes summary for *Moby-Dick* explains, "One of the ships . . . carries Gabriel, a crazed prophet who predicts doom." Dylan's version reads, "There's a crazy prophet, Gabriel, on one of the vessels, and he predicts Ahab's doom."

5 Shortly after, the SparkNotes account relays that "Captain Boomer has lost an arm in an encounter with Moby Dick. . . . Boomer, happy simply to have survived his encounter, cannot understand Ahab's lust for vengeance." In his lecture, Dylan says, "Captain Boomer—he lost an arm to Moby. But . . . he's happy to have survived. He can't accept Ahab's lust for vengeance."

Across the 78 sentences in the lecture that Dylan spends describing *Moby-Dick*, even a cursory inspection reveals that more than a dozen of them appear to closely resemble lines from the SparkNotes site. And most of the key shared phrases in these passages (such as "Ahab's lust for vengeance" in the above lines) do not appear in the novel *Moby-Dick* at all.

Dylan's Nobel Lecture	SparkNotes for *Moby-Dick*
(78 sentences appear in the *Moby-Dick* portion of Dylan's talk.)	**(At least 20 sentences bear some similarity to passages from SparkNotes.)**
"Ahab's got a wife and child back in Nantucket that he reminisces about now and then."	". . . musing on his wife and child back in Nantucket." **(The phrase "wife and child back in Nantucket" does not appear in the novel.)**
"The ship's crew is made up of men of different races"	". . . a crew made up of men from many different countries and races."
"He calls Moby the emperor, sees him as the embodiment of evil."	". . . he sees this whale as the embodiment of evil." **(The phrase "embodiment of evil" does not appear in the novel itself.)**
"Ahab encounters other whaling vessels, presses the captains for details about Moby."	". . . the ship encounters other whaling vessels. Ahab always demands information about Moby Dick from their captains." **(The phrase "encounters other whaling vessels" does not appear in the novel.)**
"There's a crazy prophet, Gabriel, on one of the vessels, and he predicts Ahab's doom."	"One of the ships . . . carries Gabriel, a crazed prophet who predicts doom." **(Neither "predicts doom" nor "predicts Ahab's doom" appears in the novel.)**

(continues on next page)

Dylan's Nobel Lecture	SparkNotes for *Moby-Dick*
"Another ship's captain — Captain Boomer — he lost an arm to Moby. But he tolerates that, and he's happy to have survived. He can't accept Ahab's lust for vengeance."	" . . . a whaling ship whose skipper, Captain Boomer, has lost an arm in an encounter with Moby Dick. . . . Boomer, happy simply to have survived his encounter, cannot understand Ahab's lust for vengeance." **(Neither "lost an arm" nor "lust for vengeance" appears in the novel.)**
"Stubb gives no significance to anything."	"Stubb . . . refusing to assign too much significance to anything." **(The phrase "significance to anything" does not appear in the novel.)**
"A Quaker pacifist priest, who is actually a bloodthirsty businessman, tells Flask, 'Some men who receive injuries are led to God, others are led to bitterness.' "	" . . . a bloodthirstiness unusual for Quakers, who are normally pacifists." "... someone whose trials have led him toward God rather than bitterness." **(The above are from adjacent entries in the character list; the Flask quote does not appear in the novel, nor does the word pacifist.)**
"Tashtego says that he died and was reborn. His extra days are a gift. He wasn't saved by Christ, though, he says he was saved by a fellow man and a non-Christian at that. He paradies the resurrection."	"Tashtego . . . has died and been reborn, and any extra days of his life are a gift. His rebirth also parodies religious images of resurrection. Tashtego is 'delivered' from death not by Christ but by a fellow man — a non-Christian at that." **(Neither "reborn" nor "non-Christian" appears in the novel.)**
"Finally, Ahab spots Moby. . . . Boats are lowered. . . . Moby attacks Ahab's boat and destroys it. Next day, he sights Moby again. Boats are lowered again. Moby attacks Ahab's boat again."	"Ahab finally sights Moby Dick. The harpoon boats are launched, and Moby Dick attacks Ahab's harpoon boat, destroying it. The next day, Moby Dick is sighted again, and the boats are lowered once more . . . Moby Dick again attacks Ahabs boat." **(In the novel, this sequence covers several pages of text.)**
"Moby attacks one more time, ramming the *Pequod* and sinking it. Ahab gets tangled up in the harpoon lines and is thrown out of his boat into a watery grave."	"Moby Dick rams the *Pequod* and sinks it. Ahab is then caught in a harpoon line and hurled out of his harpoon boat to his death." **(In the novel, this is similarly a much longer passage and is described quite differently. For instance, the verb *ram* doesn't appear at all.)**

I reached out to Columbia, Dylan's record label, to try to connect with Dylan or his management for comment, but as of publication time, I have not heard back.

Theft in the name of art is an ancient tradition, and Dylan has been a magpie since the 1960s. He has also frequently been open about his borrowings. In 2001, he even released an album titled *"Love and Theft,"* the quotation marks seeming to imply that the album title was itself taken from Eric Lott's acclaimed history of racial appropriation, *Love & Theft: Blackface Minstrelsy and the American Working Class.*

When he started out, Dylan absorbed classic tunes and obscure compositions alike from musicians he met, recording versions that would become more famous than anything by those who taught him the songs or even the original songwriters. His first album included two original numbers and 11 covers.

10 Yet in less than three years, he would learn to warp the Americana he collected into stupefyingly original work. Throwing everything from electric guitar and organ to tuba into the musical mix, he began crafting lyrics that combined machine-gun metaphor with motley casts of characters. Less likely to copy whole verses by then, his drive-by invocations of everything from the biblical Abraham to Verlaine and Rimbaud became more hit-and-run than kidnapping. The lyrics accumulated into chaotic, juggling poetry from a trickster willing to drop a ball sometimes. They worked even when they shouldn't have.

In the past several years, Dylan seems to have expanded his appropriation. His 2004 memoir *Chronicles: Volume One* is filled with unacknowledged attributions. In more recent years, he has returned to recording covers, as many legends do. In Dylan's case, his past three albums (five discs in all) have been composed of standards.

Dylan remains so reliant on appropriation that tracing his sourcing has become a cottage industry. For more than a decade, writer Scott Warmuth, an admiring Ahab in pursuit, has tracked Dylan lyrics and writings to an astonishing range of texts, from multiple sentences copied out of a New Orleans travel brochure to lifted phrases and imagery from former Black Flag frontman Henry Rollins. Warmuth dove into Dylan's Nobel lecture last week, too, and found that the phrase "faith in a meaningful world" from the CliffsNotes description of *All Quiet on the Western Front* also shows up in Dylan's talk (but not in the book).

Even many of the paintings Dylan produces as an artist are reproductions of well-known images, such as a photo from Henri Cartier-Bresson. For Dylan, recapitulation has replaced invention.

If the *Moby-Dick* portion of his Nobel lecture was indeed cribbed from SparkNotes, then what is the world to make of it? Perhaps the use of SparkNotes can be seen as a sendup of the prestige-prize economy. Either way, through Dylan's Nobel lecture, SparkNotes material may well join Duchamp's urinal and Andy Warhol's fake Brillo pad boxes as a functional commodity now made immortal.

15 It's worth mentioning that Dylan turned in his lecture just before the six-month deadline, ensuring that he would get paid. In the interest of settling any potential moral debt, I would encourage him to throw some of his $923,000 prize to whoever wrote the original version of the online summary.

In the meantime, I asked a few academics for their thoughts on whether Dylan had committed punishable literary theft. After reviewing the similarities, they gave mixed marks. Longtime Dylan fan and George Washington University English professor Dan Moshenberg told me no alarm bells went off for him while reviewing the passages. Gwynn Dujardin, an English professor from Queen's University in Kingston, Ontario, had more issues with Dylan's approach, noting the irony that "Dylan is cribbing [from] a contemporary publication that is under copyright instead of from *Moby-Dick* itself, which is in the public domain." A final reviewer, Juan Martinez, a literature professor at Northwestern University, said, "If Dylan was in my class and he submitted an essay with these plagiarized bits, I'd fail him."

Topics for Critical Thinking and Writing

1. Andrea Pitzer draws her title from the title of Bob Dylan's 1963 album, *The Freewheelin' Bob Dylan*. How does her title support her argument?
2. Is there a difference between appropriation of another's work and plagiarism? Explain your answer.
3. If "theft in art is an ancient tradition," as Pitzer writes in paragraph 8, do you think Bob Dylan's appropriations in his Nobel speech are just another example of the artist at work? Or is his appropriation of language from SparkNotes a form of "cheating"? Explain your view.
4. In the final sentence of this essay, a literature professor is quoted saying that he would fail Bob Dylan if Dylan had turned in his Nobel speech as a classroom essay. If you were a teacher, would you fail him? Why, or why not? Explain.
5. Do some research into contemporary hip-hop songs that use samples of other songs. Determine whether or not your selections credited their sources — and/or paid for them — and then argue whether or not the difference between sampling and plagiarism in hip-hop is merely a matter of money.
6. One of Bob Dylan's most famous songs, "Blowin' in the Wind," became an anthem of the civil rights movement in 1963. The song was based on the American slave spiritual "No More Auction Block." In your opinion, does Dylan's song mark an instance of popular singers in the 1950s and 1960s "stealing" from the African American musical tradition, or is it an authentic and new work of art? Explain.
7. Because folk music developed over centuries and longer, the notion of "ownership" in that genre is complicated by the inability to find the precise origins of many songs. Research a popular folk song such as "Blue Tail Fly," "She'll be Comin' 'Round the Mountain," "The Ballad of John Henry," or "Go Down Moses" — or select a song you know — and describe what is known about its origins.

22

Online versus IRL: How Has Social Networking Changed How We Relate to One Another?

JULES EVANS

Jules Evans is the author of *Philosophy for Life and Other Dangerous Situations* (2013) and *The Art of Losing Control* (2017), both of which explore emotional resilience and well-being in the modern world. Evans is also a research fellow for the Centre for the History of Emotions at Queen Mary University of London. This article was published on June 10, 2013, in the *Huffington Post United Kingdom.*

Are We Slaves to Our Online Selves?

The public rage over revelations that governments snoop on our online activity comes partly from a sense that our online selves are not entirely in our control. The more networked we are, the more our selves are "out there," online, made public and transparent to a million eyes.

On the one hand the global interconnectedness of the internet gives us a feeling of euphoria — we are joined to humanity! We are Liked! On the other hand, we get sudden pangs of paranoia — what if all these online strangers don't wish us well, what if they are stalkers or con-men or bullies or spies? How are we coming across? Are we over-exposed? Does our bum look big in this?

Growing up in today's online world must be difficult, because every adolescent experiment, every awkward mistake, is out there online, perhaps forever. This makes me glad that I was a teenager in the 1990s, before the internet could capture my adolescent fuck-wittery for posterity. Depressingly often these days, we read about a teenager who has taken their own life because someone posted an unflattering photo or video of them online.

They feel publicly shamed, desecrated, permanently damaged.

There is a word for what the internet and social media have done to us: alienation. It means, literally, selling yourself into slavery, from the Latin for slave, *alienus*. The word has its roots in ancient Greek philosophy, particularly in Plato and the Stoics, who warned that if you place too much value on your reputation or image, you enslave yourself to the fickle opinion of the public. You raise the public above you, turn it into a god, then cower before it and beg for its approval. You become dispossessed, your self-esteem soaring or crashing depending on how the public views you. This is a recipe for emotional sickness.

5 You can end up caring more about your image or reflection than your actual self. You replace actual loving human relations with the fickle adoration of the public. How many times do we see people sitting with friends or family at a pub or a restaurant, ignoring them while they anxiously check on their online selves? Our actual selves end up shriveled and unwell, while our unreal mirror selves suck up more and more of our attention. We can even turn our loved ones into props for public approval. Your fiancé proposed? Share it! Everything is done for the public, for strangers, for people who don't really care about you at all.

I remember seeing a family at the beach, in Venezuela last year. The mother was a rather curvaceous lady in a bikini, and she insisted the father take endless photos of her, standing by the sea in various outlandish poses. Literally hundreds of photos. They completely ignored their little daughter, who gazed on her mother in confusion. Occasionally the daughter would come up to get the mother's attention, and she would be given a little shove to get out of the shot. It was like some grotesque fairy-tale. The mother was so obsessed with her online self, yet so palpably ugly inside.

The internet has become a vast pool, into which we gaze like Narcissus, bewitched by our own reflection. Our smart-phones are little pocket-mirrors, with which we're constantly snapping "selfies," trying to manage how the public perceives us. It's like we have a profound fear of insignificance and nothingness, so we check the pocket-mirror every few minutes to re-assure ourselves that we exist, that we are loved. We mistake Likes for love. We look to celebrities with a million followers, and beg them to follow us. Because then we'd be real! Celebrities do this too, tweeting about the other celebrities they hang out with, to create a sort of *Hello!* magazine existence for the public to gape at. Everything becomes a pose, a selfie.

I'm probably worse than the lot of you. I worry that extensive use of social media over the last decade has re-wired the way I think, so that I now have "share" buttons installed in my hypothalamus. No sooner do I have a thought than I want to share it. In the old days, perhaps individuals quietly spoke to God in their hearts. Now I find my thoughts instantly forming themselves into 140-character epigrams. Sublime sunset? Share it. New baby? Share it. Terminal cancer? Share it. Let's live-blog death, find eternity in re-tweets.

How much of our selves we offer up to the god of Public Opinion. How devotedly we serve it. How utterly we make ourselves transparent to its thousand-eyed stare, until we suddenly feel over-exposed and try to cover ourselves up.

10 What is the antidote to alienation? The Greeks thought the cure was simple: don't put too much value on your reputation or image. Recognize that it is out of your control. Remind yourself that there is not a direct correlation between a person's image and their actual value, that the public is not a perfect mirror, that it distorts like a circus mirror. And try not to gaze into the mirror too often. Tend to the garden within, to your deeper and better self, even if it doesn't get a hundred Likes on Facebook.

This is not an easy thing to do. No sooner did I think of this, than I immediately thought, good idea: share it! Pin it! Reddit! My over-networked self needs to be reminded of the value of disconnection, of silence and contemplation, to let deeper thoughts rise up. With that in mind, I'm off on a retreat this week in the Welsh countryside (not a re-tweet, a retreat), in search of a deeper way to connect, a better Cloud to sit on. I hope they don't have Wi-Fi.

Topics for Critical Thinking and Writing

1. Jules Evans starts his article with a basic paradox of online existence: We don't have full control over our online identities, yet so much of our sense of self these days seems tied up with that identity. We resent those who snoop into our online activity, yet we get a "feeling of euphoria" (para. 2) when something happens online that confirms our existence (e.g., we get a Like!). What is the basis of this dynamic? Can something, if anything, be done to change it? Explain your response.
2. In paragraph 4, Evans cites the wisdom of the ancient Greeks: We shouldn't put too much stock in what others think of us. He calls doing so a "recipe for emotional sickness." Why is that? In your opinion, is it realistic not to care about what others think of us? Can good things result from an awareness of the opinion of others? Why, or why not?
3. In paragraph 5, Evans calls out the problem of "caring more about your image or reflection than your actual self." What is meant by "actual self"? How disparate or different are our online, public selves and our private selves likely to be? Do we have one self after all — online or in real life? — or are we always projecting different selves to different people? Provide specific examples.
4. Why does Evans include a reference to the story of Narcissus in this essay? In your opinion, is its use effective? Why, or why not?
5. Evans ends his article by stating that he's going on vacation, hoping to "be reminded of the value of disconnection, of silence and contemplation, to let deeper thoughts rise up" (para. 11). Is he correct to be worried that being overconnected somehow causes us to be separated from ourselves? Why, or why not?
6. Evans states in paragraph 8 that he's worried that the extensive use of social media has "re-wired the way I think." Research current findings on how the use of electronic media, the internet, and social media specifically are or are not changing the way we think. In an essay of 500 to 1,000 words, present your findings. What does this rewiring mean for the future?

NAVNEET ALANG

Navneet Alang is a freelance writer, journalist, and blogger who is interested in the intersection of technology and popular culture. He has contributed to magazines such as the *Atlantic*, *Hazlitt*, the *Globe and Mail*, and the *Toronto Standard*, among others. This article appeared in the *New Republic* on August 5, 2015.

Eat, Pray, Post

"This is the cause for obesity in America!" exclaims an Indian subject after eating a Pop Tart in a charming bit of viral fluff called "Indians Taste Test American Sweets." It's one of an endless video series produced by Buzzfeed, in which people from one country are filmed tasting the foods from another. They're simple, relatable, occasionally controversial, and basically engineered to go viral. I say charming, however, because this clip in particular gives us a perspective we so rarely see: young, urban people from outside the West, gently critiquing American excess. It feels, briefly, like a viral video done right — ephemeral and shareable, to be sure, but still refreshingly challenging.

More importantly, posting a video to one's social media accounts is a performative act of self-definition. *Look*, it says, *this is who I am* — at least in the terms chosen by Buzzfeed's crack viral teams who, sitting in airy, open-concept offices in California and New York, dole out content that spills out from America to fill the world's screens.

It's true that most viral stuff works this way. Yet, while perusing Buzzfeed's various international sites, I noticed a discomfiting uniformity. The listicles and the slickly edited videos center around the same ideas: relationship quirks, patriotic celebrations, food, or the usual highly specific ephemera of "only people from this city will get this." An optimist might look at this sameness as revealing a fundamental humanity, that glibly utopian notion that, underneath it all, we are the same. But perhaps viral culture is more sinister. Perhaps it isn't about universalism and it isn't just harmless fun; perhaps it is part and parcel of an inevitable Westernization.

The video that criticizes America's oddness is, after all, a bit of an anomaly. Most of the Taste Test series is about Americans testing snacks from all over — India, Singapore, Indonesia, and so on — and expressing their bewilderment and disgust at what are, to billions around the world, ordinary things. It's often uncomfortable to watch, almost the quintessence of punching down, disturbingly mimicking the disregard for non-Western cultures that underpinned colonialism (the British, for example, made it a point to denigrate Indian culture in order to replace it with their own). Even clips about Russian or European food include the word "bizarre" in the title. One is forced to ask: Bizarre to whom, exactly?

5 The tone and content of these videos are also remarkably Western. The language is that of Tumblr, Twitter, or even early Gawker: clipped, ironic, disaffected. Posts about Snapchats that only Indians will understand are peppered with American idioms — "this could be us but u playing," many mentions of "bae." GIFs of Bollywood star Aishwarya Rai are used

just like GIFs of Rihanna, as aspirational symbols meant to reassure and entertain. In the video in which those same young, hip Indians criticize American excess and Kellogg's Pop Tarts, they do so in American terms: There's even a guy who says, based solely on watching *Breaking Bad,* that candy Pop Rocks "seriously look like meth."

At the same time, though, the production of these potentially viral posts is intended to appeal to differing demographics. As someone of Indian descent, Buzzfeed India's posts have been most clearly appealing to — and targeted at — me, and the content pushed there is often distinctly, uniquely Indian. From collections of photos that show how beautiful India is to a Tumblr that uses GIFs to describe life in Delhi, the content is breezy, fun, and (when compared to the too-white nature of most pop culture) refreshingly relatable.

There's something deeply gratifying about seeing one's culture as of the moment. When so much of what is defined as contemporary explicitly caters to a Western audience, seeing something as specific (and silly) as "19 Indian foods that taste better when it's raining" — something that plays off the uniquely celebratory attitude toward rain in India — makes one feel vital, hip, and modern. To see yourself represented is to be more alive, more real.

What does it mean, however, that so much of this representation is not only so American in style, but that the nature of online virality makes its dissemination so self-reinforcing? On one hand, there is undoubtedly a case to be made that this kind of viral grammar marks a particular style as a *global* contemporary, as opposed to a Western one. Our bloggy way of speaking is a kind of international connective tissue, making people in Jakarta and Paris and Mumbai part of an emerging, connected, privileged international demographic.

On the other hand, when that global culture flows in mostly one direction — the fact that it is in English and borrows its style from Brooklyn- and L.A.-based blogs — we have a larger problem: virality starts to look like soft cultural imperialism. It's an assertion of Western values, neatly packaged as 7 GIFs You Won't Believe.

When virality becomes the dominant mode 10
of spreading culture, the content shifts depending on location — "23 Incomparable Joys of Growing Up in Chennai" and so forth — but the form remains the same. The ideology is carried along. A post about a Bollywood power couple giving us #relationshipgoals is fun, but it also implies a specific perspective.

What this means, of course, is that virality has a kind of circular function. Many of Buzzfeed India's most popular posts draw from the popularity of the *Harry Potter* series — something that, last time I checked, wasn't exactly part of the ancient Hindu texts, the Vedas. Virality predominantly functions by reproducing what is already popular, while only occasionally propelling something to popularity itself. It's rarely inventive.

The fact that Buzzfeed India's style is indistinguishable from Brooklyn blog-speak is evidence of the circular relation of capital and culture, and the non-coincidence that centers of global finance are also centers of global culture. The nature of Buzzfeed's global operations is to produce local content in its own image: replicating a business model around the world as it also replicates a cultural one.

There is some resistance, though, elements that refuse to translate. A post on Buzzfeed India of bilingual English-Hindi puns may be groan-worthy, but its very indecipherability to a Western audience is important: It marks the cultural specificity of Northern India as unable to be neatly subsumed into a binary model of Eastern and Western.

All that said: It's hard not to wonder about power, and where it fits into the global nature of virality. As theorist Homi Bhabha argued in his book *Location of Culture*, the first world is always considered the present and future on a timeline on which the third world is perpetually the past. And perhaps online virality — in the way that it tightens itself into ever smaller circles of self-referentiality — is a sign that Bhabha was correct: That someone ten thousand miles away is talking about American obesity at all is indicative of not only how things work, but a sign that perhaps it is already too late to stop the march into a Westernized, viral future.

Topics for Critical Thinking and Writing

1. Navneet Alang states in paragraph 2 that "posting a video to one's social media accounts is a performative act of self-definition." What does he mean by that?
2. In paragraph 8, Alang presents a new idea: Perhaps what is being shown is a new style he terms "*global* contemporary" [author's italics]. Do you agree with this idea? Why, or why not? Be specific.
3. Alang also uses the expression "soft cultural imperialism" (para. 9) in which Western values are asserted. Examine the concept of cultural imperialism in general. What would "hard" cultural imperialism be as compared to "soft"? In your opinion, is there anything wrong with either "hard" or "soft" imperialism, or with both in different ways? Support your answer with specific details.
4. In paragraph 11, Alang states, "Virality predominantly functions by reproducing what is already popular." Later in that paragraph he says that virality is "rarely inventive." What does he mean? Do you agree? Support your answer with examples, perhaps from your own experience with viral videos.
5. In his conclusion, Alang cites the argument of Homi Bhabha that "the first world is always considered the present and future on a timeline on which the third world is perpetually the past" (para. 14). Are Bhabha's words still true? Do we still consider the third world part of the "past"? In 500 words or more, explain, and explore any pitfalls in reasoning that the first-world represents progress while the third-world represents primitiveness or barbarism.
6. In the last line of the essay, Alang states that "perhaps it is already too late to stop the march into a Westernized, viral future." Is this march something that *should* be stopped? Why, or why not?
7. Many countries around the world were at one time colonies of European powers (or the United States), and there has always been cultural exchange between the colonizer and the colonized. Is cultural exchange different in the twenty-first century, given the era of decolonization and the emergence of the internet and social media? Do you think westernization is occurring or is the exchange of culture a two-way street? Explain using specific examples.

HOSSEIN DERAKHSHAN

Hossein Derakhshan (b. 1975) is an Iranian Canadian journalist and blogger who started his career as a writer in 1999 in Tehran, Iran, where he penned articles for the reformist newspapers *Asr-e Azadegan* and *Hayat-e-No*. In 2000, he began a Persian-language blog, *Sardabir: khodam* ("*Editor: myself*") and quickly inspired a blogging revolution in Iran — becoming known as the "blogfather." Following two visits to Israel, Derakhshan was arrested by the Iranian government and charged with "propagating against the state" and "cooperating with hostile governments." He was sentenced to nineteen and a half years in prison, served six, and was pardoned by Iran's supreme leader in 2014. After his release, he went on to write about the social and political power of the internet in a widely translated essay, "The Web We Have to Save" (2015), and, with Claire Wardle, in a report commissioned by the Council of Europe, "Information Disorder" (2017). He is currently a research fellow at Harvard University's Kennedy School. The piece reprinted here originally appeared in *Wired* magazine on October 19, 2017.

How Social Media Endangers Knowledge

Wikipedia, one of the last remaining pillars of the open and decentralized web, is in existential crisis.

This has nothing to do with money. A couple of years ago, the site launched a panicky fundraising campaign, but ironically thanks to Donald Trump, Wikipedia has never been as wealthy or well-organized. American liberals, worried that Trump's rise threatened the country's foundational Enlightenment ideals, kicked in a significant flow of funds that has stabilized the nonprofit's balance sheet.

That happy news masks a more concerning problem — a flattening growth rate in the number of contributors to the website. It is another troubling sign of a general trend around the world: The very idea of knowledge itself is in danger.

The idea behind Wikipedia — like all encyclopedias before it — has been to collect the entirety of human knowledge. It's a goal that extends back to the Islamic Golden Age, when numerous scholars — inspired by Muhammad's famous verdict of "Seek knowledge, even from China" — set themselves to collecting and documenting all existing information on a wide variety of topics, including translations from Greek, Persian, Syrian, and Indian into Arabic. In the 9th century, a Persian scholar named Ibn Qutaybah collected the first true encyclopedia, 10 books on power, war, nobility, character, learning and eloquence, asceticism, friendship, prayers, food, and women. He was followed a century later by another Persian scholar, al-Khwārizmī who, in addition to inventing algebra, produced an encyclopedia covering what he called indigenous knowledge (jurisprudence, scholastic philosophy, grammar, secretarial duties, prosody and poetic art, history) and foreign knowledge (philosophy, logic, medicine, arithmetic, geometry, astronomy, music, mechanics, alchemy). The Chinese had their own encyclopedia dating back to the 7th century.

In Europe, the quest to compile a modern 5
encyclopedia started with the Enlightenment

in the 18th century. (Immanuel Kant coined a fitting Latin motto for the movement: "Sapere aude," or "Dare to know.") French Enlightenment thinkers like Francis Bacon and Denis Diderot began compiling ambitious encyclopedias, inspiring others throughout France, Germany, England, Switzerland and the Netherlands. The religious ruling class's discomfort with the effort only helped its financial feasibility; there was an obvious market for these massive collections, often published in numerous volumes, for an increasingly secular middle-class. The first volume of Encycopedie was sold in 1751 to 2,000 subscribers, who would go on to receive the entire twenty-eight-volume set. Notable revolutionary thinkers such as Voltaire, Rousseau, and Montesquieu were involved in the editing of the work and several even ended up in prison. Only 17 years after the publication of the last volume in 1772, the French revolution began, leading to perhaps the most secular state in human history.

That trend toward rationality and enlightenment was endangered long before the advent of the Internet. As Neil Postman noted in his 1985 book *Amusing Ourselves to Death,* the rise of television introduced not just a new medium but a new discourse: a gradual shift from a typographic culture to a photographic one, which in turn meant a shift from rationality to emotions, exposition to entertainment. In an image-centered and pleasure-driven world, Postman noted, there is no place for rational thinking, because you simply cannot think with images. It is text that enables us to "uncover lies, confusions and overgeneralizations, to detect abuses of logic and common sense. It also means to weigh ideas, to compare and contrast assertions, to connect one generalization to another."

The dominance of television was not contained to our living rooms. It overturned all of those habits of mind, fundamentally changing our experience of the world, affecting the conduct of politics, religion, business, and culture. It reduced many aspects of modern life to entertainment, sensationalism, and commerce. "Americans don't talk to each other, we entertain each other," Postman wrote. "They don't exchange ideas, they exchange images. They do not argue with propositions; they argue with good looks, celebrities and commercials."

At first, the Internet seemed to push against this trend. When it emerged towards the end of the 80s as a purely text-based medium, it was seen as a tool to pursue knowledge, not pleasure. Reason and thought were most valued in this garden — all derived from the project of Enlightenment. Universities around the world were among the first to connect to this new medium, which hosted discussion groups, informative personal or group blogs, electronic magazines, and academic mailing lists and forums. It was an intellectual project, not about commerce or control, created in a scientific research center in Switzerland.

Wikipedia was a fruit of this garden. So was Google search and its text-based advertising model. And so were blogs, which valued text, hypertext (links), knowledge, and literature. They effectively democratized the ability to contribute to the global corpus of knowledge. For more than a decade, the web created an alternative space that threatened television's grip on society.

Social networks, though, have since col- 10
onized the web for television's values. From

Facebook to Instagram, the medium refocuses our attention on videos and images, rewarding emotional appeals — "like" buttons — over rational ones. Instead of a quest for knowledge, it engages us in an endless zest for instant approval from an audience, for which we are constantly but unconsciously performing. (It's telling that, while Google began life as a PhD thesis, Facebook started as a tool to judge classmates' appearances.) It reduces our curiosity by showing us exactly what we already want and think, based on our profiles and preferences. Enlightenment's motto of "Dare to know" has become "Dare not to care to know."

It is a development that further proves the words of French philosopher Guy Debord, who wrote that, if pre-capitalism was about "being," and capitalism about "having," in late-capitalism what matters is only "appearing" — appearing rich, happy, thoughtful, cool and cosmopolitan. It's hard to open Instagram without being struck by the accuracy of his diagnosis.

Now the challenge is to save Wikipedia and its promise of a free and open collection of all human knowledge amid the conquest of new and old television — how to collect and preserve knowledge when nobody cares to know. Television has even infected Wikipedia itself — today many of the most popular entries tend to revolve around television series or their cast.

This doesn't mean it is time to give up. But we need to understand that the decline of the web and thereby of the Wikipedia is part of a much larger civilizational shift which has just started to unfold.

Topics for Critical Thinking and Writing

1. Hossein Derakhshan writes in paragraph 3 that "knowledge itself is in danger." What does he mean by that?
2. In paragraphs 4 and 5, Derakhshan accounts for the evolution of the encyclopedia to its print form and then its emergence as a user-generated version like Wikipedia. Which kind of reference work could be considered more reliable — the traditional professionally edited encyclopedia or Wikipedia? Why? What are the advantages and disadvantages of each?
3. In paragraph 10, Derakhshan writes, "It's telling that, while Google began life as a PhD thesis, Facebook started as a tool to judge classmates' appearances." Explain in 300 to 500 words how that assessment connects to Derakhshan's overall argument about the ways the internet has changed information access and exchange.
4. Consider what Neil Postman said about Americans, especially his conclusion that Americans "do not argue with propositions; they argue with good looks, celebrities and commercials" (para. 7). Is this statement true? Test Postman's claim by refuting it or supporting it in an essay of about 500 words.
5. Has technology created a landscape where information is limited, manipulated, and controlled, or has it democratized the process of knowledge construction, opening it up to outsider voices, new perspectives, and expanded knowledge? Answer in about 500 words, citing specific examples to support your position.

STEPHEN MARCHE

Stephen Marche (b. 1976) has written essays for the *New Yorker,* the *New York Times,* the *Atlantic,* and *Esquire,* among others, and has written six books, including two novels, a collection of stories, and two works of nonfiction, most recently *The Unmade Bed: The Messy Truth about Men and Women in the Twenty-First Century* (2017). Marche wrote the essay presented here for the *Atlantic* in May 2012.

Is Facebook Making Us Lonely?

Yvette Vickers, a former *Playboy* playmate and B-movie star, best known for her role in *Attack of the 50 Foot Woman*, would have been eighty-three last August, but nobody knows exactly how old she was when she died. According to the Los Angeles coroner's report, she lay dead for the better part of a year before a neighbor and fellow actress, a woman named Susan Savage, noticed cobwebs and yellowing letters in her mailbox, reached through a broken window to unlock the door, and pushed her way through the piles of junk mail and mounds of clothing that barricaded the house. Upstairs, she found Vickers's body, mummified, near a heater that was still running. Her computer was on too, its glow permeating the empty space.

The *Los Angeles Times* posted a story headlined "Mummified Body of Former Playboy Playmate Yvette Vickers Found in Her Benedict Canyon Home," which quickly went viral. Within two weeks, by Technorati's count, Vickers's lonesome death was already the subject of 16,057 Facebook posts and 881 tweets. She had long been a horror-movie icon, a symbol of Hollywood's capacity to exploit our most basic fears in the silliest ways; now she was an icon of a new and different kind of horror: our growing fear of loneliness. Certainly she received much more attention in death than she did in the final years of her life. With no children, no religious group, and no immediate social circle of any kind, she had begun, as an elderly woman, to look elsewhere for companionship. Savage later told *Los Angeles* magazine that she had searched Vickers's phone bills for clues about the life that led to such an end. In the months before her grotesque death, Vickers had made calls not to friends or family but to distant fans who had found her through fan conventions and Internet sites.

Vickers's web of connections had grown broader but shallower, as has happened for many of us. We are living in an isolation that would have been unimaginable to our ancestors, and yet we have never been more accessible. Over the past three decades, technology has delivered to us a world in which we need not be out of contact for a fraction of a moment. In 2010, at a cost of $300 million, 800 miles of fiber-optic cable was laid between the Chicago Mercantile Exchange and the New York Stock Exchange to shave three milliseconds off trading times. Yet within this world of instant and absolute communication, unbounded by limits of time or space, we suffer from unprecedented alienation. We have never been more detached from one another, or lonelier. In a world consumed by ever more novel modes of socializing, we have less and less actual society. We live in an accelerating contradiction: the more connected we become, the lonelier we are. We were promised a global village; instead we inhabit the drab cul-de-sacs and endless freeways of a vast suburb of information.

At the forefront of all this unexpectedly lonely interactivity is Facebook, with 845 million users and $3.7 billion in revenue last year. The company hopes to raise $5 billion in an initial public offering later this spring, which will make it by far the largest Internet IPO in history. Some recent estimates put the company's potential value at $100 billion, which would make it larger than the global coffee industry — one addiction preparing to surpass the other. Facebook's scale and reach are hard to comprehend: last summer, Facebook became, by some counts, the first Web site to receive 1 trillion page views in a month. In the last three months of 2011, users generated an average of 2.7 billion "likes" and comments every day. On whatever scale you care to judge Facebook — as a company, as a culture, as a country — it is vast beyond imagination.

5 Despite its immense popularity, or more likely because of it, Facebook has, from the beginning, been under something of a cloud of suspicion. The depiction of Mark Zuckerberg, in *The Social Network*, as a bastard with symptoms of Asperger's syndrome, was nonsense. But it felt true. It felt true to Facebook, if not to Zuckerberg. The film's most indelible scene, the one that may well have earned it an Oscar, was the final, silent shot of an anomic Zuckerberg sending out a friend request to his ex-girlfriend, then waiting and clicking and waiting and clicking — a moment of superconnected loneliness preserved in amber. We have all been in that scene: transfixed by the glare of a screen, hungering for response.

When you sign up for Google+ and set up your Friends circle, the program specifies that you should include only "your real friends, the ones you feel comfortable sharing private details with." That one little phrase, *Your real friends* — so quaint, so charmingly mothering — perfectly encapsulates the anxieties that social media have produced: the fears that Facebook is interfering with our real friendships, distancing us from each other, making us lonelier; and that social networking might be spreading the very isolation it seemed designed to conquer.

Facebook arrived in the middle of a dramatic increase in the quantity and intensity of human loneliness, a rise that initially made the site's promise of greater connection seem deeply attractive. Americans are more solitary than ever before. In 1950, less than 10 percent of American households contained only one person. By 2010, nearly 27 percent of households had just one person. Solitary living does not guarantee a life of unhappiness, of course. In his recent book about the trend toward living alone, Eric Klinenberg, a sociologist at NYU, writes: "Reams of published research show that it's the quality, not the quantity of social interaction, that best predicts loneliness." True. But before we begin the fantasies of happily eccentric singledom, of divorcées dropping by their knitting circles after work for glasses of Drew Barrymore pinot grigio, or recent college graduates with perfectly articulated, Steampunk-themed, 300-square-foot apartments organizing croquet matches with their book clubs, we should recognize that it is not just isolation that is rising sharply. It's loneliness, too. And loneliness makes us miserable.

We know intuitively that loneliness and being alone are not the same thing. Solitude can be lovely. Crowded parties can be agony. We also know, thanks to a growing body of research on the topic, that loneliness is not a matter of external conditions; it is a psychological state. A 2005 analysis of data from a longitudinal study of Dutch twins showed that the tendency toward loneliness has roughly the same genetic component as other psychological problems such as neuroticism or anxiety.

Still, loneliness is slippery, a difficult state to define or diagnose. The best tool yet developed for measuring the condition is the UCLA Loneliness Scale, a series of twenty questions that all begin with this formulation: "How often do you feel . . . ?" As in: "How often do you feel that you are 'in tune' with the people around you?" And: "How often do you feel that you lack companionship?" Measuring the condition in these terms, various studies have shown loneliness rising drastically over a very short period of recent history. A 2010 AARP survey found that 35 percent of adults older than forty-five were chronically lonely, as opposed to 20 percent of a similar group only a decade earlier. According to a major study by a leading scholar of the subject, roughly 20 percent of Americans — about 60 million people — are unhappy with their lives because of loneliness. Across the Western world, physicians and nurses have begun to speak openly of an epidemic of loneliness.

The new studies on loneliness are beginning to yield some surprising preliminary findings about its mechanisms. Almost every factor that one might assume affects loneliness does so only some of the time, and only under certain circumstances. People who are married are less lonely than single people, one journal article suggests, but only if their spouses are confidants. If one's spouse is not a confidant, marriage may not decrease loneliness. A belief in God might help, or it might not, as a 1990 German study comparing levels of religious feeling and levels of loneliness discovered. Active believers who saw God as abstract and helpful rather than as a wrathful, immediate presence were less lonely. "The mere belief in God," the researchers concluded, "was relatively independent of loneliness."

But it is clear that social interaction matters. Loneliness and being alone are not the same thing, but both are on the rise. We meet fewer people. We gather less. And when we gather, our bonds are less meaningful and less easy. The decrease in confidants — that is, in quality social connections — has been dramatic over the past twenty-five years. In one survey, the mean size of networks of personal confidants decreased from 2.94 people in 1985 to 2.08 in 2004. Similarly, in 1985, only 10 percent of Americans said they had no one with whom to discuss important matters, and 15 percent said they had only one such good friend. By 2004, 25 percent had nobody to talk to, and 20 percent had only one confidant.

In the face of this social disintegration, we have essentially hired an army of replacement confidants, an entire class of professional carers. As Ronald Dworkin pointed out in a 2010 paper for the Hoover Institution, in the late 1940s, the United States was home to 2,500 clinical psychologists, 30,000 social workers, and fewer than 500 marriage and family therapists. As of 2010, the country had 77,000 clinical psychologists, 192,000 clinical social workers, 400,000 nonclinical social workers, 50,000 marriage and family therapists, 105,000 mental-health counselors, 220,000 substance-abuse counselors, 17,000 nurse psychotherapists, and 30,000 life coaches. The majority of patients in therapy do not warrant a psychiatric diagnosis. This raft of psychic servants is helping us through what used to be called regular problems. We have outsourced the work of everyday caring.

We need professional carers more and more, because the threat of societal breakdown, once principally a matter of nostalgic lament, has morphed into an issue of public health. Being lonely is extremely bad for your health. If you're lonely, you're more likely to be put in a geriatric home at an earlier age than a similar person who isn't lonely. You're less likely to exercise. You're more likely to be obese. You're less likely to survive a serious operation and more likely to have hormonal imbalances. You are at greater risk of inflammation. Your memory may be worse. You are more likely to be depressed, to sleep badly, and to suffer dementia and general cognitive decline. Loneliness may not have killed Yvette Vickers, but it has been linked to a greater probability of having the kind of heart condition that did kill her.

And yet, despite its deleterious effect on health, loneliness is one of the first things ordinary Americans spend their money achieving. With money, you flee the cramped city to a house in the suburbs or, if you can afford it, a McMansion in the exurbs, inevitably spending more time in your car. Loneliness is at the American core, a by-product of a long-standing national appetite for independence: The Pilgrims who left Europe willingly abandoned the bonds and strictures of a society that could not accept their right to be different. They did not seek out loneliness, but they accepted it as the price of their autonomy. The cowboys who set off to explore a seemingly endless frontier likewise traded away personal ties in favor of pride and self-respect. The ultimate American icon is the astronaut: Who is more heroic, or more alone? The price of self-determination and self-reliance has often been loneliness. But Americans have always been willing to pay that price.

15 Today, the one common feature in American secular culture is its celebration of the self that breaks away from the constrictions of the family and the state, and, in its greatest expressions, from all limits entirely. The great American poem is Whitman's "Song of Myself." The great American essay is Emerson's "Self-Reliance." The great American novel is Melville's *Moby-Dick*, the tale of a man on a quest so lonely that it is incomprehensible to those around him. American culture, high and low, is about self-expression and personal authenticity. Franklin Delano Roosevelt called individualism "the great watchword of American life."

Self-invention is only half of the American story, however. The drive for isolation has always been in tension with the impulse to cluster in communities that cling and suffocate. The Pilgrims, while fomenting spiritual rebellion, also enforced ferocious cohesion. The Salem witch trials, in hindsight, read like attempts to impose solidarity — as do the McCarthy hearings. The history of the United States is like the famous parable of the porcupines in the cold, from Schopenhauer's *Studies in Pessimism* — the ones who huddle together for warmth and shuffle away in pain, always separating and congregating.

We are now in the middle of a long period of shuffling away. In his 2000 book *Bowling Alone*, Robert D. Putnam attributed the dramatic postwar decline of social capital — the strength and value of interpersonal networks — to numerous interconnected trends in American life: suburban sprawl, television's dominance over culture, the self-absorption of the Baby Boomers, the disintegration of the traditional family. The trends he observed continued through the prosperity of the aughts, and have only become more pronounced with time: the rate of union membership declined in 2011, again; screen time rose; the Masons and the Elks continued their slide into irrelevance. We are lonely because we want to be lonely. We have made ourselves lonely.

The question of the future is this: Is Facebook part of the separating or part of the congregating; is it a huddling-together for warmth or a shuffling-away in pain?

Well before Facebook, digital technology was enabling our tendency for isolation, to an unprecedented degree. Back in the 1990s, scholars started calling the contradiction between an increased opportunity to connect and a lack of human contact the "Internet paradox." A prominent 1998 article on the phenomenon by a team of researchers at Carnegie Mellon showed that increased Internet usage was already coinciding with increased loneliness. Critics of the study pointed out that the two groups that participated in the study — high-school journalism students who were heading to university and socially active members of community-development boards — were statistically likely to become lonelier over time. Which brings us to a more fundamental question: Does the Internet make people lonely, or are lonely people more attracted to the Internet?

20 The question has intensified in the Facebook era. A recent study out of Australia (where close to half the population is active on Facebook), titled "Who Uses Facebook?" found a complex and sometimes confounding relationship between loneliness and social networking. Facebook users had slightly lower levels of "social loneliness" — the sense of not feeling bonded with friends — but "significantly higher levels of family loneliness" — the sense of not feeling bonded with family. It may be that Facebook encourages more contact with people outside of our household, at the expense of our family relationships — or it may be that people who have unhappy family relationships in the first place seek companionship through other means, including Facebook. The researchers also found that lonely people are inclined to spend more time on Facebook: "One of the most noteworthy findings," they wrote, "was the tendency for neurotic and lonely individuals to spend greater amounts of time on Facebook per day than non-lonely individuals." And they found that neurotics are more likely to prefer to use the wall, while extroverts tend to use chat features in addition to the wall.

Moira Burke, until recently a graduate student at the Human-Computer Institute at Carnegie Mellon, used to run a longitudinal study of 1,200 Facebook users. That study, which is ongoing, is one of the first to step outside the realm of self-selected college students and examine the effects of Facebook on a broader population, over time. She concludes that the effect of Facebook depends on what you bring to it. Just as your mother said: you get out only what you put in. If you use Facebook to communicate directly with other individuals — by using the "like" button, commenting on friends' posts, and so on — it can increase your social capital. Personalized messages, or what Burke calls "composed communication," are more satisfying than "one-click communication" — the lazy click of a like. "People who received composed communication became less lonely, while people who received one-click communication experienced no change in loneliness," Burke tells me. So, you should inform your friend in writing how charming her son looks with Harry Potter cake smeared all over his face, and how interesting her sepia-toned photograph of that tree-framed bit of skyline is, and how cool it is that she's at whatever concert she happens to be at. That's what we all want to hear. Even better than sending a private Facebook message is the semi-public conversation, the kind of back-and-forth in which you half ignore the other people who may be listening in. "People whose friends write to them semi-publicly on Facebook experience decreases in loneliness," Burke says.

On the other hand, nonpersonalized use of Facebook — scanning your friends' status updates and updating the world on your own activities via your wall, or what Burke calls "passive consumption" and "broadcasting" — correlates to feelings of disconnectedness. It's a lonely business, wandering the labyrinths of our friends' and pseudo-friends' projected identities, trying to figure out what part of ourselves we ought to project, who will listen, and what they will hear. According to Burke, passive consumption of Facebook also correlates to a marginal increase in depression. "If two women each talk to their friends the same amount of time, but one of them spends more time reading about friends on Facebook as well, the one reading tends to grow slightly more depressed," Burke says. Her conclusion suggests that my sometimes unhappy reactions to Facebook may be more universal than I had realized. When I scroll through page after page of my friends' descriptions of how accidentally eloquent their kids are, and how their husbands are endearingly bumbling, and how they're all about to eat a home-cooked meal prepared with fresh local organic produce bought at the farmers' market and then go for a jog and maybe check in at the office because they're so busy getting ready to hop on a plane for a week of luxury dogsledding in Lapland, I do grow slightly more miserable. A lot of other people doing the same thing feel a little bit worse, too.

Still, Burke's research does not support the assertion that Facebook creates loneliness. The people who experience loneliness on Facebook are lonely away from Facebook, too, she points out; on Facebook, as everywhere else, correlation is not causation. The popular kids are popular, and the lonely skulkers skulk alone. Perhaps it says something about me that I think Facebook is primarily a platform for lonely skulking. I mention to Burke the widely reported study, conducted by a Stanford graduate student, that showed how believing that others have strong social networks can lead to feelings of depression. What does Facebook communicate, if not the impression of social bounty? Everybody else looks so happy on Facebook, with so many friends, that our own social networks feel emptier than ever in comparison. Doesn't that *make* people feel lonely? "If people are reading about lives that are much better than theirs, two things can happen," Burke tells me. "They can feel worse about themselves, or they can feel motivated."

Burke will start working at Facebook as a data scientist this year.

John Cacioppo, the director of the Center for Cognitive and Social Neuroscience at the University of Chicago, is the world's leading expert on loneliness. In his landmark book, *Loneliness*, released in 2008, he revealed just how profoundly the epidemic of loneliness is affecting the basic functions of human physiology. He found higher levels of epinephrine, the stress hormone, in the morning urine of lonely people. Loneliness burrows deep: "When we drew blood from our older adults and analyzed their white cells," he writes, "we found that loneliness somehow penetrated the deepest recesses of the cell to alter the way genes were being expressed." Loneliness affects not only the brain, then, but the basic process of DNA transcription. When you are lonely, your whole body is lonely.

To Cacioppo, Internet communication allows only ersatz intimacy. "Forming connections with pets or online friends or even God is a noble attempt by an obligatorily gregarious creature to satisfy a compelling need," he writes. "But surrogates can never make up completely for the absence of the real thing." The "real thing" being actual people, in the flesh. When I speak to Cacioppo, he is refreshingly clear on what he sees as Facebook's effect on society. Yes, he allows, some research has suggested that the greater the number of Facebook friends a person has, the less lonely she is. But he argues that the impression this creates can be misleading. "For the most part," he says, "people are bringing their old friends, and feelings of loneliness or connectedness, to Facebook." The idea that a Web site could deliver a more friendly, interconnected world is bogus. The depth of one's social network outside Facebook is what determines the depth of one's social network within Facebook, not the other way around. Using social media doesn't create new social networks; it just transfers established networks from one platform to another. For the most part, Facebook doesn't destroy friendships — but it doesn't create them, either.

In one experiment, Cacioppo looked for a connection between the loneliness of subjects and the relative frequency of their interactions via Facebook, chat rooms, online games, dating sites, and face-to-face contact. The results were unequivocal. "The greater the proportion of face-to-face interactions, the less lonely you are," he says. "The greater the proportion of online interactions, the lonelier you are." Surely, I suggest to Cacioppo, this means that Facebook and the like inevitably make people lonelier. He disagrees. Facebook is merely a tool, he says, and like any tool, its effectiveness will depend on its user. "If you use Facebook to increase face-to-face contact," he says, "it increases social capital." So if social media let you organize a game of football among your friends, that's healthy. If you turn to social media instead of playing football, however, that's unhealthy.

"Facebook can be terrific, if we use it properly," Cacioppo continues. "It's like a car. You can drive it to pick up your friends. Or you can drive alone." But hasn't the car increased loneliness? If cars created the suburbs, surely they also created isolation. "That's because of how we use cars," Cacioppo replies. "How we use these technologies can lead to more integration, rather than more isolation."

The problem, then, is that we invite loneliness, even though it makes us miserable. The history of our use of technology is a history of isolation desired and achieved. When the Great Atlantic and Pacific Tea Company opened its A&P stores, giving Americans self-service access to groceries, customers stopped having relationships with their grocers. When the telephone arrived, people stopped knocking on their neighbors' doors. Social media bring this process to a much wider set of relationships. Researchers at the HP Social Computing Lab who studied the nature of people's connections on Twitter came to a depressing, if not surprising, conclusion: "Most of the links declared within Twitter were meaningless from an interaction point of view." I have to wonder: What other point of view is meaningful?

Loneliness is certainly not something that 30
Facebook or Twitter or any of the lesser forms of social media is doing to us. We are doing it to ourselves. Casting technology as some vague, impersonal spirit of history forcing our actions is a weak excuse. We make decisions about how we use our machines, not the other way around. Every time I shop at my local grocery store, I am faced with a choice. I can buy my groceries from a human being or from a machine. I always, without exception, choose the machine. It's faster and more efficient, I tell myself, but the truth is that I prefer not having to wait with the other customers who are lined up alongside the conveyor belt: the hipster mom who disapproves of my high-carbon-footprint pineapple; the lady who tenses to the point of tears while she waits to see if the gods of the credit-card machine will accept or decline; the old man whose clumsy feebleness requires a patience that I don't possess. Much better to bypass the whole circus and just ring up the groceries myself.

Our omnipresent new technologies lure us toward increasingly superficial connections at exactly the same moment that they make avoiding the mess of human interaction easy. The beauty of Facebook, the source of its power, is that it enables us to be social while sparing us the embarrassing reality of society — the accidental revelations we make at parties, the awkward pauses, the farting and the spilled drinks and the general gaucherie of face-to-face contact. Instead, we have the lovely smoothness of a seemingly social machine. Everything's so simple: status updates, pictures, your wall.

But the price of this smooth sociability is a constant compulsion to assert one's own happiness, one's own fulfillment. Not only must we contend with the social bounty of others; we must foster the appearance of our own social bounty. Being happy all the time, pretending to be happy, actually attempting to be happy — it's exhausting. Last year a team of researchers led by Iris Mauss at the University of Denver published a study looking into "the paradoxical effects of valuing happiness." Most goals in life show a direct correlation between valuation and achievement. Studies have found, for example, that students who value good grades tend to have higher grades than those who don't value them. Happiness is an exception. The study came to a disturbing conclusion:

> Valuing happiness is not necessarily linked to greater happiness. In fact, under certain conditions, the opposite is true. Under conditions of low (but not high) life stress, the more people valued happiness, the lower were their hedonic balance, psychological well-being, and life satisfaction, and the higher their depression symptoms.

The more you try to be happy, the less happy you are. Sophocles made roughly the same point.

Facebook, of course, puts the pursuit of happiness front and center in our digital life. Its capacity to redefine our very concepts of identity and personal fulfillment is much more worrisome than the data-mining and privacy practices that have aroused anxieties about the company. Two of the most compelling critics of Facebook — neither of them a Luddite — concentrate on exactly this point. Jaron Lanier, the author of *You Are Not a Gadget*, was one of the inventors of virtual-reality technology. His view of where social media are taking us reads like dystopian science fiction: "I fear that we are beginning to design ourselves to suit digital models of us, and I worry about a leaching of empathy and humanity in that process." Lanier argues that Facebook imprisons us in the business of self-presenting, and this, to his mind, is the site's crucial and fatally unacceptable downside.

Sherry Turkle, a professor of computer culture at MIT who in 1995 published the digital-positive analysis *Life on the Screen*, is much more skeptical about the effects of online society in her 2011 book, *Alone Together*: "These days, insecure in our relationships and anxious about intimacy, we look to technology for ways to be in relationships and protect ourselves from them at the same time." The problem with digital intimacy is that it is ultimately incomplete: "The ties we form through the Internet are not, in the end, the ties that bind. But they are the ties that preoccupy," she writes. "We don't want to intrude on each other, so instead we constantly intrude on each other, but not in 'real time.'"

Lanier and Turkle are right, at least in their 35
diagnoses. Self-presentation on Facebook is continuous, intensely mediated, and possessed of a phony nonchalance that eliminates even the potential for spontaneity. ("Look how casually I threw up these three photos from the party at which I took 300 photos!") Curating the exhibition of the self has become a 24/7 occupation. Perhaps not surprisingly, then, the Australian study "Who Uses Facebook?"

found a significant correlation between Facebook use and narcissism: "Facebook users have higher levels of total narcissism, exhibitionism, and leadership than Facebook nonusers," the study's authors wrote. "In fact, it could be argued that Facebook specifically gratifies the narcissistic individual's need to engage in self-promoting and superficial behavior."

Rising narcissism isn't so much a trend as the trend behind all other trends. In preparation for the 2013 edition of its diagnostic manual, the psychiatric profession is currently struggling to update its definition of narcissistic personality disorder. Still, generally speaking, practitioners agree that narcissism manifests in patterns of fantastic grandiosity, craving for attention, and lack of empathy. In a 2008 survey, 35,000 American respondents were asked if they had ever had certain symptoms of narcissistic personality disorder. Among people older than sixty-five, 3 percent reported symptoms. Among people in their twenties, the proportion was nearly 10 percent. Across all age groups, one in sixteen Americans has experienced some symptoms of NPD. And loneliness and narcissism are intimately connected: a longitudinal study of Swedish women demonstrated a strong link between levels of narcissism in youth and levels of loneliness in old age. The connection is fundamental. Narcissism is the flip side of loneliness, and either condition is a fighting retreat from the messy reality of other people.

A considerable part of Facebook's appeal stems from its miraculous fusion of distance with intimacy, or the illusion of distance with the illusion of intimacy. Our online communities become engines of self-image, and self-image becomes the engine of community. The real danger with Facebook is not that it allows us to isolate ourselves, but that by mixing our appetite for isolation with our vanity, it threatens to alter the very nature of solitude. The new isolation is not of the kind that Americans once idealized, the lonesomeness of the proudly nonconformist, independent-minded, solitary stoic, or that of the astronaut who blasts into new worlds.

Facebook's isolation is a grind. What's truly staggering about Facebook usage is not its volume — 750 million photographs uploaded over a single weekend — but the constancy of the performance it demands. More than half its users — and one of every thirteen people on Earth is a Facebook user — log on every day. Among eighteen-to-thirty-four-year-olds, nearly half check Facebook minutes after waking up, and 28 percent do so before getting out of bed. The relentlessness is what is so new, so potentially transformative. Facebook never takes a break. We never take a break. Human beings have always created elaborate acts of self-presentation. But not all the time, not every morning, before we even pour a cup of coffee. Yvette Vickers's computer was on when she died.

Nostalgia for the good old days of disconnection would not just be pointless, it would be hypocritical and ungrateful. But the very magic of the new machines, the efficiency and elegance with which they serve us, obscures what isn't being served: everything that matters. What Facebook has revealed about human nature — and this is not a minor revelation — is that a connection is not the same thing as a bond, and that instant and total connection is no salvation, no ticket to a happier, better world or a more liberated version of humanity. Solitude used to be good for self-reflection and self-reinvention. But now we are left thinking about who we are all the time, without ever really thinking about who we are. Facebook denies us a pleasure whose profundity we had underestimated: the chance to forget about ourselves for a while, the chance to disconnect.

Topics for Critical Thinking and Writing

1. In his first three paragraphs, Stephen Marche argues that, despite modern technology, "we have never been more detached from one another, or lonelier." What methods does he go on to use in his effort to persuade? Did his essay convince you? Explain.
2. In paragraph 6, Marche states that "social networking might be spreading the very isolation it seemed designed to conquer." Does your own experience with social media confirm or refute this assertion? Explain your response.
3. In paragraph 17, Marche speaks of "social capital." What does this term mean? How do you know?
4. In paragraph 20, Marche discusses the findings of an Australian study of Facebook users. How do you interpret the study's finding of "significantly higher levels of family loneliness" among Facebook users?
5. In paragraph 33, Marche writes: "[Facebook's] capacity to redefine our very concepts of identity and personal fulfillment is much more worrisome than the data-mining and privacy practices that have aroused anxieties about the company." In your estimation, is this claim true? In 500 to 1,000 words, support your position.

JOSH ROSE

Josh Rose is founder and creative director at Humans Are Social, a digital content agency dedicated to social media marketing. A graduate of the University of California–Santa Cruz, Rose has also worked at public relations agencies Deutsch LA and Weber Shandwick. The following article was published on Mashable.com, an online source that reports on digital innovation, on February 23, 2011.

How Social Media Is Having a Positive Impact on Our Culture

Two events today, although worlds apart, seem inextricably tied together. And the bond between them is as human as it is electronic.

First, on my way to go sit down and read the newspaper at my coffee shop, I got a message from my ten-year-old son, just saying good morning and letting me know he was going to a birthday party today. I don't get to see him all the time. He's growing up in two houses, as I did. But recently I handed down my old iPhone 3G to him to use basically as an iPod Touch. We both installed an app called Yak, so we could communicate with each other when we're apart.

The amount of calming satisfaction it gives me to be able to communicate with him through technology is undeniably palpable and human. It's the other side of the "I don't care what you ate for breakfast this morning" argument against the mundane broadcasting of social media. In this case, I absolutely care about this. I'd listen to him describe a piece of bacon, and hang on every word. Is it better than a conversation with "real words"? No. But is it better than waiting two more days, when the mundane moment that I long to hear about so much is gone? Yes.

I guess one man's TMI is another man's treasure.

5 Moments later, I sat down and opened the paper. A headline immediately stood out: "In China, microblogs finding abducted kids" with the subhead, "A 6-year-old who was snatched when he was 3 is discovered with a family 800 miles away." Apparently, the occurrence of reclaimed children through the use of China's version of Twitter — and other online forums — has become triumphant news over there. I'm reading about the father's tears, the boy's own confusing set of emotions, the rapt attention of the town and country, and I'm again marveling at the human side of the Internet.

THE PARADOX OF ONLINE CLOSENESS

I recently asked the question to my Facebook friends: "Twitter, Facebook, Foursquare . . . is all this making you feel closer to people or farther away?" It sparked a lot of responses and seemed to touch one of our generation's exposed nerves. What is the effect of the Internet and social media on our humanity?

From the outside view, digital interactions appear to be cold and inhuman. There's no denying that. And without doubt, given the choice between hugging someone and "poking" someone, I think we can all agree which one feels better. The theme of the responses to my Facebook question seemed to be summed up by my friend Jason, who wrote: "Closer to people I'm far away from." Then, a minute later, wrote, "but maybe farther from the people I'm close enough to." And then added, "I just got confused."

It is confusing. We live in this paradox now, where two seemingly conflicting realities exist side-by-side. Social media simultaneously draws us nearer and distances us. But I think very often, we lament what we miss and forget to admire what we've become. And it's human nature to want to reject the machine at the moment we feel it becoming ubiquitous. We've seen it with the printing press, moving pictures, television, video games, and just about any other advanced technology that captures our attention. What romantic rituals of relationship and social interaction will die in the process? Our hearts want to know.

In the *New Yorker* this week [February 14, 2011] Adam Gopnik's article "How the Internet Gets Inside Us" explores this cultural truism in depth. It's a fantastic read and should be mandatory for anyone in an online industry. He breaks down a whole slew of new books on the subject and categorizes it all into three viewpoints: "the Never-Betters, the Better-Nevers, and the Ever-Wasers." In short, those who see the current movement as good, bad, or normal. I think we all know people from each camp. But ultimately, the last group is the one best equipped to handle it all.

FILLING IN THE SPACE WITH CONNECTIONS

10 Another observation from the coffee shop: In my immediate vicinity, four people are looking at screens and four people are reading something on paper. And I'm doing both. I see Facebook open on two screens, but I'm sure at some point, it's been open

on all of them. The dynamic in this coffee shop is quite a bit more revealing than any article or book. Think about the varied juxtapositions of physical and digital going on. People aren't giving up long-form reading, considered thinking, or social interactions. They are just filling all the space between. And even that's not entirely true as I watch the occasional stare out the window or long glance around the room.

The way people engage with the Internet and social media isn't like any kind of interaction we've ever seen before. It's like an intertwining sine wave that touches in and out continuously. And the Internet itself is more complex and interesting than we often give it credit for. Consider peer-to-peer networking as just one example, where the tasks are distributed among the group to form a whole. It's practically a metaphor for the human mind. Or a township. Or a government. Or a family.

The Internet doesn't steal our humanity, it reflects it. The Internet doesn't get inside us, it shows what's inside us. And social media isn't cold, it's just complex and hard to define. I've always thought that you really see something's value when you try to destroy it. As we have now laid witness to in recent news, the Internet has quickly become the atom of cultural media; intertwined with our familial and cultural bonds, and destroyed only at great risk. I think if we search our own souls and consider our own personal way of navigating, we know this is as true personally as it is globally. The machine does not control us. It is a tool. As advanced today as a sharpened stick was a couple million years ago. Looked at through this lens, perhaps we should reframe our discussions about technology from how it is changing us to how we are using it.

Topics for Critical Thinking and Writing

1. In paragraph 8, Josh Rose says, "Social media simultaneously draws us nearer and distances us." Do you agree? Write a short response citing examples that may help convince a reader of the truth or untruth of this assertion.
2. In paragraph 9, Rose claims that of the Never-Betters, the Better-Nevers, and the Ever-Wasers, "the last group is the one best equipped to handle it all." Do you agree or disagree that those who see the changes brought about by the internet and social media as normal are the best equipped to handle it? Explain your answer.
3. In your own experience, what are the best parts and worst parts of social media? How do you balance the positives and negatives? What would you recommend for others?
4. In paragraph 11, Rose writes that the internet is a "metaphor for the human mind." Extend this metaphor. In what ways does the brain work like a computer? In what ways does it not?
5. Rose begins his final paragraph with these three sentences: "The Internet doesn't steal our humanity, it reflects it. The Internet doesn't get inside us, it shows what's inside us. And social media isn't cold, it's just complex and hard to define." Assume for the moment that he is correct. Go on to continue his paragraph, offering details that support these sentences.

JARON LANIER

Jaron Lanier (b. 1960) is a computer scientist, philosopher, artist, and composer who worked for Atari Games in the early 1980s before leaving to develop early research on virtual reality and later to work at Microsoft and Internet2. He has written five books, most recently *Dawn of the New Everything: Encounters with Reality and Virtual Reality* (2017) and *Ten Arguments for Deleting Your Social Media Accounts Right Now* (2018), in which the following essay appears. On Lanier's website, he informs visitors that "Jaron has no social media accounts at all and all purported ones are fake."

Social Media Is Making You into an Asshole

Let me rephrase this argument's title. I don't know you. I'm not saying that you personally are definitely turning into an asshole, but many people are, yet they seem to only see that many *other* people are. I've seen myself start turning into an asshole online, and it was scary and depressing.

So what I should really say is something like "You're vulnerable to gradually turning into an asshole, or statistically you might very well be turning into an asshole. So, no offense, but please take the possibility seriously."

SOOTY SNOW

Addicts can try to hide an addiction, especially from themselves, but often it shows. Personalities change.

The deeply addicted person's rhythm becomes nervous, a compulsive pecking at his situation; he's always deprived, rushing for affirmation. Addicts become anxious, strangely focused on portentous events that aren't visible to others. They are selfish, so wrapped up in their cycle that they don't have much time to notice what others are feeling or thinking about. There's an arrogance, a fetish for exaggeration, that by all appearances is a cover for profound insecurity. A personal mythology overtakes addicts. They see themselves grandiosely and, as they descend further into addiction, ever less realistically.

Hard-core social media addicts display 5
these changes, just like junkies or ruinous gamblers. More commonly, social media users become a *little* like this, statistically more likely to behave like an addict at any given time. There are shades of gray, just as with everything else about social media. The whole society has darkened a few shades as a result.

The most curious feature of the addict's personality is that the addict eventually seems to seek out suffering, since suffering is part of the cycle of scratching the itch. A gambler is addicted not to winning, exactly, but to the process in which losing is more likely. A junkie is addicted not just to the high, but to the vertiginous difference between the lows and the highs.

Similarly, a social media addict eventually becomes preternaturally quick to take offense, as if hoping to get into a spat.

Addicts also become aggressive, though they feel they are acting out of necessity. The choice is to victimize or be a victim. Even successful and pleasant addicts, like top social media influencers, have reported that they must not be too nice to others, for that shows weakness[1] in a highly competitive fishbowl. One must be followed more than one follows, for appearances' sake.

[1] https://www.nytimes.com/2017/12/30/business/hollywood-apartment-social-media.html

The characteristic personality change is hard to perceive or acknowledge in oneself, but easier to see in others, especially if you don't like them. When conservative social media addicts dislike liberal college students with social media addictions, they sometimes use the insult "poor little snowflake."

The poorest snowflake of them all, however, is Donald Trump, who exhibits the same behavior. I met him a few times over several decades, and I didn't like him, but he wasn't a social media addict back then. He was a New York City character, a manipulator, an actor, a master at working the calculus of chums and outcasts. But as a character he was in on his own joke. Even reality TV didn't really make him lose it.

As a Twitter addict, Trump has changed. He displays the snowflake pattern and sometimes loses control. He is not acting like the most powerful person in the world, because his addiction is more powerful. Whatever else he might be, whatever kind of victimizer, he is also a victim.

MEETING MY INNER TROLL

Many things about social media have changed over the years, but the basic form was already around when I first got into computers in the late 1970s. The social media we had back then amounted to little more than commenting, just a bunch of people adding their text. There wasn't any voting for favorite posts, nor did algorithms customize your feed. Very basic.

But I noticed something horrifying all those years ago. Sometimes, out of nowhere, I would get into a fight with someone, or a group of people. It was so weird. We'd start insulting each other, trying to score points, getting under each other's skin. And about incredibly stupid stuff, like whether or not someone knew what they were talking about when it came to brands of pianos. Really.

I'd stew between posts. "I am *not* ignorant! I know about pianos! How dare that moron say those horrible things about me? I know, I'll ruin his reputation by tricking him into saying something stupid."

This happened so often that it became normal. Not just for me, but for everyone. It was chaotic human weather. There'd be a nice morning and suddenly a storm would roll in.

In order to avoid falling into asshole behavior you had to make yourself fake-nice. You'd have to be saccharine polite, constantly choosing your words super carefully, walking on eggshells.

That sucked worse!

I just stopped using the stuff because I didn't like who I was becoming. You know the adage that you should choose a partner on the basis of who you become when you're around the person? That's a good way to choose technologies, too.

When some friends started a pioneering online community called the Well in the 1990s, they gave me an account, but I never posted a single thing. Same story much later, when I helped some buddies start an online world called Second Life.

In the early 2000s, an enterprising woman named Arianna Huffington got me to blog on her Huffington Post for a while. I have to tell you how she did it.

We were at a fancy conference for rich and influential people at a fancy little town in the Colorado Rockies. I was sitting on a bench with my arm resting on the rim of a rounded cement wall surrounding a garbage can. Arianna came along and sat on my arm, trapping it. "Arianna—oh, you didn't notice; let me get my arm out."

In her thick Greek accent: "Do you know what some men would pay for this privilege? I will release your hand if you will blog for me."

So I did it. Briefly I was one of the HuffPost's top bloggers, always on the front page. But I found myself falling into that old problem again whenever I read the comments, and I could not get myself to ignore them. I would feel this weird low-level boiling rage inside me. Or I'd feel this absurd glow when people liked what I wrote, even if what they said didn't indicate that they had paid much attention to it. Comment authors were mostly seeking attention for themselves.

We were all in the same stew, manipulating each other, inflating ourselves.

After a short while, I noticed that I'd write things I didn't even believe in order to get a rise out of readers. I wrote stuff that I knew people wanted to hear, or the opposite, because I knew it would be inflammatory.

Oh my God! I was back in that same place, becoming an asshole because of *something* about this stupid technology!

I quit — again.

I want to be authentically nice, and certain online designs seem to fight against that with magical force. That's the core reason why I don't have accounts on Facebook, Twitter, WhatsApp,[2] Instagram, Snapchat, or any of the rest. You'll see fake accounts in my name. There's even a supposed @RealJaronLanier on Twitter. But I have no idea who that is. Not me.

I don't think I'm better than you because I don't have social media accounts. Maybe I'm worse; maybe you can handle the stuff better than I can.

But I've observed that since social media took off, assholes are having more of a say in the world.

Social media platform experiences ricochet between two extremes. Either there's a total shitstorm of assholes (that's not a mixed metaphor, right?) or everyone is super careful and artificially nice.

The biggest assholes get the most attention, however, and they often end up giving a platform its flavor. Even if there are corners of the platform where not everyone is an asshole all the time, those corners feel penned in, because the assholes are waiting just outside. . . .

GO TO WHERE YOU ARE KINDEST

Of course there were assholes in the world before social media, but it wasn't as hard to avoid being one. On social media you have to fight gravity just to be decent.

The online asshole-supremacy problem could be solved rather easily simply by dumping the social media model of business. One possibility is that people could earn money more often and more fairly from what they do online; that idea will be explored in the argument about how social media is ruining economics.

What we need is *anything* that's real beyond social pretensions that people can focus on instead of becoming assholes.

In the meantime, there is something you can do personally. If, when you participate in online platforms, you notice a nasty thing inside yourself, an insecurity, a sense of low self-esteem, a yearning to lash out, to swat someone down, *then leave that platform*. Simple.

There is a spotlight on online bullying, as there should be, and you might have experienced being bullied online. Many, many people have.

But I am also asking you to notice, within your own mind, in genuine secrecy — don't share this — if you are feeling the temptation to strike out at *someone else* online. Maybe that other person started it. Whatever. It isn't worth it. Leave the platform. Don't post that insult video, don't tweet in retaliation.

[2]WhatsApp is part of Facebook; even if it sometimes feels like any other texting platform, it's in fact a primary data scooper for social media. Facebook has faced considerable legal blowback for using WhatsApp data that way in Europe (see https://www.theverge.com/2017/12/18/16792448/whatsapp-facebook-data-sharing-no-user-consent). In the United States, since the network neutrality rules are being relaxed, it's possible that *all* texting, even native texting between phones, will become part of social media, but as of this writing it doesn't appear to have happened.

If Twitter ceased operations tomorrow, not only would Trump not be able to tweet, obviously, but also I believe he'd become a nicer, better person at all hours, at least until he latched on to another social media platform.

40 I can't prove this, and a lot of people will disagree with me. That doesn't matter. Look into yourself. Seriously, are you being as kind as you want to be? At what times are you more like the person you want to be, and when do you get irritable or dismissive?

Your character is the most precious thing about you. Don't let it degrade.

Topics for Critical Thinking and Writing

1. How do you make sense of Jaron Lanier's first two paragraphs? How do they help or hurt his argument?
2. Do you find Lanier's analogy between drug addiction and social media addiction convincing? Why, or why not?
3. After Lanier took the position at the *HuffPost*, he says, "I wrote stuff that I knew people wanted to hear, or the opposite, because I knew it would be inflammatory" (para. 25). How does this statement support Derakhshan's argument (p. 533)?
4. How does Lanier *define* (see p. 85) an "asshole"? Is the definition stated or unstated? Provide your own definition of what it means to be an "asshole" in any digital communications (discussion boards, texts, emails, or anything).
5. In 2018, media reports claimed that Silicon Valley parents — some of the very people who work for the largest tech companies — were increasingly shielding their children from social media and limiting their screen time. Early in 2019, a team of doctors in England recommended limiting internet usage for adults and children, especially in bed and during meals. What do you think of prescribed limits on screen time — in general or during activities such as sports events, movies, classrooms, or dinner parties? Should phones be banned in any of these places? In 500 words or more, support or oppose these limitations.

TOURIA BENLAFQIH

Touria Benlafqih is the founder and chief executive officer of Social Impact and Development Employment (SIDE), a group that works to build public/private partnerships addressing social, economic, and environmental development issues in Africa. This essay was published in the World Economic Forum in 2015.

Has Social Media Made Young People Better Citizens?

There have never been as many young people as there are today. This is particularly true in Africa and the Middle East. Young people are a considerable asset to their countries, with a critical role to play in the political, social, economic and cultural landscape. Yet their potential is still untapped, and their contribution to their nations still hasn't been fully realized: a large part of this young population remains uneducated, unemployed or uninterested.

Youth is a pivotal period in a person's life; it's the bridge between childhood and adulthood. According to Erik Erikson's stages of psychological development, each individual experiences a phase during which they search for their identity, a phase where they blend their identity with friends and want to fit in, and a phase of "generativity," where they start wishing to build a legacy and guide the next generation.

With that in mind, we understand that the very nature of youth is to be involved and contribute. It is quite difficult for me to believe the line that young people lack engagement in society nowadays. So why is it the case, then?

There are various reasons why young people are less likely to be active citizens: the lack of effective communication between them and decision-makers, for example. Also, young people feel used instead of empowered, so they don't easily embrace the "old school mindset" in doing things. Often, they lack information and don't fully understand how political institutions, economic development, public services or social inclusion work—and nothing is more vital to a democracy than a well-informed electorate.

Ten years ago, when I began working with 5
young people, I was surprised to discover that many of them don't know where or how to get started. They had dreams, energy and enthusiasm, but no proper knowledge of how to be active, and no proper guidance to channel that energy.

Back then, the internet was a new concept in Morocco, and was still confined to a very limited population. A young person could only access information through traditional media (TV, radio, newspapers and magazines); and they could only find out about the activities of a political party or a public gathering for a social cause, through word of mouth, provided they knew the right people.

Social media is the most adapted communication tool of today's younger generation. It's easy to see why: accessible and user-friendly, platforms such as Twitter, Facebook and LinkedIn let you create and showcase your personality, develop new contacts, discuss issues and keep in touch in real time. They allow you to read, analyze and share content without any prerequisites.

Media is no longer the one-way communication channel as it used to be. With connected devices becoming ever more ubiquitous, questions can be answered and misunderstandings avoided. It has become easier to connect with people from different places and backgrounds: to benefit from their experience, to support a cause without being directly involved, to engage with organizations and movements, and to mobilize people in less time and with less cost.

Working with young people in Morocco over the years, I have witnessed a change in how they engage: they have become better and more active citizens, in both a formal and informal way. Thanks to social media's diverse platforms, young people can view content about their region, about influencers and decision-makers. They can participate in online petitions, join groups and talk to like-minded people on Facebook, contribute to the debate on Twitter, report an injustice on Instagram, or share videos and podcasts on Youtube. Social media fosters a sense of ownership and responsibility, and young people can engage directly, not just as individuals, but as part of a community in their own personal way.

While many young people in Morocco 10
are engaged in social activities outside social media, youth engagement in "real-life" organizations, projects and awareness-raising is

comparatively insignificant, and remains concentrated in major cities, where most government, civil-society and private-sector activity is focused.

How can we help the momentum of online youth engagement spread to real-world local areas? We need to provide monitoring and funding for local initiatives, organize more events and training workshops, and attract more attention to civil-society activities in smaller cities, towns and villages. We need to create local success stories that inspire and drive young people, and which they can showcase on social media to inspire others.

I believe that participation and engagement is a natural attribute of youth, and has been like this for as long as humanity and social interaction existed. Young people will continue to expand their contribution and participation for as long as they have the tools. Even though more than half of Morocco is connected to the internet, more efforts have to be made in terms of youth mobilization and participation, in order to see this contribution growing exponentially towards a better, more inclusive world.

Topics for Critical Thinking and Writing

1. Do you agree with Touria Benlafqih's assessment that young people "don't fully understand how political institutions, economic development, public services or social inclusion work" (para. 4)? Use evidence to support your response.
2. What kinds of remedies does Benlafqih advocate to get young people more involved in politics and global issues? Do you think they would be effective?
3. Does Benlafqih's essay provide a convincing counterpoint to Marche's (p. 536) and Lanier's (p. 548)? Explain in 300 to 500 words.
4. Do you think the voting age in the United States should be lowered? If so, to what age, and why? If not, provide reasons why it should be kept the same or increased.
5. Do some research on the term "hashtag activism" and discuss whether or not you think such activism is worthwhile or effective. Why, or why not?

23

Immigration: What Is to Be Done?

AVIVA CHOMSKY

Aviva Chomsky (b. 1957) is a professor of history and the coordinator of Latin American, Latino, and Caribbean studies at Salem State University in Massachusetts. She has authored six books on related topics, most recently *Undocumented: How Immigration Became Illegal* (2014), and has contributed chapters to many academic studies of immigration in the United States, Caribbean, and Latin America. She is also a regular contributor to *The Nation*, *TomDispatch*, and *HuffPost*, and she speaks around the world on topics of labor rights and immigration reform. She is the elder daughter of renowned linguist and philosopher Noam Chomsky and his wife, the late linguist Carol Chomsky. The following essay was published by *TomDispatch* on March 13, 2018.

Talking Sense about Immigration

The immigration debate seems to have gone crazy.

President Obama's widely popular Deferred Action for Childhood Arrivals program, or DACA, which offered some 750,000 young immigrants brought to the United States as children a temporary reprieve from deportation, is ending . . . except it isn't . . . except it is. . . . President Trump claims to support it but ordered its halt, while both Republicans and Democrats insist that they want to preserve it and blame each other for its impending demise. (Meanwhile, the Supreme Court recently stepped in to allow DACA recipients to renew their status at least for now.)

On a single day in mid-February 2018, the Senate rejected no less than four immigration bills. These ranged from a narrow proposal to punish sanctuary cities that placed limits on local police collaboration with Immigration and Customs Enforcement (ICE) officials to major overhauls of the 1965 Immigration and Nationality Act that established the current system of immigration quotas (with preferences for "family reunification").

And add in one more thing: virtually everyone in the political sphere is now tailoring his or her pronouncements and votes to political opportunism rather than the real issues at hand.

Politicians and commentators who once 5
denounced "illegal immigration," insisting that people "do it the right way," are now advocating stripping legal status from

many who possess it and drastically cutting even legalized immigration. These days, the hearts of conservative Republicans, otherwise promoting programs for plutocrats, are bleeding for low-wage workers whose livelihoods, they claim (quite incorrectly), are being undermined by competition from immigrants. Meanwhile, Chicago Democrat Luis Gutiérrez — a rare, reliably pro-immigrant voice in Congress — recently swore that, when it came to Trump's much-touted wall on the Mexican border, he was ready to "take a bucket, take bricks, and start building it myself. . . . We will dirty our hands in order for the Dreamers to have a clean future in America."

While in Gutiérrez's neck of the woods, favoring Dreamers may seem politically expedient, giving in to Trump's wall would result in far more than just dirty hands, buckets, and bricks, and the congressman knows that quite well. The significant fortifications already in place on the U.S.-Mexican border have already contributed to the deaths of thousands of migrants, to the increasing militarization of the region, to a dramatic rise of paramilitary drug- and human-smuggling gangs, and to a rise in violent lawlessness on both sides of the border. Add to that a 2,000-mile concrete wall or some combination of walls, fences, bolstered border patrols, and the latest in technology and you're not just talking about some benign waste of money in return for hanging on to the DACA kids.

In the swirl of all this, the demands of immigrant rights organizations for a "clean Dream Act" that would genuinely protect DACA recipients without giving in to Trump's many anti-immigration demands have come to seem increasingly unrealistic. No matter that they hold the only morally coherent position in town — and a broadly popular one nationally as well — DACA's congressional backers seem to have already conceded defeat.

GOOD GUYS AND BAD GUYS

It won't surprise you, I'm sure, to learn that Donald Trump portrays the world in a strikingly black-and-white way when it comes to immigration (and so much else). He emphasizes the violent criminal nature of immigrants and the undocumented, repeatedly highlighting and falsely generalizing from relatively rare cases in which one of them committed a violent crime like the San Francisco killing of Kate Steinle.[1] His sweeping references to "foreign bad guys" and "shithole countries" suggest that he applies the same set of judgments to the international arena.

Under Trump's auspices, the agency in charge of applying the law to immigrants, the Immigration and Customs Enforcement, has taken the concept of criminality to new heights in order to justify expanded priorities for deportation. Now, an actual criminal conviction is no longer necessary. An individual with "pending criminal charges" or simply a "known gang member" has also become an ICE "priority." In other words, a fear-inspiring accusation or even rumor is all that's needed to deem an immigrant a "criminal."

10 And such attitudes are making their way ever deeper into this society. I've seen it at Salem State University, the college where I teach. In a recent memo explaining why he opposes giving the school sanctuary-campus status, the chief of campus police insisted that his force must remain authorized to report students to ICE when there are cases of "bad

[1]Kate Steinle was a thirty-two-year-old woman who was shot and killed by an undocumented immigrant at Pier 14 in San Francisco's Embarcadero District on July 1, 2015. [Editors' note]

actors . . . street gang participation . . . drug trafficking . . . even absent a warrant or other judicial order." In other words, due process be damned, the police, any police, can determine guilt as they wish.

And this tendency toward such a Trumpian Manichaean worldview, now being used to justify the growth of what can only be called an incipient police state, is so strong that it's even infiltrated the thinking of some of the president's immigration opponents. Take "chain migration," an obscure concept previously used mainly by sociologists and historians to describe nineteenth- and twentieth-century global migration patterns. The president has, of course, made it his epithet *du jour.*

Because the president spoke of "chain migration" in such a derogatory way, anti-Trump liberals immediately assumed that the phrase was inherently insulting. MSNBC correspondent Joy Reid typically charged that "the president is saying that the only bill he will approve of must end what they call 'chain migration' which is actually a term we in the media should just not use! Because quite frankly it's not a real thing, it's a made up term . . . [and] so offensive! It's shocking to me that we're just adopting it wholesale because [White House adviser] Stephen Miller wants to call it that. . . . [The term should be] family migration."

Similarly, New York Senator Kirsten Gillibrand claimed that "when someone uses the phrase chain migration . . . it is intentional in trying to demonize families, literally trying to demonize families, and make it a racist slur." House Minority Leader Nancy Pelosi agreed: "Look what they're doing with family unification, making up a fake name, chain. Chain, they like the word 'chain.' That sends tremors through people."

But chain migration is not the same as family reunification. Chain migration is a term used by academics to explain how people tended to migrate from their home communities using pre-existing networks. Examples would include the great migration of African Americans from the rural South to the urban North and West, the migrations of rural Appalachians to Midwestern industrial cities, waves of European migration to the United States at the turn of the last century, as well as contemporary migration from Latin America and Asia.

15 A single individual or a small group, possibly recruited through a state-sponsored system or by an employer, or simply knowing of employment opportunities in a particular area, sometimes making use of a new rail line or steamship or air route, would venture forth, opening up new horizons. Once in a new region or land, such immigrants directly or indirectly recruited friends, acquaintances, and family members. Soon enough, there were growing links — hence that "chain" — between the original rural or urban communities where such people lived and distant cities. Financial remittances began to flow back; return migration (or simply visits to the old homeland) took place; letters about the new world arrived; and sometimes new technologies solidified ongoing ties, impelling yet more streams of migrants. That's the chain in chain migration and, despite the president and his supporters, there's nothing offensive about it.

Family reunification, on the other hand, was a specific part of this country's 1965 Immigration and Nationality Act, which imposed quotas globally. These were then distributed through a priority system that privileged the close relatives of immigrants who had already become permanent residents or U.S. citizens. Family reunification opened paths for those who had family members in the United States (though in countries where the urge to migrate was high, the waiting list could be decades long). In the process, however, it made legal migration virtually impossible for those without such ties. There was no "line" for them to wait in. Like DACA and Temporary Protected Status (TPS), the two programs that President Trump is now working so assiduously to dismantle, family reunification has been beneficial to those in a position to take advantage of it, even if it excluded far more people than it helped.

Why does this matter? As a start, at a moment when political posturing and "fake news" are becoming the norm, it's important that the immigrant rights movement remain accurate and on solid ground in its arguments. (Indeed, the anti-immigrant right has been quick to gloat over Democrats condemning a term they had been perfectly happy to use in the past.) In addition, it's crucial not to be swept away by Trump's Manichaean view of the world when it comes to immigration. Legally, family reunification was never an open-arms policy. It was always a key component in a system of quotas meant to limit, control, and police migration, often in stringent ways. It was part of a system built to exclude at least as much as include. There may be good reasons to defend the family reunification provisions of the 1965 Act, just as there are good reasons to defend DACA — but that does not mean that a deeply problematic status quo should be glorified.

RACISM AND THE IMMIGRANT "THREAT"

Those very quotas and family-reunification policies served to "illegalize" most Mexican migration to the United States. That, in turn, created the basis not just for militarizing the police and the border, but for what anthropologist Leo Chávez has called the "Latino threat narrative": the notion that the United States somehow faces an existential threat from Mexican and other Latino immigrants.

So President Trump has drawn on a long legacy here, even if in a particularly invidious fashion. The narrative evolved over time in ways that sought to downplay its explicitly racial nature. Popular commentators railed against "illegal" immigrants, while lauding those who "do it the right way." The threat narrative, for instance, lurked at the very heart of the immigration policies of the Obama administration. President Obama regularly hailed exceptional Latino and other immigrants, even as the criminalization, mass incarceration, and deportation of so many were, if anything, being ramped up. Criminalization provided a "color-blind" cover as the president separated undocumented immigrants into two distinct groups: "felons" and "families." In those years, so many commentators postured on the side of those they defined as the deserving exceptions, while adding further fuel to the threat narrative.

President Trump has held onto a version 20
of this ostensibly color-blind and exceptionalist narrative, while loudly proclaiming himself "the least racist person" anyone might ever run into and praising DACA recipients as "good, educated, and accomplished young people." But the racist nature of his anti-immigrant extremism and his invocations of the "threat" have gone well beyond Obama's programs. In his attack on legal immigration, chain migration, and legal statuses like DACA and TPS, race has again reared its head explicitly.

Unless they were to come from "countries like Norway" or have some special "merit," Trump seems to believe that immigrants should essentially all be illegalized, prohibited, or expelled. Some of his earliest policy moves like his attacks on refugees and his travel ban were aimed precisely at those who would otherwise fall into a legal category, those who had "followed the rules," "waited in line," "registered with the government," or "paid taxes," including refugees, DACA kids, and TPS recipients — all of them people already in the system and approved for entry or residence.

As ICE spokespeople remind us when asked to comment on particularly egregious examples of the arbitrary detention and deportation of long-term residents, President Trump has rescinded the Obama-era "priority enforcement" program that emphasized the apprehension and deportation of people with criminal records and recent border-crossers. Now, "no category of removable aliens [is] exempt from enforcement." While President Trump has continued to verbally support the Dreamers, his main goal in doing so has clearly been to use them as a bargaining chip in obtaining his dramatically restrictionist priorities from a reluctant Congress.

The U.S. Customs and Immigration Service (USCIS) made the new restrictionist turn official in late February when it revised its mission statement to delete this singular line: "USCIS secures America's promise as a nation of immigrants." No longer. Instead, we are now told, the agency "administers the nation's lawful immigration system, safeguarding its integrity and promise . . . while protecting Americans, securing the homeland, and honoring our values."

CHALLENGING THE RESTRICTIONIST AGENDA

Many immigrant rights organizations have fought hard against the criminalization narrative that distinguishes the Dreamers from other categories of immigrants. Mainstream and Democrat-affiliated organizations have, however, generally pulled the other way, emphasizing the "innocence" of those young people who were brought here "through no fault of their own."

Dreamers, TPS recipients, refugees, and even those granted priority under the family reunification policy have all operated as exceptions to what has long been a far broader restrictionist immigration agenda. Trump has now taken that agenda in remarkably extreme directions. So fighting to protect such exceptional categories makes sense, given the millions who have benefited from them, but no one should imagine that America's policies have ever been generous or open.

Regarding refugees, for example, the State Department website still suggests that "the United States is proud of its history of welcoming immigrants and refugees. . . . The U.S. refugee resettlement program reflects the United States' highest values and aspirations to compassion, generosity, and leadership." Even before Trump entered the Oval Office, this wasn't actually true: the refugee resettlement program has always been both small and highly politicized. For example, out of approximately seven million Syrian refugees who fled the complex set of conflicts in their country since 2011 — conflicts that would not have unfolded as they did without the American invasion of Iraq — the United States has accepted only 21,000. Now, however, the fight to preserve even such numbers looks like a losing rearguard battle.

Given that a truly just reform of the country's immigration system is inconceivable at the moment, it makes sense that those concerned with immigrant rights concentrate on areas where egregious need or popular sympathy have made stopgap measures realistic. The problem is that, over the years, this approach has tended to separate out particular groups of immigrants from the larger narrative and so failed to challenge the underlying racial and criminalizing animus toward all those immigrants consigned to the depths of the economic system and systematically denied the right of belonging.

In a sense, President Trump is correct: there really isn't a way to draw a hard and fast line between legal and illegal immigration or between the felons and the families. Many immigrants live in mixed-status households, including those whose presence has been authorized in different ways or not authorized at all. And most of those felons, often convicted of recently criminalized, immigration-related or other minor violations, have families, too.

Trump and his followers, of course, want just about all immigrants to be criminalized and excluded or deported because, in one way or another, they consider them dangers to the rest of us. While political realism demands that battles be fought for the rights of particular groups of immigrants, it's no less important to challenge the looming narrative of immigrant criminalization and to refuse to assume that the larger war has already been lost. In the end, isn't it time to challenge the notion that people in general, and immigrants in particular, can be easily divided into deserving good guys and undeserving bad guys?

Topics for Critical Thinking and Writing

1. Look up the word *Manichean* (para. 11) and jot down your understanding of its origins. In a few paragraphs, explain why Aviva Chomsky thinks the Manichean view of "felons" and "families" (para. 19) does not adequately account for the realities of illegal immigration and the complexities of enacting and enforcing laws related to it.
2. One frequent conservative critique of Democrats' positions related to immigration is, in the words of President Donald Trump at a June 2018 rally, that "Democrats want open borders and they don't mind crime." Does Chomsky's argument reinforce or dispute that claim? Answer using evidence from her essay.
3. Explain in your own words the notion, cited by Chomsky, of the "Latino threat narrative" (para. 18). Briefly describe it and provide an example of it drawn from American media culture.
4. Research what a "path to citizenship" for illegal immigrants already in the United States means. What kinds of pathways have been proposed and for whom, and do you think they would be effective in solving illegal immigration issues today? If so, how? If not, why not?
5. Read Jean-Paul Sartre's account of anti-Semitism in "Anti-Semite and Jew" (p. 670) or Bridget Anderson's "The Politics of Pests: Immigration and the Invasive Other" (p. 685). In 750 to 1,250 words, write an essay applying any of the key ideas you discover to the social, cultural, or political debates about illegal immigration in the United States. How does Sartre's or Anderson's analysis inform how we understand "family migration," "chain migration," or any other issues you choose to discuss related to immigrants, immigration, or illegal immigration?
6. Read Emma Lazarus's poem "The New Colossus" on page 662. Should the United States welcome the "tired . . . poor . . . huddled masses," "the wretched refuse" of other places, or should it accept, for example, only educated people and people of means? Justify your answer in 300 to 500 words.

JOSEPH CARENS

Joseph Carens (b. 1945) is a professor of political science at the University of Toronto and a fellow of the Royal Society of Canada. Before his Toronto post, he taught at various institutions, including Princeton University. He is a leading expert in questions of immigration. His most recent book, *The Ethics of Immigration* (2013), joins a list of highly praised studies by Carens along with his books *Culture, Citizenship and Community* (2000) and *Immigrants and the Right to Stay* (2010). His academic articles have been widely published in journals such as the *Boston Review*, *Political Theory*, and the *Journal of Political Philosophy*. The following essay was published in 2015 on openDemocracy.net, a nonprofit media platform for discussions of global affairs.

The Case for Open Borders

Borders have guards and the guards have guns. This is an obvious fact of political life but one that is easily hidden from view — at least from the view of those of us who are citizens of affluent democracies. If we see the guards at all, we find them reassuring because we think of them as there to protect us rather than to keep us out. To Africans in small, leaky vessels seeking to avoid patrol boats while they cross the Mediterranean to southern Europe, or to Mexicans willing to risk death from heat and exposure in the Arizona desert to evade the fences and border patrols, it is quite different. To these people, the borders, guards, and guns are all too apparent, their goal of exclusion all too real. What justifies the use of force against such people? Perhaps borders and guards can be justified as a way of keeping out terrorists, armed invaders, or criminals. But most of those trying to get in are not like that. They are ordinary, peaceful people, seeking only the opportunity to build decent, secure lives for themselves and their families. On what moral grounds can we deny entry to these sorts of people? What gives anyone the right to point guns at *them*?

To many people the answer to this question will seem obvious. The power to admit or exclude non-citizens is inherent in sovereignty and essential for any political community that seeks to exercise self-determination. Every state has the legal and moral right to exercise control over admissions in pursuit of its own national interest and the common good of the members of its community, even if that means denying entry to peaceful, needy foreigners. States may choose to be generous in admitting immigrants, but, in most cases at least, they are under no moral obligation to do so.

I want to challenge that view. In principle, borders should generally be open and people should normally be free to leave their country of origin and settle wherever they choose. This critique of exclusion has particular force with respect to restrictions on movement from developing states to Europe and North America, but it applies more generally.

In many ways, citizenship in Western democracies is the modern equivalent of feudal class privilege — an inherited status that greatly enhances one's life chances. To be born a citizen of a rich state in Europe or North America is like being born into the nobility (even though many of us belong to the lesser nobility). To be born a citizen of a poor country in Asia or Africa is like being born into the peasantry in the Middle Ages (even if there are a few rich peasants and some peasants manage to gain entry to the nobility).

Like feudal birthright privileges, contemporary social arrangements not only grant great advantages on the basis of birth but also entrench these advantages by legally restricting mobility, making it extremely difficult for those born into a socially disadvantaged position to overcome that disadvantage, no matter how talented they are or how hard they work. Like feudal practices, these contemporary social arrangements are hard to justify when one thinks about them closely.

5 Reformers in the late Middle Ages objected to the way feudalism restricted freedom, including the freedom of individuals to move from one place to another in search of a better life — a constraint that was crucial to the maintenance of the feudal system. Modern practices of state control over borders tie people to the land of their birth almost as effectively. Limiting entry to rich democratic states is a crucial mechanism for protecting a birthright privilege. If the feudal practices protecting birthright privileges were wrong, what justifies the modern ones?

THE CASE FOR OPEN BORDERS

The analogy I have just drawn with feudalism is designed to give readers pause about the conventional view that restrictions on immigration by democratic states are normally justified. Now let me outline the positive case for open borders. I start from three basic interrelated assumptions. First, there is no natural social order. The institutions and practices that govern human beings are ones that human beings have created and can change, at least in principle. Second, in evaluating the moral status of alternative forms of political and social organization, we must start from the premise that all human beings are of equal moral worth. Third, restrictions on the freedom of human beings require a moral justification. These three assumptions are not just my views. They undergird the claim to moral legitimacy of every contemporary democratic regime.

The assumption that all human beings are of equal moral worth does not mean that no legal distinctions can be drawn among different groups of people, nor does the requirement that restrictions on freedom be justified mean that coercion is never defensible. But these two assumptions, together with the assumption that the social order is not naturally given, mean that we have to give reasons for our institutions and practices and that those reasons must take a certain form. It is never enough to justify a set of social arrangements governing human beings by saying that these arrangements are good for us, whoever the "us" may be, without regard for others. We have to appeal to principles and arguments that take everyone's interests into account or that explain why the social arrangements are reasonable and fair to everyone who is subject to them.

Given these three assumptions there is at least a *prima facie*[1] case that borders should be open, for, again, three interrelated reasons. First, state control over immigration limits freedom of movement. The right to go where you want is an important human freedom in itself. It is precisely this freedom, and all that this freedom makes possible, that is taken away by imprisonment. Freedom of movement is also a prerequisite to many other freedoms. If people are to be free to live their lives as they choose, so long as this does not interfere with the legitimate claims of others, they have to be free to move where they want. Thus freedom of movement contributes to individual autonomy both directly and indirectly. Open borders would enhance this freedom.

[1]***Prima facie*** At first look. [Editors' note]

Of course, freedom of movement cannot be an unqualified right, if only for reasons like traffic control and other requirements of public order. But restrictions require a moral justification, i.e., some argument as to why the restriction is in the interest of, and fair to, all those who are subject to it. Since state control over immigration restricts human freedom of movement, it requires a justification. This justification must take into account the interests of those excluded as well as the interests of those already inside. It must make the case that the restrictions on immigration are fair to all human beings. There are restrictions on border crossing that meet this standard of justification (e.g. limiting the entry of terrorists and invading armies), but granting states a right to exercise discretionary control over immigration does not.

10 The second reason why borders should normally be open is that freedom of movement is essential for equality of opportunity. Within democratic states we all recognize, at least in principle, that access to social positions should be determined by an individual's actual talents and effort, and not on the basis of birth-related characteristics such as class, race, or gender that are not relevant to the capacity to perform well in the position. This ideal of equal opportunity is intimately linked to the view that all human beings are of equal moral worth, that there are no natural hierarchies of birth that entitle people to advantageous social positions. But you have to be able to move to where the opportunities are in order to take advantage of them. So, freedom of movement is an essential prerequisite for equality of opportunity.

It is in the linkage between freedom of movement and equality of opportunity that the analogy with feudalism cuts most deeply. Under feudalism, there was no commitment to equal opportunity. The social circumstances of one's birth largely determined one's opportunities, and restrictions on freedom of movement were an essential element in maintaining the limitations on the opportunities of those with talent and motivation but the wrong class background. (Gender was another pervasive constraint.) In the modern world, we have created a social order in which there is a commitment to equality of opportunity for people *within* democratic states (at least to some extent), but no pretense of, or even aspiration to, equality of opportunity for people *across* states. Because of the state's discretionary control over immigration, the opportunities for people in one state are simply closed to those from another (for the most part). Since the range of opportunities varies so greatly among states, this means that in our world, as in feudalism, the social circumstances of one's birth largely determine one's opportunities. It also means that restrictions on freedom of movement are an essential element in maintaining this arrangement, i.e., in limiting the opportunities of people with talents and motivations but the wrong social circumstances of birth. Again, the challenge for those who would defend restrictions on immigration is to justify the resulting inequalities of opportunity. That is hard to do.

A third, closely related point is that a commitment to equal moral worth entails some commitment to economic, social, and political equality, partly as a means of realizing equal freedom and equal opportunity and partly as a desirable end in itself. Freedom of movement would contribute to a reduction of existing political, social, and economic inequalities. There are millions of people in poor states today who long for the freedom and economic opportunity they could find in Europe or North America. Many of them take great risks to come. If the borders were open, millions more would move. The exclusion of so many poor and desperate people seems hard to justify from a perspective that takes seriously the claims of all individuals as free and equal moral persons.

Topics for Critical Thinking and Writing

1. Identify at least three reasons Joseph Carens believes it is immoral to deny entry to "ordinary, peaceful people, seeking only the opportunity to build decent, secure lives for themselves and their families" (para. 1). How would you characterize Carens's perspective?
2. In your opinion, does Carens's essay justify the frequent critique among conservatives that Democrats are for open borders and are willing to risk increased crime rates? Why, or why not?
3. Do you think modern immigration policies and border security are fundamentally inhumane? Why, or why not?
4. Do you think the idea of strong borders and selective immigration makes citizenship, as Carens argues, a "feudal class privilege — an inherited status that greatly enhances one's life chances" (para. 4)? Is being born in a Western democracy equivalent to "being born into nobility," whereas being born in some parts of the world is equivalent to "being born into the peasantry in the Middle Ages" (para. 4)? Support your reasoning.
5. One view supporting strong border security argues that a lax border and ineffective processes like "catch and release" (whereby immigrants with pending asylum claims are allowed to live with relatives or sponsors) invite people to travel to and stay in the United States illegally. In this view, harsher measures like arrest, family separation, and deportation protect people through deterrence. Explain your stance on the position and tell whether or not you think Carens would take the same approach.

REIHAN SALAM

Reihan Salam (b. 1979) is the executive editor of *National Review*, a contributing editor at the *Atlantic*, and a frequent commentator on television and radio. He has recently been named as the fifth president of the Manhattan Institute, a conservative think tank based in New York City. Salam is the author of *Melting Pot or Civil War? A Son of Immigrants Makes the Case against Open Borders* (2018), in which he argues that immigration to the United States today is fundamentally different than it was in the past: With fewer opportunities to live the American Dream and find economic advancement, immigrants today have to define themselves against privileged native classes — leading to social division and racial animosity. The following essay was published in the *National Review* on March 28, 2016.

Beyond the Wall

Mexico has been at the heart of Donald J. Trump's presidential campaign from the very start. When Trump first announced that he would be seeking the Republican presidential nomination, he warned that the Mexican government was "laughing at us, at our stupidity." Though Mexico's GDP per capita is roughly one third of that of the United States when adjusted for purchasing power, Trump insisted that Mexico was "beating us economically." One of his more provocative claims was that Mexico was, in effect, using the U.S. as a "dumping ground," sending not its best and brightest across the border, but rather its drug dealers and its rapists.

Trump's anti-Mexican remarks have not exactly been warmly embraced across the political spectrum. Liberals maintain that Trump's Mexico-bashing is designed to appeal to a dangerous ethnic chauvinism that has hitherto lain dormant. Many conservatives who favor more-vigorous border enforcement have also objected to Trump's language, on the grounds that it is needlessly inflammatory. Mitt Romney was just as committed to combating illegal immigration as Trump, and he paid a political price for it. Yet no serious person could accuse Romney of bigotry, since his objections to illegal immigration were so clearly rooted in respect for the rule of law. The same cannot be said of Trump.

Regardless of what one thinks of Trump's qualifications to be president — my own view is that he isn't qualified to serve as America's dogcatcher — there is no question that his fixation on Mexico has touched a nerve. The reason is that Trump has the germ of a point. Mexico may not be "beating us economically," but it really is true that the U.S. has served as a kind of economic escape valve for Mexico, in ways that have ill served not just the U.S. but also, in the long run, Mexico itself. Trump's Mexico-bashing notwithstanding, there is potentially a great deal of common ground between Americans on the political right who want to put an end to illegal immigration and Mexicans on the political left who want to make their country more egalitarian and inclusive.

From 2009 to 2014, the net flow of migration from Mexico to the U.S. was negative, according to the Pew Research Center. While 870,000 Mexican nationals settled in the U.S., 1 million of them returned to Mexico, a figure that includes those who returned voluntarily as well as 140,000 who were deported. Had there been no deportations, the net flow would have been slightly positive, and of course the threat of removal may have led at least some Mexican nationals to "self-deport." By way of comparison, between 1995 and 2000, when labor-market conditions for less-skilled workers in the U.S. were far stronger and the Mexican economy was in worse shape, 2.94 million Mexican nationals settled in the U.S., while only 670,000 returned home.

5 Some observers claim that because net migration from Mexico is now negative, there is no longer any need for concern. This is nonsense. There are still roughly 5.6 million Mexican immigrants illegally in the U.S., and to meaningfully reduce the size of this population, we'd need far more Mexicans to return to their native country, and far fewer to enter the U.S., every year. Had the Obama administration been more aggressive about immigration enforcement, the number of illegal immigrants in the U.S. would almost certainly be considerably smaller.

One straightforward step the federal government could take would be to aid state-level efforts to curb illegal immigration. In February 2016, Bob Davis of the *Wall Street Journal* reported that the passage of a series of immigration-enforcement measures in Arizona had contributed to a steep 40 percent decline in that state's unauthorized-immigrant population between 2007 and 2012. There were other factors, to be sure, most importantly the housing bust and the subsequent recession. But the outflow of illegal immigrants from Arizona proved far greater than that from other states that were similarly hard hit — in part, it seems, because Arizona endeavored to make it more difficult for employers to hire illegal immigrants. Other states, however, have moved in the opposite direction by extending more legal protections to illegal immigrants, and the Obama administration badly undermined state-level immigration-enforcement efforts by issuing executive orders that shield roughly half of the illegal immigrants currently residing in the U.S. from deportation.

If more-vigorous immigration enforcement can do so much to curb illegal immigration, why should Americans, least of all American conservatives, care about economic conditions in Mexico? The reason is that Mexico's poverty is the ultimate source of the migration challenge. Economic development is the only reliable way to reduce migrant outflows. Once a country's income per capita passes $8,000 or so, its residents become far less inclined to leave the country as their incomes rise. Before this threshold is reached, rising income can actually spur more migration, presumably because it gives truly impoverished people the means to pack up and leave.

If poor Mexicans had better prospects for advancement at home, far fewer of them would choose to settle in the United States. Indeed, the most important reason migration from Mexico to the United States has slowed in recent years is not more-aggressive border enforcement. Rather, it is the fact that Mexico's GDP per capita (adjusted for purchasing-power parity) has reached $18,500, which places it in roughly the same ballpark as moderately well-off countries such as Russia, Malaysia, and Turkey. This is still substantially lower than U.S. per capita income ($56,300), though, and the gap remains big enough to tempt Mexican workers northwards. Yet as Mexico's standard of living has improved, its people are less eager to leave their families and neighborhoods behind. The problem we face is that while Mexicans are better-off on average, Mexico remains a highly unequal society. Until life improves for the poorest Mexicans, migration will remain an attractive option.

When conservatives rail against illegal immigration from Mexico, they should also rail against the Mexican government for failing to provide for its own people. Illegal immigrants are at fault for violating U.S. immigration laws, but so are their home governments that have failed to create safe and prosperous environments in which they can raise their children. To lose sight of that is a mistake. The good news is that Mexico has made strides in reducing extreme poverty, thanks in part to the increased social spending that accompanied Mexico's political democratization. Two major anti-poverty programs in particular, Progresa and Oportunidades, have greatly increased household incomes among Mexico's poorest families. But social spending is not enough. Further reductions in poverty will depend on job creation for Mexicans with modest skills. One of the ironies of Donald Trump's embrace of protectionism is that if our goal is to reduce migration from Mexico, we ought to welcome the offshoring of industries that depend heavily on less-skilled immigrant labor. Why fight to keep low-wage jobs in meatpacking, general assembly, and furniture manufacturing in the U.S. if these jobs tend to be held by less-skilled immigrants, who need subsidies from U.S. taxpayers to lead decent lives?

10 In a similar vein, the U.S. ought to consider encouraging U.S. retirees to settle in Mexico. As the U.S. population ages, demand for home health aides and other low-wage service workers who can provide for the elderly is increasing, and this rising demand is often cited by advocates of higher immigration levels. But instead of admitting more less-skilled immigrants, the U.S. could allow U.S. retirees

to make use of Medicare in Mexico, a simple measure that would address a number of problems at once: It would generate employment opportunities for less-skilled workers in Mexico; it would reduce the demand for less-skilled immigrant workers in the U.S.; and it might even reduce Medicare expenditures, since the cost of offering benefits would be substantially lower in Mexico than in the U.S. If this seems unrealistic, consider that U.S. retirees have already settled in regions such as Jalisco, Guanajuato, Baja Sur, and the Mexican Caribbean in large numbers. More older Americans would join them in seeking a lower cost of living in Mexico if their Medicare benefits traveled with them.

Whether we like it or not, the fates of the U.S. and Mexico are intertwined, and securing Mexico's cooperation in curbing illegal immigration will likely require giving the Mexican government something it wants. Keep in mind that Mexico is not just a source of migrants to the U.S. — it also separates us from Guatemala ($7,900), Honduras ($5,000), and El Salvador ($8,300), all of which are much poorer than Mexico, and where migration pressures are still building. These countries are the biggest new sources of illegal immigration, and to stem the tide of illegal immigration from Central America, we must convince the Mexican government to stop turning a blind eye when Central Americans pass through its territory en route to the U.S.

The Mexican government, for all its weaknesses, is fully capable of halting Central American migrants. In 2001, for example, President Vicente Fox deployed the armed forces to prevent migrants from passing through the Sonoran Desert, out of fear that they might die of thirst in a severe heat wave. Instead of focusing solely on securing America's southern border, we would do well to secure Mexico's cooperation in halting migrants long before they reach it.

Winning over the Mexican government by helping it create employment opportunities at home might be less emotionally satisfying than trying to bully Mexico into doing our bidding, as Donald Trump would prefer. But while a bullying approach would almost certainly drive the Mexicans into taking a more adversarial stance, appealing to Mexico's self-interest would have a far greater chance of success. If we really hope to put a stop to illegal immigration, we'd be foolish not to do so.

Topics for Critical Thinking and Writing

1. In the opening paragraphs, Reihan Salam criticizes views about immigration expressed by Donald Trump, though Salam himself agrees that the number of Mexican immigrants in the United States needs to be reduced. Characterize the similarities and differences between Salam's and Trump's points of view.
2. In paragraph 4, Salam claims that "there is potentially a great deal of common ground between Americans on the political right who want to put an end to illegal immigration and Mexicans on the political left who want to make their country more egalitarian and inclusive." What kinds of solutions might please both groups? What goals do they share, and what would each group stand to gain from pursuing those shared goals?

3. Why does Salam advocate for American retirees to move to Mexico (para. 12)? Do you think his proposal is reasonable? Why, or why not?
4. What is Salam's solution for curbing immigration from Guatemala, Honduras, and El Salvador (para. 12)? Does this solution make sense to you? Why, or why not?
5. Do some research on the current conditions of migrants attempting to reach the US southern border, then select some aspect of the problem, or a potential solution, to focus on. Construct an argument of around 500 to 750 words that encourages average US citizens to pay special attention to the issue you chose. Why is the issue important? How does it inform debates over immigration? What might be done to resolve the problem or help implement your solution?
6. Compare Salam's argument to the argument made by Joseph Carens in "The Case for Open Borders" (p. 560). How do their views differ, and what concerns, ideas, or values do they share?

VICTOR DAVIS HANSON

Victor Davis Hanson, born in 1953 in Fowler, California, did his undergraduate work at the University of California–Santa Cruz and his PhD work at Stanford University. A specialist in military history, he taught classics at California State University, Fresno, where he is now a professor emeritus. A noted conservative, Hanson is a senior fellow at Stanford's Hoover Institution. This piece first appeared on realclearpolitics.com on May 25, 2006.

Our Brave New World of Immigration

In the dark of these rural spring mornings, I see full vans of Mexican laborers speeding by my farmhouse on their way to the western side of California's San Joaquin Valley to do the backbreaking work of weeding cotton, thinning tree fruit, and picking strawberries.

In the other direction, even earlier morning crews drive into town — industrious roofers, cement layers, and framers heading to a nearby new housing tract. While most of us are still asleep, thousands of these hardworking young men and women in the American Southwest rise with the sun to provide the sort of unmatched labor at the sort of wages that their eager employers insist they cannot find among citizens.

But just when one thinks that illegal immigration is an efficient win-win way of providing excellent workers to needy businesses, there are also daily warnings that there is something terribly wrong with a system predicated on a cynical violation of the law.

Three days ago, as I watched the daily early-morning caravan go by, I heard a horrendous explosion. Not far from my home, one of these vans had crossed the white line down the middle of the road and hit a pickup truck head-on. Perhaps the van had blown a bald tire. Perhaps the driver was intoxicated. Or perhaps he had no experience driving an overloaded minivan at high speed in the dark of early morning.

5 We will probably never know — since the driver ran away from the carnage of the accident. That often happens when an illegal alien who survives an accident has no insurance or driver's license. But he did leave in his wake his three dead passengers. Eight more people were injured. Both cars were totaled. Traffic was rerouted around the wreckage for hours.

Ambulances, fire trucks, and patrol cars lined the nearby intersection. That accident alone must have imparted untold suffering for dozens of family members, as well as cost the state thousands of dollars.

Such mayhem is no longer an uncommon occurrence here. I have had four cars slam into our roadside property, with the drivers running off, leaving behind damaged vines and trees, and wrecked cars with phony licenses and no record of insurance. I have been broadsided by an undocumented driver, who ran a stop sign and then tried to run from our collision.

These are the inevitable but usually unmentioned symptoms of illegal immigration. After all, the unexpected can often happen when tens of thousands of young males from Mexico arrive in a strange country, mostly alone, without English or legality — an estimated 60 percent of them without a high-school degree and most obligated to send nearly half of their hard-won checks back to kin in Mexico.

Many Americans — perhaps out of understandable and well-meant empathy for the dispossessed who toil so hard for so little — support this present open system of non-borders. But I find nothing liberal about it.

10 Zealots may chant *¡Sí, se puede!* all they want. And the libertarian right may dress up the need for cheap labor as a desire to remain globally competitive. But neither can disguise a cynicism about illegal immigration, one that serves to prop up a venal Mexican government, undercut the wages of our own poor, and create a new apartheid of millions of aliens in our shadows.

We have entered a new world of immigration without precedent. This current crisis is unlike the great waves of nineteenth-century immigration that brought thousands of Irish, Eastern Europeans, and Asians to the United States. Most immigrants in the past came legally. Few could return easily across an ocean to home. Arrivals from, say, Ireland or China could not embrace the myth that our borders had crossed them rather than vice versa.

Today, almost a third of all foreign-born persons in the United States are here illegally, making up 3 to 4 percent of the American population. It is estimated that the United States is home to 11 or 12 million illegal aliens, whose constantly refreshed numbers ensure there is always a perpetual class of unassimilated recent illegal arrivals. Indeed almost one-tenth of Mexico's population currently lives here illegally!

But the real problem is that we, the hosts, are also different from our predecessors. Today we ask too little of too many of our immigrants. We apparently don't care whether they come legally or learn English — or how they fare when they're not at work. Nor do we ask all of them to accept the brutal bargain of an American melting pot that rapidly absorbs the culture of an immigrant in exchange for the benefits of citizenship.

Instead, we are happy enough that most labor vans of hardworking helots stay on the road in the early-morning hours, out of sight and out of mind. Sometimes, though, they tragically do not.

Topics for Critical Thinking and Writing

1. As you know, speakers and writers who take care to present themselves as decent, trustworthy people are concerned with *ethos*, or character (see p. 78). What impression do you get of Victor Davis Hanson's *ethos* or character from his first two paragraphs? If you had to guess — based on these first two paragraphs — where Hanson stood on immigration, what would you say? Why?
2. Briefly discuss how *pathos* (see p. 76), or the appeal to emotion, is deployed in this essay. Is it effective? Why, or why not?
3. What does Hanson mean in paragraph 3 when he calls the labor market in the San Joaquin Valley "a system predicated on a cynical violation of the law"? Do you agree with that description? Why, or why not?
4. In paragraph 11, Hanson speaks of "the myth that our borders had crossed [the immigrants from Mexico]" rather than vice versa. What does he mean by that? Do you agree that it is a myth? Explain your response.
5. What are the differences between current immigration from Mexico and historic immigration from Europe a century ago (see para. 11)?
6. In his next-to-last paragraph, Hanson says, "We apparently don't care whether [immigrants] come legally or learn English." Do you agree with this assertion? On what evidence do you base your response?
7. Of the other essays in this chapter, which one does Hanson's support the most? Explain the reasoning for your choice.

Analyzing Visuals: Immigration Then and Now

From the mid-1800s through the early twentieth century, the average number of immigrants to America was about 600,000 per year. This large-scale movement came to be known as the first "Great Wave" of immigration. The majority of these immigrants came from Europe and intended their journey to be temporary, staying only long enough to work and save enough money to improve their prospects upon their return home. The United States was undergoing massive industrialization at the time, so there was an ever-increasing demand for factory workers. Moreover, studies have shown that the average immigrant during this time made wages comparable to people who were already in the United States, and immigrants tended to advance within their jobs at a commensurate rate.

That's a far cry from the modern immigration landscape, where people looking to settle elsewhere sometimes have to take drastic and even dangerous measures to do so. What's more, those who make it face other difficulties and challenges when they reach their destinations, especially if they have entered a new country without proper documentation. In addition to social stigmas that some people thrust upon nonnative residents, many immigrants earn much lower wages than native workers, especially if they have come from less developed countries. Yet according to the United Nations' International Migration Report, as of 2017, an estimated 258 million people — roughly 3.4 percent of the world's population — lived outside their country of origin.

Immigrants on the deck of the SS *Patricia*, an Atlantic liner. The *Patricia* came from Hamburg to New York in late 1900.

Christophe Archambault/Getty Images

Rohingya migrants swimming to collect food supplies dropped by a Thai army helicopter in the Andaman Sea in 2015. The boat was found adrift, and passengers reported that several people, including children, had died in the days before the boat was found.

John Moore/Getty Images

A Honduran mother and daughter detained by agents at the US-Mexico border.

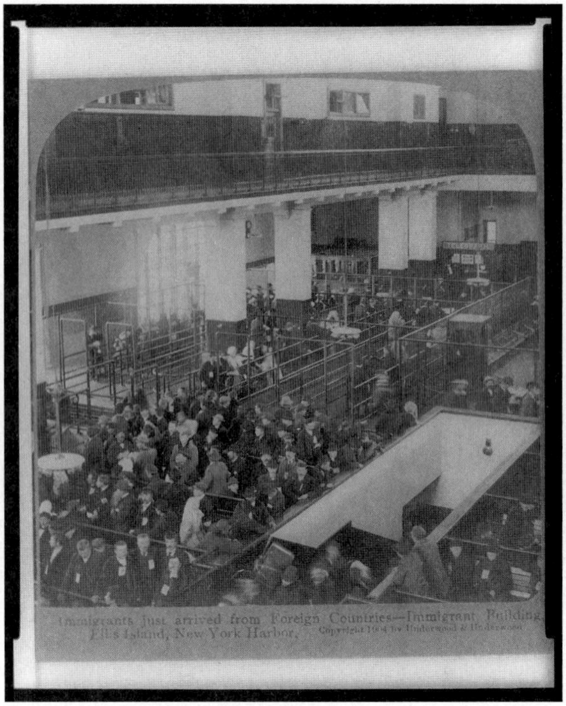

The Immigrant Building at Ellis Island, New York, circa 1904. Ellis Island opened in upper New York harbor near the Statue of Liberty in 1892 and closed in 1954, during which time it served as the main gateway for new immigrants coming to the United States.

Topics for Critical Thinking and Writing

1. Even if you knew nothing about the history of immigration, what kinds of differences would stand out to you between the early twentieth-century photos versus the pictures from 2015 and 2018?
2. Compare the two images that depict immigrants making journeys via boat. What kinds of figurative meanings, if any, do you read from each image?
3. The image of the Honduran mother and her daughter quickly spread across world newsfeeds and activist websites as a heartbreaking instance of the Trump administration's child separation practices at the US border. That week, *Time* magazine published an image of the crying two-year-old, Yanela Sanchez, alongside an image of Donald Trump, with the headline "Welcome to America." Within days, journalists revealed that Yanela and her mother had not, in fact, been separated but had been held in a detention facility together. Consider these contexts (research the case if you wish) and offer your response to the photograph. Is it fraudulent? Was *Time* unfair to Donald Trump, or did it rush to judgment about the issue of child separation?

24

#MeToo: (How) Has Society Changed for Women?

SARAH JAFFE

Sarah Jaffe (b. 1980) is a journalist whose coverage of social movements, politics, and culture has appeared in the *New York Times*, the *Nation*, the *Guardian*, the *Washington Post*, and the *Atlantic*. Her recent book, *Necessary Trouble: Americans in Revolt* (2017), examines contemporary movements like Occupy Wall Street, the Tea Party, and Black Lives Matter. In addition to being a columnist for *Dissent* magazine, Jaffe also cohosts, with Michelle Chen, the magazine's *Belabored* podcast. This essay was published in *Dissent* magazine in 2018.

The Collective Power of #MeToo

You never can tell where a social movement is going to come from. They're built of a million injustices that pile up and up, and then, suddenly, spill over. I've spent years covering movements, trying to explain how one incident becomes the spark that catches, turning all those individual injustices into an inferno.

When the *New York Times* ran a story about Harvey Weinstein's repulsive — and long — history of sexual harassment and assault in October 2017, no one knew what it would start. But soon a wave of people, most of them, though not all of them, women, began to wield their stories like weapons in a battle that, for once, they seemed to be winning. Well, if not winning, then at least drawing some blood. When #MeToo began to circulate on Facebook I was beyond cynical; I was actually angry that the men around me might be shocked to learn that yes, it had happened to me, it had happened to almost every woman I know. Yet #MeToo defeated my cynicism and became something else: a watershed moment in contemporary feminism, one that has made sexual violence into big news.

Like so many movements that appear spontaneous, the #MeToo moment is built on the work of longtime organizers. Tarana Burke has worked for decades with young women of color who survived sexual violence, and in 2006 she named her campaign "me too" as an expression of solidarity. But when she found the words trending on social media last year she worried that they were being used for something that she did not recognize as her life's work. Burke's "me too" campaign was designed to support survivors, to get them resources and help them heal; despite #MeToo hinging on survivor stories, it has, Burke noted in a recent interview, been more focused on outing the actions of perpetrators.

This focus is to some degree a reaction to a system designed to fail survivors of violence and harassment. Under the existing legal system, "justice" for sexual violence requires convincing first the police and then a court of law that what was done to you actually happened, and then that it counts as a crime. In a case of workplace harassment, the situation is similar: the person being harassed must come forward and lodge a complaint with HR (if her company has it) or her boss (if it doesn't). In the exceedingly likely scenario that the person harassing her is in fact her superior, she likely has no one to report to who does not have every incentive to side with the boss.

This is how we got to the moment when 5
sexual harassment stories are big news. The structures of the legal system and the workplace did not change. Instead, tens of thousands of women said yes, me too. Then, rather than wait for men to absorb that knowledge and decide whether to change or not, they started naming names. And making lists. And talking to each other.

That's how organizing starts, after all. It starts with people talking about the conditions of their lives, realizing that they are common, and that they want them to change. It starts with enough people joining the conversation that they begin to believe that they can win. And despite the individualizing tendency of the tales of horror flowing through the press, many of those stories became public through organizing work. The whisper network has long been a form of organizing for the powerless, sharing information quietly, person-to-person, even if it often left out exactly the people who were the most vulnerable, those who had the fewest connections. The now-infamous "Shitty Media Men" list, begun by journalist Moira Donegan, turned the whisper network into a spreadsheet, where women could add layers to each report. The crowd-sourced Google document, which collected women's anonymous stories of more than seventy men in media in the few hours it was live, was designed to collectivize the incomplete information that individuals receive based on their social networks.

I refused to look at the list when I learned of its existence — I still refuse to. Not that I blame anyone for reading to try to protect themselves, or in the case of hiring editors, for trying to learn more about the people working for them. But for me not looking was a tiny refusal of the work that is constantly forced back upon women, the work that the backlash writers — recycling the bad arguments they've been making since the 1990s at least — keep demanding that we do. *Protect yourself. Yell louder. Stop complaining, you should have known better.* Bullshit.

The viral hashtag that spread across social media asked not just about workplace harassment, but sexual assault in general. The discussion surrounding it has been broad and sprawling. But the common denominator has been, as sociology professor Christy Thornton noted, "In our culture, part of what it means to be a powerful man is to have unfettered access to women's bodies," or the bodies of others who are less powerful — transgender and queer people, and people of color are especially vulnerable to such sexual violence. The movement's opponents or even just those made slightly uncomfortable by its breadth keep attempting to narrow its parameters. But the wide scope is the point. The movement is not just about Hollywood, just about the worst of the worst, or even just about the workplace. It is a rejection of a core piece of patriarchal power — and the beginnings of imagining what a society without that power looks like.

It feels to many feminists now, in this second year of Trump, that it is not the time to accept petty reforms and good-enough moments. Why should we compromise, when our opponents refuse to? Things are rotten, and there is a significant number of people who are willing to defend the indefensible as the powerful pass it into law. Against such opponents, who care nothing for our lives, why play nice?

As Charlotte Shane wrote at *Splinter* in January 2018,

> If this past year taught us anything, it was how profoundly every system one might have hoped to improve with mere reform, every institution one might have trusted to "do the right thing," every politician who'd been positioned as a beacon of integrity, will never come to our rescue. Parity and justice and restitution are not priorities of our existing structures because those structures were designed to maintain hierarchies that make justice and parity and restitution impossible.

One of the things that it has seemed hardest for the opponents or even just the confused sideline-sitters to grasp is that people are not calling for perpetrators to go to jail. Perhaps one of the deepest assumptions of the #MeToo movement is that the society we live in provides us no real options for justice. The court system does not work for survivors and HR is a tool of the boss. The tools we need do not exist yet, so we must build from the ground up.

In fact, the thing I have heard the most from survivors (and we are all survivors, aren't we, that was the point of saying "me too") is that they want acknowledgment of what happened. If the perpetrator was in a position of power over them at work, they might want him fired. Since so much of the #MeToo conversation has revolved around workplace harassment and assault, powerful men have faced investigations and even lost jobs. Some of those were prestigious jobs those men assumed they had worked uniquely hard to win, and a perk of which was access to women's bodies.

Women's bodies — and women's work — are considered rewards for proper male behavior. The women themselves aren't supposed to find this unpleasant. Some men treated women as just another tray of canapés at a party — think of Al Franken's record of ass-grabbing. Others seemed to glory in the horror they created — Harvey Weinstein, whose story broke the floodgates open, or Matt Lauer and the button he had installed to lock his office door from the inside.

The stories are mostly not about dating, yet the backlashers worry that #MeToo will ruin dating. The men are not going to jail, but the backlashers constantly argue that they should not go to jail. They persist in using legal definitions for what, as Tressie McMillan Cottom noted, is a conversation about norms. "When we require a perfect victimless norm before we will consider the possibility of the improved lives of women," she wrote, "we are making an affirmative case about our values."

The norms #MeToo revealed are often called "rape culture," but I prefer the term "patriarchy" despite, or perhaps because of, its old-fashionedness. I write about systems, and "rape culture" is just a piece of the whole, an answer that seems only to provoke more questions. Rape culture exists to ensure a culture of male dominance, which takes many forms. By naming patriarchy, I hope that we can begin to understand the way the threads of power and dominance leak into every corner of our lives. Then we can see that violations are not purely or even mostly about sex, but instead reinforce a structure that offers power to a few by pretending to offer rewards to many. Patriarchy spreads the lie that there are rules we can follow that will keep us safe — that if we wear the right clothes, say no loudly enough, walk away, don't laugh at men, work hard, no harm will come to us.

There are not.

Well-intentioned men are now afraid that they have done harm, or that they will be accused of having done what they did not realize was harm. Because even when they are not bosses, when they might have had little tangible power over others, they have had the power of *not being required to learn* to read the people around them. That, after all, has been women's job, whether or not it is done for pay.

The reason for telling stories about men we thought were "good" is not to permanently etch their names into some list of "shitty men," though the lack of real justice means those lists are often all we get. The reason is for us to understand deep in our bones that there are no "good" and "bad" men or "good" and "bad" people. To repair the harms done is going to take change from all of us. We can't just pat ourselves on the back for not being as bad as Weinstein.

The scariest part of #MeToo is the realization, as Tarana Burke notes, that "more often than not, the reality is we live in the gray areas around sexual violence." There is a spectrum of abuses of power, some tiny and some huge, that all add up to a world where women's voices, women's work, and women's sexual desires are ignored or devalued. What most of us who've told stories want is for that to stop happening. It is a huge demand, perhaps unrealizable in our lifetimes, one that is bigger than any perpetrator outed in the media: It is not a demand for men to go to jail. It is a demand for men to do the work of learning.

What does justice and accountability look 20
like when the perpetrator is your boss?

We asked ourselves that a lot this year, and by this "we," I mean a specific group of women who worked alongside me at the online news website AlterNet and had been harassed by the organization's executive director Don Hazen. Because while we — a group of journalists — knew better than most that getting a story published in the media often doesn't change anything, we realized that if there was going to be a moment to topple an abusive boss, this was it.

And so we organized. We discussed, we planned, and we supported each other. We wondered if our stories were sympathetic enough, because we all knew how the media loves a perfect victim and how commentators will tear you apart if you don't fit that mold. We verified one another's stories and we talked, a lot, about what we wanted to happen. We wanted him out of a position of power over others, that was for sure, but what else? What did justice look like? Just having the story told is not justice but it can be wielded, occasionally, as a tool to help get there.

My former coworker Kristen Gwynne told Rebecca Traister, "[e]ven if the people who did target me were punished, I still feel like I deserve some sort of compensation. I don't want them to release a public apology — I want them to send me a check."

This comment stuck with me. When famous men are accused, some of them will release a public apology for us to hem and haw over, to try to decide if we can forgive someone with whom our only interaction has been consuming their performance on television. But really, it's not for me to forgive Louis CK or Kevin Spacey or Aziz Ansari. Such forgiveness would only serve to make me feel better about watching their films or TV shows, as if I could consume anything with clean hands.

25 Restorative and transformative justice hinges on the notion of community; that accountability can happen within and with the support of the people around us. Yes, famous people feel like they're part of our community, but they aren't, not really. And your boss? Most of us didn't want to repair or restore a relationship with our boss — we wanted him to no longer have power to affect our lives. What we want repaired is the damage to our work. Maybe part of what such restoration looks like, as Gwynne said, is a check.

A flyer from the Wages for Housework movement in the 1970s, on the cover of a new collection, declares "The women of the world are serving notice!" It lists demands for which women want wages, including "every indecent assault." Such assaults, in this framework, are part of a broader picture of exploitation that assumes that housework is a woman's role, that they are "naturally" subservient to men, and that sees this exploitation replicated in the paid workplace. The women of the Wages for Housework movement wanted to be able to refuse that work — the flyer says "if we don't get what we want we will simply refuse to work any longer!" — but they also fought for concrete support in the here and now, for abuses that have happened and are happening. Those assaults in the workplace, then, should be *compensated.*

The question of wages for assaults can seem strange, like putting a monetary value on violence, but in fact such compensation can take many forms. In the wake of the Movement for Black Lives, the framework of reparations is back in the public consciousness, as a way to try to acknowledge and make up for systematic, rather than individual, oppression. Late in 2017 I sat down with Raj Patel and Jason W. Moore to talk about their new book, *A History of the World in Seven Cheap Things.* We discussed their use of the idea of reparations, which Patel described thus: "Reparations are necessarily a collective process that demand revolutionary organizing, jolting the imagination with the historical memory of what happened, the challenge of accountability, and the invitation to dream a society that ceases the crimes on which capitalism is based." What, he asked, would reparations for patriarchy look like?

Reparations remains a fraught topic in the United States even though campaigns for reparations exist and even succeed. Organizers won reparations for police torture in Chicago — a plan that included not just cash for survivors but also recovery services, counseling, and importantly, that the story would be taught in public schools.

What would such a framework look like for sexual violence? For harassment? How do we come up with demands that move beyond naming and shaming?

30 Part of the challenge of talking about sexual harassment in the media is that stories are always told based on news value. As a reporter who has covered labor issues for years I can tell you that until recently, stories of sexual harassment at a call center or a restaurant or of home healthcare workers did not garner a lot of attention. It usually took famous

perpetrators and photogenic, famous victims for these stories to crack the media.

But something changed this time. It started, I think, with a letter from 700,000 women farmworkers of the Alianza Nacional de Campesinas, published in *Time* magazine, that expressed solidarity with the Hollywood women who had come forward. "Even though we work in very different environments, we share a common experience of being preyed upon by individuals who have the power to hire, fire, blacklist and otherwise threaten our economic, physical and emotional security."

Those women hit on the thing that has been at the core of these seemingly endless revelations: the power of the boss. Sexual harassment is just one of the many tools used to keep women compliant and their labor cheap. It drives women out of prestigious occupations and terrorizes them in subsistence occupations. It doesn't matter how hard you "lean in" if someone keeps leaning *on* you. As my former colleague Sarah Seltzer wrote, the problem was never us. "If unadorned sexism, exploitation, and harassment are the biggest problem white-collar women face, then it turns out women across most industries are actually up against some of the same enemies."

Suddenly it wasn't about being the perfect victim or being the perfect, upwardly mobile worker. The media rippled with stories of hotel housekeepers, restaurant workers, domestic workers. Women at a Ford plant in Chicago told stories to the *New York Times* of being called "Fresh meat!" on the shop floor, and of complaints to the union going unheard.

While some unions, like UNITE HERE, have made campaigns against sexual harassment central to their work and connected the dots explicitly to the Weinstein case — Chicago members wore "No Harveys in Chicago" shirts to celebrate the passage of an ordinance granting hotel housekeepers panic buttons to wear on the job — the labor movement itself has not been immune to sexual harassment. High-up officials at SEIU and at the AFL-CIO itself have stepped down after harassment allegations, including the leader of the Fight for $15 campaign in New York, Kendall Fells. "Sexual harassment is a reason women organize," Kate Bronfenbrenner, Director of Labor Education Research and a Senior Lecturer at Cornell University's School of Industrial and Labor Relations noted. "But it can be a reason women don't organize."

While unions grapple with how to handle this moment, famous women are learning what solidarity looks like. Tarana Burke walked the red carpet at the Golden Globes alongside Michelle Williams; other movie stars brought Ai-jen Poo of the National Domestic Workers Alliance and Saru Jayaraman of Restaurant Opportunities Centers United as their dates.

Five years ago in this magazine I wrote of the problems with feminism's obsession with cracking glass ceilings and "having it all." In the year following Hillary Clinton's second failed attempt at breaking "the biggest glass ceiling," we have learned that even the women we thought had it all had instead been trapped in their own personal hells. And perhaps, just perhaps, we have learned that feminism will not trickle down from the top.

Rather than advice on how to work harder and get ahead, it seems that the issue that unites women across a broad number of workplaces is being abused by more powerful men. And rather than leading from the top, famous and powerful women are accepting leadership from those at the bottom. They are putting some money where their mouths are, too. The Time's Up fund, administered by the National Women's Law Center, began with over $13 million in donations from film stars and aims to provide legal support for those facing harassment. Their launch letter read:

> To every woman employed in agriculture who has had to fend off unwanted sexual advances from her boss, every housekeeper who has tried to escape an assaultive guest, every janitor trapped nightly in a building with a predatory supervisor, every waitress grabbed by a customer and expected to take it with a smile, every garment and factory worker forced to trade sexual acts for more shifts, every domestic worker or home health aide forcibly touched by a client, every immigrant woman silenced by the threat of her undocumented status being reported in retaliation for speaking up and to women in every industry who are subjected to indignities and offensive behavior that they are expected to tolerate in order to make a living: We stand with you. We support you.

Of course, the Time's Up page links to LeanIn .org as a trusted partner organization. The progress away from such top-down, work-harder ideology is still incomplete.

Still, it is beginning to feel like a sea change in feminism has come, not from one wealthy woman almost but not quite getting elected president, but rather, from a rippling of anger that spread from woman to woman for a thousand reasons that are at once individual and deeply familiar. It even came from a few men sharing their stories. And it has brought us to this place, where we are talking, finally, about structural barriers — the way sexual harassment and violence shape women's lives at work and away from it, the way class hierarchies are brutally maintained — in a way that emphasizes the breadth and depth of the problems. Perhaps next we will grapple with the breadth and depth of the change we will need to begin to solve them.

Topics for Critical Thinking and Writing

1. Why do you think the #MeToo went viral in 2017? Why did it strike a nerve with the public? What events or conditions might have strengthened the movement?
2. In paragraph 6, Sarah Jaffe refers to the "whisper network" that "has long been a form of organizing for the powerless." What do you think she means by that? What is a whisper network, and how is it similar to, or different from, gossip?
3. Why does Jaffe refuse to look at Moira Donegan's "Shitty Media Men" list (para. 6)? Read Jaffe's explanation and then elaborate on her reasoning, connecting it to her argument.
4. In paragraph 12, Jaffe includes the parenthetical comment "and we are all survivors, aren't we." Is this claim overgeneralized? Explain.
5. In paragraph 14, Jaffe refers to people who believe that #MeToo will "ruin dating." Explain this concern. Then write an argument of 300 to 500 words about what you think the overall impact of #MeToo has had on dating.
6. Should young children be taught about "rape culture"? Why, or why not? At what age might it be appropriate, and why? What kind of messages should children of different ages be given about sexual harassment and assault in public, at school, or in the workplace?
7. In 2018, French lawmakers approved legislation making "street harassment" a crime and punishable with fines and potentially jail. Research what street harassment is, define it, and then address this question: Should states and cities in the United States have similar laws? Your essay should be between 500 and 1,000 words.

8. Jaffe quotes sociologist Christy Thornton: "In our culture, part of what it means to be a powerful man is to have unfettered access to women's bodies" (para. 8). Can you find some evidence for and against this idea? Do you believe it to be true overall? In your opinion, what does it mean to be a powerful woman in our culture today?
9. Jaffe writes that it is time "for men to do the work of learning" (para. 19). How should colleges approach teaching about sexual harassment and assault? Should they teach women how to avoid victimization? Or should they focus on educating men about sexual harassment and assault? Which approach do you think is more effective?

ASHWINI TAMBE

Ashwini Tambe is an associate professor of women's studies at the University of Maryland, where she also serves as the director of graduate studies. She has published numerous articles on feminism and women's issues in transnational contexts, and her work has focused recently on conceptions of girlhood and age-of-consent law. Her books include *Codes of Misconduct: Regulating Prostitution in Late Colonial Bombay* (2009) and the forthcoming *Defining Girlhood in India: A Transnational History of Sexual Maturity Laws*. She is also the editorial director of *Feminist Studies*, which published this essay in 2018.

Reckoning with the Silences of #MeToo

The year 2018 has been an important time for US feminism. For women's studies professors, it's been heartening to find the world outside our classrooms taking up conversations about sex and power that we've been having for decades. In this piece, I will reflect on three questions: What is going on? Why is it happening now? And what forms of feminism have been overlooked in the coverage of the #MeToo movement? I spend the longest time on the third question, because I'm concerned about how #MeToo has advanced a version of public feminism that is, in some ways, out of step with currents in academic feminism.

WHAT'S GOING ON?

Although feminists have long championed public speak-outs for survivors of sexual violence — whether in Take Back the Night open mics since the 1980s or the workshops also called "MeToo" that Tarana Burke started in Alabama in 2007 — the viral force of the hashtag #MeToo in mid-October 2017 took most people by surprise. Within the first twenty-four hours, it had been retweeted half a million times. According to Facebook, nearly 50 percent of US users are friends with someone who posted a message about experiences of assault or harassment. #MeToo was by no means just a US phenomenon: Facebook and Twitter feeds in various parts of the world, notably Sweden, India, and Japan, were rocked for days by this hashtag. Then came the slew of powerful cis-men,[1] largely

[1] **cis-men** Derived from *cisgender*, describing a state or condition in which a person's sex and gender identity match their sex at birth (i.e., people born with male genitalia who identify as men). [Editors' note]

in the US media and entertainment industries, who were forced to swiftly resign after allegations of sexual misconduct. This toppling continues and has expanded beyond the media to other industries where reputations matter: politics, music, architecture, and, somewhat belatedly, higher education. In an important way, the ground beneath us has shifted. #MeToo has tilted public sympathy in favor of survivors by changing the default response to belief, rather than suspicion; the hashtag has revealed how widespread sexual coercion is.

WHY NOW?

We need to theorize, on a cultural scale, why this movement against sexual harassment and violence in the United States has happened now rather than, say, three years ago, when Bill Cosby was accused by multiple women, or after Roger Ailes, CEO of Fox News, was deposed. #MeToo's impact may seem sudden, but it is a part of a groundswell in women's activism since the November 2016 elections. The Women's March was the largest globally coordinated public gathering in history. The 3-million strong Facebook group Pantsuit Nation saw hundreds of thousands of posts about experiences of misogyny. Unprecedented numbers of women are running for US political office this year. The signature affective note running through this political moment is a fierce rage about the election of Donald Trump.

Trump's impunity, I suggest, serves as a trigger provoking the fury at the heart of #MeToo. There are many reasons to find fault with Trump, but it is distinctly galling that he faced no consequences after acknowledging being a sexual predator. For victims of sexual trauma, it is already painful to watch perpetrators roam free because of how high the burdens of proof are in legal cases. When a person such as Trump is grandly affirmed by an election, it retraumatizes victims. Right after the election, therapists and counseling centers were flooded with patients seeking help with processing past events. The ballast provided by women's feverish organizing and the instant power of social media has facilitated a collective emboldening. Trump has made the comeuppance of all powerful men feel more urgent.

But from the inception of #MeToo, I have 5
also watched its racial and class politics with some wariness: whose pain was being centered, I wondered? A colleague recently asked aloud: is #MeToo a white women's movement? Another wondered, is this a moral panic? These questions underline the importance of feminist insights that are overlooked in dominant coverage of the movement.

WHAT'S LEFT OUT?

Critical race feminism offers important insights when exploring the question of whether this is a white women's movement. The answer is complicated — both yes and no. Obviously, sexual violence and harassment are not white women's problems alone. They have been a pervasive workplace experience for women of color — whether we are talking about enslaved women or the vast majority of women in low-wage service professions. The viral reach of the hashtag around the globe — driving changes in laws in places such as Sweden and shaking up the elite professoriate in the Indian academy — makes clear that sexual violence is not only a US white women's issue.[2] But if we look at US media coverage of the movement and the most striking spokespersons as well as casualties in recent scandals, it is certainly white women's pain that is centered in popular media coverage. There are a few exceptions, such as the *New York Times* December 2017 feature on Ford's Chicago auto assembly plant and Oprah Winfrey's Golden Globes speech about Recy Taylor, but by and large, it is young white women's complaints, such as those by victims of Roy Moore or Larry Nassar, that have the most visibility.[3] This is a familiar problem in a racist society. It has been commented on for a long time — including in Kimberlé Crenshaw's classic article about how to understand intersectionality in domestic violence cases.[4] Black women are regularly also pressured by black men not to speak publicly about harassment. Apart from the logic of protecting a community's image — the logic that dramatically shaped the Clarence Thomas hearings and the vilification of Anita Hill — it is worth keeping in mind that the primary instrument of redress in #MeToo is public shaming and criminalization of the perpetrator. This is already too familiar a problem for black men. We know the history of how black men have been lynched based on unfounded allegations that they sexually violated white women. We know how many black men are unjustly incarcerated. The dynamics of #MeToo, in which due process has been reversed — with accusers' words taken more seriously than those of the accused — is a familiar problem in black communities. Maybe some black women want no part of this dynamic.

#MeToo's affective focus on pain is also out of step with currents in contemporary academic feminism that center pleasure, play, and healing. Many lessons from feminist debates over sex and sexuality in the past few decades have not been absorbed, as #MeToo displays.

The rapid series of scandals have produced a conflation in the public imagination of different types of problem behaviors. It is pretty clear that what Larry Nassar and Roy Moore did, trapping unsuspecting younger women and girls, is predatory. But predatory sex is not the same thing as transactional sex. Charlie Rose and Harvey Weinstein's wrongs are more complicated because they involve trading promotions or film roles in exchange for sexual favors. These kinds of transactions happen frequently.

In many contexts — both within and outside marriage — sex is exchanged for security, affection, and money. So, a crucial point to keep in mind is that not all transactional sex is coerced. As sex positive feminists would argue, we need to guard against casting all transactions as coercion. The question is, how to discern coercion within contexts of transaction.

Not all seemingly consensual transactions 10
are free of coercion, of course. A common mistake of philosophical liberalism (and some sex positive feminism) is to presume that any

[2] Rick Noack, "Sweden Proposes Tough Sexual Assault Law," *Washington Post,* December 20, 2017, https://www.washingtonpost.com/news/worldviews/wp/2017/12/20/amid-metoo-movement-and-fear-of-immigrants-sweden-proposes-tough-sexual-assault-law/?utm_term=.edf02570c5b4; Elizabeth Cassin and Ritu Prasad, "Student's 'Sexual Predator' List Names Professors," *BBC,* November 6, 2017, http://www.bbc.com/news/blogs-trending-41862615.

[3] Susan Chira and Catrin Einhorn, "How Tough Is It to Change a Culture of Harassment? Ask Women at Ford," *New York Times,* December 19, 2017, https://www.nytimes.com/interactive/2017/12/19/us/ford-chicago-sexual-harassment.html; Madison Park, "Recy Taylor Is 'A Name I Know . . . You Should Know, Too,' Oprah says," *CNN*, January 10, 2018, https://www.cnn.com/2018/01/08/us/recy-taylor-oprah-winfrey-golden-globes-speech/index.html.

[4] Kimberlé Williams Crenshaw, "Mapping the Margins: Intersectionality, Identity Politics, and Violence Against Women of Color," *Stanford Law Review* 43, no. 6 (July 1991): 1241–99.

exchange arises out of, and generates, symmetry between two actors. But transacting in sex, or getting something in exchange for sex, does not mean that coercion is absent. In fact, coercion can also work in seemingly consensual ways.

We need, in this moment, a broader lens to understand coercion beyond the liberal understanding of verbal consent. Many of the scandals in the news involve women who went along with sex without saying no — but who would have preferred not to. Men such as Charlie Rose should have asked themselves: under what conditions could women have said no to their advances? Was it difficult for women to refuse? Was the men's institutional position, or age, or wealth, tilting their decision? Coercion, in other words, should be defined by more than just whether someone says yes or no. It hinges on whether one has power over that other person such that they might interpret a request as force — or even as a threat. If s/he faces negative consequences for saying no to a sexual advance, then that sexual advance is coercive.

This broad definition of coercion extends beyond contexts of sexual harassment to other abuses of power. In fact, if we take sex out of the picture for a moment, it becomes much easier for most people to recognize such coercion: most people relate to the problem of being forced to do something that they really don't want to do.

So why is it hard to take sex out of the picture? Perhaps it is not a surprise that a movement against sexual coercion, rather than, say, domestic violence, has received this level of news attention; sexual harassment stories gain traction because the details make for sensational copy. Many powerful people ask for inappropriate personal favors — such as John Conyers asking his subordinates to babysit for him — but the infractions that really seem to exercise our attention are related to sex. This predilection is not simply an outgrowth of a repressed interest in sex; it is because readers conflate sex and selfhood — many people see any experience of sexual coercion as eroding a woman's core sense of self.

We need not view sex this way, of course: equating sex with selfhood is a historically specific mandate connected to norms of middle-class respectability. Many sex workers express different understandings of their sexual activity — they don't treat their sexual encounters as signaling their virtue (or lack of it). Asexual people also protest that we give sex undue centrality in the way we define ourselves.

So, if we are to ask, what makes coercion 15
in workplaces so common, we will need to do more than just fire those who are accused of forcing sex. We will need to look at the factors that generate cis-male dominance in the workplace: historical wage discrimination, childcare policies, and the way skills are defined and valued in masculinist ways. When men are systematically privileged by workplace policies and practices, they regularly ascend to powerful positions. This is why when we see the words "coach" or "boss" or "director" or "executive," we imagine male figures first. Our goal shouldn't only be to unseat coaches, bosses, directors, and executives who have abused their power. We need to re-script misogynistic practices that make it difficult for women to inhabit these roles in the first place. And we need to create alternatives to a politics of retribution that only focuses on punishment rather than transforming workplace hierarchies.

Topics for Critical Thinking and Writing

1. Ashwini Tambe writes that "#MeToo has tilted public sympathy in favor of survivors by changing the default response to belief, rather than suspicion" (para. 2). Do you think our culture finds claims about sexual harassment less credible when made by women of different ages, races, classes, ethnicities, sexual orientations, gender identities, or occupations? Explain.
2. In the section titled, "Why Now?," Tambe connects the emergence of #MeToo to the election of Donald Trump and asks whether #MeToo is a "white women's movement" (para. 5). In the 2016 election, exit polls indicated that a majority of white women (about 52 percent) voted for Trump nationally. Use this statistic to help you answer — or complicate — Tambe's question.
3. What problem does Tambe say arises when black men are accused of sexual harassment or assault? How does identifying this problem contribute to Tambe's argument?
4. In paragraph 9, Tambe discusses the complications of "transactional" sex, such as quid pro quo encounters, in which a person performs a sexual favor in exchange for a job, promotion, or other opportunity, either agreed upon or unstated. Is that person a victim? Explain in 300 to 500 words; as you do, be sure to examine circumstances that make the concept of victimization in transactional sex so complicated.
5. In paragraph 13, Tambe claims that "sexual harassment stories gain traction because the details make for sensational copy." Do you think the #MeToo movement and the types of people and experiences the media covers is determined in any way by the allure of scandalous, salacious, or titillating details? Explain.
6. Do some research into the issue of male prison rape in the US justice system and write an essay of 500 to 1,000 words on the visibility of this problem of sexual violence, what problems prisoners face in reporting or dealing with sexual victimization in prison, and whether or not a viable #MeToo movement is possible for men in prison. (Feel free to focus on a specific group of prisoners, such as juveniles, gay or bisexual men, transgender men, or men of a specific racial or ethnic class.)
7. Do some research on how the #MeToo movement occurred in another country. In 500 to 1,000 words, tell about the movement there — how it started, what propelled it, and how supporting arguments or criticisms differ from those in the United States.
8. Examine some other kinds of "silences" in the context of the #MeToo movement. Are there any silences, voices, experiences, or perspectives that are not mentioned in Tambe's essay? If so, do you think the omission is a flaw in Tambe's argument or a sign of its success? Explain.

V. L. SEEK[1]

The following essay, written under a pseudonym by an anonymous author, appeared in *Not That Bad: Dispatches from Rape Culture* (2018), a collection of essays on rape and sexual assault and harassment.

Utmost Resistance

Law and the Queer Woman or How I Sat in a Classroom and Listened to My Male Classmates Debate How to Define Force and Consent[2]

I.

My life at twenty-one was all short skirts and red wine and big talk about life after college.

Twenty-two was a move out west and a first year of law school, going out but not staying out, annotating case law, and settling into the comfort of a long-distance girlfriend and thousands of miles and a computer screen separating our bodies. My mother never taught me to knit but somehow I taught myself and managed to deeply and expertly weave delusion and denial into the threads of the blanket I buried my feet under to keep warm in the new Colorado nights. Yes, it was cold out here, I told my friends, but not as cold as you would think.

II.

> *"There must be the utmost resistance by the woman by all means within her power."*
>
> State v. McClain, 149 N.W. 771, 771 (Wis. 1914)

That summer I was twenty-one, just before my senior year in college, I worked as an intern at a prep school in a small town in the Northeast. I took the train up from Baltimore to get there. I was the only person to get off at the stop. The train had emptied in New York and never filled back up, so I'd spent much of the ride staring out the window and romanticizing the upcoming months. My bags were spread across several seats, and I found a safety in the isolation that did not surprise me. My stop had no train station, no platform. I dragged my bags down the steps and found myself facing a one-room train depot and a gazebo draped in patriotic flags. I waited for my cab for two hours, thinking that everyone who passed me must know that I wasn't from around these parts. In the cab, the driver offered a knowing sigh when I told him where to take me. We drove up the hill.

There were parts of the job that were exactly as I imagined: taking residents of my dorm to visit the family-owned candy shop in town, teaching writing to eighth graders already primed to write their college admissions essays, supervising the Fourth of

[1]Many legal academic papers criticize the law, but to criticize academia is a different kind of purpose and a different kind of risk, especially when one is housed in its ivory tower. I think of these things when I write under my name, and when I instead choose to write under my pen name, I wonder if I am contributing to the problem or still fighting for a solution.

[2]In law school, you are taught how to write academic articles for publication in law reviews, which is the art of crafting the perfect title, of making your student analysis of strict scrutiny and constitutional law sexy, of disguising your theory-heavy piece as something that is not too political and therefore not too divisive. You are taught the art of the paragraph-long footnotes that cite obscure case law or define a seemingly obvious word with thirty-something synonyms. This is not that. Its edges are not dull and its words arguably divisive (though I struggle to think of any article about rape, legal or otherwise, that is not cause for debate). But we have wasted too much time softening the corners of our speech and blunting our legal arguments to nudge legal reformation to our desired outcome when it comes to rape. We have wasted too much.

July lawn games and cookouts (that summer was too dry for fireworks), beholding the steps and rooms boasting plaques and the names of presidential alumni.

But there were other parts I hadn't imagined. The twenty-minute walk to the single town bar that we made every night in heels. The spot under the tree where people would go to smoke, steps away from the campus perimeter. Daily breakfast with other interns who would show up with a bruised eye and smile ("I couldn't feel my face") and talk about the drugs they took last night.

Drinking on the campus was not allowed, and so those of us with IDs and nights off would make that nightly pilgrimage to the one bar. Some nights we came back early, others we returned with our heels in our hands, and a few nights we took a cab (it was the same driver every time). The drinks were cheap and I was newly twenty-one.

Our last night of work was the first night we could drink on campus: The students had left for the summer and the halls and dorm rooms were empty for the first time in six weeks. A night was planned, starting at a colleague's dorm and stopping by six others that housed us before ending up at the town bar. The crawl was themed, so we spent the day at the Goodwill crafting our costumes. We spent our last paychecks on the alcohol and I remember that liquor store and that bottle of wine so well. I remember holding it by its neck as I walked from my friend's room to the first party of the night. I remember holding it by my side for group photos. And I remember vomiting it back up the next morning.

We got to the first party at eight. By 8:30 my night was over; I never made it to the bar.

The next morning I lay on the floor of a shower stall of that first dorm under a stream of water. The hot water was turned all the way up, but it felt like ice on my skin. I didn't know how many hours I had been on that floor. I was shaking. My underwear was on the other side of the room. I was so concerned with cleaning up where I had been sick. I took off my soaking wet clothes and tried to stop shaking. I wrapped a towel around myself. It was barely the size of my torso. In the mirror I saw scratch marks on my back and bruises on my chest (I wouldn't notice the bruises on my thighs until later). I pulled my shirt back on to cover them. It was heavy and made me shake harder than before. I walked back to my building and called a security guard to let me in because I couldn't find my key in that bathroom. (My friend would return my purse later that day. "You left this behind when you left with. . . ." She trailed off with a teasing knowingness suggesting she did not know at all.) I didn't meet the security guard's eyes. I knew he was thinking that I had too much to drink last night — that I had let this happen.

For years, that night was my fault. I knew what rape was. I knew what consent was. I knew about first- and second-wave feminism. I knew queer theory. But I swallowed the blame like that bottle of red wine and repeated to myself the lies that would run on loop for years to come. *You have only yourself to blame. It was not that bad. You're okay. You're alive. At least you don't remember it all. The bruises are gone. You can forget about it. No one ever has to know.* Even now, these lies taste familiar, comfortable, in a way that the words *survivor* and *victim* never have.

III.

"In a civil case, the court may admit evidence offered to prove a victim's sexual behavior or sexual predisposition if its probative value substantially outweighs the danger of harm to any victim and

> *of unfair prejudice to any party. The court may admit evidence of a victim's reputation only if the victim has placed it in controversy."*
>
> Federal Rules of Evidence 412(A)(B)(2)

In the beginning of law school, you have a pervasive idealism about the law. Fresh off writing an essay about justice for all and changing the world using the rule of law for the admissions committee, you are thrown into classrooms with peers who ostensibly want the same — teachers and debaters, Peace Corps members and journalists. It doesn't take more than a week with the Socratic classes and the formulaic writing and the memorizing of case law for that initial unbridled idealism and passion to slip away.[3] I, however, clung to the ideal of law school despite my bad grades and the professors asking why I wasn't in law review or mock trial or moot court, despite the classes that I walked out of and in which I couldn't will my hands to stop shaking.

In Criminal Law, there was an entire chapter devoted to rape. It was my second semester, almost two years after I'd been raped. Around that time, the debate on the merit of trigger warnings was becoming mainstream, and it was present in our classrooms. My fellow law students were more than happy to chime in with a First Amendment or "slippery slope" defense; I didn't engage and I didn't care. I didn't reflect on my past experience as it interacted with my present: Trigger warnings were an academic debate, not a practical one. Distilling two pages of facts into a pithy "issue is how to define force" note was how I was going to be a lawyer, not how I was going to finally come to terms with my own rape.

We barely got to the second case in class, before the questions — repetitive and probing — began to chip away at the protective dissociation I used to stay disengaged. How do we define force? What does it mean to "resist to the utmost"? How do we define consent? From an evidentiary perspective, can we ask what she was wearing? When can we ask about previous sexual partners, experiences, and proclivities?

With each question, each case, and each eagerly volunteered comment, I got colder and colder. I could not stop shaking. The room was eighty degrees and I was wearing a winter coat. I told myself I was just angry. There was so much to be angry about: the patriarchy, the precedent of rape law, the slow strides of legal reform. I had so many reasons that were not "I was raped." I had so many reasons that were not remembered trauma. That night, I cried while talking to my girlfriend and I wasn't able to explain why.

15 In Evidence, we learned how to discredit a witness on the stand. We learned the exceptions that would allow you to introduce a witness's sexual history to undermine the idea that she was raped. How much did you have to drink that night? Would you say it was your usual custom to dress in this way when going out? And you gave him your phone number? Do you normally accept a drink from any man who buys you one? Did you have sexual relations with him in the past? How many, would you say? And all of those times were consensual? Did you ever say no? You didn't scream? And you continued to be in a relationship with him? But it's hard to remember now what happened on that day, isn't it? In Ethics, I learned that an attorney who collected money from his friends for a football game was disbarred because he kept the money for himself.

3. This is not to imply that all social-justice-minded people who go to law school become corporate-defending drones. Nor should you infer that all lawyers have subscribed to the "ask questions but only so many" mind-set with which I am familiar. But there is a reason that these are the moments I remember and the people I can't forget. It was harder to think of examples to exclude than to find ones to mention.

I also learned that a senior attorney who repeatedly sexually harassed a female attorney was not disbarred because the court did not consider his daily groping to be conduct involving "moral turpitude." In seminars, I wrote papers with facts that would not fade from my mind[4] and that made me pick fights with my girlfriend because it was easier to accuse than admit. In clinical classes, I talked with my public defender friends who told me how to make a witness seem like a "lying bitch" on the stand. In the hallways, we debriefed from classes and criticized our classmates. "I've woken up after a lot of drunk sex and regretted it, but *I* didn't say it was rape," a girl told me. She was my closest friend.

It was isolating. Maybe it was retraumatizing, but I didn't let myself use that word. Trauma was for other people, I thought. And so I did not speak often in class. I had no interest in debating the law, in briefing a case, or commenting on the intersection of trigger warnings and the First Amendment. But law school — the law as it was taught, as it was received, as my classmates minimally questioned it, and as I understood it — was a trigger warning. That night when I was twenty-one had shifted a bullet into the chamber. And I spent three years trying to move away from the line of fire.

IV.

> *"She must follow the natural instinct of every proud female to resist, by more than mere words, the violation of her person by a stranger or an unwelcomed friend. She must make it plain that she regards such sexual acts as abhorrent and repugnant to her natural sense of pride."*
>
> STATE V. RUSK, 424 A.2D 720 (1981) (COLE J., DISSENTING)

There is an art in deceiving oneself and I have always liked to be the best at everything. For me, coming out as a queer woman and a rape survivor have been inextricably linked. The way I relied on easy lies to avoid my own trauma was the same way I justified staying closeted. It was always "later" or "someday" or "no one's business at all."

But that summer when I was twenty-one, I thought that maybe "someday" was sooner than I'd initially believed, because there was a girl. I practiced saying the words in front of myself, hoping to see a more honest version staring back at me. *Queer. Lesbian. Dyke.* The words were foreign but they came from a mouth that understood them all the same. They felt wrong to say aloud but my tongue knew the shape to make and I heard my own truth pouring from a body that had spent years convincing herself otherwise. I wanted to come out. I wanted to speak my truth. I wanted to tell that girl I loved that there was a reason I named every woman in my writing after her. I was in love with her name and the way she laughed at me.

I had planned to come out my last year of college but those plans changed after the summer. What had felt so close to the surface, I once again forced back under. What I had romanticized as speaking my truth became so entrenched in doubt. Doubt about my identity, about that night, about whether it was all worth it. I was committed to shame because it was familiar. I was terrified about the questions of the men I had slept with and dated. And what about all of them? I was terrified that someone would somehow know I was

[4]These facts included: Most rapists are repeat offenders. Trauma resolution is never final. In 1825, a rape conviction required the testimony from two male witnesses. In rural America, rapes increase during hunting season.

raped and tell me that was why I was gay. I was terrified that it was true.

20 The shame and doubt that I struggled with about my sexuality was easily transferred to my trauma. I am not surprised by the statistics that show an increased rate of violence against queer people. Nor am I surprised that 46 percent of bisexual women face such violence, as compared with 14 percent and 13 percent of straight and lesbian women respectively.[5] The culture of shame and silence shrouds survivors of sexual violence, but also queer people who are so often considered other. "How did you know you were gay?" is another version of "Can I believe you?"

When your truth is so inherently questioned, it is easier to say nothing than anything at all. I know this because I live in a bastion of liberalism, I have aligned myself with open-minded people, I have spent my life devouring queer feminist theory, I have spent years in therapy, decades in yoga, and months in meditation to grow and heal and understand and yet, despite everything, when I write about that night I still worry if my story is believable.

V.

If I were trying to convince you of a legal position, this is where I would conclude. I would summarize my arguments, allude to the case law, and propose a workable solution. But a conclusion seems out of reach when we are still stuck debating the facts, deciding whom to trust and what is true. We are trapped in a legal system that has never favored women and has never believed survivors. And we are mired in a circuitous and damning dialogue, so powerful that it invalidates our experiences, our traumas, our truths — a dialogue so powerful that we begin to doubt whether our experience was ever there at all.

[5] Centers for Disease Control, "The National Intimate Partner and Sexual Violence Survey: An Overview of 2010 Findings on Victimization by Sexual Orientation" (2010).

Topics for Critical Thinking and Writing

1. As V. L. Seek tells her story about her internship at the beginning of the essay, at what moment did you realize something was about to go wrong? What clues did you take from the text as indicative?
2. In paragraph 12, Seek refers to "the debate on the merit of trigger warnings." Research the term *trigger warning* and the conversations that surround it. Then provide an account of the pros and cons of trigger warnings.
3. Studying subjects close to one's own negative experiences can be a difficult balancing act. When Seek discusses studying criminal law related to rape, she says that she distanced herself from her own traumatic experience to focus on "how I was going to be a lawyer, not how I was going to come to terms with my own rape" (para. 12). Do you think it is possible for a traumatized person to objectively study his or her own trauma?
4. In paragraph 15, Seek discusses her evidence class, in which she trained in methods to undermine an alleged sexual assault victim's testimony. What kinds of questions are taught as those that best undermine the testimony? Do you think they are fair questions? Why, or why not?

5. Seek's essay is a personal testimony, but is it a successful argument? If you think it is not, tell why the argument fails. If you think it is, tell why it is effective.
6. Why do think Seek writes under a pseudonym and leaves out the details of her assault, as well as the name of the school where it occurred and the name of her attacker? Does her anonymity help or hurt her argument? Why?

ROBIN WEST

Robin West (b. 1954) is the Frederick J. Haas Professor of Law and Philosophy at Georgetown University. Her research focuses on feminist legal theory, constitutional law, philosophy of law, and law and literature. Over her career, which includes authorship of numerous books and journal articles, West also taught at the University of Maryland, the University of Chicago, and Stanford University Law Schools. The argument presented here was excerpted from an article that appeared in *The Baffler* in May 2018.

Manufacturing Consent

OF TOUCHINGS AND TORTS

What is the legal wrong of sexual harassment? Sexual harassment is not simply boorish, immoral sexual behavior on the job. Nor is it nonconsensual — and therefore criminal — sexual assault or sexual battery. Sexual harassment is the imposition of *unwelcome* — not necessarily nonconsensual — sexual advances or behavior, either physical or nonphysical, at work or school. When it interferes with one's ability to engage in work, it's a violation of the victim's civil right to a nondiscriminatory workplace. And when it occurs at school, it likewise impermissibly obstructs a victim's right to equal and nondiscriminatory education, guaranteed by Title IX of our Civil Rights Acts. In both settings, the status of harassment as a Title VII[1] or Title IX[2] violation means that it can result in actionable claims for damages and injunctions in civil suits.

It's important to note that much of the behavior that harassment law targets, when construed under ordinary state law, is also a tort[3] — i.e., an actionable infringement on the integrity of one's person — or, if sufficiently severe, a crime. Nonconsensual sexual touching at work (or elsewhere) are batteries, and sexualized aggression that falls short of physical touching might qualify as assaults or the intentional infliction of emotional distress. Before the advent of Titles VII and IX, and before the turn to civil rights as the framing of sexual harassment, courts did at least occasionally treat these touchings or assaults as common, or garden-variety, intentional torts.[4]

However, modern courts have not developed a robust body of tort law addressing these

[1]Title VII of the Civil Rights Acts of 1964 prohibits discrimination by employers on the basis of sex, race, color, religion, or national origin. [All notes are the editors'.]

[2]Title IX legislation, prohibiting sexual discrimination at universities and education institutions, was enacted in 1972 as an amendment to the Civil Rights Act of 1964.

[3]**tort** The area of law dealing with civil law (as opposed to criminal law).

[4]**intentional torts** Actions resulting in harm to others done purposefully and intentionally and therefore possibly also criminal.

behaviors. Instead, virtually all judges and lawyers, as well as most ordinary Americans, have adopted a view of sexual harassment as primarily a form of discrimination at work or school, and for that reason only secondarily or incidentally a tortious assault or any other kind of personal injury. Sexual harassment is thus, in the eyes of law, now understood as being more akin to the group-based wrong of discrimination than it is to the "personal" wrong of assault or battery. It is an instance of treating someone differently "because of their sex" — i.e., akin to the manner in which discrimination generally is a wrong because its victims are treated differently because of their race or some other innate and irrelevant characteristic. Given this framing, the act of harassment often loses what might be termed its common-sense character as a wrongful personal injury — an assault, a battery, or an infliction of emotional distress that, because it is a violation of a person's physical sovereignty, renders it a *tort,* i.e., a private, compensable wrong, giving rise to a judicially imposed remedy.

There were good reasons that second-wave feminists of the late seventies urged the courts to rethink, or reframe, harassment as a form of Title VII discrimination, rather than (or rather than *only*) as an intentional tort, actionable under state law. As Catharine MacKinnon convincingly showed in her breakthrough 1979 book, *The Sexual Harassment of Working Women,* the older tort law of assault and battery was compromised by moralistic assumptions about the nature of sexual behavior — and even modern tort law fails to grasp the systemic and economic nature of the harm. Then as now, tort law had no language with which to express or condemn the deep connections between sexual harassment at work and women's unequal condition in American society at large.

Conceptualizing sexual harassment as a 5
form of discrimination, and therefore as a civil rights violation, occasioned a profound shift in legal and (by extension) public consciousness: it put forth the claim that this form of personal aggression and its routinely expected sufferance represent a linchpin of the subordination of women, forbidden by our civil rights acts, and not only by state tort law. The emerging consensus around harassment as a discriminatory harm elevated the legal recourse against it accordingly as a strike for women's equality — much as, say, voting-rights and anti-redlining court decisions codified a slowly emerging consensus against racial discrimination in our legal system. They couldn't be effectively waved away via legal compensation for batteries or assaults suffered by individuals, and treated as though they were no different in kind from the injuries sustained in a barroom brawl. This consensus marks a deep, qualitative shift in our understanding of equality between the sexes, and we have Catharine MacKinnon and the early lawyers and activists who framed the issue this way to thank, and to credit.

WORKED OVER

But any legal strategy can also entail opportunity costs for both aggrieved complainants and the elaboration of social consensus, and that's plainly been the case here. Some of our current public ambivalence over the wrongs of sexual harassment and the benefits of the law proscribing it can be traced to this legal framing of the wrong: the first-order definition of sexual harassment as, at heart, a form of discrimination rather than a personal injury, which might be adjudicated through tort law. First, it's simply confusing. Is sexual harassment really sex discrimination? And is it really *discrimination*? Is the harm in being treated differently, because of your sex? Is that what you think when you suffer it? "Goddamn it, I'm being treated differently because I'm female. This wouldn't be happening to me if I were a man. That's unfair." Or do you think "get your goddamned hands off of me"? The construction of sexual harassment as wrong because it's discriminatory seems at odds with our experience of it as wrong because it's *assaultive*—an unwanted touching, or battery, that violates our physical integrity at work.

But there are other problems stemming from the formulation of sexual harassment as sex discrimination—or more broadly, as a civil rights violation—that may be a little less obvious. First, that formulation seems to many, not at all without reason, as badly under-inclusive. As Yale Law Professor Vicki Schultz has persuasively argued, women often suffer harassment at work that may be unrelated to anything having to do with their sexuality but everything to do with their gender: being repeatedly referred to as a bitch or girl or stupid, being presumed incompetent, being the object of looks-based ridicule, or being required to perform non-work but gendered tasks such as babysitting, gift-shopping, and so on, may have everything to do with gender and literally nothing to do with sex. Gender harassment of this sort may be every bit as much an obstacle to advancement as sexual harassment.

The U.S. Equal Employment Opportunity Commission has now recognized as much, and treats these forms of gender harassment as discriminatory violations of a worker's civil rights. But adding the category of gender harassment doesn't cure the problem of under-inclusiveness—if anything, it underscores the basic difficulty. *All* workers—men, women, trans, cis, gay, straight, and bi—suffer harassment on the job constantly by virtue of their status *as workers*, and have absolutely no "civil right" under the law to be free of it, unless by chance it can be regarded as racially or sexually charged.

The bullying, the belittlement, the undermining, and the generally shitty, uncivil, and sometimes sadistic treatment of workers that is a part of so many workplaces goes at best unchallenged under the prevailing legal definition of harassment as discrimination. At worst, this consensus actively shores up this destructive status quo, by homing in on a civil right to be free of only some of the more egregious forms of gender harassment—and only then if it can be characterized as sexual and aimed at a victim because of sex. That some harassment at work is a civil rights violation, in other words, helps legitimate the considerable harassment that cannot be so characterized.

This is a regrettable implication of the 10
structure of virtually all of our civil rights laws, including our law of sexual harassment. *All* workers should enjoy a civil right to a harassment-free workplace. All workers should enjoy a right to be treated with dignity and respect in their place of employment. Work matters, hugely, to virtually everyone; it is often our central place of civil identity. Civil rights should not only address discrimination, regardless of how we interpret sexual harassment as an elementary mode of discrimination. Civil rights and civil equality should fundamentally sustain our rights to inclusion as equals in public spaces, which most profoundly include our work spaces. We *all* should have a right to civil treatment: in fact, that should be our absolutely non-negotiable core civil right.

Topics for Critical Thinking and Writing

1. Explain the difference between *assault* and *battery* according to Robin West. Why are the differences in these terms important legal distinctions in the context of her argument?
2. Look up some definitions of *tort law* and gather some examples of "tortious acts." How do they differ from criminal acts? Are any types of torts also criminal acts? Provide some examples. Now consider sexual harassment. What forms of sexual harassment in school or work are not crimes? When do they become crimes?
3. In paragraph 4, West refers to "the deep connections between sexual harassment at work and women's unequal condition in American society at large." Do you think there is a connection between sexual harassment in the workplace and inequality in general? Explain.
4. If you were to follow West's argument and come away thinking that sexual harassment at work constitutes an assault or battery even when it does not include touching, consider whether or not the race, religion, or color of the victim of harassment also matters. Should harassment of a racial or religious minority be a hate crime?
5. What is the difference between sexual harassment and "gender harassment" (para. 7)? Should gender harassment also be labeled discriminatory and punished in the same way as sexual harassment? Why, or why not?
6. Research the protections of LGBTQ+ individuals in schools and workplaces. What laws are and are not applicable to certain categories of people? What cases stand out to you as remarkable for bringing to light the problems with applying discrimination laws to such persons? Why? Answer in 500 to 1,000 words. Be sure to explain what was being debated and where things stand now.
7. In this excerpt, West writes about harassment in the workplace, but consider other public places (parks, gyms, concerts) where harassment may also occur. Should sexual harassment laws address these places, too? Are there any laws in place that do, and if so, are they effective?

BECKY HAYES

Becky Hayes is a graduate of the University of California–Davis School of Law. She works as a union attorney for the Screen Actors Guild and American Federation of Television and Radio Artists (SAG-AFTRA), which represents more than 150,000 actors, performers, broadcasters, and other media professionals. This essay appeared on February 16, 2018, in *The Establishment*, an online forum for cultural and political discussions.

The Critics of #MeToo and the Due Process Fallacy

The most persistent criticism of the #MeToo movement is that advocates have abandoned due process in favor of trial by the faceless internet mob. Critics accuse the women leading the movement of pursuing "vigilante justice" or worse, a witch-hunt.

These critiques have dogged #MeToo from the beginning, and now that the backlash to the movement has reached a crescendo, we're about to hear a whole lot more.

But don't listen.

Social media is exactly the right place for #MeToo to play out. In fact, it's the only place it ever could. The frequent invocation of due process ignores just how inadequate the American legal system is for protecting women against sexual violence and harassment. It is precisely because the courts of law and other traditional avenues of recourse have failed women that they've turned to the internet and the court of public opinion.

5 Due process sounds great in theory. Zephyr Teachout, former Democratic candidate for the U.S. House of Representatives in New York, defined it as "a fair, full investigation, with a chance for the accused to respond" in her recent *New York Times* op-ed on this topic. It's hard to argue with that. The concept of due process is a fundamental pillar of the American justice system and one that we pride ourselves on.

The problem with #MeToo — according to its detractors — is that women have bypassed the courts, where due process rights apply, and gone directly to the public to seek out justice. The public, in turn, has rushed to judgment. Critics argue that justice can only be served by submitting these claims through the formal legal systems that guarantee basic fairness to the accused.

We know from experience, however, that the systems currently in place to deal with complaints of sexual harassment and assault have systematically failed victims and have allowed far too many perpetrators to continue their abuse unchecked.

This is true of the nation's criminal and civil courts, forced private arbitrations, HR department investigations, and campus tribunals. There's no great mystery as to why. We have shorthand for these kinds of impossible-to-prove claims: "he said-she said."

The phrase refers to the fact that all too often the only evidence in sexual harassment or assault cases is the victim's word against the abuser's denial. The incident of alleged abuse almost always takes place behind closed doors, so there are no other witnesses. With so little to go on these claims almost never result in a successful verdict.

10 And while no database tracks the outcomes of employment discrimination cases nationwide, a review of a random sampling of cases by Laura Beth Nielsen, a professor at the American Bar Foundation and Northwestern University, revealed that only 2% of plaintiffs win their cases.

Even when there are eyewitnesses, much of the mistreatment women are complaining about falls short of the legal definition of sexual harassment. There is a big gap between what the public believes is appropriate workplace behavior and what is considered egregious enough to warrant discipline, dismissal, or legal sanction under our existing guidelines and laws.

For example, did you know that your supervisor grabbing your butt at work is not enough, on its own, to sustain a claim under Title VII, the federal law that prohibits workplace sexual harassment? The Equal Employment Opportunity Commission (EEOC) defines sexual harassment as "unwelcome sexual advances" that "unreasonably interfere with an individual's work performance," or that create a hostile atmosphere at work. Under *Meritor Savings Bank v. Vinson* the Supreme Court held that such conduct must be "sufficiently severe or pervasive" to "create an abusive working environment." As recently as 2014 a federal court dismissed the claim of an employee whose boss grabbed her butt twice in one day in front of co-workers because it was neither severe nor pervasive enough to offend the average woman according to the judge, a woman no less.

Laws protecting women from sexual misconduct are much narrower than the commentators who want to redirect all these claims into the courts seem to realize. Annika Hernroth-Rothstein argues in *National Review* that "[i]f sexual harassment is a crime, it should be fought not with hashtags but with the full force of the law" in a piece titled, "#Metoo and Trial by Mob."

Sexual harassment is not, in fact, a crime. Title VII imposes only civil liability — i.e. money damages — on employers in cases of workplace misconduct. Further, only employers with more than 15 employees are covered. Employees of small businesses have no federal protection.

The same goes for freelancers employed as independent contractors and unpaid interns. Some state and local laws are more generous, but these are few and far between. Sexual harassment claims against anyone but employers and, under Title IX, federally funded schools are not covered at all.

Even if your claim is covered and meets the *legal* definition of harassment, there are still multiple barriers to seeking recourse through the courts. First, going through the formal legal system costs money. There are court fees and lawyers to pay, in addition to the time of work required.

Second, sexual harassment claims are subject to statutes of limitations — meaning that victims cannot bring these claims after a certain amount of time has passed. In many cases, these time limits are very short. The federal statute of limitations under Title VII, for example, is only 180 days, or roughly six months.

The New York State limit is three years.

Many of the claims of sexual harassment — and worse — that are coming out now as part of #Metoo are many years, and in some cases, decades old. Victims of sexual harassment often have more pressing needs in the immediate aftermath of the experience than filing a lawsuit, including dealing with the resultant trauma and, all too frequently, job loss. For these men and women there is nowhere else to go but the internet to air the grievances that have long been buried.

The calls for due process are often tied with calls for reform to the existing laws. Reforms can take years to pass, and even when they do, they almost always apply prospectively to new claims, not retroactively. Thus, for many of the victims who posted their experiences as part of #MeToo, their options were internet justice or no justice at all.

Which would you have had them choose?

Social media has no barriers to entry. It is free and open to all. The only thing women need is an internet connection and the guts to come forward. Unlike the federal courts which are bound by the strictures of a nearly 50-year old law, the public has shown great willingness to consider the whole wide range of women's stories that run the gamut from rape to a squeeze on the waist during a photo op.

Even better, social media has allowed for a dialogue among diverse voices about what kind of behavior is acceptable and desirable in the society we want to live in, rather than just what is legal or illegal. The recent engagement around *Babe*'s account of a young woman's date with Aziz Ansari is the perfect example. That article engendered some of the most thought provoking discussions on today's sexual politics despite the general consensus that the behavior described didn't break any laws.

One of the unique advantages of social media that makes it particularly well suited to this movement is the incredible power of hashtags to connect women with similar stories. The men who have been brought down by the #MeToo movement have not been felled by individual women tweeting out isolated claims. In each case consequences have been visited upon abusers based on the strength of a large number of women coming forward with often nearly identical allegations that show a pattern of misbehavior.

25 Such is the power of #MeToo that it can aggregate the stories of women who have never met and who are separated by decades. Hashtags allow for the revolutionary possibility that sexual harassment will no longer be characterized by "he said-she said" allegations, but, as illustrated poignantly in a recent *New York Times* ad, "he said-she said, she said, she said," cases, ad infinitum. (Though, of course, even one "she said" should not be dismissed.)

For all its utility, the role social media played in the #MeToo movement has also been overstated. The stories that brought down industry giants like Harvey Weinstein, Louis C.K., Mark Halperin, and others did not originate on social media platforms, but rather in the pages of the nation's finest newspapers. The allegations were thoroughly vetted by investigative journalists bound by a code of ethics that provides its own kind of due process. Journalistic ethics require corroborating sources before going to print with a story with serious allegations such as sexual harassment. Furthermore, journalists always seek comment from the accused, giving them an opportunity to speak out on their own behalf.

Critics' insistence on due process presupposes an answer to a still open question: What is "the point" of #MeToo? The courts are best at meting out punishment for violations already committed. What if #MeToo isn't about punishment, or, more to the point, what if it's about more than punishment?

What if it's about changing the system prospectively, not seeking redress for the past? What if it's about prevention? The author of the Shitty Media Men list wrote that her goal was to warn others about men in her industry so they could protect themselves. What if #MeToo is about catharsis and about having a long overdue conversation where we all get to have a say? What if there are a multitude of points, and very few of them are well served by the courts?

The reflexive outcry about the need for due process from #MeToo critics is not well considered. It's time we stop telling women where, when, and to whom they can tell their own stories. If #MeToo is about anything, it's about the end of the era of women and other victims suffering in silence.

Topics for Critical Thinking and Writing

1. Do you agree with Becky Hayes that social media can act as a court of public opinion and compensate for the inadequacies of formal judicial processes in dealing with sexual assault claims? What are the advantages of hashtag justice over procedural justice? Do you think charges of sexual assault made through the social media hashtag #MeToo violate the standard of "innocent until proven guilty"? Cite Hayes's argument in your answer.
2. Some people have claimed that the #MeToo movement is an attack on men. Do you agree or disagree? Why?
3. Do some research to learn more about one specific case in which #MeToo was used to expose a person alleged to have committed sexual harassment or assault. Explore the social and legal consequences of the accusation. Was either type of justice adequate or inadequate? Explain.

4. The phrase "he said–she said" is often used to signify the problem with knowing the truth when two people are giving different accounts of the same event. In paragraph 25, Hayes refers to a full-page *New York Times* advertisement that ran in 2018 that portrayed the phrase "He said. She said." and then followed it with "She said." more than a hundred more times. What message does that ad convey, and how does it support Hayes's overall argument?
5. Near the end of her essay (paras. 27–28), Hayes asks about #MeToo: "What if it's about more than punishment? What if it's about changing the system prospectively, not seeking redress for the past? What if it's about prevention?" Do you think the #MeToo movement is a deterrent to future assaults? Explain.

BARI WEISS

Bari Weiss (b. 1984) is a graduate of Columbia University. She is a staff editor and writer for the opinion sections at the *New York Times*. Previously, she was the book review editor at the *Wall Street Journal* and the news and politics editor at *Tablet*, a daily online magazine of Jewish news and culture. The following piece was published in the *New York Times* on November 28, 2017.

The Limits of "Believe All Women"

Ever since Eve gave Adam that forbidden fruit, demonizing and disbelieving women has been the planet-wide policy. You don't need to reach back to the Pleistocene to see the truth of that.

"You're just a child," Roy Moore is accused of saying to Beverly Young Nelson, age 16 at the time, when he molested her in his car. "I am the district attorney of Etowah County, and if you tell anyone about this, no one will ever believe you."

Things have not changed much since 1603, when Shakespeare presaged the conversation between that Alabama district attorney and his teenage target. In "Measure for Measure," Angelo, a government official who is a strong proponent of his society's morality code, tries to get a young woman named Isabella to give up her virginity to him in exchange for pardoning her brother, who is on death row for having violated that code by having sex outside marriage.

Isabella calls out the vile quid pro quo: "Or with an outstretch'd throat I'll tell the world aloud / What man thou art."

5 Angelo replies: "Who will believe thee, Isabel? / My unsoil'd name, the austereness of my life, / My vouch against you, and my place i' the state, / Will so your accusation overweigh."

No longer.

Now, suddenly, Mitch McConnell is saying, "I believe the women."

Now, suddenly, Chelsea Handler is saying to Juanita Broaddrick, "I believe you."

This — despite, or perhaps because of, the predator in the Oval Office — is a cultural watershed.

10 The biggest sign of it in my life has been the conversations I've had with friends and family. While we women revisit our sexual histories, the men I know — old and young, liberal and conservative — are doing the same from the flip side. An older conservative

friend told me that he was considering reaching out to a girl he went on a date with in high school to apologize for kissing her in the car. She didn't say no, and she kissed him back. But he worries that she felt pressured. A close friend, a progressive, told me about a college hookup he regrets. He is spending time wondering about how the woman thinks about the experience: Did it leave a scar? Or is it arrogant to even assume she remembers his name?

This reckoning would never have happened without Gretchen Carlson and Lara Setrakian and Selma Blair and Rose McGowan and Kyle Godfrey-Ryan and the hundreds of others who told reporters their stories. They deserve our praise and our gratitude.

And hasn't the hunt been exhilarating? There's no small chance that by the time you finish this article, another mammoth beast of prey, maybe multiple, will be stalked and felled.

The huntresses' war cry — "believe all women" — has felt like a bracing corrective to a historic injustice. It has felt like a justifiable response to a system in which the crimes perpetrated against women — so intimate, so humiliating and so unlike any other — are so very difficult to prove.

But I also can't shake the feeling that this mantra creates terrible new problems in addition to solving old ones.

15 In less than two months we've moved from uncovering accusations of criminal behavior (Harvey Weinstein) to criminalizing behavior that we previously regarded as presumptuous and boorish (Glenn Thrush). In a climate in which sexual mores are transforming so rapidly, many men are asking: If I were wrongly accused, who would believe me?

I know the answer that many women would give — are giving — is: Good. Be scared. We have been scared for forever. It's your turn for some sleepless nights. They'll say: If some innocent men go down in the effort to tear down the patriarchy, so be it.

Emily Lindin, a columnist at *Teen Vogue*, summed up this view concisely last week on Twitter. "I'm actually not at all concerned about innocent men losing their jobs over false sexual assault/harassment allegations," she wrote. "If some innocent men's reputations have to take a hit in the process of undoing the patriarchy, that is a price I am absolutely willing to pay."

Ms. Lindin was widely criticized, but say this much for her: At least she had the guts to publicly articulate a view that so many women are sharing with one another in private. Countless innocent women have been robbed of justice, friends of mine insist, so why are we agonizing about the possibility of a few good men going down?

I think the worry is justified. And it's not because I don't get the impulse to burn it all down. It's because I think that "believing all women" can rapidly be transmogrified into an ideological orthodoxy that will not serve women at all.

20 If the past few weeks have shown us the unique horrors some women have faced, the answer to it can't be a stringent new solidarity that further limits the definition of womanhood and lumps our highly diverse experiences together simply based on our gender. I don't think that helps women. Or men.

I believe that the "believe all women" vision of feminism unintentionally fetishizes women. Women are no longer human and flawed. They are Truth personified. They are above reproach.

I believe that it's condescending to think that women and their claims can't stand up to interrogation and can't handle skepticism. I believe that facts serve feminists far better than faith. That due process is better than mob rule.

Maybe it will happen tomorrow or maybe next week or maybe next month. But the Duke lacrosse moment, the Rolling Stone moment, will come. A woman's accusation will turn out to be grossly exaggerated or flatly untrue. And if the governing principle of this movement is still an article of faith, many people will lose their religion. They will tear down all accusers as false prophets. And we will go back to a status quo in which the word of the Angelos is more sacred than the word of the Isabellas.

There are limits to relying on "believe all women" as an organizing political principle. We are already starting to see them.

Just yesterday *The Washington Post* reported that a woman named Jaime Phillips approached the paper with a story about Roy Moore. She claimed that in 1992, when she was 15, he impregnated her and that he drove her to Mississippi to have an abortion. Not a lick of her story is true.

It appears that Ms. Phillips was collaborating with Project Veritas, an organization that tries to expose mainstream media "bias" through undercover operations, and that the group's intent was to embarrass *The Post*—and, ultimately, to discredit Mr. Moore's other accusers.

The mission failed spectacularly, thanks to the professionalism of *The Post*'s reporters, but it's clear that Project Veritas was exploiting this moment. It's also not hard to imagine how this episode might have played out if Ms. Phillips had announced her accusations on, say, Twitter. Or even if she'd taken her story to a less fastidious news organization. In this climate, it would have caught on like wild fire.

That's exactly what happened, at least in the right-wing media bubble, in the case of an Al Franken accuser, Melanie Morgan. There are now several women who have accused Senator Franken of groping, but in the days immediately after Leeann Tweeden's original charge, Ms. Morgan, a radio host, claimed she was "stalked and harassed" by him after an appearance in 2000 on Bill Maher's "Politically Incorrect." The internet lit up with the fact that another woman had come forward to accuse Mr. Franken.

Breitbart and Laura Ingraham and Rush Limbaugh seized on her story immediately. And no wonder. Melanie Morgan has praised Sean Hannity's "tenacious search for the truth in the Roy Moore sex allegation story." Melanie Morgan has said that Bill O'Reilly was fired for "dubious reasons." Melanie Morgan is a birther.

She also claims that Mr. Franken "scared the living hell out of me" . . . because he called her three times. Do you believe that Mr. Franken stalked Ms. Morgan? I don't.

The zeal of "believe all women" can also lead down a strangely pedantic path, in which women are told how to properly understand their own pasts. The same year that Ms. Morgan claims Mr. Franken stalked her, Arianna Huffington did a photo shoot for *The New York Post* with the then-comedian, in which he is pictured grabbing her butt and her breast. Now those photos are being trotted out as evidence of his sexual predilections. An anonymous source from the shoot said: "Arianna was pushing his hands away. He was groping her. There was some fun attached to it, but she wasn't enjoying it. She definitely told him to stop and pushed him away."

But Ms. Huffington says that's not true. The notion that she was being assaulted, she tweeted, "trivializes sexual harassment because he was no more 'groping' me than I was 'strangling' him in the photo." The disturbing assumption behind the blind item is that Ms. Huffington was necessarily the victim because of her gender. In fact, as she reports, she was in on the joke and grabbing Mr. Franken right back.

Arianna Huffington isn't an uncomplicated figure: She has been accused of overlooking sexual misconduct at her company. But do we not believe that she knows what happened to her?

From time immemorial, men have been allowed to just be people while women have had to be women. I thought feminism was supposed to liberate us from this flattening of our identity. It's supposed to allow us to just be people, too.

35 What we owe all people, including women, is to listen to them and to respect them and to take them seriously. But we don't owe anyone our unthinking belief.

"Trust but verify" may not have the same ring as "believe all women." But it's a far better policy.

Topics for Critical Thinking and Writing

1. In paragraph 15, Bari Weiss raises the issue of "criminalizing behavior that we previously regarded as presumptuous and boorish" as one of the problems of the #MeToo movement. Do you agree? Why, or why not?
2. Briefly summarize Weiss's argument, identifying her thesis and main supporting points.
3. Do you agree with Emily Linden that a few false allegations are worth the price of gaining justice (para. 17)? Why, or why not?
4. Do you think the #MeToo movement is an example of "mob rule" (para. 22) or a legitimate way to expose perpetrators given the limits of recourse through the justice system? Explain.
5. Consider the argument made by Tambe on page 580. Do you think some people are more or less likely to be "believed" in their accounts or accusations of harassment or assault based on the class, race, sexual orientation, gender identity, and so forth? Explain.
6. Read the lyrics to the popular holiday song "Baby, It's Cold Outside." (If you do not know it, find an audio version and listen to it, too.) Does this song celebrate harassment or coercion (or present either as cute or romantic), as some have claimed? If so, what should be done about it? If not, explain your reading and understanding.

25

American Democracy: Is the Nation in Danger?

IAN BREMMER

Ian Bremmer (b. 1969) is a political scientist whose first book, *The J Curve: A New Way to Understand Why Nations Rise and Fall*, was the *Economist* magazine's Book of the Year when it was published in 2006. Since then, Bremmer has written, edited, and co-authored several other books, including *Superpower: Three Choices for America's Role in the World* (2015) and the *New York Times* best-selling title *Us vs. Them: The Failure of Globalism* (2018), from which this selection was excerpted. Bremmer is a professor at New York University, a contributor and foreign affairs editor at *Time* magazine, and president of the political risk consultancy Eurasia Group, which he founded in 1998.

Us vs. Them: The Failure of Globalism

Will walls kill democracy? Not for everyone. "Do walls work? Just ask Israel about walls," said Donald Trump in February 2017 in a reference to that country's four-hundred-mile security barrier on its border with the West Bank. Israel has also built walls and fences along part of its border with Egypt. Its Iron Dome, Arrow, and David's Sling missile defense systems add a ceiling to these walls by protecting citizens from incoming aerial attacks. It has invested in a floor in the form of a system designed to detect and destroy underground tunnels. Its security services have exceptional ability to track threatening communications and dangerous people through cyberspace, even in the occupied territories, where the risk of terrorist attack might otherwise be among the highest in the world.

Today, Israel appears more secure than at any time since its founding in 1948. It's the only truly stable democracy in the Middle East, one blessed with a free (often rambunctious) press, a world-class education system, rule of law, and independent governing institutions. Inside the walls, about 18 percent of Israeli citizens are Muslims, and they have the right to vote under Israeli law. Five of 120 members of the Knesset, Israel's parliament, are Sunni Muslims. Today, Israel's left struggles to rally its political base with calls for a peace settlement based on a "two-state solution," because arguments that Israel's long-term security depends on it have become more difficult to make.

In other words, Israel's walls work, if you're lucky enough to live inside them. The walls that separate Israel from Gaza and the West Bank make all the difference for quality of life. Outside them, per capita income is about $4,300. Inside, it's above $35,000. Unemployment is just under 18 percent in the West Bank and just over 42 percent in Gaza.[1] Inside the walls, it's just over 4 percent.[2] Youth unemployment outside the walls is 41 percent, but it's just 8.6 percent inside.[3] The infant mortality rate is 14.6 per 1,000 live births in the West Bank, 17.1 in Gaza, and 3.5 inside the walls. Less than 58 percent have Internet access outside the walls vs. nearly 80 percent inside.

Walls don't kill democracy. They protect democracy for "us" by denying it to "them." That's the argument that some will be making more openly in coming years in countries around the world. Walls are satisfying, and they make for good politics. They're not hard to explain, and they offer a visible (if sometimes illusory) sign of security.

5 In many ways, we're talking about attempts to reverse the flow of globalization. To create the appearance of protecting jobs and industries, we'll see a continuing increase in garden-variety protectionism. We'll see more censorship — more restrictions, both old school and more innovative, on the transmission of information and politically resonant ideas. There will also be new barriers to the movement of people. The newest kinds of walls are those that will separate people within societies.

Some of these walls will be designed to protect "national interests," an idea that will be defined ever more broadly. Others will be built to protect the interests of a ruling party or even an individual leader and his family, friends, and clients. Some will be thrown up as quickly and haphazardly as the Berlin Wall, a barrier made of cheap cement and pebbles that divided East and West for twenty-eight years. Others will be digital-age barricades that are much more difficult to climb over or tunnel under. . . .

KEEPING THEM OUT

The past decade has proven again that the cross-border flow of ideas, information, money, goods, and services can have big political implications as it undermines the illusion of control that both leaders and citizens want to protect. But the flow of people is destabilizing in a much more immediate way. Even in the land of the Statue of Liberty, where Ellis Island romanticism has become part of the U.S. national identity, immigration remains a subject of bitter debate. In Europe, the principle of free movement of people through the Schengen area has become a central political concern, and the refusal of some EU members to accept union rules on quotas for Middle Eastern refugees offer early examples of a trend that will intensify.

Whether the question of the moment is jobs, terrorism, or the protection of national identity, governments around the world will become much more selective about who is allowed to enter. Large diaspora populations within countries will use their political clout to try to ensure that doors remain open to their compatriots. But immigration overall will become tighter. As job creation becomes a

[1]"The World Bank in West Bank and Gaza," World Bank, www.worldbank.org/en/country/westbankandgaza/overview.

[2]Hagai Amit, "Israel's Unemployment Rate Falls to Lowest Rate in Decades," *Haaretz*, August 21, 2017, www.haaretz.com/israel-news/business/1.808252.

[3]www.cia.gov/library/publications/the-world-factbook/geos/is.html.

more sensitive subject in years to come, we can expect controversies over immigration even in developing countries, just as the flow of people from crisis-plagued Venezuela has already raised this issue even in Latin America.

In one important respect, future immigration debates will be different from those we've heard before. In the past, there was an obvious counterargument to immigration restrictions. Proimmigration Americans, for example, aware that practical concerns and economic incentives are more persuasive for some people than moral arguments, have asserted that immigrants are needed to take the low-skilled work that few Americans want. Long before Trump glided down the Trump Tower escalator to warn Americans that Mexico was exporting "rapists" into the United States, Ronald Reagan promised to tighten controls at the southern U.S. border, and the number of illegal immigrants temporarily declined as a result. But it wasn't long before prices, particularly for food, began to rise as the drop-off in low-wage labor made agricultural products more expensive to produce. Pocketbook pain then eased political pressure on immigration, and border controls were relaxed.

10 Today, the argument is that low-wage construction workers, many of them immigrants from Latin America, boost American industry. But we're already living in a world where a 3-D printer can construct the foundation of a building in a matter of hours.[4] Whatever the industry, demand for lower-skilled, lower-wage labor will decline sharply in coming years in countries with access to this kind of technology. The moral and cultural arguments in favor of a more open approach to immigration are as strong as ever, but the economic argument is disintegrating, even in countries with fast-aging populations like Germany and Italy that need an influx of foreign migrant labor to power their economies forward. That's bad news for the countries that immigrants come from, where governments will face even greater pressure to create more jobs at home.

There are already a growing number of literal border walls around the world. In fact, there are now more physical barriers at European borders than at any time during the Cold War. According to a 2016 report in *The Economist,* more than forty countries around the world have built fences against more than sixty of their neighbors since the fall of the Berlin Wall.[5] We see them in Asia, South America, and sub-Saharan Africa, as well as in Europe, the Middle East, and the United States. These obstacles leave poorer countries, like Jordan, and middle-income countries, like Greece and Turkey, to house huge numbers of migrants. The supply of refugees will grow as conflict, state failure, extreme climate conditions in poor countries, and the search for a better life push more and more people onto the road. The bottleneck countries can't absorb them all. As the problem builds, pressure will rise further inside wealthier countries for new walls that are higher and stronger.

In response, investment will flow toward new technologies. We can expect infrared sensors and cameras to update border controls.[6] Virtual walls will rise as well. We'll see wider use of biometric tools that allow governments to admit more of "us" and fewer of "them," however they are defined in each country. Governments will face public pressure to make citizenship

[4]Kaya Yurieff, "This Robot Can 3D Print a Building in 14 Hours," CNN, May 2, 2017, http://money.cnn.com/2017/05/02/technology/3d-printed-building-mit/.

[5]"More Neighbours Make More Fences," *Economist*, January 7, 2016, www.economist.com/blogs/graphicdetail/2016/01/daily-chart-5.

[6]Nick Wingfield, "Oculus Founder Plots a Comeback with a Virtual Border Wall," *New York Times*, June 4, 2017, www.nytimes.com/2017/06/04/business/oculus-palmer-luckey-new-start-up.html?utm_source=newsletter&utm_medium=email&utm_campaign=newsletter_axiosam&streamstories&_r=0.

harder to acquire. We'll hear more and louder calls to end "birthright citizenship," the legal right to citizenship in the country in which you are born, within countries that now honor it.

To welcome immigrants with skills and resources ahead of the wretched refuse knocking at the "golden door," citizenship will more often be for sale, and well-educated workers, particularly those with in-demand job skills, are more likely to have the money they need to buy visas.[7] In the United States, the EB-5 visa program already allows wealthy foreigners to accelerate their green card applications by investing hundreds of thousands of dollars in real estate projects.

In Europe, nearly half of EU members offer some form of investment residency or citizenship program. Today, these programs involve relatively small numbers of people, but as demand for restricted access rises within wealthier countries, these projects will expand.[8] Forced to become more creative, states will make wider use of "guest worker" programs that place new restrictions on the work that foreigners are allowed to do, their ability to change jobs, and their wages. As in apartheid South Africa, which required black and mixed-race citizens to live in townships that segregated them from the rest of the population, future "guest worker" programs will place similar restrictions on where foreign workers can live.

SORTING "US" FROM "THEM" WITHIN

We'll also see new methods of sorting citizens within states. "Identity politics" is an old story. Winning support by pitting one group of people against another is older than language. In Malaysia, discrimination that favors the ethnic Malay majority, two-thirds of the population, over ethnic Chinese, Indian, and other citizens is established in law. A day of deadly riots targeted at minorities in 1969 led to adoption of the New Economic Policy, which enshrined quotas for university admission and public-sector jobs. It's "affirmative action" for the majority, with all the positive and negative elements that come with that kind of plan. What was supposed to be temporary has become permanent, as officials in the United Malays National Organization, dominant players in the country's governing coalition, have discovered that discrimination in favor of the ethnic majority continues to win them elections. There are many other examples of this kind of politics around the world, and we'll see many more governments offering subtle and not-so-subtle changes to laws to concentrate power in the hands of those who will protect the government against "them."

There will also be new government efforts to establish greater control over the movement of people. In some countries, governments will try to establish new controls, or tighten existing ones, on the movement of people within borders. For years, Chinese citizens have lived with the *hukou* system, a registration list and internal passport that determines the opportunities and social provisions that a person can receive based on where he or she lives. Before 2014, a migrant from the countryside might pay taxes in the city to which he had moved for work, but could only receive public services and benefits in the province listed as his home. The same restrictions applied to his children, even if they were born in the city. The *hukou* was relaxed beginning in the 1980s to boost economic growth by allowing more movement of cheap labor toward urban

[7]"Golden door" is a reference to the Emma Lazarus poem featured on the Statue of Liberty.

[8]Katie Beck, "Why Citizenship Is Now a Commodity," BBC, May 30, 2017, www.bbc.com/capital/story/20170530-why-citizenship-is-now-a-commodity.

factories, filling cities with huge numbers of second-class citizens. As a result, overcrowded cities have become increasingly difficult to govern, and the system has again been tightened to avoid urban chaos and the political problems it might create.

Today, Russia is the only other country that still uses a form of internal passport—something mainly associated with defunct systems like the Ottoman Empire, Soviet Union, or apartheid South Africa. But in a world of us vs. them, technological changes that give political officials access to unprecedented streams of data on citizens and their behavior will offer governments a tool that some will use to try to control the movement of people, particularly in volatile areas of the country. And there are other ways in which governments could, theoretically, use data to increase the dependence of citizens on the state, allowing for greater political control in times of political crisis.

In the United States, divisions are growing more organically. Voting data from the 2016 U.S. presidential and congressional elections show increasingly sharp differences of political opinion depending on age, ethnicity, income, level of education, and whether the voter lives in a city or a rural area. These identities are interrelated, of course, and technological change will exacerbate these divisions in coming years by benefiting younger, better-educated people who live closer to centers of the modern job market and enjoy rising incomes as a result.

Over the years, there has also been a natural self-sorting process that separates one group from another.[9] Race is an obvious place to start. A 2013 study published in the journal *Education and Urban Society* found that "students are more racially segregated in [U.S.] schools today than they were in the late 1960s and prior to the enforcement of court-ordered desegregation in school districts across the country."[10] A 2013 study from Reuters/Ipsos found that "about 40 percent of white Americans and about 25 percent of non-white Americans are surrounded exclusively by friends of their own race."[11]

The updated 2016 edition of Paul Taylor's 20
The Next America: Boomers, Millennials, and the Looming Generational Showdown, based on a collaboration with the Pew Research Center, provides a wealth of new data and offers a sobering look at the ongoing self-sorting of the United States. First, Taylor reports that racial, social, cultural, economic, religious, gender, generational, and technological changes are pushing Americans into "think-alike communities that reflect not only their politics but their demographics." Second, he notes that the United States will soon become a majority nonwhite nation, and that the percentage of older Americans is headed for record levels. Together, he writes, "these overhauls have led to stark demographic, ideological and cultural differences between the [two major political] parties' bases." Third, political divisions in America are widening. Taylor notes that "92 percent of Republicans are to the right of the median Democrat in their core social, economic and political views, while 94 percent of Democrats are to the left of the median Republican." In 1994, those numbers stood at just 64 percent and 70 percent, respectively. The same study in 2014 also found a doubling in the past two decades in the share of Americans with a highly negative

[9]Charles Blow, "The Self-Sort," *New York Times*, April 11, 2014, www.nytimes.com/2014/04/12/opinion/blow-the-self-sort.html?_r=0.

[10]Dana Thompson Dorsey, "Segregation 2.0: The New Generation of School Segregation in the 21st Century," *Education and Urban Society* 45 (September 2013), pp. 533–547, http://journals.sagepub.com/doi/pdf/10.1177/0013124513486287.

[11]Lindsay Dunsmuir, "Many Americans Have No Friends of Another Race: Poll," Reuters, August 8, 2013, www.reuters.com/article/us-usa-poll-race-idUSBRE97704320130808.

view of the opposing party. Reinforcing the effect, "two-thirds of consistent conservatives and half of consistent liberals say most of their close friends share their political views."[12]

This self-sorting encourages both major political parties to send messages and adopt policies tailored to favored demographic groups to maximize their side's election day turnout while discouraging it on the other side, rather than to moderate core positions to draw support from centrist voters. In short, Republicans don't talk to Democratic voters, and Democrats don't talk to Republicans. The practice of gerrymandering, which allows state legislatures to draw the boundaries that separate congressional districts, has added to the us vs. them dynamic. As of February 2018, voters have given the Republican Party control of two-thirds of state legislatures and half of the nation's governorships. That allowed Republicans to win 55 percent of House seats in the 2016 congressional elections while winning just half of all votes cast.[13]

There are also efforts to use race to drive a political wedge between us and them. We saw this in President Trump's defense of white supremacists following violence during a protest over removal of Civil War statues in Charlottesville, Virginia. We saw it again with Trump's decision to pardon Arizona sheriff Joe Arpaio, who had been convicted of criminal contempt of court after refusing to comply with an order to end the harassment of people he believed, without evidence, to be illegal immigrants. We saw it again when Trump attacked the patriotism of professional football players who protested racism by refusing to stand for the national anthem before games. In each case, Trump made a deliberate decision to arouse the anger of one group of Americans at another for personal political benefit. And he used race as his weapon.

[12]See summary article at Paul Taylor, "The Demographic Trends Shaping American Politics in 2016 and Beyond," Fact Tank, Pew Research Center, January 27, 2016, www.pewresearch.org/fact-tank/2016/01/27/the-demographic-trends-shaping-american-politics-in-2016-and-beyond/.

[13]Richard North Patterson, "The Democrats' Demographic Dilemma," *Boston Globe*, February 14, 2017, www.bostonglobe.com/opinion/2017/02/14/the-democrats-demographic-dilemma/K1LM2FbTRdhk3FX1cGZG4H/story.html.

Topics for Critical Thinking and Writing

1. Why do you think Ian Bremmer opens his argument with a description of Israel and the security measures it takes to protect its people?
2. Examine how Bremmer uses "walls" as both a literal and figurative phenomenon. What is he trying to say?
3. Do some research on the concept of a nation. How is a nation defined? What characteristics must be present for a collective to call itself a nation?
4. Point to some of the forecasts Bremmer makes in his portrait of the future, especially concerning new forms of surveillance and control of the population. Do you think he is overstating things? Why, or why not?
5. Compare Bremmer's argument to the argument made by Carens in "The Case for Open "Borders" (p. 560). Do you think the two essays are complementary? In your answer, highlight any parallels or points of difference you observe in the two arguments.

6. Do some research on the terms *protectionism* and *free trade*. Why would nations choose one over the other as a basis of their economic policies? What are the benefits and drawbacks of each? Provide some examples to offer concrete cases of each type of economic policy.
7. Near the end of the essay, Bremmer examines the divisions between groups of people in the United States. Do divisions among people jeopardize democracy? Or is division the very thing that democracy resolves? Answer in about 500 words.
8. The Electronic Information Privacy Center (EPIC) is a nonprofit, nonpartisan Washington, DC–based research center focusing on privacy and civil liberties issues in the information age. Visit the center's website and use the drop-down menu on the home page titled "Policy Issues" to find the EPIC Domestic Surveillance Project. Select a news item about a policy or proposed policy or choose some other current event related to government surveillance. Explain it, evaluating its purpose and what might be said to support it or criticize it.

DAVID RUNCIMAN

David Runciman (b. 1967) is a professor of politics and history at Cambridge University. He has published numerous reviews for the *London Review of Books* and six books, including *How Democracy Ends* (2018), in which the following selection appeared.

How Democracy Ends

Nothing lasts forever. At some point democracy was always going to pass into the pages of history. No one, not even Francis Fukuyama — who announced the end of history back in 1989 — has believed that its virtues make it immortal.[1] But until very recently, most citizens of Western democracies would have imagined that the end was a long way off. They would not have expected it to happen in their lifetimes. Very few would have thought it might be taking place before their eyes.

Yet here we are, barely two decades into the twenty-first century, and almost from nowhere the question is upon us: is this how democracy ends?

Like many people, I first found myself confronting this question after the election of Donald Trump to the presidency of the United States. To borrow a phrase from philosophy, it looked like the *reductio ad absurdum* of democratic politics: any process that produces such a ridiculous conclusion must have gone seriously wrong somewhere along the way. If Trump is the answer, we are no longer asking the right question. But it's not just Trump. His election is symptomatic of an overheated political climate that appears increasingly unstable, riven with mistrust and mutual intolerance, fuelled by wild accusations and online bullying, a dialogue of the deaf drowning each other out with noise. In many places, not just the United States, democracy is starting to look unhinged.

[1]Francis Fukuyama, "The End of History?," *The National Interest*, Summer 1989 (16), pp. 3–18.

Let me make it clear at the outset: I don't believe that Trump's arrival in the White House spells the end of democracy. America's democratic institutions are designed to withstand all kinds of bumps along the road and Trump's strange, erratic presidency is not outside the bounds of what can be survived. It is more likely that his administration will be followed by something relatively routine than by something even more outlandish. However, Trump's arrival in the White House poses a direct challenge: What would democratic failure in a country like the United States actually involve? What are the things that an established democracy could not survive? We now know we ought to start asking these questions. But we don't know how to answer them.

5 Our political imaginations are stuck with outdated images of what democratic failure looks like. We are trapped in the landscape of the twentieth century. We reach back to the 1930s or to the 1970s for pictures of what happens when democracy falls apart: tanks in the streets; tin-pot dictators barking out messages of national unity, violence and repression in tow. Trump's presidency has drawn widespread comparison with tyrannies of the past. We have been warned not to be complacent in thinking it couldn't happen again. But what of the other danger: that while we are looking out for the familiar signs of failure, our democracies are going wrong in ways with which we are unfamiliar? This strikes me as the greater threat. I do not think there is much chance that we are going back to the 1930s. We are not at a second pre-dawn of fascism, violence and world war. Our societies are too different — too affluent, too elderly, too networked — and our collective historical knowledge of what went wrong then is too entrenched. When democracy ends, we are likely to be surprised by the form it takes. We may not even notice that it is happening because we are looking in the wrong places.

Contemporary political science has little to say about new ways that democracy might fail because it is preoccupied with a different question: how democracy gets going in the first place. This is understandable. During the period that democracy has spread around the world the process has often been two steps forward, one step back. Democracy might get tentatively established in parts of Africa or Latin America or Asia and then a coup or military takeover would snuff it out, before someone tried again. This has happened in places from Chile to South Korea to Kenya. One of the central puzzles of political science is what causes democracy to stick. It is fundamentally a question of trust: people with something to lose from the results of an election have to believe it is worth persevering until the next time. The rich need to trust that the poor won't take their money. The soldiers need to trust that the civilians won't take their guns. Often, that trust breaks down. Then democracy falls apart.

As a result, political scientists tend to think of democratic failure in terms of what they call "backsliding." A democracy reverts back to the point before lasting confidence in its institutions could be established. This is why we look for earlier examples of democratic failure to illuminate what might go wrong in the present. We assume that the end of democracy takes us back to the beginning. The process of creation goes into reverse.

I want to offer a different perspective. What would political failure look like in societies where confidence in democracy is so firmly established that it is hard to shake? The question for the twenty-first century is how long we can persist with institutional arrangements we have grown so used to trusting, that we no longer notice when they have ceased to work. These arrangements include regular elections, which remain the bedrock of democratic politics. But they also encompass democratic legislatures, independent law courts and a free press. All can continue to function as they ought while failing to deliver what they should. A hollowed-out version of democracy risks lulling us into a false sense of security. We might continue to trust in it and to look to it for rescue, even as we seethe with irritation at its inability to answer the call. Democracy could fail while remaining intact.

This analysis might seem at odds with the frequent talk about the loss of trust in democratic politics and politicians across Western societies. It is true that many voters dislike and distrust their elected representatives now more than ever. But it is not the kind of loss of trust that leads people to take up arms against democracy. Instead, it is the kind that leads them to throw up their arms in despair. Democracy can survive that sort of behavior for a long time. Where it ends up is an open question and one I will try to answer. But it does not end up in the 1930s.

10 We should try to avoid the Benjamin Button view of history, which imagines that old things become young again, even as they acquire more experience. History does not go into reverse. It is true that contemporary Western democracy is behaving in ways that seem to echo some of the darkest moments in our past — anyone who watched protestors with swastikas demonstrating on the streets of Charlottesville, Virginia, and then heard the president of the United States managing to find fault on both sides, could be forgiven for fearing the worst. However, grim though these events are, they are not the precursors of a return to something we thought we'd left behind. We really have left the twentieth century behind. We need another frame of reference.

So let me offer a different analogy. It is not perfect, but I hope it helps make sense of the argument. Western democracy is going through a mid-life crisis. That is not to trivialize what's happening: mid-life crises can be disastrous and even fatal. And this is a full-blown crisis. But it needs to be understood in relation to the exhaustion of democracy as well as to its volatility, and to the complacency that is currently on display as well as to the anger. The symptoms of a mid-life crisis include behavior we might associate with someone much younger. But it would be a mistake to assume that the way to understand what's going on is to study how young people behave.

When a miserable middle-aged man buys a motorbike on impulse, it can be dangerous. If he is really unlucky it all ends in a fireball. But it is nothing like as dangerous as when a seventeen-year-old buys a motorbike. More often, it is simply embarrassing. The mid-life motorbike gets ridden a few times and ends up parked in the street. Maybe it gets sold. The crisis will need to be resolved in some other way, if it can be resolved at all. American democracy is in miserable middle age. Donald Trump is its motorbike. It could still end in a fireball. More likely, the crisis will continue and it will need to be resolved in some other way, if it can be resolved at all.

I am conscious that talking about the crisis of democracy in these terms might sound self-indulgent, especially coming from a privileged, middle-aged white man. Acting out like this is a luxury many people around the world cannot afford. These are first world problems. The crisis is real but it is also a bit of a joke. That's what makes it so hard to know how it might end.

To suffer a crisis that comes neither at the beginning nor at the end but somewhere in the middle of a life is to be pulled forwards and backwards at the same time. What pulls us forwards is our wish for something better. What pulls us back is our reluctance to let go of something that has got us this far. The reluctance is understandable: democracy has served us well. The appeal of modern democracy lies in its ability to deliver long-term benefits for societies while providing their individual citizens with a voice. This is a formidable combination. It is easy to see why we don't want to give up on it, at least not yet. However, the choice might not simply be between the whole democratic package and some alternative, anti-democratic package. It may be that the elements that make democracy so attractive continue to operate but that they no longer work together. The package starts to come apart. When an individual starts to unravel, we sometimes say that he or she is in pieces. At present democracy looks like it is in pieces. That does not mean it is unmendable. Not yet.

15 So what are the factors that make the current crisis in democracy unlike those it has faced in the past, when it was younger? I believe there are three fundamental differences. First, political violence is not what it was for earlier generations, either in scale or in character. Western democracies are fundamentally peaceful societies, which means that our most destructive impulses manifest themselves in other ways. There is still violence, of course. But it stalks the fringes of our politics and the recesses of our imaginations, without ever arriving center stage. It is the ghost in this story. Second, the threat of catastrophe has changed. Where the prospect of disaster once had a galvanizing effect, now it tends to be stultifying. We freeze in the face of our fears. Third, the information technology revolution has completely altered the terms on which democracy must operate. We have become dependent on forms of communication and information-sharing that we neither control nor fully understand. All of these features of our democracy are consistent with its getting older.

Whatever happens — unless the end of the world comes first — this will be a drawn-out demise. The current American experience of democracy is at the heart of the story that I tell, but it needs to be understood against the wider experience of democracy in other times and other places. In arguing that we ought to get away from our current fixation with the 1930s, I am not suggesting that history is unimportant. Quite the opposite: our obsession with a few traumatic moments in our past can blind us to the many lessons to be drawn from other points in time. For there is as much to learn from the 1890s as from the 1930s. I go further back: to the 1650s and to the democracy of the ancient world. We need history to help us break free from our unhealthy fixations with our own immediate back story. It is therapy for the middle-aged.

Topics for Critical Thinking and Writing

1. Does David Runciman come across as "anti-Trump" in the opening paragraphs of this essay? How does he contextualize the election of Donald Trump in his framework of examining the "end of democracy"?
2. Describe in your own words what Runciman means when he claims, "We are trapped in the landscape of the twentieth century" when we imagine democratic failure (para. 5)? Why, according to Runciman, is that a problem?
3. Do you think Runciman's analogy comparing democracy to a middle-aged person having a midlife crisis is effective? Why, or why not? What further parallels can you draw to extend the analogy, or what contradictions can you show that challenge it?

4. Political commentators frequently point out that although we think of our current times as divided and hostile, the United States has always had political division at the heart of its character as a democracy (indeed, the nation had a Civil War from 1861 to 1865). Do you think the divisions today are more potent, powerful, or dangerous than other times besides the Civil War? Answer this question in 500 to 1,000 words, looking to another period or decade in US history, examining the dominant political conflicts of that time, and comparing them to today.
5. In assessing the unique character of today's crisis in democracy, Runciman writes, "Where the prospect of disaster once had a galvanizing effect, now it tends to be stultifying" (para. 15). Do Americans lack the resolve and consensus to deal with the nation's most serious threats? Either way you answer, show what pushes forward or impedes progress on one or more of the most pressing problems.
6. Do you think the digital revolution and the advent of the internet help or hurt democracy? Address this question in an essay of 500 to 750 words.

SEBASTIEN THIBAULT

Sebastien Thibault is a Canadian illustrator and graphic designer known for penetrating artwork on political and social issues. His work has appeared in numerous publications, including *Rolling Stone*, the *Wall Street Journal*, the *Guardian*, and *Time* magazine. The illustration shown here was one of several accompanying an article about political division in the United States. It was published in *The Walrus* on November 1, 2018.

America's Collapse

Anna Goodson Illustration & Motion

Topics for Critical Thinking and Writing

1. Examine Sebastien Thibault's illustration and use the strategies for seeing and looking on page 137 to discuss how its meaning is constructed. That is, inventory the elements of the image and discuss the connotative meanings of each element and how they work together to form a visual argument.
2. Consider the model for accommodating, negotiating, or resisting the meaning of a visual image (p. 146) and argue against the intended meaning of this illustration by resisting its message.
3. Do you think political divisions in the United States are overstated or exaggerated in the media? Is it fair to portray such divisions in the way Thibault does?

RUSSEL MUIRHEAD AND NANCY ROSENBLUM

Russel Muirhead (b. 1965) is the Robert Clements Professor of Democracy and Politics at Dartmouth College, where he is chair of the government department. He is a leading authority on democratic theory and political economy and has published his ideas widely, including in his 2004 book *Just Work.*

Nancy Rosenblum (b. 1947) is a professor of political science and has taught at both Harvard University and Brown University. Among her many award-winning books on political theory, her 2010 work *On the Side of the Angels: An Appreciation of Parties and Partisanship* won the Walter Channing Cabot Award for scholarly eminence at Harvard University. Her most recent book, *Good Neighbors: The Democracy of Everyday Life in America*, was published by Princeton University Press in 2016. The following was published in the journal *Dissent* in 2018.

The New Conspiracists

The conspiracist mindset moved into the White House with the election of Donald Trump as president of the United States. Trump is the most powerful person who views politics through a miasma of secret, malignant intent, but he's not the only one. Alex Jones, a syndicated radio talk show host from Austin, Texas, has become a celebrity by peddling conspiracy. Fox News is not above giving its audience the conspiracy they want to hear — even if it turns out to be false, as was "pundit" Andrew Napolitano's charge that British intelligence (on President Obama's orders) spied on Trump during the 2016 campaign. Amplifying charges by characters such as Napolitano are websites like *Infowars* (which is operated by Jones) or the *Gateway Pundit*, which, like burbling mud pots, release new conspiracies by the day. And underlying the officials, celebrities, and the fantasy news sites are online forums like Reddit, where anyone can share conspiracy theories with an audience of thousands at the click of a button.

Conspiracism has traveled from the margins to the mainstream, infusing public life and altering the bounds of what is acceptable in democratic politics. Aside from the presidency, conspiratorial designs are attributed to judges, elected representatives, and civil servants working in federal agencies. No official action is immune to being labelled a conspiracy. Rewording questions in the Census, for instance, is cast as a conspiracy to make the Affordable Care Act look more successful. Even acts of nature point to secret conspiratorial machinations: in 2012, some insisted that Hurricane Sandy was engineered by scientists at the direction of President Obama to help secure his reelection.

Conspiracism is not new, of course, but the conspiracism we see today does introduce something new — conspiracy without the theory. And it betrays a new destructive impulse: to delegitimate the government. Often the aim is merely to deligitimate an individual or a specific office. The charge that Obama conspired to fake his birth certificate only aimed at Obama's legitimacy. Similarly, the charge that the National Oceanic and Atmospheric Administration publicized flawed data in order to make global warming look more menacing was designed only to demote the authority of climate scientists working for the government. But the effects of the new strategy cannot be contained to one person or entity. The ultimate effect of the new conspiracism will be to delegitimate democracy itself.

Conventional conspiracism makes sense of a disorderly and complicated world by insisting that powerful human beings can and do control events. In this way, it gives order and meaning to apparently random occurrences. And in making sense of things, conspiracism insists on proportionality. JFK's assassination, this type of thinking goes, was not the doing of a lone gunman — as if one person acting alone could defy the entire U.S. government and change the course of history. Similarly, the brazen attacks on the World Trade Center and the Pentagon on 9/11 could not have been the work of fewer than two dozen men plotting in a remote corner of Afghanistan. So conspiracist explanations insist that the U.S. government must have been complicit in the strikes.

Conspiracism insists that the truth is not on the surface: things are not as they seem, and conspiracism is a sort of detective work. Once all the facts — especially facts ominously withheld by reliable sources and omitted from official reports — are scrupulously amassed and the plot uncovered, secret machinations make sense of seemingly disconnected events. What historian Bernard Bailyn observed of the conspiracism that flourished in the Revolutionary era remains characteristic of conspiracism today: "once assumed [the picture] could not be easily dispelled: denial only confirmed it, since what conspirators profess is not what they believe; the ostensible is not the real; and the real is deliberately malign."

When conspiracists attribute intention where in fact there is only accident and coincidence, reject authoritative standards of evidence and falsifiability, and seal themselves off from any form of correction, their conspiracism can seem like a form of paranoia — a delusional insistence that one is the victim of a hostile world. This is not to say that all conspiracy theories are wrong; sometimes what conspiracists allege is really there. Yet warranted or not, conventional conspiracy theories offer both an explanation of the alleged danger and a guide to the actions necessary to save the nation or the world.

The new conspiracism we are seeing today, however, often dispenses with any explanations or evidence, and is unconcerned with uncovering a pattern or identifying the operators plotting in the shadows. Instead, it offers only innuendo and verbal gesture, as exemplified in President Trump's phrase, "people are saying." Conspiracy without the theory can corrode confidence in government, but it cannot give meaning to events or guide constructive collective action.

The effect of conspiratorial thinking, once it ceases to function as any sort of explanation, is delegitimation. The new conspiracist accusations seek not only to unmask and disempower those they accuse but to deny their standing to argue, explain, persuade, and decide. Conspiracism rejects their authority. In the end, the consequences of delegitimation are not targeted or discrete but encompassing.

CONSPIRACY WITHOUT THE THEORY

The new conspiracist mindset posits the meaning of events with certainty, but in contrast to conventional conspiracism — the myriad accounts of JFK's assassination or 9/11, say — it has little interest in explanation. "Rigged" was a single word that in the election of 2016 had the power to evoke sinister intentions, fantastic plots, and an awesome capacity to mobilize three million illegal voters to support Hillary Clinton for president and then to cover it up. In Trump's (and Bannon's) insistence that busloads of fraudulent voters were sent to vote against him in the New Hampshire primary there are no stray facts to account for: no local officials testify to having been besieged by hundreds or thousands of new voters exiting from fleets of busses. The baseless charge of voter fraud in New Hampshire is designed to obscure the reality that Trump lost the popular vote: it is an attempt to enhance Trump's legitimacy by delegitimizing the electoral process.

The new, lazy conspiracism satisfies itself 10
with vague assertions. For instance, when a former Washington D.C. homicide investigator wrote on Facebook, referring to Justice Scalia's death: "My gut tells me there is something fishy going on in Texas." References to unnamed actors ("people are saying") are elastic; they can embrace a changing cast of public enemies and a wide but unspecified repertoire of nefarious acts. Complicity by insinuation and equivocation also evades responsibility. A telling example was Mike Huckabee's seemingly off-hand comment in relation to Obama's birth certificate in 2011: "I would love to know more. What I know is troubling enough."

The manner of coy insinuation that marks the new conspiracism both absolves the speaker of responsibility for the charge he's putting forth and invites endless investigation. As Trump said about a *National Enquirer* story that linked Texas senator Ted Cruz's father with JFK's assassination, "even if it isn't totally true, there's something there." Or, as Representative Bryan Zollinger (R-ID) said about the allegation that Democratic Party officials lured white nationalists and antifascist protestors to Charlottesville in order to manufacture a clash, "I am not saying it is true, but I am suggesting that it is completely plausible."

Where nothing is true but everything is plausible, it becomes respectable, even necessary, to insert conspiracism into the official business of democratic institutions. Trump enlisted administration officials to affirm his ungrounded claim that he was being wiretapped by former president Obama ("during the very sacred election process"), and followed up with a demand for a congressional investigation. In another example from 2013, Congress held a joint hearing to investigate ammunition purchases by the Department of Homeland Security, in response to charges that the federal government was stockpiling arms in preparation for a violent campaign against American citizens. Conspiracism simultaneously degrades and exploits Congress, the Justice Department, intelligence agencies, and the press.

The new conspiracism — conspiracy without the theory — is potent and divisive. It pretends to own reality. It carries us beyond partisan polarization to epistemic polarization, so that Americans are in conflict about nothing less than what it means to know something. And through disinterest in explanation and disregard for the logic of evidence and argument, it is energetic and all-encompassing in its targets.

THE NEW CONSPIRACISM'S PARTISAN PENUMBRA

The ultimate consequence of the new conspiracism is the destruction of the administrative state, a state with the capacity to design and implement long-term policy. The administrative state is the legacy of the Progressive era and the New Deal. To be sure, every conspiracy theory is not designed to attack the administrative state in toto. It is often only one institution (like the EPA) or one actor (such as President Obama) that is the target. But the blizzard of conspiracy theories creates whiteout conditions that obscure any perception of governmental integrity. The consequence of conspiracism is not simply distrust; it feeds the assumption that the government is staffed by those who are actively hostile to the common interest.

15 In its consequences for the administrative state, today's conspiracism is congruent with partisan Republican purposes, because it has the effect of derailing the operations of liberal policies and programs that defined national politics in the twentieth century. In its modest iteration, conservatism sought to correct the alleged excesses of New Deal liberalism while securing its core. As Ronald Reagan explained, in his youth he shared the goals of Roosevelt and the New Deal, but as he saw it, the Democratic Party became more extreme. "I didn't leave the Democratic Party," Reagan pronounced, "the Party left me." In its current, more radical iteration, conservatism seeks to reverse the New Deal legacy altogether. It was also Reagan who gave radical Republicanism its organizing principle: "government is not the solution to our problem. Government is the problem." This more radical and destructive impulse was exemplified by Rick Perry when he insisted during the presidential campaign of 2011 that he would eliminate three federal agencies, but could only name two. The specifics do not matter — what matters is that government be dismantled.

Yet once in power, radical conservatism runs into a formidable obstacle: dismantling government is not very popular. People expect government to protect them from dangerous products, to monitor the safety of the water and food supply, to assist victims of natural disasters, to ensure access to healthcare, to regulate markets, to prosecute frauds, and so on. Conspiracism helps accomplish what radical conservatives in office cannot by delegitimizing the institutions that deliver these policies. It dissolves the authority of knowledge-producing institutions inside and outside government, communities of expertise, and conventions of fact and argument necessary to make effective decisions.

Conspiracism's attack has a partisan penumbra, then, but its effects are totalizing and go well beyond what even radical conservatives want. It destroys not only liberal policies but the institutional capacities of the state wholesale. The communities of special knowledge — the doctors and economists and engineers who regulate the safety of airplanes, who steward the macroeconomy toward low inflation and sustainable growth — do not reside on one side of the partisan divide. To undermine them is not to weaken liberalism or progressivism or the left but to weaken democracy. Conspiracism is the acid that dissolves the institutions, processes, and standards of justification that make government possible.

THE DELEGITIMATION OF POLITICAL PARTIES

Political parties are among the most important institutions that conspiracism corrodes. Americans are so used to disparaging parties and partisans that we don't spring to their defense as we do to (ironically) the FBI. From George Washington to Barack Obama, anti-partisanship has been a staple of American political life. Against the background of endemic anti-partisanship and weak parties, conspiracism goes about the business of delegitimizing the democratic state.

It starts with delegitimizing opposition candidates. The most infamous case was the Republican story about a conspiracy to conceal President Obama's foreign birth. President Trump is the most notorious birther, and helped bring the conspiracy into the mainstream. The conspiracy moved quickly from the periphery of political discourse to the formal institutions of politics, and threatened to keep Obama's name from appearing on the Kansas ballot in the reelection campaign of 2012 — the state where Obama's own mother was born. Kansas Secretary of State Kris Kobach said at the time, "I don't think it's a frivolous objection." Kobach said of the charge that Obama was foreign-born: "I do think the factual record could be supplemented." This was more than a year after the White House released Obama's "long form" birth certificate.

Allegations of conspiracy extend beyond 20
this or that candidate or official to the political opposition altogether. Not content with the hyper-criticism and incivility that mark polarized partisanship, conspiracists cast the Democratic Party as a danger to the nation. The conspiracist mindset is part of a larger tendency to paint the opposition as a revolutionary party surreptitiously altering national identity and creating an alien nation. The party is said to be the agent of Muslims, Jews, blacks, immigrants — exploiting the electoral process to subvert America as a Christian nation, to "mongrelize" a white population, to empower "takers and suckers," to extend rights to outsiders, to cede sovereignty to the "new world order." As an existential threat (not merely an opponent), President Obama is cast by some, like Senator Ted Cruz (R-TX), as a "lawless" president, and by others, like conservative attorney Cleta Mitchell, as a "dictatorial tyrant."

And of course, the opposition is said to abet foreign enemies. Their foreign policy of international aggression (or failure to act aggressively) is not just ineffective or immoral but designed to undermine the United States' power and status in the world. Hillary Clinton, according to President Trump, "meets in secret with international banks to plot the destruction of U.S. sovereignty."

The objective in all this is not only defeating the opposition in an election but assuring their permanent incapacitation. That was Steve Bannon's consolation at a moment when he thought Trump would lose the election: "Our back-up strategy is to f--k her [Clinton] up so bad that she can't govern."

Senate Republicans' refusal to consider Judge Merrick Garland's nomination to the Supreme Court was tactical, of course, designed to entrench a conservative majority on the court. But the terms of refusal are telling. Stalling until the next election in order to "let the voters decide" is a public disavowal of the authority of voters who elected President Obama in 2012.

This is delegitimation — not just opposing or discrediting or defeating. When conspiracism delegitimizes regulated party rivalry, loyal opposition, and the tradition of "agreeing to disagree" it strikes at the bedrock of representative democracy.

The ultimate moment in delegitimizing democratic politics is to impugn all parties. Trump is perfectly cast to preside over such a moment. He was never loyal to a party. His presidential campaign did not have the support of the national Republican leadership, party elites, or donors. He does not call his supporters Republicans. The conspiracist-in-chief may destroy the Republican Party, but he is not reshaping it or organizing another. He is preparing the public for a politics without parties.

True, parties and partisans frustrate this impulsive personality. He would work without and around them, bully or disregard them. But more important, he and networks of conspiracists see parties as cabals. In Trump's view, Democratic/Obama "holdovers" at the National Security Council, the State Department, and other agencies are pulling the strings of the "deep state," undermining the country and his rightful authority. In this respect, the Trump administration sounds much like figures such as Alex Jones, who sees the federal government as a "Trojan horse" harboring "enemies within." And Democrats are not the only ones with nefarious, concealed aims. Republicans are complicit. The parties collude. They are all agents of (pick the conspiracy of the moment) global elites who rule the world. Both parties are responsible for the "American carnage" Trump conjured up in his apocalyptic campaign speeches.

NEW CONSPIRACISM VERSUS PROGRESSIVE ANTIPARTYISM

The United States has a history of antipartyism, but today's conspiracism deviates from its antecedents. For, in the past, a common reason for wanting to do away with parties and partisanship was democratic reform — aimed at *enhancing* democracy.

Progressivism early in the twentieth century saw political parties as "perverters of the democratic spirit," part of a system shrouded in corruption and fraud. Progressives ferreted out facts and observed patterns and wove them into detailed accounts of conspiracy; they called it muckraking. They championed nonpartisan local government and reliance on expertise. They accepted electoral democracy, but insisted on a secret ballot and primary elections in which candidates were not identified with a party and voters were independents, not partisans. And like many progressives today, they championed direct participatory democracy: initiatives and referenda, recall, and constitutional conventions.

By contrast, the new conspiracists' delegitimation of parties is not a sober confrontation with the limitations of party democracy. There is no interest in democratic reform, no prescription for institutional innovation, or any form of collective democratic action.

Rather than appeal to his fellow partisans, Trump instead appeals to "real Americans."

After all, we don't need parties if there is only one collective identity, one community, one people with only one voice. Trump gives us identity politics with a vengeance. Because unlike ethnic or racial identities, the category of "real Americans" is not just one element of the American polity.

The value of parties lies in the way they connect the pluralism of a free society to the formal institutions of politics. And though every partisan believes she is "on the side of the angels," partisans do not imagine they speak for the whole or that their victory is anything but partial and temporary. It takes humility not to claim to be the voice of "the nation" or "the people," and to recognize opposition as legitimate.

Today's antipartyism — with its virulent populist trappings and eruptions of justificatory conspiracism — is a form of malignant anti-pluralism. This is delegitimation of democracy at the deepest level, penetrating beyond the formal state to society.

THERE ARE NO ALTERNATIVES

What, exactly, the new conspiracist mindset wants to put in place of the institutions, practices, and policies it degrades is uncertain. Perhaps nothing at all. For despite its partisan penumbra — its alignment with radical conservatism — conspiracism today is not embedded in an ideology, a political program or movement, an understanding of justice or a constitutional view (this is why discerning conservatives have so forcefully resisted endorsing Trump's conspiracism). Conspiracism claims to uncover odious plots against the Constitution, the fabric of society, sacred American values, national identity — but not for the sake of upholding any constitutional theory, or affirming any vision of society, or installing any coherent understanding of American values and national identity.

Some commentators see in conspiracism an aspiration to overturn the established political order for the sake of a new regime — a populist authoritarian regime unconstrained by constitutional limitations, for example. This is wrong. To be sure, Trump has a few policies he favors, some venal, like lower estate taxes. He indulges his hostility toward immigrants, affinity for white supremacy and anti-Semitism, lust for thuggery, and disdain for legal restraints. But backlash garnished with a handful of grievances and bad policies is not a political theory. We're witness to the fact that it does not take an alternative ideology or program — communism, authoritarianism, theism, fascism, nativism — to delegitimize democracy. Sterile conspiracism does the work.

The new conspiracism is destabilizing, degrading, and delegitimizing, without a countervailing constructive impulse, as if whatever rises from the detritus of constitutional democracy is less important and less captivating than narratives of grievance, catastrophe, and humiliation.

This is striking. Fearsome fascist and totalitarian regimes, revolutionary politics, even apocalyptic movements that would destroy the world to save it all envision what the next world or our own revivified world will be like. Disregard for what might be constructed in place of what is destroyed goes against the grain of human hopefulness. It instead reveals a conspiracist mindset trapped in an angry private reality of the moment, with no next steps or better ways forward.

Contemporary politics is a lesson in what delegitimation looks like. Authorities, institutions, and reasoning based on standards of evidence and argument are held in contempt, its principals charged with malicious intent. Officials are "so-called" officials (for example, "the quote president" Obama) and can be justifiably demeaned, subverted, undermined, or declared criminal. Agencies and knowledge-producing institutions can be hollowed out. Parties can be dismissed as cabals. Delegitimation proceeds by assaulting, degrading, and violating the institutions and norms that make democracy possible.

Social scientists since Weber (or Aristotle) have studied legitimacy and how authorities gain it. The process of delegitimation, however, especially in wealthy, historically stable democracies, is much less well understood. In a sense, we are on our own.

What can be done? First, we must call out conspiracists' claim to reality. Speaking truth to conspiracy is a moral imperative. It is a sign of dangerous times that so few responsible office-holders, and barely any among conservatives, do.

40 We also need democratic narratives as compelling as the accusations conjured by conspiracists. Speaking truth to conspiracy is disarming, when it is, not because it offers facts or represents sounder reasoning but because it supports a story that makes better sense to citizens.

Yet we also need more. When conspiracism becomes a regular element of public life, we need to defend the ordinary routines of democratic politics. That means not only adherence to the customary and legal processes of constitutional democracy by both parties (and civil society groups and others) but also literally articulating them, pedagogically, so citizens appreciate the purpose of democratic norms. Citizens need to witness exhibitions of institutional integrity and regular politics at work, such as when the chair of a congressional intelligence committee announces that he will investigate as the evidence warrants rather than act at President Trump's direction. These deliberate exhibitions of institutional integrity and regular democratic politics have to be meaningful, producing recognizably fair outcomes in the public interest. With that, the conspiracist threat to democratic legitimacy may be called out and contained.

Reversing the damage already done, however, is more complicated. Conspiracism has an extended half-life. Re-legitimation will be long and arduous. The challenge is clear: as Archibald MacLeish once said, "It is not enough, in this war of hoaxes and delusions and perpetuated lies, to be merely honest. It is necessary also to be wise."

Topics for Critical Thinking and Writing

1. Explore the psychology of conspiracies. Why are conspiracies and conspiracy theories so alluring? What do Russel Muirhead and Nancy Rosenblum think? What do you think?
2. In paragraph 2, the authors argue that "conspiracism has traveled from the margins to the mainstream." Point to some evidence for this claim by drawing from Muirhead and Rosenblum or adding your own observations and examples.
3. Explain what Muirhead and Rosenblum mean by arguing against the "new" conspiracy theories (as opposed to the "old" ones). Why do they see the new conspiracists as particularly dangerous?

4. Do some research on one of the conspiracy theories mentioned by Muirhead and Rosenblum and compare what conspiracists believe to what more conventional, accepted beliefs are. In 500 to 1,000 words, write an essay in which you weigh the evidence and determine whether or not you believe the conspiracy. (Use the checklist for evaluating the reliability of sources on page 270. Which sources are more reliable, and why?)
5. Argue for or against the following claim: Muirhead and Rosenblum are part of a conspiracy to undermine the legitimacy and authority of the Trump administration. Make this argument in 500 to 1,000 words.
6. Invent your own conspiracy theory. Describe it in about 500 words and feel free to be humorous. You may be imaginative, or you might think of a time when you were paranoid that somebody or some group "had it out for you." What evidence did you have? How did you put the evidence together to support your theory?

GANESH SITARAMAN

Ganesh Sitaraman is a professor of law at Vanderbilt University Law School and a senior fellow at the Center for American Progress. He is also policy director and senior counsel advisor to Senator Elizabeth Warren. His notable books include *The Counterinsurgent's Constitution: Law in the Age of Small Wars* (2012) and *The Crisis of the Middle-Class Constitution* (2017), and he has published widely in various law reviews. The following essay was published in the *New Republic* in May 2017.

Divided We Fall

It only took a week after Donald Trump's inauguration before Democrats and the media began to warn that our democracy faces a grave and potentially fatal threat. On the second weekend of Trump's presidency, when customs officials began enforcing his hastily imposed ban on travel from Muslim nations, Senator Cory Booker dashed out to Dulles Airport and told a crowd of protesters that the American rule of law was under assault. "I believe it's a constitutional crisis," Booker declared. Two days later, when Trump fired acting Attorney General Sally Yates for refusing to enforce the ban, CNN's Wolf Blitzer practically had the question, "Are we on the verge of a constitutional crisis?" on auto-repeat. And when Trump blasted the "so-called judge" who overturned the travel ban, Senator Richard Blumenthal wasted no time in predicting the worst: "We're careening, literally, toward a constitutional crisis."

We weren't. The ban may have been illegal, and deeply un-American, but its issuance alone didn't present an existential threat to the republic. Lawyers sprang into action, and federal judges halted the ban's enforcement. Even the president's tweeted response indicated that the Constitution was still in working order: "SEE YOU IN COURT."

The alarm over the travel ban reflected the wider fear that many Americans have felt ever since Trump was elected. Indeed, the mere fact of his victory struck many on the left as nothing short of a national emergency—a threat to the very nature of American democracy. But in their vigilance, many politicians and pundits are missing a deeper and more profound peril. We aren't "careening" toward a constitutional crisis, as Senator Blumenthal feared. We've been sinking into one for years — and the Constitution isn't designed to get us out of it.

Long before Trump came along, America was already mired in a constitutional crisis — one that crept up on us gradually, as historical transformations always do. The reason is simple: Our Constitution wasn't built for a country with massive economic inequality and deeply entrenched political divisions. The three times in our history when the republic has faced a threat to its very existence — the Civil War, the Gilded Age through the Great Depression, and the present moment — the crisis arose because America had evolved in ways the Founders could only dimly imagine. In each instance, the social conditions of the country no longer matched the Constitution.

Trump is a symptom, not the cause, of the 5
crisis we now face. It is written, in fact, into the very fabric of our society. And the only way we'll avert the disintegration of our political system — as Lincoln and the abolitionists did in their day, and the Roosevelts and the progressives did in theirs — is first to understand its origins.

If you ask many Americans today, they'll tell you exactly who the Founding Fathers were: a pack of rich white men who rigged the Constitution to serve their own financial and political interests. Sure, they talked like radical egalitarians. But they also denied women the vote, slapped a specific numeric value on the political worth of slaves, and enshrined human bondage as wholly compatible with a democracy founded on "unalienable rights."

That's true enough. But it's easy to forget, at the historical distance that separates us from the eighteenth century, that America in its founding era was, in the relative terms of the time, the most economically equal place on Earth. Unlike their revolutionary counterparts in France, the Founders didn't have to account for — or break from — centuries of entrenched wealth and property. There was no hereditary nobility in America. No property rules that concentrated wealth. No history of feudalism. Instead, there were vast lands to the West, which meant that any white man could work his way into the middle class. Even William Manning, one of America's first great champions of "the many" versus "the few," acknowledged in 1799, "We are on an equality as to property [compared] to what they are in the old countries."

The Founders shaped their new republic around its economic parity. Nothing short of "equality of property," declared Noah Webster, could ensure the social stability and national solidarity that any constitutional system needs to function properly. This, Webster added, was "the very *soul of a republic*." Our Constitution, in short, was literally founded on an egalitarian distribution of wealth. Without property being "pretty equally divided," the anti-federalist Samuel Bryan warned during ratification, "the nature of the government is changed, and an aristocracy, monarchy, or despotism will rise on its ruin."

For most of the world's constitutional history, property had been anything but "pretty equally divided." Political systems were often created to accommodate economic *inequality*, and to ward off catastrophic clashes between the rich and poor; social stability was achieved, at least theoretically, by giving each class a share in governance. Think, for instance, of Britain's House of Lords (for the rich) and House of Commons (for the masses) or Rome's tribune of the plebs, which allowed poor citizens to veto the decisions of the patrician senators.

10 Our Constitution, by contrast, made no such accommodations to economic inequality. There are no wealth requirements for U.S. senators, and no cap on wealth for admission to the House. In fact, there are no provisions in our constitutional structure — not one — that account for differences in economic class. This represented an extraordinary transformation in the way countries govern themselves. Instead of drafting a constitution to resolve divisions created by wealth and poverty, the Founders asserted that all men were created equal, and established a government that depended on all men remaining economic equals.

The Founders understood full well that if severe economic inequality emerged, their democratic experiment would collapse. The rich would gradually take over the government, passing laws to benefit themselves at the expense of everyone else. When America's wealthy began to "plunder the poor," a Virginia politician warned in 1814, it would be "slow and legal." Sooner or later, the masses would respond — but not through a violent uprising. Instead, they would turn to a figure who would know how to manipulate their resentments. Of "those men who have overturned the liberty of republics," Alexander Hamilton observed in *The Federalist Papers*, "the greatest number have begun their career by paying an obsequious court to the people; commencing demagogues, and ending tyrants."

But in preindustrial America, the onset of mass inequality — and the social and political divisions that grow from it — was only a distant possibility. In a society with relative equality, the only "checks and balances" needed were between three separate — and equal — branches of government. "The Founding Fathers devised a scheme to deal with conflict," the political scientist Louis Hartz once observed, "that could only survive in a land of solidarity."

"Solidarity," of course, is also a relative term, and a fragile foundation on which to build a national government. Throughout the nineteenth century, as the regional divide over slavery grew, some Americans came to believe that the only solution was to alter the Constitution to account for the increasingly deep fractures — to find an American equivalent of the Lords and Commons. In the buildup to the Civil War, Senator John C. Calhoun of South Carolina proposed splitting the presidency in two: one president from the North, one from the South. The co-presidents would have to agree before any law could take effect. "Nothing short of this," he warned, "could restore harmony and tranquility to the union."

The Civil War, our greatest constitutional crisis, stemmed directly from the Founders' failure to create a framework for forging solidarity out of division. And in the decades after the war's brutal resolution, sweeping economic changes would lead to a second crisis — rooted in another stark social divide — at the turn of the twentieth century. With industrialization, urbanization, the closing of the frontier, and the shift from artisanal and agricultural work to wage labor in factories, the Constitution once again strained at its seams.

15 James Madison, for one, had foreseen that the republic would confront such challenges. In 1788, he estimated that America had 25 years before the population density across the entire country would match that of the Eastern states. By 1829, thanks to westward expansion, he'd revised his estimate: Within a century, Madison thought, the mass of Americans would be

"reduced by a competition for employment to wages which would afford them the bare necessities of life." As the "proportion being without property" increased, the system would have to be overhauled for representative democracy to survive. "The institutions and laws of the country must be adapted," Madison wrote, "and it will require for the task all the wisdom of the wisest patriots."

When the industrial age plunged America into its second constitutional crisis, wise patriots answered Madison's call. From the 1890s to the 1930s, populists, progressives, and New Dealers alleviated the strain on our system by passing a combination of new laws and constitutional amendments. Anti-trust measures broke up the concentration of economic power. Working hours were regulated, and labor unions offset the power of employers. The Constitution was amended to establish a progressive income tax, helping redistribute superconcentrated wealth. The people's voting power was expanded by requiring the direct election of U.S. senators, permitting citizens to float ballot initiatives to change laws by popular vote, and extending the franchise to women. These reforms were all designed to realign economic and political power — to give a fair measure of it back to the people. Only then could the Constitution work again as intended.

By the 1960s, the progressive patriots had largely succeeded. This was the age of the Great Compression: The gross domestic product soared, wages rose, and the middle class boomed. Not since the founding era had America seen such economic equality. At the same time, progressives took aim at social divisions, ending Jim Crow segregation and beginning to ensure equal rights for women, gays, and lesbians, and the disabled. As the 1970s dawned, the great American experiment faced a new challenge: Could the republic sustain an equal economy *and* an inclusive social community?

This time, however, our leaders failed us. Instead of promoting policies to continue broad-based economic growth, they passed tax breaks for the wealthy and gutted regulations that protected workers and consumers. Rather than work toward social harmony, they took advantage of growing economic anxieties and used dog-whistle politics to stir racial resentments. And if you couldn't blame "those people" for your problems, you could always blame the government, which Ronald Reagan so memorably cast in his first inaugural address as "not the solution," but "the problem."

As much as liberals would like to chalk up this disastrous state of affairs to white racism, or pin it to the rise of reactionary conservatism, Democrats have done their part to contribute to the crisis. For decades, many Democrats have gone along with economic reforms that aided the rich, and they have increasingly demonized working-class whites as ignoramuses, contributing to a destructive tit for tat that only keeps escalating.

By neglecting the economic conditions 20
necessary to sustain our republic, we've fueled a slow-burning constitutional crisis. As a battery of studies over the past decade have shown, the rich now dominate our system of governance. They participate more at every stage of the political process — from meeting candidates, to donating to their campaigns, to voting and running for office. Some scholars argue that the majority's views now have *zero* impact on public policy; all is dictated by the interests of wealthy elites. It's no wonder that trust in government has sunk to all-time lows.

Just as the Founders feared, our sense of national solidarity could not survive the rise of economic inequality. We have divided ourselves geographically, with liberals amassing in urban areas and blue states, and conservatives in rural and red. We get our news from sources that reflect our partisan assumptions, and we make our political decisions based on fundamentally incompatible ways of looking at democracy. We may be governed by a single Constitution, but we are becoming, for all intents and purposes, two countries.

The terrifying thing is that all these transformations — economic, political, and social — make reform even more difficult to achieve. As the wealthy rig the system in their favor, it gets harder to tax the rich, bust up monopolies, help working families, and reduce the influence of money in our politics. As social divisions become more entrenched, it becomes easier to keep everyone divided through fear-mongering and scapegoating. To function properly, the Constitution requires equality and solidarity — and once those are gone, it contains no mechanism to restore them.

It would be nice to think that our current crisis could be solved by getting rid of President Trump. But if he were driven from office and forced into exile at Mar-a-Lago, the conditions that created the crisis would still be with us. There's no quick fix to a problem that has been half a century in the making.

Thanks to the Constitution's checks and balances, a president alone can't fix the republic any more than he can destroy it. Only a new surge of progressive patriotism, modeled on the one that took hold a century ago, can save our democracy. Like the wise patriots of the Gilded Age, the progressive patriots of the twenty-first century will have to rebuild the bedrock of economic opportunity, stone by stone: a fair tax system, tougher financial regulations, more investments in education and infrastructure. The foundations of participatory democracy must also be rebuilt, by liberalizing election laws and enabling more Americans to vote. Only then can we hope to rediscover a sense of common purpose that the Founding Fathers knew was a prerequisite for their experiment to succeed.

It sounds impossible, of course. Donald 25
Trump's in the White House. Anti-government, trickle-down conservatives dominate Congress, the courts, and most state legislatures. How can we even dream about reversing such entrenched inequality, or of healing our seemingly bottomless social rifts?

Our hope rests partly in our history. Hard as it is to believe, we have been here before. We've stared into a dark future in which the Constitution no longer functions, in which democracy is replaced by oligarchy or tyranny. But wise patriots found a way to adapt. It took more than one election, one candidate, one party. A crisis decades in the making will take decades to resolve.

Our greatest hope, ironically, rests in the very ferocity of our political climate. Trump wasn't elected because conservative voters are unaware that America is in a mortal crisis. A socialist like Bernie Sanders didn't almost upend the Democratic establishment because liberals felt that everything was fine under President Obama. The American people might not think of what we're experiencing as a "constitutional crisis," but they understand what their leaders have failed to recognize: The system does not work anymore. Something radical has to happen. This knowledge, above all, is one thing that the citizens of our deeply divided country still have in common.

Topics for Critical Thinking and Writing

1. In paragraph 4, Ganesh Sitaraman writes, "Our Constitution wasn't built for a country with massive economic inequality and deeply entrenched political divisions." Extend his argument or argue against his claim.
2. What is a "demagogue" (para. 11), and why are demagogues considered dangerous in a democracy? What is a populist, and are they also considered dangerous? Is there a difference between a demagogue and a populist?
3. In paragraph 4, Sitaraman says that the republic has faced threats to its very existence at three historical moments, "the Civil War, the Gilded Age through the Great Depression, and the present moment." Do you think he is correct? Why, or why not? Have there been other critical moments? If so, explore one of them and tell why it does or does not measure up to constituting a threat to democracy.
4. Sitaraman argues that economic inequality is the fundamental threat to the republic and that other problems might be sourced to this one overriding problem. Make the connections yourself between a *specific* social problem that threatens democracy and its basis in economic inequality.
5. Do some research comparing measures of economic equality in the 1960s with today. What measures do economists use to make such comparisons? What do their numbers suggest has happened since then? What does Sitaraman cite as the reasons for increased economic inequality today?
6. One stereotype of the political parties today is that Republicans are "for the rich" and Democrats are "for the poor." Challenge this binary thinking in an essay of 500 to 750 words. (Consider also why it might be important to challenge the binary.)
7. In the final section, Sitaraman claims that "only a surge of progressive patriotism," such as the New Deal of the 1930s, can address the many aspects of economic inequality that threaten the republic. Do you see this surge occurring in the United States? If so, where? If not, why do you think it is not occurring?

MEGAN McARDLE

Megan McArdle (b. 1973) is a columnist for the *Washington Post*. She has also written for *Bloomberg Review*, the *Atlantic*, the *Economist*, and other publications, and she appears regularly as a commentator on news, politics, and economics on MSNBC, Fox News, and National Public Radio. In 2014, she published *The Up Side Is Down: Why Failing Well Is the Key to Success*. She operates her own blog on business and economics, *Asymmetric Information*. The following essay was published in the *Washington Post* on July 6, 2018.

The Nationalism America Needs Now

This has been the year of the national anthem. Never before have so many Americans been so passionately interested in the details of its performance.

Lengthy debates were held over whether the third verse of "The Star-Spangled Banner" was racist, most of them conducted by people who had not previously been aware that "The Star-Spangled Banner" had a third verse.

One faction decided that in a country whose Bill of Rights guarantees freedom of expression — right up front, where you can't miss it! — refusing to stand during the national anthem was a near cousin to treason. Another argued that kneeling was extremely patriotic and yet, somehow, also an excellent form of protest against American society. A third suggested that perhaps we should just stop playing the national anthem at sporting events.

There is something to be said for the first two. But there is nothing to be said for entirely getting rid of the anthem at sporting events, except that the idea is rather shockingly naive about what it takes to hold a country together.

5 "Nationalism" has become a dirty word in the modern era, having become inextricably associated with repression of minorities and imperialist ambition. We've forgotten that the nationalists actually did start out in the 19th century with a worthy and difficult project: persuading a large group of people to think of themselves as a single unit.

This was immensely hard work that took most of a century to complete in places such as Italy, Germany and Greece. We fail to appreciate it only because their efforts were so successful that we take the results for granted.

Just how much we take them for granted is reflected on the left, which utters harsh words for nationalism while also constantly engaging in nationalist projects. A welfare state, after all, is a fundamentally nationalistic enterprise, and it is frequently justified on those terms: invidious comparisons to the allegedly superior amenities offered by rival states; claims about obligations to fellow Americans that would be nonsensical without an important, and binding, national identity.

We may debate whether the US government should provide health care for all its citizens, but we are not arguing about whether we should open up an ObamaCare exchange in Chad.

Of course, there's good reason that "nationalism" ultimately became a dirty word; the quest for a strong national state sometimes resulted in internal purges of minorities and in external conquest. Thus the appeal of a cosmopolitan, denationalized political ethos that reified the individual over the group.

10 There's a lot to like about that view. But our particular species is, as social psychologist Jonathan Haidt says, "groupish." Most of us don't want to think of the place we live as merely another sort of consumer choice, and of our neighbors as nothing more than fellow consumers, for the same reasons we prefer homeownership to living in a hotel.

Nationalism channeled that groupish instinct into the nation-state. Some of those nations then used the immense power of mass group-ness to commit great horrors.

It's understandable, and perhaps inevitable, that so many people rejected any hint of nationalism in the aftermath of World War II. But the current political moment illustrates the limits of that approach: The groupish instinct has not gone away, and neither has it leveled up into a mass identification with all humanity.

Instead, it has leveled down, into a global outbreak of populist particularism. That particularism is threatening to tear the United States apart as rival tribes lose the ability to do anything, however trivial, together.

If we are to fight our way back from this soft civil war, we'll need a muscular patriotism that focuses us on our commonalities instead of our differences. Such a patriotism must not be either imperialist nor racialized. Which means we desperately need the flag, and the anthem, and all the other common symbols that are light on politics or military fetishism and heavy on symbolism.

We need much more of them, rather than 15
much less — constant reminders that we are groupish, and that our group consists of 328 million fellow Americans with whom we share a country and a creed, a song and a flag, and the deep sense of mutual obligation that all these things imply.

Topics for Critical Thinking and Writing

1. What is the controversy surrounding the third verse of the national anthem (para. 2) that Megan McArdle is referring to?
2. Examine the paradox McArdle writes about in paragraph 3. What values or perspectives are in play that make people interpret athletes' kneeling for the national anthem as either fully American or anti-American? Which do you think it is?
3. Why did "nationalism" become a bad word, as McArdle says in paragraph 5? In an essay of about 500 words, discuss some of the benefits and perils of nationalism. What is its greatest benefit or highest potential? What are its greatest drawbacks or dangers?
4. Look up the word *exceptionalism*. In about 250 to 300 words, explain your understanding of what that term means in relationship to nationalism.
5. In paragraph 8, McArdle writes, "We may debate whether the US government should provide health care for all its citizens, but we are not arguing about whether we should open up an ObamaCare exchange in Chad." Rephrase her claim here. How does it assist her argument?
6. The United States is a pluralistic, multicultural society rooted in differences. What role does McArdle see in "the flag and the anthem, and all the other common symbols" of nationalism (para. 14)? Do you think these symbols are enough to hold Americans together? Why, or why not?
7. It is sometimes said that a nation is a type of family. What are the strengths and weaknesses of the nation-as-family metaphor?

PART SIX

Enduring Questions

Essays, Poems, and Stories

26

What Is the Ideal Society?

THOMAS MORE

The son of a prominent London lawyer, Thomas More (1478–1535) served as a page in the household of the Archbishop of Canterbury, went to Oxford University, and then studied law in London. More's charm, brilliance, and gentle manner caused Erasmus, the great Dutch humanist who became his friend during a visit to London, to write to a friend: "Did nature ever create anything kinder, sweeter, or more harmonious than the character of Thomas More?"

More served in Parliament, became a diplomat, and after holding several important positions in the government of Henry VIII, rose to become lord chancellor. But when Henry married Anne Boleyn, broke from the Church of Rome, and established himself as head of the Church of England, More refused to subscribe to the Act of Succession and Supremacy. Condemned to death as a traitor, he was executed in 1535, nominally for treason but really because he would not recognize the king rather than the pope as the head of his church. A moment before the ax fell, More displayed a bit of the whimsy for which he was known: When he put his head on the block, he brushed his beard aside, commenting that his beard had done no offense to the king. In 1886, the Roman Catholic Church beatified More, and in 1935, the four-hundredth anniversary of his death, it canonized him as St. Thomas More.

More wrote *Utopia* (1514–1515) in Latin, the international language of the day. The book's name, however, is Greek for "no place" (*ou topos*), with a pun on "good place" (*eu topos*). *Utopia* owes something to Plato's *Republic* and something to then-popular accounts of voyagers such as Amerigo Vespucci. *Utopia* purports to record an account given by a traveler named Hytholodaeus (Greek for "learned in nonsense"), who allegedly visited Utopia. The work is playful, but it is also serious. In truth, it is hard to know exactly where it is serious and how serious it is. One inevitably wonders, for example, if More the devoted Roman Catholic could really have advocated euthanasia. And could More the persecutor of heretics really have approved of the religious tolerance practiced in Utopia? Is he perhaps in effect saying, "Let's see what reason, unaided by Christian revelation, can tell us about an ideal society"? But if so, is he nevertheless also saying, very strongly, that Christian countries, although blessed with the revelation of Christ's teachings, are far behind these unenlightened pagans? Utopia has been widely praised by all sorts of readers — from Roman Catholics to communists — and for all sorts of reasons. The selection presented here is about one-twelfth of the book (in a translation by Paul Turner).

From *Utopia*

[A DAY IN UTOPIA]

And now for their working conditions. Well, there's one job they all do, irrespective of sex, and that's farming. It's part of every child's education. They learn the principles of agriculture at school, and they're taken for regular outings into the fields near the town, where they not only watch farm work being done, but also do some themselves, as a form of exercise.

Besides farming which, as I say, is everybody's job, each person is taught a special trade of his own. He may be trained to process wool or flax, or he may become a stonemason, a blacksmith, or a carpenter. Those are the only trades that employ any considerable quantity of labor. They have no tailors or dressmakers, since everyone on the island wears the same sort of clothes — except that they vary slightly according to sex and marital status — and the fashion never changes. These clothes are quite pleasant to look at, they allow free movement of the limbs, they're equally suitable for hot and cold weather — and the great thing is, they're all home-made. So everybody learns one of the other trades I mentioned, and by everybody I mean the women as well as the men — though the weaker sex are given the lighter jobs, like spinning and weaving, while the men do the heavier ones.

Most children are brought up to do the same work as their parents, since they tend to have a natural feeling for it. But if a child fancies some other trade, he's adopted into a family that practices it. Of course, great care is taken, not only by the father, but also by the local authorities, to see that the foster father is a decent, respectable type. When you've learned one trade properly, you can, if you like, get permission to learn another — and when you're an expert in both, you can practice whichever you prefer, unless the other one is more essential to the public.

The chief business of the Stywards[1] — in fact, practically their only business — is to see that nobody sits around doing nothing, but that everyone gets on with his job. They don't wear people out, though, by keeping them hard at work from early morning till late at night, like cart horses. That's just slavery — and yet that's what life is like for the working classes nearly everywhere else in the world. In Utopia they have a six-hour working day — three hours in the morning, then lunch — then a two-hour break — then three more hours in the afternoon, followed by supper. They go to bed at 8 p.m., and sleep for eight hours. All the rest of the twenty-four they're free to do what they like — not to waste their time in idleness or self-indulgence, but to make good use of it in some congenial activity. Most people spend these free periods on further education, for there are public lectures first thing every morning. Attendance is quite voluntary, except for those picked out for academic training, but men and women of all classes go crowding in to hear them — I mean, different people go to different lectures, just as the spirit moves them. However, there's nothing to stop you from spending this extra time on your trade, if you want to. Lots of people do, if they haven't the capacity for intellectual work, and are much admired for such public-spirited behavior.

[1] **Stywards** In Utopia, each group of thirty households elects a styward; each town has two hundred stywards, who elect the mayor. [Editors' note]

After supper they have an hour's recreation, either in the gardens or in the communal dining-halls, according to the time of year. Some people practice music, others just talk. They've never heard of anything so silly and demoralizing as dice, but they have two games rather like chess. The first is a sort of arithmetical contest, in which certain numbers "take" others. The second is a pitched battle between virtues and vices, which illustrates most ingeniously how vices tend to conflict with one another, but to combine against virtues. It also shows which vices are opposed to which virtues, how much strength vices can muster for a direct assault, what indirect tactics they employ, what help virtues need to overcome vices, what are the best methods of evading their attacks, and what ultimately determines the victory of one side or the other.

But here's a point that requires special attention, or you're liable to get the wrong idea. Since they only work a six-hour day, you may think there must be a shortage of essential goods. On the contrary, those six hours are enough, and more than enough to produce plenty of everything that's needed for a comfortable life. And you'll understand why it is, if you reckon up how large a proportion of the population in other countries is totally unemployed. First you have practically all the women — that gives you nearly 50 percent for a start. And in countries where the women *do* work, the men tend to lounge about instead. Then there are all the priests, and members of so-called religious orders — how much work do they do? Add all the rich, especially the landowners, popularly known as nobles and gentlemen. Include their domestic staffs — I mean those gangs of armed ruffians that I mentioned before. Finally, throw in all the beggars who are perfectly hale and hearty, but pretend to be ill as an excuse for being lazy. When you've counted them up, you'll be surprised to find how few people actually produce what the human race consumes.

And now just think how few of these few people are doing essential work — for where money is the only standard of value, there are bound to be dozens of unnecessary trades carried on, which merely supply luxury goods or entertainment. Why, even if the existing labor force were distributed among the few trades really needed to make life reasonably comfortable, there'd be so much overproduction that prices would fall too low for the workers to earn a living. Whereas, if you took all those engaged in nonessential trades, and all who are too lazy to work — each of whom consumes twice as much of the products of other people's labor as any of the producers themselves — if you put the whole lot of them on to something useful, you'd soon see how few hours' work a day would be amply sufficient to supply all the necessities and comforts of life — to which you might add all real and natural forms of pleasure.

[THE HOUSEHOLD]

But let's get back to their social organization. Each household, as I said, comes under the authority of the oldest male. Wives are subordinate to their husbands, children to their parents, and younger people generally to their elders. Every town is divided into four districts of equal size, each with its own shopping center in the middle of it. There the products of every household are collected in warehouses, and then distributed according to type among various shops. When the head of a household needs anything for himself or his family, he just goes to one of these shops and asks for it. And whatever he asks for, he's allowed to take away without any sort of payment, either in money or in kind. After all, why shouldn't he? There's more than enough of everything to go round, so there's no risk of his asking for more than he needs — for why should anyone want to start hoarding, when he knows he'll never have to go short of anything? No living creature is naturally greedy, except from fear of want — or in the case of human beings, from vanity, the notion that you're better than people if you can display more superfluous property than they can. But there's no scope for that sort of thing in Utopia.

[UTOPIAN BELIEFS]

The Utopians fail to understand why anyone should be so fascinated by the dull gleam of a tiny bit of stone, when he has all the stars in the sky to look at — or how anyone can be silly enough to think himself better than other people, because his clothes are made of finer woollen thread than theirs. After all, those fine clothes were once worn by a sheep, and they never turned it into anything better than a sheep.

Nor can they understand why a totally useless substance like gold should now, all over the world, be considered far more important than human beings, who gave it such value as it has, purely for their own convenience. The result is that a man with about as much mental agility as a lump of lead or a block of wood, a man whose utter stupidity is paralleled only by his immorality, can have lots of good, intelligent people at his beck and call, just because he happens to possess a large pile of gold coins. And if by some freak of fortune or trick of the law — two equally effective methods of turning things upside down — the said coins were suddenly transferred to the most worthless member of his domestic staff, you'd soon see the present owner trotting after his money, like an extra piece of currency, and becoming his own servant's servant. But what puzzles and disgusts the Utopians even more is the idiotic way some people have of practically worshipping a rich man, not because they owe him money or are otherwise in his power, but simply because he's rich — although they know perfectly well that he's far too mean to let a single penny come their way, so long as he's alive to stop it.

They get these ideas partly from being brought up under a social system which is directly opposed to that type of nonsense, and partly from their reading and education. Admittedly, no one's allowed to become a full-time student, except for the very few in each town who appear as children to possess unusual gifts, outstanding intelligence, and a special aptitude for academic research. But every child receives a primary education, and most men and women go on educating themselves all their lives during those free periods that I told you about. . . .

In ethics they discuss the same problems as we do. Having distinguished between three types of "good," psychological, physiological, and environmental, they proceed to ask whether the term is strictly applicable to all of them, or only to the first. They also argue about such things as virtue and pleasure. But their chief subject of dispute is the nature of human happiness — on what factor or factors does it depend? Here they seem rather too much inclined to take a hedonistic view, for according to them human happiness consists largely or wholly in pleasure. Surprisingly enough, they defend this self-indulgent doctrine by arguments drawn from religion — a thing normally associated with a more serious view of life, if not with gloomy asceticism. You see, in all their discussions of happiness they invoke certain religious principles to supplement the operations of reason, which they think otherwise ill-equipped to identify true happiness.

The first principle is that every soul is immortal, and was created by a kind God, Who meant it to be happy. The second is that we shall be rewarded or punished in the next world for our good or bad behavior in this one. Although these are religious principles, the Utopians find rational grounds for accepting them. For suppose you didn't accept them? In that case, they say, any fool could tell you what you ought to do. You should go all out for your own pleasure, irrespective of right and wrong. You'd merely have to make sure that minor pleasures didn't interfere with major ones, and avoid the type of pleasure that has painful aftereffects. For what's the sense of struggling to be virtuous, denying yourself the pleasant things of life, and deliberately making yourself uncomfortable, if there's nothing you hope to gain by it? And what *can* you hope to gain by it, if you receive no compensation after death for a thoroughly unpleasant, that is, a thoroughly miserable life?

Not that they identify happiness with every type of pleasure — only with the higher ones. Nor do they identify it with virtue — unless they belong to a quite different school of thought. According to the normal view, happiness is the *summum bonum*[2] toward which we're naturally impelled by virtue — which in their definition means following one's natural impulses, as God meant us to do. But this includes obeying the instinct to be reasonable in our likes and dislikes. And reason also teaches us, first to love and reverence Almighty God, to Whom we owe our existence and our potentiality for happiness, and secondly to get through life as comfortably and cheerfully as we can, and help all other members of our species to do so too.

15 The fact is, even the sternest ascetic tends to be slightly inconsistent in his condemnation of pleasure. He may sentence *you* to a life of hard labor, inadequate sleep, and general discomfort, but he'll also tell you to do your best to ease the pains and privations of others. He'll regard all such attempts to improve the human situation as laudable acts of humanity — for obviously nothing could be more humane, or more natural for a human being, than to relieve other people's sufferings, put an end to their miseries, and restore their *joie de vivre,* that is, their capacity for pleasure. So why shouldn't it be equally natural to do the same thing for oneself?

Either it's a bad thing to enjoy life, in other words, to experience pleasure — in which case you shouldn't help anyone to do it, but should try to save the whole human race from such a frightful fate — or else, if it's good for other people, and you're not only allowed, but positively obliged to make it possible for them, why shouldn't charity begin at home? After all, you've a duty to yourself as well as to your neighbor, and, if Nature says you must be kind to others, she can't turn round the next moment and say you must be cruel to yourself. The Utopians therefore regard the enjoyment of life — that is, pleasure — as the natural object of all human efforts, and natural, as they define it, is synonymous with virtuous. However, Nature also wants us to help one another to enjoy life, for the very good reason that no human being has a monopoly of her affections. She's equally anxious for the welfare of every member of the species. So of course she tells us to make quite sure that we don't pursue our own interests at the expense of other people's.

[2]*summum bonum* Latin for "the highest good." [Editors' note]

On this principle they think it right to keep one's promises in private life, and also to obey public laws for regulating the distribution of "goods" — by which I mean the raw materials of pleasure — provided such laws have been properly made by a wise ruler, or passed by common consent of a whole population, which has not been subjected to any form of violence or deception. Within these limits they say it's sensible to consult one's own interests, and a moral duty to consult those of the community as well. It's wrong to deprive someone else of a pleasure so that you can enjoy one yourself, but to deprive yourself of a pleasure so that you can add to someone else's enjoyment is an act of humanity by which you always gain more than you lose. For one thing, such benefits are usually repaid in kind. For another, the mere sense of having done somebody a kindness, and so earned his affection and goodwill, produces a spiritual satisfaction which far outweighs the loss of a physical one. And lastly — a belief that comes easily to a religious mind — God will reward us for such small sacrifices of momentary pleasure, by giving us an eternity of perfect joy. Thus they argue that, in the final analysis, pleasure is the ultimate happiness which all human beings have in view, even when they're acting most virtuously.

Pleasure they define as any state or activity, physical or mental, which is naturally enjoyable. The operative word is *naturally.* According to them, we're impelled by reason as well as an instinct to enjoy ourselves in any natural way which doesn't hurt other people, interfere with greater pleasures, or cause unpleasant aftereffects. But human beings have entered into an idiotic conspiracy to call some things enjoyable which are naturally nothing of the kind — as though facts were as easily changed as definitions. Now the Utopians believe that, so far from contributing to happiness, this type of thing makes happiness impossible — because, once you get used to it, you lose all capacity for real pleasure, and are merely obsessed by illusory forms of it. Very often these have nothing pleasant about them at all — in fact, most of them are thoroughly disagreeable. But they appeal so strongly to perverted tastes that they come to be reckoned not only among the major pleasures of life, but even among the chief reasons for living.

In the category of illusory pleasure addicts they include the kind of person I mentioned before, who thinks himself better than other people because he's better dressed than they are. Actually he's just as wrong about his clothes as he is about himself. From a practical point of view, why is it better to be dressed in fine woollen thread than in coarse? But he's got it into his head that fine thread is naturally superior, and that wearing it somehow increases his own value. So he feels entitled to far more respect than he'd ever dare to hope for, if he were less expensively dressed, and is most indignant if he fails to get it.

Talking of respect, isn't it equally idiotic to attach such importance to a lot of empty gestures which do nobody any good? For what real pleasure can you get out of the sight of a bared head or a bent knee? Will it cure the rheumatism in your own knee, or make you any less weak in the head? Of course, the great believers in this type of artificial pleasure are those who pride themselves on their "nobility." Nowadays that merely means that they happen to belong to a family which has been rich for several generations, preferably in landed property. And yet they feel every bit as "noble" even if they've failed to inherit any of the said property, or if they have inherited it and then frittered it all away.

Then there's another type of person I mentioned before, who has a passion for jewels, and feels practically superhuman if he manages to get hold of a rare one, especially if it's a kind that's considered particularly precious in his country and period — for the value of such things varies according to where and when you live. But he's so terrified of being taken in by appearances that he refuses to buy any jewel until he's stripped off all the gold and inspected it in the nude. And even then he won't buy it without a solemn assurance and a written guarantee from the jeweler that the stone is genuine. But my dear sir, why shouldn't a fake give you just as much pleasure, if you can't, with your own eyes, distinguish it from a real one? It makes no difference to you whether it's genuine or not — any more than it would to a blind man!

And now, what about those people who accumulate superfluous wealth, for no better purpose than to enjoy looking at it? Is their pleasure a real one, or merely a form of delusion? The opposite type of psychopath buries his gold, so that he'll never be able to use it, and may never even see it again. In fact, he deliberately loses it in his anxiety not to lose it — for what can you call it but lost, when it's put back into the earth, where it's no good to him, or probably to anyone else? And yet he's tremendously happy when he's got it stowed away. Now, apparently, he can stop worrying. But suppose the money is stolen, and ten years later he dies without ever knowing it has gone. Then for a whole ten years he has managed to survive his loss, and during that period what difference has it made to him whether the money was there or not? It was just as little use to him either way.

Among stupid pleasures they include not only gambling — a form of idiocy that they've heard about but never practiced — but also hunting and hawking. What on earth is the fun, they ask, of throwing dice onto a table? Besides, you've done it so often that, even if there was some fun in it at first, you must surely be sick of it by now. How can you possibly enjoy listening to anything so disagreeable as the barking and howling of dogs? And why is it more amusing to watch a dog chasing a hare than to watch one dog chasing another? In each case the essential activity is running — if running is what amuses you. But if it's really the thought of being in at the death, and seeing an animal torn to pieces before your eyes, wouldn't pity be a more appropriate reaction to the sight of a weak, timid, harmless little creature like a hare being devoured by something so much stronger and fiercer?

So the Utopians consider hunting below the dignity of free men, and leave it entirely to butchers, who are, as I told you, slaves. In their view hunting is the vilest department of butchery, compared with which all the others are relatively useful and honorable. An ordinary butcher slaughters livestock far more sparingly, and only because he has to, whereas a hunter kills and mutilates poor little creatures purely for his own amusement. They say you won't find that type of blood lust even among animals, unless they're particularly savage by nature, or have become so by constantly being used for this cruel sport.

There are hundreds of things like that, which are generally regarded as pleasures, but everyone in Utopia is quite convinced that they've got nothing to do with real pleasure, because there's nothing naturally enjoyable about them. Nor is this conviction at all shaken by the argument that most people do actually enjoy them, which would seem to indicate an appreciable pleasure content. They say this is a purely subjective reaction caused by bad habits, which can make a person prefer unpleasant things to pleasant ones, just as pregnant women sometimes lose their sense of taste, and find suet or turpentine more delicious than honey. But however much one's judgment may be impaired by habit or ill health, the nature of pleasure, as of everything else, remains unchanged.

Real pleasures they divide into two categories, mental and physical. Mental pleasures include the satisfaction that one gets from understanding something, or from contemplating truth. They also include the memory of a well-spent life, and the confident expectation of good things to come. Physical pleasures are subdivided into two types. First there are those which fill the whole organism with a conscious sense of enjoyment. This may be the result of replacing physical substances which have been burnt up by the natural heat of the body, as when we eat or drink. Or else it may be caused by the discharge of some excess, as in excretion, sexual intercourse, or any relief of irritation by rubbing or scratching. However, there are also pleasures which satisfy no organic need, and relieve no previous discomfort. They merely act, in a mysterious but quite unmistakable way, directly on our senses, and monopolize their reactions. Such is the pleasure of music.

Their second type of physical pleasure arises from the calm and regular functioning of the body — that is, from a state of health undisturbed by any minor ailments. In the absence of mental discomfort, this gives one a good feeling, even without the help of external pleasures. Of course, it's less ostentatious, and forces itself less violently on one's attention than the cruder delights of eating and drinking, but even so it's often considered the greatest pleasure in life. Practically everyone in Utopia would agree that it's a very important one, because it's the basis of all the others. It's enough by itself to make you enjoy life, and unless you have it, no other pleasure is possible. However, mere freedom from pain, without positive health, they would call not pleasure but anesthesia.

Some thinkers used to maintain that a uniformly tranquil state of health couldn't properly be termed a pleasure since its presence could only be detected by contrast with its opposite — oh yes, they went very thoroughly into the whole question. But that theory was exploded long ago, and nowadays nearly everybody subscribes to the view that health is most definitely a pleasure. The argument goes like this — illness involves pain, which is the direct opposite of pleasure, and illness is the direct opposite of health, therefore health involves pleasure. They don't think it matters whether you say that illness *is* or merely *involves* pain. Either way it comes to the same thing. Similarly, whether health *is* a pleasure, or merely *produces* pleasure as inevitably as fire produces heat, it's equally logical to assume that where you have an uninterrupted state of health you cannot fail to have pleasure.

Besides, they say, when we eat something, what really happens is this. Our failing health starts fighting off the attacks of hunger, using the food as an ally. Gradually it begins to prevail, and, in this very process of winning back its normal strength, experiences the sense of enjoyment which we find so refreshing. Now, if health enjoys the actual battle, why shouldn't it also enjoy the victory? Or are we to suppose that when it has finally managed to regain its former vigor — the one thing that it has been fighting for all this time — it promptly falls into a coma, and fails to notice or take advantage of its success? As for the idea that one isn't conscious of health except through its opposite, they say that's quite untrue. Everyone's perfectly aware of feeling well, unless he's asleep or actually feeling ill. Even the most insensitive and apathetic sort of person will admit that it's delightful to be healthy — and what is delight, but a synonym for pleasure?

They're particularly fond of mental pleasures, which they consider of primary importance, and attribute mostly to good behavior and a clear conscience. Their favorite physical pleasure is health. Of course, they believe in enjoying food, drink, and so forth, but purely in the interests of health, for they don't regard such things as very pleasant in themselves — only as methods of resisting the stealthy onset of disease. A sensible person, they say, prefers keeping well to taking medicine, and would rather feel cheerful than have people trying to comfort him. On the same principle it's better not to need this type of pleasure than to become addicted to it. For, if you think that sort of thing will make you happy, you'll have to admit that your idea of perfect felicity would be a life consisting entirely of hunger, thirst, itching, eating, drinking, rubbing, and scratching — which would obviously be most unpleasant as well as quite disgusting. Undoubtedly these pleasures should come right at the bottom of the list, because they're so impure. For instance, the pleasure of eating is invariably diluted with the pain of hunger, and not in equal proportions either — for the pain is both more intense and more prolonged. It starts before the pleasure, and doesn't stop until the pleasure has stopped too.

So they don't think much of pleasures like that, except insofar as they're necessary. But they enjoy them all the same, and feel most grateful to Mother Nature for encouraging her children to do things that have to be done so often, by making them so attractive. For just think how dreary life would be, if those chronic ailments, hunger and thirst, could only be cured by foul-tasting medicines, like the rarer types of disease!

They attach great value to special natural gifts such as beauty, strength, and agility. They're also keen on the pleasures of sight, hearing, and smell, which are peculiar to human beings — for no other species admires the beauty of the world, enjoys any sort of scent, except as a method of locating food, or can tell the difference between a harmony and a discord. They say these things give a sort of relish to life.

However, in all such matters they observe the rule that minor pleasures mustn't interfere with major ones, and that pleasure mustn't cause pain — which they think is bound to happen, if the pleasure is immoral. But they'd never dream of despising their own beauty, overtaxing their strength, converting their agility into inertia, ruining their physique by going without food, damaging their health, or spurning any other of Nature's gifts, unless they were doing it for the benefit of other people or of society, in the hope of receiving some greater pleasure from God in return. For they think it's quite absurd to torment oneself in the name of an unreal virtue, which does nobody any good, or in order to steel oneself against disasters which may never occur. They say such behavior is merely self-destructive, and shows a most ungrateful attitude toward Nature — as if one refused all her favors, because one couldn't bear the thought of being indebted to her for anything.

Well, that's their ethical theory, and short of some divine revelation, they doubt if the human mind is capable of devising a better one. We've no time to discuss whether it's right or wrong — nor is it really necessary, for all I undertook was to describe their way of life, not to defend it.

[TREATMENT OF THE DYING]

As I told you, when people are ill, they're looked after most sympathetically, and given everything in the way of medicine or special food that could possibly assist their recovery. In the case of permanent invalids, the nurses try to make them feel better by sitting and talking to them, and do all they can to relieve their symptoms. But if, besides being incurable, the disease also causes constant excruciating pain, some priests and government officials visit the person concerned, and say something like this:

"Let's face it, you'll never be able to live a normal life. You're just a nuisance to other people and a burden to yourself — in fact you're really leading a sort of posthumous existence. So why go on feeding germs? Since your life's a misery to you, why hesitate to die? You're imprisoned in a torture chamber — why don't you break out and escape to a better world? Or say the word, and we'll arrange for your release. It's only common sense to cut your losses. It's also an act of piety to take the advice of a priest, because he speaks for God."

If the patient finds these arguments convincing, he either starves himself to death, or is given a soporific and put painlessly out of his misery. But this is strictly voluntary, and, if he prefers to stay alive, everyone will go on treating him as kindly as ever.

[THE SUMMING UP]

Well, that's the most accurate account I can give you of the Utopian Republic. To my mind, it's not only the best country in the world, but the only one that has any right to call itself a republic. Elsewhere, people are always talking about the public interest, but all they really care about is private property. In Utopia, where's there's no private property, people take their duty to the public seriously. And both attitudes are perfectly reasonable. In other "republics" practically everyone knows that, if he doesn't look out for himself, he'll starve to death, however prosperous his country may be. He's therefore compelled to give his own interests priority over those of the public; that is, of other people. But in Utopia, where everything's under public ownership, no one has any fear of going short, as long as the public storehouses are full. Everyone gets a fair share, so there are never any poor men or beggars. Nobody owns anything, but everyone is rich — for what greater wealth can there be than cheerfulness, peace of mind, and freedom from anxiety? Instead of being worried about his food supply, upset by the plaintive demands of his wife, afraid of poverty for his son, and baffled by the problem of finding a dowry for his daughter, the Utopian can feel absolutely sure that he, his wife, his children, his grandchildren, his great-grandchildren, his great-great-grandchildren, and as long a line of descendants as the proudest peer could wish to look forward to, will always have enough to eat and enough to make them happy. There's also the further point that those who are too old to work are just as well provided for as those who are still working.

Now, will anyone venture to compare these fair arrangements in Utopia with the so-called justice of other countries? — in which I'm damned if I can see the slightest trace of justice or fairness. For what sort of justice do you call this? People like aristocrats, goldsmiths, or moneylenders, who either do no work at all, or do work that's really not essential, are rewarded for their laziness or their unnecessary activities by a splendid life of luxury. But laborers, coachmen, carpenters, and farmhands, who never stop working like cart horses, at jobs so essential that, if they *did* stop working, they'd bring any country to a standstill within twelve months — what happens to them? They get so little to eat, and have such a wretched time, that they'd be almost better off if they *were* cart horses. Then at least, they wouldn't work quite such long hours, their food wouldn't be very much worse, they'd enjoy it more, and they'd have no fears for the future. As it is, they're not only ground down by unrewarding toil in the present, but also worried to death by the prospect of a poverty-stricken old age — since their daily wages aren't enough to support them for one day, let alone leave anything over to be saved up when they're old.

Can you see any fairness or gratitude in a social system which lavishes such great rewards on so-called noblemen, goldsmiths, and people like that, who are either totally unproductive or merely employed in producing luxury goods or entertainment, but makes no such kind provision for farmhands, coal heavers, laborers, carters, or carpenters, without whom society couldn't exist at all? And the climax of ingratitude comes when they're old and ill and completely destitute. Having taken advantage of them throughout the best years of their lives, society now forgets all the sleepless hours they've spent in its service, and repays them for all the vital work they've done, by letting them die in misery. What's more, the wretched earnings of the poor are daily whittled away by the rich, not only through private dishonesty, but through public legislation. As if it weren't unjust enough already that the man who contributes most to society should get the least in return, they make it even worse, and then arrange for injustice to be legally described as justice.

In fact, when I consider any social system that prevails in the modern world, I can't, so help me God, see it as anything but a conspiracy of the rich to advance their own interests under the pretext of organizing society. They think up all sorts of tricks and dodges, first for keeping safe their ill-gotten gains, and then for exploiting the poor by buying their labor as cheaply as possible. Once the rich have decided that these tricks and dodges shall be officially recognized by society — which includes the poor as well as the rich — they acquire the force of law. Thus an unscrupulous minority is led by its insatiable greed to monopolize what would have been enough to supply the needs of the whole population. And yet how much happier even these people would be in Utopia! There, with the simultaneous abolition of money and the passion for money, how many other social problems have been solved, how many crimes eradicated! For obviously the end of money means the end of all those types of criminal behavior which daily punishments are powerless to check: fraud, theft, burglary, brawls, riots, disputes, rebellion, murder, treason, and black magic. And the moment money goes, you can also say goodbye to fear, tension, anxiety, overwork, and sleepless nights. Why, even poverty itself, the one problem that has always seemed to need money for its solution, would promptly disappear if money ceased to exist.

Let me try to make this point clearer. Just think back to one of the years when the harvest was bad, and thousands of people died of starvation. Well, I bet if you'd inspected every rich man's barn at the end of that lean period you'd have found enough corn to have saved all the lives that were lost through malnutrition and disease, and prevented anyone from suffering any ill effects whatever from the meanness of the weather and the soil. Everyone could so easily get enough to eat, if it weren't for that blessed nuisance, money. There you have a brilliant invention which was designed to make food more readily available. Actually it's the only thing that makes it unobtainable.

I'm sure that even the rich are well aware of all this, and realize how much better it would be to have everything one needed, than lots of things one didn't need — to be evacuated altogether from the danger area, than to dig oneself in behind a barricade of enormous wealth. And I've no doubt that either self-interest, or the authority of our Savior Christ — Who was far too wise not to know what was best for us, and far too kind to recommend anything else — would have led the whole world to adopt the Utopian system long ago, if it weren't for that beastly root of all evils, pride. For pride's criterion of prosperity is not what you've got yourself, but what other people haven't got. Pride would refuse to set foot in paradise, if she thought there'd be no underprivileged classes there to gloat over and order about — nobody whose misery could serve as a foil to her own happiness, or whose poverty she could make harder to bear, by flaunting her own riches. Pride, like a hellish serpent gliding through human hearts — or shall we say, like a sucking-fish that clings to the ship of state? — is always dragging us back, and obstructing our progress toward a better way of life.

But as this fault is too deeply ingrained in human nature to be easily eradicated, I'm glad that at least one country has managed to develop a system which I'd like to see universally adopted. The Utopian way of life provides not only the happiest basis for a civilized community, but also one which, in all human probability, will last forever. They've eliminated the root causes of ambition, political conflict, and everything like that. There's therefore no danger of internal dissension, the one thing that has destroyed so many impregnable towns. And as long as there's unity and sound administration at home, no matter how envious neighboring kings may feel, they'll never be able to shake, let alone to shatter, the power of Utopia. They've tried to do so often enough in the past, but have always been beaten back.

Topics for Critical Thinking and Writing

1. Thomas More, writing early in the sixteenth century, was living in a primarily agricultural society. Laborers were needed on farms, but might More have had any other reason for insisting (para. 1) that all people should do some farming and that farming should be "part of every child's education"? Do you think everyone should put in some time as a farmer? Why, or why not?
2. More indicates that in the England of his day, many people loafed or engaged in unnecessary work (producing luxury goods, for one thing), putting an enormous burden on those who engaged in useful work. Is this condition, or any part of it, true of our society? Explain.

3. The Utopians cannot understand why the people of other nations value gems, gold, and fine clothes. If you value any of these items, can you offer an explanation as to why such things are valued?
4. What arguments can you offer against the Utopians' treatment of persons who are incurably ill and in pain?
5. What aspects of More's Utopia do not sound particularly "utopian" to you? Why?
6. In three or four paragraphs, summarize More's report of the Utopians' idea of pleasure.
7. More's Utopians cannot understand why anyone takes pleasure in gambling or in hunting. If either activity gives you pleasure, explain why in an essay of 500 words, offering an argument on behalf of your view. If neither activity gives you pleasure, tell whether it accords with the Utopians' views.
8. As More makes clear in the part called "The Summing Up," in Utopia there is no private property. In a sentence or two, summarize the reasons he gives for this principle and then, in a paragraph, evaluate them.

NICCOLÒ MACHIAVELLI

Niccolò Machiavelli (1469–1527) was born in Florence at a time when Italy was divided into five major states: Venice, Milan, Florence, the Papal States, and Naples. Although these states often had belligerent relations with one another as well as with lesser Italian states, under the Medici family in Florence they achieved a precarious balance of power. In 1494, however, Lorenzo de' Medici, who had ruled from 1469 to 1492, died, and two years later Lorenzo's successor was exiled when the French army arrived in Florence. Italy became a field where Spain, France, and Germany competed for power. From 1498 to 1512, Machiavelli held a high post in the diplomatic service of the Florentine Republic, but when the French army reappeared and the Florentines in desperation recalled the Medici, Machiavelli lost his post and was imprisoned, tortured, and then exiled. Banished from Florence, he nevertheless lived in comfort on a small estate nearby, writing his major works and hoping to obtain an office from the Medici. In later years, he was employed in a few minor diplomatic missions, but even after the collapse and expulsion of the Medici in 1527 and the restoration of the republic, he did not regain his old position of importance. He died shortly after the restoration.

This selection comes from *The Prince*, which Machiavelli wrote in 1513 during his banishment, hoping that it would interest the Medici and thus restore him to favor; but the book was not published until 1532, five years after his death. In this book of twenty-six short chapters, Machiavelli begins by examining different kinds of states, but the work's enduring power resides in the discussions (in Chapters 15–18, reprinted here) of qualities necessary to a prince — that is, a head of state. Any such examination obviously is based in part on assumptions about the nature of the citizens of the realm.

This selection was taken from a translation by W. K. Marriott.

From *The Prince*

CONCERNING THINGS FOR WHICH MEN, AND ESPECIALLY PRINCES, ARE PRAISED OR BLAMED

It remains now to see what ought to be the rules of conduct for a prince towards subject and friends. And as I know that many have written on this point, I expect I shall be considered presumptuous in mentioning it again, especially as in discussing it I shall depart from the methods of other people. But, it being my intention to write a thing which shall be useful to him who apprehends it, it appears to me more appropriate to follow up the real truth of the matter than the imagination of it; for many have pictured republics and principalities which in fact have never been known or seen, because how one lives is so far distant from how one ought to live, that he who neglects what is done for what ought to be done, sooner effects his ruin than his preservation; for a man who wishes to act entirely up to his professions of virtue soon meets with what destroys him among so much that is evil.

Hence it is necessary for a prince wishing to hold his own to know how to do wrong, and to make use of it or not according to necessity. Therefore, putting on one side imaginary things concerning a prince, and discussing those which are real, I say that all men when they are spoken of, and chiefly princes for being more highly placed, are remarkable for some of those qualities which bring them either blame or praise; and thus it is that one is reputed liberal, another miserly, using a Tuscan term (because an avaricious person in our language is still he who desires to possess by robbery, whilst we call one miserly who deprives himself too much of the use of his own); one is reputed generous, one rapacious; one cruel, one compassionate; one faithless, another faithful; one effeminate and cowardly, another bold and brave; one affable, another haughty; one lascivious, another chaste; one sincere, another cunning; one hard, another easy; one grave, another frivolous; one religious, another unbelieving, and the like. And I know that everyone will confess that it would be most praiseworthy in a prince to exhibit all the above qualities that are considered good; but because they can neither be entirely possessed nor observed, for human conditions do not permit it, it is necessary for him to be sufficiently prudent that he may know how to avoid the reproach of those vices which would lose him his state; and also to keep himself, if it be possible, from those which would not lose him it; but this not being possible, he may with less hesitation abandon himself to them. And again, he need not make himself uneasy at incurring a reproach for those vices without which the state can only be saved with difficulty, for if everything is considered carefully, it will be found that something which looks like virtue, if followed, would be his ruin; whilst something else, which looks like vice, yet followed brings him security and prosperity.

CONCERNING LIBERALITY AND MEANNESS

Commencing then with the first of the above-named characteristics, I say that it would be well to be reputed liberal. Nevertheless, liberality exercised in a way that does not bring you the reputation for it, injures you; for if one exercises it honestly and as it should be exercised, it may not become known, and you will not avoid the reproach of its opposite. Therefore, anyone wishing to maintain among men the name of liberal is obliged to avoid no attribute of magnificence; so that a prince thus inclined will consume in such acts all his property, and will be compelled in the end, if he wish to maintain the name of liberal, to unduly weigh down his people, and tax them, and do everything he can to get money. This will soon make him odious to his subjects, and becoming poor he will be little valued by anyone; thus, with his liberality, having offended many and rewarded few, he is affected by the very first trouble and imperiled by whatever may be the first danger; recognizing this himself, and wishing to draw back from it, he runs at once into the reproach of being miserly.

Therefore, a prince, not being able to exercise this virtue of liberality in such a way that it is recognized, except to his cost, if he is wise he ought not to fear the reputation of being mean, for in time he will come to be more considered than if liberal, seeing that with his economy his revenues are enough, that he can defend himself against all attacks, and is able to engage in enterprises without burdening his people; thus it comes to pass that he exercises liberality towards all from whom he does not take, who are numberless, and meanness towards those to whom he does not give, who are few.

5 We have not seen great things done in our time except by those who have been considered mean; the rest have failed. Pope Julius the Second was assisted in reaching the papacy by a reputation for liberality, yet he did not strive afterwards to keep it up, when he made war on the King of France; and he made many wars without imposing any extraordinary tax on his subjects, for he supplied his additional expenses out of his long thriftiness. The present King of Spain would not have undertaken or conquered in so many enterprises if he had been reputed liberal. A prince, therefore, provided that he has not to rob his subjects, that he can defend himself, that he does not become poor and abject, that he is not forced to become rapacious, ought to hold of little account a reputation for being mean, for it is one of those vices which will enable him to govern.

And if anyone should say: Caesar obtained empire by liberality, and many others have reached the highest positions by having been liberal, and by being considered so, I answer: Either you are a prince in fact, or in a way to become one. In the first case this liberality is dangerous, in the second it is very necessary to be considered liberal; and Caesar was one of those who wished to become pre-eminent in Rome; but if he had survived after becoming so, and had not moderated his expenses, he would have destroyed his government. And if anyone should reply: Many have been princes, and have done great things with armies, who have been considered very liberal, I reply: Either a prince spends that which is his own or his subjects' or else that of others. In the first case he ought to be sparing, in the second he ought not to neglect any opportunity for liberality. And to the prince who goes forth with his army, supporting it by pillage, sack, and extortion, handling that which belongs to others, this liberality is necessary, otherwise he would not be followed by soldiers. And of that which is neither yours nor your subjects' you can be a ready giver, as were Cyrus, Caesar, and Alexander; because it does not take away your reputation if you squander that of others, but adds to it; it is only squandering your own that injures you.

And there is nothing wastes so rapidly as liberality, for even whilst you exercise it you lose the power to do so, and so become either poor or despised, or else, in avoiding poverty, rapacious and hated. And a prince should guard himself, above all things, against being despised and hated; and liberality leads you to both. Therefore it is wiser to have a reputation for meanness which brings reproach without hatred, than to be compelled through seeking a reputation for liberality to incur a name for rapacity which begets reproach with hatred.

CONCERNING CRUELTY AND CLEMENCY, AND WHETHER IT IS BETTER TO BE LOVED THAN FEARED

Coming now to the other qualities mentioned above, I say that every prince ought to desire to be considered clement and not cruel. Nevertheless he ought to take care not to misuse this clemency. Cesare Borgia[1] was considered cruel; notwithstanding, his cruelty reconciled the Romagna, unified it, and restored it to peace and loyalty. And if this be rightly considered, he will be seen to have been much more merciful than the Florentine people, who, to avoid a reputation for cruelty, permitted Pistoia[2] to be destroyed. Therefore a prince, so long as he keeps his subjects united and loyal, ought not to mind the reproach of cruelty; because with a few examples he will be more merciful than those who, through too much mercy, allow disorders to arise, from which follow murders or robberies; for these are wont to injure the whole people, whilst those executions which originate with a prince offend the individual only.

And of all princes, it is impossible for the new prince to avoid the imputation of cruelty, owing to new states being full of dangers. Hence Virgil, through the mouth of Dido, excuses the inhumanity of her reign owing to its being new, saying, "against my will, my fate / A throne unsettled, and an infant state, / Bid me defend my realms with all my pow'rs, / And guard with these severities my shores."[3] Nevertheless, he ought to be slow to believe and to act, nor should he himself show fear, but proceed in a temperate manner with prudence and humanity, so that too much confidence may not make him incautious and too much distrust render him intolerable.

Upon this a question arises: whether it be better to be loved than feared or feared than loved? It may be answered that one should wish to be both, but, because it is difficult to unite them in one person, it is much safer to be feared than loved, when, of the two, either must be dispensed with. Because this is to be asserted in general of men, that they are ungrateful, fickle, false, cowardly, covetous, and as long as you succeed they are yours entirely; they will offer you their blood, property, life, and children, as is said above, when the need is far distant; but when it approaches they turn against you. And that prince who, relying entirely on their promises, has neglected other precautions, is ruined; because friendships that are obtained by payments, and not by greatness or nobility of mind, may indeed be earned, but they are not secured, and in time of need cannot be relied upon; and men have less scruple in offending one who is beloved than one who is feared, for love is preserved by the link of obligation which, owing to the baseness of men, is broken at every opportunity for their advantage;

[1] **Cesare Borgia** The son of Pope Alexander VI, Cesare Borgia (1476–1507) was ruthlessly opportunistic. Encouraged by his father, in 1499 and 1500 he subdued the cities of Romagna, the region including Ferrara and Ravenna. [All notes are the editors']

[2] **Pistoia** A town near Florence; Machiavelli suggests that the Florentines failed to treat dissenting leaders with sufficient severity.

[3] In *Aeneid* I, 563–64, **Virgil** (70–19 BC) puts this line into the mouth of **Dido**, the queen of Carthage.

but fear preserves you by a dread of punishment which never fails.

Nevertheless, a prince ought to inspire fear in such a way that, if he does not win love, he avoids hatred; because he can endure very well being feared whilst he is not hated, which will always be as long as he abstains from the property of his citizens and subjects and from their women. But when it is necessary for him to proceed against the life of someone, he must do it on proper justification and for manifest cause, but above all things he must keep his hands off the property of others, because men more quickly forget the death of their father than the loss of their patrimony. Besides, pretexts for taking away the property are never wanting; for he who has once begun to live by robbery will always find pretexts for seizing what belongs to others; but reasons for taking life, on the contrary, are more difficult to find and sooner lapse. But when a prince is with his army, and has under control a multitude of soldiers, then it is quite necessary for him to disregard the reputation of cruelty, for without it he would never hold his army united or disposed to its duties.

Among the wonderful deeds of Hannibal[4] this one is enumerated: that having led an enormous army, composed of many various races of men, to fight in foreign lands, no dissensions arose either among them or against the prince, whether in his bad or in his good fortune. This arose from nothing else than his inhuman cruelty, which, with his boundless valor, made him revered and terrible in the sight of his soldiers, but without that cruelty, his other virtues were not sufficient to produce this effect. And short-sighted writers admire his deeds from one point of view and from another condemn the principal cause of them. That it is true his other virtues would not have been sufficient for him may be proved by the case of Scipio,[5] that most excellent man, not only of his own times but within the memory of man, against whom, nevertheless, his army rebelled in Spain; this arose from nothing but his too great forbearance, which gave his soldiers more license than is consistent with military discipline. For this he was upbraided in the Senate by Fabius Maximus, and called the corrupter of the Roman soldiery. The Locrians were laid waste by a legate of Scipio, yet they were not avenged by him, nor was the insolence of the legate punished, owing entirely to his easy nature. Insomuch that someone in the Senate, wishing to excuse him, said there were many men who knew much better how not to err than to correct the errors of others. This disposition, if he had been continued in the command, would have destroyed in time the fame and glory of Scipio; but, he being under the control of the Senate, this injurious characteristic not only concealed itself, but contributed to his glory.

Returning to the question of being feared or loved, I come to the conclusion that, men loving according to their own will and fearing according to that of the prince, a wise prince should establish himself on that which is in his own control and not in that of others; he must endeavor only to avoid hatred, as is noted.

CONCERNING THE WAY IN WHICH PRINCES SHOULD KEEP FAITH

Everyone admits how praiseworthy it is in a prince to keep faith, and to live with integrity and not with craft. Nevertheless our

[4]**Hannibal** The Carthaginian general (247–183 BC) whose crossing of the Alps with elephants and full baggage train is one of the great feats of military history.

[5]**Scipio** Publius Cornelius Scipio Africanus the Elder (235–183 BC), the conqueror of Hannibal in the Punic Wars. The mutiny of which Machiavelli speaks took place in 206 BC.

experience has been that those princes who have done great things have held good faith of little account, and have known how to circumvent the intellect of men by craft, and in the end have overcome those who have relied on their word. You must know there are two ways of contesting, the one by the law, the other by force; the first method is proper to men, the second to beasts; but because the first is frequently not sufficient, it is necessary to have recourse to the second. Therefore it is necessary for a prince to understand how to avail himself of the beast and the man. This has been figuratively taught to princes by ancient writers, who describe how Achilles and many other princes of old were given to the Centaur Chiron[6] to nurse, who brought them up in his discipline; which means solely that, as they had for a teacher one who was half beast and half man, so it is necessary for a prince to know how to make use of both natures, and that one without the other is not durable. A prince, therefore, being compelled knowingly to adopt the beast, ought to choose the fox and the lion; because the lion cannot defend himself against snares and the fox cannot defend himself against wolves. Therefore, it is necessary to be a fox to discover the snares and a lion to terrify the wolves. Those who rely simply on the lion do not understand what they are about. Therefore a wise lord cannot, nor ought he to, keep faith when such observance may be turned against him, and when the reasons that caused him to pledge it exist no longer. If men were entirely good this precept would not hold, but because they are bad, and will not keep faith with you, you too are not bound to observe it with them. Nor will there ever be wanting to a prince legitimate reasons to excuse this non-observance. Of this endless modern examples could be given, showing how many treaties and engagements have been made void and of no effect through the faithlessness of princes; and he who has known best how to employ the fox has succeeded best.

But it is necessary to know well how to disguise this characteristic, and to be a great pretender and dissembler; and men are so simple, and so subject to present necessities, that he who seeks to deceive will always find someone who will allow himself to be deceived. One recent example I cannot pass over in silence. Alexander the Sixth[7] did nothing else but deceive men, nor ever thought of doing otherwise, and he always found victims; for there never was a man who had greater power in asserting, or who with greater oaths would affirm a thing, yet would observe it less; nevertheless his deceits always succeeded according to his wishes, because he well understood this side of mankind.

Therefore it is unnecessary for a prince to have all the good qualities I have enumerated, but it is very necessary to appear to have them. And I shall dare to say this also, that to have them and always to observe them is injurious, and that to appear to have them is useful; to appear merciful, faithful, humane, religious, upright, and to be so, but with a mind so framed that should you require not to be so, you may be able and know how to change to the opposite. And you have to understand this, that a prince, especially a new one, cannot observe all those things for which men are esteemed, being often forced, in order to maintain the state, to act contrary to fidelity, friendship, humanity, and religion. Therefore it is necessary for him to have a mind ready to turn itself accordingly as the winds and

[6]**Chiron** (Kī'ron) A centaur (half man, half horse) who was said in classical mythology to have been the teacher not only of Achilles but also of Theseus, Jason, Hercules, and other heroes.

[7]**Alexander the Sixth** Pope from 1492 to 1503; father of Cesare Borgia.

variations of fortune force it, yet, as I have said above, not to diverge from the good if he can avoid doing so, but, if compelled, then to know how to set about it.

For this reason a prince ought to take care that he never lets anything slip from his lips that is not replete with the above-named five qualities, that he may appear to him who sees and hears him altogether merciful, faithful, humane, upright, and religious. There is nothing more necessary to appear to have than this last quality, inasmuch as men judge generally more by the eye than by the hand, because it belongs to everybody to see you, to few to come in touch with you. Everyone sees what you appear to be, few really know what you are, and those few dare not oppose themselves to the opinion of the many, who have the majesty of the state to defend them; and in the actions of all men, and especially of princes, which it is not prudent to challenge, one judges by the result.[8]

For that reason, let a prince have the credit of conquering and holding his state, the means will always be considered honest, and he will be praised by everybody; because the vulgar are always taken by what a thing seems to be and by what comes of it; and in the world there are only the vulgar, for the few find a place there only when the many have no ground to rest on. One prince of the present time, whom it is not well to name, never preaches anything else but peace and good faith, and to both he is most hostile, and either, if he had kept it, would have deprived him of reputation and kingdom many a time.

[8]**one judges by the result** The original Italian, *si guarda al fine*, has often been translated erroneously as "the ends justify the means." Although this saying is often attributed to Machiavelli, he never actually wrote it.

Topics for Critical Thinking and Writing

1. In the opening paragraph, Niccolò Machiavelli claims that a ruler who wishes to keep in power must "know how to do wrong" — that is, must know where and when to ignore the demands of conventional morality. In the rest of the excerpt, does he give any convincing evidence to support this claim? Can you think of any recent political event in which a political leader violated the requirements of morality, as Machiavelli advises? Explain your response.
2. In paragraph 2, Machiavelli claims that it is impossible for a ruler to exhibit *all* the conventional virtues (trustworthiness, liberality, and so on). Why does he make this claim? Do you agree with it? Why, or why not?
3. Machiavelli says that Cesare Borgia's cruelty brought peace to Romagna and that, in contrast, the Florentines who sought to avoid being cruel in fact brought pain to Pistoia. Can you think of recent episodes supporting the view that cruelty can be beneficial to society? If so, restate Machiavelli's position, using these examples from recent history. Then go on to write two paragraphs, arguing on behalf of your two examples. Or if you believe that Machiavelli's point here is fundamentally wrong, explain why, again using current examples.
4. In *The Prince*, Machiavelli is writing about how to be a successful ruler. He explicitly says that he is dealing with things as they are, not as they should be. Do you think that one can, in fact, write usefully about governing without considering ethics? Explain.
5. In the next-to-last paragraph, Machiavelli declares that "in the actions of all men, . . . one judges by the result." Taking account of the context, do you think the meaning is (a) that

any end, goal, or purpose of anyone justifies using any means to reach it or (b) that the end of governing the state, nation, or country justifies using any means to achieve it? Or do you think Machiavelli means both? Or something else entirely?

6. In about 500 words, argue that an important contemporary political figure does or does not act according to Machiavelli's principles.
7. Read the selection from Thomas More's *Utopia*, and write an essay of 500 words on one of these two topics: (a) why More's book is or is not wiser than Machiavelli's or (b) why one of the books is more interesting than the other.
8. More and Machiavelli wrote their books at almost exactly the same time. In 500 to 750 words, compare and contrast the two authors' arguments about the nature of the state, examining their assumptions about human beings and the role of government.

THOMAS JEFFERSON

Thomas Jefferson (1743–1826) was a congressman, the governor of Virginia, the first secretary of state, and the president of the United States, but he said he wished to be remembered for only three things: drafting the Declaration of Independence, writing the Virginia Statute for Religious Freedom, and founding the University of Virginia. All three were efforts to promote freedom.

Jefferson was born in Virginia and educated at William and Mary College in Williamsburg, Virginia. After graduating, he studied law, was admitted to the bar, and in 1769 was elected to the Virginia House of Burgesses, his first political office. In 1776, he went to Philadelphia as a delegate to the second Continental Congress, where he was elected to a committee of five to write the Declaration of Independence. Jefferson drafted the document, which was then subjected to some changes by the other members of the committee and by the Congress. Although he was unhappy with the changes (especially with the deletion of a passage against slavery), his claim to have written the Declaration is just.

The Declaration of Independence

When in the course of human events, it becomes necessary for one people to dissolve the political bands which have connected them with another, and to assume among the Powers of the earth, the separate and equal station to which the Laws of Nature and of Nature's God entitle them, a decent respect to the opinions of mankind requires that they should declare the causes which impel them to the separation.

We hold these truths to be self-evident, that all men are created equal, that they are endowed by their Creator with certain unalienable Rights, that among these are Life, Liberty and the pursuit of Happiness.

That to secure these rights, Governments are instituted among Men, deriving their just powers from the consent of the governed.

That whenever any Form of Government becomes destructive of these ends, it is the Right of the People to alter or to abolish it, and to institute a new Government, laying its foundation on such principles and organizing its powers in such form, as to them shall seem most likely to effect their Safety and Happiness. Prudence, indeed, will dictate that Governments long established should not be changed for light and transient causes; and accordingly all experience hath shown that mankind are more disposed to suffer, while evils are sufferable, than to right themselves by abolishing the forms to which they are accustomed. But when a long train of abuses and usurpations pursuing invariably the same Object evinces a design to reduce them under absolute Despotism, it is their right, it is their duty, to throw off such government, and to provide new Guards for their future security.

Such has been the patient sufferance of 5
these Colonies; and such is now the necessity which constrains them to alter their former Systems of Government. The history of the present King of Great Britain is a history of repeated injuries and usurpations, all having in direct object the establishment of an absolute Tyranny over these States. To prove this, let Facts be submitted to a candid world.

He has refused his Assent to Laws, the most wholesome and necessary for the public good.

He has forbidden his Governors to pass Laws of immediate and pressing importance, unless suspended in their operation till his Assent should be obtained; and when so suspended, he has utterly neglected to attend to them.

He has refused to pass over Laws for the accommodation of large districts of people, unless those people would relinquish the right of Representation in the Legislature, a right inestimable to them and formidable to tyrants only.

He has called together legislative bodies at places unusual, uncomfortable, and distant from the depository of their Public Records, for the sole purpose of fatiguing them into compliance with his measures.

He has dissolved Representative Houses 10
repeatedly, for opposing with manly firmness his invasions on the rights of the people.

He has refused for a long time, after such dissolutions, to cause others to be elected; whereby the Legislative Powers, incapable of Annihilation, have returned to the People at large for their exercise; the State remaining in the mean time exposed to all the dangers of invasion from without, and convulsions within.

He has endeavored to prevent the population of these States, for that purpose obstructing the Laws of Naturalization of Foreigners; refusing to pass others to encourage their migration hither, and raising the conditions of new Appropriations of Lands.

He has obstructed the Administration of Justice, by refusing his Assent to Laws for establishing Judiciary Powers.

He has made Judges dependent on his Will alone, for the tenure of their offices, and the amount and payment of their salaries.

He has erected a multitude of New Offices, 15
and sent hither swarms of Officers to harass our People, and eat out their substance.

He has kept among us, in time of peace, Standing Armies without the consent of our Legislature.

He has affected to render the Military independent of and superior to the Civil Power.

He has combined with others to subject us to jurisdictions foreign to our constitution, and unacknowledged by our laws; giving his Assent to their acts of pretended Legislation:

For quartering large bodies of armed troops among us:

For protecting them, by a mock Trial, 20
from Punishment for any Murders which they should commit on the Inhabitants of these States:

For cutting off our Trade with all parts of the world:

For imposing Taxes on us without our Consent:

For depriving us in many cases, of the benefits of Trial by Jury:

For transporting us beyond Seas to be tried for pretended offenses:

For abolishing the free System of English Laws in a Neighbouring Province, establishing therein an Arbitrary government, and enlarging its boundaries so as to render it at once an example and fit instrument for introducing the same absolute rule into these Colonies:

For taking away our Charters, abolishing our most valuable Laws, and altering fundamentally the Forms of our Governments.

For suspending our own Legislatures, and declaring themselves invested with Power to legislate for us in all cases whatsoever.

He has abdicated Government here, by declaring us out of his Protection and waging War against us.

He has plundered our seas, ravaged our Coasts, burnt our towns and destroyed the Lives of our people.

He is at this time transporting large Armies of foreign Mercenaries to compleat the works of death, desolation and tyranny, already begun with circumstances of Cruelty & perfidy scarcely paralleled in the most barbarous ages, and totally unworthy the Head of a civilized nation.

He has constrained our fellow Citizens taken Captive on the high Seas to bear Arms against their Country, to become the executioners of their friends and Brethren, or to fall themselves by their Hands.

He has excited domestic insurrections amongst us, and has endeavored to bring on the inhabitants of our frontiers, the merciless Indian Savages, whose known rule of warfare is an undistinguished destruction of all ages, sexes and conditions.

In every stage of these Oppressions We Have Petitioned for Redress in the most humble terms: Our repeated petitions have been answered only by repeated injury. A Prince, whose character is thus marked by every act which may define a Tyrant, is unfit to be the ruler of a free People.

Nor have We been wanting in attention to our British brethren. We have warned them from time to time of attempts by their legislature to extend an unwarrantable jurisdiction over us. We have reminded them of the circumstances of our emigration and settlement here. We have appealed to their native justice and magnanimity and we have conjured them by the ties of our common kindred to disavow these usurpations, which would inevitably interrupt our connections and correspondence. They too have been deaf to the voice of justice and of consanguinity. We must, therefore, acquiesce in the necessity, which denounces our Separation, and hold them, as we hold the rest of mankind, Enemies in War, in Peace Friends.

We, therefore, the Representatives of the United States of America, in General Congress, Assembled, appealing to the Supreme Judge of the world of the rectitude of our intentions, do, in the Name, and by Authority of the good People of these Colonies, solemnly publish and declare, That these United Colonies are, and of Right ought to be, Free and Independent States; that they are Absolved from all Allegiance to the British Crown, and that all political connection between them and the State of Great Britain, is and ought to be totally dissolved; and that as Free and Independent States, they have full power to levy War, conclude Peace, contract Alliances, establish Commerce, and to do all other Acts and Things which Independent States may of right do. And for the support of this Declaration, with a firm reliance on the protection of Divine Providence, we mutually pledge to each other our lives, our Fortunes and our sacred Honor.

Topics for Critical Thinking and Writing

1. According to the first paragraph, for what audience was the Declaration of Independence written? To what other audiences do you think the document was (in one way or another) addressed?
2. In the Declaration of Independence, it is argued that the colonists are entitled to certain things and that under certain conditions they may behave in a certain way. Make explicit the syllogism that Thomas Jefferson is arguing.
3. What evidence does Jefferson offer to support his major premise? His minor premise?
4. In paragraph 2, the Declaration cites "certain unalienable Rights" and mentions three: "life, liberty and the pursuit of happiness." What is an unalienable right? If someone has an unalienable (or inalienable) right, does that imply that he or she also has certain duties? If so, what are these duties? John Locke, a century earlier (1690), asserted that all men have a natural right to "life, liberty, and property." Do you think the decision to drop "property" and substitute "pursuit of happiness" improved Locke's claim? Explain how or why you think Jefferson changed the phrase.
5. The Declaration states that it is intended to "prove" that the acts of the government of George III had as their "direct object the establishment of an absolute Tyranny" in the American colonies (para. 5). Write an essay of 500 to 750 words showing whether the evidence offered in the Declaration "proves" this claim to your satisfaction. (You will want to define *absolute tyranny.*) If you think further evidence is needed to "prove" the colonists' point, indicate what this evidence might be.
6. King George III has asked you to reply, on his behalf, to the colonists. Write this reply in 500 to 750 words. (Caution: A good reply will probably require you to do some reading about the period.)
7. Write a declaration of your own, setting forth in 500 to 750 words why some group is entitled to independence. You may want to argue that adolescents should not be compelled to attend school, that animals should not be confined in zoos, or that persons who use drugs should be able to buy them legally. Begin with a premise, then set forth facts illustrating the unfairness of the present condition, and conclude by stating what the new condition will mean to society.

ELIZABETH CADY STANTON

Elizabeth Cady Stanton (1815–1902), a lawyer's daughter and journalist's wife, proposed in 1848 a convention to address the "social, civil, and religious condition and rights of women." Responding to Stanton's call, women and men from all over the Northeast traveled to the Woman's Rights Convention held in the village of Seneca Falls, New York. Her declaration, adopted by the convention — but only after vigorous debate and some amendments by others — became the platform for the women's rights movement in the United States.

Declaration of Sentiments and Resolutions

When, in the course of human events, it becomes necessary for one portion of the family of man to assume among the people of the earth a position different from that which they have hitherto occupied, but one to which the laws of nature and of nature's God entitle them, a decent respect to the opinions of mankind requires that they should declare the causes that impel them to such a course.

We hold these truths to be self-evident: that all men and women are created equal; that they are endowed by their Creator with certain inalienable rights; that among these are life, liberty and the pursuit of happiness; that to secure these rights governments are instituted, deriving their just powers from the consent of the governed. Whenever any form of government becomes destructive of these ends, it is the right of those who suffer from it to refuse allegiance to it, and to insist upon the institution of a new government, laying its foundation on such principles, and organizing its powers in such form, as to them shall seem most likely to effect their safety and happiness. Prudence, indeed, will dictate that governments long established should not be changed for light and transient causes; and accordingly all experience hath shown that mankind are more disposed to suffer, while evils are sufferable, than to right themselves by abolishing the forms to which they were accustomed. But when a long train of abuses and usurpations, pursuing invariably the same object, evinces a design to reduce them under absolute despotism, it is their duty to throw off such government, and to provide new guards for their future security. Such has been the patient sufferance of the women under this government, and such is now the necessity which constrains them to demand the equal station to which they are entitled.

The history of mankind is a history of repeated injuries and usurpations on the part of man toward woman, having in direct object the establishment of an absolute tyranny over her. To prove this, let facts be submitted to a candid world.

He has never permitted her to exercise her inalienable right to the elective franchise.

He has compelled her to submit to laws, in the formation of which she had no voice.

He has withheld from her rights which are given to the most ignorant and degraded men — both natives and foreigners.

Having deprived her of this first right of a citizen, the elective franchise, thereby leaving her without representation in the halls of legislation, he has oppressed her on all sides.

He has made her, if married, in the eye of the law, civilly dead.

He has taken from her all right in property, even to the wages she earns.

He has made her, morally, an irresponsible being, as she can commit many crimes with impunity, provided they be done in the presence of her husband. In the covenant of marriage, she is compelled to promise obedience to her husband, he becoming to all intents and purposes, her master — the law giving him power to deprive her of her liberty, and to administer chastisement.

He has so framed the laws of divorce, as to what shall be the proper causes, and in case of separation, to whom the guardianship of the children shall be given, as to be wholly regardless of the happiness of women — the law, in all cases, going upon a false supposition of the supremacy of man, and giving all power into his hands.

After depriving her of all rights as a married woman, if single, and the owner of property, he has taxed her to support a government which recognizes her only when her property can be made profitable to it.

He has monopolized nearly all the profitable employments, and from those she is permitted to follow, she receives but a scanty remuneration. He closes against her all the avenues to wealth and distinction which he considers most honorable to himself. As a teacher of theology, medicine, or law, she is not known.

He has denied her the facilities for obtaining a thorough education, all colleges being closed against her.

He allows her in Church, as well as State, 15
but a subordinate position, claiming Apostolic authority for her exclusion from the ministry, and, with some exceptions, from any public participation in the affairs of the Church.

He has created a false public sentiment by giving to the world a different code of morals for men and women, by which moral delinquencies which exclude women from society, are not only tolerated, but deemed of little account in man.

He has usurped the prerogative of Jehovah himself, claiming it as his right to assign for her a sphere of action, when that belongs to her conscience and to her God.

He has endeavored, in every way that he could, to destroy her confidence in her own powers, to lessen her self-respect, and to make her willing to lead a dependent and abject life.

Now, in view of this entire disfranchisement of one-half the people of this country, their social and religious degradation — in view of the unjust laws above mentioned, and because women do feel themselves aggrieved, oppressed, and fraudulently deprived of their most sacred rights, we insist that they have immediate admission to all the rights and privileges which belong to them as citizens of the United States.

In entering upon the great work before 20
us, we anticipate no small amount of misconception, misrepresentation, and ridicule; but we shall use every instrumentality within our power to effect our object. We shall employ agents, circulate tracts, petition the State and National legislatures, and endeavor to enlist the pulpit and the press in our behalf. We hope this Convention will be followed by a series of Conventions embracing every part of the country.

[The following resolutions were discussed by Lucretia Mott, Thomas and Mary Ann McClintock, Amy Post, Catharine A. F. Stebbins, and others, and were adopted:]

Whereas, The great precept of nature is conceded to be, that "man shall pursue his own true and substantial happiness." Blackstone in his Commentaries remarks, that this law of Nature being coeval with mankind, and dictated by God himself, is of course superior in obligation to any other. It is binding over all the globe, in all countries, and at all times; no human laws are of any validity if contrary to this, and such of them as are valid, derive all their force, and all their validity, and all their authority, mediately and immediately, from this original; therefore,

Resolved, That such laws as conflict, in any way, with the true and substantial happiness of woman, are contrary to the great precept of nature and of no validity, for this is "superior in obligation to any other."

Resolved, That all laws which prevent woman from occupying such a station in society as her conscience shall dictate, or which place her in a position inferior to that of man, are contrary to the great precept of nature, and therefore of no force or authority.

Resolved, That woman is man's equal — was intended to be so by the Creator, and the highest good of the race demands that she should be recognized as such.

Resolved, That the women of this country ought to be enlightened in regard to the laws under which they live, that they may no longer publish their degradation by declaring themselves satisfied with their present position, nor their ignorance, by asserting that they have all the rights they want. 25

Resolved, That inasmuch as man, while claiming for himself intellectual superiority, does accord to woman moral superiority, it is preeminently his duty to encourage her to speak and teach, as she has an opportunity, in all religious assemblies.

Resolved, That the same amount of virtue, delicacy, and refinement of behavior that is required of woman in the social state, should also be required of man, and the same transgressions should be visited with equal severity on both man and woman.

Resolved, That the objection of indelicacy and impropriety, which is so often brought against woman when she addresses a public audience, comes with a very ill-grace from those who encourage, by their attendance, her appearance on the stage, in the concert, or in feats of the circus.

Resolved, That woman has too long rested satisfied in the circumscribed limits which corrupt customs and a perverted application of the Scriptures have marked out for her, and that it is time she should move in the enlarged sphere which her great Creator has assigned her.

Resolved, That it is the duty of the women 30 of this country to secure to themselves their sacred right to the elective franchise.

Resolved, That the equality of human rights results necessarily from the fact of the identity of the race in capabilities and responsibilities.

Resolved, therefore, That, being invested by the Creator with the same capabilities, and the same consciousness of responsibility for their exercise, it is demonstrably the right and duty of woman, equally with man, to promote every righteous cause by every righteous means; and especially in regard to the great subjects of morals and religion, it is self-evidently her right to participate with her brother in teaching them, both in private and in public, by writing and by speaking, by any instrumentalities proper to be used, and in any assemblies proper to be held; and this being a self-evident truth growing out of the divinely implanted principles of human nature, any custom or authority adverse to it, whether modern or wearing the hoary sanction of antiquity, is to be regarded as a self-evident falsehood, and at war with mankind.

[At the last session Lucretia Mott offered and spoke to the following resolution:]

Resolved, That the speedy success of our cause depends upon the zealous and untiring efforts of both men and women, for the overthrow of the monopoly of the pulpit, and for the securing to woman an equal participation with men in the various trades, professions, and commerce.

Topics for Critical Thinking and Writing

1. Elizabeth Cady Stanton echoes the Declaration of Independence because she wishes to associate her ideas and the movement she supports with a document and a movement that her readers esteem. She must have believed that if readers esteem the Declaration of Independence, they must grant the justice of her goals. Does her strategy work, or does it backfire by making her essay seem strained? Explain your response.
2. When Stanton insists that women have an "inalienable right to the elective franchise" (para. 4), what does she mean by "inalienable"?

3. Stanton complains that men have made married women, "in the eye of the law, civilly dead" (para. 8). What does she mean by "civilly dead"? How is it possible for a person to be biologically alive and yet civilly dead?
4. Stanton objects that women are "not known" as teachers of "theology, medicine, or law" (para. 13). Is that still true today? Do some research in your library and then write three 100-word biographical sketches, one each on well-known female professors of theology, medicine, and law.
5. The Declaration of Sentiments and Resolutions claims that women have "the same capabilities" as men (para. 32). Yet in 1848 Stanton and the others at Seneca Falls knew, or should have known, that history recorded no example of a woman philosopher comparable to Plato or Kant, a composer comparable to Beethoven or Chopin, a scientist comparable to Galileo or Newton, or a mathematician comparable to Euclid or Descartes. Do these facts contradict the Declaration's claim? If not, why not? How else but by different intellectual capabilities do you think such facts can be explained?
6. Stanton's declaration is more than 165 years old. Have all the issues she raised been satisfactorily resolved? If not, which ones remain?
7. In our society, children have very few rights. For instance, a child cannot decide to drop out of elementary school or high school, and a child cannot decide to leave his or her parents to reside with some other family that he or she finds more compatible. Whatever your view of children's rights, compose the best Declaration of the Rights of Children that you can.

MARTIN LUTHER KING JR.

Martin Luther King Jr. (1929–1968) was born in Atlanta and educated at Morehouse College, Crozer Theological Seminary, and Boston University. In 1954, he was called to serve as a Baptist minister in Montgomery, Alabama. During the next two years, he achieved national fame when, using a policy of nonviolent resistance, he successfully led the boycott against segregated bus lines in Montgomery. He then helped organize the Southern Christian Leadership Conference, which furthered civil rights, first in the South and then nationwide. In 1964, he was awarded the Nobel Peace Prize. Four years later, he was assassinated in Memphis, Tennessee, while supporting striking garbage workers.

The speech presented here was delivered from the steps of the Lincoln Memorial, in Washington, DC, in 1963, the hundredth anniversary of the Emancipation Proclamation. King's immediate audience consisted of more than two hundred thousand people who had come to demonstrate for civil rights.

I Have a Dream

I am happy to join with you today in what will go down in history as the greatest demonstration for freedom in the history of our nation.

Five score years ago, a great American, in whose symbolic shadow we stand today, signed the Emancipation Proclamation. This momentous decree came as a great beacon light of hope to millions of Negro slaves who had been seared in the flames of withering injustice. It came as a joyous daybreak to end the long night of their captivity. But one hundred years later, the Negro still is not free. One hundred years later, the life of the Negro is still sadly crippled by the manacles of segregation and the chains of discrimination. One hundred years later, the Negro lives on a lonely island of poverty in the midst of a vast ocean of material prosperity. One hundred years later, the Negro is still anguished in the corners of American society and finds himself in exile in his own land. And so we have come here today to dramatize a shameful condition.

In a sense we have come to our nation's capital to cash a check. When the architects of our republic wrote the magnificent words of the Constitution and the Declaration of Independence, they were signing a promissory note to which every American was to fall heir. This note was the promise that all men — yes, black men as well as white men — would be guaranteed the inalienable rights of life, liberty, and the pursuit of happiness.

It is obvious today that America has defaulted on this promissory note insofar as her citizens of color are concerned. Instead of honoring this sacred obligation, America has given the Negro people a bad check, a check which has come back marked "insufficient funds." But we refuse to believe that the bank of justice is bankrupt. We refuse to believe that there are insufficient funds in the great vaults of opportunity of this nation; and so we have come to cash this check, a check that will give us upon demand the riches of freedom and the security of justice.

5 We have also come to this hallowed spot to remind America of the fierce urgency of *now*. This is no time to engage in the luxury of cooling off or to take the tranquilizing drug of gradualism. *Now* is the time to make real promises of democracy. *Now* is the time to rise from the dark and desolate valley of segregation to the sunlit path of racial justice. *Now* is the time to lift our nation from the quicksands of racial injustice to the solid rock of brotherhood. *Now* is the time to make justice a reality for all of God's children.

It would be fatal for the nation to overlook the urgency of the moment. This sweltering summer of the Negro's legitimate discontent will not pass until there is an invigorating autumn of freedom and equality. Nineteen sixty-three is not an end, but a beginning. And those who hope that the Negro needed to blow off steam and will now be content will have a rude awakening if the nation returns to business as usual. There will be neither rest nor tranquility in America until the Negro is granted his citizenship rights. The whirlwinds of revolt will continue to shake the foundations of our nation until the bright day of justice emerges.

But there is something that I must say to my people who stand on the warm threshold which leads into the palace of justice. In the process of gaining our rightful place, we must not be guilty of wrongful deeds. Let us not seek to satisfy our thirst for freedom by drinking from the cup of bitterness and hatred. We must forever conduct our struggle on the high plane of dignity and discipline. We must not allow our creative protest to degenerate into physical violence. Again and again we must rise to the majestic heights of meeting physical force with soul force. And the marvelous new militancy which has engulfed the Negro community must not lead us to a distrust of all white people; for many of our white brothers, as evidenced by their presence here today, have come to realize that their destiny is tied up with our destiny, and they have come to realize that their freedom is inextricably bound to our freedom.

We cannot walk alone. And as we walk we must make the pledge that we shall always march ahead. We cannot turn back. There are those who are asking the devotees of civil rights, "When will you be satisfied?" We can never be satisfied as long as the Negro is the victim of the unspeakable horrors of police brutality. We can never be satisfied as long as our bodies, heavy with the fatigue of travel, cannot gain lodging in the motels of the highways and the hotels of the cities. We cannot be satisfied as long as the Negro's basic mobility is from a smaller ghetto to a larger one. We can never be satisfied as long as our children are stripped of their selfhood and robbed of their dignity by signs stating "For Whites Only." We cannot be satisfied as long as the Negro in Mississippi cannot vote and a Negro in New York believes he has nothing for which to vote. No, no, we are not satisfied, and we will not be satisfied until justice rolls down like waters and righteousness like a mighty stream.[1]

I am not unmindful that some of you have come here out of great trials and tribulations. Some of you have come fresh from narrow jail cells. Some of you have come from areas where your quest for freedom left you battered by the storms of persecution and staggered by the winds of police brutality. You have been the veterans of creative suffering. Continue to work with the faith that unearned suffering is redemptive.

10 Go back to Mississippi, and go back to Alabama. Go back to South Carolina. Go back to Georgia. Go back to Louisiana. Go back to the slums and ghettos of our Northern cities, knowing that somehow this situation can and will be changed. Let us not wallow in the valley of despair.

I say to you today, my friends, even though we face the difficulties of today and tomorrow, I still have a dream. It is a dream deeply rooted in the American dream. I have a dream that one day this nation will rise up and live out the true meaning of its creed: "We hold these truths to be self-evident, that all men are created equal." I have a dream that one day, on the red hills of Georgia, sons of former slaves and the sons of former slave owners will be able to sit down together at the table of brotherhood. I have a dream that one day even the state of Mississippi, a state sweltering with the heat of injustice, sweltering with the heat of oppression, will be transformed into an oasis of freedom and justice. I have a dream that my four little children will one day live in a nation where they will not be judged by the color of their skin, but by the content of their character.

I have a dream today. I have a dream that one day down in Alabama — with its vicious racists, with its governor's lips dripping with the words of interposition and nullification — one day right there in Alabama, little black boys and black girls will be able to join hands with little white boys and white girls as sisters and brothers.

I have a dream today. I have a dream that one day every valley shall be exalted and every hill and mountain shall be made low, the rough places will be made plain and the crooked places will be made straight, and the glory of the Lord shall be revealed, and all flesh shall see it together.[2]

This is our hope. This is the faith that I go back to the South with. And with this faith we will be able to hew out of the mountain of despair a stone of hope. With this faith we will be able to transform the jangling discords of our nation into a beautiful symphony of brotherhood. With this faith we will be able

[1]**justice . . . stream** A quotation from the Hebrew Bible: Amos 5:24. [Editors' note]

[2]**every valley . . . see it together** Another quotation from the Hebrew Bible: Isaiah 40:4–5. [Editors' note]

to work together, to play together, to struggle together, to go to jail together, to stand up for freedom together, knowing that we will be free one day.

15 And this will be the day — this will be the day when all of God's children will be able to sing with new meaning:

My country, 'tis of thee,
Sweet land of liberty,
  Of thee I sing;
Land where my fathers died,
Land of the Pilgrim's pride,
From every mountainside
  Let freedom ring.

And if America is to be a great nation, this must become true.

And so let freedom ring from the prodigious hilltops of New Hampshire. Let freedom ring from the mighty mountains of New York. Let freedom ring from the heightening Alleghenies of Pennsylvania. Let freedom ring from the snow-capped Rockies of Colorado. Let freedom ring from the curvaceous slopes of California.

But not only that. Let freedom ring from Stone Mountain of Georgia. Let freedom ring from Lookout Mountain of Tennessee. Let freedom ring from every hill and molehill of Mississippi. "From every mountainside let freedom ring."

And when this happens — when we allow freedom to ring, when we let it ring from every village and every hamlet, from every state and every city — we will be able to speed up that day when all of God's children, Black men and white men, Jews and Gentiles, Protestants and Catholics, will be able to join hands and sing in the words of the old Negro spiritual: "Free at last! Free at last! Thank God Almighty. We are free at last!"

Topics for Critical Thinking and Writing

1. Analyze the rhetoric — the oratorical art — of the second paragraph. What, for instance, is gained by saying "five score years ago" instead of "a hundred years ago"? By metaphorically calling the Emancipation Proclamation "a great beacon light of hope"? By saying that "Negro slaves . . . had been seared in the flames of withering injustice"? And what of the metaphors "daybreak" and "the long night of . . . captivity"?
2. Do the first two paragraphs make an effective opening? Why?
3. In paragraphs 3 and 4, Martin Luther King Jr. uses the metaphor of a bad check. Rewrite paragraph 3 *without* using any of King's metaphors and then in a paragraph evaluate the differences between King's version and yours.
4. King's highly metaphoric speech appeals to emotions, but it also offers *reasons*. What reasons, for instance, does King give to support his belief that African Americans should not resort to physical violence in their struggle against segregation and discrimination?
5. When King delivered the speech, his audience at the Lincoln Memorial was primarily African American. Do you think the speech is also addressed to other Americans? Explain.
6. The speech can be divided into three parts: paragraphs 1 through 6; paragraphs 7 ("But there is") through 10; and paragraph 11 ("I say to you today, my friends") to the end. Summarize each of these three parts in a sentence or two so that the basic organization of the speech is evident.

7. King says (para. 11) that his dream is "deeply rooted in the American dream." First, what is the American dream, as King seems to understand it? Second, how does King establish his point — that is, what evidence does he use to convince us — that his dream is the American dream?

8. King delivered his speech in 1963, more than half a century ago. In an essay of 500 words, argue that the speech still is — or is not — relevant. Or write an essay of 500 words in which you state what you take to be the "American dream" and argue that it now is or is not readily available to African Americans.

W. H. AUDEN

Wystan Hugh Auden (1907–1973) was born in York, England, and educated at Oxford University. In the 1930s his witty left-wing poetry earned him wide acclaim as the leading poet of his generation. In 1939 he came to the United States, becoming a citizen in 1946 but returning to England for his last years. Much of Auden's poetry is characterized by a combination of colloquial diction and technical dexterity. The poem reprinted here was originally published in 1940.

The Unknown Citizen

(To JS/07/M/378
This Marble Monument
Is Erected by the State)

He was found by the Bureau of Statistics to be
One against whom there was no official complaint,
And all the reports on his conduct agree
That, in the modern sense of an old-fashioned word, he was a saint,
For in everything he did he served the Greater Community.
Except for the War till the day he retired
He worked in a factory and never got fired,
But satisfied his employers, Fudge Motors Inc.
Yet he wasn't a scab or odd in his views,
For his Union reports that he paid his dues,
(Our report on his Union shows it was sound)
And our Social Psychology workers found
That he was popular with his mates and liked a drink.
The Press are convinced that he bought a paper every day
And that his reactions to advertisements were normal in every way.
Policies taken out in his name prove that he was fully insured,
And his Health-card shows he was once in hospital but left it cured.
Both Producers Research and High-Grade Living declare
He was fully sensible to the advantages of the Installment Plan
And had everything necessary to the Modern Man,
A phonograph, radio, a car and a frigidaire.
Our researches into Public Opinion are content
That he held the proper opinions for the time of year;
When there was peace, he was for peace; when there was war, he went.

He was married and added five children to the population,
Which our Eugenist says was the right number for a parent of his generation,
And our teachers report that he never interfered with their education.
Was he free? Was he happy? The question is absurd:
Had anything been wrong, we should certainly have heard.

Topics for Critical Thinking and Writing

1. Who is the narrator in W. H. Auden's poem, and on what sort of occasion is the narrator speaking? How do you know?
2. France, Great Britain, and the United States all have monuments to "The Unknown" (formerly "The Unknown Soldier"). How is Auden's proposed monument like and unlike these war memorials?
3. The poem ends by asking "Was he free? Was he happy?" and the questions are dismissed summarily. Is that because the answers are so obvious? What answers (obvious or subtle) do you think the poem offers to these questions?
4. What does it mean in line 23 that the unknown citizen "held the proper opinions for the time of year"? Explain and tell why this attribute is presented as something lamentable.
5. Read the selection from Thomas More's *Utopia*, and write an essay of 500 to 750 words setting forth More's likely response to Auden's poem.
6. Reread the section on author-based, text-based, and reader-based approaches to literature (pp. 376–78). Select one type of approach, and evaluate Auden's poem using that approach.

EMMA LAZARUS

Emma Lazarus (1849–1887) was born in New York City as the fourth of seven children in a well-established family. Her parents provided her with a private education, and her father supported her writing: When Lazarus was just seventeen, her father had a collection of Lazarus's poetry, called *Poems and Translations: Written between the Ages of Fourteen and Sixteen*, printed for private circulation. In addition to poetry, Lazarus wrote essays, plays, several highly respected translations, and a novel, going on to become part of the literary elite in late nineteenth-century New York. Lazarus is probably known best for the poem that follows, "The New Colossus." She wrote this sonnet in 1883 as a donation to an auction held to raise money to build the pedestal for the Statue of Liberty. The poem was installed on the base of the statue in 1903, nearly two decades after Lazarus's death in 1887.

The New Colossus

Not like the brazen giant of Greek fame,
With conquering limbs astride from land to land;
Here at our sea-washed, sunset gates shall stand
A mighty woman with a torch, whose flame
Is the imprisoned lightning, and her name
Mother of Exiles. From her beacon-hand
Glows world-wide welcome; her mild eyes
command
The air-bridged harbor that twin cities frame.
"Keep, ancient lands, your storied pomp!"
cries she
With silent lips. "Give me your tired, your poor,
Your huddled masses yearning to breathe free,
The wretched refuse of your teeming shore.
Send these, the homeless, tempest-tost to me,
I lift my lamp beside the golden door!"

Topics for Critical Thinking and Writing

1. In the opening line of the poem, Emma Lazarus alludes to the Colossus of Rhodes—a statue of the Greek titan-god of the sun Helios that was erected in the city of Rhodes in 280 BC. The Colossus was 98 feet tall, making it one of the tallest statues of the ancient world. Compare the language Lazarus uses to describe this "brazen giant of Greek fame" (l. 1) to the language she uses to describe the Statue of Liberty, the "Mother of Exiles" (l. 6). If both statues are symbols for nations, what kind of argument does Lazarus make by describing the two statues as she does?
2. Lazarus refers to the Statue of Liberty as the "Mother of Exiles." Do you think this description still holds up today in light of current debates about immigration laws? Write a brief essay of about 500 words using both historical evidence and current events to support your argument.
3. Notice the description of the Statue of Liberty's eyes as "mild" in line 7. Do you think it is an accurate depiction of how "the homeless, tempest-tost" are generally seen in the United States today? Why, or why not?
4. Do some research into immigration in the United States today and then write an essay in which you judge whether or not the current immigration debate lives up to the ideals of "The New Colossus."

WALT WHITMAN

Walt Whitman (1819–1892) is one of the most renowned poets in the American canon. He was born in Huntington, New York, as the second of nine children to Walter and Louisa Van Velsor Whitman. He attended public school until age eleven, at which time he concluded his formal schooling and took a job as a printer's assistant. He quickly learned the printing trade, and at age seventeen, he became a teacher. He continued to teach until 1841, when he became a full-time journalist. Whitman founded and served as editor of the *Long-Islander*, a weekly Huntington newspaper, and went on to edit several other newspapers in the New York area before leaving the newspaper business in 1848. He moved back in with his parents at that point, working as a part-time carpenter and beginning work on *Leaves of Grass*, his most enduring and famous collection of poems. He first published *Leaves* at his own expense in 1855, although he continued to revise it several times throughout the rest of his life. "One Song, America, Before I Go" first appeared in the 1900 edition of *Leaves of Grass*.

One Song, America, Before I Go

One song, America, before I go,
I'd sing, o'er all the rest, with trumpet sound,
For thee — the Future.

I'd sow a seed for thee of endless Nationality;
I'd fashion thy Ensemble, including Body and
  Soul;
I'd show, away ahead, thy real Union, and how
  it may be accomplish'd.

(The paths to the House I seek to make,
But leave to those to come, the House itself.)

Belief I sing — and Preparation;
As Life and Nature are not great with
  reference to the Present only,
But greater still from what is yet to come,
Out of that formula for Thee I sing.

Topics for Critical Thinking and Writing

1. Walt Whitman identifies his poem as a song for America. What kinds of songs do you usually think of when you think about America? How does Whitman's tone compare to other songs about the country?
2. Why is the future important in this poem? What argument is Whitman making about the present and past of the country?
3. "One Song, America, Before I Go" was originally published in 1900. If Whitman were alive today, how do you think he would assess the state of the country? Do you think he would think that the "Belief" and "Preparation" (l. 9) he advised had been heeded? Why, or why not?

URSULA K. LE GUIN

Ursula K. Le Guin (1929–2018) was born in Berkeley, California, the daughter of a distinguished mother (Theodora Kroeber, a folklorist) and father (Alfred L. Kroeber, an anthropologist). After graduating from Radcliffe College, she earned a master's degree at Columbia University; in 1952, she held a Fulbright Fellowship for study in Paris, where she met and married Charles Le Guin, a historian. She began writing in earnest while bringing up three children. Although her work is most widely known to buffs of science fiction, it interests many other readers who normally do not care for sci-fi because it usually has large moral or political dimensions.

Le Guin said that she was prompted to write the following story by a remark she encountered in William James's "The Moral Philosopher and the Moral Life." James suggests there that if millions of people could be "kept permanently happy on the one simple condition that a certain lost soul on the far-off edge of things should lead a life of lonely torment," our moral sense "would make us immediately feel" that it would be "hideous" to accept such a bargain. This story first appeared in *New Dimensions* 3 (1973).

The Ones Who Walk Away from Omelas

With a clamor of bells that set the swallows soaring, the Festival of Summer came to the city Omelas, bright-towered by the sea. The rigging of the boats in harbor sparkled with flags. In the streets between houses with red roofs and painted walls, between old moss-grown gardens and under avenues of trees, past great parks and public buildings, processions moved. Some were decorous: old people in long stiff robes of mauve and gray, grave master workmen, quiet, merry women carrying their babies and chatting as they walked. In other streets the music beat faster, a shimmering of gong and tambourine, and the people went dancing, the procession was a dance. Children dodged in and out, their high calls rising like the swallows' crossing flights over the music and the singing. All the processions wound towards the north side of the city, where on the great water-meadow called the Green Fields boys and girls, naked in the bright air, with mudstained feet and ankles and long, lithe arms, exercised their restive horses before the race. The horses wore no gear at all but a halter without bit. Their manes were braided with streamers of silver, gold, and green. They flared their nostrils and pranced and boasted to one another; they were vastly excited, the horse being the only animal who has adopted our ceremonies as his own. Far off to the north and west the mountains stood up half encircling Omelas on her bay. The air of morning was so clear that the snow still crowning the Eighteen Peaks burned with white-gold fire across the miles of sunlit air, under the dark blue of the sky. There was just enough wind to make the banners that marked the racecourse snap and flutter now and then. In the silence of the broad green meadows one could hear the music winding through the city streets, farther and nearer and ever approaching, a cheerful faint sweetness of the air that from time to time trembled and gathered together and broke out into the great joyous clanging of the bells.

Joyous! How is one to tell about joy? How describe the citizens of Omelas?

They were not simple folk, you see, though they were happy. But we do not say the words of cheer much any more. All smiles have become archaic. Given a description such as this one tends to make certain assumptions. Given a description such as this one tends to look next for the King, mounted on a splendid stallion and surrounded by his noble knights, or perhaps in a golden litter borne by great-muscled slaves. But there was no king. They did not use swords, or keep slaves. They were not barbarians. I do not know the rules and laws of their society, but I suspect that they were singularly few. As they did without monarchy and slavery, so they also got on without the stock exchange, the advertisement, the secret police, and the bomb. Yet I repeat that these were not simple folk, not dulcet shepherds, noble savages, bland utopians. They were not less complex than us. The trouble is that we have a bad habit, encouraged by pedants and sophisticates, of considering happiness as something rather stupid. Only pain is intellectual, only evil interesting. This is the treason of the artist: a refusal to admit the banality of evil and the terrible boredom of pain. If you can't lick 'em, join 'em. If it hurts, repeat it. But to praise despair is to condemn delight, to embrace violence is to lose hold of everything else. We have almost lost hold, we can no longer describe a happy man, nor make any celebration of joy. How can I tell you about the people of Omelas? They were not naïve and happy children — though their children were, in fact, happy. They were mature, intelligent, passionate adults whose lives were not wretched. O miracle! But I wish I could describe it better. I wish I could convince you. Omelas sounds in my words like a city in a fairy tale, long ago and far away, once upon a time. Perhaps it would be best if you imagined it as your own fancy bids, assuming it will rise to the occasion, for certainly I cannot suit you all. For instance, how about technology? I think that there would be no cars or helicopters in and above the streets; this follows from the fact that the people of Omelas are happy people. Happiness is based on a just discrimination of what is necessary, what is neither necessary nor destructive, and what is destructive. In the middle category, however — that of the unnecessary but undestructive, that of comfort, luxury, exuberance, etc. — they could perfectly well have central heating, subway trains, washing machines, and all kinds of marvelous devices not yet invented here, floating light-sources, fuelless power, a cure for the common cold. Or they could have none of that: it doesn't matter. As you like it. I incline to think that people from towns up and down the coast have been coming in to Omelas during the last days before the Festival on very fast little trains and double-decked trams, and that the train station of Omelas is actually the handsomest building in town, though plainer than the magnificent Farmers' Market. But even granted trains, I fear that Omelas so far strikes some of you as goody-goody. Smiles, bells, parades, horses, bleh. If so, please add an orgy. If an orgy would help, don't hesitate. Let us not, however, have temples from which issue beautiful nude priests and priestesses already half in ecstasy and ready to copulate with any man or woman, lover or stranger, who desires union with the deep godhead of the blood, although that was my first idea. But really it would be better not to have any temples in Omelas — at least, not manned temples. Religion yes, clergy no. Surely the beautiful nudes can just wander about, offering themselves like divine soufflés to the hunger of the needy and the rapture of the flesh. Let them join the processions. Let tambourines be struck above the copulations, and the glory of desire be proclaimed upon the gongs, and (a not unimportant point) let the offspring of these delightful rituals be beloved and looked after by all. One thing I know there is none of in Omelas is guilt. But what else should there be? I thought that first there were no drugs, but that is puritanical. For those who like it, the faint insistent sweetness of *drooz* may perfume the ways of the city, *drooz* which first brings a great lightness and brilliance to the mind and limbs, and then after some hours a dreamy languor, and wonderful visions at last of the very arcana and inmost secrets of the Universe, as well as exciting the pleasure of sex beyond all belief; and it is not habit-forming. For more modest tastes I think there ought to be beer. What else, what else belongs in the joyous city? The sense of victory, surely, the celebration of courage. But as we did without clergy, let us do without soldiers. The joy built upon successful slaughter is not the right kind of joy; it will not do; it is fearful and it is trivial. A boundless and generous contentment, a magnanimous triumph felt not against some outer enemy but in communion with the finest and fairest in the souls of all men everywhere and the splendor of the world's summer: this is what swells the hearts of the people of Omelas, and the victory they celebrate is that of life. I really don't think many of them need to take *drooz*.

Most of the processions have reached the Green Fields by now. A marvelous smell of cooking goes forth from the red and blue tents of the provisioners. The faces of small children are amiably sticky; in the benign grey beard of a man a couple of crumbs of rich pastry are entangled. The youths and girls have mounted their horses and are beginning to group around the starting line of the course. An old woman, small, fat, and laughing, is passing out flowers from a basket, and tall young men wear her flowers in their shining hair. A child of nine or ten sits at the edge of the crowd, alone, playing on a wooden flute. People pause to listen, and they smile, but they do not speak to him, for he never ceases playing and never sees them, his dark eyes wholly rapt in the sweet, thin magic of the tune.

He finishes, and slowly lowers his hands 5
holding the wooden flute.

As if that little private silence were the signal, all at once a trumpet sounds from the pavilion near the starting line: imperious, melancholy, piercing. The horses rear on their slender legs, and some of them neigh in answer. Sober-faced, the young riders stroke the horses' necks and soothe them, whispering, "Quiet, quiet, there my beauty, my hope. . . ." They begin to form in rank along the starting line. The crowds along the racecourse are like a field of grass and flowers in the wind. The Festival of Summer has begun.

Do you believe? Do you accept the festival, the city, the joy? No? Then let me describe one more thing.

In a basement under one of the beautiful public buildings of Omelas, or perhaps in the cellar of one of its spacious private homes, there is a room. It has one locked door, and no window. A little light seeps in dustily between cracks in the boards, secondhand from a cobwebbed window somewhere across the cellar. In one corner of the little room a couple of mops, with stiff, clotted, foul-smelling heads, stand near a rusty bucket. The floor is dirt, a little damp to the touch, as cellar dirt usually is. The room is about three paces long and two wide: a mere broom closet or disused tool room. In the room a child is sitting. It could be a boy or a girl. It looks about six, but actually is nearly ten. It is feeble-minded. Perhaps it was born defective, or perhaps it has become imbecile through fear, malnutrition, and neglect. It picks its nose and occasionally fumbles vaguely with its toes or genitals, as it sits hunched in the corner farthest from the bucket and the two mops. It is afraid of the mops. It finds them horrible. It shuts its eyes, but it knows the mops are still standing there; and the door is locked; and nobody will come. The door is always locked; and nobody ever comes, except that sometimes — the child has no understanding of time or interval — sometimes the door rattles terribly and opens, and a person, or several people, are there. One of them may come in and kick the child to make it stand up. The others never come close, but peer in at it with frightened, disgusted eyes. The food bowl and the water jug are hastily filled, the door is locked, the eyes disappear. The people at the door never say anything, but the child, who has not always lived in the tool room, and can remember sunlight and its mother's voice, sometimes speaks. "I will be good," it says. "Please let me out. I will be good!" They never answer. The child used to scream for help at night, and cry a good deal, but now it only makes a kind of whining, "eh-haa, eh-haa," and it speaks less and less often. It is so thin there are no calves to its legs; its belly protrudes; it lives on a half-bowl of corn meal and grease a day. It is naked. Its buttocks and thighs are a mass of festered sores, as it sits in its own excrement continually.

They all know it is there, all the people of Omelas. Some of them have come to see it, others are content merely to know it is there. They all know that it has to be there. Some of them understand why, and some do not, but they all understand that their happiness, the beauty of their city, the tenderness of their friendships, the health of their children, the wisdom of their scholars, the skill of their makers, even the abundance of their harvest and the kindly weathers of their skies, depend wholly on this child's abominable misery.

This is usually explained to children when they are between eight and twelve, whenever they seem capable of understanding; and most of those who come to see the child are young people, though often enough an adult comes, or comes back, to see the child. No matter how well the matter has been explained to them, these young spectators are always shocked and sickened at the sight. They feel disgust, which they had thought themselves superior to. They feel anger, outrage, impotence, despite all the explanations. They would like to do something for the child. But there is nothing they can do. If the child were brought up into the sunlight out of that vile place, if it were cleaned and fed and comforted, that would be a good thing, indeed; but if it were done, in that day and hour all the prosperity and beauty and delight of Omelas would wither and be destroyed. Those are the terms. To exchange all the goodness and grace of every life in Omelas for that single, small improvement: to throw away the happiness of thousands for the chance of the happiness of one: that would be to let guilt within the walls indeed.

The terms are strict and absolute; there may not even be a kind word spoken to the child.

Often the young people go home in tears, or in a tearless rage, when they have seen the child and faced this terrible paradox. They may brood over it for weeks or years. But as time goes on they begin to realize that even if the child could be released, it would not get much good of its freedom: a little vague pleasure of warmth and food, no doubt, but little more. It is too degraded and imbecile to know any real joy. It has been afraid too long ever to be free of fear. Its habits are too uncouth for it to respond to humane treatment. Indeed, after so long it would probably be wretched without walls about it to protect it, and darkness for its eyes, and its own excrement to sit in. Their tears at the bitter injustice dry when they begin to perceive the terrible justice of reality, and to accept it. Yet it is their tears and anger, the trying of their generosity and the acceptance of their helplessness, which are perhaps the true source of the splendor of their lives. Theirs is no vapid, irresponsible happiness. They know that they, like the child, are not free. They know compassion. It is the existence of the child, and their knowledge of its existence, that makes possible the nobility of their architecture, the poignancy of their music, the profundity of their science. It is because of the child that they are so gentle with children. They know that if the wretched one were not there snivelling in the dark, the other one, the flute-player, could make no joyful music as the young riders line up in their beauty for the race in the sunlight of the first morning of summer.

Now do you believe in them? Are they not more credible? But there is one more thing to tell, and this is quite incredible.

At times one of the adolescent girls or boys who go to see the child does not go home to weep or rage, does not, in fact, go home at all. Sometimes also a man or woman much older falls silent for a day or two, and then leaves home. These people go out into the street, and walk down the street alone. They keep walking, and walk straight out of the city of Omelas, through the beautiful gates. They keep walking across the farmlands of Omelas. Each one goes alone, youth or girl, man or woman. Night falls; the traveler must pass down village streets, between the houses with yellow-lit windows, and on out into the darkness of the fields. Each alone, they go west or north, towards the mountains. They go on. They leave Omelas, they walk ahead into the darkness, and they do not come back. The place they go towards is a place even less imaginable to most of us than the city of happiness. I cannot describe it at all. It is possible that it does not exist. But they seem to know where they are going, the ones who walk away from Omelas.

Topics for Critical Thinking and Writing

1. The narrator suggests, "Perhaps it would be best if you imagined it [Omelas] as your own fancy bids . . . for certainly I cannot suit you all" (para. 3). Do you think leaving the description of Omelas to the reader is an effective strategy for storytelling? Why, or why not?
2. Consider the narrator's assertion in paragraph 3 that happiness "is based on a just discrimination of what is necessary." Do you agree? Why, or why not?
3. Summarize the point of the story — not the plot, but what the story adds up to, what the author is getting at. What do you think is the intended meaning of the story?
4. Why do you think the citizens of Omelas hold a child captive, and why do you think they refer to the child as "it"?
5. Do you think the story implies a criticism of contemporary American society? Explain.

27

How and Why Do We Construct the "Other"?

JEAN-PAUL SARTRE

Jean-Paul Sartre (1905–1980) was a French philosopher, playwright, novelist, critic, and political activist whose influence on post–World War II intellectual life is significant. As the first philosopher of what he called "existentialism," Sartre drew from the notions about the individual and society established by Søren Kierkegaard and Friedrich Nietzsche; in his many philosophical treatises and artworks, Sartre addresses what he called "the phenomenon of being," a concept he articulated most prominently in *Being and Nothingness* (1943). In that work—and others around the same time, such as the plays *Nausea* (1938) and *No Exit* (1944) and the essay "Existentialism Is Humanism" (1944)—Sartre explored the limits and possibilities of individual consciousness in relation to knowledge and experience. His ideas inspired many of the countercultural trends of the postwar period, especially those that advocated nonconformity as a means of discovering personal authenticity and freedom. Further, they were politically salient: The concept of the individual liberated from social pressures to conform undermined cultural assumptions about the social order and gave weight to claims by women, African Americans, and others that their identities and experiences were inherently valuable and legitimate. Such views found articulation in much European and American art, literature, and theater, especially of the 1950s and 1960s.

Sartre was awarded (but declined) the Nobel Prize in Literature in 1964. The following selection is from his book *Anti-Semite and Jew* (1946).

Anti-Semite and Jew

If a man attributes all or part of his own misfortunes and those of his country to the presence of Jewish elements in the community, if he proposes to remedy this state of affairs by depriving the Jews of certain of their rights, by keeping them out of certain economic and social activities, by expelling them from the country, by exterminating all of them, we say that he has anti-Semitic *opinions.*

This word *opinion* makes us stop and think. It is the word a hostess uses to bring to an end a discussion that threatens to become acrimonious. It suggests that all points of view are equal; it reassures us, for it gives an inoffensive appearance to ideas by reducing them to the level of tastes. All tastes are natural; all opinions are permitted. Tastes, colors, and opinions are not open to discussion. In the name of democratic institutions, in the name of freedom of opinion, the anti-Semite asserts the right to preach the anti-Jewish crusade everywhere. . . .

A man may be a good father and a good husband, a conscientious citizen, highly cultivated, philanthropic, *and* in addition an anti-Semite. He may like fishing and the pleasures of love, may be tolerant in matters of religion, full of generous notions on the condition of the natives in Central Africa, *and* in addition detest the Jews. If he does not like them, we say, it is because his experience has shown him that they are bad, because statistics have taught him that they are dangerous, because certain historical factors have influenced his judgment. Thus this opinion seems to be the result of external causes, and those who wish to study it are prone to neglect the personality of the anti-Semite in favor of a consideration of the percentage of Jews who were mobilized in 1914, the percentage of Jews who are bankers, industrialists, doctors, and lawyers, or an examination of the history of the Jews in France since early times. They succeed in revealing a strictly objective situation that determines an equally objective current of opinion, and this they call anti-Semitism, for which they can draw up charts and determine the variations from 1870 to 1944. In such wise anti-Semitism appears to be at once a subjective taste that enters into combination with other tastes to form a personality, and an impersonal and social phenomenon which can be expressed by figures and averages, one which is conditioned by economic, historical, and political constants.

I do not say that these two conceptions are necessarily contradictory. I do say that they are dangerous and false. I would admit, if necessary, that one may have an opinion on the government's policy in regard to the wine industry, that is, that one may decide, *for certain reasons*, either to approve or condemn the free importation of wine from Algeria: here we have a case of holding an opinion on the administration of things. But I refuse to characterize as opinion a doctrine that is aimed directly at particular persons and that seeks to suppress their rights or to exterminate them. The Jew whom the anti-Semite wishes to lay hands upon is not a schematic being defined solely by his function, as under administrative law; or by his status or his acts, as under the Code. He is a Jew, the son of Jews, recognizable by his physique, by the color of his hair, by his clothing perhaps, and, so they say, by his character. Anti-Semitism does not fall within the category of ideas protected by the right of free opinion.

Indeed, it is something quite other than an 5
idea. It is first of all a *passion*. No doubt it can be set forth in the form of a theoretical proposition. The "moderate" anti-Semite is a courteous man who will tell you quietly: "Personally, I do not detest the Jews. I simply find it preferable, for various reasons, that they should play a lesser part in the activity of the nation." But a moment later, if you have gained his confidence, he will add with more abandon: "You see, there must be *something* about the Jews; they upset me physically."

This argument, which I have heard a hundred times, is worth examining. First of all, it derives from the logic of passion. For, really now, can we imagine anyone's saying seriously: "There must be something about tomatoes, for I have a horror of eating them"? In addition, it shows us that anti-Semitism in its most temperate and most evolved forms remains a syncretic whole which may be expressed by statements of reasonable tenor, but which can involve even bodily modifications. Some men are suddenly struck with impotence if they learn from the woman with whom they are making love that she is a Jewess. There is a disgust for the Jew, just as there is a disgust for the Chinese or the Negro among certain people. Thus it is not from the body that the sense of repulsion arises, since one may love a Jewess very well if one does not know what her race is; rather it is something that enters the body from the mind. It is an involvement of the mind, but one so deep-seated and complete that it extends to the physiological realm, as happens in cases of hysteria.

This involvement is not caused by experience. I have questioned a hundred people on the reasons for their anti-Semitism. Most of them have confined themselves to enumerating the defects with which tradition has endowed the Jews. "I detest them because they are selfish, intriguing, persistent, oily, tactless, etc." . . . A young woman said to me: "I have had the most horrible experiences with furriers; they robbed me, they burned the fur I entrusted to them. Well, they were all Jews." But why did she choose to hate Jews rather than furriers? Why Jews or furriers rather than such and such a Jew or such and such a furrier? Because she had in her a predisposition toward anti-Semitism.

A classmate of mine at the lycée[1] told me that Jews "annoy" him because of the thousands of injustices that "Jew-ridden" social organizations commit in their favor. "A Jew passed his *agrégation*[2] the year I was failed, and you can't make me believe that that fellow, whose father came from Cracow or Lemberg, understood a poem by Ronsard or an eclogue by Virgil better than I." But he admitted that he disdained the *agrégation* as a mere academic exercise, and that he didn't study for it. Thus, to explain his failure, he made use of two systems of interpretation, like those madmen who, when they are far gone in their madness, pretend to be the King of Hungary but, if questioned sharply, admit to being shoemakers. His thoughts moved on two planes without his being in the least embarrassed by it. As a matter of fact, he will in time manage to justify his past laziness on the grounds that it really would be too stupid to prepare for an examination in which Jews are passed in preference to good Frenchmen. . . . To understand my classmate's indignation we must recognize that he had adopted in advance a certain idea of the Jew, of his nature and of his role in society. And to be able to decide that among twenty-six competitors who were more successful than himself, it was the Jew who robbed him of his place, he must a priori have given preference in the conduct of his life to reasoning based on passion. Far from experience producing his idea of the Jew, it was the latter which explained his experience. If the Jew did not exist, the anti-Semite would invent him. . . .

The anti-Semite has chosen hate because hate is a faith; at the outset he has chosen to devaluate words and reasons. How entirely at ease he feels as a result. How futile and frivolous discussions about the rights of the Jew appear to him. He has placed himself on other ground from the beginning. If out of courtesy he consents for a moment to defend his point of view, he lends himself but does not give himself. He tries simply to project his intuitive certainty onto the plane of discourse. I mentioned awhile back some remarks by anti-Semites, all of them absurd: "I hate Jews because they make servants insubordinate, because a Jewish furrier robbed me, etc." Never believe that anti-Semites are completely unaware of the absurdity of their replies. They know that their remarks are frivolous, open to challenge. But they are amusing themselves, for it is their adversary

[1]**Lycée** school (Fr.). [Editors' note]

[2]Competitive state teachers' examination.

who is obliged to use words responsibly, since he believes in words. The anti-Semites have the *right* to play. They even like to play with discourse for, by giving ridiculous reasons, they discredit the seriousness of their interlocutors. They delight in acting in bad faith, since they seek not to persuade by sound argument but to intimidate and disconcert. If you press them too closely, they will abruptly fall silent, loftily indicating by some phrase that the time for argument is past. It is not that they are afraid of being convinced. They fear only to appear ridiculous or to prejudice by their embarrassment their hope of winning over some third person to their side.

10 If then, as we have been able to observe, the anti-Semite is impervious to reason and to experience, it is not because his conviction is strong. Rather his conviction is strong because he has chosen first of all to be impervious.

He has chosen also to be terrifying. People are afraid of irritating him. No one knows to what lengths the aberrations of his passion will carry him — but he knows, for this passion is not provoked by something external. He has it well in hand; it is obedient to his will: now he lets go the reins and now he pulls back on them. He is not afraid of himself, but he sees in the eyes of others a disquieting image — his own — and he makes his words and gestures conform to it. . . .

The anti-Semite readily admits that the Jew is intelligent and hard-working; he will even confess himself inferior in these respects. This concession costs him nothing, for he has, as it were, put those qualities in parentheses. Or rather they derive their value from the one who possesses them: the more virtues the Jew has the more dangerous he will be. The anti-Semite has no illusions about what he is. He considers himself an average man, modestly average, basically mediocre. There is no example of an anti-Semite's claiming individual superiority over the Jews. But you must not think that he is ashamed of his mediocrity; he takes pleasure in it; I will even assert that he has chosen it. This man fears every kind of solitariness, that of the genius as much as that of the murderer; he is the man of the crowd. However small his stature, he takes every precaution to make it smaller, lest he stand out from the herd and find himself face to face with himself. He has made himself an anti-Semite because that is something one cannot be alone. The phrase, "I hate the Jews," is one that is uttered in chorus; in pronouncing it, one attaches himself to a tradition and to a community — the tradition and community of the mediocre.

We must remember that a man is not necessarily humble or even modest because he has consented to mediocrity. On the contrary, there is a passionate pride among the mediocre, and anti-Semitism is an attempt to give value to mediocrity as such, to create an elite of the ordinary. . . .

Besides this, many anti-Semites — the majority, perhaps — belong to the lower middle class of the towns; they are functionaries, office workers, small businessmen, who possess nothing. It is in opposing themselves to the Jew that they suddenly become conscious of being proprietors: in representing the Jew as a robber, they put themselves in the enviable position of people who could be robbed. Since the Jew wishes to take France from them, it follows that France must belong to them. Thus they have chosen anti-Semitism as a means of establishing their status as possessors. . . .

15 By treating the Jew as an inferior and pernicious being, I affirm at the same time that I belong to the elite. This elite, in contrast to those of modern times which are based on merit or labor, closely resembles an aristocracy of birth. There is nothing I have to do to merit my superiority, and neither can I lose it. It is given once and for all. It is a *thing*. . . .

Whatever [the anti-Semite] does, he knows that he will remain at the top of the ladder; whatever the Jew does, he will never get any higher than the first rung.

We begin to perceive the meaning of the anti-Semite's choice of himself. He chooses the irremediable out of fear of being free; he chooses mediocrity out of fear of being alone, and out of pride he makes of this irremediable mediocrity a rigid aristocracy. To this end he finds the existence of the Jew absolutely necessary. Otherwise to whom would he be superior? Indeed, it is vis-à-vis the Jew and the Jew alone that the anti-Semite realizes that he has rights. If by some miracle all the Jews were exterminated as he wishes, he would find himself nothing but a concierge or a shopkeeper in a strongly hierarchical society in which the quality of "true Frenchman" would be at a low valuation, because everyone would possess it. He would lose his sense of rights over the country because no one would any longer contest them, and that profound equality which brings him close to the nobleman and the man of wealth would disappear all of a sudden, for it is primarily negative. His frustrations, which he has attributed to the disloyal competition of the Jew, would have to be imputed to some other cause, lest he be forced to look within himself. He would run the risk of falling into bitterness, into a melancholy hatred of the privileged classes. Thus the anti-Semite is in the unhappy position of having a vital need for the very enemy he wishes to destroy. . . .

We are now in a position to understand the anti-Semite. He is a man who is afraid. Not of the Jews, to be sure, but of himself, of his own consciousness, of his liberty, of his instincts, of his responsibilities, of solitariness, of change, of society, and of the world — of everything except the Jews. He is a coward who does not want to admit his cowardice to himself; a murderer who represses and censures his tendency to murder without being able to hold it back, yet who dares to kill only in effigy or protected by the anonymity of the mob; a malcontent who dares not revolt from fear of the consequences of his rebellion. In espousing anti-Semitism, he does not simply adopt an opinion, he chooses himself as a person. He chooses the permanence and impenetrability of stone, the total irresponsibility of the warrior who obeys his leaders — and he has no leader. He chooses to acquire nothing, to deserve nothing; he assumes that everything is given him as his birthright — and he is not noble. He chooses finally a Good that is fixed once and for all, beyond question, out of reach; he dares not examine it for fear of being led to challenge it and having to seek it in another form. The Jew only serves him as a pretext; elsewhere his counterpart will make use of the Negro or the man of yellow skin. The existence of the Jew merely permits the anti-Semite to stifle his anxieties at their inception by persuading himself that his place in the world has been marked out in advance, that it awaits him, and that tradition gives him the right to occupy it. Anti-Semitism, in short, is fear of the human condition. The anti-Semite is a man who wishes to be pitiless stone, a furious torrent, a devastating thunderbolt — anything except a man.

Topics for Critical Thinking and Writing

1. Early in the essay, Jean-Paul Sartre examines how anti-Semitism can be a feature even of a good person's character. What, to him, is the source of such anti-Semitism? Is the individual responsible for his own views on the Jews? Explain.
2. Reread paragraphs 5 and 6 and explain why Sartre views anti-Semitism as a form of "hysteria."

3. Use ideas, examples, and evidence from the text to explain Sartre's claim, "If the Jew did not exist, the anti-Semite would invent him" (para. 8). What benefits does the anti-Semite derive from these attitudes about Jews?
4. Explain what Sartre means by "the passionate pride among the mediocre" (para. 13) and discuss how this type of pride relates to conformity. Do you see the passionate pride of the mediocre operating today? Explain.
5. Sartre remarks that anti-Semites "know that their remarks are frivolous" but nevertheless, they "have the *right* to play" (para. 9). Define the term *white privilege*—especially as the concept is understood in our society today—and then compare it to anti-Semitism. Are the terms similar in character, or are they different? Explain.
6. In the final paragraph of this selection, Sartre compares anti-Semitism to the nature of racism elsewhere against "the Negro or the man of yellow skin." These words—"Negro" and "yellow skin"—are today considered to be offensive terms in the United States. Do you think Sartre's argument is undermined by his own use of the words? Explain.
7. Write a 500- to 1,000-word argument built on the following Sartrean conception: Anti-Semitism is an assault not only against people but against *reason* itself.

HANS MASSAQUOI

Hans Massaquoi (1926–2013) was a German of African descent (his mother was German; his father Liberian) who grew up in Hamburg, Germany, during the rise and reign of the Nazi Party. Although he was not Aryan by Hitler's definition of the term, Massaquoi was German-born and non-Jewish, and thus his family managed to remain German citizens despite the increasing persecutions against nonwhite "others." However, after the 1936 Olympic Games in Berlin, where African American athlete Jesse Owens embarrassed Hitler by winning four gold medals over his German opponents, blacks in Germany became increasingly targeted by the regime. Massaquoi was forced into an apprenticeship and labor during World War II; shortly after the war, he immigrated to the United States. He served in the Korean War and then studied journalism at the University of Illinois at Urbana-Champaign, eventually becoming a writer at *Jet* magazine and editor of *Ebony* magazine, both lifestyle magazines created specifically for African American audiences. Massaquoi's autobiography, *Destined to Witness: Growing Up Black in Nazi Germany*, was published in 1999. This selection, reprinted in *Lapham's Quarterly* in 2015, is from that work.

Destined to Witness

With arch-Nazi Principal Wriede at the helm, my school aggressively pursued the indoctrination and recruitment of young souls for the *Jungvolk*, the Hitler Youth's junior league for ten- to thirteen-year-olds, whose members were known as *Pimpfe* [cubs]. Hardly a day went by without our being reminded by our teachers or Wriede himself that for a German boy, life outside the movement was no life at all. Pursuing his objective with characteristic single-mindedness, Wriede was tireless in thinking up new gimmicks to further his goal. One day, he announced his latest brainchild, a school-wide contest in which the first class to reach 100 percent *Jungvolk* membership would be rewarded with a holiday.

The immediate effect of the announcement was that my new homeroom teacher, Herr Schürmann, became obsessed with the idea of winning the coveted prize for our class and some brownie points for himself. Toward that end, he became a veritable pitchman, who spent much of his — and our — time trying to persuade, cajole, or otherwise induce our class to join the Nazi fold. The centerpiece of his recruitment drive was a large chart he had carefully drawn on the blackboard with white chalk. It consisted of a large box divided into as many squares as there were boys in the class. Each morning, Herr Schürmann would inquire who had joined the Hitler Youth. After a show of hands, he would count them, then gleefully add the new enlistees' names to his chart. Gradually the squares with names increased until they outnumbered the blank ones.

Up to that point I had followed the contest with a certain degree of emotional detachment because quite a few of my classmates, including some of my closest pals, had let it be known that they had no interest in anything the Hitler Youth did and would not join, no matter what Wriede or Schürmann had to say. That suited me fine since I, too, had no intention of joining. But under the relentless pressure from Schürmann, one resister after another caved in and joined.

One morning, when the empty squares had dwindled to just a few, Herr Schürmann started querying the holdouts as to the reasons for their "lack of love for Führer and *Vaterland*." Some explained that they had nothing against Führer and *Vaterland* but weren't particularly interested in the kinds of things the *Jungvolk* were doing, such as camping, marching, blowing bugles and fanfares, and beating on medieval-style drums. Others said they didn't have their parents' permission, whereupon Herr Schürmann instructed them to bring their parents in for a conference. When it came to what I thought was my turn to explain, I opened my mouth, but Herr Schürmann cut me off. "That's all right; you are exempted from the contest since you are ineligible to join the *Jungvolk*."

The teacher's words struck me like a bolt of lightning. Not eligible to join? What was he talking about? I had been prepared to tell him that I hadn't quite made up my mind whether I wanted to join or not. Now he was telling me that, even if I wanted to, I couldn't. Noticing my bewildered expression, Herr Schürmann told me to see him immediately after class.

Until the bell rang, I remained in a state of shock, unable to follow anything that was said. I felt betrayed and abandoned by my friends and terrified at the prospect of being the only person in class whose name would not appear on the chart. At age ten, I was as tough as any of my peers, able to take just about anything they dished out in the course of rough-and-tumble schoolboy play. What I couldn't take, however, was feeling that I didn't belong — being treated like an outcast, being told, in effect, that I was not only different but inferior.

Schürmann invited me to take a seat beside his desk. "I always thought you knew that you could not join the *Jungvolk* because you are non-Aryan," he began. "You know your father is an African. Under the Nuremberg Laws, non-Aryans are not allowed to become members of the Hitler Youth movement." Charitably, perhaps to spare at least some of my feelings, he omitted the much maligned and despised Jews from his roster of ineligibles.

"But I am a German," I sobbed, my eyes filling with tears. "My mother says I'm German just like anybody else."

"You *are* a German boy," Herr Schürmann conceded with unusual compassion, "but unfortunately not quite like anybody else."

Having gotten his point only too well, I made no further plea.

"I'm very sorry, my boy," Schürmann concluded the conference. "I wish I could help you, but there's nothing I can do; it's the law."

That evening, when I saw my mother, I didn't tell her what had transpired in school. Instead, I asked her to come with me to the nearest *Jungvolk Heim,* the neighborhood *Jungvolk* den just one block up the street, so I could join. Since I had never expressed the slightest interest in joining the Hitler Youth, she had never felt it necessary to burden me with the thought that I would be rejected. Thus, my sudden decision to join took her completely by surprise. When she tried to talk me out of it, even hinting that there was a possibility of my not being accepted, I grew frantic. I told her that I simply had to join since I could not be the only one in my class who was not a member. But she still didn't think it was a good idea. "Please take me," I pleaded, almost hysterically. "Maybe they'll make an exception. Please!"

Against her better judgment, my mother finally relented and agreed to do whatever she could to help me join. When we arrived at the *Jungvolk Heim*, a long, solidly built, one-story stone structure, the place was buzzing with activities and paramilitary commandos. Through the open door of a classroom-like meeting room, I could see a group of boys, most of them about my age, huddled around a long table, apparently listening to a troop leader's lecture. They wore neat uniforms, black shorts, black tunics over khaki shirts, and black scarfs that were held together at the neck by braided leather knots. Most of them, I noticed with envy, wore the small black *Dolch* [dagger] with the rhombus-shaped swastika emblem of the Hitler Youth. Ever since seeing it displayed in the window of a neighborhood uniform store, I had secretly coveted this largely ceremonial weapon. Even the words *Blut und Ehre* [blood and honor] that were engraved on its shiny blade, and whose symbolic meaning had totally eluded me, stirred my soul. I knew that once my membership had been approved, nothing would stand in the way of my becoming a proud owner of a Hitler Youth *Dolch.* I wanted it so much, I could almost feel it in my hand.

After one *Pimpf* spotted me, I immediately became the subject of snickers and giggles until the troop leader, annoyed by the distraction, shouted "*Rube* [Quiet]!" and closed the door. When my mother asked a passing *Pimpf* to show us to the person in charge, he clicked his heels, then pointed to a door with the sign HEIMFÜHRER. Upon my mother's knock, a penetrating male voice shouted, "Enter!"

"*Heil Hitler!* What can I do for you?" asked the handsome, roughly twenty-year-old man in the uniform of a mid-level Hitler Youth leader who was seated behind a desk.

My mother returned the mandatory Nazi salute, then asked, "Is this the right place to apply for membership?"

The young man looked incredulous. "Membership for whom? For *him*?" he inquired, his eyes studying me as if they had spied a repulsive worm.

"Yes, for my son," my mother responded without flinching.

The Nazi recoiled. "I must ask you to leave at once," he commanded. "Since it hasn't occurred to you by now, I have to tell you that there is no place for your son in this organization or in the Germany we are about to build. *Heil Hitler!*" Having said that, he rose and pointedly opened the door.

For a moment I thought my mother would strike the man with her fist. She was trembling and glaring at him with an anger I had never before seen in her eyes. But she quickly regained her composure, took me by the hand, and calmly said, "Let's go." Neither she nor I spoke a word on the way back home. I felt guilty for having been the cause of her anguish and humiliation, and I was afraid she would be angry. Instead, when we reached our apartment, she just hugged me and cried. "I'm so sorry, I'm so sorry," was all she could say.

Seeing my mother like this was more than I could bear. "Please don't cry, *Mutti*," I pleaded while tears were streaming down my cheeks. It was a rare occurrence, since usually we outdid each other in keeping our hurt to ourselves. We were Germans, after all.

Topics for Critical Thinking and Writing

1. What explains Hans Massaquoi's initial reluctance and then growing interest in becoming part of the *Jungvolk* group at his school? Refer to the text in your explanation.
2. Explore the conundrum of Massaquoi's teacher who apologizes to him by saying, "I wish I could help you, but there's nothing I can do; it's the law" (para. 11). How, in our own time, is the law used to define and exclude "others"?
3. Do some research and write about the purpose and the activities of the *Jungvolk*. Why was it established? How did it contribute to the ideologies of the Nazis?
4. Examine the final paragraph of the selection and tell why the last sentence is effective.
5. Write an essay of about 500 words in which you integrate Massaquoi's experience with Sartre's theories in "Anti-Semite and Jew." How do the authorities in Massaquoi's piece reflect Sartre's ideas about racism?
6. In the United States, there are many organizations and groups that children can join for fun, leisure, and community. Select one and discuss the nature of its activities and its underlying principles. What values does the organization teach through its activities? Is it open, or does it exclude any class of people? Would you call your selected organization or group "ideological" — that is, committed to indoctrinating children into a particular belief system? If so, is it for good or ill? Explain.

W. E. B. DU BOIS

William Edward Burghardt Du Bois (1868–1963) was born in Great Barrington, Massachusetts, was educated at Fisk University, and was the first African American to earn a doctorate degree from Harvard University. He held fellowships and appointments at the University of Berlin, Wilberforce College, and the University of Pennsylvania. Du Bois wrote his first book, *The Philadelphia Negro*, in 1899. It was the first systematic study of urban conditions for African Americans and one of the first examples of sociology as a modern social science. In 1903, he published *The Souls of Black Folk* and became a prominent voice in American social thought. Du Bois was highly critical of the most well-regarded black American social theorist at the time, Booker T. Washington. Where Washington argued for a program of economic advancement for blacks through industrial education and gradual change, Du Bois argued strenuously for traditional liberal arts education and immediate reformation of laws disadvantaging the racial group. In 1905, along with other black activists, Du Bois started the Niagara Movement, and in 1909, he was among a handful of leaders who established the National Association for the Advancement of Colored People (NAACP). He became the editor of *The Crisis*, the official magazine of the NAACP. In the 1950s, Du Bois's socialist sympathies, internationalism, and peace activism put him squarely in the sights of the US government's anticommunist campaign, and he was indicted and put on trial in 1951 for refusing to register as a communist under new, restrictive laws in the United States intended to quash communist subversion. Incensed by the US Supreme Court's decision in 1961 to uphold the McCarran Act, a piece of anticommunist legislation, Du Bois moved to Ghana, where he was given a state funeral following his death in 1963. The following selection is the first chapter of *The Souls of Black Folk* (1903).

Of Our Spiritual Strivings

O water, voice of my heart, crying in the sand,
All night long crying with a mournful cry,
As I lie and listen, and cannot understand
The voice of my heart in my side or the voice of
the sea,
O water, crying for rest, is it I, is it I?
All night long the water is crying to me.

Unresting water, there shall never be rest
Till the last moon droop and the last tide fail,
And the fire of the end begin to burn in the
west;
And the heart shall be weary and wonder and
cry like the sea,
All life long crying without avail,
As the water all night long is crying to me.

—ARTHUR SYMONS

Between me and the other world there is ever an unasked question: unasked by some through feelings of delicacy; by others through the difficulty of rightly framing it. All, nevertheless, flutter round it. They approach me in a half-hesitant sort of way, eye me curiously or compassionately, and then, instead of saying directly, How does it feel to be a problem? they say, I know an excellent colored man in my town; or, I fought at Mechanicsville; or, Do not these Southern outrages make your blood boil? At these I smile, or am interested, or reduce the boiling to a simmer, as the occasion may require. To the real question, How does it feel to be a problem? I answer seldom a word.

And yet, being a problem is a strange experience,—peculiar even for one who has never been anything else, save perhaps in babyhood and in Europe. It is in the early days of rollicking boyhood that the revelation first bursts upon one, all in a day, as it were. I remember well when the shadow swept across me. I was a little thing, away up in the hills of New England, where the dark Housatonic winds between Hoosac and Taghkanic to the sea. In a wee wooden schoolhouse, something put it into the boys' and girls' heads to buy gorgeous visiting-cards—ten cents a package—and exchange. The exchange was merry, till one girl, a tall newcomer, refused my card,—refused it peremptorily, with a glance. Then it dawned upon me with a certain suddenness that I was different from the others; or like, mayhap, in heart and life and longing, but shut out from their world by a vast veil. I had thereafter no desire to tear down that veil, to creep through; I held all beyond it in common contempt, and lived above it in a region of blue sky and great wandering shadows. That sky was bluest when I could beat my mates at examination-time, or beat them at a foot-race, or even beat their stringy heads. Alas, with the years all this fine contempt began to fade; for the worlds I longed for, and all their dazzling opportunities, were theirs, not mine. But they should not keep these prizes, I said; some, all, I would wrest from them. Just how I would do it I could never decide: by reading law, by healing the sick, by telling the wonderful tales that swam in my head, — some way. With other black boys the strife was not so fiercely sunny: their youth shrunk into tasteless sycophancy, or into silent hatred of the pale world about them and mocking distrust of everything white; or wasted itself in a bitter cry, Why did God make me an outcast and a stranger in mine own house? The shades of the prison-house closed round about us all: walls strait and stubborn to the whitest, but relentlessly narrow, tall, and unscalable to sons of night who must plod darkly on in resignation, or beat unavailing palms against the stone, or steadily, half hopelessly, watch the streak of blue above.

After the Egyptian and Indian, the Greek and Roman, the Teuton and Mongolian, the Negro is a sort of seventh son, born with a veil, and gifted with second-sight in this American world, — a world which yields him no true self-consciousness, but only lets him see himself through the revelation of the other world. It is a peculiar sensation, this double-consciousness, this sense of always looking at one's self through the eyes of others, of measuring one's soul by the tape of a world that looks on in amused contempt and pity. One ever feels his two-ness, — an American, a Negro; two souls, two thoughts, two unreconciled strivings; two warring ideals in one dark body, whose dogged strength alone keeps it from being torn asunder.

The history of the American Negro is the history of this strife, — this longing to attain self-conscious manhood, to merge his double self into a better and truer self. In this merging he wishes neither of the older selves to be lost. He would not Africanize America, for America has too much to teach the world and Africa. He would not bleach his Negro soul in a flood of white Americanism, for he knows that Negro blood has a message for the world. He simply wishes to make it possible for a man to be both a Negro and an American, without being cursed and spit upon by his fellows, without having the doors of Opportunity closed roughly in his face.

5 This, then, is the end of his striving: to be a co-worker in the kingdom of culture, to escape both death and isolation, to husband and use his best powers and his latent genius. These powers of body and mind have in the past been strangely wasted, dispersed, or forgotten. The shadow of a mighty Negro past flits through the tale of Ethiopia the Shadowy and of Egypt the Sphinx. Throughout history, the powers of single black men flash here and there like falling stars, and die sometimes before the world has rightly gauged their brightness. Here in America, in the few days since Emancipation, the black man's turning hither and thither in hesitant and doubtful striving has often made his very strength to lose effectiveness, to seem like absence of power, like weakness. And yet it is not weakness, — it is the contradiction of double aims. The double-aimed struggle of the black artisan — on the one hand to escape white contempt for a nation of mere hewers of wood and drawers of water, and on the other hand to plough and nail and dig for a poverty-stricken horde — could only result in making him a poor craftsman, for he had but half a heart in either cause. By the poverty and ignorance of his people, the Negro minister or doctor was tempted toward quackery and

demagogy; and by the criticism of the other world, toward ideals that made him ashamed of his lowly tasks. The would-be black *savant* was confronted by the paradox that the knowledge his people needed was a twice-told tale to his white neighbors, while the knowledge which would teach the white world was Greek to his own flesh and blood. The innate love of harmony and beauty that set the ruder souls of his people a-dancing and a-singing raised but confusion and doubt in the soul of the black artist; for the beauty revealed to him was the soul-beauty of a race which his larger audience despised, and he could not articulate the message of another people. This waste of double aims, this seeking to satisfy two unreconciled ideals, has wrought sad havoc with the courage and faith and deeds of ten thousand thousand people, — has sent them often wooing false gods and invoking false means of salvation, and at times has even seemed about to make them ashamed of themselves.

Away back in the days of bondage they thought to see in one divine event the end of all doubt and disappointment; few men ever worshipped Freedom with half such unquestioning faith as did the American Negro for two centuries. To him, so far as he thought and dreamed, slavery was indeed the sum of all villainies, the cause of all sorrow, the root of all prejudice; Emancipation was the key to a promised land of sweeter beauty than ever stretched before the eyes of wearied Israelites. In song and exhortation swelled one refrain — Liberty; in his tears and curses the God he implored had Freedom in his right hand. At last it came, — suddenly, fearfully, like a dream. With one wild carnival of blood and passion came the message in his own plaintive cadences:—

"Shout, O children!
Shout, you're free!
For God has bought your liberty!"

Years have passed away since then, — ten, twenty, forty; forty years of national life, forty years of renewal and development, and yet the swarthy spectre sits in its accustomed seat at the Nation's feast. In vain do we cry to this our vastest social problem:—

"Take any shape but that, and my firm
nerves
Shall never tremble!"

The Nation has not yet found peace from its sins; the freedman has not yet found in freedom his promised land. Whatever of good may have come in these years of change, the shadow of a deep disappointment rests upon the Negro people, — a disappointment all the more bitter because the unattained ideal was unbounded save by the simple ignorance of a lowly people.

The first decade was merely a prolongation of the vain search for freedom, the boon that seemed ever barely to elude their grasp, — like a tantalizing will-o'-the-wisp, maddening and misleading the headless host. The holocaust of war, the terrors of the Ku-Klux Klan, the lies of carpet-baggers, the disorganization of industry, and the contradictory advice of friends and foes, left the bewildered serf with no new watchword beyond the old cry for freedom. As the time flew, however, he began to grasp a new idea. The ideal of liberty demanded for its attainment powerful means, and these the Fifteenth Amendment gave him. The ballot, which before he had looked upon as a visible sign of freedom, he now regarded as the chief means of gaining and perfecting the liberty with which war had partially endowed him. And why not? Had not votes made war and emancipated millions? Had not votes enfranchised the freedmen? Was anything impossible to a power that had done all this? A million black men started with renewed zeal to vote themselves into the kingdom. So the decade flew away, the revolution of 1876 came, and left the half-free serf weary, wondering, but still inspired. Slowly but steadily, in the following years, a new vision began gradually to replace the dream of political power, — a powerful movement, the rise of another ideal to guide the unguided, another pillar of fire by night after a clouded day. It was the ideal of "book-learning"; the curiosity, born of compulsory ignorance, to know and test the power of the cabalistic letters of the white man, the longing to know. Here at last seemed to have been discovered the mountain path to Canaan; longer than the highway of Emancipation and law, steep and rugged, but straight, leading to heights high enough to overlook life.

Up the new path the advance guard toiled, slowly, heavily, doggedly; only those who have watched and guided the faltering feet, the misty minds, the dull understandings, of the dark pupils of these schools know how faithfully, how piteously, this people strove to learn. It was weary work. The cold statistician wrote down the inches of progress here and there, noted also where here and there a foot had slipped or someone had fallen. To the tired climbers, the horizon was ever dark, the mists were often cold, the Canaan was always dim and far away. If, however, the vistas disclosed as yet no goal, no resting-place, little but flattery and criticism, the journey at least gave leisure for reflection and self-examination; it changed the child of Emancipation to the youth with dawning self-consciousness, self-realization, self-respect. In those sombre forests of his striving his own soul rose before him, and he saw himself, — darkly as through a veil; and yet he saw in himself some faint revelation of his power, of his mission. He began to have a dim feeling that, to attain his place in the world, he must be himself, and not another. For the first time he sought to analyze the burden he bore upon his back, that dead-weight of social degradation partially masked behind a half-named Negro problem. He felt his poverty; without a cent, without a home, without land, tools, or savings, he had entered into competition with rich, landed, skilled neighbors. To be a poor man is hard, but to be a poor race in a land of dollars is the very bottom of hardships. He felt the weight of his ignorance, — not simply of letters, but of life, of business, of the humanities; the accumulated sloth and shirking and awkwardness of decades and centuries shackled his hands and feet. Nor was his burden all poverty and ignorance. The red stain of bastardy, which two centuries of systematic legal defilement of Negro women had stamped upon his race, meant not only the loss of ancient African chastity, but also the hereditary weight of a mass of corruption from white adulterers, threatening almost the obliteration of the Negro home.

A people thus handicapped ought not to be asked to race with the world, but rather allowed to give all its time and thought to its own social problems. But alas! while sociologists gleefully count his bastards and his prostitutes, the very soul of the toiling, sweating black man is darkened by the shadow of a vast despair. Men call the shadow prejudice, and learnedly explain it as the natural defence of culture against barbarism, learning against ignorance, purity against crime, the "higher" against the "lower" races. To which the Negro cries Amen! and swears that to so much of this strange prejudice as is founded on just homage to civilization, culture, righteousness, and progress, he humbly bows and meekly does obeisance. But before that nameless prejudice that leaps beyond all this he stands helpless, dismayed, and well-nigh speechless; before that personal disrespect and mockery, the ridicule and systematic humiliation, the distortion of fact and wanton license of fancy, the cynical ignoring of the better and the boisterous welcoming of the worse, the all-pervading desire to inculcate disdain for everything black, from Toussaint to the devil, — before this there rises a sickening despair that would disarm and discourage any nation save that black host to whom "discouragement" is an unwritten word.

But the facing of so vast a prejudice could not but bring the inevitable self-questioning, self-disparagement, and lowering of ideals which ever accompany repression and breed in an atmosphere of contempt and hate. Whisperings and portents came borne upon the four winds: Lo! we are diseased and dying, cried the dark hosts; we cannot write, our voting is vain; what need of education, since we must always cook and serve? And the Nation echoed and enforced this self-criticism, saying: Be content to be servants, and nothing more; what need of higher culture for half-men? Away with the black man's ballot, by force or fraud, — and behold the suicide of a race! Nevertheless, out of the evil came something of good, — the more careful adjustment of education to real life, the clearer perception of the Negroes' social responsibilities, and the sobering realization of the meaning of progress.

So dawned the time of *Sturm und Drang:* storm and stress today rocks our little boat on the mad waters of the world-sea; there is within and without the sound of conflict, the burning of body and rending of soul; inspiration strives with doubt, and faith with vain questionings. The bright ideals of the past, — physical freedom, political power, the training of brains and the training of hands, — all these in turn have waxed and waned, until even the last grows dim and overcast. Are they all wrong, — all false? No, not that, but each alone was over-simple and incomplete, — the dreams of a credulous race-childhood, or the fond imaginings of the other world which does not know and does not want to know our power. To be really true, all these ideals must be melted and welded into one. The training of the schools we need today more than ever, — the training of deft hands, quick eyes and ears, and above all the broader, deeper, higher culture of gifted minds and pure hearts. The power of the ballot we need in sheer self-defence, — else what shall save us from a second slavery? Freedom, too, the long-sought, we still seek, — the freedom of life and limb, the freedom to work and think, the freedom to love and aspire. Work, culture, liberty, — all these we need, not singly but together, not successively but together, each growing and aiding each, and all striving toward that vaster ideal that swims before the Negro people, the ideal of human brotherhood, gained through the unifying ideal of Race; the ideal of fostering and developing the traits and talents of the Negro, not in opposition to or contempt for other races, but rather in large conformity to the greater ideals of the American Republic, in order that some day on American soil two world-races may give each to each those characteristics both so sadly lack. We the darker ones come even now not altogether empty-handed: there are today no truer exponents of the pure human spirit of the Declaration of Independence than the American Negroes; there is no true American music but the wild sweet melodies of the Negro slave; the American fairy tales and folk-lore are Indian and African; and, all in all, we black men seem the sole oasis of simple faith and reverence in a dusty desert of dollars and smartness. Will America be poorer if she replace her brutal dyspeptic blundering with light-hearted but determined Negro humility? or her coarse and cruel wit with loving jovial good-humor? or her vulgar music with the soul of the Sorrow Songs?[1]

[1]**Sorrow Songs** Music originating among African slaves, especially slave spirituals. [Editors' note]

Merely a concrete test of the underlying principles of the great republic is the Negro Problem, and the spiritual striving of the freedmen's sons is the travail of souls whose burden is almost beyond the measure of their strength, but who bear it in the name of an historic race, in the name of this the land of their fathers' fathers, and in the name of human opportunity.

And now what I have briefly sketched 15
in large outline let me on coming pages tell again in many ways, with loving emphasis and deeper detail, that men may listen to the striving in the souls of black folk.

Topics for Critical Thinking and Writing

1. In his opening paragraph, W. E. B. Du Bois talks about the implied question, "How does it feel to be a problem?" Do some research on the social conditions for black people around the turn of the twentieth century. What were the problems? Why?
2. In paragraph 2, Du Bois juxtaposes his own ambitions with those of "other black boys" whose "youth shrunk into tasteless sycophancy, or into silent hatred of the pale world about them . . . or wasted itself in a bitter cry." How would you characterize these three responses?
3. In paragraph 3, Du Bois coins the phrase "double-consciousness, this sense of always looking at one's self through the eyes of others." Describe what he means in relation to the experience of being African American at the time. Then attempt to apply your concept of double-consciousness to a group or class of people today and examine whether or not individuals of that group or class may see and evaluate themselves "through the eyes of others."
4. Examine the dilemma of the black artist outlined by Du Bois in paragraph 5. Explain what Du Bois means in this paragraph and also tell whether or not you think it applies in the present day.
5. Why do you think Du Bois delves into the history of Africans in America in paragraphs 6 through 10? How does this background help his argument?
6. Write a brief analysis of Du Bois's use of metaphor and poetic language in making his argument. Is it an effective strategy for his argument? Why, or why not?
7. In paragraph 11, Du Bois writes, "A people thus handicapped ought not to be asked to race with the world, but rather allowed to give all its time and thought to its own social problems." Do some research on affirmative action in the United States today and determine whether or not Du Bois's claim could still be used to justify a specific aspect of affirmative action policies.
8. In paragraph 11, Du Bois writes that people often "learnedly explain it [prejudice] as the natural defence of culture against barbarism, learning against ignorance, purity against crime, the 'higher' against the 'lower' races. To which the Negro cries Amen!" How might it happen that an oppressed group comes to agree with forms of prejudice against its own members? Can people be taught to hate themselves? Explain.

BRIDGET ANDERSON

Bridget Anderson is director of the University of Bristol Institute on Migration and Mobility Studies in Bristol, England. With her doctorate in sociology, she has produced a formidable body of interdisciplinary research on immigration, citizenship, and economics, including more than a dozen book chapters, six edited books, twenty journal articles, and two authored books, *Doing the Dirty Work? The Global Politics of Domestic Labour* (2000), and *Us and Them? The Dangerous Politics of Immigration Controls* (2013). The piece below was excerpted from an article published in *Social Research*, a scholarly journal, in 2017.

The Politics of Pests: Immigration and the Invasive Other

The United Nations High Commissioner for Refugees (UNHCR) estimates that more than one million people crossed into Europe by sea in 2015. At least 3,700 of those attempting to enter drowned. The vast majority of these travellers were from the world's top 10 refugee-producing countries, including Syria, Iraq, and Afghanistan. Like the apocryphal story about the Haitian slave revolutionaries who greeted the repressive French army by singing "La Marseillaise," so some people walking along the motorways of Hungary and Austria were carrying the European flag, as if to say "We share your respect for justice, freedom, and human rights, and here we are! We belong!"

This situation was labelled a "crisis," and the responses were schizophrenic. Widespread "Refugees Are Welcome" demonstrations were met with nationalist counterdemonstrations and fire-bombings. As autumn arrived amidst mutual recriminations of xenophobia and hypocrisy, Europe rebordered: checkpoints were instituted between Austria and Germany, Italy and France, Sweden and Denmark, Croatia and Austria, Macedonia and Greece. Thus the crisis brought into question not only the principles of asylum and free movement within the European Union, but also Europe's very idea of itself as a space of liberal values, freedom, moral equality, and human rights. As well as a migration crisis confronting Europe, what started to unfold was a *European* crisis confronting migrants: a multidimensional crisis of solidarity between member states, many of which are struggling with austerity and rapidly diminishing state capacity. This crisis was effectively called out by migration (Kriss 2015).

The media coverage of these events and their consequences reflected these tensions. Hostility toward mobile people, concerns about security, and demands on resources collided with the unavoidably human face of catastrophe, and for a time negative responses were mitigated by the photograph of drowned toddler Alan Kurdi. This contradiction was encapsulated in an editorial in *The Times* of January 21, 2016: "compassion is the right response but unconditional welcome is the wrong way to express it."

The relation between media coverage, policy, and public opinion is highly complicated, particularly in cases that are depicted as some kind of "crisis." Press coverage is not a neutral mirror of public opinion, nor does it simply shape public attitudes — news organizations are businesses, concerned with building relationships with their readers rather than challenging their views. The relation between media, public attitudes, and policymaking is complex and mutually constitutive, and there is a growing interest in this triangular relation in the case of how migration and asylum are covered (Matthews and Brown 2012). This question has received more attention post-2015, and there continues to be considerable debate about the role of the media in the representation of migrants/refugees, and its relation to public opinion. . . .

5 The use of imagery and metaphor of natural disasters permeates the coverage of migration. The particular ways in which migrants are portrayed offer insights into the nature of popular anxieties about the foreigner as invasive other and clues as to the political responses that can help to counter these anxieties. One metaphoric trope that has emerged as particularly powerful in the coverage of the 2015 events is the migrant as invasive insect, a metaphor that has been deployed by politicians as well as press commentators and reporters. . . .

However, metaphors are at their most effective when they are surreptitious and uncontested — not when they are applauded or called out, but when they pass unremarked into our language, when they shift from simile to metaphor suggesting the horror lurking beneath reason. In the press, migrants routinely scurry, scuttle, sneak, and they often swarm, too. Migrants are invaders, but invasion usually suggests a state or at least an authority that controls the invasion. In the case of migrants this invasion is a force of nature, of war without sovereignty and of agency without individuality.

ANIMAL MAGIC

Metaphors matter. "They are figures of thought as much as they are figures of speech" (Steuter and Wills 2008, 7), or to paraphrase Otto Santa Ana (1999), they do not simply color the poetic but shape the prosaic. They are a crucial element in the structuring of our conceptual systems, providing cognitive frames that make issues understandable. They bridge the gap between logic and emotion, exposing and shaping our feelings and responses and acting as both expression and legitimation (Mio 1997).

The comparison of foreigners and outsiders with animals has a long history. Noncitizens and those regarded as outsiders or subhuman have been called animal names, treated like animals, and forced to behave like animals. This has contemporary twists — in 2013, the Tripoli Zoo was turned into an immigration detention center — but it is not new. In Ancient Greece, Herodotus compares slaves to cattle, while more recently in the American South, slaves were commonly equated with domestic animals — oxen, hogs, calves, and colts (Jacoby 1994). Santa Ana analyzed the coverage in the *Los Angeles Times* of the referendum on Proposition 187 and found the key metaphor discerned to be "immigrants are animals" (1999), while O'Brien (2003) describes the metaphors deployed during the immigration debate in the United States of the early twentieth century, showing that the immigrant as invader and as animal were even then common tropes. O'Brien's analysis finds that in contrast to the depiction of slaves — who were imagined as beasts of burden to be whipped, branded, and controlled — migrants, whose entry must be controlled, are compared to "parasites or 'low animals' capable of infection and contamination" (243). Similarly, those seeking to enter Europe are not depicted as beasts or brutes but as vermin, forms of nonvital life, low down on the animal phyla.

Rats, cockroaches, and insects are urban — they are not considered wild animals. Unlike beasts of burden, these are not perceived as productive animals. They are alive but not perceived as truly sentient. Considered more closely, there are three interrelated connotations of invasive vermin that are of relevance to anxieties about asylum: waste, numbers, and threats to the home. . . .

Vermin are ubiquitous, and cockroaches, rats, and "swarms" are everywhere indigenous. The horror is not simply that the "sneaky little creatures" do not respect borders or boundaries. They are not invasive of a *territorial* space.[1] What vermin are invasive of is the civilized space of the home. Thus comparing migrants to insects and vermin invokes what Walters (2010) has called "domopolitics," the aspiration to govern the state like a *home*. Indeed, Merkel's policy has been dubbed her "open door" policy and is in contrast to Cameron's stance that we need to stop migrants "breaking into Britain," both metaphors associated with the home. The home is our place, the space where "we" are native. In recent years in Europe there has been a striking resurgence of language of nativity and indigeneity. . . .

When they are in the home, insects must be dealt with, and while "exterminate all the brutes" is not acceptable, "exterminate all the bugs" is. Indeed, this is the solution to an infestation of pests. The lives of insects do not matter — they are not "grievable" (Butler 2009). Indeed, the relation between the development of pesticides for agricultural and domestic use and chemical technologies for the mass killing of humans has been well documented. During the Second World War, for example, the German chemical company IG Farben bought the patent for Zyklon B, which was used in the extermination camps of the Holocaust. Its original use was as an insecticide, and it had previously been licensed for delousing Mexican migrants to the United States in the 1930s.

There is no proposal to exterminate people at the borders of Europe (though Katie Hopkins' piece titled "Rescue Boats? I'd Use Gunships to Stop Migrants" came perilously close). However, "letting die" is a different matter. . . .

The etymological origin of "exterminate" is to put beyond the boundary or the frontier. The question is: where shall they be removed to? What to do with Bauman's "human waste," the "collateral casualties of progress" (Bauman 2003, 15)? . . .

Perhaps we can look to metaphor for political inspiration, for ways of reframing the relationship between embedded citizens and mobile populations. Teiko Tomita was a Japanese woman who came to the United States in 1921. Throughout her life she wrote beautiful *tanka*, a particular form of Japanese short poetry, expressing her struggles and hopes. When her poetry was published as part of a collection of Issei poetry, she entitled her section "Tsugiki," meaning "graft" or "grafted tree," a depiction of her and her children's relation to their lives in the United States (Nomura 2005).

Carefully grafting
Young cherry trees
I believe in the certainty
They will bud
In the coming spring
(Teiko Tomita)

---

[1]The Israeli army has opened small tunnels in the separation wall to allow migration, in part because of the separation of animal families caused by the wall (http://www.dw.com/en/israeli-army-opens-west-bank-barrier-for-animals/a-16351700). This of course is not deemed necessary for vermin like rats who live on both sides of the wall.

REFERENCES

Bauman, Z. 2003. *Wasted Lives: Modernity and Its Outcasts.* Oxford: Wiley.

Butler, Judith. 2009. *Frames of War: When Is Life Grievable?* London: Verso.

Hopkins, Katie. 2015. "Rescue Boats? I'd Use Gunships to Stop Migrants." *The Sun*, April 17.

Jacoby, Karl. 1994. "Slaves by Nature? Domestic Animals and Human Slaves." *Slavery & Abolition* 15 (1): 89–99.

Kriss, Sam. 2015. "Building Norway: A Critique of Slavoj Žižek." https://samkriss.wordpress.com/2015/09/11/building-norway-a-critique-of-slavoj-zizek/.

Matthews, J., and A. R. Brown. 2012. "Negatively Shaping the Asylum Agenda? The Representational Strategy and Impact of a Tabloid News Campaign." *Journalism Criticism, Theory and Practice* 13 (6): 802–17. http://jou.sagepub.com/content/13/6/802.

Mio, J. S. 1997. "Metaphor and Politics." *Metaphor and Symbol* 12 (2): 113–33.

Nomura, Gail M. 2005. "Tsugiki, a Grafting: The Life and Poetry of a Japanese Pioneer Woman in Washington." *Columbia Magazine*, Spring, 19:1.

O'Brien, G. 2003. "Indigestible Food, Conquering Hordes and Waste Materials: Metaphors of Immigrants and the Early Immigration Restriction Debate in the United States." *Metaphor & Symbol* 18 (1): 33–47.

Santa Anna, Otto. 1999. "'Like an Animal I Was Treated': Anti-immigrant Metaphor in US Public Discourse." *Discourse & Society* 10 (2): 191–224.

Steuter, Erin, and Deborah Wills. 2008. *At War with Metaphor: Media, Propaganda, and Racism in the War on Terror.* Plymouth: Lexington Books.

The Times. 2016. "Reality Check: Expecting European Union States to Accept Refugee Quotas Is Wishful Thinking. Brussels Must Focus on its External Borders and on the Territories Beyond." Editorial, January 21. http://www.thetimes.co.uk/article/reality-check-c7t930g5j7g.

Walters, William. 2010. "Secure Borders, Safe Haven, Domopolitics." *Citizenship Studies* 8 (3): 237–60.

Topics for Critical Thinking and Writing

1. Under European Union (EU) rules, people may travel between EU countries without going through customs. How do you think this policy contributed to Europeans' sense of a "crisis" given that so many immigrants were arriving in Europe from countries like Iraq, Afghanistan, and Syria? How did this situation challenge "Europe's very idea of itself as a space of liberal values, freedom, moral equality, and human rights" (para. 2)?
2. In paragraph 3, Bridget Anderson refers to "hostility toward mobile people." Do you think, in general, that people have negative attitudes toward mobile people? Provide an example of a mobile population and examine the challenges they encounter.
3. Describe Anderson's understanding of the relationship between media portrayals of immigrants and public opinion about immigrants. Then consider the ways some group — an immigrant or a minority group, in any place or time — was affected by the way that group was portrayed in the media. What do you think is the best way to counteract stereotypical or misleading representations of people?

4. Paragraph 7 begins with a claim, "Metaphors matter." Think of some instances in the United States today in which a metaphor or figurative language is used to describe a group or class of people. What is suggested by the language — that is, what feelings are associated with the words used? What do you think are the consequences of such language use?
5. Construct two definitions of *civil disobedience* and explain whether and to what extent it is easier (or harder) to justify civil disobedience, depending on how you have defined the expression.
6. Do some research to discover which countries allow the most immigrants and which ones have the tightest controls. Choose one and explain why that country has more welcoming or less welcoming processes, what public attitudes about immigrants are like there, and how those attitudes are demonstrated in public (or in public media).
7. Imagine that someone your age from Syria, Iraq, or Afghanistan were moving into your hometown or starting classes at your school. Write a letter of about 500 words to the imagined person telling them what to expect, what to look forward to, and what to look out for.
8. In a previous selection, W. E. B. Du Bois, writing about a typical African American man, says that he would not want to "Africanize America," but neither would he wish to "bleach his Negro soul in a flood of white Americanism." Consider this idea from the perspective of foreign immigrants to the United States: Should they be expected to "assimilate" by ridding themselves of the language and customs of their culture, or should they be appreciated for bringing more diversity to the nation?

JOHN BARTH

John Barth (b. 1930) is an American novelist decorated with numerous major writing awards and honors, including three nominations for the National Book Award for his novels *The Floating Opera* (1956), *Lost in the Funhouse* (1968), and *Chimera* (1972), the last of which shared the prize. The author of over twenty books and story collections, Barth is recognized as one of the most important postmodern literary writers, whose experiments in style and form expanded the boundaries of creative expression in the twentieth century. Some of his theories are present in the landmark essays "The Literature of Exhaustion" (1967) and "The Literature of Replenishment" (1980), both considered manifestos of postmodern literature. Barth is also a literary scholar who taught at Penn State University, SUNY–Buffalo, Boston University, and Johns Hopkins University. His latest books include *Every Third Thought: A Novel in Five Seasons* (2011) and a collection of stories, *Collected Stories* (2015). The short story included here is from *The Development* (2008), a collection of nine interlocking stories set in a fictional Chesapeake Bay gated community, Heron Bay Estates.

Us/Them

To his wife, his old comrades at the *Avon County News*, or his acquaintances from over at the College, Gerry Frank might say, for example, "Flaubert once claimed that what he'd *really* like to write is a novel about Nothing." In his regular feature column, however — in the small-town weekly newspaper of a still largely rural Maryland county — it would have to read something like this:

FRANK OPINIONS, by Gerald Frank
Us/Them

> The celebrated 19th-century French novelist Gustave Flaubert, author of *Madame Bovary,* once remarked that what he would *really* like to write is a novel about Nothing.

After which he might acknowledge that the same was looking to be the case with this week's column, although its authors still hoped to make it not quite about Nothing, but rather ("as the celebrated Elizabethan poet/playwright William Shakespeare put it in the title of one of his comedies") about Much *Ado* About Nothing.

There: That should work as a lead, a hook, a kick-start from which the next sentences and paragraphs will flow (pardon Gerry's mixed metaphor) — and voilà, another "Frank Opinions" column to be e-mailed after lunch to Editor Tom Chadwick at the *News* and put to bed for the week.

But they *don't* come, those next sentences — *haven't* come, now, for the third work-morning in a row — for the ever-clearer reason that their semiretired would-be author hasn't figured out yet what he wants to write about, namely: Us(slash)Them. *In Frank's opinion,* he now types experimentally in his column's characteristic third-person viewpoint, *what he needs is a meaningful connection between the "Us/Them" theme, much on his mind lately for reasons presently to be explained, and either or all of (1) a troubling* disconnection, *or anyhow an increasing distinction/difference/whatever, between, on this side of that slash, him and his wife — Gerald and Joan Frank, 14 Shad Run Road #212, Heron Bay Estates, Stratford, MD 21600 — and on its other side their pleasant gated community in general and their Shad Run condominium neighborhood in particular; (2) his recently increasing difficulty — after so many productive decades of newspaper work! — in coming up with fresh ideas for the F.O. column; and/or (3) the irresistible parallel to his growing (shrinking?) erectile dysfunction* [but never mind *that* as a column topic!].

Maybe fill in some background, to mark time while waiting for the Muse of Feature Columns to get off her ever-lazier butt and down to business? Gerry Frank here, Reader-if-this-gets-written: erstwhile journalist, not quite seventy but getting there fast. Born and raised in a small town near the banks of the Potomac in southern Maryland in World War Two time, where and when the most ubiquitous Us/Them had been Us White Folks as distinct from Them Coloreds, until supplanted after Pearl Harbor by Us Allies versus Them Japs and Nazis (note the difference between that "versus" and the earlier, more ambivalent "as distinct from," a difference to which we may return). Crossed the Chesapeake after high school to Stratford College, on the Free State's Eastern Shore (B.A. English 1957), then shifted north to New Jersey for the next quarter-century to do reportage and editorial work for the *Trenton Times*; also to marry his back-home sweetheart, make babies and help parent them, learn a few life lessons the hard way while doubtless failing to learn some others, and eventually — at age fifty, when those offspring were off to college themselves and learning their own life lessons — to divorce (irreconcilable differences). Had the immeasurably good fortune the very next year, at a Stratford homecoming, to meet alumna Joan Gibson (B.A. English 1967), herself likewise between life chapters just then (forty, divorced, no children, copyediting for her hometown newspaper, the *Wilmington* [Delaware] *News Journal).* So hit it off together from Day (and Night) One that after just a couple more dates they were spending every weekend together in her town or his, or back in the Stratford to which they shared a fond attachment — and whereto, not long after their marriage in the following year, they moved: Gerry to associate-edit the *Avon County News* and Joan ditto the College's alumni magazine, *The Stratfordian.*

5 And some fifteen years later here they are, happy with each other and grateful to have been spared not only direct involvement in the nation's several bloody wars during their life-decades, but also such personal catastrophes as loss of children, untimely death of parents or siblings, and devastating accident, disease, or other extraordinary misfortune. Their connection with Gerry's pair of thirty-something children, Joan's elder and younger siblings, and associated spouses and offspring is warm, though geographically attenuated (one couple in Oregon, another in Texas, others in Vermont and Alabama). Husband and wife much enjoy each other's company, their work, their modest TINK prosperity (Two Incomes, No [dependent] Kids), and their leisure activities: hiking, wintertime workouts in the Heron Bay Club's well-equipped fitness center and summertime swimming in its Olympic-size pool, vacation travel to other countries back in more U.S.-friendly times, and here and there in North America since 9/11 and (in Gerald Frank's Frank Opinion) the Bush administration's Iraq War fiasco (U.S./"Them"?). Also their, uh . . . friends?

Well: No F.O. column yet in any of *that*, that Gerry can see. While typing on from pure professional habit, however, he perpends that paragraph-ending word above, flanked by suspension points before and question mark after: something to circle back to, maybe, after avoiding it for a while longer by reviewing some other senses of that slash dividing Us from Them. Peter Simpson, a fellow they know from Rockfish Reach who teaches at the College and (like Joan Frank) serves on the Heron Bay Estates Community Association, did a good job of that at one of HBECA's recent open meetings, the main agenda item whereof was a proposed hefty assessment for upgrading the development's entrance gates. As most readers of "Frank Opinions" know, we are for better or worse the only gated community in Avon County, perhaps the only one on Maryland's Eastern Shore. Just off the state highway a few miles south of Stratford, Heron Bay Estates is bounded on two irregular sides by branching tidal tributaries of the Matahannock River (Heron and Spartina Creeks, Rockfish and Oyster Coves, Blue Crab Bight, Shad Run), on a third side by a wooded preserve of pines, hemlocks, and sweet gums screening a sturdy chain-link fence, and on its highway side by a seven-foot-high masonry wall atop an attractively landscaped berm, effectively screening the development from both highway noise and casual view. Midway along this side is our entrance road, Heron Bay Boulevard, accessed via a round-the-clock manned gatehouse with two exit lanes on one side, their gates raised and lowered automatically by electric eye, and two gated entry lanes on the other: one on the left for service vehicles and visitors, who must register with the gatekeeper and display temporary entrance passes on their dashboards, and one on the right for residents and nonresident Club members, whose cars have HBE decals annually affixed to their windshields. So successful has the development been that in the twenty-odd years since its initial layout it has grown to be the county's second-largest residential entity after the small town of Stratford itself — with the consequence that homeward-bound residents these days not infrequently find themselves backed up four or five cars deep while the busy gatekeepers simultaneously check in visitors in one lane and look for resident decals in the other before pushing the lift-gate button. Taking their cue from the various E-Z Pass devices commonly employed nowadays at bridge and highway toll booths, the developers, Tidewater Communities, Inc., suggested to the Association that an economical alternative to a second gatehouse farther down the highway side (which would require expensive construction, an additional entrance road, and more 24/7 staffing) would be a third entry lane at the present gatehouse, its gate to be triggered automatically by electronic scansion of a bar-code decal on each resident vehicle's left rear window.

Most of the Association members and other attendees, Joan and Gerry Frank included, thought this a practical and economical fix to the entrance-backup problem, and when put to the seven members for a vote (one representative from each of HBE's neighborhoods plus one at-large tie-breaker), the motion passed by a margin of six to one. In the prevote open discussion, however, objections to it were raised from diametrically opposed viewpoints. On the one hand, Mark Matthews from Spartina Pointe — the recentest member of the Association, whose new weekend-and-vacation home in that high-end neighborhood was probably the grandest residence in all of Heron Bay Estates — declared that in view of HBE's ongoing development (controversial luxury condominiums proposed for the far end of the preserve), what we need is not only that automatic bar-code lane at the Heron Bar Boulevard entrance, but the afore-mentioned second gated entrance at the south end of the highway wall as well, and perhaps a third for service and employee vehicles only, to be routed discreetly through the wooded preserve itself.

In the bluff, down-home manner to which he inclined, even as CEO of a Baltimore investment-counseling firm, "Way it is now," that bald and portly, flush-faced fellow complained, "we get waked up at six a.m. by the groundskeepers and golf course maintenance guys reporting for work with the radios booming in their rusty old Chevys and pickups, *woomf woomf woomf,* y'know? Half of 'em undocumented aliens, quote unquote, but never mind *that* if it keeps the costs down. And then when we-all that live here come back from wherever, the sign inside the entrance says Welcome Home, but our welcome is a six-car backup at the gate, like crossing the Bay Bridge without an E-Z Pass. I say we deserve better'n that."

"Hear hear!" somebody cheered from the back of the Community Association's open-meeting room: Joe Barnes, I think it was, from Rockfish Reach. But my wife, at her end of the members' table up front, objected: "Easy to say if you don't mind a fifty percent assessment hike to build and staff those extra entrances! But I suspect that many of us will feel the pinch to finance just that automatic third entry lane at the gatehouse — which I'm personally all for, but nothing beyond that unless *it* gets backed up."

A number of her fellow members nodded 10
agreement, and one of them added, "As for the racket, we just need to tell the gatekeepers and the maintenance foremen to be stricter about the no-loud-noise rule for service people checking in."

Mark Matthews made a little show of closing his eyes and shaking his head no. The room in general, however, murmured approval. Which perhaps encouraged Amanda Todd — a friend of Joan's and an Association member from Blue Crab Bight — to surprise us all by saying "Gates and more gates! What do we need *any* of them for, including the ones we've got already?"

Mild consternation in the audience and among her fellow members, turning to relieved amusement when Joan teased, "Because we're a gated community?" But "Really," Ms. Todd persisted, "those TCI ads for Heron Bay are downright embarrassing, with their 'exclusive luxury lifestyles' and such. Even to call this place Heron Bay *Estates* is embarrassing, if you ask me. But then to have to pass through customs every time we come and go, and phone the gatehouse whenever we're expecting a visitor! Plus the secondary nighttime gates at some of our neighborhood entrances, like Oyster Cove, and those push-button driveway gates in Spartina Pointe . . . Three gates to pass through, in an area where crime is practically nonexistent!"

"Don't forget the garage door opener," Mark Matthews reminded her sarcastically. "That makes *four* entrances for some of us, even before we unlock the house door. Mindy and I are all for it."

"Hear hear!" his ally called again from the back of the room, where someone else reminded all hands that we weren't *entirely* crime-free: "Remember that Peeping Tom a few years back? Slipped past the main gatehouse and our Oyster Cove night gates too, that we don't use anymore like we did back then, and we never did catch him. But still . . ."

"You're proving my point," Amanda argued. Whereupon her husband — the writer George Newett, also from the College — came to her support by quoting the Psalmist: "Lift up your heads, O ye gates! Even lift them up, ye everlasting doors, and the King of Glory shall come in!"

"Amen," she said appreciatively. "And *leave* 'em lifted, I say, like those ones at Oyster Cove. No other development around here has gates. Why should we?"

"Because we're *us*," somebody offered, "with a community pool and tennis courts and bike paths that aren't for public use. If you like the other kind, maybe you should move to one of *them*."

Mark Matthews seconded that suggestion with a pleased head-nod. But "All I'm saying," Ms. Todd persisted, less assertively, "— as Robert Frost puts it in one of his poems? — is, quote, 'Before I built a wall, I'd ask to know what I was walling in and walling out, and to whom I'm likely to give offense,' end of quote. Somebody just mentioned *us* and *them:* Who exactly is the Them that all these walls and gates are keeping out?"

To lighten things a bit, I volunteered, "That Them is Us, Amanda, waiting at the gate until we get our Heron Bay E-Z Pass gizmo up and running. Shall we put it to a vote?"

"Not quite yet, Gerry," said Peter Simpson — also from the College, as has been mentioned, and chairman of the Association as well as its member from Rockfish Reach. "Let's be sure that everybody's had his/her say on the matter. Including myself for a minute, if I may?"

Nobody objected. A trim and affable fellow in his fifties, Pete is popular as well as respected both in the Association and on campus, where he's some sort of dean as well as a professor. "I'll try not to lecture," he promised with a smile. "I just want to say that while I understand where both Mark and Amanda are coming from, my own inclination, like Joan's, is to proceed incrementally, starting with the bar-code scanner gate and hoping that'll do the trick, for a few years anyhow." He pushed up his rimless specs. "What's really on my mind, though, now that it's come up, is this Us-slash-Them business. We have to accept that some of us, like Amanda, live here because they like the place *despite* its being a gated community, while others of us, like Mark, live here in part precisely *because* it's gated, especially if they're not fulltime residents. The great majority of us, I'd bet, either don't *mind* the gate thing (except when it gets backed up!) or sort of like the little extra privacy, the way we appreciate our routine security patrols even though we're lucky enough not to live near a high-crime area. It's another Heron Bay amenity, like our landscaping and our golf course. What we need to watch out for (and here comes the lecture I promised I'd spare you) is when that slash between Us and Them moves from being a simple distinction — like Us Rockfish Reach residents and Them Oyster Cove or Spartina Pointers, or Us Marylanders and Them Pennsylvanians and Delawareans — and becomes Us not merely *distinct* from Them, but more or less *superior* to Them, as has all too often been the case historically with whites and blacks, or rich and poor, or for that matter men and women."

Up with the glasses again. Mark Matthews rolled his eyes, but most present seemed interested in Pete's argument. "At its worst," he went on, "that slash between Us and Them comes to mean Us *versus* Them, as in race riots and revolutions and wars in general. But even here it's worth remembering that *versus* doesn't always necessarily mean inherently superior: It can be like Us versus Them in team sports, or the Yeas versus the Nays in a debating club, or some of the town/gown issues at the College that we try to mediate without claiming that either side is *superior* to the other."

Here he took the glasses off, as if to signal that the sermon was approaching its close. "I'm sure I'm not alone in saying that some of Debbie's and my closest friends live outside these gates of ours."

"Amen," Joan said on his behalf. After which, and apologizing again for nattering on so, Pete called for a vote authorizing the Association to solicit bids and award a contract for construction of an automatically gated HBE Pass third lane at our development's entrance. When the motion passed, six to one, Amanda Todd good-naturedly reminded Mark Matthews, the lone dissenter, that "Us versus You doesn't mean we don't love you, Mark." To which that broad-beamed but narrow-minded fellow retorted, "You College people, I swear."

"Objection!" Amanda's husband called out.

"Sustained," declared Peter Simpson, rising from his chair and gathering the spec sheets and other papers spread out before him. "No need to pursue it, and thank you all for coming and making your opinions known." Offering his hand to Matthews then, with a smile, "Here's to democracy, Mark, and parliamentary procedure. Agreed?"

"Whatever."

And that had been that, for then. But en route back along sycamore-lined Heron Bay Boulevard to our condominium in "Shad Row," as we like to call it (punning on that seasonal Chesapeake delicacy), we Franks had tsked and sighed at Mark Matthews's overbearing small-mindedness versus Pete Simpson's more generous spirit and eminently reasonable review of the several senses of Us/Them. "Like when people born and raised in Stratford talk about 'us locals' and 'them c'meres,'" Joan said, using the former's term for out-of-towners who "come here" to retire or to enjoy a second home. "Sometimes it's a putdown, sometimes it's just a more or less neutral distinction, depending."

"And even when it's a putdown," her husband agreed, "sometimes it's just a good-humored tease between friends or neighbors — unlike Lady Broad-Ass's Us/Thems in our condo sessions," he added, referring to his Shad Run Condominium Association colleague Rachel Broadus, a hefty and opinionated widow-lady who, two years ago, had vehemently opposed the sale of unit 117 to an openly gay late-middle-aged couple from D.C., early retired from careers in the federal government's General Services Administration — even letting the prospective buyers know by anonymous letter that while it was beyond the Association's authority to forbid the sale, homosexuals were not welcome in Heron Bay Estates. A majority of the Association shared her feelings and had been relieved when the offended couple withdrew their purchase offer, although most agreed with Gerry that the unsigned letter was reprehensible; he alone had spoken on the pair's behalf, or at least had opposed the opposition to them. When in the following year Ms. Broadus had similarly inveighed against the sale of unit 218 to a dapper Indian-American pharmacist and his wife ("Next thing you know it'll be Mexicans and blacks, and there goes the neighborhood"), he'd had more company in objecting to her objection, and the Raghavans had come to be well liked by nearly all of their neighbors. "Even so," Gerry now reminded his wife, "Broad-Ass couldn't resist saying 'Mind you, Ger, I don't have anything against a nice Jewish couple like you and Joan. But *Hindus*?' "

Joan groaned at the recollection — who on first hearing from Gerry of this misattribution had said, "You should've showed your foreskinned shlong already. Oy." Or, they'd agreed, he could have quoted the Irish-American songwriter George M. Cohan's reply to a resort-hotel desk clerk in the 1920s who refused him a room, citing the establishment's ban on Jewish guests: "You thought I was a Jew," said the composer of "The Yankee Doodle Boy," "and I thought you were a gentleman. We were both mistaken." Rachel Broadus, they supposed, had heard of Anne Frank and had readily generalized from that famed Holocaust victim's last name, perhaps pretending even to herself that the Them to which she assigned the Shad Run Franks was not meant pejoratively. It was easy to imagine her declaring that "some of her best friends," et cetera. Gerry himself had used that edged cliché, in quotes — "Some of Our Best Friends . . ." — as the heading of a "Frank Opinions" column applauding the progress of Stratford's middle-class African Americans from near invisibility to active representation on the Town Council, the Avon County School Board, and the faculties not only of the local public schools but of the College and the private Fenton Day School as well.

All the above, however, is past history: the HBECA lift-gate meeting and us Franks' return to Shad Run Road for a merlot nightcap on our second-story porch overlooking the moonlit creek (where no shad have been known to run during our residency) before the ten o'clock TV news, bedtime, and another flaccid semi-fuck, Gerry's "Jimmy" less than fully erect and Joan's "Susie" less than wetly welcoming. "Never mind that pair of old farts," Joan had sighed, kissing him goodnight before turning away to sleep: "They're Them; we're still Us." Whoever *that's* getting to be, he'd said to himself — for he really has, since virtual retirement, been ever more preoccupied with his approaching old age and his inevitable, already noticeable decline. To her, however, he wondered merely, "D'you suppose they're trying to tell us something?"

"Whatever it is," she answered sleepily, "don't put it in the column, okay?"

The column: Past history too is his nattering on about all the above to his computer for four work-mornings already, and now a fifth, in search of a "Frank Opinions" piece about all this Us/Them stuff. By now he has moved on from Joan's "Us Franks" as distinct from "Them body parts of ours," or the singular "I-Gerry/Thou-'Jimmy,' " to Gerry's-Mind/Gerry's-Body and thence (within the former) to Gerry's-Ego/Gerry's-Id+Superego, and while mulling these several Us/Thems and I/Thous of the concept Mind, he has duly noted that although such distinctions are *made* by our minds, it by no means follows that they're "all in our minds."

Blah blah blah: Won't readers of the *Avon County News* be thrilled to hear it?

Yet another Us/Them now occurs to him (just what he needed!): It's a standing levity in Heron Bay Estates that most of its male inhabitants happen to be called familiarly by one-syllable first names and their wives by two-: Mark and Mindy Matthews, Joe and Judy Barnes, Pete and Debbie Simpson, Dave and Lisa Bergman, Dick and Susan Felton — the list goes on. But while we Franks, perhaps by reflex, are occasionally fitted to this peculiar template ("Ger" and "Joanie"), we're normally called Gerry and Joan, in exception to the rule: an Us distinct from, though not opposed to, its Them.

So? So nothing. Has Gerald "Gerry" Frank mentioned his having noticed, years ago, that his normal pulse rate matches almost exactly the tick of seconds on his watch dial, so closely that he can measure less-than-a-minute intervals by his heartbeat? And that therefore, as of his recent sixty-eighth birthday, he had lived for 24,837 days (including 17 leap days) at an average rate of 1,400 pulses per day, or a total of 34,771,800, give or take a few thousand for periods of physical exertion or unusual quiescence? By which same calculation he reckons himself to have been mulling these who-gives-a-shit Us/Thems for some 7,200 heartbeats' worth of days now, approaching beat by beat not only his ultimate demise but, more immediately, Tom Chadwick's deadline, and feeling no closer to a column than he did five days ago.

Maybe a column about that? Lame idea.

Tick. Tick. Tick. Tick. Tick.

He believes he did mention, a few thousand pulses past, that the Shad Run Franks, while on entirely cordial terms with their workmates and with ninety-nine percent of their fellow Heron Bay Estaters, have no *friends,* really, if by friends one means people whom one enjoys having over for drinks and dinner or going out with to a restaurant, not to mention actually vacation-traveling together, as they see some of their neighbors doing. They used to have friends like that, separately in their pre-Us lives and together in the earliest, pre-Stratford period of their marriage. Over the years since, however, for whatever reasons, their social life has atrophied: annual visits to and from their far-flung family, lunch with a colleague now and then (although they both work mainly at home these days), the occasional office cocktail party or HBE community social — that's about it. They don't particularly *approve* of this state of affairs, mildly wish it were otherwise, but have come to accept, more or less, that outside the workplace that's who they are, or have become: more comfortable with just Us than with Them.

As if his busy fingers have a mind of their own, *To be quite frank, Reader,* he now sees appearing on his computer screen, *old Gerry hasn't been being quite Frank with you about certain things. E.g.:*

— He and his mate share another, very different and entirely secret life, the revelation whereof would scandalize all Stratford and Heron Bay Estates, not to mention their family.

— Or they *don't,* of course, but could sometimes half wish they did, just for the hell of it.

— Or they *don't* so wish or even half wish, for God's sake! Who does this nutcase columnist take us for, that he could even *imagine* either of them so wishing?

— Or he has just learned that the precious, the indispensable Other Half of our Us has been diagnosed with . . . oh, advanced, inoperable pancreatic cancer? While *he* sits scared shitless on his butt counting his heartbeats, her killer cells busily metastasize through that dearest of bodies. Maybe a dozen thousand ever-more-wretched tick-ticks to go, at most, until The End — of her, therefore of Us, therefore of him.

— Or he's just making all this crap up. Trying it out. Thinking the unthinkable, perhaps in vain hope of its exorcism, or at least forestallment. But such tomfoolery fools no one. While his right hand types *no one,* his left rummages in a "drawer of the adjacent inkjet-printer stand for the reassuring feel of the loaded nine-millimeter-automatic pistol that he keeps in there for "self-defense": i.e., for defending Joan and Gerry Frank yet a while longer from murder/suicide — which they agree they'd resort to in any such scenario as that terminal-cancer one above-invoked — by reminding himself that they have the means and the will to do it, if and when the time comes.

But they don't — have the means, at least; at least not by gunfire. There is no pistol, never has been; we Franks aren't the gun-owning sort. Should push come to shove *chez nous,* in our frank opinion we'd go the route that Dick and Susan Felton went last year: double suicide (nobody knows why) by automobile exhaust fumes in the closed garage of their empty-nest house in Rockfish Reach, with not even a goodbye note to their traumatized, life-disrupted offspring.

Well, we guess we'd leave a note.

Maybe this is it?

Nah. Still . . .

45 Deadline a-coming: Tick. Tick.

Deathline? Tick.

FRANK OPINIONS: Us/Them
or
Much Ado About

Topics for Critical Thinking and Writing

1. What do you think is the point of distinguishing at the start of the story the differences between how Gerald Frank would speak to his friends compared to his audience? What does the difference tell you?
2. John Barth is famous for his language games and unique grammar and syntax. Locate three moments in the story that were most unique to you. What effect did the language have on you?
3. Look up the term *metafiction* and tell whether or not you think it is an effective strategy for writing fiction. Why, or why not?
4. Examine some of the self/other dualities in Barth's story and extrapolate how groups define and divide themselves through the processes of inclusion and exclusion. Draw on any of the theories of "othering" from other selections in this chapter to assist in your description.
5. When Barth published "Us/Them," he was eighty-eight years old. Discuss the significance of the author's age, the age of the characters, and your own experience living and reading this story. Is there an "us/them" division — an othering process — at work between the young and old in the United States today? Explain.
6. Examine your own neighborhood, town, or school, and attempt to understand how the people who are "insiders" (neighbors, residents, or students) define themselves against "others." Describe the dynamic: Is it hostile or friendly, part of a long tradition or something new, something at the forefront of awareness or more subtle? Now, describe an experience you had in encountering the other. What was it like? What did you learn — about yourself or about the other, or about the othering process?
7. In 250 to 500 words, describe the role of Mark Matthews in this story.
8. Consider the "edged cliché" (para. 30) commonly used by people insisting that they do not disparage the other because "some of my best friends are X." Is it possible to have prejudice or bias against a racial, cultural, or ethnic group despite having "friends" who are of that origin? Explain.

JACOB RIIS

Jacob Riis (1849–1914) was a social reformer, journalist, and photographer who emigrated to the United States from Denmark in 1870 in one of the first waves of European immigration that brought around 12 million people to the country in the following three decades. After working as a carpenter, miner, and farmhand in western Pennsylvania and New York, Riis moved to New York City, where he trained as a journalist and eventually became the city editor of the *New York Tribune*. Riis, having lived among the swelling immigrant communities in lower Manhattan, witnessed the abject poverty and dire living conditions in the tenements of New York City where, according to one report, more than 335,000 people were crammed into a single square mile on the Lower East Side, making it the most densely populated place in the world. Conditions in the tenements — or slums — were abhorrent. Immigrants were packed into buildings whose interiors, modified to maximize the number of tenants, were often dark, dank, and disease-ridden, left to fester by mostly indifferent landlords who viewed the occupants as inferior races whose squalor was largely seen as their own responsibility. Riis became a crusader in exposing these conditions to the general public and working with other reformers to improve the conditions of the tenements. He was among the first Americans to use flash photography, and he included disturbing photographs of his subjects alongside the articles and books he wrote advocating for humanitarian responses to poverty in New York City. In 1890, he published his most famous work, *How the Other Half Lives*, a lurid account of tenement living conditions and an argument for philanthropic, legislative, and tax-based solutions to the public housing crisis. The images presented here are from that work.

Street Arabs in "sleeping quarters"

"Five Cents a Spot"—Lodgers in a crowded Bayard Street tenement

Topics for Critical Thinking and Writing

1. Explain how the first image (showing children sleeping an alley) makes an argument. What kind of appeal does it make? To whom does it make the appeal?
2. It is known that Jacob Riis asked the boys in the first photograph to pose for this photograph. Do you think this fact undermines the integrity of the photograph? Why, or why not?
3. Examine the second image, which shows lodgers who rented space in a tenement, and account for the denotative and connotative meanings of the elements within the frame.
4. An exposé is a type of representation that "exposes" a certain truth or reality to people who might not otherwise be aware of it. Think of an instance when photography has been used today to expose something. Was it effective? Explain your answer.

SIMONE DE BEAUVOIR

Simone de Beauvoir (1908–1986) was a French writer and philosopher whose work had a significant impact on feminist thought and social thought. Her dictum, "One is not born but becomes a woman," from her 1949 tome, *The Second Sex,* is one of the most quotable instances of the social constructionist perspective of gender development. She defined women as the second sex in a bivalent, or dualistic, symbolic system that relegated women to the status of "other." This symbolic system, spanning myth, language, and culture, resulted in the disenfranchisement of women in political, economic, and material realms. Her work is a foundational feminist tract and remains in print now seventy years since its initial publication. "The Woman as Other," excerpted below, is from *The Second Sex.*

The Woman as Other

Throughout history [women] have always been subordinated to men, and hence their dependency is not the result of a historical event or a social change — it was not something that *occurred*. The reason why otherness in this case seems to be an absolute is in part that it lacks the contingent or incidental nature of historical facts. A condition brought about at a certain time can be abolished at some other time, as the Negroes of Haiti and others have proved: but it might seem that natural condition is beyond the possibility of change. In truth, however, the nature of things is no more immutably given, once for all, than is historical reality. If woman seems to be the inessential which never becomes the essential, it is because she herself fails to bring about this change. Proletarians say "We"; Negroes also. Regarding themselves as subjects, they transform the bourgeois, the whites, into "others'." But women do not say "We," except at some congress of feminists or similar formal demonstration; men say "women," and women use the same word in referring to themselves . . . They have gained only what men have been willing to grant; they have taken nothing, they have only received.

The reason for this is that women lack concrete means for organizing themselves into a unit which can stand face to face with the correlative unit. . . . Male and female stand opposed within a primordial *Mitsein*,[1] and woman has not broken it. The couple is a fundamental unity with its two halves riveted together, and the cleavage of society along the line of sex is impossible. Here is to be found the basic trait of woman: she is the Other in a totality of which the two components are necessary to one another.

[1]***Mitsein*** a concept developed by twentieth-century German philosopher Martin Heidegger meaning "being-with," or the essential characteristic of humanity that is the need to be with other humans, a social fact that influences our individual behavior. [Editors' note]

Topics for Critical Thinking and Writing

1. Leading up to this passage, Simone de Beauvoir writes in *The Second Sex* that the category of the Other is "a fundamental category of human thought." If that is true — if otherness is a natural condition in human cultures — does it justify or excuse forms of devaluing other racial, cultural, or ethnic groups? Explain your response.
2. De Beauvoir wrote this piece in 1949. Do some research into the balance of rights and privileges of women and men during that time and explain if you agree with her that there was a condition of "male sovereignty."
3. Part of the problem with the empowerment of women, de Beauvoir suggests, is that women "do not say 'We' " (para. 1). What does she mean? How is the "We" spoken by other cultural and ethnic groups different from the ways women think of themselves collectively?
4. Research the concept of "intersectionality" and describe what challenges it poses to the notion of otherness as put forth by de Beauvoir.
5. Think of another group of people who do, or do not, have a strong sense of a collective "We." How did it develop or disintegrate — or was it ever present at all?
6. What are the benefits of unity within a group and what are the drawbacks? Explain using examples of more cohesive and less cohesive identity categories.

RUDYARD KIPLING

Rudyard Kipling (1865–1936) was an English journalist, poet, and writer of fiction. His most well-known work, *The Jungle Book* (1894), has been adapted in a wide variety of literature, music, and film, including the Walt Disney films of the same name. In his lifetime, Kipling was one of the most popular writers in the United Kingdom, publishing poems such as "Gunga Din" and "The White Man's Burden" in addition to short stories, children's books, travel books, military histories, and two autobiographies. In 1907, he won the Nobel Prize in Literature.

As an Englishman born in India, Kipling's work is suffused with Indian culture; as such, it has been criticized for representing India through the eyes of the colonialist. Indeed, Kipling's views were imperialistic. They accorded with attitudes of the time about the civilizing effects of empire — to many, a moral justification for exploitation in the colonies. In these views, natives of India were seen as backward, naïve, and almost childlike — beneficiaries, not victims, of colonization. This poem, "We and They," was published in 1926.

We and They

Father, Mother, and Me,
Sister and Auntie say
All the people like us are We,
And every one else is They.
And They live over the sea,
While We live over the way,
But — would you believe it? — They look upon We
As only a sort of They!

We eat pork and beef
With cow-horn-handled knives.
They who gobble Their rice off a leaf,
Are horrified out of Their lives;
While they who live up a tree,
And feast on grubs and clay,
(Isn't it scandalous?) look upon We
As a simply disgusting They!

We shoot birds with a gun.
They stick lions with spears.
Their full-dress is un-.
We dress up to Our ears.
They like Their friends for tea.
We like Our friends to stay;
And, after all that, They look upon We
As an utterly ignorant They!

We eat kitcheny food.
We have doors that latch.
They drink milk or blood,
Under an open thatch.
We have Doctors to fee.
They have Wizards to pay.
And (impudent heathen!) They look upon We
As a quite impossible They!

All good people agree,
And all good people say,
All nice people, like Us, are We
And every one else is They:
But if you cross over the sea,
Instead of over the way,
You may end by (think of it!) looking on We
As only a sort of They!

Topics for Critical Thinking and Writing

1. Do you think the "We" and "They" in this poem are presented equally and relatively, or is there an implied superiority in the speaker's words or tone? Using evidence from the poem, argue one way or the other.
2. On pages 146–48, we talked about accommodating, resisting, and negotiating the meanings of images. Apply those concepts to this poem: Determine what kind of approach to take and write an analysis of 300 to 500 words in which you accommodate, resist, or negotiate the meaning of this poem.
3. Write about an American practice "we" assume to be a normal, reasonable, right, or correct practice and then compare the practice of a different culture that "we" might (at least at first) consider to be inferior in some way. Now, assess the question of which practice is "better." What standards are you using? Do you have a basis for evaluating which is better or worse? What would an opponent say? How would you respond?

EMARI DIGIORGIO

Emari DiGiorgio is poet and professor of writing at Stockton University. She is a Geraldine R. Dodge Foundation Poet and the author of two poetry collections, *The Things a Body Might Become* (2017) and *Girl Torpedo* (2018), which won the Numinous Orison, Luminous Origin Literary Award. DiGiorgio has received many poetry prizes including, in 2016, the Auburn Witness Poetry Prize and a New Jersey State Council on the Arts poetry fellowship. She is also the senior reviews editor for *Tupelo Quarterly*. In "The Brownest White Girl," reprinted here, DiGiorgio, an Italian American woman, explores the intersectional aspects of racial, ethnicity, and identity.

When You Are the Brownest White Girl

Someone will call you spic. And you won't know what to say
because you're a Ferrucci-DiGiorgio from the region of Molise

where olives become oil, and there are slurs for your kind, too:
Guinea, WOP, grease ball, so maybe, the sting is being slapped

with another's epithet. When you're the brownest white girl
at CCD, no one lets you play the Virgin Mary, even if you

look the most like her and have memorized all the prayers.
When you're the brownest white girl, you know you need

to run fast, leave their pink tongues flapping. Though you're
not as dark as the girl who just moved from Queens, or Javi

and Nando, and Keisha and Tasha have made it quite clear
that *you're a white girl, white girl.* Though someone tugs

at your kinky hair and says, *Mami, you got a little black in you.*
And if there was, some big reveal on the Maury show, what

would it change? When you are the brownest white girl
at field day, you're a piñata and the blindfolded stick swinger.

One minute you use your hands to block their wild swings,
the next, you beg for your turn to beat on someone else.

Topics for Critical Thinking and Writing

1. Research the terms *intersectionality* and *intersectional identity.* How do these conceptions challenge the We/They, Us/Them, Self/Other constructions? Explain your response.
2. Why do you think "fitting into" a racial category is important to the speaker in the poem? Answer in 100 to 200 words.
3. Why do you think Emari DiGiorgio uses the piñata as an image in this poem? Is the usage ironic in any way? If yes, explain.
4. Have you ever been mistaken for a different identity group? If so, tell about the circumstances and how it made you feel. If not, what is it about you that made such an experience unlikely?
5. When the poet is told that she looks like she's "got a little black" in her (l. 13), she wonders — if she had, what would it change? Think through this question and try to answer it yourself. If something would (or could) change, what might it be? If you think otherwise, explain.

28

What Is Happiness?

Thoughts about Happiness, Ancient and Modern

Here are some brief comments about happiness, from ancient times to the present. Read them, think about them, and then write on one of the two topics that appear after the last quotation.

> *Happiness is prosperity combined with virtue.* — ARISTOTLE (384–322 BCE)

> *Pleasure is the beginning and the end of living happily. . . . It is impossible to live pleasurably without living wisely, well, and justly, and impossible to live wisely, well, and justly without living pleasurably.* — EPICURUS (341–270 BCE)

> *Very little is needed to make a happy life.* — MARCUS AURELIUS (121–180)

> *Society can only be happy and free in proportion as it is virtuous.* — MARY WOLLSTONECRAFT SHELLEY (1759–1797)

> *The supreme happiness of life is the conviction that we are loved.* — VICTOR HUGO (1802–1885)

> *Ask yourself whether you are happy, and you cease to be so.* — JOHN STUART MILL (1806–1873)

> *A lifetime of happiness! No man alive could bear it: it would be hell on earth.* — GEORGE BERNARD SHAW (1856–1950)

> *We have no more right to consume happiness without producing it than to consume wealth without producing it.* — GEORGE BERNARD SHAW (1856–1950)

> *If only we'd stop trying to be happy, we could have a pretty good time.* — EDITH WHARTON (1862–1937)

Happiness makes up in height for what it lacks in length. — ROBERT FROST (1874–1963)

Point me out the happy man and I will point you out either egotism, selfishness, evil — or else an absolute ignorance. — GRAHAM GREENE (1904–1991)

Those who are unhappy have no need for anything in this world but people capable of giving them their attention. — SIMONE WEIL (1909–1943)

Happiness is always a by-product. It is probably a matter of temperament, and for anything I know it may be glandular. But it is not something that can be demanded from life, and if you are not happy you had better stop worrying about it and see what treasures you can pluck from your own brand of unhappiness. — ROBERTSON DAVIES (1913–1995)

Topics for Critical Thinking and Writing

1. If any one of these passages especially appeals to you, make it the thesis of an essay of about 500 words.
2. Take two of these passages — perhaps one that you especially like and one that you think is wrong-headed — and write a dialogue of about 500 words in which the two authors converse. They may each try to convince the other, or they may find that to some degree they share views and they may then work out a statement that both can accept. If you do take the position that one writer is on the correct track but the other is utterly mistaken, try to be fair to the view that you think is mistaken. (As an experiment in critical thinking, imagine that you accept it and make the best case for it that you possibly can.)

DANIEL GILBERT

Daniel Gilbert (b. 1957) is the author of *Stumbling on Happiness* (2006), a book that has sold six million copies worldwide and that won the prestigious Royal Society Prize for Science Books. Hearing of the award, Gilbert said, "There are very few countries (including my own) . . . where a somewhat cheeky book about happiness could win a science prize — but the British invented intellectual humor and have always understood that enlightenment and entertainment are natural friends."

A high school dropout, Gilbert was nineteen when he visited a community college, intending to take a writing course but enrolling instead in the only course still open — a psychology course. He is now a professor of psychology at Harvard University and has shared his views on happiness in various essays and television appearances. In 2010, he co-wrote a six-hour television series for *NOVA*, "This Emotional Life," and in 2013, he gave one of the twenty most-viewed TED talks, "The Surprising Science of Happiness."

The following essay originally appeared in *Time* a few days before Father's Day in June 2006.

Does Fatherhood Make You Happy?

Sonora Smart Dodd was listening to a sermon on self-sacrifice when she decided that her father, a widower who had raised six children, deserved his very own national holiday. Almost a century later, people all over the world spend the third Sunday in June honoring their fathers with ritual offerings of aftershave and neckties, which leads millions of fathers to have precisely the same thought at precisely the same moment: "My children," they think in unison, "make me happy."

Could all those dads be wrong?

Studies reveal that most married couples start out happy and then become progressively less satisfied over the course of their lives, becoming especially disconsolate when their children are in diapers and in adolescence, and returning to their initial levels of happiness only after their children have had the decency to grow up and go away. When the popular press invented a malady called "empty-nest syndrome," it failed to mention that its primary symptom is a marked increase in smiling.

Psychologists have measured how people feel as they go about their daily activities, and have found that people are less happy when they are interacting with their children than when they are eating, exercising, shopping, or watching television. Indeed, an act of parenting makes most people about as happy as an act of housework. Economists have modeled the impact of many variables on people's overall happiness and have consistently found that children have only a small impact. A small negative impact.

5 Those findings are hard to swallow because they fly in the face of our most compelling intuitions. We love our children! We talk about them to anyone who will listen, show their photographs to anyone who will look, and hide our refrigerators behind vast collages of their drawings, notes, pictures, and report cards. We feel confident that we are happy with our kids, about our kids, for our kids, and because of our kids — so why is our personal experience at odds with the scientific data?

Three reasons.

First, when something makes us happy we are willing to pay a lot for it, which is why the worst Belgian chocolate is more expensive than the best Belgian tofu. But that process can work in reverse: When we pay a lot for something, we assume it makes us happy, which is why we swear to the wonders of bottled water and Armani socks. The compulsion to care for our children was long ago written into our DNA, so we toil and sweat, lose sleep and hair, play nurse, housekeeper, chauffeur, and cook, and we do all that because nature just won't have it any other way. Given the high price we pay, it isn't surprising that we rationalize those costs and conclude that our children must be repaying us with happiness.

Second, if the Red Sox and the Yankees were scoreless until Manny Ramirez[1] hit a grand slam in the bottom of the ninth, you can be sure that Boston fans would remember it as the best game of the season. Memories are dominated by their most powerful — and not their most typical — instances. Just as a glorious game-winning homer can erase our memory of eight and a half dull innings, the sublime moment when our three-year-old looks up from the mess she is making with her mashed potatoes and says, "I wub you, Daddy," can erase eight hours of no, not yet, not now, and stop asking. Children may not make us happy very often, but when they do, that happiness is both transcendent and amnesic.

Third, although most of us think of heroin as a source of human misery, shooting heroin doesn't actually make people feel miserable. It makes them feel really, really good — so good, in fact, that it crowds out every other source of pleasure.

[1]**Manny Ramirez** Ramirez (b. 1972), a former professional baseball player, played for the Boston Red Sox from 2001 to 2008. [Editors' note]

Family, friends, work, play, food, sex — none can compete with the narcotic experience; hence all fall by the wayside. The analogy to children is all too clear. Even if their company were an unremitting pleasure, the fact that they require so much company means that other sources of pleasure will all but disappear. Movies, theater, parties, travel — those are just a few of the English nouns that parents of young children quickly forget how to pronounce. We believe our children are our greatest joy, and we're absolutely right. When you have one joy, it's bound to be the greatest.

10 Our children give us many things, but an increase in our average daily happiness is probably not among them. Rather than deny that fact, we should celebrate it. Our ability to love beyond all measure those who try our patience and weary our bones is at once our most noble and most human quality. The fact that children don't always make us happy — and that we're happy to have them nonetheless — is the fact for which Sonora Smart Dodd was so grateful. She thought we would all do well to remember it, every third Sunday in June.

Topics for Critical Thinking and Writing

1. How would you define the "empty-nest syndrome" (para. 3), and how do you respond to Daniel Gilbert's suggestion that it was "invented"?
2. Do you believe the "studies" that Gilbert mentions in paragraph 3? Why, or why not? Similarly, do you believe the "psychologists" of paragraph 4? Explain your response.
3. What does Gilbert mean when he describes the happiness that children cause their parents as "transcendent" (para. 8)? Are there other, nontranscendent kinds of happiness that parents experience? Explain your response.
4. Let's assume that even if you don't fully accept Gilbert's view about fatherhood and happiness, you're willing to grant that it is just possible that there may be something to what he says. Are you willing to take the next step and say that what he says of fatherhood may also be true of motherhood? Why, or why not?
5. What do you think Gilbert's chief purpose is in this essay? To inform? To persuade? To entertain? Something else? Support your answer with evidence.
6. You may have been told not to write paragraphs consisting of only a sentence or two, but Gilbert's essay includes two such paragraphs, 2 and 6. Should Gilbert have revised these paragraphs? Or does their brevity serve a purpose? Explain your response.

HENRY DAVID THOREAU

Henry David Thoreau (1817–1862) was born in Concord, Massachusetts, where he spent most of his life ("I have travelled a good deal in Concord"). He taught and lectured, but chiefly he observed, thought, and wrote. From July 5, 1847, to September 6, 1847, he lived near Concord in a cabin at Walden Pond, an experience recorded in *Walden* (1854). He is also the author of the renowned essay "Resistance to Civil Government" (1849), sometimes called "Civil Disobedience," in which he forcefully argued against the institution of slavery with ideas later adopted by social reformers such as Mahatma Gandhi and Martin Luther King Jr.

This selection below, "As for Clothing" (the editors' title), comes from *Walden*, Chapter 1. "We Do Not Ride on the Railroad; It Rides upon Us" (also the editors' title) is from *Walden*, Chapter 2.

Selections from *Walden*

[AS FOR CLOTHING]

As for Clothing, to come at once to the practical part of the question, perhaps we are led oftener by the love of novelty and a regard for the opinions of men, in procuring it, than by a true utility. Let him who has work to do recollect that the object of clothing is, first, to retain the vital heat, and secondly, in this state of society, to cover nakedness, and he may judge how much of any necessary or important work may be accomplished without adding to his wardrobe. Kings and queens who wear a suit but once, though made by some tailor or dressmaker to their majesties, cannot know the comfort of wearing a suit that fits. They are no better than wooden horses to hang the clean clothes on. Every day our garments become more assimilated to ourselves, receiving the impress of the wearer's character, until we hesitate to lay them aside, without such delay and medical appliances and some such solemnity even as our bodies. No man ever stood the lower in my estimation for having a patch in his clothes; yet I am sure that there is greater anxiety, commonly, to have fashionable, or at least clean and unpatched clothes, than to have a sound conscience. But even if the rent is not mended, perhaps the worst vice betrayed is improvidence. I sometimes try my acquaintances by such tests as these, — Who could wear a patch, or two extra seams only, over the knee? Most have as if they believed that their prospects for life would be ruined if they should do it. It would be easier for them to hobble to town with a broken leg than with a broken pantaloon. Often if an accident happens to a gentleman's legs, they can be mended; but if a similar accident happens to the legs of his pantaloons, there is no help for it; for he considers, not what is truly respectable, but what is respected. We know but few men, a great many coats and breeches. Dress a scarecrow in your last shift, you standing shiftless by, who would not soonest salute the scarecrow? Passing a cornfield the other day, close by a hat and coat on a stake, I recognized the owner of the farm. He was only a little more weather-beaten than when I saw him last. I have heard of a dog that barked at every stranger who approached his master's premises with clothes on, but was easily quieted by a naked thief. It is an interesting question how far men would retain their relative rank if they were divested of their clothes. Could you, in such a case, tell surely of any company of civilized men which belonged to the most respected class? When Madam Pfeiffer,[1] in her adventurous travels round the world, from east to west, had got so near home as Asiatic Russia, she says that she felt the necessity of wearing other than a traveling dress, when she went to meet the authorities, for she "was now in a civilized country, where . . . people are judged of by their clothes." Even in our democratic New England towns the accidental possession of wealth, and its manifestation in dress and equipage alone, obtain for the possessor almost universal respect. But they who yield such respect, numerous as they are, are so far heathen, and need to have a missionary sent to them. Beside, clothes introduced sewing, a kind of work which you may call endless; a woman's dress, at least, is never done.

[1]**Madame Pfeiffer** Ida Pfeiffer (1797–1858), author of travel books. [All notes are the editors'.]

A man who has at length found something to do will not need to get a new suit to do it in; for him the old will do, that has lain dusty in the garret for an indeterminate period. Old shoes will serve a hero longer than they have served his valet — if a hero even has a valet — bare feet are older than shoes, and he can make them do. Only they who go to soirées and legislative halls must have new coats, coats to change as often as the man changes in them. But if my jacket and trousers, my hat and shoes, are fit to worship God in, they will do; will they not? Who ever saw his old clothes — his old coat, actually worn out, resolved into its primitive elements, so that it was not a deed of charity to bestow it on some poor boy, by him perchance to be bestowed on some poorer still, or shall we say richer, who could do with less? I say, beware of all enterprises that require new clothes, and not rather a new wearer of clothes. If there is not a new man, how can the new clothes be made to fit? If you have any enterprise before you, try it in your old clothes. All men want, not something to *do with,* but something to *do,* or rather something to *be*. Perhaps we should never procure a new suit, however ragged or dirty the old, until we have so conducted, so enterprised or sailed in some way, that we feel like new men in the old, and that to retain it would be like keeping new wine in old bottles. Our moulting season, like that of the fowls must be a crisis in our lives. The loon retires to solitary ponds to spend it. Thus also the snake casts its slough, and the caterpillar its wormy coat, by an internal industry and expansion; for clothes are but our outmost cuticle and mortal coil. Otherwise we shall be found sailing under false colors, and be inevitably cashiered at last by our own opinion, as well as that of mankind.

We don garment after garment, as if we grew like exogenous plants by addition without. Our outside and often thin and fanciful clothes are our epidermis, or false skin, which partakes not of our life, and may be stripped off here and there without fatal injury; our thicker garments, constantly worn, are our cellular integument, or cortex; but our shirts are our liber,[2] or true bark, which cannot be removed without girdling and so destroying the man. I believe that all races at some seasons wear something equivalent to the shirt. It is desirable that a man be clad so simply that he can lay his hands on himself in the dark, and that he live in all respects so compactly and preparedly, that, if an enemy take the town, he can, like the old philosopher, walk out the gate empty-handed without anxiety. While one thick garment is, for most purposes, as good as three thin ones, and cheap clothing can be obtained at prices really to suit customers; while a thick coat can be bought for five dollars, which will last as many years, thick pantaloons for two dollars, cowhide boots for a dollar and a half a pair, a summer hat for a quarter of a dollar, and a winter cap for sixty-two and a half cents, or a better be made at home at a nominal cost, where is he so poor that, clad in such a suit, *of his own earning*, there will not be found wise men to do him reverence?

When I ask for a garment of a particular form, my tailoress tells me gravely, "They do not make them so now," not emphasizing the "They" at all, as if she quoted an authority as impersonal as the Fates, and I find it difficult to get made what I want, simply because she cannot believe that I mean what I say, that I am so rash. When I hear this oracular

[2]**liber** Inner bark of a tree.

sentence, I am for a moment absorbed in thought, emphasizing to myself each word separately that I may come at the meaning of it, that I may find out by what degree of consanguinity *They* are related to *me*, and what authority they may have in an affair which affects me so nearly; and finally, I am inclined to answer her with equal mystery, and without any more emphasis of the "they" — "It is true, they did not make them so recently, but they do now." Of what use this measuring of me if she does not measure my character, but only the breadth of my shoulders, as it were a peg to hang the coat on? We worship not the Graces,[3] nor the Parcæ,[4] but Fashion. She spins and weaves and cuts with full authority. The head monkey at Paris puts on a traveller's cap, and all the monkeys in America do the same. I sometimes despair of getting anything quite simple and honest done in this world by the help of men. They would have to be passed through a powerful press first, to squeeze their old notions out of them, so that they would not soon get upon their legs again; and then there would be some one in the company with a maggot in his head, hatched from an egg deposited there nobody knows when, for not even fire kills these things, and you would have lost your labor. Nevertheless, we will not forget that some Egyptian wheat was handed down to us by a mummy.

5 On the whole, I think that it cannot be maintained that dressing has in this or any country risen to the dignity of an art. At present men make shift to wear what they can get. Like shipwrecked sailors, they put on what they can find on the beach, and at a little distance, whether of space or time, laugh at each other's masquerade. Every generation laughs at the old fashions, but follows religiously the new. We are amused at beholding the costume of Henry VIII, or Queen Elizabeth, as much as if it was that of the King and Queen of the Cannibal Islands. All costume off a man is pitiful or grotesque. It is only the serious eye peering from and the sincere life passed within it which restrain laughter and consecrate the costume of any people. Let Harlequin be taken with a fit of the colic and his trappings will have to serve that mood too. When the soldier is hit by a cannon ball rags are as becoming as purple.

The childish and savage taste of men and women for new patterns keeps how many shaking and squinting through kaleidoscopes that they may discover the particular figure which this generation requires today. The manufacturers have learned that this taste is merely whimsical. Of two patterns which differ only by a few threads more or less of a particular color, the one will be sold readily, the other lie on the shelf, though it frequently happens that after the lapse of a season the latter becomes the most fashionable. Comparatively, tattooing is not the hideous custom which it is called. It is not barbarous merely because the printing is skin-deep and unalterable.

I cannot believe that our factory system is the best mode by which men may get clothing. The condition of the operatives is becoming every day more like that of the English; and it cannot be wondered at, since, as far as I have heard or observed, the principal object is, not that mankind may be well and honestly clad, but, unquestionably, that the corporations may be enriched. In the long run men hit only what they

[3]**Graces** In Greek mythology, the Graces were three minor goddesses who were patrons of earthly pleasures such as happiness, creativity, beauty, and fertility.
[4]**Parcæ** Goddesses of fate in Roman mythology.

aim at. Therefore, though they should fail immediately, they had better aim at something high.

[WE DO NOT RIDE ON THE RAILROAD; IT RIDES UPON US]

Still we live meanly, like ants; though the fable tells us that we were long ago changed into men; like pygmies we fight with cranes; it is error upon error, and clout upon clout, and our best virtue has for its occasion a superfluous and evitable wretchedness. Our life is frittered away by detail. An honest man has hardly need to count more than his ten fingers, or in extreme cases he may add his ten toes, and lump the rest. Simplicity, simplicity, simplicity! I say, let your affairs be as two or three, and not a hundred or a thousand; instead of a million count half a dozen, and keep your accounts on your thumb nail. In the midst of this chopping sea of civilized life, such are the clouds and storms and quicksands and thousand-and-one items to be allowed for, that a man has to live, if he would not founder and go to the bottom and not make his port at all, by dead reckoning, and he must be a great calculator indeed who succeeds. Simplify, simplify. Instead of three meals a day, if it be necessary eat but one; instead of a hundred dishes, five; and reduce other things in proportion. Our life is like a German Confederacy, made up of petty states, with its boundary forever fluctuating, so that even a German cannot tell you how it is bounded at any moment. The nation itself, with all its so-called internal improvements, which, by the way are all external and superficial, is just such an unwieldy and overgrown establishment, cluttered with furniture and tripped up by its own traps, ruined by luxury and heedless expense, by want of calculation and a worthy aim, as the million households in the land; and the only cure for it as for them is in a rigid economy, a stern and more than Spartan simplicity of life and elevation of purpose. It lives too fast. Men think that it is essential that the *Nation* have commerce, and export ice, and talk through a telegraph, and ride thirty miles an hour, without a doubt, whether *they* do or not; but whether we should live like baboons or like men, is a little uncertain. If we do not get out sleepers,[5] and forge rails, and devote days and nights to the work, but go to tinkering upon our *lives* to improve *them*, who will build railroads? And if railroads are not built, how shall we get to heaven in season? But if we stay at home and mind our business, who will want railroads? We do not ride on the railroad; it rides upon us. Did you ever think what those sleepers are that underlie the railroad? Each one is a man, an Irishman, or a Yankee man. The rails are laid on them, and they are covered with sand, and the cars run smoothly over them. They are sound sleepers, I assure you. And every few years a new lot is laid down and run over; so that, if some have the pleasure of riding on a rail, others have the misfortune to be ridden upon. And when they run over a man that is walking in his sleep, a supernumerary sleeper in the wrong position, and wake him up, they suddenly stop the cars, and make a hue and cry about it, as if this were an exception. I am glad to know that it takes a gang of men for every five miles to keep the sleepers down and level in their beds as it is, for this is a sign that they may sometime get up again.

[5]**sleepers** The woody ties beneath railroad rails.

Topics for Critical Thinking and Writing

1. What, according to Henry David Thoreau, are the legitimate functions of clothing? What other functions does he reject or fail to consider?
2. Many of Thoreau's sentences mean both what they say literally and something more; often, like proverbs, they express abstract or general truths in concrete, homely language. How might these sentences be interpreted?

   a. We know but few men, a great many coats and breeches.
   b. Dress a scarecrow in your last shift, you standing shiftless by, who would not soonest salute the scarecrow?
   c. If you have any enterprise before you, try it in your old clothes.
   d. Every generation laughs at the old fashions, but follows religiously the new.
   e. The head monkey at Paris puts on a traveller's cap, and all the monkeys in America do the same.

3. We have just quoted some of Thoreau's epigrammatic sentences. Is this style effective or not? Explain your response.
4. Notice that Thoreau writes in long paragraphs. (The first of them runs to more than 450 words — the length of many respectable essays.) Can such long paragraphs do their job effectively? What is the job of a paragraph? Or is there no one such job? Explain your response.
5. Toward the end of paragraph 2, we meet the cliché "new wine in old bottles." Do you think this sentence is effective? Why, or why not? Was this expression already a cliché in Thoreau's day? Complete the following definition: "A word or phrase is a cliché if and only if . . ."
6. In paragraph 7, Thoreau criticizes the factory system. Is the criticism mild or severe? Explain. Point out some of the earlier passages in which he touches on the relation of clothes to a faulty economic system.
7. Apply Thoreau's ideas about clothing and fashion to conditions today, judging whether or not contemporary readers can draw wisdom about their relationship to clothes and fashion.
8. In paragraph 8, Thoreau asserts that "Our life is frittered away by detail." Is it possible to argue that "Yes, our life is frittered away by detail, but, perhaps oddly, attention to detail — studying for examinations, grading papers, walking the dog — is largely responsible for human happiness"? Explain your response.

DARRIN M. McMAHON

Darrin M. McMahon received his Ph.D. in 1997 from the University of California–Berkeley. The author of *Happiness: A History* (2006), McMahon has taught at Columbia University, Yale University, and New York University. He is currently a professor of history at Dartmouth College and a Guggenheim Fellow (2016). His most recent book is *Divine Fury: A History of Genius* (2013). The following essay was first published in the *New York Times* on December 29, 2005.

In Pursuit of Unhappiness

"Happy New Year!" We seldom think of those words as an order. But in some respects that is what they are.

Doesn't every American want to be happy? And don't most Americans yearn, deep down, to be happy all of the time? The right laid out in our nation's Declaration of Independence — to pursue happiness to our hearts' content — is nowhere on better display than in the rites of the holiday season. With glad tidings and good cheer, we seek to bring one year to its natural happy conclusion, while preparing to usher in a happy new year and many happy returns.

Like the cycle of the seasons, our emphasis on mirth may seem timeless, as though human beings have always made merry from beginning to end. But in fact this preoccupation with perpetual happiness is relatively recent. As Thomas Carlyle observed in 1843, " 'Happiness our being's end and aim' is at bottom, if we will count well, not yet two centuries old in the world."

Carlyle's arithmetic was essentially sound, for changes in both religious and secular culture since the seventeenth century made "happiness," in the form of pleasure or good feeling, not only morally acceptable but commendable in and of itself. While many discounted religious notions that consigned life in this world to misery and sin, others discovered signs of God's providence in earthly satisfaction. The result was at once to weaken and transpose the ideal of heavenly felicity, in effect bringing it to earth. Suffering was not our natural state. Happy was the way we were meant to be.

5 That shift was monumental, and its implications far reaching. Among other things, it was behind the transformation of the holiday season from a time of pious remembrance into one of unadulterated bliss. Yet the effects were greater than that. As Carlyle complained, "Every pitifulest whipster that walks within a skin has had his head filled with the notion that he is, shall be, or by all human and divine laws ought to be, 'happy.' "

Carlyle was notoriously cranky, but his central insight — that the new doctrine of happiness tended to raise expectations that could never possibly be fulfilled — remains as relevant today as it was in 1843. Despite enjoying far better living standards and more avenues for pleasure than before, human beings are arguably no happier now than they've ever been.

Sociologists like to point out that the percentage of those describing themselves as "happy" or "very happy" has remained virtually unchanged in Europe and the United States since such surveys were first conducted in the 1950s. And yet, this January, like last year and next, the self-help industry will pour forth books promising to make us happier than we are today. The very demand for such books is a strong indication that they aren't working.

Should that be a cause for concern? Some critics say it is. For example, economists like Lord Richard Layard and Daniel Kahneman have argued that the apparent stagnancy of happiness in modern societies should prompt policymakers to shift their priorities from the creation of wealth to the creation of good feelings, from boosting gross national product to increasing gross national happiness.

But before we take such steps, we might do well to reflect on the darker side of holiday cheer: those mysterious blues that are apt to set in while the streamers stream and the corks pop; the little voice that even in the best of souls is sometimes moved to say, "Bah, humbug." As Carlyle put it, "The prophets preach to us, 'Thou shalt be happy; thou shalt love pleasant things.' " But as he well knew, the very commandment tended to undermine its fulfillment, even to make us sad.

10 Carlyle's sometime friend and long-time rival, the philosopher John Stuart Mill, came to a similar conclusion. His words are all the more worth heeding in that Mill himself was a determined proponent of the greatest happiness for the greatest number. "Ask yourself whether you are happy, and you cease to be so," Mill concluded after recovering from a serious bout of depression. Rather than resign himself to gloom, however, Mill vowed instead to look for happiness in another way.

"Those only are happy," he came to believe, "who have their minds fixed on some object other than their own happiness; on the happiness of others; on the improvement of mankind, even on some art or pursuit, followed not as a means, but as itself an ideal end. Aiming thus at something else, they find happiness by the way." For our own culture, steeped as it is in the relentless pursuit of personal pleasure and endless cheer, that message is worth heeding.

So in these last days of 2005 I say to you, "Don't have a happy new year!" Have dinner with your family or walk in the park with friends. If you're so inclined, put in some good hours at the office or at your favorite charity, temple, or church. Work on your jump shot or your child's model trains. With luck, you'll find happiness by the by. If not, your time won't be wasted. You may even bring a little joy to the world.

Topics for Critical Thinking and Writing

1. Who or what gives us the "order" to be happy — or is the whole idea silly? (See paras. 1 and 9.) Explain your response.
2. What's the difference between happiness and pleasure, or are they two different ways of saying the same thing? Explain your response.
3. Has Darrin McMahon persuaded you to think of happiness in a fresh way? Why, or why not?
4. McMahon's article was originally published on December 29, so it's not surprising that in paragraph 2 he says that his readers are preparing "to usher in a happy new year." Try to recall how you spent the most recent New Year's Eve. Was it a happy evening? Or was it tinged with melancholy, perhaps even with sorrow as you remembered sad things and hoped that the next year would be happier? If you can't remember New Year's Eve, think of the last year as a whole: Was it predominantly happy or unhappy? Or can't you judge it in such terms? Explain your response.
5. McMahon says (para. 4) that since the seventeenth century, a shift in thinking has occurred: "Suffering [is] not our natural state. Happy was the way we were meant to be." Assume you are speaking to someone who has not read McMahon's essay. How would you explain this point?
6. John Stuart Mill (para. 10) is often described as a hedonist. What do you have to do or believe to be a hedonist? What are the positive and negative aspects of hedonism? Explain why you think the way you do.
7. Are you likely to take the advice McMahon offers in his final paragraph? Why, or why not?
8. Do you believe that Americans are happier today than they were three centuries ago? How would you go about arguing for your belief?

EPICTETUS

Epictetus (pronounced Epic-TEE-tus) was born in Phrygia (now southwestern Turkey) some sixty years after Jesus and died about 135 CE. His mother was a slave, and he was brought to Rome as a slave. At an uncertain date, he was given his freedom, and he went to Nicopolis in northwestern Greece, where he taught philosophy. One of his students, a Roman named Flavius Arrian, recorded the teachings of Epictetus in two books written in Greek, the *Discourses* (or *Lectures*) and the *Handbook* (or *Manual*, often known by its Greek title, *Enchiridion*). Our selection is from a translation by Helena Orozco.

The doctrine that Epictetus taught is stoicism, which can be briefly characterized thus: The goal of life (as other philosophers of the period would agree) is "happiness" or "a flourishing life" (*eudaimonia*). The way to achieve this condition is to understand the nature of the good. Such things as health, wealth, and rank are not good because they do not always benefit those who possess them. True, such things are "preferred," and sickness, poverty, and low social status are "not preferred," but all of these are "indifferent" when it comes to being good or evil. The only true good is virtue. Yes, wealth can be useful, but it is not good or bad. What is good or bad is the way in which one makes use of what one has. The life that is happy or fruitful (*eudaimôn*) is the virtuous life. Of course, some things are beyond our power, but we are able to judge whatever comes to us, to see that what is "not preferred"—for instance, poverty—is not bad but is morally indifferent (just as wealth is morally indifferent). And we also have the power to adapt ourselves to whatever comes our way. A slightly later contemporary reported that Epictetus said that if one wanted to be free from wrongdoing and wanted to live a peaceful life, then one should endure and abstain.

From *The Handbook*

1. Some things are in our control, and some are not. Our opinions are within our control, and our choices, our likes and dislikes. In a word, whatever is our own doing. Beyond our control are our bodies, our possessions, reputation, position; in a word, things not our own doings.

Now, the things that are within our control are by nature free, unhindered, unimpeded, but those beyond our control are weak, slavish, hindered, up to others. Keep in mind, then, that if you think things are free that by nature are slavish, and if you think that things that are up to others are yours, you will be hindered, you will suffer, you will complain, you will blame the gods and your fellows. But, on the other hand, if you take as yours only what in fact is yours, and if you see that what belongs to others belongs to others, nobody will compel you, nobody will restrict you; you will blame nobody, and you will do nothing against your will. No one will harm you, you will have no enemies.

5. People are not disturbed by what happens but by the view they take of what happens. For instance, death is not to be feared; if it were to be feared, Socrates would have feared it. The fear consists in our wrong idea of death, our idea that it is to be feared. When, therefore, we are disturbed or feel grief, we should not blame someone else, but our [false] opinion. An uneducated person blames others for his misfortunes; a person just starting his education blames himself; an educated person blames neither others nor himself.

6. Do not take pride in any excellence that is not your own. If a horse could be proud, it might say, "I am handsome," and such a statement might be acceptable. But when you proudly say, "I have a handsome horse," you should understand that you are taking pride in a horse's good. What has the horse's good to do with you? What is yours? Only your reaction to things. When you behave in accordance with nature, you will take pride only in some good that is your own.

7. As when on a voyage, when the ship is at anchor, if you go ashore to get fresh water, you may amuse yourself by picking up a seashell or a vegetable, but keep the ship in mind. Be attentive to the captain's call, and when you hear the call, give up the trifles, or you will be thrown back into the ship like a bound sheep. So it is in life: If instead of a seashell or a vegetable, you are given a wife or child, fine, but when the captain calls, you must abandon these things without a second thought. And if you are old, keep close to the ship lest you are missing when you are called.

9. Sickness impedes the body but not the ability to make choices, unless you choose so. Lameness impedes the leg, but not the ability to make choices, unless the mind chooses so. Remember this with regard to everything that happens: Happenings are impediments to something else, but not to you.

15. Remember, behave in life as though you are attending a banquet. Is a dish brought to you? Put out your hand and take a moderate share. Does the dish pass you by? Do not grab for it. Has it not yet reached you? Don't yearn for it, but wait until it reaches you. Do this with regard to children, a spouse, position, wealth, and eventually you will be worthy to banquet with the gods. And if you can forgo even the things that are set before you, you are worthy not only to feast with the gods but to rule with them.

17. Remember: You are an actor in a play that you did not write. If the play is short, then it is short; if long, then it is long. If the author has assigned you the part of a poor man, act it well. Do the same if your part is that of a lame man or a ruler or an ordinary citizen. This is yours to do: Act your part well (but picking the part belongs to someone else).

21. Keep in mind death and exile and all other things that appear terrible — especially death — and you will never harbor a low thought nor too eagerly covet anything.

36. At a feast, to choose the largest portion might satisfy your body but would be detrimental to the social nature of the affair. When you dine with another, then, keep in mind not only the value to the body of the dishes set before you, but the value of your behavior to your host and fellow diners.

43. Everything has two handles, one by which it can be carried and one by which it cannot. If your brother acts unjustly, do not take up the affair by the handle of his injustice, for it cannot be carried that way. Rather, take the other handle: He is your brother, he was brought up with you. Taken this way, it can be carried.

Topics for Critical Thinking and Writing

1. Consider Epictetus's words in paragraph 1: "Our opinions are within our control, and our choices, our likes and dislikes." Does Epictetus exaggerate the degree to which these things are under our control? Do we, in fact, control opinions, choices, likes, and dislikes? Explain.
2. Epictetus advises us not to fear death. What is his argument?
3. It is often said when bad, wrongful, or immoral actions are taken, even for a good cause, that "the ends do not justify the means." Think of an instance that makes this claim concrete and write about 250 words on why the ends do not justify the means.
4. Choose one from among the eleven paragraphs by Epictetus that best expresses your own view of life — or are you entirely at odds with what Epictetus believes? Explain your response.

"If I won the lottery, I would go on living as I always did."

Mischa Richter The New Yorker Collection/The Cartoon Bank

BERTRAND RUSSELL

Bertrand Russell (1872–1970), British mathematician and philosopher, was born in Wales and educated at Trinity College, Cambridge, where he later taught. His pacifist opposition to World War I cost him this teaching appointment and earned him a prison sentence of six months. In 1940, an appointment to teach at the College of the City of New York was withdrawn because of his unorthodox moral views. But he was not always treated shabbily. He won numerous prizes, including a Nobel Prize in Literature in 1950. Much of his work is highly technical, but he also wrote frequently for the general public. The following passage comes from one of his most widely read books, *The Conquest of Happiness* (1930).

The Happy Life

The happy life is to an extraordinary extent the same as the good life. Professional moralists have made too much of self-denial, and in so doing have put the emphasis in the wrong place. Conscious self-denial leaves a man self-absorbed and vividly aware of what he has sacrificed; in consequence it fails often of its immediate object and almost always of its ultimate purpose. What is needed is not self-denial, but that kind of direction of interest outward which will lead spontaneously and naturally to the same acts that a person absorbed in the pursuit of his own virtue could only perform by means of conscious self-denial. I have written in this book as a hedonist, that is to say, as one who regards happiness as the good, but the acts to be recommended from the point of view of the hedonist are on the whole the same as those to be recommended by the sane moralist. The moralist, however, is too apt, though this is not, of course, universally true, to stress the act rather than the state of mind. The effects of an act upon the agent will be widely different, according to his state of mind at the moment. If you see a child drowning and save it as the result of a direct impulse to bring help, you will emerge none the worse morally. If, on the other hand, you say to yourself, "It is the part of virtue to succor the helpless, and I wish to be a virtuous man, therefore I must save this child," you will be an even worse man afterwards than you were before. What applies in this extreme case, applies in many other instances that are less obvious.

There is another difference, somewhat more subtle, between the attitude toward life that I have been recommending and that which is recommended by the traditional moralists. The traditional moralist, for example, will say that love should be unselfish. In a certain sense he is right, that is to say, it should not be selfish beyond a point, but it should undoubtedly be of such a nature that one's own happiness is bound up in its success. If a man were to invite a lady to marry him on the ground that he ardently desired her happiness and at the same time considered that she would afford him ideal opportunities of self-abnegation, I think it may be doubted whether she would be altogether pleased. Undoubtedly we should desire the happiness of those whom we love, but not as an alternative to our own. In fact the whole antithesis between self and the rest of the world, which is implied in the doctrine of self-denial, disappears as soon as we have any genuine interest in persons or things outside ourselves. Through such interests a man comes to feel himself part of the stream of life, not a hard separate entity like a billiard ball, which can have no relation with other such entities except that of collision. All unhappiness depends upon some kind of disintegration or lack of integration; there is disintegration within the self through lack of coördination between the conscious and the unconscious mind; there is lack of integration between the self and society, where the two are not knit together by the force of objective interests and affections. The happy man is the man who does not suffer from either of these failures of unity, whose personality is neither divided against itself nor pitted against the world. Such a man feels himself a citizen of the universe, enjoying freely the spectacle that it offers and the joys that it affords, untroubled by the thought of death because he feels himself not really separate from those who will come after him. It is in such profound instinctive union with the stream of life that the greatest joy is to be found.

Topics for Critical Thinking and Writing

1. In paragraph 1, Bertrand Russell says, "The happy life is to an extraordinary extent the same as the good life." First, how do you suppose Russell knows that? How might one confirm or refute the statement? Second, do you agree with Russell? Explain in detail.
2. In his final paragraph, Russell says that it is through their interests that people come to feel that they are "part of the stream of life, not a hard separate entity like a billiard ball, which can have no relation with other such entities except that of collision." Does this sentence strike you as (a) effective and (b) probably true? Why, or why not?
3. In the final paragraph, Russell says that happy people feel connected to themselves (do not feel internally divided) and connected to society (do not feel pitted against the world). Describe in some detail a person who seems to you connected to the self and to society. Do you think that person is happy? Explain. Describe two people, one of whom seems to you internally divided and one of whom seems to you separated from society. Now think about yourself. Do you feel connected to yourself and to the world? If so, are you happy? Why, or why not?

THE DALAI LAMA AND HOWARD C. CUTLER

The fourteenth Dalai ("ocean-wide") Lama ("superior person"), Tenzin Gyatso, is the spiritual leader of the Tibetan people but has lived in exile in Dharamsala, India, since 1959, when China invaded Tibet. In 1989, he was awarded the Nobel Peace Prize. In 1982, Howard C. Cutler, a psychiatrist who practices in Phoenix, Arizona, met the Dalai Lama while visiting India to study Tibetan medicine. Cutler and the Dalai Lama had frequent conversations, which Cutler later summarized and submitted to the Dalai Lama for approval. The material was then published in *The Art of Happiness* (1998). Here is one selection from that book.

Inner Contentment

Crossing the hotel parking lot on my way to meet with the Dalai Lama one afternoon, I stopped to admire a brand-new Toyota Land Cruiser, the type of car I had been wanting for a long time. Still thinking of that car as I began my session, I asked, "Sometimes it seems that our whole culture, Western culture, is based on material acquisition; we're surrounded, bombarded, with ads for the latest things to buy, the latest car and so on. It's difficult not to be influenced by that. There are so many things we want, things we desire. It never seems to stop. Can you speak a bit about desire?"

"I think there are two kinds of desire," the Dalai Lama replied. "Certain desires are positive. A desire for happiness. It's absolutely right. The desire for peace. The desire for a more harmonious world, a friendlier world. Certain desires are very useful.

"But at some point, desires can become unreasonable. That usually leads to trouble. Now, for example, sometimes I visit supermarkets. I really love to see supermarkets, because I can see so many beautiful things. So, when I look at all these different articles, I develop a feeling of desire, and my initial impulse might be, 'Oh, I want this; I want that.' Then, the second thought that arises, I ask myself, 'Oh, do I really need this?' The answer is usually no. If you follow after that first desire, that initial impulse, then very soon your pockets will empty. However, the other level of desire, based on one's essential needs of food, clothing, and shelter, is something more reasonable.

"Sometimes, whether a desire is excessive or negative depends on the circumstances or society in which you live. For example, if you live in a prosperous society where a car is required to help you manage in your daily life, then of course there's nothing wrong in desiring a car. But if you live in a poor village in India where you can manage quite well without a car but you still desire one, even if you have the money to buy it, it can ultimately bring trouble. It can create an uncomfortable feeling among your neighbors and so on. Or, if you're living in a more prosperous society and have a car but keep wanting more expensive cars, that leads to the same kind of problems."

"But," I argued, "I can't see how wanting or 5
buying a more expensive car leads to problems for an individual, as long as he or she can afford it. Having a more expensive car than your neighbors might be a problem for them — they might be jealous and so on — but having a new car would give you, yourself, a feeling of satisfaction and enjoyment."

The Dalai Lama shook his head and replied firmly, "No. . . . Self-satisfaction alone cannot determine if a desire or action is positive or negative. A murderer may have a feeling of satisfaction at the time he is committing the murder, but that doesn't justify the act. All the nonvirtuous actions — lying, stealing, sexual misconduct, and so on — are committed by people who may be feeling a sense of satisfaction at the time. The demarcation between a positive and a negative desire or action is not whether it gives you an immediate feeling of satisfaction but whether it ultimately results in positive or negative consequences. For example, in the case of wanting more expensive possessions, if that is based on a mental attitude that just wants more and more, then eventually you'll reach a limit of what you can get; you'll come up against reality. And when you reach that limit, then you'll lose all hope, sink down into depression, and so on. That's one danger inherent in that type of desire.

"So I think that this kind of excessive desire leads to greed — an exaggerated form of desire, based on overexpectation. And when you reflect upon the excesses of greed, you'll find that it leads an individual to a feeling of frustration, disappointment, a lot of confusion, and a lot of problems. When it comes to dealing with greed, one thing that is quite characteristic is that although it arrives by the desire to obtain something, it is not satisfied by obtaining. Therefore, it becomes sort of limitless, sort of bottomless, and that leads to trouble. One interesting thing about greed is that although the underlying motive is to seek satisfaction, the irony is that even after obtaining the object of your desire, you are still not satisfied. *The true antidote of greed is contentment.* If you have a strong sense of contentment, it doesn't matter whether you obtain the object or not; either way, you are still content."

So, how can we achieve inner contentment? There are two methods. One method is to obtain everything that we want and desire — all the money, houses, and cars; the perfect mate; and the perfect body. The Dalai Lama has already pointed out the disadvantage of this approach; if our wants and desires remain unchecked, sooner or later we will run up against something that we want but can't have. The second, and more reliable, method is not to have what we want but rather to want and appreciate what we have.

The other night, I was watching a television interview with Christopher Reeve, the actor who was thrown from a horse in 1994 and suffered a spinal cord injury that left him completely paralyzed from the neck down, requiring a mechanical ventilator even to breathe. When questioned by the interviewer about how he dealt with the depression resulting from his disability, Reeve revealed that he had experienced a brief period of complete despair while in the intensive care unit of the hospital. He went on to say, however, that these feelings of despair passed relatively quickly, and he now sincerely considered himself to be a "lucky guy." He cited the blessings of a loving wife and children but also spoke gratefully about the rapid advances of modern medicine (which he estimates will find a cure for spinal cord injury within the next decade), stating that if he had been hurt just a few years earlier, he probably would have died from his injuries. While describing the process of adjusting to his paralysis, Reeve said that while his feelings of despair resolved rather quickly, at first he was still troubled by intermittent pangs of jealousy that could be triggered by another's innocent passing remark such as, "I'm just gonna run upstairs and get something." In learning to deal with these feelings, he said, "I realized that the only way to go through life is to look at your assets, to see what you can still do; in my case, fortunately I didn't have any brain injury, so I still have a mind I can use." Focusing on his resources in this manner, Reeve has elected to use his mind to increase awareness and educate the public about spinal cord injury, to help others, and has plans to continue speaking as well as to write and direct films.[1]

[1]Christopher Reeve died on October 10, 2004. [Editors' note]

Topics for Critical Thinking and Writing

1. In paragraph 1, Howard Cutler says that he had long wanted a Toyota Land Cruiser. Exactly why might a person want such a vehicle? Do you think most people buy vehicles for the purpose of efficient transportation or as status symbols? How do you think identity is linked to the kind of car you drive?

2. At the end of paragraph 8, Cutler reports that the Dalai Lama suggests that the best way to achieve inner contentment "is not to have what we want but rather to want and appreciate what we have." In the next (final) paragraph, Cutler cites the example of Christopher Reeve. Drawing on your own experiences — which include your experience of persons whom you know or have heard about — can you offer confirming evidence? Explain your response.
3. The Dalai Lama refers several times to the ways satisfying certain desires can lead to "trouble" (paras. 3, 4, and 7) or "danger" (para. 6). What kinds of trouble and danger does he mean? What other kinds of trouble or danger can come from materialism or with "keeping up with the Joneses"? Think of examples — real or imagined — of such trouble or danger.
4. Compare the Dalai Lama's views with those of Epictetus. Would you say they are virtually the same? Why, or why not?

C. S. LEWIS

Clive Staples Lewis (1898–1963) taught medieval and Renaissance literature at Oxford University, his alma mater, and later at Cambridge University. In addition to writing about literature, he wrote his own fiction and poetry, including the children's series *The Chronicles of Narnia*. Lewis became an atheist at age thirteen and held that view until he was about thirty-one years old. He wrote numerous essays and books on Christianity from the point of view of a believer. This essay reprinted was published in the *Saturday Evening Post* on December 11, 1963.

We Have No "Right to Happiness"

"After all," said Clare, "they had a right to happiness."

We were discussing something that once happened in our own neighborhood. Mr. A. had deserted Mrs. A. and got his divorce in order to marry Mrs. B., who had likewise got her divorce in order to marry Mr. A. And there was certainly no doubt that Mr. A. and Mrs. B. were very much in love with one another. If they continued to be in love, and if nothing went wrong with their health or their income, they might reasonably expect to be very happy.

It was equally clear that they were not happy with their old partners. Mrs. B. had adored her husband at the outset. But then he got smashed up in the war. It was thought he had lost his virility, and it was known that he had lost his job. Life with him was no longer what Mrs. B. had bargained for. Poor Mrs. A., too. She had lost her looks — and all her liveliness. It might be true, as some said, that she consumed herself by bearing his children and nursing him through the long illness that overshadowed their earlier married life.

You mustn't, by the way, imagine that A. was the sort of man who nonchalantly threw a wife away like the peel of an orange he'd sucked dry. Her suicide was a terrible shock to him. We all knew this, for he told us so himself. "But what could I do?" he said. "A man has a right to happiness. I had to take my one chance when it came."

I went away thinking about the concept of 5
a "right to happiness."

At first this sounds to me as odd as a right to good luck. For I believe — whatever one school of moralists may say — that we depend for a very great deal of our happiness or misery on circumstances outside all human control. A right to happiness doesn't, for me, make much more sense than a right to be six feet tall, or to have a millionaire for your father, or to get good weather whenever you want to have a picnic.

I can understand a right as a freedom guaranteed me by the laws of the society I live in. Thus, I have a right to travel along the public roads because society gives me that freedom; that's what we mean by calling the roads "public." I can also understand a right as a claim guaranteed me by the laws, and correlative to an obligation on someone else's part. If I have a right to receive £100 from you, this is another way of saying that you have a duty to pay me £100. If the laws allow Mr. A. to desert his wife and seduce his neighbor's wife, then, by definition, Mr. A. has a legal right to do so, and we need bring in no talk about "happiness."

But of course that was not what Clare meant. She meant that he had not only a legal but a moral right to act as he did. In other words, Clare is — or would be if she thought it out — a classical moralist after the style of Thomas Aquinas, Grotius, Hooker, and Locke. She believes that behind the laws of the state there is a Natural Law.

I agree with her. I hold this conception to be basic to all civilization. Without it, the actual laws of the state become an absolute, as in Hegel. They cannot be criticized because there is no norm against which they should be judged.

The ancestry of Clare's maxim, "They have a right to happiness," is august. In words that are cherished by all civilized men, but especially by Americans, it has been laid down that one of the rights of man is a right to "the pursuit of happiness." And now we get to the real point.

What did the writers of that august declaration mean?

It is quite certain what they did not mean. They did not mean that man was entitled to pursue happiness by any and every means — including, say, murder, rape, robbery, treason, and fraud. No society could be built on such a basis.

They meant "to pursue happiness by all lawful means"; that is, by all means which the Law of Nature eternally sanctions and which the laws of the nation shall sanction.

Admittedly this seems at first to reduce their maxim to the tautology that men (in pursuit of happiness) have a right to do whatever they have a right to do. But tautologies, seen against their proper historical context, are not always barren tautologies. The declaration is primarily a denial of the political principles which long governed Europe: a challenge flung down to the Austrian and Russian empires, to England before the Reform Bills, to Bourbon France. It demands that whatever means of pursuing happiness are lawful for any should be lawful for all; that "man," not men of some particular caste, class, status, or religion, should be free to use them. In a century when this is being unsaid by nation after nation and party after party, let us not call it a barren tautology.

But the question as to what means are "lawful" — what methods of pursuing happiness are either morally permissible by the Law of Nature or should be declared legally permissible by the legislature of a particular nation — remains exactly where it did. And on that question I disagree with Clare. I don't think it is obvious that people have the unlimited "right to happiness" which she suggests.

For one thing, I believe that Clare, when she says "happiness," means simply and solely "sexual happiness." Partly because women like Clare never use the word "happiness" in any other sense. But also because I never heard Clare talk about the "right" to any other kind. She was rather leftist in her politics, and would have been scandalized if anyone had defended the actions of a ruthless man-eating tycoon on the ground that his happiness consisted in making money and he was pursuing his happiness. She was also a rabid teetotaler; I never heard her excuse an alcoholic because he was happy when he was drunk.

A good many of Clare's friends, and especially her female friends, often felt — I've heard them say so — that their own happiness would be perceptibly increased by boxing her ears. I very much doubt if this would have brought her theory of a right to happiness into play.

Clare, in fact, is doing what the whole western world seems to me to have been doing for the last forty-odd years. When I was a youngster, all the progressive people were saying, "Why all this prudery? Let us treat sex just as we treat all our other impulses." I was simple-minded enough to believe they meant what they said. I have since discovered that they meant exactly the opposite. They meant that sex was to be treated as no other impulse in our nature has ever been treated by civilized people. All the others, we admit, have to be bridled. Absolute obedience to your instinct for self-preservation is what we call cowardice; to your acquisitive impulse, avarice. Even sleep must be resisted if you're a sentry. But every unkindness and breach of faith seems to be condoned provided that the object aimed at is "four bare legs in a bed."

It is like having a morality in which stealing fruit is considered wrong — unless you steal nectarines.

20 And if you protest against this view you are usually met with chatter about the legitimacy and beauty and sanctity of "sex" and accused of harboring some Puritan prejudice against it as something disreputable or shameful. I deny the charge. Foam-born Venus . . . golden Aphrodite . . . Our Lady of Cyprus . . . I never breathed a word against you. If I object to boys who steal my nectarines, must I be supposed to disapprove of nectarines in general? Or even of boys in general? It might, you know, be stealing that I disapproved of.

The real situation is skillfully concealed by saying that the question of Mr. A.'s "right" to desert his wife is one of "sexual morality." Robbing an orchard is not an offense against some special morality called "fruit morality." It is an offense against honesty. Mr. A.'s action is an offense against good faith (to solemn promises), against gratitude (toward one to whom he was deeply indebted) and against common humanity.

Our sexual impulses are thus being put in a position of preposterous privilege. The sexual motive is taken to condone all sorts of behavior which, if it had any other end in view, would be condemned as merciless, treacherous, and unjust.

Now though I see no good reason for giving sex this privilege, I think I see a strong cause. It is this.

It is part of the nature of a strong erotic passion — as distinct from a transient fit of appetite — that it makes more towering promises than any other emotion. No doubt all our desires make promises, but not so impressively. To be in love involves the almost irresistible conviction that one will go on being in love until one dies, and that possession of the beloved will confer, not merely frequent ecstasies, but settled, fruitful, deep-rooted, lifelong happiness. Hence *all* seems to be at stake. If we miss this chance we shall have lived in vain. At the very thought of such a doom we sink into fathomless depths of self-pity.

25 Unfortunately these promises are found often to be quite untrue. Every experienced adult knows this to be so as regards all erotic passions (except the one he himself is feeling at the moment). We discount the world-without-end pretensions of our friends' amours easily enough. We know that such things sometimes last — and sometimes don't. And when they do last, this is not because they promised at the outset to do so. When two people achieve lasting happiness, this is not solely because they are great lovers but because they are also — I must put it crudely — good people; controlled, loyal, fairminded, mutually adaptable people.

If we establish a "right to (sexual) happiness" which supersedes all the ordinary rules of behavior, we do so not because of what our passion shows itself to be in experience but because of what it professes to be while we are in the grip of it. Hence, while the bad behavior is real and works miseries and degradations, the happiness which was the object of the behavior turns out again and again to be illusory. Everyone (except Mr. A. and Mrs. B.) knows that Mr. A. in a year or so may have the same reason for deserting his new wife as for deserting his old. He will feel again that all is at stake. He will see himself again as the great lover, and his pity for himself will exclude all pity for the woman.

Two further points remain.

One is this. A society in which conjugal infidelity is tolerated must always be in the long run a society adverse to women. Women, whatever a few male songs and satires may say to the contrary, are more naturally monogamous than men; it is a biological necessity. Where promiscuity prevails, they will therefore always be more often the victims than the culprits. Also, domestic happiness is more necessary to them than to us. And the quality by which they most easily hold a man, their beauty, decreases every year after they have come to maturity, but this does not happen to those qualities of personality — women don't really care twopence about our *looks* — by which we hold women. Thus in the ruthless war of promiscuity women are at a double disadvantage. They play for higher stakes and are also more likely to lose. I have no sympathy with moralists who frown at the increasing crudity of female provocativeness. These signs of desperate competition fill me with pity.

Secondly, though the "right to happiness" is chiefly claimed for the sexual impulse, it seems to me impossible that the matter should stay there. The fatal principle, once allowed in that department, must sooner or later seep through our whole lives. We thus advance toward a state of society in which not only each man but every impulse in each man claims *carte blanche*. And then, though our technological skill may help us survive a little longer, our civilization will have died at heart, and will — one dare not even add "unfortunately" — be swept away.

Topics for Critical Thinking and Writing

1. Having read the entire essay, look back at C. S. Lewis's first five paragraphs and point out the ways in which he is not merely recounting an episode but is already conveying his attitude and seeking to persuade his readers.
2. Do you want to argue: If I have a right to happiness, you or someone has a duty to see to it that I'm happy (see para. 7)? Or do you want to argue: No one has a right to happiness because no one has a duty to make anyone happy? Argue one of these positions in 250 words.

3. What's the difference between being happy in a marriage and being content in a marriage? Explain the difference in an essay of 250 words.
4. What is absurd about the idea (para. 6) of having "a right to be six feet tall"? Explain in 100 words or fewer.
5. What, if anything, do the absurd candidates for rights (para. 6) have in common?
6. What's the difference between having a legal right to something and having a moral right to that thing (see paras. 8 and 9)? Give an example of each.
7. Do you agree with Lewis (paras. 26 and 29) that "a right to happiness" really means "a right to sexual happiness"? Why, or why not?
8. Do you agree with Lewis that monogamy is "a biological necessity" for women (para. 28)? Explain in an essay of 250 words.

DANIELLE CRITTENDEN

Danielle Crittenden (b. 1963), founder of the *Woman's Quarterly*, is an author and journalist who has written for numerous publications, including the *New York Times* and the *Wall Street Journal*. A selection from her book *What Our Mothers Didn't Tell Us: Why Happiness Eludes the Modern Woman* (1999) appears here.

About Love

From a feminist view, it would be nice, I suppose — or at the very least handy — if we were able to derive total satisfaction from our solitude, to be entirely self-contained organisms, like earthworms or amoebas, having relations with the opposite sex whenever we felt a need for it but otherwise being entirely contented with our own company. Every woman's apartment could be her Walden Pond. She'd be free of the romantic fuss and interaction that has defined, and given meaning to, human existence since its creation. She could spend her evenings happily ensconced with a book or a rented video, not having to deal with some bozo's desire to watch football or play mindless video games. How children would fit into this vision of autonomy, I'm not sure, but surely they would infringe upon it; perhaps she could simply farm them out. If this seems a rather chilling outcome to the quest for independence, well, it is. If no man is an island, then no woman can be, either. And it's why most human beings fall in love, and continue to take on all the commitments and responsibilities of family life. We *want* the warm body next to us on the sofa in the evenings; we *want* the noise and embrace of family around us; we *want,* at the end of our lives, to look back and see that what we have done amounts to more than a pile of pay stubs, that we have loved and been loved, and brought into this world life that will outlast us.

The quest for autonomy — the need "to be oneself" or, as Wurtzel declares, the intention "to answer only to myself" — is in fact not a brave or noble one; nor is it an indication of strong character. Too often, autonomy is merely the excuse of someone who is so fearful, so weak, that he or she can't bear to take on any of the responsibilities that used to be shouldered by much younger but more robust and mature souls. I'm struck by the number of my single contemporaries — men and women in their early to mid-thirties — who speak of themselves as if they were still twenty years old, just embarking upon their lives and not, as they actually are, already halfway through them. In another era, a thirty-three-year-old man or woman might have already lived through a depression and a world war and had several children. Yet at the suggestion of marriage — or of buying a house or of having a baby — these modern thirtysomethings will exclaim, "But I'm so young!" their crinkled eyes widening at the thought. In the relationships they do have — even "serious" ones — they will take pains to avoid the appearance of anything that smacks of permanent commitment. The strange result is couples who are willing to share *everything* with each other — leases, furniture, cars, weekends, body fluids, holidays with their relatives — just as long as it comes with the right to cancel the relationship *at any moment.*

Unfortunately, postponing marriage and all the responsibilities that go with it does not prolong youth. It only prolongs the illusion of it, and then again only in one's own eyes. The traits that are forgivable in a twenty-year-old — the constant wondering about who you are and what you will be; the readiness to chuck one thing, or person, for another and move on — are less attractive in a thirty-two-year-old. More often what results is a middle-aged person who retains all the irritating self-absorption of an adolescent without gaining any of the redeeming qualities of maturity. Those qualities — wisdom, a sense of duty, the willingness to make sacrifices for others, an acceptance of aging and death — are qualities that spring directly from our relationships and commitments to others.

A woman will not understand what true dependency is until she is cradling her own infant in her arms; nor will she likely achieve the self-confidence she craves until she has withstood, and transcended, the weight of responsibility a family places upon her — a weight that makes all the paperwork and assignments of her in-basket seem feather-light. The same goes for men. We strengthen a muscle by using it, and that is true of the heart and mind, too. By waiting and waiting and waiting to commit to someone, our capacity for love shrinks and withers. This doesn't mean that women or men should marry the first reasonable person to come along, or someone with whom they are not in love. But we should, at a much earlier age than we do now, take a serious attitude toward dating and begin preparing ourselves to settle down. For it's in the act of taking up the roles we've been taught to avoid or postpone — wife, husband, mother, father — that we build our identities, expand our lives, and achieve the fullness of character we desire.

5 Still, critics may argue that the old way was no better; that the risk of loss women assume by delaying marriage and motherhood overbalances the certain loss we'd suffer by marrying too early. The habit of viewing marriage as a raw deal for women is now so entrenched, even among women who don't call themselves feminists, that I've seen brides who otherwise appear completely happy apologize to their wedding guests for their surrender to convention, as if a part of them still feels there is something embarrassing and weak about an intelligent and ambitious woman consenting to marry. But is this true? Or is it just an alibi we've been handed by the previous generation of women in order to justify the sad, lonely outcomes of so many lives?

What we rarely hear — or perhaps are too fearful to admit — is how *liberating* marriage can actually be. As nerve-racking as making the decision can be, it is also an enormous relief once it is made. The moment we say, "I do," we have answered one of the great, crucial questions of our lives: We now know with whom we'll be spending the rest of our years, who will be the father of our children, who will be our family. That our marriages may not work, that we will have to accommodate ourselves to the habits and personality of someone else — these are, and always have been, the risks of commitment, of love itself. What is important is that our lives have been thrust forward. The negative — that we are no longer able to live entirely for ourselves — is also the positive: *We no longer have to live entirely for ourselves!* We may go on to do any number of interesting things, but we are free of the gnawing wonder of *with whom* we will do them. We have ceased to look down the tunnel, waiting for a train.

The pull between the desire to love and be loved and the desire to be free is an old, fierce one. If the error our grandmothers made was to have surrendered too much of themselves for others, this was perhaps better than not being prepared to surrender anything at all. The fear of losing oneself can, in the end, simply become an excuse for not giving any of oneself away. Generations of women may have had no choice but to commit themselves to marriage early and then to feel imprisoned by their lifelong domesticity. So many of our generation have decided to put it off until it is too late, not foreseeing that lifelong independence can be its own kind of prison, too.

Topics for Critical Thinking and Writing

1. Do you agree or disagree with Danielle Crittenden's argument that women can be happy only if they put aside what she describes as misleading feminist ideas about independence?

2. In paragraph 2, Crittenden quotes a writer who speaks of "the need 'to be oneself.' " What does "to be oneself" mean? Perhaps begin at the beginning: What is "oneself"? In *Hamlet*, Polonius says to his son,

   > This above all, to thine own self be true,
   > And it must follow, as the night the day,
   > Thou canst not then be false to any man.

   What is the "self" to which one should be true? Notice that in paragraph 4, Crittenden says that "it's in the act of taking up [certain] roles . . . that we build our identities, expand our lives, and achieve the fullness of character we desire." Does that make sense to you? Explain your response.

3. In paragraph 3, Crittenden talks about "postponing marriage and all the responsibilities that go with it." What responsibilities go with marriage? Might these responsibilities *add* to one's happiness? Explain your response.

4. In paragraph 6, Crittenden says, "What we rarely hear . . . is how *liberating* marriage can actually be." Consider the married people you know best. Does Crittenden's statement apply to some? To most? Does your experience — your familiarity with some married people — tend to offer evidence that confirms or refutes her assertion? Why, or why not?

JUDY BRADY

Born in San Francisco, Judy Brady (1937–2017) married in 1960 and two years later earned a bachelor's degree in painting from the University of Iowa. Active in the women's movement and in other political causes, she worked as an author, an editor, and a secretary. The essay reprinted here, written before she and her husband separated, originally appeared in the first issue of *Ms.* magazine in 1971.

I Want a Wife

I belong to that classification of people known as wives. I am A Wife. And, not altogether incidentally, I am a mother.

Not too long ago a male friend of mine appeared on the scene fresh from a recent divorce. He had one child, who is, of course, with his ex-wife. He is looking for another wife. As I thought about him while I was ironing one evening, it suddenly occurred to me that I, too, would like to have a wife. Why do I want a wife?

I would like to go back to school so that I can become economically independent, support myself, and, if need be, support those dependent upon me. I want a wife who will work and send me to school. And while I am going to school I want a wife to take care of my children. I want a wife to keep track of the children's doctor and dentist appointments. And to keep track of mine, too. I want a wife to make sure my children eat properly and are kept clean. I want a wife who will wash the children's clothes and keep them mended. I want a wife who is a good nurturant attendant to my children, who arranges for their schooling, makes sure that they have an adequate social life with their peers, takes them to the park, the zoo, etc. I want a wife who takes care of the children when they are sick, a wife who arranges to be around when the children need special care, because, of course, I cannot miss classes at school. My wife must arrange to lose time at work and not lose the job. It may mean a small cut in my wife's income from time to time, but I guess I can tolerate that. Needless to say, my wife will arrange and pay for the care of the children while my wife is working.

I want a wife who will take care of *my* physical needs. I want a wife who will keep my house clean. A wife who will pick up after my children, a wife who will pick up after me. I want a wife who will keep my clothes clean, ironed, mended, replaced when need be, and who will see to it that my personal things are kept in their proper place so that I can find what I need the minute I need it. I want a wife who cooks the meals, a wife who is a *good* cook. I want a wife who will plan the menus, do the necessary grocery shopping, prepare the meals, serve them pleasantly, and then do the cleaning up while I do my studying. I want a wife who will care for me when I am sick and sympathize with my pain and loss of time from school. I want a wife to go along when our family takes a vacation so that someone can continue to care for me and my children when I need a rest and change of scene.

5 I want a wife who will not bother me with rambling complaints about a wife's duties. But I want a wife who will listen to me when I feel the need to explain a rather difficult point I have come across in my course of studies. And I want a wife who will type my papers for me when I have written them.

I want a wife who will take care of the details of my social life. When my wife and I are invited out by my friends, I want a wife who will take care of the babysitting arrangements. When I meet people at school that I like and want to entertain, I want a wife who will have the house clean, will prepare a special meal, serve it to me and my friends, and not interrupt when I talk about things that interest me and my friends. I want a wife who will have arranged that the children are fed and ready for bed before my guests arrive so that the children do not bother us. I want a wife who takes care of the needs of my guests so that they feel comfortable, who makes sure that they have an ashtray, that they are passed the hors d'oeuvres, that they are offered a second helping of the food, that their wine glasses are replenished when necessary, that their coffee is served to them as they like it. And I want a wife who knows that sometimes I need a night out by myself.

I want a wife who is sensitive to my sexual needs, a wife who makes love passionately and eagerly when I feel like it, a wife who makes sure that I am satisfied. And, of course, I want a wife who will not demand sexual attention when I am not in the mood for it. I want a wife who assumes the complete responsibility for birth control, because I do not want more children. I want a wife who will remain sexually faithful to me so that I do not have to clutter up my intellectual life with jealousies. And I want a wife who understands that *my* sexual needs may entail more than strict adherence to monogamy. I must, after all, be able to relate to people as fully as possible.

If, by chance, I find another person more suitable as a wife than the wife I already have, I want the liberty to replace my present wife with another one. Naturally, I will expect a fresh, new life; my wife will take the children and be solely responsible for them so that I am left free.

When I am through with school and have a job, I want my wife to quit working and remain at home so that my wife can more fully and completely take care of a wife's duties.

My God, who *wouldn't* want a wife? 10

Topics for Critical Thinking and Writing

1. If one were to summarize Judy Brady's first paragraph, one might say it adds up to "I am a wife and a mother." But analyze it closely. Exactly what does the second sentence add to the first? And what does "not altogether incidentally" add to the third sentence?
2. Brady uses the word *wife* in sentences where one ordinarily would use *she* or *her.* Why? And why does she begin paragraphs 4, 5, 6, and 7 with the same words, "I want a wife"?
3. In paragraph 2, Brady says that the child of her divorced male friend "is, of course, with his ex-wife." In the context of the entire essay, what does this sentence mean?
4. Complete the following sentence by offering a definition: "According to Judy Brady, a wife is . . ."
5. Try to state the essential argument of Brady's essay in a simple syllogism. (*Hint:* Start by identifying the thesis or conclusion you think she is trying to establish and then try to formulate two premises, based on what she has written, that would establish the conclusion.)
6. Drawing on your experience as observer of the world around you (and perhaps as husband, wife, or former spouse), do you think Brady's picture of a wife's role is grossly exaggerated? Or is it (allowing for some serious playfulness) fairly accurate, even though it was written in

1971? If grossly exaggerated, is the essay therefore meaningless? If fairly accurate, what attitudes and practices does it encourage you to support? Explain your response.

7. Whether or not you agree with Brady's vision of marriage in our society, write an essay (500 words) titled "I Want a Husband," imitating her style and approach. Write the best possible essay and then decide which of the two essays — yours or hers — makes a fairer comment on current society. Or if you believe Brady is utterly misleading, write an essay titled "I Want a Wife," casting the matter in a different light.
8. If you feel that you have been pressed into an unappreciated, unreasonable role — built-in babysitter, listening post, or girl (or boy or man or woman) Friday — write an essay of 500 words that will help the reader to see both your plight and the injustice of the system. (*Hint:* A little humor will help to keep your essay from seeming to be a prolonged whine.)

TEXT CREDITS

Navneet Alang, "Eat, Pray, Post," *New Republic,* August 5, 2015. Copyright © 2015 Navneet Alang. Used with permission.

Bridget Anderson, "The Politics of Pests: Immigration and the Invasive Other" (excerpt), *Social Research: An International Quarterly* 84.1, Spring 2017, pp. 7–8, 14–16, 18–19, 25, 26–28. Copyright © 2017. Reproduced with permission of Graduate Faculty of Political and Social Science at the New School for Social Research, in the format Republish in a book via Copyright Clearance Center.

Kwame Anthony Appiah, "Go Ahead, Speak for Yourself," *New York Times*, August 10, 2018. Copyright © 2018 by The New York Times. All rights reserved. Used by permission and protected by the Copyright Laws of the United States. The printing, copying, redistribution, or retransmission of this Content without express written permission is prohibited.

Robert Applebaum, "Debate on Student Loan Debt Doesn't Go Far Enough," from *The Hill,* May 8, 2012, is reprinted by permission of the publisher.

W. H. Auden, "The Unknown Citizen," copyright © 1940 and renewed 1968 by W. H. Auden; from *W. H. Auden Collected Poems* by W. H. Auden. Used by permission of Random House, an imprint and division of Penguin Random House LLC. All rights reserved. Electronic use by permission of Curtis Brown, Ltd.

John Barth, "Us/Them," from *The Development: Nine Stories* by John Barth. Copyright © 2008 by John Barth. Reprinted by permission of Houghton Mifflin Harcourt Publishing Company. All rights reserved.

Helen Benedict, "The Military Has a Man Problem," from *Politico Magazine,* July/August 2015. Copyright © 2015 by Helen Benedict. Reprinted with the permission of The Jennifer Lyons Literary Agency, LLC for the author.

Touria Benlafqih, "Has Social Media Made Young People Better Citizens?," from *World Economic Forum*, January 16, 2015. Reprinted by permission of the author.

Richard Blanco, "One Today: A Poem for Barack Obama's Presidential Inauguration, January 21, 2013." Copyright © 2013. Reprinted by permission of the University of Pittsburgh Press, Pittsburgh, PA 15260.

Derek Bok, "Protecting Freedom of Expression on the Campus," was originally published as "Protecting Freedom of Expression at Harvard," *Boston Globe*, May 21, 1991. Copyright © 1991 by Derek Bok. Reprinted by permission of the author.

K. Tempest Bradford, news report titled "Commentary: Cultural Appropriation Is, In Fact, Indefensible," was originally published on npr.org on June 28, 2017. Copyright © 2018 K. Tempest Bradford for National Public Radio, Inc. Used with the permission of NPR. Any unauthorized duplication is strictly prohibited.

Judy Brady, "I Want a Wife," *Ms. Magazine*, 1972. Copyright © 1970 by Judy Syfers. Reprinted by permission.

Ian Bremmer, excerpt from Chapter 4, "Walls," in *Us vs. Them: The Failure of Globalism* by Ian Bremmer, copyright © 2018 by Ian Bremmer. Used by permission of Portfolio, an imprint of Penguin Publishing Group, a division of Penguin Random House LLC. All rights reserved.

Paul Butler, "The Chokehold," from *The Guardian,* August 11, 2017. This excerpt originally appeared in *Chokehold: Policing Black Men,* published by The New Press. Copyright © 2017 by Paul Butler. Reprinted by permission of The New Press. www.thenewpress.com.

Joseph Carens, "The Case for Open Borders," *openDemocracy,* June 5, 2015, https://www.opendemocracy.net/beyondslavery/joseph-h-carens/case-for-open-borders. Copyright © 2015. Reprinted by permission.

Steve Chapman, "Are Blacks to Blame for Police Actions?," *Chicago Tribune*, December 5, 2014. Copyright © 2014 Chicago Tribune. All rights reserved. Used by permission and protected by the Copyright Laws of the United States. The printing, copying, redistribution, or retransmission of this Content without express written permission is prohibited.

Aviva Chomsky, "Talking Sense about Immigration," originally published on *TomDispatch*, March 13, 2018. Copyright © 2018. Reprinted by permission of the author.

Ed Conard, "We Don't Need More Humanities Majors," *Washington Post*, July 30, 2013. Copyright © 2013 Ed Conard. Used with permission.

Danielle Crittenden, "About Love," from *What Our Mothers Didn't Tell Us: Why Happiness Eludes the Modern Woman*. Copyright © 1999 by Danielle Crittenden. Reprinted with the permission of Simon & Schuster, Inc., and ICM Partners. All rights reserved.

Justin Cronin, "Confessions of a Liberal Gun Owner," *New York Times*, January 28, 2013. Copyright © 2013 by The New York Times. All rights reserved. Used by permission and protected by the Copyright Laws of the United States. The printing, copying, redistribution, or retransmission of this Content without express written permission is prohibited.

Dalai Lama and Howard C. Cutler, "Inner Contentment," from *The Art of Happiness: A Handbook for the Living* by Dalai Lama and Howard C. Cutler. Copyright © 1998 by His Holiness the Dalai Lama and Howard C. Cutler, M.D. Used by permission of Riverhead, an imprint of Penguin Publishing Group, a division of Penguin Random House LLC. All rights reserved.

Andrew Delbanco, "3 Reasons College Still Matters," first published in the *Boston Globe*, March 4, 2012, is reprinted from *College* by Andrew Delbanco by permission of Princeton University Press; permission conveyed through Copyright Clearance Center, Inc.

Hossein Derakshan, "How Social Media Endangers Knowledge," *Wired*, October 19, 2017. Copyright © 2017 Condé Nast. Reprinted by permission.

Emari DiGiorgio, "When You Are the Brownest White Girl," from *Rattle* 58 (Winter 2017). Copyright © 2017. Reprinted by permission of the author.

Nora Ephron, "The Boston Photographs," copyright © 1975 by Nora Ephron. Reprinted by permission of ICM Partners.

Jules Evans, "Are We Slaves to Our Online Selves?," *Huffington Post*, October 6, 2013. Copyright © 2013 Jules Evans. Used with permission.

Nina Fedoroff, "The Genetically Engineered Salmon Is a Boon for Consumers and Sustainability," from *The New York Times*, December 2, 2015 issue. Copyright © 2015 by Nina Fedoroff. Used with permission.

Conor Friedersdorf, "A Food Fight at Oberlin College," *The Atlantic*, December 21, 2015. Copyright © 2012 The Atlantic Media Co., as first published in the *Atlantic Magazine*. Distributed by Tribune Content Agency, LLC.

Robert Frost, "Mending Wall," from *The Poetry of Robert Frost*, ed. by Edward Connery Lathem. Copyright © 1930, 1939, 1969 by Henry Holt and Company. Copyright © 1958 by Robert Frost. Copyright © 1967 by Lesley Frost Ballantine. Reprinted by permission of Henry Holt and Company. All rights reserved.

Daniel Gilbert, "Does Fatherhood Make You Happy?," from *TIME Magazine*, June 11, 2006. Reprinted by permission of the author.

Nick Gillespie, "Millennials Are Selfish and Entitled, and Helicopter Parents Are to Blame," *TIME.com*, August 21, 2014. Copyright © 2014 Time Inc. Used under License. TIME.com and Time Inc. are not affiliated with, and do not endorse products or services of, Licensee.

Kenneth Goldsmith, Excerpt from *Uncreative Writing: Managing Language in the Digital Age*. Copyright © 2011 by Columbia University Press. Reprinted with permission of the publisher.

Adam Gopnik, "The Caging of America," *The New Yorker*, January 30, 2012. Copyright © 2012 Adam Gopnik. Used by permission.

Ronald M. Green, "Building Baby from the Genes Up," *Washington Post*, April 13, 2008. Reprinted by permission of the author.

Sanjay Gupta, "Why I Changed My Mind on Weed," *CNN.com*, August 8, 2013. Copyright © 2013 Turner Broadcast Systems. All rights reserved. Used by permission and protected by the Copyright Laws of the

United States. The printing, copying, redistribution, or retransmission of this Content without express written permission is prohibited.

Victor Davis Hanson, "Our Brave New World of Immigration," *realclearpolitics.com,* May 25, 2006. Reprinted by permission of the author.

Caroline Harper, "HBCUs, Black Women, and STEM Success," from *Higher Education Today*, May 14, 2018. Copyright © 2018. Reprinted by permission of the American Council on Education.

Becky Hayes, "The Critics of #MeToo and the Due Process Fallacy," as first published on *The Establishment,* February 16, 2018. Copyright © 2018 by Becky Hayes. Used with permission.

Richard Hayes, "Genetically Modified Humans? No Thanks," *Washington Post*, April 15, 2008. Reprinted by permission of the author.

Jeff Jacoby, "Bring Back Flogging," *Boston Globe*, February 20, 1997. Copyright © 1997 by Boston Globe Media Partners. All rights reserved. Used by permission and protected by the Copyright Laws of the United States. The printing, copying, redistribution, or retransmission of this Content without express written permission is prohibited.

Susan Jacoby, "A First Amendment Junkie." Copyright © 1978 by Susan Jacoby. Originally appeared in *The New York Times* (January 26, 1978). Reprinted by permission of Georges Borchardt, Inc. on behalf of the author.

Sarah Jaffe, "The Collective Power of #MeToo," *Dissent Magazine*, Spring 2018. Copyright © 2018. Reprinted with the permission of the University of Pennsylvania Press.

Martin Luther King Jr., "I Have a Dream," reprinted by arrangement with The Heirs to the Estate of Martin Luther King Jr., c/o Writers House as agent for the proprietor, New York, NY. Copyright © 1963 by Dr. Martin Luther King; copyright renewed 1991 by Coretta Scott King.

Rudyard Kipling, "We and They" from *Debits and Credits* by Rudyard Kipling, copyright © 1926 by Rudyard Kipling; renewed copyright © 1953 by Elsie Bambridge. Used by permission of Doubleday, an imprint of the Knopf Doubleday Publishing Group, a division of Penguin Random House LLC and A.P. Watt/United Agents. All rights reserved.

Alfie Kohn, "The One-Sided Culture War against Children," from *The Myth of the Spoiled Child: Challenging Conventional Wisdom about Children and Parenting* by Alfie Kohn, copyright © 2014. Reprinted by permission of Da Capo Lifelong Books, an imprint of Hachette Book Group, Inc.

Nicholas Kristof, "For Environmental Balance, Pick Up a Rifle," *The New York Times*, December 14, 2005. Copyright © 2005 by The New York Times. All rights reserved. Used by permission and protected by the Copyright Laws of the United States. The printing, copying, redistribution, or retransmission of this Content without express written permission is prohibited.

Jaron Lanier, "Social Media Is Making You into an Asshole," from *Ten Arguments for Deleting Your Social Media Accounts Right Now.* Copyright © 2018 by Jaron Lanier. Reprinted by permission of Henry Holt and Company. All rights reserved.

Charles R. Lawrence III, "On Racist Speech," *Chronicle of Higher Education*, October 25, 1989. Copyright © 1989. Reprinted by permission of the author, Professor of Law and Centennial University Professor at Univ. of Hawaii, Manoa.

Ursula K. Le Guin, "The Ones Who Walk Away from Omelas." Copyright © 1973 by Ursula K. Le Guin. First appeared in "New Dimensions 3" in 1973 and then in *The Wind's Twelve Quarters*, published by HarperCollins in 1975. Reprinted by permission of Curtis Brown, Ltd.

C. S. Lewis, "We Have No Right to Happiness," from *God in the Dock* by C. S. Lewis. Copyright © C. S. Lewis Pte. Ltd. 1967. Extract reprinted by permission.

Heather Mac Donald, "The Myth of Criminal Justice Racism," from *City Journal*, October 22, 2015. Copyright © 2015. Reprinted by permission.

Christian Madsbjerg and Mikkel B. Rasmussen, "We Need More Humanities Majors," *Washington Post*, July 30, 2013. Copyright © 2013 Christian Madsbjerg. Used with permission.

Kenan Malik, "The Bane of Cultural Appropriation," from *Al Jazeera*, April 14, 2016. Copyright © 2016 by Al Jazeera; permission conveyed through Copyright Clearance Center, Inc.

Stephen Marche, "Is Facebook Making Us Lonely?," *Atlantic Monthly*, May 2012. Copyright © 2012 The Atlantic Media Co., as first published in the *Atlantic Magazine*. Distributed by Tribune Content Agency, LLC.

Hans J. Massaquoi, pp. 98–102 from *Destined to Witness*. Copyright © 2000 by Hans J. Massaquoi. Reprinted by permission of HarperCollins Publishers.

Megan McArdle, "The Nationalism America Needs Now," originally published under the title "America Needs More Patriotism" in the *Washington Post*, July 6, 2018. Copyright © 2018 by the Washington Post. All rights reserved. Used by permission and protected by the Copyright Laws of the United States. The printing, copying, redistribution, or retransmission of this Content without express written permission is prohibited.

Darrin M. McMahon, "In Pursuit of Unhappiness," *The New York Times*, December 29, 2005. Copyright © 2005 by The New York Times. All rights reserved. Used by permission and protected by the Copyright Laws of the United States. The printing, copying, redistribution, or retransmission of this Content without express written permission is prohibited.

James E. McWilliams, "The Locavore Myth," *Forbes*, August 3, 2009. Copyright © 2009. Reprinted by permission.

Alex Miller, "Why Do We Care So Much about Explainable Algorithms? In Defense of the Black Box," from Alex Miller, *Towards Data Science*, January 11, 2018. Copyright © 2018 by Alex Miller. Used with permission.

Russell Muirhead and Nancy Rosenblum, "The New Conspiracists," *Dissent Magazine*, Winter 2018. Copyright © 2018. Reprinted with the permission of the University of Pennsylvania Press.

Safiya Umoja Noble, "Missed Connections: What Search Engines Say about Women," from *Bitch, The Frontier Issue*, Spring 2012. Copyright © 2012. Reprinted by permission of Bitch Media.

Suzanne Nossel, "The Pro–Free Speech Way to Fight Fake News," *Foreign Policy*, October 12, 2017. Copyright © 2017. Reprinted by permission.

Lynn Stuart Parramore, "Fitbits for Bosses," from *Al-Jazeera America*, September 18, 2015. Used with permission of the author.

Andrea Pitzer, "The Freewheelin' Bob Dylan" (text and illustration), *Slate*, June 13, 2017. Copyright © 2017 by The Slate Group. All rights reserved. Used by permission and protected by the Copyright Laws of the United States. The printing, copying, redistribution, or retransmission of this Content without express written permission is prohibited.

Plato, from *The Republic*, trans. with an introduction by Desmond Lee (Penguin Classics 1955, Fourth Rev. Edition 2002). Copyright © 1953, 1974, 1987, 2002 by H. D. P. Lee. Reproduced by permission of Penguin Books Ltd.

Charles Rangel and James Lacey, "The Argument: Should America Reinstate the Draft? (yes and no)," *Saturday Evening Post*, January/February 2013. © SEPS licensed by Curtis Licensing Indianapolis, IN. All rights reserved.

Nausicaa Renner, "How Do You Explain the 'Obvious'?" *The New York Times*, August 21, 2018. Copyright © 2018 by The New York Times. All rights reserved. Used by permission and protected by the Copyright Laws of the United States. The printing, copying, redistribution, or retransmission of this Content without express written permission is prohibited.

Carl Rogers, "Communication: Its Blocking and Its Facilitation." Copyright © Rogers Trust. Reprinted by permission of the Natalie Rogers Separate Property Trust.

Josh Rose, "How Social Media Is Having a Positive Impact on Our Culture," *Mashable.com*, February 23, 2011. Copyright © 2011 by Josh Rose. Used by permission.

Carlo Rotella, "No, It Doesn't Matter What You Majored In," *Boston Globe*, December 24, 2012, is reprinted by permission of the author.

David Runciman, excerpts from "Preface: Thinking the Unthinkable," and "Conclusion: This Is How Democracy Ends," in *How Democracy Ends* by David Runciman (Basic Books, 2018), pp. 1–7, 8–9. 216–18. Copyright © 2018 by David Runciman. Reprinted by permission of Basic Books, an imprint of Hachette Book Group, Inc.

Bertrand Russell, "The Happy Life," from *The Conquest of Happiness* by Bertrand Russell. Copyright 1930 by Horace Liveright, Inc., renewed © 1957 by Bertrand Russell. Used by permission of Liveright Publishing Corporation. Electronic use licensed by Bertrand Russell Peace Foundation. Copyright The Bertrand Russell Peace Foundation Ltd.

Carl Safina, "Never Mind Theory," from *Beyond Words: What Animals Think and Feel.* Copyright © 2015 by Carl Safina. Reprinted by permission of Henry Holt and company. All rights reserved.

Reihan Salam, "Beyond the Wall," *National Review,* March 2016. Copyright © 2016 by The National Review. Used with permission.

Bernie Sanders, "We Must Make Public Colleges and Universities Tuition-Free," from *Vice Impact*, October 9, 2017. Used with permission.

Jean-Paul Sartre, excerpt(s) from *Anti-Semite & Jew* by Jean-Paul Sartre, translated by George Becker, translation copyright © 1948, copyright renewed 1976 by Penguin Random House LLC, copyright 1954 by Editions Gallimard. Preface copyright © 1995 by Michael Walzer. Used by permission of Schocken Books, an imprint of the Knopf Doubleday Publishing Group, a division of Penguin Random House LLC and Editions Gallimard. All rights reserved.

V. L. Seek, "Utmost Resistance," from *Not That Bad: Dispatches from Rape Culture* by Roxanne Gay (HarperCollins, 2018). Used with permission from the author.

Julia Serano, "Free Speech and the Paradox of Tolerance," from *Medium*, February 6, 2017. Copyright © 2017 by Julia Serano. Used with permission.

Zachary B. Shemtob and David Lat, "Executions Should Be Televised," *The New York Times*, July 29, 2011. Copyright © 2011 by The New York Times. All rights reserved. Used by permission and protected by the Copyright Laws of the United States. The printing, copying, redistribution, or retransmission of this Content without express written permission is prohibited.

Max Shulman, "Love Is a Fallacy." Copyright © 1951 by Max Shulman, renewed 1979. Reprinted by permission of the Harold Matson Co., Inc. All rights reserved.

Ganesh Sitaraman, "Divided We Fall," *New Republic*, April 10, 2017. Copyright © 2017. Reprinted by permission of the author.

Ronald Takaki, "The Harmful Myth of Asian Superiority," *The New York Times*, June 16, 1990. Copyright © 1990. Reprinted by permission of the Roam Agency.

Ashwini Tambe, "Reckoning with the Silences of #MeToo," was originally published in *Feminist Studies*, Volume 44, Number 1 (2018): 197–203, by permission of the publisher, Feminist Studies, Inc.

John Tierney, "The Reign of Recycling," *The New York Times*, October 3, 2015. Copyright © 2015 by The New York Times. All rights reserved. Used by permission and protected by the Copyright Laws of the United States. The printing, copying, redistribution, or retransmission of this Content without express written permission is prohibited.

Matthew Walther, "Sorry Nerds, Video Games Are Not a Sport," from *The Week*, May 4, 2018. Copyright © 2018 by The Week Publications. Used with permission.

Bari Weiss, "The Limits of 'Believe All Women,'" *The New York Times*, November 28, 2018. Copyright © 2018 by The New York Times. All rights reserved. Used by permission and protected by the Copyright Laws of the United States. The printing, copying, redistribution, or retransmission of this Content without express written permission is prohibited.

Robin West, "Manufacturing Consent," from *The Baffler*, Issue No. 39. Copyright © The Baffler. Used with permission.

Edward O. Wilson, "Letter to a Southern Baptist Minister," from *The Creation: An Appeal to Save Life on Earth* by Edward O. Wilson. Copyright © 2006 by Edward O. Wilson. Used by permission of W.W. Norton & Company, Inc.

James Q. Wilson, "Just Take Away Their Guns," *The New York Times*, Magazine Section, March 20, 1994. Copyright © 1994 by The New York Times. All rights reserved. Used by permission and protected by the Copyright Laws of the United States. The printing, copying, redistribution, or retransmission of this Content without express written permission is prohibited.

Justin Wolfers, "Forgive Student Loans? Worst Idea Ever," from *Freakonomics*, Sept. 19, 2011, is reprinted by permission of the author.

Yo Zushi, "What's Mine Is Yours," from *New Statesman*, October 12, 2015. Copyright © 2015 by The New Statesman. Used with permission.

Index of Authors, Titles, and Terms